The Complete Book of ASTROLOGY HOROSCOPE AND DREAMS

MODERN PROMOTIONS
A Division of Unisystems Inc., New York, New York 10022

Copyright © 1979 Ottenheimer Publishers, Inc.
A to Z Dreams and Lucky Numbers
Copyright © 1940, 1958, 1979, by
Books, Inc.
All Rights Reserved.
Printed in Canada.

CONTENTS

ASTROLOGY: The Science of the Stars	1
Introduction to Astrology	3
History of Astrology	5
Astrology, Horoscopes, and Astrologers	9
Astrology and Your Career	14
Sun Sign Messages	14
What the Stars Have to Say About Your Boss	15
Astrology and Your Home Environment	18
Astrological Guide to Home Decorating	18
Cosmic Cues for Home Happiness	20
Astrological Hints for Health and Happiness	22
Astrology and Diets	22
Revealing Facts About Your Health	24
Astrology and Your Love Life	26
The Many Faces of Love	26
How to Rate Your Sex Appeal	27
Twelve Signs to Married Happiness	29
Astrological Hints for Getting Along Better With Others	31
How to Better Understand Your Children	31
Bridging the Generation Gap	33
Relating to Other People	34
Your Friendship Guide	36
NUMEROLOGY: The Science of Numbers	38
Overview and History	38
Basic Numbers and Their Meanings	40
GRAPHOLOGY: The Language of Handwriting	44
The Historic Evolution of Graphology	44
Graphology as a Diagnostic Tool	45
The Methods of Graphology	46
The First Impression	46
Zonal Balance	47
Writing Size	49
Expression of Force	50
Handwriting Examples	52
Some Specific Graphic Indicators	52
Analysis and Synthesis of Handwriting	54
PALMISTRY: The Study of the Hand	56
History of Palmistry	56
The Relationship of Astrology to Palmistry	57
The Thumb	57
The Fingers	59
The Hand	60
Fingerprints and Palmar Loops	61
The Major Lines	62
The Minor Lines	65
The Psychic Indicators	66
Incidental Signs and Markings	66
HOROSCOPES: A Year's Forecast	67
Aries	69
Taurus	88
Gemini	107
Cancer	126
Leo	145
Virgo	164
Libra	183
Scorpio	202
Sagittarius	221
Capricorn	240
Aquarius	259
Pisces	278
A TO Z DREAMS AND LUCKY NUMBERS	297
How to Interpret Your Dreams	475
How to Use Your Dream Number	475
GLOSSARY	476

ASTROLOGY: THE SCIENCE OF THE STARS

INTRODUCTION TO ASTROLOGY

Astrology offers the only recipe for living in which we may "eat our cake, and have it too."

Similar magic has been promised by other occult studies, and modern book-shelves are piled with various designs for living wisely and well; but no new theory for the manufacture of success and happiness can show the practical results that even a remote knowledge of Astrology can produce.

The "Starry theory for success" is no heavenly fantasy, for it bears the stamp of antique culture and the seal of ancient authority.

If this book were simply a history of Astrology, instead of a self-help book, many pages could be filled with the story of famous seers from Chaldean civilization in the ancient land of Ur up to the present day who ruled the destiny of nations by the way of the stars.

From those venerable times to the present, great minds have noted the influence of each planet in its dominance over the lives of men, and no living being is too remote for this control.

This book, planned for the average person to whom Astrology may be a new thought, offers a simple analytical guide based on modern accepted conclusions, all of which will answer everyday questions.

People search the stars to find out if they are going to make lots of money, enjoy good health, and indulge in a glamorous love affair. They want specific answers to concrete questions, such as:

Are the Newlyweds going on a Southern Cruise?
Is Mother getting the mink coat?
Will Mary Ellen win a scholarship?
Is it going to be profitable for Junior to major in chemistry?
Will Father get a bonus next year?
Is Aunt Mamie's operation a real necessity?
Will stocks go up?
Will the rent go down?
Will Uncle Jonas leave me his money?
Will Florrie's new young man propose, and is his father really rich?

Material questions? Perhaps. But all of these and thousands more clamor for answer. Astrology will illuminate the path.

The easiest way to apply Astrology is to see it as a great searchlight trained on life, and in its radiance, once we have learned the code, the past is explained, the present clarified, and the path of the future outlined.

It is false to believe that the Astrological plan sets the final hand of fate upon events and people, or that such a thing as bad luck is ordained. This is not true. Astrology never says, "It can't be done," or "You are completely out of luck." Rather, it tells us what can be done, how and when; and in the words of an old Astrological quotation, "The stars incline, but they do not compel."

By all this is meant that the stars in their courses and the planets in their signs and heavenly houses have each a different influence upon our earthly life. These rays or vibrations cause us to be hasty or slow, bright or dull, calm or explosive, according to their force. The planets bring conditions to us, conditions of wealth or poverty, atmospheres of joy or sorrow, conflict or expansion.

All of these astrological forces help to shape our thoughts, which in turn direct our actions. Rash explosive attitudes that suddenly overwhelm can always be justified by the person afflicted.

"The occasion demanded that outburst," the person involved will declare.

It is such conditions that can be averted through a knowledge of Astrology. If we are warned that rash actions will be the result of certain planets in their relation to the life, no matter how deceptively right that behavior appears to us at the time, we can hold a powerful check-rein on our emotions, and save the situation.

There is no combination of circumstances or emotions that is not conveyed to us by the heavenly bodies. When we know what to expect from these forces, we can use the energy and take advantage of the opportunities offered us by the stars.

With few exceptions, everyone seeks health, love, wealth, and power. Astrology deals out favorable conditions generously, to be absorbed by each individual according to his scope and capacity.

Many who are reading these words will exclaim at this point, and feverishly cite cases of persons dogged through life by hardship and tragedy. However true these tragic histories may be, they would have been less terrible had the subject been able to use Astrology as a guide.

Somewhere in every maze of wretchedness are dotted helpful periods, that recognized, understood, and used, will turn the tide of unhappiness. The key is here in this book.

First of all, clear every image out of your mind's eye and look up at the heavens.

Try to see it as a huge map of another world, with continents, countries, and principal cities, for that is what it really is; another World, made up of twelve Heavenly Houses, twelve signs of the Zodiac, and the ten major Planets.

Astrology, Horoscope, and Dreams

The Heavenly Houses, twelve in number, are like continents. They are stationary, and each house has an environment, or a special atmosphere all its own.

Traveling in and out among the Heavenly Houses are the twelve Signs of the Zodiac. Each sign has its own influence which combines in meaning with whatever House it happens to be in at the time of the transit.

Lastly, the ten Planets, weaving around the Zodiac, add their mighty influence to the Signs and Houses.

Therefore, every individual's character is a combination made up of House, Sign and Planet, according to the picture of the heavens on the day of his or her birth.

Some people are mirrors of their sun sign; others, where the moon is well aspected, take dominant characteristics from the moon. Still others are influenced by the ascendant.

The following chapters will describe the meaning of each House, Sign and Planet. After that, individual birthdays will be analyzed.

In order to get a complete horoscope, the following is necessary:

A Solar reading, which is based on the individual birthday.

A Lunar reading, which is based on the position of the moon according to the year, month and day of birth.

A reading of the Ascendant, which is based on the hour of birth.

This book contains all of this material, with charts, and detailed explanations. But the special mission is to make a highly technical subject understandable and helpful to the layman.

Astrology has much to offer the average man and woman, but it is quite useless to the uninitiated when it is in a complicated mathematical state. The following chapters will analyze the astrological plan for you, translate it into understandable language, and cover forecasts for all types of persons.

A glossary of Astrological terms, phrases and words will be found at the end of this book. When you meet something you do not understand, you will find an explanation in that section.

HISTORY OF ASTROLOGY

Celestial observation has been a primary function of civilization throughout the known history of man. The earliest records showing the phases of the moon were made on bone on animal tusks. Early architects and artisans in every part of the globe erected huge structures dedicated specifically to stargazing. Wherever these astrological and astronomical records exist, reference is made to correspondence between the celestial and terrestrial worlds. An active science emerged to study the effects in nature, cycles of weather, agriculture, civilizations, and the destiny of kings. Influences on healing the ill and preparation of precious metals were everyday tools of educated people in these early societies.

The practical application of astronomical information, using apparent positions of the sun, moon, and the planets against the background of the stars, is known as *astrology*. Meanings were derived from these symbolic omens and applied to the affairs of man and nature. The underlying concept of astrological thinking is that happenings in the celestial sphere are reflected in events on earth and in human activities.

All mythological dieties are tied to this planetary lore. Thor, or Zeus, is Jupiter; Apollo is the sun; and fast-moving Mercury was known as Hermes, messenger of the gods. Deified human form was a symbolic way of understanding their influence in daily life. The circle of animals that evolved into the present-day zodiac were created with the same purpose in mind. The astrological alphabet of planets and signs furnished the basic tools of study for this ancient science.

The ancients realized that life in the earth was tied to the eternal law of change—cycles of day and night, spring and winter, abundance and famine. This law is best reflected in the Biblical commentary from Ecclesiastes 3:1-8.

1. For everything there is a season, and a time for every matter under heaven; 2. A time to be born, and a time to die; a time to plant and a time to pluck up what is planted; 3. A time to kill, and a time to heal; 4. A time to weep and a time to laugh; a time to mourn and a time to dance; 5. A time to cast away stones, and a time to gather stones together; a time to embrace and a time to refrain from embracing; 6. A time to seek, and a time to lose; 7. A time to rend and a time to sew; a time to keep silence, and a time to speak; 8. A time to love, and a time to hate; a time for war and a time for peace.

Records of planetary motion, the sun, and the phases of the moon exist in every culture on earth. Bone, stone tablets, papyrus, and huge monoliths, such as Stonehenge and the Great Pyramid of Giza, were used to record these events. The grand gallery of the Giza pyramid utilized a reflecting pool at the bottom, similar to the pool of reflective mercury utilized by the Naval Observatory in Washington, D.C., to observe the passage of celestial bodies across the meridian.

The ancients as well as modern-day physicists study man's tie to the universe. Science states that the entire universe is composed of the same basic building blocks. We live in a celestial environment of planets, solar system, galaxy, the universe, etc. . . . A new celestial consciousness is emerging with the many discoveries of our space probes. Unacceptable concepts are being rapidly vindicated. Venus, at one time thought to be a twin planet of the earth, is now known to be a searing, cloud-covered inferno whose rotation is in reverse direction compared to that of the earth. The list goes on and on.

The basic questions that stimulate this climb beyond the atmosphere with rockets, radar probes, radio, infrared detectors, telescopes, spectographs, satellites, etc. . . . etc. brings cherished notions of astronomy, physics, archeology, philosophy, and religion to the brink of breakthrough—or disaster.

And yet, out of this chaos of modern thought, stand the basic principles of astrology, surviving the ravages of time as a ragged refugee of the ages. As Carl Jung conjectured, astrology is a composite reflection of the breadth of human development . . . part of the mysterious imagination of the subconscious reflected in daily living. With great stamina and vitality, it has challenged the greatest thinkers as the longest-lived legend in man's cultural development next to the legend of Atlantis. The general notion that anyone interested in the subject of astrology is tainted with lunacy and charlatanism is rapidly deteriorating in the light of a variety of new discoveries resulting from modern-day research. The world of impossible possibilities is upon us.

A new concept of ourselves as extraterrestrials, harbored in an electro-chemical "space suit" appropriate for life on planet earth, is rapidly emerging. Through the various centers of the endocrine system within the body, cells seem to respond in sympathy with the celestial environment. Even the air we breathe is charged with positive and negative ions in sympathy to the solar flare activity of the sun. Positive ions create discomforting, irritable responses and ground the individual. Negative ions in the atmosphere usually create a cheerful relaxed mood, a feeling of well-being. The cause of solar flares themselves seems to be related to the positions of the planets in relation to one another in the solar system. The vision of all life forms, including man, as being linked with the activity of the celestial environment is not a new one.

Historical Survey

The priests of old were not unlike the scientists of our own day. They were the intelligentsia of their age. They did not relate their secrets to the general class of people. Language using the terms of their craft separated them still further from those of the masses. Knowledge is power, an equation that has not changed with our own era. Huge libraries around the world—Alexandria, Peking, the Vatican in Rome—attest to the fact that vast information resources were effective tools for controlling civilization. Religion, science, mathematics, music, medicine, and cosmology, were each a part of the vision of body, mind, and spirit in luminous synthesis.

All major cultures of the ancient worlds were tied by a common esoteric language in symbolic form. India, China, Persia, Chaldea, Egypt, the Mayans in South America, and Hopi Indians in North America all had extensive use of symbols, including numbers and glyphs to denote ruling influences in the experiences of individuals. Rituals involving the activities of the heavens and energy from the sun and stars were created to give meaning to the mysteries of life. These ancient systems pervade the religious holidays of every world culture, including the Christian ones.

The celebration of Christmas was moved to the date of the pagan Saturnalia, winter solstice date of December 21, to make it more acceptable to new converts. Easter alays falls in accordance with a prescribed astronomical formula, that is, the first Sunday after the first full moon following the spring equinox, March 21. The number of examples linking signs of the zodiac and the twelve prophets and the twelve disciples is contained in the Judeo-Christian tradition. The list can go on and on.

According to Cicero, in his book on divination, Chaldeans and Babylonians had records of celestial motion (used for navigation by both land and sea), which encompassed 370,000 years of history. Much of these priceless data were either destroyed or stolen by the many invading hordes. Even this information suffered still further in the fires that eliminated the great libraries of Alexandria and Peking. A good example of a still existent calendar of that ancient information is that of the Mayas, who recorded the motion of the planets to an exactness of six decimal places! This is a feat that can only be duplicated by modern computers.

The great pyramid of Giza, itself reputed to be a calendar of thousands of years recorded on the inner walls of the interior chambers, is one of the few remaining remnants of the ancient records. According to Peter Tompkins' research as reported in his book, *Secrets of the Great Pyramid,* the very shape and dimension of the pyramid is in exact proportion to those of the earth. The pyramid duplicates in its outer dimensions the distortion of the earth—flat at the poles and bulging at the center. The height is less than the width. To acquire such knowledge, to build a structure oriented to true north and south, whose corners are correctly oriented to the solstice points and the polar axis of the planet, would require 2200 years of celestial observation.

The Egyptians used the planets and references to fifth-magnitude stars, almost invisible to the unaided eye, to orient this edifice of stone. It is reflective of reasoning beyond much of our capability to duplicate. Performed systems of math, engineering, and astronomical science without an apparent source were used to create this forty-story structure covering the equivalent area of seven square city blocks. Two-and-one-quarter million stones, carefully cut and dressed, each weighing between 4,000 and 24,000 pounds, were used in an engineering feat impossible to duplicate with our most advanced technology. Located at the center of all land masses on the earth—the 30th parallel of latitude and longitude—it represents a geological survey comparable in accuracy only to that recently accomplished via modern satellite. Some have inferred that possibly a technology totally unfamiliar to us was involved here.

As mentioned previously, the ascending passageway of the grand gallery creates a meridian slot for observing the culmination of any celestial body within a twenty-four-hour period. It catches the exact moment that a planet or star passes across the local meridian, an imaginary line that runs north and south at the locale, intersecting the ecliptic or path of the planets and sun. This technique is paramount in developing any body of astronomical knowledge.

Measurements around the pyramid have also revealed the expertise of the Egyptians in recording celestial motion. According to David Davidson, author of *The Great Pyramid, Its Divine Message,* the pyramid measures 365.2242 cubits around its base from corner to corner. This number corresponds exactly to the *solar day,* or time it takes the sun to move across the earth's equator through one year to again cross the earth's equator during the spring equinox (approximately March 21). With the advent of photography, it was discovered that the pyramid was not exactly square but slightly indented along the sides. By measuring these indentations back out to the corners around the entire circumference of the pyramid, Davidson discovered that this equalled 365.25636 cubits of Egyptian measure. This number corresponds to the sidereal day as compared to the solar day of the previous number. This increment of time is the time it takes a star to appear at the same spot in the sky at the same time of year. It is approximately twenty minutes longer than the solar day and plays a vital part in the precession of the signs every 2,160 years, which equals one age.

The period of time it takes the earth in its orbit to make its closest approach to the sun is known in astronomical terms as the anamolistic day. This figure also appears in the measurements around the great pyramid. The many correspondences to mathematical formulae, the *golden section,* and *pi* are too numerous to elaborate on here.

Much of what comes to us today as the ancient tradition of astrology is from the Persian and Egyptian sources. Even modern astronomers have used the Egyptian texts to locate other planets. Such was the case with Pluto, rediscovered February 18, 1930. According to the Egyptians there are three additional planets yet to be discovered in our solar system. The Hamburg School of Astrology claims to have discovered these additional bodies plus five other sources of energy in our solar system.

The builders of Stonehenge understood that, by using a series of stakes coupled with the large stones, precise measurements could be made of the rising and setting of celestial bodies. Solar and lunar eclipse points could be predicted as well as the seasonal occurrences of equinoxes, as well as the spring and winter solstice points. Each stone is placed at 30° intervals, or moon stations, which record the daily motion of the moon.

Though there are only a few of these ancient observatories remaining for our investigation, certain deductions can be made. Gerald S. Hawkins, in his book, *Stonehenge Decoded,* states: ". . . many facts, for example, the fifty-six year eclipse cycle, were not known to me and other astronomers but were discovered (or rather *re*-discovered) from this decoding of Stonehenge.

"There can be no doubt that Stonehenge was an observatory; the impartial mathematics of probability and the celestial sphere are on my side. In form, the monolith is an ingenious computing machine, but was it ever put to use? As a scientist I cannot say. But in my defense, a similar skepticism can be turned toward other probers of ancient humanity. Do we need to see lipmarks on a drinking cup, blood on a dagger, and sparks from a flint striking pyrites to convince us that these things were, indeed, used?"

Hawkins and his team, using a large computer as well as the Smithsonian Astrophysical Observatory, Harvard College Observatory, Boston University, and the sight of Stonehenge itself, showed that the builders of Stonehenge had a classic concept of astronomical observation that today is called 'astrophysics'!

Advanced study of cycles provided the timing factors for raising crops and conducting their activities in attunement with natural rhythms. The High Tor at Glastonbury, which is supposedly the center of "King Arthur's Round Table," is generally translated with each Knight representing one of the twelve zodiac signs. Each of these twelve signs is carved out in a five-mile circle in the surrounding landscape.

The complicated ley system, described in *A View Over Atlantis* by John Michell, is apparently tied to many of the ancient centers all over the entire globe. The Mound of Ching, the Dragon Paths, and the Great Wall of China, the temples of India and Greece, and the Pyramids in Egypt and South America *are all linked* through the ancient astronomical study with astrological interpretations. Records of the study of the heavens comprising centuries of observation correspond historically whether one researches the Mayans, Incans, Egyptians, or Chinese!

There are many other ancient resources available to the modern researcher, even manuscripts of the early Christian church. The Vatican Library in Rome probably contains the most extensive references to astrology and lost knowledge of any information center in the world. The gathering of its resources is due in part to the many inquisitions conducted by the Dominican Order, themselves expert astronomers and astrologers. In order to have an influence over the masses, these early church fathers believed in keeping them ignorant. They did not want knowledge disseminated but felt it should be kept in the hands of the few— knowledge is power.

The architecture, glass work, and sculpture of the churches in Europe still reflect the Masonic secrets in symbolic form. An example is the Chartres cathedral and its incorporation of the twelve zodiac signs rendered in various forms throughout. The appearance of the four fixed signs on each side of the Christ figure in the stone of the entrance speaks words of wisdom. It also bespeaks of the high esteem in which astrology was held by these early Christian church-builders.

These sculptured symbols and their representations are here listed:

Symbol:	Angel	Lion	Bull	Eagle
New Testament:	Matthew	Mark	Luke	John
Old Testament:	Isaiah	Daniel	Jeremiah	Ezekiel
Fixed Signs:	Aquarius	Leo	Taurus	Scorpio
Elements:	Air	Fire	Earth	Water

The Pope's bathtub is said to have the twelve signs enscrolled on its sides. Whether this tub is tucked away in some storeroom or is in use, I can't say, but the bathtub has been mentioned by several writers.

The challenge of astrological concepts has vascillated back and forth throughout history, but it is also noted that most of the great minds throughout the ages seem to have taken some interest in the subject. St. Thomas Aquinas (1225?-1274), Dominican monk, had as one of his duties the job of overseeing astrological activities for the Church. Copernicus (1473-1543) re-established the sun as the center of the solar system. Nostradamus (1503-1566), noted astrologer and seer, made predictions known to be accurate today. Tyco Brahe (1546-1601), brass-nosed Danish astronomer/astrologer, was responsible for the first astronomical observatory in the western hemisphere. Johannes Kepler (1571-1630), student of Brahe, whose laws of planetary motion are references for modern science, did extensive work to create a new astrology. These are just a few of the list of luminaries of the past who studied and practiced astrology, the oldest science.

In 1666 A.D., astrology was officially banished from the Academy of Sciences in France and from the universities. Yet, many mental giants of later dates still undertook to learn astrology. The world renowned poet, Goethe (1749-1832), pursued the study of astrology. Citations such as this might go on and on and would include most of the great minds of history.

The investigation of natural phenomena fostered by Aristotle and now heralded by the twentieth century of skepticism, has come full circle. The dilemma facing modern man is that we have investigated to the point of disproving all that our science seemed to prove in the beginning. Jacques Bergier and Louis Pauwels in their book, *Morning of the Magicians,* comment that science, theology, and philosophy, all dissimilar disciplines in their approach, are rapidly converging to the point of merging as one science. Skepticism faces destruction by its own hand; division and arbitrary judgment have given way to a holistic vision of the universe.

Kepler most appropriately heralded the increased interest in astrological principles of our own age by stating . . . "a warning to certain physicists, theologians and philosophers, who while rightly rejecting the superstitions of the astrologers, ought not to throw out the baby with the bathwater. Because it should not seem incredible that from the stupidities and blasphemies of the astrologers, a new, healthy and useful learning may arise."

The first signs of these new sciences began with the cycles of plant growth and weather. Svante Arrhenius (1859-1927), Nobel Prize-winning chemist from Sweden, undertook the first statistical investigation of the influences of the moon on weather and living organisms. The study of the effect of sunspots on human life soon followed during the period 1920-1940, conducted in part by A. L. Tchijevsky and Drs. Faure and Sardou. The frequency of sudden illness occurring in rhythm with sunspot cycles led to research in 1941 by a Japanese investigator, Maki Takata, using human blood serum. With the publication of *The Season of Birth* by E. Huntington of Yale University, the principles of the ancient science of astrology again reappeared as a reputable subject of investigation. Out of the remnants of lore and lost knowledge, a new science is emerging. Research in one area is being spearheaded by Frank A. Brown, Professor of Biology at Northwestern University, Evanston, Illinois. For the last fifteen years, his studies of exogenous rhythms have shown conclusively that plants and animals respond directly or indirectly to the position of the sun and moon. A whole new field of astrobiology or bio-magnetics has been started. Brown's research began with his study of oysters.

He found that the oysters, taken from the Atlantic ocean, continued to open and close their shells in sequence with the tides on the Atlantic seaboard, even though they had been taken inland to Evanston, Illinois, along the shores of Lake Michigan. The pattern continued for two weeks, stopped for twenty-four hours, and then resumed in sequence to the tides [sic] corresponding to the moon passing the local meridian at their New Evanston location.

Rats sealed in closed environments, with constant food, constant light, and constant temperature were found to be *more active when the moon was below the horizon than when above it.* This illustrates that rats seem to be more aware of the moon's cycles than humans are.

Other recent research in physiological rhythms and social stress has revealed that human beings, though unaware, are extremely sensitive to the moon, too. These scientific studies promise profound impact on our day-to-day living, especially if we heed these natural, cyclic fluctuations. Illness, response to medical treatment, learning abilities, and job performance are likely to be affected by these cycles. Timing, in all our affairs, is of utmost importance, and a crucial key to evolutionary survival. It is certainly time for man to heed the work of these investigators of biomagnetism. Scientists have so far failed to come up with the most important discovery of all, which is the exact mechanism used to interpret these geomagnetic signals. As Brown points out, this is not unusual, as science has yet to discover the mechanism with which we identify smells.

As Shakespeare said, "There is a tide in the affairs of men, which taken at the flood, leads on to fortune; omitted, all the voyage of their life, is bound in shallows and miseries. We must take the current when it serves, or lose our ventures. . . ." *Julius Caesar,* Act 3, Scene 3.

The introduction of statistics and computers has aided the validation of many of the ancient principles. We are basically aware of the cycle of night and day, which has been extended with the use of modern electricity. Spring and winter have been altered by air-conditioning and modern heating systems. Studies of these broader cycles, such as those being done by the Foundation for the Study of Cycles, will certainly make us more the masters of our fate. In rescuing some of the old truths from obscurity and utilizing them along with newer discoveries, we will be harnessing more of the life forces available to us for our planet.

The movement of the moon has defied the greatest mathematical minds in predicting with infinitesimal accuracy precisely its orbital position. Only with recent discoveries made by our lunar probes, have we been able to make these precise calculations, which were necessitated by our venture into space. We now understand more about the moon's movement around the earth than we do about its geomagnetic effect on life.

The most obvious effect of the moon on the earth is related to the tides. The tide effect is a result of gravitational pull on the earth's surface by the sun and the moon. The new moon and the full moon create the greatest tidal conditions. The tides occurring on the side of the earth closest to the moon are the highest; so, the lowest tides are experienced on the side of the earth away from the moon. But did you know that there is an equal rise and fall of the landmass during maximum tidal periods?

Perhaps this phenomenon has some influence related to the occurrences of earthquakes and volcanic eruptions. So much is not known, that astrological explanations are as valid as mere conjectures by theorists; at least, there are some data available to astrologers.

The variety of research—in medicine and physiology, meteorology and biomagnetism, heredity and child birth, crime, and economics—is pointing to a new dimension for the use of natural cycles for the future. Man, armed with computers, statistics, space probes, etc., has revealed that astrological principles are a valuable human tool. Bergier and Pauwels in their work, *Impossible Possibilities,* state that by 1984 . . . "more and more scientists will be seeking to prove the theory of synchronization postulated by Carl Jung and Nobel Prize- winner Pauli. This theory, which gives the ancient concept of fate a scientific underpinning through the idea that every man can be the master of the destiny determined for him through genetic and social factors, will form the axis of completely new sciences combining cosmology, psychology, and mathematics. Young people will dream of becoming cosmic observers or destinologists. These professions will be very difficult, but they will form the hub, the most significant orientation of science." Obviously the basic foundation stones of such an occurrence have already been laid.

It is important to keep this entire concept in a context of exactly *what astrology is insofar as affecting our destiny is concerned. Forecasts made regarding the celestial environment must always be treated as weather reports. There is nothing that can dominate the will of man once he chooses to use this great source of creative action. Environment, heredity, and celestial influence are the dominant structures of life on the earth*. If we allow them to rule us, we subject our will to a material view with no recourse. *Should we decide that we wish to utilize these astrological tools at our disposal to enhance our own growth, then we truly partake of our inheritance as "children of the universe."* The analogy of the space prober, or the deep-sea diver, putting on special attire to explore an alien environment is not far removed because our mind and spirit clothe themselves in the veil of flesh, a "space" suit, for the exploration of this three-dimensional world.

ASTROLOGY, HOROSCOPES, AND ASTROLOGERS

It is possible to give only a rudimentary survey of astrology within this brief chapter. Rather than imparting definitions and terms, showing the steps necessary to create and translate an astrological chart will be far more interesting.

The word astrology comes to present usage from the Greek, astrologia, *which combines* astron, *meaning star, and* logia, *from* legein, *meaning to speak, or word.* Literally, this is *the science or doctrine of the stars, formerly equivalent to astronomy. Astrology and astronomy were one and the same science until 1200 A.D., when the two began to grow out of each other. Astronomy* derives from the same Greek root word *astron* (star), but adds *nomos,* from the word *nemein,* meaning to arrange or distribute. We know astronomy today as the science that gives us a description of the motions, figures, periods, of revolution, and other phenomena of the heavenly bodies—fixed stars, planets, satellites, and comets—their nature, distribution, magnitudes, motions, distances, periods of revolution, eclipses, etc.

Comparing the two studies, it is easy to see that *astronomy is an observational science and astrology an applied science.* Astrology is the form and practice of translating astronomical information by studying its influence on human affairs. It is not the many sun sign horoscopes read in so many newspapers, or sun sign forecasts sold on bookstands. *Astrology is applied Astronomy.*

Your response may be, "but that is difficult to study!" My reply is that it *is a complex study,* created by people to be understood by other people. There are many people all over the world actively pursuing the study of astrology on both amateur and professional levels. Each of these individuals may pursue a variety of branches of astrology. Natal or genethliacal, for example, uses the day, month, and standard time of birth moment, as well as the place in terms of latitude and longitude, for an individual person. In this approach, the astrologer also studies the effect of subsequent movements of all of the planets in relation to the *natal horoscope.* This is the most commonly pursued branch of astrology.

Other branches of astrology are:

HORARY—casting a chart for the birth moment of an idea, question, or an event.

ELECTIONAL—application of Horary astrology as a means of choosing the most propitious moment for starting a new enterprise, business, marriage, or journey.

MUNDANE or JUDICIAL—a study of the current positions of the planets with respect to their influence upon entire populations, countries, cities, and locations during the period of eclipses, new and full moons, or major changes of planetary positions.

MEDICAL—a diagnostic aid for unusual symptoms of disease, and unusual ailments.

METEOROLOGICAL—also known as Astro-Meteorology, which deals with forecasting weather conditions, earthquakes, and severe storms. (It is interesting to note that a great deal of progress in this area has occurred in recent years. NASA utilizes a forecasting service which uses planetary positions related to the dangerous solar flairs from the sun that threaten the lives of our astronauts. Weather prediction in this branch of the science can be extremely accurate, and a most useful study.)

AGRICULTURAL—the application of astrology to planting and harvesting crops, using the phases of the moon, etc.

Many modern-day astrologers are utilizing the services of computers in their study of these various branches of astrology. This greatly reduces the time required to construct an individual chart for each event. Specialized services exist exclusively for calculations of charts for astrology students; still others attempt to replace the astrologer with the computer. The computer cannot replace the interesting encounter that the client experiences with a competent astrologer.

Choosing the astrologer to cast your natal horoscope is important. It is actually better for the individual to study his or her chart himself after some instruction. Let us assume that you have found a competent astrologer. You know by his or her reputation that he or she qualifies as a cosmic psychologist, ready to evaluate your individual horoscope, or map of an hour, listen to your story, and offer options or possibilities for new action. The astrologer's code should be similar to that developed by Hippocrates, the most revered of physicians and the first cosmic psychologist: "I will not give 'readings,' 'tell fortunes,' or make predictions to satisfy the morbid cravings of the curious, nor will I seek to astound or mystify; but will give consultations only to those who have a problem regarding which they know they need help and seek it; and instead of prophesying a prognosis, I will endeavor to instill the right thinking that will contribute to avoiding or mitigating an unfavorable condition which I see in operation, interpreting such in terms of influences rather than events, and at all times teaching a philosophy of *free will* and emotional self-control that is the antithesis of fatalism and predestination.

"I will not give counsel contrived to assist any person in working injury to or taking unfair advantage of another.

"I will never make an utterance or inference that will reflect in any degree upon any other practitioner; nor will I treat a client of another practitioner, except as called in consultation by such practitioner.

"I will never relax in my efforts to add to my knowledge of the science, to impart it to such as I deem worthy to follow in my footsteps and to devote my efforts without stint toward the improving of human understandings and personal relationships, and in rendering service to humanity and society.

"And may the Creator who placed the planets in their orbits as His means of guiding the Destinies of men, preserve and sustain me in proportion to the fidelity with which I exemplify the laws I am ordained to teach."

At this point we must clarify that it is not necessary to prove astrology, only to *improve* it. Astrologers operate on this premise when they meet the client. They have studied and prepared for a number of years to master their craft. They have also been engaged in two to six hours of work of preparation for each meeting with a client.

The astrologer must start with *accurate data,* which includes the *day, month, year,* and *time of the client's birth. The place of birth and any important dates, including the dates of siblings' and parents' births, as well as important events such as marriages, children, etc...* Most astrologers agree that the "first cry" of the new-born child determines the basic cosmic "patter" to which the child responds throughout life. According to Michel Gauquel in his book, *Cosmic Influences on Human Behavior,* the results of extensive statistical analysis of thousands of drug-induced and natural births have produced some startling results. If we view the astrological chart as a chromosome picture of the new-born child, we find that drug-induced births reflect weakened family patterns which show up in the parents' charts of birth. Natural births usually reflect the strong points of the family traits. How you were born is important.

The first step, before the astrologer even meets the client, is to construct the Natal horoscope. In doing this, he or she utilizes a variety of tools: First, an epemerides for your year of birth, which includes the positions of the sun, moon, and planets in the solar system. Each planetary position is carefully calculated for its exact position in degrees of longitude on the ecliptic. *The ecliptic is the path along which the planets appear to move as we view them from earth. This path has been divided into twelve sectors, or signs of the Zodiac, each with its appropriate symbol. Each sector has 30 degrees of celestial longitude (360 degrees divided by 12).*

These signs are as follows:

ARIES, sign of the Ram	*LIBRA*, sign of the Scales
TAURUS, sign of the Bull	*SCORPIO*, sign of the Eagle
GEMINI, sign of the Twins	*SAGITTARIUS*, sign of the Centaur
CANCER, sign of the Crab	*CAPRICORN*, sign of the Goat
LEO, sign of the Lion	*AQUARIUS*, sign of the Water Bearer
VIRGO, sign of the Virgin	*PISCES*, sign of the Fishes

The sun, moon, or planets can be in any one of these respective twelve sectors of the zodiac. To facilitate this process, both the planets and signs have been given symbols as follows:

Houses and Keywords		SIGNS			PLANETS	
		Symbols and Names	Status and Element	Keywords	Symbols and Names	Keywords
1	One's self	Aries	Cardinal Fire	I Am	Mars	Dynamic energy
2	Personal assets	Taurus	Fixed Earth	Have	Venus	Beauty, Harmony
3	Brethren Basic education	Gemini	Mutable Air	Think	Mercury	Daily communications
4	Family, Home	Cancer	C Water	Feel	Moon	Emotions
5	Speculations	Leo	F F	Will	Sun	Life
6	People and Services	Virgo	M E	Analyze	Mercury	Communicate with people
7	Partnerships	Libra	C A	Balance	Venus	Calculated harmony
8	Partners assets	Scorpio	F W	Desire	Pluto	Either — Or (No middle)
9	Higher education Philosophy	Sagittarius	M F	See	Jupiter	Expansion
10	Professional and Social status	Capricorn	C E	Use	Saturn	Catalyst of truth
11	Expectations (Friends, hopes)	Aquarius	F A	Know	Uranus	Revolution — Humanity
12	Soul	Pisces	M W	Believe	Neptune	Utopia

Figure 1

Notice that the symbol for each planet includes extensive data associated with each planet. Whether the astronomical information, motions, dignities and rulerships, some of the people, or traditional keywords, each symbol is a condensed cuneiform of information to stimulate the mind to all information associated with that planet, a key word. These key words are the primary letters in the astrology's alphabet.

The astrologer must next determine where the earth is placed within this scheme of things in order to produce the astrological dial. This procedure is comparable to a ship's navigator locating his position from celestial positions. The mathematics required for this procedure are as simple as the everyday mathematics of addition and subtraction. Just as we are able to pinpoint any street in the city of Chicago, such as Michigan Avenue and Ohio Street, so also we can pinpoint a location on the earth using *latitude* and *longitude*. Longitude is a line between the North and South Poles. Latitudes are lines dividing the earth into horizontal slices or parallels of latitude, just as east/west streets in a particular city.

If you were to say that "We will meet on February 14, 1976, at 10:35 A.M., Central Standard Time, 41 N 52 and 87 W 39, at the corner of Ohio Street and Michigan Avenue," we have just agreed to meet in Chicago. This is a time and space measurement similar to that used to calculate the specific moment of birth.

In order to make the calculations for the horoscope, you would need the following items:

Ephemeris—a book containing astronomical information for the individual year to be studied.
Table of Houses—a book showing the exact mathematical factors necessary to calculate the path of the ecliptic around the earth for the specific moment of time, the Ascendent Sign, etc. . .

Time Changes—a book showing the laws affecting the recording of birth data for various locations as well as variations in time keeping, such as when Daylight Savings Time was in effect, etc. . .

Looking at a horoscope, we see that it is subdivided into twelve sectors of a circle. Starting at the Easter Horizon, these divisions—or Houses—are distributed in an uninterrupted sequence, counter-clockwise, around the chart.

These twelve heavenly houses are often called "Palaces of the Sky." At birth, each planet is in a sign, and both planet and sign are posited in a heavenly house. The law governing this is as follows:

The first house belongs to the first sign, which is Aries. The second house to Taurus. The third to Gemini, the fourth to Cancer. The fifth to Leo. The sixth Virgo. The seventh to Libra, the eighth to Scorpio. The ninth to Sagittarius, the tenth to Capricorn. The eleventh to Aquarius, and the twelfth, to Pisces.

The Houses never change their position, and the planets and signs move through them and can be placed anywhere in the chart.

These house and sign relationships are harmonious to each other, and lucky is the person who is born with the signs posited in their rightful houses. Each house rules over a specific area of life in the earth as follows:

The first house	Personal self, appearance, temperament, health
The second house	Possessions, finances, and values of a personal kind
The third house	Mental expression, short trips, communication, and brothers and sisters
The fourth house	Home environment, old age, land, father or mother
The fifth house	Children, romance, speculation, entertainment, and creative projects
The sixth house	Service to others, illnesses, food, elderly relatives, employees, small animals, and obligations
The seventh house	Partnerships, marriage, relations with others, open enemies, public relationships
The eighth house	Taxes, insurance, finances, and possessions of other people, inheritance, death, regeneration
The ninth house	Abstract mind, education, long journeys, philosophy, religion, faith, communication of ideas
The tenth house	Reputation, honor, profession, employer, mother or father
The eleventh house	Friends, hopes, wishes, social contacts, social organizations
The twelfth house	Confinement, hospitals, institutions, secret enemies, the fruits of past action

These heavenly houses influence life in the following way:
At birth the signs and planets are posited in various houses.

The atmosphere of the house blends with planet and sign to make an influence. In addition, the planets make what is known as aspects to each other. The house, as well as the sign and planet, is affected by these aspects.

Aspects are forces that give energy to the original meaning of the sign, house, planet combination. These aspects are benign or explosive, and are called trines, squares or oppositions. The trines are slow motion, but harmonious, while the squares are explosive, and create conflict. Sometimes the violent square results in greater fortune and richer results than the happy trine.

There are also conjunctions, where two planets are found in the same sector of the sign, or in conjunction. This aspect combines the meaning of both, the stronger planet infecting the more variable. There is also the harmonious semi-sextile, and the sextile.

If a heavenly house in an individual horoscope suffers from an explosive aspect at birth, the person feels activity in that particular department of the life throughout their span of years. For instance, if at birth the fourth house, holding Uranus makes an opposition to the native's sun, the home life of that person will always incline toward lightning changes, because Uranus is the planet of upheaval and violent reorganization. The individual, learning this fact, must recognize that changes can be made for the best, but quick action is essential.

Every aspect has a positive and a negative reaction. It is the force behind the influence that is valuable. An explosive aspect has that very useful energy, which to some of the passive signs and planets is just the needed impetus to make progress.

Never be frightened by a square or opposition. Frequently right thinking, and correct action applied to these violent forces result in success.

The promising trine often lulls us into a dreamy, inactive mental attitude. Then the favorable period passes without result from the good opportunity presented, and is followed by a violently antagonistic period that could never be used for gain, but is energy that might after all, be useful in another field.

Thus completes the third section of our astrological alphabet of planets, signs, and houses. *It is important to understand that the sun, moon, and planets are placed in the sky, or celestial world, and the earth rotates beneath them. Thus the chart of houses is representative of the time of day that will determine where the sun, moon, or planets will be distributed around the*

Astrology, Horoscope, and Dreams

dial. The horoscope dial shows the way time is related to the chart. For example, the sun rising in the east at 6:00 A.M., would put it on the left side of the chart near the dividing line between the twelfth and first house. At twelve noon the sun would be at the top of the diagram. Since the sun is in one of the signs of the Zodiac, it would appear to be pulling the twelve signs around through the houses. We might refer to the sun as the hour hand of our celestial clock.

Thus we have established our astrological alphabet using the *Houses, Signs,* and *Planets.* The *Reference Table* of key words indicates the meanings that are drawn from these symbols as we approach the interpretation of an astrological chart.

* * *

The complete delineation of a horoscope is a symbolic representation of the life of the individual with respect to the past, present, and future. No astrologer is able to give in a few hours of consultation what you and the cosmos have created by your interaction. Astrologers can cover important events, trends, cycles, potentials, and opportunities for change as they appear in their interpretations. No one astrologer will give you the same delineation as another from the same mathematical calculations, just as no doctor will necessarily give you the same diagnosis from the same examination. Principles and parallels are of utmost importance when comparing one astrologer's work to that of another. All should consistently give a similar analysis of the situation.

To do an astrological evaluation the astrologer must now consider the details of his work. The planets are the key to this interpretation; that is, *planets in signs indicate character . . . . Planets in houses indicate destiny.* The two worlds of the celestial and terrestrial are integrated by the planets in this statement. A parallel to this is that the spiritual and the material worlds are integrated by the function of the mind. Again, this is a potential diagram of how man will express his *will.* Some of us may utilize the same design for a house, but one will build a house of straw, another a house of wood, and a third a house of bricks. Two people may be born at the exact same time and yet live totally dissimilar lives, one in the slums and another in a wealthy suburb.

The factors that astrologers must consider in this subject are environment, hereditary factors, and the celestial environment. This we will call the raw data. The variable that changes all of this is a function of the mind and soul expressing itself in the earth. This we will term *Creative Willpower.* To illustrate, let me chart a small graph.

RAW DATA	FACTORS	POTENTIAL
25%	Environmental	10%
25%	Heredity	10%
50%	Celestial	20%
00%	Creative Willpower	60%

As you can see from these data, we have tremendous capability to weld the forces in nature into creative synthesis. This is what the counselor's role is—to bring more of these potentials to the point of expression. This role is spoken of in all religious teachings—man is a potential "co-creator" with God. This gives us all the open option and responsibility to create our own lives . . . quite a challenge.

This philosophical perspective must always be maintained as we again turn to the diagrams of the astrologer. The subject for our study will be a horoscope for February 14, 1976 at 07:45 P.M., in Chicago, Illinois, 41 N 52 and 87 W 39. The chart that would be drawn up for this date would look like this:

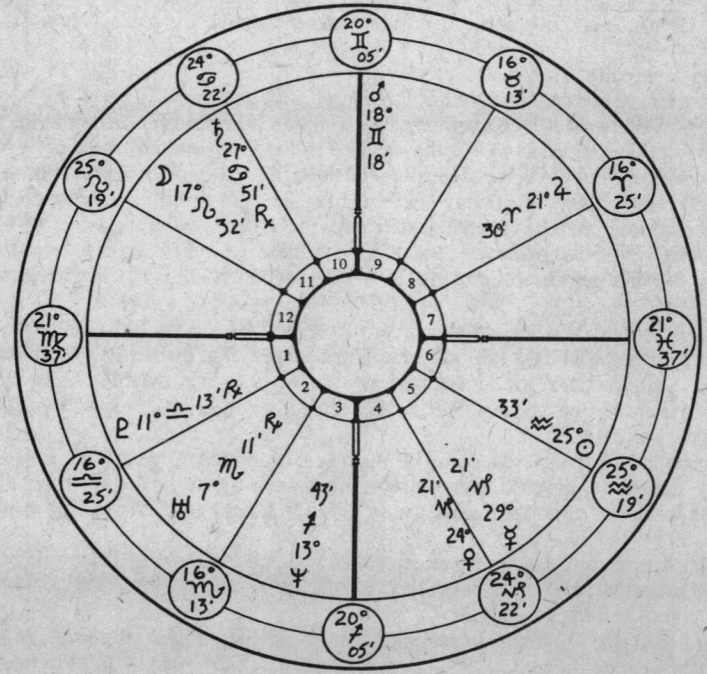

Figure II

12

Astrology, Horoscope, and Dreams

After a horoscope has been drawn, the astrologer would proceed to break down the various planetary patterns, etc. in sequential order. This process begins with the Eastern Horizon, or Ascendant, and proceeds in counter-clockwise fashion around the entire diagram. Each house is described in a key word fashion, such as those illustrated in the previous *reference table,* that is, house one = Virgo = Analyze

Pluto + Libra + First House = Either – Or, Balance, One's self.

The astrologer might comment that individual perspective of balance was necessary to prevent extremes in behavior. This process continues through the chart until an extensive commentary is formulated.

Other factors the astrologer will consider are *how the planets relate to one another.* The often-mentioned invisible lines of force connecting one planet to another. These are called *Aspects,* which are the measurement in degrees of celestial longitude by which any two celestial bodies are separated. These degrees are given key words as well, just as the planets, signs, and houses were. A table referencing these interpretations will give you the idea:

PLANET	SUN ☉	MOON ☽	MERCURY ☿	VENUS ♀	MARS ♂	JUPITER ♃	SATURN ♄	URANUS ♅	NEPTUNE ♆	PLUTO ♇
ELEMENTS										
Distance from Sun (in miles)	93 Million (from Earth)	240,000 (from Earth)	36 Million	67 Million	142 Million	484 Million	887 Million	1,784 Million	2,795 Million	3,675 Million
Diameter (in miles)	865,400	2,162	3,000	7,848	4,268	89,329	75,021	33,219	27,700	3,600
No. of Moons			0	0	2	12	10	5	2	0
Solar Orbit Period			88 Days	225 Days	687 Days	12 Years	29-1/2 Yrs.	84 Yrs.	165 Yrs.	248 Yrs.
MOTIONS, APPROX.										
Average Daily Motions	59'08"	13°10'35"	1°23'	1°12'	31'27"	4'59"	2'01"	42"	24"	15"
Av. Time in a Sign	1 Month	2 to 2-1/2 Days	14-20 days (When not Rx)	23-24 Days (When not Rx)	45-47 Days (When not Rx)	1 Yr.	2-1/2 Yrs.	7 Yrs.	14 Yrs.	20 Yrs. Av. (Varies)
Misc. Approx. Motions	2-1/2' per Hr.	1/2° per Hr.			± 20° per Mo	2-1/2° per Mo.	1° per Mo.	± 4° per Yr.	2° + per Yr.	1° per Yr. (Libra only)
Period of Rx & Stat.			20-24 Days	40-42 Days	58-81 Days	4 Months	4-1/2 Mos.	5 Months	5 Months	5 Months
Dignities & Rulerships										
Signs Ruled	Leo	Cancer	Gemini & Virgo	Libra & Taurus	Aries Scorpio	Sagittarius Pisces	Capricorn Aquarius	Aquarius	Pisces	Scorpio
Signs Co-Ruled										
Detriment	Aquarius	Capricorn	Sag. & Pisces	Aries & Scorpio	Libra & Taurus	Gemini & Virgo	Cancer & Leo	Leo	Virgo	Taurus
Exaltation	Aries	Taurus	Virgo	Pisces	Capricorn	Cancer	Libra	(Scorp. Gem. Aq)	(Can. Leo Sag.)	(Aries, Leo)
Degree of Exaltation	19	3	15	27	28	15	21	Exaltations of the three outer planets are ascribed variously as above and placement is controversial.		
Fall	Libra	Scorpio	Pisces	Virgo	Cancer	Capricorn	Aries			
Day	Sunday	Monday	Wednesday	Friday	Tuesday	Thursday	Saturday			
Metal	Gold	Silver	Quick-silver	Copper-Brass	Iron - Steel	Tin	Lead			
Anatomy	Heart & Spine	Pituitary Gland Digestive	Nervous S., Brain, Tongue	Skin, Venous S.	Muscles, Generative Organs	Liver, Arterial System	Bony System, Teeth			
Some of the PEOPLE Signified	Real Self Father Husband Males Head of a group Employer	Self--Personality & Subcons. mind Mother Wife Females The Public.	Self--Objective awareness Children Young people of both sexes Messenger	Females Loved ones Artists	Males Soldiers Surgeons Mechanics	Prof. Men Judges, Lawyers Clergymen Lawgivers Sportsmen Mature Men of benefic nature	Older Males in authority Older People Statesmen Administrators Teachers	Inventors Reformers Altruists Rebels Psychologists Humanitarians	Mystics Prophets Promotors Actors Seafaring Men Recluse	Groups Organizations Spiritual Leader Gangster Monopoly
TRADITIONAL KEYWORDS	Vitality Individuality Will Power Leadership Vigor Ego Masculine Prin. Creativeness Authority	Fluctuation Change Domestic Adaptability Instinctual Impressionable Nourishing Receptivity Feminine Prin. Fecundation Response	Communication Expression Adaptability Intellection Perception Self-Expression Alertness Thought Skill Dexterity	Association Harmony Attraction Cohesion Ease Love Pleasure Affection Mildness Decoration	Energy Initiative Action Aggression Assertion Courage Protection Construction & Destruction Passion Independence	Expansion Benevolence Vision Abundance Devotion Prudence Optimism Justice Prosperity Generosity	Contraction System Limitation Restriction Tradition Framework Crystallization Persistence Discipline	Uniqueness Disruption Originality Unexpected Eccentric Altruism Renunciation Non-Conformist Progressive Invention	Visionary Utopian Mystic Idealistic Illusion Confusion Mediumistic Imaginative Vagueness Inspiration	Regeneration Mutation Transformation Integration Collectivity Coercion Inversion Annihilation Domination Alteration

PLANETARY ELEMENTS, MOTIONS & KEYWORDS

Figure III

As you can see by the description we have given you of chart construction using mathematical calculations and key word delineation, the astrologer's job is a complex one. Other steps and procedures utilized will take a number of hours to understand fully the dynamics of your individual chart. Your astrologer will evaluate where the planets moved after your birth, where they are at the present time, and will project their movement into the future. This will signal the major events in your life and through interview, your astrologer will determine how you handled those situations. You can now understand why Carl Jung considered *astrology,* scientifically used, as *an excellent psycho-diagnostic tool.*

The study of astrology, whether you learn it yourself or select a competent astrologer to do your chart, is always a rewarding experience. In the words of Dr. Zipporah Dobyns, prominent researcher and practicing astrologer, "As a map and compass, clock and calendar, the sky has long been used by humanity for orientation in space and time. But its greatest value is as a mirror to let us see ourselves while we create our lives. Self-knowledge is the beginning of wisdom."

ASTROLOGY AND YOUR CAREER
Sun Sign Messages

Your Special Career Approach

In this day of cybernetics and the disappearance of many of the old-line jobs, it is more than ever necessary to know how you fit in and what is your best approach for a gratifying career. Many feel animosity toward automation and with some justification, for until the world becomes totally automated, the transition period is going to cause doubt, confusion and suffering from lack of work. Many will find they have just nothing to do.

It is wise to learn these new skills. Get a good training in some phase of the newly automated world. To be a skilled worker, hard work is necessary, but the skills to be learned will be satisfying and profitable ones, nothing like the old routine, tedious labors.

The Sun Sign messages ahead are intended to help you find the right way to assure yourself of a job that is congenial and also fits in with the new world in the miraculous age of Aquarius.

Aries:

You enjoy competition and so long as work is not monotonous you can enjoy it, too. You want to take on the big jobs, be supervisor. Before you can do that you have to learn the rudiments, may have to spend quite some time with training. You need to have command of all details of your field, for a supervisor, more than anyone else, must be knowledgeable of every small bit of detail included in a job. You must be able to organize things from the bottom to the top. You'll dote on the machine age, the push-button ease, but you must understand the machinery in every particular. Seek to work in a brand new field.

Taurus:

Your determination to count in the world will lead you to adapt well and to learn what must be learned to cope with the new. Age will not stop you from fitting in with the world ever. Your ideal is to be complete and accurate. You know that you must be realistic and wherever your work is, you will accept the new as it replaces the old. Whether it's the "new math" or the machines used in language training now, you will master the processes necessary to have a meaningful career that fits in. You may well take a course in computer skills and win a high paying position due to your ability to be logical and exact.

Gemini:

You can be a whiz in mastering skills of communication or transportation in this world which keeps very busy with both. It's part of your artistry to be able to learn quickly the demands of the day. You like to be stimulated in your career, so do choose one which keeps your mentality challenged. Ideally you like to have several careers going at once or at least to have a career plus a hobby that may pay off, such as decorating. Be cautious of moving around too much in your career search, for you might not even stay around to learn anything thoroughly if you allow impulses to rule you. Find work so that you may use words, for that is your basic need.

Cancer:

Cancer is threatened with career trouble, for it is not so easy to adapt to the new, and you incline to looking with a grim eye at change which others accept easily. Actually you should have a leading position, for your talents are entirely equal to it. You may do very well in work with food which now has many amazing opportunities in processing. You will work well with furnishings and equipment for home. There are schools springing up all over the country now to help with domestic services and goods, and it would be well for you to embark on a course in one of these. Motel management could be the thing and you'd adapt.

Leo:

You have your eye on leadership from youth on but you might want it all handed to you. This is not because you are not industrious; it is just that your regal nature assumes things will be given to you. You feel people will sense your royalty and ability to manage and thus catapult you into a top position. Not likely to be so! Show your abilities to handle emergencies, whatever your work is. Always get along harmoniously with work associates, and do not display arrogance or an attitude of superiority to them. Keep in mind that those in authority want the best one for each job and that diplomacy with subordinates is a basic requirement for any top job.

Virgo:

You see to it that you have good training and you know that starting with a detail at the bottom is necessary to make a good executive in the long run. Never let yourself get bogged down in a trivial position, though. You will make a marvelous instructor for use of modern machines, and can thrive on the details you must know about them. Get training so that you can set up the machines for their work as well as handle the work itself as it needs. You will always keep control, for your memory will retain work at the bottom of the ladder. Working with words or research, statistics and charts will please you. Fulfill yourself.

Libra:

You want to follow a career that allows you to feel harmonious with many. You can be an excellent boss because you believe in treating all people well and yet have a mind of your own that will control situations. You will do well in personnel management, counselling, public relations. You may have artistry that would fit in well in a decorator shop of your own. You might become head of the advertising department for a large concern and might be window-dresser for a huge store that always keeps beautiful windows as ads. You need to have a bit more willingness to compete; you like too well to stay a bit aloof and need to lessen pride.

Scorpio:

You will not work where any executive does not have your esteem. You like the situation to be one in which you can learn. When you feel you are no longer learning anything, you may change your job or take a business of your own. A partnership is fine for you, if you find the one you have respect for the one who will work along with you. You like to be creative in your work, to feel that you are benefitting the world or its people. You can innovate and lead but you are just as happy in quiet work behind the scenes where you may be directing without the public knowing it. You could be a TV cameraman or director of the performing arts.

Sagittarius:

You're happier the more you feel you are working in the spirit of the day, so what is new attracts you. You will study assiduously to learn the new skills. You want to show expert efficiency, to have all angles of your work very clear in your mind and under your control. You would like a career in writing or teaching, editing or publishing. You are fortunate with Jupiter as your ruler, and you may go to a top job more quickly than others. You might create envy around yourself. Be particularly cautious not to offend your peers or subordinates. You must feel that you can make changes for progress for to you the world moves—daily!

Capricorn:

You will work hard but you want it to count. Everything you do in your career must contribute to some future attainment of the top position. If possible you want your own business, to be able to organize and direct with no one to hinder you. You can be pleased working for the government or for a major firm, if you have a position of leadership. You need a little time to get used to the new and must be patient with these swiftly changing days, and also must keep learning each day. You can teach well, take charge of a large office, be an excellent minister if you will go along with the very young who are changing church practices today.

Aquarius:

You are aspiring rather than ambitious. You want a leading role in ushering in the new age which should bring happiness and love for all. You must get in with a cause or work that will let you feel you are a vital person in the new world that you see coming when old ills are erased for good. You want to see everyone fitted into work perfectly so they will be happy with what they are doing. You want to see payment enough for all to live pleasantly. You may work with labor and accomplish great things. You may have several careers for you do not feel bound to stay with any where progress cannot be made and seen. You may accomplish much with art or invention to brighten the world.

Pisces:

You start in any work rather nebulously, feel your way around in it. Some of the newer machinery may alarm you; on the other hand, you may achieve perfect mastery of machinery if you are attracted to it and you might become an important person in the creation of even newer machines. You may work best for the law, for medicine, perhaps as a medical technician. You will be happy where you are helping people as in welfare work or the peace corps. You collect much knowledge and know that it is to be passed on, so teaching may attract you whether in an academic or trade school. You could be very attached to work in a trade school for it would involve your sympathies.

What the Stars Have to Say About Your Boss

When you go off each day to work, do you find your boss is a joy to work for? Or is he too demanding or quite a tyrant? Perhaps you have not studied his birthsign to learn a bit about him, how to handle him when the going gets rough, or what kind of an atmosphere he needs to have around him. According to Astrology, the Stars line up each boss into one of 12 categories—the 12 sunsigns of the zodiac. Find out where your boss fits, and learn something about him with the following hints.

Aries:

Your Arien boss is a *real* go-getter, moving at a very *fast* pace, and he will expect you to move just as quickly, and to be just as enthusiastic about your work as he is. But it should prove a real joy, for his never-ending pep and enthusiasm can be catching. However, don't expect to loll around; he will never allow that. You have to work, and he will expect you to give your *all*. He won't watch the timeclock to see if you are a mite late, and he should be generous with raises when you deserve it. He'll hire you quickly, point out your errors quickly (with no beating around the bush), and he will fire you just as quickly if you do not live up to his expectations. Show him you are loyal and dedicated; you won't be sorry.

Taurus:

Your gentle, sweet Taurean boss is such a joy to work for, but do learn at least three lessons quickly. *Never* take advantage of his sweet nature by *not* doing your work properly. *Never*, but *never* try his patience by waving a red challenging flag before him, because he'll turn into a raging bull before you realize what has happened, and then it is *too late!* And don't expect to earn more money than you are worth! And remember, too, this guy never forgets anything you do, good or bad, and you can never change his mind about anything once he has made it up. Especially if he has decided to fire you. So give this sweet guy lots of comforting attention, loyalty, and a fair deal. You'll be glad you did!

Gemini:

Your airy Gemini boss will prove to be an education on wheels, as he turns his interest from one project to another faster than you can bat an eye! Be on your toes, quick to catch his moods and changing interests. He can be up in the air today, breezing through with much enthusiasm and, tomorrow, restless, watching every move you make! He doesn't like responsibilities, as a rule, so be ready to carry *many* for him. Do not let him down, and keep his interests going strongly in his work; do not allow it to falter. If you do, that is when he will become quite critical of *you*.

Cancer:

Although your Cancerian boss can be emotional and moody and quite sensitive, he generally is all-business, similar to his polar opposite Capricorn. He will expect you to be neat in appearance, and to keep his office "Home" just as neat and very "comfy" for him. He has a great sense of humor, and can use it at times, but don't count on it. Loyalty is another characteristic you will need, and if you do your homework correctly, with a neat appearance, "comfy" office, loyalty, good work, as well as show your desire to help him make money for himself or his company, your salary will grow and grow and grow! He'll appreciate you greatly!

Leo:

To be a long-time, well-paid employee of a Leo boss, you must be an exceptionally good "listener," as well as a captive audience as he dramatically goes through his working day. Each word and action seems to be embellished with drama or elegance. Be prepared, too, to write his letters for him, and to be able to write *just* what *he* wants you to say without him telling you. If you have any interesting ideas to help him, be sure to tell him for he will appreciate that. And you should love working in the office occupied by this guy, with all its rich, beautiful furnishings.

Virgo:

This boss never misses anything; he will see every mistake you make, and everything out of place as well. He wants his office tidy—everything categorized, labeled and precisely in its place. He is very conscious of minute detail, and will expect you to be. He can be critical if you fall down in your work. He is also very service conscious and will work long hard hours to do his work properly. Many times, he takes on far more work than he can safely handle, so be prepared to assist him in *many facets* of his work.

Libra:

So your boss is a marvelous Libran? And many employees are in love with this gorgeous creature—even *you* a bit? Well, I am certain you enjoy your working day in the environment created by this Libran, a beautiful place, no doubt. However, your Libran tends to sit on the fence when it comes to making decisions, finds it very difficult to make up his mind about an issue. He will take you into his confidence and ask your opinion and this should make you feel somewhat important. You may have to listen and point out all of the points to a question from both sides to help him come to a decision—get off that fence. He may be restless at times, and very active, rushing here and there, but can always manage to communicate volumes with his gentle smile and charming ways! A great boss.

Scorpio:

Your boss may be soft-spoken, creating the appearance that he is easy, but think again! He puts tremendous *power* behind every word, thought, act. He seeks out *all* of your secrets; you might as well tell him from the beginning. Many times he can look directly in your eyes and read all of the secrets you have been trying to keep from him. He is eternally curious about everyone and everything. Always seeking knowledge in some manner. He can be very stubborn however, and you can be sure you will never change his mind when it is made up; and believe me, when he issues an order, you had best obey it! A Four-Star General is he! If he likes you, however, he will go the limit for you!

Sagittarius:

Sagittarius is the frankest, most out-spoken boss in the entire zodiac! One day you will love him dearly for all the nice, honest flattery he has paid you, and another day, you'll be ready to fly the coop when his frankness hits the mark and wounds your pride. When you make an error, you can be certain he will be brutally frank about it, and expect you not to make it again. Don't, by the way, reverse the process and tell him frankly what's wrong with him, for he doesn't want to hear it. He thinks he is just about perfect anyway! But if you can catch his enthusiasm and honesty, do a good job for him, he will surely reward you handsomely!

Capricorn:

Capricorn is one of the greatest organizers in the world; he can sit behind a desk and pull his puppet strings all over the world, in complete harmony with his rhythmic tune! He can handle anything and anybody, though he prefers generally to remain behind the scenes, be the power behind the throne. He wants *complete* organization in his office, and all files, papers, desks neatly kept. He also wants the comforts of home, so you can become his favorite if you can manage to swing into action when he issues an order. If you do, you can find he is a kind, most appreciative fatherly boss!

Aquarius:

Your Aquarian usually doesn't like to be confined behind a desk; he likes to be out doing things, going places. He is completely unpredictable, can make complete changes in *your* routine or office programs and spring them on you quite casually. He is very fixed in nature, so don't expect to change his mind once he makes it up. And he is money-conscious; don't expect a raise from him in salary unless you truly deserve it! But even though he may be odd, changeable or unpredictable, he is generally a true "love" of a person; you should enjoy working for him, especially if you like an unpredictable helter-skelter type of life.

Pisces:

This boss is quiet, and his feelings run very deep. He makes a great manager especially in matters requiring deep concentration or investigation. Don't mistake his quietness and sweetness for lack of discipline, for this guy can smile sweetly at your too-frequent mistakes and walk right into his office, fill out your dismissal notice and silently hand it to you and go on his way! He likes to travel, and will not be averse to taking you along. Give this man loyalty, and much creative attention!

* * *

Perhaps your boss is a composite of more than one sign, but regardless, you should recognize some of his traits. Why not clue yourself in on *your* boss and make both of your lives happier?

ASTROLOGY AND YOUR HOME ENVIRONMENT

Astrological Guide to Home Decorating

How often we have said: "What interesting living quarters. I enjoyed being there but I would never decorate in such a manner." The differences in personal taste are reflected in our homes and our preferences are usually guided by the stars. Astrology tells us that no two people are precisely alike because no two persons can be born at the same time at the same place. Even identical twins are minutes or seconds apart. The tendency to surround oneself with certain colors and styles will help you understand the homes which you visit and may help you select the type of decor best suited for the astrological you.

Aries:

Natives of Aries, a fire sign, are pioneers rather than fashion-followers. They care little about their environment if it makes them happy. They prefer bold warm colors and often mix them with careless free abandon. Furniture and artifacts are often blunt and heavy. You should not be surprised to find iron candlesticks or brass andirons. Because of their driving force, Aries people readily open their homes for political rallies, campaigns, drives and, as host or hostess, unconsciously become the center of attraction.

Among the clan of famous Aries people are Charlie Chaplin, Charlotte Bronte, Albert Einstein, Joan Crawford and Doris Day.

Taurus:

Those born under the sign of Taurus are practical, basic and have a keen eye for the value of money. Their homes are not filled with frills but with things that last. The furniture is solid and meant to be handed down from generation to generation. They search for "bargains" but only good bargains which will endure. Being an earth sign, you can expect a garden and if not that, many house plants which are carefully tended and nurtured. Taureans are especially fond of heavy wood and, being collectors, their homes usually contain wooden bowls, chairs and pictures in wooden frames.

Renowned Taureans include the names of Lionel Barrymore, Celeste Holm, Barbra Streisand.

Gemini:

Gemini, an air sign of the twins, tends to produce people who are alert, eager to travel and revolt against monotonous regularity. These characteristics evince themselves in their environment. They enjoy changing the position of their furniture, collect unusual things which usually have no particular central theme but are interesting or conversation pieces. Theirs is a tendency to discount money if the article fulfills a whim. It has been said that the Gemini personality may be a headache but it is seldom a bore. Their homes reflect this imagination, duplicity and broad interests in many things rather than a deep interest in one.

Outstanding Gemini names are Marilyn Monroe, Sir Lawrence Olivier, Louis Armstrong, John Wayne and President John F. Kennedy.

Cancer:

Those born under the sign of the Crab, a water sign, are referred to as Cancerean or Moon Children. Of all the zodiac these people are usually the most home-living and protective of their family and its sanctity. They tend to be extremely romantic, which shows in their surroundings which are often filled with antiques, dainty laces and frilly curtains. Their choice of color falls into the pastels. The male Moon Child prefers elegance which is not splash and his den is likely filled with perhaps fencing swords and rare old books rather than a case displaying modern rifles and a desk covered with risque magazines.

Famous Moon Children include Anne Morrow Lindberg, Empress Josephine of France, Pearl Buck, Ann Landers and Gina Lollobrigida.

Leo:

The fire sign of the Lion produces strong personalities. Natives of Leo will fight to the death for their homes and those they love but they are not sheltering as are the Moon Children. Their personalities are usually paternal or maternal, showy, and can be melodramatic. This shows in their choice of decor. They prefer furniture that is massive, opulent and regal. Warm colors, gold, red and orange attract them and gold, in addition to its intrinsic value, is their favorite metal, a contrast to Moon Children, who prefer placid silver. They usually entertain lavishly whether they can afford it or not because they want to make themselves happy by making others happy.

Those who are born under the sign of Leo are typified by Jacqueline Kennedy Onassis, Napoleon Bonaparte, Princess Margaret of England, Mata Hari and George Bernard Shaw.

Virgo:

Those born under the sign of the Virgin, an earth sign, are neat, tidy, with a place for everything and everything in its place. Their homes reflect their ability to catalog and to buy only good things which are unbroken and without a flaw. In all likelihood tables will be carefully placed with an ashtray on each so guests will not drop ashes and coasters readily available to avoid marring the furniture. Virgonians decorate their homes in good but modulated taste, preferring blues, greys, sleek easy-to-clean fabrics rather than velvets or chiffon.

Greta Garbo, Ingrid Bergman, Verdi and Leonard Bernstein are on the list of notable Virgonians.

Libra:

Natives of the air sign Libra, the Scales of Justice, are very aware of the needs of others in planning their home or environment. Tactful and peace-loving, they are deeply interested in the artistic side of life which is reflected in the way they live. Their homes are well-arranged, with a good balance between furniture and fixtures, the outdoors and the indoors. Librans enjoy people and often entertain in an informal, sincere way but they are deeply concerned about the comfort of others. Usually natives of Libra prefer cool colors, blue, mauve, purple or soft greys.

Famous Librans are: Grace Kelly and Helen Hayes.

Scorpio:

Those born under the water sign of Scorpio have quick observance and curiosity. They know a good thing when they see it and often find treasures for a small sum at auctions. Their homes, which are important in their lives, reflect these interests. Very often they will carefully unwrap something they cherish just for you to see it but not for the eyes of everyone. The real secrets of the home of a native of Scorpio lie below the outward surface. They are avid do-it-yourselfers and they work painstakingly well. In all probability, since natives of Scorpio are researchers, you will find many books and dictionaries in their homes. By choice they usually prefer paisley prints, quiet but unusual patterned fabrics from which they find a hidden meaning.

The natives of Scorpio, known to most of us, are Voltaire, Mark Twain and Walt Disney.

Sagittarius:

Those born under the fire sign of the archer reflect their interests in their homes which, if they have a choice, are rambling and have room for activities both of an intellectual and physical nature. Their environment likely includes books, maps, things they have collected on hikes or camping trips. The garage may be filled with hunting and fishing equipment. He or she is fond of people and pets but the Sagittarian places living things over and beyond neatness; comfort is more important than style. Their homes are usually a mixture of modes, patterns and eras. Purples, deep blues, woodsy browns and greens usually predominate the scheme.

Sagittarians include Sir Winston Churchill, Mary Martin and Frank Sinatra.

Capricorn:

Those born in this 10th and earth sign of the zodiac are industrious and authoritative. Their environment is usually solid and stolid, featuring family heirlooms and, being time conscious, they usually have a clock of some kind in every room. The Capricorn, whose astrological symbol is the goat, tends to be active outside the home as well as in it. This drive often leads them to have a family room for committee work and community or church activities. In general they are happiest when surrounded by attractive but dark, somber hues.

Noted Capricorns include Benjamin Franklin, Joan of Arc, Charles Dickens and Charles Lindberg.

Aquarius:

Those under the air sign of the waterbearer are independent thinkers, always ready to help others even if it means letting affairs of housekeeping run down. Being thoughtful people, they need a room for their own privacy and their own activities, which are usually many and varied. While they appreciate stately mansions of others, they choose more functional environments for themselves. Neatness is a means of better functioning rather than an end in itself. They are fond of electric blues and bright greens, solid colors to busy prints.

Aquarian names we all know include Abraham Lincoln, Jules Verne, George Washington, John Steinbeck, Eartha Kitt and Tallulah Bankhead.

Pisces:

This water sign of two fish tied together tends to produce people who disregard fads or "tricky" things in their environment. However, their decor is often filled with exotic pieces of furniture or art work. They do not buy bargains just because they are cheap but are pleased when they find something they really need at a low price. They are happiest when they are by the sea or some other place of quiet. Apartment living is not their forte. Their choices of colors are usually muted and natural, with sea green being a favorite.

Famous Pisceans include Elizabeth Taylor, Vincent van Gogh and Casanova.

Cosmic Cues for Home Happiness

There is more accent on the home lately than there has been for some time. So much is this true that many people desire to have a second home—a rural retreat usually—where they can escape from the urban atmosphere, far enough to forget it at least for brief periods.

Many developments have come into existence for the very purpose of providing the chance for a happy hideaway, and these are so popular that they stand in danger of being just another crowded place with all the conveniences of city living.

Your home, whether it be one or two, must answer to your needs and desires. This is the place you like to think of as your castle and in it to show your tastes and reflect your chosen pursuits is desirable. Each Sun Sign has a particular spirit of home which is the particular base of your home-making which you hope will render your ideas and ideals in a fashion to make you and your loved ones happy.

Aries

You have the combined beauty and lived-in ideal for your home. You want the busy spirit of the city or a popular suburb for your home but you also want room to stretch out, to run and shout if you feel like it. Two homes are ideal for you, therefore. Beauty exists for you in the very modern, the shiningly metallic, or a kitchen full of the latest electric marvels.

You want the decor to be bright but lines to be simple. Ornate furnishings will never do. Your spirit is best off in an atmosphere of durable woods, such as oak, especially if you have children. Mars, ruler of your Sign, gives you a liking for bronze and you may want a picturesque display of guns, oriental weapons, military artifacts or such and display them in a special place in a den. You *must* have a rumpus room.

Taurus

Venus rules gives you desire for beauty but of a soft, muted type which will be restful, never harsh. Colors should be somewhat smoky in tone. You will want to make many of the items in your home. You want the best quality but at the least expense. Your home will be comfortable; guests will be at ease in it immediately, for entertaining is a major objective for you.

You will learn to do everything possible yourself; painting, carpentry and even plumbing may come within your money-saving projects for your home. You will be able to repair electrical items, even do some wiring. You prefer a traditional home, one with plenty of space, suburban and without pavements, full of nooks and crannies and interesting architecture.

Gemini

You are adept at home decoration, helpful with your skills to anyone in need of suggestions or aid with their home decor. Yet, you may never settle down in one home simply because so many different types attract you and you like to keep moving around anyhow. Mercury, your ruling planet, gives you a good sense of real estate value, as well as the skill to create a charming home.

Efficiency of home arrangement is a prime consideration with you. You want to be near all kinds of public facilities, too, so your preferred location will be a busy one. Rural scenes don't attract you much, but you do want a neat and unusual garden in which to exercise your talent for creating a lovely scene. You want everything in perfect running conditon and will check for perfection.

Cancer

You are devoted to home, prefer an older building with an air of grandeur, a strong hint of many traditional feasts and parties. You will also lean to a strong consideration of family health when choosing your home. There must be room for exercise, a large and beautiful lawn if possible. You will much prefer furniture that is rare and antique. You are willing to work long hours putting it into good shape.

You will want to entertain much and should have a formal dining room, none of those little cramped corners for dining. A beautiful china closet, perhaps a hutch, is a must for your home. And the kitchen may be the center of attention for much will take place there while excellent meals are being prepared for family and guests. You definitely want to own your own home and make it your castle.

Leo

Appearances mean a lot to you, so your home must look good to all who enter. There must be a sense of both beauty and welcome, plus a tinge of drama through some art work or a collection of fabulous artifacts. All within your home must be well-dressed, for you have pride in the family and this is where it begins, you think. You will entertain frequently and usually with a touch of splendor.

Your home must have a palatial air, be set back from any street and surrounded by gracious lawns, lovely trees. A swimming pool is desirable—a tennis court if possible. You'll be happy in a home that you feel suggests a regal atmosphere and in which your family can be the center of your pride. All who enter will be treated with affectionate esteem and must pay you respect in turn.

Virgo

Your spirit of home happiness demands cooperation from the family in bringing about perfection in every corner and cupboard. The home may be moderate in size and cost, but it must shine with attention and be spotless. All that goes on in your home must follow a sensible pattern and lateness for meals is practically unheard of. You're not lenient with children about such things.

Your home is regarded as an investment, as security, and as a place to express a private desire for perfection. You can become so concentrated on your home that you're in danger of never letting it be really lived-in at all. An ash on the rug, a careless upset of a teacup by a guest can be almost disastrous to you. Your taste is excellent but may be operating in a vacuum.

Libra

You like to have a home which offers a chance for variety, so you can be rearranging furniture, putting up and taking down pictures and plaques, planning and working for a grand piano to give a special look to the place. But you want good times there and above all a sense of love and romance which is unremitting. You'll have artistic taste, in all arrangements.

A large oriel, pleasant dining quarters, a picturesque fireplace can provide the atmosphere you want. You will know just what colors to choose for everything and may bring about unusual effects with drapes, cushions and lovely small tables. Venus is your ruler and gives you a sure hand with beauty, also the affection to cherish guests and make them feel at home.

Scorpio

You want a home that is practical; this includes practicality in price and running it easily. Good quality must be seen in everything and you do not care much for flimsy, light effects but tend to go in for the darker woods and colors—too much perhaps. Your home will mirror some of your own secretiveness and may have many secret shelves, unexpected closets and hidden passageways.

You will watch over expenditures of everything in the home, may be intolerant with loved ones who exceed a budget. More relaxation in this direction may be necessary if you are to hold your home together. Add a touch more of comfort, too, for you tend toward the austere, even the bleakly forbidding in your tastes.

Sagittarius

Jupiter as your ruler makes you desire a home with splendor, spacious rooms in which you can entertain crowds if you wish. You want it a touch formal, but also a bit casual. It must be lived-in and some may even criticize you for not being much of a housekeeper. You're a sporadic one, but don't like to take too much time for cleaning from your busy day.

You want a home near a large city. You don't incline toward the rural. You have so many activities that you need to be near the heart of things, with easy access to the theatres, museums and glamor spots. You're not very domestic. Better hold yourself a little more to regular meals served, particularly if you have children.

Capricorn

You want a home that lacks nothing, yet you don't want things to be costly. You choose locale for prestige, a good outer appearance, land enough to have a pool and tennis court, but you shop around for a bargain and convert some older place instead of buying a new one. Actually you can spend more that way.

You want to make it impressive to entertain the boss, important members of the community, perhaps to make it a center for some community group. Yet you hold cost down, buy such things as used Persian rugs for their grandeur. You are not domestic at heart and your home may show a certain coldness. You want happiness in your home, though, and may create the relationships to make it so.

Aquarius

You're unpredictable about home as about all else. You tend to rent or buy a home on impulse, for some one little thing that pleases you. You will take moderately good care of it. You are somewhat the "sometimes I live in the country, sometimes I live in town" type. People have trouble keeping up with just what your address is at the present.

Style may be lacking in your home, you may mingle unimaginable items of furniture, colors and pieces of art. The most modern and the most traditional combine, sometimes even the primitive ways prevail in your utensils and the like. So long as you feel "at home" you care little what is actually there and somehow you create comfort and peaceful atmosphere for others.

Pisces

Home for your spirit is a place of softness that takes off the hard effects of the world when you retire into its cushioned and draped beauty. Neptune, your ruling planet, gives you a taste for the subdued but comfortable and there is always unique atmosphere in your home. You do ingenious things to make it artful.

You like to make love the theme of your home and to somehow express this in furnishings. There is little formality about the furniture, although you may encourage formality in attitudes of guests due to your quiet, evasive ways. Altogether your home is a unique place, a unique experience for others. You may tend to let it get cluttered for you enjoy many little things around you due to the sense of security they give. You're no housekeeper but somehow the family and guests enjoy the lived-in creation you have achieved.

ASTROLOGICAL HINTS FOR HEALTH AND HAPPINESS

Astrology and Diets

Why is it some people can engage in such delightful pastimes as eating lots of pastries and rich chocolates, while others have only to whiff these enchanting foods and literally seem to gain? This may not be fair, as many will agree, but it does seem to be the way the Stars decree it.

While doctors may point to metabolism, and explain in medical terminology why our enzymes do not convert our food into energy as fast as someone else's, and give us a diet to follow, it just isn't that easy to follow the diet. Many fall short of the goal our doctor has set for us, mostly because we are individuals, and we try to tailor the diets our doctor gives us to fit our individual appetites.

Astrology has some clues as to why we are different, one from another, and while it is not considered an authority, the science of it is being felt and respected more and more every day. There seems to be a cosmic plan, all relating us to sunsigns and the type of energy our sign has given us to burn. If a sign tends to retain water, or doesn't burn energy readily or easily, this sign would find it hard as a rule to lose weight, and very easy to gain. But if a sign burns energy quickly, that sign would be more apt to stay slim.

The cosmic plan for us is aimed at helping us maintain good health, which of course includes staying slim and vital. If we use this cosmic plan wisely we have a tremendous power, all within our subconscious mind, ready to act automatically by giving us suggestions and commands designed to help us maintain a good physical and mental fitness.

To follow this path, it is wise to know and understand our sunsigns, our weaknesses and strengths, and to maintain harmonious thoughts around us as much as possible. Get rid of the negative and take on the positive, for we must first control our minds and emotions *if* we wish to slim or fatten, either one, for our minds control us. However, we should not try to be our own doctor and select our own diet, but should consult first with our own doctor for any health or diet problem we may have. Here are some hints for the sunsigns.

Aries:

With your impulsive nature you burn a great deal of energy, and, as a rule, should not be overweight. Your diet should emphasize wholesome foods that nourish as well as satisfy. Keep away from liquor or tobacco and cut down on the coffee and tea. Avoid bolting your food and try to keep the digestive tract free of distress. Avoid heavy breakfasts—cut it down to 1 or 2 poached or soft-boiled eggs and fresh fruit. Keep lunch light with perhaps a fresh salad, and follow with a good protein meat dinner *minus* potatoes.

Taurus:

You tend toward plumpness for you truly like to eat, especially all of the rich foods and sweets. It is easy for you to gain, hard to lose. Best way for you to lose would be to cut down on the portions of food you eat, and this way you can have your cake and eat it too. Don't eat between meals unless it might be an apple, peach, carrot or piece of celery. Try to eat a good breakfast with 1 or 2 poached or boiled eggs, and some fresh fruit, or you might once in a while have cornflakes with a nice scoop of vanilla ice cream. Lunch should be light with a fresh vegetable salad followed by a good protein dinner. You generally need exercise, as you are prone to sit a lot and the circulation can become sluggish.

Gemini:

You have a nervous, busy temperament, and are rarely overweight. But if you want to lose weight, try cutting out all of your heavy starches, and when you have to nibble, try apples, carrots, celery and raisins. You should really find it easy to diet. However, the best way for you to lose is to find yourself a new interest and voila! Food should become less important to you! You need sufficient rest and relaxation, for you can suffer exhaustion at times if you do not relax enough or get balanced meals. For breakfast, you might have an egg omelet or hard boiled egg, plus some wheat germ coated with honey and skim milk. Try a raw vegetable salad for lunch with some juices, and a good, nourishing protein evening meal.

Cancer:

You are inclined to be emotional, sensitive, moody. You do love to prepare food and to eat it as well, but tend to retain water, as well as gain weight. Nervous stomach upsets can occur due to eating while upset. Avoid, too, emotional food binges. You should exercise better self-control; eat a good breakfast with eggs, fresh fruits. If your doctor agrees, go on a 2 or 3 day liquid diet to try to shrink the stomach. Let sweets and starches alone, and eat lots of fish or seafood, salads made with fresh vegetables, and fresh fruits. Swimming can be a good exercise for, as well as tennis or golf, to gain control of stomach muscles.

Leo:

You are rarely fat, for you burn energy too quickly for that. I do not believe you find it hard to diet, but rather that it is easy. Best to use coffee and cigarettes sparingly since Leo rules the heart. Keep down the calories and get lots of protein, fresh vegetables and fruits. Get fresh air and sunshine, proper exercise. You love the gourmet type of foods and sweets, and you generally eat too fast. Try to slow this down and maintain a healthy well-balanced diet.

Virgo:

You are usually health and diet conscious, so rarely are too fat. But if you wish to lose, try to cut down the portions you eat and leave the table before you are full. Your nerves can make you frustrated at times and send you on a snack binge, sure to add the pounds. Instead of eating the wrong snack foods at these times, be prepared with snacks of celery, carrots, apples, peaches. Have a good breakfast with eggs and fruit, a light lunch of salads and fresh vegetables and a good protein dinner.

Libra:

Due to your desire for pastries and sweets, it is very difficult for you to stick to a diet. You continually say, "Just one more" and always break training. Try reaching for a peach, apple or pear when you have an immense desire for a sweet. Or for breakfast have a melon, wheat germ with honey. For lunch a fancy, fresh vegetable salad could be a delight for you, and for dinner a good protein *meat* meal with fresh vegetables and fruit for dessert. Avoid at least an excess of starches and potatoes. You should drink plenty of water and juices. A balanced diet makes for better harmony within the body. Leave the calorie-laden sweets alone.

Scorpio:

I believe you have all the willpower necessary to go on a diet; all you have to do is *decide* and you can do whatever you decide to do. Use lots of protein—chicken, turkey, fish, eggs, cottage cheese, and fresh vegetables. For dessert fresh fruit is great! You do love *rich* foods and can be quite a gourmet when it comes to preparing or dining on the finest foods. Fruits are necessary for you, and alcoholic beverages should be avoided.

Sagittarius:

You are a fire sign with much energy and drive, yet you do love to eat, especially exotic foods and generally eat quite a lot. Once you decide to diet, though, you should have no trouble sticking with it. Your main problem generally stems from improper circulation, although you have strong recuperative powers. Best for you to decide to begin a new *food* program; learn to eat differently with less calories in the amounts you eat. Chicken, fish, turkey, eggs, cottage cheese, fresh vegetables and fresh fruit for dessert should assist you. Keep a calorie counter handy.

Capricorn:

You do not generally generate much body heat, can be gloomy and depressed at times—all tending to send you on a food binge. Be more optimistic about your life, what you can do. You should organize your diet well, in a business-like manner. But try to maintain a good balanced diet with plenty of fresh vegetables and fresh fruits. Being earthy in nature you generally like a meat and potatoes diet, but should eat lighter, using skim milk, cottage cheese, eggs. Avoid depressive moods that can send you to the cookie jar or ice box!

Aquarius:

Being of a nervous temperament, you tend to like to nibble a lot. Doubt if you can stop this. However, try nibbling on less calorie-filled foods. Try nibbling on carrots, apples, celery, raisins, peaches and pears. Leave off alcoholic drinks, fattening snacks, creamed foods or rich foods. Get out and be more active. You can gain weight easily so you should do your best to limit fattening foods of all kinds. Use more protein, fresh vegetables and fresh fruits. Try some soft boiled eggs for breakfast and fresh fruit. For lunch, fresh vegetable salad, and perhaps some cheese toast; and follow with a good protein meat dinner, leaving off creams, and potatoes. Fresh fruit for dessert.

Pisces:

You do love to eat, and can indulge in a bit of emotional snacking. You are somewhat psychic and retain influences reaching you from others. For this reason, it may be difficult for you to stay on a diet. Try eating chicken, sea foods, fresh vegetables and fresh fruits. Omit all of the rich creams, gravies, sauces, candies, sweets and pastries. For dessert try some fresh fruits, even a banana once in awhile. You need protein foods for energy. You tend to retain water and can gain weight easily. Best for you to avoid tobacco and alcoholic beverages.

* * *

Most of the ills affecting man might well be controlled by the mind, if it were called upon with good positive thinking. Sometimes we retain bad thoughts in our minds too long, and this is negative thinking. It is good to give the subconscious mind the opportunity to promote good thoughts for you as well as good body reactions, consequently, building instead of destroying. This is truly a key to *good health*—maintaining a good mental, emotional and physical response to life. When one is healthy, not *too* fat and not *too* lean, then true happiness can reign!

Revealing Facts About Your Health

Your Sun Sign strengths & weaknesses

The ages have many a story to tell about the determination of people to attain perfect health through some magic or semi-magic means. Some people think that if they ignore trouble it will go away. Others try incantations and various mysterious means of attaining good health. Medical attention of the skilled professional is the source all should turn to, though.

While Astrology does not diagnose or prescribe, it can reveal basic health inclinations which are inherent in your Sun Sign traits. When trouble shows up Astrology urges you to seek a physician quickly.

The following messages sketch out some of the strengths and weaknesses in the health of people according to Sun Sign birth.

Aries

Aries rules the head in the cosmic figure. Your health attentions may be needed most frequently in this region. And of course it is wise to be protective of this area. You may suffer more sinus trouble, frequent headaches, eyes and ears give you cause for complaint. Tension headaches may require a complete change of career and sinus trouble a change of climate.

You are strong in general health, for Mars is your ruling planet and gives you abundant energy and many health advantages. The Ram is your zodiacal emblem and indicates that you may forge ahead in strenuous activities, sports and work. In spite of fine natural health, never get up or return to work too soon after an illness.

Taurus

The throat is your region of greatest concern; it may also be your gift for a career as a singer or lecturer. Protect your neck and throat, but dress them up attractively. Scarves and necklaces will give pleasing effects for you. Venus as your ruler helps you fulfill the promise of a beautiful voice.

Your general health is excellent but make sure all is well with tonsils, glands, other throat conditions. You need B complex vitamins and lots of calcium. Seafood is good for you but you should shun hot and spicy foods. Move your head slowly, not quickly, for you could damage tendons in the throat. Do not remain in places that are damp. Never let a sore throat go without immediate care.

Gemini

Your nervous system, arms and hands along with the respiratory tract are regions of stress for health. You keep going on nervous energy which allows much accomplishment. It can also cause a break down from sheer exhaustion when the momentum lets you down. Eat regularly, avoid snacks, do not drink stimulants which put your nerves more on edge than ever.

You hate to go to bed with illness; you might miss something. But without rest you become subject to emotional troubles, wrought up states. You may develop allergies of a respiratory nature and these could indeed require professional medication. You rush too much and may have accidents for this reason. Dress up your hands and arms attractively; also guard them from machinery and other possible dangers.

Cancer

Body fluids, lymph glands, the digestive process and the stomach are under Cancer rule. You love good food and may overload your digestive system frequently as well as becoming overweight. A diet should be established for you by a good physician. If your stomach is not given proper care, you will suffer from the spleen, liver, kidneys and gall bladder.

Avoid heavy foods, be cautious with alcoholic drinks and stimulants. Stay with the fruit juices. Beef, chicken, fish, liver are meats best suited to your constitution. Never rush with meals or try to eat when under emotional stress. Place your life on an orderly schedule and you'll have good health effects.

Leo

You have exuberant health and vitality but since the heart is Leo's organ of rule, you must guard against any ill to this susceptible region. You have strength and stamina, but strain for the heart can be catastrophic. You need not be out in the air, to be active and pursuing a career which provides this environment is best. Your appetites are lusty, indulge them with restraint.

Keep your life paced evenly, avoid neurotic worries about health, try not to suffer emotional shocks. Tension can be hazardous so do not remain in situations which are conducive to it. Avoid fat in the diet, protect the aorta and all organs connected with digestion. Your blood pressure must remain well adjusted due to its important role with the heart.

Virgo

The intestines are ruled by Virgo and some of the lymph glands. You are vitally interested in health and keep up with the latest news. You may be too prone to take up diet fads which really do you no good. Chances are your work is sedentary, long hours without motion. You can develop colitis easily. Your nerves and emotions can be under strain from rigorous work; too much calcium can cause bursitis, allergies, liver ailments.

Mercury endows you with intellect for your work but makes you tense, also. You can invite much intestinal trouble from tension. In your concern for food avoid too much protein, eggs or an overload of raw greens. Use a lot of vegetables, cooked cereal, fruit juices, chicken, fish, liver and tongue. Vitamin C is beneficial.

Libra

The nerves, emotional channels and the kidneys are the domain of Libra. Therefore ought to be given special attention by you. Feminine sexual organs are linked with Libra through Venus, its ruler. You must have emotional peace, live a well-balanced life. Your health is only moderately good but don't humor yourself too much due to this fact.

If you let emotions prevail they will throw your system off balance, cause depletion of energies, lethargy, true ill health. When you have love and feel secure in it, your health can be steadily good. Avoid rich food, hard liquor, too much raw green salad. Eat protein foods, vegetables, dairy products plentifully.

Scorpio

The organs of birth and sex are associated with Scorpio and tissue destruction and construction also belong under rule of this Sign. Life and death are closely linked with this segment of the Zodiac. You have stout health, unfailing energies. On the debit side you are susceptible to ailments and inflammation of the genitals. Protection for the pelvic region is mandatory.

You can work tirelessly, but emotions can build up to volcanic propensities. You need to keep your health under the careful observation of a physician. Avoid excess in sex, alcohol, food. Make sure you get plenty of vitamin C. Your wisdom will attract you to balance in life and that will maintain high health for you.

Sagittarius

The thighs, sciatic nerve, hips and arteries are the areas of Sagittarius rule. You have a bright and vivacious personality that makes you seem extremely healthy but the fact is you can be quite delicate in health. Also, Jupiter rules the liver and so you must take good care of diet for the sake of this planetary link. You may have arthritis in the hips, can easily fall prey to sciatic nerve injury. You should never be obstinate about seeing a doctor.

If you dose yourself with advertised remedies, you may make matters worse. In a happy environment, feeling affection from friends you can be quite healthy. Eat lightly but intelligently, get moderate exercise but forego the strenuous. Get plenty of rest.

Capricorn

The bone structure, knees, teeth, and functions of the body are under Capricorn and Saturn rule. Your legs may be painful for almost no reason at all. Your nervous system is easily disturbed, you tend to imagine ills and be neurotic. Your moping and melancholy can set up bad relationships with those near you and this goes in a vicious circle to make you melancholy and bitter over again.

Your emotions can keep your health run down. Your posture can slump when you are busy pitying yourself, the bone structure be upset and your entire health pattern adversely affected. The preventive medicine a physician can give may help you much. Keep teeth checked, include calcium in your diet and don't eat under rushed or emotional circumstances. Good health in your case is easily upset.

Aquarius

Legs, calf muscles, Achilles tendon, blood circulation and chemistry are under Aquarius rule. Tension occurs easily, nerves are highly susceptible to shocks. You need to have a blood count taken frequently. Cramps in the legs are a warning sign of blood chemistry trouble, possible lack of calcium.

You are temperamental, may ignore weather, fail to protect yourself. You do not heed health rules and tend to go beyond the limits your nervous system will allow. Uranus keeps you aware when there is real need to see a physician. Never fail to heed such psychic nudges. Make variety in eating and drinking a habit, and don't make a habit of too much of anything. Celery is fine for soothing nerves. Vitamin C is a necessity.

Pisces

The glands, alimentary canal, body fluids and the feet are under Pisces rule. Your feet may swell, edema be present. This threatens coronary troubles. Glands may become infected and need surgical care. You are very emotional, have little or no protection for the emotions. You may go to excess to try to forget your troubles, which only makes more and worse ones.

A psychiatrist may be more helpful than any other type of physician for you. It is also good not to lead a sedentary life. Move around, get exercise; sloth threatens and fat can build up, overweight be dangerous. Never worry about health neurotically. Be sure your shoes are of fine fit. Avoid alcohol and drugs, eat much protein and balance your diet well.

ASTROLOGY AND YOUR LOVE LIFE
The Many Faces of Love

Love is a nun kneeling at her nightly devotions; it's a mother holding her new-born infant. But love also can be a lonely sailor in a foreign city, reaching out for the touch and comfort of some street girl. It is wife greeting tired husband after a long day's work, wife thinking all day as she goes through her interminable chores that soon he will be home and they will find fulfillment together, husband anxiously closing that door against the world as he enters his home because in the arms of this woman, he is hero, a god.

Love can be the basis of sex just as sex often is the means of expressing an overwhelming love that can't be expressed in other ways. Love is the basis of Christianity, and when asked to put all into a nutshell, the Divine Master told his followers: "Love your God with your whole mind, your whole heart, your whole soul. And love your neighbor as yourself."

How simple then is faith, following the Divine Law, for to love should be much easier than to hate. You are following the law when you make your contributions to charitable ventures, when you love the old enough and the poor enough, the children enough to want society to meet their special needs.

Love stimulated by the Sun is love of self, often a form of self-indulgence, but it is also pride in your self, your loved ones, your work, your other achievements. It is the love that makes you a good person, a good citizen, a human being.

Love stimulated by the Moon is a more sensitive, complex, subtle, day-to-day harmonious instinct to be one with your fellow men.

Love stimulated by Mars is aggressive love, cock-sure love, the lust of the male, who must have a female partner, for in this he finds that masculine self-fulfillment he can not find otherwise. Mars-ruled love takes men to the frontier and women are never far behind them. This is a pioneering love, an explorative, investigative love. It is the compulsive sex of young men, love of battle, love of knowing self and of accepting those challenges that help young men know themselves.

Love stimulated by Venus, is radiant, emotional love, bubbling but fragile love, love gone seeking, love in need of response, it is warm, glowing, embering love that is always beautiful. It is very much that enchanting love of a young girl. It is puppy love, but it also can become very possessive love. It is the love that makes everybody glamorize their appearance when they go searching for love and all the happiness it can bring.

Love stimulated by Mercury is very much puppy love, highly creative, the love that wants to help you grow up, the day-to-day affections, the special momentary attachments a youngster can develop for a playmate, a comrade, a cherished friend, a kindred spirit, a schoolmate, and in the presence of this person, one is always young no matter how many years pass between meetings. Love that is sweet, enjoyable between two young boys or two young girls and yet still innocent is ruled by Mercury.

When that love is no longer innocent, Mercury forces are buttressed by star-crossed Pluto and Neptune forces. Then you have the love between the same sexes, some of which can be steady, heart-rending, even beautiful love, but there is never that peace of mind that Mars or Venus might bring.

Love stimulated by Saturn is love of older people, it's love between senior citizens, the love of marriages that surprise people because one or both parties are really up in years. Saturn ruled love is love of traditions, of the Establishment, of what one knows to be right and deserving of love.

Love stimulated by Jupiter is bountiful love, exciting, demanding, compulsive, unusual love. This is the love of the big tycoon for his secretary, the love by which husband and wife make a better team than they do individuals, the marital love on which high success is founded, the wife pushing her husband on to greater glory. It is the love of the older man for the younger woman.

When an older woman loves a younger man, Neptune forces are very much at work. This is exotic, subtle, reclaimed, once lost love. Neptune-ruled love is mysterious, elusive, often evasive, it is mist-aura love, love that can't be explained away, demanding love that wants another chance, that won't take no for an answer this time.

Uranus-ruled love is the new alert to love, the reminder that one doesn't stop loving because the loved one is not present. It is second and third loves, the force that says you never really stop loving, that each can love many others and that under no circumstances was it ordained that you could only love one person in life. Love's reawakening after disappointment, despair, disillusionment is ruled by Uranus.

Pluto-ruled love is love's instincts, love's awareness, that thread within self that makes you attracted to one person and unable to respond to another. Pluto is separative love, discriminating love. A girl on this corner says no to the man, but the girl on the next corner says yes—why? Because Pluto is at work in this discriminating way. Everybody wonders what John really sees in Mary and what Mary sees in John. The special force of Pluto in their charts could explain what the special attraction is and chances are it is something outsiders could not understand or recognize, but John and Mary understand it.

First-House love is love of self, desire to be popular. Second-House love is love of possessions. Third-House love is love of studies, travel, hobbies, creative effort and achievement. Fourth-House love is love of home, family, parents, traditions, ancestors, community, nation. Fifth-House love is love of offspring, love of new friend, somebody you just met today. It is a strongly undeniably creative force, warm, glowing, fiery.

Sixth-House love is love of health, ability, vitality, stamina, love of that feeling of being in control, able to do. It is love of work, the ability to settle down and get a job done.

Seventh-House love is marital love, respect for the contract of marriage, avoidance of infidelity and divorce. Seventh-House love is living up to alliances, contracts, agreements, promises, doing the right thing to which you have committed yourself. It is standing by your word.

Eighth-House love is love of inheritances, riches, and the ability to discipline self so that money is saved. It is love and need of future and long-range security. It is the way you make changes in your life so that you become a more secure person. It is love of those who are dependent on you. It also is a strongly geared sexual pattern that demands new love experiences. Strange you may say that these trends are grouping or lumped under one part of your horoscope, but then through sex and physical experiences one often finds emotional security, or loses it when the Eighth-House is sorely pressured.

Ninth-House is love of long-distance travel, of church, faith, knowledge. It also can be love of larger and beautiful animals.

Tenth-House love is love of God, of Divinity, of the spiritual. It is claiming prestige and status, it is achievement to which you feel entitled, never anything that comes to you in a crooked, unreal, undeserved manner.

Eleventh-House love is love of groups to which you belong, special membership and activities, love of friends. It is the most social type of love, an expansion that takes in many, it is humanitarian endeavor as a way of expressing love.

Twelfth-House love is love of the past, appreciation of self, of latent and dormant talents, of special strengths, of the knowledge of what you can do under attack, under pressure. It is the sense of belonging and needing and loving that feeling.

These are a few of the many faces of love.

How to Rate Your Sex Appeal!

Give yourself an aptitude test to find your sex score

Never belittle the power of your sex! Your ability to use sexuality effectively can win you almost anything—a seat on a crowded bus, a job at the top as supervisor! Every individual has special traits of sex but your Sun Sign shows you the most relevant and probable facts of your own sex potential.

From the following Sun Sign discussions of your characteristics, you can answer to yourself whether you are using them to be a winner or not. You will also receive stimulating advice or hints about making better use of your natural sexual gifts and appeals. Your sex image is traced lightly for you here, see if you can fill it in and make it come alive!

Aries

Mars gives you courage and persistence in winning what you want in the way of a sexual companion. You tend to take what you want, in fact, may just push aside obstacles and competitors quite ruthlessly. You might say with Julius Caesar, "I came, I saw, I conquered!" for that's just what you're capable of doing through use of sex appeal.

You feel capable of any struggle necessary to win what you want. Your radiant health glows, zest of the sexual conquest gleams in your eye. You're a forbidding fact to any who try to oust you in matters of sex. You step in and take charge whether you are man or woman. Romance and sex are your field and you know it. Little chance you need to be told how to use your sex gifts from the stars. Early in life you start perfecting them and using them—sometimes relentlessly.

Taurus

Venus rule gives you an inside place in the sex world, for your nature is very romantic, your sexuality deep and easily felt by others. You are sensuous, no matter how practical and industrious you may seem from a distance. Whether male or female, you were made for love and must have it. You feel you're truly nothing at all until the right person loves you.

Once your sexuality finds an ideal person you will be completely loyal; promiscuity is not for you in spite of your deeply felt sex urges. Your deep emotions give you just as deep an enjoyment of sexual relationship. This begins early in life, but you may not marry early for you are cautious, knowing that you want it all to be love and beauty in marriage—no false starts. You are aware sexually, need little urging.

Gemini

You have a superficially attractive sexual nature and it commences its display early in life with enchanting little messages, obvious little flirtations. As you grow older you make this a little more subtle but not too much so, for really you're not too much interested. Your mentality gets in the way; your need for novelty moves you on from one light love to another.

Mercury gives you ability to handle your sexuality much as you would the kitchen faucet—turning it on and off as it pleases you. You have emotions but not much actual physical desire for sex. You would disappoint one of such a Sign as Taurus if you married, so be cautious in this respect. Romance is delightful to you so long as it is breezy—that's about it!

Cancer

You have a quite deep well of silent sexual emotion from which your appeal rises and may attract many. You tend to regard sex as a rather sacred matter and would never like levity to enter the sexual relationship. The Moon causes your emotions to waver often; sometimes is difficult for the exquisitely gracious Cancer to accept the realities of sex. You need much caution in choice of a lifemate.

Love and sex in the case of Cancer must intertwine to make a charmingly acceptable beauty. Pure sex you tend to regard with a dim and rather shocked view. Don't hang on to outworn notions about sex. Learn more about its facets, bring it more to the surface of your charm if you want true happiness in sex.

Leo

You feel fully in command of your sexuality and like to use it whenever you can to win rewards of any kind for which you have a fancy. Your posture and bearing can make you the very embodiment of sex that shines out like a beacon. You can win many conquests, too many—be wise. It is a good thing that you have a basic desire to be loyal to a chosen lifemate and to be dutiful to a family. Otherwise you might just go drifitng from one sensuouf relationship to another, for you can have just too many opportunities.

It is difficult for people to resist you when you turn on the full sexuality in your eyes. You are dynamic and almost hypnotic in the sex spell you can exert. Also, people of the opposite sex fall for you heavily for you manage to convey the idea that you will be steady and a source of protective security. This can be true if you marry ideally.

Virgo

You tend to ignore and fail to cultivate you sexual nature which is as deep and enthralling as anyone else's. You may ignore anyone seeking to know you better. You can have the idea that sex must be repressed and this is an idea from which you must free yourself. When you let awareness of sex run through you in sensous ways, you can discover a real predilection for sexual ability, find you can attract more than you can handle.

You have a dynamic store of sexual energy and desire; take a look at it honestly. Use it! Dress to bring it out, use cosmetics as a further lure, and by all means have a scent that is subtle but unforgettable. Study up on sex a little! You'll become as efficient in using sex appeal as in adding a column of figures.

Libra

Your appearance may be a delight and suggest sexuality of a natural, healthy type. Your features may be sensuous. You like embraces, kisses, adoration from one attracted to you, and you know how to win all this. But—beyond it you really have little interest. You are not, if typical Libra, a highly sexual person but are one who prefers just the demonstrations of romance in a poetic way.

You want many little acts of love and romance, but very scant actual sexual intercourse. You may be called a "cheat" by some who take your enjoyment of the beginnings of romance to mean you are really fond of sex. Give this some thought and when you attract others don't imagine it will end in nothing—or you'll fail to win happiness in marriage and disappoint lovers constantly.

Scorpio

Scorpio is the sexiest Sign of the Zodiac. Your sensuality reaches depths unthought of by others. You are always serious about sex and it can mar your life when your sexuality is disappointed. You wouldn't be happy with the light or cool type of sexuality in a mate, so be cautious not to marry one to whom sex is not important. When you give your sexual attention, it is forever and it is an act of taking possession. It takes much control to turn off your sexual nature and if you must do so for awhile you can become irritable, entirely belligerent. Emotional and sensual fulfillment are necessary to you and you know it!

Sagittarius

You are an idealistic person in love and do not tend to separate sex from love as some do. You want it all one big package of perfection. Although your disposition is often breezy, you really have an ardent sex nature. You may not let others know about it, but you really rate sex quite high and know your own tendency to be strongly for it. You also tie up mental congeniality with sex and romance. Be cautious in choosing a lifemate, for this person must fulfill all your high demands that go along with sexual happiness for you. You may seem light of speech but underneath this you are searching and testing constantly to find the right person for ideal sexual union. It is difficult to fool Sagittarius in sex.

Capricorn

You are another of the deeply sexed people and this can be unfortunate. Ambitions may be sidetracked when you are in the midst of sexual attraction to someone who does not care about your career. When you are alone your mentality may get busy worrying about sexual trends, being afraid they may dominate and ruin your life. You may try to keep all sex out of your life, turn yourself into an automaton of work and carving out a life of prestige. Your sex appeal is terrific, you'll be unfulfilled if you don't use it. Things may turn to ashes for you if you go after ambition alone, or if you take sex as just an occasional enjoyment. You need to give this matter deep thought.

Aquarius

You take a rather superior view toward sex, may be a walking encyclopedia of knowledge about it but have little actual experience. You prefer to live a mental life and may regard sex as an intrusion. This is, of course, up to you to decide, but if you decide in favor of a love life that includes sex, you have a deep and idealistic source of sensuousness that many may not realize you have. Any time you care to get busy and turn on the sex interest, you may win a conquest of another. Since yours is an Air Sign your sexual nature partakes more of the soaring ecstasy type of experience than of the more earthly type which some Signs know. Your nature in sex is subtle and can be used very artfully when you wish to interest someone of the opposite sex.

Pisces

You present an exotic and mysterious sexual allure. You are languid, tend to invite attentions. If you are masculine you may take delight in causing women to make overtures. Your dreamy disposition can have quite a bit of mischief to it when it comes to sex. It's all so easy for you that you may entice people just to break a few more hearts. However, when you become serious and want to marry, you are very solemn about sex and hold it as a vital part of marriage. Your sexuality is soft and deep, somewhat passive but nonetheless strong. You are just the type to become a dream for many people, for there is quite a bit of the unreal in your charm; you may have beauty which belongs more in the world of art than in the factual world. All of this can bring on sexual arrogance once you know and practice your full sex skill.

Twelve Signs to Married Happiness

Avoid the pitfalls; embrace the benefits

How unfortunate it can be to marry when you are actually in love with someone else, but quite a few people do this—a pitfall to be avoided. Some marry on the rebound, a source of trouble usually. Be sure you are truly ready for marriage before undertaking this step which has problems connected with it. Be sure your emotions and interests are really attached to the one you marry. Motivations that are questionable such as marrying for money or for security create only a dubious chance for marriage and happiness. Be sure that you are willing to face and live through troubles together without losing love for one another. Be sure you can discuss things intelligently together and that emotional flare-ups will not take control in your married life. Suggestions for each of the 12 Signs follow and indicate areas of trouble, areas to stress for benefit and happiness.

Aries

Your ruling planet, Mars, can cause a tendency to tantrums on your part and these can be so childish they endanger marital happiness. Your lifemate cannot work with intelligent good will to create harmony if you insist on yielding to high temper and putting everything on an emotional basis that leads nowhere. Make a point of cultivating mature wisdom, helping to keep in-family harmony and avoid quarrels, spiteful actions, emotional reactions to matters that should be handled mentally. Endure through dull periods, be steadfast, not too changeable in views or too demanding in personal desires. Unselfishness is needed, toning down of your own will.

Taurus

With Venus as your ruler love and marriage are primary needs in your life. If you marry young, remember that people do change with advancing years. There may be adjustments to make as time goes on. You are very concerned with money, might pinch pennies too close for the comfort of your lifemate. You have vast resources of emotional strength and ability to fulfill a lifemate's sexual desires. You want to be proud of lifemate, home, children. Don't regard these just too much as your own possessions. You can be jealous when there is no real basis for it. Cultivate an attitude of granting others their rights with good nature.

Gemini

You may neglect your lifemate for personal interests and activities which are not shared happily. Desire to feel free can cause you to be a sporadic companion, leave your lifemate alone too much. You can be careless about money, spend extravagantly on passing fancies, be too lenient with children and go broke on big installment debts. Mercury makes you volatile in your relationships, your affections tend to waver and alter. Be prepared to face a long future with a loved one or the marriage may self-destruct on your fickle attentions that turn elswhere quickly. Cultivate steady appreciation, deeper affections.

Cancer

You might build up resentments, harbor unhappy emotional trends about a lifemate. You may complain and criticize unreasonably, make the marriage one of tension and unhappiness. You may attempt to change a loved one's entire personality and views. This can lead to an explosion ultimately and much grief. You must honor and love your lifemate's individual nature, cease to fret and feel sorry for yourself if you feel your opinions are slighted. You can view the home as your personal possession, be tyrannical in it. You must look upon material things as mutual possessions, avoid trying to take over the life of another totally.

Leo

Your Sun-ruled disposition makes you tend to take the lead in marriage, want to be consulted about everything, rule the family sternly. You love intensely and will be an excellent parent where provision and protection are concerned, but relax in your attitude to all in your home. You can be full of vanity, demand attention of almost humble type from those around you. Try to outgrow this characteristic enough to share in mature views and discussions of quiet nature. You can maintain radiant romance and joy in marriage when you extend generosity of spirit to those who love you. You are romantic and lovable; stay that way.

Virgo

Be very attentive to the real needs of marriage and don't just concentrate on a meticulous home and neurotic attentions to children's diets, manners, learning and the like. You may have trouble settling into marriage, for you feel you are right about everything and can be officious, coldly despotic and even shut romance out of picture when you get engrossed with other matters connected with home life. Relax and you'll have far fewer problems, far more likelihood of a happy marriage. Do not take a superior attitude toward sexual romance, for this is an essential area of marital happiness; don't downgrade it or you'll lose much, possibly wreck your marriage.

Libra

Venus is your ruler, your Sign is the one always associated with love and marriage. Romance is the breath of life to you and your ideals about it are high, sometimes unreasonably so. You tend to make a lifemate fit into your ideals and when this doesn't work, you may go off in disillusionment to other places to continue your search for love. It isn't easy for you to attain the perfect marriage you desire; the greatest part of the struggle is for you to accept and to value what you have enough to want to keep it instead of just criticizing and demanding. Be sure to check your own capricious moods, avoid selfish whims and bring affection to your view of your lifemate at all times.

Scorpio

Never imagine that sexual compatibility if all there is to marriage. Far from it. Two people may fight like tigers about everything else and get along well sexually. This does not make for a good marriage and break up is almost certain. Sometimes marriage succeeds well with only a minimum of sexual interest and activity. You need a companion who can go with you in intellectual regions. It is necessary for you to value the opinions and views of a lifemate. You must also realize that if you marry the doormat type you will have no esteem for your lifemate and this will defeat happiness in the long run. Do not be tight-mouthed with a lifemate; that way you undermine trust and love itself.

Sagittarius

You are generous and an energetic worker in marriage, full of romantic ideals, wishing to keep all the glamor of the first star-filled night of love. You are proud in marriage, do not like to admit flaws that may exist in it. You can be dismayed if separation is suggested. You like to think that the one to whom you've given your life is perfect and thus you are loyal sometimes to the point of being ridiculous in praise of your lifemate. You have many interests; if your lifemate does not share them there can be trouble. There must be great intelligence in your lifemate or you can feel badly fooled and disillusioned. Exhilarating conversations are necessary for you.

Capricorn

You examine and test out people methodically. You can have many doubts about love and romance; your emotions worry you and make it difficult for you to decide about marrying. You do not tend to look ahead and realize that there will be changing circumstances. You judge purely on the present and can be a harsh judge. You have strong ideas about what a lifemate should be but must recognize that you will never know what this person has in store for you until actual marriage shows up the facts in daily life. Take an honest look at yourself and realize you have flaws. Be just as lenient with a lifemate in the matter of imperfections as you are with yourself.

Aquarius

Your greatest stumbling block to a happy marriage can lie in your absolute independence, insistence on liberty which you take for granted. Your ruling planet, Uranus, keeps you alert to any damage to personal freedom and you can become defiant if you feel oppressed by marital bonds. You simply must heed the fact that there are two people in a marriage and that utter freedom for either one is impossible if marriage is to succeed. Romantic attraction can disappear quickly if there are serious differences and no compromises or attempt to understand and accept each other. If you think children can hold the marriage together, how wrong you are. They increase problems vastly.

Pisces

You let emotions gnaw at you and may build up discontent, take on a nagging tone of personality. Your charm can vanish under such conditions. You may not be very reasonable in your demands, may expect far too much from love. Selfishness can grow and poison your relationship, causing you to see no reason why you can't always have your way in every little thing. There is no place for selfishness in marital happiness and it will be noticed quickly by a lifemate. No one is likely to want to be a martyr to your will and emotional craving to have things all your way. See yourself honestly and correct this trend, use good humor and wit, relax about what you want and don't want.

ASTROLOGICAL HINTS FOR GETTING ALONG BETTER WITH OTHERS

How To Better Understand Your Children

Many pyschiatrists, parents and teachers feel that a knowledge of astrology gives insights in dealing with children—whether their own or those of others. There are no straight lines to be drawn, no astrological rule-of-the-thumb, but each sign of the zodiac which hovers over the birthdate of a child tends to indicate certain characteristics. Wise adults can channel these natal drives for better rather than for worse.

Aries

Those born under the sign of the ram will likely be children who need a loose rein and they will go far with proper guidance. Because natives of Aries have the planet Mars as its ruler, they can be active pioneers and overly aggressive, energetic and impatient, constructive and even cruel.

Their attitude toward life can usually best be defined as "Me first." Therefore adults should not be surprised if he pushes ahead in line or the fact that he wants this or that should not be considered selfishness but part of the child's natal personality. If you find him climbing a tree or walking a fence, this too fits into his scheme.

In most cases, when the tremendous energy of these children is dammed, they become hostile, but when they are given safe and challenging vents to blow off steam, they are creative and untiring.

Taurus

Children born under the sign of the bull have a tendency to be stubborn and possessive. It is best to allow them to have a place of their own for their belongings and the sharing of toys, books, clothing is not a part of their natal scheme. A Taurean child, even at a very early age, would like his own garden—or at least his potted plant which he can care for.

If properly understood, these youngsters are reliable, steadfast and hang on to their friendships like pieces of gold.

Because a Taurean characteristic is hospitality, he may often bring his friends into his home to see what he has. To this end, he may be a bit vain, to wish to keep his hairbrush out of the hands of others and to be neat and tidy at all times.

Gemini

While it is seldom explained even in serious astrology books, natives of Gemini are "handy". It is also said by serious astrologers in Asia that they are ruled by monkeys. Curiosity is a part of a Gemini nature and most children born under this sign want to feel with their hands, make things. Their attention span is short because the next move is more interesting than the last.

With this as a characteristic of the Gemini pattern, keep away from his hands anything that could be dangerous. Encourage reading, looking, and the creative arts.

The Geminian child is usually lively, quick to pick up new ideas and just as quick to toss them down if they bore him. He is easy to teach, provided he is interested. For him "variety is the spice of life."

Cancer

Most of the Moon children are home-loving, affectionate and extremely discriminatory. Home is their Heaven and Heaven is their Home. They are usually highly sensitive. The sense of beauty is a part of their being. There is a tendency to shyness so it helps when a parent goes with the child when he first enrolls in school, be at graduations and, constructively, "push him out of the nest" when the time is right.

The sign of the crab is appropriate for those born under this sign for they seem hard-shelled but are easily hurt under their protective shell. In general they respond best to feelings rather than reason. Their frequent requests to "Tell me a story" should be answered whenever possible because the Cancerian's vivid imagination needs paths on which to wander.

Leo

Children born under this constellation are the first of the Sun signs. Never, if possible, tell, rather suggest, to this child what to do. They tend not to enjoy menial chores and will not be a member of "the group" but a leader. Usually Leonine children are cheerful, bright and charming. They prefer to nap rather than to sleep on a regular schedule. Easily bored with stupidity, they will knuckle down under responsibility.

The tendency to be "bossy" with other children should be gently restrained but not killed. He should be directed into activities where he can "show-off" in a positive manner.

Generous by nature, the child of Leo will quite literally "give the shirt off his back." This is not to buy friendship but simply because he likes to give.

Virgo

As a child, the Virgo will be lively, busy and ready to do little tasks. There is a tendency for them to be shy so they do not seek the limelight. Both at home and at school natives of Virgo are happiest when expressing themselves in some creative way—with words, drawing, painting, making things or working in a garden.

The true Virgo nature is a purist. At school their work is usually neat and tidy. At home they take readily to picking up their toys and keeping their room in order. Don't be surprised if they constantly pester their parents for clean clothing, a new dress or trousers. Because of their inborn drive for cleanliness and perfection, your Virgo child will probably not be the "snuggly" type and their teachers should avoid such gestures of approval as patting them on the head.

Libra

While the Aries child thinks in terms of "me-first," the child born under the sign of Libra seeks out unison, harmony and partnership. With Venus as their ruler, they tend to use their charm and, if permitted, will exploit their parents and teachers. He is rarely rude or rough and is probably the most popular child in the zodiac.

Because those born during this period have a great sense of fairness, parents and teachers should not be surprised if he resents unjust accusations or punishments which he thinks are undeserved. He responds more to praise and affection than to sternness.

Scorpio

Children born under this sign burn with energy and it is often noted that they, along with the Leo children, are the most active and tireless of the zodiac. Their ability to search for what is hidden makes it wise *not* to be disappointed or surprised if he finds his birthday present ahead of time when you think you did a masterful job of putting it out of reach.

This tendency is of great value to teachers who can guide this characteristic into research projects such as science, minerology, oceanography. It is wise for adults around him to recognize that he is deeply emotional, can be easily hurt, and like the Water sign itself, is the type best described by the well-worn statement "Still water runs deep."

Sagittarius

Children born under this sign are usually alert, good at games and usually athletic. In early days of astrology the sign of Sagittarius was a strange animal—the head and torso of a man, arrow and bow in hand, with the body of a horse. As a child he may tend to be overly-jovial, overly-expansive, a prankster. However, when a parent or teacher attempts to curb his native drives, he can become sulky and ill-tempered. He should be given means of letting off his exuberance, especially in outdoor physical activities.

Sagittarians are usually not only intelligent but intellectual. These children can rapidly learn facts but often drive adults frantic with their constant question "why?"

Capricorn

Capricorn children seem to take life more seriously than those of other signs. When scolded or left with a feeling of failure they can become despondent, stubborn and morose. With proper guidance, he is practical, cautious, responsible and ambitious. Being an Earth sign and ruled by the planet Saturn, natives of this tenth sign of the zodiac are often likely to make "heavy weather" of life and to live solemnly.

Given encouragement, he will unleash his desires to "get somewhere." He will constantly aspire to higher and higher positions. A Capricorn will be highly popular by some and highly disliked by others.

Aquarius

The predominately Aquarian child is freedom-loving or obstinately disobedient, original and independent. With disruptive Uranus as his ruling planet, parents and teachers may find that he sometimes is a trouble-maker but they should understand that, in most cases, he is merely trying to find a better way of doing or thinking about a subject. He will have inventive ideas and is quick to see the solution to a problem especially those of a mechanical nature.

The Aquarian develops best when his natural urges can be safely expressed. Therefore he functions at his top ability away from mental, scholastic or personal restrictions of a hidebound or conventional nature.

It is of little use to make an emotional appeal to an unemotional aloof child, but once his *heart* is won, he will be a sincere friend.

Pisces

Children born under the sign of Pisces are usually gentle and cuddlesome. Being overly- emotional and overly-sensitive, parents and teachers should make allowances for floods of tears which come easily for these youngsters. The sign of Pisces is predominant in the charts of most great painters, poets, musicians and artists who create in moments of inspiration. The same is true with scientists who, in a dream or while waking, get the solution to a problem which has eluded them.

With these characteristics, teachers and parents should encourage, rather reprove, when a Piscean child tells long and perhaps implausible accounts of his dreams. These dreams sometimes take the form of "really-truly" stories which are not "lies" but a natural tendency of a Piscean to "up in the clouds."

Bridging The Generation Gap
The Bridge is Over Your Solar 7th House

From time immemorial, adolescent people have rebelled against parental and government authority. They have been cocksure that given the chance they could instantaneously create a better society. They conclude early in life that they know more than their parents. In this sense, then, there always is a so-called generation gap.

Every adult realizes that he learned the most important lessons of life the hard way—through experience. The theories given to him by highblown professors in classrooms were interesting; out in life, such theories run into all forms of natural opposition and unless one goes around with a gun and ignores the rights of others, the theories are rarely workable. People as they grow older become more like buckwheat than like Biblical wheat. They learn the value of compromise, they learn a lot about the rights of their neighbors through having neighbors. Children and those on the sunny side of 30 have yet to learn these lessons. So, there is a fantastic difference between the older generation and the up-and-coming youngsters.

Aries
Bridge the generation gap by opening your mind to ideas that go counter to what you really believe. Listen to the advice that is available to you through marriage and business partners. Don't lose your temper with youngsters until you have the whole story. Don't give up on the set ways of older people until you understand how they arrived at them. People are not just spontaneous critters, who automatically know what is right and wrong. They learn these truths only by living. Through Oriental philosophies, you can find the golden keys that unlock understanding.

Taurus
Bridge the generation gap through generosity and through showing that you can make up your mind and adhere to it through thick and thin. Be less possessive of younger and older relatives. Accept Feuchwanger's theory that each generation says: "Sleep in peace, Father; I shall be different from You." Ponder this idea, cogitate on it and you will come into greater understanding of those who are coming after you and seeking the reins of leadership you hold in your hands.

Gemini
Bridge the generation gap through spending greater amounts of time out of doors, with the baffling generation. Don't let youngsters believe you are in total agreement with them just because you agree with many of their basic ideals. Discuss at length how you personally arrived at a more conservative approach toward life and why this is necessary if the race and Earth are to survive. The more you rap with youngsters, the better your opportunities for coming to a more generous understanding. Give and take is a wonderful route.

Cancer
The bridge to greater understanding of the younger generation is in your case Saturn ruled. Stick to what you really believe and the younger generation will respect you. Even if they don't agree with your ideals, they will admire the way you adhere to them. Support law and order as the basis of civilization and do not depart one iota because youngsters would have you respect only certain laws and flagrantly violate those you don't particularly like. You have enormous power for setting a good example for the young.

Leo
Much of the above advice also applies to Leo. But your bridge to understanding the younger generation is Uranus ruled. You are in a good position to groove and rap with kids because one side of you remains forever youthful. You know when and how you fell into settled ways and more importantly why. Let the kids know your story. Show how your generation acted and reacted to the philosophies of those who were the managerial generation when you were a student.

Virgo
The bridge to understanding the young in the case of Virgo people is Neptune ruled. Youngsters have great allure for you. But it often is difficult to understand their rebellion because you are by nature the last who could ever become an anarchist. But weren't you rather rebellious when you were young? And many of these commune ideas, these desires to be self-sufficient, outside the Establishment are in truth Virgo-Mercury ruled. Like the young, you too once wanted more of a return to Nature, to the Natural, and you can spurn many of the so-called advances of your generation that in your mind really set the natural back.

Libra
You should have less difficulty than many parents in bridging the so-called generation gap, because Libra is by nature the Cosmic Bridge between East and West, Oriental and Occidental, between male and female, right and wrong, day and night, and between one generation and another generation. You have strong drive to create bridges of understanding in everything. You have enormous Mars-ruled powers for instigation and for beginning programs that bring warring and feuding factions together. Your bridge is the bridge of peace. It calls for honest exchanges between both groups.

Scorpio
You do not take the generation gap as seriously as most solar groups. Probably because you are by nature one that expects each generation to be different. If you do not bridge the gap well in working matters, in political philosophy, nobody can bridge it so well in love, sex, in bed than can Scorpio. You find much to admire in the younger group and you like to be

their teacher, especially in things physical. Beyond this, you have the potential for being their teacher in just about everything else. Love bridges the gap, for, in your case, the bridge is ruled by Venus.

Sagittarius

Your bridge to the younger generation is Mercury ruled, and this gives you many advantages. Mercury rules students and youths in general. You have special insight into what youngsters really want and often it is greater discipline from older people. More than most, you realize the disadvantages of growing up in a permissive society. Nobody knows how to vocally apply chastisement better than you. You have great cosmic ability for bridging the generation gap through talk.

Capricorn

Your bridge to understanding the younger generation is Moon ruled. You have great sensitivity to when the younger generation requires parental and adult guidance and when they deserve to be pulled up short for their offenses against society and civilization. More than most, you realize how thin is the fabric and veneer of civilization and you excel in showing youngsters that they may pull down some institution that existed more to protect them than to harass them. Youngsters, who cry against the police, have great need of police protection when they talk out of turn before the angry adults of today.

Aquarius

Your bridge to understanding the younger generation is Sun ruled. Because of this, you make a good parent, and you have enormous ability to sacrifice self in the interest of the inexperienced. You lead, inspire and encourage younger people better than most. You're a life long searcher for the ultimate in freedom and independence and few can explain to youngsters that the very technology of the times detracts from personal liberties more than you can. You can explain the basis of society and civilization to others.

Pisces

Your bridge to understanding the younger generation is Mercury ruled. This puts you in good position to bend, adjust, and come quite close to such understanding. You understand the spirit of the times, thanks to Neptune trends near your natal Sun. You can interpret for other adults just what it is these youngsters are complaining about, what it is they want from society and from life. You are a good viewer of the scene, a good recorder, and you have enormous sympathy for idealists who are in the last defense of ideals before their next birthday makes them an adult, mature, less idealistic, more experienced, more knowing.

Relating To Other People

There Are People You Automatically Groove With, Others Who Turn You Off

The explanation for your ability or your failures in the matter of relating to other people is in your horoscope and in the mathematical and psychological analysis of your Sun Sign and the favorable aspects or adverse strictures existing between your Sun and the Sun of those with whom you are attempting to relate.

There is nothing mysterious here. Everybody you meet can be represented in your own horoscope. They fit into one of your Twelve Angles. People who fit into your solar 1st House, for instance, share many of your assets and liabilities, those who fit into your solar 2nd House can relate to you financially at least. You are going to relate more to a sibling who shows up in your solar 3rd House than to one who shows up in your solar 12th House.

When your Sun is sextile or in trine position with the Sun of another person, you can groove instantly. But you will find rapping with somebody whose Sun is in your solar 7th, 4th, or solar 10th House rather difficult.

The following messages will give you basic pointers.

Aries

You are attracted to Libra because opposites do attract. You relate quite easily to Gemini, Leo, Sagittarius, and Aquarius people. You will find the going rough with those whose Sun is in Cancer and Capricorn. There's financial relativity with Taurus, good co-worker potential with Virgo, a security motif with Scorpio. In a sense, it is Pisces who can undo you and upset your apple cart. You are one of those who will form lasting impressions upon first meeting. It is difficult to get you to change your mind once it is made up about a person.

Taurus

You empathize with Scorpio for despite the vast difference between you and this dynamic Water Sign Scorpio, there will be a kind of love at first sight attraction. You relate well to Cancer, Virgo, Capricorn and Pisces people. Gemini is something of a mystery but can make a good financial contribution to your life. With Leo, the sparks can fly, particularly if you live under the same roof. You work all right with Sagittarius. You can know some envy of the unrestricted Aquarius and this is returned in equal measure.

Gemini

You polarize with Sagittarius the attraction is there, it vocalizes, it brings problems. You are at your best with Libra and Aquarius, at your worst with Virgo, Capricorn, and Pisces. The effort to relate to Cancer is often not quite worth

Astrology, Horoscope, and Dreams

it. You relate beautifully to Leo and Aries. You do change your opinions about people as you get to know them better, and being a highly social as well as intellectual being, you work overtime to come to some community of interest even with those who don't like you.

Cancer

You automatically groove with Scorpio and Pisces, who share your Water Element base of personality and character. You polarize with Capricorn and despite all the differences, there is common desire for effort and achievement. You are turned off by Libra and Aries. With Leo, there is the possibility of a fiery exchange and of joint achievement financially. You do well in any relationship with Taurus and Virgo.

Leo

You polarize with Aquarius, and can find great happiness over the long pull of time. There is a love-at-first-sight attraction between you and Aquarius. You are at your worst trying to relate to Taurus and Scorpio. You groove well with Gemini and Libra. Your closest sibling is usually somebody with Sun in Libra. Nobody extends self as much as the Leo-born father to groove with his sons, but he usually has more success in an attachment for the oldest daughter.

Virgo

You can relate to Pisces over the long pull of time although at first glance, you two seem to have nothing in common. You are attracted to Pisces because this Sign is so different. You relate well to Cancer and Scorpio. You are at your best with Taurus and Capricorn, at your worst with Gemini and Sagittarius. You financial association with Libra can go far and produce for both of you.

Libra

With Aries, there is automatic and instantaneous attraction, because the two of you are complete opposites. Where this relationship will end up is always anybody's guess. You relate beautifully to Gemini and Aquarius, almost as well with Leo and Sagittarius. You are at your worst with Cancer and Capricorn. Closest sibling over the long pull of time will turn out to be Sagittarius or one with a strong Jupiter trend in his or her chart.

Scorpio

With Taurus, there is a strong possibility of one of those up and down simmering love relationships. You relate well with Cancer and Pisces, who share your Water Element base of personality and character. You also groove with Virgo and Capricorn. You are at your worst attempting to groove and rap with Leo and Aquarius. There's a brotherly affection for Capricorn. There can be favorite teachers and employers all along the way, but Scorpio women do not like to work for men who know less then they do.

Sagittarius

You can have a strange attraction for Gemini throughout life without ever really understanding what this is all about. You work well together, you talk well together, but there is a big void just the same and marriage to Gemini always will present many problems for Sagittarius. You are at your best with Aries, Libra, Leo, another Sagittarius, and Aquarius. With Pisces, there are problems and hangups but initial attraction. You are at your worst with Virgo, with in-laws, and with staid, critical, ultra conservative people.

Capricorn

You harmonize with Cancer and this relationship usually works out well over the long pull of time. You find another Capricorn competitive and boring. You are at your best with Taurus and Virgo people, who share your Earth Element base of personality and character. You are at your worst with Aries and Libra. Leo can give you strange security, so can your father, and older men generally. You are exceptionally loyal to those for whom you work and will bend over backwards in an effort to rap effectively with them. With Gemini and Sagittarius, there is little empathy.

Aquarius

You are drawn to Leo and this association can lead to something worthwhile after an initial setback or several misunderstandings. You are at your best with Gemini and Libra, who share your Air Sign base of personality and character. You don't do well with Capricorn, Pisces, and especially with Taurus and Scorpio people. There's a sharing of a humanitarian bent with Pisces. Capricorn can ultimately undo you. Your favorite sibling and the one you are closest to in life will turn out to be an Aries or a Mars-ruled brother. With Sagittarius, you can groove instantly.

Pisces

You polarize with Virgo and this association after many initial setbacks can turn into something valuable for both of you. You are at your worst with Gemini and you find Sagittarius elusive, high flying and difficult at times. You are at your best with Cancer and Scorpio, who share your Water Element base of personality. You can groove well with Taurus and Capricorn. You tend to be more suspicious of Gemini and even of Sagittarius than you should be. You sense great attraction for these Signs and you don't want to admit it.

Astrology, Horoscope, and Dreams

Your Friendship Guide

What to Expect From Your Friends

Myth and literature always occupied themselves much with friendship. Castor and Pollux are a well known pair from Greek myth. Cicero and many others have written philosophically about friendship. Only the cynics denied any value to friendship. A poet of our time, John Masefield, proclaimed that friends make darkness bright.

The Sign Aquarius rules friendship, and this is an indication that you must accept your friends as they are and be loyal to them even when their independence seems a bit too much for you to approve. Friendship must be enjoyed as a voluntary concern.

Astrology allows you to know facts about each person in the variety of your friendships. Their horoscopes, Sun Signs, show you their traits and faults which you need to be philosophical about. The following twelve messages may help you a great deal in understanding your friends and thus making association more pleasant and harmonious.

Aries

Rely on your Aries friend when something needs to be done quickly. They will plunge in, help and complete things in a hurry. They are generous and sincere of spirit. Yet, you may find this friend impulsively taking unsound risks. They need self-control to check their impetuous activity. Be very diplomatic if you want to help an Aries friend win this control. You will enjoy the optimistic nature of Aries, find that it often lifts you from the doldrums. Joy in living is part of the nature of your Aries friend and this can often lift you into enthusiasm when you have been tired and bored. Aries is a spark for your life.

Taurus

The friend of Taurus birth likes to share sports, good food and good talk with you. You find the person and environment of this friend lovely and soothing. Wonderful advice can come your way, particularly in money and other practical concerns, from this friend. Taurus is one of the most staunch friends, loyal to the last degree. There is a tendency to appreciate wealth and social prestige, so you might occasionally find a bit of snobbery in this friend. You will also find an obstinate nature for Taurus makes plans and doesn't give them up. If obstacles appear this person can be irritable.

Gemini

You will admire the versatile artistry of your Gemini friends. It seems there is literally nothing that such a friend can't do. They'll help you out with problems that require clever good taste, will enjoy aiding in choice of clothes or home decoration. Such a friend is eloquent; watch out you do not get into something that is against the grain for you just due to the persuasive speech of a Gemini friend. You have a wonderful travel companion in a Gemini friend who will step up your appreciation of new sights and experiences. You may become weary of the ceaseless change your Gemini friend seeks; you may cleverly help this nature be more serene and steady.

Cancer

The most gentle and affectionate of your friends may be born under Cancer. There is intense loyalty and you can expect to be defended when need be by this person who holds on to ideals and high values perpetually. The longer you have known your Cancer friend, the more you are valued; you indeed become part of the life of this person. Sometimes Cancer holds on to traditional beliefs when it is not advantageous. You can encounter a silent obstinacy in your friends of Cancer birth at such times. You may show your loyal affection to a Cancer friend when troubles and worries come. Sincere encouragement may lift this friend from gloom.

Leo

The Sign Leo also represents another of the most loyal friendships you'll ever know. This friend will be a source of inspiration when courage is needed, and you will find that whenever you are in real need the generosity of this friend is right on the spot to help in realistic ways. Show your admiration for the talents and appearance of a Leo friend; these people need a certain amount of ego boosting and the feeling that they're being observed. However, never try to do this insincerely for Leo is very sensitive and you can't deceive in this way. You may get excellent, objective advice from a Leo friend who will enjoy being consulted often.

Virgo

Be straightforward and honest in all you say to Virgo and you will find a trust-worthy friend who will stop at nothing to help you when you're in need. Mercury gives the Virgo personality much alert intelligence and ability to see flaws easily. You can expect some constructive criticism from such a friend. Be patient with it, but if it becomes too constant show your displeasure in an honest way. You may help decrease Virgo's tendency to be too critical. Appreciate your Virgo friend, help restore optimism when gloom arrives from seeing the many flaws in the world. You'll find an excellent, prudent mind in this friend.

Libra

Your Libra friend will enjoy your companionship when you are a good conversation-alist, also when you are affectionate and do many little things to show affection. Be a good listener, too, for Libra likes to talk and to advise, feeling instinctive good judgment possible on almost any matter. Your Libra friend may point out other angles in problems and troublesome situations, may even sometimes find you sharing the blame where you think only another is guilty. Learn to accept this all-around view of Libra thought. Libra will soon come to your aid when troubles besiege, so build up a loyal and affectionate relationship here.

Scorpio

This friend is a worker, a realist, courageous and determined. Never imagine you can sway this Scorpio friend, for the Scorpio mind is highly independent and rules his or her own life totally, may even try to rule yours. The Scorpio person may work in solitude but when work is done wants some glittering social life. You'll need to get accustomed to the outbursts of Scorpio which can be highly sarcastic or ironic, sometimes painfully outspoken. Try to avoid argument with your Scorpio friend. You will gain much of value from association with this dynamic person of high intelligence; avoid vexation, be patient, develop a deep understanding.

Sagittarius

Your Sagittarius friend enjoys your appreciation of the many things generously done for you. This friend will find unique ways to be helpful and will enjoy giving unique gifts. Admire the idealism of this honest person and respect the love for learning and discussion of deep philosophical problems, for your friend of Sagittarius likes conversation based on abstract matters, the spirit, the occult. Here is the friend who will know the exact touch to bring you out of your depression, help you to fulfillment of your talents and show loyalty which cannot be topped. Accept an occasional temper spell with good nature.

Capricorn

Capricorn will be a reliable friend. It is not very easy to become one of the inner circle of Capricorn's friends but you can make it if you show practicality, love for conventions and good behavior, and are always mannerly. Capricorn is quite a stiff judge and will want friends who are serious workers, will steer away from much pleasure-seeking. If you are radical in thoughts and inclination, you can just forget Capricorn—you'll never make a real friend from that Sign if you are non-conformist. If you do develop a friendship with Capricorn you'll need to be helpful, dependable and preferably someone who is a very solid citizen indeed.

Aquarius

Here is the very spirit of friendliness. The friend from Aquarius is honorable about keeping promises and expects you to be. This is *the* unpredictable one among your friends. It may also be the radical one, the friend to accept or even comprehend. However, Aquarius will value you as an individual, even when in disagreement with you will acknowledge your full right to your opinions. The Aquarius friend is almost totally forgiving and may expect you to be, too. Sometimes Aquarius may seem intolerant, but when you show you can forgive even so, Aquarius is your friend for life.

Pisces

The mental pattern and intuitive sense of your Pisces friend always keep working. No matter what you are talking about, you can be sure there is a type of inner dialogue going on in deep secret of Pisces own brand. The Pisces friend can help solve your problems due to the gift of psychic insight. Peace and harmony must be obvious in your relationship; honesty and freedom from petty matters must also be present in your nature if you are to win this friend's confidence. You may sometimes be astounded at a sudden emotional eruption which is entirely unjustified. Pisces lets imagination build up and no matter how wrong it is may become wrought up over nothing.

Astrology, Horoscope, and Dreams

NUMEROLOGY: THE SCIENCE OF NUMBERS
Overview and History

A brief look into the past reveals that the ancients were much preoccupied with the study and workings of symbolism, particularly in areas of astrology and numerology. A search of ancient writings—the scrolls, texts and the like—of the ancient Chinese, Hindus, Hebrews, Greeks, and Egyptians makes this obvious.

From the Greeks there was Pythagoras of Samos, about 600 B.C. He is generally credited with being the father of numbers and mathematics. Pythagoras had an elite school; only the chosen few were allowed to attend. Perhaps this restriction was related to the establishment of a brotherhood in which the metaphysical mysteries of life were revealed to these select students. Some of the mysteries were explained through the symbolism and use of numbers. Pythagoras is credited with first saying, "All things have form, and all forms can be defined by number." For the scientific student there is a note of sadness, however, because no known physical records of his teachings have been found. One can only guess as to the authenticity of his teachings and philosophies.

For the serious student the most exciting and perhaps most convincing account to the merit of numbers may be found in a careful reading of the Holy Bible. The Bible is rich in number references, starting with the book of Genesis and continuing throughout to Revelations. Psalm 90, for example, says:

"Teach us to number our days so that we may apply our hearts in wisdom."

An extensive search in the reading of the late clairvoyant Edgar Cayce will tell of many occasions where numbers were used for signs, signals, and omens to point the way toward a better universal understanding. Cayce is probably the world's most accurately-and completely-recorded mystic.

The modern era has also produced "Cheiro," Count Louis Hamon, who spent a lifetime in seeking out these truths. He was world traveled and spent much time in India, where the Brahmin sect welcomed him and gave him their secrets. His approach to numbers is far different from the use that Edgar Cayce gave, yet the learning from both sources gives one insight and understanding.

The word, *numerology,* according to Webster, simply means "a system of occultism built around numbers, especially those giving birthdates, those which are the sum of the letters in one's name, etc.; divination by number."

The word *numerology* is derived from the Latin *numerus* (number) and the Greek *logos* (word).

From a study of numerology one will learn that throughout our entire universe all forces are moving and are in vibration. These vibrations can be defined or expressed and communicated through the language of numbers. In essence, there are nine elemental descriptions symbolized through the use of the numbers one through nine. Each compound set of digits also holds a particular meaning. Reference to this fact is found in passages of the Bible and in the Kabbalah. Yet, within the frequency of one through nine, all that is manifest, all that is thought, abstract or concrete, negative or positive, may be explained.

The concept of good and evil, positive or negative, is the most simplified attempt at universal understanding. It is the basic approach to atomic structure as well as to principles of morality, religion, and social order.

Each of these nine basic numbers represent the following:

One	Aspects of creation and the self
Two	The principle of gestation and union
Three	All aspects of self expression
Four	Self discipline, creative direction
Five	Recreation and changes in cycles of activity
Six	Aspects of social consciousness
Seven	Intellectual and spiritual development
Eight	Principles of material accomplishment
Nine	Selflessness and universal awareness

To apply these meanings, letters must first be translated into numerical values. This alphabet is shown as recommended by the Cayce readings. It is also the most commonly used alphabet.

1	2	3	4	5	6	7	8	9
A	B	C	D	E	F	G	H	I
J	K	L	M	N	O	P	Q	R
S	T	U	V	W	X	Y	Z	

Astrology, Horoscope, and Dreams

In the ancient Chaldean alphabet, nine was considered to be sacred; therefore, it was not used. "The Highest Sphere," nine, represented the nine-lettered word of God. An adaptation of that ancient alphabet is shown here.

1	2	3	4	5	6	7	8
A	B	C	D	E	U	O	F
I	K	G	M	H	V	Z	P
J	R	L	T	N	W		
Q		S		X			
Y							

Some numerologists say that the letter *K* has a value of eleven and the letter *V* has a value of twenty-two. They consider that the more master numbers found, the more profound are past life experiences of the person. Eleven, twenty-two, thirty-three—numbers compounded by eleven—are said to be master numbers.

A further division of basic numbers is based on whether or not they are odd or even. The odd numbers—1, 3, 5, 7, 9, 11—tend to be related to thoughts and ideas. They are *active* in nature.

The even numbers—2, 4, 6, 8, 22—tend to be related to practical realities and are sometimes passive in nature.

In analyzing, once the number values have been listed, a brief explanation of numerology is needed. In briefest form, there are four parts which must be considered. They are: destiny; subconscious self; conscious self; and inspiration. These four are found by the added total numbers of various components of the person's name and birthdate. In simple chart form, they line up as follows:

1. Total of Month, Day, Year = DESTINY
   This number gives the analyst the birth path and birth force and shows what the soul came to earth to accomplish.
2. Total of Vowels in the Name = SUBCONSCIOUS SELF
   This number gives the soul urge, the motivation, and thus gives the basic motivating forces.
3. Total of the Consonants in the Name = CONSCIOUS SELF
   These letters recount impressions, outer self, and fantasy side of the person. The total number shows what you dream about and how you impress others.
4. Total of the Complete Name = INSPIRATION
   The expression of self is shown by this total number. It determines, along with the Destiny number, the person's vocation. It is the key to the person's abilities as well as an indication of the soul's grade level.

When a chart is made in numerology, showing all the numbers and total numbers present in an individual's name and birthdate, some numbers sometimes are not present anywhere in the chart. These missing numbers are very significant and point to areas where the subject should cultivate and expand those missing qualities.

These missing elements are:

1. Friendliness; interest in individuals
2. Strength for decisions
3. Concentration; self expression
4. Broader viewpoint; ability to organize a firm foundation
5. Patience; purpose of mind
6. Balance in emotions; less personal attitude
7. Ability to avoid fear
8. Tolerance; fairness
9. Emotional control; balance

Individuals who have more odd numbers in their basic numbers are usually inspirational, spiritual, artistic, and intuitive. Individuals who have more even numbers are practical, analytical, self-reliant, materialistic, skeptical of psychical truths, and they reason by intellect alone.

Basic Numbers and Their Meanings

One

Each of the basic numbers will be considered here separately.

Key word — Ambition

One is: Sunday
    Masculine in its expression
    Positive and mental
    Its element is fire.

A One person must:
    learn to become independent in thought and action
    learn tolerance of others, their opinions and their feelings
    broaden their outlook and be more progressive
    lose their pride in the personal ego

One's spiritual lesson for Destiny is: Unity with God.

Positive Vibrations
One gives originality in thought and action, mechanical ability, quickness in all things, ability to take command and make decisions, is personified in the pioneer spirit.

Negative Vibrations
Aggression, laziness, stubbornness, arrogance, and too much independence characterize the negative side of One. The destructive side of the One vibration is *dominance*.

One rules the head.

One's dominant characteristic is aggression.

Best vocations for individuals with a One vibration are: pioneers, builders, contractors, managers, professors, generals or captains, designers, operators of art galleries, museums, antique stores or their own business.

Two

Key word — Duality

Two is: Monday
    Feminine in expression
    Negative and mental
    Psychic
    Emotional
    Its element is water.

A Two person must:
    develop wisdom and love for wisdom
    have consideration of small opportunities and details that are important
    be a diplomat, a peacemaker
    have self-control

Two's spiritual lesson for Destiny is: Love expressed through peace.

Positive Vibrations
Two gives ability to form partnerships; be affectionate and good natured; be sympathetic, patient, and understanding; gives musical talent.

Negative Vibrations
Two fosters emotional dependence, self-delusion, cowardice, shyness, and pettiness. The destructive side of the Two vibration is *indifference*.

Two rules the kidneys.

Two's dominant characteristic is balance.

Best vocations for individuals with a Two vibration are: secretaries, diplomats, musicians, companions or homemakers, politicians, bankers, bookkeepers, and teachers.

Three

Key word — Expression

Three is: Thursday
    Masculine in its expression
    Emotional
    Its element is fire.

A Three person must:
    keep things as they are; not worry
    learn tolerance and emotional control
    not scatter efforts
    find expression through the arts

Three's spiritual lesson for Destiny is: Awaken the joy of the soul.

Positive Vibrations
Three gives artistic ability through oratory, writing and acting; makes living an art; gives inspiration and imagination; freedom from worry; good taste in dress, and the ability to be a grand host or hostess

Negative Vibrations
Worry, vanity, criticism, impatience, extravagance, conceit, antisocial attitudes. The destructive side of the Three vibration is *intolerance*.

Three rules the liver.

Three's dominant characteristic is entertainment.

Best vocations for individuals with a Three vibration are: orators, writers, performers, dancers, dressmakers, welfare workers, society organizers, decorators, fashion designers, social secretaries.

Four

Key word — Justice

Four is: Sunday
    Feminine in its expression
    Positive and mental
    Its element is earth.
    (it is the lowest power of the numbers 4, 8, 9, and 22)

A Four person must:
    learn lessons in honesty, sincerity, faithfulness, truth, persistance
    bear responsibilities for others
    learn discipline for self in work, play and life
    learn concentration and attention to detail

Four's spiritual lesson for Destiny is: Understanding materiality before the soul can raise itself spiritually.

Positive Vibrations
Four gives responsibility and ability to carry the burden for others, build homes and communities, and has powers of endurance

Negative Vibrations
lazy, stubborn, bad temper, contrary, tight-wad with finances. The destructive side of the Four vibration is *discontent*.

Four rules the intestines.

Four's dominant characteristic is steadfastness.

Best vocations for individuals with a Four vibration are: business enterprises, accountants, chemists, economists, technicians, organizers, mechanics, biologists, bankers.

Five

Key word — Change

Five is: Wednesday
    Masculine in expression
    Negative and mental
    Psychic and spiritual
    Its element is air.

A Five person must:
    govern the five senses
    not fear or resist change
    learn to develop the spiritual mind

Five's spiritual lesson for Destiny is: Freedom from mental bondage.

Positive Vibrations
Five gives elasticity of character, speculation, advertising, curiosity, and investigation, utilization of new opportunities, love of change and travel.

Negative Vibrations
Five gives addiction to change resulting in irresponsibility, impulsiveness, overindulgence (in sex, food, drugs, drink, etc.), proscrastination. The destructive side of the Five vibration is *indulgence*.

Five rules the stomach.

Five's dominant characteristic is adventure.

Best vocations for individuals with a Five vibration are: salesmen, business promoters, mining or electrical specialists, detectives, editors, actors, senators, civil service; opportunities in all directions.

Six

Key word — Harmony

Six is: Friday
    Masculine and feminine (dual) in expression
    The cosmic guardian
    Its elements are earth and air.

A Six person must:
    learn to live for others and not for self alone
    learn business and art, coupled with a home environment
    take responsibility and be of service

Six's spiritual lesson for Destiny is: Soul unfoldment.

Positive Vibrations
Six gives concern for harmony, truth, and justice; ability to heal, teach, and counsel; love of home, family, groups, and mankind; poise, stability, idealism, and balance.

Negative Vibrations
Six has misplaced sympathy, mistaken ideals, anxiety, interference, unwilling service. The destructive side of the Six vibration is *interference*.

Six rules the womb.

Six's dominant characteristic is responsibility.

Best vocations for individuals with a Six vibration are: teachers, counselors, lawyers, healers, doctors, dealers in food or home necessities, dramatic actors, professional guardians.

Seven

Key word — Intuition

Seven is: Monday
    Psychic
    Negative and mental
    Spiritual
    The number of the mystic
    Its element is water.

A Seven person must:
    be calm and patient
    develop the inner sources of supply
    acquire understanding of the unseen world

Seven's spiritual lesson for Destiny is: Development of the spiritual mind.

Positive Vibrations
Seven gives wisdom to the soul, love of nature and animals, mystery and philosophy, refinement and dignity, mental analysis.

Negative Vibrations
Melancholy, coldness, dishonesty, escape into drugs. The destructive side of the seven vibration is *turbulence*.

Seven rules the heart.

Seven's dominant characteristic is mystery.

Best vocations for individuals with a Seven vibration are: scientists, electrical or electronic specialists, astronomers, occultists, watchmakers, editors, clergymen, horticulturists.

Eight

Key word — Leadership

Eight is: Saturday
    Positive and mental
    Feminine in expression
    The second power number
    The number that vibrates to God.
    Its element is earth.

An Eight person must:
    develop a larger outlook
    dispense justice in all forms
    link itself with the commercial world
    use wealth for humanity

Eight's spiritual lesson for Destiny is: Material freedom.

Positive Vibrations
Eight gives power of authority, management ability, understanding of man and conditions, self-reliance, discrimination, and material freedom.

Negative Vibrations
Worship of the material, demand for recognition, abuse of power and authority, desire for revenge. The destructive side of the Eight vibration is *impatience*.

Eight's dominant characteristic is success.

Best vocations for individuals with an Eight vibration are: bondsmen, bankers, executives, corporation heads, manufacturers, judges, lawyers, consultants, promoters, mathematicians, investment counselors.

Nine

Key word — Universal

Nine is: Tuesday
    Emotional in expression
    Spiritual
    Negative and mental
    Masculine
    The third power number
    Its element is fire.

A Nine person must:
    learn lessons in humanity
    learn to be intuitive and visionary
    attract all things but hold onto nothing

Nine's spiritual lesson for Destiny is: Forgiveness and development of brotherhood.

Positive Vibrations
Nine gives fulfillment of self by giving of oneself, a prejudice-free view of life, love and compassion for all, tolerance and forgiveness.

Negative Vibrations
Extremes in emotion, waste, bitterness, and aimless dreaming. The destructive side of the nine vibration is *desire*.

Nine rules the nervous system.

Nine's dominant characteristic is power.

Best vocations for individuals with a Nine vibration are: spiritual teachers, specialists, artists, writers, doctors, surgeons, humanitarians, criminal lawyers.

    Just as in mathematics each number has its value, so in numerology each number has its corresponding vibration. Some people are in harmony with a particular number, others are not. Plato regarded numbers as the essence of harmony, and harmony as the basis of the Cosmos and of man.
    In a world of materialism and science, man knows least about himself. The study of oneself and the numbers which unlock the mysteries of that self is but a small link in your chain of life. Cheiro believed that every link in life has its number and its place. Make the patterns in your own life easier to understand; the study of numerology can help you to do it. Just as the square peg cannot fit into a round hole, neither can a Four operate in the vocation of a Five.

GRAPHOLOGY: THE LANGUAGE OF HANDWRITING

Most people wish they knew more about themselves and the people around them. Many wonder why they feel as they do when certain things happen and why they respond as they do. To the avid seeker of this kind of information and knowledge, graphology provides the means, because graphology speaks loud and clear to these questions.

From the earliest times, there has been an awareness of the relation of handwriting to character and personality. The Greek Philosopher, Aristotle, in the fourth century B.C. wrote, "Spoken words are symbols of mental experience; written words, the symbols of spoken words. Just as all men do not have the same speech sounds, neither do they all have the same writing." Handwriting is a symbolic language, and its meanings can be learned.

The Historic Evolution of Graphology

Through the years of recorded history, many famous people have expressed a seriouf interest in handwriting analysis but made their evaluations without formal rules or principles. The first known work on this subject was written in 1632 by an Italian physician, Camille Baldo, who wrote a treatise entitled, *How to Know the Nature and Qualities of a Person by Looking at a Letter He Has Written.*

Through the next two hundred years, curiosity about the possible revelations in handwriting began to stir the imagination of poets, artists, and philosophers. In 1820, Goethe said in one of his letters, "There can be no doubt that the handwriting of a person has some relation to his mind and character; that from it one may conceive at least some idea of his manner of being and acting, just as one must recognize not only appearances and features, but also bearing, voice and bodily movements as being significant and congruent with the total individuality." Edgar Allen Poe, the Brownings, Thomas Mann, Sir Walter Scott, Alexander Dumas, and Emile Zola, among others, studied handwriting, often arriving at keen observations and personality portraits of amazing accuracy.

Graphology in its modern form began in the nineteenth century when a search was started to find correlations between isolated character traits and specific graphic signs in writing. Around 1830, a group of French churchmen composed of Cardinal Regnier, Archbishop of Cam-Brai, Bishop Soudinet of Amiens, and the Abbe Louis J. H. Flandrin, were involved in handwriting interpretations, and the success of their investigations gave them recognition throughout France. Their disciple, Abbe Jean-Hippolyte Michon of Paris, carried on this work and not only gave graphology (meaning the science of writing) its name but, by studying thousands of handwriting specimens, also discovered certain constants, or signs, in writing that were indicative of character traits. Publication of his books in 1872 and 1878 not only caught popular fancy but also furnished material for research in tme decades to come.

Michon's ascribing fixed and definite meaning to graphic signs in writing was to be challenged by one of his successors, Julee Crepieux-Jamin. Jamin broke away from Michon's "school of fixed signs," as it was later called, and shifted emphasis from the elements of handwriting—isolated fragments such as the form of i-dots, t-bars, hooks, and flourishes, etc.—to its overall, more integrated aspects. He made the point that a handwriting must be perceived as a whole, and stressed that ejch trait contributes in a varying degree and with differing emphases. This concept, much like the Gestalt point of view in psychology, is referred to as the *holistic* approach, as contrasted to Michon's which is known as the *atomistic* approach.

Jamin made another important contribution to the field of graphology by enlisting the interest of Alfred Binet, founder of the intelligence tests, who made investigations of handwriting analysis at the Sorbonne. Binet tested the assumption that specific character traits correlate with specific handwriting traits; the affirmative results achieved, with respect to the graphic indices of honesty and intelligence, brought new esteem to graphology.

Whereas French investigators had dominated the field of theoretical and applied graphology during the nineteenth century, toward the end of the century German scientists took the lead.

Wilhelm Preyer, a child psychologist, was the first to deal with the relationship of graphic movements to mental processes. In research with handicapped people, he had taught a person with no arms to write with a pen held in the mouth or between the toes, and found the same signs in the writing as would have appeared had the person been holding a pen. As a result, the concept that handwriting is really "brain writing," a centrally organized function, was formulated by Preyer in 1895.

Georg Meyer, a psychiatrist, made a further important contribution by undertaking to analyze writing movement, particularly with emotionally disturbed persons. He held that the character of handwriting is determined not by the anatomy or strength of the writer's hand but by the "psychomotor energies." While underlining what he considered the three main factors of writing movement—extension, speed, and pressure—Meyer regarded unity of expression as the decisive feature of psychomotor functioning. Furthermore, Meyer recognized that problems of expression cannot be treated apart from what he called the "character" of the writer.

Meanwhile, a German philosopher, Ludwig Klages, was developing a metaphysical approach to graphology based upon many of these findings which he termed a "science of expression." He postulated two forces within man: "mind," which binds and inhibits; and the "soul," which frees and allows for creative development. Klages felt these two forces, always dynamically at variance, influence all of man's behavior and become crystallized in *expressive movements* such as walking, gesturing, speaking, and writing, etc. All such bodily movements, actualizing the tensions and drives of the personality, have a common *form level* or style that is consistent with the individual's general motor behavior and rhythm of movement. Because handwriting preserves the record of these movement, it was considered the most accessible for study and interpretation.

During the mid-1920s significant advances were being made in Switzerland under the leadership of Max Pulver. Pulver extended Klages' graphological system by applying psychoanalytic concepts. Working in research with the famous psychoanalyst, Carl Jung, Pulver developed a theory of the symbolic meaning of the writing space, and gave handwriting a third dimension. To the previously accepted dimensions of height and width, he added depth in the form of pressure—those movements that actually seek to penetrate the paper.

The extension of graphology to the United States has not been very broad at this point in time, but there has been a growing interest in many areas. American psychologists and psychiatrists still tend to neglect its study largely because of the strong influence of the behavioral-school system. The over-concern with the idea that behavior is caused and aroused by external stimuli rather than inner direction has left such inquiries as graphology out of consideration in analysis and therapy programs in this country. There have been programs of research, such as the one Gordon Allport and Philip E. Vernon of Harvard made in the 1930s which concluded that there were meaningful interrelations to be found in handwriting that could be correlated in the total expressive movement of any given individual. In 1942 the Lewinson-Zubin experiments developed a system of scales which they applied in a clinical manner to the handwriting of normal and abnormal individuals.

In spite of graphology's long history and the wealth of information on the subject, its study and application is largely separated from the field of psychology. Its use by certain businesses in personnel work and by counselors in vocation guidance, for example, is extensive. Its use in crime-detection applications—especially in document examination—is well established, and many police departments use graphologists for specialized work. By and large, however, graphology is still in its infancy in the United States, and this is due in large part to the fact that professionals in psychological areas have not as yet recognized the great value of graphology as a diagnostic tool.

Graphology as a Diagnostic Tool

Graphology, the art and science of handwriting analysis, as a psychological method is primarily a diagnostic tool for examining and measuring the many facets of character and personality that contribute to drawing a personality portrait of an individual. It is also used in grapho-therapy, which postulates that changing of one's handwriting in certain ways will bring about corresponding changes in character and personality. There are also other specialized applications such as in document examination, but we will be primarily concerned with graphology as a diagnostic tool.

As a diagnostic tool, graphology is of potential value to anyone interested in self-improvement as well as those engaged in helping people through applied psychology. With a basic knowledge, almost anyone can benefit and gain greater self-knowledge. For in-depth applications, however, considerable experience both in graphology and psychology are needed.

The basis for graphology is movement and expression. The act of writing is a finely coordinated gesture of human expression that records the human brain-and-body-in-action by means of a graphic form that normally combines the movement of a writing instrument and the human hand. Because handwriting is an expressive movement, the individuality of the writer is revealed through a study of a person's writing. This is the method of graphology. Integral to graphology as a method is the fact that every handwriting is unique and never duplicated by anyone else. No two handwritings are exactly alike, and each of us has handwriting as distinctive as our fingerprints.

Handwriting begins as a learning process. We are taught to imitate an imposed standard model, and because it requires conscious attention, the first writing is hesitant, forced, and disorganized. As the graphic skills are improved to a point of being organized, emphasis shifts from attention centered on the act of writing to emphasis on the act of expression as it is needed for communication. This brings into play the coordination of the brain with muscles, nerves, and body organs with the manipulation of a writing instrument.

As we become less conscious of how we write, the act of writing tends to become more spontaneous and automatic. So as the writing instrument moves across the paper and down the page, a picture is drawn and our individuality unfolds. During the act of writing, our "true inner natkre" surfaces and is recorded in our handwriting. Even with conscious effort, it is difficult to hide completely that which lies deep in our person.

Because of this brain-and-body-in-action movement that is a closely coordinated process, our handwriting reflects not only the essences of our character and personality, but also indicates the changes that take place as we react to the things taking place in our environment.

To the common question, "If I write differently at different times, how can you tell anything about me?" the answer is that change is normal because we live in a dynamic and changing world. Fluctuations and variables are a part of every handwriting, but there is also a continuity. Within each script there are "constants" which do not change, unless we, of course, change our lives drastically. It is upon these constants as they relate to change that the principles of handwriting analysis are built.

Fluctuations and variables in handwriting will follow specific patterns of reaction. For one conditioned to change, the deviations will be rhythmic and fluent; for those who function from a rigid view of reality, change is erratic and lacking in spontaneity. Within all of us, there is a conditioned response pattern which determines how we react to change, and this will vary from very conscious control to that which we cannot seemingly control in spite of our desire to do so.

Handwriting is a process and a reflection of our brain-and-body-in-action relationship. Part of it is determined by our conscious response structure; part resides within the unconscious, which is expressed spontaneously. One part tends to be static, whereas the other part tends to be dynamic and changes as our lives change in their daily response to environment.

As a method, graphology examines and measures our expressive movements as we contract and release our vital energies. It is therefore a dynamic method, and must take into account the whole person as he or she responds to the society in which he or she lives. As we proceed to examine the basic principles of graphology, we will be looking at these factors of movement and expression as they characterize human activity.

The Methods of Graphology

All schools of graphology rely heavily upon the discoveries of the early French and German graphologists, but each has developed its own method of interpretation according to different psychological concepts. And, because graphology is both an art and a science, its application will be determined largely by the individual graphologist. There is no right way of application, only many ways of arriving at the same goal.

Because there is a vast amount of literature available on graphology, the beginner has a wealth of resources to draw upon. But ultimately the most important teacher will be experience. It is an applied science that needs to be exercised.

To the beginner, there are a number of things to consider when approaching the study of graphology. First, and *probably most important,* is the need for objectivity. This is not easy, because it is very tempting to the beginner to be carried away with a little knowledge. With the insight possible through this knowledge goes a need for using it responsibly. One must not attempt to play the role of God and pass judgments.

It is not our place to decide whether what we see in another's handwriting is "good" or "bad," but rather to assess the writing in terms of qualities that may be affecting a person's ability to cope in a given environment and to achieve personal objectives. With this responsibility goes the need to reveal the possible insights in such a way as to be helpful, and all such information must be kept as confidential.

In approaching an analysis, apart from having the needed samples of writing it is necessary to know certain things. First, you must know the age and the sex of the writer because neither can be determined with accuracy from handwriting. Age is a matter of maturity, and the years lived may or may not have contributed to an individual's growth in this area. Sex as a psychological quality, in like manner, is a matter of personal adaption. We all have feminine and masculine qualities, and a dominance of one over the other is not necessarily a matter of gender. Another factor to consider is whether the writer is left- or right-handed. A left-handed writer, depending upon training and environment, may write in a way that differs somewhat from the right-handed writer—certain motions being unnatural to the positioning of the paper, etc., so that it is awkward. Depending on whether the "leftee" writes overhand or underhand, such things as slant may be distorted from that of a right-handed writer.

In setting up a sample, or in selecting one already written, writing should be on plain, unlined paper. Line and margin rules will create artificial barriers that will prevent the writer from making natural handwriting.

Another factor is country of origin, which is not as important in this country as it is in Europe. Different countries teach different writing styles and use standard models that vary conscderably from those taught in the United States.

The First Impression

While there are some systems of graphology that disregard or play down the analyst's first impression, it is generally accepted as the first step in examining a person's writing. Take a look at the sample and record your first impressions. You must be careful to be objective, but there are certain factors that will be apparent. Does it look neat or messy? Is it organized, or is unity lacking? Is the writing large or small, simple or embellished? Do you feel strength or weaknesses, warmth or coldness, etc.? It is this type of impression that will give you a feel for the writing, but you must bear in mind that this is only the beginning and that you must consider other factors.

From your overall impression, you can categorize the writing as tending to be either positive or negative, noting again that these categories are only general classifications and not absolute. In other words, writing will tend to one of these directions.

Positive Writing

Positive writing tends to be legible and uses the writing space neatly. The margins and line spacings tend to form a pattern that is easy to read. There is an overall harmony to the writing, though it may vary considerably from a standard copybook model. It may have a flair and a quality of excitement, or it may be small and compact, but at this level we are just thinking in terms of its positive or negative qualities and not trying to judge the writing beyond this level.

Negative Writing

Negative writing, on the other hand, will tend to have an unpleasing appearance. Be careful at this point to be sure the sample is representative of the person's normal writing. Most of us will scribble in haste and not take care in writing, particularly if there is no need to be more careful. A shopping list or an office note to yourself are examples of such instances. But, if this is normal writing and it is unpleasing, messy, and disorganized with lines intermingled and spacings disorderly, then it may fit the negative category. In general, negative writing is difficult to read because it lacks harmony, rhythm and unity; and it represents a person who doesn't care or who is emotionally unstable to the point of having great difficulty in communication. Many creative people often will have unconventional writing, so care must be exercised in making the distinction between negative and the unusual. For the beginner, this will be very difficult.

Zonal Balance

Upon making this initial assessment, the next step will vary with teachers, depending upon their particular approach. I personally next look at the zonal balance in writing. By zonal balance, I mean the vertical height of individual small letters, omitting the capital letters at this time.

The English alphabet is made up of twenty-six letters with thirteen letters falling within the middle zone, as follows:

Six letters are written using both the middle zone and upper zone, as follows:

Six letters are written using both the middle zone and lower zone, as follows:

Only one letter is written using all three zones, as follows:

As can be seen from this classification, all letters move within or through the middle zone of writing. Movement to and from the upper and lower zones to the middle zone tends to be a vertical movement, whereas the movements within the middle zone tend more in a horizontal direction. The middle zone symbolizes the area of coordination that accepts the influences coming from above or below and translates them into forward movement as the writing proceeds across the page from left to right. The middle zone is the zone of action and of doing.

The upper zone represents the zone of the conscious mind and the activity of the intellect. Projections upward symbolically indicate a movement out of self into contact with external thought and influence. Our conscious mind is conditioned by the external influences found in our culture and environment. People who have become conditioned and disciplined into working with intellectual ideas will show tall extensions of their upper-zone letters, often to the lessening of their lower-zone extensions.

Astrology, Horoscope, and Dreams

The lower zone represents the zone of the unconscious and activities that are sensory in origin. Projections downward symbolically indicate a movement into the inner self and into contact with our feelings and other impressions coming into our nervous system. It is the zone of sensory appetite, which may be manifest in such things as sex, love of color and strongly favored foods, material wants, and other manifestations characteristic of strong energy flow. It is also the zone of psychic and spiritual impressions that feed into the emotional structure of the human psyche.

By examination of a handwriting sample for its zonal proportions, we are able to visualize the foundations of a person's attitudes and other factors that contribute to and become responsible for human motivation. The copybook standard as taught in school tries to develop a zonal balance in writing with a slight emphasis given the upper zone in comparison to the lower zone. Standard proportions as taught are: a middle zone of 3 mm. (or 1/8 inch) in height, with an upper zone approximately one and one-half to two times the middle zone.

Developing of a zonal balance as taught in school rarely happens in practical reality; and in a large majority of people there will be an emphasis upon one or two zones giving rise to a number of possible combinations.

When you look at the writing for zonal balance, you must view this aspect as a relationship. As has been noted, the standard calls for an upper zone approximately two times the middle, and the lower about one and one-half times the middle zone. The standard copybook model also assumes a middle zone of about 3 mm., or 1/8 inch. In small writing, the middle zone may be 2 mm. or less, so in judging the zonal relationships you would have to think in terms of what the middle zone actually measures and judge the upper and lower zones accordingly on the basis of the given proportions. This adjustment also applies when writing is larger than the copybook model.

When a strong middle zone is present, you know that there is a potential for action and for achievement; when it is minimized, there will be a tendency to be impractical or unrealistic depending upon the other factors of influence. In Freudian terms, the middle zone symbolized the Ego drives, so when there is excessive height to the middle zone with the upper and lower zone minimized, the writer is driven by the need to achieve projected goals and will be a subjective person who finds it difficult to relate to abstract ideas or to emotional impressions. Action is based upon what is going on *now,* and it's full speed ahead!

Large middle zone writers function well in areas that are structured and well defined, because they are operational people. They follow a prescribed standard, and plow ahead without being detracted by their own thoughts or feelings.

When you add a well-developed lower zone to the large middle-zone writer, you will find the influence of feelings and emotions. The strong drive to act will be accented by the drives of the instinct. This type of writer is often very independent in action and does not need the stimulation offered by people. This is not to say that it is not welcome, because there is a natural and spontaneous quality about this writer, and there is a ready willingness to cooperate which can be very productive. In Freudian terms, the lower zone symbolized the Id or the "soul" qualities which, because they are dynamic, are often at odds with the Super-Ego, which tends to be static and absolute.

the meantime I'll be in

Example of a Strong Middle Zone

the Evanston Store must win!

Strong Middle Zone With Upper Zone Influence

office yesterday afternoon

Strong Middle Zone With Lower Zone Influence

These examples and brief descriptions should begin to give you a feel for the type of evaluations that comes from analyzing handwriting. They are but three of many possible combinations with zonal relationships and provide some indication of the effect attitudes and motivation have upon the action of a person. Zones indicate movement inward and outward and how this vertical movement relates to action. When there is excessive emphasis of one zone over another, there is bound to be resultant imbalances, which is not to say this is good or bad. In many fields of activity, it is beneficial to have a strong drive to the exclusion of other drives, so evaluations from zonal relationships is just one factor of the personality profile to be constructed.

Astrology, Horoscope, and Dreams

Writing Size

Closely allied to zonal relationships is the factor of writing size. Whereas zones indicate vertical movement, writing size indicates the writer's view of the size world in which he or she is operating. The writing that is close to the standard copybook model as taught in school, would indicate a person who quite readily accepts that which is presented. They are followers and tend not to be aware of choices. They do not venture out far beyond the accepted norm as they have come to know it.

Example of Smaller-than-Average Size Writing

Example of Average Size Writing

Example of Larger-than-Average Size Writing

The writer whose writing is noticeably smaller than the average, or norm, is one who has chosen to contract his or her world into a smaller segment and finds interest and satisfaction in having limited areas in which to work. Such writers prefer to keep their action within close range and desire to be in closer contact and control of what they are doing than one who has a larger writing size. They often aspire to perfection and will pay attention to fine details.

The large writer, in contrast to the small writer, expands his or her world beyond the norm as structured by the standard. Such writers view their world as vast and expansive, and do not expect to be limited by movement in space. They tend to develop and expend considerably more energy than the average person, and build expectations that carry them into areas of opportunities more than do the smaller writers. Whether such expectations are realistic is another matter and cannot be determined from writing size alone.

In putting these elements of zonal relationships and writing size into a perspective, we begin to see the correlation between elements in handwriting and expressive movements. We can determine the inner and outer movements from zones—those directed from our conscious thoughts and those coming from the unconscious level of feelings into an area of expression—or their restraint, which would be a repression of such directives. From size of writing, we can determine a spatial projection of the writer: is it outward and expanding, or inward and contracting.

Astrology, Horoscope, and Dreams

Expression of Force

Adding to these elements of expression, one being to determine the origin of motivation that results in action and the other being one that sets forth the size of the area for expression, we now can add the *expression of force*. This concerns two factors in handwriting.

Writing Pressure

First, there is the energy development factor that is measured by pressure in writing. Because we are currently dominated by ball point pens as writing instruments, the visualization of writing does not readily reveal pressure, and it is necessary to examine the back side of the writing sample. Strong pressure will emboss the paper, and this can be felt by running the fingers over the back side of the paper. Another method is to provide a writer with a choice of writing pens, such as a fine point, medium, or broad—such as a felt pen. The pen selection when freely made becomes an indicator of energy force to be expressed by the writer.

Example of Light Writing Pressure

Example of Medium Writing Pressure

Example of Heavy Writing Pressure

50

Writing Slant

Pressure is the expression of energy development, and is manifest as a depth dimension in handwriting. As a vital force, it flows in all directions. Restraint or release of energy tends to be controlled by our conscious mind, even though the process tends to become automatic. The degree of control indicates our capacity for expression and restraint, and this *conscious control of our energy force* is measured in the slant of our writing.

Strong pressure, or energy flow, with a minimum of control will result in fast writing with a far forward slant; with maximum control, the writing will be slower and more vertical. Lighter pressure will be indicated by right slant when controls are released; but the writing will be slower, and attempts at faster writer will make the writing less legible. While pressure in writing flows in all directions, slant becomes a measurement of its control because of the need for handwriting to move from the left to right.

The right, vertical, or left slant in writing then becomes an important indicator in revealing the amount of control one is exercising on the release of vital energy. Therefore slant becomes an important link between one's private inner world and the world revealing this relationship as it is extended into one's environmental position.

Measurement of slant is accomplished by drawing a baseline with a straight edge to connect the points where the strokes touch the bottom position in the middle zone.

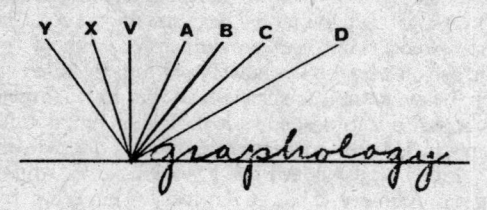

Vertical projections are determined by using the base-line as the horizontal and drawing a vertical line through each letter along an axis that follows the slant of the letter.

Various charts have been drawn to give a symbolic meaning to slant that generally refer to the right-slanted writer as being an extrovert and the extreme left as being introverted.

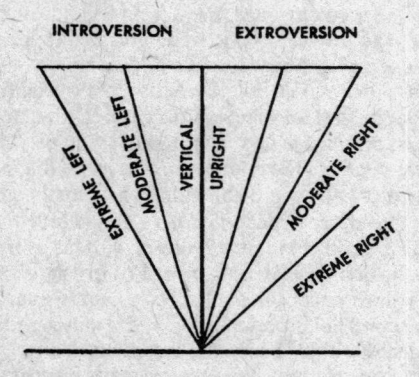

The terminology, unfortunately, carries with it the inference that the extrovert, who is one whose interest and energy is directed outward to things and events outside the self and is concerned chiefly with what is external and objective, is a "positive" person, whereas the introvert, whose direction is inward to self and concerned chiefly with thoughts of self, is a "negative" person. To the extreme, either quality can be quite negative, whereas within a framework of balance each tendency has its pluses and minuses. One cannot, therefore, generalize and arrive at absolute conclusions. It is much more realistic to look at these qualities in terms of control and release. The right slant writer allows the energy flow to extend outward to others, so in a social sense the writer is an outgoing person. From a psychological frame of reference, the extrovert is being affected by his or her environment and in that sense is also giving up self-control in varying degrees to become dependent upon circumstances, many of which then are out of the person's control.

The more vertical writer, on the other hand, is more of a controlled person. In some cases, the control results from awareness of the energy flow as being so strong that it requires control. But this awareness may not be that clearly defined. With most people, it is probably the result of environmental conditioning by parents and social institutions. In any case, the vertical writers apply the brakes when extending outward to others, and it takes a period of time for them to feel comfortable enough to extend from self to others. So in a social sense, the vertical writer is not objective and friendly. But as far as being in control is concerned, the vertical writer may be far better adjusted than the writer with a forward slant.

Handwriting Examples

Dr. Benjamin Spock

Putting the factors we have covered so far into a type of simple evaluation, let's discuss the signature of the famous Dr. Benjamin Spock.

Several factors are immediately obvious. One is a heaviness that indicates a strong pressure, and the writing slants far forward, meaning that there is a free flow of feelings. Add to that the large size middle zone, measuring 5 mm., compared to the copybook standard of 3 mm., and the small extenders into the upper and lower zones.

These characteristics indicate a dynamic person who thinks and acts aggressively based upon his desire to achieve his goals. He is what you might call a "now" person; what he wants to achieve *he wants now*. He relates to circumstances rather than to directives from either his conscious or subconscious minds, so he is motivated by his feelings and his sympathies for those whom he touches in his reaching out from self. He believes strongly about his objectives and will be willing to fight for them when necessary. He possesses a dynamic spirit which can be felt just by looking at his writing. He is positive and direct, as can be discerned from the fact that his writing is simplified and has no unnecessary embellishments. It flows smoothly and is quite legible in spite of the fact he writes with a swift movement of his pen.

George Bernard Shaw

Looking at another example, that of the late famous author, George Bernard Shaw, one sees a sharp contrast to the writing of Dr. Spock.

Mr. Shaw's writing is smaller than the copybook average, measuring less than 2 mm., and though there is an indication of strong pressure, still it is vertical writing. The middle zone is small and the upper zone quite large by comparison. There is some indication of a lower zone, but it is not brought back into the middle zone.

Using the information we have learned, we can infer that Mr. Shaw had strong force that was held in tight control and expressed largely through his intellect. The large, well-developed upper zone shows his deep interest in using his conscious mind to explore philosophical and abstract ideas; and, while he was in contact with his feeling levels of the unconscious, he did not allow them to detract from his conscious thoughts. His small writing indicates that he liked to work at close range on his ideas and he worked methodically in his explorations to keep them within his mental control. There is a narrowness to his writing which shows he compressed his thoughts into narrow ideas, and his small middle zone indicates a tendency to idealism rather than to putting his ideas into action. While he hoped to impress others with his expressions through writing, he himself would not be the activator of his ideas. The long, final extender at the end of his signature is a symbolic gesture that says, "Keep your distance; I am a cautious person." This extender can almost be visualized as an arm holding Shaw away from the action.

I think you can see by using the simple principles presented that you can gain insights into character and personality by adapting them to various examples of handwriting. From the beginning I have purposely avoided getting into the many specific elements that are factors in handwriting analysis, because too many elements tend to confuse. To the beginner it is too much input that prevents practical application. I will proceed to add to what has been discussed, but up to this point we have looked at just a few simple basics that form the structure upon which to build.

Some Specific Graphic Indicators

In approaching the numerous graphic indicators that are to be found within the framework of expression and therefore in handwriting, we must always bear in mind the general principles we have been discussing. Handwriting forms a graphic record of our movements and expressions at a given time and provides a symbolic picture. Strokes that move upward and to the right are outward and forward moving; those that go downward and to the left are inward and backward moving. Experience in working with this symbolic picture will demonstrate the truths it represents, and you will begin to realize that upon this structure many details can be added for greater definition and depth. Because they are numerous, I have placed them in an alphabetical sequence.

Alignment refers to the direction of the baseline, which is the invisible line upon which the bottom of the middle-zone letters rest, and the space between the baselines. Good alignment is pleasing to the eye and expresses a sense of order and control. An unsteady baseline indicates changeableness, indecision, possible emotional conflict, and lack of self-discipline. Ascending lines express cheerfulness and optimism; descending lines express pessimism and possible depression. Adequate spacing between lines to prevent tangling of lower with upper loops shows good organization, whereas entanglement can indicate confusion and too many interests for clear judgment.

Beginning strokes refer to the initial strokes of words. Rigid, braced strokes indicate resentments; when proceeding from the lower zone, they are deeply engrained from early childhood. Beginning strokes coming from the upper zone may indicate fantasy or humor. Long initial strokes can mean hesitancy or timidity; small tight circles, jealousy; and hooks upturned, selfishness. An absence of beginning strokes shows directness and simplicity.

Capital letters when tall indicate pride and dignity; when inflated, imagination had possible pretense and there is a need to impress others. Small capitals indicate modesty and timidity—or objectivity when they are about the same size as the middle zone.

Connectedness of letters shows continuity of thought and systematic, logical thought patterns. Breaks between letters if the strokes flow and seem to connect, although not actually there, would indicate intuition and perception. If letters stand separately, hesitation, isolation, and timidity in social relationships are indicated. If separation is excessive, egotism and selfishness are possibilities.

Dots for *i's, j's,* and periods, when round and well-centered close to stem of the letter, indicate order and attention to details; if high, they signify idealism and optimism. Missing dots indicate poor attention to details, and maybe absentmindedness. Dots made as dashes, often are placed to right of letter and show haste, impatience, and impulsiveness. To the left of the letter, they indicate hesitation and possible procrastination. When made as slashes, they show frustration and emotional disturbance. Circle dots in teenagers are a fad; in older people, they are an indication of a desire to be unique or unusual.

Elaboration and flourishes are embellishments to the standard copybook style and often indicate interest in dramatics, art, and music, or in ornate objects. When extreme, they might signify loss of balance, or uninhibited or unrestrained behavior. Circular movements symbolize a desire to claim attention, with small circles indicating jealousy, and hook-like forms depicting grasping movements to acquire and hold on to possessions or past achievements. Over-developed embellishments may indicate vanity, boastfulness, or impulsive action; and some may be loud of voice and extreme in mode of dress.

Fluency in writing is the flowing movement in continuous and unbroken progression and relates to fluency of thought and speech. It is indicated in letter forms such as a *g* made like a figure *8*. It indicates resourcefulness, ingenuity, and creativity.

Individualized forms are departures from the copybook style and represent independence, creativity, and nonconformity. They may be simplifications or elaborations and embellishments, but, they should not take away from legibility and good form. Distorted or bizarre configurations, though individual, would not be positive aspects in a writing sample.

Loops in writing refer to inflation of letters normally looped as well as to those not looped in copybook style. Upper-zone loops have to do with intellectual imagination, idealism, and abstract thought. When increased at the expense of the middle and lower zone, excessive attention is paid to intellectual matters, and attention to social and environmental relationships may be neglected or dealt with unrealistically. Disturbed, jagged, or broken areas in upper loops may indicate physical problems in the head and heart areas; in lower-zone loops, problems in the legs and feet. Looped *d's* indicate sensitivity to criticism about the self, while looped *t's* relate to one's ability to perform in daily activities. Inflated lower-zone loops refer to concerns about physical activities, money, and other material values and to above-normal need for sexual satisfactions. Absence of loops in normally looped letters indicate a lack of imagination and a suppressing of one's emotional need to express, especially when found in the lower zone. Loops at the bottom of *m's* and *n's* suggest insincerity.

Margins reflect the writer's regard for relationships with environment or with the person to whom he or she is communicating. If the writing is surrounded by wide margins, the writer may be expressing formality, or is extravagant and has a tendency to snobbishness. If the margins are narrow, the writer is not concerned with esthetic tastes or balance, and may indicate a tendency to monopolize situations and exclude others. In small or formal writing, narrow margins may show a tendency toward thrift or economy. Increasing left-hand margins indicate aggression and momentum in forward motion, whereas a decreasing left or right-hand margin shows regression and withdrawal from social relationships. Zig-zag or irregular margins reflect instability in movement and development of fears in relationships.

Rigidity in writing indicates an dxcess of regularity and a lack of spontaneity. There is overcontrol, and the writing will reflect a sameness in size, slant, and spacing. There is a lack of flexibility in dealing with others and with one's environment.

Rhythm refers to consistency of movement within the writing, and one measurement is in the letter placements. By drawing a vertical line perpendicular to the baseline at the point where middle-zone downstrokes touch the baseline, you will see the rhythm pattern. If the spacings are regular and of even distance, there is consistency within the writing movement.

Signatures represent the writer's self-concept and the way he or she desires to be represented. Signatures are very personal and individual. Size, elaborations and embellishments, simplicity, and underlinings have special meanings in the signature. Large writing indicates a feeling of self-importance and strong ego strength; small writing is a sign of conformity and compliance. Excessive elaborations and embellishments indicate a desire to inflate openly one's self-concept or to seek recognition that may or may not be deserved. It is a dramatic and artistic type of expression. Simplicity indicates a direct approach without adornment or ornamentation, and shows self-confidence. Underlinings, if they end in a forward motion, show self-reliance. The initial letter of the first name, when larger than that of the family name, shows a feeling of greater importance to self than to family ties; this will often be found in a woman's writing when she is unhappily married. Also, size of the signature can be related to the size of the writing other than the signature. A signature made larger than the regular writing indicates that the self-concept is not being manifest in daily living; expectations are greater than realizations. Same-size writing shows that expectations are being met; whereas a smaller signature than the writing of the body script shows a self-concept that is below what is actually being achieved and often will indicate a person that is under-achieving. Excesses in size in either direction can mean imbalances that can become emotional disturbances.

Simplicity in writing forms represents clarity of thought, directness of approach to life and work objectives; and an avoidance of pretense. Plainness, leanness, and the absence of embellishments and unneeded strokes are signs of simplicity. To the extreme, simplicity can mean meagerness and a lack of expression of emotional warmth. If legibility is reduced or absent, a personality disorientation might be indicated.

Spacing between letters and words adds special significance to an analysis. Wide spacings mean expansiveness, ease in relationships, liberal outlook, and ability to communicate freely. Extremely wide spacing could mean a wasting of energies and resources due to a lack of caution. Tight spacing shows an expression of fears and inhibitions that restrict communication; it may be evidence of hostility and resentment and selfishness, and an inability to be at ease in personal social relationships. In word spacing, large, even spaces may indicate an ability to remain aloof from people and not to join in with regularity. Close word spacings means almost the opposite, indicating a person needing involvement, particularly when letter spacing is not compressed. When there are discrepancies between letter spacing and word spacings—where one is tight and the other is open, for example—imbalances with relationships to self and specific individuals, as well as to society in general, can be expected.

Terminal strokes express an attitudinal and motivational direction in communication with others. Terminals that are short and end at the baseline indicate a writer who is decisive and definite in purpose, and not easily swayed from pursuing specific goals. When terminals end above the baseline, indecisiveness and a lack of self-confidence deter the writer from goals. Longer terminal strokes that move forward indicate aggressiveness, but with a note of caution. If they move upward and curl to the left, self-criticism colors and detracts from goal achievement; if downward, goals are primarily concerned with self interest. Long horizontal endings show caution and a desire to keep one's distance.

Analysis and Synthesis of Handwriting

From this list of specific graphic indicators comes a wealth of information that is needed in making an analysis and synthesis of handwriting that will yield the subject's personality and character profile. When combined with the basic principles outlined at the beginning of this article, anyone who will take the time to study and apply this material can benefit from such information. As one progresses in interest in and use of graphology, there are many additional indicators that will be helpful, but at the outset too much information can be confusing and so reduce the efficiency of the beginning graphologist. With time and application there will also develop new combinations that will become meaningful as the student progresses.

As we have seen, the graphological procedure has involved progressions or steps which begin by viewing the writing pattern as a whole to grasp its essential overall expression. A closer examination of the pattern reveals certain components which are differentiated further into primary factors and individual features which become the basis for correlations into the personality factors they represent. By ordering these factors into related groups, an integrated, dynamic picture begins to emerge.

It should be emphasized at this point that it is never the form of a single letter, nor any one particular factor that forms the picture; rather it is the combination and interaction of all parts of the writing pattern that reveal the personality portrait. The graphologist sees all of this, first as communication, then, looking deeper, he or she becomes concerned with the underlying motivations and unconscious factors that become a language of their own in revealing the writer's essential nature.

These levels of concern may be divided into three categories:

1. *The informative category or level,* which is the conscious level; the objective is to convey a message by means of written words. This is the first and most obvious level of functioning by the graphologist.
2. *The unintended communication level,* which conveys information without words to color and shape the writing very much the same as voice and expressive gestures color speech. It is the sub-verbal communication that is expressed through involuntary tensions and motions that accompany the act of writing.

3. *The unconscious projection level,* which contains certain forms, twists, and slips of the pen, that tend to be hidden within the graphic patterns and escape the untrained eye. Though this level closely relates to the second level, the trained graphologist can readily make the distinction between the two.

The beginner will operate largely in the first level; but as skill increases, a progression is made into the other two levels. It is as this progression deepens that the graphologist becomes more and more intuitive and psychic in drawing the personality and character profile. It is the dynamic interplay of conscious observation with the unconscious factors that brings forth the impressions that are to be useful and meaningful in the broadest sense possible.

Psychometry is another factor that those who are attracted to graphology often possess and use, although many are not aware of its possibility to obtain information from the energy in writing. As one writes, energy is expended and is left embedded within the writing. Those who have developed a sensitivity to this part of the "sixth sense" and who are aware of it will find that upon touching and handling the writing, sample impressions come into the mind. These impressions will often take the form of symbols, much as in dream analysis. The individual graphologist must give meaning to these symbols.

An example of this form of symbolization is one that I experienced in working on an analysis. The picture that came through my consciousness as I felt the writing was that of a medium-sized box that was tied shut with ribbon in a criss-cross fashion. And as I visualized the box, projections came through the top and then returned into the box. As I interpreted the symbols, I saw this man as one who had been controlled by his environment (the box) which was one that contained much harmony and affluence (the ribbon ties), and though he was trying to get out of confinement, the gestures to do so were sporatic and momentary (projections through the top), and he then would retreat back into the shelter and comfort of his confinement. This interpretation was confirmed by further analysis of his writing. His background was one in which family relationships had been important but stifling, and because of newly found interest he was drifting away from close family ties. He found conflict between the comfort of what had been and what he sought apart from his family relationships. Realization of this dichotomy allowed him to re-examine his relationships and provided new alternatives that removed the conflict, which was largely on unconscious levels.

While progression into this stage of graphological analysis comes only from in-depth experience, it is a potential that the beginner should know about because it tends to strengthen the importance of impressions, particularly first impressions. Learning to make distinctions between actual unconscious impressions and conscious prejudices is where the skill develops. We are all subject to feelings that are not objective but mainly subjective; and, if these contain excessive prejudice, the ability to be aware is lessened.

As can be seen from the material presented, graphology can be a meaningful inquiry into human nature. Inasmuch as handwriting is expressive as a movement that reflects how a person is feeling and acting at the time, its analysis can be a valuable diagnostic tool. Graphology, the language of handwriting, speaks for itself.

PALMISTRY: THE STUDY OF THE HAND

History of Palmistry

> God caused signs or seals on the hands
> of all the sons of men, that the sons
> of men might know their works.
> Orig. Hebrew, Job: Chap. 37, V. 7

The origin of the art and science of palmistry is lost in the dim mists of pre-history. We do know, however, that it occupied a place in the mysteries of the Hebrew Kabbalah, and played an important role in the religion and philosophy of the ancient Greeks and Hindus. Indeed, the famous analyst, Cheiro (Count Louis Hamon, 1866-1936), tells us of personally examining in India an extremely ancient book on the markings of the hand. The book was perhaps the greatest treasure of the Brahmans who possessed it, and it was zealously guarded in one of the cave temples of the ruins of ancient Hindustan. This book, of enormous size, was made of human skin, pieced together, and it contained hundreds of illustrations well-drawn with a red liquid which had failed to spoil or fade. Surely a grisly document by modern standards, but nonetheless one which serves to give us some idea of the antiquity of the practice of palmistry.

The study of the hand has never been the province of the weak mind or poor intellect. We find among its early practioners such men of learning as Aristotle, Pliny, Paracelsus, Cardomis, Albertus Magnus, and others of equal stature. Down through the ages there have marched billiant observers of human nature as it is recorded in the human hand. Alongside them have marched the scoffers and skeptics, mindless of the observations of ancient philosophers and modern scientists who have considered the subject worthy of their time and attention.

The basis of palmistry is not contrary to the dictates of reason, but is wholly in accordance with natural law. The human hand is a network of motor and sensory nerves. The first two fingers, half the third finger and the area of the palm beneath, and part of the thumb are served by the median nerve. That part of the hand is related to the conscious self. The ulna nerve expresses the subconscious self; it occupies the outer, or percussion, side of the hand, and the little finger and the other half of the third finger. The thumb shares branches from the radial nerve. Thus, it is through this complex network of nerves that the hand is the servant of the brain.

It has been observed that the lines in the hand change in unison with changes in the mental attitude of the individual when these changes are great enough to alter his temperament and characteristics. The lines also change in response to changes in health and constitution. Therefore, we may state with certainty that the lines of the hand are the direct result of the subject's mind and that his mind produces, controls, and alters them. Accordingly, the skilled analyst is well-nigh infallible in reading the history of past events because those events have already been impressed upon the brain.

It is in the accuracy of the lines to forecast future events that we come upon some difficulty. It is the opinion of this author that divination by the sole means of reading the lines and signs of the hand is a virtual impossibility. Only those events which have already cast their shadow in either the conscious or subconscious levels of the mind will be found to have impressed themselves upon the hand. For example, those subjects who have contemplated divorce or suicide, or have strong desires for travel, will be found to have registered these "thought forms" on the hand, whereas no sign will appear to warn of sudden and unanticipated events. It should be added that those lines appearing as a result of desire will be seen to disappear if action does not follow thought.

Any palmist who accurately forecasts such events does so by means of intuition and not by the evidence at hand. The author is acquainted with one such lady who persists in calling the Heart Line the Head Line and vice versa; to her, the Mount of Luna is where we send the astronauts out to play. For dependable analysis one must follow circumscribed rules. The rules work at all times and under all circumstances, whereas intuition comes and goes according to its own whim.

Hand analysis is indeed a key factor in the detection of human nature, revealing not only the good and bad aspects of character, but also the latent talents and energies whose discovery is necessary if a subject is to have the opportunity to develop his highest potential. "Know thyself," the adage of the ancients, applies even today; for by knowledge of self we master self, and by improvement of self we improve mankind, and so the race is advanced.

The Relationship of Astrology to Palmistry

Astrology and palmistry share a common nomenclature which has come down to us from the earliest chiromantical writings. The naming of each finger and palmar zone was not done in a haphazard manner. This fact indicates that analysts of an earlier time, even as today, regarded the hand as a miniature zodiac which served as the "horoscope" of the subject. In addition to the zodiacal naming of the parts of the hand, there are four basic hand types which are analogous to the four elements. The Practical Hand is related to Earth, the Intuitive to Fire, the Intellectual to Air, and the Sensitive Hand to Water.

In cooperative research between astrologers and palmists, it has been shown that the casting of a natal chart and the reading of the hand results, a large percentage of the time, in two forecasts which agree on the major events in the subject's life. There appears to be no question that the two arts are compatible. The skilled palmist, however, has the advantage over the astrologer in that the palmist can give an accurate analysis anywhere, anytime, without the need for time-consuming and exacting mathematical calculations.

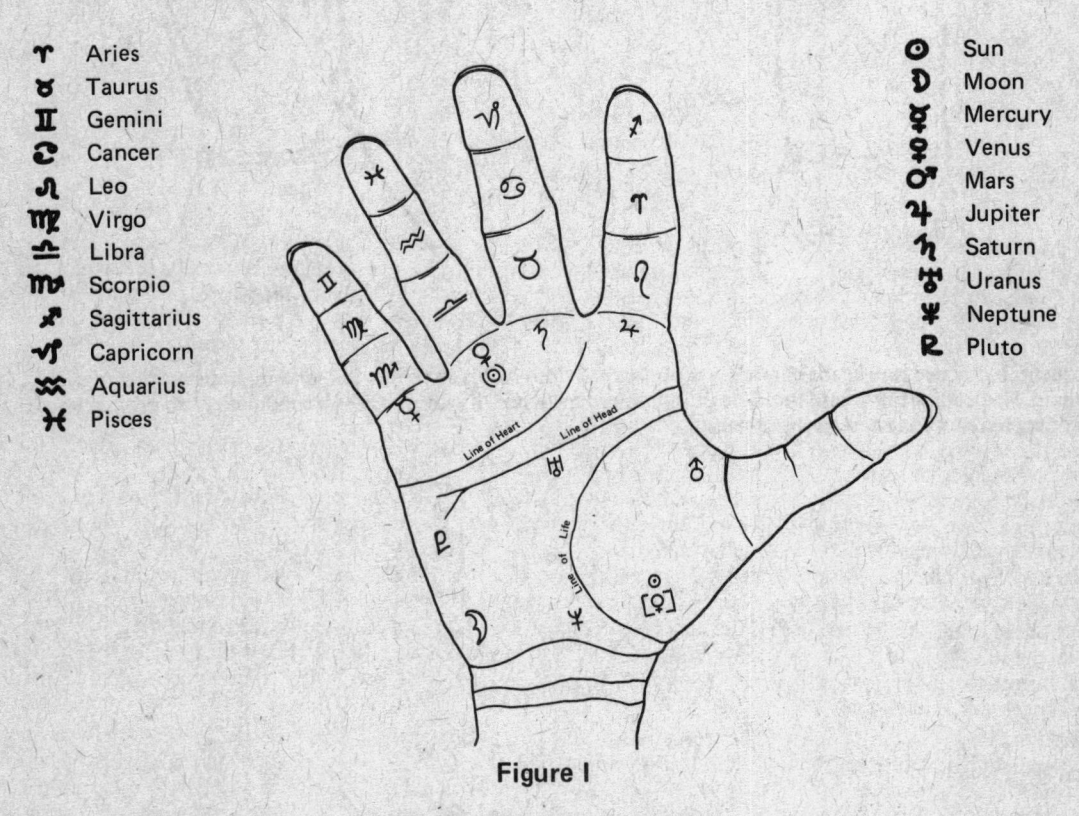

♈ Aries
♉ Taurus
♊ Gemini
♋ Cancer
♌ Leo
♍ Virgo
♎ Libra
♏ Scorpio
♐ Sagittarius
♑ Capricorn
♒ Aquarius
♓ Pisces

☉ Sun
☽ Moon
☿ Mercury
♀ Venus
♂ Mars
♃ Jupiter
♄ Saturn
♅ Uranus
♆ Neptune
♇ Pluto

Figure I

The Thumb

The thumb is a human development. In addition to being among the most useful of tools, it is also the indicator of the ability to find purpose and direction in life. The thumb is usually described as the significator of will power, which may be misconstrued to mean determination, stubbornness, aggression, or self-will. In the case of a properly developed thumb, we define the will as the ability to live the life in accordance with a greater will, the will of God. In this sense, the thumb esoterically represents the will force of the cosmos, Shamballah.

The base of the thumb springs from that section on the Mount of the Sun, having to do with that most vital of human functions, the sex drive. If this section of the thumb is found to be over-developed in comparison with the other segments, we have a subject whose animal passions may dominate the will and logic. If proportionately flat and thin, it shows the absence of vital force needed to balance and regulate determination and reason.

The second section is the field of logic. When full and thick, we find a domineering personality, prone to force itself upon others. Moderately full, the subject is direct and sees no reason to gild the lily when what is reasonable and true should be able to stand on its own merits. When this section is very thin, we see the type of mind that is unable to reason effectively. Consequently, the subject is wishy-washy and easily led to accept whatever opinion is currently prevalent. This phalange, when slightly slimmed or "waisted" (Figure II) shows a balanced and logical mind, inclining to instinctive tact.

The nail phalange is the flowering of what has passed before, the will emerging triumphant from the arena of reason, culminating in a desire to work with the cosmos, nature, and self to achieve the life purpose. If this phalange is thin and underdeveloped, the subject is weak-willed and has little or no sense of responsibility. If overdeveloped, we find strong willfulness and a self-centered disposition. On rare occasions, a subject is found to have a "clubbed" thumb. When the deformity is not due to accident or thumb-sucking as a child, we may expect an overwhelming ego, highly willfull and materialistic. In the event of opposition, the subject yields to violence, and it is no accident that this formation has been dubbed the "Murderer's Thumb."

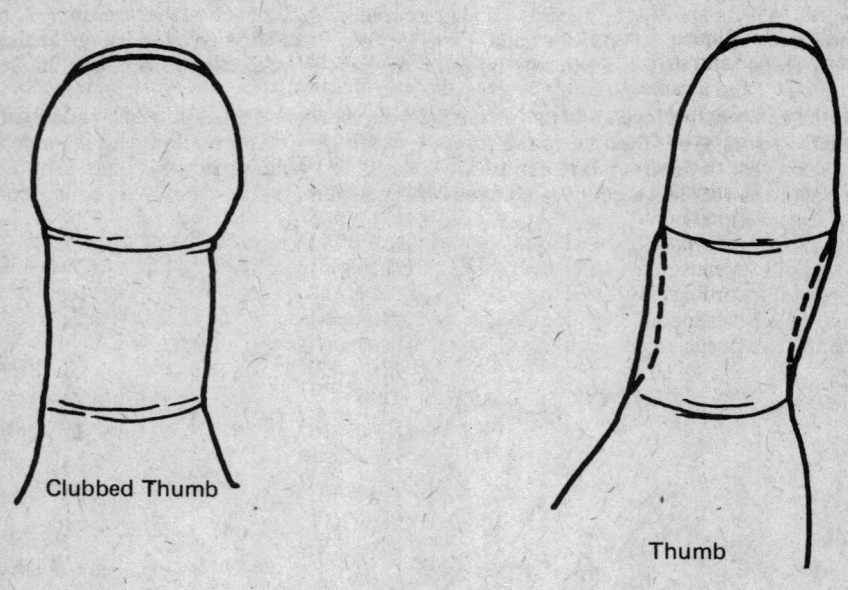

Clubbed Thumb

Thumb

Infrequent, but not so rare as the clubbed thumb, is the thumb that is so thin, weak, and infantile as to appear out of place on the hand. The author has found this type of thumb on the hands of women with "round heels," so promiscuous that it is apparent they have no control over themselves.

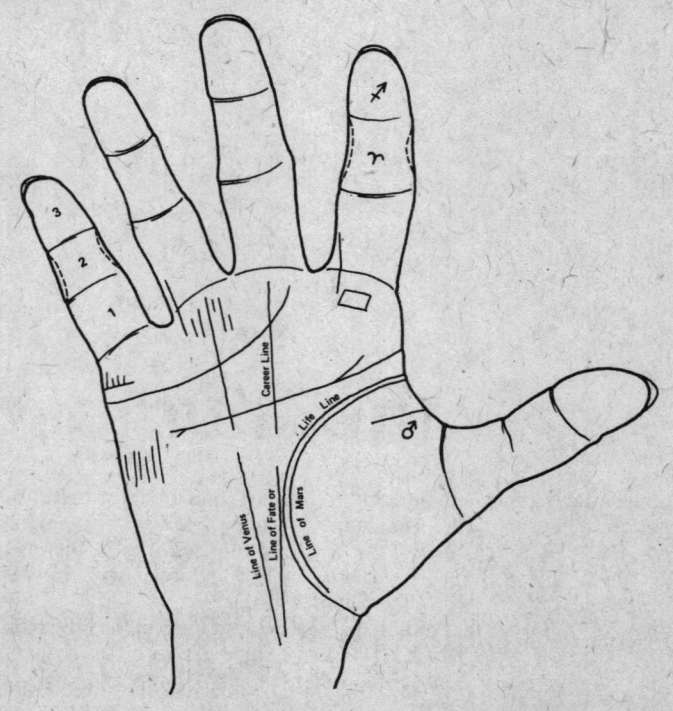

Figure II

The Fingers

The time-worn method of numbering the finger phalanges is from the tip to the base, with the nail phalange being number one, the middle phalange number two, and the base of the finger being number three. Presumably, this system arose from the idea that the fingers act as antennas for gathering vital ethers of the atmosphere to the body for its use and revitalization. Nevertheless, this author prefers to view the fingers as the branches on our symbolic Tree of Life, springing as they do from the rootedness of the palm, and, as messengers to the world, conveying that inner essence which is wholly individualistic and ours alone.

The first finger is named for Jupiter, Lord of the Visible World, and it is here that we find awareness of our status in the world around us. A well-shaped and strong Jupiter indicates a subject who has a good evaluation of his own position, coupled with a sense of responsibility, and a capacity for leadership. The first phalange applies to leadership, the second to ambition, and the third to philosophy, which may manifest in religious form. A long third phalange (the Sagittarius tip) is often seen on the hands of ministers. A waisted second phalange (Aries) (Figure II) is indicative of lack of desire for self-advancement.

The second, or Medius, finger rises from the Mount of Saturn. Overall it has to do with duty and service to others. The first phalange relates to the ecology, agriculture, outdoor life, and generally the gifts of Mother Earth. The second phalange deals with the emotions and the childhood home, while the third phalange relates to economy.

The Venus, or ring, finger has overall to do with the artistic side of life, fame, publicity, and success in the arts. A strong line rising from the Mount of Venus in to the first phalange of the finger indicates a devotion to one of the arts. The first phalange also encompasses, according to its development, love of riches and personal vanity. The second phalange relates to idealism and the senses of brotherhood and justice. The third phalange is assigned to the water sign Pisces and when well-developed gives tendencies to a poetic, sentimental nature, which is often mystical in its expression.

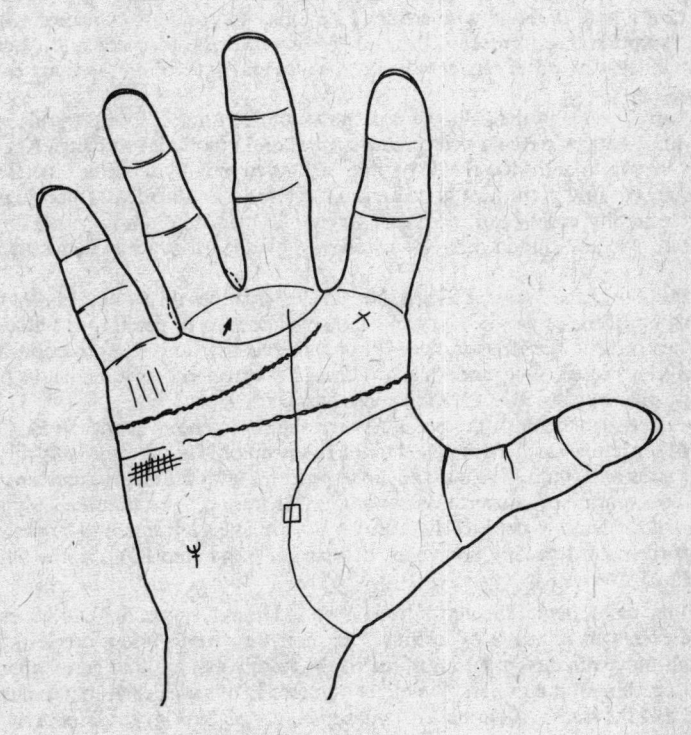

Figure III

The first phalange of the Mercury finger deals with feminine-masculine aspects and is an important indicator of the subject's sexuality. On the hand of a man impotent for many years, although not advanced in age, the author found this phalange entirely absent on one hand and barely present on the other. The second phalange has to do with the critical faculties and love of detail. As a health barometer, it is an excellent reflector of the condition of the digestive system. A thin and waisted Virgo phalange may well signal that the subject suffers from nervous indigestion. As stated before, the tip of the Mercury finger has to do with the powers of expression and communication of ideas. A gentle wilt towards Venus is known as "the tip of sacrifice" and is found on the hands of subjects who give of themselves to create happiness for others. A sharp bend or kink in the same direction, unless inherited as a genetic trait, reveals a tendency to color the truth or to exaggerate and fantasize to the point of believing one's own tall tales. It is definitely not a desirable trait.

The Hand

The twelve phalanges of the four fingers are named for the twelve signs of the zodiac. The shape and size of the phalanges reveal much to the observant analyst. For example, the little finger rises above the Mount of Mercury (planetary ruler of communications) and the third phalange is assigned to the sign of Gemini, ruled by Mercury. If this phalange is long and accompanied by a well-developed Mount of Mercury, the reader may well surmise that the subject is a gifted communicator. However, in the absence of supportive evidence, the long Gemini tip may merely signify gabbiness; perhaps telephonitis or "hoof-in-mouth" disease.

The mounts of the hand are named for the planets. Here the author flies fearlessly in the face of tradition and suggests that the assignment of Venus to the mount in the thumb area and the Sun to the mount under the third, or ring, finger should be reversed. The reasons for the suggestions are: The life line encircles the thumb and is indicative of the vitality and health of the subject. It therefore appears more logical to assign this area to the giver of life itself, the Sun, which symbolizes and rules the life principle. Likewise, that area beneath the third finger is the indicator of the subject's interest and capabilities in the arts. Accordingly, that area should more appropriately be assigned to Venus, the ruler of the fine arts, crafts, and creativity. In addition, the sign of Libra, ruled by Venus, has been assigned to that phalange of the ring finger which rises directly out of the Mount.

In the "web" area of the thumb, just above the Mount of the Sun, is the Mount of Mars. It seems fitting that the area designated to the planetary ruler of dynamic energy should lie inside the life line adjacent to the Mount of the Sun. Here we find attributes of vigor and temperament. This area of conscious energy reveals physical courage especially so if, when the thumb is held closely to the hand, a "puff" of flesh obtrudes. As might be expected from the god of war, this is where we also find tendencies to quarrelsomeness. Interestingly, the author has observed that if the Mount of Mars is red, the subject has recently quarreled. The redder the area, the more recent or intense the quarrel. A straight, short line extending in from the edge of the hand toward the life line signifies an intense approach to the activities of life.

Occasionally, one finds a Line of Mars rising on the mount itself and running side by side with the Life Line. This line denotes robust health and, if found with a faint Life Line, it appears to reinforce and support the life inasmuch as it adds vitality to the constitution. Healthwise, the Mount of Mars rules the adrenal glands, small endocrine glands which are located just above each kidney. The clever reader will take the hint and note the connection between physical courage, aggressiveness, and adrenal output.

On the lower outside edge of the palm we find the Mount of Luna (Moon). In this subconscious area of the hand, we find the qualities of imagination, psychic ability, and mental and emotional stability. Again, it appears logical to place the two "lights" of astrology (Sun and Moon) side by side, separated only by the Life Line. The second largest mount on the hand, we might here expect to find in the Mount of Luna a large variety of incidental markings and signs, and indeed this is the case. The Moon rules fecundity, child-bearing organs, and female disorders, among other things. Any defect in these functions will be registered. Here also are found symptoms of allergy, bladder disorders, edema, and lymphatic system ailments, to name just a few.

Between the Mounts of the Sun and Moon, next to the wrist, lies the Mount of Neptune. This mount is very rare and consists of a building up of the center of the palm next to the wrist as opposed to the hollow space usually found between Luna and the Sun. When present, the effect is one of strong magnetism, and this formation is often found on the hands of medical personnel and psychic healers. One modern analyst may be correct in her belief that its presence signifies qualities of spirituality, psychic agility, divine protection, and God consciousness.

Traditionally, the entire center of the palm between the commencement of the Head and Life Lines and extending to the percussion side of the hand, has been assigned to the rulership of Mars. Presumably this classification predates the discoveries of the planets Uranus and Pluto. The author, however, is not a traditionalist, and several years ago teamed up with another non-conformist in a venture of cooperative exploration. It seemed to us that the assignment to one of the smaller planets of such a large area of the hand to the exclusion of two other planets left much to be desired. Accordingly, we assigned Uranus to that hollow of the palm formerly known as the Plain of Mars, and Pluto to the outer side of the hand, previously called Upper Mars or Passive Mars.

The hollow of the palm, herein theoretically assigned to Uranus, has to do with life changes and inner motivations. Uranus rules unexpected events and changes of fortune. Hence, if we were to find a break in the Fate Line or the Line of Venus as they pass through the area ruled by Uranus, we might readily assume that some unexpected turn of events occured in the career or financial affairs of the subject. We might also find in this area clues to nervous ailments and convulsions. It is in this area of the hand that the victim of Grand Mal will sometimes register jagged lines raying from the Head Line which resemble the form of lightning flashes. Uranus is the planetary ruler of epilepsy.

On the outer side of the hand above the Mount of Luna is the newly named Mount of Pluto. Pluto is astrologically the higher octave of Mars and rules psychology, disorders of the prostate, virus diseases, and arthritis. A veiling of many fine vertical lines in this area is indicative of the type of arthritic complaint that responds well to cortisone. A grille (Figure III) in the same area signifies an irritable nature. A line coming into the mount from the side of the hand is the sign of the natural psychologist.

Beneath the little finger we find the Mount of Mercury. Mercury rules commerce, communications, medicine, and many of the practical endeavors of life. A well-developed Mount of Mercury gives strength in the business world and those marked with the medical stigmata are unequalled in the field of medicine.

We have already touched upon the Mount of Venus at the base of the Venusian finger (traditionally, Apollo). It is here that we find the capacity for success in the arts, whether it is fine arts, design, architecture, or engineering—all of which are ruled by Venus. The Line of Venus, when it is present in the hand terminates at this mount. Short, vertical lines at the top of the mount signify the designer, the "idea" man. A long vertical line traversing the whole of the mount indicates a subject with creative imagination and the ability to carry out his ideas with his own hands. Short lines at the bottom of the mount indicate one who does hand work based on another's design, whether it be carpentry or knitting, or needlepoint (See Figure II). The Venus Line is somewhat of an enigma since it does not always appear in the hand; even the hands of highly successful people may be characterized by its absence. In this case, there are three possibilities: 1) the subject has overcome tremendous obstacles to achieve success, 2) the subject is a perfectionist who is never satisfied with his work, or 3) the subject is truly modest and unassuming to the point of not caring for the plaudits of the world.

Under the middle finger lies the Mount of Saturn, which concerns itself with service to others, the vocations rather than the professions or business, fate, and duty. Healthwise, Saturn rules the hearing, the teeth, diseases of or broken or dislocated bones. This is one instance where the absence of the mount is the preferred characteristic. The subject with a well-developed Mount of Saturn is inclined to hermitism, bitterness, melancholy, and depression. A heart line ending under this finger indicates possessiveness and jealousy in love.

Under the first finger, and lending its name to the finger, is the Mount of Jupiter. Jupiter is associated with abundance and position in life, philosophy, religion, sports, philanthropy, and prosperity. Well developed and properly placed, the mount gives the subject a healthy self-confidence, an easy, outgoing manner, and considerable warmth of personality. From an overdeveloped mount in combination with an extremely long Jupiter finger, we find arrogance and tyranny. A strong, clear line running from the mount up the Jupiter finger (Figure II) signifies a strong sense of responsibility for other people. This line is often seen on the hands of social workers, ministers, teachers, and reformers. A square on this mount (Figure II) is called the "teachers' square" and is found on the hands of those sufficiently secure in knowledge of their material that they are able to transmit this information to others in an intelligible manner. A cross on the mount (Figure III) represents the ability on the part of the subject to make a happy and successful marriage.

Fingerprints and Palmar Loops

The name given to the study of skin patterns is dermatoglyphics; from the Greek derma (skin) and glyphe (carve).

In a universe filled with unique things, the snowflake and the fingerprint hold star billing. No two of either are ever alike. With regard to fingerprints, it is this quality of singularity that visibly brands us from birth to death with the stamp of individuality. Fingerprint patterns fall into five basic formations (Figure IV). However, there are numerous sub-patterns and an endless variety of combinations abounds. The five types, at a glance, are: 1) the loop, an adaptable outlook, good for group

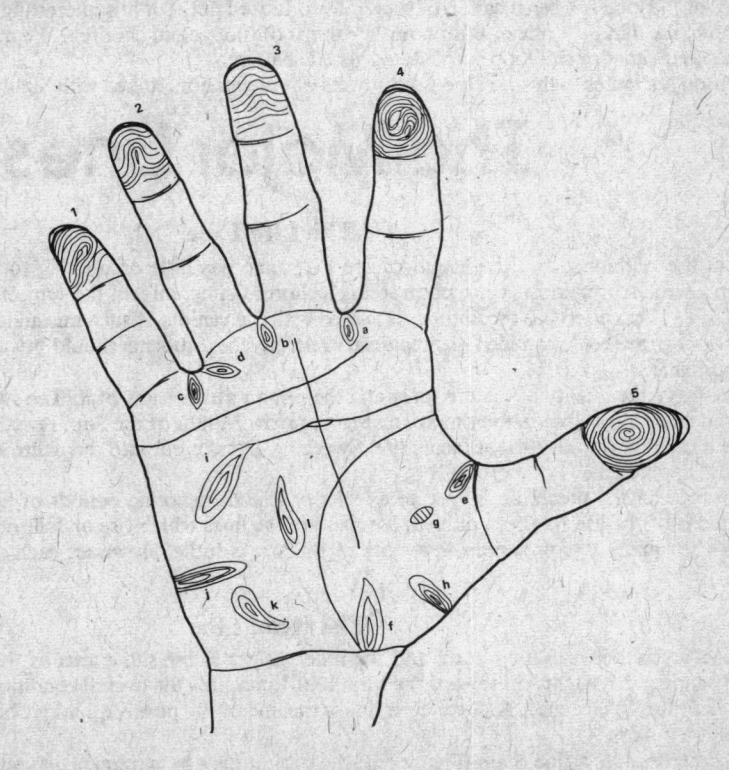

Figure IV

work; 2) the tented arch, fixed ideas, the reformer who expects "them" to change the system; 3) the simple arch, practical and reliable; 4) composite loop, the "double thinker" who sees both sides of the question; and 5) the whorl, the hide-bound individualist who approaches life situations in an unorthodox manner. The reader is cautioned to bear in mind that these definitions are basic only and are modified by the finger on which the pattern occurs. Conversely, the qualities of the finger itself are modified by the type of fingerprint found thereon.

For example, a weak thumb will be strengthened by the presence of a whorl; the presence of a tented arch on an otherwise good third phalange of the ring finger may signify one whose religious ideals are so fixed as to border on intolerance for the beliefs of others. A composite loop on a good Jupiter finger is a definite asset on the hands of judiciary personnel because it signifies the ability to see both sides of a problem; whereas if the finger is poorly developed, it may signify problems with decision making. These modifications of characteristics is difficult to explain, but much practice will lend facility of interpretation.

Certain loops and whorls make their appearance on the palm. A highly regarded scientific text dealing with interpretations of loops and whorls is Beryl Hutchinson's *Your Life In Your Hands*. A basic interpretation of palmar loops is as follows:

a. Royalty loop, found rarely between the first and second fingers. According to Indian tradition, this is the sign of a Rajah and is supposed to show royal descent. In the western world, the analyst may be more inclined to interpret this as a sign of leadership and executive ability.
b. A loop situation between the second and third fingers indicates common sense and a serious purpose in life.
c. A loop between the third and fourth fingers indicates a sense of humor, and the possessor thereof can be counted upon to enliven his or her surroundings. If, however, this inclines itself under the ring finger, we find a sense of humor that is marred by vanity and the subject cannot take a joke aimed at himself.
d. The loop of courage is found on the Mount of Mars, augmenting the qualities thereof. The author knows of one subject on whose hand this loop appears to have worked diligently throughout the lifetime to conquer an irrational fear of reptiles and small closed spaces.
e. The loop of music arises from the wrist up the Mount of the Sun and tells us that the subject will have great love of music. This small figure, resembling the body of an insect, is related to the ability to play stringed instruments, including the piano. It is the inborn ability that is revealed and not necessarily that the subject does in fact play a stringed instrument.
f. A well-pronounced bulge on the lower edge of the Mount of the Sun is indicative of a good sense of time and rhythm. A loop at this point generally denotes a love of military music with its strong, rhythmic beat. The subject is usually a good dancer.
g. The loop most frequently found on the Mount of Luna is the memory loop. Not only do subjects having this loop seem to have an active memory for everyday details, but they also seem to remember the unseen and previously unknown. Strongly intuitive, these people seem able to reach into the past for answers to today's problems.
h. The loop that enters the palm from the ulna side is known as the "nature lover's loop." Subjects having this loop are often gifted and enthusiastic gardeners, campers, and ecologists. The Swiss psychologist, Dr. Hugo DeBrunner, is said to have found this mark on ninety-five percent of the Mongoloids he examined. This is not to say that the presence of the loop is a certification of mongolism. Indeed not, but it is interesting to note that the author has found this loop in the hands of one or both normal parents of mongoloid children. We might be justified in suspecting that the true significance of this loop is an altered genetic pattern.
i. Hutchinson attributes to this rare loop the powers of imagination, linked with highly developed intuition.

The Major Lines

The Life Line

Let us state at the beginning that the length of the Life Line has little or nothing to do with the length of a person's life. A pox upon all amateur palmists who, upon seeing a short life line, inform the subject that he is doomed to die an early death! No such thing! Too often has the author counseled with the victims of such misguided and cruel prophecy, never quite successfully uprooting the seed of an idea planted deep in the psyche. Students should beware of predicting the length of life; that is *not* their province.

The Life Line shows the quality of the life force and the person's awareness of it. The sweep of the line is important to interpretation. A line that hugs close to the thumb, giving a narrow Mount of the Sun, reveals introversion, a clinging to home and hearth, and a peculiar timidity about facing life. Sweeping grandly out into the palm, the life is extroverted and marked with an enthusiastic approach.

The Life Line may have a break, an island, or a series of islands denoting periods of poor health or excessive worry. In some way, the tenor of the life has been altered. Myriad are the lines which rise or fall, or cross, over the Life Line. To attempt to classify their many interpretations in a work of this size is futile. However, each of these lines has a meaning all its own.

The Head Line

The Head Line begins between the thumb and the index finger in the same area as the Life Line and continues across the palm, usually ending in a slight wilt toward the Mount of Luna. It is the overall condition of the Line, and not necessarily the length, that indicates intelligence. A deep, clear line is the line of the positive thinker, blessed with a good memory and a capacity for decision making.

If the Head Line resembles a fine chain (Figure III), the subject may be extremely nervous and inclined to excessive worry. When only a portion of the line is chained, the indication is that during that phase of the life represented by this part of the line the subject was confused or under strain. Tiny breaks in the line show shock of some type or a change in philosophy. If the correct answer is shock, a "tracer" line running to the Life or Heart Lines will cut in at that specific point.

Astrology, Horoscope, and Dreams

An island on the Head Line indicates a breakdown in the mental processes. If the island is marked on each end by bars (Figure IV), the subject has probably undergone psychiatric treatment. If the treatment has been effective, the condition of the line improves thereafter. Small hair lines sweeping up and down from the Head Line indicate that the mentality has registered new lines of thought or has been exposed to the higher truths of life.

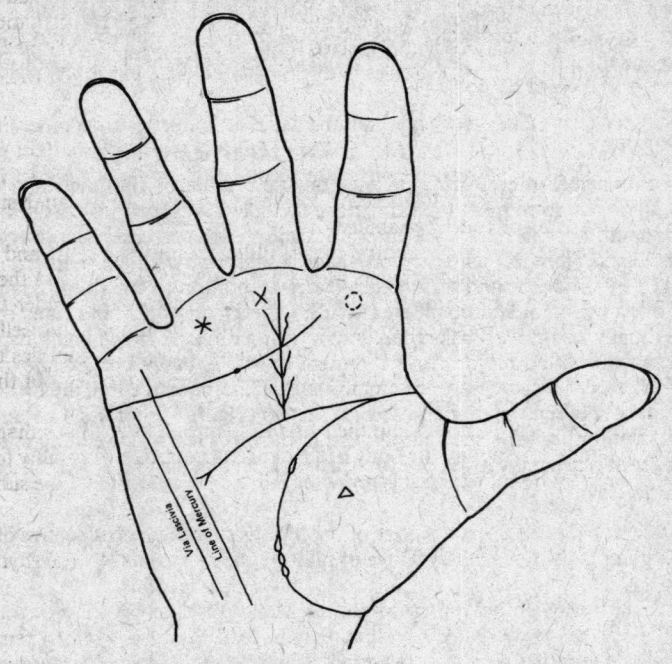

Figure V

When the Head Line commences from the Life Line (Figure V), the subject is usually a traditionalist and almost certain to be conservative in moral, religious, and political matters. Home ties are strong with this type, and the skilled analyst can gauge with great accuracy the age at which the subject departed from the family unit.

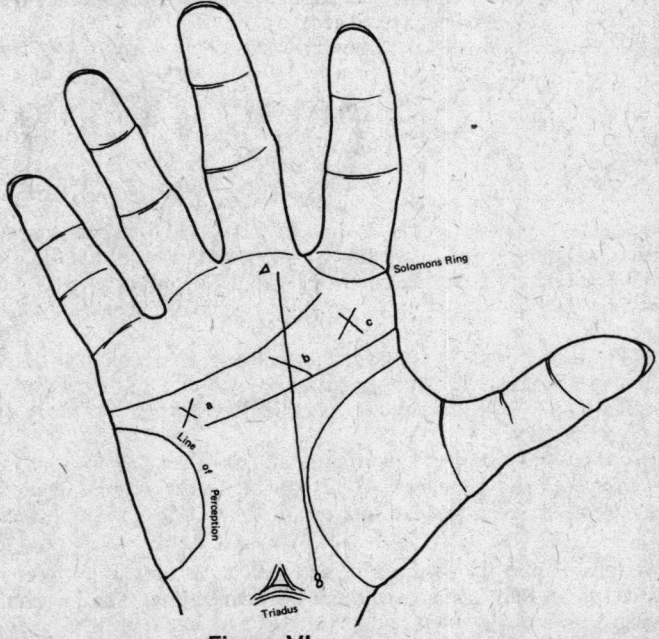

Figure VI

If the Head Line is separated slightly from the Life Line, the subject's actions are less inhibited and less controlled by the sphere of influence. If the two lines are more widely separated, the subject is more independent in thought and more liberal in action. In such a subject, social consciousness is developed, and the qualities of humanitarianism are expressed. If the separation of Life and Head Lines is extreme, impulsiveness reigns; and, all other indications being equal, the subject is true nonconformist.

A Head Line ending on the Mount of Luna is indicative of qualities of creativity and imagination. If the Head Line ends on the Mount of Luna with a small "writer's fork," we might expect to find the subject to be a writer of poetry or fiction. If the Head Line ends deep on Luna (Figure VII), the subject might suffer much from over-sensitivity. The exaggerated imagination would find slights in the most commonplace occurrences, and the subject would be the victim of sudden sharp swings in mood. This is especially so if the Head Line is found in combination with a poor Line of Heart. When the Head Line ends on the outer side of the hand, the approach is more practical, and the mentality is more logical and well organized. A writer's fork on this ending signifies the gift of factual reporting or technical writing. A large fork on this ending signifies the practical humanitarian who works toward his goals.

The Heart Line

Analysts differ on whether the Heart Line rises on the outside of the hand and crosses to the Mount of Jupiter, or vice versa. It does, however, seem more logical to have the emotional energies transmitted from the subconscious to the conscious region of the hand. For this reason the author has adopted the percussion as the rising point for the Line of Heart.

A chained Heart Line (Figure III) signals emotional instability and perhaps an inferiority complex. The subject has an emotional nature marked by problems and difficulties. If only a portion of the line is chained, with the rest clearly defined, the subject has undergone a period of emotional unrest during the length of time indicated by the length of the chained part.

The Heart Line usually has more breaks than does any other line. A single break usually indicates trauma associated with the loss of a loved one or with a major disappointment in life. A badly broken line can, physiologically speaking, indicate some form of heart disease. The analyst, upon finding such a line, should check the Life Line for further indications.

A Heart Line ending between the first and second fingers (Figure I) signifies a balanced emotional nature, with a healthy sexuality and good relationship with one's family and friends. A Heart Line ending under the index finger indicates idealism in love and the danger of placing the loved one on a pedestal, from which he or she dare not fall.

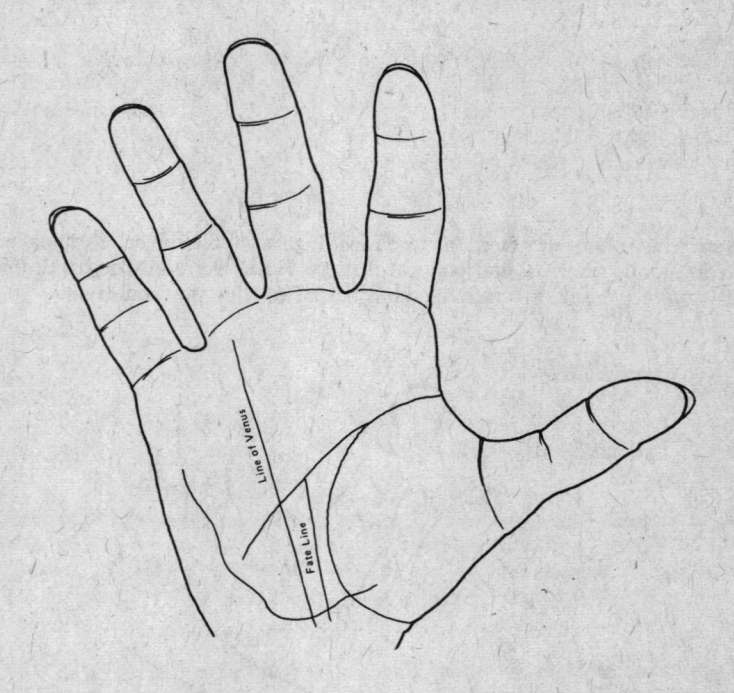

Figure VII

The Fate Line

The Fate Line, variously called the Saturn Line and the Career Line, is not present on every hand. When missing, this fact seems to place the subject fully in charge of his or her own destiny. If and when the subject makes good, it is due to his own merit and striving.

This Fate Line, like the other major lines on the hand, has various starting points and points of termination, each of which has its own special meaning. The Fate Line that starts from the wrist and runs straight and true, unmarked by adverse signs, to the Mount of Saturn (Figure II) indicates a smooth path in life and a successful career. The Fate Line commencing from the Life Line (Figure III) indicates that the early environment gave the subject little chance to develop his natural gifts, or that circumstances had a restricting effect on the course of the life. That point on the Life Line from which the Fate Line springs symbolizes the moment of independence, when the subject launched out for himself.

The Fate Line that starts at the Head Line and runs unchecked to the Mount of Saturn (Figure IV) indicates that, after hard struggle, the subject became successful at about the age of thirty-five. The Fate Line curving upward from the Head Line bespeaks a life of continual labor and struggle.

When the Fate Line rises from inside the Life Line on the Mount of the Sun (Figure IV) this fact indicates that family influence played a helpful part in the subject's life. From a secure childhood filled with love, the subject received substantial help and encouragement from the family throughout life.

The Mount of Luna so typifies the creative imagination that we cannot fail to make the connection between a Fate Line rising in this area and success in the arts for actors, writers, lecturers, singers, etc.

The owner of a Fate Line ending at the Heart Line must guard against loss due to his own errors of judgment or poor organization. A Fate Line curving over or throwing a branch to the Mount of Jupiter indicates ambition, and the owner will probably reach a position in life where he has influence or authority over others. The Fate Line branching to the Mount of Venus serves the purpose as a Line of Venus and constitutes a forecast of good fortune, popularity, and success. When it is branch line to the Mount of Mercury, it symbolizes high achievement in commercial or scientific endeavors.

Tiny branches sometimes run upward off the Fate Line (Figure V) and promise that prosperity will gradually come to the subject. However, if the lines run downward, they warn of loss of money or property.

The Fate Line may be marked with crosses, squares, stars, islands, breaks, or bars. The possible indications of these incidental markings are too numerous to permit their discussion here.

The Line of Venus

The lucky possessor of a clear, straight Line of Venus has a sunny disposition and radiant charm. The ideal Line of Venus starts close to the wrist between the Mounts of Luna and the Sun and ends on the Mount of Venus. The Line of Venus promises a golden shower of success, good luck, financial reward, and a good reputation. Alas, an unblemished Line of Venus is extremely rare, and the line itself is frequently absent.

The Line of Mercury

The Line of Mercury has many other names, such as Line of Hepatica, Line of Health, and Line of Liver. Traditionally, absence of the line indicates a strong constitution. When present, the line should be narrow, straight, and clear. The old interpretation of this line is that if the line is uneven or broken, there is a tendency to poor digestion. Modern analysts, however, have suggested that this line is the indicator of certain psychic powers and that its owner will experience strong intuitions and an active dream life. The experience of the author lends credence to this theory.

The Minor Lines

The Racettes or Bracelets

The three lines separating the wrist from the palm are known as the Racettes or Bracelets. They do not assume much importance in the analysis of the hand except that, as Cheiro points out, when the first bracelet rises in an arch almost into the palm (Figure I) in the hands of women, the subject will experience difficulty in child bearing. Personal observation supports this interpretation. The author has also found this formation in the hands of sterile males.

The Girdle of Venus

The Girdle of Venus is a semi-circle between the first and second finger and the third and fourth finger (Figure III). The line may be continuous or a series of broken lines, which breaks up the intensity imparted by the Girdle. The structure is often seen on the hands of sensitive, idealistic people, who can rise to the heights of ecstacy or plunge to the depths of despair. Quite often highly intelligent, these subjects are almost always interesting and stimulating personalities.

The Via Lascivia

The Via Lascivia may appear as a straight line running parallel to the line of Mercury on the side nearest the edge of the hand, or as a curving line rising from the Mount of the Sun. In neither case is this a desirable line, but of the two, the straight line (Figure V) is preferable. Since the structure is an indicator of lax morals, the subject having it must take great care to avoid scandal in his or her life. The curved line (Figure VII) is the sign of self-undoing, and subjects having it are their own worst enemies. It is extremely difficult for them to avoid the lure of stimulants or sexual excess.

Line of Marriage and Children

The so-called Lines of Marriage enter the edge of the hand between the base of the little finger and the Heart Line and cross a short distance into the Mount of Mercury (Figure II). These lines more accurately signify deep emotional attachment than participation in a formal contract. Several of these lines may appear on a hand, but they do not by any means indicate that the subject will enter into a series of marriages. Strong clear lines suggest a marriage, whereas faint, weak lines represent minor affairs of the heart. Other factors, such as termination point, determine interpretation.

The child lines, which rise from the Marriage Line toward the base of the little finger, are supposed to predict the number of children born to the person. The appearance of these lines can be deceptive, for I have seen them on barren subjects. Hence, they may be taken to signify the way the subject feels about children; the indicated children may be dearly loved nieces and nephews. In the case of one woman, the children lines were so numerous it was physically impossible for her to have borne so many children. Inquiry revealed that the subject was a kindergarten teacher by profession and emotionally a mother to her small charges.

The Psychic Indicators

Psychic gifts or powers are those which one possesses in addition to those derived from the five senses. The indicators for the "sixth sense," or extra-sensory perception, are plainly visible on the palms of those so gifted. One mark is sufficient to brand the subject, as "psychic" and two strengthen the power. If all indicators are present, the analyst may be sure he is in the presence of a competent occultist, perhaps even an adept.

The Line of Perception

Rarely found, the Line of Perception appears on the hands of subjects who are perceptive and in tune with their surroundings. Sometimes they are mediumistic. Occultism holds strong appeal for such subjects, and they are frequently precognitive. Oddly enough, the subjects whose hands the author has been priviliged to examine are also musically gifted. Whether or not there is any connection, or if it is merely coincidence, remains to be seen.

The Mystic Cross (Croix Mystique)

The Mystic Cross lies in the Great Quadrangle between the Head Line and the Heart Line. If found in the center of the quadrangle (Figure VI), the subject has psychic powers and uses them in the everyday life. Such subjects are serious students of occult lore, especially so if one leg of the Cross is formed by the Fate Line. If the Cross is found under the Mount of Mercury (Figure VI), the subject often has telepathic powers and an uncanny insight into human nature. If it is found in connection with medical stigmata, the subject may also be a psychic healer. When located under the Mount of Jupiter, (Figure VI), the Cross may lose its strength and be frittered away for self-interests only. Occasionally, the Cross may be found in more than one location.

Ring of Solomon

A ring around the Jupiter finger is known as the Ring of Solomon and is traditionally recognized as the sign of great wisdom. It denotes a deep love of the occult; and, according to some analysts, it indicates the spiritual power of a master or adept. In this connection the shape of the hand itself is significant. The fingertips may have fleshy pads known as the Teardrops of Isis, which contribute much to psychic sensitivity and may be found on more than one hand type. The Psychic hand is usually quite beautiful in form and graceful in use. In addition, there is sometimes a fine skin pattern known as a "triadus" on the Mount of Neptune. A figure 8, formed by two islands at the start of the Fate Line, are said to denote clairvoyance or second sight. A well-developed Mount of Luna or a triangle on the Mount of Saturn are both indicators of intuitive qualities.

Incidental Signs and Markings

A brief description only will be given for the incidental signs on the hand, inasmuch as their full interpretation and significance will be altered in accordance with their position on the hand and their relationship to other evidence.

Circle—Misfortune, unless found on the Mount of Jupiter (Figure V). In this position the circle denotes personal success. This mark is almost never seen as an unbroken circle; most often it appears as a series of lines forming a circle.

Spot—Usually a sign of temporary illness (Figure V). A series of tiny dots on the Heart Line may warn of active diabetes or a hereditary predisposition toward this disease.

Island—Not a fortunate sign, the island warns of weakness in the area in which it is found (Figure V).

Square—Considered fortunate. It offers protection at the point where it occurs (Figure III).

Star—A fortunate sign with few exceptions. It is not desirable on the Mount of Saturn (Figure IV).

Cross—Seldom favorable. An interesting little gimmick is that a cross on the side of the index finger near the nail indicates a love of animals—small cross for small animals and a large cross for large animals (Figure V).

Grille—Found most frequently on the Mounts of the hand, the grille indicates obstacles brought on by the subject's own character (Figure III).

Triangle—A good mark, giving emphasis to the mount on which it is found (Figure V).

Tripod and Spear—Either indicates success on whichever mount it is found (Figure III).

HOROSCOPES: A YEAR'S FORECAST

Aries
March 21—April 20th

Inspiration leads you
to seek new worlds
to conquer.
Your happiness lies
in a victory over limiting conditions.
The conquest
is your source of greatest happiness,
and you cheer
when you win.
Once that's accomplished
you're bored
and seek some new way to find challenge
and get the best of it.
You rejoice at overcoming hindrances,
defeating obstacles and opposition.
This goes for love, too;
watch out a bit
for this happiness trend,
preferably by marrying someone
who gives you a constant sense of challenge.
You can be joyous
when striving
to win political position
and each step upward
in this field
can provide splendid challenge.

Aries

JANUARY

1—Start now to accomplish something you have long wanted to achieve. Friendly guidance and inspiration from others can help you obtain cherished desires more readily. Reversals and setbacks you encounter should prove to be of only minor importance.

2—Let others do and say as they wish so that harmony can prevail. Be practical in money matters and give special attention to budget limitations. Refrain from being forceful and aggressive or exerting pressure on other people.

3—Think things over carefully before saying what is on your mind. Do not let yourself be drawn into an argument involving a money matter. Review facts carefully before acting on them and do not make hasty decisions.

4—Do not allow yourself to relax too completely, since you may have to double your efforts at a later period. Determination and faith in yourself may prove instrumental in overcoming obstacles. Avoid restlessness and do not anticipate trouble before it actually appears.

5—Refrain from taking chances that might jeopardize your income or savings. Apply yourself diligently to carrying out obligations and completing required duties. Strive for worth-while goals and do not let up in your efforts.

6—Seek competent guidance and avoid conversations that may foster emotional conflicts. Your poise and diplomacy may strengthen the admiration and respect others have for you. Do not ignore your duties for more interesting activities.

7—Extravagant or impetuous whims may lead to more trouble than you anticipated. Smoothing over differences of opinion may start you on a new period of lasting harmony and friendship. Face each household problem squarely as it arises instead of giving in to an attitude of pessimism.

8—Allow yourself ample time for the tasks you undertake. Ward off undesirable criticism by keeping your personal affairs to yourself. Meet your problems face to face rather than try to postpone decisions or responsibilities.

9—You may overcome present limitations by adhering to conservative policies. Control impetuous feelings and beware of emotional conflicts. Remain in the background and observe what is going on around you.

10—Be reserved in your approach, rather than aggressive. Settle matters with diplomacy, and do not let the impatience of others exhaust you. An indifferent attitude on your part may prove helpful in getting what you want.

11—Give consideration to household problems and what is needed to make the domestic scene more harmonious. Clear up minor tasks so that you will be in a better position to tackle more important assignments. Seek solid advice before making important career or business adjustments.

12—Let your desire for recreation and pleasure wait for the time being. Steer clear of any enterprises that have risks attached to them. Refuse to be discouraged if the results of your efforts are ignored by others at first.

13—Participate in activities that can facilitate your release from dull and boring routines. Travel in connection with your job or for pleasure may be unusually enjoyable. Arrange to use your time profitably by tackling jobs from which you can expect to derive financial benefit eventually.

14—Attend to personal and home needs and make every effort to keep things running smoothly. Refrain from entrusting personal responsibilities or duties to another. Handle temperamental people in your most diplomatic manner.

15—Take the initiative and make needed changes in your job or business. Do not let temporary pressures put you in a gloomy mood, even though you are likely to be bothered by minor disappointments. Patience and calm understanding are needed to produce satisfactory results.

16—Adapt yourself quickly to changing trends and new situations. Regardless of how slow things may be going, do not try to speed up events. Do what you can to maintain harmony among your circle of friends.

17—Personal happiness and contentment are indicated from successful results at work. Clear and logical programs are essential for satisfactory progress. Your versatility in handling a business matter may prove effective in offsetting antagonism.

18—Abrupt changes that you make in your home are likely to prove unsatisfactory. Prudent and conservative actions are particularly essential today. Pay attention to matters associated with your business, property, or savings.

19—Concentrate on fulfilling present obligations and duties before considering new projects. Regardless of how irritated you may feel, refrain from becoming involved in an argument. Go forward on your own initiative, but do not take things for granted.

20—Do not ignore an irksome task, even though you may be anxious to break away from restrictions. Use inexpensive measures to gratify your desire for pleasurable activity. Arrange your work program carefully so that you will be able to use every minute of time to good advantage.

21—Tempers may be frayed unless a calm attitude is maintained. Keep ideas and opinions to yourself, especially if they concern money. Control restless feelings and the desire to make changes.

22—Look to the future with enthusiasm and optimism. Seek opportunities that may prove helpful in augmenting your income. Do not overlook trifles which may become important later.

23—Use the hours you have effectively but do not press for achievements that are out of reach. A cautious approach is desirable when settling household matters. Guard against attempts to separate you from your money.

24—Keep your intentions to yourself until you can put plans into effect. Adapt yourself quickly to new changes and thoughts rather than offer open resistance. Ignore apprehensive feelings and gratify some of your present desires.

25—You may benefit from taking a new and aggressive approach to achieve results. Aim for worth-while goals and do not relent until you have realized them. Discard outdated equipment and appliances for more modern innovations.

26—Arrange to demonstrate your skills and resourcefulness to others. Direct your attention to clearing up matters you had previously neglected. Refrain from taking a chance that might adversely affect your money or job standing.

27—Do not let anyone or any situation deter you from the progress you can make. This can be a period of multiple activities that should prove enjoyable. Face problems in a realistic manner, especially when your income or savings is concerned.

28—There should be little need for pessimism, even though your plans may not work out exactly as anticipated. Fulfill major responsibilities and financial obligations with care. Do not force an issue or try to evade a duty that you are required to perform.

29—Get essential tasks done well ahead of time so that you will have ample opportunity for recreation. Build up a solid foundation for your future security by working conscientiously. New ideas and approved methods for completing laborious duties may bring benefits.

30—Make use of opportunities that can give you increased prestige and popularity. Plan to do something different from your usual program of recreation. See that cash and jewelry are in a safe place where there is little chance of your losing them.

31—Guard against becoming involved in unnecessary emotional entanglements. Avoid taking hasty action, even though you may feel that what you are doing is correct. Refuse to give in to your doubts or let others discourage you, even if you encounter a disappointing experience.

FEBRUARY

1—You may have to live up to some major commitments. Do not let anyone or anything disrupt your program. The evening is fine for social relationships, but there may be one flaw in the form of a personality clash.

2—If you are married or deeply in love, do not allow any intruder to disrupt your love. A mischievous acquaintance might start a very unpleasant situation and make a serious effort to end the happiness in your romantic life.

3—Have a long conversation with someone you would like to know better. If you give your trust and confidence, you are likely to win the trust of another. Avoid any plans that prevent early retirement.

4—You may be introduced to something new in the way of adventurous pleasure. Don't go in for this so happily that you soon make a habit of it. It might be a form of gambling that could be disastrous to your pocketbook.

5—This is a good time to make a decision about a move of residence. Keep any promises you make. If you are going to move, you should start plans and begin getting things together quickly. A new horizon is appearing before you.

6—Family troubles may grow irksome. There can be some vexing arguments, and all problems may be deepened by the trend toward disagreement. Try not to add extra fuel to this scene of quarrelsome temperaments and selfish wills.

7—You will have much more physical energy and serenity of mind today. You will accomplish your aims now. Everyone may show you affection and you can be quite proud of how popular you are. Someone may be jealous and stand aloof though.

8—A talk with an executive may bring out some facts of which you do not really approve. You'll have to accept things of this type, keep quiet about it and let your feelings remain unknown, even if asked for advice by this person.

9—You may be suspicious that someone is trying to play a romantic game with you and that it could be dangerous. A state of alarm won't help. Use common sense and note that you are in a safe position, anyhow.

10—A person who is very serious about career matters may come to you for advice about a major concern. Unfortunately, while you may be sincere, you could give the wrong advice, so be careful in this matter.

11—You could be in the mood for following fashion strictly; you may buy some new clothes just to make your ego feel at ease with the world at this moment. Do this and enjoy it. At a party tonight, you'll shine more than you usually do.

12—Keep good health habits, avoid eating weight-increasing foods, and be cautious about drinks if you go out this evening. You're in a genial mood and might give in to immoderation just to be sociable.

13—You may try to figure out a mechanical matter without any help. This can intrigue you and you may succeed. Most strange of all is that the answer may come to you during your sleep and be clear the next morning.

14—Keep a promise you have recently made to yourself. Also fulfill any work aims you set yourself for the day. You'll enjoy being particular, thorough and efficient. This evening is good for restful companionship.

15—Someone new entering your life can seem very serene and pleasant. This can be the highly deceptive appearance of a person who is adept at deception about personality and character. Be on guard now; take no chances.

16—Keep the family in mind and do not neglect anything you have promised them, especially the children. It is a good evening for social life or going to the theatre. Music might hit the spot for you now.

17—Do not be too friendly with anyone after leaving work. You could, without meaning to, delay and frustrate a younger person. Be considerate throughout the day and expect the same treatment from others.

18—You may be excited over news about your career. The type of chance you have waited a long time for may come. However, do not talk too soon about this matter to others. Wait until it is officially announced.

19—Not much of a day, and you can wish for other times, other places. Someone may catch you brooding and startle you out of it with more immediate concerns. The evening has a happy surprise ending for the day.

20—Your answers about important problems are much desired. Help an executive who has expressed a need for your views. Be calm and quiet to help soothe and assure this person. A casual entertainment at home is best for tonight.

21—You can go through quite an emotionally disturbed cycle, much different from what Aries usually experiences. You feel as though a plot were being formed to do harm in your life, but you're far off base now.

22—A young relative may come to you with a problem and expect you to be handing out some money. This person is quite hypocritical, and also sly, so do as you deem best but be wary of the consequences.

23—Don't expect perfection. You may praise someone who works neatly and efficiently and then discover this person has a terribly narrow view and a great intolerance about others and their views.

24—Take nothing for granted. Show love and be generous with family members. Avoid taking any harsh financial positions. You'll find work inspiring, aims easily reached, and you can set your new targets much higher.

25—Because someone seems in-the-know and superficially sophisticated, you may imagine this friend is a deep and bold thinker. You may be surprised later to learn that this new acquaintance is really a retiring recluse-type of person.

26—Take a new look at a financial proposition; you may want to move some funds in another direction. Aspects are excellent for a major financial change if you use sharp thought and all the latest information about investment opportunities.

27—Good news comes early and keeps the day exciting. You may be traveling over the weekend in connection with your career. All is favorable for your advancement and the tackling of new responsibilities in your career.

28—Have sympathy for a young person who is quite alone and feels the need of talk. Avoid being impatient; be prepared to give time and thought to others today. Your shopping can wait for a free moment this evening.

29 (Leap Year Only)—Your excellent reputation and the affection people have for you will pay off today. This is a time when kindness will be remembered and you will receive rewards and gratifying messages that are entirely unexpected. Plan on an evening at home.

MARCH

1—Let yourself get to know a new person better before you form opinions. Make sure there is no envy in your attitude and approach this person with fresh and impartial view. You may find a loyal lifetime friend here.

2—You may be invited to join a social club, a cotillion or a square dance club. You really have your pick of some good things going on today. Make social life your interest and extend your present range of acquaintances.

3—Take another look at your job and see where you can improve your methods a little for better results. Much cooperation today and a romantic promise for tonight should brighten your spirits. Look your very best this evening.

4—A very active mind may show you where you can bring improvements to your life. Taking on some extra work is just the thing to get your financial accounts straightened. Such work can be enjoyable, really recreational.

5—An unsociable and self-centered mood may keep you in the house, uncommunicative and resentful. You may be dreaming of other days, doing too much wishful thinking about yesterday. You'll just have to settle for what is *now*.

6—A very clever person may enter your life and cause you to be puzzled. You are in too much of a hurry to put this person in a category. You may be dealing with someone who has mystical insight, strong intuition.

7—A bit of wisdom to stay with the tried and true, the familiar and trustworthy. You can get in much trouble by following up curiosity. Dissatisfaction with your romantic life can bring about a very bad marital situation.

8—Difficulty with work can arouse your temper. The trouble is you are just looking for an excuse to lose your temper and this won't work very well. Others may just laugh at you and where will you be then?

9—Be cautious of companionship today; think first of reputation and also consider that you aren't really happy with people who do not share your interests. Get out and walk this evening, cultivate health habits tonight.

10—You may have some inspired thought but must check it over before seeking a conference about it. Let everything proceed slowly and sensibly today. Avoid impetuous actions and any possible social blunders through haste.

11—An older relative may say something that upsets you a lot. Your reactions can be strong, defiant and quite lacking in true affection. You are on the verge of a big blunder that will have resounding consequences.

12—Home might be depressing today. You could enjoy seeking out a different household or neighborhood and visiting it. If you do any entertaining, make it entirely spontaneous. A telephone conversation tonight may be the beginning of a new friendship.

13—Time will speed by and you must not be left behind. A good bargain may come your way. Check for safety in career and domestic life. It may be better to discard an article that has outworn its use in order to be safer today.

14—A good day for any plans. Financial transactions go over big, moving your residence can bring joy and new comfort, getting married may be the best thing you ever did. Evening is warm and cheery in relationships.

15—Another fine day for any project you have going. You can make real strides in creative work. You may win some favorable publicity for what you do today. It is a good time to ask for higher wages and get them.

16—Do your best to please someone who is very particular and trusts you. Work can be strenuous so you'll need a peaceful evening, but do enjoy a romantic telephone call that comes through contrary to your expectations.

17—Take your time in reaching a decision. If you have accepted an invitation for tonight, do not cancel out. Please those around you but also protect yourself from those who impose. Let your thoughts be known to these.

18—Novelty may enter your life in the form of a very attractive new acquaintance. Although this person just passes by in your life, there can be lasting effect from the encounter. Be very firm and loyal in your attitude.

19—Do nothing to startle a very conventional person. Keep your conversation within limits indicated by the companionship you have. Be very kindly with an older friend. In the evening find solitude, reflect, care for grooming.

20—A hope may come true and you can get started on something which has suffered much delay. Be sure to eat well, don't skip any meals. Your good care of a dependent person will be rewarding and much appreciated tonight.

21—Best to hold a slow, steady pace. Your health is a bit disturbed but if it doesn't get worse you may find it improved after a good night's rest. Do not plan on attending any meeting this evening, though pressed to do so.

22—You may meet someone you haven't seen for a long time and be shocked by the change in both appearance and general life. This person may be of importance to you in the future so do not reject the association of today.

23—An older neighbor may be unpleasant and you may have to cut out help you have been giving this person. Do not tolerate ingratitude or some sarcasm on top of it. Keep working quietly, don't brood about the unpleasant.

24—A happy day and a good one for shopping. Buy clothes for the coming season, buy a painting or art object for the home, send a toy to a child you love. Expand, follow impulses, take new people into your friendship without criticism.

25—Today you may know it's love that makes the world go 'round, love that keeps your life going. The pace is fast, the joys are intense and you may forever remember this time. Things will sparkle for your love and you.

26—Excellent to get out and see people you've been neglecting for awhile. Go along harmoniously with ideas of others, expand your social interests. You can please someone a lot by an invitation to dine out with you now.

27—Be practical, work with all your skill and concentration, avoid the gossipers and be helpful rather than troublesome to others. You may discover a new source of income during a conversation over the telephone tonight.

28—Put a little pressure on to get things completed. It is against the grain with you to work this way, but prove you can do it. You may have a fascinating encounter with someone of the opposite sex. You will derive much enjoyment from a chat.

29—A day to sum up the good things in your life and be appreciative of them. You will find someone in business deals with you very honorably. The evening may hold a romantic date about which you are happy but somewhat dubious.

30—Surprise someone by offering to do a routine chore and relieve them of a burden. Making yourself useful is the best way to enhance social life and community standing. Be faithful to a cause or work in your church. Be helpful!

31—Make sure that any work you have done today is done expertly and conscientiously. The evening is good for spontaneous entertainment but not for planned events. In romantic matters let discretion be your guide in speech.

APRIL

1—You may have to do twice as much work as usual due to some adverse complications in your work atmosphere. Don't rely on haste for it can set you back. Rely on your industrious attitude and clear mind. If too tired this evening, break a date about which you may have had a previous understanding.

2—A new outlook can come to you when you listen to those around you. A talk with an executive can put matters on the table clearly and help you make a decision. More affluence and honor may come to you soon as a result of your thinking today. Talk with a relative about your change of mind.

3—You might be too impatient with a person who deserves better treatment from you. Keep emotions under control and your most affectionate views out in front. A new honor may come to you that can win you some publicity. This may stir up more envy and resentment than it is worth, so think about it.

4—Be very attentive to youngsters in the family, make sure their welfare is what it should be. Do not be selfish with your time but devote it where needed. In the evening a little treat for children can make a memorable time for them. Enjoy the little ones and their ways, speech, affections.

5—News that comes in this morning can be cheering. In a matter where you almost gave up hope there may be new avenues to success opening. Value a loyal friend who has through many years kept in touch. That which is rare is in evidence strongly in your life and shows you favorable guidance.

6—You are not much in the mood for companionship. A leisurely walk in a garden, thoughtful meditation and a chance to rest are what will please you. Have no plans and don't let anyone talk you into activity that doesn't appeal. In the evening a family member may jolt your happiness.

7—You can be worried about finances, feel that you have undertaken too many installment type buys. There is no use brooding upon this; just don't keep on doing it. You'll work things out gradually and time itself will take care of them, so don't mar your work by silly worry.

8—An unfortunate health situation can arise and you may find that a physician or dentist urges some immediate care of special nature. If you ask for time to get used to this, you may just bring on more trouble. Be a good sport, have faith and take the word of an expert about it all.

9—Not a good day for work, shopping or any real estate deal. You find it difficult to give your mind to making choices and you may feel that you're all thumbs at work that takes manual skill. Slow down, don't brood, seek cheer in company of associates around you who have their problems.

10—You may suddenly wish to make a major change in your life. This can bring on complications when you let others know about it. If you wish to move your residence, there is little chance that you will carry out a plan of your own about it. You may move, all right, but not where you thought.

11—Trust someone new to you and all will work out for a good relationship. Whether this is romantic or not does not matter just now. You may have much instruction today, find yourself able to do things efficiently that you thought were beyond your skills. A day of change for the better.

12—People, people, people. Every time you turn around there may be one on the telephone; every time you turn around there may be one at the door. And so it goes. You may get nothing done that you planned and have to make a last minute rush trip out to the grocery for food for evening and tomorrow.

13—You wish you were on vacation and never had to return to work. Well, everyone has a right to dream a little today. Outdoors may be damp and dispiriting yet you can feel too confined if you stay inside. Having the family for dinner can help a little by keeping you too busy to fret.

14—Be very honorable about debts and pay off as many as possible. You may even take on a small extra job to hasten getting rid of your bills. You have learned a new lesson recently and will have a more mature view of money from now on. You are entering a phase of new, clearer thought.

15—An associate may ask help that you do not really want to give. However, for the sake of a good relationship, do as asked. You can win undying loyalty and admiration by doing your very best. A romantic trend may be established late in the day and you may have a date you didn't expect to have.

16—An older person may try to tell you things that you already know. Try to avoid showing an impatient, vexed reaction. Honor the older ones around you, have appreciation for experience. In the evening follow your impulses and you may go to some place that is new and utterly charming.

17—Be thrifty but not miserly. You are on a new budget, perhaps, and must stay with it even though it means more shopping around to get things at your price. Don't become irritable with the difficulties of this cycle; they're really nothing unusual. Try to get lots of rest and sleep tonight.

18—Trust the powers that be to see you through a busy day, one with many new demands, and a lot of work to do for an evening party you've planned. You can get wound up and tense; try to prevent this by a pause for refreshment when possible. You'll have fun out of it all before it's over.

19—Someone who does not understand you may offend you by underestimating your knowledge and abilities. Be amused at this. Show the humility that the intelligent always feel when it comes to surveying the vast field of knowledge they do not have. Quiet and reasonable ways are best.

20—A romantic message may come to you and you may be going places with someone special. It could be a day that leads up to an engagement, but don't do anything to rush these affairs. If you can, stop in and visit an older friend who is ill. Take a small gift but don't linger long at this place.

21—Your financial situation is showing improvement; have faith that it will improve farther. A good day to get essential repairs made in the home, to shop for clothes, jewelry, cosmetics and a new hair style. Even buying a wig can do something beneficial for this day. Enjoy life now!

22—An older person you admire may injure your feelings somewhat. Perhaps you have failed to understand a certain matter. Well, don't let it weigh you down. Avoid emotional reactions today and follow a course of cool mentality. Balance advantages and disadvantages of a change you are considering.

23—Though others around you delight in gossip, keep clear from it. No one has all the facts and everyone is willing to make them up with malice. Someone could be badly injured, so don't add your bit to this campaign of calumny. Sympathize with an older person who is bored with life tonight.

24—A neighbor may be kind and thoughtful. Rejoice in all the good you find around you today. Your path will lead you among the righteous, the honest and sincere. Keep your own character at its best. A request tonight may have to be turned down but the one who asks will understand.

25—An unexpected telephone call can hold too much emotional content to please you. Someone may speak words of love when you couldn't possibly respond. You'll do well to ignore or forget this; don't let it worry you. Have a happy time tonight with someone you do love and perhaps hope to marry.

26—Do something positive about your habits and health. Starting with today go on a rigid health plan. Halt a habit which you know has weakened you in some respects. Be cautious about medication you take under your own jurisdiction. In the evening enjoy entertainment at a friend's but leave rather early.

27—Make it to church if you can. A sermon can lift your mood, dispel some doubts. A cycle when thinking things through is favored. Be happy that a new neighbor comes to you for companionship and comfort. Home will be a pleasant place and you'll be appreciative of your blessings.

28—A good day to repay obligations, help people. Lend your talents to the community and church. If you have things to discard, think twice before you do so. You might sell a few items at prices that would amaze you. A garage sale might be the answer you need; don't be too lethargic to try it.

29—Worry about a young relative may all be in vain. You incline to let emotions take over and pester you with imaginative build-up. Handle money carefully today; also be cautious when walking across streets. An old friend may get in touch with you tonight and you'll find this very stimulating.

30—You'll need your most magnanimous spirit today for someone or maybe two people are going to do and say things that are difficult to overlook or forgive. If you can walk straight on through without speaking, you'll be doing well. Let evening find you reading spiritual or philosophical literature.

MAY

1—Everything may go contrary to what you expect. A sense of humor will get you through disturbing circumstances. You will be pleased to see people you've been missing for some time and it is a good day to become more sociable, accept some invitations which come spontaneously.

2—A new neighbor may show signs of pleasure to be living near you. You can find that any loneliness you felt before will be relieved by this neighbor's friendly presence and outgoing personality. Be outdoors as much as possible. If you are on vacation, take a lot of challenging pictures.

3—You can be rushed and might speak hastily to someone who needs your consideration. Be generous and patient for you will regret it if you're not. Be ready to accept what comes and do your best where help is needed.

4—Someone in your work environment may malinger and get by with it. You can have quite a dislike for such a person. You will benefit most from going your way and refusing to harbor bad attitudes toward anyone. Make the evening one of rest, enjoy TV light shows for a bit of laughter.

5—Someone may get in touch with you about an important job opportunity. This deserves your best attention and thought. Postpone making a decision, ask for time to sleep on matters before giving an answer. Take heed for other family members in your meditation about this.

6—Be generous in spirit to others now and take no offense at anything that is said. You may be called upon to do some new work; don't let timidity hold you back. Feel capable and you'll be capable. Don't be smug about accomplishments, though, even if they are more than adequate.

7—An older friend may get in touch with you—be lonely for your companionship. Make an opportunity to see this person and you'll bring cheer to the day. Entertainment in your home can be pleasant if you take it easy and avoid hard work to please guests. They come to see *you*.

8—A totally uninhibited person may seem strange to you. Don't show any harsh criticism; you may find this person a friend beyond value. There is need for you to be gracious and respectful toward others. Avoid all snobbish trends in a social gathering during the evening.

9—You might become gloomy about money. Instead of letting this build up get out and take a walk. Drop in on a neighbor and you may find some excitement. A romantic introduction may be made if you're in the right place. Let youthful spirits prevail at this time.

10—Ignore a sharp remark made by an influential person who is highstrung and temperamental. You can win esteem by being pleasant, philosophical and unwilling to take offense. A new work associate may become quite attached to you; be helpful in giving instructions.

11—You may not be able to do anything to alleviate a family problem. Try to get this concern out of your mind so that you can live your own life fully and attentively. You may have a financial opportunity that calls for clear thought, swift decision and action late in the afternoon.

12—A good clue may come to you through a new social acquaintance who speaks casually of things that interest you. You may have a better chance in career matters by following up the suggestion of this casual acquaintance. If you attempt something you may gain something.

13—A hope may dim due to delays and thwarted plans today. Postpone action and then be optimistic. Things may be shaping up behind the scenes for your benefit in the near future. Avoid making long distance calls this evening when you're in a somewhat confused state of mind.

14—You may receive good news from someone you were trying to help lately. A debt may be repaid and other money may come in unexpectedly. Don't splurge but do have a quiet celebration with family members or a loved one over your good fortune and happy spirits tonight.

15—Cut down your work load, don't be too ambitious. There is a chance of interruptions which you must not let irritate you. Better to give your time to one who needs it than to get a lot of chores done that can wait until later. Your judgment can be good in solving a problem for another.

16—Protect your health today, avoid driving if possible, be sure to have enough cash in case of a minor emergency. You may have an obligation you must fulfill. Don't shirk anything. You'll have more joy by helping others and mixing freely than by staying shut in today.

17—You may have to revise your work schedule so you can take care of a special demand. Passing out a small amount of money to help a person who comes to you is in order. Don't be in so much of a rush you refuse to listen to such a person. Patience does it for this cycle.

18—Work is monotonous and tiring. You may have an appointment to keep and find yourself quite weary by mid-afternoon. Cancel any plans for this evening and resolve on quiet and peace for a good rest. Read something light tonight to allow relaxation and good humor in spirits.

19—You can be disappointed about a shopping trip. It is difficult to find what you want and the price may be very high when you find it. This is a matter that may need more thought before actual purchase. Find a way to delay a decision and consult others before you act.

20—Romantic hopes may rise and you can be happy about a date for this evening. You're optimistic about this relationship which may indeed finally become the answer to your ideals. Take a neighbor into your confidence about happiness and you'll win a new friend.

21—Someone may speak quite bluntly to you and you can be wise to answer just as bluntly. Let someone know that you can criticize sharply—give it as well as take it. The whole matter may end in good nature on both sides and might even mean a new and deep friendship.

22—The day promises sheer happiness, gratitude for benefits, cheerful relationships, promising conditions within the family. Look your best today for romantic trends can lead to a more serious relationship and love which is growing stronger. You may be headed toward marriage.

23—You may have some explaining to do in connection with a person who doesn't understand you well. An honor may come to you through participation in a group with a constructive cause. Be happy in a bit of limelight today; it will give you an occasion to remember very fondly.

24—A certain condition in your neighborhood may not be pleasing but you'll use diplomacy when you try to correct it. Keep working with determination today, let nothing stop you in what you feel is right. You may win a lot of admiration through being loyal to your own convictions.

25—Someone may irritate you by trying to persuade you to do something against the grain with you. Do not become unpleasant in these conditions but do explain slowly and clearly why you are not interested. You may be called upon for a decision in romance this evening.

26—You may be at your most efficient and it's a good day for work in general. You'll also keep a good pace, enjoy fine health and pleasant relationships. You may change your mind about a move you've been considering, decide to go on just as you are. This appears to be wise.

27—Be conventional, conservative, cautious. In handling money be sure of accuracy. Communications may be disturbing and you may feel duty bound to some generosity when you would rather not give. However, evening will bring peace of mind, deeper understanding about this.

28—Someone may be delightfully frank with you, honest about acknowledging facts. You'll feel you have someone you can really talk to about some important matters that have been kept silent. Your neighborhood may be a pleasant, sociable area this evening, share in activities.

29—You may find that a mistake you thought you made was not made. Many things cheer you and lift your spirits. A romantic mood prevails late in the day and you can feel that all is well with love concerns. You'll be happy and have a memorably enjoyable evening with a loved one.

30—Don't be confidential with anyone except your loved one. Avoid talk if you are out in a crowd. You can gain some pleasure from artistic trends, may be consulted about matters of taste. Avoid the company of a know-it-all who provokes you but make sure you do not have that flaw.

31—Someone new in your work area may be interesting and a worthwhile relationship can develop. Admiration for your talents may lead this associate into doing you a favor which is connected with a hope. Good fortune is here when you take what comes and use it wisely.

JUNE

1—You might lose your temper suddenly today and with a person who is entirely innocent of any accusation you make. If you take an arbitrary attitude you will make trouble that can bring embarrassment and regret. Try to keep calm, be reasonable, shun all sharp speech today.

2—A romantic trend may surprise you. You can be amazed when you analyze your own interest in someone near you at work. This is a serious love and may develop quickly from the beginning. Possible marriage can come from the relationship and be very happy henceforward.

3—Be kindly to a younger person even where you do not approve some of this person's ways. You may find a business transaction disappointing but if you hold the course for a time matters may become more profitable. Use your own judgment in all financial activities now.

4—Much friendship is offered you, help will come for any matter in which you need it. You can be surprised to find how many friends you have. A good evening to talk over plans for a coming vacation. Family members may have something useful to say about this upcoming event.

5—It is not wise to travel today or to spend any large sum. Avoid all expense possible. If you have plans of romantic nature make sure that harmony reigns. Do not be easily upset emotionally in a social situation tonight. Keep poise and calm at your command.

6—You may have to deal with someone who is hostile and has a basic dislike for you. It may be possible to find a way out of any future arrangement with this person. Seek out those who are congenial late in the day and you'll get needed soothing for ruffled emotions.

7—Value your talents highly, put in a bid for more income. It is time to think of a change if you do not get recompensed properly. Shopping for wardrobe is well aspected but avoid any major purchase such as a car, furniture or appliances. Keep the evening quiet, read something light.

8—You may as well face a matter which is going to have to be taken care of. Further evasion of facts can cause trouble. This can be connected with health, perhaps dental needs. Investigate expenses and scan your budget to see how you can manage; then go straight ahead.

9—You may not be in a good humor—may show much temperament. If you treat people badly you'll get the same back. Strive for amiable relationships, be helpful and generous where you can. Best to avoid anything in the way of entertainment or group activities tonight.

10—You have excellent taste today and all you buy or do will bring about improvements. You may hear some good news that will allow you to turn a hobby into profit soon. Don't brush away suggestions, give them some good thought. Examine your own ideas for benefits, too.

11—Your nerves may get unsettled due to friction in relationships. It is a dangerous time to drive; keep your concentration on the law if you must drive. You may have a social engagement you would rather skip for tonight but go anyhow and you will be glad you did.

12—You may want to spend much time getting things done around the home. Don't be brusque with someone who visits this afternoon. Keep yourself open for suggestions about tonight and you may have a very romantic date. You may be elated with love's trends this evening.

13—You can be very restless, bored and prone to follow questionable impulses. Too much ability to discern flaws and criticize makes companionship dubious. Do something creative and the tensions of the time may be lifted suddenly. A talk on the telephone may cheer you later.

14—You may take a new view of an opportunity and decide on the spur of the moment to follow it up. This could lead to a real change, move of residence, more income. Be thoughtful about obligations and very dutiful to family members, particularly small children who are dependent.

15—You might insist on too much perfection in what others are doing. You could become angry when there is a mistake or accident of some kind. Best to be tolerant, show that no real harm is done. Be encouraging rather than discouraging to those in your vicinity today.

16—Love can take over even though you feel it is not a wise trend to follow. You can find yourself in love and at the same time unhappy with the personality of a loved one. Trying to tie down someone who naturally loves freedom may be the core of difficulty in this romance.

17—Be very conscientious in work, follow instructions cautiously, go slow and you'll come through with praise won for your accomplishments. Keep lunch and dinner both light, resist all dubious things which could cause digestive flare-up for you during the evening.

18—Be helpful and sociable to someone new in your environment. The main things you may give generously are comfort and a chance for another person to talk freely. Be absolutely tolerant and sympathetic. If you go out this evening for social life, make sure you look your best.

19—You may cross swords with someone quite insolent and belligerent. Stand up for your own rights, do not let any one take over and domineer. It is possible to end a relationship now but that can be for the best in the long run. Do not look back in sentimental fashion.

20—You can be gloomy about something you want to do in which you are getting opposition. If you ignore this matter, refuse to be obsessed by it, all may turn out for your happiness finally. Be cheerful with an older friend, dine out, enjoy a short walk to window shop.

21—Don't let a little extra expense hold you back from something beneficial to your career. It is worth devoting time and money for the purpose of enhancing earning trends. Be steadfast in a new pursuit you take up today; let nothing stop you from learning thoroughly.

22—A good time to buy something to add cheer to your life and home. A pet is just the thing. Please little children, older relatives and a loved one. You can be quite ingenious in thinking of things to do that will make others happy and add a glow to your own emotions also.

23—A telephone call can cause a change in your plans. Advice you get about money can be all to the good. Be courageous, take a small risk, have faith. There is an atmosphere of upheaval this evening; don't let it make you feel insecure and uncertain; keep your cool now.

24—A delightful event may occur today. It could be an engagement starting over the luncheon table. If this happens a wedding will follow quite soon. Do not let age make too much difference in any relationship. Enjoy companionship that comes, don't question trends.

25—All that you do to make your appearance more glamorous will have good results so long as kept within bounds, of course. Don't be glaringly artificial. A good time to read for instructions on latest cosmetic trends and buy some items to get in step with the times.

26—The mail can bring news you have been wanting and all will appear more favorable for your major plans. The day in general holds excitement and surprise, all of the happy kind. You can be effervescent in social life and add to your popularity in an enduring way tonight.

27—There is danger of jumping to conclusions about someone new to you. Wait until you get facts; above all do not make any blunt statements. Offending the feelings of an innocent person can bring much regret. Try to speak with praise to all instead of criticizing harshly.

28—The trend is emotional and difficult to get through without a quarrel. Someone may try to make you feel inferior and such a person must be ignored. Go your own way as much as possible; when with others keep your temper, make an effort to understand matters on practical basis.

29—Time to have things repaired, make sure all is running smoothly. Do not take risks about fire. Someone may speak scornfully of your caution but don't let that stop you from being cautious. Show your independence, do as you feel right and all will be well with this cycle.

30—Someone who is irritable and unpleasant may cross your path. You can be a little sad to see the changes in this person's nature. You might be able to stir up some good humor if you try and it's worth trying. Make no romantic commitment during the evening.

JULY

1—Be pleasing to relatives and friends, do little favors, make others happy. You may encounter someone new in a strange situation. It could be wiser to let the encounter stop right there. The evening can bring a problem to solve in connection with the family; don't back out on your responsibility.

2—There is not a very good health trend today. Avoid rush, store up energies, take it easy. Do nothing rash in connection with social or romantic life tonight. You may find yourself exhausted and have to retire before you planned. Heed only your inner feelings and cater to health needs.

3—A very unpleasant person may threaten you in a way that is ridiculous. However, the threatening type of person must always be viewed with caution. Best to break up circumstances in which you associate with a gossip who is vindictive and determined to have the last "say" about matters.

4—Today can bring a problem. A conversation with someone outside the home may bring another problem. The day is so full of unexpected trends that you may feel as though you're on a merry-go-round that just doesn't stop. Make plans for the evening and keep them; do not let anything interfere with being punctual.

5—Someone you trusted and loved may prove entirely unworthy, disloyal and insincere. You may get an "earful" of unpleasant information from this person and find it is the parting of the way for you. You may not know how lucky you are for some time but the fact is you are well off.

6—There is really more nonsense in the air today than you can handle. Curious people may pry; those who are resentful may start talking about legal action. Go your way independently and ignore all the bickering and silliness. Enjoy something unusual this evening with friends who are enduringly loyal.

7—A happy day, good for shopping, travel and romance. You may be interrupted in work many times but still can come out ahead with demands. Your shopping expedition can yield something very becoming to wear for a big date tonight. Spending the evening with someone new can be an important prelude.

8—Be sure not to repeat anything you are told today. You can be happy with your personal life, so don't get involved in other's lives. A telephone call you make to an older relative tonight will be cheering and much needed. Don't spare the expense of long distance to bring happiness to the lonely.

9—Don't make a harsh judgment about anyone today. Be an influence for a kindly attitude, generous spirit and friendly ways. Social changes are taking place and it is time you caught up with them. You may have this opportunity in what you hear tonight about neighbors. Be patient and tolerant.

10—Do constructive things, get the home in good order, arrange for needed repairs. You may make a big decision about your residence. Don't complain this evening if you are asked to give special help for a major social event. Do all you can for a friend who has always been generous.

11—If you are not alert the competition will get the best of you today. You may have some special obligation to fulfill and if you fail in this, a rival can take your place in an important organization. You can be inclined to dream romantically, and let the practical aspect of life pass you by today.

12—Someone may try to play a clever but petty trick on you. Be sure not to speak about matters where you do not know the facts well enough. Circumstances you discover today through a telephone call may show you that a trouble-maker is at work. End your part of this business immediately.

13—Avoid jumping to conclusions. Keep abreast of current news in the papers but don't make any guesses about reading between the lines. A big surprise may arrive this afternoon and you may have to make a quick decision in this connection. You can get help by making the right telephone call.

14—You may make a new friend through today's conversation. Practice the ideal sense of freedom that you preach. You may have a special conference this afternoon that will serve as a guide to you about your future. Acknowledge the admirable honesty with which an executive speaks to you.

15—Not a good day for health affairs. You can feel that you have some kind of "bug" and may have to leave work early. Take no risk with food that is rich, stay with liquids of healthful nature to a large extent. A telephone call tonight may astound you and anger you a bit into the bargain.

16—You can go ahead with a major pursuit of creative nature due to the good news you get now. Much elation and high spirits will show you the way by giving inspiration and encouragement. A fine day for ambitions and friendships which are beneficial for spurring you on to high attainments.

17—Someone who is given to making errors about facts may try to get you involved in some tricky gossip. Stay away from this completely. Get out and don't be at home. That way you'll miss some adverse events and be able to stay free of threatened trouble. Dress quite glamorously for evening.

18—A good natured person may try to cultivate friendship. Don't be in one of your snobbish moods where you judge by appearances. Open your mind and affections to all today and don't make people feel shut out. A good evening for conversation about spiritual affairs that interest you.

19—There are obstacles in your way now. Advice you get from a professional person may urge you to forge right through the obstacles. If you accept this view and follow it with determination, you will be wise. Make your decision, act upon it and then never look back or even dream of regret.

20—A younger person can make life difficult for you without meaning any harm. Your finances need to be taken care of, and you must devote some time to getting them straightened out today. Make sure your arithmetic is correct. You can feel restless tonight; nerves can keep you awake.

21—Use your best judgment in all you do. Hesitate and think before each step you take. You can make quite a bit of money through today's pursuits, but there may be risk involved. If you are willing to take the risk, you must never back down on it or show bitter blame toward another person.

22—You could be in one of your more selfish moods and cause financial trouble to one who loves you. You tend to want everything you see and to be determined to have it. This childish trait is very bad when carried into adult activity. Control your desires and don't be demanding in these matters.

23—Someone who enters your life today can cause much mischief in the near future if you let any type of relationship develop. You are advised not even to treat this person as you would a friendly acquaintance. Keep at a good distance, be cool, even chilly. Issue no invitations tonight.

24—Sum up your career picture, see if you have attained the position you want. If not, then it is time to begin making plans for another approach or a complete change of locale. Be ambitious and resolve to follow your ambitious nudges. In matters of romance this evening can be quite circumspect and prudent.

25—You may not like what you hear but you may as well accept it without saying anything. You may be admired more than you know. Don't assume that someone is not your friend just because of a little sharp speech. Keep the evening for a walk, some meditation, and restful early retirement for health.

26—Be kindly toward an older work associate who seems to treat you rather badly. There may be fear in this person that you will take away a coveted job. Make allowances for people today and take their failings into account without harsh judgment. Recognize the fact of human frailties.

27—The day can seem long, dull and dreary. Your work is monotonous and moves slowly. Health is not up to its best and you may need to change your diet a little. Be cautious about taking any type of medication after making self-diagnosis. Be careful with temper toward loved ones tonight.

28—You may be asked to do something for the community which will allow you to put your talents to work in such a way that you draw valuable attention to them. This could be an opening into just the kind of situation you want, so don't turn the request down even if it carries no remuneration.

29—You are in danger of underestimating someone. It is never wise to do this and in the particular instance of today it can cause you much embarrassment. Go along calmly, take nothing for granted. Children may play quite a role in your life this evening. Do not try to do the impossible.

30—Neighborhood events can grow quite hazardous and you may have to play the part of a guardian in some unpredictable fashion. Your place of work also holds dangers and the entire situation under these aspects threatens to be a harmful one. Do your best by following cool, steady logic.

31—Information you get may be all wrong or you may interpret it wrongly. Communications are snarled today. Don't make it worse by talking to others in an effort to clear things. All speech and writing will just make things more tangled. Relax and realize it's sometimes a mad, mad world.

AUGUST

1—A major change may commence in your life. Be ready for what comes and also do not put up opposition to it. This would just tear up your own nervous system and accomplish nothing. A good time is here to get to yourself to make decisions; decide what you want, yes and no, for good results.

2—Try something new today. A hair style that is different can be fun and also attractive. A new neighbor who comes your way now may be entirely different from what you envisioned. You may find yourself very ready to engage in spontaneous evening affairs and this is good for the introductions it brings.

3—You might be offended at what an influential person has to say. It is not wise to let this go to extremes for you could cut yourself out of some desirable personal situations. There is a chance you will be introduced to someone of importance to your future life if you hang in with your friends.

4—A tendency to sit down and be serene will be here. No matter what comes you will have the genius to overcome it. It is a good day to shop in desultory fashion, to give gifts to youngsters in the family, to be genuinely generous. Think twice before you accept an invitation for the evening.

5—Someone from a distance may aggravate you over a small matter. It is up to you to arise and keep your head above such trivialities. Avoid all those who are noted for their gossip, keep your slate clean when it comes to repeating words of no real interest to you. You could end up in the hash.

6—It can be difficult to face financial matters today but you should do this and get unpleasant matters out of the way. A time when you can meet fascinating people through social engagements, so do not turn down invitations or stay to yourself this evening. A desirable romance might get its beginning.

7—An exciting day is here and you may know it from the moment you arise. Your social calendar is full, you feel like a million when it comes to being out and doing things. Avoid letting anyone bluff you into doing something you do not want to do. Be cautious if you go out of town this evening.

8—You can be in for a killing as far as the stock market concerns go. If you're not so involved, you are advised to sell real estate or put anything of value on the market. The way is yours all the way when it comes to finances. Even a personal shopping trip can yield wondrous, desired results.

9—You may waste money today. Things that seem of importance to you may not seem that way to others. If you are wise you will advance only step by step and be very thoughtful. Avoid talking about personal matters to those outside the family. Also, avoid talking about the family to those outside.

10—A neighbor may prove very kindly, intelligent and understanding. This is one of those times when it is good to take what is offered and refuse to put pressure on for that which is not offered. Try to get an evening of freedom for watching TV, reading and reflection on your own course through life.

11—You may be amazed at the attitude that relatives and friends take today. Yet, when you think things over you may see where relatives are in the right. Friends are in a mood to gamble and you'll lower the esteem they have for you if you fit in with this picture. Cudgel your brain and come up with clever and practical answers.

12—There are some mysterious things going on in your chart and very little reasons for them. Your telephone calls may go astray, your correspondence can cause some trouble. A good time to get yourself to rights and keep everything in order. You may end the day on a happy medium then.

13—It may be one of those uppety-down days which brings more telephone calls than you can handle and more advice-asking than you like. Back away from it all a little and you'll get a refreshing atmosphere. Avoid going into debt for anything today; you're better off paying cash for all purchases.

14—Disappointment may come to your attention and it can be hard to take. One of those times when you need your sternest manner and a firm personality in order to endure the trouble that seems to be seeking you. Avoid neighbors, conversation with them can be nothing but troublesome.

15—A major change may come about in your life due to a decision made today. This is a good time to write letters, postcards and anything that can bring special remembrance to someone you love. Let little children enter into your life more fully. You can regain spirit of youth by association with them.

16—A telephone call you make can be expensive beyond your expectations. A romantic or affectionate gesture can be costly. On the other hand, you may be better off showing where your true sentiments are rather than trying to hide them. Be particularly kind and understanding with younger people in the neighborhood.

17—Difficulties may arise one after another and your mental attitude can be assaulted. If you become excited and show your worry about these matters, they can become all the worse. Do be sure to show prompt attention to a person who is ill. You can do much good with a token of remembrance in this circumstance.

18—A day when you can bring balance into your life and be happy about it. You may find yourself going here and there, doing this and that. If you don't let yourself become worried over physical stability and strength, you'll have good health and spirits.

19—Impulses to do things today can be very difficult to resist. Let yourself drift a little and don't worry about impetuous actions. You may begin to think about a drastic change in your life late in the day. This can be all to the good and should by no means be held up due to alarms.

20—Something may happen in the family that you do not think is desirable. It is better to keep silent and take all this as it comes. Be cautious about spending money now; any large expenditure could whittle down your savings and this you wouldn't want at all. You can have trouble making a contract.

21—Go out and spend a small fortune buying clothes that will make you feel the most glamorous in the town. Your sophisticated charm will show and when you get dressed up for the evening you may be the knock-out of any social affair. An entirely delightful cycle is here.

22—Some facts may come your way that dismay you. It is better to take a logical stand than to go in for some selfish ideas. Your romantic life may take a turn for the better and still demand some thought. Don't endanger your own happiness by making an off-beat decision about tonight.

23—Do not talk much today. When it comes to neighbors, friends, business associates, try to remember that silence will be your most valuable ally. Avoid getting involved with someone new this evening. Keep to yourself, read, write letters and make a long distance call that you think deserves attention.

24—Face hard work with determination knowing that the hours will not be long. Get in touch with a younger relative and give all the advice you can. You may be rebuffed but in the end you will realize why. Good nature will help a lot and understanding of the younger generation will help more.

25—It can be a slightly wild day with a chance for you to do your best and still not profit. Avoid extreme extravagance and generosity. Hold on to the almighty dollar and you will see why this is good advice. Avoid conversation with neighbors that can turn into gossip before you know it.

26—A mischievous and malicious person may try to make you pay for an inconvenience. Shut yourself off from conversation, refuse to talk about anything except impersonal matters. Answer no questions and volunteer no information about public affairs. You may win some special laurels from wisdom today.

27—You can feel quite alone and forsaken today because some people neglect you. It is not worthwhile to nurture grudges and unhappiness just because of a few people. Be courageous, don't stop in a personal attempt just because you feel you do not have much support. Be generous financially as well as other ways.

28—A message you get today may change your entire attitude about another person. Try to be reasonable and do not alarm anyone with your altered outlook. If you go shopping be moderate and above all buy only what is in keeping with your own style. Desire for new fashion could lead you astray badly.

29—There can be some outstanding troubles today and they may be mostly personal. You can be in the depressed stage, very unhappy with those you contact. An older friend may try to do something for you and may just make matters worse. It is time to think of your responsibilities and not be selfish.

30—A very difficult task may be assigned to you and it can take you time to get on to it so that you are efficient. Too much worry and tension can ruin your day. Come up out of the depths of depression and talk to someone whose philosophy will show you a light and cheerful way to proceed henceforward.

31—A day on which to be generous in every way imaginable. Let your personality flow out toward others, give them your best wishes, make no effort to impose your beliefs. Difficulty in communications this evening may set the tone for tomorrow. Best to give up where it is just too difficult to win through talk.

SEPTEMBER

1—Splendid hours for achieving a goal. Promotion in your career is highly possible, if you use your initiative and put matters clearly before an executive. Direct action will win direct results, and you will have reason to be proud by evening. Share your happiness tonight.

2—A leisurely day with friendship stressed. Conversations will be pleasant and full of ideas for future use. Have lunch with an associate who is lonely. The good cheer your companionship brings to another will be returned in your own life. Accept an invitation for tonight.

3—Surprising news may cause a change of plans. A journey today will have favorable results, and long distance communications can mean an increase in income. Your talents will be in demand at more than one place. Excellent hours for signing contracts and winding up transactions.

4—Don't hesitate to accept a role in a special project. You may be asked to take the lead, and your talents will bring pleasure to others. A happy and busy day. Family life will bring joy and a loved one will prove deep affection. Entertain at home this evening.

5—Try not to give in to moodiness and irritability. Go out for a walk where you can be alone and concentrate on trying to solve problems reasonably. Conclusions you arrive at may not be pleasant, but responsibility must be recognized and accepted. Avoid going out tonight.

6—You may have news of legal or business troubles early in the day, but matters may turn out better than you expected in the end. Remain poised and friends will bring you comfort before evening. A gay romantic interlude tonight will make you forget worries. Dress up and go out happily.

7—Constructive plans can be made today. Consult with others and find inspiration in their attitudes. A day for deep thought and clear insight. Your intuition may show you a path which lies open. Decisions can be made wisely. Harmonious family circumstances bring joy.

8—Changes are likely, and if you have plans of your own to make a drastic change in environment, this is a day to get busy and start. Buying a new home is favored, and all transactions involving purchasing will bring good bargains as well as personal satisfaction.

9—Your hopes may soar with a surprise message about your career. Put plans into action and endeavor will pay off handsomely. Telephone calls and correspondence will bring excellent results. A friend will have cheerful news this evening. A sociable atmosphere.

10—A new firmness and self-assurance will come to you, if you felt inadequate formerly. Grasp matters clearly and take them in your own hands. A day when taking care of things yourself will prove beneficial. Your family and loved ones will bring happiness this evening.

11—A disappointing day when things go wrong and all seems futile. There will be many slips in any work you try to do. Interruptions will be most unwelcome, but try to be gracious to friends who visit when you don't enjoy having them. If possible seek solitude this evening.

12—Strenuous activity but happiness in your work will mark the day. A new idea can be discussed profitably, at lunch perhaps or in the office of an executive. Progressive trends are noticeable, and you may have suggestions which mean much improvement. A family evening.

13—Talk will be raging around you. Try to ignore the fact that you sense malicious gossip. Put personal feelings out of your mind and keep busy with work. Ill temper might cause loss of your position, and at least would lower your prestige. Read and stay in this evening.

14—Keep on the go today. Sociable trends and romantic happiness will fill life with activity of the most pleasant nature. A picnic can be engineered happily, and refreshments you provide will delight others. Consider children today and do things to make them happy.

15—A day when you may do much wishing and little acting. Bitterness and dreams can struggle with each other in your mind. Idleness will be noticed, and you may be criticized sharply. Health is not at its best, but try to remain at work through the day. Eat little and retire early.

16—A much happier day when a new point of view will show you the advantages of your situation. Harmonious conditions at work will bring new affection to many. You may attract the eye of a person you admire. The evening promises romantic adventure and quiet pleasure.

17—Not very auspicious hours for business. Be careful with money, in general. Resist extravagant impulses. Otherwise there will be quite a bit of personal happiness. Friends, family and romantic interests fill the latter part of the day with good cheer and gaiety.

18—Favorable trends for romance under the current influences. You may meet an interesting person of the opposite sex in a casual introduction and find it the beginning of a lifelong love. Make no plans for the evening, since it will take care of itself and bring adventure your way.

19—Security will be augmented by happy financial conditions today. An increase in salary or a new source of income is indicated by these favorable influences. Emphasis upon money will give you little time for leisure or relaxation. You will enjoy the brisk business activity.

20—Emotional serenity will make this a peaceful day. Relationships are more important than business matters today. Plan an entertainment for this evening with attractive refreshments. Good conversation.

21—A day of persuasive speech and personality. Put your ideas and yourself across with an important person under these very favorable influences. By later afternoon, you may receive the word that you have been hoping for. Take your good news to those who love you and celebrate.

22—Get up a little early and allow yourself time to enjoy music and news before you go to work. Have breakfast slowly, and enjoy the serene atmosphere you start the day with. Trends for activity later will be stepped up and you will be given a new important responsibility.

23—First impressions will count a great deal today, so be dressed in the best of taste and watch your grooming. Speak slowly and after second thought. You can win new admiration and honor from these influences. The evening is favorable for small social gatherings.

24—Avoid speed and handling of any dangerous element. Make sure that appliances are in good repair. Lock doors carefully and wear no valuable jewelry. Litigation threatens those who are reckless in the later part of the day. Do not share in family plans for going out.

25—Avoid going out if you can help it. Conflict can arise even between yourself and a stranger. Many will have chips on their shoulders and feel mistreated. If you must go out, be very quiet, for quarrels can arise suddenly. Do not enter into disputes about family matters.

26—Another day when it is a good idea to avoid people. If you do go out, be very brief in greetings and do not express opinions in any group. The afternoon can bring a mild pleasure if you read or keep busy with personal matters such as revising the budget. Retire early.

27—Rewards for industrious work are part of the day's pleasant events. You may be praised by an important person. Friends will be happy about your good fortune, and you may be the guest of honor at a cheerful party this evening. Buy something new for your wardrobe.

28—The aspects signify the desire for change and excitement. Express this by going out with dependable people. Avoid getting caught in an emotional scene with someone who is unstable. The desire to travel and visit is quite strong, but be sure that others will be ready to welcome you.

29—Exceptionally good news. Adventure is in the air, and relationships are back on a happy plane. You may be kept busy with a new line of activity. Excellent for buying or selling. A major change in environment can be made with good results. Engagement is possible tonight.

30—Personal uneasiness and whimsical action may cause you to waste the day disastrously. If you give in to desires not to work, you will regret it soon. Keep with the job, even though you feel you are not accomplishing anything. Be careful of diet. Read or watch TV later.

OCTOBER

1—Don't hold high hopes for good results from social plans. There is a cloud over artistic and music affairs, frustrating circumstances that chill amiability. It would be wise to tidy up at home, or catch up on needed sleep. For safety, avoid the unorthodox.

2—Plans shape up and much can be accomplished by taking others into your confidence, gaining their views and decisions. There is a cheery outlook concerning the outcome of long-range plans. You may meet some intriguing, talented people under the current magnetic influences.

3—An unfortunate finish for the work week, with a gloomy morning causing depression and dissatisfaction. Avoid having lunch with an associate, but try not to be rude. Any conversation with an executive will end unhappily if you complain. Silence is the best policy throughout.

4—Wishful thinking can be a real hazard. Be sure to talk things over with a practical-minded person before going ahead with anything important to your work, money or personal happiness. There is excessive optimism and a tendency to argue. Avoid an unconventional tangent tonight.

5—Friendly influences prevail for art, music, luxury and travel. This day and evening may see the solving of some emotional problem, the beginning of happier conditions, more peaceful associations. Take care that idle comments do not lead to carping criticism as the day comes to a close.

6—Keep alert for personality difficulties. The cycle is adverse for social matters. Your manner may antagonize people and strife may follow your slightest words. A domineering tone can cause breaks in friendships which are just beginning to mature. Spend time finishing up leftover matters.

7—Cooperation rules the day. Mutual profit from listening to the ideas of others is possible, due to the current aspects. Have a full day; enjoy the sense of worthwhile contacts which you can make. Make each moment count, because what you do may have far-reaching effects.

8—The aspects favor your prestige. A spur to action will come from success early in the day. Use all resources to accomplish a great deal where it will count the most. Ask favors wherever you feel they can best be filled. You probably won't be turned down today.

9—Necessity to use imagination and foresight crops up when you find yourself blocked in ordinary procedure. Put on your thinking cap and ideas will flood in. Forget personal interests for the time being and good fortune may accompany your activities.

10—The day may be lit brilliantly with a touch of social glamor. Your personality may sparkle. Put on your best array and sally forth for pleasure. A time to drift into the spotlight for a while and let people see how interesting you are. The planetary influences are your boosters today.

11—Criticism will irritate you today. If you feel you are in the right, use tact in explaining your point of view. Think twice before speaking and be willing to discuss calmly whatever is suggested. Don't bet on a sure thing. If you do, it is a sure thing that you will lose.

12—A difficult day in social relationships. Don't let it bother you, you can't please everybody. Take it easy. Let new ideas float around in your mind and see what is useful among them. Business considerations of major proportions can fill a large part of the day. Have some fun tonight.

13—Cooperate where you are needed, but don't become involved personally with anyone. Let your interest in young people be apparent and devote some time to them today, even though they are not your own. A few worries may bother you, but you will find ways to get your mind off your own problems.

14—An excellent time for telephone calls, interviews, writing letters. Attend to all the paper work necessary. The practical issues should be most important during the day, but in the evening hours relaxation can be enjoyed in the company of friends or loved ones. Dine in a new place or on a new recipe tonight.

15—Make solid investments. An excellent cycle for building up financial security. You may be asked to perform services for which you have little time. Try to work in as much as you can. You will have intuition which can be followed throughout the day. Trust your feelings about all vital things.

16—Opportunity may knock more than once today. Remain alert and grab every moment for its possibilities. Work in harmony with those around you; the day is fine for progress of a personal nature if cooperation is given. Keep your ears open today.

17—With friendly aspects in power, you may have a lot of places to go today. Your phone may ring often and you may be at sixes and sevens; many people will seem to be demanding your time and attention. Devote yourself to those of your family who need you, and let romance wait.

18—The unexpected and swift changes can give this cycle an air of chaos, with today bringing a marked or radical breaking with the past. Don't depend too much on what is said or written today as becoming a permanent condition. Be careful in travel, taking no risks with machinery or moving objects.

19—If you divide your problems into detailed portions you probably will be able to manage them more efficiently. Take care of one thing at a time and don't look ahead into the next problem you must tackle. Take time off tonight for enjoyment of friends and those close to your heart.

20—The only measure of victory to be gained today is simply to keep plodding through thick and thin. It probably will be mostly thin, for the scales are not really tipped in your favor and competition may give you a few jolts. Yet all is not lost if you ignore annoyances and work diligently.

21—The day calls for a state of inner serenity. School yourself to accept what comes along without showing a sign of being ruffled. This will get you through any difficulty which will arise. Disturbances will be temporary and trifling if you follow this pattern.

22—Visit friends who can give you serious topics for conversation. A day on which you can gain much insight into reality by discussing over the past and making plans with those close to you for the future. A day wasted in idleness or vain pleasures will give cause for regret.

23—Adhere to details today, finishing everything in the best style possible. Check your work and then check it again. Perfection will pay off. Let large-scale planning go for now; the workings of your ideas will be clearer as time passes by. Go out for some fun tonight.

24—Nervous tension might make you abrupt. Romance which beckons and finds you unresponsive may not beckon again. Wounded feelings are difficult to repair and a word cast needlessly against the sensitivities of another can never really be called back.

25—You may feel limited in scope today. The wide fields of your imagination are indeed more alluring to rove, but bide your time, hold to plans and you probably will get a chance to try some of the things which are dear to you. Cope with demands of routine.

26—People may feel that you are impractical today. The less you say, the better you will feel in the end. Make your plans, take stock of your assets. Otherwise spend the time in meditation of larger truths; read and learn. Happiness lies in quiet, solitary pleasures today. Take no risks.

27—Don't believe everything you hear today. Even authentic tales should be ignored. A day of gossip and rumor which will do no credit to anyone who takes part. Adverse cycle for gambling, traveling, writing, debating, contesting, marrying, flying, interviewing.

28—Finish up things which have been hanging and perhaps bothering you. It is a time for conclusions. Perhaps romance can come to a favorable culmination. Glamour is in the air. Have beauty treatments, and buy attractive clothes and jewelry. View the world through rosy glasses.

29—If people annoy you, try to get away for awhile, if possible. Arguments can arise where you least desire them. Make plans, retrieve hopes and see where optimism can be fruitful. Organize well for the days to come and let no loose ends impede your march to personal success.

30—Your plans can mature rapidly under the force of the current aspects. Get into work which is creative or educational in an experimental mood. Mistakes made now can serve as reminders for future efforts. Try to attend a small gathering in the evening hours.

31—Some adjustments may be necessary in your home. If you are neglectful you may have to pay for more than your share in money and comfort. Show thought and affection for those nearest you, iron out problems concerning all; you will find gratitude cheerfully paid to you.

NOVEMBER

1—Go slow since hazards and recklessness can cause serious difficulty. Focus your attention on work that has to be done rather than waste time dreaming about what you would like to do. Prepare for worthwhile achievements, and do not be satisfied with half-way measures.

2—You should be able to hurdle barriers by making well planned changes. Regardless of what project occupies your time, place emphasis on doing something practical. Insure effective use of available resources by keeping your whims separate from actual requirements.

3—Make this an enjoyable day for yourself, even though others around you may be in a disagreeable mood. Do not let unpreparedness be the cause for delays in your work. Avoid any situation which might jeopardize your prestige or popularity.

4—Make sure you are getting adequate value for your money and efforts while shopping. Forcefulness, instead of diplomacy, would be best in dealing with a contrary person. You can avoid frustrated feelings by depending on your own resources rather than on expected assistance.

5—Stay out of the way of people who can disrupt the things you are trying to do. Be especially careful in the use of mechanical or electrical equipment. Do not sacrifice accuracy for speed regardless of how anxious you may be to complete your assignments.

6—Do not risk unfavorable results in your work from guesses or impulsive action. Concentrate on a hobby or other form of activity from which you can obtain diversion. Give thoughts to long-range plans about your future security.

7—Devote yourself to duties which can be of value to others today, as well as to yourself. Careless use of money may give a bad impression that would be difficult to overcome. Listen eagerly to criticism that is offered to you rather than resent it.

8—Be very cautious in a business transaction and do not make a rash agreement during the current adverse aspects. Remain in the background so far as domestic squabbles are concerned. Take events as they come and do not let them upset an otherwise enjoyable day.

9—Adhere to accepted procedures and have complete confidence in your abilities. Take care of disagreeable problems as they arise instead of postponing them for later action. Remain optimistic regardless of the little things that could go wrong and cause inconvenience.

10—Use this day for arranging to get things accomplished as scheduled or ahead of time. Attend to all obligations without delay to remove the burden of worry from your mind. Be patient and wait for the things you want. They will come to you.

11—Use your time to good advantage by improving the efficiency and attractiveness of your home. Take an active interest in the things that are going on around you now. Be consistent in formulating a savings plan to build up your cash reserves.

12—This is not a good time to start a new assignment, unless you can complete it quickly. Be prepared to cope with difficulties that may arise as the result of trivial mistakes. A policy of caution in matters connected with large-scale spending would be appropriate.

13—You can gain far more than you anticipate by being conciliatory rather than by forcing an issue. Keep business and pleasure activities separate regardless of sympathetic inclinations. Rather than complain about monotonous situations, do things to liven the day.

14—Give encouragement where it is needed and express your confidence in others. A slow and cautious pace may prove the best way to make satisfactory progress. Regardless of how strongly you believe in your own viewpoints, let others do the talking and acting.

15—Let your thoughts dwell on new scenes and situations that can distract your mind from customary worries. Refrain from expressing yourself in anger regardless of how exasperating the circumstances. Do not become so engrossed in your own personal matters that you neglect the need of others.

16—Understanding and patience are needed to offset what could otherwise be a major difference of opinion. Be optimistic about the future and do not worry about the problems you expect to encounter. Heed suggestions which are made for your benefit rather than ignore them entirely.

17—By being persistent in your efforts you can reap the benefits of a job well done. Go out of your way to prevent animosity and antagonism while dealing with others. Arrange your work schedule so that there is plenty of time for pleasure and recreation.

18—Obtain accurate directions before attempting to do something with which you are unfamiliar. Be diplomatic and courteous even though you may feel in a contrary mood. Do not let over-confidence in your abilities be the source of an expensive mistake.

19—Forge ahead today despite opposition, and hurdle obstacles which have been slowing you down recently. Seek cooperation from family members in keeping your budget within practical limits. Avoid trying to get things done in a hurry merely to show progress.

20—Depend on steady toil, rather than on inspirational impulses, to show worthwhile progress. Discussing your plans too far in advance may create trouble rather than avoid it. Do not magnify the trivial details of your work beyond their worth.

21—Get the loose ends of your duties cleared up even if you have to work long and hard to do it. Alert thinking and acting may enable you to transform an adverse situation to your advantage. Avoid unpleasant surroundings rather than permit a gloomy atmosphere to bother you.

22—Do not place too much faith in extravagant promises that are made to you this day. Control any temptation to give advice to another since it may cause antagonism. Be patient if things seem to drag and proceed at a leisurely pace. They will pick up.

23—Despite all the alluring temptations, make every effort to hold on to your cash. Seek out pleasurable activities, but not at the expense of neglected responsibilities. Take each new problem in your stride, and do not shun distasteful tasks.

24—Make necessary revisions in your work program, and arrange to bring everything up-to-date. For satisfactory results, seek expert guidance when trying to solve a difficult problem. You may be able to sidestep trouble by deferring a discussion about finances.

25—Avoid changing your mind because of an annoying or temporary pressure which plagues you at the present time. Make sure you fully understand the instructions you receive to avoid costly mistakes. Work alone rather than attempt to get others to help you.

26—Expressing your feelings in a blunt manner could result in strained relationships. Although things may proceed in a rapid manner, reject the urge to slow down the pace. Tackle each task with determination, and do not revert to slip-shod methods.

27—Although you may be slowed down by petty annoyances, do not let things get the best of you. Enjoy your friends and present surroundings rather than seek unfamiliar scenes. Give yourself ample time to get things done without having to rush.

28—Do not over-estimate your capabilities by taking on increased responsibilities. Your willingness to compromise in matters of importance may help you to make larger gains. Be careful in what you say since your words may be distorted by repetition.

29—Get all your important duties done now to avoid delaying matters. Do not allow a temporary setback to disrupt your plans completely. Be practical in matters concerning money, and do not let emotions interfere with your logic in any way.

30—Time and effort can be saved by correspondence or telephone calls. Avoid antagonizing those around you by being forceful in the expression of your opinions. Follow all safety precautions before handling equipment with which you are unfamiliar.

DECEMBER

1—Clear up pending matters and prepare for new events and activities. Dispose of assignments that could impede your progress. Efficiency and careful attention to detail can pay off in financial rewards. Also, your good example may inspire another.

2—Care is needed wherever personal or business risks are involved. This can be especially true if you have to drive in areas of heavy traffic or are conducting large-scale negotiations. Stick to routines you know best.

3—Shelve non-essential tasks temporarily. Stick to projects that have a practical purpose. Make yourself work hard so that at the end of the day you have a satisfied feeling of accomplishment.

4—Regardless of your plans for the weekend, you should have a pleasant time. Disregard petty inconveniences, and you will discover that no problem exists which patience cannot solve. Cultivate new acquaintances whenever the opportunity presents itself.

5—A contemplated change in your home may prove unsatisfactory if it concerns redecorating. You may not feel comfortable in new surroundings that are different from the accustomed ones. Also, your inability to achieve a special effect may prove annoying. Seek the advice of experts before making alterations.

6—To attain the position you desire, be willing to make small concessions. By doing this, you may create a more favorable impression. Regardless of doubts you may have, be optimistic and encouraging in dealings with others.

7—Since arguments are likely to crop up for little apparent reason, be particularly alert to avoid them. This is not a good day for money matters. Employ persuasion rather than beligerence to gain your ends.

8—Rash and impetuous action may lead to more difficulty than expected. Guard against doing anything that might have an unfavorable effect on your friends. Resentment that you stir up might be difficult to smooth over. It would be unwise to fight antagonism openly.

9—Make every effort to keep trivial mistakes and confusion to a minimum. Unanticipated trouble caused by others may also prove a special source of annoyance. Keep your temper under control, and your many problems will work out their own solutions.

10—This is a particularly adverse day to make major changes in your job or career. Uncontrolled vacillation may prove costly, as well as time-consuming. Refrain from doing anything that would jeopardize your reputation. Closely adhere to conservative practices.

11—Insisting on having your own way may arouse stubborn opposition. Do not take unnecessary chances in dealing with others, stay away from situations that could develop into a display of temperament. Your calmness may act as a soothing balm.

12—You should find it a pleasant change to ignore routine duties. Spend most of your time doing things you enjoy. Allow some time in your weekday program for recreation and rest and you should find that you work with greater efficiency.

13—This would be a good time to give your wardrobe some special attention. Keep up with current trends and prepare for changes in the weather. However, listen to the viewpoints of others before deciding on the style and the cost of your purchases.

14—You should feel encouraged and happy about the serenity in your home. Limitations and obstacles which have been causing you to have a hectic time should disintegrate. Domestic harmony prevails now.

15—If you want to make good headway, do one job at a time. You may save energy by setting a definite routine for each assignment that you have to complete. Also, by doing this you can perform your work more rapidly and increase your rate of production.

16—Regardless of your enthusiasm to embark upon new enterprises and seek new fields of accomplishment, engage only in undertakings which are likely to reward your efforts. A shift from your normal goals at this time might have an undesirable result.

17—This is a good time to gratify a long-standing desire for a special luxury. Even though it might temporarily upset your budget, you should find that the pleasure you receive is well worth the expense. As long as you do not place yourslef in the position where you will have to depend on borrowed cash, you might indulge yourself a little.

18—Keep alert against an attempt to impose on you. Do not let anyone take advantage of your generosity or become so obligated to you that a strained and unfriendly relationship is likely to follow.

19—Contact people personally. Your presence may create a better impression than letters or phone calls. Put your charm to work for you in the business as well as social world.

20—Do not rely on guesswork, but follow customary procedures, especially where money or business matters are concerned. Analyze each problem carefully before making a decision. Also, do not ignore assistance or guidance that is offered to you.

21—Matters pertaining to love, romance, and friendship are particularly highlighted. Arrange it so that recreational and social activities can occupy some portion of your time. Pleasure is indicated regardless of where you are or what you are doing.

22—Show little hesitation in accepting all challenges designed to test your capabilities. Your efforts could be well rewarded. The excellent results of your work at this time may lead to assignments from which you can obtain splended financial benefits.

23—Do not make any decisions without giving considerable forethought to the facts at hand. You could place yourself in a serious predicament, if you rely solely on your intuitive impressions. Also, trouble that you encounter now can last for a long time.

24—A strong sense of satisfaction may be obtained through doing something thoughtful for a loved one. Demonstrate your generosity and affection openly to someone you hold dear. Arrange a surprise or give a party so that others may share your happiness.

25—Your effort to make others happy can put you in a good humor, as well as having a cheering and pleasant reaction on the Christmas guests you entertain. Cheerfulness is an exceptionally powerful force today.

26—This can be an ideal day to plan a party or sponsor another form of social gathering. Devote your efforts and enthusiasm to putting the people around you in a happy frame of mind.

27—Do not let interference from others or your own apprehensions interfere with matters that pertain to your job or business. Be bold and aggressive and let those around you know that you intend to achieve your goals.

28—Do not depend entirely on advice you receive from another, even though you respect the source. Instead, act only after you have drawn your own conclusions. While you may receive valuable pointers that you can use to advantage, erroneous information that you receive now could be costly.

29—Concentrate on matters which form your present concern. Go after goals you have long wanted to achieve, instead of daydreaming about what you would like to do. Make any changes in your present setup you feel will prove helpful in obtaining your desires.

30—Although you may encounter differences of opinion, do not let this upset you. Instead, take setbacks in your stride, and redouble your efforts to make things run smoothly. Determined efforts on your part may soon cause bothersome situations to right themselves.

31—Today you may have to prove your devotion. In strange ways the real basis of your relationships will be brought to the test. Look hopefully ahead to next year and all that it holds for you.

Taurus
April 21st—May 20th

You are quite steadfast
in your view
of happiness.
To win and hold an ideal,
cherished lifemate,
to rear a family
of which you can be proud,
to hold valuable property
and have a solid savings account
are all in the nature of happiness for you.
You like the applause of friends and associates
for work well done
and for careful thought
which allows you
to give good advice.
It pleases you
to be consulted frequently.
You are happy
when you feel
your life is secure
with the benefits you have won.
You have no objection
to some fame and honor of wider type
and may strive for it.
You are a worker
and just rewards give you happy gratification.

Taurus

JANUARY

1—Diplomacy and poise are essential if you expect to get along well with others. Strive for topnotch results, regardless of the project with which you are occupied. Make arrangements to enjoy future luxuries by starting to save for them now.

2—Confide only in those people whom you know to be trustworthy. Use your ingenuity to make profitable use of your leisure hours. Your efforts to help someone out of a difficult situation should be received with appreciation.

3—Guard against making a decision that might create an unnecessary drain on your finances. Your resourcefulness can help to make a favorable impression on others. Clear up pending obligations without delay before diverting your attention to other things.

4—Rely on yourself rather than on the promise of an associate. Take extra precautions to safeguard your cash and valuables. Avoid requesting a favor unless you are in a position to repay it without delay.

5—Start on a household project that you have been especially anxious to get underway. Do not act on hunches, particularly where job or money matters are concerned. Express your thoughts to others but avoid putting on pressure to get your own way.

6—Regardless of how annoyed or depressed others may feel, see that your own attitude is one of cheerfulness. Gratifying results from your efforts are possible through diligent and unyielding determination. Rather than worry over previous mistakes, make the best of existing situations.

7—Your popularity and circle of acquaintances may show a marked increase. Plan your purchases carefully and aim for maximum usage of your cash. Settle matters with finality, rather than leave them open for later negotiations.

8—Plan each move you intend to make carefully in order to prevent confusion and interference. Take an interest outside your usual sphere of activities for a stimulating change of pace. Display patience rather than irritability if you expect to sidestep difficult situations.

9—For best results, follow customary procedures and do not try to be different. Take time out from arduous duties for fun, romance, and friendship. Let home and family matters occupy the major portion of your thoughts, regardless of the other problems you have to face.

10—Take difficulties that you encounter in your stride rather than give in to self-pity. Refrain from participating in any activity where there is possibility of your conduct or motives being criticized. Despite boring activities, refrain from making sudden changes in your routine.

11—You can forestall strained relations by ignoring remarks of a critical nature. Sticking to established procedure may be your most effective means of achieving satisfactory headway. Cope with one problem at a time and do not try to get everything done at once.

12—Make every effort to smooth-over differences of opinion as quickly as possible. Work at a slow and conservative pace, wasting little time on matters of minor consequence. Remain poised despite a display of temper from another.

13—See that minor disturbances and disruptions do not prevent you from achieving required goals. Avoid risking a clash of temperament with someone who is in a position to discipline you. Refuse to become upset about difficulties that are not of your immediate concern.

14—Take time to evaluate facts, particularly where your future or income is involved. Hold on to what you already have rather than take an unnecessary chance. Depend on your own resources to get what you want; do not count on the efforts of an associate.

15—Guard against saying or writing anything that, if repeated, might be misinterpreted. Discuss in detail your plans about things you would like to do in the future, but temporarily defer action. Allow time to fit recreational or social activities into your schedule.

16—Do not allow yourself to be imposed on, regardless of close associations. Clear up the loose odds and ends of your duties before taking time out for pleasure. Refrain from forcing an issue about a household matter no matter how correct you feel you are.

17—Utilize available opportunities to demonstrate your creative and artistic abilities. Concentrate on your own personal problems instead of worrying about the needs of others. Adjust yourself quickly to existing situations rather than offer opposition.

18—Insure a trouble-free day by steering clear of arguments that are not your immediate concern. Do what you can to apply your capabilities and interests toward greater accomplishments. Pay attention to the minor details of your work—you may find that they can cause the most difficulty.

19—Put the finishing touches on uncompleted tasks rather than leave loose ends for later consideration. Seek competent counsel before investing your cash or adopting a new financial policy. Ignore discord and say things you feel can promote cheerfulness and optimism.

20—Use your money effectively while shopping by aiming for quality and practicability. Be flexible in your plans, so that you can make changes and keep up with new situations. Be prepared to face inconveniences or unwelcome interference with your ambitions.

21—Exercise special care while working or doing something that is unfamiliar to you. Do not let business matters keep you from the pleasures that are offered. Gratifying a desire to shop for an expensive article may turn out to be a discouraging experience.

22—Live up to what is expected of you, even though doing so may entail extra effort. Careless spending might lead to emotional conflicts and cause criticism. Efficiency and accuracy should be emphasized; mistakes that you make now may prove difficult to rectify.

23—Offset gloom and pessimism in others by being humorous in your remarks. A display of friendliness in a business matter may help you remove an imposing obstacle. You can attract the attention you desire by demonstrating a special ability.

24—Abrupt changes that you make in your present setup might lead to obstacles that would be difficult to overcome. Seek from others suggestions that you feel can supplement your own experience and ideas. Accede to the wishes of associates and do all you can to maintain harmony.

25—Do not press your viewpoints too vigorously; doing so could stir up antagonism. Maintain an optimistic attitude even though things may develop more slowly than expected. Your patience, friendliness, and generosity can have a favorable effect on those around you.

26—Keep on the lookout for errors and do not take any chances with work that is unfamiliar to you. Make plans that you feel can help promote financial and career advantages. Your participation in a conversation may result in a misunderstanding, so be careful.

27—Take time out to enjoy the friendliness and companionship of those around you. Benefit from mistakes made by others—see to it that you do not run into the same trouble yourself. Look for inspiration in the fine results achieved by a successful acquaintance.

28—Splendid benefits are possible from working on a method by which you can reduce the time it takes to do a specific task. The degree of success you obtain may depend on your willingness to cooperate with others. Clear and logical thinking is essential if you expect to minimize confusing circumstances.

29—Draw your own conclusions rather than expect someone else to do your thinking for you. Even though you may have to work under pressure, do not place the burden of your duties on another. Patience instead of aggressiveness can net you desirable results.

30—By combining mental and manual activities, you should be able to produce satisfying results. Do not allow yourself to become upset or annoyed by things of minor consequence. Your enthusiasm can be a valuable asset, provided you keep it headed in the right direction.

31—Do not incur extra expenses, regardless of temporary whims. Display your sympathy and understanding, but make sure that you will not place yourself in an inconvenient position. Do not let friendship interfere when making a necessary decision about money.

FEBRUARY

1—You may try your hand at something new with great success. It's a grand day to buy something artistic that has gripped your imagination, perhaps a recording of an appealing song. Be unusually pleasant with friends.

2—There is no reason to become upset by a little opposition. If you are subtle and turn on the charm, obstacles will be swept away. Evening is a good time to get out and walk around. If it is possible to have a garden, plan one for the spring.

3—You may be much liked by younger people, and this can make you joyous. A happy time for conversations, and work will go with a whiz. You may have an evening date that makes you want to be at your very best.

4—You can have some mechanical trouble if you're driving. Be on guard and have your automobile checked for safety if possible. Avoid unfamiliar places and don't let whims lead to unwise activities and companionship.

5—Someone at work may take advantage of your generosity. Keep alert for a person who is unscrupulous about money; be very close-fisted today. This evening is excellent for attending a glittering party.

6—Go over your financial and social position; find ways you can improve. Put your home into excellent condition—make things shine. You may have a surprise visitor and make a fine impression with a clean and polished home.

7—Although you may really like and admire an older person, you may be in the mood to say unpleasant things about this person's ways. Curb your speech, stay friendly and agreeable and show your best nature to the world today.

8—This is a good day for major activities involving finances, but be sure to deal only with reputable people. You may invest in a marvelous new venture that is going to do extremely well. Evening will give a feeling of contented relaxation.

9—Overlook small defects; even let someone hoodwink you a bit. Life is amusing today and good nature wins. Be ready to laugh, even at yourself for a foolish error. Not a good time for romance to begin, so watch out!

10—You may receive an exciting letter. Your day-dreaming self might be forced into action by this letter. Try to avoid neglect of your work duties; don't let a supervisor catch you dilly-dallying on the job.

11—From lack of belief in your trustworthiness, an older relative may make you unhappy by refusing a request. Don't mope or sulk about this. Today may be the pointer for some things you have to learn.

12—You can become suddenly very determined about a romantic matter and may make overtures to someone you've just been seeing around lately. This may develop into something quite serious but never very pleasant for you.

13—Pleasure and sport may be all you want to give your time to, but you'll have to find a way to handle a responsibility first. Be cautious with little children today; avoid temper which might injure them.

14—Historic places can be pleasant, and visiting a new one could be most enjoyable. Neighbors are friendly, but you may find in the long run that their friendship is only a foundation for continuous borrowing, much to your expense.

15—Something may come your way today to make you very happy. A big change can be made; you may be put in a more prestigious position. Be proud and happy with work that is demanding and requires more use of your mentality.

16—Consider seriously the advice of someone close to you who wants to help with a health problem that is worrying you. You may need expert advice more than any medicine for ailment.

17—You may suddenly want to take a trip to see a young relative who is in a special situation, possibly about to be wed. If finances do not allow this trip, do not become angry, but try to be reasonable with all involved.

18—A very generous person may do something for you that should win eternal gratitude. Don't take things for granted or show any sign that you expected even more to be done for you. A calm wisdom is needed tonight.

19—You can be so wrapped up in a date you are to have tonight that you speak sharply to those who break into your thought. Try to be more mature, more tolerant and patient. Your evening, in fact, may be a total flop.

20—A favorable time to get out and visit some nearby places of interest. Good to travel briefly and perhaps stay overnight with friends at a little distance. Go along with the day; be ready to do unplanned things.

21—An influential person may speak to you in a way you find offensive. This is undoubtedly just a bit of high-class teasing, which you need to take in a witty rather than angry way. Think before you speak.

22—An unusual day, when plans can go awry. But it won't matter because of the good things that are happening. Sudden changes may come about and you can have a very pleasant adventure. Excitement keeps you glowing.

23—A hope you have been cherishing may come true. You may be engaged and even have a ring before evening. Romance is the big thing for Cancer today and the already married will find it a time of receiving renewed affection.

24—Avoid being too swift and impatient. Your work can suffer and you may be called for a conference about errors you are making. It could be a humiliating day for you, and loss of temper could also cause the loss of your job.

25—Your education may win a new chance today. If you are given the ability to improve your talents with more polish, by all means take it. Do not let sloth and pleasure-loving keep you from accepting opportunity.

26—A day you will always remember. Excitement, adventures and new contacts fill the day with activity you can enjoy. This evening is very brilliant socially; be cautious to be diplomatic if occasion demands it, though.

27—News from a former friend can make you somewhat envious. Beware of those tricky and swift emotions of yours. Do not destroy anything worth-while or in any way set a bad example for children during meals of this cycle.

28—An important telephone call may come and it can change the whole direction of your life. Your ability to adapt to the new may be needed. You can be in exotic circumstances you never experienced before. Use your mentality.

29 (Leap Year Only)—Go out of your way to make contacts. Business opportunities seized now will mean future profit. You can also go through with transactions successfully, talk to those in charge of work, and make appointments for further conferences.

MARCH

1—A conference may be lengthy and can give you some new things to think about. Have your own defense in mind when you answer questions. Avoid being too straightforward in talk with a younger person tonight.

2—Expenditures may be made on emergencies and you can be highly worried about this trend. Make sure to keep up your credit reputation. Finances are emphasized but before the cycle ends can turn more favorable to you.

3—Let nothing keep you from carrying out plans. Avoid arguments, especially with a lifemate. If unmarried do not become engaged this evening, for it would lead only to an unsuccessful union that should never happen.

4—You can be very surprised at the mail, a telephone call, visitors who drop in out of a blue sky. It's an exciting day with a generally beneficial trend for you. Family matters improve through your wisdom tonight.

5—An error on your part may be laughed at by others but you can feel embarrassed. No use taking things so seriously you make yourself unhappy. Avoid the kind of pride that can never tolerate a joke on one's self.

6—Keep busy, avoid letting your mind wander, and do not be interrupted by people who want to chat and gossip. Stay clear of any questionable group of conversation. Avoid heavy eating foods or staying up late tonight.

7—Let no one upset your poise, remain good-humored even though you realize a younger person is trying to bait you and upset you. Avoid all types of bigotry in actions and speech. Make the evening restful rather than active.

8—You can have an inspiration to shop for something pleasant that will brighten your life. Of course obligations go with almost everything, but don't let these stand in the way of adding a touch of happiness to the domestic scene.

9—A most unexpected person may come to see you briefly on an errand. You can become interested in this person and if unmarried you may later enter romance with the one mentioned. A good evening for pleasant dreaming.

10—Do not forget an important anniversary or birthdate. Be sure to buy a card or a gift which is appropriate. Let your generosity show today and in evening entertainment reign in your life.

11—You may waste time over someone who is undependable. This should be a good lesson for a decision you need to make. Use your firmest character and be very determined in your dealings with a person of doubtful scruples.

12—Driving is hazardous, relationships are tense. In general the day is displeasing. You feel oppressed and depressed. Best not to see an older friend who just might make some remarks to cause you to feel more gloomy.

13—Your interest in the arts can form an important part of your happiness now. A good day for cultural matters, creative projects. Evening will become somewhat tedious if you spend it with a new romantic acquaintance.

14—Be very careful of arithmetic today. Check all totals you get, don't trust anyone else to do mathematics for you. A new situation may crop up late in the afternoon and you may devote your evening hours to hashing it over.

15—A decision you make this morning may have to be altered when new facts show it up as impractical. A very enchanting person may enter your life today, but the charisma might be deceiving.

16—Your affection for an older executive may waver some due to talk that goes on today. A very loyal friend will stand by you no matter what the circumstances. Value true friendship first of all in life today.

17—Give attention to a matter which you have been ignoring. You have special talents for solving and handling this matter and others expect you to do so. End a war with your own emotions and get busy to do as required.

18—You may be on the grouchy side, particularly with children if you have them. You can be longing for freedom that seems to be impossible to attain. A good day to start thinking about buying birthday gifts and cards.

19—Try not to show disapproval of anyone. You can be most scornful of those who make mistakes because they follow no plan. What help will your scorn be? Show more sympathy than criticism to others now.

20—You may be numbered with the snobs today due to your attitude toward culture, your insistence on just the right aesthetic effects. Well, you don't object to being put in this category, and maybe even secretly enjoy it.

21—A letter may dismay you and you might try to avoid responding. That may bring a long distance call eventually. Better get busy and communicate as expected. What you have to say can be helpful whether you're sincere or not.

22—Someone of influence and charm may let you down. The discovery that such a person doesn't keep promises may sadden you. One of those days you will learn more about the world you live in. Don't be too pessimistic.

23—Someone may attack you out of the blue. This person may be very irrational, swift to lose temper. Have some pity because the health of this person is questionable; there may be serious illness setting in.

24—Shopping, beauty care, music, pets and neighbors are all favorably aspected for you. You can keep busy with these matters, buying or enjoying, adding glamor. Be helpful to an older neighbor tonight with your many talents.

25—Do as the family wishes and be dutiful in all your chores for loved ones. If you plan a party tonight, make sure all is approved by relatives who will be there. Have consideration for an in-law in what you do, above all.

26—You may rest most of the day, prefer to stay in and lounge around. Don't let anyone move you out against your will. You can do some essential thinking, get your wardrobe in better shape, tending to family needs efficiently.

27—Delay can make you almost frantic and this is not becoming or healthy. Slow down, be patient with others, and all will work out. Your wish to change residence may be fulfilled by what you do and talk about today.

28—There may be an important matter you need to free your mind from. This will involve finances, no doubt. Best to consult an expert and by evening have a festive mood to celebrate the end of your problems.

29—A neighbor's personality can vex you beyond words. If you yield to brooding over this matter, you're the one who will suffer. It could get so bad emotionally that you'd have to see a physician about it at much cost.

30—Be practical, swift of decision, very precise in work. Expect the same kind of action from others and you'll get it. A young relative may have a request you can fulfill; don't give advice along with aid.

31—Excellent hours for change you've been planning. You can move residence, have health work done, make an investment of almost any kind. Your social life can be glamorous but do not keep late hours or you'll regret it.

APRIL

1—Slow down, take stock of your situation, find ways to improve production. If you own a business put money back into it. Avoid any shady dealings, schemes proposed by people you do not trust. Keep diet simple and meagre. Spend the evening with someone who cheers you and is a good listener.

2—Subscribe to magazines, buy books, records, equipment such as typewriters, pens, paper and the like. Enjoy shopping at leisurely rate. Don't let anyone hurry you. Your health will profit from a slow pace. You'll be happy with results of following a few of your impulses during evening.

3—What you want to do may be expensive but can be worth it. Your mind is not on material things but on matters of the spirit and emotions which you want to be clear about and to find happiness in. A very successful day for follow-up urges that can give deep inner cheer to your spirit.

4—If you are surprised by an attack an associate makes, keep your own temper. In fact you may not be angry at all except that your feelings may be jolted and injured a little. A quiet manner is your best answer, but you might also be stirred to a little laughter; that could be irritating to another.

5—Very romantic inclinations are here and while you are out browsing around in a book or music store you may encounter someone you met formally quite awhile ago. It might suddenly be apparent to both of you that romance could be quite pleasing. Go a little easy with this; it's dubious.

6—Be cautious in the home, around all machinery and fire, do not drive unless you must. A quiet walk can do you good, help get your thoughts straightened out. A telephone call late in the day can be surprising but from it you may make a valuable new friend in the near future.

7—You can be feeling sorry yourself, if married and might even look for a way to get out of it beneficially. Wisdom will lead you to acceptance, appreciation and shame at your own selfish trends. Be particularly generous and kindly with the family that you basically love and value.

8—An older person can aggravate you by appearing to have an answer to everything. Laugh at this rather than getting upset and irritated. Treat people with esteem today and you will win their esteem. Do your work very methodically, get a little ahead of requirements and you'll be pleased.

9—Romantic matters claim your attention but you may wish they didn't. Someone may show attention and be outright in speech about love for you. Since you cannot return the sentiment you need much diplomacy. Fortune may smile upon you and give you a perfect way out of the dilemma.

10—A good day to aid others, visit the lonely and shut-ins, give little gifts to show affections. Be attentive to little children and their needs. Keep the home life quiet and seek an evening to devote to doing things to improve the home, start an attractive do-it-yourself project.

11—You may be occupied with mathematics all day and feel quite vexed about it. Work to balance all money concerns may be essential. You may think about quitting the job due to the trivial matters you must trace down to their initial point of error. Don't do anything reckless tonight.

12—An unlearned person may make a disparaging remark. Actually, although this is meant to injure you, you can take this as a compliment due to unusual circumstances. All is a matter of individuals involved, so take heart and realize that learned people will have just the opposite to say.

13—You could waste the day brooding too much over destiny and the quirks of life that come along no matter how you labor to stave them off. Actually, you may be living in a place temporarily that is very depressing to you and you can be living just to escape from it in the near future.

14—Someone from your past may come back under the intuitive urge of being needed by you. This is a delightfully touching event but you may not want to associate with this person again. A certain clash of values exists and you know it will never end. Find a wise way to explain this clearly.

15—Don't work to the point of exhaustion. Your health is a bit on the delicate side and needs good care. A visit to a physician can be in order. You may need special diet items to give a correct balance in your system, possibly more calcium. Avoid any pleasure-seeking with friends tonight.

16—You may arrive at facts you cannot deny and this can be a puzzling circumstance, one which worries you. Any attempt to evade or change things simply will not work. Buckle down, make the day pay financially, keep everything you do on the practical side. Avoid family arguments tonight.

17—You may cross the path of someone who is very imperious, demanding and self-righteous. If you see that you must do so, yield pleasantly and with poise to a dictum of such a person. The time is not long and will be over shortly. Relax totally this evening; love can soothe ruffled spirits.

18—Some of your acquaintances may be too diplomatic and well-versed in courtesy to bring up certain subjects, but a neighbor who is just the opposite may bring up a subject that can cause you much dismay. You may feel torn by emotional troubles and the need to be forgiving today.

19—Dealing with younger people can be stimulating and teach you quite a bit and yet it can be exhausting, too. Do not let your weariness show until you are safely at home and can rest. Social life later tonight may hold a moment of tension that no one present will ever forget.

20—Do not let disillusionment and unhappiness keep you from attending church. It can be very inspiring and comforting, giving you a new and refreshing outlook. Spend much of the afternoon outdoors, attend a picnic if you can, do nice things for little children in the family or neighborhood.

21—Seek a leisurely pace, go about work slowly but methodically. Let no one share you or rush you. Haste can be disastrous. Protect your pocketbook and all credit cards or anything of value that can be lost or stolen. Best not to spend at all; be content with window-shopping.

17—You may cross the path of someone who is very imperious, demanding and self-righteous. If you see that you must do so, yield pleasantly and with poise to a dictum of such a person. The time is not long and will be over shortly. Relax totally this evening; love can soothe ruffled spirits.

18—Some of your acquaintances may be too diplomatic and well versed in courtesy to bring up certain subjects, but a neighbor who is just the opposite may bring up a subject that can cause you much dismay. You may feel torn by emotional troubles and the need to be forgiving today.

19—Dealing with younger people can be stimulating and teach you quite a bit and yet it can be exhausting, too. Do not let your weariness show until you are safely at home and can rest. Social life later tonight may hold a moment of tension that no one present will ever forget.

20—Do not let disillusionment and unhappiness keep you from attending church. It can be very inspiring and comforting, giving you a new and refreshing outlook. Spend much of the afternoon outdoors, attend a picnic if you can, do nice things for little children in the family or neighborhood.

21—Seek a leisurely pace, go about work slowly but methodically. Let no one share you or rush you. Haste can be disastrous. Protect your pocketbook and all credit cards or anything of value that can be lost or stolen. Best not to spend at all; be content with window-shopping.

22—You may find a new friend in a person you once believed was hostile to you. Actually this person is only temperamental and you should be able to understand that. You get along beautifully in sharing a mutual pursuit such as a hobby. A sociable day and evening add up to happiness.

23—One of those times for big-scale enterprise, aiming high in financial goals. Your astute knowledge of money matters is at work for you. You'll get encouragement from a loved one and today may be the commencement of a real accumulation of fortune beginning from a small project.

24—You can be suspicious about the motives of a person at a distance with whom you are in communication. Actually, you probably are just building up this feeling due to some outside consideration. You can feel your security jeopardized by this person and chances are that is ridiculous.

25—Emotions may be touchy and you could be unpleasant with just about everyone. You can have a health matter developing that might put you out of circulation for a few days. You may find that you can't avoid seeing a doctor. Don't let fear be any part of your reactions. Relax tonight.

26—Cooperation is difficult to get, family members may be no help at all. On the other hand, your mail can be interesting and may hold an idea worth following through. Shopping today can be enjoyable if by yourself or with a good friend, but keep family members out of it, if you possibly can.

27—An old friend may do you a favor that is much needed. You'll get a big surprise when you find out where loyalty is shown and where it is not shown. Everything that happens today and everyone you talk to will give you something to think about. Your wisdom may reach a new level of maturity as a result.

28—You can be tempted to buy a large new item. It is not a good day for this but you may feel pressure of need. If you make a real effort to put off this purchase until tomorrow, you may find that the pressure to buy it is off. For your own financial well-being make an effort to try this stalling.

29—A day for beauty, romance, travel, enjoyment of life. If you are on vacation it's wonderful. You can go to the splendid places, eat delicious food, have a gorgeous time with the right companions. Those who love you are generous and help you enjoy this cycle all the way.

30—Someone you admire may show equal esteem for you. This can be the beginning of a profitable friendship, possible partnership. There is a chance, quite slim though, of romance entering your life as the result of a meeting today. It may be a very fleeting matter, so don't hope for a great deal.

MAY

1—Someone may make you a gift of something you desire. Be appreciative of this gracious gesture. The day is peaceful and calm, happy in a quiet way. You may discover some mutual interests in conversation with a new acquaintance. Strong bonds may be forged in this relationship.

2—There are hazards to health and accidents are entirely possible. Be cautious what you say to a lifemate if married. If unmarried do not become entangled in a new romance now. Let the day go by rather inactively, be alert to dangers, eat moderately and avoid stimulants firmly.

3—You may hear good news about hopes that are dear to you. You may receive word that a promotion is going through for you soon. The evening can bring contact with a friend at a distance and some encouraging, affectionate talk. All is well for your personal plans and ambitions.

4—Major efforts will have to be made to carry out work that is more difficult than it appeared at first. You will win rewards but it is difficult to stop concentrating on the strenuous side of affairs. Win your way to more optimism and cheer by simple determination to do so.

5—Make a real effort not to think about yourself and some unhappiness you're nurturing. Cultivating good habits of thought rather than depressing ones is necessary. You can accomplish what is essential only if you devote yourself to it entirely, forge right ahead.

6—If you stick to work too long, you'll become exhausted, nervous, unhappy. Take time off now and then, slight changes will prove refreshing. You may be presented with a large problem to solve this evening. Family members may depend upon you and take too much for granted.

7—Your financial situation is under some dubious influences now. You might be hit hard with an unexpected bill. Do not let despair creep into your thought. Be glad you can handle things with your money resources and don't keep your eyes on what you must pay out dutifully.

8—Let your day be as quiet as possible. Avoid any people who are upsetting for your tranquility. Come to some conclusion about romance or marriage. Your sense of security is your best guide now. Do as seems best about social life tonight; don't linger long if you are tired.

9—You may be given new ideas to think about if you attend church. What you hear can be encouraging and brighten all your views. Stay out a lot, see many people, seek stimulating companionships today. Dining out with an older friend is favored; be a little luxurious.

10—Disconcerting news may arrive and can take your mind off work disastrously. A mistake you have to correct may be frustrating to plans. Protect yourself against error by close checks. Think your way through some confusing circumstances during the evening at home.

11—A new situation may develop which calls upon you to do something against the grain. You may have to make plans to move to a distance when you do not want to. Put trust in those who love you and are willing to help in these new circumstances. Be courageous in facing necessity.

12—Avoid letting an older neighbor impose upon you or pry into your personal life. A curious and meddlesome person can be difficult to discourage but turn on the ice and aloofness and do it thoroughly. Romance may call for some meditation and consulting of true feelings tonight.

13—You may win high praise, perhaps be in the public spotlight due to facts connected with your talents and knowledge. Be sure to live up to the expectations others have of you and do not resent the need to do so. You may be entering a fascinating new phase of work activities now.

14—Your generosity will be more than appreciated. The favor you do for someone may be returned in a strange way later. A good evening to entertain in your home, but be moderate about all provisions. Avoid excess in your own indulgence in party life; be wise about what you say tonight.

15—Stop to think before you make a promise or commit yourself in any way. Do not let anyone know you are carrying on an analysis of another person's character. You could be embarrassingly wrong about such a matter. Keep equanimity of spirit and enjoy a good show tonight.

16—An influential person may make a remark you do not understand. Do not show disturbance, keep your poise, walk right on through circumstances today. Be helpful to a new neighbor who comes to you for friendship. Provide companionship for a lonely person who is affectionate.

17—Keep yourself on a concentrated course with work or you won't fill expectations of an executive. Be cautious about what you say to one who loves you. You could lose the happiest most rewarding love in your life. Be dependable, gracious and appreciative in love tonight.

18—Treat all children very well, be generous in buying them things to please. Avoid a squabble with relatives or an in-law. Keep harmony in all relationships, be kindly and patient. You may have something to say that will be helpful to a person in doubt about emotional matters.

19—Don't encourage anyone to enter an organization just because you think it is worthwhile. Let everyone be independent in coming to such decisions. Your work will be rewarding and new ideas about handling it can have a touch of genius. Do nothing to make a loved one unhappy tonight.

20—You may need to check with a physician about a minor ailment. Don't worry if the condition is not what you expected. Arrange to keep it a quiet day and evening, do not accept any invitation for tonight and be very quiet in all pursuits; listen to music, read.

21—Be considerate of someone who is a hard worker but may irritate you personally. Make allowance for pressures in this person's life. You may meet someone new in social life this evening, be wary if you feel highly attracted at once. This person may be an experienced heartbreaker.

22—Shop with a good companion, enjoying the appeal that frivolous merchandise has for you now. Buy a few small items just for fun, brighten the home. Entertain tonight on a casual level, provide plenty but make it inexpensive. Good nature prevails and guests are happy.

23—Be sure to follow out plans you have made; let no one lead you away from this course. Write a letter that is due, let someone know how much you appreciate attention. You may come to a beneficial decision about financial activity that attracts you. Be daring in plans.

24—The day can be trying and dull. You may have to listen to comments of an executive you consider overbearing. If you walk out on this situation you will regret it soon. Be self-disciplined; think of financial necessity and go your way in quiet and pleasant relationships.

25—A neighbor may ask favors and be offensive on top of it. You might as well realize that such a person is only trying to use you and has no consideration for you. Break off any such relationship for good and make it clear you are through being helpful and generous.

26—Sum up your money circumstances, get things in orderly shape in your mind. Do nothing whimsical and irresponsible today. Be careful of your companionship and do not make a loved one jealous by a reckless flirtation. Your evening can bring surprises, unusual communications.

27—Be accurate in all you say and do. Don't make statements if you don't have facts. Avoid trying to persuade a younger person to follow your advice. You could be blamed very much later. Guard your valuable possessions, keep doors locked when you are away from home.

28—You may find someone unfriendly, so it is best not to make any approaches to new acquaintances. Keep to yourself and do not plan on a big evening socially. Someone who visits you casually may be your best companion for the evening. Avoid any temperamental trends tonight.

29—What you discover today may put you in a good mood. The time is favorable for making a decision about a big change, an investment, things you wish to buy for home improvement. You'll get help from an unexpected source and this will cut down expenditures considerably for you.

30—Protect yourself today, follow health rules, be alert if driving. Don't spend too much just because luxury attracts you and glamorous places lure you. You may come to the end of a romantic relationship which will linger in the form of fond friendship when the break-up is over.

31—A wonderful opportunity may come through the mail and provide the way for you to spend your vacation soon. Give thought to the suggestions of a friend at a distance. Take your time in making up your mind. You'll be happy with outcome of a cooperative venture in the near future.

JUNE

1—You can be unhappy with work today, feel you are wasting talents. Avoid any restless trend that urges change, keep the status quo and be conscientious. Evening may bring an unusual telephone call that supplies facts of importance. Your emotions may be upset by this.

2—Keep a steady pace, don't complain or be unpleasant in any way. Be particularly thoughtful about one who loves you, a small gift is in order for your lifemate or other romantic companion tonight.

3—You may find much fault with your living conditions and make an effort to change your residence. It is best not to make any final decision about this or pay any money down on a lease or the like. Talk things over with your family before you make any decision about this.

4—Be cautious with health, keep regular meals as a basis for avoiding troubles, don't go in for stimulants. In the evening if you go out socially, don't indulge in anything questionable for health although you may be tempted. Be helpful to someone who needs a friend.

5—Don't risk money on something that may not be of any use to you. Make practicality the basis of all you do. You might become upset with the manner of a loved one; don't speak too quickly for wisdom. Value what you have and do nothing to disturb affections in the family.

6—Getting in touch with an old friend may not be wise although no immediate trouble is seen. You could be remembering happiness of former days but it would not be your advantage to follow up this trend. Give your attention to your situation of current times.

7—News may filter through that you are due for a pay raise, perhaps a more responsible position. Don't be afraid of new trends, be courageous, feel capable and keep your mood one of ambition and worthwhile effort. Go easy with any spending you do during the evening hours.

8—You may find family life a snarl of mixed attitudes and undercurrents of hostility. Don't contribute to this trend. An in-law may also irk you but don't show any bad temper in this direction. Seek a peaceful evening with some light, pleasant reading or television watching.

9—A good day for gaining extra money, also good for large investments. If you want to move your home, this is the day to do it. It will be a happier situation for you if you gain conveniences which your former home did not have. Optimism prevails and you are happy.

10—Sudden weariness and sloth may be due to a physical condition that needs care from your doctor. Don't delay going for a check; delay could make things really bad. You may hear some surprising news in a diagnosis. Be thoughtful and considerate with your family.

11—You may acquire a valuable possession in a unique way. There are surprises in the atmosphere. Social life can provide experience of interest. Do not answer personal questions if a curious friend meddles in your life tonight, but do keep good-humored about this trend.

12—There is a major romantic trend but it could prove to be illusory in the near future. You may have the idea that someone cares for you much more than the facts warrant. Best to take a middle course, don't make promises or commit yourself to any specific line of action.

13—Irritating circumstances in your work environment may be due to some envy and hostility that are being hidden from you. There is a chance that an associate may break into the open with criticism and accusations before the day is over. You must not heed this trend seriously.

14—You may be criticized for a relationship which means quite a lot to you. Be silent but don't let anyone sway you in attentions you feel are merited by a friend. Generosity will bring happiness and good spirits.

15—Be courteous today even though you have to struggle to be so. You feel that you'd like to speak harshly to a person who has never harmed you. Your imagination and tendency to blame others must be curbed. A temperamental outburst can have very bad results.

16—It is best to stay in familiar regions, and in fact best to stay near home. Going shopping can be frustrating and you might buy the wrong thing as a substitute for what you really want. Avoid involvement with a neighbor who might impose on you during the evening.

17—An executive may give you a chance to prove abilities that have been held back. Enter wholeheartedly into any creative enterprise you are asked to tackle. This could mean a much more satisfactory job if you carry through with skill and enthusiasm for the task.

18—You could meet someone new today and a serious romantic trend might lead to marriage soon. This is not a favored time for romance, though, and any such person you become interested in now could bring much unhappiness later. Try to make a keen analysis in this matter.

19—A favor you do for someone will be rewarded many times over. Be friendly even if you feel aloof to others. Social life can be happy if you'll participate fully. Spending to entertain in your home is favored; invite someone new and develop a very loyal friendship.

20—Discussion with a family member will lead to an agreement if you are willing to compromise a bit. Don't be harsh with a young relative who wants to show independence. In fact, give credit to this person who is trying hard to carve out a self-dependent life from now on.

21—Expenses can be terrific and make you very unhappy; nevertheless, you must bow to necessity and have things repaired or buy new ones which are vital for your daily life. A better trend comes after dark when you can relax and find rest that will bring serenity.

22—Someone with a desire to rule and dictate may show up. Resolving to avoid relationship with this person is wise. If you go anywhere and are driving, do not take along any companion outside of the family. Dining out can be a pleasure and you can be a bit luxurious.

23—Let others come to you today; don't make any approaches yourself. There can be a romantic trend but it won't last long, possibly a week. A good day is here to sign documents, close a transaction of importance. It is also good to start a vacation, travel far.

24—Do not let anyone undermine your abilities, knowledge or hopes. Seek companions who will be encouraging and avoid those who have resentment toward you. Do nothing to risk your job. Be very pleasant and unselfish with a loved one during the later hours.

25—Difficult conditions may arise due to a misunderstanding. Ask questions in any matter where you are uncertain. Don't let an irritable trend grow. Be pleasant to guests in the home this evening even though you have moments you'd like to speak quite sharply to them.

26—Be circumspect in activities, don't eat or drink heavily or pile up large debts. It is better to skip shopping altogether if possible. Be friendly with someone new in your neighborhood but don't get involved for evening when you'll want quiet and seek early retirement.

27—Your career can take an upward swing that will be gratifying. Efforts bring good results and you'll be praised. A day for happiness, a little light shopping, some conversation which may reveal splendid compatibility. You may have a surprise visitor some time this evening.

28—Mistakes are possible, check things, be thorough and accurate. You may decide upon a change that you have been considering lately. It is a good time to get in touch with those at a distance who can help you. Be outspoken about your desires and you'll win surprise aid.

29—Do not commit yourself to anything of romantic nature. Don't nurture dreams of romantic type, either. Be sensible and value your present situation too much to want a change in personal relationships. Be truthful but also tactful with family members during the evening.

30—New circumstances may crop up in your work situation and this may mean a slight change of scene for you. It is possible to find more congenial associates around you due to this trend. The day augurs well for health, wishes, work and some minor shopping tonight.

JULY

1—You may by chance fall in with someone who will fall in love with you quickly. While you like this person you may be totally unable to respond to love with love. You need tact and just about anything else you can use today. Go easy and you may somehow get the idea across with no harm done.

2—Work worries may assail you, you can be criticized by a grouchy executive. At home you may be criticized by everyone in the house. It just isn't your day but perhaps you can manage to laugh at it and be the winner somehow in the end, social life tonight may make you feel shut out in the cold.

3—A new friend may call and show interest. This person is undoubtedly very loyal and will always be. A most important day is here for your personal life due to this new friendship. You can be discouraged about work and your home life. Be cautious not to go to excess tonight in any way.

4—You won't enjoy any of the usual activities of this day but don't hinder the rest of the family from doing so. This is a good time to plan what you really want to do and you may arrive at a decision which you may soon follow. Keep calm even though you are irked at the attitude of a relative.

5—Good news may greet you first thing in the morning. A younger relative about whom you are concerned can be out of a danger that was faced. Find a way to celebrate just a little, spread your happiness today. A good discussion with a loved one tonight about your future can help you a great deal.

6—An unexpected telephone call can be somewhat embarrassing. You really haven't anything to say and yet feel under pressure to come up with something. Well, such things happen to everyone from time to time, so don't be too grim about it. Evening brings a calm, peaceful, restful atmosphere.

7—A legal matter can call for consultation with a professional expert. Be very cautious about any steps you take in a new venture. Love becomes important later in the day; you can have some happy thoughts about a person who attracts you now. Keep these to yourself for best results.

8—Health is not at its best and you may even have to leave work and go home for the afternoon. You may have a rare condition that is not very serious but painful, perhaps a virus settled in an unusual place such as the jaw. Take care of yourself with professional advice.

9—A new neighbor may be friendly and this could develop into one of your favorite relationships. There might be jealousy from a lifemate if you are married, though, and that could complicate things, make you unhappy and bitter. Evening social life is promising if you can stay good-natured.

10—Do something to help a lonely person who cannot get around easily. A shopping trip with such a person would be very kind. You may have a surprise in the evening. A visitor who arrives without notice may make life gay and show you how to look upon emotional matters with less disturbance.

11—Don't take on new duties that another should assume. Protect yourself and your finances. Go for a brief trip if someone invites you but do not be out after dark. You would not be safe away from home; accidents are likely when the sun has set. Be happy with loved ones.

12—An unreasonable boss can call you to account for something that is not your mistake at all. Try to maintain your good nature but don't let this unpleasing scene go too far without showing your irritation. This might be the beginning of the end for your present work and that could be good.

13—Getting out today will help lift rather dull spirits, but don't linger or get into gossipy circles afterward. Best to turn down invitations for the afternoon, since your personal correspondence, telephone calls and details of work at home need attention. A brief walk in the evening will cheer you.

14—Be sure to eat regularly and balance your menu. Be cautious if you are not at home, make sure the drinking water is pure. There are some menacing health aspects today. A good idea to take your lunch to work even though you don't usually do that. Do not spend the evening with a depressing person.

15—Fine time for travel, a wedding, shopping or a change of job. You can find your destiny becoming much happier due to being active today. There can be excitement in talk with a new friend, possibly a new romance from an introduction made by a friend. The day is totally unclouded.

16—Be sure to have your financial situation firmly in control. Don't be miserly but do be thrifty. You may be entertaining at home this evening; keep provisions abundant but not expensive. You'll be at your best with fixing good food at little expense and your guests will marvel about it.

17—Investigate some educational opportunity that has interested you for some time. You might be able to lay the foundation for future permanent security if you enroll in a course. Read all literature available, talk to someone who knows about the institution you are considering attending.

18—Bad news may come from a family member but you can't do a thing about it. Don't make futile long distance calls trying to persuade someone to have a change of heart. Get out and walk, go somewhere with a friend, avoid solitude. It is necessary to get your mind off matters that are troublesome and sad.

19—A work associate may do something very generous and pleasing for you. Look for the good in the life around you and you will find a lot of it at work. Pass on the benevolence and good cheer. Be one of those who do nice things today and you'll have a role in a chain of good things for others.

20—Do not intrude on anyone who is busy. You could get a burst of temper from someone who means you no ill at all. Be careful if you drive, stay within speed limits, don't insist on having your rights. Much trouble can come from your inflexible attitudes during the evening, so be ready to bend a bit.

21—A good time for action in business. Investment is favored, security will be bolstered. You can enter business for yourself or with a partner who admires your skills much. Your romantic life also takes a change for the better. Someone ideal is with you all the way in your efforts now.

22—You will be very pleased with a new friend, but don't show too much elation or you'll arouse jealousy. Go out shopping, buy some clothes for yourself and children but not for a spouse. Your taste might not please your lifemate. Be independent and let others around you be independent.

23—The day is swift-paced and a lot will be accomplished. Make sure you are one of those who use these beneficial vibrations for practical matters. You may be tempted to go off on a pleasure spree and let duties go. That could be disastrous and pretty quickly you might find it out.

24—Take a mature attitude about family matters. Do not criticize a young relative when you have done the same things in your own youth. Have understanding and try to be tolerant of all. Don't get in a political argument or any discussion of religion during social affairs this evening.

25—A good day to get out and unwind. Just keep going and enjoy the refreshing trend of having no real plans. You can meet with strangers who are delightful to chat with. In the evening try to relax at home with a book. Don't encourage any visitors; you need freedom from others.

26—New circumstances can come about in your work position and they may demand that you make a change. Your willingness to cooperate will be appreciated. You soon may find yourself with more congenial companions due to alterations in work environment and the group surrounding you. All looks good.

27—Don't be too proud to learn a little from someone younger who has had a different experience than you. Enjoy the day by remaining good natured, turn everything to humor if it threatens to be too serious. This is no time for excess in emotions. Evening may bring you a surprise visitor.

28—Be cautious all day. Accidents are many and you could be among the victims. Machinery must be handled with great care, sharp instruments and fire are better not handled by you at all. In the evening you may have a casual, attractive invitation; think twice before you accept it.

29—A fine day for travel, going to unfamiliar places, meeting new people. Your financial situation is better than it has been for some time. Don't spend too much but do allow yourself some pleasure from extra resources. Romantic happenings this evening should not be taken seriously at all.

30—A conversation can be pleasing and make you think you have found a new affinity. However, matters may not go that far; you may just be agreeable on one level and may discover mutual hostilities in other areas. Handle money carefully, don't lend anything you cherish or put value on.

31—This is the day for love. You may spend most of your time being elated due to a letter you receive. Dress up in your most becoming just to fit your happy mood. Social life isn't very attractive tonight but go along and spread the cheer of your happy spirits. Keep your secrets well hidden.

AUGUST

1—It is time to tell a younger person to show independence and not rely so much on you. This can be difficult for you have a very protective attitude, but in the long run it will benefit your young relative. A good day for quiet and peaceful occupations, a walk, some reflections on career.

2—News from afar can be exciting and yet you feel a little apprehensive about it. When things go too smoothly you are inclined to be suspicious and this time you may be right. What looks like a good development in the family can turn into a very bad one eventually. Don't speak about this.

3—Someone who comes to you for advice might not be able to take cold facts very well. Be tactful, therefore, and express your opinion in a way that leaves interpretation up to the other person. It would not be doing a service to another to be too dogmatic in your opinion or self-expression.

4—You may be faced with the necessity of taking a trip that is repugnant to you. This can mean staying for awhile at a place that is hostile and has no attraction for you. Much of this is a highly personal matter and therefore it is up to you to control your personality and thinking for your own good.

5—Financial matters go very well and you'll feel more affluent before the day is over. Someone who values your talents will see to it that you get a fair chance to use them and profit from them. You can be elated and this might cause extravagance, so watch out for harmful, foolish trends.

6—Becoming angry about a friend's speech will do no good. You are urged to hold on to your friends and value them. Your emotions may be in a tangle today and it's up to you to straighten them out as much as possible. Selfishness is dangerous and it is not worthy of you in connection with a friend.

7—Be charitable, mindful of human frailty today. Do not expect miracles from anyone. Be kind and helpful to a young member of the family and don't take the stern parent attitude if you have children of your own. A good evening for social life on quite a formal scale, so enjoy it.

8—Rest as much as you can, don't let demands of others rush you or anger you. Reading will be beneficial today and you may add a major new thought to your spiritual or philosophical views now. Be willing to talk a little this evening with a lonesome person who asks your company briefly.

9—A hazardous day for you when almost anything can trigger your emotions and cause an outburst of irreparable nature. Someone very loyal may not be able to do anything for you if you break up your life now. Strive for serenity, silence, diligence and refuse to yield to impetuous emotional urges.

10—Family news can be disturbing in fact excessively so. However, there is no use taking the blame yourself about any of this, for that will not help. Avoid making plans for the evening and avoid anything harmful to your health. A good idea to watch TV and then retire quite early.

11—You may be on the verge of a major change in your life. There could be some dispute about this with a lifemate or other loved one. You are urged to consider other people's attitudes and not to do anything to inconvenience them radically. A cycle in which to be unselfish and very reasonable.

12—Your thoughts can be taken up by a romantic trend you have begun to notice. It could be a mistake to let yourself get into this any further. You may be dealing with a tricky, deceptive and entirely unpredictable person. You could lose out in the game of love and find it merely a game.

13—An associate may be in error but you must resist the inclination to contradict or point out facts. Keep relationships harmonious for any other trend can bring fireworks you wouldn't like at all. Social life should be taken quietly. If trouble is stirred up by anyone, do not take sides.

14—The mail can bring financial good fortune. You can be inclined to spend the rest of the day in celebration, forget about chores and not even go shopping for family provisions. Better get the practical done and out of the way and then go in for the gala time your spirit will enjoy this evening.

15—A good family day but don't let a relative take over your life if you see any trend in this direction. If you have children let it be known you will make decisions about them. If you drive today be very cautious. There is a reckless atmosphere in general on the road, so allow for it; be defensive.

16—Keep busy today, attend to your own affairs and don't give advice even if asked. Try to take a humorous attitude even when it's difficult. You might come under fire from a grouchy executive and answering angrily might be quite natural. This must be checked and curbed, however.

17—Something that happens may be beyond your control even though it involves and concerns you deeply. Undoubtedly you will suffer some emotional trouble. This will vanish rather quickly and by the end of the day you may have arrived at the point of calm, cool mental observation to your advantage.

18—Think the best of people today, let your view be optimistic. You can spread some sunshine and win new affections yourself. Fall in with the plan of an old friend about this evening's pleasure. it is a good time to join a new group, get busy with some service for your community.

19—Shopping is happy, but count your change. Do not carry your check book, just set a limited amount of cash for yourself to spend and try not to go over it. Gift buying goes well now. If a friend visits this evening you may be weary and it would be wise to be frank about needing to retire.

20—Rumor that comes to you may have a grain of truth in it, but don't be too gullible. Also, it's best not to spread this news. If you are entertaining in your home, avoid too much hard work for it. If you have a romantic date you can be overjoyed and may find this is the night you fall in love.

21—In family affairs, suppress your true feelings. Be tactful with an in-law, silently endure things that make you nervous and tense. This is a day when people in general may be hiding their true feelings. In a way this is good for it will prevent painful quarrels and unpleasant unheavals.

22—A good day in every way. Work goes well, you are inspired and efficient, much admiration may be won. Pleasure in shopping will be enjoyed and a happy little evening gathering can be just right when it is done casually. Romance may hold a surprise, perhaps in an unexpected telephone call.

23—You may find exactly what you need and want today. It will take a little search, some questioning. When this is done you can find yourself in ideal conditions and freedom which you have not enjoyed in the past. Don't let panic about finances cause you inner misery. Keep cheerful about money.

24—Try to visit a friend, a concert or go to church, talk to others afterwards, accept a dinner invitation. Take what life offers today and you'll find it pleasant. Your faith is strong and minor worries won't get to you now. Be a little cautious if you drive after dark; there are some accidental trends at work then.

25—Your career is going well and praise may come your way. Difficulties you have been having will not be overlooked by an executive and you may get a high compliment for the way in which you have handled troubles. Be thrifty, don't indulge in any selfish desire to buy a whimsical item now.

26—This can be a day of wonderful serenity, just the type that induces emotional health for you. A younger person may show admiration and you may find yourself embarked on a new trip with a whole new circle of friends. Just the right touch of affection and admiration will be shown.

27—A neighbor can become interested in you, perhaps try to be influential in your life. Put a stop to that at once but be affectionate also. You'll be esteemed when you are firm about your mental attitude and independence. You may have to turn down a request of a young relative tonight.

28—You may devote the day to shopping, taking care of correspondence, writing and mailing checks and enjoying romantic trends in the evening. These are full hours and very gratifying ones when you get chores taken care of and then are happy in romance. You'll feel it's a day well lived and memorable.

29—Be prudent. Think things over. If you feel you need an expert of any type, money will be well spent on such service. If you must ask for a loan do it promptly. Chances are that things will go your way. A fine evening to get plans completed and start a new course of life and thought.

30—A work associate can show malice and make a heavy-handed attempt to put you down, make you feel inferior. It is best to ignore all this. You'll be moving on soon and needn't worry over this person's harmful influence. Do your work well for that is what counts most in the right places today.

31—Health is just a bit under par; don't imagine major ailments for they are not likely. Keep a slow pace, avoid emotional reactions, don't brood on any circumstance of your life. Others have difficulties to bear; you're just one of them and should be strong enough to endure things silently.

SEPTEMBER

1—A day when new talents can be used and personality will brighten. Your aggressiveness will allow you to go after profits and a position which you want. The hours will bring real rewards for influences and are favorable all the way. Spend time with the family this evening.

2—A day of good will, kindliness, generosity. You will be expansive in spirit and have affection for those around you. A warm glow of relationship with others will make this a notably happy day. Entertain in your home this evening, for you will create a lovely atmosphere.

3—A quiet day of serene emotions. Cancer can feel the ebb and flow of well-being which is good fortune in itself. You will be able to reason and come to wise conclusions. This may mean the beginning of a change in your career for you will see things clearly.

4—There may be confused atmosphere, many disturbed plans, but soon you will recognize that you have high spirits to match the hectic atmosphere of the day. You will find pleasure in the activity which comes on the spur of the moment. A brilliant invitation for tonight.

5—Gloom and a sense of defeat may overwhelm you. You can spend the entire day brooding over mistreatment which you conjure up from this depression. Try to get your bearings and be realistic. No one is trying to oppose you or injure your feelings. Treat the family affectionately.

6—The aspects bring you a day of action, but you can expect a minor misfortune or two. Be careful handling sharp instruments. Avoid over-zealous groups this evening. Choose your companions among those whose affection is sincere and will make you happy.

7—A busy day with opportunity all around. It may be difficult to grasp all that is offered, for you can't be everywhere at once. Make wise selections, swift decisions. Influences are in favor of those who know their own minds and speak quickly and to the point.

8—Financial gain may be considerable. Unexpected sources of income or gifts will appear on many horizons. Litigation is favored, and where money was due, you will be able to collect. Your manner will be at its most gracious best, and your speech will be persuasive throughout.

9—A day when romantic or domestic matters may consume most of your attention. Don't be surprised if you make the decision to propose or accept an offer of marriage. Married life will take on new happiness and children will bring pride. Celebrate with loved ones tonight.

10—Your reputation for industrious work will soar. Accomplishments will be rewarded and your position may take on new authority. Do not shy away from such responsibility. You will be quite adequate, and a future increase in salary is indicated by events.

11—Avoid disputes with neighbors. You may feel your rights infringed upon, but talk will only make matters worse. Show by example how to be a good neighbor. Friends may intrude in the evening when you hoped for quiet with the family. Be patient but not too cordial.

12—Make plans for a special outing today. Hours will be jovial and pleasant with the family and friends. Be leisurely, though, for influences call for good cheer at a slow pace. The relaxation will be what you need for health and mental outlook. A comfortable evening.

13—Best to be very careful as far as social life is concerned. Frivolous persons who mean you no good may try to interrupt your schedule. If they succeed, it can mean a long and serious trouble for you. Be very firm, deny your self-pleasure, and stay at home tonight.

14—A good day for giving a dinner party or for accepting an invitation. Joy will reign supreme and conversation may be beneficial in your career. Watch for ideas and opportunities to get future plans working. Keep reasonable hours and be happy.

15—You may have emotional disturbances today. Members of the family may seem to try to compel you against your will in a direction you feel is unwise. Your obstinacy may win, but at a great price to you. Best to try to stay to yourself as much as possible today.

16—Use initiative and boldness. Make yourself get out and enter the competition. You will find good fortune for the courageous. A message late in the day can cause a change of plans which is very favorable and will bring additional pleasure. Evening promises romance.

17—You will be in a luxurious mood of sociability and probably pleasure-seeking festivity. Keep this within control and the day will bring happy results, particularly in a romantic direction. Evening will be softly gay and perhaps mark the beginning of courtship.

18—A favorable period for personal and domestic matters. The aspects bring emotional happiness where marriage is concerned. Family plans will thrive and harmony will be found where discord threatened formerly. Be sure to entertain this evening. Neighbors bring cheer.

19—A good day to start a journey, specially with a companion. A wedding trip might well commence now. Associations are favored. Business contracts may be signed, partnerships discussed. You may find excellent financial backing, if you talk to a new acquaintance today.

20—An ambitious streak marks the morning. You will be unusually willing to talk to people with frank expression of your opinions and desires. A conference with one in a high place may put you on a new path. The evening holds exciting messages for Cancer.

21—Spendthrift ideas and high spirits—but these are the very traits to guard against now. Quick action and hilarity may bring swift reactions of a very unpleasant type. Try to control yourself step by step through a hazardous day with danger lurking where least expected.

22—Dreams and hopes may possess your mind. Romantic life is stressed and there may be happy moments, unusual messages. It isn't likely that anything definite will mature today, but this can be the foundation of what leads to engagement and marriage. Dress attractively.

23—A slow day which may be vexing with problems which seem to have no solution. Associates will be on edge and you may offend unintentionally. Best to eat lunch alone, avoid making telephone calls. In the evening guard against accidents from speed and carelessness.

24—You will get a lot done along lines which you have planned. There may not be much time for thought or relaxation, but you will be happy and have good news for the family. A change is indicated from today's opportunities. A good time to arrive at an important decision.

25—Watch out for deceitful, tricky conversation today. Someone may try to make you the victim of probing which has a harmful motive. Best to avoid intimacies even with old friends. Keep to yourself when possible. Do not give neighbors cause for complaint. Retire early.

26—Steady progress, interesting discussions, good opportunities to buy or sell. Investigate what you hear about major investments. This is a day which can bring profits from large sums of money. Be wise, but not afraid to increase your income in this way. A family evening.

27—A fortunate day for those who are in love. From early morning, happy surprises will pile up. Engagement may be in the air, and, if so, marriage will follow soon and bring permanent happiness. Your personality is at its best. Friends and family will all be in happy accord.

28—Spendthrift ideas and rather selfish whims for luxuries must be avoided if you want to get through the day wisely. Avoid even looking at that which is beyond your budget. Listen to the family, leave your checkbook and large bills at home. Sign no business transactions.

29—Some contact with unfamiliar realms of life, either by means of travel or through studies, is a potent factor in making you reach new levels of consciousness and a new sense of fulfillment. Financial and business matters, however, might pose problems.

30—End the month with a cautious eye to your health. Eat sparingly, and don't expose yourself to any risks. Best not to travel with eccentric people or allow them to influence your plans in any way. Be firm about spending the evening at home even if tempted by an invitation.

OCTOBER

1—You may imagine yourself the victim of discrimination today. Don't feel offended since a subsequent explanation might prove that you are mistaken. Take in a movie tonight, or stay at home and watch TV. Let the day pass without any dramatic fuss.

2—You may have some difficulty in determining your line of action because there are mixed planetary aspects in force. It is safer to follow normal courses than take chances with the strange and uncertain things. Pay no attention to flattery. It may cost you cash as well as heartache.

3—You may get a glimpse of the dream you have been striving to make true, or your social contacts may bring you an introduction to a person whose friendly interest will be invaluable. If you pause before jumping a hurdle you may not make a successful jump.

4—Abdicate a minor right rather than work excessively hard to win an unimportant advantage. A sense of proportion and humor should enable you to rise above petty abstractions. If you plan to travel by car today, see to it that everything has been checked for mechanical defects.

5—An old friend may bring you an unusual opportunity. Do not allow inattention to cause you to pass up a chance for future gain. But conversely neither should you rush things. Undue aggressiveness could destroy the enthusiasm of someone who really wishes to help you with future plans.

6—Avoid impulsive action. Reduce everything to a practical basis, and guard against personal entanglements. Balance your budget and pay off all the debts you can. You will feel better and at the same time preserve your credit. The influences call for ethical integrity.

7—Your inventive ability should be given scope. Work quietly to create and originate. Revamp old things and old methods. Concentrate on that which is practical. A friend or member of your family may have a usable idea for you. A time for personal achievement.

8—You have every reason to be hopeful where your desires and ambitions are concerned. But do more than wait—work to achieve your goals. This is a vital planetary period, for use of ingenuity and courage toward definite objectives. Take time off for love and admiration of beauty.

9—Show that you are willing to make a correction if you have made a mistake. Though being called to account for an error may disturb you, you may receive valuable pointers on how to improve your technique. Follow the path of least resistance, and you will come out on top.

10—This is a favorable time to write, travel, execute contracts and buy clothes. Make every effort to accomplish all that you plan for. Do not find fault with persons lacking enthusiasm or animation. Be sure your own humor is kept at high peak when criticism is aimed at you.

11—Make changes or revisions in connection with home and property matters. Devote some time to salvaging or making an inventory of your possessions. Psychic studies, occult lectures, and creative matters are excellent outlets today. Toward evening, someone may tell you about a broken engagement.

12—Do not spread your attentions over diverse interests. There will be a lot of confusion if you do. Even a little carelessness or forgetfulness could cause unnecessary expense, delay, or an accident. Haste will be accompanied by waste now.

13—Invitations and telephone calls may give evidence that you are a popular person. Consciousness of this fact may stimulate your interest in others. You cannot be self-centered and expect your friends and acquaintances to continue their kind attentions. Add to the pleasure of others.

14—You have first call on inspiration. Start your ideas working at once. The splendid influences enable you to express yourself with clarity and fluency. This may be the day when a bolt from the blue takes you out of the red. So start early, and work late.

15—You are gifted inherently with sufficient foresight to see that things you reach for are gained through persistence rather than wishing. But do not hurry the march of events. Allow time to bring its benefits in an orderly schedule. You may be in for a surprise.

16—This is no time for doubting your abilities. You have hidden potentialities. They can come to the surface through proper direction. Dig persistently through the covering layer and uncover "pay dirt." The aspects favor traveling, writing, working, planning and winning.

17—Welcome new ideas and suggestions. Keep your mind flexible. For instance, you can learn about electronics, inventions, travel, literature, play acting, preaching, photography, history, and many subjects that could prove useful later, by asking questions and listening to the answers.

18—Perhaps the temperature of your hopes and aspirations has dropped to zero, but being disagreeable will only react to your detriment. Use psychology and wait patiently for the clouds to disperse. The aspects are thwarting signals for getting what you want.

19—Seek variety without sacrificing your main interests. There are adequate experiences and subsidiary interests within your chosen sphere to provide the means to freshen your outlook. You can be a great discoverer in a close area.

20—Adhere to facts. Do not waste time theorizing. Take a long time to make up your mind, because if you jump to conclusions, you may find you will have to unscramble the whole job and do it all over again. The influences call for tact, patience, understanding and cooperation.

21—Neither make nor rely on promises, because the aspects indicate that they may not be kept. Also, be conservative in romance and money matters. Do not be lured to attempt things with which you are unfamiliar. See to it that your valuables are locked away carefully.

22—If you have something important to do, do it with dispatch; don't fool around or the opportunity will pass. See those in authority, deal with the public, make decisions. However, if you are restless and have nothing planned, you could end up with aggravation at the end of the day.

23—Refuse to fall victim to talk aimed to lull you. Be shrewd in estimating everyone and everything so that no one can hand you something phony wrapped in a bundle of compliments. Your emotional and intellectual perceptions need to be well-balanced if you meet strange conditions and jittery people.

24—Being too friendly with some people may prove expensive, due to the influences being in opposition. Wastefulness and extravagance would follow in the wake of too many social pleasures, if you accept invitations or suggestions from a frivolous person.

25—Don't be caught off guard. Someone may endeavor to be inquisitive. Close the door against intrusion into your private concerns by controlling the direction which the conversation takes. Do not attempt to settle the problems of an older person, and do not buy expensive heavy-duty equipment.

26—Be polite if you wish to receive courtesy in return. Should you speak sharply, others will do the same. Do not permit friendly relations to become antagonistic just because of carelessness. With the mixed planetary influences, there is imperative need for docility, respect and patience.

27—Do not become careless while the aspects are opposed. If you give a party, arrange all the details with care. If you are lax in the preparation, the praise will be just as sparse itself. Be careful that you do not lose your keys, and avoid a strange pet.

28—Think of safety when rushing to keep an appointment. Better a few minutes late than laid up for repairs. Finances should go well today provided you keep sound in health and limb. Music, drama, literature and the other arts should yield joy and satisfaction during the evening.

29—It is hard to correct an error now. Do your work thoroughly so as to minimize the possibility of having to do it again. This may seem a slow process, but in reality it will save time. Do what you can to clean the slate as you get ready for next month's vibrations.

30—You must be careful that everything is done with the utmost accuracy or you may be caught in a network of fraud as a result of planetary opposition. Don't accept anybody's word for anything today. Insist on receipts and written instructions. When you give orders, do so in signed memorandums.

31—The gate to progress that resists pressure may swing open easily if you oil its hinges with tact. Luck may operate in your favor under the present friendly influences. Perhaps a small amount of speculation will prove profitable. Do not risk money needed for essentials.

NOVEMBER

1—Complete what is expected of you before gratifying your desires for pleasure. An impatient attitude may become a barrier to the successful completion of your aims. Refrain from being arbitrary or attempting to tell other people what to do.

2—Do not intensify a difficult situation that never should have arisen in the first place. Keep alert and be prepared to make changes so that you will not lose pace with new developments. Work on projects which will enable you to utilize your capabilities in the most effective manner that you know.

3—Be sure that you are correctly informed before voicing your opinion about a controversial issue. Take obstacles in your stride, rather than allow yourself to become upset. Plan a definite program for your daily activities and stick to it as closely as possible.

4—What you do now can be the groundwork for important gains in the very near future. Adapt yourself to changing situations without delay and without fuss. Ignore pessimistic thoughts and give full attention to available opportunities.

5—Focus your mind on things that will give you a feeling of serenity rather than make you anxious. Despite time-consuming duties keep friendship intact through phone calls, short visits or letters. Spend money only on things for which you have a definite use and practical purpose.

6—Avoid being aggressive since you may give the impression that you are domineering. Give particular attention to the details of your work regardless of how trivial you may consider them. Avoid making promises or committing yourself to long-term obligations.

7—Set a rapid pace for your work so that whatever has been pending may be completed in short order. Do not allow a feeling of restlessness or boredom to cause you to lapse into a period of inactivity. Take definite steps toward achieving a highly desired job or business goal.

8—Avoid any situation where emotional conflict is likely to arise during the current adverse influences. The consideration you show a loved one would be deeply appreciated. Defer making important decisions concerning business, money or property.

9—A few well-planned changes should help you overcome difficulties and make things work out to your advantage. Do not let petty arguments or minor differences of opinion upset you. Constructive changes in your work should help you save time and money.

10—Your ambitions can be furthered now but it will require hard work, as well as planning. Showing a determined attitude would be all that is needed to win over the opinions of others. Good results should be obtainable through original and imaginative thinking.

11—Make a definite effort to catch up with all your neglected tasks, instead of just worrying about them. Get busy on new undertakings you have been waiting to start. Keep personal feelings separated from practical considerations where your work is concerned.

12—Arrange to take care of needed repairs about your home, instead of allowing things to go neglected. Undertake only those projects which you can complete rapidly with a minimum of confusion. Avoid placing yourself in a position where you might become the target of another's criticism.

13—Go after the things you want and you should find that the barriers you have to overcome are not as serious as anticipated. Do not let friendship interfere with making a necessary decision about money. Make effective use of the assistance that others offer to you.

14—Satisfaction is possible only if you depend on the results you get and not on the ones you anticipate. Avoid unnecessary trouble by steering clear of worries which are the concern of others. Use care when making changes and do not take things for granted.

15—You should be able to overcome tense situations with a patient and diplomatic approach. Show a willingness to listen to the opinions of others, even though you may not agree with what is being said. Do not give in to feelings of pessimism, merely because you fail to achieve a particular goal.

16—The application of diligent efforts should enable you to realize your ultimate aims. Aim to keep things running smoothly and guard against trouble that impatience can cause. Stick to prudent procedures and refuse to take chances where money is concerned.

17—Let experience and reason, rather than impulse, dictate your course of action. Take ample time to think and plan what you are going to do, rather than rush around aimlessly. Be conciliatory in your approach if you meet with sturbborn opposition to your ideas.

18—This can be an active and productive day providing you put your resourcefulness to good use. Avoid taking on extra responsibilities or making plans which might be hard to follow through. Although you may feel some concern about financial problems, do not let it completely disrupt your schedule.

19—Face reality and do not lull yourself into complacency by ignoring difficult problems which present themselves now. Calm presentation of facts during a lively discussion should prevent friction. This is a favorable period in which to put your skills to better use.

20—Guard against letting enthusiasm cause you to become extravagant at this time. Although haste may save you time now, it may prove more expensive in the long run. Better delay than guess about something of which you are unsure. Spend the evening with the family and relatives.

21—Regardless of how much you disagree with another, avoid showing your dissatisfaction. Occupy yourself with pastimes which you find physically and mentally stimulating. Kind and reassuring words on your part can do much to promote congeniality.

22—Attend to your own responsibilities, but do not completely ignore those around you. Keep yourself busily occupied and do not complain about monotonous tasks you have to do. The results of determined efforts may pay off in handsome dividends for you.

23—Take a firm stand in dealings with others, particularly in matters which involve money. Correct mistakes and rectify wrong impressions which you have created. Arrange your work schedule so that you can compensate for the numerous distractions which you are likely to encounter.

24—Waste little time worrying about trifles since you may be throwing away good opportunities. Start things on your own initiative but be sure that what you do is constructive. Take care of personal obligations and duties before giving thought to diversion.

25—Avoid putting yourself in the position where you can be provoked by the actions of another. Regardless of what you start see that it does not result in wasted action. Care should be taken to protect advantages and gains which are already yours.

26—Use a straightforward approach, rather than concealed strategy, to achieve the most favorable results. Your words could be misinterpreted unless you choose your comments carefully. Aim for maximum achievements and apply yourself diligently to each task you undertake.

27—Give consideration to plans and ideas which you feel might prove useful in augmenting your income. Refrain from doing anything which might invite antagonism from associates. Although you may feel energetic, do not undertake more than you can comfortably handle.

28—Use your time profitably by working on a hobby which you find enjoyable. Guard against impulsive decisions which could deplete your cash reserves. Your awareness of new and favorable situations should help you to achieve unexpected advantages.

29—You should be able to overcome aggravating circumstances with a calm, levelheaded approach during the current adverse aspects. Avoid unnecessary loss or damage by keeping valuable articles in a safe place. Reflect carefully on what you are doing to avoid mistakes.

30—Prevent confusion by letting others know your thoughts and the action you plan to take. Avoid taking things for granted, regardless of how well your projects seem to be working out. Do not shirk an irksome duty, even though it may be distasteful to you.

DECEMBER

1—Good day for headway in your job if you work fast. Take the initiative rather than wait for others to be of assistance. Although the progress you make may not be spectacular, you can pave the way for substantial gains later.

2—Insist that any business agreements of an important nature be put in writing. Place emphasis on a careful analysis of the facts, particularly where your resources are concerned. Plan in detail each move you make, and discuss your intentions only with those whom you trust.

3—Since what you do or say now can have quite an effect on your reputation, choose your words and actions carefully. Try to be agreeable with others, regardless of the viewpoints they express. Accept criticism in the spirit in which it is intended, and do not be sarcastic in your comments.

4—Spending money for personal needs can give you a vibrant feeling of inner satisfaction. Whatever you buy yourself should prove pleasant and satisfying. Add to your wardrobe or get something that can enhance the decorative appearance of your home.

5—Rather than give in to a feeling of restlessness, attend to incompleted tasks. Refrain from letting your mind dwell on irrelevant subjects. Much can be accomplished now, provided you do not waste time worrying or fretting about minor problems.

6—You are likely to have a strong feeling of optimism about your job and income. Regardless of how well your plans seem to be materializing, keep your thinking and actions on a realistic level. Regardless of what changes you may have to make in your work, you should have little difficulty in adapting yourself to new situations.

7—Activities around your home may cause you some concern. Despite this, try to remain in an amiable mood, and do not give others cause for argument. Treat contrariness and selfishness with a diplomatic attitude and refrain from forcing issues.

8—Intuitive impressions that you have are likely to prove incorrect. Therefore, base important decisions on a logical analysis of the facts rather than on hasty impulses. Do not take things for granted; act only on verified information.

9—Although existing conditions may not be exactly what you want, do the best you can rather than let circumstances get the best of you. Refrain from making changes in established procedures and employ prudent methods. Give full attention to the details of your work, and emphasize methodological completion of all tasks.

10—Keep clear of bickering and quarrels. If your ideas conflict with those of others, remain silent for the time being. Listen to what others have to say rather than continue a discussion that will intensify differences of opinion.

11—Traveling in connection with business and pleasure is highlighted. Even though you may have duties that are arduous and tie you down, try to get away from everyday routine. Spend savings only if absolutely essential.

12—Keep on the lookout for worthwhile hobbies or other activities that can help to keep you occupied. Also, use your leisure time effectively to catch up with your reading, letter writing, or visiting. Keep your hands and mind busy on a multitude of stimulating tasks.

13—Clear up routine assignments so that you can devote some of your leisure time to recreational activities. You should find enjoyment in whatever you attempt to do. Ignore current problems and responsibilities temporarily; keep yourself occupied with pleasant pastimes.

14—Use extreme care in making agreements which concern your home or its furnishing. Be particularly reticent about scheduling decorative changes and alterations at this time. Considerable control is also needed now to keep your spending within budgetary limits.

15—Conversation and business planning should develop into profitable results. Arrangements that you make should quickly develop into personal advantages for you. However, take on only those assignments which you can finish without encountering last-minute rushing and confusion.

16—Do not let emotions or sympathy divert you from making a decision which requires practical and logical forethought. Calmness and patience are needed to keep emotional tension to a minimum. Regardless of how others react, refrain from saying anything which can develop into a quarrel.

17—This is a splendid day in which to make headway in your work. Get an early start on whatever project you intend to do. Make every effort to place yourself well ahead of the crowd, as far as achievements are concerned.

18—Remain in the background, and observe what is going on around you. Let others talk and take action. You may find it better to limit yourself to a program of inactivity rather than become enmeshed in limitless confusion. Above all, keep your enthusiasm within practical bounds.

19—To insure a pleasant atmosphere avoid controversial discussions about money. Be jovial and friendly with family members but do not take an act of extravagance too seriously. Friendships and entertainment are especially favored.

20—Focus your thoughts on the present rather than on what you expect to accomplish in the future. Do not ignore your current duties to daydream about what you expect to do. Organize a program designed to protect and increase your income.

21—Since events may be occurring at an excessively rapid pace, be prepared to make sudden and unexpected changes. Take things calmly, and accept upheaval of your plans with good grace. You should find that what occurs now will ultimately work out to your best advantage.

22—Quick, but well-planned changes in business or property matters can prove to your advantage. Action that you take designed to enhance your job advancement should work out in accordance with your expectations. Think things out carefully, and do what you feel is correct rather than rely on the conclusions of others.

23—Refrain from taking chances with your money in a speculative enterprise. Although, from all external appearances, a promising deal looks financially safe, it would be desirable to adhere to conservative and economical principles. Beware of taking the chance of a monetary loss.

24—You may find unexpected advantages in utilizing valid suggestions and hints you receive from others. However, you will probably find that the difference between success and failure in the achievement of your aims will depend on the self-confidence and determination you display. Be guided by others, but act for yourself.

25—An agreeable turn of events can result in a delightful family reunion and indeed a "Merry Christmas." Intellectual accomplishment and creative expression are favored.

26—Engage in activities that will enable you to demonstrate your qualities as a host. Show thoughtfulness and be appreciative of what others have done for you. This can be an ideal day for returning favors and repaying social obligations.

27—Things should work out according to your plans regardless of apprehensive feelings. Adjust yourself to current trends and thinking so that you can make the most of existing opportunities. You can do much in the way of securing a job or business advantage by getting others to conform to your ideas.

28—Do not be so stubborn in your attitude that you ignore wishes of others. Listen to any suggestion that is made to you. Avoid antagonizing any adversary, even though you may feel that there can be no compromise of opinion.

29—If you have a burning major ambition, this is the time to try to make it a reality. What you desire can be yours, provided you are willing to work long and hard to obtain it. Waste little time on insignificant details and settle only for first-class results.

30—With patience and understanding, you should be able to transform a scene of emotional tension into one of mutual accord. Emphasize subjects that are cheerful so that you can put people around you in a pleasant, optimistic mood. Enjoy your surroundings, but refrain from doing so or saying anything that would invite trouble.

31—Your enthusiasm and vitality will allow you to enter the swift pace of events. Make positive decisions. Then enjoy the merry-making cycle of the evening. Next year has good things in store for you!

Gemini
May 21-June 20th

Your dual nature,
symbolized by the Twins in the zodiac,
finds happiness
in using swift wit
to solve problems ingeniously.
Your skills also being happiness
in artful endeavors,
You enjoy using eloquence to charm,
perhaps to win fame in your career,
A busy life keeps you happy
and the more variety
the greater is your elation.
Idleness or loneliness
depresses you.
You are happy on a journey,
entering a new group,
trying some new use
for your talents.
A new romance
exhilarates and pleases.
Be wary of
too much change,
scattered use of talents,
for these can lead to futility,
lack of joy.

Gemini

JANUARY

1—Refrain from taking action on decisions made under the pressure of emotions. Keep clear of trouble, since it can come near you without much effort on your part. Before making an important decision, be sure you know all the facts.

2—Let others handle their own problems, regardless of your own interests. Avoid making large-scale changes in your present setup but improve on whatever exists. Confide only in those people whom you know to be trustworthy.

3—You may incur needless expense by not adhering to prudent procedures. Give helpful suggestions and encouragement rather than risk dissension by criticizing another. Find constructive things to do around your home instead of wasting time in idle recreation.

4—Planning things well in advance, you can create spare time for many of the projects you have been wanting to do. Clear up pending obligations before giving your attention to other things.

5—Avoid future trouble by insisting that important agreements or promises be put in writing. Displaying a cooperative attitude can prove more of a help than you expect. Attempt a new approach if methods and procedures you are now using appear unsatisfactory.

6—Rather than worry about mistakes that have been made, make the best of existing situations. Do not ignore duties or obligations for the purpose of taking part in recreational activities. Refuse to tackle an assignment unless you are sure you possess the ability to complete it satisfactorily.

7—For a stimulating change in pace, take an active interest outside your usual sphere of activities. Keep yourself occupied with tasks that you find interesting as well as remunerative.

8—Avoid acting on intuitional impressions, particularly where job or money matters are concerned. Express your thoughts to others but avoid using pressure to get your own way. Wise planning and prudent action can prove effective in helping you to achieve a desired goal.

9—Harness your resourcefulness and determination to clear up pending obligations. Give attention to necessary home repairs and make sure that all equipment is in serviceable condition.

10—Heeding the advice of an experienced person may prove more to your advantage than relying on your own judgment. Work at a slow and conservative pace, not wasting time on matters of minor consequence.

11—Personal sacrifices you make now may create the way for unlimited opportunities at a later period. A cheerful disposition can make it easier for you to achieve goals you have set for yourself. Take care of all personal obligations and duties before seeking diversion.

12—Discuss openly plans and ideas you feel can prove useful in augmenting your income. Cope with one problem at a time rather than try to get everything done at once. Think things out for yourself instead of depending on guidance from another.

13—Plans to improve the attractiveness of your home can be especially gratifying. Acting on impulse may prove to be an expensive move in a special matter. Do not let minor upsets throw you into an unhappy frame of mind.

14—Refuse to become disturbed about conditions that are not of your immediate concern. Diplomacy may be more effective than forcefulness in your dealings with others. Avoid risking a clash of temperaments with someone who is in a position to discipline you.

15—Work on a project that you feel can give you pleasure as well as a sense of accomplishment. Refrain from saying or writing anything that, if repeated, might be unintentionally misinterpreted.

16—You can make this an enjoyable day by promoting friendliness and understanding wherever you may be. Waste little effort on impractical activities and concentrate on doing something that can promote lasting results. You may find it a pleasurable experience to take an interest outside your usual sphere of activities.

17—Utilize available opportunities rather than waste time and effort looking for new ones. Do not let sympathetic inclinations interfere with decisions that require impersonal logic. Your resourcefulness can have a stimulating effect on your work production.

18—Remain patient, even though you may be burdened with work that requires tedious effort. Do not let indecision cause you to miss out on opportunities that are available.

19—Seek wise counsel before investing your cash or adopting a new financial policy. Let others do the talking and acting, regardless of how strong your viewpoints may be. Pay attention to the minor details of your work, since you may find they can cause the most difficulty.

20—Insure a trouble-free day by steering clear of arguments that are not of your immediate concern. Concentrate on your own personal problems rather than worry about the needs of others. Give irksome duties your primary attention in order to clear them up and get them out of the way.

21—Take it on your own to spread cheerfulness and harmony among those around you. Do not let business matters keep you from enjoying the pleasures that are offered to you. Refuse to become upset or confused by the occurrence of rapid changes.

22—Give top priority to your own needs before catering to the wants of someone else. Gratifying a desire to shop for an expensive article may turn out to be a discouraging experience. Take minor setbacks in your stride and refrain from making unnecessary comments.

23—Offset gloom and pessimism in others with humorous remarks and witty conversation. A carefully-planned variation from your normal routine may result in a stimulating release from monotony.

24—Fulfill your own desire for happiness by doing and buying the things you like. Refrain from saying anything that might arise as a point of disagreement. Do not take on additional responsibilities that might act as a drain on your own financial resources.

25—Be particularly attentive about handling money or working with numbers, to avoid serious difficulty. Do not request a favor unless you are in a position to return it immediately.

26—Use to advantage constructive criticism you receive rather than resent or ignore it. Adhere closely to established methods and do not experiment or take chances. You might be inviting trouble if you try to speed things up past their normal limitations.

27—Certain unpleasant elements at work will have to be ignored. If anyone tries to stir up your dissatisfaction, ignore their remarks, but smile pleasantly. Work diligently and have an eye to the coming evening when you can enjoy those who are waiting for you at home.

28—Do what you can to keep the atmosphere pleasant and congenial through well-planned humor. Keep dissension to a minimum by refusing to discuss money, business or property matters. Clear and logical thinking are essential if you expect to minimize confusing circumstances.

29—Consider the ultimate consequences before making a promise with regard to your services or cash. Do not let minor hindrances deter you from fulfilling your responsibilities. Patience rather than aggressiveness can net you better results.

30—Go at a slow and easy pace, even though your thoughts may be racing at top speed. Keep clear of bickering and petty quarrels, regardless of how annoyed you may feel about the actions of another. Rather than take things too seriously, be jovial and friendly in your attitude.

31—Go slow when considering the purchase of a large item for your home. By shopping carefully, you may discover a bargain. Keep your social life moving at a fast tempo, but at the same time watch expenses very carefully.

FEBRUARY

1—Someone very cautious may hide the impression gained at first meeting you. You can be certain that this person has many reservations about you. Don't lead the talk into personal channels; that would not work out well for you.

2—A disappointment may darken your day and cause you to waste time brooding. While your habits are good and you have high principles, you can make a mistake by insisting on these things for others. Exercise more tolerance now.

3—A message from a loved one who is far away can make the day pleasant. You may yearn to be near this person, but that is quite impossible now and for some time to come. Settle down to contentment with work and family.

4—Be firm with yourself about following a decision. Guard your money carefully and lend none of your valuable possessions. It is not a good idea to invite a guest you know, but who does not like you, for a party in the evening; be wary.

5—You may have to take on a family burden, but do not object. Your home will be adequate for another person, if that is necessary. Be cautious this evening and avoid any excess in your life tonight.

6—This may be a lazy day for you, and lounging at home can seem quite heavenly. You need this rest and freedom from responsibilities, so enjoy it fully. A pet can be the best companion; take heed for safety throughout this cycle.

7—An unscrupulous person may be active in your vicinity. A telephone call you make can reveal amazing news. The day is a bit chaotic, with everything seeming to contribute to that condition; you'll need to be highly alert.

8—Necessary repairs must be made. Do not begrudge the money for work that has been done well. A misunderstanding in communications can occur this afternoon. Try to remedy this before it can do harm. You'll need a quiet evening, possibly with a good book.

9—Get in touch with someone who can do you a favor and let them know what you want. It is your day to use as a prelude to major success. Friends are loyal and you have much to be thankful for, so do not be critical tonight.

10—Keep your fingers crossed about a financial risk; it may come through with big winnings. Avoid any snub to someone you knew a long time ago who now appears briefly in your life. Be tolerant, democratic and understanding.

11—You can be tired today for no apparent reason. You may need to check with your physician and may discover a new fact about your entire system. Seeing a good show, after dinner in a restaurant, can be really pleasing.

12—Don't let the day become too active. You could use up energies you can't spare tonight. A telephone call can be romantic and that's just about all you need tonight.

13—A brief trip out of town can do a lot for you—stimulate your interest and give you new experiences. Have a companion who is cheerful and likes to investigate the new. You may become interested in worth-while real estate.

14—You can be in an unusually whimsical mood and not inclined to work. You may be drawn to buy some frivolous items. Enjoy this trend, even if it is not profitable. You might find yourself deeply involved in romance.

15—Avoid too much haste; you could have a humiliating fall. This is a day that can bring accident, theft, loss and disappointment. Nothing works out well today, and you may give up in anger and great chagrin.

16—Do not judge another or even start coming to conclusions about them. This person may be a very good actor who has cooked-up some sheer nonsense just because you are so critical.

17—Be ready for a big change. It will come to you in such a way that you cannot prevent or moderate it. Your finances have command today and you must follow where they lead. Don't despair; things are good.

18—Be kind to someone new in your vicinity. Help to instruct, but do not give any orders. Have your grooming taken care of in the evening. This promises to be a big-time social evening and you can shine in a new hair style tonight.

19—Someone may startle you with their amazing insight. Trust what you hear; it is not fraudulent. The day can be full of surprises and the evening may bring a romantic one that you would prefer to avoid. It will be difficult to do that.

20—Be very protective of loved ones today. There are dangers that are difficult to discern. If you travel you must be certain your car is in good shape mechanically. News over the telephone may be pleasant during the evening.

21—A fine time for a business of your own, expansion, a new partnership or just becoming chairman of an important concern. All financial well-being is taken care of admirably under these aspects. Give a gift to a child tonight.

22—Do not rush with work. A steady pace will be best. Your imagination may be vivid late in the day and might have a tinge of the neurotic to it. Don't build up the idea that someone new dislikes you.

23—Work you do today will probably not be appreciated as it should be. However, your conscience drives you and you want to do your best. Keep your speech highly discreet during an evening walk.

24—An undependable person may also be deceptive. Do not waste time clearing your life of such a companion. Let no weakness in your own nature prevail. You could become emotionally upset or unhealthy due to this person.

25—An excellent day to follow impulses, shop, start a new diet, or give a new romance a chance to thrive. You may be surprised at a new pleasure this evening because it is so unexpected.

26—Keep your mind on the present; don't look back with nostalgia on vanished days. You can become ill with longing for the past and also be a wet blanket for several people who are looking for a happy social evening now.

27—Keep to yourself to a large extent. Telephone conversations should not be lengthy. You can become weary if a visitor talks a lot. Protect yourself today even though it calls for a little blunt speech and firm action.

28—A gift may arrive to surprise you very much. Someone at a distance is thinking of you with love. You can be proud of a young relative who has won a new position. This will be a happy day that ends too quickly.

29 (Leap Year Only)—A jovial spirit will have you fully in its grip. If you don't get an invitation that is exciting enough you should probably plan some festivity on the spur of the moment. Any such idea will succeed remarkably.

MARCH

1—In spite of your best intentions, you may find you get little done. Too late a start, too little inertia and not enough genuine desire to work make the day fairly unsuccessful. Tomorrow's aspects will allow you to do a lot better.

2—You may excel today, win a prize, have your name and picture in the paper as a result. It's a good day for activity, creative work, sports and romance. You enjoy the full quality of this cycle and in gifts to you.

3—Get into contact with someone at a distance who can put your mind at ease about an important matter. Keep the evening for a romantic companion. Make yourself as glamorous as possible, enjoy a time of magical happiness.

4—Be out a lot, exercise adequately, keep to your diet and don't let temptation get started. Be cautious with friends who are extravagant. If you are out socially this evening, do not get drawn into certain dubious activities.

5—This is not an 'indoors' day. It's a good day to be out, take care of a yard if you have one, enjoy nature in general. A treat for little children can bring happiness, so have a little outing of some kind.

6—Your financial situation needs attention. Seeing an expert about investment may be best in the long run. Do not pile up big bills even though there are things you need. Be independent about money; don't let relatives help now.

7—Spiritual matters come under stress. Someone may criticize you for being too non-comformist in your views. This is your own business and you may well point out the fact. Don't let others trample upon you and your ideas.

8—You may have information and also intuition about how to use it. You will have to employ discretion, also, or you might get in some minor legal trouble. Be very cautious if driving in fast traffic after dark tonight.

9—You can work wonders with younger people today, for you have much understanding of them and patience with them. Work you do in connection with the community can be rewarding and give joy. Make it an unselfish cycle.

10—Do not be too friendly with a neighbor who moves near today. You could find everything you have being borrowed or simply taken over. Avoid acquisitive people, those who want to "use" others for base motives.

11—Someone may pay you a high compliment that is deserved. Pass on the happy atmosphere this brings and be ready to have a good word for every friend. Romantic matters can come to a very serious state during the evening.

12—A good day for plans about a trip you have been thinking of taking. Let your desires dictate where to go and then anticipate many pleasant activities. You may want to visit a relative far away, enjoy carefree days.

13—A young relative may let you down in hopes. Remember the young are very busy with their own plans and also difficult to pin down. Be forgiving and forget the matter. Keep your evening for reading something that benefits you.

14—A good day to shop for home decorations, new materials for drapes and slipcovers, lamps, small tables and the like. Your color sense is wonderful, your ideas about quality won't let you down. Money will be spent well.

15—Be a little on the humorous side today, make speech witty or inconsequential. It is a time to avoid the serious approach. Be an inspiration for merriment among your associates. An evening surprise may overwhelm you.

16—A change you contemplate will probably not be made. You're restless today and feel as though you need a whole new climate for your entire life. An impractical mood must not be followed. Be helpful to the young this evening.

17—You may suffer a letdown by someone who is very snobbish and unsettled in attitude. This is the signal to drop such a person, for you will now see that you rate about zero in this relationship. Give a small party for old friends.

18—Keep yourself to a strict routine so you can catch up with domestic demands. Do not let the mail or telephone disturb you so much that you drop all work. Keep the evening for family affairs, helping in-laws a bit.

19—Make promises that you mean to carry out; say nothing that is not basically true. It will be easy for others to detect any slight deception or insincerity in your manner. Not a very sociable evening, better for rest.

20—Someone of the opposite sex can prove to be a most loyal, unselfish friend. Your generosity of today will always be remembered. This is a memorable day in a deep respect and it may make you a little sad in the future.

21—Get facts very correct, keep them filed neatly in your mind. Use instructions carefully, follow the letter of the law. Caution as a pedestrian is needed. Your evening may be so surprising that you're in a dream world.

22—Do what is required but don't volunteer more. Avoid stressing a talent which might tempt someone to take advantage of your abilities without remuneration. Be prudent, self-protective and practical throughout this cycle.

23—Be very true to your commitments and don't even dream of being heedless of one of them. In any connection with children in the family, be dutiful but not possessive. Realize that your own life is different from theirs.

24—Something unusual may arrive today, possibly a present of considerable value. Avoid talking about older relatives to anyone else. Be loyal to the family and also do not trouble friends with your personal emotional worries.

25—You may have to talk your way out of something into which you recently found yourself. Bear your fair share of this matter justly. Do nothing that could be considered deceptive. A romantic evening is most likely.

26—Give help to a person who is lonely or ill or afflicted in some way. Don't expect too much of relatives or small ones in the family. Avoid intruding into a marriage involving a relative. Follow high philosophy now.

27—Be pleasant with an older person who may have said something offensive lately. Forgiveness is the keynote today and you must mean it from your heart. Plan something good for a loved one and make it a beautiful treat.

28—Take your time about a long task. If you rush you can create a terrible snarl instead of fulfilling aims. Be as accomodating as you can with the little leisure you have. Take care of a community obligation tonight.

29—You may get some surprise publicity today. If you are honored in the papers, you can draw much envy. Be wise in decisions, give up something that is merely ego. An evening visitor may intrude on plans but be gracious.

30—You may listen to a long tale of trouble. Give serious attention and thought to this, but make no judgment. Your hint of advice may not be taken, but give it anyway if you feel inspired to help in this fashion.

31—An old friend may get in touch with you just for the pleasure of it. This is not a relationship to be followed up and can cause trouble if either of you tries to do so. Find newer friends to spend happy evenings with.

APRIL

1—Don't cater to yourself in emotional whimsies and peculiar dislikes. Try to be practically one hundred per cent conservative and conventional, fit in with groups of most conforming attitudes. Your disposition needs to be firmly controlled and no one else but you can do this vast work.

2—Someone new in your environment may be very outspoken, honest and attractive. You might consider the pleasure of romance with such a person and yet be held by obstacles which are too unattractive to deal with. Evening can bring a call which fills you with sense of adventure.

3—Unfamiliar people and unusual events may occupy you and your time today. You may be asked to take charge of something you know little about. Live up to expectations of others and prove to yourself you are fully capable and adequate in an emergency. Be ready for unexpected expenses.

4—Neighbors may be fretful and you had best avoid them. If you let yourself in for criticism, you can become emotionally disturbed, you may put on a terrible scene of unrealistic complaint and attack upon others. Control yourself and the day's happenings in your life by being wise.

5—Health can give you some painful moments. You can find you will have to cut an item from your diet or halt use of a stimulant totally. If you go out socially tonight, be rather quiet. If you have a romantic date, think over just how serious you want this relationship to become finally.

6—Write a letter you have been neglecting. Make sure that what you write shows mature wisdom and kindliness. Be as diplomatic as possible. Get out and walk around but do not linger to talk to anyone long. Reading can give you a sense of well-being this evening and you'll enjoy quiet peace.

7—Your work may cause you trouble and you may feel you have gone too far in a field that you do not really like. Thoughts of further training may come back into your head and you may decide to do something about getting help for an educational course. The time is ripe to make a special request.

8—A relative will be prompt and faithfully keep a promise. You can be quite excited that your life is going to have a radical change. There may be some argument with a loved one but you'll stay with your decision in an unyielding way. Keep your mind centered on career interests and tastes.

9—You may be living in a state of happy anticipation and could let your work slip today. Best to focus on demands of the present and get them completed efficiently. You may have an interesting invitation this evening but have to turn it down due to previous plans and other requirements.

10—Accidents may happen but turn out to be only minor in results. Try to watch where you are going, be very cautious climbing anywhere, even on a very small ladder. Take good care of valued possessions, do not be ostentatious about jewelry or money in any way. Avoid all boasting.

11—Emotions may cause you trouble, lead you to speak in hostile fashion to someone who has always been kind to you. You may be hipped on a certain subject and under its spell today. If you go out tonight you may endanger your poise by letting emotions break you up and cause a distasteful scene.

12—Someone you care for very much may welcome your attentions and show deep understanding. You may spend part of the time shopping together for things to brighten life and the rest in a delightful conversational trend with a gourmet-type dinner in a restaurant to round out a perfect day.

13—A very young member of the family may ask something you do not think it wise to grant. Make sure that your affections are known but also be firm about refusing request. Get outdoors, walk or drive around a little, but do nothing of any importance. Do not face making a big decision.

14—Today may be the start of a new phase in your life. Someone kindly may bring convenience to your life with offer of help. A strange environment will please you and you will rapidly "catch on" to new things you are doing. You feel very serious about your opportunities; relax for better results.

15—Money can be quite short but you're tempted to spend. Not much thought for the future is here and you may have a youthful view that is not practical. Surprise mail can arrive and you may not know what to think of its content. You're too busy to respond and need to think things over anyhow.

16—Difficult to be happy today because of a turn in the romantic pattern. A separation may occur but it will only be temporary. Do not let such matters distract you from your goals. Resolve to learn and perform well in order to benefit from your new training. Be very mature, thoughtful and precise in all you do.

17—Travel is favored and you may go where you'll find much enjoyment and some new experiences. You may be in a place that is famous in modern-day history. The evening can continue a pleasant trend but watch out for excesses in food and drink. Also be thoughtful about the motivations of others.

18—You may get a practical bit of advice from someone very experienced who is concerned about you. Don't be scornful of this. Your efforts will bring good rewards today and you will be happy with ability to use new talents quite well. Evening may be needed for study to fix things in mind.

19—A telephone call in the morning may give you the news that money is coming your way unexpectedly. There is much to rejoice about in your life. Romantic matters may be good for the unmarried. You may meet someone who will bring romance into your life and be very generous and kindly.

20—Think twice before making a long distance call to someone who has snubbed you recently. Try to keep occupied with things in your immediate vicinity. Get out and walk around a region that is new to you. You can learn some facts today from talking to near neighbors who are experienced.

21—You may tend to take too harsh and cold an attitude with a younger relative. Remember that things are changing and old patterns breaking up. Be as generous as possible, show that you are truly concerned. Evening is good for making plans, looking ahead to the type of career you really want.

22—Much fraud in the air today; don't fall for sales talks and affected ways of speaking. Buy just what you intend to buy and then leave the shop. You can be far too tempted by shoddy things, fleeting fads. Be courteous and gentle in speech with a romantic person who calls on the telephone tonight.

23—Do not express your opinion on a matter that is someone else's concern. Someone who confides in you may want just that—a confidant. Avoid giving advice or showing disapproval. You may think the other person unwise but don't reveal that. Have a happy laugh about the whole subject.

24—The unexpected will occur or arrive. You may get results of communications made recently. All is well except that there is a health threat seen in your chart. You may have to see a physician about a throat condition that may be caused by fumes. Be cautious about respiratory matters.

25—A generous person may make an offer that is kindly but not very useful to you. A good day to shop for clothes and do things to put bright accents to your appearance. A romantic companion tonight may displease you in a minor way. Strive for more tolerance and sheer human warmth.

26—Even your subtle understanding may not plumb the depths of another person's love for you. It is difficult to accept what you cannot understand, but try your best. You will find this is a peculiar day with communications which are more interesting than you would ever have guessed they could be.

27—Be kindly and helpful with neighbors' troubles. You can do something to turn the whole day to gladness for an older person. Your mental ingenuity and occult wisdom will be appreciated. Any tendency to be too wrapped up in family affairs should be discouraged, for relatives don't want advice.

28—Something you buy today will give joy for a long time to come. Keep an optimistic view. If married you may be a little discontented, feel that the romance is slipping away. Try to discourage such thoughts and turn your attention to other things. Travel is hazardous in this cycle.

29—You can find a clever way to use something that is in need of repair. Your artistic skills can come in handy and you have a right to be proud of your work. You may receive a surprising invitation which you cannot accept though you'd like to. Evening is peaceful, a bit dull for you.

30—Be sure to keep your word to a relative who is waiting for news. Your success in a project is fervently hoped for by one who loves you. A chance event may bring you an opportunity but you must think about this for awhile. It is not a good day for practical efforts to bear fruit. Be patient.

MAY

1—You may become very angry with a task that is mandatory, dull and energy-sapping. A good day to hatch some new ideas, make plans about following them up. Social life will be pleasing this evening if you keep emotions under control and avoid staying out too late.

2—A friend who is slightly older may have a good suggestion. You tend to resent advice now but you can cut your own nose off to spite your face if you refuse to heed it. You are due for an effort to brighten your life and the directions you receive now are valuable.

3—Glamor is the good keynote to strike now. Be at your best; have self-confidence; let that mysterious personality of yours have freedom. You may meet someone who will soon become the one and only. Courage is here and you will appreciate having it to make decisions with.

4—Rest today. Read, watch TV, listen to soothing music. You can find the cycle very refreshing and healthful if you avoid crowds and stay at home except for a brief walk to exercise. Avoid showing too much interest in a neighbor; chances are that this person wants to impose.

5—Get in touch with a relative who likes to hear from you and be reassuring about your concern. You can do much good today by being unselfish, thinking of others and their needs. Avoid any big plans for tonight, you may want the time for yourself, solitude, meditation.

6—Take it easy, schedule your activities for convenience and saving time. Be very attentive to anyone dependent upon you—to a pet—to your chief concerns. A solemn view and serious endeavor pay off today. Be very brief when interruptions appear, cut them short.

7—Someone utterly unscrupulous may intend to get all the cash possible from you and work you to death if possible. Protect yourself; be courageous, daring and faithful about your beliefs. You may turn the tables on another person and find your path much smoother tonight.

8—The cycle is romantic in general but not a good one in which to resolve upon marriage or express yourself in a serious vein. Just enjoy the good times in store, the light banter and romantic chat. You may want to sleep on this before you have even one more date.

9—Expenses can mount quite high but you are optimistic due to funds you know will come in. Have faith in life now and follow your routine without worries. You may have a romantic date tonight and find your interest growing in your companion. Don't stay up late though.

10—Splurge a little with your money. Shopping is great fun and brings satisfactory results. Your need to get repairs for home items. You may want to switch the place with which you do business in concerns with your car. A good time for changes.

11—A family matter can give much concern and make you unhappy. Avoid thinking too much about finances or taking an unhappy view. Build up a more unselfish attitude starting with now. You can form the habit of happy thought and unselfish attitude which will make you happy.

12—Make sure you have good provisions for all that you desire. What you spend today will be beneficial but you will also be called upon to help another financially. Get your budget into good shape and handle cash with efficiency; all will turn out well in spite of worries.

13—Be generous with a new acquaintance. Welcome anything that comes into your life today, including long distance calls and letters that are unexpected. Do not get on a high horse with anyone. Take it easy tonight, aim at restful activities.

14—You may get a new opportunity in career matters. Think twice about the chances that come your way. However, where a promotion and more money are concerned the dice are loaded in your favor. Do not be timid about exposing your talents to someone who admires you.

15—You cannot depend upon a person who has romantic interests that are not your affair. Live independently and make your own decisions. Divide your time as you see fit. Do not allow anyone else to steer your romantic life. Avoid emotional outburst wherever you go.

16—There are mystic trends today and a chance that a new relationship can begin on very subtle and quiet lines. Be alert to those around you, heed anyone who speaks to you. You can have charming thoughts upon which to dwell tonight and should save late hours for your own use.

17—Get things done to make yourself more attractive. Buy bright new clothes, be in with the fashion scene. Have some work done on hair and finger nails, shine out in good grooming. Your boss can be very impressed and what you leave in your wake today may bring benefits.

18—Someone who is biding time and waiting to see what happens to you can be quite malicious. You will be able to thwart the ill-will of this person so don't take the trend seriously. Do as you please in romantic matters no matter what is stacked against you today.

19—A very hidebound and hostile person may take you to task in career matters. Contemplate a change in your work picture. Investigate conditions and possibilities with government work. Resolve to use your talents more fully in the future and to part with your past.

20—You may be near someone who is boastful and tries to make you feel discredited. Be clever and tactful about all this and you'll find a way to do a little ostentatious acting yourself. A good-humored trend is here although it takes some peculiar ways. Be ready to laugh at it all.

21—You may be whimsical but you must not cater to your own fantasies. There are disturbing trends in romantic matters and a person you are greatly interested in may take off for other regions this evening. You can be left alone with your thoughts which must be turned to the future optimistically.

22—Do not find fault with a younger member of the family but do show support which will encourage this young person. Avoid encounters with the law by being very conservative and cautious. If you are forced to face a legal issue, find some way to circumvent and remove it.

23—This is a dull day—dull thoughts—dull activity. You may follow a dutiful trend and yet wonder why. It's one of those times that demand a philosophical view. Do not fall behind in the concerns of unselfishness. Be generous with anyone who comes to you for help in finances.

24—The road ahead looks difficult today. You may incline to sulk and be quite unattractive. If you're wise you will go after what you want and be brave, full of faith and initiative. You can please an executive very much and be started on new success trends in your career.

25—It is a good idea to get out, mix freely with people and avoid indulging your own views and fears. Attend church and a luncheon afterwards. Be very kindly to older people today and also take a good look at a romantic situation which becomes serious as soon as it starts.

26—You may be prompted by intuition to buy some gifts today. It is a wonderful cycle to be extravagent on behalf of younger people in the family. Make sure everyone in your world is able to be happy. Entertain someone who is lonely tonight but don't burn the midnight oil over this.

27—Do not be obstinate and persistent about something you want to do. You will come out better in the end by being cooperative. Avoid saying pessimistic things to those close to you. All will be well if you hide your sensitivity and prophetic sense. Go your own way.

28—Work can be strenuous, boring and very nearly impossible. Stay along with the situation but look ahead to better times which are near. All is clearing for you nicely and you will be able to get rid of detriments which took over the past. Be very happy in romantic circumstances.

29—You may be open to suspicions and doubts, achieve a real dislike of someone due to imaginative trends you allow to build up. This foolish streak can be conquered only by subjecting yourself outright to companionship of the person you are discrediting in your imagination.

30—An older friend may be mischievous and could get you in trouble. Avoid spending time with the idle and those who seek pleasure with no regard for consequences. Make a telephone call tonight to glean information. What you learn now can change your plans for the better.

31—This is a day of suspicion and distrust. Try to overcome your feelings. Work through routine diligently. You may be on the list of someone who has dubious motives. Avoid letting yourself be influenced by emotional trends. Keep secrets and be as trustworthy as possible.

JUNE

1—Someone in the neighborhood may speak with malice of you if you do not perform a favor that is asked. Best to endure this circumstance rather than become involved by doing a favor. Intuition will inform you of trends that are not visible during the evening; secrets are uncovered.

2—Do not let anyone downgrade you in work concerns. Keep your poise and put up a struggle to have your rights observed. You'll win a victory which may surprise you. Be very helpful to subordinates today for popularity among all is important for your success trends.

3—Emotions may get you into a situation difficult to escape when you want to. Best to be very honest and straightforward with another; this will prevent undesirable circumstances from building up. Be clear in all you say over long distance telephone during evening.

4—Be friendly rather than aloof today; hide a mood of criticism and disappointment with others. Romantic affairs may grow more important during a glamorous evening but don't commit yourself to any course just yet. Think about relatives and their views in this matter.

5—You can be in error about another person. If you jump to conclusions you'll be doing someone a wrong. Try to take matters very lightly, let the time pass over without a serious trend for judgment and the like. Eat sparingly if you go out tonight, keep everything moderate.

6—This is a busy day with people coming and going and the telephone ringing almost constantly. It is difficult to get any rest or do the things you planned to do. You may just have to skip out and avoid matters around home. Seeing an older friend can put you in a good mood for evening.

7—Your work can please you today; you'll feel you've made a mark set by yourself some time ago. The mail can hold an interesting item but in the long run you can be irked by this correspondence so do nothing to encourage it. Strive to keep good-natured with the family.

8—Someone might step into your life and tend to take it over from the start. Make it plain you will go your own way. Don't share information with someone who is curious. You may be at your most aloof today but that's the way it is wise to be at this time.

9—This can be one of your thrifty days when a bargain delights you. Be lenient with youngsters in the family, though, and don't refuse them some small gift for happiness in play. Silence and meditation may bring some facts to light that are valuable for your career.

10—A neighbor may disparage you in petty ways. If you hear of this through a third person, just laugh a little about the matter. Envy is probably at the base of trouble now and that is not worth heeding. You may consider a change in residence but don't carry one out today.

11—A wonderful opportunity to improve your career is indicated. What you aim for now will not be too difficult to attain and you will receive support from influential people when you express desires, show confidence about talents. A jubilant mood this evening brings harmony.

12—Someone who misunderstands you should be tolerated. If you show dislike to such a person, you will be doing the wrong thing for there is much simple affection here. Do not be abrupt over the telephone this evening even though you are going out to a big party.

13—Share your time with someone who needs your quiet companionship. You can make the heart of another ring with joy by showing concern, helping with a bit of philosophical speech. Don't give direct advice today but make small suggestions without a dogmatic approach.

14—Events in the neighborhood may disturb your sense of serenity. Change is the order of the day. Finances may come under a cloud due to market trends connected with your hopes. Do not become gloomy for this is a passing state of affairs. Avoid strenuous activity tonight.

15—A relative can be demanding and unreasonable. Your loyalty will cause you to endure inconvenience and other unpleasant trends. However, do try to get away from the scene as soon as possible. You may find the evening irritating with inconsequential telephone calls.

16—You may contact someone you have not seen for awhile and find it a pleasant experience. Whether it is romance or friendship you can enjoy renewal of the association. Do not be penny-pinching in anything you do. Buy something to improve appearance in modern styling.

17—Be very steady in work, complete your aims and win a feeling of freedom. If someone tries to get something without paying for it, simply turn off your generosity. Ability to recognize motives of others will see you through the day successfully without regrets.

18—Major plans for entertainment may keep you busy during all moments free from other work. Shopping at your lunch hour may be necessary for last-minute items. Eat enough to keep your energies up, though, for weariness would ruin the evening you intend to be a merry event.

19—Guard your reputation today, seek companionship only with those who are responsible good citizens. You may have to devote some time to a neighborhood project of importance. However, this could bring you into contact with a person who will be lastingly loyal and helpful.

20—You may turn down an invitation due to some psychic sensitivity to the person who gives the invitation. You may feel there is an undercurrent of hostility. Obstinacy about your mood might be injurious to hopes for the future. Best to think twice before making decisions.

21—Someone may give unasked-for advice; this is sufficient signal for you to turn away from the relationship, discourage it absolutely. Hold out for what you want in the way of money now, follow through good plans for obtaining extra funds. Be a little thrifty in all things.

22—News that comes in may elate you and fulfill a wish you've nurtured for a long time. Avoid being impulsive about celebration, sit back and think of beneficial things to do with your windfall. Someone in the family will be very proud of you, perhaps too boastful about you.

23—Danger of accident here. You can be preoccupied, fail to be alert enough. Make an effort to control it all, keep your mind on what you are doing. Even if you get some disappointing news from an executive, keep your concentration on driving and all hazards.

24—It can be difficult to disregard the words of a person who wishes to annoy you, the attempt to be above all this nonsense. You're better off associating with younger people than with older ones today. Some mischief is in the air from all of them, though.

25—You may feel the need of a rest and still have vacation far off. The evening can be anticipated most happily if you have no social obligations. Also, it is best to avoid a romantic date if you are unmarried. You'll profit from solitude and sheer relaxation in your own home.

26—Strong inclinations to do what is not wise are present today. Your chart is chaotic and clouded. Make an effort to follow sensible plans, perform chores. Keep a desire to run off on a pleasure-seeking spree under firm control. Be cautious about welcoming visitors tonight.

27—An inconsiderate and unreasonable person may vex you. Showing impatience and intolerance will not be wise. Consider that such a person may have troubles you do not know of and be as kindly as possible. Get in some walking this evening, good to have a neighbor accompany you.

28—Much injustice in attitudes of others can plague you. You may feel unfairly treated, singled out for criticism. This can be the signal for a big change in your life. There is no need to remain under unpleasant circumstances. Seek your own happiness and protection.

29—An intolerant person who doesn't really know the score may attack you on personal matters. Say nothing, smile and walk away. Keep in command of every situation today and show no emotions. People may be trying to "bait" you; don't play into their hands. Be chilly and aloof now.

30—Be thoughtful about an older person who has befriended you. Don't be irritated if such a person does a little checking up to make sure you are well. Be more outgoing than usual, avoid a mood that suggests solitude. Appreciate your friends highly.

JULY

1—Your inner thoughts are becoming more realistic and mature. The day can be memorable for a philosophical fact you note for the first time. It is best not to make long distance calls though prompted to do so. Write a letter instead; that way you won't be just catering to your own sloth.

2—Discontentment with your romantic or marital life can be hazardous today. You are in danger of breaking up when you had a good thing going. It's the Gemini unpredictability and mysterious ways at work today. You could be in a better condition if you take a firm, decisive manner with yourself.

3—Not much chance for a wish to be fulfilled. The more you ask of others, the more obligations you acquire. Do not be dishonorable in attitude toward those who help you. Show your finest rather than your weakest qualities. Evening speeds up and you may have an exciting date with a new person.

4—You may feel free, victorious over hostility and other troubles. A mood for shopping may arrive and should be indulged somewhat. New cosmetics can make you particularly happy. Avoid any arrangements for the evening that include companionship you are dubious about.

5—Keep within bounds on all food and drink. Eat nothing that adds weight, drink nothing that affects the nerves adversely. Be wise and avoid a neighbor who usually imposes on others. Also, avoid gossip wherever it is going on in your vicinity. Be thoughtful about a young relative at a distance.

6—You may encounter someone you would rather not see. It will be more awkward if you show your feelings. Try to be polite, friendly within bounds. You may find there are things to admire in this person and should give credit where it is due. Make no big plans for the evening. Spend some time in reflection.

7—A need for more money can be your entire motivation today. There can be slow going in this direction but if you keep your mind active about it, you will hit on the exact thing to bring in the financial rewards. Make sure your home is in good order; a surprise visitor may drop in during the evening.

8—Good to shop, look around for a new residence, interview someone about your career. If you travel any distance today be sure you have ample funds for things that may come up. Companionship with a family member can be pleasant; you may be proud of a young person who has won some fame.

9—Emotional conditions are bad everywhere. People are on edge, easily vexed, inclined to brusque speech. You're in the same boat. Try to get through the period without any major explosion of nerves and emotion. Be guarded in what you say during a long distance call that is inconvenient tonight.

10—Try to realize that everything has some value; even a misfortune you have today can hold an important lesson. Be very careful about having a date with anyone this evening. You might be in with someone very deceptive and unreliable. Best to be by yourself rather than with the wrong person.

11—You may be kept occupied by "busy work" today and you can resent it. A very good chance here that you will begin thinking positively about getting a new job. Your talents can go to rust in what you are doing. Think of enrolling in some course to polish a talent that can be more profitable.

12—You may turn your career in a direction which it will follow permanently. For the first time you may realize what you truly want to do. A relative can be disappointed in you but if you explain things clearly you'll get some sympathy. Go over your budget and make sure it accounts for everything.

13—Things move slowly, interruptions are inconvenient. Do not encourage an intruder to stay. Be cautious about handling machinery, crossing streets, climbing ladders—no matter how small they are. You can be accident-prone so you need a sharp watch over your own welfare throughout cycle.

14—Good for shopping, changing residence, taking a trip, or even having a wedding. You'll find things go smoothly in relationships. A business partnership can begin with good auspices now. However, it is best not to buy a home or a major purchase today; that is do not put any money down for an option or otherwise.

15—Take an amiable attitude toward a neighbor even though you feel some tension in the relationship. Look for the best everywhere and encourage optimistic thoughts. Your work will be somewhat different from usual and you may acquire a new skill by a little practice you get in today.

16—Do not make yourself available for social life this evening; turn down an invitation. Exciting things are going to happen around your home and that's where you will want to be. However, do be dressed attractively and well-groomed, for this could be a romantic evening that will be outstanding.

17—You may have strange experiences today. Your psychic abilities are turned on at just about full force. It may be wiser not to mention such things to anyone else. You'll probably meet skepticism if you try to talk things over. Keep your dignity and be a bit aloof though smiling tonight.

18—A difficult problem in family matters can be solved by time only, so don't worry yourself about it. You could become emotionally very upset if you let things prey on your mind. A good idea to work with your own plans, adjust your budget, make a sacrifice so that you can buy a needed item.

19—Someone very superficial and not in possession of facts may try to analyze you and have it all wrong. Don't let this annoy you. Depart from such companionship quickly and try to avoid it in the future. You can have a good evening just getting out and around in immediate neighborhood.

20—A romantic possibility may arise today. You can be of two minds about this. The wisest thing to do is the most honest thing to do. You may have a unique conversation which will lead to the announcement that you really have no interest in the person who shows a romantic interest in you.

21—Much patience is needed. Co-workers are slow, some seem inadequate for their jobs and much depends upon you to get matters straightened out. Be firm, decisive and quick to act. Today you may earn a reputation that will soon put you right at the top in a position that holds prestige and honor.

22—Don't drive yourself too hard at work; you could have a minor breakdown from sheer exhaustion. Your mind may need a rest, so seek to do that which you can do automatically without calling upon mental resources. Best to keep evening open, make no plans. You'll want rest throughout evening.

23—An older person may intrude into your personal affairs in a way which is inexcusable. This is one time you will be justified in speaking out openly about the way you feel, in telling such a person to stay out of your life. Not very pleasant and yet you may feel much better once you've delivered yourself.

24—Get out and stay out as much as possible. Shop for unusual items, your taste will be excellent and you'll be all set for an evening of glamor due to new clothes. Your unique style can be expressed well tonight and you'll get many compliments. A wonderful time for sheer enjoyment and sparkle.

25—The day may seem long and hopes may seem to have little chance. This is mostly due to the fact that you are personally a little tired and need to relax in leisure. Optimism will return if you get enough rest. Do not let yourself dwell on anything unpleasant or imagine that you have health troubles.

26—This is the time for big things, a major transaction, a wise investment. You will profit from what you do with money today. Your intuition is a good guide but so is the word of an expert who wants to help you along. Quite a brisk time for work and at the end of the day companionship is pleasant.

27—Be alert today, listen closely to all conversation. You may analyze someone's speech and find it full of subtle power of suggestion. You could become quite angry or you may just nurture a strong ill-will toward this person. Best to get it over with and avoid storing up troubles.

28—A new acquaintance may vex you and your manner might be very hostile. This is a plain personality clash and there is no good reason to let hostility show. Just try to keep things going as usual and don't be temperamental. Help someone in the neighborhood tonight and you'll win deep gratitude.

29—Money may come in that you didn't expect. Be careful what you do if you feel elated. You could throw a large sum away on something you'll never use or even continue to like. It's a mixed day. Handle good fortune with prudence and you'll get all the advantages and defeat the disadvantages.

30—Be attentive to work needs and as accurate as possible. Your attention may be on a glamorous date for tonight but you must not let this ruin your work output. Avoid dressing in an elegant fashion for evening party, be more casual, have a feeling of freedom about your appearance and grooming.

31—Many messages in the mail, many telephone calls. Strive for good nature, be helpful to those around you. Put correspondence aside for it brings up matters about which you need time to solve. Don't be out too late tonight on a romantic engagement.

AUGUST

1—A problem that is left up to your decision can be difficult. It is suggested that you solve it on the courageous side rather than trying to forestall hard work and taking the easiest choice. You may rate much more highly with an important executive when you show daring and ability to take a risk.

2—Don't talk about your special professional skills and training with someone outside the field of your career. It is never wise to do this and can lead to some bitter resentments, perhaps outright anger. Change the subject if it tends to go in this way; keep all your personality gracious.

3—Romantic trends may be a major surprise to you today. You'll have a lot to think about and scarcely know where to start except that you know you may as well admit to yourself that you are attracted by a new acquaintance. Perhaps this is as far as you should try to go in analyzing the matter now.

4—You may travel today, might even be starting a vacation. This could bother you a little in the light of dawning romantic interest. Well, being away for awhile could be just the thing to get proper perspective on the situation. Evening can be somewhat long, boring, unhappy.

5—In any financial undertakings, make sure that you are paid well for your schooling and time. Do not let a friend flatter you in such a way as to throw your mind off practical concerns. You need to be on guard, self-protective in all money matters, so keep your mind fixed on such affairs.

6—A health matter which has needed attention for some time should be given consideration. Although it is costly, get your mind set on paying for it. Although it takes courage, get your daring ready for it. Nothing at all is gained by procrastination; you'll feel better when this is over.

7—Go shopping, buy things for children, have luncheon out with a good friend. Don't let the day and evening become too much in the way of social life. You need to retire early and should not attend any party where late hours are the thing and excess might keep you going for too long.

8—You can take a dislike to an older person and encourage it by turning the darkest thoughts toward this person. This is not worthy of you and is in fact malicious. You may let your emotions take over and keep convincing you that harm is meant by this acquaintance. How wrong you can be.

9—Do something special for a person who has a special occasion today. Could be a birthday or a birth, wedding anniversary or some such. Be original in your thoughts for a gift and you'll give much enjoyment. A good evening for a chat with an older person who is somewhat depressed.

10—Your obligations can seem too many and you may have to cut down a bit. Others will sympathize and so you needn't feel guilty of neglect. Be cautious what you eat today; don't go in for any heavy meals. Try to walk around a little; fresh air and exercise can work wonders with swift health recovery.

11—Don't let an inconsiderate person take advantage of you or waste your time when you need it for something important. Be a little cool to everyone today; you won't care much for conversations so don't encourage them. You may get a message by phone or mail that will give you something to think of.

12—This is a good day to have health corrected, to get into the finest condition possible. Go through what needs to be done, don't worry about the outcome or the bills connected with it. Your welfare comes first and you must approach matters very intelligently and bravely to see them through.

13—A neighbor may show up in true colors today. Someone who knows you could use a little comforting companionship may stay away due to lack of interest in your condition, although friendship was falsely expressed formerly. Well it's usually good to get things classified and sorted efficiently.

14—Something new in your life can take your interest. Romantic trends are changing and becoming more hopeful. In fact, you can become quite excited about romance. On the other hand, it will be necessary to stay in now and nurture your health along in accordance with its improvement now.

15—Someone in your family may be going through a difficult time. It is up to you to honor this person's silence, to avoid intruding upon emotional matters. Be industrious, thrifty and cautious today. There is some accident-potential of tricky nature after 6:10 P.M. so walk carefully and keep your eyes open during the evening.

16—There can be a family decision that will have an effect on your plans. Be cautious about all legal matters. If you don't know the facts, get them before you act. Don't try to outwit someone; you can be dealing with someone who doesn't miss a trick. If your answers are evasive, this will be known.

17—Mapping out a new program of reading for yourself is a good idea. It's high time to become familiar with some of the world's outstanding writers or people who are written about. Biographies are an especially good field into which to turn attention. Educational opportunities abound and are desirable.

18—A good day to move your residence, improve your living standards starting with location. Be cautious about prejudices you may harbor, and do nothing to build them up. What you need may be more information. Good to take an interest in community projects, join a group doing worthwhile things.

19—The day can become marvelously romantic and your entire thought-trend may be taken over by your happy love for someone fairly new in your life. You may have a date for the evening which keeps you in suspense. There are many things to wonder about your new love; fascinating things.

20—An excellent chance for a better job may come along. This can be dependent upon your answers to questions put by an executive. Be very calm, cool, use your wit. Keep emotions out of the picture when talking. There is every chance you will win higher position and quite a lot more affluence.

21—Dangers are rather abundant today. If married, you may find yourself on the verge of a break-up which is none of your doing. Traffic is perilous; home is the safest place. Even there, be very cautious about what you do. Be cautious in reaching for things which are up high. Avoid social life.

22—Someone may try to force a straight answer from you about some of your beliefs. No one has a right to bludgeon you over the head with questions about personal matters. On the other hand, it is desirable that you remain gracious, say nothing angry. Keep your temperament under complete control.

23—A busy day when you may be pleased with the variety of things you have to do. The hours speed by, there is no boredom possible. You can be joyous because of the way romantic matters are going and yet a little worried due to family attitudes. Everyone has those to contend with, so cheer up.

24—A bit of mystery in the atmosphere today may not have much meaning, so don't be apprehensive or worry about anything that seems to threaten happiness. It is best to avoid talk with a work associate who is new. Your role might be instructive and that could be resented, so just keep quiet.

25—Financially the picture looks good, dividends may come in for larger sums than you expected. A little shopping trip for items to make home more attractive is in order. Where clothes are concerned do mostly window shopping and some thinking about things you'd like for the coming season.

26—Good fortune may almost literally fall from the skies for you today. There is much good cheer, you feel the affection others have for you and everything seems harmonious. Evening is excellent for a casual get-together with a few choice friends but don't prolong hours too late for your own comfort.

27—A new acquaintance may have much charm. Avoid being intolerant, harsh of view. The world is growing mentally and spiritually; you grow with it. Take your time if you are buying a large item such as a car. That can wait for tomorrow while you make a decision so don't let a salesman pressure you.

28—A friend from a distance may call and have an unusual idea. You'll probably turn this down mostly due to uncertainty and some fear for your security. This could be just the wrong attitude and might result in conditions in the future which could bring regret. Be cautious of reactions now.

29—Avoid the family unless someone in it just insists on seeing you. There can be disputes, quarrels, very tense and unpleasant scenes. Someone may expect you to give up all your desires and intentions. This is ridiculous and you should not have to point out that you know your own mind firmly.

30—Be certain not to criticize or accuse an older person or an in-law. You can ruin a perfectly good relationship if you show irritability and doubt about another today. Better to get clear out of town if you think you can't control emotions and find a better set of charitable thoughts for others.

31—A long distance call can be more important than you know now. Things are not just what they seem. Looking beneath the surface may do little good. You can protect your financial situation, though, and this you should do at every moment. Loss is threatened and schemes are subtle, dangerous.

SEPTEMBER

1—Gemini starts the month splendidly with a new opportunity to meet people and gain public approbation. Responsibility may seem large to you, but you will carry out duties superbly. Rejoice in these happy auspices for your benefit. Career and personal life alike are improved.

2—A day when pleasure lights your eyes. You will enjoy the vibrations for sheer sociability and relaxation in the artistic side of life. Music and good humor will cheer the hours, and you will have happy plans for a gay evening. Romance is behind much of your joy.

3—Popularity is stressed. People who haven't noticed you before may be attracted suddenly. Your charm of appearance and affectionate understanding will win their way. You may have more invitations than you can handle. Choose according to your true feelings.

4—Energy and ideas spark the day. You will want to go in for brisk activity and accomplishment, perhaps on the domestic scene, perhaps not. Educational fields offer excellent opportunity and you may embark on a new project to gain information or enhance a talent. Entertain tonight.

5—Stay at home and rest today, if you have the inclination. Your health may be under depressing influences. Have a good book or magazine handy, and don't force yourself to think of problems. Try to avoid people who might be stimulating in a way that would exhaust you.

6—Rather mixed influences, but on the whole, good aspects under current conditions. Best to resist temptations to spend a lot or make changes. Try to remain on schedule, watch your diet and keep good hours. Otherwise you will be happy in the knowledge that you have affection you want.

7—The stars bring you personal happiness and affectionate relationships today. If you are married, domestic life may blossom with new romance. If you are not married, it is a good day to plan marriage or become engaged. Friendship also will bring joy.

8—You may be surprised at your independent spirit and initiative. You will be able to solve a personal problem efficiently under these influences, and the opinion of family or friends will slide into the background where it belongs. All will end harmoniously tonight.

9—Another good day, and this time finances are stressed, too. Investment may be recommended and safely made. Courage to put a sum of money into a promising venture may bring rewards in the future which pass expectation. Friends will bring happiness and affection this evening.

10—Exhilarating influences which make a brisk whirl of activity and speech. Happy hours with much accomplished easily. You will enjoy your work, perhaps be asked to take on a slightly new duty which your talent makes possible. The evening may have an unexpected romantic atmosphere.

11—Family and neighborhood strife. You may feel much mistreated, perhaps dominated by a member of the family. If you can yield temporarily to these influences, you may find that your unhappiness is ended automatically very soon. A large party this evening will bring sorrow.

12—Changes and surprises may greet you in the morning. The mail or telephone calls will bear exciting messages which can take you on a journey. Profit and pleasure in the excitement of life will keep you busy and happy. There won't be much time for idleness.

13—A day on which to be very careful about speaking your opinion or letting emotion show. At any cost hold back words of complaint. In romance, also, maintain a quiet reserve. If you do go out this evening, make your hour of return early. Unfortunate auspices for engagement.

14—A day when routine will move ahead steadily and you will be contented with your work. A sense of fitting into the universe will make you serene. Count on an afternoon with a cheerful conversation which is promising to your hopes. The evening will be happiest if quiet with loved ones.

15—Convention is ruler today, and you may have some eccentric tendencies which bring sharp criticism. Be particularly careful to please the family and close friends or their words may injure you deeply. Think first of others, follow the line of duty and postpone selfish indulgence.

16—A spirit of independence and determination will make this a noteworthy day. You may gain a favor you scarcely hoped for in the past. Be bold and go right ahead with your plans. Don't let anyone discourage you; by evening you will have a victory to celebrate with a harmonious family.

17—The morning will be cheerful. Your sense of gaiety and enjoyment of life will fill the hours. An associate may try to bring your spirits down with carping remarks in your presence. Ignore any such slights or jeers. They will pass and be forgotten quickly. Entertain tonight.

18—Get out and mix with others. Particularly you may find pleasure in neighbors you scarcely knew before. A day for sociability of a warm type. Also good for buying. Let yourself spend more than usual. Buy new items for wardrobe. The aspects favor romantic hopes.

19—Your career may take a jump ahead because of a contact you make today in the social world. Important plans which are underway for a community project may appeal to you. Let your ambition soar and make your way around in a crowd which is sparkling and has prestige.

20—Rather favorable for personal matters. Plan no major business projects for the day, however. You may have a surprising message in the afternoon, but chances are your good sense will handle it reasonably in the long run. Save the evening for a special party and dress up.

21—Very favorable hours for educational and artistic pursuits. You may find an opening to use a talent profitably. Don't be surprised if a friend has an amazing idea. Sift matters thoroughly. You will win cooperation on several important items.

22—Good messages through several mediums. You may be kept very busy and have surprises which fill the day with excitement. The ability to keep calm, take care of responsibility and still enjoy the pleasure of the day will be noticeable. Plan on an evening out tonight.

23—There won't be much time for anything but routine work. However, you may be watched by a very important person. A day when you will come up to expectations of those who have faith in you and are thinking of promoting you. Good news may come before evening. A gay night.

24—Many misfortunes threaten the unwary or overfriendly. Keep to yourself, share no secrets or plans. Guard possessions and spend little money. Watch your diet, also, for temptation to excess can lead to illness and depressed spirits by evening. Resist invitations for tonight.

25—Not good for business or financial hopes. Avoid buying or selling. A promise made about finances or a purchase today may be broken and cause bitterness. Retreat into philosophy and meditation for the evening if possible. Avoid quarrels and accusations in speech with family.

26—Selfishness is prevalent, and it may be best to stay away from people today. Do not take your troubles anywhere, even though tempted. Also, it will be wisest to avoid giving sympathy to an acquaintance who has a long sob story. Do not saddle yourself with other people's troubles.

27—A confused atmosphere in the morning will amuse rather than vex you. Your sense of humor will lend happiness to the hours, and a clarity of mind will enable you to see the nonsensical actions of many. Have a good day, work as necessary but don't overdo. A sociable evening.

28—Romantic matters may hang fire and give you personal concern. Whatever the difficulty try to avoid worrying about it or even solving it at present. Best to keep your mind on practical matters, watch your budget and talk but briefly to others. Read or watch TV tonight.

29—A chance to earn new laurels will be elating. Your happy spirits will also be contagious and those around you will feel their share in the favorable influences guiding your day. Participation in major events is your share, and a rise in popularity is at hand.

30—A severe reversal in the morning may make you bitter and start thoughts about quitting your job immediately. Use control, be realistic. Avoid all excess or any reckless action throughout these hours. A hope of a legacy may fall through and bills may mount up threateningly.

OCTOBER

1—Do not be flattered by a romantic avowal. If you accept this seriously, you may be chagrined to learn that the person who made it is untrustworthy. The intention to impose on your good nature is indicated by the adverse influences which abound.

2—Do your own thinking today, come to your own conclusions and do not listen to foolish notions. If you have what it takes, you might do something about creating a demand for it. Your theories combined with good technique should bring you substantial results in the not too distant future.

3—Do not be persuaded to make plans against your will. Judgments are apt to be biased because the Luminaries are opposed, so do not make any decisions for yourself or others, and refuse to be snared into accepting prejudiced edicts. Relax at home throughout the day.

4—Don't work so hard in the morning that you are too tired to enjoy the leisure for which you have prepared. In the afternoon a delicate situation may need all your discretion and tact. Don't let it overwhelm you. The opposing aspects call for the wiser use of time and effort.

5—A friend may kindle your enthusiasm and give you the incentive to do creative work. Let yourself be infused with new ideas and start off with a bang to do something unique and original. Do not let the thought of failure deter you since strong planetary allies are backing up your efforts.

6—This is not a favorable day to take risks in journeys, so keep within a short distance of the home portals. Stay alone, if possible, and do not ask for special privileges or favors from relatives or friends. The aspects call for discretion, diplomacy, dependability and diligence.

7—Should you have the opportunity to get work that provides an outlet for personal recognition, do not waste time, weighing pros and cons. Today's aspects signify new, deep-rooted connections. The trend also favors gaining new friends, enjoying surprises and bright ideas.

8—Do not be too meek today or else someone may run away with the honors that belong to you. Concentrate your efforts on producing the work that is expected of you and if the merit system prevails you may get first choice when promotion time comes along.

9—A friend may have the solution for an immediate problem. Try not to feel discouraged and say to yourself, "How did I ever overlook that?" Look forward to cooperation and good will. Your turn to do a good favor will come sooner than you may think.

10—Be gay and enjoy yourself, as the configurations are congenial. It is the sort of day when you can be charming and gracious in manner and attractive in appearance. Vitalize the evening with novel, original entertainment. Wear your best clothes, and let yourself go, as the saying goes.

11—Do not hold on to unnecessary mental strain or go through temperamental phases. Try to dodge trouble by side-stepping old issues. Discard what you do not need. Do a thorough job of emotional housecleaning. Avoid fast-moving vehicles.

12—This is a favorable day to show others your true worth and also to take part in vital issues of the community you live in. You are on an important cog in the wheel of existence, so do not neglect your public duties. Attend church services, a concert or religious discussion today if possible.

13—There are planetary indications that impulsive people will wish to rush into business entanglements unnecessarily today. Do not follow the crowd. If you stumble with those who are unable to decide which course is best, you may endanger your energy and your profits. Be steady, true and brave.

14—Let this be a day of rejoicing. Put aside old grievances. Invite others to cooperate with you. Rekindle the light of enthusiasm in yourself and see the reflected glow in others. Be kind and temperate because life is not so harsh as you surmise it to be. Wear your most becoming outfit.

15—Your success depends upon your judgment and ability to use your mental resources to the best advantage. Be original in theory and practice while the favorable aspects prevail. Do nothing that is cut and dried. Get rid of cluttering debris around the home, as well as at your place of business.

16—You can accomplish what you set out to do today. Arrange your work systematically and do not allow problems to loom too big in your imagination. Keep a mental balance and you can make fine headway with the pile of details you have to handle.

17—If others seem self-centered, determined and secretive today, do not try to force issues because the planetary aspects are in a position where lack of enterprise, caution and reserve manifest themselves in most deals. Take it easy, and let the cycle go by without trying to direct it.

18—The planetary influences may start a chain of circumstances that test your patience and fortitude. Prove your worth by not going to pieces. Keep pace with changing events. Do not go off on a tangent over a minor annoyance. Watch the speedometer if you are driving.

19—Avoid running around in circles. Watch the actions of others, but do not initiate them. There may be a rift in the lute so far as domestic and emotional matters are concerned. Do not allow them to jar you. Try to be serene and refuse to argue. Find solace through meditation and prayer.

20—You may be upset by a friend or your lifemate. Try to be conservative. The unfavorable opposition are forcing conditions and playing with mental gunpowder. If you are in the wrong, admit it. If you believe you are right, hold on to your opinions.

21—The morning vibrations are unfavorable for discussing money matters, business plans and legal trends. The afternoon and evening hours favor general work, family gatherings, neighborly accord and news from friends. If you have an important issue to settle today, try to handle it late in the day.

22—Itemize your money-earning possibilities. If you cannot put your plans into actions right away, make a record of them for future reference. But above all try to be philosophical in thought and action. Forget strong likes and dislikes for the time being.

23—Your affairs may require routine attention, so turn your mental searchlight to clearing up old details. A moderate day for ordinary duties, and yet there is a definite trend toward forcing issues. Let things slide if you find an argument in the making. Wait for a more serene day to act.

24—Cast no stones into the well that gives you water. Be careful that the sources of your income are not jeopardized and handle your affairs judiciously so as not to be cut off from your bread-and-butter supply through sudden impatience. The practical, down-to-earth method is best today.

25—Acts of omission and commission need balancing today, and if you have private plans keep them so. Do not take the public into your confidence because the aspects are adverse for privacy and mutual trust. Do one thing at a time, and do it well. Go to bed earlier than usual.

26—Hold your energies under rein because if directed wrongly, they can create irritations. The influences can make this a nervous, unreliable day. Do not pin others down to make final decisions. Keep away from anyone who is depressed and subject to moods of bad temper.

27—If you feel defeated and upset, it is due to the disorganizing influences present. Discuss plans and ideas with those fortunate enough to be in a success cycle. Try to sidestep annoyances, confusions, and imaginary afflictions by loosening your sense of fear.

28—There is only one beneficient aspect today, but it may create an important matter which requires lively manipulation. If you feel full of zest and ready to conquer the world, make this a day for achieving grand results. Keep your enthusiasm high and your production quota above capacity.

29—Rely on your plans rather than on the counsel of others. Your schedule might be upset if you fail to follow your own ideas. Do not complain if you have more to do than you can handle. Do your best and meet your obligations. Justice will take care of the rest.

30—The cosmic design indicates stabilized business, and the need for giving serious attention to vital issues. Handle everything with cool assurance. Whether you want a raise in pay or need to make another important decision, do not bungle or hold back. Forget past failures and welcome new opportunities.

31—Even if you feel safe, do not defy any authority today. Today is what you make it. Potential evil and potential good can be aroused at the pull of your mental lever so guard your speech and action. Stay at home tonight. Tidy up your home. Then watch television this evening.

NOVEMBER

1—Do not become upset over minor mistakes than can be straightened out easily. Seek things you want on your own initiative, instead of waiting for others to help you. Self-control and logical planning are necessary to come out ahead in the face of obstacles.

2—Avoid the subject of finances in your discussions now since you could give a wrong impression. Keep the atmosphere pleasant by staying away from anyone who appears to be in an unpleasant or quarrelsome mood. Take care of the things you have been neglecting, rather than waste time in useless conversation.

3—Do not expect too much from others if you want to avoid disappointment. Avoid making changes in your job or business, unless they are absolutely necessary. Look ahead to the future, instead of wasting time reminiscing about previous accomplishments.

4—Try a new approach if you feel that your efforts and progress are being slowed down. Avoid letting enthusiasm to get things done in a hurry be the cause of careless errors. Do not let your emotional impulses stand in the way of making a decision which requires impersonal logic.

5—Control feelings of restlessness by putting your hands and mind to work on a project from which you can derive practical benefit. Accomplish things well ahead of time, rather than force yourself to struggle under pressure. Be willing to compromise on a difference of opinion since concessions made now may be valuable sources of good will later.

6—Disregard all ideas for leisure until you have given full attention to responsibilities. Ambitions can be furthered now through careful planning and alert thinking. Handle routine matters quickly so you will have time for pleasant recreation.

7—Do not let minor worries interfere with the enjoyment and pleasures available. Invest your cash in worthwhile purchases, rather than on temporary pleasures. Attend only to matters which involve you, rather than be concerned with the problems of others.

8—Make room for new things by disposing of accumulations of useless possessions. Take part in activities that may increase your popularity and circle of friends. Do not press advantages too hard, even though things may be working out well for you.

9—Put your originality and ability to effective use on a project from which you might derive financial gain. Take conditions as you find them since attempts to change things might cause setbacks. Keep moody or depressed feelings to yourself, rather than discourage those about you.

10—Take disappointing conditions in your stride and think about favorable prospects that may be available to you in the future. Guard against becoming involved in an activity which could jeopardize your job or financial resources. Obtain the benefit of experienced advice before putting a new business policy into effect.

11—Rather than worry about the things you do not have, utilize to full advantage possessions that are already yours. Work on a project which can be of benefit to others, as well as to yourself. Help foster friendliness by reciprocating for a favor you have received recently.

12—Take conditions as they are rather than agitate for changes that might prove disappointing. Organize your plans carefully to prevent possible mix-ups and confusion. Do not openly show that you are provoked, even though your patience and temper may be put to test.

13—Preserve pleasant conditions by ignoring petty matters that might start trouble. Devote time to the repair or replacement of defective appliances in your home. Be particularly conservative in matters associated with work, money and real estate.

14—Do not allow yourself to become emotionally upset if something disagreeable occurs to disrupt your plans. Control any inclination you may have to go places and do things outside your usual routine. You should benefit from making use of helpful criticism aimed in your direction.

15—Enjoy your surroundings, ignore petty annoyances and you should find that things run smoothly. Regardless of how anxious you are to get things done, do not act on the spur of the moment. Arrange to invest your cash safely, rather than use it for temporary pleasures.

16—Be straightforward in your answers while dealing with others, rather than resort to subtle means. Create a closer bond of friendship by offering your assistance to someone who is in need of it. Meet each problem as it arises since letting them pile up might cause trouble.

17—Take things as they come, rather than try to force matters to an early conclusion. Conscientious efforts should help you achieve your goals, regardless of the obstacles you have to face. Choose your words and actions carefully since decisions you make now may have a lasting effect.

18—Deviations from accepted procedures could meet with disappointment. Stick to things you know best and can do well if you expect to make satisfactory headway. Do not attempt to evade irritating conditions since doing so might lead to further complications.

19—A little extra patience on your part should enable you to straighten out misunderstandings. Avoid forcing your opinions on others in the face of opposition to your ideas. Be courteous in your remarks, even though you may not care for the people around you.

20—Splendid headway in your work is possible but keep your enthusiasm within practical bounds. Be diplomatic in your approach and adjust disagreements before they get out of hand. Do not let business or money worries mar what could otherwise be a pleasurable day.

21—Do not ignore obligations, regardless of the pleasure anticipated from social activities. Say what is on your mind and then refrain from further discussion to avoid being drawn into an argument. Devote your attention to worthwhile projects, instead of dwelling on ventures of nebulous value.

22—Let others do and say what they wish this day without your offering interference in any way. Extra caution should be taken to prevent delays in your work. Take part in activities where you can utilize your initiative and resourcefulness to advantage.

23—More can be achieved now by compromising on money matters, than through forcing issues. Let others take the initiative while you remain in the background and take things easy. A mistake could make you the target of criticism, so guard against careless errors.

24—Prevent future difficulty by insisting that all arrangements be clear and definite at the beginning. Do not engage in an argumentative discussion, since your interference might aggravate the situation. Prove you are equal to the results expected of you by getting things done quietly and efficiently.

25—Concentrate on things which need your immediate attention, rather than worry about problems you expect to encounter in the future. Eliminate many annoying difficulties by paying attention to the minor details of your work. Let others do the talking and acting, while you mull things over.

26—Keep personal activities separate from job or business matters wherever possible. Avoid becoming involved in the emotional problems of another and maintain a cheerful mood. Your ability to cope with exasperating situations may have surprisingly effective results.

27—Be generous with your assistance to someone who is in need of it, but only if it is requested. Despite provocation, control the impulse to give undiplomatic expression to your thoughts. Let others be in on your plans so that you may get the benefit of others' points of view.

28—Even though you may be sure of your capabilities, exercise much caution in everything you undertake today. Take an active interest in the things going on around you, and be prepared to reap the available benefits.

29—Making arrangements for a temporary change from your work surroundings may be a splendid source of inspiration. A calm and patient attitude may be necessary to offset the confusion that is likely to prevail. Aim your conversation toward areas of agreement, rather than points of discord.

30—Regardless of what others say, do not worry about difficulties until you actually encounter them. Take troubles in your stride since bothersome situations should soon right themselves. Regardless of what you are called on to do, make every effort to produce what is expected of you.

DECEMBER

1—Do not let a contradiction of your ideas sidetrack you. Instead take criticism seriously and incorporate its wisdom into plans already formulated. Do not try to get the opinions of others to coincide with your own.

2—Do not attempt anything of a spectacular nature. Otherwise, you may expose yourself to trouble, and receive the blame even when you are not at fault. Make sure that little attention will be directed toward you, regardless of what you do.

3—An open display of sincerity and friendliness on your part can be used as a successful tool in obtaining the results you desire. In a social matter, it may be especially beneficial. Show others that you have faith and confidence in them if you seek cheerful cooperation in return.

4—Social activities, romance and entertainment are favored. Do something thoughtful which can prove enjoyable to friends or members of your family. By expressing words of affection, you should be able to bring yourself closer to a person of whom you are fond.

5—Take care of personal matters yourself and carry out domestic responsibilities conscientiously and efficiently. Avoid depending on anyone else to perform your duties. Also, do not settle for second-best, regardless of what you undertake.

6—To make successful headway in your work now, patience and conscientious effort is necessary. Despite the limitations you have to overcome, attention to details and adherence to customary methods should see you through. Keep ambitions alive, even though you may experience a difficult time in achieving your desires.

7—Although disturbing incidents may tend to upset the domestic scene, do not let them get the best of you. Concentrate on clearing up the source of annoyance rather than permit heated emotions and tempers to predominate. Avoid making a fuss over matters which are inconsequential.

8—Since your plans may go awry because of conditions over which you have no control, maintain a patient attitude. Avoid undertakings for which you do not possess the necessary experience or skill. You may encounter several unhappy moments if you attempt something you are not completely qualified to handle.

9—Draw your conclusions from facts whenever you have to make a decision. You may invite more trouble than you anticipate if you let your emotions be the deciding factor. Also, do not let irrelevant issues high-pressure your thinking in the wrong direction.

10—Be careful that you do not say anything that would intensify a difference of opinion between yourself and a member of your family. An open quarrel may place you at a disadvantage. Even though you may try to make amends later, you may find that friendship will be strained.

11—Keep business and pleasure in their respective portions of your daily schedule providing ample time for fun as well as accomplishment. Spend time, rather than money, in promoting social recreations. Use your resourcefulness to create diversion.

12—Get the most out of the facilities within your neighborhood. Do not go too far afield for amusement. You should find ample stimulation and congeniality with your family and friends.

13—Try a change of pace from your normal duties even if it is only time out for relaxing. Shopping for clothing and personal accessories may prove especially enjoyable. Gratify your personal desires, provided you do not place yourself under a severe financial strain.

14—You should find this an excellent day to visit or write persons with whom you have been out of touch for a long time. Club activities may prove interesting. Emotional and inspirational happiness is emphasized regardless of what program you schedule for yourself.

15—This is a good day to formulate ambitions and plan in detail your expected future accomplishments. However, do not be impulsive or try to attain distant goals too fast. Instead, work slowly and methodically so that you can achieve maximum results from your efforts.

16—Be cautious about accepting new plans or ideas where there is the likelihood of depleting your cash reserves. Be unusually conservative regarding property and valuables. Avoid financial risks of any kind and do not embark upon business expansion at this time.

17—Utilize opportunities available to you, rather than waste time or energy looking for new ones. Your enthusiasm can also be a valuable asset. Harness your initiative and resourcefulness to achieve the advantages that are now possible.

18—Avoid participating in any project that would subject you to adverse criticism. Unfavorable publicity that you receive may prove more damaging than you realize. A patient and cautious attitude would be more to your advantage than putting up a bold front.

19—Despite a feeling of intense enthusiasm, stay out of the way of trouble. It would be easy to get involved in difficulties now, especially where your job or savings are concerned. Keep within practical bounds, regardless of what goals you have set for yourself.

20—Go after the things you want, but aim your thoughts and efforts in practical directions. Work at something which you find enjoyable. Make effective use of your originality, skills and determination. Work hard, but not to excess.

21—For best results, stick to established facts and accustomed routines. Avoid guesswork and follow procedures which have proved practical. Refrain from taking chances. Rash action could be costly and also detrimental to your prestige.

22—You can attract favorable notice by doing more than is expected of you. Perform a favor or grant a request without having to be prompted. Express your feelings to others, but in a kindly and constructive manner.

23—You may find yourself burdened by unwanted obligations if you attempt to do too much for others now. Be on guard against an open attempt to place obstacles in your path. Do not let emotions or sympathies influence you when impersonal logic is needed.

24—Keep your mind on tasks which require your immediate attention. Choose a goal that is within your means and concentrate on its realization. Do not worry about difficulties until you actually encounter them.

25—The mystical splendor of Christmas should be apparent to you of the Sign, Gemini. Try to impart the strange magic of this day to those who need a cheer-up.

26—Working conditions may turn out better than your expectations. You may discover the cause of your concern is not so serious as had first appeared. Benefit through making long-term plans while placing emphasis on accuracy and efficiency.

27—Do not cling to outmoded procedure if you feel that you are not making sufficient progress in your work. Instead, look for more efficient and up-to-date methods. Success in your job is possible through a combination of resourcefulness and cooperation.

28—Do not take things more seriously than you should. Instead, replace anxiety with confidence. Although events may not turn out as anticipated, accept setbacks in your stride and make the best of existing situations.

29—Do not try to place a governor on your imagination. Even though some of your ideas may appear to be impractical or illogical, try them out. Do not discount a thought as being impractical until you have given it a chance.

30—Do not leave loose ends of your work for later consideration or action. Instead, get things done quietly and quickly by yourself rather than look to others for help. This is not the time to sit back and wait for someone to take over your responsibilities.

31—A high-voltage day, so get ready for it. Excitement is in the air—everyone appears to be in a big rush. Apportion your time and efforts in order to enjoy fully the ushering of a Happy New Year! Next year heralds many triumphs for you.

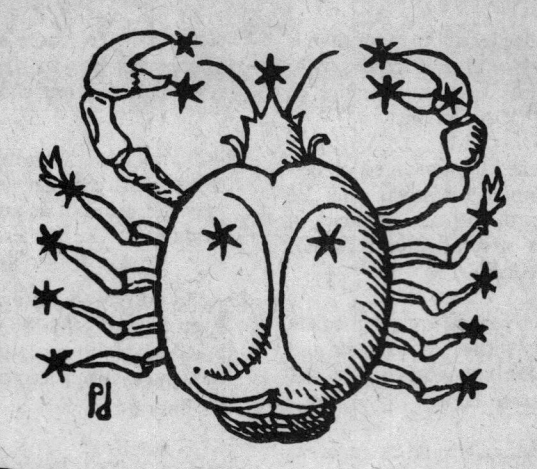

Cancer

June 21st-July 22nd

When you are happy
in home and family conditions,
you really ask little beyond that
in the way of pleasure.
Good friends
and frequent entertainment
in your home
add to happiness.
You find joy
when preparing delicious meals in the kitchen,
in children whom you can instruct
and bring up in fine tradition.
When your children
do things
to make you proud,
you are in your glory
with radiant happiness.
Taking part in community events
fills you with happiness.
and being able to help others
with sympathetic understanding
also rates your happiness list.
Travel pleases when the family is along.
You are happy
in work with home essentials in your career,
working with food,
furnishings,
running a motel.

Astrology, Horoscope, and Dreams

Cancer

JANUARY

1—Congenial thoughts and harmonious relationships are emphasized, so you should be able to get along well with others. Arrange your household routine so that you can finish a maximum of work and yet have sufficient time for enjoyable diversion. Regardless of activities in which you are participating, do not ignore prudent policies.

2—Harmony can prevail if you let others talk and act as they wish. Pleasant experiences are possible from taking a short trip or attending an outing. Friendly guidance and inspiration from a close association can help you to obtain cherished desires.

3—Arrange your schedule of tasks so that you will not have to work under pressure. Seek a change of pace and locality, even if it is only temporary. Clear up obligations without delay so that you will not be impeded in the quest of your goal.

4—Act only after considerable forethought, since errors in judgment and careless mistakes are possible. Place emphasis on getting things done quietly and efficiently. Yielding to emotional tension can invite trouble that would prove annoying to yourself and to those around you.

5—Rather than sidestep distasteful responsibilities, take care of them before they become an excessive burden. The poise and diplomacy you display can help strengthen the respect others have for you. Do not let temporary whims culminate in wasted efforts.

6—Put aside any desires for pleasure until you have completely caught up with your work. Strive for first-rate goals and do not let up in your efforts. Realistic thinking and practical action with regard to your job can pay off handsomely.

7—Refrain from showing your curiosity about things that are of no concern to you. Tackle only those assignments within the limits of your capabilities. Avoid making a promise until you have given full consideration to the consequences.

8—Take whatever precautions are necessary to eliminate entanglements and delays in your work. You can do much to keep things running smoothly by observing carefully what is going on around you. An optimistic attitude should enable you to achieve the results for which you are aiming.

9—Be reserved in your attitude; do not demonstrate an aggressive personality. Give complete attention to advice you receive, particularly from someone who is qualified by experience. Work slowly and accurately rather than at an excessively rapid pace.

10—Keep your conversation at a cheerful level and emphasize harmonious relationships with others. An indifferent attitude on your part may not prove as helpful as you expect. Work out household problems to logical conclusions rather than depend on intuitive impressions.

11—Do not be too generous with your time and money, regardless of sympathetic inclinations. Defer making an attempt to break away from conditions that have been restricting you. You can protect your prestige and popularity by remaining silent.

12—Refuse to be discouraged if the results of your efforts are at first ignored by others. Catch up with uncompleted tasks without delay. Make sure that generous efforts will be appreciated and that someone is not purposely taking advantage of you.

13—Practical accomplishments are possible, provided you do not crowd too many activities into a limited time. Tackle jobs from which you can derive financial or other down-to-earth benefits. Do not ignore responsibilities, even though you may feel an obligation should be handled by someone else.

14—Instead of avoiding a discussion about money, express your viewpoints clearly and back them up. Avoid entrusting personal matters or duties to another. Arrange to take some time during the day for needed relaxation.

15—Patience and calm understanding of your problems are needed to produce satisfactory results. Avoid becoming enthusiastic about projects that are of no consequence. Take care of arduous duties without complaint.

16—Discipline yourself to an exacting schedule of accomplishment and do not let your self-control lapse. Any attempt you may make to keep things running smoothly for others might be considered interference. Place emphasis on economy and refrain from giving in to extravagant desires.

17—Take things slowly, despite psychological pressure that others may try to put on you. Listen carefully to the words of associates before revealing your thoughts and making final decisions. Refuse to allow yourself to be inconvenienced by an associate.

18—Keep your intentions to yourself until you can actually put them into effect. Attend to matters associated with letter writing, studying and education. Your versatility in handling a social matter can prove effective in offsetting antagonism.

19—Realistic thinking is needed rather than taking a chance on the unknown. Settle bills and straighten out budget matters without delay so that you can take part in pleasurable activities. Do what you can to remain on agreeable terms with others.

20—Keep emotions under control, even though the actions of some person may give you good cause to lose your temper. Go forward on your own initiative but do not take things for granted. Do not relent in your determination to keep quarrels and confusion to a minimum.

21—Concentrate your efforts on new and profitable ideas from which you can gain financially. Work out a consistent savings program to build up your cash reserves. Take whatever action you feel is necessary for increased production.

22—Do not look for new diversions, despite the fact that you might be bored. Keep ideas and opinions to yourself, especially if they concern money. Tempers can be frayed and mixed emotions may prevail unless a calm attitude is maintained.

23—Differences of opinion can lead to estranged relationships that would be difficult to overcome. Refrain from accepting new responsibilities without first giving them careful consideration. Unnecessary tension and worry can be eliminated by ignoring interference with your plans.

24—A favorable day in which to attract attention to yourself and your capabilities. Plans associated with visiting and entertainment should work out enjoyably. Although this can be a pleasant day, you may be disappointed if you spend an excessive amount of cash.

25—False impressions you create would be hard to overcome. Get your work program organized quickly and concentrate on tasks that have a useful purpose. Take a new and aggressive approach to achieve effective results.

26—Keep in a cheerful frame of mind and do not let yourself become upset about the problems of another. Decide each issue on the facts presented rather than let prejudice sway your decision. Give consideration to new ideas and make contemplated changes in your work.

27—This can be a day of multiple activities that should prove enjoyable. Although plans may not work out as anticipated, there should be little need for pessimism. Attend to important matters personally instead of depending on someone else.

28—Remain within your own neighborhood rather than travel afar for diversion. Buy needed household maintainance items but keep your spendings and savings in balance. Share your hobbies and other forms of pleasures with the members of your family.

29—Do not let emotional interests interfere with matters that require logical attention. A conscientious attitude can help you build up a solid foundation for your future security and job advancement. Gear your efforts for speed as well as quality in your work.

30—Before making any decision with regard to money, be sure you are in possession of correct information. Dissension is likely if you neglect your household duties. Keep your personal life separate from business and job activities.

31—Get your plans for the day organized well in advance and adhere closely to schedule. Refrain from purchasing anything that would cause open conflict with other members of your family. Have confidence in your own conclusions and back them up with appropriate actions and words.

FEBRUARY

1—You will have unusual chances for making decisions that can put your life on a new purposeful plane. Frustrations will be removed and you will be free to act. A telephone call this evening must not be allowed to affect your life.

2—Your endeavor today may be praiseworthy but can be too exhausting in the long run. It is best to aim for moderate accomplishments rather than to strive unrealistically forward. Avoid a pleasure-seeking friend tonight.

3—A surprise can come in the mail and a response be required. Think over this matter for a couple of days before replying. Be cautious if you are in an unfamiliar place during the evening; there could be a loss.

4—Good financial opportunities are present and you may have the courage to grasp one with risk attached. A good day to settle bills. Count up your financial advantages and start making choices about future investments.

5—You may take a new view toward someone you have been hoping would ask you for a date. Today you may realize there is more you dislike than you like about this person. You may get some measure of amusement from this fact.

6—A good time for serious discussion with an older member of the family. Explain your ambitions and the ways you hope to achieve them. Sympathy you gain can be very helpful, and you may also be encouraged financially.

7—You may learn something that astounds you and it can throw you off the track for a short while. Try to recognize the limits to which this knowledge affects your own life and you may find it really makes no difference.

8—An executive may disclose some new ideas with much enthusiasm, but the whole matter may fill you with dismay. It is possible that today's discoveries will lead you to look for a new job. Be careful in this matter.

9—In general there is too much tendency to try to force the day to take on a romantic hue. You may be one of those who are doing too much wishful thinking. Call a halt to dreams and desires; just protect yourself practically.

10—Disappointment about something expensive you recently bought may be overcome once you get in touch with the dealer. You will be given an honest deal and your good spirits will return for the good of your family happiness.

11—At work a new burden may be placed on your shoulders. You may be put through a course of instruction that does not really interest you. This evening a thoughtful mood may reveal that you really want to change your job.

12—Your total environment--all your relationships--may seem undesirable. You may become morose and unpleasant; you should try to prevent such an outcropping of your inner moods. Let things happen rather than try to force them.

13—Take your mind from serious things; you need to relax. Go shopping and buy things to brighten your environment. Stay out quite awhile if the weather is right. You'll profit from being by yourself in shopping and other pursuits.

14—Your attitude may puzzle someone of the opposite sex who might want to have a romantic relationship. Chances are it has never really occurred to you at all. This is one of those days when diplomacy may be needed, and quickly.

15—A message in the mail can cause you to be disturbed about a younger relative. Avoid too much interference in this matter; don't keep the airwaves busy with long distance calls. You cannot run things or change them, so write an encouraging letter.

16—A neighbor may take an unpleasant attitude. Do not let this bother you. Be crisp and cool in greeting when you meet; otherwise, forget the whole thing. Buy some books and magazines for evening reading.

17—Good news in your career interests and perhaps a financial dividend you did not expect. Someone who has taken much interest in you may now prove their true affection by aiding you when you most need it and in a most-needed form.

18—Your feelings are easily injured today and you are advised to strive for good sense in this direction. If you brood over things that are said or attitudes that are shown toward you, you'll grow nothing but a crop of unhappiness.

19—It is unfortunate but true that today is a good time to do some trimming of relationships. Go through your list of acquaintances and see exactly where you want to terminate these relationships. Polish up your life a little.

20—Accident is prevalent and great care is needed. Be particularly cautious in large public buildings with escalators and elevators. You're best off on the ground floor. Temptation to spend a lot for certain pleasures needs curbing.

21—If married, go out of your way to please your lifemate and to make life sunny. You must conquer a tendency to criticize. A good day to plan a little spring flower garden if you have the space for it near home.

22—There will be little sympathy from an executive today, although you try to put speech on a common-sense basis. You may get a word of discouragement when you need encouragement. You'll need to be philosophical and do some laughing tonight.

23—If you complain about your home life, you can start a long trend of unhappiness. Also, don't pull any sly tricks to make it possible to change your environment in any way. Your health is good, don't pretend otherwise.

24—An excellent day for major financial matters, purchases, transactions, partnerships and new insurance policies. Sign papers, close deals and get a clear picture of your funds on hand. Today has a busy sparkle.

25—You can struggle with yourself over circumstances that both anger and puzzle you. If you ask questions, you may seem too concerned. Seek wisdom in meditation; holding off all action and speech may be best.

26—Get in touch with someone who can advise you about a financial idea you have. You'll undoubtedly be in the midst of bright social life this evening. Do not show any dislike or boredom with your circumstances now.

27—Try to be thoughtful and considerate; don't act on impulse or intrude where you know privacy is desired. The day is somewhat dull for Cancer, but try to spice it.

28—Be very poised today. You can find yourself in the midst of people who try to influence your mind. If you are angry, do not show it; get away as quickly as it is possible to do gracefully. Avoid brooding over others.

29 (Leap Year Only)—Your best interest today will be served by paying specific attention to loved ones. Don't let anyone detract from the time you give to those nearest your heart. You will win great happiness by spending the hours with a romantic companion.

MARCH

1—Avoid unethical actions, make no excuses to yourself about honor and trustworthiness. In personal affairs be unselfish and avoid any explosion about your desires that are not fulfilled. Make the evening peaceful and quiet.

2—A long distance telephone call can bring excellent news and encourage you in a worthwhile endeavor. Your financial status has a chance of rising sharply. Be very kindly and uncritical where neighbors are concerned.

3—Rather a dull day and some discomfort possible. You may have the beginning of a cold or even virus. Best to plan on staying at home and resting this evening. Social life could endanger your condition a bit too much.

4—Intuition may guide you in the right path today. A person you know who has done something unexpected may come to you for affection and comfort. Do what you feel is right even if it means some very critical comments must be made.

5—Someone who has good intentions toward you may win deep affection from you. However, it should be a day of quiet trends and little speech. You can nurture satisfying knowledge inwardly and be quite happy with all your relationships now.

6—Someone who has entirely different values from yours can show open disapproval. You may be dealing with someone very narrow, whose life has been limited in scope. Employ tolerance but don't linger over any conversation.

7—You may have a financial problem and be almost afraid to make any move to meet it. Think it through carefully and then do what is most realistic on your part. All will turn out well if you are true to honest standards.

8—You can be forgetful and cause yourself some inconvenience. Don't get impatient although the tempo of the day tends to rush at you. Be unselfish in doing something that will aid another and don't count the cost to yourself.

9—Keep your diet wholesome, live a little leisurely, keep your appearance up to best standards. A good day for general welfare and cultivating of good habits. Avoid conversation with a new neighbor whose talk is one-track type.

10—You can succeed in any financial endeavor today, sign papers, for any transaction. It is an exciting day and you'll be very popular. Telephone calls can come in thick and fast. Make a careful choice of invitation for evening.

11—No use being annoyed about a family situation in which you can do nothing. Try to forget the whole thing and live just as though nothing were wrong. Unreasonable jealousy plays a part; possessive people will seem to take over.

12—Your understanding is needed; be very affectionate with an older person who shows loyal friendship even though your attitudes are very different. Find what can be mutually enjoyed and agreed upon to make another happy now.

13—Take a firm grip on essentials connected with your job. You may have to check over some work before turning it in, since there absolutely must not be error allowed to go through today. Do not make a remark that shows prejudice.

14—The day may be quite ordinary and enjoyable, particularly where younger people are concerned. However, evening can bring a telephone call that will be rather startling. Best to just let it go; it will be safer that way.

15—A good time to enjoy the companionship of a very compatible person of the opposite sex. You can just have a good time even when busy. Much exchange of wit will keep you cheerful. Make the evening menu quite light tonight.

16—A suggestion made by a younger person can have value. Do not be obstinate or haughty. Think over everything others have to say. You may come out with a brilliant inspiration and inspire several ideas of others to help it along.

17—Impulses are not good today and you are very likely to follow them. Undesirable circumstances can result and you may also undermine your health. A good chance that there will be a major quarrel at home this evening.

18—Be considerate of others, help out as requested, go shopping, and be at your most attractive for social life tonight. Be discreet and do not ask questions about anyone's personal life. That could bring on a critical attack.

19—You may make a new contact with a person of great charm who will turn out to furnish much heartache for you. You may find this person is a sponger without scruples, someone with no consideration of anyone at all.

20—Do not forget to mail something of importance. Also get bills paid up today and don't put off a matter of taxes that annoys you but must be handled. Try to get the unpleasant out of the way so that you can relax tonight.

21—Not much chance for doing any personal chores today. You can be tied up with routine work right up to the last minute. An executive with no sentiment can keep everyone working slightly overtime and win much disapproval.

22—You can resolve to go on a diet and be determined to lose 5 or 10 pounds. A fine start can be made with today's lunch. It won't harm health at all to figure out a simple diet for yourself and it won't be hard to follow.

23—You can be bored with a situation which arises today in connection with one of the opposite sex. Someone may pursue you when you don't want to be pursued. Much persistence in this matter can cause you to be rude.

24—Let no one persuade you to invest money in a project linked with friendship. Be quite miserly today, in fact. What you spend may only bring bad results. It is not a good evening for social or romantic engagements.

25—Keep your mind on finances and all will go well. Do not let yourself dwell on personal relationships. If you have a social gathering this evening, you may be startled at the questions a snoopy person asks. Be prepared.

26—You will thrive better indoors today. Avoid anything strenuous, and don't sit out in the sun. You need to eat very lightly. Have a leisurely day, look through old papers, discard things no longer of use or worth.

27—A chance encounter can be more important than you know. Much will arise out of today's conditions. Be conscientious, be sure you look your best, employ quiet ways to win the most admiration. Supply serenity others need now.

28—A dull day, mostly just routine and a passing of time. Things are building up behind the big scene but you won't know what they are until people get ready to speak. Avoid trying to persuade or influence anyone at all.

29—A request you make should be honored but perhaps it won't be. There can be too many on a waiting list or some other condition may serve to thwart your desires. Be gracious about this, show no impatient anger.

30—A good day for a wedding if that's the way you incline. Or, if romance is just starting, this can be the day that gets it off the ground for a real flight. You may be in the most glamorous and glittering of nightspots; don't let this illusion of magic make your love go wrong.

31—Do not be willing to give up your plans in order to follow those of another person. Even if criticized by the family tonight, remain independent and follow your own instincts. This can make life interesting, indeed.

APRIL

1—Today you may be moving into new quarters and very happy about it. In your high spirits don't speak in offhand fashion to someone who loves you. It is easy to breed distrust and that is your danger now. If words of love are spoken to you, don't turn them aside as so much nonsense tonight.

2—Your intelligence rates high but your emotions can rate zero. You may be hostile toward a harmless person who has never done you anything but favors. You may also deceive someone who loves you by being attracted elsewhere. Make some kind of effort to control flighty emotions.

3—A neighbor may do something you do not like and you could flare up about it. It's much better to smile and have a light attitude about this matter, then go on as though nothing had happened. Keep evening for brief entertainment of older people you have known a long time and liked.

4—Try not to be absent-minded today. Recalling a fact might prevent much trouble for you. Avoid shopping for any major items. Things you buy today would prove full of faults. Keep track of where the money goes now.

5—Someone who tries to help you may only aggravate you. An older person who is accustomed to taking over may take over part of your life in a firm way. You're advised to wait this out, let it die of sheer inattention. Attend a large party tonight or enjoy a family gathering harmoniously.

6—A very pretentious person in your neighborhood may earn your dislike. Keep it to yourself, be poised and gracious of manner. You may have a happy afternoon if you can get in some outdoor activity. You need this refreshment and must stir yourself to action for sake of total health.

7—Gossip, envy, threat of accident and some money loss all hang over you today and form quite a dense cloud. You can feel deluged by bad fortune by evening. Minimize these possibilities by working quietly by yourself, being cautious with money and abiding by traffic laws and driving defensively.

8—You may go in too much for self-expression today and that could be the end of a job you've held for some time. An executive who is criticized may turn upon you and fire you point blank. Other possibilities of harm may come through a neighbor who carries tales in a vicious way about you.

9—You may accidentally get involved in the emotional problems of a friend. Do not give any advice, make it plain you would rather not even hear about these matters. You might be asked to help as a witness in litigation and this is best avoided. Try to relax, read something light tonight.

10—You may feel lonely and shut out in your home area. People today are just too cool to the newcomer and if you have moved recently you may feel that you are unattractive to them. It isn't that; it's just the modern way of being too busy to be hospitable or to cultivate acquaintances.

11—You may buy a luxury. It is all right to treat yourself to something very nice once in awhile. Today's big buy will be an enduring one, giving you pleasure for years. Select colors carefully in anything you buy. You'll be best off with old friends tonight or a trusted lover.

12—You might get some criticism today which could be on the subject of something vital to you. Do not show any anger. Keeping harmony with all people is the word for today. If you attend a glamorous affair tonight, have a new hair style to show off and wear your most sophisticated outfit.

13—You may try to impress a neighbor and this is rather childish of you. Just be yourself, be honest and you'll make a much better impression than by taking on elegant airs and florid speech. An older member of the family may call upon you for help in a problem; don't get too deeply involved.

14—You're in one of those gay, impractical and careless moods. Watch out or you will lose something of great value. Your speech to others may be too superficial and fail to take into consideration when you are expected to be serious. This is an adverse cycle; you're warned to be wary.

15—Someone you meet now can be more superficial than you are in romantic relationships. This can intrigue you. If you do not have regard for your reputation, you can lose it in a hurry through this person's companionship. Worst of it is you may become desperately in love to your sorrow.

16—There is a mysterious air to cope with today. People may seem evasive, you can't get cooperation, and any travel you do can be frustrating. If you are in sales work you can find the day one of the worst slump periods you've known and most frustrating. Just relax and do your best.

17—An older person may do you an injustice through gossip and the notion that you lack wisdom. Such a person may try to guide you and none too subtly either. If you take umbrage you will be playing false to your own wisdom. Be serene and too poised to let anything aro your anger now.

18—This is a money day all the way. Investments a rewarding, bargains are many if you shop, real estate can have true value for you if you are courageous about it, and in general the money picture is fine. You may find money and be free to keep it, spend it and fulfill a desire.

19—A person with hidden motives may seem very pleasant to you. The day shows it is not a good time to take on any new friendships. There is much deception in the atmosphere, some knife-in-the-back tactics going on. Best to avoid social life if you value peace and happiness tonight.

20—You may be impatient with an elderly person who wants to talk to you after church. Try to control this urge of your nervous system. Be cautious in afternoon activities; pleasure-seeking can bring costly regrets. Choose your companions wisely and with solid discretion in mind today.

21—You may fall in with someone narrow, prejudiced, bigoted and snoopy. This you will learn too slowly for your own good. However, the person may also be the forgiving type, intelligent in a certain way, and prove to have an excellent memory. In the long run, he or she may be a staunch friend to you.

22—Educational matters should be given some attention. A solid ambition you have had for some time may be fulfilled if you are bold enough to ask for financial help in the right place. You'll get moral support, so go right ahead. Time runs swiftly and this is the time to act swiftly, too.

23—An unavoidable parting with a friend may be here. Someone you have learned to count on for good companionship may have to move far away. By evening you can be in a sorrowful mood. Call a cheerful person on the telephone and it will help considerably. For once you really don't like change.

24—A health check may be necessary due to conditions that arise and alarm you. Be serious about your health whether this happens or not. Resolve to add some high-protein items to your menu, try some health routine recommended by a friend who is loyal and wants the best for you.

25—High praise may come to you and the promise of a pay increase can be included. Don't spend money you don't have. Be happy but keep actions and pleasures wise. In evening social life is agreeable, don't argue with someone who has differing opinions from your own.

26—You may have a puzzling problem that requires deep thought. Don't try to win freedom from this unfairly. With your temperament you should be happy with a challenging problem but this one just isn't the type you like to cope with. Resist temptation to share troubles with a loved one.

27—You may come to a conclusion that makes you quite bitter. If you are married you may begin to think about divorce. This is a situation for which there is no outside help. You'll have to go your way as all indications direct. Don't be afraid to acknowledge a bad mistake now.

28—Adventure may befall you and take you out of a glum mood. This is just the kind of day Cancer lives for. You may go to new places, meet enchanting new people, be taken in with a circle that exhilarates you mentally and emotionally. Surprises rule and the unpredictable may happen.

29—Do a favor for a neighbor and don't expect any return. Show that you do not want your neighbor to feel obligated. You may be curious late in the day about a trend your work is taking lately. Perhaps someone is putting you through a rugged test and will tell you so by the end of the day.

30—Aim at perfection now if ever. Your wit is quick and sharp, your skills more than adequate to fulfill demands. Much success in career at this time should be your only goal and you must be dedicated to it. You may be starting a course that will be lengthy, difficult but rewarding.

MAY

1—Be gracious with people in your neighborhood and don't show hostility to an older person no matter how you feel. A good day to keep busy, shop with pleasure, buy a pet and home additions of interest. Make your environment happier and you'll benefit for a long time to come.

2—You may spend the day in romantic companionship and be delighted with the way it is going. Enjoy the cycle but don't look ahead. You may learn some things later that will put a different color on romantic matters. Conversation will be witty and pleasing throughout this cycle.

3—Shopping for clothes can be a pleasure and you'll find just what you want with a little looking around. Keep all activities on the light side; this will be beneficial for health and spirits. Be friendly with a newcomer in your environment and you'll find much congenial happiness.

4—Much enjoyment from reading and what you learn may delight you. A long telephone conversation may be the prelude to a new friendship. You are alert and able to follow up new leads and ideas profitably. There's a slightly mystic atmosphere to the day's events and talk.

5—You can be interested in a romantic trend that promises much pleasure. Your conversation will delight someone of the opposite sex. Be very sure not to be deceptive and don't be late for any appointment with the one who attracts you. This is quite a deep romantic influence.

6—There can be much competition in your career situation. Someone may try to get your job by subtle ways with an executive. Guard what is yours, keep right on the ball in defending what you wish to keep. You'll win in the end so don't let nerves get ragged or be irritable.

7—A monotonous day when you might feel like letting out a healthy scream. Maybe you can take off for a rural scene to spend the weekend and be able to utter that scream as you unwind. Avoid getting intimate with anyone new today. Do not make promises or get tied up in any way.

8—You may prefer just to rest and follow whims around home rather than tackle shopping or the social situation. You need time to meditate, listen to music, enjoy leisure. If you are invited out for dinner, think twice before you accept. The evening is interesting at home.

9—There is a chance of hopes going astray now and some of your best ideas will bring no results. If you have dependent children, do your best to care for them. Have medical and dental check-ups, be dutiful in all responsibilities. Put self-interest in the background for now.

10—Difficulty in understanding a work requirement can be irritating. Come right out with questions so that you get everything clear before tackling a new type of endeavor. You are favored in romance this evening and may find yourself happy to be tied down to one person.

11—Get out, attend church, make a good impression with appearance and personality. You can enjoy becoming better known. In other activities be practical. You may have to think through a plan and make it more practical. Let ambitious thoughts provide background for plans.

12—Make plans and follow them conscientiously, do not waste time with interruptions. Make it plain you have demands you intend to meet. Avoid temptation about food and drink, keep health rules in mind throughout cycle. Do not be temperamental and difficult in home tonight.

13—A marvelous idea may show you just how you can achieve a creative effect easily. You will be able to change all high-flown thoughts into practical use. A day to remember for good opportunities and clever ways of following them. You'll win praise for your work today.

14—Appreciate the pleasant things in your life and let nothing disturb your quiet happiness. A letter you receive might hold a tendency to be bitter. Perhaps you have injured someone who was romantically inclined. If so, answer such a letter with a friendly, helpful attitude.

15—Be thoughtful and generous, carry out the wishes of another person and you'll be pleased with results. You may receive a small but pleasing gift. Social life is very attractive this evening but don't ask questions of personal nature. People can resent such intrusions.

16—Avoid mistakes; they can be costly and vexing. A good day to shop for luxurious items. Try to pay for what you buy rather than venture on installments. A friendly neighbor can make the evening pleasant but it's best not to get closely involved until better acquainted.

17—You can make a mistake about someone's motives and may thus owe an apology. Be generous of spirit and friendly rather than having a chip on your shoulder. Avoid a snobbish attitude, don't snub anyone in any way. Accept a favor that is done for you with gratitude.

18—There may be a surprise which is somewhat of a jolt to your hopes. Someone who was very attracted to you sexually, perhaps really in love with you, may now turn down opportunity to see you again. Think back over your conduct and you may find you have been too undependable.

19—Be relaxed in efforts and you'll accomplish more. A day when haste can cause trouble. Have a pleasant companion for lunch, let conversation be casual and straightforward. You can find something to laugh about happily tonight and that's a healthy, rewarding trend of events.

20—Be meticulous in appearance, in all you do and in relationships. Don't be deceptive even about small matters. Show understanding for someone with emotional troubles but don't get involved beyond a bit of sympathy. Keep the evening for yourself and personal chores.

21—Avoid judgments about others. You may feel a younger person is being unwise, but don't mention this. You could win a lot of hostility by expressing yourself. You may have to comfort someone in a social dilemma this evening; if so go all out for giving solace and sympathy.

22—An event in the family may be disturbing but don't add your bit to the general confusion. Keeping quiet may be the best thing you can do today. Find some errands to get you out of the house and keep busy outdoors. Shopping can bring inferior purchases and regrets to you.

23—Don't complain or feel sorry for yourself about progress that is lagging. Your ambitions can be unrealistic and you may fret too much about what others are doing; you can feel held back. If you voice discontent you can bring on a quarrel of most unpleasant nature tonight.

24—Be thoughtful and you'll find good reason to do as another person wishes you to. Don't be evasive. The straight-forward approach is required if you want success today. A chance to take on a new responsibility and new use of talent can be very worth taking up quickly.

25—You may feel like quitting cold, just walking out on everything today. The weather may lure you to take a trip, urge you to get away and enjoy balmy breezes. But you'll stick with demands and see things through. Just dream a bit about freedom that seems enticing now.

26—Do not be harsh with a child or any loved one who wins your disapproval. Take a lenient attitude for you may need such treatment yourself before the cycle is over. Be on the beam to be helpful where a deserving person needs advice and some encouragement to act firmly.

27—You may be very speedy with work but the pace can be exhausting. Slow down at least during the afternoon. Be considerate of associates and don't ask any favor that you wouldn't want to grant someone else. Reason and logic are your best allies in all you do at this time.

28—Health may be in a slump and emotions may bother you. You can be very unhappy over a romantic trend while at the same time you are much in love. For self-protection it can be best to break off this romance, get over it all and be yourself again in a cheerful, breezy way.

29—You may have glamorous social life to anticipate for evening. Spending on some extra beauty-salon work is in order and so are your most becoming clothes. Take great pains with grooming, be at your best in appearance. You can win attention of a person important to your life.

30—Take it easy, be harmonious with family members or in-laws. You can enjoy having some relatives for dinner if you make it casual, don't work hard on it. Discussions may yield some worthwhile ideas, and you may be praised in a way that soothes your ego and brings confidence.

31—Handle money cautiously, count your change, do not carry a large sum. Avoid temptations in shopping, keep expenditures down within reason. You may have an opportunity connected with use of talents. It's a good time to find a market for a hobby of creative. nature, win new profit.

JUNE

1—Please a friend who has been loyal to you by going to church. It may be very pleasant to enjoy a special outing this afternoon, perhaps a picnic with children as the center. A good day in general for unselfish and helpful gestures toward others. You'll have peace of mind.

2—A person with petty attitudes may irritate you but don't let a quarrel develop. By changing a minor habit you may be able to avoid further encounter with this person. Avoid being deceptive with yourself or anyone else where romance is concerned during the evening hours.

3—A good chance can arrive to help you over a financial difficulty. The pace speeds up around noon and you can find yourself deluged with work assignments. Avoid a feeling of chaos by tackling one thing at a time with concentration. You will need a restful evening, early retirement.

4—An older relative may be domineering and could cause you some difficulties in romance or marriage. You will need to get out from under this influence which may be quite subtle and therefore very effective. Aim at independence in your personal affairs and be firm about it today.

5—You will probably keep busy with chores, shopping, some unexpected demands that arise in the neighborhood. Take a generous view toward an older neighbor who means well. Don't let yourself be critical and sharp of speech. Evening social life is favored but not late hours.

6—The day favors a major move, change of residence or job. You may meet new people, find your personality working well for new friendships. There may be disappointment late in the day due to a money expectation that doesn't come through. Be patient for this may be only delay.

7—Financial enterprise goes along well today and there is no hitch to your plans and hopes. Large sales or purchases bring some elation and you can feel your living standards are on the upgrade. Find some way to show appreciation to a person who has been helpful all along.

8—The main trend today is connected with romance. It can be the beginning of a relationship that may lead to marriage or it can be the end of a relationship that has begun to bore you. Try to be thoughtful about all that you say to a romantic companion or lifemate at this time.

9—Good news may come in about a career hope; you may get the chance to use a talent which will bring in more money soon. Be cautious in driving today; there will be a somewhat reckless atmosphere prevailing for drivers, but don't be one of those so affected.

10—Avoid being changeable today and don't let alarm about any matter take over. You may find yourself interested in a newcomer to work environment. Be helpful and instructive with such a person. This could develop into a fine relationship of endurance and affection.

11—You may be criticized by someone who has high ability to analyze and see through superficial matters. It can repay you to take this trend seriously and with good nature, for you might find criticism is justified and improvement of value can be made because of it.

12—You can feel weary today, may cancel a social engagement for tonight and seek relaxation throughout the cycle. There is need to protect health. Don't be in a rush about anything, for this could add to health hazards. A telephone call tonight may be interesting.

13—Do not become involved with a neighbor who has favors to ask. It could become inconvenient if you let yourself in for helping this person, so don't get tied down. Enjoy some outdoor activity, find pleasure in a small group of people who have much good will.

14—Be sure to be accurate in all financial reckoning, do not forget a big installment bill. You may be somewhat dreamy today, tend to be anticipating happy activities in the near future. Be sure to check work before you let it out of your hands, for a mistake could be embarrassing.

15—Be patient with those around you, particularly any relatives who are near. Don't chide someone for being slow; have sympathy with those who simply aren't as alert as you are. Don't contradict anyone who has false information or an opinion at variance with yours today.

16—You may have a big decision to make and need some help about facts involved. If you consult anyone it will be wisest to see an expert rather than talking it over with a friend. Be careful with money today; loss is possible or being short-changed can be quite a mixup.

17—A good day to do essential things connected with a vacation. Getting clothes ready, having the car checked, making sure you have good maps can all be handled efficiently. In matters connected with career, relax and take it easy. Don't exhaust yourself over anything today.

18—A good day to start a vacation, get away from home and unwind. Safety is featured and all will go well with your plans. Be considerate of your lifemate if married. Avoid being self-centered and prone to displease others. Taking a high hand about matters which must be avoided.

19—An excellent morning for a wedding ceremony and a luncheon reception afterwards. You may start a trip for honeymoon or other purposes. Be trustful of people today and all will go well. If you show doubts of others you may create tensions and gain some bitter hostility.

20—A new neighbor may be friendly and this can be a pleasant relationship. Generosity is good today so don't hesitate to do kindly things, be helpful with material matters. A young relative may call and have good news. There is a busy and somewhat festive atmosphere today.

21—Follow your personal desires, do things that will help get your life into more orderly condition. You'll work best by yourself now so discourage intruders, those who simply hang around for idle chat. Communications can be full of misunderstanding so avoid them mostly.

22—Mechanical difficulties can make the day frustrating and worrisome. Vexation can make you impatient and nervous, prone to be sharp with others. If you snub someone even slightly today you can create a bad impression that will last. Make every effort to be pleasant to all.

23—You may have a unique point of view that is not liked by others. If you express yourself in straightforward ways you can make an enemy. Do not ask any favors today, for there is not a good atmosphere for gaining requests. Plan to be by yourself for a restful evening.

24—You may have to do some work that is rightfully the duty of another. Don't show resentment but be as efficient as you can. If you shop today you'll have excellent taste for clothes. Now is a good time to switch to some new cosmetic line which is deluxe and quite costly.

25—Be sure to keep personal secrets quiet. Someone may have a subtle way of trying to pry them out of you. Also do not talk about others' confidential remarks to you. The day requires quiet wisdom. Avoid driving if you possibly can, for there is a personal accident trend.

26—You may receive a letter which causes a change in plans. A good day to follow impulse, resolve on some new action that will bring about a major change in circumstances. Give some thought to your career and to desires to find time for a creative project that interests you much.

27—You may encounter much bigotry in the attitudes of others. Best not to argue about any of this. Make a good impression with your appearance; the afternoon can bring a surprise romantic trend. This evening you may have some personal matters to mull over in depth.

28—Small children may delight you today. Your personality is excellent for enjoying the company of little ones. It is also a good time to buy a pet or something else to bring more cheer to the home. What you spend today will be well spent due to bringing new happiness.

29—Be reserved, uncommunicative to some extent. Someone older may be searching for scandal and try to find it in your life, so "clam up" about personal affairs. Be pleasant, though. You may have a lonely time late in the day but a walk by yourself can help clear your mind of unnecessary problems.

30—Keep your pace slow and you'll avoid accidents. Do not climb up on any rickety piece of furniture. In shopping do not humor yourself too much where luxuries are concerned. Be very pleasant and gracious to someone who calls long distance tonight. Show much simple affection.

JULY

1—Take your time today, shop at leisurely pace, don't let bright colors and fads lure you to spend. Be cautious about how you speak to a neighbor who is older. You could make a very unpleasant enemy of such a person. Telephone conversation tonight can be boring but don't cut it short in crude fashion.

2—Your career can take a new direction, become more technical than formerly. You may be asked to take instruction from someone who is leaving a job for you to step into. Be good-natured and don't worry that your plans were upset. You'll find value and progress in changes that get started now.

3—Be very conscientious about a relative who has a right to rely on you. A good day to buy small gifts, perhaps a pet for a child who wants one. Avoid big crowds in social life tonight, enjoy some small group with whom you feel intimate and at ease. You will profit from ease for your emotions.

4—Don't cross swords with an associate who has entirely different views from yours. Hostility aroused today can have damaging effects. You may have a conference in which an executive has some wise things to say about your career and your financial expectations from it.

5—You will not be content, monotonous work will make you restless. You are in danger of quitting and walking out without so much as a word. Try self-control to the utmost and get through this day. Have dinner out, see a good show with a friend. You'll forget what a dull day you've been through.

6—A surprise may come this morning but it may not be desirable. Someone who professes to love you may just be looking for selfish advantages. Best to keep cool and calm, avoid letting emotions get in your way at all. Keep busy in evening outside or with a hobby of artistic nature.

7—You may find delight in a new personality that comes into your work scene now. Someone of the opposite sex attracts you and has all the right things to say to please you. You're in with a very clever one now and it looks as though you may get in deeper and stay there even against good judgment.

8—Financial difficulties can take over, cause you to worry and possibly even send you to the physician soon for nerves and insomnia. Fact is probably that you've just over-spent and now are beginning to pay for it. No real worry is necessary if you'll just economize a little each day.

9—If married you can have quite a dispute with your lifemate about where the vacation is to be spent. This is foolish and may indicate you should take separate vacations. You may just be a little weary of one another briefly. If unmarried you may be saying goodbye for a short while to a romantic companion.

10—An unpleasant person can be in your vicinity and you may not realize just how unpleasant this person can be. If you accept an invitation for evening, you may find out. Not very good signs here for your favor. Nothing much turns out right. You'll be glad when the cycle is over and it's time to sleep.

11—A surprise may come your way, someone may show much affection. A good day to be out, drive around, have dinner somewhere unfamiliar. Conversation will be both enlightening and pleasing to your ego. Watch out if you detect any romantic sexual drift in the talk of your companion, though.

12—Keep your pace leisurely. Accidents are possible and all caution should be used with any type of machinery. A conference today can leave you not knowing whether to laugh or cry. You may be in for a change of jobs soon and this can be the beginning of an adventurous path you are destined to follow.

13—Church or meditation may not help to cure the doldrums you are in for today. Buy some reading material, go for little walks, chat with the neighbors. Still it's a day you'll feel at a loss. Your spirit is low but you have no really pressing trouble. Evening may bring sudden uplift and exuberant happiness.

14—A friend from your past may come back into your life and try to renew the relationship. Chances are this wouldn't appeal to you at all. Be kind but don't encourage this person. Be very attentive to anyone dependent on you today. Accidents can be quite bad for small children in the family.

15—Hard work can vex you and yet you may come through without a mistake and win much praise. Value yourself highly enough to make an approach about more earnings. It's the kind of a day to take a slight risk. Good chances of winning are here but there's also good sportsmanship if you lose.

16—Don't listen to hearsay. Don't repeat gossip. You may be questioned by someone very clever at winning facts from others even when they try to keep secrets. Be prepared to walk away if such a barrage of subtle questioning starts. A quarrel would be undesirable, so silence is golden about all this.

17—Wonderful day to get out into a rural region. Do something refreshing. The healthy things of life appeal more than the sophisticated today. You'll like the country better than the town. A telephone call this evening can be interesting in line with some of your creative work.

18—A large responsibility may come your way. You can be asked to handle finances for an older relative. You may receive a gift that you would rather not have. A sense of humor will help some but also keep your habits healthy. Avoid snacks and don't skimp on well-balanced, wholesome meals today.

19—Let prudence rule. Steer clear of any financial plans of others, particularly a neighbor. Don't talk too much to children, for they will repeat your words in the wrong context and distort your meanings. The evening is best spent at home, enjoying a restful atmosphere and recalling what you have to appreciate.

20—A fine day for creative projects, optimism and new insight into how to go about getting the effects you wish to achieve. You may encounter someone you haven't seen for a long time and this can be an inspiring meeting. Don't prolong conversations when you see others ready to bring them to an end.

21—Handle tax, insurance, savings and charge account matters today. It is also a favorable time to move into a new home, particularly one at some distance from a former residence. You will get much cooperation and good will from anything you do connected with domestic matters and help you need.

22—Don't be gullible today. Also, don't encourage a mood you may have for nostalgia. Try to work ahead steadily without being introspective. You may enjoy some unusual favor from an executive who has been observing you quietly. A good evening to be out and enjoy friendships of close nature.

23—New romance may enter your life unexpectedly and in an unusual way. There is little chance this will become anything permanent but it could give pleasure for a month or so. On the other hand, if your loyalty belongs elsewhere, you are urged to turn down romantic invitations of anyone new in your life.

24—A neighbor may want to borrow too much and you can learn to your sorrow that this is not the type of person who is returning what is borrowed. Try to get through the day without making a mistake of this or any other kind. Evening is purely sociable and very pleasant in a romantic way.

25—Your interest in a certain subject may be the source of a new friendship. A telephone call you make to get information can eventually lead into this ideal friendship. A day when things happen behind the scenes and bring about changes you won't be fully aware of for some time to come. Quite pleasant.

26—Something you expected in the mail may be delayed. Don't let your temper get out of hand. You may also find you have made a mistake of a personal type and that you would have to make a major upheaval in your entire life style in order to rectify this trouble. You need the best philosophy you can evoke.

27—You'll waste time and mental effort if you let yourself become afraid of some new circumstances in your life. Let things pass on over and you'll find there is no threat to your safety. Trust an older neighbor. You may have a chip on your shoulder and this will simply never do.

28—Your personality is working at its best, you'll win new admiration, make new friendships and possibly enter upon a really serious but slow-moving romantic experience. Someone at a distance may call you tonight and conversation can be delightful. Much affection is shown you throughout cycle.

29—You may have only yourself to blame for a blunder that has tied you down in a way you dislike. To escape from this complicated situation may take time and thought. Don't do it just by impatient, tactless behavior. Do some reading tonight and you may achieve some new, useful ideas.

30—Don't worry about what other people think. You must protect yourself today and think of your future security. Avoid asking favors of any neighbor. You could be denied such a favor and into the bargain have some embarrassing things said about your attitude. Be wise, serene, honorable.

31—Take it easy with romance or marriage. There can be some tension, jealousy, and angry accusations. If you can keep these things from maturing, you'll do well. Getting out of town by yourself for awhile might serve, but the mere act of going might cause emotional upheaval from your loved one.

AUGUST

1—A lovely day when you will be at ease, find money difficulties disappearing, enjoy your work and be able to buy something you want at a bargain price. You are favored for major changes now. A friend may have news for you this evening that will end the cycle with complete happiness.

2—You may find that an expensive possession has lost its appeal to you because of changes the times are bringing. Don't take this too much to heart; it isn't like you to be materialistic anyhow. Take good care of what you have and don't pay attention to the latest style or other news.

3—Church or a philosophical chat is a good idea, but don't express yourself too freely when talking to a friend afterwards. You'll get little but rebuff for remarks you might make. Get outdoors this afternoon, do something nice for neighborhood children. A little picnic can please everyone, provide a happy memory.

4—Someone might try to start a quarrel over literally nothing at all. Laughter is the answer you can give, but that can create real anger in your antagonist. Well, that's the way it is and you may find some pleasing excitement in the attitude of another even though you deplore it at the same time.

5—Be speedy today or you'll really fall behind. The day is one that whizzes past and you must whiz right along with it or your reputation for talented work can suffer. Be friendly with a newcomer on the work scene but don't interrupt your activities to talk a lot about conditions and problems.

6—You may be in one of your most restless, unreasonable and aggravated moods, might even walk out on your job. This tendency is one to get a grip on and be more mature about. Try something new for social life tonight and be anticipating that rather than tearing up the scene at your place of work.

7—You can make a new and loyal friend if .you wish. Unfortunately, Cancer always has it in the back of the mind to keep moving on, so you don't worry too much about constancy and loyalty. You'll be doing yourself an injustice if you take a flippant and superficial mood about anyone today.

8—Make sure that all you say is truthful. Someone with an excellent memory can easily catch you in a falsehood if you change a story today. Keep busy with work; your diligence will be noticed favorably and that is your best bet for the entire day's activities.

9—Buy something that attracts you, perhaps a pet. Do not go too far in this direction, though, such as buying two of them. It's a day when being rational isn't exactly your mood and you could load yourself down with a burden if you yield to impulsive desires and impulses that arise suddenly.

10—You may prefer to rest, stay at home and see no one today. Thinking over the future can make you a little glum for you don't see much progress to be made. This could lead to some inspiring idea about your career, perhaps the thought of further training to develop a basic skill profitably.

11—Good news from a distance may bring you extra money that will come in very useful just now. If your car needs special repair, get it done today, don't delay. Keep up your style and general appearance; a trip to the beauty salon is good. Accent your glamor and you may attract a new love.

12—You may have a large favor done for you; don't feel obligated, for that would embarrass the donor. Your life is going through subtle transitions now and you may sense the fact that the atmosphere is changing for your thought and attitudes. This is all to the good so don't struggle against what is new to you.

13—Someone may be very unfriendly, and this can tempt you to try your skill in creating friendliness out of this chilly atmosphere. You'd be foolish to waste your time; you can't win; look forward to seeing good friends tonight or having a date that is really the big time where you're concerned.

14—Mail and telephone calls may deluge you. You can become highly nervous due to many interruptions, many requests for help. Do what you can but don't force yourself to go on helping when exhaustion sets in. Going to a friend's home for a party is all right tonight, but don't give one in yours.

15—A good day to move your residence. You can get help and save expense, find yourself in much more desirable quarters. If you want to buy attractive things to furnish this place, do some planning about it first and make sure choices of color are right. Cultivate a new neighbor's friendship.

16—Cheer up an older person who is gloomy with some sincere compliments. You can do a lot of good today just by being yourself since your disposition is a real ray of sunshine now. You'll find, indeed, that if you laugh the world laughs with you and what more could you ask for than this healthy virtue.

17—An irritable and self-centered person may be very hostile to you today. You may feel that this person deeply dislikes you but could be wrong about that. Don't adapt any strong attitude yourself, just smile and drift with the tide. No harm will be done in the long run if you remain pleasant.

18—A wish may come true this morning. You can be astounded at the way life fits in with your mental pattern and hopes. Excitement, adventure, profit and romance may all be here. Real-estate transactions go just as you wish them; all investments you consider can bring worthwhile rewards.

19—Health may be somewhat delicate and you may have to keep activities to the minimum. Even though you have little appetite be sure to eat enough for vitality. There could be a low-grade infection making you feel weak. Work can be difficult, your eyes may seem to burn, you may have to go home early.

20—An older relative may do something very pleasing for you. The work day is a happy one for your spirits are lifted and health returned. You may issue some spontaneous invitations for this evening and find a charming group of guests making the day perfect. Your best nature is showing now.

21—Romantic interests may mount a bit higher and you may learn more about a person in whom you are concerned. Whatever you think today, chances are it won't be your thought for very long. A friend may try to play Cupid but you can laugh that off. Be yourself, enjoy the cycle, but don't make decisions.

22—Keep up with the news, accept an invitation to a special show. The day is one for culture and the arts, so enjoy your opportunities in this direction. A family member can be unpleasant this evening. Someone very possessive and tyrannical may try to direct your life in a subtle way.

23—Don't go out of your way for anything today. Keep a well-planned course and allow no one else to interrupt it. You may have a neighbor who imposes upon you; see to it that this doesn't happen today. You may be amazed at the petty gossip going on in your neighborhood this evening; it's amusing.

24—A sudden new romantic turn may arrive. You can be taken completely by surprise by someone who expressed admiration for you in an appealing way. However, things may not be so pleasant if you get to know this person better, and that is unadvisable. Go your way without being influenced at all.

25—Word from a distance may bring help you need for a financial matter you think will not lose. You can be very happy over a risk you take today. It may require a few weeks before you see the direction your luck is headed but keep courage and faith; they're useful no matter what happens.

26—A small child may please you very much and you may plan a surprise for this child. It is a wonderful time to give your attention to little ones. Make your home a scene of festivity for a little while tonight. You'll be repaid by sheer fun and your natural affinity for the little ones.

27—Where your efforts don't succeed don't waste much time. The world is full of a lot of things today, so take your pick and make it one that will really bring rewards. A glamorous date tonight may be pleasant but you can find reasons you won't want to see your companion again, so be a little chilly.

28—A wonderful day for travel, adventure, money and romance. You have a cornucopia of good fortune tumbling its contents out for you now. Enjoy life and don't seek to go farther than that. Live for the present, make the evening sparkle a little with glamorous clothes and your own charming personality.

29—A very crude person may make a remark you consider inexcusable. Maybe you're just being tested for some reason; perhaps someone wants to find out how thin your skin may be. It's a good idea to be sophisticated enough to take everything the day offered without a visible sign of noticing it.

30—A good day for changes of the major type. You may invest wisely, tie up your money as security so that you cannot get at it easily. The time is good for changing your job, finishing up an old one or starting a new one. You may travel quite far to take up a better position in your career.

31—Difficult to get stirred into action. You're in the mood to be exquisite in detail of your appearance and this is good. It's possible your name and picture may be in the paper as the result of today's events and talk. You may feel a little on guard about all this and you could be right at that.

SEPTEMBER

1—An emphasis on communication will bring some splendid messages of good news. Perhaps the result of a former inquiry will come in very favorably. Before the day is over you will have cause to rejoice, for your career is on an upward trend along most congenial lines.

2—A good day for planning, and getting your mental picture clear and firm about future activities. Put down in writing any rather detailed matters. You can see advantages and disadvantages better this way. The late afternoon and evening are excellent for companionship and conversation.

3—A day which is busy, swift, but happy. Many people will come and go in your life, some contacts being pleasant surprises. You may encounter old friends and commence associations formerly broken by circumstances. The evening holds romantic promise and gay social life.

4—A good day to get personal chores done, go shopping, plan a party which will allow you to use your originality. People will be very pleased and your popularity will soar. Concentrate on unusual refreshments served in attractive new ways. A very pleasant evening.

5—Not a good time to venture far from home. If you must travel, take all precautions and avoid any thoughtless or pleasure-seeking tendencies. Plan carefully, do not be friendly with strangers. Try to humor members of the family whose health is not at its best.

6—Good aspects are mingled with tricky ones. Trust your emotions, follow your impulses. The influences can bring you some happiness where you had not planned. However, avoid business, litigation, chats with people whom you do not care for. Save the evening for loved ones.

7—A good day for beginnings. Partnerships will flourish if commenced today. Marriage will be permanently happy; new friendships get off to a favorable start. Sincere relationships are stressed, and you can trust your own judgment in all dealings with people. A surprise may come.

8—Another good day to make progress, especially in business. You will have a keen sense of values and a practical point of view to guide you in transactions. Be courageous today and investment can bring a good profit. Your self-confidence will communicate itself to the family.

9—Financial trends continue in your favor. You may receive an exciting gift or legacy. Make no plans to dispose of it as yet, and don't let generosity or desire to spend ruin this favorable period. Be wise, slow to act, and take thought for solid security. A happy evening.

10—An expansive day for many interests. Personality will bring you to the attention of an important person. You may gain new prestige by a brief speech you make to a group. Your poise and attractive appearance may catch the eye of a person of the opposite sex tonight.

11—There may be problems to solve before the day is over. Apply yourself seriously to any domestic difficulties which arise or which you know have existed. Be reasonable, discuss matters without heat or bitterness. You may arrive at a satisfactory conclusion by night.

12—Outdoor activity will interest you today. If you attend a gathering, you will probably be given the opportunity to take part in a progressive plan to gain more pleasure and benefits for others. Lend all your talent gladly, for you will find happiness in this way. A day for unselfishness.

13—There may be many temptations today. Frivolous people can lead you away from your best interests and possibly into real danger. Avoid all recklessness or companionship with reckless persons. Refuse invitations for the evening, and plan to be with the family, TV, reading.

14—Adventure can bring excited pleasure today. You won't find plans being kept, for spur-of-the-moment action and change will be more important than any scheduled actions. You will find harmonious help in carrying out ideas which come to you through imagination tonight.

15—Unhappy hours for friendship, love and domestic life. There may be sad breaks in close relationships. Words will be spoken which will be regretted. Do your utmost to guard against taking part in this trend, but, on the other hand, do not struggle too much against odds.

16—A return to cheerful spirits. Many doubts will solve themselves automatically. You can talk to people without a barrier of preoccupation or selfish interests interfering. Expect affections to be shown, for you will be pleased with gifts or messages bearing love.

17—A fairly good time for business and surprise in romantic matters. You may learn that what you planned on cannot take place. Try to be philosophical and gracious. By evening emotion may calm down. Retire rather early this evening if you can possibly do so.

18—The aspects bring influences for your personal life. Make it a day to take care of your grooming, dress well, buy a few new clothes and accept a pleasant invitation for the evening. You may meet a new romantic interest and love at first sight is possible now.

19—Unusually good hours for starting a journey, planning a special treat for a group, giving pleasure to friends. Any enterprise will bring successful happiness today. You will feel zestful, energetic and imaginative. Rewards will be abundant for the job you bring today.

20—Go out after what you want today. You will find the atmosphere congenial and win respectful ears. Your personality will be assured but tactful. You may gain more than you expect. However, it is a rather romantic day later on, and the evening will be sociable.

21—There may be a major change in your life because of today's favorable events. An opportunity can be very unexpected but exceptionally beneficial. A time when swift decision will be wise and trends just as swift to show you how right you were. Celebrate tonight.

22—A happy day for family matters. You can know a great deal of harmony, enjoy plans which you share, and have the warmth of affection which is expected from ideal love. Financial increase is indicated by these influences, also, and this may be in a surprising form.

23—You may follow an impulse and find profit, but do be wise and follow the right impulse. Take thought for family security, and be sure that investments are not proposed by those with false motives. Do as the family wants this evening and all will be very harmonious.

24—Keep to your schedule today, and avoid unconventional behavior. A day when reputations will suffer, even from chance words with no particular meaning. Choose speech carefully, and even then realize that there will be misunderstandings. Try to maintain good nature.

25—Neighbors, in-laws, children and even strangers can be quite irritating today. A young member of the family may cause expense which seems needless. Try to be understanding. If a neighbor complains, be reasonable and you may win new understanding. Best to stay home tonight.

26—Home territory is best again, but avoid too much conversation with the family. Work on a hobby or some minor chore which makes the home more pleasant. The later hours may find you exhausted and feeling a sense of strain. A quiet walk nearby will do you much good.

27—A quiet day, but one on which a conference may bring promise which gives you pleasant anticipation. Good fortune for those who are in love is also indicated. You will probably have rather important plans for the evening. A good time to accept invitations.

28—If the world seems dreary, hunch up your shoulders and take a long walk to get the proper perspective. It should be easy to reach Olympian heights in your thinking now. Thumb through the classics for dramatic reading, or invite a neighbor in to watch television.

29—Happiness awaits you today. You will feel the good cheer if you rise early and take your time to enjoy breakfast, the news and leisure. Adventure will come naturally, and a change which you desire may be made with great benefit today. Absolute accord among loved ones.

30—End the month on a note of silence, if possible. Your words will be misconstrued, perhaps deliberately distorted. Eat lunch alone, avoid speaking your opinions to associates. Your job may be in jeopardy. Patience is your strongest ally today. Guard your health tonight.

OCTOBER

1—Guard against a clash with an emotional person. Annoying disturbances could upset you while the aspects are in conflict. Do what you think is best, guided by your own integrity. Watch TV shows, or catch up on your rest. By all means, try to stay by yourself at this time.

2—Avoid any show of ostentation while mixed planetary aspects vie for supremacy. Be generous and cordial, but restrain every inclination to be excessively lavish. To be truly hospitable, give your guests food instead of cause for envy. Be careful not to misplace your wallet. Avoid an unfamiliar pet.

3—A business reversal may be bad news in the morning. In fact there will probably be several messages which disturb your serenity and make you restless. Avoid urges to rush off and leave duty for another day. Take care of routine matters, work slowly and carefully, and avoid mistakes.

4—Dare to be unique in your ideas while favorable influences prevail. Let the glow of your inventiveness blaze. This is not a pep-talk but an interpretation of personal potentialities. Under proper direction you should be able to make profitable use of them.

5—The aspects sponsor happiness in thoughts. Gather inspiration from a radio program; take a friend to hear an interesting speaker, or invest in a popular novel. Fill your mind with optimism and hope for material gain. Make this an action-plus day.

6—Avoid unfamiliar places while the aspects are unsettled. A chance acquaintance may try to inveigle you into something not quite "above-board." Or, you may take it upon yourself to repeat a story that is not founded on fact. Don't buck celestial odds.

7—The aspects generate the type of vibrations that are useful to improve the foundation of a brilliant future. Business expansion, a better job or recognition of your ability may be the way to do this. Also endeavor to make this a gala day for your beloved. Contact a pal you haven't seen lately.

8—A different way of looking at things may increase your sympathy and understanding for others. Perhaps you will find your preferences changing from expenditures for personal luxuries to disbursements for the relief of the suffering.

9—Do not dream away precious hours of wishfully picturing that something will turn up. The influences are fine to estimate reality, and to work with vim and purpose. Be diligent and inspire others. The greatest philanthropy is to share courage, extend sympathy and promote good cheer.

10—Talk, think, and work. Apply yourself to a task that requires inspiration. If you need a special favor, ask for it. If you wish to audition for a special role, go ahead. Make important decisions about your future. The stars favor the Cancer-born today.

11—Arguments now can do no more than defeat their own purpose. If a close friend or relative tries to fasten an opinion on you, change the subject. If you must travel, go by well-routed highways. If you stay home, keep to yourself. Easy does it today.

12—Do not permit your ambitions to wander too far afield because disappointment may lurk even for a normal wish. Nor should you indulge in anticipation of calamities that will never happen. A middle-of-the-road policy is best for you today.

13—Help for promoting a cherished idea which has lodged in your mind for sometime may come while the aspects are favorable. Since two heads are better than one, discussion may prove to be a source of inspiration. Also excellent to buy a TV set, or to go on a trip.

14—The influences are wonderful today for attracting popularity instigated by your own initiative. Knowing that you are esteemed can help achieve wonders, and make you willing to share your bounty with those who have faith in you. Entertain in a small way this evening.

15—The trend is potent for the propagation of original and inspiring ideals. Whether you have a remarkable conception of your own or whether you cull it from the consensus of contemporary thought—find a way to put it to wider circulation. The day calls for originality and courage.

16—Focus your mind on a great ideal. The aspects are conducive to inspired thoughts and the spread of harmony. You can be a militant altruist whether you belong to a philanthropic organization or do private welfare work. You should have a deep sense of obligation toward humanity today.

17—While the present influences prevail, your faith may be inspired to victorious heights, for these celestial spheres are like spiritual mentors which guide you in tolerance and justice. A remarkable friendship may be made today. Or, you may be singled out for special applause. Hold your place with dignity.

18—Buckle down to work and forget any inner turmoil and discord that prevails. Make no attempt to force your ideas about how cash should be spent, nor insist on having your way while walking or driving on a crowded highway. Let others act for themselves.

19—Discuss, debate, argue, if someone who is imaginative or emotional is trying to influence you unduly. Beware also of inflated egoism usually superseding deflated vanity. Unless you maintain your sense of proportion, you may become jittery during the current aspects.

20—Good fortune is in a smiling mood. You may be able to find peace, harmony and satisfaction in your work today. A business vacancy for which you are qualified may come your way. Or if you merit promotion, speak up. What you say should help you to get what you want.

21—Determine to get what you want—then make a definite advance toward getting it. Caution plus initiative is an unbeatable combination for satisfactory results. The evening hours favor initiative.

22—Old conditions may be adjusted, terminated, or be the means of promotion. New and inspiring vistas may open up and idealistic or practical work may be crowned with success. However, do not cloud your effectiveness by selling your self-confidence short. Faith still moves mountains, you know.

23—You may have to make some tentative or even vital changes, but do so only after mature deliberation. If you are tempted with bargains, be careful not to pay too much for them, because the aspects are not good for speed, impetuosity or expensive tastes. Do not admit a stranger to your home.

24—Keep away from the unfamiliar now. It would not matter a great deal other than if you should listen to glittering promises and heed suggestions, it might cost a lot more than you can afford in cash, time, reputation and integrity. Only sorrow lies at the end of the primrose path of dalliance.

25—Be honest and truthful, but not needlessly frank for you may have to differentiate between nefarious influences and authentic conditions. Build for the future instead of arguing about the present, and keep at it, because steady application will bring steady returns. Take everything in your stride.

26—Do not come to quick conclusions as the aspects are under pressure and it is discouraging to go back over ground you traversed before. Take care that your personal belongings are safe and hold aloof from anyone with whose integrity you are not familiar. "Safety-first" is today's useful motto.

27—Do not fight Fate or speak out of turn today. You might cut off a valuable business connection if you are too opinionated. Say nothing controversial either, in what you write, and if you travel make sure that your car is in excellent condition.

28—Merit progress through the exercise of good judgment and efficiency. You may feel gay, contented and ready to lead or follow toward the "mount of enlightenment." Splendid cycle also for beauty treatments, purchasing jewelry, cosmetics, clothing and plastic surgery.

29—Set a high standard and believe in its attainment for the influences generate splendid help to pick out the best fruits in the mental and psychological farms, despite stubbles and weeds. Push your plans with confidence as you seek to trap success in its lair.

30—The planetary opposition is a warning signal against family arguments, business dissension, gloomy attitudes, useless complaints, greedy demands, rancid gossip and lovers' quarrels. Silence will be the best prevention against giving offense.

31—Listen to sincere advice but do not jump to conclusions or allow others to force their opinions on you. Be careful of what you say, because the simplest expressions might be so garbled on repetition as to be unrecognizable. Be careful of electrical hazards, and watch out for lighted candles.

NOVEMBER

1—Despite a busy working schedule allow ample time to fit recreation into your routine. Keep discussions on an impersonal basis rather than risk inviting discord. Although you may worry a lot, events should work out to your satisfaction.

2—Make needed repairs or replacement to prevent future trouble with mechanical or electrical equipment. Set a goal and work toward it regardless of the obstacles you have to overcome. Unless you adhere to prudent policies, you may be tempted to buy something now which would be better to resist.

3—Avoid any obligation which involves the use of credit or borrowed cash. Direct your efforts along constructive lines by doing something which is both practical and profitable. Be prepared to make changes in your present work setup if you expect to make satisfactory progress.

4—Insist on adhering to the correct procedure when negotiating a business matter. Let your actions speak for themselves rather than try to impress someone with words. A little extra forethought and planning may enable you to make substantial gains in your work.

5—You can find inner satisfaction from aiming for and fulfilling a cherished desire. Work with optimism rather than waste time worrying about failure of your efforts. Be exacting and avoid rushing to show satisfactory progress.

6—Refuse to agree with a financial transaction unless you are in full possession of all viewpoints and facts. Proceed cautiously and avoid letting hasty inpulses cause you to act unwisely. Do not completely depend on assistance from others regardless of what has been promised to you.

7—Be careful of what you say since the meaning of your words may not be interpreted as you intended. Seek recreational activities that will give you an opportunity to make new friends and find interesting diversions. An excellent day to participate in pastimes that will develop your social prestige.

8—Your personal problems may require more attention than the demands of others. Sympathy and consideration while dealing with others would be appreciated just as much as financial generosity. Despite your anxiety to get things done, avoid taking any chances that would jeopardize your present position.

9—For best results, adapt yourself to the plans of others instead of insisting that things be done your own way. Turn your personality into a useful asset while striving for the things you want. Look ahead to the future progress that is possible for you instead of worrying about your past mistakes.

10—Be accurate and cautious in matters which concern your job or income. Take immediate care of your obligations rather than put them off for later attention. Obtain all pertinent facts before making a promise or taking on a new responsibility.

11—Be particularly careful in your conversation to avoid saying something that you might have to retract later. Go out of your way to maintain a cheerful attitude as long as you keep those around you in a pleasant mood. Do not let an argumentative discussion get out of hand despite your interests in the issues at stake.

12—Arguing with an arbitrary person may prove to be an unnecessary waste of time and effort. Insure satisfactory headway in your work by checking each detail and leave nothing to chance. Control any desire you may have to spend money lavishly merely for the sake of showing-off.

13—Rather than rush around aimlessly, catch up with your letter-writing or reading. Instead of showing resentment to criticism, put the suggestions you receive to good use. Take situations and events as they are without becoming unduly annoyed.

14—Make good use of your abilities by working on something that can show them off to advantage. Spend your leisure hours in restful relaxation, instead of rushing around with nothing practical accomplished. You should find that today can be as pleasant as you are willing to make it.

15—Be conservative in your approach, rather than yield to over-optimistic thoughts. Do not volunteer advice since your unsolicited opinions may be received with resentment. Do not worry about expected inconveniences until you actually experience them.

16—Reserve your opinion in a controversial issue since your comments might not be appreciated. Offset a feeling of personal frustrations by keeping your aspirations within practical limits. Do not be hesitant in asking for a favor to which you feel you are entitled.

17—Be particularly careful while handling and performing responsibilities entrusted to you. Prevent possible trouble by limiting your transactions to people whom you know to be reliable. Before purchasing anything new, check it over carefully for flaws.

18—Let others tackle their own problems if giving assistance means that you will be placed at an inconvenience. Make your requests in a firm manner so that there will be no room for erroneous impressions about your wishes. Do what you can to sponsor mutual accord and promote harmony for all.

19—Take ample time to think things out before saying what is on your mind. Avoid making hasty decisions. Refrain from purposely participating in any activity that could antagonize someone who is in a position to help you. You can obtain better results through friendly understanding than by voicing strong criticism.

20—Seek guidance from an experienced person if you doubt your own judgment concerning a difficult problem. You can find increased enjoyment by making inexpensive plans to improve the attractiveness of your home. Avoid attempting anything for which you do not already possess the required skill.

21—Do not place yourself in a disadvantageous position by ignoring a promise you have made. Do not allow your progress to be slowed or allow yourself to become sidetracked by petty details. Handle routine matters quickly, and do not give them a chance to pile up and cause confusion.

22—Keep a close watch on finances, and control any temptation to part with your cash assets. Maintain a calm attitude and do not let present disturbing situations get the best of you. Use effectively the hours you have by pressing for achievements that are within your reach.

23—Adhere to well-regulated schedule so that time will not slip away without giving satisfaction. Keep thoughts to yourself so that you can prevent interference with your plans or wishes. Be particularly careful to guard against the loss or misplacement of anything of value.

24—Trifles can seem tremendous now so avoid magnifying the importance of something that has gone wrong. Take time out to enjoy things, regardless of how enmeshed you are in your work assignments. Maintain a congenial attitude while dealing with others no matter how irritable they appear.

25—Set aside ample time for thinking and planning despite the pressure of arduous tasks. Arrange your schedule of tasks so that you can get the best results with the least amount of effort. Take care of responsibilities without delay rather than yield to a feeling of restlessness.

26—Contribute effective suggestions, instead of risking antagonism with words of criticism. A humorous and friendly approach on your part should prove helpful in getting what you want. Adhere to regular activities since considerable annoyance is likely to result if you seek variety.

27—Concentrate on expected accomplishments for the future rather than dwell on what you have done in the past. Do not let your preoccupation with one problem detract your attention from other important matters. Refuse to let a momentary whim cause you to part with the major portion of your cash assets.

28—Face responsibilities with the determination to see them through despite obstacles. Do your best to offset inefficiency and loss of time by keeping things running on schedule. Avoid acting in too much of a hurry even though your thoughts may be racing at top speed.

29—Do not let the discouraging remarks of a dissatisfied associate spoil your enthusiasm. Take immediate steps to clear up any mistaken impression others may have about you. Guard against being placed in a difficult position by the actions of an unreliable person.

30—Be conciliatory in your attitude, and adjust disagreements before they get out of hand. Go out of your way to avoid unpleasant surroundings and temperamental people. Do not take a chance on something unknown or that is outside the limits of your capabilities.

DECEMBER

1—Revive a dormant financial ambition which has a good chance of success. Unless routine jobs require prompt attention, devote your efforts toward practical future achievements.

2—Regardless of how restless you may feel or how anxious you may be to get things done, do not let your emotions dominate you. Be patient rather than assertive. Avoid anything that would be considered startling or unconventional. Shun publicity of any kind.

3—Engaging in social pleasures can help pass the hours pleasantly. Since a good time might entail a considerable cash outlay, strive to keep costs to a minimum. Watch your budget to avoid exceeding your allowance for amusement.

4—Take time off for fun, romance and friendship. Rather than concern yourself with problems and worries over which you have no control, enjoy life and all that goes on around you. Adapt your plans to those of others and join in a pastime which can prove mutually pleasing.

5—Regardless of how irritated you may feel, try to prevent any cause for a dispute in your home. Keep objections to yourself, and refrain from making antagonistic retorts, even though you may not agree with the way someone is handling a situation.

6—A discussion of household matters with members of your family can help to clear up reasons for dissension. By making compromises on important issues, things should work out to your benefit.

7—Give little heed to the emotional troubles of another. Instead, concentrate on keeping away from scenes of tension. Do not stir up an unnecessary fuss and keep away from persons and situations where trouble is likely to develop.

8—Too much assertiveness on your part could develop strong opposition to your plans and give rise to serious antagonism. Maintain a patient attitude until the pressure against you subsides.

9—Refrain from making any changes in your work program or taking financial risk, if there is the possibility of jeopardizing your career. Foolhardy moves and vacillation may prove costly, as well as time-consuming. You may find that the wisest and most remunerative policy is to adhere to conservative practices.

10—Control an inclination to do things in a big way, regardless of how enthusiastic you feel. Avoid forcing yourself along at a pace that is more rapid or of a greater magnitude than the one to which you are accustomed. Fast progress can be made through slow, careful action.

11—Aim your thoughts away from personal matters rather than give into a feeling of pessimism. Bolster your self-confidence by thinking of the future and what it has in store for you. Help others around you who are experiencing difficulties. You may find that your own worries will minimize and that you will have reason to be cheerful.

12—Do not take anything for granted, regardless of what others promise. You may encounter selfish motives that will quickly reverse your trend of thinking. However, seek competent guidance where a matter of money, property, or business is involved.

13—Investigate carefully the projects you wish to undertake and the goals you desire to achieve. Get rid of the feeling of doubt and frustration and respond to your goals with all the initiative and enthusiasm and confidence of which you are capable.

14—Whether you are engaged in conversation or writing a letter, avoid saying anything where you could place your prestige or popularity in jeopardy. If you feel you must express exactly what is in your mind, do so with the utmost diplomacy. Avoid stirring up trouble merely to have your own way.

15—Do not let present setbacks in your work interfere with your optimism over gains you expect to make. Let courage and confidence be the basis for your actions. You should find that actual and anticipated obstacles may vanish. Good work, well done, at this time can bring you unexpected compensation.

16—Organizational and property matters may bring a hectic day. However, place emphasis on clearing up present responsibilities before giving further consideration to new undertakings. Pay bills and collect debts, even though such action may not be to your liking.

17—Make a break away from conditions which have been restricting you if you feel that a change will prove advantageous. A well-planned shift in your plans should produce expected results. If things do not work out at first, do not lose confidence. Renew your efforts with greater determination.

18—Employing slipshod methods and taking hasty action could result in more trouble than you had anticipated. Calm deliberateness is necessary to keep your work program running smoothly. Friends and neighbors can offer helpful financial advice.

19—Demonstrate your affections for someone who is close to you by discussing your inner feelings. Feel free to express yourself since your sentiments will be appreciated. Favors or courteous action that you can offer others can help to make this a day of genuine pleasure for you.

20—Concentrate on tasks from which you can derive financial benefit. Do not lose time through idle or inefficient efforts. Take adverse reactions and impressions you encounter in your stride, rather than look for trouble by fighting back.

21—Prevent unnecessary complications, confusion and dissension by adjusting your plans so that they will conform with those of others. Take arduous duties in your stride, and do not complain about extra hours or work that may be required of you. Make changes.

22—Keep your mind and imagination busy by planning for a successful future. By combining your originality and creative abilities, you can do much toward attaining much progress in your career. Methodical and well-coordinated efforts can pay substantial dividends, providing you do not give in to periods of temporary laxity.

23—Your going on a shopping tour to complete your Christmas shopping could yield satisfaction. You should be able to obtain choice articles at substantial savings. Forget about personal worries, and do some of the things which can keep you in a happy frame of mind.

24—You can do much in the way of practical accomplishment in your job, provided you do not crowd too many activities into a limited period. Allow sufficient time to complete each task without having to hurry or be under pressure. Keep an eye on details.

25—Due to the complex aspects both solemnity and merriment should characterize this day. Let festivity reign, but be mindful of those less fortunate. Kindness will be repaid at a later date.

26—A multitude of pleasurable moments is emphasized through association with family and friends. You can find relaxation and satisfaction in being with others. Rather than take part in solitary endeavors, seek the stimulation and entertainment possible through spending your time with congenial companions.

27—Traveling in connection with your job or business can prove to be a profitable venture. Also, taking a short trip for pleasure could be enjoyable. Ignore worrisome situations, and plan to make this a period of worthwhile gains. Recreation can be stimulating.

28—Regardless of how anxious you may be to help someone having a difficult time, take care of personal needs first. Let others attend to their own problems, if it means that by giving assistance, you will be placed at an inconveneince. If, however, you feel you are in a position to be of help, altruistic projects are favored.

29—A good day to demonstrate your talents if you feel you have abilities which are not being put to full use. Use your accumulated knowledge and previous experience to advantage. Show a willingness to accept guidance from someone who is in a position to give you a helping hand.

30—Prevent discord and frustration by carefully adhering to a well-regulated schedule. Everything should go according to your expectations, provided you do not participate in extraneous activities. Whether you want to buy something or complete a project, work toward the realization of your ambitions with courage and optimism.

31—Social excitement, novel ideas and romantic charm activated. Hours may be rewarding personally. Enjoy life as it is offered to you. Greet the New Year with hope, faith and trust.

Leo

July 23rd-August 22nd

A high, leadership position,
the center of the stage,
the applause of the crowd
are matters of happy delight for you.
You love to manage things,
to be an authority.
Warm generosity
allows you to help many
and this gratifies your need for happiness.
You like your opinion
to be the basis for action by others,
your word to be law
in family matters.
A responsible position
in community or church concerns
make you happy
and you do your best
to win honors thus.
You're at the peak of happiness
when you know
you have a band of admiring,
loyal friends.
Using talents
to entertain and win praise
is another source of happiness
for you to tap.

Astrology, Horoscope, and Dreams

Leo

JANUARY

1—Take things as they come rather than jump to hasty conclusions. Seek recreational activities that are close at hand, instead of going far afield. Settle disagreements about money before they get out of hand.

2—Seek a change of pace. Promote an atmosphere of friendly companionship and congeniality among your family and friends. Make the best of difficult conditions rather than risk more trouble by trying to dodge them.

3—Rapid headway can be made in your work but do not fail to stress accuracy. Budget your working time carefully so that you can get the maximum from each hour. Keep occupied with something that challenges or stimulates your mind.

4—Yielding to the whims of an imposing acquaintance can prove costly. Work things out for yourself instead of acting on the advice of another. Spend time on budget matters and adjust your spending program to meet current needs.

5—Determined efforts can help you smooth over the strain caused by mental and financial burdens. Make arrangements to replace worn-out possessions with attractive new ones. A conciliatory attitude could prove helpful in almost any type of activity with which you are occupied.

6—Clear up unfinished tasks, even though you may not feel in your most energetic mood. Take obstacles in your stride rather than cause dissension by complaining about them. Minimize wasted motions and meaningless conversation so that you can make this a day of practical accomplishments.

7—Proceed slowly and cautiously, even though a splendid rate of advancement is possible now. Give consideration to the future and what you can do to provide for your financial security. Emphasize efficient procedures and plan each move before you act.

8—You can achieve extra benefits by adjusting your plans to conform with those of others. Unselfishness can pay off, so help your friends all you can. Avoid taking anything for granted, particularly where your job or income is concerned.

9—Settle money matters with finality rather than allow allow them to drag on. New ideas and improved methods of doing things can prove unusually effective. Pay attention to the suggestions offered to you, since they will probably be to your advantage.

10—Adhere closely to prudent policies, to prevent quarrels and emotional tensions. Guard against mistakes, because any that you make now might place you in an embarrassing position. Remain diligent in your efforts, even though tempers may be frayed under the strain.

11—Refuse to let emotional or sentimental feelings affect your judgment in a financial matter. A bold expression of your ideas may lead to more trouble than you would care to handle. The purchase of an expensive article is likely to give you less satisfaction than was anticipated.

12—Concentrate on getting cumbersome routines cleared up so that you can pave the way for more enjoyable activities. Tackle responsibilities with determination regardless of how distasteful they may seem. Have complete confidence in your own conclusions where money is concerned.

13—Keep a close watch on your possessions, particularly cash and small articles of value. Devote time to a hobby or other activity that can keep you away from annoying persons. Keep your thoughts cheerful and your enthusiasm at a high level so that those around you can share your enthusiasm and optimism.

14—Show little hesitation in insisting on having your own way. You should be able to get what you want. Pay close attention to minor details despite the swiftness of events moving around you. Devote attention to needed repairs and alterations in your home or place of business.

15—Satisfactory results are possible from following customary procedures; do not try to be different. A patient attitude is needed to prevent temperamental outbursts. Concentrate on major issues of your work instead of wasting time on minor matters.

16—Be cautious while handling electrical and mechanical equipment, to prevent the possibility of an accident. By forcing an issue, you may only succeed in turning an advantage into a loss. Disregard thoughts of social pleasures until you have taken care of your duties.

17—Make your purchases carefully and do your best to get maximum value for your cash. Plan to do something that can serve as an outlet for inspirations and be a worthwhile goal for your ambitions. You may find it wise to listen rather than to take an active part in a controversy.

18—Do not shun your duties or avoid taking care of necessary obligations. Extravagant or impetuous moves may lead to more trouble than you anticipate. Take disappointments in your stride and think about advantages that may soon be available to you.

19—The poise and diplomacy you display can help strengthen the admiration others have for you. Refrain from taking any chances that might adversely affect your income or savings. Seek competent guidance about a problem rather than take things for granted.

20—This can be a favorable day of entertainment, ambitious thoughts, and fulfilling your desires. Place emphasis on achieving first-class results in whatever project you undertake. Keep yourself occupied with tasks that offer immediate financial benefit.

21—Do not be discouraged if your plans fail to mature as rapidly as you would like. Control restless feelings and beware of emotional entanglements. Regardless of how annoyed you feel, do not let your irritation affect others.

22—Remain in the background. Be reserved in your approach rather than aggressive. Refrain from making drastic changes and keep your energies in reserve.

23—This is not a favorable day to break away from conditions that have been restricting you. Hold firm to your purpose, even though others may persistently attempt to disrupt you. Do not be discouraged if the results of your efforts are at first ignored by others.

24—Avoid taking any chances with money that is entrusted to you. A strong feeling of pessimism about household matters can dominate the scene unless you personally take charge. Aim your attention toward keeping associations with others on a pleasant level.

25—Arrange to take time out during the day for relaxation. Express your viewpoints about money clearly and back them up rather than avoid discussion. Give attention to personal and home needs and make every effort to keep things running smoothly.

26—Avoid entrusting personal responsibilities or duties to another. Schedule your tasks so that you will have time to complete each one without having to rush or work under pressure. Practical thinking and conservative action are necessary if you expect to make satisfactory headway.

27—Your resourcefulness and skill should enable you to accomplish a difficult task without trouble. Patience and calm understanding of your problems are needed to produce gratifying results. Discipline yourself to a rigid schedule for accomplishment and do not allow your self-control to lapse.

28—Any attempt you may make to keep things running smoothly for someone else may be considered as interference. Do not let minor problems detract from what could otherwise be an enjoyable day. Do what you can to instill harmony among those in your close circle of friends.

29—Take necessary action on job matters that are pending. Do not allow yourself to be inconvenienced by another. Changes that you make in your home should prove to be pleasing.

30—The achievement of a cherished ambition can come as a surprise. Increased pleasure is likely through association with family and friends. Take part in social or recreational activities that can be shared by those around you.

31—Conservative action can help to keep things running efficiently in your home. Steer clear of hectic situations and let others handle their own problems. Give consideration to your future as well as to your present duties.

FEBRUARY

1—Strange events and unexpected telephone calls can keep you busy today. You may be curious about one telephone call and decide to follow up on it to discover more. This could lead to a new, exciting relationship.

2—An old acquaintance you encounter today may prove more interesting than in the past. Friendliness is in the atmosphere and you may be more outgoing than usual. Entertainment in the home of a new acquaintance will be pleasing.

3—You can be dissatisfied with work because you feel unable to use your true talents and are being kept too much on routine. Your manner can be sullen and may win disapproval. It would be best to put your case to an executive for a clear explanation.

4—You may feel like shopping for some expensive item, but it is a day when you can easily waste money through faulty judgment. Look around more and check prices. Avoid any type of action during both the day and night.

5—A valuable possession can be damaged. It is better not to handle prized items that cannot be satisfactorily repaired. also avoid an ostentatious manner when among associates and neighbors. You could lose the respect of an intelligent person.

6—Much excitement may be in the air for you. A new romantic situation may just begin to blossom a bit. However, before you even think of letting this go any further, make sure your affections are sincere and meaningful.

7—Be slow and sure with work; concentrate on the present. Temptation to let your mind wander in anticipation of dreams coming true can be harmful to your interests. Complete tasks efficiently and then get ready for a big evening, perhaps a brand-new date.

8—Disappointment about a domestic matter can make you sad. This is one of those days when you feel as though nothing goes right for you and that this is because of some discrimination against you by the gods. Strive to maintain an even keel and common sense.

9—Be very pleasant in conversations; do not bring up troubles that are nagging at your mind. You can dispel much of your gloom by listening to others, trying to be helpful and viewing your own life optimistically.

10—Use your best business sense today; you may get somewhere with an idea you've been milling-over. You can be inspired today, but you need to pick up and choose carefully among the products of your imagination.

11—The details count today; take good care of them and an executive will favor you. Have an eye for things others miss and an ear for remembering some interesting things someone else has said. A surprising reward here!

12—You may have to go back over some work and fill in facts more concretely. Do not let idlers interrupt or consume your time. This evening a telephone conversation with someone of the opposite sex may bear fruit.

13—You can err in thinking that something that happened in the past is entirely over. In fact, you may be in for a new start that is just the real beginning for a fine relationship. Avoid having inflexible ideas today.

14—A good day for shopping, but examine items thoroughly for quality and workmanship. It is a good evening for social affairs and romantic happiness. Don't get involved at all, though, in a dispute that may arise suddenly.

15—Today there could be an upheaval in the family. There is a threat of incompatibility, and although you feel it strongly, you will probably keep silent. One of your silent, obstinate moods may take over tonight and it's just as well.

16—An experience of the day can be baffling but have some charm. Your romantic life is a busy one now and your chart is filled with signs of difficulty in making choices. Allowing things to drift will not work out well.

17—You may have to give up an inspired thought for the present due to practical needs. Your inabilities as a worker and earner are under examination and you are urged to be as solid in your efforts as possible. Appreciation will be shown.

18—Avoid any type of complaint or criticism today. You may not have much sympathy with the actions of an associate, but your criticism can make things worse. Avoid any big plans for the evening; family members need you.

19—Be generous, helpful and cheerful. Let your best nature shine out and be an inspiration. In a romantic situation show nothing but affection. Even if a little cool, you can lighten the heart of one who loves you.

20—Someone may take unjust advantage of your position and try to make your life unhappy by stealing an idea and using it before you get a chance to act on it. Total silence may do some good later.

21—You could feel that you are not really important to anyone today, and that can bring bitterness. Express yourself to a true friend and you may get words of help and encouragement. You need the strength of philosophical thought.

22—A visit or call from an old friend may revive a companionship that was always pleasant. Today and this evening you may find conversation the most fascinating ever. Be sociable and show loyalty to friends throughout the day.

23—You may be in a lethargic mood and even cancel a dining-out arrangement. You might be indulging your own sloth too much, thus allowing happiness to pass you by while Moon is square on Jupiter.

24—Be open to new ideas, avoid insisting on tradition, and cooperate in work that is a new endeavor for you. In these changing times you can count on a change in work schedules as beneficial. Write a letter this evening.

25—You may be asked to undertake a task that will put you in the public spotlight. If you feel too timid or nervously worried, consult a physician quickly and you'll get aid. A certain sense of pride in what you do this evening may develop.

26—Trouble with machinery can make the day bleak. Make a telephone call and you will get everything corrected without further cost to yourself. Be courageous tonight for you may be faced with a situation that calls for faith.

27—Punctuality is the big thing today. Some very good things may be passed around, and, if you're not present, you'll be left with only the less desirable things. People have a certain amount of the unscrupulous in them now.

28—You may have a big party in the making for tonight and must not get tired beforehand. Take it easy with work; avoid all rush. Things will turn out beautifully and everyone will be happy—pleased at the care you show for them.

29 (Leap Year Only)—Your neighbors are important to your happiness today, and you will find substantial profit from sharing views and activities with them. Do not hold aloof, even from neighbors with whom you do not feel quite in accord. All activities in your own community can bring rewards.

MARCH

1—Being too practical is not always good and this is one of the days when it is beneficial to heed more mystic and enchanting influences. It is a time for mental and spiritual growth, new faith and much generous tolerance.

2—You may suffer a minor defeat. A relative or in-law can cross you up in aims or desires. You may be quite angry but are urged to act in a mature and understanding way. Admit that you are not always in the right in your motives.

3—You can be too anxious about certain matters and this can bring on illness of such degree that you'll need to see a physician. A sleepless night signals that you must get some expert help to calm your nerves quickly.

4—A good day to get out and mingle freely, meet new people, take part in community affairs, spread your reputation for service and hard work on behalf of others. Someone of much interest may contact you this evening.

5—Prayer or religious meditation is almost mandatory and your companionship is needed by another this afternoon. Let the day carry you along, be harmonious with what it brings and unselfish with your sympathy. You can wind up a good day by evening.

6—Take no chances now. Do your work but don't take on extra burdens. Avoid making a telephone call that is motivated by curiosity. Do not be too out-going if a new neighbor calls on you this evening and is quite talkative.

7—You may be given a chance you have long wanted. Your excellent taste, powers of discrimination and ability to organize things for best effect will be used advantageously. You will win new admiration, possibly an increase in earnings.

8—Be sure to do something to cheer a person who is in the midst of misfortune. Take consideration of the young today and try to adapt your personality so that there will not be any possible communications difficulty.

9—A telephone call you make can bring information you need. Financial affairs will go well and it is a good cycle for a new investment in something substantial. Evening can have an experience that you would rather do without.

10—A problem can arise about helping a younger relative. If you are too helpful you can dull the edge of ambition. It may be best to consider yourself first. In social life protect your personal views if they are attacked.

11—A neighbor may not be at all the kind of person you think. Treating someone as young and innocent can be quite a mistake. It is best not to become involved today and to skip a social invitation or become involved with romance tonight.

12—Use your memory to salvage a creative project. Yot can be quite wrapped up in what you are doing today. A product you make can be very attractive so that there is a large market for it at some time in the near future.

13—Your health needs protection. If you have any type of cold or virus it is wisest to stay at home until your health returns in full. If you are well, avoid the company of those who are not so well. A hazardous day here.

14—A good day for shopping if you keep your mind and eye on quality. Avoid rushing into a purchase just because it seems to be a bargain. Write a letter to someone at a distance who is having trouble. Be very encouraging.

15—Someone may warn you in a subtle way about something undesirable that could happen. Be wary of your own obstinate optimism. You can have startling results if you persist in ignoring facts about other people at this time.

16—Go out of your way to help an associate who is mixed in some tangled work mistakes. You will be able to see the core of other thinking about appropriate birthday gifts, considering prices and the like. The later part of the day is excellent for making a few brief visits where you know people are lonely and gloomy.

17—Your day will be busy and successful in career affairs but you may be regretting the fact that you accepted an invitation tonight. It is best to keep promises and also to control your impulses to criticize.

18—A fine day to shop, begin thinking about appropriate birthday gifts, considering prices and the like. The later part of the day is excellent for making a few brief visits where you know people are lonely and gloomy.

19—Sacred music or a quiet social gathering will please you and conversation afterwards should not be cut too brief. Give your time to others a little more freely today. Ignore it if someone makes a remark about the way you use your time.

20—Your estimate of a person may not be very pleasant. You can be right but you must not show it. If you ignore this person it will be noted and you will invite hostility. Better find a tactful but brief subject to discuss for times when you meet.

21—Tackle a long, monotonous job and it will be completed sooner than you think. Avoid day-dreaming and too much going off on tangents of any kind. Your evening may be adventurous due to someone new who enters your life now.

22—Health may be a problem now. It is possible that you may eat something not properly preserved or drink something that is contaminated. Be very cautious where water comes from; it can be best to carry a thermos of it for quenching your thirst.

23—Good news from a distance will made you proud and happy with a member of the family. Be generous in giving a gift; make someone else feel free from financial worry. Keep your mind far above all petty selfishness.

24—A long talk with an executive may persuade you that you should do something to improve earnings. A special training may be acquired without expense. Go along where you see there is wisdom and benefit for you today.

25—You may have to rush quite a lot and this can make you angry. Younger relatives are inconsiderate and may keep you on the go too much. When evening falls make it clear you are not going to do anything further today.

26—Someone envious may speak in spiteful fashion. Do not heed this brazen and ill-willed person. You may be able to enjoy a healthful walk. Stay aloof from others somewhat, keep your meditations at work and uninterrupted.

27—A good day for clothes buying; you can pick out a luxury to bring much pleasure. Keep a romantic companion or lifemate in mind when you choose colors for clothes. Buy a surprise gift for a child you love deeply.

28—Routing may be unbearable but your determination to carry out a project will keep you on the track. Your personal life is taking on a new interest and all you can really think about is your romantic attitude and opportunity.

29—Be more straightforward than usual, do not try to hedge about anything or to keep secrets from a loved one. You could bring about an unpleasant situation if you insist too much on having a life of your own selfishly.

30—Be ready to take what comes even though a change is not what you want. Be patient with today and later you can work out things more as you desire them. If you have a romantic date tonight, you may have to make a decision.

31—Be very honorable, keep promises, make your word as good as gold. Use your strongest character to avoid the temptations which friends hold out to you. Someone may be wanting to get you to fall into a trap now.

APRIL

1—You may be called upon to do some supervising which will make you proud but can be quite difficult. Concentrate on the task and not upon your own feelings. There may be a visitor tonight who tries to give advice you do not want. Find a way to remain pleasant even though bored.

2—A romance or any type of partnership formed today can have great success, lead to an enduring relationship and happiness. Be your own out-going self and show your pleasure when introduced to someone new who attracts you. A day when many things in your life may undergo change.

3—A wonderful day for success in work and a chance to use skills that have been in need of polish for some time. You may receive most sincere praise. Bask happily in the light of approval from influential people. Do some shopping, if possible, for your taste is at its best, though costly.

4—Get in touch with someone from your past that you would like to see. You might find this happening before you know it, due to a long-distance call you make. Interest you show in another person is important, but it's most important to know your own mind and be guided by it entirely.

5—Instead of resenting dull chores and brooding about them, let yourself daydream a little while you are doing domestic tasks that are somewhat automatic. A party you plan for evening can turn out well, bring an enduring friend into your life but don't be extravagant about food.

6—New circumstances in your neighborhood can make you quite contented. You'll be happy in a relationship, feel more secure due to friendship that is given you now. Best not to talk too much with a lifemate or romantic companion. You might talk about all the wrong things, bring on a quarrel.

7—A conference can make you rather unhappy about a choice you must make quite soon. Although your thoughts may wander about and try to escape essential facts, you'll no doubt end up realizing there is only one real choice—the one connected with cold, hard facts, about money, your financial standing.

8—Try to be very courteous to an associate even if you feel envious and unfriendly. If you show hostility in your work area, you will regret it soon. Do your very best work for an executive who asks a special favor. Avoid becoming involved in anyone else's emotional life tonight.

9—Keep your thought clear, your speech brief. An associate may be watching for a chance to trap you in an error. Check everything you do before handing it in; think twice before every word you speak. You can have serious consequences from today's adverse aspects if you fail anyone.

10—You can be in one of your very light and heedless moods. Inclined to sit around and chat without any real thought behind it all. You're after pleasure and this may show up so much at work that you are highly criticized and even threatened with losing your job due to malingering.

11—This cycle is good for domestic matters, shopping for decorative materials, using your skill to make things for the home and save money. You will get a lot of admiration from guests this evening if you give a very small party. Be cautious about one who seems romantically fascinated now.

12—Do some repair work where your own skills are adequate and then make a mental list of repairs that you must get a professional to do soon. Check everything in the home for safety. Be cautious about pets, don't trip over one. Also, be careful if out walking with a youngster today.

13—If you attend church try not to linger afterwards. Also do not feel offended by anything that is said while you are at church. You can feel somewhat defiant and inclined to show obstinate independence this afternoon. Perhaps you are on the verge of a romantic separation and showing it this way.

14—A task you have no taste for may be dumped in your lap by someone who doesn't care in the least about your feelings. You can be kept on a monotonous routine throughout this cycle and be ready to explode at quitting time. In fact, you may consider quitting for good and actually do so as a result.

15—There are some fine aspects for you in the financial world. If you'll control desires to spend and start saving for a special investment, the information you get today is excellent. Find some pleasure in saving even though you never have before. A good time to start this habit.

16—Your natural good manners and the courtesy in which you were trained in home background show up very much to your credit today. You can be in a tense situation yet manage to keep serene and polite, poised and attractive. This is your clue for handling surprises destined to arise now.

17—An excellent time to travel, to make money in a spot distant from home and to get a promise that will be kept about financial affluence in your future. You will never forget this day because of the aura of success and the facts that follow your efforts to succeed. Looks good all the way.

18—The cycle can be romantic almost from the time you arise this morning. You feel sparkly and gay, ready for something new in the way of romance. There is every chance you will get it and be surprised at the manner in which a new relationship gets its start. You're definitely attractive today!

19—Avoid putting focus on trivial things; you need to put important things in the foreground of your thought. Don't hesitate to talk things over with an older neighbor you believe is wise. On the other hand don't rush to take advice, for remember your life is its own separate entity.

20—Take it easy today, get outdoors, if possible be around a calm body of water. Your health will benefit from a change of scene and invitation from a rather new friend can be just the thing to give you this welcome change for the afternoon. Best to keep evening free so you can retire early.

21—Give full credit to someone who has a good mind even if it is not trained. Show esteem for those who deserve it and be willing to listen carefully. Latter part of the day is attractive for shopping and bargains can be found. In the evening do not be too generous in giving things away to a neighbor.

22—You may find yourself daring enough to tackle a big venture without telling anyone else about it. Go slow with this! It might win so much disapproval that you'd have to do everything all over again backwards. You may be wise to stay away from home as much as possible during this strange cycle.

23—A letter you receive can have news that makes you a little envious of a member of the family. You want too much today, as is often the case with Leo. You are not likely to get fulfillment of a desire about travel, so don't build up hopes or be belligerent about the impossible now.

24—Treat all elderly people courteously. You may be surprised by the consequences of being nice to older ladies who may admire you and find your personality delightful. This is an evening when romance may bloom, a relationship you thought was ended may be started again and make you happy.

25—You can be sluggish in your attitude toward all work today. A slow start, no enthusiasm and some cynical remarks to associates can create a lot of gloom in your atmosphere. Be more realistic, work hard, smile and be pleasant. Evening holds marvelous romantic anticipation, so enjoy it.

26—Do not make any promises or take on any new responsibilities impulsively. You're too generous with yourself and your time. Avoid a neighbor who likes to visit and chat inconsequentially. Do not let anyone pry into your personal life, your past or your intentions for the future.

27—A know-it-all who lives nearby can become hostile to you because you don't accept the words of wisdom offered. You can laugh about this in private but if you laugh at the other person face-to-face you can bring on a lengthy feud you do not want. Make it a cycle to be moderate, discreet.

28—Some change in your environment may be cheerful. If you are working in the vicinity of a new group you may find them much more congenial than former co-workers. There is a good chance you will be given the opportunity to learn the operation of a brand new piece of machinery. Grasp this quickly.

29—Investments made today will prosper and flourish, aid your security for a long time to come. You have an astute attitude toward money and although it doesn't show, this is the central concern you are dedicated to now. Be gracious and pleasant with all neighbors tonight, avoid dispute.

30—You feel like a million and would just love to be off to a distant point. You may be before the day is over! A surprise will arise and change your plans, free you from burdens. It's an exciting day one which promises vast change in your life. You can welcome all this with open arms.

MAY

1—Take a close look at your position with an eye for improving it. Your thought is clear today and will allow you to make excellent plans for the near future. Take a loved one into your confidence this evening and discuss things of practical nature. You can be excited with results.

2—Don't go in for strenuous activity today but be content with neighborhood affairs, some people dropping in casually. A very generous person may give you something useful and your appreciation will be in order. Talk pleasantly to relatives or in-laws over the telephone this evening.

3—News about finances may be good but may have a catch also. Don't be resentful about hard work that is left to your responsibility. Be glad of a chance to express your opinions and use talents independently. There is promise of a romantic message coming through during the evening.

4—Control your inclination to be on edge with associates. Don't let your speech be irritable. Keep the good will of everyone around you. If a favor is asked, grant it quickly. You may need to consult an expert in legal matters about a problem that has been puzzling you in recent days.

5—Someone new in your vicinity may prove very delightful in companionship, honest in speech and view, generous in material ways. Cultivate such a relationship and you may have much gratification in a loyal friendship. Be thoughtful about the good things in your life this evening.

6—Worry about trivial matters can warp your day. An effort to control such a trend will be rewarding. Avoid letting a habit of unhappy attitude grow now. Be cheerful with cheerful companions. A good idea to have dinner out with congenial friends and take in a show afterwards.

7—An opportunity that comes your way can be more valuable than it appears. Think things through and do not jump to any conclusions. Social life or a trip this evening will be pleasant. There may be a romantic trend that puts things on a new and more serious basis in love matters.

8—Listen well to what is said in your presence. You can pick up an inspiring idea from a business acquaintance. If you feel depressed this afternoon, it can be a good idea to talk over your situation with an older person. Heed a suggestion that is made even though it doesn't appeal.

9—Be wary of safety hazards in the home. Walk carefully, keep your eyes open. If you drive stay well within speed limits. If married there may be an argument threatening late in the day; don't encourage such a trend by too much self-expression about dubious desires you have.

10—Give sympathy to someone with an emotional problem rather than being bored with the story. Your optimistic views may help someone else get over a bad situation. In romantic matters this evening, guard your reputation, be careful about activities, avoid all excess in eating and drinking.

11—An introduction that is made today can be quite exciting. You're just ripe for falling in love at first sight, but make sure that the love is based on the person rather than on affluent circumstances of which you are aware. Avoid being materialistic in inclinations now.

12—Deception may be in the atmosphere at work. A person who is envious may be gossiping about you and you can sense it. Do not let this matter come to a showdown, but pass right on through it with poise and serene spirits. Nothing can harm you during this cycle.

13—Monotony and discontent may fill the day. Do not be slothful in work but fulfill demands and complete an assignment of importance. Complaint about money may not win you much, but "nothing attempted is nothing gained." You're rather caught in the middle about finances.

14—Someone whose thinking is not clear or exact can make a mistake that involves you and your hopes. Find a tactful way to mention this and all will turn out well. Use a pleasant approach in all conversations, be agreeable and you'll discover the benefits good nature has for you.

15—You can be very happy about circumstances in the family. News is all to the good. It's a fine time to buy gifts for those you love, be thoughtful and considerate in shopping instead of selfish about purchases. The evening is best spent in a restful way; avoid big plans.

16—Great effort may be needed to get through vital tasks. Be conscientious and thorough in what you do to improve conditions. Take good care of children dependent on you. In the evening you may be torn between two choices, let true desires dictate your course for tonight.

17—Don't give anyone a false impression. If you are not interested in a romance, don't encourage it. Making a friend of someone who does not appeal romantically is a good idea. You are at your wisest today and all decisions will be based on practical and true facts of your life.

18—A wonderful chance for new training may arrive and you can be happy with work that comes easily to you. You will be keeping very up-to-date with work matters and the chance to increase your earnings will be part of today's package. Enjoy domestic life this evening, relax thoroughly.

19—Neatness counts a lot today, aim for perfection in all you do. Someone rather new to you may show much affection. Follow up what promises to be a good romantic trend. Be independent in judgments and course of action. An older relative may interfere; try to keep good natured.

20—A difficult task may be faced and you can feel weary just thinking of it. Bestir yourself, keep busy and it will be all over before you know it. Praise and encouragement will compensate for strenuous efforts. Follow an opportunity to be generous with a neighbor tonight..

21—Don't neglect seeing a physician if your nerves are bad and you feel exhausted. The trends show possible need for medication. Relief from troubles will be gratifying when you get professional help. Do nothing to worry a romantic companion about your loyalty this evening.

22—There are restrictions today and you may have to compromise instead of following your desires. Show how well you can cooperate when necessary. A large social gathering this evening can be delightful. Make a good impression with your most becoming clothes, shining grooming.

23—Follow your whims and moods a bit now. Do pleasing things, be luxurious. Conversation of casual nature can be enjoyable and may hold a surprise bit of information you can use in a practical way. It is wisest not to make any promises in connection with a new romantic trend.

24—Fall in harmoniously with plans of others. The day is neutral but pleasures will be gratifying though quiet in nature. New acquaintances may want to know you better, so give them a chance, insight about your personality. Keep evening restful for health's sake.

25—The day may be slow, dull, vexing. An executive may seem to single you out during an angry mood. Don't show resentment for that may cause trouble in the future. Be in control of emotions, don't talk much, avoid all temptations of a restless type tonight.

26—You may get help from a family member in connection with something you want to do. Take nothing for granted but show gratitude for what others do for you. You may find yourself free to follow plans you cherish. Be slow and thoughtful, progress steadily, not in spurts.

27—There may be some sharp criticism of unjust type for what you do to help another person. You can feel the world is against you; don't nurture self-pity. It is not a good evening for any romantic companionship. Quarrels and even a break-up threaten. Marriage is also pressured.

28—Show respect for older people, listen to them and think about what they say. You can find much benefit in following the suggestion of an older neighbor who is wise and practical. Think of your financial future, do nothing to undermine your own chances for financial security.

29—A happy day with carefree spirits and enjoyment of all you do. Relationships are harmonious and you'll like witty conversation about small matters. Show generosity to a new friend this evening and create a stronger bond of understanding with this ethical and pleasant person.

30—Get facts before you act in an important matter. Do nothing which you think a loved one might disapprove. Use your wisdom, avoid any action that could cause a state of upheaval. Get out some and walk around, enjoy companionship of a breezy personality that is new to you.

31—Be attentive to people who come to you for good cheer and help. On the other hand, avoid those who are irresponsible and unpredictable. You may learn something of value this evening and it may put you in touch with a new friend for the future. Be frank and open in speech.

JUNE

1—There may be something unusual to think about today. There is a good chance you will need costly repairs and find conditions helpful to your needs. This is a time to come to some wise conclusions about your own life and those around you. Be calm and slow to speak about your feelings.

2—You may receive an unusual gift and be very happy with outcome of things today. Avoid becoming too intimate with someone who seeks you out and tries to cultivate your acquaintances: You can be better off when you keep your own plans and ideas to yourself.

3—Bring yourself up-to-date in clothes and grooming. Get out some of the jewelry you have been neglecting and find a happy attitude in dressing up and showing off a little. No trouble at all when you show your sensuous and romantic nature. Have fun and you'll get an invitation.

4—Let time take care of things today and this evening. You may find that the day is much more pleasant than you expected if you just wait and let people come to you. There can be some interesting telephone conversations tonight, much better than going out in social life.

5—There can be some romantic trouble in your life today. You may find yourself completely discontented with the one you have been seeing lately, completely desirous of making connections with someone new. Take things as they come and do some analysis to get them clear.

6—You can be in a mood to discard all of your present life, your acquaintances, and your career position. You may think today in terms of the future and come to some good conclusions. You will be happiest if you uphold the dreams you have, fight for the wishes you cherish now.

7—Take things slowly and do not let anyone rush you. You need calm thought to make a decision. Someone in your territory may try to rush you, persuade you when you are not at all ready. Be adamant in your ideas and trends: all will be well if you follow personal concepts.

8—Be generous with young people in the family, take a lenient trend and do not let anything turn you to harsher movements. Be church-going and very loyal to your religious body today so that you can win full benefit from the current tides that urge a cosy friendship.

9—Be moderate in all you do, eat only wholesome food, avoid things that can upset your health. Do not let a dislike of someone connected with you in business ways grow. Be logical about all you do and say. Keep the evening for personal chores that must be done.

10—Affairs may go against the grain with you but you can have a chance to carry out highly personal desires if you tackle things in the way you know is intelligent. Be in control of whims and desires, a selective trend can bring you all that is good for your welfare.

11—Be very independent. Issue invitations as you feel prompted. An older person may try to wrangle a way into your life, but you must shut this person out. Some good directives on the way to manage your own life can be given and help this older person much in emotional matters.

12—Guard your reputation in every direction. You may feel that you are impelled to do something but must take an easy way out. You can be protecting your own welfare when everything seems stacked against you. Be very firm in the direction you take this evening.

13—Many active things are going on in your life and you do not have too much control over them. Anger with a loved one can make the day unpleasant. Why not aim for harmony and amicability? Don't press your own desires too much or you will lose out before evening falls.

14—The day can hold troubles and you may become very resentful of the trend which a work associate follows. If you are wise you will make no complaints, ask for no changes. Just follow along routine and you will find that a very observant person gives you credit where it is due.

15—You may have a very special request to make of an influential person. Be bold about such a matter and let nothing hold you back from expressing your attitude. Young people in the family may be demanding. Listen to the needs of such people and do not turn them down.

16—You will be in on the essential activities today and haven't a thing to worry about. Do not let yourself become involved in a family matter, avoid giving advice to anyone close to you. Take time off to walk a bit, get exercise and start a new health regimen if possible.

17—A romantic trend is deep and persuasive yet you may have difficulties that hold you back. It is a good time to seek advice from an expert and see where your best life trends are for the near future. Think things over yourself after you get advice, for safety lies here.

18—Someone very enchanting may enter your life but the relationship you strike up could be detrimental to your future. Do not become too friendly with anyone new today. Think over relationships and be discriminating so that you hold the upper hand in all doings today.

19—Pay debts, get finances straightened out and be proud of your credit reputation. Make a long distance call when you feel urged to do so. Be quick to accept charges from anyone younger who calls you tonight.

20—Some amusing things may happen today but it will be wiser not to laugh at them until nightfall. Keep your life balanced in all ways. Eat wholesome meals. If you dine out do not go in for the gourmet things but be sensible and you'll come out happier in the long run.

21—Family circumstances can mean a severe drain on your budget. You'll be happier with the outcome if you draw a limit to your generosity and benevolence. Take thought about the demands made upon you and don't go over the border in a sheer desire to help and alleviate.

22—There can be some emotional wear and tear, you may be trying to analyze someone who defies description. Best to give yourself up on the difficult matters today. Get in touch with someone who supports you all the way. You can begin to plan a radical change in your life.

23—Be very attentive to pets, children and a loved one. Your life may undergo a big change late in the day but do not heed to much of this. Be sure you keep your menu wholesome and do not skip any meals. The cycle is an unusual one and cannot be predicted easily.

24—You are favored for financial affairs, signing papers, following your desires in the realm of money. You will be very practical and able to manage your own affairs today. Take advantage of these aspects to get the most you can from trends of this time.

25—News that comes through today can be the utmost in excitement and pleasure. You may be driven to use your talents to the utmost and this can be the very best for your own success. Give credit where it is due in communications.

26—Someone very honorable may get in touch with you today. Do not turn down any visitor who may have meticulous relationship today. Keep your thought reasonable and be accessible to those who come to you for help. The time is amenable for your projects. Courtesy and graciousness will pay off.

27—You may get many calls today, have your program interrupted several times. Try to keep calm mental attitudes and do not let yourself be upset about financial trends. You can come out ahead if you exert your mentality in the right way tonight and wake up whole in the morning.

28—The day is very romantic and you will be happy if you keep your role in this trend. Be cautious not to speak in an angry or criticizing fashion to anyone. Be particularly careful with older people. Avoid thoughts about money and general security which may work themselves out.

29—You may undergo a tendency to undermine every position you make. When trying to be pleasant with children in the family you may find you can't carry things through. Retreat into modesty and general pleasantness. You'll stack up more advantages by accepting things now.

30—Avoid older people, keep all conversation in an amicable mood. You may be asked to take on an extra duty; do not turn down such a chance for it may be full of advantages for you. Be very kindly and dutiful in any matter connected with home or religious matters during this cycle.

JULY

1—You will be very busy, have little time for talking to others. Don't let yourself be distracted from work by idlers who want to gossip. The evening can bring special happiness with good friends and relatives who share your tastes. Pursuit of hobbies can be pleasing, bring you closer together.

2—You need understanding from a loved one. If there is a lack of romantic attention shown to you, don't be angry. Express yourself freely and you'll clear up a situation that could otherwise lead to a sad separation. When you both speak out clearly, you'll arrive at mutually gratifying sympathy.

3—Difficult to get started; you don't really want to work today. Trying any mischief to escape chores won't help you. It's best to get things done quickly and then leave the time for freedom and fun. You may have an exciting time tonight with someone romantic who challenges you in a form of sport.

4—Accept an invitation which will give you a new experience. You'll be surprised how much you enjoy a special group. Music just hits the spot with you today. Your spirits are good and you feel you have done the right thing about love. Evening can bring much happy exchange of romantic sentiments and affections.

5—An unjust accusation may be made. Someone is watching you too closely. You can erupt angrily and may walk off the job. Being too hasty can bring regrets. There is a personality clash at work in your environment; it could be costly for you if you don't control your emotions.

6—A new relationship in which you get involved can bring you unhappiness in the end. Someone may just be passing time with you while waiting for other conditions to develop. If you're wise you'll be quite aloof from new acquaintances. Don't make big plans for the evening; you'll need to retire early.

7—Money can be your big concern today. You must be conscientious about paying bills. Do nothing to upset your lifemate, if married, when it comes to spending. You could bring on a real upheaval in your environment if you insist on having your own way regardless of the funds available to you.

8—You may have a chance to see someone as they really are. A big pretense and an artificial disguise may be penetrated by you today. Seeing such facts can make you feel lucky you got out of the relationship as quickly as you did. Cheer up the evening with some unusual entertainment.

9—Big things are happening in your life. You may have a conference with an executive that shows you how high you rate. You can be unusually pleased with the way matters go for your practical benefit. Don't be on a high horse with one you love tonight. There could be a quarrel that would be just plain silly.

10—Spread cheer and sunshine around, be at your most shining-eyed and friendly. A telephone conversation may bring a marvelous invitation for evening enjoyment. If you need to take an escort, you'll have no trouble getting the one you want. It's joy all the way for you and your activities during this cycle.

11—Someone older may have a worthwhile friendship to give you. Be happy with the admiration and praise that comes your way. Circumstances may put you in the center of the stage in social life this afternoon. Don't talk about personalities or trivial matters, find some large general subject in which all are interested.

12—Analyze a romantic problem of recent days and you may find good answers to troubles. An older relative may find something to say that is just the right word for encouragement. However, do not act in a rush about anything. Let the course of events go on without interruption and you'll be pleased.

13—Make an attempt to get to church, a museum or a park even though you feel lethargic. An older person would like to see you there today and may have an invitation to extend. Take a vacation from romance for the time being; it will be a healthy change and also send you back to a loved one with a refreshed attitude and a new love.

14—Not much chance for a wish you've been nurturing. You have much working against you and a victory is probably impossible. Your friends may be right when they discourage you from a certain romantic path. Be cautious of speech with older relatives; do nothing to get them upset about your romantic life.

15—A good chance to get ahead in your work, today, and to get a head-start over others. You may hear word of a supervisory job that could come your way. Keep your fingers crossed and don't talk about this to anyone. Keep evening for some casual and brief entertainment with good friends as company.

16—You can become so busy you get temperamental and irritable. That will never do since you have fine social chances to look forward to for evening and being in a bad frame of mind can ruin the whole evening. Be very cautious not to express yourself in an ill-natured way about a future in-law.

17—You may get a chance to buy some things you have been wanting for the home. Excellent to brighten the atmosphere with new carpeting, use some decorative covering for bathroom and kitchen walls. You can make things look bright and new, find much gratification from the praise of friends and a loved one.

18—There may be a long, dull and discouraging task ahead of you. You can conquer it only by tackling it head on and forging right through. Get the best of your own feeling of monotony. Be cautious if you travel today. Driving laws must be respected; stay well within the speed limit, also drive defensively.

19—A wish may come true today! but you can be rather sorry when it does. A new friend you have made may visit you. Chances are the conversation may bore you. Be careful of drifting off into daydreams, for that way you could miss something important that will be said by someone who has an inside track.

20—Take a good look at your financial picture and consider a sound investment. No matter how small it is to start with, it will be worthwhile in the end. Be practical, think of security, listen to the advice of an experienced person. Keep health in mind today; avoid a heavy diet or snacks this evening.

21—Try to see the view of another person. You may be called upon to cooperate and having your mind in a flexible condition is desirable. Avoid obstinacy about a matter that concerns others as much as it concerns you. Put aside every selfish inclination and be generous, considerate, and tolerant of friends today.

22—You can make a loyal friend for life by accepting a person without criticism. This is a good trend and is part of your naturally generous spirit anyhow. A wonderful day for shopping, buying bargains for the home, using excellent taste to select everything. You may have an unusual message tonight.

23—Best to go slow and steady with work. There are good trends for travel after 3:00 P.M. and you might find it desirable to start a vacation then. Be sure to pay your own way wherever you go, don't expect others to shoulder a lot of financial burden. Dress very becomingly to please someone in love with you.

24—You could have a minor health upset, find your nerves on edge. It could be wise to plan a thorough check of your health for some day next week. If any emergency arises in your family, be ready to take over quickly and do the right thing. Telephone calls can be vital in your affairs during the evening.

25—A hunch you have today can lead straight to the discovery that you were right. Make sure your behavior complies with the ideas of older persons. Do nothing to upset a romance—your own or someone else's. Don't be too curious about romantic matters of a sister or brother. Above all, avoid being envious.

26—A good chance for career change may come along. Being asked to learn something new should be taken as an honor. You are considered capable of receiving training in a worthwhile field. Shop for small items today. Subscribe to a magazine, buy books and records, perhaps a plant of beauty for a special nook.

27—You can find yourself in a position that requires much tact to avoid. Don't blame anyone else; this is all your doing and you shouldn't expect another to pull your chestnuts from the fire. Be thoughtful, slow to speak, courteous and add a touch of formality. This will do the desired trick for you.

28—A surprise may brighten the morning and you may begin big plans to spend more money. It will be much better to make plans for saving first, and then use whatever is left over for some finery you want to add to your wardrobe. If married, be quite attentive to an in-law. This will bring you good fortune.

29—Try to be relaxed today and don't let tensions mount to the point where they cause sharp speech. You may have a glamorous date for tonight but it can turn out disappointingly so it is best not to even think of of any enduring relationship. Look your best, though, and be very pleasant.

30—Avoid brooding about a matter you resent. Also if you have an active social life tonight, do not ask questions that could embarrass or irritate another. Very easy for a quarrel to start and it could be a thoroughly unpleasant matter. Silence will provide your best bet, so control the talk tonight.

31—You will be given much sympathy in a practical matter at which you have tried and failed. Chances are the affection of an older relative will find a way to compensate for your troubles. This can put you on a good new path for career and affluence. Evening may have a surprise in the way of romance.

AUGUST

1—Don't even think of making a big change. Your judgment may be swayed too much by emotion. Your best bet today is to go along with a loved one's ideas and avoid resentment about it. Have some neighbors in for a game or two, perhaps some delightful snacks that you fix yourself for evening.

2—Work can be demanding and you can get angry with an associate. Better watch your temperament a little and control it. Don't feel you can get by with just anything, for it won't work that way. Be sure to show respect for your elders even though you don't really feel they are so groovy.

3—Resolve to save money for what you want. Be willing to work for the luxuries you are tired of doing without. You may receive some mail that worries you today. No use worrying for that won't help. Get busy and think of a way you can alter the circumstances that are an emotional problem.

4—It can be difficult to make connections in a trip you take today. Don't get irritable, be patient. Conversation with someone else in the same boat can help. Keep things cheery and they will work out that way. Be very careful about safety of youngsters in your charge at this time.

5—An in-law may upset you and cause you much anger. Better look again at this situation and be honest with yourself about it. It can be a question of just not getting your own way. And after all, that happens to everyone quite frequently. Don't be childish about such matters; show intelligence.

6—You may enter upon a new romance as a result of a contact today. Someone may charm you with bright and witty personality, also excellence at sports. You may feel an immediate urge toward marriage and could be quite unrestrained about this desire. Be wary! This may not be what you think it is.

7—You may be asked to handle some intricate machinery. Don't plunge in hastily; you could be injured. Ask advice of those who are older and wiser. If you have an important date tonight, don't be unhappy about a limited wardrobe. After all a new loved one hasn't seen your clothes before.

8—Parents may enter into your life in a big way and there can be a family hassle. Avoid any gesture of violence. It is not worthy of you. Be independent, though, and explain just why you feel you are right in the course you are taking. Keep all activity wise and don't eat or drink too much.

9—Be thoughtful and tactful in speech. You could say something unkind about an older person without realizing it. Probably there will be no harm done because the older person is understanding and wise. Avoid being extravagant, going in for large debts just to cater to your whims at this time.

10—Be good-natured. If married, you may need more tolerance for an in-law. Don't be offended if you are given a little unasked-for advice. Plan a new style of hair-do, get busy and seek to improve your natural appearance. A neighbor may help you tonight in a do-it-yourself project.

11—You could be accident-prone today, also too strenuous about sports or work under the sun. Best to take it easy, shelter yourself as needed. Keep food light, drink plenty of juices and don't keep late hours. Company may not want to go home at a reasonable hour; you'll have to be forceful.

12—There can be some gossip in the neighborhood that is more amusing than anything else. However, it is not good for you to get involved however funny this situation is. You may have a happy date tonight; don't put on any pressure about an engagement. Let your loved one be the one to decide the progress.

13—Facts you didn't have formerly may now arrive and allow you the chance to make a wise decision. Don't be too materialistic about anything. A relative is not to be trusted in an offer that is made today. Think about a trip that interests you and get ready to make a decision about it.

14—There may be a flurry of activity in your vicinity; you can be getting ready for something big—a journey. Excitement and anticipation will take over and keep you elated. The evening will bring help and you can get everything important under control, ready to go at a moment's notice.

15—Your generosity will be beneficial today so let it shine forth. You'll have a good time with a congenial group of pleasure-seekers this afternoon. A member of the family may object to your friends and this can make you very obstinate and loyal-as you have every right to be.

16—Go slow in all that you do. Being taken off guard could cause a drastic error and setback. Be ready for what comes with an answer that is well thought out. Make sure to tune in on the mental today and keep physical matters in the background. You may win new laurels.

17—Money is accented. If you lend it you'll never get it back. Think of your loved ones; don't deprive them of anything rightfully theirs. Do not be vexed if a loved one criticizes you justly. A good cool discussion can be quite helpful to married life if you are married; be willing to talk.

18—An interruption may set you back in plans. Don't be angry, this just means about an hour more of work later. An argument could arise with a neighbor this evening; don't let that happen. Be practical, steady and dependable today. Put all nonsense out of your thoughts about romance.

19—You might become unhappy about a choice made recently and you could stir up trouble if you don't curb your temper. You have no right to assume things about another person, so don't just take for granted someone else should follow your lead. Avoid being on your high-horse all evening, too.

20—Good news can come from a distance. The trouble is it can make you desirous of a luxury. Envy can ruin your day; don't let it. A good evening for entertainment at home but don't be extravagant about it. Give a loved one a voice in your decisions and you'll keep everything happy and harmonious.

21—Avoid financial transactions today, shop only for needs and even at that be thrifty. Do not go overboard for buying things for small children just because they ask for them. You may look forward to a glittering evening and spend much time getting yourself ready to attract admiration.

22—You will regret it if you are too outspoken. Best to go into everything slowly, think before you speak or act. You may meet someone very influential who will soon be a big help to you in your search for a better job. Be pleasant with all, accept uninvited visitors graciously this evening.

23—Extreme caution about money is needed. It can be lost, stolen, mislaid or have almost anything happen to it. Keep your mind on practical matters today; don't let a foolish person lead you into pleasure seeking that is not wise or healthy tonight. A walk in your own neighborhood is best tonight.

24—Aspects are not good for your physical welfare. A tendency to be nervous can lead to ways with children that are harmful and unjust. Best to keep yourself under complete control, avoid all violence. Don't try to make a loved one jealous for that would only be inexcusable mischief on your part.

25—Someone may have a poor memory about money borrowed from you. Just be persistent and you'll get it back. A time to stand up for your rights, collect what is due. Shopping is favored if you keep it keyed to wardrobe items that are necessary for the coming cooler season.

26—Legal troubles could arise or you might be asked to testify in a matter where it would be most unwise. Be blunt with a neighbor and refuse to let yourself in for a dubious and put-up job involving the law. Call a good friend on the telephone tonight and your day will be cheered immensely.

27—You may be totally innocent in a matter for which you are harshly criticized. Be intelligent and let this all pass over your head. Keep your mind on work requirements; someone will be watching closely. If you entertain tonight be clever about it. Enjoy your talent for making things attractive.

28—Be careful not to endanger yourself with speed or careless handling of fire, sharp instruments, or machinery. Follow instructions in everything you do. A rather quarrelsome atmosphere exists in both love and marriage. Be forewarned and forearmed about this; strive for harmony everywhere.

29—Make it a day of rest and leisure. You need a change from those you usually see. If you can get solitude, fine. For once, Leo won't mind quiet meditation, planning and simple rest from the rigors and activities of life. Above all, don't take part in any strenuous sport, though tempted.

30—A new associate may ask help and you could be a little obstinate about giving it. Envy could be your trouble and if so, it will really create trouble for you. Best to be kind, patient and affectionate with all. Avoid spending money selfishly; think of the family if you go shopping now.

31—Good news about money may come and one of your hopes seem much nearer to coming true. Don't jump the gun on anything and be sure to wait so that you can act harmoniously with a loved one's approval. Do not talk to strangers or go to unfamiliar places in pleasure-seeking activities tonight.

SEPTEMBER

1—Look for progress in these hours when your energy and eagerness will keep you forging ahead. Contacts made today will prove profitable in the near future. Discuss plans with a person who may be able to help more than you expect. Excellent time for partnerships and domestic life.

2—Your ideas will prove imaginative and beneficial when you talk them over. All will be harmonious among associates and sincere affection will be shown by loved ones and relatives. Personal relationships are favored. Engagement may commence this evening. Plan on romance.

3—The aspects usher in a trend which can bring you profit and rewards for former activity. A cycle for fruition of plans. Get all in good order and control your impulses which might take you off on a tangent. Not very good for romantic relationships tonight.

4—Worthwhile advice can be gained by listening closely to others. Neighbors may plan an important part in the happiness of the day. A shopping tour can win you bargains. Look for an appliance you have been needing. You may find a rare buy and be greatly pleased. Entertain at home tonight.

5—A lack of understanding may prevail in the family. Difficulty in seeing other peoples' points of view may make it a day of tension and conflict. Try to restrain impatience and temper about plans which seem senseless to you. If possible, go your own way and let others do likewise.

6—The hours will go swiftly in pursuit of new interests. A day of adventure and surprise. You will be able to satisfy your desire for action and progress. Romance, too, may take an exciting turn. Be dressed attractively, use your personality intelligently. Things will happen.

7—Today opens on a high note for good fortune in the life of Leo. Surprises which bring you closer to an important goal will occur. Messages may mean the beginning of a new phase in your career. All attempts to grasp opportunity will meet with unusual success.

8—Another good day for social life, career progress and a turn of events which may mean a change in your environment soon. Talk over opportunities, but postpone decisions. Seek expert help if need be on a problem which may turn out very profitably. Litigation is favorable.

9—The hours tend to involve you with financial plans which will mean a lot for your future security and affluence. Chances of investment are excellent. You will use your courage and do what is necessary to win new income and bank account augments. The family is harmonious.

10—Your plans may undergo a last-minute alteration which is pleasing. Travel is favored today, and the start of a journey connected with business will bring pleasure also. You will be willing to go along with the needs of others and find a suitable reward for efforts.

11—According to the ephemeris, it is all right to seek advice, but be careful that you do not let it make you too optimistic. Excess enthusiasm may prove costly if misapplied. Be particularly watchful while moving through congested traffic, and put out lighted matches with care.

12—Make this a day of unselfish interest in those who need your companionship. Your vivid conversation and genuine affection can do a lot to cheer a lonely or ill person. If a friend has emotional problems, your point of view may settle down in a pleasing way. Rewards will come.

13—Best to call a halt to activities, avoid speaking of your hopes, seek solitude and be thoughtful as much as possible. You may find emotional confusion about problems entering the picture. Impossible to see your way clear in certain personal matters. Stay home tonight.

14—You can count on good news today. Conversation will be pleasant, too, and all means of communication are favored. The atmosphere is one of pleasure rather than laborious work. Take time out to enjoy the companionship which will be available. Accept an invitation for tonight.

15—Trends do not favor business enterprise. Be very cautious, and don't let any reckless urges cause accident or litigation. Avoid speech with neighbors, for everyone may have a chip on his shoulder. Be very gentle with children and use tactful means if they are mischievous.

16—Make strides in career plans. You may be in for a promotion, but it will be a good idea for you to make sure that you get it. Seek conference with an important person, and express yourself clearly. Your merits will win recognition when you show your ambition.

17—The morning may be a bit gloomy and your disposition rather on the unpleasant side. Avoid intolerance of associates, for any show of scorn can bring much trouble later. The afternoon will bring more cheer, and perhaps a desired promise. Spend the evening with the family.

18—This is a favorable day under the present auspices. Leo can expect personal happiness, emotional serenity, romantic events. This is a time when your dreams can come true if you have been hoping to win the love of a certain person. New romance can begin this evening.

19—A favorable period for enterprises which take a bit of daring. Visit someone of extreme importance, make long distance calls, send telegrams. There will be a speedy and favorable response to your needs. Family and friends will bring much happiness in social occasions tonight.

20—A rather pleasant day when you may hear good results of conversation with an executive. You may be starting a climb upward when it may be slow, but it will suddenly catapult you into a high bracket. Your pleasant nature and personality will win romantic laurels tonight.

21—Avoid neglecting family duties. Church or meditation can be a source of irritation and even of conflict, if you linger to talk to people. Relatives may seem to be vexing and far too demanding. Do what you know is right, but refuse to let others trample upon your freedom.

22—Blessings of an unusual nature may come your way today. Exceptional contacts may start you on a new road to prestige and honor. Accept all conversation in a serious spirit and be ready to cast your lot with a new group. You can gain great rewards through your ideas.

23—Be very sure to take care of responsibilities, and the day will go well for your projects. Carelessness is not tolerated today, so handle details efficiently and thoroughly. You may meet a new acquaintance of the opposite sex who will prove to be a sincere friend. Write letters.

24—Unfortunate hours for physical welfare. An accident may cause financial loss as well as painful and perhaps hospitalized injury. Avoid speed, refuse to travel with those who are careless or eccentric. Abide by the letter of the law and avoid all excesses rigidly.

25—Go out of the house as little as possible, hold tight to money. Many people may be trying to gain false profits and you can find your generosity imposed upon even by a good friend. Make no large loans and promise no aid to anyone who approaches you. Watch TV tonight.

26—Another very favorable day for Leo. Get out early, use your assets. You will strike just the right note when a business transaction is in question. Your high ethics and sparkling personality will win a new friend who is very valuable. Give time to society tonight.

27—It may be wisest to let others take the lead today. You can hear some interesting news, but do not become involved in circles of gossip. A rather good day for personal projects and any plans for entertainment will come off well. Be a bit of a spendthrift to make friends happy.

28—Do not be critical about the inattention of fellow auditors at church or a lecture you might attend. You might lose sight of the magnificent thought expressed by the speaker. With the aspects in full power, find a tactful way to prevent personal involvement in the schemes, plans and acts of others. Say "No" and mean it.

29—There may be a special surprise in today's correspondence. A relative may send a gift which is just what you wanted. There are going to be unusual incidents which promise much profit. Enjoy the day but also be alert, for surprises can elude you if you are not there to grasp them.

30—Be very careful in conversation with an associate. You may find yourself saying things which can lead to severe trouble about your job. Do not criticize executives or other important people. Avoid talk of a controversial nature and keep opinions to yourself. Retire early.

OCTOBER

1—If you feel that you must talk about a private matter, do so with an understanding friend or a sympathetic neighbor. Do not confide in anyone who can misinterpret or repeat what you say. You might be penalized or balked while the current aspects prevail.

2—Tackle work that you can accomplish alone. Assistance on which you had reason to depend, might be refused. Don't wait for reluctant help. Emphasize the humorous rather than the exasperating side of a domestic situation. Tonight, watch TV shows or go to the movies.

3—A very slow pace is required. Your health can be injured from nervous tension and too much activity. Refuse to let anyone talk you into a rather reasonless plan. Avoid anything that might lead to litigation. Be very polite, lock up valuables and look forward to a quiet evening.

4—The stimulating vibrations created by the planets should arouse your ambitions. You should be willing to undertake extra work or deny yourself pleasure in order to accomplish a definite purpose. Plan for long-range security rather than for immediate gains.

5—Keep your aims within reasonable limits. Wait for your plans to work out according to your expectations before you begin to boast about them. Caution is necessary not to overestimate your capacity for carrying out big things in a big way since the influences are in opposition.

6—Place no faith in the honeyed words of those who seek only your assistance for ulterior advantages. If you meet with objections or refusals, your natural resourcefulness should help you find a suitable corrective. Shop for dress accessories, purchase phonograph records, and write letters.

7—If one thing peters out, try another. Variety is the spice of today's contribution to your career, so do not allow hindrances to stand between you and attainment. With the aspects mixed, have two smiles for every frown you meet. Think, act and dream success.

8—Your magnetism might be strong today, since the current aspects are very active. However, do not allow your imagination to lead you to useless expenses, which you certainly cannot afford at this time. Do one thing at a time today, and do it well.

9—Combine entertainment with education by arranging a party that will give your friends an opportunity to prove their knowledge. This can be a means of enlarging your fund of facts, particularly with dynamic influences in power. Wear your best clothes tonight.

10—You might bask in the spotlight of popular approbation today due to the harmonious planetary influences. Friendships might lead to new professional progress. Go to the local cinema tonight, or tidy up at home. Chart next week's course with confidence.

11—According to the ephemeris, it is all right to seek advice, but be careful that you do not let it make you too optimistic. Excess enthusiasm may prove costly if misapplied. Be particularly watchful while moving through congested traffic, and put out lighted matches with care.

12—Try to sidestep unnecessary obligations and debts, but meet each payment cheerfully. Handle the most important part of your program before noon. If others are short-tempered tonight, do not let it affect you. Keep serene and confident since there are better cosmic vibrations on the way.

13—An inspiring appeal may prompt you to open your pocketbook for those in distress in this period when the aspects are uncertain. Also, a meeting to discuss a publicity campaign will not prove very valuable. Watch for the unsuccessful signals which loom nearby.

14—Forceful planetary influences prevail. You may be able to get what you want if you are clever and sincere. Matters associated with love, adventure, romance, home and plans for the future are under star-friendly approval. Start early and turn in a revenue-yielding performance.

15—An excellent day that calls for collaboration with a friend. Business or professional associates may be unusually cooperative, so put forth your best efforts for achievement. Also, favorable to subscribe to your favorite magazines and to watch thrilling TV presentations tonight.

16—Your inspired thoughts can be worth a king's ransom. Concentrate on work that requires "trigger-quick" calculation. An associate may suggest a brilliant and profitable idea. Your combined efforts should enable one of you to attain a measure of fame and fortune.

17—A favorable outlook prevails for spiritual meditation, discussing important matters with the members of the family, planning business strategy, writing letters to executives, asking for special favors and concentrating on career matters. Elegant grooming goes along with the tempo of the day.

18—Impatience may cause your good judgment to take a faulty slant. Do not make a reckless promise or you may toss away a rosy chance by being too impulsive. The trend is favorable, however, for buying toiletries and hobby material.

19—There is cosmic promise of success in matters associated with traveling, teaching, acting, painting, sculpting, singing, designing, working, playing, experimenting and debating. You may meet a wonderful person destined to be a life-long friend. This is your day to enjoy the limelight.

20—With the current influences in opposition, you might have a tempestuous flareup about a mistake you have made. Instead of losing your temper, convert your impatience into energetic work. Hold fast to the job that brings you regular pay.

21—Take no business risks this day. Also, postpone travel plans. There is a signal warning against extravagances, spur-of-the-moment promises, listening to romantic overtures of a stranger, risking cash on a sure thing and frequenting unfamiliar places. Catch up on your rest.

22—Study a technique that can help you apply your creative talent to a practical enterprise, in collaboration with a friend who has imagination and intuitive sagacity. Fluency of speech and articulate expression of thought may enable you to attain an inspired wish. Keep on your mental toes.

23—Be sure that you are aware of a responsibility that you accept while current aspects exist. If you do it lightly, belated regret about the extra duties might follow. The more you think of yourself today, the better it is for your immediate future. Take no useless risks.

24—Love is getting short shrift today. Emotional tantrums, broken friendships, unrequited love and conjugal infidelity are possible under this Garden of Eden aspect. Discretion and diplomacy will help to ward off unpleasant complications today.

25—Be patient with a relative who seems anxious to run your life. This desire, though misguided, may be sincere. Also, avoid a money dispute. Even winning the argument would hardly compensate you for resultant exasperation. Tact and patience are needed now.

26—Do not allow yourself to be goaded to anger by a selfish person. If you keep your temper you should be able to control even the most hectic situation. Relax with creature comforts tonight. An illustrated magazine, a new best-seller, radio music or TV presentations are in order.

27—Be vigilant in preventing personal rifts, yet retain the right to do your own thinking and acting. Allow others the same privilege. This is one tested way of preserving the peace. You can also contribute to the cause of harmony by not injecting yourself into other people's affairs.

28—Romance may be aroused today, and if so, it will be all right to go along with it. But do not expect a whirlwind heart affair to follow. Yet a little sentiment experienced now could have some effect on your life for some time to come. Keep alert because Dan Cupid is scurrying by fast.

29—Do nothing to incur the displeasure of those who work with you. You might be in the right but find it difficult to convince them of the justice of your position. Antagonisms aroused today could endure long after the point in question has been settled. "A word to the wise" should be more than sufficient today.

30—Your mental outlook should be extremely realistic under today's planetary setup. You may be able to estimate values correctly, or to see through sham and flattery. Pay attention to your pillow dreams. They may reveal accurate events of things to come.

31—There are some people who are too smart for their own good. Do not put yourself in this class by being unnecessarily self-assertive in seeking attention. If you try to boost your own stock, others may attempt to sell you short. Take it easy. Try to end the month on a harmonious note.

NOVEMBER

1—Keep personal plans to yourself to avoid interference. Sustained efforts should help you to make a success of almost everything you want to try. Budget your hours so that you can complete necessary duties and yet have time for fun and relaxation.

2—Avoid wasting or abusing possessions by making maximum use of each article. Follow the pattern of your normal routine rather than seek a change. Insure satisfactory results by basing your decisions on logic rather than on emotional impulses.

3—Be diligent, but cautious in your efforts to avoid accidents. Do not let momentary reverses slow down your rate of work progress. Tackle without delay disagreeable problems that you have been avoiding. Tell what you really think when requested to do so, but only in your most diplomatic manner.

4—Try to be agreeable with others even though they may express viewpoints that are different from yours. Avoid taking unnecessary chances, regardless of anticipated gains. Your impatience to get things done in a hurry may prove more of a handicap than a help.

5—Stick to a carefully worked-out schedule instead of experimenting with untried ideas. Be firm in your desire not to let anything interfere with the headway you can make in your work. More can be gained through diplomatic methods than by a display of force.

6—Temporarily defer making decisions or changes that can directly affect your financial status. Despite your interest in social activities, this is not the time to let them interfere with your work. You should be able to overcome resistance to your ideas by using a new and different approach.

7—Remain calm even though you may have to work in the midst of confusion. Arrange to start setting aside a small sum of money now if you have hopes of buying an expensive article. You should be able to find enjoyment entertaining in your home or when visiting.

8—Do not let anyone dissuade you from aiming for goals you have set for yourself. Insist on taking care of personal obligations and duties before seeking diversion. Do not lose your feeling of optimism even though things may not work out exactly as you expect.

9—You can find more pleasure now by associating with others by remaining in seclusion. Arrange to dispose of time-wasting distractions and concentrate on matters that are important. Avoid worrying about errors that cannot be rectified. Make an effort to put others in a cheerful mood.

10—Adjust yourself quickly to the current trend of events so that you can make prompt use of available opportunities. Move at a slow enough pace to insure a minimum of errors and yet not cause any unnecessary delays. Let others take the initiative, but do not ignore assignments you have undertaken.

11—Patient and prudent efforts can prove fruitful, particularly with regard to money matters. Give prompt attention to work and duties even though you may have a strong inclination to shirk them. Rather than waste time, get busy with odds and ends which you had previously left undone.

12—Be patient even though you may have to resist others who are against you. Regardless of how anxious you may be to buy something, do not let your enthusiasm lead you into extravagance. Let others handle their own problems and avoid arguments that do not concern you.

13—Refuse to take anything for granted regardless of how satisfactorily things may appear to be running. Avoid bickering and petty quarrels even though your ideas may conflict with others around you. Give special attention to matters of practical importance instead of letting your thoughts dwell on fantasies.

14—Give assistance only where you are sure it will be of help and appreciated. Insure harmonious relationships by compromising rather than arguing about insignificant points. You should be able to obtain the results you desire by uniting your efforts with the work of others.

15—Take plenty of time to think things out carefully before acting. Keep on the lookout for bargains, particularly those articles for which you have an immediate use. Fulfill obligations without delay, and make arrangements to return whatever you have borrowed.

16—Display your generosity while dealing with others, but not to the point of allowing anyone to take unfair advantage of you. Do things which you can handle adequately yourself instead of seeking outside assistance. Despite minor disturbances, do your best to make this a period of practical production.

17—Avoid making important decisions now unless you leave a loophole which will enable you to change your mind later. Remain silent while in the company of others, rather than open yourself to question. Take things as they come instead of insisting on having your own way.

18—An excellent day to do some of the pleasurable things you have been postponing. Any attempt you may make to speed things up could have the opposite effect. Wait for someone else to make the first move; do not take the responsibility yourself.

19—Industrious efforts can reduce the difficulty of your duties into relative insignificance. Take plenty of time for whatever you do, and let no one force you into making quick decisions. Be careful that a display of temperament or impetuous actions does not result in costly mistakes.

20—Despite your sympathetic understanding, do not become involved in the emotional problems of another. Arrange to avoid boredom by making changes and putting variety into your work. Do not take chances with your cash, particularly when you are not sure of the outcome.

21—Wait for things to happen by themselves rather than take aggressive action. Adhere to conservative policies since trouble may spring from sources where least expected. Steer your attention away from matters that are not of your immediate concern.

22—Devote the major portion of your efforts toward work that has a constructive purpose. Despite your anxiety to accomplish a variety of tasks, control the inclination to do too many things at once. Express optimism and cheerfulness, if only to keep those around you in a happy frame of mind.

23—Be aggressive in your own attitude to help overcome the slowness and obstinacy of others. Get the benefit of various viewpoints by discussing your ideas with associates. You may invite trouble if you yield to your emotions instead of sticking to facts and logic.

24—Offer constructive suggestions instead of openly criticizing the actions of another. Unless you can satisfactorily complete a duty yourself, avoid undertaking it. Patience is required while dealing with others since temperaments might not be at their best.

25—Avoid possible disappointment by building your plans for the future slowly and methodically. Follow your own conclusions, instead of being swayed in your views by outside opinions. Avoid possible trouble by being scrupulous and exacting when handling a money matter.

26—Be careful in what you say since your comments might be interpreted in an unfavorable light. Obstinacy in dealing with others could have undesirable repercussions. Do your own research for uncertain facts rather than depend on the efforts of another.

27—Combine your plans with those of others for the most effective and harmonious results. Avoid giving anyone a chance to hinder or delay you through a display of emotions. Regardless of adverse comments about your work, have confidence in your abilities.

28—Despite a feeling of restlessness, keep busy and dispose of tiresome tasks about your home. Steer clear of arguments that involve others since intervention on your part might arouse further antagonism. By being flexible in your plans you should experience little difficulty in obtaining advantages that are open to you.

29—Despite temporary discouragements, do not give up on a project that still has a chance of success. For best results, confine your attention to familiar things and routine efforts. Work with optimism and enthusiasm, and refuse to waste time worrying about possible failure.

30—A discussion of business or money matters with an associate may prove to your advantage. Instead of wasting time being sorry for mistakes you have made, do something practical to correct them. Rather than try to evade issues, be realistic in facing problems which confront you.

DECEMBER

1—Get things done and go where you want. Clear up the loose ends of your work so that nothing can hold you back from accomplishing your aims. Gratify your impulses, provided they do not act as an imposition on others.

2—Headstrong action involving a business or job agreement, can lead to considerable difficulty. Unguarded words and deeds might also result in your receiving adverse publicity. Make every effort to keep out of a controversy resulting from the quantity and quality of your work.

3—Although you may be requested to do a favor for a friend, your efforts on behalf of another should be genuinely appreciated. Do what you can for others who can benefit from your actions, but do not ignore your own responsibilities.

4—Devote your attention to a hobby or other project which will enable you to pass the hours of the day enjoyably. If possible get together with friends who find pleasure in the same recreational activities as you. Temporarily forget about work problems and concentrate on being happy.

5—Be careful of what you say or write, particularly where your reputation is involved. Also do not force an issue or bring pressure on others to get things done. Instead, only tactfully observe what is going on, regardless of how anxious you may be to take the initiative.

6—Harmony should predominate in your household. Discuss and make arrangements for decorative changes in your home. Alterations made now should prove very beneficial in the future.

7—Be cautious while dealing with others, since emotions are likely to get out of hand. Remain alert for deception and trickery. Care should especially be taken against misappropriation or the misplacement of a valuable article.

8—Avoid disturbing domestic conditions even though this may mean that you will have to temporarily absent yourself from the scene. You may have to be unusually patient to overcome disorganizing situations. Keep critical remarks to yourself, despite an ample reason for making them.

9—Although what you are doing may not meet with the approval of others, adhere to procedures and policies which you feel are correct. Face each problem as it arises, and try to handle it alone, rather than depend on another for assistance. This is a good day to demonstrate your resourcefulness and independence.

10—Let things remain the way they are though you may be dissatisfied with the way things in your home are running. Do not make any changes in your present set-up, and place emphasis on making the best of existing situations. You may only increase your present difficulties if you try to make too much of trivial inconveniences.

11—Refrain from starting a quarrel, even though you may have good cause to be in an angry mood. Do not let emotions interfere with your normal diplomacy, and keep relationships with others on a friendly basis. An argument now could have undesirable repercussions.

12—For an enjoyable day, visit scenes from your neighborhood. Call on a friend or relative who lives at a distance from your home. It may be a pleasant experience to look for new and interesting sights that you have previously overlooked.

13—Do not become so engrossed in your work that you ignore social matters and domestic life. Maintain harmony within your family and accede to the wishes of others when arrangements for recreation are being made. Ignore trivialities and concentrate on things which you find pleasurable.

14—Do not jump to conclusions, regardless of what others say or because of the information you possess. Allow plenty of time for making up your mind before you reach a decision or take action.

15—Avoid taking any action that will increase the burden of your present duties. This is not a favorable day to increase your expenses. Before agreeing to a large expenditure, be sure that you will be in a position to fulfill the obligation. Any shift from prudent procedures can have an undesirable effect.

16—Do not give in to a feeling of restlessness. Avoid starting any project now unless you are certain you can complete it satisfactorily. Take precautions against making mistakes since an error can cause you to be a target for menacing criticism.

17—Spending money for personal needs, such as clothing and accessories, can prove to be an enjoyable experience. Increase your inventory with things you have long been wanting to buy. Do not have any qualms about an expensive purchase if you feel you can derive enjoyment from it.

18—Although you encounter gloom in others, it is not necessary that their attitude remain that way. Promote congeniality by being humorous and adding wit to your conversation. You may also find it enjoyable to do something from which your community can derive benefit.

19—This can be a good day to settle an argument or a clash of opinion, particularly where money matters are concerned. A conciliatory attitude on your part can do much to cement friendly relations. Although there may have been dissension and antagonism, mutual accord should prevail.

20—Although someone may purposely try to interfere with your plans, take immediate aggressive action to obtain your goals. Do not let obstacles or psychological pressures deter you from your desires. However, make sure that you have a constructive purpose in mind before starting out.

21—A stimulating source of inspiration is indicated from attending church or listening to religious services over the radio. Pleasant experiences are also possible from taking time out to enjoy the companionship of family members and neighbors. A good time to increase your friendships.

22—Move swiftly and keep up with rapidly changing events. However, you should be able to take things in your stride. If you want to make a decorative change or begin alterations in your home, take the necessary actions.

23—Regardless of a multitude of obstacles that you may have to face in your work, do not let your outlook be dimmed. You can forestall frustrated feelings and prevent temperamental displays by showing patience and understanding. Overcome barriers by refusing to let adverse situations get the best of you.

24—Arrange to keep busy with tasks that can provide you with mental and physical stimulation. Do not allow yourself to become bored or stuck in a rut of dull routines. Pleasure is indicated from working on projects of a constructive nature.

25—Despite tense aspects, let a spirited "Merry Christmas" be your greeting to all you meet today. Further the holiday mood by telephoning friends and acquaintances this evening.

26—Set a detailed schedule for the use of your time, and do your best to adhere to it. Also determine the amount of effort needed in your work to get ahead and expenses you expect to encounter. By using this knowledge effectively, you can gain advantages that would otherwise not be yours

27—Although you may feel apprehensive about exceeding your budget, allow sufficient funds for entertainment and recreation. This can be an enjoyable period, provided you do not worry about cash spent on pastimes. However, you may be able to discover much pleasure by developing an inexpensive hobby.

28—Take an active interest in the things that are going on around you. Listen to others for ideas and advice from which you feel you can derive benefit. Since you should find it easy to get along with others, take part in activities which can be enjoyed by your circle of friends.

29—Careful handling of friendly relationships, particularly in a business or job matter, may be required. Emotions could flare up with devastating effects unless you make every effort to keep things running smoothly. Use your most gentle, persuasive approach while dealing with others to avoid anger and disputes.

30—Make certain that what you speak or write will be clearly understood. In doing this, you can forestall possible criticism and interference. Since someone could easily misinterpret your thoughts, give careful consideration to the meaning of each word you use.

31—Mingle with people. The Star trend indicates bright conversations, charming plans, sympathetic ideals and general good will. Make a merry time for all. See the new year in with loved ones.

virgo

August 23rd-September 22nd

You are happy
when reading informative material,
gaining educational goals.
You never cease to learn,
never cease to win improvements
in your work and environment.
Happiness comes
with each step
you feel is successful,
but you go right on
toward even further steps
to help create perfection.
Happiness is never a stagnant matter
but you seek it
further on
in making new efforts.
You actually find happiness
in monotonous,
difficult work
as you keep control of its complexities.
Fame does not attract you
but you will win much praise
for capabilities and tireless effort
of diligent nature.
This will bring quiet happiness,
mental joy.

Virgo

JANUARY

1—You can make this a more enjoyable day by doing something at variance with your routine. Meet each new problem squarely and take prompt action when necessary. Complete one assignment at a time rather than risk failure by starting too many.

2—Take care of delayed correspondence and obligations, and thus avoid possible embarrassment. Learn lessons from errors you have made previously rather than worry about them. Rely on your own efforts and do not depend on promises made to you until they are fulfilled.

3—Once you start something, get it completed and out of the way. Spend time on projects that have the possibility of future benefit rather than waste precious hours. Seek the things you want yourself; do not wait for others to help you.

4—Make more effective use of the things you already own instead of yearning for new possessions. Do not let anyone provoke you into saying anything that might result in a controversy. Stick closely to the suggestions and guidance of someone who is interested in your welfare.

5—Let things go unsaid rather than voice strong criticism. Do not take on increased obligations, you may assume a greater burden than anticipated. Keep dissension to a minimum, since the results of an emotional outburst may be felt for a long time.

6—You can prevent possible aggravation and confusion by adhering closely to accepted methods. Arrange to save time and money by planning things carefully before starting action. Insure harmonious relationships by refusing to let minor disturbances go further than they should.

7—Avoid the purchase of household equipment for which you have no urgent need. Give practical aid as well as reassurance to someone who is in need of it. Avoid taking any chances that might jeopardize your present position or prestige.

8—Finish what you are doing regardless of the time or difficulties entailed. State your objectives rather than be secretive if you expect to secure needed cooperation. Confine your attention to familiar things and routine duties instead of trying to be different.

9—Avoid counting on goals you have yet to achieve. This can be a pleasant day if you adhere to customary routines. Emphasize efficient procedures in your work by planning each move before you act. Despite your interests in the issues at stake, avoid joining a quarrel that concerns others.

10—Arrange furniture, write letters, make changes and otherwise attend to neglected duties. Purchase something you find pleasing, even though it might not be considered practical. Waste little time on unessential activities by making effective use of each hour of the day.

11—Meet hasty issues with determination and be willing to accept responsibilities that are rightfully yours. Through determined efforts, you can remove obstacles that have been retarding your progress. Be prepared to spend extra work, time, and cash to obtain desired results.

12—Emotional tension concerning money may flare up unless an attitude of diplomacy is indicated. Despite arduous duties, keep friendship intact through short visits and phone calls. Do not let anything interfere with the harmony that is possible now.

13—Plan the details carefully before starting action on a new project. Control an inclination to buy luxury articles that have little practical value. Despite your desire to get things done, keep your aspirations within practical limits.

14—Go over your home carefully and remove anything that might be the cause of an accident. Keep a cautious eye on your income and expenses so that you can maintain a correct balance of the two. Do not let your emotions be the influential factor in a financial matter.

15—Maintain your amiability with acquaintances, even though you may not particularly care for their company. Listen carefully and familiarize yourself with any instructions you may receive. See that your generosity by way of a promise does not place you in an embarrassing position.

16—Maintain a cheerful attitude, even if only to keep those around you in a pleasant mood. Spend time on a hobby or other form of diversion from which you can derive relaxation. Be polite but firm in adhering to a decision once you have made it.

17—Do the best you can under existing conditions rather than let them upset you. You can find more enjoyment with others than in seclusion. Focus your attention on enjoyable activities and do not let minor problems upset you.

18—Refuse to be hurried or forced into making hasty decisions. Despite your irritation, control an impulse to exert pressure on someone who is interfering with your plans. Do not let friendship interfere with your making a necessary financial decision.

19—Accuracy is needed more than speed, so take things easy. Wait for others to make the first move rather than personally taking the initiative. Refrain from offering advice to associates unless you are expressly requested to do so.

20—Take care of unfinished tasks rather than begin new things. Despite ambitious plans, keep entertainment and visiting to a minimum. Refrain from discussing any subject that might form the basis for a quarrel.

21—Do not let the pessimistic viewpoints of someone else be a discouraging influence. Follow customary procedures rather than try to be different.

22—Depend on perseverance, rather than haphazard efforts, to get things done. Let situations develop at their normal speed instead of trying to hasten events. A diplomatic approach when dealing with others is needed for maximum results.

23—Keep temperamental displays to a minimum, even though you may have a difficult time counteracting the impatience of others. You can make substantial headway, provided you keep emotions and personal feelings separated from decisions that require practical action.

24—Do not take any chances where the feelings or finances of others are concerned. Seek useful suggestions and ideas that can improve the plans you already have. Contribute cheerful and encouraging words to stimulate the enthusiasm of people around you.

25—To show a satisfactory rate of progress, be exacting and avoid doing things in a hurry. A display of progress can greatly enhance your personal popularity. Depend on your own resources when accomplishing something rather than rely on someone else.

26—Avoid emotional discord by keeping discussion on an impersonal basis. Concentrate your efforts on projects by which you can further your ambitions or increase your income. Contribute cheerful conversation to enliven the spirits of someone who is in need of an emotional boost.

27—Concentrate on getting things done, since distractions are likely to hamper your progress. Be conciliatory in your attitude and make every effort to adjust disagreements before they get out of hand. Keep your aspirations for the day within practical limits and strive to produce the best results.

28—Go out of your way to avoid unpleasant surroundings and temperamental people. Be patient and persistent in your efforts, so that you can reap the benefits of a job well done. Do not let your desire for pleasure distract you from tasks that must be done.

29—Stick to regular activities, since annoyance is likely to result if you seek variety. Put your time and effort to effective use rather than dissipate them through inefficiency. Place emphasis on accuracy instead of speed; aggressiveness can lead to trouble.

30—Enjoyable companionship and affection can prove stimulating and inspiring. Do not let the discouraging remarks of a dissatisfied person spoil your enthusiasm. Adhere to your usual activities, since annoyance is likely to result if you seek variety.

31—Steer clear of any situations where there is the possibility of an emotional conflict arising. Take care of responsibilities without delay rather than yield to a feeling of restlessness. Do not let your preoccupation with one problem distract your attention from other important matters.

FEBRUARY

1—The pace of the day will suit you with its speed and mixture of pleasure with chores. There is no very heavy burden on you now, so your best humor is released and all will find you enjoyable company, particularly tonight.

2—People you may meet today can become vital in your life. This is an important cycle for your social prestige. By showing a generous will to help others in the community, and being unselfish and cooperative, you will generate harmony and happiness.

3—Don't let your more selfish trends enter into a family discussion. Don't voice ideas that would be disadvantageous to others while they helped you a great deal. In other words, don't be demanding or grasping.

4—You may get a chance to go somewhere new that you will find exciting. There is a festive air about the day and you'll enjoy it more with each passing hour. Evening may find you among a new group and having lots of fun.

5—There are concerns that transcend the practical and material by a great margin. These are what you must consider today. Love is one of them, of course, but there are other spiritual matters to consider now.

6—You may be much affected by a dream you had recently and you will see ways in which it is proving true. Quite a mysterious day and you may be entranced by discoveries you make about the workings of your own mind.

7—Health can be troublesome and require rest that you do not feel like taking. You may have to be confined to bed because of dizziness and a bug that really has gotten to you. Avoid being sullen; a loved one will console you.

8—The time goes quickly with some amusing things you have to do. If still on the sick list, you'll get a kick out of a jig-saw puzzle someone has brought you. Some lovely flowers may also come from one who loves you.

9—You may make one of your instantaneous decisions and refuse to listen to reason about it. You can bring a heap of criticism upon yourself and find no benefit in carrying out your ideas, which are really outlandish.

10—Much happier hours. You feel highly affectionate toward older relatives and get some help from them about a trivial matter which is of importance to you. The evening is fine for going out and for seeing a good show.

11—Fine for enjoying the outdoors, getting a bit away from home. A dinner invitation can bring much pleasure and you'll receive compliments from someone you admire. The evening gives you a lot to think about.

12—Do nothing to risk a fall or an injury from fire or sharp instruments. Do not handle mechanical items with which you are not familiar. Follow carefully all instructions about the use of anything and about driving laws.

13—Don't listen to someone who tempts you to cater to pleasure-seeking ways. You have work to do and must be industrious. There are sharp eyes watching you and sharp temperaments are triggered and ready to be unleashed.

14—Good advice can come through casual conversation and you may conserve it for future use. You have some worries about your nerves, your diet and your emotions. These things must be solved in the most effective, though expensive, way.

15—An unreasonable person can go through too many mental changes and make you feel insecure. You might give up in disgust and stalk out in fury. Destiny may have something better to offer you soon, anyhow.

16—Go in for some new high style for hair and dress. Be as glamorous as possible. You'll get fun out of this and may win many compliments for the way you can carry off the ultimate in the moment's fashion now.

17—The social and romantic are emphasized. You may be in a brilliant gathering this evening and need to be rested and in good shape for it. A romantic adventure may await you due to a friend's invitation and introduction.

18—Protect yourself today, particularly from those who are idle chatterers. You need to reflect on your career, your financial situation and your hopes. A journey you are planning for your vacation may give delight now.

19—Be magnanimous to those around you; do something to please a new neighbor or associate. Cultivate your best qualities; seek to achieve more serenity and poise. The day helps you mature in wisdom and graciousness.

20—Good news about money may come and you may have reason to be very thankful. Avoid spending before the money is actually in your hands. Also, do not boast or even talk about your financial situation to anyone at all now.

21—You can be slowed down by some scarcity of materials today. Don't let this anger you; practice your new poise and show superior tolerance, even for those who have caused the delay. Avoid excesses this evening or you'll be ill.

22—An excellent day, well-aspected for investments, buying or selling, doing something to further your career, moving your home or taking a new job. You may also become engaged or married under these most favorable aspects.

23—Respect others and win respect from them. The dignity of the inner human being must be regarded in every association. People are feeling a bit aloof and haughty. This will show up at a party which is quite formal.

24—A hostile person may let fly a barrage of accusations in your direction. Ignore such matters even though you have to close your ears totally. Seek joyous and affectionate companions for evening pleasure tonight.

25—You can be a bit miffed at an older person who tries to detain you. There just aren't many people being considerate today. You'll need to keep to your schedule, so be prompt for every appointment.

26—One of those happy days when you look and feel radiant. Your health shines out, your smile attracts and everyone finds you pleasant, helpful and affectionate. Spread your friendship widely among associates.

27—Time may fly and keep you rushed. You might get a tension headache—a signal to slow down and relax. Make no rigid plans for this evening; the best activity will be one which comes along of itself and provides romantic delight.

28—You may complete plans for your vacation, which you can be starting in a few days. You're enthusiastic and eager to get going. Don't let this cause slipshod work. Keep up your reputation for energy and diligence in your career.

29 (Leap Year Only)—Friendly gestures made at this time might be genuinely appreciated by someone with whom you have been at odds. The vibrations generated today are beneficial for happy emotions and social pleasures. The aspects also spotlight attainment of your hopes and wishes.

MARCH

1—Get the last of plans settled for the coming holidays. If you are going to travel be sure to have your mind made up about the mode of transportation. Do not alter any plans made today, for your insight is at best now.

2—If you are a parent think twice before doing something quite arbitrary and outside of your true rights. You may seriously limit the future of a child by being too determined and keeping the upper hand in everything.

3—A happier day with gloom brushed aside and a social affair to be anticipated. Be sure to look your best no matter how much trouble it takes. You can make an impression on a very attractive person you may later wed.

4—Remembering that there is more than one way to skin a cat will be very helpful. You can bring an end to an undesirable situation indirectly, making it look as though someone else were the one to end it.

5—Decorating home, polishing up some things to be used for entertaining can make the day full. An unexpected visitor may stay a little too long tonight. You'll just have to speak up in order to get proper rest.

6—There is very fortunate atmosphere for you now. You may receive a large sum of money, be given a new position and honor, find life treating you royally. Be appreciative of what the stars toss to you just now.

7—If you are going on a trip this is a good day to take off. Make your trip as light as possible, don't take a whole lot of clothes. Pleasant anticipation will keep you cheerful and delightfully happy.

8—The day is active, things move swiftly and there is a very exciting air for you. A romantic meeting may take place. It is a good day on which to become engaged. Practical affairs come to a standstill for the most part.

9—The spirit of the season dominates your personality now and everyone will be attracted to you in a friendly way. Nice to talk with people on a long journey or in an unfamiliar place during this cycle.

10—Be very helpful wherever you are; take a major hand in work to be done. Also, attending to small children can be helpful and will make you happy. This evening you may find something a bit wrong in the health region for you.

11—An inconvenience should be cleared up quickly; be generous with money where younger relatives are concerned. Make sure everyone is as happy as you can make them and be pleased doing things for others.

12—An incident of the day may rankle but you must not mention this. There can be some tension in the air. Try to help settle it all, with an evening of love and happiness. You may have visitors to share this happy time with.

13—All will go like clockwork, with much happiness when you help to do little things. The day is quite busy and you may be dining in a home that is new to you, among people who are almost strangers, perhaps in-laws.

14—You may encounter a situation that surprises you. Be poised, keep serene no matter how you feel inwardly. Show only affection and if your feelings are injured, hide it with a pleasant attitude. No other change in manner is advised.

15—It may be back to work for you and you can be glad of it, for you need to get away from a bit too much of family life, too much food, and too much idleness. You have something to plan for tomorrow, so keep busy.

16—A neighbor may totally misunderstand you. Let this go, for if you correct the person as to your meaning, you will make an enemy. Just a big communication gap in your life today, and it's somewhat laughable.

17—Your holiday plans should be completed whether going out or staying at home. If you entertain, make sure all things are purchased by end of today so that you can relax and be ready to prepare a pleasant party.

18—You can make a discovery today that will please you. A telephone call has good news both in personal relationships and in money that will soon come in to augment your income. You're in a bright and fortunate cycle here.

19—You'll have all under good control, be joyous with the people you see today and tonight. Your security is firm, you will end the year optimistically. Let yourself go a bit tonight in a social engagement and display affection for all.

20—Do not pass on any news or gossip today. Keep clear of the troublemakers, those who thrive on spreading gossip. The evening is good for making plans about an educational program which you intend to enter in the near future.

21—If you drive yourself too much today, you can be good for nothing tomorrow. Find and keep a steady, healthy pace and don't just go on nervous energy. Be sure to follow good health rules throughout the cycle prevailing now.

22—An older person may accuse you ridiculously of some things that don't matter much. You may get a laugh out of this but don't let on you feel it's funny or you'll get more of the same attack thrown your way.

23—News from a distance can cause a change in plans. You may be urged so much to take a trip you decide you should do it. Be very considerate of everyone today and particularly during the evening in social affairs.

24—An excellent day to shop, to get started on a birthday gift list. Buy something needed for the home. You can have inspiring ideas and find them just wonderful. Someone who loves you very much has a surprise for you tonight.

25—Good fortune continues to be your lot and all that takes place will increase your happiness. You may find that you have a new companion of much varied interest tonight. Accept an unusual invitation in order to enjoy this person.

26—A good day to be thoughtful, solve a problem or two, help the family with some difficulties. Be generous and invite a relative to live with you for awhile. Don't think too much about your own convenience in this matter.

27—Unusual conditions at work can cause you to fret over delay. Relax and enjoy the chance to do nothing for awhile. Do not eat or drink too much of anything, protect yourself from inclement weather in this cycle.

28—Another good shopping day and you may find something that is difficult to find in the stores. Think of a grand surprise for a small child in the family. Don't strain the budget too much but do enjoy being a little extravagant.

29—You may need a little extra boost from vitamins or a visit to a physician for some kind of treatment to give you more energy. Possibly your blood pressure is low or your diet deficient. Don't take on extra chores but do finish what you have started.

30—You may very much want to buy something you consider cheerful, such as a new pet. A good day for such enterprise and you will find just what you want. Avoid being too lenient with a teenage relative who imposes on you.

31—You may discover sudden interest in a person who you haven't thought of for years. It could take some time to get in touch with this person but may be well worth the trouble. Evening can bring a surprise due to a neighbor's visit.

APRIL

1—Getting some time to yourself to think things out is necessary. Contributions that a loved one gives toward solving a problem may also be of value. It's a serious day for you and it will be beneficial for health if you can read something light. Watch a comedy show for laughter tonight.

2—You may be the focus of attention for an executive who has a promotion in mind for you. Your work must be done efficiently today, leave no loose ends. Be sure to keep harmony with associates, go out of your way to be pleasant to one about whom you do not really feel to be truthful.

3—Do not talk about personal affairs, and do not give away secrets of others. This is a good day for money affairs and looking for a new job if you are so minded. There are not beneficial aspects for shopping but you can be tempted to buy something luxurious that would not be practical.

4—Do not look ahead at the pile of work you must do. Simply forge right through today's demands and be as efficient as possible at each moment. You may rather dread going to a social affair tonight but it won't be nearly as dull as you anticipate. Dress to make a good impression.

5—You may get out a lot, perform many small errands. It is possible to meet someone who will be romantically interested, but this can be a very casual and dubious kind of meeting. If you are asked for a date it is wisest to turn it down. No new romance is likely to be a happy one today.

6—You can be in an adventurous mood and bored with all possible companions or activities. Don't encourage this mood; get out and walk, call someone up and in general keep active for this may bring on enough excitement to make the day not quite a total loss. Be generous with a new neighbor.

7—A request made by an official should be granted. By being obstinate you will only injure your own chances. Do some concentrating on plans which can make your life more constructive for the community and broaden your reputation and status. A good evening for talking with a loved one.

8—Be cautious about your relationship with a younger relative. By being too dictatorial you can lose the trust of this person, possibly cause some deep injury that will have bad results for you as well as for your relative. Make a point of taking a kindly view and being tolerant today.

9—Keep a leisurely pace, don't think about time, focus attention on requirements. If you shop and visit the beauty salon you will be able to take on a new appearance and style that can be highly pleasing. Try to avoid making any telephone calls tonight; be brief if you are called.

10—You may be asked to pass judgment, make a choice. Some deep humility in your nature can make you hesitate about this. You do not really feel that you are adequate to make such a choice. Go ahead, however, for destiny demands this special action from you today and what you do will be right.

11—You may be in the spotlight, have to make a brief speech to a group of people to inform them of a new situation. Keep this quite informal. If asked to write anything special, be very clear, concise and to the point. It is a good day for anything connected with words, for all communications.

12—An unusual person may enter your life through a social introduction. You may be enchanted by the appearance of this new acquaintance but not inclined to understand the speech clearly. There is a chance you are dealing with someone very knowledgeable whose vocabulary is beyond you at present.

13—You can be easily vexed today, and may be so if you attend church particularly. If you do attend, get out as quickly as possible after the services. You are on edge today, worried about a family or marital concern. If unmarried you may feel very bleak and depressed about your lonesome state.

14—A neighbor may do a favor, try to make you feel at ease and give affection to you freely. You may be of divided mind about this person but are urged to be broad and to accept what are facts without judging people. The more expansive your tolerance, the better a world you'll make for yourself.

15—A know-it-all type may criticize you and say things that are ridiculous. Since they are ridiculous, laugh. You may add to the hostility of this person but don't let it bother you for a lack of reasonable attitude is the trouble; you're dealing with an emotionally unstable and illogical person.

16—Don't rush through a job for you can make many errors. Be sure your mathematics are corrected when working out any addition. You may be a little hazy mentally today; there are some dreams and wishes going on in the back of your mind and trying to push forward. Make an effort to concentrate.

17—Something new enters your life, a big change may come about today. Excitement, financial gain, a new bright outlook can be yours as a result of these fortunate aspects. You may find yourself the center of attention in an important matter, perhaps find your name in the headlines now.

18—Pleasure and sociability with possible romance make the day a marvelous one to remember. You may attend a party at the home of new acquaintances and be introduced to someone who will provide your romantic inspiration for a long time to come. Dress with great care and attention to grooming tonight.

19—You may want to talk over some problems with an older neighbor who seems wise and practical. Just because the neighbor is more experienced and wise you may receive no advice at all. Recognize that others can't solve your problems, although you may get some comfort and sympathy about them.

20—Do not be too anxious to get out today. There are dangers mingling with crowds and the highways are very difficult to manage if you drive. Be pleasant to neighbors and chat awhile with one, but then get busy with things that need to be done at home. An evening telephone call can delight.

21—Don't let emotion over something that happened in the past overwhelm you. Do not let nostalgia get a start. Be busy, keep busy, be sure you have other people around you at all times. This day threatens brooding that could make you quite emotional and very unhappy with present life.

22—A wonderful day for financial projects, real estate, insurance sales, studying the market situation and acting upon your knowledge. It's a favorable time for quick decisions; don't tarry too long about any decision connected with money. Accept the encouragement of one who loves you today.

23—Avoid all extremes and excesses. A firm resolution to lose weight and the commencement of some new diet restrictions will be good indeed. Look upon your associates, friends and family with much benign good will. Avoid talking a great deal for peaceful harmony and quiet are healthful.

24—Romantic matters must be handled wisely. Be very discreet about any romantic meeting you have scheduled. You might be surprised at the bad fortune that can overtake you if you are the least bit deceptive. Younger people play a role in your life tonight; be aware of this and cope with it.

25—You can win hostility from a malicious person who may start gossip going right away. There is a lot of envy mixed in with sheer ill will that motivates your enemy. Try to forget this matter and go right ahead as usual. Look forward to a special party at the home of a good friend tonight.

26—Have sympathy for someone who is disadvantaged financially and unable to achieve a wish which would be expensive. Although you can't help in material ways, your understanding will do a lot good. If you entertain at home tonight, limit guests to just a few, play some new games.

27—An interesting experience may cause this day to be a turning point in your life. What is done by a younger person has much consequence for you although you don't see it at this time. A new friend may be made, you may be given more understanding and help than ever before in your life. Express gratitude.

28—A rather bad day. Memory can play you a trick that causes an emotional upheaval. Someone you love and trust may not believe you when you tell your story. You are frustrated at every turn. If you can manage to find some laughter here, no matter how grim, by all means laugh without stint.

29—Marvelous things may happen to you. You may get extra money from something you did long ago, inheritance can come your way, an executive may praise you and give you an immediate lift in position that puts you in the supervisory category. Hard to get to sleep tonight thinking over good things.

30—A day for quiet, diligent labor, learning a few new things and working harmoniously wherever it is called for. Be at your best in sunny, dynamic nature but don't overdo it, that is don't be loud and press forward too much. Keep evening for some communications with those who want news of you.

MAY

1—Unusual measures may be needed to protect your practical interests and financial situation. An expert will give you the right suggestion and it should be followed promptly. A romantic turn to the day may be provided through a chance encounter with a new acquaintance tonight.

2—Demands can be impossible to fulfill. You are on the spot and may have to strive against futility for all you are worth. Do your best and no one can validly complain. The day is frustrating but it may hold a lesson which will keep you away from such trends in the future.

3—Keep speech and manner with loved ones gentle and do not show harshness to young people in the family. Your views may be too stern and traditional; loosen up and accept what is modern, don't be hostile to youth. The evening should be spent in quiet ways, watching TV.

4—Keep secrets closely and do not talk about financial plans at all. You might be imposed upon if you let it be known you have a sufficient sum for a large investment. Your plans to invest could be undermined as a result. Older people will not be cooperative today.

5—You may have to face a condition you do not like. Realize what you must do and be firm in determination to do it. Do not let your motives be known, keep an air of mystery in connection with people you talk to today. Your opinion could bring enmity if you express them.

6—Big changes can be made successfully today and mean better circumstances for your future. Be persistent about getting what you want. You may take a lease on a new residence, be quite happy about outcome of your efforts. You're in a transition phase of your life now.

7—Take all that comes in your stride, show how firm you can be in fitting into circumstances that are demanding. You can win admiration and esteem for your intelligent handling of difficult matters. Set a good example for younger people who will be alert to follow you now.

8—If you make a large purchase today, you will be disappointed. Postpone such a purchase even though impulse is strong to carry it through immediately. Control all your impulses and you will have good results. Be cautious about social life and romantic trends this evening.

9—Someone may be too full of advice and you can take umbrage under these conditions. Show that you mean to be independent and use your own judgment. You may lose the interest of an acquaintance but it's worth it to keep your plans and activities as you feel they should be.

10—Onerous work may keep you in a vexed frame of mind. You can resent the day's trends and think of a big change you will make soon. You might be impelled to make it ahead of time due to the pressures of this unpleasant day. Better think twice before you speak today.

11—Try to carry out requirements even though they seem unreasonable. If you do your best you will win rewards and praise. The afternoon can bring a surprise message and may cause you to change plans radically. Talk over your new ideas with loved ones during the evening.

12—The cycle is very romantic and you might embark on a romance that will keep you in dubious mood for a long time to come. Someone may make you very unhappy even though you have much love for the person. Don't struggle against trends; let time and the tide come to your rescue.

13—A relative may ask a favor that you cannot perform conveniently. It is best to say so and explain why. You may find some bitterness due to this situation but that is better than risking all you have on a dubious matter. Be wise, cool and practical in all you do today.

14—Shop for something you need. Look around, compare quality. Saving a dollar isn't necessarily the wisest course. Take into consideration the reliability of the place where you do business, and make your purchase under conditions you know will be honorable, thrifty in the end.

15—The mail can be vexing and hold strange news. You may be unpleasantly surprised with the talk during a telephone call, too. A person who is extravagant may turn to you to help with funds. You can be in the midst of a dilemma, give much cool thought to the whole problem.

16—Don't pattern your behavior on that of others today. Much heedlessness and lack of consideration is in the atmosphere. Keep your role kindly, considerate and helpful. Don't turn down someone who comes to you to ease lonely hours. Avoid putting too high a value on your time today.

17—Do what you can and don't drive yourself beyond such limits. Trying too hard can have bad results in the end. You need to keep health, strength and good spirits in store for tomorrow. If a guest stays too late this evening, find a tactful way to say goodnight quickly.

18—Your health may need attention and you can be inclined to postpone this. That is a dangerous thing to do right now. Act swiftly to get a diagnosis and be faithful about taking prescribed medication. You may have to cut some item from your diet and find this dismaying.

19—An act of generosity can have good consequences. Do not let things go to waste that could be used by others. You are in a happy mood and that will see you through a large pile of uninspiring work. Be cheerful in speech and others will profit from your good companionship at work.

20—Avoid the unfamiliar, drive carefully, do not talk to strangers. Avoid being too friendly with someone who may turn out to have romantic interest. This wouldn't be anything you would want to encourage so a cool attitude from the start is the only wise course you can follow.

21—You may be of a double mind about a new acquaintance. Look on the best side of things, assume the best. Think a bit about your own imperfections rather than being harsh in judgments. You may have a wonderful time at a large social gathering tonight; make sure you are well-rested before going.

22—You can be tempted to buy a luxury you know will not fit in with other items in your home. Let an older person dissuade you from this purchase and do not let a younger one coax you into it. Be sensible and you'll end the day happy. Welcome casual visitors during the evening.

23—You may have to spend the cycle doing something you formerly neglected. You can feel driven to get things in good order and to make resolutions to keep them that way. You may be quite exhausted by evening and may have to close your door, not answer the telephone at this time.

24—Difficulties can arise, a personality clash may have an actual physical affect on your digestion. Analyze the situation and you will understand it, although that will not change anything. Be patient and a chance to escape this environment will come in a short while.

25—If married your lifemate may persuade you to take a trip you do not really want to take. Rather than resenting this it can be wisest just to refuse firmly from the start. Silence in work and home environment can be best. Little use in trying to employ a sensible approach.

26—You may be depressed over your financial situation and see no way to improvement for a long while. Being resigned and courageous will bring best results. Things aren't so bad as you think and imaginative alarm is at work too much. Have a quiet evening with books and TV.

27—You may have to clear up a misunderstanding with a younger person. Be sure to express yourself clearly. In a long distance telephone conversation also be very clear and do not risk misinterpretation of what you say. You'll need to meditate on career matters tonight.

28—Be patient with older people, try to please a relative who is up in years. Avoid being too possessive of anything. There may be an unexpected romantic invitation for evening. Take your time to look your best for this can turn into a serious matter if you make a good impression.

29—Go slowly, take it easy, allow nothing to ruffle you. Serenity is healthy and fluster is unhealthy. Keep emotions under control and they will cease to bother you. Seek a cheerful companion tonight but don't talk about personal matters. Have dinner out and see a show if possible.

30—You may change your mind about an important matter. Get in touch with someone who can help you in a practical way. You may find you have more loyal friends than you realized when you express your needs today. Keep diet sensible and do not stay up very late tonight.

31—An executive who is superficial in relationships may irk you considerably. Keep good humor in store and be ready to enjoy a laugh in private. Not much accomplished today but you are not in the mood to worry. You may reach a wise decision in pondering during the evening.

JUNE

1—Avoid risking money and don't give anything away that could irk your family. Be conservative, conventional and cautious in all you do. Show perfectionist quality in work, use energies which are good. Avoid pleasure seeking with irresponsible companions tonight.

2—A younger relative may play an important role in your life today. Value loyalty shown by such a person. Resist any desire to criticize a family member and keep things tranquil in the home. You could be in one of your more tyrannical moods during this cycle.

3—Do not underestimate a work associate or neighbor. Wait for facts to come in, don't judge things superficially. A good trend is here for acquiring new wisdom when you think about things in detail. Be reasonable and don't let emotions have any say in what you do now.

4—You may sense dislike in another person and seek a way to change this circumstance. It will do no good to make such an attempt. Take things the way they are, be serene and go your way without worry. Discourage company this evening for you are not in a sociable mood.

5—Do not be impatient with a family member. Carry out chores you have planned, follow through on all intentions. Do not spend selfishly or buy an item that would just be a costly plaything. The evening can be very romantic and pleasing if you are not yet married.

6—You may receive an interesting invitation which should be accepted. An older friend may value your intelligence sincerely. You can be elated with conversational trends and find the day permanently rewarding. Relax, enjoy all that comes and you'll learn important knowledge.

7—You can be in high spirits, want to be out and about. Difficult to stay in a building for your work; maybe a benefit will come in the way of an errand that takes you out for a while. Think about domestic changes you would like, check the budget before planning.

8—Attending church can be pleasant, you'll enjoy seeing people and chatting afterwards. A good idea is to go along for a lunch, even with a small group bound for a special art show or other public entertainment feature. You'll appreciate a restful evening, a short walk.

9—Work can be difficult, monotonous, tiring. A bad mood may arrive in the afternoon and you could be disagreeable with work associates. Help someone who has a plan that will benefit others. Be cooperative, don't talk much but get things done, complete a rough assignment.

10—Extravagance today can bring deep regret. Do not carry much money, leave your check-book at home. Your emotions may be somewhat mixed about a new relationship which has romantic promise. Look beneath the surface to the personality of someone vividly attractive.

11—Protect your health; there are hazards here. You may be exposed to an illness someone else has if you visit anyone this evening. Best plan to stay at home, eat lightly, find relaxation with TV and magazines tonight. Do not fall into a dispute with a lifemate.

12—A letter can bring welcome news, and you may develop plans that have been tentative. Casual encounters this afternoon can bring happy opportunities for a pleasant evening. Good to follow a casual course without any rigid plans. Your personality is splendid tonight.

13—Surprising events, perhaps an introduction of interests. Don't be too frank about your personal life, avoid those who pry. You'll be happy with people of good will but unhappy with someone you believe is deceptive. Your doubts and suspicions may be quite correct.

14—Be kindly to a newcomer in your area but don't get intimately involved. You may be in with someone very critical who doesn't show it at first. Avoid inviting blame by avoiding advice-giving. Work goes well and there may be some minor change in your career.

15—A reflective attitude takes over now and you can solve some problems by meditations. Make a good appearance today and you'll find rewarding compliments that lift your spirits. A younger neighbor may outwear welcome late in the day; get around this situation cleverly.

16—Do not speak unkindly of an older relative. Avoid gossip, be charitable in all views. Come to grips with yourself about a worry and find a way to diminish it. There are hidden trends here that will bring a more optimistic mood in the evening and allow a tranquil mind.

17—Accident hazards abound. Take a public conveyance instead of driving if possible. Be sparing with food and do not overload your digestive system in any way. Nerves can be edgy by evening and you'll need to control them in your association with your loved one tonight.

18—Someone may try to advise you and win your resentment. Strive to keep silent about this. Don't be independent in a fashion similar to cutting off your nose to spite your face. Why not take a hint of advice which you yourself can see will bring benefits in the future!

19—Someone at a distance may get in touch by telephone and have an idea that interests you. You may make up your mind suddenly about following through on this idea. A big change is on the way for you and today can be the time that sets the direction this change will take.

20—Do not look ahead in dread of something that must be done. Keep your mind on the moment, concentrate on duties. If you shop keep the needs of family members in mind and don't be selfish in spending. However, you are favored to buy an item or two of clothing for yourself.

21—If you are in a new place be cautious about drinking water. Your career may be undergoing changes. Keep health good by sensible ways and don't let excess enter the picture. This is a good time to buy a gift, remember an anniversary, show affection to those at a distance tonight.

22—Turn down a request for your help in an area that does not interest you. Do not let yourself be imposed upon by anyone today. Get outdoors, chat briefly but avoid lengthy conversations. Get some home chores done late in the day and attend to grooming needs this evening.

23—You may be quite intuitive now and see through the superficial personality of a neighbor. Keep things to yourself. Be wise and avoid further involvement with such a person. Your romantic life is accented tonight and there may be a marriage possibility building up for you.

24—Be slow and steady, avoid haste and errors. A conference can bring out pleasing facts. An executive will be very honest with you. You'll be happy in general and quite exuberant in the home tonight. You appreciate love and the interest that others show in you now.

25—Someone may envy you and try to make you feel inferior. Don't rise to any bait or be ruffled by attitudes of others. Do what is expected of you in work, but don't go beyond your strength. Get a little rest before going out for pleasing social life this evening.

26—There are possibilities of a break up in romance, difficulties in marriage. Getting away from home and staying away can help avert such troubles. Take a trip and visit friends a few miles away. You'll be happy and safe seeing people that you miss from daily environment.

27—You may be asked to do something difficult. Don't feel incapable or inadequate but face up to the situation and do your very best. Good things may come from your work today and you may get a promotion sooner than expected. Avoid being brusque with a new work associate.

28—Money is the big thing today and you may receive some of it by surprise. A gift deed could come or news of a legacy arrive. You are also favored for sound investment; it's a good idea to heed the inspiration of a loved one about money and how to attract it soon.

29—See the views of others, not just your own. Be generous of spirit, somewhat flexible in mental trend. If you show obstinacy where you are wrong, you can lose the esteem of an important person. Avoid being arrogant, and aloof. Be friendly and sociable.

30—Some tricky aspects here and you may have a small shower of misfortune. Money may have to be paid for an unexpected matter, family news can be unhappy. Try to just get through this cycle without too much dismay. Evening will bring enjoyable pleasure, relaxation.

JULY

1—There can be expense, worry and trouble due to the blunder of another person. You need all your control and much ability to forgive. Don't nurture the least resentment but be sincere in your efforts to overlook this matter. Then turn to the good things of life and think of tomorrow's new chances particularly.

2—Not a very good day for money concerns although there may be a necessity to sign certain papers. A young relative may have some difficulty; be understanding and avoid reproof for this person. Entertainment for the evening will be pleasant but should be just a small group who all know each other.

3—The mail can bring a delightful new suggestion from a friend at a distance. When you think this over you can become more and more enthusiastic about it. However, let some time pass before you give your response. Don't be in a rush about anything today and don't be extravagant in buying clothes.

4—An influential person can show loss of temper and impatience with you. The only good way to deal with this is to ignore it and cut conversation short. Avoid large crowds today; you'll be safer and healthier in your own neighborhood with simple occupations and philosophical reflections.

5—Good news about money is in the aspects for your chart. You may also have a strange and interesting encounter. Chances are it would not be wise to follow this up, but enjoy it for the moment. You may have to make a big decision about your residence; get help from a person who loves you about this.

6—This is the time for you to halt aid you have been giving to a younger relative. Let this person learn to stand on his own feet. You'll meet with no resistance for all will be understood. Beware of strangers of the opposite sex today, no matter how harmless and pleasant they look and speak.

7—You could get yourself into trouble by following an impulse connected with romantic ideas. Too much tendency to look backward when actually good fortune and happiness lie ahead. Do not make a telephone call to someone you haven't seen for years. Stay busy this evening chatting with neighbors.

8—You may find yourself getting some publicity. Your name and picture may be in the paper for special work you are doing. Remember that anything of note such as this may stir up envy and that can be dangerous. Don't be surprised if a person or two begin to show hostility and try to belittle you.

9—A new neighbor may seem ideal, be able to share many tastes. You can have a good conversation about reading material you both like. Stay away from talk about the personal side of life where you are concerned though. Have a couple of friends in for a brief but pleasant bit of social life.

10—Difficult to find what you want when you shop but if you go to some place off your usual track you may discover it quickly. It's worth paying to have a quality item, so don't begrudge money to cover this need and desire. Guard your reputation this evening; some people are ready to gossip.

11—Anything you do for small children today will give delight. Give up your time and work for the little ones. A picnic would be just great, some special occasion may be here to celebrate, perhaps a birthday of a child. Your talents for knowing youthful tastes and joys serve you well now.

12—An executive may show interest in your work and it can be advantageous to discuss plans with this person. Make it plain that you are aiming for more money and don't intend to wait very long for it in any one place. You may get cooperation on this sooner than you expected if you are forthright.

13—You may be unwilling to socialize and prefer to see any of the usual people today. A long walk can be good if the weather permits. You'll get mental refreshment and emotional serenity this way. Don't stay cooped in the house during this cycle, even though tempted to do so.

14—Complaints may be made by someone just trying to cause difficulties for you. Your personality may be under attack now. Don't say anything about this; let things go on as though you didn't notice them. Nothing to get excited about, just stick to routine and don't permit a chance for a quarrel to arise.

15—The day may become romantic suddenly due to a telephone call you get. Don't leap into anything connected with romance, though. You need time and good judgment to mull over this matter. Avoid conversation with an older person in your neighborhood who is curious and noted for gossip.

16—Time can go so swiftly today, you'll be amazed and only partially through the work goals you set for yourself. Don't worry, it's just one of those days and many others will feel its frustrating effects. See a good show with a loved one, dine out, be happy and carefree and make the evening a healthy one.

17—You'll need much tolerance and patience today; you also need to put aside any tendency to judge harshly or mete out scolding and punishment for a child. Be sympathetic with one who needs help rather than rushing in with blame and a stern attitude. Don't dwell on unpleasant matters.

18—Make it a day to take it easy, enjoy what you do and be friendly with all around you. It will be fun to take a younger person out shopping with you this evening and buy something special to please them. It could be that a pet is just the thing. Also make the evening a bit festive in dining.

19—Financial news is wonderful and can mean a considerable chance to save more or spend on a few luxuries. Share your good fortune with a loved one in the family who needs the encouragement of a little extra money. Work diligently; don't take too much time just enjoying your feeling of elation.

20—A great disappointment may come and you can be told some harsh truths about yourself. Even though the truth is spoken it would be better if it were not. You will see quickly that one who pretended love has been doing little but stir up grievances against you. Life's like that sometimes.

21—A day which can bear fruit of various varieties. It is good for shopping or finding a new job. Keep a positive thought about your desires and intentions. You'll be busy in a happy way; don't spend extravagantly on an item that would be just a big and unusual plaything in the long run.

22—Travel plans can be made today and please everyone connected with the project. You'll be in much harmony with the family. Let someone know in plenty of time if you expect to make a visit. Your health is good and you may work overtime trying to keep your slate free from accumulated demands.

23—A younger neighbor may criticize you and you can become quite intolerant of this person. Better think twice, the criticism may be so true it angers you. Be mentally honest today and you will turn the cycle into a beneficial one. Admiration and affection you gain now will be permanent.

24—The early part of the day goes slowly with a few small tasks getting done. You can be restless in the afternoon but too slothful to get out and do anything about it. An invitation for the evening can find you accepting though bored at the thought. You are mostly just plain lazy today.

25—Social life today is more important than appears on the surface. An introduction made to you now may lead to a marriage in the not-so-distant future. Be rather silent today; let others talk and you'll learn a lot. Also your quiet manner will be appealing to those you meet during the cycle.

26—You may find yourself suddenly making a final decision and actually getting busy on it immediately. It is possible you will walk out on a job today. You may be in search of more freedom and not quit until you find such a position. There is possibility of a long-distance move due to this.

27—Excitement is in the air, you're very pleased about family matters. Temptation to be extravagant in buying gifts must be moderated. Your generous nature is all to the fore but it must be curbed. Be patient with a loved one who is a little slow in falling in with your joyous mood.

28—You can be depressed over general conditions and what you see in the papers. Emotional health can be jeopardized by your attitude. Find something to keep you busy and take up your thoughts so nothing else can intrude. Get in touch with cheerful and sensible friends this evening.

29—You may acquire a large item, possibly an automobile today. It is a time when wishes come true and your circumstances become more ideal. You may be relieved of a hardship which was beginning to affect your health somewhat. It's a smooth cycle for you and you will make others happy with your gay mood.

30—Someone you haven't seen for a long time may get in touch and want to visit you. Probably you will encourage this even though you don't know exactly why. You could be headed for a complex emotional situation. Remember, it will be up to you to take the consequences courageously for your acts.

31—An older relative may pressure you about certain trends in your life. This person may be the type who thinks everyone else is wrong if they don't agree. Say little but don't even consider letting yourself be persuaded. You must live your own life and get happiness from it in your own way.

AUGUST

1—There can be some high jinks in your neighborhood. Someone spiteful may try to involve you in a fray that is ridiculous. Protect yourself by silence, refuse to repeat a word that anyone says. One of those times when you scarcely know whom you can trust, so be on guard all day.

2—Be leisurely, get out into rural districts if possible, enjoy sports. You're not in the mood for work and nothing much will go right with it if you have to be on the scene. Don't worry about errors. Nobody is going to be in much of a work mood or inclined to worry about the other person now.

3—Await developments. Matters in which you are deeply concerned can take much longer than you think to come to a meaningful point. Be neighborly; your judgment will be very good and you will know just the people to stay away from, those with whom to enjoy a good conversation and better acquaintance.

4—Do not get involved with a highly talkative person. Such a situation could cause an accident that would be costly. Keep your companionship limited to those of good sense and good will, avoid anyone you suspect of being malicious. The family trend tonight is good and problems can be solved.

5—You may require some special help on a matter of personal nature. Don't begrudge a lawyer's fee for something that you must do. Don't be bitter about any conditions today, but do protect yourself sensibly. Finances may be a large part of your problems but not the largest in the long run.

6—There may be some mix-ups on the social and romantic front. Misunderstandings, hostilities and some sheer obstinacy can make relationships unhappy. It may seem pleasant to go out this evening but before a party is through you may wish you had never gone to it. Strive for good thoughts now.

7—Someone younger who lives near you can cause a complicated situation. There can be threat to your happiness due to conditions in the neighborhood. Perhaps this is one of those conditions that only time can heal. Be patient, avoid having a chip on the shoulder.

8—Welcome a new neighbor, be tolerant, generous and just today. You can find some situations that bothered you formerly will be alleviated during the day. You can be at your best with a way to handle things with more expediency that will please the boss.

9—Something you are waiting for may not come through. There can be a delay at the basis of matters and you're the one to suffer for it. Don't be bitter even though the delay can cost you a small sum of money. Evening may take a special turn for romance which is very surprising to you.

10—Don't let your philosophy be contaminated by that of a younger person near you either at work or at play. Maintain your high principles. Evening is a good time to come to some decisions about this whole matter. Although affections and tolerance are at war with facts, let them win out a bit.

11—Don't turn on your most persuasive manner with anyone in the family. You could get some very unpleasant answers if you take on the role of authority for the concerns of someone else. Avoid quarrels, keep your speech pleasant and attend strictly to your own affairs no matter how difficult.

12—Shopping can be pleasant and have some rewards to make you happy. An inspiration about buying something to make the home more cheerful can carry you along with pleasure. A generally good day with light work demands, harmony among associates. You may like home best this evening though.

13—Keep your good humor, let wit win through the day. Where troubles threaten it is good to be strictly honest. You can put an end to some resentful attitudes if you show that your own spirit is on the side of a peaceful agreement to let everyone enjoy personal rights without question.

14—Excellent financial advantages are here. You may have an informal meeting with someone who wants to enter a financial venture with you. You will be delighted with the trust shown in you and today could actually be the start of beginning your own business as ambition has always urged you to.

15—Your guardian angel may seem very close to you all day. Misfortunes you miss by a hair's breath can tell you that you are being watched over constantly. Your faith increases due to the tensions which arise but always find a happy ending. There is a new note to your relationship with neighbors now.

16—Try to avoid going to any unfamiliar place, talking to unfamiliar people. There is strange danger for you in such things, and little protection available. Keep up with work demands, be helpful to associates, make the day one of unselfish activity. Evening can find you weary so make no big plans.

17—You will have no difficulty finding what you want. Your personal life is accented and good fortune in it will be the big thing of the day. Otherwise make sure that all you do is legal; an infringement of the law could cause embarrassing trouble. Be kindly to older relatives tonight.

18—You will find happiness in life stressed. Part of this trend is due to your affection for nature and your ability to understand its workings. You may not get much work done, technically speaking, but you'll have a day to remember as successful. A wish may come true and delight you tonight.

19—Communications with a distant point center around financial matters. You may get some advice and information which makes a swift investment desirable. Trust those who are your friends and have always been willing to support you. By evening you may be happy you took a daring risk.

20—Let impulse guide you some today for intuition is good and what seems whimsical on your part may have a lasting benefit. Avoid anyone who criticizes you simply because you do not heed their personal opinions or change your way of living to fit theirs. Be independent and self-reliant now.

21—Make it a restful day. If you have something important on your mind such as moving your residence, this is a good time to look around and find the ideal spot to fulfill your desires for a change. Evening is a wonderful time for social life. Look your best, be exotic and glamorous tonight.

22—A neighbor can be irresponsible and cause you some trouble. Difficult to avoid those who are thoughtless; the day may seem filled with them. Be a recluse if possible, get away on a walk that will be healthy and allow meditation. This is much better than getting into lengthy conversations.

23—People who are much younger are important in your life today. Help you give will be appreciated and may be the only way in which some young people can save their situation. In other directions, be very thoughtful about your work associates. You may note that one of them is envious of you.

24—A joyous event can befall you. Someone you haven't seen for a long time may return into your life. This could be by correspondence or a long distance telephone call. You may find yourself happy to know that this person is still around and has the same delightful wit as always.

25—Someone may mean to do you good, encourage you in a direction which is different from the one you are taking now. You must realize that each has a personal life to live and that one person's meat is another's poison. Make it plain that you have no intention of weakly yielding to another's ideas.

26—You may be planning a trip which combines business and pleasure. You'll need to take into account the amount of money that may be needed, not just that which will barely get you through circumstances. Evening can have a special message for you and it can be difficult to know your true reactions.

27—A day for great caution. Avoid climbing on objects that are flawed and rickety. Handle fire with greatest care. Do not talk about what is not your business; you might be taken to court for even a slight word. However, evening is a good romantic time; your chart shows pleasure here.

28—A neighbor may show good will and that will make you happy. Do not rush into a friendship, however. It is best also not to express your personal attitude too boldly or persuasively. You could be mistaken for a know-it-all and someone who wants to dominate another's life.

29—Make it a day to do and say nice things to others. You may be extremely happy in the love you feel turned in your direction by a person you admire. It's a time to be magnanimous. You will reap rewards in due time, but just now sincerity is the big thing in your life, so avoid deception.

30—Be cautious in all matters pertaining to health. Keep your diet light, make sure it includes some fresh greens. Do not go in for fads in food or drink. Stay with the wholesome and the balanced. Evening may demand some of your time for an organization getting started in your community.

31—Avoid actions that are highly decisive. Much of what you do today could be undesirable if you try to make a final decision. Try to avoid making decisions. If another asks you to come to conclusions, politely turn down the idea unless you feel it is mandatory for you to concur.

SEPTEMBER

1—Read the news carefully in the morning. There may be something of great personal interest to you on this very favorable day. Friends will play an important role in your happiness, and a surprise is waiting for you at home in the evening. Popularity is at a height.

2—Enthusiasm will spark your plans and you will get into action so that results are seen before the day is over. A cooperative atmosphere will make it possible for you to achieve what you scarcely hoped for. Plan a special treat for the family or a romantic companion.

3—Many changes may be necessary today, but they will be minor and improve your schedule pleasantly. You will find leisure to relax as you need, and the rest will be beneficial. Accept the good influences which will add to your well-being and health through the day.

4—Your leadership abilities will be called upon unexpectedly. A generous desire to help others can bring honor and perhaps financial reward, although you do not seek it. A day of life in the public domain. You won't have spare time until the evening, but do accept an invitation.

5—You may be in deep need of rest and solitude. Stick to plans to read, take a walk alone, meditate. Activity of any strenuous nature should be avoided, and long conversations are risky. Even members of the family can be firmly and tactfully avoided. Settle for a book and early retirement.

6—Rather unfortunate trends for those who want to get a lot done. Companionship is favored and there will be much pleasant chatter of a harmless nature. You can make a new friend today, perhaps begin a discussion which will later lead to a partnership of profit.

7—The pressure of domestic matters may be relieved, and emotional happiness found in a new attitude. Spend the hours with loved ones. Ignore all troubles of yesterday, and set your mind on future plans. Change is in the air, and a definitely new arrangement is called for.

8—You can get in a lot of accomplishment today. Happy hours for the fulfillment of plans to finish up detailed work which has been pending. Your sense of freedom from these matters will make the late afternoon and evening very pleasant socially. Relax and enjoy yourself.

9—Another good day, but more for romantic matters. Business may seem boring and work not interesting. No need to worry, for the hours do not demand much down-to-earth effort. Let yourself bask in the light of affection a loved one showers. A happy surprise in the form of a gift or news.

10—A good time to start a journey upon career matters. Changes can be made, a new position accepted with assurance of happier surroundings and greater financial opportunities. Discussion will prove profitable, also. If you are at home, accept an invitation this evening.

11—Relatives will be provoking and probably demand what you are unwilling to do. Whatever stand you take, be firm about it. This may be a day upon which difficult decisions will have to be made. A permanent effect upon your future can be the outcome. Relax at home tonight.

12—Virgo has a sparkling day of brisk business activity. You will concentrate on practical matters, and make real headway with career plans. Pleasant anticipation of future happiness will be in the back of your mind, and your present objectives and motives for work will spur you.

13—A day of nervous tension, strained relationships and the hint of quarrels in the air. If you are intimate with an associate, do not rely upon affection to carry you safely through conflict. Keep back words of resentment, if you do not want to start a serious rift.

14—Zest for your work, happiness over romantic matters, and pride in children are part of Virgo's day. All the dramatic vividness you crave can enter your life when you are asked to perform a special task of an honorary nature. Spend the evening with this new, pleasant chore.

15—Unfortunate tidings about a loved one may make the day gloomy. Be very careful to concentrate on what you are doing, and don't let preoccupation or worry cause accidents or mistakes. Any slip can be very expensive. Health will suffer if you do not keep on schedule.

16—You will be very sensitive to the possibilities of the day's incidents. Alertness and enthusiasm will spark your efforts, and you will be noticed by an important person. This can be the start of a new trend in your career. First impressions will carry much weight.

17—A sense of foreboding may darken the morning, but probably without justification. Keep working, and don't let mental images disturb you. Look at reality and by noon you will find the atmosphere clearing of falsely imaginative fears. A happy evening at home.

18—A favorable day for all plans which include loved ones, friends, associates. A good idea to plan an outing, provide an interesting picnic and entertainment. Include young people and sports which will give an invigorating air to the day. Activity and sociability are stressed.

19—A splendid day to get out, be inspired both spiritually and sociably. People will be very charming, and your own personality delightful. New friends and congenial relationships. Very favorable for entertaining.

20—A rather good day for personal projects, shopping, even buying major items. A friend may tell you of an excellent opportunity to gain an appliance you have needed. Plan to entertain at home this evening and be quite lavish with refreshments. Good cheer in society.

21—Sources of friction in the family may mount as the hours go by. Try to be considerate, but do not expect much understanding. A day of confused purposes and plans which go astray. Try to find time for rest in the afternoon. Even at the cost of strife avoid going out tonight.

22—Advantages for investment, selling, travel and new contacts are splendid. Schedule conferences, go after something you want. All is favorable for gaining along financial lines and career promotion. Don't be surprised if your dreams have started to come true by evening.

23—A rather slack day for business interests, but personal matters have a favorable and rather lively trend. New romance can begin slowly but adventurously today. Avoid jumping to conclusions, be casual and enjoy the hours. Look your best and be friendly to a member of the other sex.

24—Misfortune and loss may follow you through most of the day. Avoid speed, angry words, ill temper. Keep motion under control, for a chain of troubles can ensue from one unreasonable moment. Remember family affections and take advice of loved ones. Put selfishness aside.

25—Best to stay close to home. Leaving shopping to be done by others is best today. You will be tempted if you go near stores, and extravagance can make you rueful before nightfall. Avoid long conversations and refuse invitations tactfully. A book or TV is best for evening.

26—A benevolent trend in which you can be swept upward and find yourself in a new position. You may be asked to assume authority which means a promotion. Be dressed well, show your willingness, and use tact in new surroundings. All will give you reason to celebrate tonight.

27—News from a distance can be very promising. Take time to think carefully before making a decision. Make sure that all correspondence is clear, and you may receive a profitable answer. Accept an invitation for tonight even though it means special expense. A happy, romantic night.

28—Spend the day with friends and loved ones. High-flown speech can arouse your emotions and bring about a sad letdown later in the day. Best to avoid groups, public meetings, the theatre. Rest and take care of correspondence, your wardrobe and grooming and minor repairs of small objects.

29—A sudden change in your life may bring great happiness. A very busy day but a very profitable one for the future. Your romantic happiness may hinge upon seizing the opportunity of a moment today. All will be harmonious, your mind clear and your emotions happily adjusted.

30—A series of minor accidents, annoying delays and a perturbed mental state may make the day unpleasant. No lasting disaster will come to this mischievous period, if you maintain your poise and do not rush into impulsive action or speech. Avoid making vital decisions.

OCTOBER

1—An inclination toward being self-centered should be avoided today. You may find yourself voicing your opinion loudly and strenuously, wanting to make a fuss over the least little thing and becoming angry when others make mistakes. It will be your mistake if you let the tendencies run away with your better judgment.

2—It is a wise policy not to believe everything you hear today. Fraud and deceit will be on the loose, and you can be taken in even by the most seemingly sincere person. Flattery can charm you to the extent where you part with cash, so just smile at words of effusive praise.

3—A business disappointment or litigation which comes to a standstill can cause you anxiety. Financial news may be gloomy. Try to hold on with industrious work, little talk and solitude when you can get it. Best not to talk over problems with anyone. Postpone solving them.

4—It may be best to spend the day in solitude as much as possible. Reflect rather than act. Action today can bring financial loss. Plans and ideas, however, can be viewed impartially and will show up their weak and strong points, so survey your own scheme for your career, home and environment.

5—A stepped-up tempo for the day will find you in a whirl during the early hours. Gear yourself calmly to the rapid pace and you will whiz happily through to a cheerful luncheon. Conversation will be witty, quick and full of teasing repartee. Plan a light entertainment for the evening.

6—Hesitation and caution will be the wisest guiding words today. Any action commended without thorough thought will result in loss. Watch over your private possessions, for it is a day of deprivation. Hazards can meet you at several points, so be prepared to deal with unforeseen obstacles.

7—Ambition can bring large rewards today. Financial security is attainable by taking thought and making your budget watertight. Make sure you know exactly what you want, stand aside from personal emotion and be self-confident. This is a day for major improvement.

8—A rush to finish up scheduled work will find you able to achieve your aims. A good day for industrious effort, and no special endeavor will go unrewarded. Responsibilities will not be irksome, but will give you a sense of being able to take your place in the world reliably.

9—Conservative aid may be obtained from an unconsidered source. An old friend may provide you with the key to the solution of an emotional snarl, making it possible for you to find new harmony and satisfaction in your social life. Good deeds have cumulative value under the current aspects.

10—Keeping your chin up will overcome much more than a double chin. Should you feel that time is hanging too heavily on your hands, devote a few hours a week to charitable or social work, not the professional variety, but just good old-fashioned neighborly helpfulness.

11—It will be difficult to win a free objective view today. Your emotions will cloud the real issues of practicality and your tendency will be to act impulsively on the strength of momentary feeling. Best to take as few steps as you can and let the day go by without any radical changes.

12—It will be difficult to make harmonious adjustments with your associates. Your personality and disposition may suffer various feelings during the day, but it is important to control yourself in all ways and find amiable relationships rather than to submit to the pressures of your own feelings.

13—If you are attempting to govern your thinking by another's philosophy, some of your thoughts and writings may not sound convincing because you yourself are not convinced. Give your mind the opportunity to free itself from the psychological straitjacket imposed by single direction reading and thinking.

14—Listen to suggestions because they may be laden with nuggets of wisdom. If you apply for a favor from someone who is in a position to help you, you may be fortunate enough to get what you want. The rays particularly favor love, marriage, travel and money.

15—The more articulate you are today, the better. Without being aware of the reason, your friends will be exceedingly interested in the wisdom of your utterances. Make yourself heard and listened to. Write letters, and express your opinions. A partial settlement of an important matter could give you great satisfaction.

16—Relegate to the past all your heartaches, forlorn ambitions and fears. Let a new vision flower. Stimulating rays may bring you a full and fruitful day, which you can help along by attending to details, which are too often neglected. Get to some fun tonight.

17—Good fortune tips to the other end of the scales sometimes, as does adversity. If accomplishment does not reach up to your expectations, do not be disturbed. That may merely be a signal for you to bestir yourself to greater effort. The aspects should be an aid to success.

18—There is no sense in averting your mind from unpleasant facts. Face and solve them. The quicker you apply yourself to eliminating annoyances, the sooner you will have the time and the disposition to do the things you want. Keep out of arguments with older people, and watch out for accidents.

19—Make decisions about money, home, business, travel, career, pleasure and aspirations while friendly aspects operate in your favor. Cooperation, enthusiasm, and tolerance should get a good response. The higher your ideals and wishes, the greater will be the final victory.

20—There are discordant vibrations generated today, so beware of psychological difficulties. Do not be influenced by nebulous ideas that might set you on the wrong side of the fence in family matters, nor let anyone pull the wool over your eyes. Be realistic.

21—Dispose of any past obligations before taking on new responsibilities, not so much as a matter of policy or as a precaution against loss, but because you may be drawn into a series of controversies that might lead to notoriety, rather than favorable prominence.

22—Exchange ideas with someone whose thoughts and aims run along the same channels as your own. Your conversation may be so stimulating that your cleverness will be gladly recognized. Get out and around. These are not aspects under which to vegetate at home. Buy something nice for your room.

23—A possible opportunity to take an interesting trip may be the very incentive you need to wake up your flagging ambition and increase your self-confidence. Do not neglect your work though. It is never pleasant to wake up some fine morning and find yourself without revenue-yielding employment.

24—Pick your way as cautiously as time and circumstance permit else you may get jarred mentally or physically. Adjust yourself to any breaks in your ordinary routine. Not a favorable cycle for social gatherings, writing letters, visiting neighbors or traveling.

25—Be careful what ties you discard. If you are too impetuous, a close relationship might be broken, much to your later regret. If you sense indifference in someone who once was an appreciative companion, make sure the fault is not yours. The influences warn against indiscretion.

26—Sidestep irritations or unpleasant confusion, by being gallant rather than assertive. If others appear ungrateful for what you have done, refuse to let that depress you. Keep plugging right along. There is no greater solace or panacea for life's ills than hard work. See a movie thriller.

27—Look out for errors in judgment in your work or career so that you will not be misled by too much optimism. There is possibility of misjudgment, detriment and physical mishap since the planetary influences are in opposition. Take it easy, and do one thing at a time.

28—Beware of false promises. The planetary vibrations are weak for the fulfillment of casually-made vows. Do not allow trivialities to unbalance you. Locks can keep away marauders but they are little use against waste of time and opportunity. Keep the pendulum of personal effort moving in rhythmic cadence.

29—Do not expect perfection today. If someone is inquisitive about your personal life, do not be resentful. It is human to be curious at times. Keep steadily on, and do the work that is required of you. Get in a little relaxation tonight.

30—Try not to be disturbed by events over which you have no control, nor give anyone half a chance to antagonize you. This may be more apparent in social and domestic matters than in business or professional matters. Let others beat the drums today, while you sit on the sidelines.

31—You may feel stimulated by a surge of enthusiasm. Obstacles, real or fancied, may fade away. Splendid influences augment your personal popularity. Take stock of what you have accomplished so far this month, and you may find that you have added a lot to your reputation and credit.

NOVEMBER

1—Avoid unnecessary frustration by not wasting your cash resources on extravagant purchases. Although routine work may prove bothersome, its successful completion may release you from restrictions. Do not allow yourself to become upset by a person who makes unreasonable demands on you.

2—Take advantage of present opportunities to widen the scope of your daily activities. Even though you may feel you are producing good results, do not expect immediate appreciation of your efforts. Taking unnecessary chances or giving in to impulse may lead to trouble.

3—You may invite trouble if you antagonize family members or friends. Future financial benefits are possible by making long range budget adjustments. Concentrate on solving difficulties which have restricted the attainment of your desired goals.

4—Concentrate on the major issues and forget petty matters if you expect to make this a day of progress. An aggressive attitude may help you break through restrictions, but planned action is needed to make real headway. Rather than dream about what you would like to do, get busy achieving a desired goal.

5—Pleasant happenings and enjoyable emotions are likely, provided you avoid scenes of tension. Keep busy at remunerative tasks and do not waste time on frivolous pasttimes. Pay little attention to the opinions of others who may be prejudiced or incorrect.

6—Taking needless risks with your money may be the source of unpleasant experiences. Display affection subtly and take things easy when it comes to emotional matters. Keep your ambitions channeled in the right direction by undertaking only those tasks which you can handle efficiently.

7—Even though you may desire to take time out for recreation, clear up pending duties first. You may encounter resistance that would be a long time subsiding if you press your viewpoints too strongly. A patient attitude, rather than a critical one, should help you to receive cooperation desired from others.

8—Attend to matters associated with your future, but do not completely ignore present responsibilities. Be conservative in your approach so that you will not give anyone an opportunity to take advantage of you during the current planetary vibrances.

9—Rather than avoid difficult tasks, tackle and complete them as rapidly as possible. Adhere to a pre-arranged schedule of activities; do not experiment with new ideas if you expect to achieve favorable results. Avoid making any agreement or promising something which you cannot fulfill with relative ease.

10—Retain your courage and optimism despite obstacles that you may encounter. Be persistent in doing the things you want, and refuse to let anyone stand in your way. A favorable day to write letters or return favors you have received in the past.

11—Sticking to your viewpoints despite strong opposition may result in lasting hard feelings. Petty disagreements are likely, so be cautious in everything you say or do. Be open and above-board in your dealings with others to protect your reputation.

12—Keep your work in good order and your obligations up-to-date so that you can face the future with a clear conscience. Look at things realistically, particularly with regard to financial matters. Use your ingenuity to advantage by turning ideas into practical and valuable realities.

13—Let things develop at their normal pace, instead of attempting to hasten the progress of events. You can achieve better results by being somewhat impersonal than by yielding to emotions. Be cautious when offering your services since your assistance might be misused.

14—Adjust yourself to the moods of associates rather than risk trouble by appearing to be contrary. Check over everything you put in writing to make sure that your meaning will be understood as intended. Spend the evening hours in the company of good friends.

15—Changes in your job or home should work out well for you provided you coordinate your plans with those of others. Get down to the routine of your work as quickly as possible and do not let anything disturb you. Seek sound advice before making any decision with regard to your career.

16—Do not allow a well planned work program to be jeopardized by a temporary feeling of restlessness. Rather than struggle under last-minute pressure, aim to get your assignments done in advance. Take part in activities which can provide you with mental stimulation as well as physical exercise.

17—Clear thinking is essential to keep things running smoothly and overcome interference with your plans. Any deviation from accepted procedures and customs may stir up more trouble than you can handle. Arrange to work on assignments which you find enjoyable yet productive.

18—Be firm when making a decision, and do not leave any unsettled arrangements that may require later consideration. Regardless of questions that you may have on your mind, it may be undesirable to discuss controversial issues. Be quick to take care of domestic conditions that are particularly annoying.

19—Mistakes that you make now may be hard to overcome, particularly if you let carelessness get the best of you. Enjoyable experiences are possible from disposing of old possessions and replacing them with new ones. Do not give in to your doubts or let the pessimistic words of others discourage you.

20—Aim for accuracy rather than speed in your work so that you can avoid time-wasting repetition of effort. Regardless of disturbing incidents, do not allow them to completely upset your daily routine. Make every effort to promote congeniality among associates through friendliness and humor.

21—This is a period for hope and anticipation rather than pessimistic fears. Your plans for the future should work out well so long as you do not try to get everything done at once. Unwise spending may lead to an emotional conflict that would be difficult to overcome.

22—Waste little time on recreational activities that are without practical purpose today. Follow your own conclusions even though others may offer you a wide variety of advice. This can be a pleasant day provided you stick to light subjects in your conversation.

23—Be optimistic and encouraging when dealing with others even though you may encounter upsetting conditions. Concentrate your attention on one task at a time to prevent wasted effort. Let logic and reason dictate your course of action.

24—Keep your ambitions within limits, and do not undertake more than you can effectively handle. Refuse to take any risk where there is the possibility of losing your money or possessions. Do not dwell on previous accomplishments, but focus your attention on the future and what you expect to do.

25—Rely on yourself to get things done instead of depending on the efforts of another. Look for and make practical use of methods to improve your home or business. Conscientious efforts are essential to rapid progress, so concentrate on your work.

26—Errors in judgment are a strong possibility unless you pay careful attention to detail. Give others an opportunity to express themselves first before voicing your own opinion. A conciliatory attitude on your part can do much to prevent a difficult situation from becoming worse.

27—Stick closely to pre-arranged plans in order to avert confusion in your work. Control an inclination to be generous since it will probably not be appreciated. Do not place yourself in a vulnerable position by spending too much time and cash on amusements.

28—Regardless of how inconsequential you may consider them, take domestic responsibilities seriously. Adjust yourself to the tempo of rapidly moving events and keep alert for the opportunities available. Do not become so engrossed in clearing up your obligations that you neglect your desire for happiness.

29—Set the pace for yourself today, rather than wait for others to initiate action. Make effective use of things you already have and take advantage of existing benefits. Industrious effort on your part can help you transform a wish into reality.

30—Since tempers can be short, allow others ample opportunity to express their ideas. Make an effort to proceed at an uninterrupted tempo by avoiding arguments and criticism. Maintain a neutral attitude rather than become involved with the trouble of another.

DECEMBER

1—Your work assignments should prove more interesting and stimulating. Even though you may consider some of your tasks rather tedious, concentrated effort may help you to revise your attitude.

2—Keep your thoughts to yourself, especially in a business or job matter. To voice your opinion or take bold action against the will of others could lead to serious trouble. Increase the efficiency of systems employed in your home or place of business.

3—Take time out from your normal routine to give concentrated thought to your future and what you can do to make it more secure. Put to practical application ideas that you conceived. Do not relent in your efforts to achieve desired goals.

4—Social activities and hobbies from which you can derive mental and physical relaxation are favored. Arrange to take some time out for fun, regardless of where you may be or what you are doing. However, keep business and pleasure separate.

5—Quarrels and bitter clashes of emotions are possible, unless you are careful in your conversation and actions. You can keep the atmosphere serene. Keep your temper under control, regardless of how trying the circumstances you are required to endure.

6—Since losses through speculation, fraud and poorly made plans are possible, keep a tight hold on your present cash assets. Watch your spending and investments. However, exert every effort to fulfill promises and obligations for which you are responsible.

7—You may have to be constantly on the alert to keep up with the thoughts and actions of those around you. Prevent confusion by refusing to become upset if things do not work out to your expectations. Adjust yourself to the present pace of events.

8—This is not a good day to take the initiative nor expect cooperation from someone else. You can make revisions and changes in your present set-up now, but do not take immediate action or expect quick results.

9—Do not take chances where the feelings or emotions of others are concerned. A combination of impatience and curt remarks can upset what would otherwise be a pleasant day. To foster animosity by engaging in a quarrel might result in repercussions that are lasting and of serious consequence.

10—You may find it difficult to focus your full attention on the tasks at hand. However, strive for the highest possible achievements of which you are capable, regardless of momentary impulses of interference caused by others.

11—A calm and meditative mood is essential to prevent the emotional tension that is likely to prevail. Seek a place where you can relax in an atmosphere of quiet. Do not take any action or make a promise that would place you under financial obligation.

12—Devote time to taking care of your own personal needs, but do not ignore entirely the wishes of others. Go out of the way to help a friend or relative who can benefit from your assistance. Your efforts should be well rewarded.

13—Take on new job responsibilities if you feel that it will ultimately benefit you. Purchase clothing and household equipment that are necessary. Also, settle bills and straighten out budget matters without delay so that you will feel free to take part in more pleasant activities.

14—Do not take anything for granted, particularly in dealings with strangers. Refrain from becoming involved in risks of any kind. This is a time for realistic thinking, rather than taking chances on the unknown.

15—Do not force an issue despite the fact that things may not work out exactly as you had planned. Take temporary setbacks in stride. Hold off on achieving your ambitions for the time being.

16—Do not make a strong attempt to get away from confining conditions. Instead, discuss your thoughts with people whom you feel can help you. Correct an adverse situation without running away from it. Yielding to your emotions could prove annoying to yourself, as well as to those around you.

17—Not only is this a good day to make ambitious plans, but it is also a favorable time to take definite action toward their realization. Give a well formulated plan your complete consideration and attention. Splendid headway can be made by demonstrating initiative to get things done.

18—Do not let your sympathies interfere with matters that pertain to job or business. Decide each issue on merits, and do not let prejudiced feelings sway your decisions. Self control is essential if you expect to obtain desired results.

19—Regardless of the swift pace around you, relax and take full advantage of the recreation and comforts within your home. Do not permit existing problems to upset you. Keep travel and expenses for entertainment to a minimum.

20—Patient and well-planned moves, rather than haphazard efforts are required if you expect to achieve effective results. Although you may find it difficult to keep things running smoothly, do not allow yourself to become upset if something does go wrong. Press for the results you wish to obtain quietly, but relentlessly.

21—Sponsoring an impromptu party or social group can lead to some happy moments. Entertain friends or relatives whose company you enjoy. If possible, join a club or group activity where you can be with others who are in a cheerful frame of mind.

22—A splendid day to make decorative changes in your home or to shop for additions to your Christmas list. Talk over your ideas with someone who is qualified to give you practical advice. By doing this, you may be able to save a substantial amount of cash.

23—Since arrangements that you have made may suddenly go away despite your most careful planning and attention, try not to let your temper get out of hand. Instead, counteract difficulties by observing prudent policies and adhering to conservative practices.

24—Refrain from making a drastic change. Do not do anything in haste or make quick decisions. Instead, restrict yourself to familiar places and accustomed activities.

25—Pleasant conversation at breakfast may set the tempo for the day. And while it is all right to look back to glorious tradition, look ahead to an exciting future. And have a happy holiday.

26—Take stock of your mental talents and physical skills, and plan to capitalize on them. This is a good time to embark upon a program of creative production. Utilize opportunities available to you since what you undertake now can prove of benefit in the future.

27—Rather than let frustration cause you to feel limited, increase your self-confidence through hard work and practical accomplishment. Although you may not be able to achieve all you desire, you can make splendid progress, provided you are earnest in your ambitions.

28—You can turn discord into harmony, but you must make a concerted effort to do so now. Do not place yourself in a position where someone else will be able to take advantage of you. Be on guard against strangers.

29—Get the fullest value from your resources. Make every effort to advance your present position and increase your financial assets. Prepare yourself for important tasks and get started on them.

30—Patient analysis of a financial problem should help you to avoid conditions which might otherwise prove annoying. Conclusions based on intuitive impressions may lead you in the wrong direction. Do not risk a setback by acting on impulse.

31—Some surprising change is possible though it isn't of your own making, go along with it as it may bring eventual good fortune. Happy New Year to you of the Virgo solar group.

Libra

September 23rd—October 22nd

You enjoy using artistic talents
or talking about art
with people
who are in the know.
Advanced ideas please you
and good conversation about them
makes you happy.
When beauty and harmony
are strongly in evidence in your environment,
you glow with a happy light.
You love being consulted
on matters
and may often settle disputes among friends
very amicably.
You need love
and a lifemate
who brings you
into practical use of your talents;
otherwise you might dream
and be too inactive.
Real happiness is achieved finally
by active work
and results that are admired.
Never bury
or hide your talents.

Libra

JANUARY

1—Use a straightforward approach rather than involved methods to achieve the results you want. For greatest efficiency, rely on correspondence or the telephone in preference to personal visits. Avoid placing yourself under obligation by making promises or accepting needless responsibilities.

2—Romance and social activities are favored, so get together with congenial companions. Almost anything you plan should work out well, providing it does not require forceful or rapid action. Avoid risking a clash of opinions with someone whose viewpoints do not coincide with yours.

3—Attend to your own problems rather than give anyone an opportunity to create upsetting conditions. Avoid discussion about your intentions until they become realities. Be firm in your attitude and adhere to your conclusions.

4—Defer making abrupt changes, since the results might be hard to undo. Any attempt to find variety or to do something different may not prove as satisfactory as anticipated. Regardless of what you start, carry it through to completion.

5—Do not let over-confidence in your abilities cause you to lose sight of possible results. Get things done well ahead of time and call on others for assistance when you need it. Seek the advice of someone whose judgement you respect rather than take chances.

6—Be clear and definite in your statements in order to avoid a misunderstanding. Put humor and cheer into your day to promote a feeling of congeniality. Set a schedule for work accomplishment and adhere closely to it.

7—Refrain from acting on any information or statements without first checking all the facts. Adjust your finances to allow for future as well as current expenses. Keep on the lookout for errors and do not take any unnecessary chances.

8—Complete with finality whatever obligations are placed on you. For maximum results in your work, seek the help or cooperative efforts of others. Regardless of how busy you are, allow ample time for attending to details.

9—Your silence may prove more beneficial than expressing your thoughts. Whatever your obligations, perform them without complaints or delay. Seek constructive criticism about your ideas and make effective use of valid suggestions.

10—An unguarded comment might undo an otherwise favorable impression. Refrain from doing anything that might place your job or reputation in jeopardy. Be careful of property, particularly if it belongs to someone else.

11—A calm approach to your problems should yield the most satisfactory results. Take action on your plans where necessary to offset interference but avoid discussing it. Remain within your usual surroundings rather than venture into new area.

12—Get things organized quickly so that you can travel toward a definite objective you have in mind. Keep on the lookout for hazards and possible causes of accidents. Avoid divulging matters that are only your concern, since your words are likely to be repeated.

13—Be complimentary in your words if you can, but silence would prove better than criticism. Have patience with others, even though you may feel there is cause to be annoyed. Look for ways to get around restrictions that have been hampering you.

14—Be content to let things work out at their own pace, without rushing matters. Time-wasting conditions can dissipate the hours, so concentrate on that which is important. Utilize your knowledge and skills to greater advantage by doing more than is expected of you.

15—Seek competent advice rather than take unnecessary chances. Overlook petty inconveniences and do not let minor annoyances shatter your peace for the day. Remain optimistic in your atitude, even though things may occur more slowly than expected.

16—Any attempt to give advice or be aggressive may be met with opposition and resentment. Rely only on what you can do, not on the promises of others. Use to advantage what you already have rather than give up everything for something untried.

17—Consider your plans for the future and make arrangements to fulfill them. Refuse to take action on decisions you have made under the pressure of emotions. Use your ingenuity to make profitable use of your leisure hours.

18—Give your full attention to needed home improvements. Arrange to replace worn-out or outmoded possessions with more modern innovations. Start only those things that can be completed in a short time.

19—Tackle each task with determination but make time to do the things you like. Eliminate the subject of business and finances from the conversation so that you can enjoy a calm and peaceful day. Refuse to take part in an argument that does not concern you at all.

20—Wait for problems to straighten out of their own accord, despite a feeling of intense impatience. Handle mechanical or electrical devices with care, since damage or accidents are possible. Keep expenditures under close control, and schedule the fulfillment of tasks to a definite time.

21—Be particularly attentive when handling money or working with others. Spend the time with a hobby or other project from which you can obtain relaxing diversion. Diplomacy and tact are needed rather than giving vent to arguments.

22—Take the initiative in completing matters that have been postponed or delayed too long. Carry out duties for which you are responsible, regardless of how troublesome they may be. Too frank expression of your opinions may invite trouble instead of respect.

23—Go out of your way to keep a prevailing atmosphere of harmony in your household. Organize your work schedule so that tasks can be completed swiftly and efficiently. Benefit from the errors of others so that you will avoid trouble yourself.

24—Keep on the lookout for the attempt of another to take advantage of you. Rely on established facts rather than on intuition when making a decision. Avoid wasting valuable time and money looking for bargains on articles for which you have no real need.

25—Keep your mind alert for possible trouble and mistakes in your work. Make changes in your schedule so that you will have time for many of the things you have had to neglect. Do not invite setbacks in your work by being too exacting in your demands.

26—Give consideration to your own responsibilities before worrying about those of another. Patience and understanding are needed to keep things running smoothly. Over-confidence and carelessness could result in undesirable setbacks.

27—Make needed corrections of errors before they cause difficulty. More can be accomplished through completing one task at a time than by trying to get everything done at once. Do not give in to the temptation to boast, even though your plans may be working out successfully.

28—Arrange to buy things that can add to your personal comfort and happiness. You can overcome minor difficulties and temporary hindrances through determined efforts. Better results can be achieved by appealing to the logic rather than the emotions of another.

29—Misplaced confidence in an associate or taking chances could undo the progress you have already made. Avoid trying to speed up events, even if they appear to be moving too slowly. Seek cheerful surroundings and friends to help make this day an enjoyable one.

30—Make your plans for recreation well ahead of time to avoid delays. Defer decisions concerning money and possessions to insure making this a harmonious day. Generosity and congeniality can create a highly favorable impression.

31—Prepare the foundation for future gains by doing the necessary planning now. Adjust yourself to the temperaments of others instead of taking exceptions to existing trends. Accept words of criticism and advice you receive with appreciation rather than with resentment.

FEBRUARY

1—Be very patient now. You can be longing to get out and to avoid work and responsibilities. It will be impossible, and the sooner you quit the wishful-thinking, the sooner your unhappiness will end. Keep the evening for solitude.

2—Kindliness to a neighbor may bring more impositions and no appreciation. See old friends and avoid your immediate neighborhood today. This evening you need to go over your financial status and make it clearer.

3—Keep a good pace so that you will not fall behind. If a problem about a young child comes up be tolerant and lenient. You may be dealing with a young genius.

4—Be attentive today; you could miss out if you do not heed those who speak. In work you can be proud that you have mastered something new. You are on the road to extra earnings, and the future looks pleasing for your affluence.

5—A good time for shopping (keeping warmer weather in view) and enjoying the day in a relaxed fashion. A letter that comes today may seem strange, but you will become accustomed to what it says and get in touch with its writer.

6—This is a day of danger. Your romantic tendencies are at a height; someone new may take your interest. You can be quite "gone" on someone for whom you shouldn't waste a thought. A good friend may issue a subtle warning.

7—You can be in an excellent mood, your eyes sparkling with your best nature. You'll just love to entertain, particularly if you have a special place in which to do it. Jump the season a bit and visit a lake resort today.

8—Someone who enters your life will be a cause of much concern and some trouble. If you gossip about this person, you will be sorry. Also, you will regret it if you come to conclusions. Keep the evening on the quiet side; stay in.

9—You may get into the car or onto a bus or plane and just keep going. That's what you feel like doing, anyhow. If you have to stay near home, do so; otherwise, get out and follow your impulses for adventurous travel enjoyment.

10—Go about it the right way and you'll get exactly what you want. Gracious ways, endearing speech and absolute truth about amibtions are needed, in addition to approaching the right person. You may pass a big test today!

11—Do not criticize anyone; you can get it back even stronger than you give it. People are not very tolerant and you will be wise to note this. Make a good impression through your appearance at a meeting tonight.

12—Praise someone who has a remarkable memory. Give credit where it is due now. If you are expecting to go out socially tonight, have a brief rest beforehand. A surprise romance may get its start tonight!

13—Shop for that special purchase you need and want. If you find a bargain, examine it thoroughly—there could be subtle but important flaws. Anything that looks too good to be true must be investigated thoroughly before it is bought.

14—Your wisdom is at its best and will allow you to make a decision for your best interests. You can win new esteem today and find that someone really appreciates you—someone you had believed to be hostile and arrogant.

15—Do your best and make no excuses for being lethargic; just get on with the chores. Small children can be a delight this afternoon, and fixing up a little treat for them can be a rare pleasure. Don't work too hard, though.

16—Take good care of all that belongs to you; do not lend and do not part with money. A young relative may have an impractical idea and may be angry if you do not help with it. That is too bad, but let it go at that.

17—Your fashion sense is at its best and things you buy now for a wordrobe will be enchanting. It is a good day to take someone to lunch—perhaps a new associate. Don't let anything mar your efficiency in work during this cycle.

18—Stay with your responsibilities and don't take time out for other things. Be at your best, make no mistakes, and you will pave the way for an improvement in your position. Let your evening be sociable and harmonious.

19—Be cautious of your manner with a younger person. Do not demand too much respect for something that is just part of your nature. Avoid imagining that another person will want to see things in the same practical light that you do.

20—You may receive an invitation that perplexes you. If you doubts are too strong, do not accept it. A good day to join a physical-culture class, attend a spa and get started on some muscle-toning exercise.

21—You'll be called on to be fast and also accurate. Avoid being angry at the pressure. Do not talk with associates. There can be some subtle things going on and they will not benefit you. Be patient about this.

22—You may be in an aloof mood and come across someone who stirs you out of it. You may marvel at the wisdom of an acquaintance and find this person to be a deep well of occult knowledge. A happy relationship can grow.

23—You may be too busy to make it to a meeting. If someone visits this afternoon, be kindly, but remark about the many things you must do today. Relatives and in-laws come first; if married, your lifemate is at top.

24—You may have doubts about a new neighbor right from the beginning. You'll have a difficult time with this person and the law might even be involved later. However, do not let your arrogance gain the ill-will of anyone now.

25—A fine day to close a real estate transaction, sign up for a new investment or sign a marriage certificate. You'll be happy and lucky. Today's favors may include a surprise benefit late in the evening. Love prevails for you.

26—Go shopping, enjoy buying light or small things, a book or two, some stationery, a pet, records or a decorative object for home. Follow your impulses a bit now; they'll bring happiness and be practical.

27—You are in line for a big lift in position, with more money coming in. Surprises and pleasures may come one right after the other today. Call someone at a distance tonight and share the good news. Offer help that may be needed.

28—Do as much as you can, but don't press on when you begin to feel exhausted. Your diet may need some supplementary vitamins. Do what is needed to keep in the pink of condition; enjoy social life in moderate style tonight.

29 (Leap Year Only)—Business will summon you to use all your efforts. Sales can be good today and new partnerships can flourish, but there may be quite a long period of effort. Patience and understanding of the views of others will be needed. Accept an invitation.

MARCH

1—Not much activity today and most spirits are low. You may be thinking back over past matters, wondering about different choices you once had. This can be the most futile of all pursuits, so try to switch off the past and live in the present.

2—You can develop frustrations with a mechanical object, possibly a machine you work with. Call an expert for help and do not attempt amateur repairs. You could get injured. In fact, the present cycle calls for much caution.

3—Someone who does not like or understand you may be quite blunt about it today. You will have your choice of reactions, for you won't really care at all. Walking away with a smile might be as good as anything else in this situation.

4—A surprise letter may have some sad news for you but it may also offer you some interesting new relationship. Ponder this matter well, for you should look at the disadvantages as well as advantages and weigh all possibilities quite carefully.

5—Take a visitor walking with you, enjoy being outdoors, take a little trip to a place of beauty, roam around this afternoon. Casual conversation may turn up some wonderful ideas and might be the beginning of a profitable venture.

6—Try to keep your disposition as serene and steady as possible. Avoid yielding to an attitude of giving up. There is a certain sense of disappointment about life in general that may attack your spirits. Defend yourself.

7—Someone may try to steal a brilliant idea from you; keep very quiet even though you feel elated. It may be the start of a new technique for which you will win a fine reward. In home life tonight be agreeable, avoid argument.

8—A good day to buy anything from a mousetrap to a house. Buy vacant land which may soon become a center of building activity. Survey your possibilities of some maneuvering on the market. It's all yours financially.

9—You'll discover true affection in an old friend who wants to see you after a long time apart. Avoid making any assumptions, however, Keep your life running smoothly today and in the evening be hospitable.

10—You may hear from someone at a distance who needs help. Your conscience may cause you to send such help immediately but don't let it be taken for granted. Make sure the relative to whom you are generous knows your difficulties.

11—A big surprise and then several small ones can come your way in daylight hours. A visitor just passing through town on vacation can be the highlight of the day. Social life may be fun tonight but you'll be tired early.

12—Do not let anyone imagine you are interested romantically when that is farthest of all from your thoughts. Your cool should be turned on in a pleasant fashion for all contacts at meeting or wherever else you are.

13—Shopping yields rewards, particularly in supplies for home such as linens and dishes. You can be proud of today's acquisitions when you take advantage of sales. Do a little artistic work on kitchen decorations tonight.

14—You can be tempted to have luxuries. Your ego is quite busy today but some of this spending may be due to need for compensating in other matters which did not go well for you. Try to draw a line somewhere in spending.

15—New circumstances in your life can prove the best thing that ever happened for your health's sake. You can be very pleased to be among associates who are not envious or worried about your ability to steal jobs from others.

16—Conditions that surprise you may not seem desirable once you have the chance to take stock of them. You are urged to be tactful and not to follow up on first words that come to you. Utter only your second thoughts.

17—You can be very popular today; if masculine you may be lionized a bit or even more than a bit. You may have to turn down some invitations because so many are rolling in for the weekend. Be prudent and strategic now.

18—This is a good time to go on a vacation, particularly if that means a visit to relatives at a distance. If you stay at home today be sure to surround yourself with congenial people, give a small but merry party.

19—News over long distance telephone can be exciting but you can't quite analyze your feelings otherwise. Avoid thinking in material fashion and view the situation in a larger manner. Do not let trivialities annoy you.

20—Work is under trying circumstances. You may be closely observed, notes may be taken on your efficiency and there can be talk that is embarrassing to to you between two executives. Hold on to your temper like fury now.

21—Emotions may take over, you are just ripe for romantic trends and they may come in a surprising fashion. The charm of life is noteworthy and it puts your spirits on high plane. Love commencing now can be enduring forever.

22—Someone very whimsical and grouchy may speak out of turn. You're not in the mood to exchange argumentative remarks. Walk on by and don't notice if someone is trying to bait you and arouse your anger now.

23—You may find you have a rival in love and may feel like retreating silently. It's up to you, of course, but if you really are attracted, don't give up so easily. What is worth having is worth struggling for a bit.

24—A letter may seem friendly but if you read between the lines you may note hostility of indirect nature. It might be best to discourage this correspondence for good by never answering again. Social life may hold some peculiarity.

25—An ironic person can stir your enmity and you may lash back with a few telling words yourself. However, the day grows more balmy, love comes in strong during the evening and you'll end the day with great contentment.

26—You can be full of delight over a plan that is working well. Be cordial with all you meet, stop and talk a bit if called upon to do so, make it obvious that you are interested in people. Evening can bring a charming experience.

27—Be ready for the unexpected. You may be making a move to new work environment. Do not brood on the words of others now; they probably mean much less than you imagine. You may get a chance to use a talent for the first time.

28—Be kindly, pleasant, unruffled. Your emotional calm can be inspiring to others. Those who are older will gain particular benefit from your manner. It is a good evening to buy a new book and get lost in it.

29—Social situations can be embarrassing. Something you never thought may happen. You may protect your own dignity and honor by calling people and telling them what has happened. Don't try to keep anything quiet.

30—Avoid a clash with someone you simply cannot tolerate. It is foolish to waste words when there is a deep mutual dislike. Go your way as calmly as possible after your paths cross. Look forward to a cheerful, friendly evening.

31—Be wary in shopping today. You can be highly tempted to put much money into clothes. This is not a very ethical attitude for money is needed elsewhere. Your self-centered view now can do some permanent harm in family.

APRIL

1—Slow and easy does it today. You want to get into the act with a lot of industrious activity, but you'll have a more important role if you are thoughtful and follow a gradual but perfect course in your undertakings. You'll climb, but do it without rushing or getting confused in your objectives.

2—Something good may come your way and cause you some happy emotional excitement. Avoid neighbors who irritate you. Recognize a personality clash when it is present. You may have quite a time of it if you attend a meeting of importance tonight. You may be elected to high office.

3—Discard some old beliefs that are no longer valid in this age of the computer. These may be somewhat philosophical in nature—ideas such as the job being more important than the worker, for instance. Don't follow lesser lights, switch to fact and get on the train of now.

4—If you become friendly with a new associate you may regret it soon. Every word may be carried to the place where it can do the most harm, and all may be distorted as much as possible to make it even worse. You'll need self-protection and forewarning should be adequate for help.

5—You can feel too weary to get going on chores. Some kind person will help you and they'll be over before you know it. In the evening's plans you may have a large role and thus need to spend time and thought on appearance. Be right up in style and a little daring in every way possible.

6—Some concern about an older relative may make the day gloomy. You may know that you are going to have to part with a large sum of money and that can make you despondent. Buck up and be your own brave, intelligent and philanthropic self. A guest may surprise and cheer you tonight.

7—A romantic day when you can fall deeply in love just by walking past someone on your way elsewhere. Chances of meeting the person again are very good but events can be mysterious and have a strange aura. One of the most exciting trends of your life is present and will unfold gradually.

8—Health care may be needed and you may tend to neglect it. A toothache means trouble; don't put off a dental appointment. If you've been having frequent headaches over the eyes, see an optometrist or optician quickly. Spend in order to keep your health and happiness at their best.

9—You can become vexed with the attitude of a younger person and may speak scathingly. That will do no good. In fact, nothing will do any good in this relationship and it will come to an end with no consequences whatever. Try to be good natured at home with a loved one and family tonight.

10—Give full credit to someone who has predicted an event you didn't believe would happen. It happened all right and today's the day there is quite a shake-up as a result. This can be one of the roughest days you've ever known, yet challenges are exciting and you are happily keyed up.

11—If you refuse to confide in a loved one, you may lose out on this love completely. Well, perhaps it was meant to end, you may say. Don't let the first shock cause you to do something unworthy of your intelligence. Also, today you may get good news from a friend. Much mixture in aspects.

12—A neighbor may have a request that will be easy for you to fulfill, so don't back down arrogantly. Avoid heavy expenses of a selfish type. Take good care of anything or anyone in your charge. Be very good to pets. The evening may hold a discussion of importance to spiritual life.

13—Church may depress you a little, an older friend may bore you. Try to endure for that is a large part of the adult attitude. Read something instructive in either philsophy or the occult today and you can find mental growth beginning to take place as the result of a startling new thought.

14—Wonderful for any financial transaction you have in mind or for following impulse about money and various dealings. You may get a rare bargain. A good day for creative activity also and things you make can be both stylish and money-saving. Let your artistic taste go a little far out.

15—Be kindly and give encouragement to an older associate. You can support another spiritually with good effect. Industry pays off but not as much as proper investment will. Be active financially, take a calculated risk, then be willing to wait patiently while things ripen beautifully.

16—A wonderful day for relationships, pleasure, fun activities and talk. Games are enjoyable, new companions are exhilarating. If you entertain tonight be very casual about it so that you can have full enjoyment. Heed the words of a new younger acquaintance whose appearance attracts.

17—You may feel let down by a friend who totally forgets to keep a promise. Don't wait too long for anyone or anything, value your time. If you have a decision to make about a young relative, today is the day to make it boldly. You'll probably please this person very much with your verdict.

18—Don't be timid about getting involved with someone quite radical, youthful and enthusiastic. This can be a stimulating source of new spirits for you. Enjoy what is up to date and forget some of the traditions you once thought important. A romantic aura is around tonight but will be elusive.

19—Be generous, sympathetic and pleasant to everyone. If asked for a loan, try to grant it. You'll get everything back, for today brings you nothing but good and honest relationships. If you have something a younger friend can use, be swift to give it. Your role is to help and please others now.

20—New experiences, a surprise trip, romantic opportunity are all here. You can be quite pleased and entertained by the way things proceed. Put a high value on yourself and you will give other people new light about your character. There's nothing petty about you or events at this time.

21—Good time for a big change. You can start a new job, move your residence to a far location, buy furniture, install something right up-to-date to make the home more comfortable and clean. In the evening enjoy your new trends and have friends drop in to share your pleasure.

22—It will be foolish to be alarmed at what a casual acquaintance has to say or to make accusations to this person about obtaining knowledge falsely. You'll be in the wrong if you do these things. What you need is to raise your estimate of this person much higher and have more esteem.

23—Circumstances in your work environment may change for the good. You may find your place among more congenial people doing more important things. Your talents will give you a chance for greater earnings and you will be instructed in how to carry out a vital job. A day for progress indeed.

24—Someone very intolerant and conventional may enter your life and attract you sexually. This can be quite a problem. If you make the slightest overture, you may as well count upon being betrayed. Keep your personal life unsullied; do not talk about it with anyone during a party tonight.

25—Rest, walk around, talk with an older neighbor a little but don't let yourself in for a closer relationship. You'll be busy in afternoon straightening out some affairs connected with finances, taxes, savings and insurance. Get everything balanced and know just where you stand with money.

26—Someone may do something spiteful due to envy of you. You can be harmed. Those who are loyal will come to your aid and all will be ironed out by the end of the day. Nevertheless, this experience will leave a mark; try not to be too distrustful but resolve also to be more watchful in future.

27—Perform a service for a neighbor. You will be more than rewarded but above all it will enhance the relationship and make it one of warmth and deep affection. If you have a date for evening, make it brief for you need to get as much rest and sleep as possible. Set limits and keep them.

28—A splendid day for a journey and you may take one for a special purpose. An interview at a distance may land you the job you want. You may be moving soon. Be thoughtful today but also enjoy the spirit of zest and fun in the atmosphere. Feel free to express yourself verbally.

29—Extravagance threatens. You may buy hobby items of high cost, spend much on beautifying the home, and in the long run win much disapproval from a lifemate. If unmarried of course it's your own affair, but you'd be unwise to jeopardize your solid finances and good credit rating today.

30—If you make a mistake, do things over cheerfully. Be very just to all you deal with. Trying to play Cupid for a friend during an evening party may not succeed and could embarrass someone quite a lot. Be sensitive to the moods and feelings of others and you'll make no such error.

MAY

1—A surprise may be delightful. You'll be in a cheery mood, win new affection, and help someone who is very deserving. Let nothing stop you from following kindly impulses. Common sense might direct you one way, but intuition is a better guide throughout this cycle.

2—New work ideas can be successful if you make plans about using them in a practical fashion. Get in touch with someone by telephone and you may be encouraged to go ahead with a bold course. Thoughtful ways and giving time to problems will have positive results in near future.

3—Be very kindly to people in your environment and also with pets. You could become irritated and do something which is not worthy of you. Have patience with all and sundry. Work with precision, go slow, keep high goals in mind. A telephone call tonight can be disappointing.

4—An outspoken person may say something that amazes you and tends to rouse your temper swiftly. Keep in control, try to understand. You will make a fine impression if you are quiet and pleasant in the face of some unpleasant remarks from others. Give thought to this matter tonight.

5—Take your time in making plans, include a change that has attracted you for some time. This is a cycle in which new trends can take over and be beneficial. Don't look back once you have made decisions about career desires. You will get support from loved ones this evening.

6—Be practical about money, do not lend it or any possession of value. If you want to give something away that is another matter. Do not let anything go to waste, there's always a place it can be used. Good friendship may commence from a conversation with a neighbor tonight.

7—Neatness and good order are required to keep the day from becoming chaotic. You may have a social engagement that pleases you but something you disapprove of may happen this evening. Someone may pry into your personal life, make remarks that are uncalled for about it.

8—Do not indulge in regret which is futile. Take a firm stand, follow plans carefully, be moderate in all you do. Your appetite may be slight, you could have some nervous stomach troubles. Don't eat more than appeals to you. Seek early rest, avoid large gatherings tonight.

9—A neighbor may call with the intention of imposing upon you. Someone who merely wants to use you for convenience must be turned away or you'll get yourself tied down to a very unpleasant set of circumstances. Do not let yourself be used by a shrewd and malicious person.

10—A confidence may be given to you and you must be willing to keep it secret no matter how much someone else may try to pry it out of you. Use your highest character traits and prove you are worthy of a beneficial friendship that is getting underway. Silence is golden.

11—You may focus all thought on a decision that must be made. Be watchful in work, for preoccupation may cause an error that would be aggravating. You may make a promise late in the day that is vital to your future welfare. Don't make it until you are sure of your own mind.

12—You can feel quite weary and not like yourself. Consulting a physician may be necessary and you may be surprised to learn the source of your trouble. There may be need for certain measures to be taken in connection with blood pressure. It's good to know the facts now.

13—Be patient and generous with a younger person who turns to you for friendship. You may have experience which is valuable in helping another today. Be cautious of activities and companionship in the evening. You are better off at home than out anywhere at all.

14—News may be encouraging about a financial hope. You are also favored for big spending today. A very good time to buy furniture, appliances, even a car. All clothes and cosmetics bought now will be successful in making you feel at your best in a social gathering tonight.

15—Do not snub a neighbor who has vexed you in recent days. Strive for understanding, be forgiving and charitable in view. Avoid all gossip, people who are extravagant and those whose motives are suspicious. Evening can be a mixture of joy and emotional disturbance.

16—Be thoughtful and resolve to make a sacrifice in order to help someone you love. Be cautious in speech with a neighbor; your least word could be distorted later. Realistic attitude and approaches are needed, so avoid anything imaginative or not based on facts.

17—Avoid anger over the remark of a person who is not well known to you. You may be in the company of someone very wise but unable to understand you. Keep to yourself as much as possible in work. If you shop be sure you are alone; a friend would tend to sway your intentions.

18—Do something lovely for an older friend whose loyalty you appreciate. A gift of flowers or even something more lasting is a good idea. Be generous and a bit luxurious in doing things for others. You'll be happy, know you've done the right thing in reflecting tonight.

19—Show consideration for the rights of others; be tactful with young persons. Show that you can think young no matter what your age. You can win admiration from an executive when you finish a difficult task. This day's trend could lead to a desired promotion soon.

20—A wonderful day for financial activities and an unexpected romantic adventure. You can buy or sell whatever you wish and there are good prices in both directions. You may be prompted to speak unwisely about romance tonight; this inclination must be curbed.

21—Correspondence may be troublesome today. You may have a letter from someone who is in a quarrelsome mood. Do not sit down and respond in anger. The longer you let response go, the better for all concerned. Plans for the evening can be cheerful; look your best wherever you go.

22—Show ability to understand a neighbor who has some health problems that are discouraging. Don't expect too much of such a person. Nerves can be on edge late in the day and might bring need to cancel an evening social engagement. However, go if you possibly can do so.

23—Be courageous, do what is asked of you no matter how it disturbs your own plans. A young relative may visit and ask a favor. You may have to be very lenient in order to handle this matter. It is essential that you do your best so that your conscience will be in the right.

24—A grouchy executive may anger you. Although your temper is seething be quiet. You may be planning a big change but don't let your emotions cause you to speak of it now. Get work completed and keep to a steady course. Take time to read some informative literature tonight.

25—A neighbor can be malicious, try to injure your feelings. Actually, you cannot be wounded by by this person and you might as well let it be known by a cheery laugh. Avoid all arguments, make no accusations, criticize no one. Wisdom must rule throughout this cycle.

26—An excellent time to shop for personal items, buy clothes, perfume, anything needed to make your life more convenient. Let yourself be a bit extravagant in following up a time of excellent taste. Enjoy the evening with a loved one, let romance reign in your heart now.

27—You may slow down in work due to thoughtfulness about a personal matter. There are conflicting trends for your emotions. Try to put off any decision and let this cycle go by in somewhat routine fashion. Avoid talking too much to an older person during the evening.

28—Someone may have information you do not know about and on the basis of this may make an attack on your personal life. You may guess at the state of affairs, sense gossip in the air. If you are quiet and pleasant you will trample down all adverse factors in the air today.

29—Show appreciation of a kindness in a concrete way. You may feel cheerful, need some activity to get you out in the fresh air and do a little walking. A good time to refresh health. A sport might occupy you this evening and you could win honors with your adept play.

30—Difficult to gain understanding from a person who does not have your mental complexity of depth. Don't try too hard if you find you are just not congenial with another. A good day for a drive in rural regions, take an older friend along for such an outing, then dine away from home.

31—Conditions can be difficult for work progress and you may become impatient with an innocent person. Better go slow, see that good-will prevails. Make no plans for the evening; you will need to be alone to rest and recover a more tolerant attitude toward your entire world.

JUNE

1—An argument will be futile. You can be tempted to give advice when it is not asked; struggle against this trend. Not a very good day and your personality can be somewhat marred by these trends, so it is best to avoid social life—even a romantic meeting for tonight.

2—Extra money may come in, you may collect a debt of long standing. All goes well in career and a short talk with an executive may hold promise for improvement in your future. A good friend may visit this evening, but don't put off retirement.

3—Be very protective toward anyone dependent on you and toward pets. You may have some health difficulty bothering you that could cause lack of heed to the needs of others. Win out over the tendency, be dutiful and affectionate in your environment for the cycle.

4—This is a good time to cut out a habit which is not beneficial, also to start a diet for weight loss. Your own ideas about the matter can be the best to follow. If you have a social engagement this evening, it's best not to take any kind of refreshment, count yourself out.

5—A letter which arrives this morning may disturb you. Someone may be in a romantic mood when you are not. In general it is difficult to find congenial circumstances today and you may want to be alone for an evening of reading, music, thought about vital matters of career.

6—Be cordial with a new neighbor, enjoy a talk and getting to know each other. There may be natural affinity with such a person. If you drive today, try to stay out of the heavier traffic even though it means taking back streets in slower zones. An accident can be vexing and expensive.

7—You may learn that you will have to cancel a vacation plan due to matters that come to attention today. Be sure to let anyone else involved know about this quickly. Keep the evening for quiet activities and win serenity through relaxation, clearing mind of troubles.

8—You can be worried over financial hope that is slow in bearing fruit. Patience is the ticket. It can be just a classic care of delay and slowness on the part of others. Look your best today for a romantic trend might crop up suddenly and be very enticing to you tonight.

9—Avoid all gossip. Refuse to comment on other people even though strongly tempted. Be kind to all who work with you, to neighbors near your home and to relatives. You can be criticized by an older person tonight; don't take this too seriously or show umbrage.

10—This is a restless day; you may feel you do not know what you want. You may meet a younger person new to you and be enchanted with personality. It can be easy to misjudge this person, though, so be cautious in that direction. Avoid extravagance in shopping during this cycle.

11—Be tolerant with a loved one and very loyal in speech. You could put the final touch to a break-up if you criticize someone in public. It is possible to lose someone's affections and that could cause much unhappiness. Be thoughtful of all others at a social gathering.

12—You might be rash and daring and create a situation that would not be desirable and would be difficult to escape. Courtesy to those in your neighborhood is needed. Do not show dislike or a superior attitude toward someone with whom you find it difficult to communicate.

13—An older person may ask too much of your generosity today. Don't get involved in this matter. Get away from home and attend some meeting or show that interests you. Today it is possible to gain new philosophic insight and wisdom which will be very helpful to you in the future.

14—Avoid working too strenuously and don't let any circumstance cause you to rush. Guard your health, be moderate, heed traffic signals and be careful when working in the kitchen this evening. Members of the family are the best companions for you in hours after dark.

15—Turn down invitations today, pursue a leisurely course of following whims, You'll appreciate this free time doing small things that attract you. This is not a good day on which to make a romantic decision, so if asked to do so postpone it in a pleasant manner.

16—Do not let anyone influence your views or actions today. Independence is best and in following it you will profit unexpectedly. A decision you make can have good effects for your future. You gain a feeling of having everything under control, spirits and health are good.

17—Be lenient with someone younger in the family who does something a little out of line. Try to see the very youthful view. Shopping is pleasant if you limit it strictly and buy small items that are needed in the home. Avoid selfish spending on unnecessary items.

18—If you dislike someone intensely do not tell anyone. Your words will be carried around, distorted and capable of causing much trouble. Be tactful and say nothing if you can't speak well of others. It is best to cultivate a new acquaintance made in social life tonight.

19—You may see beneath the surface of someone who is quite deceptive. Don't reproach the person with your knowledge. You could win a powerful and tireless enemy that way. Keep your evening free for there may be a surprise to take advantage of during the late hours.

20—You may yield to an urge to have a luxury item that has attracted you for a long time. Go ahead and then get this matter off your mind. You'll be able to make up for expenses soon, be optimistic financially. Evening can be pleasant with light telephone chats.

21—You may be asked to tackle something new which is a challenge to your talents. Perfectionist work is desirable so keep with it until you achieve this goal. No extra money is seen but you will have personal pleasure from achievements and some fame may come to you now.

22—Attend church if you possibly can. You may hear a good sermon and find some wisdom that is useful in it. The afternoon is good for a gathering such as a picnic. Arrange some special treat to please others. Romance can play an unusual role in your life today.

23—Someone may not know your motives for a unique act. You can enjoy having this as a type of secret which is harmless. You can do some deep thinking today, arrive at a conclusion, find benefit in a situation that arises. Talk with a good friend tonight will be pleasant.

24—Your natural inclination toward being a recluse may be in full force today and you may try to keep to yourself in all you do. Watch out that temperament does not show in unpleasant way with a younger friend who admires you. You could lose esteem of this person through anger.

25—Health can be troublesome and difficult to care for. Diagnosis may take some time. Don't postpone seeing a physician if anything at all is wrong. Make sure all food and drink is preserved properly, handled properly. Keep your ways moderate and use good sense in all.

26—Someone new in your neighborhood may be attracted romantically by you. This is not a good trend to follow. The doors of many friends are open, so be sociable, go visiting. A sudden desire to entertain at your home tonight can bring pleasant results for all.

27—Unfamiliar places can be hazardous. Stay close to home. If you must travel take all safety precautions, also be sure you have adequate cash for unforseen troubles. Do not be blunt in speech with anyone. Avoid talk to a stranger beyond mere amenity.

28—Try to read the writing on the wall. You may get a hint from someone you don't know very well who feels that things are not right in your area. This could be correct. Keep your eyes open, analyze circumstances. You may make a discovery that startles you but must be heeded.

29—Keep all your activities highly ethical, do nothing questionable in the financial realm. There is definite change slated for today in your life. You may have to accept a condition that is difficult to face. New strength of character will aid you about this.

30—Ask no favors, be self-reliant, think things through on practical basis and then make plans. Buy something pleasant to lift your spirits a bit. It is best not to attend a large gathering or be out in public tonight. Seeing a loyal friend is beneficial, though.

JULY

1—You may not be your usual energetic self. Thoughts going on in the background of your mind may actually take more of your attention than outside duties and requirements. Not a very good day for practical work; watch for errors. The evening may find you developing a plan that is quite exciting.

2—A disappointment in your personal affairs can have a deep effect. Don't look back or you'll spend the day moping. Get on with the present obligations, make sure your appearance is excellent for social life tonight. What takes place now and good hopes for tomorrow are the important things.

3—You may fall in with someone who is new in the neighborhood. This relationship will probably never have anything pleasant to offer, so it is wise to say little, keep the acquaintance from ripening. Romantic matters can be disappointing tonight due to the unreliable ways of a loved one.

4—You may change plans and then not quite know what to do. You actually need rest and a chance for reflection. Making plans that take some daring can work out well. Keep your personal life very much to yourself this evening. You may have visitors who are curious, but don't talk about yourself at all.

5—A good day for the small things that make life happy. Your spirits can soar suddenly when you receive news about a young relative. Your work will go efficiently and leave you time to have a conference of importance for your future. You may be surprised at the speech of an executive this afternoon.

6—Someone younger than you may have more intuition about affairs concerning you than you do yourself. Best to listen even though what you hear is not at all what you want to hear. Disagreement will accomplish nothing in the face of facts that are developing. Wishful thinking will not halt progress of facts.

7—Shopping is favored and spending money can get your mind away from troublesome subjects. Have lunch with someone who is always encouraging. Be very loyal to one you love, say nothing but good about others today. An amusing incident may happen this evening and neighborhood tension may be high.

8—Do not imagine that you are more intelligent than someone new in your area. Appearances are very deceptive today and someone highly innocent in appearance may be anything but that underneath. Someone may telephone from a distance this evening and try to learn facts you are keeping to yourself.

9—Even though you do not like some of the present trends, it's wise to catch up on them and find some reason for approving them. The mere fact that you object to changes will have no power to prevent them. Be tolerant of the young even though you do not personally care to go in their direction now.

10—Minor home chores, a little shopping for staples and some chatting with those you encounter casually will fill most of the day. It is not a good evening to entertain in your home but it is favorable for going to someone else's home where you can meet a new person who may interest you deeply.

11—A major event may take place in your life and turn it upside down. You can find independence is forced upon you and that you have no way to control what is going on otherwise. Do not say much for you are sure to regret your speech later. Keep your pride and dignity in first place today.

12—Someone you didn't know was hostile may suddenly attack you. Envy and a feeling of inferiority may lead a neighbor or work associate to speak harshly to you. Don't let this lead to a quarrel. Walk silently away. If you are amused, that could make things worse, so don't show an amused attitude.

13—Someone who crosses your path today may have enormous effect on your thought and emotions. Best to avoid talk about this. You may be destined to meet again but not for some time. This is a highly romantic day and you may be just too far out in unknown clouds for your good at this time.

14—Someone new to you can be charming and attract you romantically. It would not be wise to speak about this matter. Make no overtures when it comes to romance. Today you need all your prudence and keen insight. Be tactful and pleasant but keep an impersonal atmosphere in all your conversations.

15—Your financial hopes may be realized today, and a start may be given by a major project. You will be very serious about this matter and might speak sharply to someone who doesn't take it as seriously as you think it should be taken. Try to be reasonable and let good wit rule, not tension.

16—News that comes in concerning your vacation may be pleasing. You may get more time than you thought you would to enjoy a lengthy trip and visit. New conditions in your life will be a source of interest to relatives but don't talk too much for there is no sense in revealing your secret ambitions.

17—Let enjoyment rule the cycle. Buy something that attracts you, perhaps a pet. Let plans for entertainment this evening be quite luxurious. Guests will never forget your abundant provisions and attractive way of serving them. Don't worry about a thing now; take it easy, have fun.

18—There may be some financial injustice in your life and little you can do about it. It may be time to seek better paying work, change your whole trend to a more ambitious one. Special study can be the answer to your needs. There are changes ahead that you will find valuable to your desires.

19—You may get some inside information that allows you a remarkable investment. Your genius for taking a calculated risk can come into play advantageously. You'll be courageous enough to undertake this gamble and also have faith in it. Don't let an older relative discourage you about money.

20—A day that calls for caution in the physical sense. Your chart shows a tendency to accident and chances of ill health from some activity that isn't well managed. Do not stay out in the heat too long or undertake strenuous tasks outside. Be careful both in walking and working at home or elsewhere.

21—A troublesome situation you thought was over for good may arise again. This could make a brief trip necessary, cause you to waste some time with people who do not really belong in your social world. Try to be pleasant and reasonable even though you blame someone for injustice and meddling.

22—Activity will be pleasing today and you'll enjoy companionship of someone who interests you due to a certain amount of mystery in personality. Shop for important things and get reactions from the friend who is with you. Your combined good taste may result in some remarkable decorative purchases.

23—If you criticize anyone for superficial matters, you will regret it. Your philosophy should tell you to look beneath the surface. Lack of using your wisdom today may upset a relationship permanently and give you cause for unhappiness. Evening is very glamorous but don't act too superior.

24—A heavy load of burdens may be upon you now. You may have to do things for both younger and older members of the family and this can keep you going at a brisk pace. You may be in the midst of someone else's emotional troubles even though you didn't try to be there. Do your best to be helpful.

25—No use wasting time, or being moody about a change over which you have no control. Your best bet is to forget family troubles and go right on with your personal interests. A loyal friend may invite you out to dinner and that can be happy. Don't rush around, take everything serenely today.

26—Financial matters are in the lead and you may decide to invest more money in a place which has already shown good results with dividends. A younger relative may feel that you should have been more generous with money rather than just using it to enhance your own financial accumulation.

27—You might fall quite hopelessly in love with someone you see every day. Your spirit is like that of first love and you marvel at your own feeling of affection. There is every chance that attraction is mutual and there is no chance at all that anything can ever come of it. Don't be sad.

28—There can be gossip, malice, some real threats to your position. Someone will remain loyal and thoughtful about you; you can count on winning due to the help of this friend. It may be some time before you get the whole story but it will gradually come out and can be quite startling.

29—Be very efficient at work but also aim for a higher position. Let your ambitions show, ask for a conference, make your plan known. If you are willing to be patient you may get just what you want. You have been saved for a special position that requires your unique and powerful mental abilities.

30—A very busy day but you'll need to work in time to get something done for your appearance. You want to be at your most attractive this evening. You will probably be going to a festive event, possibly with an air of formality to it. Some conflict is in the scene for you during the evening.

31—You'll need rest and a chance to get away from your own emotions. An experience of yesterday evening may leave you feeling very unhappy. Shop around, see a show, join people who are stimulating in conversation. Keep moving around and you won't let yourself in for hopeless brooding about anything.

AUGUST

1—You need as much self-assurance as you can muster today. You may do something unusual which you very much want to do. It will take daring and you must be ready for results that might be contrary to your hopes. However on the other hand results may be quite pleasing and make you happy.

2—Do not react with hasty emotions to what you hear now. Danger of spending too much on something that will not be appreciated as a gift. Help make a happier life for an older person by the attention you give rather than by any gift of material nature. This is your wise course, leave no regrets.

3—You may have a new and younger neighbor who will be quite interested in cultivating your acquaintance. Keep this within limits for you really do not share the same principles and philosophy. In fact, you may discover deception and falsehood in the person before this day comes to a close.

4—Safety features should be checked or added to your home or your car. It is not a time to take chances with wiring that may be faulty. Be sure to have someone really trustworthy look over your car. Avoid large bills for repair; find the necessary people who are reasonable in their charges.

5—You can do some foolish things if you let emotions get their way. This might include some unpleasant speech of criticism to one who has never harmed you. Avoid carrying forward any petty gossip. It might not be dangerous to do so, but it could be very foolish and trivial, unworthy of you.

6—You may have to deal with some complex mathematics. Be very careful not to make an embarrassing mistake. Best to get a wise friend to check over this important matter. This may hold some news that lets your hopes soar further up. Evening is excellent for social life and a new friendship.

7—An unfortunate emotional upheaval in the home can change things forever. Try to be willing to see your own flaws in an intimate relationship and be willing to make amends for them. It may not be possible to put things together again but it is worth a try before it is too late.

8—You may be concerned about the speech of someone who seems to persist in trying to belittle you. Don't worry much about it. Actually the person who is causing this trouble may be just treating you like one of the family and being blunt in the way that only intimacy can excuse.

9—An excellent day to shop for things you want. Let your impulse play its role today and you'll be happy with new acquisitions. Make your wardrobe more colorful; try something more youthful than your usual choices. After all, this is a day when youthfulness is possible for all ages.

10—A younger friend can be difficult to understand. What you say may be taken angrily and resentfully by this person. Chances are you cannot correct this relationship for you are dealing with an inflexible person who is almost obsessed by inner imagination and built-up resentments.

11—You can find yourself lacking in spirit, feeling exhausted. There may be adequate cause to see a physician without delay. A younger person may call and you can enjoy the conversation. Avoid the subject of religion throughout this cycle; many people are quite easily upset in this area.

12—You can become very interested in some major purchase you have investigated lately. Take one more good look, think once more before you negotiate further. The word of a friend might be useful in pointing out something you had overlooked. Keep the evening a quiet one near home.

13—Do not take on detailed chores which are not justly your own. Let each person take care of burdens individually. You are in one of your moods for hard work and use of talent. These can show up in preparations for a party tonight and energies can be exhilarated all the way through the cycle.

14—There is almost certain to be a romantic theme running through the day. Someone close to you may be eligible and a relation may try to play Cupid between the two of you. There is little chance that anything will come of this due to the fact that your interests are poles apart.

15—Buy something appropriate for a going-away present. This might be the day for the retirement of a fellow employee who will very much appreciate your exquisite taste in choosing an item both pleasant and useful. Your evenings may be taken up helping someone else in a problem. Be very conscientious in this.

16—This period can be tiresome. It is a good time to be on vacation, to take a trip you have always wanted to take. If you must be at work dullness can possess you and you may wish you had done things differently when you had a chance. Be cautious in speech with a lifemate tonight, if you have one.

17—You may discover a more efficient way to do something that has always been an onerous chore. As reward for this you may be put in a new position, perhaps your genius for organization will get a chance to prove itself. Make good impressions on others by your serious attitude toward work.

18—You may be blind to attitudes and flaws in someone you love greatly. This could be costly to you but your affections are so great that you do not even care about that. Well, it may be part of the scheme of things that you should benefit this younger person and have no selfish regrets about it.

19—You'll find out how deeply loyal a friend is by a voluntary offer to help you in a major achievement. The world will be a brighter place for you from now on because this person exists. If you go shopping be sure not to be lured by flashing things; seek quality first, appearance second.

20—A splendid day to enjoy life, not to take things too seriously. An encounter with someone you've known a long time may lead to an invitation to go along to a glamorous place, a country you've never visited before. Too bad that the person who gives invitation is not ethical enough.

21—Be very tolerant with family members and also use your energies to help them. An older relative may be unreasonable but you just need to smile and stay serene. Forget your own desires and be unselfish in everything. At a party tonight, avoid becoming angry at a trivial matter.

22—Some unfortunate physical fact can befall you today. Don't make a fuss about this in front of others. Wait until tomorrow and you can get an appointment with an expert who will fix things up for you at least temporarily. Be of good cheer this evening, don't dwell on personal misfortunes.

23—Be practical and prudent in all you do. Shopping is favored but it must be carried out with penetrating insight and good attention to budget limits. Be a little cautious about something to add to a hobby. You could be called wasteful and foolish for such an expenditure if it is a luxurious one.

24—Take things slowly, don't commit yourself to any large gatherings, avoid younger people somewhat. You can easily be upset by trends and therefore need a quiet atmosphere and not too much activity. A grandparent might try to interfere and thus cause you need for wise tact in speech.

25—Talk can be dangerous today; watch out for a malicious neighbor who never rests until a way is thought up to get revenge on anyone who has displeased this person. Keep yourself aloof, do not even talk on the telephone to your neighbor. You'd be surprised how vicious and petty a person can be.

26—You may be surprised at a gift you receive from someone you hadn't been thinking of. There can be a little remorse for your former coolness with this person. Just be yourself now and you'll soon establish the fact of your good will. In any romantic date tonight look your best but keep at a distance.

27—Your career gets a boost from someone very influential and you may be told about a rise in your position very soon. Be gracious to all who telephone this evening even if you are quite busy. Family affairs may demand you aid; your thought processes can open up unique ways for relatives to win help.

28—News you get may be bittersweet. You'll get the chance to do something you want to do, but it will be marred by other factors present. Avoid a harsh remark to anyone. Make your own resolutions about the future, realize that you have an individual life to live and that is what you must concentrate on.

29—You may be going someplace interesting in connection with a brief work assignment. Matters are shaping up in your career life and by the end of the day you may be asked to take a new position in a different line of work. Your decision now is vital in directing future trends in career.

30—A day for work progress, happy relationships, a delightful luncheon with a new companion, and possibly invitation to join a worthwhile organization. Avoid brooding over your finances; the future will amend some flaws in your savings and investments. Be ready for what comes tonight.

31—Disappointment about romance may darken the day for you. Be a good loser, and face matters intelligently rather than letting emotional disturbance rule. By evening your philosophical attitude may improve and you can enjoy reading or watching TV. Eat sparingly throughout the day.

SEPTEMBER

1—You are in clover today. Influences will bring many surprises, all of them good. Expect new contracts, romantic interest, vivid experiences which add to knowledge and pleasure. Business aspects are excellent, too, and you may add to your income by a large sum.

2—Investigate opportunities a friend mentions to you. A new career field may open up through use of a special talent. Sincerity and good wishes from friends will bring happiness. A good day to make a start on plans which have been forming during the past days.

3—A day for practical concerns. Optimism about your future will be a spur to accomplish a great deal. Your talents and efficiency will be noticed where they pay. Waste little time in conversation, for influences favor industry. A happy evening with the family.

4—You may become friendly with a neighbor you hadn't known before. Mutual interests will give you interesting topics of conversation. Exchange of ideas may be very profitable. Shop for major items, since bargains are to be had. Entertain at home quietly but generously.

5—Many benefits come to you now. You win the affection of a person who attracts you romantically. You may be honored at work and pleased at the value others put upon you. Don't let any tensions with a lifemate mar this otherwise good day. Be generous with young relatives; give them pleasure.

6—Try to start the day on a relaxed note. If you rush you will forget necessary items. Be sure you have a little extra cash on your person, for an emergency may demand it. The day brightens and becomes more serene toward evening. Attend a party with congenial guests.

7—A gay atmosphere in the midst of busy and purposeful activity will make you happy. Your personality will be at its most open and cordial. Many who felt they didn't understand you will appreciate your wit and wisdom. New friends will be made and old ones bring joy.

8—A day to make important decisions. Changes may come about for improvement in your circumstances under these favorable influences. Courage and initiative will be emphasized. You can obtain all that you seek by being direct, ethical and poised. Entertain tonight.

9—Personal happiness is stressed. Romantic joy will fill the day with dreams and hopes. The favorable influences of this period allow you to shop for luxury items you have wanted. Buy new clothes, accept an invitation and give the evening to pleasure with a loved one.

10—Finances are stressed. You may receive news of a legacy entirely unexpected. Rejoicing, but practical views will allow you to do the wisest thing about money. Good for investment, selling, signing contracts. A new contract may result in a profitable partnership.

11—Quarrel, self-pity and envy may make the horizon gloomy. Avoid conversation with neighbors, and try to steer clear of in-laws. Conflict today may result in feelings permanently injured. Best not to see a loved one particularly if you are engaged. Watch TV and retire early.

12—A good day for inspiring messages. You can profit greatly from conversation with new acquaintances. Surprising messages may come this afternoon. Entertain with a dinner, if possible. Company will give good cheer and enjoy your home throughout the evening.

13—Forced retreat where you had hoped to make progress can bring bitterness. Opposition, delays, errors can cloud the day so that you feel home is a better place for you than work. If your health seems low this afternoon, leave early and take care of yourself with complete rest.

14—A surprising adventure can befall you as the result of attendance at church or other group gathering. An unusually exciting trend keeps you on your toes today. Much of your time can be spent outdoors very happily. Congenial people and much romantic interest will make you emotionally elated.

15—Unkind words may hurt more than you reveal. A day when blunt speech can end relationships. An argument with an old friend may show that true affection has never existed where you trusted it. Give no confidences and betray no secrets. Avoid all excesses.

16—Trends are favorable for enterprise, imaginative ideas, promotion due to special contributions to work conditions. Be alert, remain active and helpful. You will be appreciated where it counts most. Consider the family first this evening, and plan an unusual treat for them.

17—A clash between duty and desire can give you quite a problem during the morning. Don't let your mind wander from work too much or error will be costly. By noon the day brightens and troubles will be solved. The evening may bring the start of a new romance.

18—A rather hectic but quite happy day. Many plans and much to do will keep you in a whirl. There won't be time for solitude or leisure. Social matters fill the later part of the day. These are important, for you may find new prestige in your role this evening.

19—A problem will be solved happily. Relationships with relatives can improve by your willingness to see other points of view today. Generosity with money will be rewarded. Sincere friends will appreciate your help, and you will win new recognition from employers.

20—The day may be somewhat slow, but on the whole profitable and pleasant. A leisurely luncheon with a friend can add to the good atmosphere of enjoyment. Don't count on rushing work, but finish up details carefully. Go out to a vivid social gathering this evening.

21—You will hear what you have wanted to hear. More than one exciting message is coming your way. Long distance communication is favored and will bring excellent results. Keep busy, make plans for the evening with friends who are engaged in a beneficial project with you.

22—Listen to the news this morning. Have a slow and pleasant start to the day. You will find the family very affectionate and willing to cooperate on your personal plans. If litigation commences today it will turn out favorably for you. Be courageous and you will win.

23—Rewards from industrious activity will come in today. Be alert, accept new responsibility and you will win new attention from higher up. Keep secrets well, and this will be appreciated. You may be selected for a special and very prominent role. Look your best tonight.

24—Poor aspects for money matters. Make no transactions, or loans. Be very careful if you must carry a lot of cash. Loss and other misfortune to possessions is likely. Frivolous people may be very annoying in late afternoon or early evening. Get rid of them swiftly.

25—Avoid quarrels. Try to yield to the wishes of others, particularly in the immediate family. Your wisdom can get in your way today. Put it in the background and let sincere affection have first place. Be tolerant or the evening will bring great unhappiness.

26—An unpleasant tendency to be hostile and unfriendly may pervade the air. Try not to frustrate the attempts of others to win your affections. Restlessness and boredom may be at the root of your problems. Find an interesting hobby to work with, avoid travel and all types of speed.

27—You will probably dispense with work worries today and devote yourself to personal happiness. Good social climate and romantic possibilities. Dress well, wear something new and let your personality express itself freely. The evening may be the beginning of permanent love.

28—Fraud, theft and all manner of loss is indicated for those who are unwary. Stay as near home as possible, guard possessions, sign no papers. If you confide a secret to an old friend you may be in for a siege of misery. Keep to yourself, avoid criticizing others tonight.

29—Gaiety reigns supreme. You will emerge from your usual reticence and charm people with your ability to join the fun. Many will admire you, and a new romance may begin slowly. Work interests will thrive without much effort, and you may receive a financial bonanza.

30—Tension, opposition and interruption of important matters. Try to hold your tongue and temper, but do maintain your rights. Firmness of purpose may win out over odds. Be very careful about companions throughout this period, and refuse invitations for tonight.

OCTOBER

1—Today's emphasis is on a pixie sense of humor and on the saying and writing of things which may not be so. Watch it. There may not be an intent to deceive but that will be the end result. The day may be better spent finishing up odds and ends, or relaxing from the fast pace.

2—Those in positions of authority may hand out a little advice or discipline. Be on time, be prompt and willing to work on practical issues, if you wish to get credit from those who are important in your scheme of things. If the discipline seems a little harsh, be patient and say nothing.

3—Avoid gossip. Most of what you are told today can be discounted. Naturally, things are likely to be a little confused with so much falseness around. This is the moment when the magician fools you.

4—There may be a tendency to feel depressed today, also temptation to be negative. Positive denial is good for the soul, but just negation is depleting physically and not a good mental state. Follow the old adage about "denying one's self every once in a while just to strengthen one's will."

5—A glamorous atmosphere may prevail today, due to the magnetic aspects. You might meet new and interesting people, unexpectedly. Informality and originality are the keywords for hospitality today. Make a list of what you want and be just as positive of what you don't want.

6—It might seem that you are having a little more to contend with than you deserve, but don't blame the other fellow for not being more understanding. Your lifemate or business associate can be rather restricting or critical today, or you may be burdened by the problems of an older person.

7—A sincere compliment is always welcome. Try to find something nice to say today. You will no doubt have the favor returned double. This is a time when you can write, telephone, talk, or even sing pleasant words. Go on a shopping spree. Or dine in a new restaurant. Try to make this day unique.

8—Messages which come from a distance can upset you. Needless worry over several things may make the day a bedlam of unhappiness. Get a clear perspective of known facts, calm down and don't let your imagination run riot. Seek cheerful companions for your free hours. Avoid regret.

9—Try to use your own knowledge to determine how you can best help anyone who is in need of your assistance. Do all you can in this direction. Avoid strife in the home, and also use firm but tactful strength in making plans for alterations of domestic matters.

10—A splendid cycle for friendship and entertaining. Extend hospitality. You might have some letters to write which would be appreciated. It would be a mistake to allow melancholy to take over. Find pleasure in some novel sports and different ways today.

11—A tendency toward holding financial strings too tightly can cramp your prospects for profit. Take a proper view about cash and realize that it is doing no good when lying fallow. Get an early start today, and give serious thought to all opportunities. Use the phone, and write letters.

12—Keep your feelings under strict control today. Otherwise you might upset members of your family. A day of tension which can be relieved by resorting to meditation and quiet reading. Take a walk where you cannot be disturbed, or write a letter to a friend who is far away.

13—Under prevailing aspects, it is a time when careful deliberation will be rewarding. An interesting conversation should find you speaking with well-considered and tactful intelligence. If you should become belligerent, you might be sorry. Perform duties as swiftly and well as possible.

14—Look your best and be on your best behavior, for this is a day on which you may be accepted and valued on superficial impressions at first glance. You may be in a situation of passive onlooker at important events. Remember to be interested, however remote from your personal concerns.

15—It is possible that you will be stunned by the swift succession of events and changes going on around. Try to remain calm and see the opportunity inherent. You may ask for valuable advice. A club or other organization can give you pleasure as the aspects are favorable today.

16—Entertainment, the acceptance of a social invitation should bring you nothing but pleasure today. Try to relax. You may find that there are more effective ways to do the things which are necessary. Look for real gain in your ordinary pursuits, and don't hesitate to take on new work at home.

17—Correspondence and all messages should be handled successfully today. A friend of more experience can help you with a rather difficult problem. Your future is vivid, and you can be cheerful in contemplating it, particularly since the influences in power rule your thinking.

18—There may be some rather unpleasant remarks flying around now. Try to disregard these, unless they merit your honest consideration in a constructive way. You may have to be content with routine, minor details, but these should prove to be valuable in the future.

19—Try to maintain a steady level of speed and deed, follow no rash impulses in any direction, and you should find others conforming to this pattern. It will be best not to plunge into any responsibilities which might be quite difficult to fulfill. Pay no attention to braggarts.

20—A time to steer clear of arguments, particularly any which might come up at work. Don't hesitate to grant a favor. You will be rewarded gratifyingly. Work with care and yet don't waste time. A feeling of discontent and desire for change may overtake you. Ignore it as far as possible.

21—Take it easy. Error from impulsive action could resound down the corridors of your life. Words of encouragement and cheer to a friend in distress will not be amiss. If you can, get away from your routine for a while, if only in the evening hours.

22—You may look down on a path of fulfillment of aims today. Efficiency and competence brings great achievements and progress for you. Fortitude and perseverance are your best bets, whatever incidents befall you during the day. Indulge your favorite hobby, or see a movie.

23—Firmness and courtesy should be mingled in your efforts to win your desires. Intelligently laid plans will probably give you the most satisfactory consequences. Rashness or lack of foresight in planning might cause disappointment. Better not go in for last-minute ideas, either.

24—A time in which it will be wisest to accept circumstances, be self-reliant and follow your own judgment. Also, it will be little use looking for assistance from anyone. Go ahead and work things out yourself. You may feel depressed at lack of cooperation, but this will soon clear away.

25—It would be unwise to risk anything on hazardous financial projects or schemes. You might lose seriously. A tried and tested pursuit will be best to continue with. It will be best to avoid all innovations and make sure that everything is approved throughly before you go ahead with it.

26—Whatever duties may come your way it will be better not to complain, but to assume their care with as much grace as possible. A splendid cycle on which to begin to put into effect plans for an enterprise which may bring you enduring success, particularly in financial matters.

27—Enthusiasm in another person might fire you to believe that you can get in on the main floor of a good thing. Think twice and use your best common sense. Don't allow emotions to sway you. Advantages and disadvantages should be weighed accurately.

28—A sociable day. It is possible that you might be distracted by hope of fast financial gains, so that you don't accomplish work you wish to do. Better remain faithful to solid work. You can cheer and encourage others today. Mingle with others.

29—There is no time to take a chance or risk anything on possibilities. Make certain of all outcomes of what you do. Read all legal and business papers thoroughly. Errors can only lead to ineradicable trouble today, so avoid them by painstaking care of every moment.

30—A good day for accomplishment of routine work while the aspects are favorable to this. You may be commended later for this. Take things as they come with self-assurance and realize how well off you are. Coordinate all your desires and plans for the future.

31—Delays may plague you today. Interruptions and other irritating factors mustn't be allowed to deter you from your aims. Let trivial tasks slide for a while and devote yourself to major issues. Be sure to thoroughly plan any new enterprise, and by all means don't let enthusiasm carry you away.

NOVEMBER

1—Fulfill all your current responsibilities to avoid undesired repercussions. Confidence and courage in your abilities are needed to minimize difficulties. Plan your work program well in advance to avoid last-minute pressure.

2—Stick to practical procedures and do not experiment with new ideas. Be patient, rather than in a big hurry, and adapt yourself to existing situations. Adjust yourself to changes as they occur, rather than offer open opposition.

3—Be unusually alert for slow-moving events since they can be particularly important. Seek experienced and qualified advice, instead of taking a chance on something with which you are unfamiliar. Do not depend on the efforts of others, regardless of what assistance you have been promised.

4—Do not let criticism or other forms of disapproval discourage you now. For best results, use methods and procedures acceptable to all concerned. Do not insist on having your own way in the face of determined opposition. Let others have the floor today.

5—Aim for the completion of pending projects, rather than start new enterprises. Look over every phase of your work for errors and do not leave any room for criticism. Keep your ideas within practical bounds since it would be easy to go off on a tangent now.

6—Emotional discord may become serious today if you let it develop. Face difficulties realistically and do not leave anything to chance. Take part in a program which you feel can help increase your popularity and prestige. Spend the evening in quiet leisure.

7—Turn your thinking in new directions and give your resourcefulness a chance to express itself. You may achieve surprising benefits for yourself if you go out of your way to help others. Decisions and actions now can have more favorable results than are first indicated.

8—Avoid placing yourself in a position where you will have to work under pressure. Do not worry about inconveniences you may have to endure until you actually experience them. Avoid participation in an activity that could adversely affect your reputation.

9—Aim for satisfactory achievements, regardless of minor setbacks. Guard against making any statements or voicing any comments which you may have to retract later. Sustained effort may be the only formula you can use to achieve successful results.

10—Maintain your enthusiasm about your work, even though some phases of it may seem tedious. Stick to the pattern of your normal work routine, rather than seek a change. Prevent confusion by following directions closely, even though you may disagree with them.

11—Extra patience may be needed to cope with annoying delays that are a potential source of trouble. You may put yourself in a precarious position by being aggressive or by making changes. Do not leave anything to chance, particularly where your income or financial security is concerned.

12—Although you may appear selfish, devote attention to personal needs, rather than cater to the whims of others. Sort through old clothing and other articles to dispose of things which no longer have practical value. Defer making decisions or taking action which might have an adverse effect on your financial status.

13—Generosity shown to a person in need may be returned under similar conditions. Despite existing situations, keep business and friendships separated. Avoid making critical comments, even though you may not agree with the way others are doing things.

14—Vigorous determination should enable you to overcome barriers that have been standing in your way. Rather than sit around and wait for things to come to you, exploit the opportunities available. Do something practical, instead of wasting your time in meaningless conversation.

15—Do not expect to gain much or create a favorable impression from a display of force. Go out of your way to promote a friendly cooperation, rather than let a feeling of discord take over. Concentrate on jobs that you can do best and make effective use of your capabilities.

16—Take time out to relax from arduous duties and forget about worries. Do not let anything interfere with the enjoyment that is possible now. Overlook any feelings of annoyance you may have about the actions of other people.

17—Arrange to spend time with your hobby or other activity you find interesting. Do not let discouraging thoughts, whether your own or those of another, mar the pleasantness of this period. Do something unusual that can add variety and interest to your spare time.

18—Discuss and work out practical methods to obtain the things you want. What you accomplish now will be directly related to the amount of initiative and ingenuity you display. Go out of your way to improve relationships with others, both for business and social purposes.

19—Avoid participating in anything that calls for a large investment of your cash. You may find it desirable to attend to matters yourself if you want things done. Satisfaction is possible from seeking improvements over everything you have done previously.

20—You may invite trouble of some sort if you force an issue about a business or financial matter. You may have to use forceful methods to overcome opposition that has been holding you back. Any attempt you make to provide yourself with an unusual form of entertainment may culminate in a costly experience.

21—Spend time with your family and friends, rather than seek seclusion during your leisure hours. Efficiency and planning are required to keep things in your home running smoothly. Refrain from incomplete personal plans about the future.

22—Go out of your way today to avoid arguments and prevent temperamental displays of any kind. Do not take things for granted and exercise the utmost caution in all activities. Produce superior results by adopting conservative policies, rather than by being aggressive.

23—Analyze business and household obligations carefully to avoid unnecessary complications. Despite rosy appearances, do not rely on a favor promised you until it has actually materialized. Stick to scheduled assignments which you can accomplish with a minimum of difficulty.

24—Approach your problems from a realistic viewpoint rather than indulge in self-deception. Completely ignore petty jealousies and apparently rude remarks aimed at you. Rather than fight back openly if your efforts are being obstructed, divert your attention.

25—You can find just as much satisfaction in helping others as you can in spending time devoted to yourself. Considerable patience may be required to overcome mistakes that can occur under pressure. Rather than be arbitrary, arrange your plans so that they coincide with those of others.

26—Instead of pushing ahead at a rapid pace, set aside ample time for thinking and planning. Refrain from doing or saying anything that would attract unfavorable publicity. Keep emotions under control, particularly when dealing with an obstinate person.

27—Be careful that your feelings do not become upset through the lack of consideration of another. Alert thinking and well planned action may help you to break away from restrictions. Utilize more effectively the talents you possess, rather than try to learn new skills.

28—Give helpful suggestions and guidance to someone who can benefit from your efforts. Apply your ingenuity and resourcefulness toward the achievement of worthwhile goals. For best results, stick to well established rules and regulations.

29—Do not let indecision cause you to miss out on the opportunities which are available to you now. Take on new responsibilities with the enthusiasm and determination to see them through. Regardless of expected benefits, do not tie yourself down with a long-term obligation.

30—Quarrels and antagonism may take the spotlight if you give them a chance. Potential trouble is possible from attempting something outside the limits of your capabilities. This is not a favorable time to voice your criticism or let others know how you feel.

DECEMBER

1—Give special consideration to the details of your work. Guard against making many of the minor mistakes that could arise through carelessness. It would be easy for you to be placed at a disadvantage if you were to overlook small pitfalls.

2—Make sure that what you say is clearly understood and that the stand that you take is a bold one. Do not give anyone an opportunity to distort your meaning, particularly in a matter that relates to money or your income.

3—It would be an open invitation to trouble to argue about, or to ignore, your responsibilities. Take care of obligations without delay. You can protect yourself against financial difficulty by devoting your full attention to present duties.

4—New ideas and improved methods for performing difficult tasks are worthy of your consideration. Any revisions and changes that you make at this time should be worth while. Regardless of the extra work entailed, do not hesitate to press ahead toward your goal.

5—This is not a favorable day to increase expenses or take on new obligations; rather than give thought to new things you would like, utilize more fully the possessions that are already yours.

6—Although domestic responsibilities are likely to dominate your activities, they should be easier to handle. Do not get stirred up about things of little concern to you.

7—This can be an ideal day to work out difficulties which have been hampering you. Regulate your time so that you will have ample opportunity to deal effectively with problems, and eliminate causes that have been retarding headway. The attainment of cherished ambitions is possible through following a well coordinated program.

8—Avoid wasting time and risking dissension. You may find it is desirable to express your opinion briefly and then refrain from further comment. Concentrate on points of agreement rather than on notes of discord.

9—Make every effort to hold onto your money. Unless you are careful, you easily could be parted from your cash, with little possibility of obtaining the benefits you expect from it. Be sure that any monetary outlays made are used for essential purposes.

10—Although your actions may encounter disapproval from acquaintances, disregard those who are bitter and cynical in their remarks. Stick to the principles which you feel justified in maintaining. However, control any impulses you may have to give caustic expression to your thoughts.

11—Seek a secluded spot where you can find quiet and spend time with a favorite hobby. Get away from business and financial worries. However, to insure a peaceful day, stick to familiar scenes, methods and procedures. Do not engage in any activity which is conducive to excitement or confusion.

12—Avoid becoming involved in any activity which can become boring or tiresome. Steer clear of pessimistic moods which could keep you at odds with others. Spend time with family members and friends with whom you can share an enjoyable day of recreational pastimes.

13—Go out of your way to fulfill promises you have made, regardless of the expenses or difficulty entailed. Doing this can help to release you from obligations and also keep your reputation in good standing.

14—Depend on slow but sure methods to get things done. Avoid being too strong in your demands upon others. Overlook the faults and mistakes of another that can easily be rectified.

15—Quick decisions and rapid actions may prove troublesome, especially where your job or income is concerned. Adhere to a cautious and exacting pace, instead of trying to achieve lightning results. Pay full attention to the minor details of your work and refuse to let imaginary obstacles annoy you.

16—You may find that the best way to insure harmony among your associates is to keep ideas to yourself and let others have their way. Restrain an inclination to assert yourself, and keep alert for suggestions which you can put to practical use. Avoid unnecessary arguing or clashing of opinions.

17—Do not give way to doubts or let others discourage you. Instead, get your thoughts and plans well organized, and adhere to a definite schedule. Spend little time on unessential tasks and emphasize projects from which you can derive immediate financial benefit.

18—Regardless of how much you have to get done, avoid placing yourself in a situation where you will have to rush or work under pressure. You can lose out if you act hastily. Patient and well aimed efforts are needed to come out on top in difficult problems.

19—Do not become upset by trivial domestic inconveniences. Even though you may be particularly displeased by several little things that have gone wrong, do not give minor hardships undue attention. Instead, take advantage of the many pleasurable activities available to you.

20—Differentiate between facts and assumptions before making a decision which affects your job or career. Think things out clearly so that you can avoid every possibility of mistake. Imprudent action at this time could lead to difficulties which would be hard to rectify.

21—This can be a happy and stimulating day, provided you do not attempt to crowd too many activities into a limited period. Allow sufficient time for each porject so that you can make every effort count toward practical accomplishment. Use your leisure hours to advantage by spending them in the company of congenial companions.

22—Pay attention to overtures of friendship, rather than devoting all your time to practical duties. Attend to obligations and responsibilities, but do not entirely neglect recreation. Instead, regulate your day so that you will have ample time to find enjoyment.

23—Do not let present obstacles thwart your ambition. By showing patience and understanding, you can overcome frustrated feelings and prevent temperamental displays. Apparently insurmountable odds can be conquered by determined efforts.

24—Depend on slow, but sure methods if you expect to make maximum gains. You may find that experimenting with new ideas and procedures will prove costly. Be prepared to work hard now if you expect to achieve an expected goal.

25—Be optimistic and generous today while Christmas bells chime the tuneful message. There is no valid reason to fear the future. Guide all activities with a steady hand and a cheerful frame of mind.

26—By keeping alert, you can transform an adverse situation into one that is to your advantage. Move forward quickly toward your desired goal, and do not waste time waiting for others to assist you. Your initiative and resourcefulness can prove a valuable asset.

27—Go out of your way to look for an assignment from which you can derive increased income and prestige. What you do now can help build a solid foundation for future job security and career advancement. Ignore minor setbacks and maintain an optimistic attitude.

28—Do your best to keep up with an accelerated program. Move quickly and waste little time on nonessential details. Emphasize definite and practical results, regardless of what you are doing.

29—This can be an excellent day to make changes involving your household. Rather than let things remain the way they are, give expression to ideas for innovations. To shelter an existing situation can prove stimulating and practical.

30—Emphasize points of agreement rather than notes of discord in your conversations. By doing this, you may foster better understanding with associates. Unless you purposely avoid them, quarrels and disputes are possible. Be diplomatic when making suggestions.

31—Rise early and clean the slate of the day's chores. Relax a bit and then spruce up to enjoy the Happy New Year ahead of you. Know that next year will bring you most of the things you want.

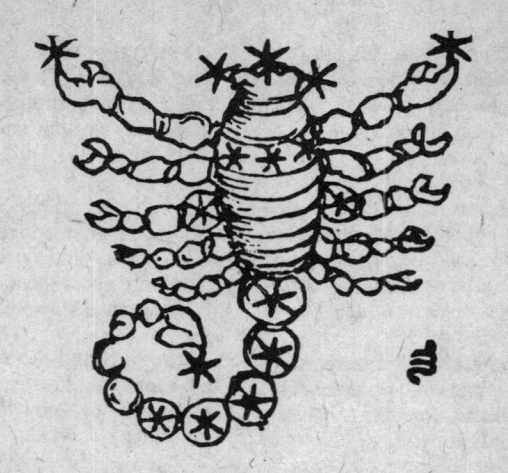

Scorpio

October 23rd—November 22nd

You are
quite a force in the world,
bring splendid skills and mentality
to all you do.
You are a worker,
happy when busy
with worthwhile tasks.
You like to feel
a sense of power
over everything in your environment
and this means
you must get the confidence of others.
Working alone
behind the scenes
pleases you
but to win greatest happiness
you should aim for
coming out a little more with personality
and results of endeavor.
You are intense when in love
and emotional gratification
is your highest form of happiness.
Winning affluence
through use of your unequaled financial wisdom
is a challenge
that also makes you intensely happy.

Scorpio

JANUARY

1—Look for new duties that differ from your customary routine, so that you can enjoy a stimulating change of pace. A short friendly conversation may help you pass the time enjoyably. Keep yourself in an ambitious and cheerful mood and refuse to let distractions disturb you.

2—Wait for problems to settle themselves instead of pressing for immediate answers. Seek constructive suggestions from an experienced person before taking action on your own initiative. Refrain from taking chances that directly involve your cash or prestige.

3—Work on a project that has practical value rather than waste time on trivialities. Devote attention to your own difficulties instead of becoming involved with the problems of someone else. Do not deviate from practices and procedures that you know to be sound and prudent.

4—Avoid letting yourself be drawn into an argument, regardless of how interested you are in the points of difference. Complete required duties without delay, despite your desire to participate in more pleasurable activities. The cooperative reactions you obtain from others may depend on your mood.

5—Refusing to compromise may cause you to lose out on an advantage that otherwise might be yours. Prevent the possibility of trouble by keeping away from anyone who appears to be irritable. Schedule your work duties so that they can be completed quickly and efficiently.

6—Refuse to let a minor difference of opinion interfere with a friendship of longstanding. Devote attention to practical matters instead of allowing your thoughts to dwell on idle fancies. Your efforts to rush matters beyond reasonable limitations may prove costly.

7—You gain more by being silent and persistent than by being openly aggressive. Do not allow skills and aptitudes that you possess go to waste. Keep your work up-to-date, regardless of how burdened you are with duties.

8—Optimism can help you maintain your poise through a troublesome financial situation. Do not let yourself be concerned with errors that cannot be rectified now. You may find enjoyment in returning favors and repaying social obligations.

9—Stick to established rules and regulations rather than insist on having things your own way. Stay away from people whom you feel have been hindering you. Do not take a chance on the unknown.

10—Concentrate your efforts on new and interesting projects from which you may gain financially. Give extra attention to personal and home needs that have been neglected. Settle matters with diplomacy and do not let impatience of an acquaintance trouble you.

11—Rely on practical thinking and conservative action to make satisfactory headway. Observe precautionary measures while handling mechanical or electrical equipment. Personal gains may be possible through increased development of your skills.

12—Get the most out of available opportunities instead of looking for something new. Refuse to allow the discouraging thoughts of others to depress you. Approach difficult emotional situations with an unusual amount of care.

13—Work things out for yourself instead of depending on the advice of another. Use a logical approach to your problems if you expect to dispose of them wisely. Budget your working hours carefully so that you can get the most done with a minimum of effort.

14—Think and act independently but be careful that you do not antagonize an associate. Do one thing at a time and limit yourself to a slow and cautious pace. Your generosity in helping a friend in difficulty may do much to increase your prestige.

15—Ignore fanciful desires and concentrate on actual needs when shopping. Regardless of the difficulty involved, take a realistic viewpoint of each situation and face things squarely. Avoid discussing intentions openly, particularly when they concern your job or money.

16—Turn your attention in new directions but emphasize diplomacy to keep conditions harmonious. You may be able to overcome hindrances by being extra diligent and aggressive in your work. Arrange a program of recreation that can be shared by all the members of your family.

17—Guard against spending an excessive amount of money on unnecessary purchases. Keep antagonistic thoughts to yourself and ignore a burst of temper from another. Guard against placing yourself in a position where it would be possible for someone to take advantage of you.

18—Avoid giving undue attention to events that have not occurred. Rely on your own resources and avoid having to depend on the use of borrowed cash. Prepare to do something pleasant for someone you love, but do not allow someone to impose on you.

19—Seek the assistance of someone who is capable of giving you practical help rather than mere advice. Do not let indecision cause you to lose out on an opportunity that might be yours. Limit your activities to a reasonable pace to prevent being swamped.

20—Avoid placing too much confidence in a promise made on the spur of the moment. Any attempt to get things done in a hurry may result in a series of needless mistakes. Approach difficult emotional situations with an extra amount of diplomacy.

21—Steady and patient efforts are required for effective progress in your work. Emphasize tact and courtesy to others, even though you may feel in a contrary mood. Refrain from attempting anything that might exceed the limits of your normal capabilities.

22—Wait and see how things are progressing around you before taking drastic action. Take care of responsibilities well ahead of time and do not ignore any obligations. Avoid wasting time on daydreaming or minor details.

23—Keep out of petty squabbles, particularly controversies that do not concern you. Be as demanding of yourself while at work as you are of others. Avoid risking a clash of opinions with someone whose viewpoints differ sharply from yours.

24—Arrange to enhance the beauty of your home by purchasing a few inexpensive decorations. You may encounter stubborn opposition if you insist on having your own way in a job matter. Be cautious when adopting any plans that might deplete your cash reserves.

25—Extra patience on your part may be required to prevent an emotional outburst. Ask for constructive criticism and make use of good suggestions. Regardless of what you have to do, let it be with caution and a conservative approach.

26—Attend to one task at a time and aim for perfection in everything you do. By avoiding money and business discussions, you may help promote a harmonious atmosphere. Remain silent about important intentions until they become realities.

27—Consistent and conscientious effort should pay off with worth-while results. Concentrate on getting things done and use your ingenuity to overcome difficulties. Discuss exactly what you intend to do but do so in your most diplomatic manner.

28—Live up to the fullest scope of your capabilities, regardless of previous accomplishments. Promote congeniality among those around you by putting humor and cheer into your words. Seeking a short-cut in your work may prove quite time-consuming in the end.

29—Make plans for home improvements that can provide greater convenience for you. Keep moving forward at a comfortable pace instead of risking mistakes by rushing. Devote the major portion of your time and effort to familiar things.

30—Let others take care of their own mistakes and keep the desire to criticize under control. Although you may have to put up with inconveniences, take temporary setbacks in stride. You can overcome a feeling of restlessness by taking part in activities where you can meet a variety of people.

31—Make arrangements to buy new clothes or other articles that can give you pleasure. Stand by your own conclusions and refuse to be swayed by the arguments of others. Give your imagination an opportunity to be expressed in a practical enterprise.

FEBRUARY

1—You may give much admiration and trust to a person who is not worthy of it. Listening to a friend can save you from the worst of a difficult time ahead. You may fail to be alert enough; heed another's insight.

2—Your work will be impeccable and your concentration given to details, so that all comes out in a smooth and flawless state. Yet, you are looking ahead and are happy with the anticipation of the social life promised for the evening.

3—Disappointment with the mail can cause some bitterness today. A personal plan will have to be changed to fit in with this delay. It is best not to have ideas about entertaining tonight; you won't feel up to it.

4—You may suddenly realize that you have not been treating a certain person, possibly your lifemate, well enough when it comes to social gatherings. You may regret the neglect and the sharp tongue you have recently displayed.

5—A younger person may show sympathy and give you quiet companionship. You must expect nothing else from this person, though, so do not ask favors. Things are not what they seem on the surface; try to see beneath it.

6—Considerable expense and work may be given to a project that just won't work. Your ideas are too grandiose; you are also too willing to make efforts on behalf of someone who does not care about you in the least.

7—An important telephone call may come through and please you greatly. News you have been waiting for will break now and allow you to proceed with an ambition involving money. New affluence looms ahead for you.

8—Some trivial and pointless demands may be made today, but perform them quietly and say nothing. Time will go fast and you will be free to go shopping for awhile for special items that you have been thinking about lately.

9—Someone quite clever may try to point out facts to you, but you may incline to be unrealistic and heedless of these facts. Be very cautious in your romantic life; do not say or do anything that could be repeated by a disloyal person.

10—This is a good day for your philosophy to work and for your mentality to reach new heights of understanding. You can be aloof now and it is not wise to entertain, for your mind will not be on guests or provisions for their happiness.

11—Do not talk much to someone you have met just recently in your neighborhood. Keep secrets; show that you can be trusted with confidential matters. A good day to be outdoors, to exercise moderately and to refresh yourself.

12—You could be easily misled today, so check things thoroughly, and particularly talk about good investments. Do not ask a favor from an older relative. Keep your pride and dignity, but be pleasant in an impersonal way with all.

13—Be sure to keep your word about a career matter. Keep your mind from anything purely selfish and devote yourself to the outside world. There is a romantic trend that is not beneficial for you; try to end it today.

14—A conference may be just the thing to help clarify your ideas about what you want. You may now be free to aim at long-term work that will make your future more interesting and be more in line with your natural talents.

15—Take a risk with money today. You have good fortune on your side and can make a pretty penny when the results come in. Travel is not favored now and even if you are visiting it is wise to stay close to your accommodations.

16—You may refuse to believe what you hear or what is hinted today. You may feel that your own judgment and reactions are reliable; this is not the case. You will be wise to heed what you hear and to analyze it carefully for your own benefit.

17—Be very conscientious, make everything you do a work of perfection. You may entertain a new neighbor briefly, but guard your speech. Your gracious ways will make a hit, but if you are sarcastic you'll win only scorn.

18—Be very methodical and keep your schedule precisely. You may have an engagement you wish you had not accepted. Don't show any boredom or lack of harmony. It is not wise to be out after dark, particularly if you are driving.

19—You will do well in any undertaking—shopping, moving your home, arranging new conditions for children, or getting married—today. It's good fortune straight through. No blight is on your horizon during this period.

20—You may have a major protest to air but you are in danger of making it to the wrong person. There is quite a lot of hostility in the air and a large share may be directed to you, your desires and your opinions in general.

21—Now is the time to be moderate in all things. Take no chances with health, through excess; avoid too much intensity in your views. Do not let emotions take over concerning a romantic situation; choose your companions wisely.

22—An old neighbor may show friendliness never hinted at before. This could be due to the hope that you will perform a special favor. Be a little on the cool side with everyone. Shop carefully during the evening.

23—You may be irritated by the attitude of your lifemate, if married. Resist the temptation to tell others about the situation. If you are unmarried, this is not a good day for romance and it may end with a quarrel and a separation.

24—Be as sympathetic as possible even though you do not really understand the view of another and the deep disappointment about it. Arrange some kind of rather fancy party for the evening; please younger people particularly.

25—This may be your chance to do as you wish about someone of importance to you. Your speech may be glowing when you refer to this person. However, all this may fall a little flat because of someone who disagrees with you now.

26—Respect the pride of others, and do nothing to deflate an ego, even if you are tempted. Be pleasant and helpful; give your services freely. In fact, it is a good time to start an unremunerated service-type of task.

27—Avoid heavy expenditures. You're in the mood to buy clothes and luxury cosmetics. You might even take a liking to a highly expensive item for dining. Employ your basic good sense and see that it wins over all.

28—Take your time today, guard your health and set a good example for all. Your ability with finances may have a chance to show up well, and this could lead to an unexpected offer of a higher position in the near future.

29 (Leap Year Only)—Litigation that arises today can be settled favorably if you step right in and follow indicated directions. Money may not be so bountiful, but you will still come out with more than you expected. A party in your honor will make you proud and happy.

MARCH

1—Harmony will reign for you today. It's grand for clothes shopping, choosing new cosmetics, buying an entrancing piece of jewelry. Don't leave out a young one who likes nice clothes. Be generous in expenditures for others.

2—You may have little time to think and need to act with swift precision. An emergency may fall entirely into your hands. Avoiding trying to seize too much glory for handling this properly, just acknowledge your duty.

3—You may have difficulty with your car or electronic equipment today. Let an expert do the repairs and don't try it yourself; you could be injured. Don't feel too sorry for yourself because of expenses and lesser trouble.

4—You may want to work but find health troubles intervening and have to stop in order to protect yourself. You can have a bad attack of sinus and need special care. This may be an acute infection, a physician may be needed.

5—You can still be feeling quite wretched and not up to much of anything. Stay indoors, for the weather might be inclement for your condition. Do not encourage any visitor to stay. In family relationships, avoid being jealous.

6—Let things go their natural way today. You can take pleasure in seeing the way patterns form. A contact late in the day may bring about a romantic situation which surprises you. This is not likely to last long or go far.

7—Do not expect much of others, avoiding asking for cooperation. You'll get no favors done, no help given without protests. You may retreat into introspective reflection and find it quite restful to do so this evening.

8—Make some new plans about saving and resolve that you are going to turn over a new leaf in this matter. Look over the family budget, if married, and make changes even though others may howl a bit about being denied.

9—Big changes can take place, good news come through, your position be altered and much admiration given to you. It is a good day to go all the way and that's all the more reason to comfort yourself well, plan intelligently.

10—The work day goes well and you can hum along with the speedy pace and good quality of what you do. A telephone call from a distance tonight may startle you. Someone has romantic affections when you least expected such a reaction.

11—A day to devote to home and family. Avoid gadding off on selfish errands. Give yourself freely, take care of children if asked. Be very kind to a pet, and in general guard the welfare of those who are close to you.

12—Best not to miss a meeting and also be congenial about staying afterwards to talk and meet new people. You may have a duty about a sick friend this afternoon. Do not shirk this; it will be more pleasant than you anticipate.

13—You can be very swift on the uptake today, make others feel amazed at your powers of insight. You have a good idea of the way trends are shaping up and now is the time for that big investment you know instinctively can't lose.

14—Be ready for a change not of your own making. An executive who relies upon your intelligence may speak to you confidentially and explain things. Honor the person who is straightforward and ethical with you.

15—Do not be a dupe or gullible. A good day to be aloof from those with too much imagination and enthusiasm for spurious ventures. Buy some books and magazines, spend the evening quietly at home with good, light reading.

16—Be friendly but also use good judgment with those around you. No one will welcome your wisdom which is on the pessimistic side, so do not talk about things of which you are apprehensive. Let talk of yours be encouraging.

17—Guard your valuable possessions and that includes your car. Do not lend valued things. Be careful about your relationship with younger people; avoid being didactic and domineering. Social life is peculiar, varied.

18—Someone may realize your talents but be too mean-spirited to acknowledge it. You are most likely to be around people who think very highly of themselves and underestimate others. You need tact, humor and high wisdom.

19—You feel happy, carefree, affectionate. It is a good day to have a simple but attractive dinner for relatives and in-laws. If you can make it outside entertainment, by all means do so. Avoid heavy work in entertaining.

20—If you show a critical attitude toward anyone for speech, you may get some perfectly cutting speech hurled back at you. A day to be cautious if you do not want to woo the unpleasant, but there is a note of humor in it, also.

21—Get all kinds of chores finished up, pay bills, get appointments out of the way, buy what is needed for home and kitchen use. You'll enjoy the evening much in just relaxing in the company of a quiet loved one.

22—Have little to do with money today. Carry a minimum and be careful of that little bit. It can do some good to be a trifle miserly, especially with teenage children who are spoiled about material possessions and wishes.

23—An associate may be envious and try to undermine you in subtle ways. There may be an innate air of superiority about your own personality today and that can draw hostility from several people, so be a little wary.

24—An unusual streak of good fortune is here. You can win the unexpected. Take a full part in social life and show your prowess in various games. You can have your arms loaded down with things to take home after winning them.

25—Today means extra duties for you and your time may be so taken up with work that when day is done all you want is rest. However, it may be rewarding to attend a social gathering if only for awhile to meet someone new.

26—There may be a sharp exchange of words between you and an influential person. You are in no mood to endure any arrogance and thus may be quite scathing in your speech to one who acts haughty. Come to some conclusions this evening.

27—How well the day goes for you depends much upon your own attitude and efforts. It is not a good time for shopping or for being outdoors much. Be industrious but do not take chances with strenuous tasks, particularly outdoors.

28—Excellent for improving appearance, getting some articles lined up and ready for a trip. If you buy clothes, avoid letting your eyes tempt you too much. Evening can be utterly happy in a simple way making plans with a loved one.

29—It will require stamina to continue through with a detailed and difficult task. There is a good trend, though, for when you do use persistence in endeavors you can win something in the way of promotion.

30—Be sure to check things as you go along and thus you may not have to do over a large batch of work. A old friend may call from a distance this evening. Little point in talking much to such a token of the past.

31—Someone who seems aloof and unfriendly may be merely shy and slow to overcome it. Your own gentle and sympathetic manner can do a lot to loosen up such a person. Social life has special glitter this evening; you are popular.

APRIL

1—If you let one of your melancholy moods get a foot in the door today, you're lost for all good and constructive activity. Best to turn on your sense of humor and be sure to banish all self-pity. Hard work is here to do and you're just the one who can carry out major tasks perfectly, so get busy.

2—You may meet someone who is so charming that before long you'll be practically idolizing this person. You're in for a spell of joy mixed with unhappiness. Both are extremely powerful in this case. Don't build up your own feelings but chances are they'll have an irresistible element anyhow.

3—Do not try to force or persuade a younger person to follow your desires. You could be a warping influence in the life of this person due to your iron will toward a certain matter. Live and let live, be kindly to all, acknowledge rights of all, particularly your younger relatives.

4—You may have an invitation to a quite merry party and not know exactly whether you should go or not. You are urged to go—with bells on! Even if your emotions are turned elsewhere you'll enjoy brilliant social doings tonight and an air of freedom with good will all around.

5—An older neighbor may be helpful and you can be quite drawn to this person. The relationship may become somewhat permanent even though one of you moves away within a year. You encounter more tolerance than you ever knew before plus a view which inspires you in strange ways.

6—Keep it quite a restful day. Going to church can be helpful in renewing faith and stimulating inspiration. Your home may seem comfortable and a few changes you plan to make in it can be worked out on a do-it-yourself level. Don't talk long to someone who calls on telephone tonight.

7—A fortunate day for finances and travel. An item you have had your eye on for investment purposes can be purchased now and prove that your hunch was right. There are possibilities in activities today that can lead on to new affluence such as you never anticipated in your highest dreams.

8—Avoid letting sentiment get the better of your wisdom in any matter, including marriage or romance. A problem you have can be quite shocking and may require that you take a whole new look at your circumstances and life in general. Think things out clearly and thoroughly, make no decision.

9—Go ahead as your life leads you just now and let major affairs stay in the hands of destiny more or less. You may bring about results just by being very busy, not talkative, and inclined not to be around much. You may take up a hobby that keeps you away from home and a lifemate.

10—You may be proud of an achievement today but don't let pride be source of downfall as you know it often is. Don't answer questions of someone who presses you for knowledge of where you have been and what you've been doing. Be individualistic, independent, follow your own desires just now.

11—You may have large and expensive plans for the weekend that take up most of your thought now. Be sure your work does not suffer from this trend. You may be entering an entirely new phase of you life, not quite knowing where you are going yourself, even though you feel ambitions leading you on.

12—You may be taking a trip for a special purpose. Any companion you have may be one to stir up controversy in several places. The day is a crucial one. Chances are you will encounter a person you once knew well and learn something that is startling in the way of news about the past.

13—The fact is you are dubious about the rightness of your recent actions. Only time will tell and there is no profit in wondering or in chiding yourself or anyone else. You are truly caught up in a trend that is quite far-reaching and you will not be out of it just by worrying about it.

14—Sensitivity allows you to feel that your world is being overturned somewhat and that things will never be the same again. You are on the verge of drastic change in career world and business matters are becoming more important to you. Taking a risk is part of it all; be courageous.

15—Not much security in your feeling now, but you'll move ahead as indicated. You may quit your job before the afternoon is over. A discussion you intend to bring about may never get off the ground due to lack of significant communication. An air of mystery seems to surround the atmosphere.

16—You can be somewhat numb emotionally today and rather glad of it. Things may start to move fast but still you'll have the sensation that much is out of your control. If you have an interview for a new job, you will succeed. Money expectations may be a little lower than you like, though.

17—You can feel you are driving on toward circumstances you do not yet know. Some loneliness may be here and living conditions may be bare and stark, make you stay away from your residence as long as possible. Be sure to get enough rest and don't plague your mind with worries.

18—Take the day off, be thoughtful and not emotional. If you are driving home try to keep your mood pleasant. Fight down any desires to antagonize or criticize in the home. When you are with your family avoid becoming gloomy and uncommunicative. Don't rate your wisdom too highly today.

19—A surprise may come and your finances may get a boost. A relative may get in touch with you by long distance phone and have good news. Get a lot of relaxation today, go out and walk around a park or garden, visit the art gallery, chat with neighbors but don't dwell on personal affairs.

20—You may have a very important talk with someone to whom you have been introduced recently. This can be the nebulous beginning of a very solid fortune for you. The impression you make, the knowledge you show may mean much for your future benefit. Be slow to speak, think about every word first.

21—You may know that you have come into the midst of an opportunity you have often dreamed of. You can get cold feet when you think of all that is required in a very responsible position you may be taking on soon. You are excited but rather fearful, too. Well, that's your modesty at work now.

22—You'll learn how to develop more and more self-confidence as you plan and arrange things in your mind. Determination to win is a big factor today. News that comes late in this cycle may give you the go-ahead signal and all finances that are needed may be provided forthwith.

23—Your romantic and business life seem to be tied together very strongly. This helps you in self-assurance for you get excellent support from a loved one who is ideal. Happiness though, is combined with irritation for you are not satisfied with arrangements connected with relatives.

24—You may do or say something to irritate a person with a very bad temper. You can stir up a storm if you don't watch your words carefully. This is a good day to shop for things needed in career matters. Even large machinery can be bought now if that is what your work demands.

25—You may complete major concerns linked with opening your own business. Your good fortune holds and seems almost too good to be true. You are merely following the path that destiny holds for gratifying your ambitions and you have chosen it whether you think so or not, even in negative ways.

26—You may become very enthusiastic in conversation with friends and a loved one. You are planning ahead and can be more ambitious than ever. Well this is good for stoking up the fires of endeavor and determination. Evening can be extremely romantic; you may be setting a wedding date.

27—Church is indicated and don't be surprised if you find some troubles in connection with going to church. You'll get a lot of help and cooperation, everything will work out just beautifully. You can chalk up some gains in understanding. Take a tolerant attitude now.

28—Launch into the day as though into a land of magic charm! In a sense the world really is your oyster or you are trying your wings. Look at it as you will, this day is the crucial one for career, future, affluence and family hopes. Be at your most pleasant and cordial with all around you.

29—All goes like clockwork, but nerves can bother you a little due to your insistence on perfection and your efforts to supervise things too closely. Avoid arousing antagonism by concentrating on watching someone too closely. You could stir up some lasting resentment and lose esteem that is important.

30—Many telephone calls of importance can keep you from getting other things done. You can be living in a whirl today but will manage to keep up. Plan nothing for evening except staying at home quietly and resting. Talking things over with a loved one will calm you, bring early sleep.

MAY

1—You might act unwisely in connection with family affairs. By no means should you take on extra work today. Organize matters according to current conditions and make no changes of major type. You may win admiration for your cool mental ability to handle circumstances.

2—You can feel at rest and at peace with your mind, find that some worries about right and wrong are disappearing. This is because your life is becoming more beneficial than ever before and you are able to relax tensions which formerly made you emotionally troubled.

3—Make amends to a neighbor if you have caused inconvenience. Be friendly and do not allow an aggravated emotional trend to get underway. Work slowly, finish one thing at a time and you'll succeed with a difficult job. Good advice may come from one who loves you.

4—Morning can hold a puzzling event. Have lunch with someone cheerful and wise, you can get a good suggestion to clear your scene for more efficient action. Someone who drops in or telephones this evening may have much need of your friendship and encouraging speech.

5—You can discover that someone dear to you has been acting in disloyal way. This can be the beginning of the end; don't fight trends which have an inevitable nature. Be resigned and take a new outlook toward your own life. Avoid emotional upheaval, too much talk.

6—Shop for things that will make you happy, please any others in the home. Concentrate on the small but cheerful things of life today. Buying a small gift for someone who has been kind is suggested. Be thoughtful of others, make the evening pleasant for a loved one.

7—Take your time about all you do, avoid rush which can cause accidents today. Do not cancel social plans even though tempted to do so. Be lenient with a child in the family or neighborhood. Do not criticize anyone if you are out in a social gathering this evening.

8—You may be in one of your melancholy moods and could forget to do something of importance. Better have a string around your finger about all essential chores today. Do not be unfriendly with someone who turns to you for companionship, be generous with such a person.

9—There may be a change of plan that is mandatory due to new conditions that arise in the family. Don't run up an expensive long distance phone bill. It will avail you nothing. Have faith that things will turn out well even though today looks bleak for your fotrunes. Enjoy companions who are near.

10—Protect your health, eat regularly, do not overwork for any reason. Good advice may come your way; do not be too proud to take it. Save all the money you can and make the budget more watertight for future trends. Give realistic thought to your entire situation.

11—Your personality can be much admired today and you may make a new friend through your forthright speech. Be very truthful with a new acquaintance and you'll be rewarded for it. A romantic trend may be slow to develop but shows some good signs during evening conversation.

12—Make no decisions that could be dubious. Be slow to come to conclusions, hold on to your money, and do not be insistent with others. The day holds little benefit but you must see your routine work through even though you are somewhat glum of spirits now.

13—Do something thoughtful for a friend or relative who is ill. Do not be hasty in any relationship. Keep the trend slow, thoughtful and generous in all aspects. Evening plans may be broken up by a visitor; don't be resentful about trivial things in your own life now.

14—You may have an enticing invitation and look forward to a glamorous evening. There is sparkle all right but there can also be danger. If you are in an unfamiliar place, a quarrel of serious nature could commence. Do not let such trend get any foothold; use swift wisdom.

15—Be kindly to someone who has a favor to ask. You may be able to grant part of it but not the other part. All that you do will bring gratitude and lasting loyalty. Be sure your companions tonight are responsible and conventional; avoid all that is radical.

16—Examine personal plans carefully. You may find a change needed in your financial outlook. Try to organize a schedule that will be beneficial. Do not turn down the words of an experienced person about money trends in your life. You may save yourself a lot by heeding advice.

17—Work diligently, aim for a goal that is getting closer, be very realistic in talking with an executive. You may be made a good offer today, think quickly and grasp opportunity. You are favored in career matters but romantic ones can be tangled and cause you some anxiety.

18—Rest, read, walk a bit, chat idly and avoid all serious matters today. Your emotions would only be highly disturbed by thinking of troubles, trying to solve problems. You'll be able to handle all this later in the week if you get refreshing relaxation during the day.

19—Take an optimistic view of all that happens in your vicinity. Show willingness to be friendly with someone new. Do not be demanding or arrogant in manner with anyone. Keep all petty trends out of your personality. Be frank in talking with a relative this evening.

20—You may see the end of a long difficult task and be quite proud of what you've done. Plan something relaxing for the evening. Do not take on any extra chores for the family; you need leisure and restful hours after regular work. Dining out is a good idea for tonight.

21—You may be disillusioned in a romantic matter and this could have detrimental result in your work. Try to keep your mind clear, avoid self-pity, worry and regret. Get in touch with someone who loves you and is waiting for news tonight. Social life is not pleasant; avoid it.

22—Take it easy throughout this cycle. Do what appeals to you, turn down that which does not. Don't have a feeling of responsibility in a matter which is none of your business. Be serene, know that you are right in what you do and don't do. See only old friends tonight.

23—Good fortune will attend any financial move you make today. The time is also favorable for acquiring a more attractive residence. You may be delighted and want to celebrate, unwind a little with cheerful friends this evening. Nothing wrong with that desire.

24—A surprise decision may be made and bring you swift promotion. You can be joyous about career and financial trends, begin to see your way out of a money difficulty. Share your happiness with those who love you tonight. Get in touch with a good friend far away.

25—New love can enter your life today. You may be introduced to someone charming who measures up to appearance and personality in every way. Fortunate trends exist that may lead to marriage. You may need patience for things can be slow in developing through an obstacle course.

26—Show consideration of a work associate and do things to make work easier for this person. Check up on a rumor before you give it credence. It may sound too good to be true and turn out to be just that. There is some deception around today, someone may put on an "act."

27—Your abilities will shine out today and allow splendid accomplishment. You will justify the faith of executives in your capacity to handle new responsibilities. Your position is one of leadership and management in which you will achieve mastery almost immediately today.

28—A good time to take off for a week-end of fun when the day's work is done. You will find much relaxation and happiness in a spot away from home. Congenial people of your own age will be best companions over the week-end. Show your skills in cooking for a small group.

29—Much enjoyment and close understanding will make the day pleasant to remember. Be very leisurely; you need rest. Your emotions get a chance at healthy serenity which is worth more than gold. The understanding and encouragement you get will save you much trouble later on.

30—New experiences may come to you now and although you worry at first, you'll find all turns out well. Finances can be rather difficult but have faith in the future to straighten these troubles out. Keep evening quiet, be thoughtful but seek early retirement for health.

31—A compliment you get must not be allowed to go to your head. If you keep a modest attitude toward yourself, you will be happy. A moment of pride and arrogance could be costly. Do not upset anyone's good opinion of you. Be firm but kindly with children in your environment.

JUNE

1—Do not take an arrogant and superior mood to someone you encounter in church or afterward. You might be assuming far too much about another person. Look at your own flaws rather than those of others, analyze your motivations and you may see you should change your attitude.

2—Take good care of possessions of others if you are using them on loan. Damage to an item could cause you much trouble while trying to replace the item. You might attend an important meeting today. Look your best, be sure your manner is pleasant and enthusiastic.

3—Avoid rush throughout cycle. Do not let someone else cause you to speed up operations. Be cautious with food and drink, for nervous indigestion could easily result. If you are out with friends this evening, be moderate in all you do including your conversation.

4—You may have a romantic encounter, meet someone who will become your lifemate eventually. You can be very happy and find a refreshing quality to the personality of such a person. Do not be impatient for things to develop; allow time to bring maturity to you.

5—Chores can be difficult and boring, you may be out of temper with a relative. Do not show ingratitude to someone who has been helpful. When shopping avoid indulging whims. If you are out socially tonight be tactful in speech; don't injure feelings of anyone at this time.

6—You may be taking a trip today and can be overjoyed in a sense of freedom, anticipation of seeing friends. You have good fortune all the way and a happy mood continues. The evening may bring calm pleasure in the companionship of congenial friends who have missed you.

7—New work may come along and give you a wonderful opportunity to show what you can do with really difficult assignments. Your creative abilities may come to the front and you can discover ability even you did not know existed. Pleasant surprises, favorable trends are here.

8—Any door you approach will open in welcome for you. It's best not to be alone today. If you can't be with a loved one, be philosophical about it. Make no accusations to others about any lack of sense of duty. Be of service where you can but don't be arrogant about it.

9—You might conceive a deep dislike for someone today and this could prey on your mind so much it would warp your personality at least temporarily. It is better to be charitable and refuse to dwell on emotional reactions. Keep the evening for relaxation, music, peace of mind.

10—News from a distance can be contrary to what you want to hear. Depression might set in as a result of a hope that has failed. You'll be better off getting busy and looking for some other way to solve problems. Do not sign any important papers during this cycle.

11—You may be in an extravagant mood due to desire to compensate for disappointments. Romantic concerns may take over the late part of the day and the evening. Much harmony is shown in conversation, mutual interests show up. There may be the hint of an agreement on engagement.

12—Possiblity that you will feel too independent and try to go it alone too much. Best accept help and even advice that are at your service. If married do not let an intruder have any effect on your love and the pattern of your life. An envious person may visit tonight.

13—Someone may shift a duty onto your shoulders in a very inconsiderate way. It is best not to explode wrathfully. In fact, cheerful performance in this connection may put you in line for a promotion. If you go anywhere tonight do not carry much cash, regard all laws strictly.

14—This is one of those days when nothing goes smoothly and plans may have to be revised. You may be thinking of financial matters in connection with your vacation and find money less abundant than you hoped it would be. An emergency bill can make you unhappy about this.

15—Remember that the race is not always to the swift and this will cheer you, help you be patient. Keep an optimistic view about the future, maintain faith and hope. Avoid talking too much, make the evening quiet and one in which you help solve a family problem for elders.

16—Let nothing rush you or give you a sense of chaos. An associate may be inconsiderate and work can be held up unduly. Don't speed things up if you fall behind. In your home this evening a neighbor may pry too much; beware of becoming bluntly rude to this person.

17—Protect all who are dependent on you; it's a good time for medical check-ups for children, some dental work or eye exams. Do not postpone seeing a physician for any personal worry that may be too much on your mind. You'll feel gratified during evening hours.

18—An executive may have good news for you. You may be given a supervising position you have wanted for a long time. A new outlook on finances will come and you can once more smile about vacation plans. Break the good news to those involved and be a bit festive tonight.

19—Do not encourage any new acquaintance now. You can get tied up in undersirable way with someone who is lonely and will take your time thoughtlessly. Make it plain that you have many things to keep you busy. You must protect yourself. Social life is glamorous tonight.

20—You may be impatient today and a sensitive person can be injured by your brusque manner. Better slow down, be tolerant, give time to someone who needs it. Afternoon may bring a surprise telephone call. Be cautious in what you say to someone at a distance; don't urge changes.

21—You may be winding up important chores, getting in the vacation mood. You can be anxious to see people far away, dreaming of revisiting scenes of pleasure. Take it easy and be diligent, conscientious about work. Evening may be restless and emotions hard to control.

22—You may brood too much on something a loved one says. This could be the start of unfortunate trends if you are married. Best to take a good view of a loved one rather than a critical view. Do not let an older relative sway you in your attitude toward marriage.

23—It is easy to be depressed and you must keep yourself above this by direct control of thought. The habit of being melancholy should be discarded and this is a good day to start on that project. Someone cheerful may call and show affection for you tonight.

24—Avoid spending too generously on someone else. You aren't at your most practical and might regret money that leaves your hands during this cycle. A major question can come up about love and marriage; don't brush it aside easily. It can be a crisis in love matters, quite urgent.

25—Tackle work willingly even though it dismays you to see the amount of it to get through today. Hard work can be followed by a delightful evening of getting ready to start travel. A good mood will take over when the work day is done, happiness prevails this evening for you.

26—A friend may show generous interest, do a favor that is appreciated highly. You may be getting a start on a new success trend. There can be pleasure in social life but don't be impulsive in speech. Be cautious in romantic trends; don't make anyone jealous this evening.

27—You will feel happy outdoors, attending some group affairs, perhaps being entertained royally by a relative. Your mood is one of cheer, popularity rises and you feel everyone is very generous to you. Don't neglect someone who is alone and needs your companionship tonight.

28—Ignore the view of someone who urges you to "use" people and otherwise take a harsh attitude toward relationships. Keep your own opinions as guides, be optimistic about human nature and contribute your share of good to it. Your advice may aid someone in financial matters.

29—Someone new may cultivate your acquaintance. This is not entirely desirable but don't worry about it just now. Accept what comes, be pleasant in conversation, but let nothing keep you from fulfilling obligations. Cut short companionship tonight, retire early.

30—Do not take the gloomy view of anything. Delay in the morning will yield to a better tempo in the afternoon. Do not talk to someone who seems bent upon undermining you and your abilities. Make the evening a pleasant one for family life or entertain loyal friends happily.

JULY

1—A vivid new personality may come your way. You'll do well to get to know this person better. You can trust your secrets to your new acquaintance and will be able to sense the loyalty which is quite deep in this personality. Things you need to talk over with someone else will find an excellent outlet in this person.

2—A telephone call may surprise you and be even more marvelous because someone had formerly predicted that the caller would get in touch with you. Do not rush into anything but on the other hand do not close any doors which you might want to use a little later. In other words, be prudent.

3—Romance is a major concern to your today. You will indubitably have a problem, perhaps a big decision to make. Don't let anyone pressure you about this, though, take your own good time. Just because someone else is impatient is no reason for you to leap before you take a good look.

4—You may be swift to sense deception in someone's attitude and actions. Best not to speak of what you observe, though. Your intuition is working in high gear and there is little that can be hidden from you today. Try to find companionship with people who are straightforward and trustworthy.

5—It can be the dawn of a new day in your life. Your chart shows surprises coming up, an opportunity to turn in a new direction. Someone influential will put the cards on the table and give you a chance to make the best decision. This evening you may want to celebrate a little with relatives.

6—Word from an older relative may be very encouraging and helpful. You can overcome an emotional problem by following the thoughtful words of this person. You may get some financial help which sets you free from worry. The evening is good for enjoying your happy fortune, appreciating it.

7—Be prompt and on the spot. There are big rewards to be gained from being very orderly and efficient. It's a day for serious advancement, showing your very best abilities. After the work day is over be cautious about your own emotions. You could be guided in the wrong direction by an emotional impulse.

8—Shopping is highlighted and you can be happy with any purchase you make. It's fine for buying high quality clothes, that which takes your eyes immediately, and things you know are just right for your style. Be pleasant with someone who loves you and make no unkind remarks during evening.

9—You can settle some real estate matters successfully today. If a closing deal takes place, you'll be on the winner's side whether you see it that way or not. In all business relationships be pleasant but also do some fast mathematical calculations to make sure you are not being bilked of your due.

10—Be very cautious if you shop today. You can too easily be persuaded to buy what attracts your eye only. One of those times when things may even be marked up for a sale. Keep evening free for what comes. That will be better than accepting an invitation you know would lead to boredom.

11—Be patient in getting to know more about a younger person who has befriended you. Your very practical mood today could make you insensitive to the kindness of others. Let courtesy and appreciative affection guide you in all relationships. Something you read tonight can be of great value.

12—A big change may come about. You may choose a new residence, be eager to move into it. Some difficulties are seen and obstacles may not be removed for quite a while. You need to calm down and find some way to be contented until the time is ripe to carry out your desires. Don't fret or be angry.

13—Try to read a philosophical book or go to church even though you feel lethargic. What you read or hear there may interest you greatly. Afternoon is good for family affairs; be sure to call on elderly relative at a distance who is concerned about your welfare. Think through some personal problems in quiet meditation tonight.

14—You can be in an extravagant mood and reckless far beyond your usual way. You want to live like royalty. It's up to you whether to follow such impulses or not. Delusions of grandeur from time to time do grip Scorpio. Handle yours now as you wish but be able to take consequences whatever they may be.

15—You may be asked to cooperate in a special work project you do not believe will succeed. It may turn out that you are right but don't be smug about it. You may have a serious discussion with an executive before the day is over. Surprise company may come tonight; cut the visit very short!

16—An older person may be attractive to you and you won't know why. Just accept things as they are. A quiet sociable evening with this new friend can be enjoyable. You may find much affinity and perhaps form a lifelong friendship. Enjoy social trends of this intimate kind without any doubts.

17—News you want may not come through. You can be quite angry that others cause delay. Best to get out and do some shopping, cease to be irritated. You need a calm philosophy and control of your emotions. A telephone call this evening may worry you though the caller expresses affection strongly.

18—Someone who doesn't understand you at all may be quite unshakeable in opinion. The less you have to do with this person the better off you'll be. Do not gossip even though you know others are doing so. Your sense of humor may come out at its finest today and with applause from intelligent friends.

19—You may have an unfortunate encounter with a former romantic companion. Your good decisions could go down the drain. There may be much pressure put upon you to name a wedding date for the near future. You will probably be skeptical and prefer to skip this whole matter, get clear away from it.

20—You should get out a lot, go to church, a museum or a concert. Chat with a friend afterward, accept an invitation. Avoid being alone today, for brooding that would set in could be difficult to escape. Talk over creative plans you have and you may get good suggestions about how to carry them out more effectively.

21—Your taste is good so it's a fine day to do a little shopping for clothes, home decorations, a set of dishes, some lamps or floor covering of interest. Enjoy the day; work pressures are light and you're in an enviable position. Affluence is the keynote; be generous with family too.

22—Beauty can reign in your life today. You may be in love, pleased with praise you get, and have the feeling you are really needed and wanted. A new friend may do a favor without being asked. Your world is full of good things and there isn't a hitch anywhere. Evening is wonderful for pure enjoyment.

23—Get work out of the way easily and you'll have a few free hours to get ready for a trip. You may leave at night for a week-end trip, possibly very late at night. Happiness rules the cycle in your chart and there is not a cloud on the horizon. Love may be part of all the joy today.

24—An unfortunate situation in the family may come to your attention through a long distance call. Nothing you can do about this and it is best not to talk about it. Avoid all forms of excess; don't let personally elated emotions lead you into unwise activity. Be very cautious with strangers now.

25—Excellent spirits, good financial opportunities and a rare chance for advancement in your career may keep you busy and happy. You tend to put personal matters out of your thought and to be very cool and thorough in your mental processes. You are at your best in abilities and will be admired greatly.

26—This is a fortunate day financially. You may receive money you never imagined would be yours. A legacy from someone at a distance can be most surprising. Your loved one will be loyal and happy that you have good things in your life. Return affection and good will, keep the world turning.

27—Try to see the core of truth in what you hear today. You'll get nowhere by thinking in generalities, so get down to particulars. A new person in your social circle may draw your admiration for talents but there can be some subtle hostility also. You may get some more facts about this person.

28—Go shopping for small things, books, a new pen, work materials, records, even a pet. Please small children in your family. Their delight will come back to you in a lovely warm glow. It is best not to sign any important documents today, including a marriage certificate or partnership contract.

29—A neighbor may be probing for information about gossip that is going on. The whole thing may amuse you but others may take it so seriously your smile would make them disapprove of you. Try not to offend anyone. Your conservative views will be your best bet. Silence is golden!

30—Your business chances are excellent, your career will sail ahead. An executive may inform you that you have been chosen for a special assignment. You could scarcely ask for more in your world of ambition. Be wary in romantic matters tonight, though. Your personal life holds a mysterious threat.

31—No trouble seen unless you spend too heavily. You can be rather avaricious for yourself, want new clothes that you don't need and that are very luxurious. Turn away from such things and by evening you'll be glad you did. You may come to a very serious point in romantic matters during the evening.

AUGUST

1—A rare opportunity can come up and you must grasp it. If you don't do this you are almost certain to be bitterly frustrated in the future. Do not be too rigorous with very young people in the family. You could make demands that would cause quarrels even violent reactions. Consider other's attitudes.

2—You may be going somewhere today with the definite aim of finding a way to earn more. You can be very successful but this can mean a course of too much work for your health's sake. You are ambitious and feel that you can win enough money to have a luxury you want very much. Be careful.

3—Someone you meet today can bring immediate ideas of romance into your mind. You may cultivate this acquaintance and find many interests shared. There is a chance you can be very quick to arrive at a situation which is quite romantic. Be thoughtful rather than letting outside facts influence you,

4—A happy day and you'll be singing while you work for you feel new love in your life. It's as though you were in a beautiful, strange new land. You get recognition from an executive that you are one of the best workers ever. That's what love does for you; it stimulates your ambitious efforts.

5—Do nothing to antagonize a work associate who may not care much for you or the ways you have. Keep to yourself at work, don't get involved in gossip or express yourself too freely. Very easy to stir up hostile forces and that could be an unfortunate, costly trend for you once it happens.

6—Take nothing for granted during this cycle. You may have the wrong ideas about a parent's intentions. You can assume too much in romance this evening. Jealousy lies close to the surface with you and you are urged to keep it from bursting out if your companion talks about other romances.

7—You may be invited to a very entertaining affair. Be sure to go. If you feel you lack a proper dress for the ocassion, go out and shop wisely for the right thing. Be serene and optimistic today. You are much liked among certain new people and can be the center of attention during the evening.

8—Get as much rest as possible, lounge around and read something both informative and interesting. Get out in the afternoon and take a little drive around or go for a walk. You may conceive a new idea about what you want out of life and it can turn you in a more worthwhile direction soon.

9—Don't forget an anniversary of any type in the family. Remember birthdays, send cards, small gifts. It's your day to be thoughtful and generous. Give service or instruction where it is needed by people new in your vicinity. Make plans about a change but don't mention them to others.

10—A new romantic interest may arise before the day is very old. You're in a good position to meet people today. Someone may even do the right thing and introduce you to a charming romantic companion who may develop into a lifetime love. If married, your romance is reawakened joyously.

11—Someone restless may have a bad nervous system. Try to be understanding and to overlook unwise remarks of such a person. You may set a good example by your own calm and methodical ways but don't speak about such things. Your work is of perfectionist caliber and will win much praise today.

12—A fine time to move into a new home, buy a new car, appliances or furniture. If married don't cater to your lifemate's material desires too much, though, for you could let yourself in for painful debts. Be self-protective in dealing with any loved one; they can be quite selfish today.

13—Your neighborhood may be buzzing with scandal. Do not get mixed up in it. Things could go to the point of a legal suit. Turn down any request to be a witness for a matter you know is a put-up job. Take good care of your property today, insist on having your rights. This may mean a struggle.

14—Your family can be very demanding, unreasonable and quite irritable. You can wish you were miles away. Avoid showing a better face. Turn your thoughts onto larger fields such as abstract and world puzzles. You'll come through serenely if you dwell on the vastness of your world.

15—A good day to shop for anything from a mousetrap on up through a new home. Be slow to make decisions in buying but once you've decided it could be wise to sign papers immediately. You are in for a good bargain if you have faith and follow your tastes as perfectly as possible in your purchases.

16—Be very honorable. If you owe a debt, pay it. Do not try to hang on to money when it really belongs elsewhere. You may be criticized by a work associate unjustly. Do not heed this person inwardly. The matter is not deserving of any place in your mental or emotional processes.

17—Travel will please you today and you can feel proud if you are setting out for a faraway place you've never seen. You may be entrusted with a major responsibility which should also elate you. The day is entirely good but be a little careful with your menu tonight at dinner. Too much is ill-advised.

18—An unusual stroke of luck may come your way and you may be given an elevated position which comes as a complete surprise. You may have to go through a brief instructional period but added knowledge makes you worth more now and forever. Do no boasting to arouse the envy of associates.

19—Be heedful of what a young child has to say. Your sympathy for the small ones is needed. Your affections may grow during the day. Evening can bring an important message, stir up a new hope. You can see your way to possible new affluence but do not rush anything, control yourself.

20—Let no one and nothing make you pessimistic today. You have a happy date or social situation for evening. Be at your most glamorous, take much care with your hair style and make-up. You can be one of the most delightful guests. It is possible that new competition for your affections will arise.

21—A know-it-all in your vicinity can mar your happiness. You may sink into one of your melancholy cycles and be miserable for no good reason. Avoid jumping to conclusions or making final judgments. Try to find diverting light entertainment, something to make you laugh in evening shows.

22—You may be puzzled by a remark of someone you like. Be calm and let it go, don't even try to understand. Take what is good and discard what you don't want today. Don't let undesirable attitudes, opinions or ideas build up. A loved one may make you happy tonight; be appreciative.

23—Possibility of starting a cross-country trip is here. Don't take anything too fast or hard. A relaxed tempo is good and you should try to enjoy every moment of this day. A new relationship may come into being; you may become the most loyal and honored friend of one who is a good judge.

24—Don't make a telephone call to someone you know is highly emotional and undependable. Talk with those who take responsibility seriously and are cautious with money. You may get praise because someone knows your head will not be swollen. A good day for common sense, conventional behavior.

25—You'll feel you've earned every penny you get today and you could start thinking in terms of finding ways to make more money. An investment is the most sensible thing but be very cautious if there is anyone in on it with you. You need your wits about you, cold fact to be considered.

26—Do not cultivate a new acquaintance. You could fall in with an unscrupulous, selfish and vain person, someone who demands praise for appearance at all times. You can do better than that when it comes to friends. Avoid joining anything new today; keep busy at home tonight.

27—Keep your habits all healthy, eat balanced meals, be cautious in handling dangerous objects. Watch out you do not trip over an object left where it should not be. In the evening take time out for social life and be cheerful company. Your tendency is to brood alone, ignore this.

28—A telephone call can surprise you and flatter you quite a lot. You deserve the praise you get. In romantic matters, take more thought about a difference in age. That can be quite a problem, more serious than you realize. Do not be miserly about your money now, avoid pinching pennies.

29—A casual kind of day when you'll be happier if you just accept and go along with whatever happens. Relatives may drop in. It could occur to you that they do that a little too much and do it for the purpose of giving advice. It won't hurt to give them a hint you want to be independent.

30—You may be informed that a residence you want to live in will be free for your occupancy soon. You can be overjoyed and grateful to the person who put you in touch with this property. Begin plans, let a loved one have a voice in it, and be happy all evening with this anticipation.

31—Put things to rights if you have injured any feelings or feel you have spoken out of turn. You'll be accepted and forgiven without further thought. Tension could arise over an ambition; best to curb this and relax. Time will bring you what you want without any struggle being necessary.

SEPTEMBER

1—A day of placid and serene emotional mood. You will be able to accomplish a great deal because of your state of mind and feeling. Very favorable hours for putting transactions across. Start in business for yourself, make major plans and follow them through with zest and vigor.

2—Imagination and intuition can combine to give you excellent ideas today. Your aggressive spirit will come to your aid and may bring you to the attention of a very important person. Be prepared for surprises and probably a raise in position. Promises made today will be carried out.

3—The family and domestic life are stressed. New arrangements will be favored and you will be able to solve problems which have been bringing discord. Use this day to concentrate on happiness for loved ones and yourself. Private life will be improved immensely at this time.

4—A day for going out and meeting people. You may be asked to do much work for a community project. Let your heart rule your head, and tackle the work even though it seems impossible. Your schedule will be full but a sense of satisfaction will come. Plan on entertaining tonight.

5—Your usual adherence to convention may desert you today. It will be best to stay at home and avoid society, for bitterness may creep in at unexpected moments. Try to find excuses to stay away from the telephone, write no letters. Seek solitude and philosophical literature.

6—A bit of confusion in the morning will not have serious consequences. Today you will find much happiness. Romance is stressed under current influences. A sacrifice will be well worthwhile this evening.

7—You will discover a way to use talents and perhaps uncover new ones today. An inspiring period with imagination running high. Be courageous and use the opportunities which present themselves. You may be entering a new phase in your career and personal life. A surprise may come tonight.

8—Happiness will greet you in the morning. Serene spirits and a zest for the day's activities give you a good start. Enjoy your breakfast and lunch in a leisurely fashion. Read the news, magazines, chat with associates. Favorable influences for ideas and good social contacts.

9—A day of many events, some of them unscheduled and surprising. You will be able to adjust yourself to circumstances admirably. New honors and prestige from the way your personality impresses people. Get out early and keep going, for these good influences must be used energetically.

10—Money is emphasized, and indications are that Scorpio will receive an extra amount or be given news of a pay raise today. Projects which entail financial profit are also stressed. All investments will turn out profitably if ventured upon today. Talk with the family tonight.

11—Disappointment and delay will beset you today. Whatever plans you had may automatically be cancelled. The family will present new problems and romance be under fire. Try to go your own way, but don't expect much under these influences which are almost entirely negative.

12—You will be in excellent spirits and show the gayest, most charming side of your personality to people. Entertain or accept an important invitation, for much good can come from mixing freely in society. A day of inspiration and new promise. A surprise contact will be made.

13—An unfortunate period when you may suffer an accident which hospitalizes you. Be extremely careful at work if you handle any dangerous instrument or material. At home be cautious about metal and fire. Avoid heights and crowds. Refuse to go out with reckless people this evening.

14—Get out and enjoy life today. Talk to people, for you will find them stimulating and profitable ideas will be going around. Romance is noticeable, too, and you may become engaged as the result of a meeting today. Sparkling influences for personal happiness and future profit.

15—Friends may prove insincere and even loved ones give you cause for suspicion and worry today. Melancholy which assails you over flaws in others may plunge you into a deep mood of unpleasantness. Try to avoid voicing any of your feelings. You may be wrong about most of them.

16—A better day with problems solved easily. You will be able to see your next step clearly and know how to go about making it. Expert advice can be obtained today, so do not hesitate to ask questions. Splendid for planning on a large scale. Have a happy evening which will please the family.

17—It may be difficult to get started this morning. Don't rush yourself, for taking time will give you the best chance to win profit from the good influences later. Be light-hearted rather than let problems weigh on your mind. Afternoon is good for buying and selling, or investments.

18—A good day for romantic plans, personal relationships and all domestic matters. You can begin a journey pleasantly and safely today. Be sure to include loved ones in all you do, and your emotional happiness will mount. The evening is splendid for conversation in groups.

19—The day is busy and hopeful. You may have a long distance call which offers unusual opportunity. Learning that your value is going up will be cause for enthusiasm and great efficiency. You can impress others with your opinions and special knowledge. Promotion is in the air.

20—Talk over plans with an executive. You may find yourself able to realize a dream today. New responsibilities will give you a sense of assurance. Plan on entertaining this evening, and make the family happy by something special that they will like. Dress in your best, for romance is afoot.

21—Your talents will show at their best today. Creative activity is stressed, and you will win great admiration for your own abilities. A new means of gaining income may come to your attention. You will be able to meet all requirements, more than ably. Romantic joy tonight.

22—Your imagination and intuition will guide you right today. Do not hesitate to follow promptings of a psychic nature, for influences are good in this direction. Money can be gained by investment which follows a hunch. A gift may come to you through your services to a special person.

23—You will be able to change a circumstance which you have found inconvenient or irritating. Get busy on such matters and improve your present personal environment as you wish. Influences are favorable for minor changes which make major differences to your peace of mind.

24—You may have to face an unpleasant situation with in-laws squarely. Be courageous and do what must be done. Any postponement of duty and necessity will make matters worse. Be considerate of others even though you are vexed with them. Try to avoid all selfish impulses tonight.

25—Gossip may really be aimed at injury today. If you feel that you are suffering from the talk of others, do not show it or become belligerent. Temper must be controlled or you may land in serious trouble and perhaps litigation. Avoid all social engagements for this evening.

26—Expect little in the way of serenity today. In the early hours people of whom you disapprove may call and try to tempt you from your plans. Unpleasant words may be exchanged several times during the day, and the family may oppose all your ideas and actions. Retire very early.

27—A fairly good day for business, but don't make any big financial gestures. Talk over plans rather than take action. You may be able to get financial backing for a favorite idea. People will be reasonable and interested. Best not to entertain on a large scale or keep late hours.

28—Try to keep your mind from personal matters. Buckle down to work, expect no opportunities or pleasant surprises. You will be fortunate if you do not make serious errors. Mischief is in the air, and the least careless mistake can cause lasting difficulty. Watch TV tonight.

29—Extremely good hours for getting plans into effect. Make changes, large investments, drastic moves. You will find happiness in the alterations which come about today. A community project may sweep you to new honor by requesting your talents. Social prestige broadens tonight.

30—Snarls, disappointments and true difficulties arise easily. Avoid swift traffic and conversations with those who vex you. There may be illness in the family which will drain your finances severely. Put on your philosophical armor and hold the course. A disappointing message tonight.

OCTOBER

1—It would be unwise to start the month with attempting to control or criticize others. Retaliation would be swift and sure. Keep a tight rein on your pocketbook, and avoid contact with a stranger. Stay home, read, watch TV, or catch up on your rest.

2—Early morning discord may plague you. For instance, you may be awakened suddenly by a loud noise. Or your telephone may ring before rising time. Breakfast may not go well, and the mail may bring dull news. However, the afternoon and evening hours favor mental elation and social pleasure.

3—Matters related to business, the law, your lifemate and recently made contacts may come to the fore. Keep alert. Listen, and make no promises that are difficult to fulfill. It is a time to think, meditate and evaluate events and people in your life.

4—Don't allow your vivid imagination to magnify what may, after all, be but minor troubles. Little things like idle chatter can never be more than pinpricks. Keep a sense of humor throughout the day. View life philosophically.

5—With harmonious influences in force, you may discover in yourself capacities and psychological qualities of which even you were not aware. Cultivate your inner confidence, for the structure of your being is permeated with vibratory force of magnetic cosmic currents.

6—Don't lend money, and don't go on an expensive shopping spree. The tendency is toward useless extravagance. Go about your daily tasks with methodical efficiency, and turn in a good day's work. In the evening, call on a friend, or watch new television shows.

7—This is your day to get going. The aspects are extraordinary for success. Personal initiative and dealing with other people's assets on the credit side of the ledger. Write letters that you owe. Call people on the phone, ask for interviews, see people in authority.

8—The limelight continues to shine on you. There are helpful influences generated now. Good cycle to travel, write, plan, work, shop, perform or compete for a prize. Young people may be a source of pleasure, and a special gift may come to you from someone you hold in high regard.

9—Get a fresh grip on your beliefs today. You can depend on friends of long standing. Look ahead with optimistic hope, and making plans for the long- range future. Subscribe to magazines, and buy something new for your room. Put your wonderful thoughts on paper.

10—Cash in on your ideas while the influences favor you. Splendid for bringing matters to a successful climax. You might put over a business deal in a manner to exhilarate you. Or there may be a potential opportunity offered by a sincere and talented friend.

11—Your dreams may be filled with exotic scenes and tinted in technicolor, due to the influences abounding. The waking and working hours, however, are under cosmic bombardment. Do what is expected of you, and do it well. Take no risks, and keep away from anyone who has exaggerated notions.

12—Say "no" right off the bat to any proposition you consider risky. The aspects are adverse for speculation, risks, betting or wild chances. Stick to the steady path, and you will be better for it. Find time to read a classic novel, or watch TV tonight.

13—Early morning travel is favored. Also, financial transactions before noon are under friendly approval. From midday on, the tide turns backward and you may have to contend with quarrels, minor accidents, misbehaving youngsters, cranky neighbors and unreasonable demands.

14—A wonderful day to get what you want. The world is your oyster today. Start early. Call on those who can assist you, financially. Get your wardrobe in order, and buy things needed for the home. Smile.

15—Things should go along well enough, for there is a friendly aspect in power. The outlook is bright for friendship, pledges, entertaining, buying metallic objects, traveling by air, asking for favors, meeting up with surprises and attaining a long-held goal.

16—If your interests are tied up with occult or psychic research, you could find no better time this month for pursuing your studies. Be receptive to illuminating ideals. Do what you can to advance altruistic work. The Zodiacal scene also favors home matters, job activities and amusements.

17—Give new ideas full consideration before you dismiss them as being without value. The aspects favor personal initiative. Remember that many great achievements had their origin as a germ of thought. Today is favorable for formulating plans with future value.

18—Before you take on added responsibilities, be sure they are not going to be a burden. Delay any important project and do not commit yourself to anything that may tie you down indefinitely. Laxity may extol a huge sum of time and money today.

19—Your judgment should be sound and your mind clear under the favorable aspects. You might be particularly qualified to decide matters with a money angle. Do so, instead of listening to others. You probably will arrive at useful, accurate conclusions.

20—It would be unwise to rely entirely on your personality to "put yourself across." Find some means of demonstrating your capabilities. Sometimes there are people who are loathe to accept others at face value, so prove that you are competent as well as charming. Otherwise, you might lose out.

21—You may have to cope with an unpleasant experience involving two friends today. It may be necessary to show preference for one. If such a dilemma confronts you, try to meet it with velvet diplomacy and you probably will get over the hurdle with no hard feelings all around. See a show tonight.

22—Publicize your wares, if you have anything marketable, whether metal output or something more material. Your instinct may show you how you can make them appealing. The influences are favorable for public contacts, either personally, or by means of the written word.

23—Prestige and exhilaration may come with the current favorable aspects. Now and then it appears that Destiny demands tremendous effort to achieve success, but sometimes this dynamic force also scatters coveted prizes with seeming profligacy. Enjoy current planetary favors.

24—Emotional outburst, accidents, fever and fire are possible now. Also, scandal and gossip may run riot. Spend time in contemplation or praying for divine guidance. Later, attend to domestic duties and clear the way for next week's efforts. Silence pays off today.

25—Do not attempt to turn your household upside down and make things over, even if you have the best of motives. If you are a bit concerned about how things are being handled, sit quietly and plan a new system. Keep your ideas to yourself, however, for the time being.

26—One of the great themes of savants is that discipline develops character. Therefore, though you may find it difficult to remain calm under the thwarting influences, act according to the dictates of your conscience. Self-control and precepts of faith can save you from discord.

27—There might be some slight tension, so that trifles can become irritating and suddenly appear to assume gigantic proportions. The desire to make sarcastic remarks can easily become as devastating as a roundhouse blow. Relax. Go to a movie, or stay at home and enjoy creature comforts.

28—Love is favored today, but matters associated with friends and business are under a cosmic cloud. If you are depressed call on your loved one for comfort. Be tactful with business associates and make no unusual demands on your pals. Let the day go by without friction.

29—The influences are adverse for impatience, faultfinding, suspicion, doubt, chicanery and gossip. Keep away from anyone who is prone to create trouble. Carry out your expected tasks with methodical dispatch. If you shop, watch out for inferior products. Be careful not to lose your wallet.

30—You may feel particularly exuberant today because the influences are very favorable for success in many ways. Because of the quick and efficient way you dispose of accumulated duties, someone may turn up with an unusual opportunity for worthwhile profit.

31—That you may be right nine out of ten times is possible, but look out for the tenth time today. Keep your emotional balance so that you do not swing too much to the moody or to the too elated side. Catch up on neglected rest, and discourage visits from friends, if they call.

NOVEMBER

1—Make detailed preparations for the things you intend to do, rather than follow haphazard methods. Refrain from taking immediate action on decisions made under the pressure of emotion. Clear up pending obligations before giving your attention to other things.

2—Give helpful suggestions and encouragement, rather than cause dissension by criticizing another. Keep yourself occupied with creative tasks that will enable you to express your ingenuity. Work slowly, patiently and cautiously for the most satisfactory rate of progress.

3—Rather than try to avoid troublesome situations, do what you can to eliminate them. Let others handle their own difficulties, regardless of your interests. Aim for accuracy now, since errors made could have a long-lasting effect on you.

4—Do not let your enthusiasm to get things done in a hurry be the cause of careless errors. Be conciliatory in your attitude, rather than create antagonism by holding out for what you want. Avoid letting impatience place you in a position where you may have to depend on others for help.

5—Handle routine matters quickly so that you will have time to take care of the more important things which will require your attention. Express your viewpoints clearly and be prepared to back them up. Foster a stimulating change of pace by taking an interest in projects outside your usual sphere of activities.

6—Rely on yourself today, rather than on the promise of an associate. Arrange to spend some time among friends with whom you can share pleasant exchanges of thought. Do not let depressing thoughts about others put you in a disagreeable mood.

7—Do what you can to eliminate unnecessary interruptions and keep things running at an even pace. Be systematic and thorough in your work to minimize the possibility of wasted efforts. Seek assistance from others if you find it difficult to make headway on your own.

8—Despite a large variety of arduous duties, place emphasis on doing first-class work. Arrange to acquire new equipment and appliances designed to eliminate tiresome tasks. Plan each move you intend to make carefully to prevent possible confusion and interference.

9—Regardless of how boring you find your activities, refrain from making impulsive changes in your routine. Resourcefulness and perseverance on your part may be instrumental in making your ambitions a reality. Follow your own thoughts and judgment, instead of depending on guidance from another.

10—Regardless of how upset you are about the results of your effort, do not let your emotions dominate you. A cheerful disposition should make it easier for you to achieve the goals you have set for yourself. Do not alter your personal or work plans, merely to suit the whim of another.

11—Do not allow yourself to be imposed upon regardless of friendly associations. Avoid attempting undertakings which might subject you to criticism. Control your restless feelings and devote all your efforts to the most practical endeavors.

12—Avoid postponing disagreeable tasks, merely to participate in more pleasurable activities. Any attempt you make to assert yourself vehemently may result in discord. Straighten out matters as efficiently as possible, instead of making an issue over a mistake.

13—Follow customary procedures and do not try to be different if you expect to make satisfactory headway in your work. Keep yourself attuned to current trends so that you may make the most of available opportunities. Get busy on projects that you feel will be useful in augmenting your income.

14—Do not voice resentment openly if your actions meet with opposition from others. Prevent possible trouble by placing your confidence only in those whom you know to be reliable. Use your leisure hours to relax and take advantage of recreational activities open to you.

15—Arrange to make necessary household repairs and buy items that will keep things running efficiently. See that minor disturbances and disruptions do not cause you to overlook desired goals. Do not allow yourself to become upset about difficulties that are the concern of someone else.

16—Evaluate carefully facts that are presented to you, particularly when your future or income is concerned. Avoid a clash of temperament with someone who is in a position to benefit you. Make the most of your abilities, instead of being self-conscious about your faults.

17—Insure harmonious associations by keeping thoughts to yourself unless you are requested to voice your opinion. Try something at variance with your usual routine, rather than allowing yourself to become bored. Improved methods for handling job matters are worthy of consideration today.

18—Prevent remorse and regret by limiting yourself to activities well within your normal capabilities. Do not deviate from accustomed procedures, even though you may feel somewhat upset by present conditions. Take time out to evaluate facts before making a decision with regard to your job or home.

19—Give heed to creative urges and clear up neglected duties. Present a cheerful attitude in the company of others, even though you may encounter some temporary reverses. Assume the initiative in maintaining harmony among those around you.

20—Keep out of controversial discussions since it would be easy to cause a rift in friendship. Despite your irritation over the actions of another, sharp words may only make a situation worse. Do your best to solve your own problems, rather than depend on someone else.

21—Do not let indecision cause you to miss out on opportunities that are available to you at this time. See that wastefulness does not occur as a result of yielding to impatience. Say things that promise cheerfulness and optimism with others.

22—Make up your mind carefully and stick to it once you have determined your course of action. Take part in activities which you are sure can bear productive results Do not let business matters keep you from the pleasures that you have planned for yourself.

23—Develop progressive ideas which may be instrumental in making your career plans a reality. Do not neglect present obligations or attempt to break away from them. See that your emotions do not interfere when making a decision that requires an impartial viewpoint.

24—Close adherence to prudent procedures should enable you to achieve a financial advantage. Vigorous efforts should substantially reduce the number of difficulties encountered. Do not allow odds and ends of work to pile up on you now.

25—Use a straightforward approach to get what you want, rather than rely on subtle methods. Avoid making the mistake of underestimating the capabilities of a determined individual. Be particularly attentive when handling money matters to avoid serious misunderstandings.

26—Buy things today which will add to your personal comfort and happiness. Live up to the fullest scope of your capabilities, even though doing so may require extra effort on your part. Clear up distasteful tasks quickly and in your efficient manner.

27—Use to advantage the constructive criticism you receive, rather than resent it, especially during the current favorable aspects. Keep plans to yourself in order to avoid interference. Do not request a favor unless you are in a position to repay it immediately.

28—Despite unexpected delays and interruptions, aim for the completion of whatever you have started. Keep in a cheerful mood, despite the presence of aggravating conditions. Make plans which you feel can help promote financial and business successes.

29—Follow the accepted procedures, instead of risking difficulties by doing something which is different. Adjust differences of opinion quickly before they get completely out of hand. Liven things up by cheerful conversation, rather than succumb to boredom.

30—Your enthusiasm can be a valuable asset, provided you keep it headed in the right direction. Go at a slow and easy pace, even though your thoughts may be racing at top speed. Be slow about making household changes, particularly if they involve a large cash outlay.

DECEMBER

1—Activities which offer mental stimulation are favored. Concentrate on work that you like to do best. Make effective use of your capabilities and aim toward practical accomplishments.

2—Regardless of how strong your viewpoints may be, let others do the talking. Steer clear of situations which you know to be fraught with trouble. Moving at a slow, cautious pace can have more potential benefit than presenting a bold front.

3—A realistic approach to a realistic problem would yield better results than relying on impressions. Allow ample time to work on scheduled tasks since delays are possible. Clear up odds and ends to pave the way for new projects.

4—Do something unusual that can provide you with variety and diversion in your spare time. This is also an appropriate day for parties and other enjoyable social activities. Get together with friends whose company is stimulating.

5—Irritating, but minor incidents could easily mar a pleasant day if you give them the opportunity. Therefore, avoid most of these disturbing situations by ignoring sarcastic remarks and keeping your own expressions cheerful. Spend time on interesting diversions.

6—You may find it desirable to make small, but important, decorative changes in your home. This is also an excellent day to replace old and worn-out possessions with new ones. Rearrange furniture, make small repairs, and otherwise get things in good shape.

7—Letter writing, hobbies, and home entertaining are favored. Rather than rushing around, this is a period for leisure and meditation. Get away from fast-moving events and adjust yourself to a tempo which is more relaxing.

8—Your own impatience to get things done in a hurry may prove a serious handicap. Trying to move at top speed, or making impulsive changes could result in errors that might result in loss of valuable time and effort. Do not disrupt well founded systems because of momentary whims.

9—Regardless of how heavy your responsibilities, or arduous your work, bear your burdens without complaint. You would probably receive little sympathy and assistance, even though your complaints are justified. You can accomplish more by yourself than working with others.

10—Be on guard against conflicts, especially at home. Dissension could easily develop as a result of strongly opposed viewpoints. Prevent needless friction by restricting your conversation to subjects that are pleasant and mutually congenial.

11—Place particular emphasis on keeping your work up-to-date. Organize the details of your daily program to get the most done in the shortest amount of time. Follow reliable methods rather than experimenting with new procedures.

12—Control the temptation to splurge on items which have little practical value. Plan each purchase before you buy, and stress efficiency and economy. Also place emphasis on keeping business and pleasure activities separated.

13—Advice and guidance that you receive now may prove more beneficial than you had first anticipated. Listen carefully to someone whose wisdom and experience you hold in high regard. Use to advantage suggestions that might prove helpful in your home or work.

14—Although events may go contrary to expectations, refuse to become upset. Ignore feelings of apprehension and look to the future with confidence. Adjust yourself to each new situation without delay.

15—Property matters, financial transactions, savings and activities associated with money should be watched closely. Refrain from investing your money at this time, regardless of how reliable the enterprise appears. Also, hold off on buying expensive household equipment.

16—An inner compulsion may make you want to do something generous for a loved one. There can be pleasure for you in this as well as for the person who receives your attentions. Provided you refrain from rash action, whatever you do now can be pleasant and satisfying.

17—You may overcome situations that have been limiting your income through quick and well-planned action. However, if you expect to make satisfactory gains, it will take hard work. You may reap substantial benefits if you put forth diligent effort.

18—You may find it desirable to remain secretive about money matters rather than disclose your plans. Otherwise your intentions could be mistaken and trouble result. Avoid misunderstandings by acting with discretion at all times.

19—Devote your day to activities that you find interesting. Make changes you feel necessary to relieve a monotonous routine. Seek a different hobby, visit friends or attend an exciting movie. Plan to have fun regardless of what you do. Limited funds should not restrict your pleasure.

20—Although everything that occurs may not be to your liking, today should be stimulating. An attitude of complacency would be out of place since this is an interval of change. Keep abreast of what is going on around you so that you may take advantage of favorable situations.

21—Demonstrate your courage and initiative to take on important projects. Assert your independence; make your own decision; and work towards the goals you have in mind. Do not avoid new responsibilities.

22—Get an early start, regardless of what projects require your attention. Please others, as well as yourself, by being ahead of time. Put in extra effort so that you will have free moments when you are really in need of them.

23—Keep clear of bickering and petty quarrels. Rather than risk animosity by venting your emotions, direct your thoughts toward matters which can keep you in a cheerful frame of mind. Sidestep dissension by helping to initiate enjoyable activities.

24—Purchase personal items, such as clothing, accessories and articles for good grooming that enhance your personality and attractiveness. Seek ideas and suggestions from those competent, as well as willing, to give them.

25—You might be delightfully anticipative and excited. Perhaps you will be awaiting the arrival of a long-absent relative or friend. You can make Christmas merrier than ever today.

26—You may find that this is an ideal day to make travel plans or start on a trip. There can be much pleasure in visiting new places and taking part in interesting activities. Get away from your neighborhood, if possible.

27—Resourcefulness, optimism, and popularity are highlighted. By exerting an encouraging influence on others, you can overcome delays and setbacks. Start things moving, rather than wait for progress to happen of its own accord.

28—Unless you place a restraint on your enthusiasm, your ambitions may race far ahead of your ability to make them realities. Formulate plans to achieve progress, but keep them within reasonable limitations. Future gains will be in direct proportion to the amount of effort exerted.

29—Although you may have to make some quick changes to keep things running smoothly, new conditions should work out in your favor. Despite the fact that you may find it difficult to make a break from your present routines, retain your enthusiasm and optimism. Show that you are capable of taking on any task which is given.

30—Discuss personal problems with other people to get different viewpoints. Show a willingness to accept the help and suggestions given. Doing this should enable you to iron out difficulties before they develop into serious trouble.

31—A swift tempo, but you can handle it. Messages, situations and people may tax you a bit, but you can handle it all. Greet the New Year with a big smile. There are favorable trends for Scorpio in next year.

Sagittarius

November 23rd—December 21st

You are happy
in mental encounters
with others,
in discussing high issues
and ideas you feel stimulating.
Your enthusiasms take you
hither and yon
and you enjoy the changes and variety
that thus spice your life.
To be socially popular,
attend glittering affairs
delights you.
Impulsive travel pleases
and you often just throw a few things
into a traveling case
and leave for some point
that interests you suddenly.
Your work must be happy,
that means
variety and challenge to your ingenuity
must be involved.
You love adventure
and all new personal contacts
give you a sense
of starting an adventure
as does romance.

Sagittarius

JANUARY

1—Do not let impatience or a pessimistic attitude in others interfere with your recreational plans. Seek out new interests rather than let dull matters depress you. Encourage cheerfulness and harmony among the members of your family despite existing problems.

2—Take advantage of available opportunities to gain many of the things you want. Maintain a cheerful disposition and refuse to become concerned about unimportant matters. Demonstrate your generosity but do not gratify whims of another.

3—Use persuasive methods rather than force if you expect to achieve favorable results. Concentrate on clearing up routine duties and getting them out of the way in a hurry. Make the best of conditions as they are rather than attempt to make drastic changes.

4—Rely on yourself to get things done rather than on the efforts of another. Stick to procedures that have proved successful in the past instead of experimenting with new methods. Refuse to let the quality of your work be upset by occasional interruptions.

5—Regardless of the goals you have set, do not be satisfied with halfway measures. Take minor reversals in your stride, without displaying resentment. Go out of your way to steer clear of any activity that appears to be underhanded.

6—Tackle personal responsibilities by yourself, even though this may completely disrupt your plans. Stick to one assignment at a time, with emphasis placed on accuracy and efficiency. Realistic thinking and practical action may help you win opportunities for job advancement.

7—Keep yourself busy on projects that require alert thinking and vigorous action. Seek help when you need it rather than carry an extra burden alone. Utilize to the fullest extent things you already own, before giving consideration to new purchases.

8—You can offset possible confusion by cautious thinking and detailed planning. Giving in to temporary whims may prove costly later. Adhere closely to conservative policies so that you can keep personal prestige and popularity at a high level.

9—Adjust yourself to changing trends as quickly as possible rather than let existing situations get the best of you. A diplomatic approach rather than forcefulness may be most effective in your dealings with others. Concentrate on a project that can produce lasting and effective results.

10—Let matters coast along as they are to avoid arousing undesirable reactions. A cooperative attitude on your part may prove more of a help than you realize. Make sure you can fulfill present obligations before taking on new expenditures.

11—Avoid participating in any activity that could result in loss of harmony at home. Refrain from rushing matters regardless of how long events may seem to drag. Arrange to do something practical toward solving work problems rather than sit around in idleness.

12—Assert yourself strongly when you feel it necessary but do so in your most diplomatic manner. Decorative additions to your wardrobe can increase the interest of others in your appearance. Use existing resources to better advantage for obtaining the things you want.

13—Refuse to let events over which you have no control spoil your day. Keep active and be willing to help others who are in need of it. Prevent unnecessary emotional friction in your household by shopping only for what you need.

14—Refrain from saying anything that might create cause for later regret or apology. You may find it a serious mistake to use forceful methods in overcoming obstacles. Avoid investing in anything from which you cannot derive immediate benefits.

15—A few thoughtless words may lead to more antagonism and animosity than you would care to handle. Go after the things you want but be sure you thoroughly understand the problems that have to be overcome.

16—Give extra attention to the details of your work so that you can overcome existing drawbacks. Carry through present projects without leaving loose ends for later consideration. Guard against overestimating your own capabilities by taking on an assignment that you will have difficulty in handling.

17—Proceed cautiously in money matters, as it would be easy to incur harsh criticism. Arrange to promote business and friendship simultaneously. Regardless of the issues at stake, stay away from controversy.

18—Follow your own conclusions for best results rather than seek advice. A little forethought may enable you to make more effective use of your opportunities. Take a realistic view of matters when handling budget problems, and leave nothing to chance.

19—Avoid interference and delays by keeping personal plans to yourself. Adhere to practical and tested methods rather than experiment with something new. Guard against waste and loss of possessions by making maximum use of each article.

20—Let others do the talking and acting, since it would be easy to create the wrong impression. Have other members of your household in complete accord before making a decision about money. Insure maximum efficiency from your efforts by planning your activities in advance and leaving nothing to chance.

21—Devote attention to personal duties rather than be concerned with the demands of others. You can achieve successful results by being diligent and aggressive in your efforts. Prevent any possibility of disappointment by keeping business and friendship apart.

22—Base decisions on a business or financial transaction on logic rather than emotions. A conciliatory attitude on your part might turn a hostile person into an ally. Prevent possible disappointment by keeping your job matters and personal business separated.

23—Spend a quiet day away from fast-moving activities to insure obtaining needed relaxation. Prevent disappointment by keeping your plans for the future on a moderate scale. Do something you feel can increase congeniality among the members of your family.

24—Be cautious in what you say, since a harsh remark could create antagonism. Do not be bashful about asking for a favor or privilege to which you feel you are entitled. Careful attention to the details of your work may prove well worth the time and trouble entailed.

25—Do not let anyone dissuade you from achieving goals you have set for yourself. Refuse to let minor problems upset what could otherwise be a pleasant day. More can be gained through employing diplomatic methods than by an open display of force.

26—Refuse to be hurried or put under pressure with regard to money matters. Stick to an established schedule of work instead of experimenting with untried ideas. Refrain from displaying your irritation openly, even though you may have good cause to feel annoyed.

27—Move at a cautious pace, even though your thoughts may be racing at top speed. Regardless of what you start, stay with it until its successful completion. Hard work and sincere effort can make this a day of worth-while gain.

28—Adjust yourself quickly to the current trend of events so that you can make prompt use of opportunities that are available. Be careful with whom you deal when making a financial transaction. This is not a favorable day to give unsolicited opinions.

29—Seek that which is different by adding variety to your activities. This is a time for decisions based on realistic thinking and practical actions. Avoid being hasty, since the need for patience and prudence is emphasized now.

30—Your cooperation and assistance toward someone in trouble could yield you benefits later. Look for opportunities in new fields which you have been neglecting. Observe new trends and valuable achievements that can benefit you.

31—Give encouragement to those who need it but let others have their own way. Make the best of existing circumstances despite interruptions. A diplomatic approach could help you obtain results that work alone could not accomplish.

FEBRUARY

1—Be understanding, kindly and generous with younger people. Avoid any excess of food or drink yourself, but if you entertain serve it lavishly. A large dinner party is ideal if you can possibly afford it.

2—It is difficult to control your temper today; you are in danger of letting go with some severe barbs of intemperate speech. A lifemate will not endure this. In fact, if you are not cautious with your tongue today, you'll be sorely criticized.

3—It's a good day for your hopes and wishes, but you will obstinately strive to fulfill them. You could find yourself with a financial setback if you are too intent on doing as you wish. This evening holds the threat of a quarrel at home.

4—Extreme frustration may set in as the result of a faulty purchase of a costly nature. If you show very bad temper, you can make things worse. It is best to choose your own repair service rather than return the item to the original firm.

5—Be very persistent in work; set yourself limits and reach them. Your word is important today and you must build up the trust of others in it. Evening may bring a telephone call that bores you; be patient.

6—There can be a good chance to make extra money in a big way. Listen to what goes on around you and you may hear of some opportunities that your talents can fulfill. Don't hesitate to be a little aggressive about doing this work.

7—Make your attire and grooming as sharp as possible; get a new hairdo if you feel it is needed. The day will become increasingly romantic and you will be happy if you know you are at your best. Silence is alluring, too.

8—Pressures, restrictions and disappointments may fill the day and make your mood an unpleasant, gray one. You may retreat in typical Sagittarius fashion and just give up the whole thing. If a loved one urges otherwise, then do otherwise.

9—A telephone call today can seem ordinary enough at the time, but you'll discover hidden possibilities in it. You may be on the verge of a new friendship which will be helpful and also be very encouraging at this point in your life.

10—There is a lot of competition in your career, and you should guard your job strongly. Don't minimize the importance of your work or your earnings. Avoid worrying a lifemate—adhere to your agreed upon budget; be thrifty.

11—Excellent news may come about an old plan, and this could mean travel in the near future. However, don't let a festive mood take over and ruin your work plans for the day. Tonight, follow the advice of one who loves you.

12—Avoid the more sentimental part of your nature. Get busy and do some practical thinking about a new relationship. You should notice flaws that irritate you before you offer your friendship to anyone.

13—Difficult tasks lie before you and you can find the entire day tedious. Use your best skills and keep at work constantly; there is no other way to handle it. Beware of too much of any one food at dinner tonight.

14—Work will go well today; your good taste plays a part in all you do and wins much success. It is a good time to shop—buy a major item or an expensive gift. Evening social life can make you wish you had stayed at home.

15—You may determine to drop someone from your list of friends, and this may be just as well. There can be a terrific personality clash and no remedy for it. You will be happiest with members of your family this evening.

16—You may meet someone new who appears very fascinating to you. However, you may judge this person to be less intelligent than you, and that can bring about difficulties and prevent you from heeding facts when it is needful.

17—An excellent day for financial interests of any type. Activity with money will bring big rewards. You can also be generous with a friend in difficulty and never regret it. You'll be weary and ready to retire early.

18—You may meet someone in a surprise situation, and perhaps a little romance will flare up. There are no signs of this amounting to anything or being desirable. Do not go out of your way to be pleasant to someone pursuing you now.

19—A fine day to buy the type of clothes in which you are most glamorous. Add to a hobby collection, also. If you are criticized by a loved one this evening, take it in good nature and do not let any quarrel ensue.

20—Be realistic about career matters; don't imagine you can soar right to the top. You must pause at some steps along the way. Someone may remind you of this rather sharply. Don't take this reminder with ill nature.

21—A good day for planning, looking around, window shopping and thinking about your ideas and clarifying them so that you can work with them effectively. Be happy with others; try to accompany people when you are asked.

22—Try to make the day cheerful and light; avoid thinking of work. Get some help with any rather long task, and don't slave in the kitchen if you are giving a party. A fine time to use a good catering service.

23—Because of someone's friendly ways, you can become more tied down than you like. It is difficult to resist the affectionate hold that an older friend has on you; this can be costly in time and weary you a lot.

24—Money can be the big conversation today and ideas you exchange can be profitable. However, do not give away plans you have had for a long time and which you intend to follow soon. Be cautious about giving any advice tonight.

25—Some honor may come to you today—a really impressive recognition may be extended. When conversing with a younger person, be modest about this and you will win extra admiration. Allow nothing to frighten you tonight.

26—A broken promise of a business person may disillusion you for good. Don't be so intolerant; realize the pressures under which others labor at this time. Do not lose your temper with children at home.

27—Work steadily and feel that you are more than earning what you get. It is a good day for repair work in home and for making decisions about buying new appliances. Your wisdom is practical and thrifty just now.

28—There is much fraud in the atmosphere but you'll not be deceived by any of it. Don't let a quarrel get started with anyone in the business world, however. With neighbors show discretion and refuse to gossip on a very low level.

29 (Leap Year Only)—Don't expect to plunge back into business too early today. All may be in confusion, and you will only be made impatient if you attempt to get others back into the swing. You might as well go along with the spirit of indifference toward work. Nurse ideas along so that they have a chance to grow, but don't expect active production from anyone.

MARCH

1—You can be at your best in appearance, personality and sense of humor. You attract many people today, and among them you may find one who becomes romantically entranced with your dynamic sexual nature and magnetic strength.

2—Someone you have not seen for a long time may call due to some surprises that have taken place in your own life. You can be tempted to turn this call into a romantic matter, but if you do it will not last or be pleasing.

3—Take a tip from someone older and more experienced in financial matters. You can use this in your own way when it comes to investing. An excellent day for activity with money, real estate transactions, all major purchases.

4—Please others today, do nice things for neighbors, help someone who is shut-in, take a gift to an elderly friend. Keep busy now but save time to carry out family requests, too. In general this is a good day for helping others.

5—People can be stimulating, and do linger afterwards to talk a little. It is good to build up relationships with them. Your thought can become cheerful this afternoon and you are in the mood to stroll, count blessings.

6—There may be a delay of aggravating nature that you will have to endure. If you become angry with a business associate, it will do no good and can lower their esteem for you. Be as serene as possible, strive to be ingenious in your work.

7—Be very reliable, punctual and businesslike in your activities. Show someone who is in command that you can be every bit as prudent and realistic as any one else. No time for dreams and romantic guesswork here.

8—The mail can bring you a wonderful surprise, tell you of success you once hoped for. The end result of this may be some need for a new attitude toward finances and your career in general. You will need to make a choice.

9—Danger of getting mixed up with a playful character who is deceptive and undependable. Be cautious of your emotions now and do not let them get out of hand. Be prudent in all you do if out on a date tonight.

10—Use all the patience you can muster, help a newcomer in your business environment. If you envy an associate you alone will suffer for it, of course. Be courteous with an executive even if you really do not like this person.

11—Be highly considerate of others, do your very best in all chores. Avoid companions who are spendthrifts and excessive in pleasure hunting. Be willing to endure a little dullness this evening for the sake of good health.

12—There is need for strict honesty even when it is difficult. Be outspoken with an executive you talk to after work, for any deception will be noted. Your intelligence and integrity needs to be at work throughout the cycle.

13—Make no excuses for any error or unwise action that occurs today. If you malinger on the job it will be known. A relative may be unpleasant to deal with. Be as silent as possible when criticized and accused today.

14—An encounter today may result in a lifetime relationship which is rather unusual. You may attract someone to whom you are not attracted at all. A good day for shopping, making decisions about educational matters.

15—Your work can be monotonous and there may be a heavy load of it. Chances are you will get cooperation and sympathetic understanding from those near you. Free your mind from worry and all goes well throughout cycle.

16—You probably will miss religious services. You may be away visiting loved ones, and the day may be somewhat dull. Weather can account for this and so you mustn't blame others if you feel bored and a little on edge with them.

17—Take your work at an easy stride and you'll accomplish marvels. Get your mind off of impossible dreams and concentrate on what is before you. In social life this evening there may be an embarrassing moment you can handle.

18—Do not be harsh with little ones who are rather troublesome today. They may be feeling some deep frustrations and be emotionally upset. Show love and kindness, buy a little gift, fix up a little treat for them.

19—Someone childish may play a trick that causes trouble. Try not to harbor a bitter feeling about this. Go your own way as much as possible. Shopping is favored and also the start of a vacation journey is auspicious.

20—An unreasonable person can expect too much and most of it quite unnecessary. You will be wise to stay in harmony with this person no matter how you feel. It's up to you to make the day cheerful under mixed aspects.

21—Try your best to fulfill a requirement and do not complain about it. Show respect to those who are older, for if you don't you'll get a black mark against your record. It's rather a trying day with some frustrations.

22—Events can be upsetting and bring about an entirely new situation for you. What you hear through the mail can give you a big problem. You may feel emotional trouble and need someone wise to talk things over with.

23—Be very cautious and gracious with all. Do not let personal feelings enter into matters. You may have an unusual invitation to fulfill for the evening, do not have qualms about it or try to back out in any way.

24—Do not get involved in a scheme a neighbor has for pooling finances to buy a convenience. Keep to yourself where money is concerned. A romantic trend to the evening may not have good results; separation may be final.

25—Someone unscrupulous may be swift to grasp something that by rights should come to you. You'll find rewards elsewhere and they may be an improvement over original opportunity. You may have a laugh about it tonight.

26—You must be dutiful, give up personal plans, help out where your abilities are needed. Work you do for an organization will make you better known in the community. Avoid being too hasty about fulfilling demands made now.

27—A rare opportunity may come to enjoy a new experience you have often wondered about. A day for learning, practicing new skills, finding pleasure in new people around you. What you do today increases the influence for good.

28—Be helpful to someone who has an emotional problem that simply can't be solved. There is need to wait for an automatic solution to this problem through time alone. Point out the wisdom of simple patience.

29—Buy something to boost your ego, a splendid new costume, lovely new shoes, some glamorous cosmetics. Expense is worth it today, for you are having a case of the doldrums and can lift this mood only by shopping.

30—An older friend can irritate you through being just too traditional and oppressive about rules and the like. Get away from such a person swiftly. You need gay and cheerful people, so find them for evening happiness.

31—Even if you know you are right, do not be insistent. Let people learn things for themselves; don't get the reputation of being a know-it-all which might be built up by those who envy your knowledge and experience.

APRIL

1—You may find you have hidden resources that can be used now to see you through a difficult circumstance. There is some injustice in the atmosphere and nerve-wracking experiences can get you down. You may fight your way through depression by thinking clearly, resting, avoiding social life.

2—You'll accomplish a great deal of solid work today. A marvelous cycle for building up your reputation as accurate and thorough in everything you do. An executive who is observant may commend you in forthright fashion. Enjoy the evening's rest which has been well won. Music will appeal.

3—An older neighbor may irritate you with some prudish view you cannot tolerate. Best to be aloof, get away from such a companion as quickly as possible. Your life style is your own and you need not listen to criticism from one who is entirely different. Try to make this obvious.

4—You may be asking yourself how important can it be about a matter which holds some risk or fear for you. Trying to get your ego down to proper size will work and allow you to go right ahead with this awesome project. Your creative instincts are aroused to hope by a friend's speech.

5—A new neighbor can soon become a friend due to ability of both to speak out and accept each other. This is the kind of friendship you like best which leaves you free in every sense of the word. Just good companionship on occasion, some laughter together now and then, and all is perfect.

6—You can be pleased to go to church and then find yourself vexed and troubled by a remark you hear. Keeping your mind on such an irritation can bring on emotional troubles. You may make a decision which brings better emotional health and clears the way to new and wise understanding of another.

7—A health problem may nag you as you keep putting off care of it. There may be some necessity causing this delay but try to shorten it and get busy with improving your health. Telephone calls are exciting. You may get several unexpected invitations and have a difficult time choosing among them.

8—A person with an honestly tolerant view may show you new attitudes which you admire. Take something for your own philosophy from this person's wisdom. Be industrious at work and try to please a boss who is not very generous with praise and can be cranky often. Keep your conscience clear.

9—A generous act today will ring on down through the years in the minds of acquaintances. Your most magnanimous spirit is in action and even where hostility is shown to you your spirit is too large to be annoyed. You have plans of your own that give you hope; share them with no one.

10—Guard possessions and money, be cautious in movements, try not to be around large machinery. This is not a favorable day for any big change, financial transaction or talking with executives. Keep it quiet, be diligent and have no plans for evening except where a loved one is involved.

11—Shopping is favored but you can be too extravagant, buy things you won't use. Your eyes are taken by too many displays and you can easily fall prey to desire for a larger wardrobe than anyone needs, particularly when it comes to shoes. Oh well, if you do buy too much don't worry, just enjoy it.

12—A delightful visitor who is unexpected may change the course of your day. You may battle your way through a disagreeable situation in your neighborhood, but do try to be quiet about the friction and results. If you go out socially or romantically tonight, you'll enjoy every minute of it.

13—You need to give some thought to weight control and general health. Make plans about these matters; a decision to take advantage of a health spa can be a good idea, but it's also good to start today with watching your diet; avoid those treats that are not for you. In the evening take a walk with a friend.

14—Someone very ambitious, snobbish and desirous of the spotlight may take an arrogant, condescending attitude with you. Be lighthearted about this for many such people inhabit the world and the sun and rain fall on them just as on you. Evening may bring new inspiration about a previous goal.

15—A telephone call may bring a marvelous opportunity. Be ready to make a triggerquick decision and do the work necessary to follow it up. A loyal friend may show up and you may realize it's a good time to separate the wheat from the chaff when it comes to friends.

16—Even your philanthropic spirit may be pushed to the exploding stage. Someone who simply imposes and then wastes what is done may pull an act on you to impress you and succeed only in bringing the end of your kindliness. That's all right. It's good to take a hard line about such a person.

17—Humor can be the atmosphere of the day and you may be right at the front in cheering others with remarks that bring lighthearted laughter. You've reached a point of depression where you realize there's no way to go but up, so you're stretching to make the climb out of your little pit.

18—Buy clothes, get hair styling done, try new cosmetics and make it a day of glamorous luxury for yourself as far as you can. Good news that comes in late in the day can make you very happy that you got yourself fixed up in ravishing style, for you're to have wonderful company tonight!

19—A favorable day for doing new things, going to unfamiliar places, meeting people and perhaps being on the fringe of a new romance. Happy and adventurous hours are here, but don't make promises today for there are signs these would not be wise and you would not want to keep them.

20—Your intuition may spur you to act upon a matter connected with the family. This can be a necessary action although it makes you unpopular. Don't mingle with new acquaintances, don't call anyone long distance, and don't get discouraged with your own inspirational plans and creative hopes.

21—Be very cautious, don't stop, avoid being imposed upon in work demands. The day is a difficult one, the aura not favorable for much of anything. Routine work is exhausting and not very rewarding but make the best of it. Buy some magazines to look through to brighten your evening hours.

22—A know-it-all may enter your life and start talk which is going to be unceasing. You may as well take a humorous attitude toward this person who really means well enough. Your true thoughts may be on some issue which concerns you deeply in your private romantic life at this time.

23—You may hear from a relative about whom you have been concerned lately. This can be a matter of seeking you out due to a special need. Don't play too much of the bountiful helper now; use your wisdom to put limits to your affectionate desire to help. Protect yourself as well as you can.

24—Keep your mind off financial pressures and stay with thoughts of beauty, originality and your dreams which might some day be fulfilled. Someone romantically inclined may call you this evening. It can take all your diplomacy to turn this person down without injuring feelings seriously.

25—If someone seems unkindly, bend over backwards to show good will and trust. You can make a friend out of an enemy by being charmingly light and refusing to be offended. Work goes well today and in social life tonight you will be well liked and happy with popularity that comes your way.

26—You may be accident-prone today. Watch handling of sharp instruments, be cautious when doing any cleaning in the home. Avoid going to new places or talking to strangers. It is best to stay within a two-mile radius of home. Do not stop to pet stray animals if you are walking anywhere.

27—Do your best to be conventional when with other people. It would be painful to an older person to hear you express far-out views. You may work at something creative this afternoon with good results. Try not to be irritated if someone interrupts you for inconsequential reasons this evening.

28—Lethargy and sloth may be your atmosphere in the morning. It can take a happy event to shake you free from these intruding moods. Afternoon brightens and the request of an executive can make you happy. Do not talk much to work associates who may regard you as a privileged person.

29—Do not give pain to anyone. You might be in the mood to deflate idols, undermine the beliefs of others without realizing what you are doing. You can feel an air of coolness and even dislike growing around you. Think over such things in the evening and make some kindly resolutions.

30—Travel is well aspected and you may get away on a vacation. Romance is favored too and a wedding date now or the start of an engagement can be auspicious. If alone, you may meet someone who will fill your summer with love tinged with a bit of worry and feeling that you are deceived.

MAY

1—Don't take anything too seriously today. You may be approached by several people for help but not feel like living up to the occasion. Do nothing which is contrary to your principles or plans. You may seem obstinate to others but that's the way it's best now.

2—A plan and hope may fail. You can have surprising results from following what you think is a good course practically speaking. A large sum may have to be expended. Try not to worry about this but find the ray of sunshine falling in through the surrounding mist and trouble.

3—Legal snarls are possible; protect yourself. It is worthwhile spending on professional help. A good friend may lift your spirits during the afternoon and you can be pleased with the way your efforts go. Evening may bring an interesting and encouraging conversation.

4—Do not be too materialistic in thought and plans today. You can find your wishes thwarted if you undertake a project just for the sake of personal well-being. Let your spiritual light shine and be unselfish in this cycle. You can help someone through your practical outlook.

5—A contact you make will cheer you much. Be very dutiful with those dependent upon you. You can think big in financial matters and must not let any petty worry creep in. Be sure to keep up appearance, buy some new cosmetics, try something more luxurious in this line.

6—A new acquaintance may give you a new outlook. Listen to someone who is pleasant and full of healthy laughter. You'd be surprised how your life can be changed when you let the ideas of others sink in. Do not downgrade yourself and your abilities for any reason whatever.

7—Big financial deals can be undertaken with confidence. Progress with self-assurance about money, sign papers, make definite transactions. Be daring in your romantic hopes during the latter part of this cycle. You may have a chance for a new companion who is desirable.

8—Don't let anyone take over your life even in suggestions. Your independence is the only good course to follow. You may have to struggle through some social situations that bother you tonight, but don't let that cause trouble in your personal situation. Be friendly now.

9—Be sure to check everything you do for accuracy. You may be engaged in an important assignment. Build up your reputation for accuracy, let nothing in error escape your attention. Be blunt with someone who tries to take up your evening hours in idle chat and complaint.

10—A new advantage may come your way. Be quick to see the benefits in your situation. There are interesting trends for romance. There can be a type of love at first sight. The interest you inspire in another can be permanent. Be cautious in your speech and manner now.

11—Make sure all mechanical items you handle are in good repair. There could be accident and trouble through a faulty appliance or machinery of some kind. Caution is the word if you want to avoid costly danger. You need your most practical wits about you today.

12—Avoid driving yourself beyond the point of exhaustion. You can have major work demands and it is not profitable to try to fulfill them. Give some thought to your earnings and you may see they are not sufficient for work put out. Be reflective this evening.

13—Don't count on others today, use your own wits and be ready for almost anything that comes. Your career situation may undergo quite a change due to official attitude and requests. You may find yourself in a more congenial group of people as a result of today.

14—New circumstances in your neighborhood may be attractive and you can benefit from acquaintance with someone who is tuned in to the vital qualities of life. Take a hint from what is said to you this evening during social life and you can enhance your future personal welfare.

15—Avoid going to great expense for anything. If you shop for entertainment in your home this evening, buy things that are inexpensive but pleasing. Provide more than just gourmet items for snacks during the evening. Be outgoing and enjoy guests in your home.

16—Don't rush around. Don't drive at high speed. Don't linger long in talk with anyone. You need relaxation and the opportunity to think things over. Avoid being discouraged with some expense that is unexpected. Do not be hostile to an older person who has divergent attitudes.

17—You can make a new step today, enter a new phase of your life. Success trends are here and your talents are right up to the demands. Don't object to a little extra effort that may be asked in a creative matter. Your abilities will be appreciated and win your future benefit.

18—You might find some unusual gifts coming in from people who like and admire you. Flowers and other tokens of esteem may come your way. Be very patient with those around you now, there are signs that an emotional person may irritate you.

19—Take good note of all that happens and you will see that a pattern works throughout your life. Be sociable with someone new in your neighborhood, open your door to someone who feels shut out. The spiritual things are more important than the material by a wide margin.

20—You may have a grudge against someone in your vicinity. Think twice and you'll see how senseless this is. Give credit where it is due and refuse snap judgments about anyone. It is a good day to seek a new residence and make a decision but do not act in haste about this matter.

21—This is one of those times you wish you had never made a certain statement about desires. You can find your wishes fulfilled and seek to get out of the situation this puts you in. A lesson is here and you won't miss it. Keep your eye on current events, try to control them.

22—You may be more attractive than you know and sweep someone right off base by your romantic attractiveness. Becoming more friendly with someone can be a mutual aid. Do not turn down an invitation or discourage someone who wants to talk to you about serious matters.

23—Take care of personal matters now. Buy clothes, have your hair restyled, investigate some new cosmetics. You are in line for benefits from making the most of your appearance. Do not just dawdle along with what you're used to; get out and get a new and shining look.

24—You may make a new acquaintance who is to be of importance in your life for some time. Be very hospitable and give time to people who turn to you. Your personality is comforting to others; your suggestions will be used wisely. Also be generous with material items.

25—Be cautious and take very good care of pets you love, also of small children that may be in your environment. Do nothing that could be criticized by a conventional person. Try to understand the more conservative views and do not shock anyone with your speech this evening.

26—Some troubles can arise unexpectedly. Be prepared and able to handle an emergency which concerns finances. You may be much admired due to decisions you make and to your swift action. Be unselfish when helping a family member make a wise decision during the evening.

27—Take your time about work, make sure it is accurate. If you find it essential to buy something today, shop around first. Do not let any salesperson take command and persuade you to buy against your better judgment. Think of past experiences as a guide now.

28—Keep habits healthy, avoid excess, turn down an invitation you know might lead to a wild party. This is a cycle when pleasure can lead to regret and undermine your health. You need to be in the home and able to retire early. Rest up from exhausting circumstances tonight.

29—If you are too arbitrary and impulsive, you will lose the esteem of a person you value. The cycle can take a romantic trend late in the day and you will enjoy the companionship of someone interested in you this evening. Look your best, give a chance to new romance.

30—There is possibility of brooding and unhappiness due to the fact that you cannot control matters as you would like to. Avoid expenditures. Do not drive unless you must. Be tolerant and kindly to an older friend even though this person vexes you and stretches your gullibility.

31—Get in touch with someone from whom you want news. One of those times when nothing at all will come to those who simply wait. You must be active, follow up ideas and desires. You can win all you want if you follow your true feelings and natural bent at this time.

JUNE

1—Be pleasant to an older person who gets in touch with you. Taking someone to lunch can be happy event. The afternoon may offer inspiration in connection with fulfilling a wish. The evening is best spent in connection with fulfilling a wish. The evening is best spent in reading, watching TV briefly and retiring at a healthful hour.

2—Someone difficult to pin down may finally make a promise. You can be irked by the attitude of this person but don't let an unpleasant tone creep into your speech. You can end the day with much satisfaction about financial trends that are improving at present.

3—Live up to your reputation for abilities of creative or inventive nature. Your ingenuity may help another who is under pressure to get something done. You can handle complex matters, solve problems of intricate nature. Service to others is the best use for this ability.

4—Health may demand that you cancel an engagement for social life tonight. Talking on the telephone to a loved one can lift some of the gloom. You may need nothing but rest and a light diet which will put nerves in better state. Seek serenity this evening and all will improve.

5—A new acquaintance may visit. Deception, contradictory statements in this person's speech. Better go slow and avoid becoming involved until more facts come in. Be patient with loved ones in the home during the evening.

6—Someone may take you to task for certain attitudes you have, for pursuits which are a major part of your life. Don't heed such criticism and accusation. Go your own way and know that this is right for the present. People are on edge today, likely to say almost anything; overlook it.

7—This is a good day to buy clothes, cosmetics, small things for the home. You'll find it cheerful to browse around a little; you might find a treasure in a used-book store. Be leisurely but conscientious. Conversation at dinner time can become vexing; excuse yourself if this happens.

8—A disappointment in the romantic area may occur and be somewhat amusing. You may find that someone you admired greatly has turned into a grouch. That's the way it goes and you can have a little smile about it all. The evening is good for walking around, meditating.

9—Avoid that which is unfamiliar, including people. Be companionable only with the tried and true friends and associates. Keep speech to others on a very objective level. Best not to have social plans for evening, the family may need your company to make a big decision about money.

10—You'll be happy and cheerful with something purchased recently. A good mood pervades you and you can inspire others with cheer. Lift the lonely and depressed mood of a neighbor with your companionship this evening. Be generous with encouragement to all in this cycle.

11—Keep all activities healthy, avoid rich foods, do not rush, and do not go along with irresponsible pleasure-seekers. Make the day count for practical work interests and finances. You must be alert to seize an advantage which may come over the telephone during the evening.

12—Domestic chores can be bothersome, but get them out of the way quickly and then turn to activities which lure you. Shopping can be fun and a companion will make it more interesting. Attending a party at a friend's home will be pleasant tonight but be wary of a new romance.

13—You may be irritable, impatient with children, unsociable and bleak of view. This is one of those times for temperamental moods that are not reasonable. Keep to yourself, don't spread this blight. Read. Seek a calmer outlook. Do some minor things in the home. Retire early, tonight.

14—You may encounter someone who was once romantically inclined. Don't let this relationship start up again; you'd only end up at the same old stalemate. Be independent, shop for some inexpensive items, enjoy the evening writing a letter or two, making a telephone call.

15—You can become very determined to do exactly as you want to. Danger of acting in a way that is harmful to a family member is here. Better be cautious and circumspect, do nothing to mar your good situation. Be thoughtful about family children in all you do today.

16—Inwardly you may be criticizing someone when outwardly you seem to approve. This type of duplicity is not like you, but then, it wouldn't pay to speak out, either. Chances are the relationship just isn't a good one and you should not cultivate it to the point of intimacy.

17—Financial transactions are favorably accented and it is a good day to complete a real estate deal. You can also buy a car, a boat, almost any large item for the home. Don't worry about installment payments; you'll be able to live up to the bargain you make easily.

18—Drive slowly, be very alert, do not speak hastily to an official of the law. There can be costly consequences for rash activities and speech. If someone is hostile, disregard it as far as possible. Be courteous; leave no room for accusation by others.

19—You can be at the point of real dilemma where romance is concerned. There may be someone you can't live with and can't live without. Don't tie yourself down in any way today, keep the cycle for thought and assessing your own true desires, feelings and needs. Silence pays.

20—Don't let anyone persuade you to change your plans. Show the firm side of your nature, be obstinate in the face of enticements of any type. Know your own mind and let others see that you intend to follow it only. Go out a bit tonight in order to evade an uninvited guest.

21—A major responsibility can be costly but you must follow your conscience. Make a personal sacrifice if that is necessary. Stay within customary environment today and don't seek any off-beat places even though urged by pleasure seeking friends. You're best off alone tonight.

22—Someone may disappoint you bitterly, be disloyal and gossip about you. Your trust in the intelligence of such a person can be blighted. You will gain nothing by a remark about this situation. Don't dwell on what others do, for that is not worthy of your intelligence.

23—You may delay making a decision about a romantic matter, and it's probably best if you delay it forever. Signs indicate a very undesirable trend for romance and avoiding it is the best thing you can do. A relative may have a demand you must fulfill during the evening.

24—An invitation may be unexpected. If you are speedy in turning it down, you will injure feelings. Make the effort to be considerate of all today but on the other hand don't be pressured into things you do not want to do. A surprise may come tonight and be pleasing.

25—Do something for a friend. Where there is a will there is a way—remember. You'll find the way and be able to accomplish your desire easily. Now is a good time for communications at a distance. Social life is stimulating and new friends may develop from introductions now.

26—You may take a risk that does not work out well. You can be at your most impulsive and daring. Gain control over this mood and try to do only the things for which you know the outcome. Make no promises in romantic matters, keep your sense of freedom high and enjoyable.

27—New light may be gained about a career problem that is crucial with you. Discussion with a person of serious mental trend can turn up new ideas and allow progress with a major venture once you have made basic plans. Mental ability is accented favorably throughout cycle.

28—Don't go into details of explanation to a person who is curious about facts connected with your life. Disregard speaking about the intricate matters, change the subject and show you intend to keep things to yourself. A good idea to discourage this person in the future.

29—Avoid anxiety about any situation. You may later find a change of plan necessary but for the present follow along as though all were possible. You may get some honor for your accomplishments today when you settle down to defeat problems connected with work essentials.

30—If you can't say anything good about an associate, don't say anything at all. Keep your ideals high, value yourself and do nothing to lose esteem of others. A rather difficult day in relationships but you'll get through with tact. Keep the evening quietly restful.

JULY

1—You're in good health today, feeling like a million, and that can make you somewhat mischievous. High spirits need an outlet but be a little wary where you find this. Avoid flirtation that might create a situation you don't really want. No fair leading someone on just to play games today.

2—A decision you reach can be quite unwise. Let others behave as they will but by no means follow them. Act for yourself and your ideals even though you find deception and disloyalty in those you formerly trusted. It is best not to do much talking to anyone at this time. Meditate and be philosophical.

3—A new neighbor may try to be friendly. If you are aloof you can be discouraging a very nice person. Better let this relationship get off to a pleasant start by responding in friendly fashion. You may find your first impression or snap judgment turns out to be in total error.

4—It would be foolish to take umbrage at a slight remark of an influential person. Make your character too strong to be affected by what others say. Avoid any situation that threatens to bring on quarrelsome trends. It is good to retreat this evening and keep time for yourself and thought.

5—Money may flow from your hands like water. Remember it doesn't come back once it's gone. Turn away from your extravagant temptations and don't let buying one thing lead to buying another just so you'll have everything to match. You could end up with dismayingly large installment debts.

6—Be diplomatic with an older neighbor. There is no sense in speaking your mind when it might lead to some vicious hostility. If you are somewhat self-centered today you will only be protecting your rights. Sometimes one has to think of oneself first, and this is one of those days.

7—Good news may come from a friend at a distance who is trying to do something extremely generous for you. However, if money is involved don't spend it before you get it. There are some obstacles and unpredictable circumstances standing between you and ultimate success, so be very patient.

8—Keep your appearance up to its best, show what you can do when you really want to be glamorous. It's a good day for a new and unique hair styling. A romantic trend this evening can be very interesting. Don't be in a rush or make any promises. You need to get much better acquainted.

9—Don't count on any relative for anything today. If you make a request of a relative you love, you will probably be turned down flat and your feelings much injured. You must be self-reliant, make your own choices, set your direction according to the way your feelings point. It requires courage.

10—You may have a very busy day starting to get ready for a major change. An inspiration that comes to you about making a long distance telephone call can work out very well. Trust your good fortune, your wisdom of an inner nature for making the right contact and getting the most desirable results.

11—You can expect a difficult day for family matters or in-laws. This is not a good time to hash through a problem but someone may be insistent. Do not try to pressure anyone, avoid being too persuasive. It will be best for you if your opinion is not accepted, so that you can never be held to blame.

12—A happy day for work. All goes well and your talents show an unusual range. You may be given a promotion due to the way you handle work of someone who is ill today. Promotion might also be dependent upon the fact that an older worker is moving residence and you may be the one to take over.

13—You may be observed closely when you are not aware of it. It is a day with an exciting undercurrent which you may know about by evening. Try to avoid being restless. If you drive be extremely cautious. If you have a companion make sure of safety for that person by seat belts and the like.

14—An expert may be what you need today. It's worthwhile to spend a little in order to avoid a lot of tension and nervous strain. Be thoughtful about a young relative at a distance and do something to help progress for this person. A very gratifying telephone message may come through tonight.

15—You may not exactly like the way things are going in your neighborhood but if you want to keep the peace, you'll keep quiet. Avoid curiosity about what is going on among other people. Chances are it has nothing to do with you. Don't worry about gossip or any petty actions of others now.

16—It can be difficult to get information you need about an investment. Be persistent and you'll finally get through to the right contact. It is a rewarding day for work, and you'll be happy looking back on accomplishments tonight but don't leave yourself out of the happy spirit of social life.

17—You can be quite temperamental today and it can be difficult to endure conditions as they are in your home. Don't do anything to cause resentments to rise even higher. Sacrifice a bit of your own desire in order to preserve harmony and pleasant relations with everyone around you.

18—There can be some upset about financial matters, perhaps papers that do not come through on time. Make sure your arithmetic is correct in any figuring you may do. Don't assume correctness, check back over carefully. Evening may find you dull and weary, ready for early retirement.

19—You can be disillusioned with part of your career and this can show to your disadvantage. Find some cheerful people who will put verve into your life. You may have a choice about dates tonight; think it over well and you may decide to have none at all. Your wisdom is working well in your relationships.

20—A friend who wishes to express gratitude may do something very nice for you. You are fortunate in material ways now and can be quite surprised at what comes your way. Be kindly to others and pass on some of your fortune. It's a day for sharing, love and affection for all around you and your area.

21—A telephone call may abruptly change your plans for the day. Don't be irritated with a person who must have your help immediately. Be glad you are able to improve things for this person and you'll find a surprising reward. Evening can be exciting but somewhat inclined to bring on arguments.

22—Someone may help you with a complex problem. It is your day to live and learn. Don't resent another person's intrusion into your life for this is entirely well-intentioned and benevolent. Be patient with a small child in the family, don't let your nerves get upset if you are asked to baby-sit awhile.

23—There are surprises, big changes and some interesting conversation in your area. You may have a heart-to-heart talk with an executive who has always been honest with you. A decision may have to be made about your career but you'll be given adequate time to think over all angles and needs.

24—Travel may be on your day's schedule and it can be excellent travel indeed. Situations you encounter may be instructive, strangers may bring new realities to your attention. Fit in with changing tempo and places. You'll find real pleasure in an evening spent at an entirely new place.

25—Avoid any type of strenuous exercise or unwise lifting of heavy objects. Be sure to remember a birthday or anniversary of some kind. Make an appropriate telephone call or take a small gift. Feelings can be injured if you are forgetful or overlook the special occasion someone else cherishes.

26—The mail can bring a surprising letter and may bring a question that you prefer not to answer. Take your time about responding, but do respond. Make your treatment of others very honest and affectionate today. Be more concerned about mental and spiritual thoughts than about material advantages now.

27—Some excitement around your house and neighborhood will enliven the day. Be generous but not too generous. Better not to give anything you might regret. A telephone call can be rather vexing and you may find difficulty in saying anything to a person you are not at all interested in.

28—Someone may play on your sympathies, put on a helpless "act." You'd be foolish to come to the aid of a person who is just being lazy and deceptive. Keep aloof today, attend to your own affairs, avoid a mix-up in anyone else's emotional tangles. Your own may be bad enough.

29—Be cautious about diet and drink. Your nerves can become ragged by too much rich food that is not basically for your digestive system anyhow. Avoid talking of personal matters with anyone. Keep alert in traffic whether walking or driving. It is best to be safely at home after dark descends.

30—Someone may not be friendly to your ideas. You can find opposition and disbelief from a person who is too narrow to comprehend your meaning. Don't talk to such a person as you would to your own friends. You just don't belong together and the sooner you realize this, the better off you will be.

31—You'll be kept busy most of the day and this is unfortunate because of an important social engagement for which you need all of your sparkling personality. Try to get in a little nap before you go out for the evening. Someone may introduce a person who is to be your future lifemate at tonight's party.

AUGUST

1—Shopping is favored and major financial transactions can be put through successfully. Buying or selling real estate can be particularly rewarding. You may have need to get advice from an attorney, and it's best to choose someone well known rather than a stranger to you. A victory may be won this way.

2—Avoid rush, worry, fear about the future. Some misfortune you may feel pending will probably never befall you. Get your mind onto the moment and do just what is required instead of letting your thoughts roam all over. Practicality is the thing now and from it your success will come.

3—You can have ingenious ideas about clothes today but the snag may come in working them out. Get advice or some help from a neighbor who is clever that way. A gift can come most unexpectedly and please you beyond measure. A little caution about dining and wining is needed for the evening hours.

4—Financial matters may take most of your attention now. You can have an excellent chance to invest in a venture of friends that is very practical and brings large dividends. Avoid any worry about this matter, let it go along automatically once you have thrown your lot in with friends.

5—On a shopping trip don't go completely wild about having the best of everything. Better stick to prices you have fixed in your mind approximately before you went out. A mood of luxury could overtake you and you might also have a rare day of wanting to keep up with the neighbors.

6—Romantic matters may come to the surface and use up all your time and thought. You have a choice, possibly including even more than two romantic admirers. If you can relax about it all, you may see that there is no real reason to hurry through a decision. You can hang on to all affections.

7—A neighbor may be a source of annoyance without meaning to be so. Don't let this feeling build up for it could lead to a temper outburst that would embarrass you. Also avoid all gossip in the neighborhood. Someone may turn to you for information; just state that you don't know and stay in the clear.

8—If you travel be cautious in heavy traffic. Don't try to set any time records. A gift may come your way and be very charming but watch out for motives behind it. Do some thinking about your wardrobe and plan it for the season that is coming soon. Give a style a chance.

9—In any question of beliefs in mental or spiritual matters; do not give a clearcut answer to questions. Everyone must decide upon personal beliefs and you'd make a mistake to be persuasive about such things with a friend. Keep evening open for surprises that may have far-reaching consequences.

10—Temptation to write a letter in angry style must be overcome. Make no accusations or criticisms today. It is essential that you be at your best in pleasant personality, agreeable and harmonious. You may not really feel this way but acting it can induce the mood by later tonight.

11—Today may start a new phase in your career thinking. You may come to a conclusion, make a decision about your job. It is time to be moving on you think, but you have a contract to carry through for awhile yet. However, being firm in your decision can have an effect on a dispute that comes up soon.

12—A neighbor may be very friendly and in a way you like this, in a way you don't. You tend to be a little selfish with your time. In addition to the money it may mean to you, it also means opportunity to meditate and that you regard very high in the ranks of desirable, useful activities.

13—Strange little misfortunes may befall you. Although nothing is highly serious, some of these can be highly aggravating. Your ego may sink a bit under today's burdens. Don't bore others by talking of these things much. Don't let anything ruin and depress your more youthful spirits.

14—Money and career issues get most attention. You may be given something that will prevent having to spend a lot. Your good luck holds quite well today. In career matters you may be praised by someone normally hard to please. Keep your thoughts about all executives kindly, affectionate, charitable.

15—You may still be in high spirits but your nerves can be in need of rest. Don't make any plans that include going out or entertaining for today. An older relative may annoy you by taking up time you need for rest. It can be best just to speak out clearly about this for the sake of health.

16—Chance to have a really good time may be here and you may travel somewhat to enjoy it. A party you attend can be quite a bit of revelry, the spirit of fun can be high and attractive. Be bright and bold in dress, ahead a little in hair styling. This event calls for your best efforts.

17—Don't show any kind of superior feelings to an older person who is hostile to you to begin with. Your gracious manners will prevent an unpleasant scene. Be very firm in your pleasant ways, do not let the slightest thing disturb you. Character strength is important in all you do.

18—Be independent, go your own way and make plans strictly on your personal intentions. Someone may try to pry information from you. Steer clear of people who gossip constantly, are very curious and tend toward malicious talk. Also, avoid anyone who seems intent upon injuring your own feelings.

19—Be thoughtful about an invitation of casual type that you get today. Someone interested in you romantically might be highly unappropriate as an escort. Such a person may also be persistent. Analyze your own views, be very honest about your motivations. Try to act with wisdom about this.

20—Your social life may take you into a new realm by this evening. You can be charmed by the wit and knowledge of the people you meet. However, there can be drawbacks to associating with these people. They may be heedless and flippant about some serious part of life, tend to go to excess.

21—Avoid setting yourself too many chores to complete. You need leisure and rest, should do things slowly and thoughtfully. If shopping don't rush into anything big; you can go back for it next week if it's that attractive to you. Don't let an evening's entertainment make you temperamental, brusque.

22—The day favors a major purchase. This could be real estate. Make sure all legal matters are in the clear before you sign important documents. There can be some events in the family that worry you. A younger relative may be taking a trend that you feel is wrong. Advice will accomplish nothing now.

23—Go out of your way to be attractive in appearance. You may have an interview with someone who rates the superficial high. "If it looks good, it is good" tends to be the view this time. Don't show too much intellect.

24—A very cheerful person may say something you don't understand, may seem to be attacking you. This can be far from the case. Actually you're being given a chance to show how magnanimous you are. Intelligence will win out. Emotions are not to be trusted; you must be thoughtful all the way.

25—An older relative can be very angry with you due to your generosity. While this is your own affair, it is wise not to antagonize your relative further by pointing this out. Do take thought for obligations, though, and make sure you will be able to carry them out when the time comes.

26—A good day to shop for small, pleasing things, buy a pet, some records, a pretty set of dishes, some pleasant little knicknacks. Don't take work so seriously that you become upset in digestive matters. Avoid lengthy conversation with a person who is a non-stop talker and very tiresome.

27—Attend to financial interests promptly, pay bills, make sure insurance is in good state, go over your budget with an eye to improving it so you can buy a desired item. The evening may be fascinating socially, but don't get too cheerful from imbibing too much. Draw a line somewhere.

28—A neighbor may be very confidential with you and this can somewhat alarm you. You don't exactly like being the respository of secrets because it is such a tricky kind of situation. Try to turn the talk to impersonal matters, discussion of books, theatre, travel and the like.

29—A good day for travel, visiting relatives far away, enjoying recreation and a spirit of freedom. If you must be at work, that is too bad. You can be lethargic, not very efficient and in general discontented. Be cautious what kind of exhilarating pleasure you seek tonight and with whom.

30—Not much doing today. You can feel kind of let-down, be bored with just about everything. Blood pressure may be low and cause you to be weary for no other reason. Seeing a physician might help this condition. Don't let friends or neighbors keep you up too late tonight. You need rest.

31—A day of surprise and pleasure. You will enjoy every moment with physical health being at its best and all worries ceased for the time. By the end of the day you may find that your personal life is much altered for the better. Romance is promised under these influences.

SEPTEMBER

1—Someone who has been watching you may now be ready to speak about important matters. This could be a willingness to invest money in you due to certain talents. Opening a business could be the subject and you might have difficulty reacting to this for it is probably far from your mind.

2—Aggressive spirits and progressive ideas will get you far today. An opportunity can be grasped and a new position become available through your ingenuity. Use every talent. Your personality will take care of the rest. You are on the way upward under favorable vibrations.

3—A gay mood when you may want to let work go for a time. This is all right, but don't overdo it. Spend a bit, seek the pleasure you are ready for, but keep reasonable hours. People will be friendly and you will make new contacts which are valuable for later days.

4—Affection is stressed today, and you will be secretly happy with the signs you receive of new affection. Members of the family will prove their loyalty, and altogether the day will be rewarding in a very personal way. Your own generous personality will be much in evidence.

5—Avoid strangers and in fact, play it safe all the way by not engaging in any unnecessary conversation. Family quarrels can make the afternoon bitter. The end of romance or domestic life may come as a result of quick speech which you regret soon. Read and watch TV.

6—The day brings you favorable aspects, but also some confusing trends. You may not find your pace until afternoon, and the morning may hold conflicting emotions about a personal matter. Let the day iron itself out and by evening you may know new happiness in romance.

7—Talk over plans with loved ones. You can find happiness this way as well as arrive at beneficial conclusions. Listen carefully to everything you hear today, since there are some excellent ideas going around. Influences favor imagination and interesting conversation tonight.

8—A day for practical progress along scheduled lines. Good plans will pay off. Former ideas can be used and you will be able to function at your most efficient. Intelligence is high, so use it to impress in the right places. Be sure grooming is excellent and use your personality.

9—A stroke of good luck seemingly from out of the blue will make the day adventurous and profitable. Follow along with trends, don't worry about previous plans; they can be cancelled without trouble. The evening may be very sociable and you can take a new spot in the limelight.

10—Self-assurance will win you new laurels today. You can prove your true ability and gain for the future as well as the present. Be firm in your decisions, for they will be based on good judgment. The evening may take an unexpected turn, particularly in romantic matters.

11—Be on guard against people who approach you with pleas for loans or other aid. You may make promises which you will regret in haste. Even old friends are to be avoided when it comes to handing out money. The evening can be very distressing if you become enmeshed in a gathering.

12—Psychic powers are stressed. You may make a decision as the result of unusual insight. Favorable trends for desirable changes in your career. Be active, follow impulses, keep working. You will be appreciated in new quarters, and perhaps hold an important conference late in the day.

13—Many conflicting influences, much mischief and idle chatter which can bring real trouble. Try to make your way through these hazardous hours with good sense. Follow no rash impulses. Avoid writing letters and making telephone calls. Lock up valuables securely. Retire early.

14—Splendid and rather mystic influences for happiness and wellbeing. You may arrive at new philosophical understandings, share a rare moment or two of communication with a new friend. Harmony reigns and hours in the outdoors are particularly favored for relaxed enjoyment.

15—Seek the solitude you need. Remain wrapped up in your own thoughts and plans. If you emerge and talk over matters with others you will regret it. There is much envy in the atmosphere. Deceit and trickery may betray you, if you let yourself be sociable. Read tonight.

16—Aggressive spirits and progressive ideas will get you far today. An opportunity can be grasped and a new position become available through your ingenuity. Use every talent. Your personality will take care of the rest. You are on the way upward toward favorable vibrations.

17—There may be some disappointments early in the day. Do not let them dim your outlook. Giving in to depression will prevent you from gaining the rather happy tendencies of later hours. Brighten up by having lunch at a very good restaurant and thinking of pleasant associations.

18—The aspects are favorable for ventures you have had in mind. Get dressed up and go out. Excellent for buying home items, looking at large appliances, cars, jewelry. You may find just what you want. Loved ones will be cooperative and affectionate. Entertain neighbors tonight.

19—Sagittarius will find great pleasure in the little surprises which happen today. Messages, gifts and general good fortune will keep the hours busy and exciting. Spend a bit on your wardrobe. Finances are favored and a few whims can be indulged happily. Good spirits for the evening.

20—Your best disposition will bring a certain happiness to these hours. Nothing will trouble you much, and even if there is little accomplishment you won't worry. A relaxed atmosphere with good relations among loved ones and associates. Accept an invitation from a new acquaintance.

21—A gloomy morning, with a message which may mean extra duty when you feel little like assuming it. Try to shoulder burdens graciously. Your mental outlook will improve later in the day, but there is danger of accident and illness from trends toward excess and impulse.

22—Legal matters, business transactions, major changes are favored. You may receive a surprise legacy, a gift, a new source of income. The day is almost unpredictable in its good fortune, for influences indicate various windfalls and successes. A telephone call will be pleasant tonight.

23—Best not be very active today. Make the morning leisurely. Read the news, chat with the family and have a relaxed start to the day's work. You may have hints about good fortune, and a promise from an executive. Do not build on a promise from an executive. Do not build hopes too high. In the evening quiet entertainment is best.

24—It may be necessary to work beyond your strength to fulfill demands of duty. Bolster your health by careful eating and slowing down a bit. Keep at it steadily and the seeming mountain of work will diminsih. Be sure to retire early, and suffer no change of plan.

25—Unfortunate auspices for relations with those closest to you. Plan to be away from home, if possible, at least the major part of the day. The least said, the soonest mended. You may seem very selfish, even to friends, so avoid them, also. Take stock of your own personality.

26—You will be kept busy with your work. Many events and incidents to lend zest to career routine. Excitement over news in the afternoon may make your personality glow and attract new admirers. Share your happiness with loved ones by doing something very special for them.

27—The day has a rather tense atmosphere, but you will thrive under the pressure, probably. You should feel physically more fit than on the previous day. Buy a few personal items, keep your spirits high, and accept an invitation which may mean a new group of friends for you.

28—If old ideas and old ways hamper you, formulate a way to throw them off for the influences generated by the Luminaries are excellent for bringing matters to a head and for a change of viewpoint. You can find solace and inspiration at church.

29—All will go well today. Surprising changes in plan may be forced upon you, but you will welcome them. A journey may be started most auspiciously. Good friendship is in the air, also. Enjoy conversation at luncheon, and plan on an evening of romantic fascination.

30—Many mistakes, perhaps danger from associations which are tense and hostile. Avoid a quarrel in the morning and the rest of the day may hold no particular threat. Do your work thoroughly, with many checks for errors. Keep secrets firmly and avoid seeking conferences to gain ends.

OCTOBER

1—Throwing caution to the winds, and making sudden changes in emotional and career matters are aspected adversely. Though you feel restless and adventuresome, it would be wise to evaluate froth and fivolity as the trimming and note the foundation of a well-rounded existence.

2—Don't travel during the morning hours. The late afternoon and evening hours, however, favor travel—especially long trips. If you shop, look for worthwhile bargains. If you entertain, do so in the evening. The planets are in a beneficient mood tonight.

3—A business transaction may fall through or be delayed vexingly. If you lose your temper you may also lose a good financial chance. Keep silent even though you feel unjustly treated. Watch your own ethics and avoid possibility of criticism. Seek solitude this evening.

4—Be patient and understanding with someone in your family who needs encouragement and useful advice. Offer it willingly for it may do a great deal of good in proportion to the problem involved. Stick to your basic philosophies and principles today, and avoid tangents.

5—Almost everything you do today might bring you recognition, due to the friendly influences. Much of what is happening may be the result of previous hard work. Don't allow adulation or applause to give you the "big head." This would be contrary to the usual dignity of the Sagittarius born.

6—Make an effort to avoid a misunderstand. Keep a song in your heart and activate your work with persistence and willingness. Keep out of heavy traffic and don't lend cash. This is one of those days when you will not get something for nothing.

7—You may be filled with verve and high spirits today, all set to go on with your ambitions. Your instincts may be right, and opportunity might open from the last place you would expect it. Steer your way with skill.

8—Your daily program may be given a reviving injection of new ideas since the harmonious influences favor purposeful ambition. Should an opportunity of solid worth arise, embrace it eagerly, glad of a new outlet for your energy. A time to exchange favors.

9—Telephone, or write to make appointments for interviews. Something in which you are deeply interested may be brought to a successful climax. You might put over a business deal that elates you, or other opportunities might be hovering near. The aspects favor you all day.

10—The happiness essential for the full enjoyment of life may come to you while you are listening to fine music, a learned lecture or an earnest sermon. Devote thought and time to helping others solve their problems, but do not neglect your own. Entertain a few close friends this evening if possible.

11—Errors which rarely occur might turn up disconcertingly today. Do your work with that in mind and save yourself the annoyance of costly mistakes. Most important, do not allow any small variations to make you moody. The aspects call for tact, diplomacy, cooperation and understanding.

12— This day is particularly appropriate for peace and relaxation. Contemplation of nature's wonders and great ramifications might give you deep satisfaction, whether you attend church or stay at home to meditate. The whys and wherefores of existence should be clear.

13—Exciting dreams about extravagant riches and exotic places may prevail. The working hours of the day may present unexpected problems, and contentious people. The evening trend also is tense with friends at sixes and sevens with your opinions. Pace your way with care throughout the day.

14—The exhilarating rays favor new ideas, profitable decisions, earning power, family felicity and amusement pleasures. Start early today, and do what you can to extract the milk from the cosmic coconut. Success signals gleam brightly for you now.

15—If your enthusiasm is controlled reasonably you may open the way to new markets for your particular branch of work. You can accomplish more by allowing others to boost you than by self-exploitation. The planetary powers may lift you out of humdrum with one full sweep.

16—You may meet an old friend and renew pleasant memories. This should be a pleasant tonic. The harmonious influences also lead to a greater understanding of cosmic truths. Also favored on today's cosmic tapis are traveling, writing, composing, debating, acting, singing.

17—Postpone decisions if you have not made up your mind and what you really wish to do. Furthermore, do not quarrel with a friend because it would be difficult to patch up later. The aspects are adverse for writing letters, traveling, and dealing with affairs of older people.

18—It may not be easy to adhere to your program and to push your work through on schedule. But you can force yourself to be prudent so that your emotions are not inflamed, nor your tempers burst out of control. Only thorns are to be plucked on today's primrose path.

19—There can be too much of a good thing, particularly if all your friends seem to call at once. If you are not in a hospitable mood, it is because the planetary influences are opposed today. An inspiring radio broadcast of spiritual truths may put you back on the track.

20—If you have an important problem pending, it might come to a crisis under today's aspects. Be philosophical no matter which way the wind blows, instead of trying to resist the course of events. Whatever happens, happens for the best. Face the future with courage and faith in divine guidance.

21—Do not attempt to do everything at once today. You probably can get more satisfaction by holding yourself down to completing things smoothly and efficiently. The network of vibrations in the sky carries the broadcast of a friend-to-friend program. Tune in with your personal beam.

22—You may be quite thrilled by a unique and pleasing experience as well as the pleasure of entertaining an unusual visitor. Perhaps someone might make a special call at your home to explain something that has puzzled or mystified you. Accept the information with trust.

23—Iron out the wrinkles in your private problems. If you do not quite "hit it off" with a neighbor, think up some tactful way in which you can break the ice, and begin anew on friendly terms. You probably will find the other person ready to meet you more than halfway. Have some fun tonight.

24—Under prevailing aspects, it would be unwise to ask inappropriate questions or for a raise in salary. You might get a disappointing answer and a setback in your hopes for increased funds. Be patient a while longer. The cycle ahead favors your plans.

25—If you feel touchy or moody, don't take it out on your friends or your lifemate. Your close kin have enough troubles and burdens of their own without having to buttress themselves against your controversial hours. The aspects call for peace, understanding, good will, cooperation, kindness and tact.

26—Your prime wish may be to go ahead with a self-development plan. Do not be irritable or discontented if you are held up temporarily. The best laid plans often scatter wildly. But you can always make new ones. Don't give in to the dampening influences being created.

27—Go it alone in whatever you attempt, since the opposing influences make it difficult to concentrate. Hold to a single purpose that is not objectionable to a pal, relative or a business associate. A one-track mind works best for you today.

28—You might glimpse a bright vista, but if you consider journeying toward it, take care of sudden impediments. Have great care for your well-being, for no matter how many monitors there are in the world, you are the entity charged with taking care of yourself.

29—Do not lose confidence in yourself and your ability if little things tend to make you petulent. They may be friendly prods to keep you in top form. Differentiate between the right thing and the less advisable, since the opposition calls for accurate thinking and accurate work.

30—You may enjoy a full day of wholesome activity and bright cheer. The friendly rays are an indication of radiant contentment. Broadcast happiness and be cheerful in your outlook. If you are in a position to replenish your wardrobe, this is a good day for it.

31—Stay clear of risk and extravagance, but above all do not allow the depressed and gloomy to stampede you into a riot of self-pity. The influences can make even a gleaming jewel appear dull and unattractive. Revive your spirits through pleasant music.

NOVEMBER

1—During this period of favorable influences, utilize your skills effectively and let others see what you can do. Lending or borrowing money could be an open invitation for trouble. Refrain from discussing subjects which are controversial.

2—Regardless of how long your tasks take, do not use short cuts to speed things up. Avoid compromising on any matter where your integrity is concerned. Tackle things which can keep you busy rather than allow yourself to become bored by dull conversation.

3—Follow prudent procedures since money can be lost through impulsive action at this time. You can clear away obstacles to future progress by attending to details now. Guard against losing your temper, regardless of how irritated you may feel.

4—Keep striving for goals you wish to obtain, despite criticism from others. Be methodical and thorough in your work, and correct any mistakes made promptly. Listen attentively to advice you receive even though you may disagree with it.

5—Once you formulate a plan of action for your work, avoid changing it. You can save yourself much anxiety by facing facts as they actually are, and not as you would like them to be. Do not let the discouraging remarks of an associate diminish your optimism.

6—Attend to problems associated with your home or money, rather than ignore them. Seek experienced and qualified advice instead of taking a chance on something that is unfamiliar to you. Give consideration to the future and the promise it holds for you rather than worry about past events.

7—You can overcome those things which have been retarding your work progress by being determined in your efforts. Tempers are likely to clash so make allowances for the opinions of others. Refrain from taking on increased responsibilities that belong to someone else.

8—Considerable patience and persistence will be needed to keep your work program running smoothly. Fulfill your own desires, but do not neglect the needs of others around you. Refrain from buying something which is likely to place you under a heavy obligation.

9—Set a long-range work schedule for yourslef and make every effort to adhere to it. Stick to your own conclusions instead of taking a chance on the guesswork of another. You can achieve better results with others by seeking friendly cooperation rather than trying to give orders.

10—Base your conclusions on established facts rather than on nebulous assumptions. Utilize your capabilities effectively by concentrating on the things you can do best. Prevent unwarranted interference with your plans by avoiding discussion of them.

11—Allow ample time in your daily work schedule since unanticipated delays are likely. You can reap extra benefits by applying your ingenuity and resourcefulness to practical purposes. Make arrangements to do something which would please a person who is dear to you.

12—Do not try to force yourself to do more than you possibly can manage well, despite your unbounded enthusiasm. Restlessness may prove expensive, so keep impatience under control. Use persuasive conversation to get what you want rather than resort to forceful methods.

13—Do not show your annoyance to an acquaintance even though you may have good cause to feel irritated. You should be able to attract major opportunities by making the most of the minor ones that are available. Keep personal feelings and practical money decisions separated to prevent trouble.

14—Stronger efforts than usual may be required to accomplish desired objectives. Your giving aid to others may help you to find the solution to many of your own difficulties. Tackle many of the things you have in mind and get started without loss of time.

15—Avoid trying to speed up events or bypass problems, merely to escape annoyance. Make the most of your leisure hours, if only in pursuit of a new hobby. Preserve peace of mind by shunning any activity that involves the use of your money.

16—Take plenty of time for whatever you undertake so that your efforts will not have to be repeated. Clear the way for anticipated pleasures through an application of methodical efforts. Patience and understanding are required, rather than criticism, while dealing with associates.

17—A few humorous remarks can brighten up the atmosphere and help obtain desired results. Put your time and effort to practical use, and be efficient in doing so. Be sure that you can finish whatever you start, whether for pleasure or for your livelihood.

18—Maintain pleasant relations with everyone, even though doing so may require special efforts on your part. Do not let anyone or any circumstance distract your attention from tasks which have to be completed. Despite your interest in the issues at stake, do not let petty arguments or differences of opinion continue.

19—Give your full attention to responsibilities rather than try to evade them. Be diplomatic, but insist on maintaining decisions which you feel are correct. Remain content with the progress you are now making; do not increase the tempo.

20—Take an inventory of your present assets and put everything you possibly can to good use. Refrain from saying or doing anything hasty. Do not let anyone take advantage of the privileges or opportunities which are rightfully yours now.

21—Choose your words carefully so that you will not give anyone an opportunity to misinterpret what you say. Initiative and determination should enable you to break away from restricting conditions. Do not participate in any activity which might jeopardize your prestige and popularity.

22—Regardless of anticipated events, do not take any chances with your money. Organize your work schedule so that you can accomplish each assignment with a minimum of time and effort. Do not take on more duties than you can handle physically or emotionally.

23—Keep words of criticism to yourself since being frank could arouse antagonism. Adhere to established procedures since doing something different might culminate in disappointment. Govern impetuous feelings which might cause you to say something that could result in later regret.

24—Have faith in your own convictions but be willing to listen to the ideas of others with an open mind. Express your affection freely, but do not give anyone an opportunity to impose on you. Regardless of your anxiety to get things done in a hurry, keep your enthusiasm in check.

25—Do not ignore the details of your work, despite pressure that is brought to bear on you. Avoid rash actions or other methods which might cause you to lose prestige and popularity. Spend time on work that will have lasting value rather than emphasize short-term accomplishments.

26—Stick to tested and improved methods in your work instead of attempting something new. Remain silent rather than argue if you run into an obstinate person. Regardless of what stand you take, give others a chance to express their own views.

27—You can improve your economic standards by budgeting your expenses and adhering to a rigid schedule of savings. Let logic, rather than personal feelings and intuitions, be the source of decisions you make now. Obstacles that blocked your progress can be obviated if you do not force matters.

28—Be willing to adjust yourself to changing conditions, regardless of how much you resent them. Have faith in your own abilities despite what others say. Look for a well-rounded schedule that will give you ample time for both work and recreation.

29—Use your time effectively now on projects which can enhance your financial status. You can do much to make this a pleasant day by adapting yourself to the plans of others. Aim for top-notch results in your work and do not settle for anything else.

30—Avoid anything that can upset you emotionally. Stay clear of anyone who appears to be in a belligerent or argumentative mood. By keeping opinions to yourself, you will not give anyone an opportunity to contradict you.

DECEMBER

1—Your intuition may be unusually keen. Even though your hunches can prove surprisingly accurate, exercise discretion before taking action. Make sure that your popularity and cash will not be affected adversely by decisions you make now.

2—A desire for aggressive action may prove costly. You could pave the way for serious difficulties if you go out of your way to do more than is expected of you. Maintain a neutral attitude in dealings with others and seek a minimum of publicity.

3—Although at first things may appear to be in a disorganized state, you should have little difficulty straightening matters out. Put forth your best efforts, and you should encounter little trouble. Keep a cheerful attitude and make every effort to impart that feeling to others.

4—Let nothing interfere with the recreational pleasures you can derive from this day. A congenial gathering with friends would be appropriate. Whatever you do, or wherever you go, let your cheerfulness and generosity shine.

5—Take the initial step in clearing up difficulties which have made you unhappy. Do not buy anything or make an agreement that could place a heavy drain on your funds. Avoid wasting time and effort in quest of something that is not readily available to you.

6—Possible disappointment is indicated if you attempt to settle a business matter through correspondence. You may find it advantageous to get in touch with people personally. This is a good time to capitalize on your personality.

7—Make every effort to keep out of a vulnerable position. Be particularly wary of anyone who promises to help you or tries to collect in advance. Avoid risks of any type, particularly with your money.

8—Regardless of the thoughtful purpose, your efforts to be generous could go unappreciated by the person whom you had intended to benefit. Therefore, take care of your own needs before putting yourself out for another.

9—Refuse to be handicapped by your own impatience. Rather than try to move at top speed, adopt a policy of caution. Control the impulse to rush ahead by being methodical. Give careful attention to details.

10—No matter how urgent your desire to change something which does not satisfy you, check the impulse. To make a change now might place you in an awkward position. Ideas which appear to have merit may prove basically unsound.

11—Focus your attention on getting things done which are worthwhile. Even though others may be relaxing or wasting time, this is your day for making progress. Once you begin a project, carry it through to completion.

12—Make use of any opportunity which will enable you to view interesting changes of scenery. Visiting, short pleasure trips, picnics and outings are favored. Do something where there can be mutual accord and enjoyment for all.

13—Kindness, understanding and affection may prove more effective weapons than force. You may keep dissension to a minimum if you are tactful in your approach. Conditions may take an unexpected turn so cultivate the good will of others.

14—Depend on yourself to get things done. Do not allow another to undertake your responsibilities. An associate, though well meaning, may prove incompetent. Brief periods for relaxation can pay off.

15—Review household money matters and work out a program to increase the effectiveness of your budget. You can alleviate further financial difficulties through wise actions during periods of inactivity. Arrange to put away cash reserves for future needs.

16—You may expose yourself to undesirable criticism and create an adverse impression if you discuss a troublesome situation in public. Do not be too confiding, regardless of how well you know the person with whom you are dealing.

17—This may be an excellent day to clear up obligations and duties which are potential sources of trouble. By giving these matters full attention now, you may find that you can prevent your plans for recreation from becoming upset. Overlook worries and make this an interval of inspired enthusiasm and productivity.

18—Do not force an issue, regardless of how irritated you may feel. Even if events are not working out as you had anticipated, refrain from saying or doing anything rash. Stick to your accustomed pace, and make every effort to keep away from troublesome situations.

19—Regardless of how arduous your duties, take time out for needed diversion. You should find that a period of relaxation may prove more instrumental in keeping things running on an even keel than anything else. Even though you may be under emotional strain, diversions may provide temporary release.

20—If you attempt to get too many things done at once, you may achieve nothing but confusion and a multitude of unfinished projects. Concentrate on one task at a time, and do not look for trouble. Unless you can do something well, let it alone for the time being.

21—Give needed attention to your possessions. Go over equipment and appliances in your home that need servicing. Keep everything in good repair and arrange to replace those things which no longer give you satisfactory service.

22—You may find that you will have to rely on your own resourcefulness and ingenuity to extricate yourself from a difficult situation. Help that you may have expected might fail to materialize. However, sustained optimism and self-confidence should enable you to come out on top.

23—Keep alert for a possible adverse trend, despite the fact that conditons may appear rosy on the surface. Unless you are careful, unforeseen circumstances can arise to upset your plans. However, there should be no reason for pessimism to dominate your attitude.

24—A demonstration of understanding, instead of a display of criticism, would be of benefit. Even though you may not approve of the actions of another, you may find it wise to remain silent. Give advice only when it is requested and then in your most diplomatic manner.

25—Be sure you have not overlooked some necessary duty which might interfere with your promptness at yuletide festivities. Allow for some delay. Prayers and smiles will sustain you. Have a Merry Christmas.

26—Happiness in your home and work emphasized. You should feel a strong sense of security in family relationships and business associatons. Give thought to doing things that those who depend on you can find of value and pleasure.

27—You may feel a strong desire to help someone close to you who is beset by adverse circumstances. You might be able to improve a trying matter. Your comfort and moral support may be all that is necessary to sustain a friend.

28—Anxiety and restlessness may influence your outlook today. Rather than give in to needless worry about events that have not yet occured, concentrate on the present. Do not aggravate conditions by giving them more attention than is necessary.

29—Clear and logical thinking combined with personal initiative may speed up headway in your work. Obstacles and interference can be overcome by well-planned action. Set a goal for yourself and do not relax your efforts until you have attained it.

30—Your willingness to face problems squarely may be more beneficial than an attempt to evade issues. Discuss what is on your mind. However, temporarily hold off on arrangements concerning money until matters are organized to your satisfaction.

31—Your own plans will succeed but follow them through to a "T." See the old year out and the new year in with those you esteem. Resolve to win what you want.

Capricorn
December 22nd—January 19th

Rewards you receive
from ardent effort
make you happy.
You like to show
unusual capacity
for work of worthwhile type.
Building up a business of your own
can be the epitome of happiness for you.
You like to feel you are in charge,
a person of authority.
Some lust for rulership is here
and you can be happy
when you know
you do control others
and have their esteem.
You may be
an ardent worker
for community improvement,
giving your concern to public matters
and being recognized for your value
brings happiness.
A family
of which you can be proud
is another source of joy.
Opportunities to win affluence
make you happy
and are not lost
for you seize them quickly.

Capricorn

JANUARY

1—A calm and meditative mood can help to offset emotional tension. Do not let your desire to get something done in a hurry cause you to make costly errors. Take plenty of time whatever you do and refrain from exerting pressure.

2—Your generosity may be received with more enthusiasm and appreciation than you had anticipated. Regardless of setbacks, do not lose confidence in yourself or your abilities. Take part in activities that can help increase your popularity.

3—Start doing things on your own behalf that you have postponed for too long. Let others have their own way instead of offering oppostiion. Let the merits of your personality stand out but at the same time try to be modest.

4—Exploit the opportunities available to you, without wasting precious time on idle conversation. Steer clear of people and situations that might disrupt the things you are trying to do. Refrain from depending on possible gains until they have materialized.

5—Emphasize pleasantness and optimism. Do what you can to spread cheer. Avoid the discussion of a personal problem to eliminate unwanted interference. Follow the dictates of your own impressions rather than be swayed by the opinions of another.

6—Seek practical advice from an experienced person before buying household or business equipment. Complete routine tasks rapidly so that you will have ample time for diversion and relaxation. Insure harmonious results by having others in full agreement before getting your cash involved.

7—Keep discussions on an impersonal basis rather than openly invite discord. Proceed cautiously in any matter that involves others. The quality and consistency of your efforts should attract favorable attention for you.

8—Use subtle methods in preference to a direct manner in the accomplishment of your objectives. Despite provocation, refrain from saying anything that might be the basis for a quarrel. You should be able to achieve desired results by presenting your ideas in a convincing manner.

9—Be patient when events move slowly, since rushing things may result only in needless delay. Keep alert for someone who may try to pass on to you responsibilities which should be avoided. You may be able to benefit from mixing business with pleasure if the opportunity presents itself.

10—Make use of the advantages that are available, whether for your job or for recreation. The progress you make while dealing with others can hinge on your personality and popularity. Accept conditions as they exist, since any attempt to alter things may create an adverse reaction against you.

11—Contribute cheerful remarks to brighten and encourage those who are around you. Discuss budget problems with members of your family so that you can make better use of your funds. Do not let the objectives or interference of someone else throw you off your stride.

12—Make needed revisions and changes in your work to bring everything up to tee. You can find an enjoyable experience in doing something that will be useful to others. Do not let your quest for pleasure distract you from tasks that must be done.

13—Use to advantage ideas and suggestions you feel will prove helpful to your job. Defer actions on any assignment about which the outcome is doubtful. Stick to routine duties that can be handled with relative ease and that entail a minimum of effort.

14—Particular care is needed in matters that involve emotions. Participate in activities you feel can offer an interesting form of diversion. Devote a major portion of your efforts to solving difficulties that have been retarding your work progress.

15—Give full attention to home repairs and other neglected duties without delay. Refrain from participating in any activity that involves the risk of a large amount of cash. Insure making steady and satisfactory headway in the completion of household duties.

16—Be practical and utilize advantages you already possess instead of dreaming about those you expect to attain. Approach your routine duties in a slow, methodical manner rather than in a hit-or-miss fashion.

17—Give attention to routine tasks such as shopping and making minor household repairs. Get things done by yourself and do not expect too much assistance from others. Be liberal with encouraging words and compliments.

18—Extra patience may be required to keep this a period of harmony. Obstacles can be overcome through diligence and conscientious efforts, so ignore minor setbacks. Be tolerant with annoyances and remain silent.

19—Adjust yourself to the present tempo of things and aim for major achievements. Heed suggestions made for your benefit and utilize all advantages available to you. Give attention to the completion of your own duties and obligations.

20—Do not take part in any enterprise that can be a drain on your financial resources. Keep a close watch on your dealings with others and put your confidence in someone you know to be reliable. Since confusion is possible, proceed slowly and reduce the possibility of errors.

21—Personal sacrifices that you make now may pave the way for unlimited opportunities later. Regardless of how familiar you are with your duties, guard against overconfidence. Your ability to think things out clearly may enable you to solve a difficult household problem.

22—Handle financial obligations with care, since you may be under close observation. Steer clear of extraneous duties that might interfere with the more important work you have to do. Your personality and initiative should be a big help in attaining things you want.

23—Take disappointments as well as pleasures in your stride. Keep busy on practical projects and waste little time on inconsequential conversation. Refrain from making a business or financial agreement until you are completely satisfied on all points.

24—Do not attempt anything with which you are unfamiliar unless you are given expert guidance. A tactful suggestion to another could prove more effective than force. Remain satisfied with your usual diversions and surroundings rather than seek something new.

25—Do not let the discouraging remarks of another deter you from doing what you believe is correct. Keep words of criticism to yourself, since being frank can arouse antagonism from others. Demonstrate your generosity or show your gratitude to someone who has been helpful.

26—You can make satisfactory headway, provided you concentrate your complete attention on details. Any deviation from a carefully scheduled program could easily develop into wasted time. Patient understanding and diplomacy can help offset what would otherwise be a major difference of opinion.

27—Make every effort to fulfill obligations on time and do not mix business with pleasure. Make better use of the things you already own, even though you can find enjoyment in the purchase of new household equipment. Emphasize accuracy by basing your decisions on facts rather than on hasty guesses.

28—Arrange your work schedule so that it will be flexible enough to cope with unexpected difficulties that might arise. Take whatever steps you feel are necessary to keep things running smoothly. Despite temporary setbacks, do not let your optimism wane.

29—Do not waste time in needless arguing. Avoid any subject that would foster dissension. Refuse to worry about the future and attend to each problem as it arises. This can be a day of satisfactory accomplishment, but persistence and industriousness are needed.

30—Take active interest in the things going on around you and benefit from the arguments of others. You should be able to achieve effective results from your efforts but you may find it unwise to take a new approach. Adhere to a precise and exacting pace, even though rapid action may appear to be advantageous.

31—Solve your own difficulties rather than count on others for assistance. Do not be satisfied with halfway measures but aim for goals that are both practical and remunerative. Take care of obligations without complaint and refrain from delaying action.

FEBRUARY

1—Do not talk confidentially to someone who gossips liberally. Keep too busy for talk; make it a day of achieving high aims. The evening may be excellent for a walk and the refreshment such exercise brings.

2—It can be a nerve-wracking day with relatives and in-laws, a dangerous day for health, an accident-prone time for you. Caution is the word, and do not lose your temper with children. Play it as safe as you can at every moment of this cycle.

3—Information that comes through the mail can cheer you a lot. A cause that you believed was lost may prove to have much vigor. You're a bit ahead of the times with your ideas but you may put them across to a wise person.

4—Keep on schedule, be prompt for any appointment, pay bills that are due, and keep your life orderly. It's a full day and a good one, so long as you do your part. Best to avoid any plans for the evening; keep it flexible.

5—Avoid haste, be patient and endure without pacing the floor. Your fortune is so-so today. But you will improve it by being gracious and courteous. Be cautious of your diet tonight at a party where there is an excess of everything.

6—Get in touch with someone who can give you facts in a concern of interest to you. Keep the day and evening free for personal activities connected with your welfare. Long-distance calls serve important purposes now.

7—Be ready to welcome a newcomer; do not be envious in any fashion. Be respectful to an executive but do not be a sycophant. Keep your dignity and proper pride; this will bring you esteem and keep your position good.

8—Listen patiently to the troubles of an associate and offer help of a realistic nature. It is your time to serve others. Take on a task for church or community; be ready to confer at a meeting for the evening.

9—Remember only the good things you know about a person and forget other things you have heard or observed. You can be dealing with a complex personality that is difficult to know and that will never be known fully by anyone.

10—A full schedule, some changes and minor financial good fortune await you today. Start the day with zest, be pleasant about what it brings, and use your ideas well. Don't be angry if an associate robs you of an idea outright.

11—You may be doing something new and different and have your day spiced with chances to make a big and advantageous change. Avoid shopping, if possible, for you will not be content with what is bought. Retire early.

12—All goes well, your emotions are cool and unruffled and you see everyone in a good light. Work is not heavy and you can be very rested when you embark on a social or romantic engagement for the evening. Happiness prevails!

13—Abide by a bargain you've made even though you would like to be out of it. This can be a good day if you are dependable, but a bad one if you are not. Entertainment tonight may be a little too boisterous for your taste; be polite.

14—You can be in an irritable mood, not very loving and also inclined to dangerous haste. Staying in or walking near home is best, avoid chatting. You need a bit of fresh air so don't stay completely shut in now.

15—Be patient with someone who has nervous habits that waste time. Someone may be quite fussy and that can be dangerous if you are driving this person somewhere. A good day to observe facts and make changes for the future.

16—Be patient with all older relatives no matter how vexing they may be. Your role is to show sympathy and to try to help, but not to be insistent. Be dutiful in your career, but let ambitions rest. Avoid a romantic quarrel tonight.

17—Do not harbor any suspicions today. Being wrong in even the smallest way can be humiliating. Be cheerful, inspire others and let your wisdom shine a little. A meeting you attend tonight can be important for your future.

18—You may encounter a ceaseless talker and have a hard time getting away. Remain good-natured but keep edging your way out of this situation. Evening may demand a decision in your marital life; difficulty prevails.

19—A fine day for shopping, beauty work and making a good impression. Keep your personality charming; live up to your best ideals. In romantic matters, there may be a big change that is inevitable. Do not struggle against this.

20—Work slowly and take time out now and then. You can be eager to get your home clean and shining, but if you become exhausted you won't enjoy it much. You'll have company tonight and will please guests a lot by your thoughtfulness.

21—A day for caution and conventional actions. It is best to have no plans for things are going to happen when you stay at home. A telephone call from a new acquaintance may be the base of a lifetime friendship. Retire early tonight.

22—Your irritability could be due to a minor health problem for which you need a physician. An infection may need medication. Don't try home remedies; have a professional appointment. Do not build up unwarranted anxiety.

23—You may win the attention of a charming person of the opposite sex, but you may both know that nothing can ever come of this. It may be one of the most exciting days of your life, but one that can really live only in memory.

24—A confusing day; chaos may rule in your place of employment. Much of this is because of the failure of one person to attend to responsibilities; but don't voice blame. Keep the evening for a friend who wants to talk things over with you.

25—A good time to discard some of your opinions and attitudes that are not valid in this new age. You can win the esteem of others by being up on current news and able to talk about any major issue or personality with intelligence.

26—Shopping, travel, financial transactions and romance all go well. Work can be sluggish, but do what must be done. You can anticipate a time of joy. Dress very becomingly for the evening events; show a touch of luxury.

27—Try to understand and overlook the ways of an older neighbor. Stay on the good side of everyone today. Making an enemy can be serious afair. Be cautious if you travel, and avoid talking to strangers in an unfamiliar place.

28—Be thankful today, observe family ritual and call on friends. Dine out and do some roving around town. This is a fine day for companionship, new ideas, and assurance of strong faith.

29 (Leap Year Only)—Don't relax today or let pleasure tempt you. A day for busy activity on your career. You will discover the way in which you can get what you want, and a new start with a clear road to your goals will probably be offered. Alertness, ability to change plans and go along with trends will bring splendid luck.

MARCH

1—A letter can fill you with cheer and the anticipation of a surprise visit excites you. Be dutiful in work, don't get any reprimands for malingering; that would make you angry. Keep a steady course throughout the cycle.

2—Your health may not be very good and you can further endanger it by catering to a diet of rich things taken at irregular times. Better follow suggestions of an older person about your habits and perhaps the need for a doctor.

3—You can be left up in the air about an important matter. Make extra telephone calls to get the facts straight in your head. If you are attending a glamorous party tonight dress effectively but quite simply.

4—You might be guilty of trying to make a false impression today, say on a future in-law. It probably won't work at all. Don't underestimate the wisdom and alertness of other people during this cycle.

5—Be cautious with those you love. Make sure there is little likelihood for accident to them. Play no games today for you could injure someone badly if you participate. Be adult, mature and use good sense throughout.

6—You may have to slow down a lot in order to do your best. An executive can become very enraged at a sloppy job. Go over work before it is turned in, weed out errors. You may need to rest, be alone during the evening.

7—An excellent day to shop but also one on which to avoid temptation of buying too much. Don't buy two of anything, for instance. One pair of shoes only, even though another attracts you. Be prudent and you'll be happy.

8—Slow down, keep relaxed, take medicine if instructed. Do nothing to put heavy weights on your back. Let others do the lifting. Avoid falling into a sullen mood; be wise enough to realize that this is foolish.

9—You may be invited upon a date you do not want at all. Be most tactful, make sure you injure no feelings. On the other hand manage to show that you just aren't interested. You'll have your own party tonight.

10—Help out in a community affair or any local action group where you can do some good. This is a favorable day for moving your residence, or for improving it with new possessions which add color and excitement.

11—A good chance can be here to improve your position and earnings. You might turn it down due to defiance and indifference. You can be in one of the most harmful moods. Forewarned is forearmed and you can prepare to prevent it.

12—Go visiting happily and well dressed, chat with older people afterwards. Consider having dinner with one of these loyal friends later. It's a good day for spiritual matters and also for learning the ways of tact.

13—Opportunity for a new career direction may tempt you a lot. Yet you have a sense of duty toward your current situation and may just keep the status quo. This is not good if you think you may regret it in the future.

14—You can be too optimistic about work, feel you can sail through it without hindrance. You may have a different story to tell when the day is done. In fact, there may be an obstacle left you simply couldn't clear away.

15—Take your time, think in cool fashion, do not let emotions dictate what you do or say. You'll win admiration for using most practical reasoning abilities. Much happiness is seen for you with closer relatives tonight.

16—An older person may attack you without warning. Let this be a lesson to you about this person for all future relationships. Even the animals give warning before attack if they are good animals. Think a bit about this.

17—Let someone take charge and change your beauty style. You will be charmed with a new look for your hair that will change your entire personality. Go out awhile this evening and enjoy the crowds at shopping centers.

18—If you do a favor for a neighbor you may be called upon to do the same for a long time to come. In this situation there is little true gratitude and trouble may develop. Be cautious, wary, protect yourself today.

19—Avoid brooding about some things that bore you and may make you want to quit a certain organization. Be of service and then forget it. Put no limit to your patience with others today; you'll need it throughout the cycle.

20—Do not let an associate disturb you. Someone envious and ambitious can put trouble in your way. With an executive be tactful, say no word against anyone else. Keep the day smooth and cheerful all the way.

21—A fine time to make desired changes, carry out plans about domestic life that will make for more convenience. It is also fairly good to buy furniture, appliances, clothes and perhpas decorative objects for the home.

22—You will work at a speedy clip and get a lot done but this can deplete energies and bring great weariness. Better slow down, save strength. There's a new day coming. In romantic matters refuse to make a choice this evening.

23—Remember to do something you've been thinking of lately. Get many little chores out of the way. A good evening is here to go through your wardrobe and take out the things you no longer use for a charitable purpose.

24—Work may hum along, relationships improve, your spirit be elated at thought of tonight's romantic date. Avoid spending too much for an elegant little dinner you plan. Make use of those gourmet recipes you've been collecting.

25—Difficulties can arise early and stay late. You may get messages and meetings crossed up, suffer from being tardy for a special appointment. Your temper can become thoroughly bad by evening so watch it closely.

26—Best to ignore a neighbor who vexes you. One of those days when you find it impossible to look at the bright side. You need to struggle with your own feelings now and bring them into wise control with affectionate thought.

27—A person who does not understand you may take a dislike to you. Even though you sense this lack of affinity, say nothing and do nothing. Try to get your mind and feelings on past this cycle; look forward to new events.

28—Be helpful in the troubles of others and forget your own. Visit a sick friend, take a gift to a lonely person, do something to help a young person having difficulties. You can be an influence for constructive things now.

29—Legal matters may enter into your consideration now. Take thought for the request of someone who needs a witness but chances are it is wise to refuse. Do not take any role which you know at heart is bound to be phony.

30—Avoid working too steadily for this can tire you, ruin your nervous system and make you emotional in unpleasant ways by evening. If unmarried you may come under quite a lot of pressure to get married in the future.

31—A very interesting conversation can take place and may indicate a path toward partnership for the near future. Your talents can be so admired and trusted that someone influential wants to invest in them. Celebrate tonight!

APRIL

1—This will be a serene day and you will be gratified with a sense of having done right to help someone. Be tolerant in accepting someone new who comes into your life and neighborhood. You can find good use for the highest of your philosophical principles when you apply them to circumstances.

2—Good fortune is here but you may have to do a little looking for it, around corners and the like. Don't let it be a stagnant day, in other words. Keep going, be dutiful but let your impulses guide you at times. Evening may bring a surprise that will create a knotty question for you.

3—There is little chance of financial transactions working out well. Make no large investment, avoid buying real estate, and don't sign business papers which might involve you in large debts. Do not heed ideas of a neighbor about going into some improvement and sharing expenses with him.

4—Tension can get the better of you if you let it. No one seems to want to cooperate, accept your ideas or do as you ask them to. You might fly off the handle. Social life may find you expressing yourself too freely tonight and you may become impatient or angry with a romantic escort's attitude.

5—You need to slow down the hectic pace, get some rest. Turn down an invitation, do not talk at length on the telephone. Be very courteous to anyone who drops in for a minute, though and be helpful with information if asked. Best to keep evening for staying at home.

6—You may learn quite a lot today due to the people you contact or the group you join. An event of the afternoon can put you in touch with someone who will become a lifelong friend. You are eager to listen and take in new points of view from people you meet now; a youthful spirit prevails.

7—Tackling an arduous task too hastily is a mistake. Take your time today, be a little leisurely, pause for momentary rest at times. A good cycle for shopping when you can work it into your schedule. Be right up to date and don't buy things that are on their way out of the fashion world.

8—A younger friend may aggravate you by not following your advice. You feel very right about everything today and cannot accept or understand views that do not agree with yours. Try to relax this attitude by evening or you may have to face a big quarrel with a lifemate or romantic companion.

9—Look on the best side of things, take a small risk in money and enjoy the gambling spirit. News of some gossip about you may come to your ears. You may be astounded and able to laugh about this distorted report. Sheer falsehoods may abound and you could be the center of a few.

10—Not much of a day for anything. You may feel that you would like to back out of vacation plans made with another person. Don't act on any big decision today for tomorrow you may want to change it drastically. Keep expenses down, don't follow any extravagant impulse or buy on installment.

11—Use your skills to do something nice for a friend, neighbor or lifemate. You'll be appreciated greatly when you do things for others which they cannot easily do for themselves. In the evening dress glamorously and try something a bit new with arranging your hair for glamor.

12—Take good care of your close ones or a pet that is in your care. Keep your eyes open, your wits working so that you can prevent accidents to those you love. Show off a bit this evening with a small party for which you cook something quite exotic. You'll glow under praise and this is good for one's ego.

13—If married you may be upset that your lifemate does not accept a rare opportunity. There is a chance you can accept this yourself. New responsibility may come today and you'll need quite a lot of ambition to live up to chances that are given you. Show willingness and get ready to start.

14—You face a schedule that is difficult and may become more so. However, money earnings can soar. The future may hold need for even more work, but since this will be something at which you are adept you should have no complaints. Your practical wisdom is at work full force and urges you ever onward.

15—A wonderful day for anything connected with money, some life and domestic affairs. You may move your residence successfully at this time. Much help may come to you through neighbors who are generous and of good will. Find some unique way to express your appreciation during the evening.

16—Beware of your own point of view today about a family situation. Hypocrisy can creep into the way you regard a newcomer to the family. Develop a liberal attitude and hang on to it. Be generous with finances in helping a younger relative and don't brood on this generosity.

17—A delightful new personality may enter your life and be a good companion for many years to come. Shared enjoyments, brisk talk between you, and a background somewhat similar make this a good relationship. There is also an element of charming coincidence connected with your meeting.

18—A dream you have never quite given up may renew its force in your imagination and you can decide with much determination that you are going to do all possible to make it come true. This can call for some risk and much courage, like stepping out into space. Your sense of adventure is challenged.

19—Light shopping, some delectable food items and a pleasant young relative make your day good. If going out to a party tonight, have your hair done a different way. Be a little cautious in conversation with your loved one for you might take a view too radical to be accepted. A quarrel could arise.

20—A day for rest, outdoors, enjoying a small garden if you have one. Look through magazines and get ideas for making your residence more up to date. You may get inspiration for a do-it-yourself job that will work out well. You can be the envy of neighbors and friends with your artistry.

21—Don't expect too much of others, including small children. Work efficiently but slowly. An idea about changing your job may come and you may get to work on it quickly. Letting others know you value your knowledge and experience highly is a good idea even though it may provoke them a bit.

22—Temperament will rule unless you curb it. You can be too outspoken, too easily bored, too impatient with everything and everyone around you. Sit back and think for a minute and you'll see how futile this attitude is. Evening brings peace of mind, contentment with your chosen course.

23—An older neighbor can be in the mood to pry and snoop. If you encourage this meddling in any way you can be in for a relationship that will be very unhappy for you. Simply don't answer questions based on curiosity that is idle and might become malicious. Keep aloof as possible.

24—A day for enjoyment, getting out as much as possible, if possible, in a rural atmosphere. You'd love to be near a lake and may get the chance. It's also an excellent cycle for buying a large, luxury item such as a boat or a new car, even a lakeside cottage for your summer pleasure scene.

25—Be considerate of someone who is emotional and difficult to work with. There may be envy and fear in this person's attitude, fear that you might steal away a coveted job. It won't be easy, but try to settle this person's mind. and show that you will not offer any competition now or ever.

26—Take stock of your financial situation before doing anything today. If you have travel in mind, make sure the budget allows for it. Do not ask anyone to lend you money, even a relative you know would comply. Keep expenses pared down to match your wherewithal.

27—A slow day and one when you may be out of sorts with your world. Someone may fail to keep a promise and you can be cynical about everyone. If you have a visitor you may raise an argument just because you're in the mood. You could lose a possible new friend if you are arbitrary now.

28—Romance is in the air and that may worry someone who is closely connected with you. Someone new who is charming can take your interest so intensely that you accept the idea of a date immediately. You could regret this later, but you aren't inclined to listen to advice of any kind now.

29—Good day for buying small things, gifts that you have been wanting to give, and items to make the outside of your home more attractive. Best to be by yourself in shopping so that you will depend on your own taste and judgment. Evening may bring a telephone call you do not like.

30—Anything you entrust to a friend confidentially may leak out by accident. This is a time that calls for silence except in the case of purely impersonal matters such as current news. Even then, don't express your opinions. Some hostility can be found in your chart; try to avert it.

MAY

1—Don't be hasty in relationships, give others the time they ask. Rush is your enemy, leisure is your friend. Take a calm attitude throughout the cycle and let nothing cause you to speak unpleasantly. Be cautious during the evening; don't let curiosity cause unwise speech.

2—The day can be dull, spirits low, a tendency to vexation can prevail. Be sure not to do anything to worry one who loves you. Be protective of any younger people dependent on you or closely related to you. Let nothing move you to do things contrary to family interest.

3—You may discover that someone is wiser than you thought or is showing more maturity than ever before. Give credit where it is due. Someone may speak out of turn during your work hours; avoid brooding over this. Chances are intentions are good but emotions difficult to handle.

4—You might do something risky to health, incline to form new habits that are not consistent with your welfare. Think two or three times before letting such a thing happen. Avoid going into anything new too enthusiastically; you could suffer a dreadful letdown by evening.

5—Be attentive to an executive who always deals honorably with you. In answering questions be factual, avoid mention of nervous troubles. You'll get a promotion and more money if you show strength of character. Do not be critical of a loved one during the evening.

6—You might go skyrocketing into a position you have desired for a long time. Don't let elation cause you to lower your efficiency or accuracy. You may have new work companions who are delightful and a source of personality clash may be removed from your environment.

7—Splurge a little on buying clothes, pick up some cheerful things for the home, buy materials to make a luxurious item and save money. Social life is happily anticipated. Someone may come to your aid in an unpleasant moment tonight. There is a romantic aura for the evening.

8—Take your time, complete chores before going out, then enjoy getting around a little to visit. You may have a spontaneous invitation for evening, don't turn it down just because it comes so suddenly. There is an excellent friendship trend if you accept today's happenings.

9—Someone might downgrade your intelligence or speak in other slurring attitude. Be too generous of spirit to notice this. You'll win admiration where formerly there was doubt of you. Your alertness is your mainstay in this cycle. Evening may become extremely romantic.

10—Do nothing that you would criticize if another person did it. Think things through well, don't be in a rush about anything. Resist temptations in the way of rich foods and all excess trends. Don't startle someone elderly with a radical remark during evening.

11—You can be happy doing things with little children today—a good time to take over a group. You'll be ingenious and very personable. Your popularity with older people can rise, too. Your most sociable and charming ways are at the front now and sheer pleasure is yours.

12—Listen to what you hear but don't be too quick in being persuaded to change a view. Your independent thought may lead you to conclusions that vary from those of another person. Use your privileges wisely and you'll turn the day into a big success for your mental operations.

13—Good for any kind of business activity no matter how major. You may sign papers with confidence. This extends to marriage documents or any partnership concern. A chance to bask happily in your actions will come this evening and you'll relax in knowing things are underway.

14—Avoid involvement in anyone else's emotional tangles. The trend can be a sorry one if you get mixed up with the life of another. You don't have enough facts and guessing is not wise. You will be much blamed if you give advice or urge any course of action now.

15—A neighbor can be vexing even offensive. Don't bother turning the other cheek, just walk away for good. There can be a major lack of congeniality. Do not borrow or lend, be circumspect in social and romantic matters. It is wise not to talk of personal affairs at all.

16—Chance of some frustrating trends, a breakdown of mechanical nature, necessity to spend on a new item for repair. Plans can be all mixed up and you may suffer emotionally from the chaotic efforts of the day. Maybe you can laugh about it when telling your story tonight.

17—You can be in error about judgment of a younger person. The trend you set in relationships now can be unfortunate if you yield to suspicions and doubts. Avoid a domineering manner. Be very pleasant with a loved one this evening, don't let a dispute get started.

18—An ill-advised remark to a person of influence can bring a shower of wrath down upon your head. There is a tendency to make mountains out of molehills today and to brew tempests in teapots. Try to stay clear of this influence and be good humored about others who yield to it.

19—Health can be troublesome, you may have some digestive flare-up or perhaps some discomfort in legs or feet. Calling a physician may be necessary in the end just to reassure yourself that it is all minor. Be very wise in your menu for the evening, avoid stimulants.

20—A neighbor may complain about something that is not your fault. Do not become angry but be philosophical about being blamed. You can come to a pleasant agreement when you are determined to keep relationship good. Romance or marriage will be close and happy tonight.

21—News about a trip, a vacation or something linked with such activity may come through and allow you to complete your plans with happy anticipation. Relative and in-law can be the most important people in your life today. Avoid any excessive party life during evening.

22—You may find that someone is quite hasty and inattentive. You may realize that this is a habitual manner of the culprit. Let time take care of the matter, don't speak up about it now. The evening can be enjoyable with an older friend who sincerely admires you.

23—Unforseen expense can darken the day but may be all to the good in the long run. Do not complain about a surprise emergency which means that you must buy a new item. Takes things in your stride and keep good natured. Guard your reputation in companionship choices tonight.

24—Trouble may be followed closely by help from an unexpected source. Any difficulty you undergo today will bring swift relief. Looking back on it all you can see a marvelous pattern which is reassuring to your beliefs and faith in the ultimate justice inherent in matters.

25—Make up for an inconvenience you cause someone. Be generous, thoughtful, analyze things carefully. Be appreciative of a new circumstance in your life even though you were becoming doubtful about it. All is to the good when you are reasonable and think deeply.

26—You may go to an unfamiliar place today in line with work. There can be good financial conditions connected with such an action. Be determined, straightforward and ambitious in all you do. Count up the benefits this evening and be appreciative for life's benefits.

27—Be cautious and don't let careless ways cause accidents. You could have legal trouble today, perhaps difficulty with insurance matters, also. This is not a good time for action and can be quite bad for companionship and pleasure-seeking during the evening hours.

28—Do not be so arrogant that you reject wise advice and good information. Independence can be high and can get you into unforeseen trouble. Keep alert but also be slow to act. If you contemplate moving your residence, look over a new location but don't decide now.

29—You may become exhausted by undertaking too many tasks, sticking with work too long. This creates hazard for your relationships tonight. You can be on edge sharply, be tyrannical just because your nerves are jangling. Slow down, think before speaking tonight.

30—Go slow in work, be cautious, avoid mistakes. Check over all work before it leaves your hands. Be tolerant with a new work associate. Do not let envy tinge any of your relationships. If you are deceptive or evasive, someone may accuse you justly.

31—A surprise in the way of money may come. A hope may be fulfilled and you can be encouraged by a change in circumstances. Your career is under fortunate auspices and your personal life is improving. Be courteous with all, show esteem for one in a high position in the community.

JUNE

1—You may sense that there is somewhat of a shake-up in your life, a trend for change in matters about which you have little or no control. Avoid becoming upset at what you notice, hang on and things may work out very well at a future date because of the trend for change.

2—Be patient about important matters such as your mail, your financial interests and your career ideas. You may not be able to put through a plan that attracts you today. This gives you more time to work on it for practicality, so be optimistic about the delay just now.

3—A newcomer on your scene may be quite appealing but do not become involved quickly. Your friendly ways can encourage this person and then you may be sorry when you find your time taken up too much. Best to turn on a bit of pleasant aloofness, discourage things a bit.

4—Avoid criticizing others for being selfish today; you might be told a bit that you don't want to hear about your own self-centered trends of recent times. Keep your emotions as calm as possible, don't nurture dislike of anyone. In social life keep speech objective.

5—A good chance may arise to acquire a possession that you want and need. However, be slow to put any cash on the line, make sure that the item is in good condition and the price right. You can be quite happy about your purchase tonight but don't be boastful with friends.

6—Someone may be too outspoken and cause you a moment of deep concern. Be prepared to take things in your stride, don't let poise be disturbed. In the long run you'll be wise to ignore displeasing speech of others. Use your best philosophy about such matters in this cycle.

7—Keep ideas to yourself, be independent, make it plain you are not changing an opinion to suit someone else. A persuasive person may try to sway you. Do not become angry but be very firm about your course through life just now. Keep the evening for quiet pursuits and thought.

8—There is a romantic note in the day but it may not be the one you really want. You may spend time with one person while thinking about someone more glamorous for whom you cherish more romantic views. Best to accept what comes and stop yearning for the impossible now.

9—There are splendid influences for your financial wishes and you may go ahead with a transaction you had to delay formerly. You are justified in feeling you are right about money aims now even though someone close to you may object to your procedures or a risk you are taking.

10—This is a good day to shop, to have things done to improve your appearance. Be thoughtful about style when buying clothes, make sure that a new trend is favorable for your particular personality and type of attractiveness. You have a good sense of color today.

11—Do not be insistent about anything with a younger friend. You could win out in an argument and then find your victory is hollow and hat you'll lose more than you win in the end. If you entertain at home tonight do not have a guest you know always gossips about your ways.

12—You can feel cheated about affairs in the family today. Someone who has been holding out for selfish and possessive reasons may now yield and compromise. A good chance to solve a problem exists and a word of help can bring about wonders in your own mental attitudes.

13—An inconvenience can be annoying but don't build it up into a mountain when it's really quite small. There may be a surprise conference; don't make the mistake of showing nerves when talking with an executive. Be practical, realistic about all that you say during the day.

14—A letter may please you and bring a humorous outlook to you for the day. Your manner with others will be light and attractive. Make the most of this and you may receive attention of romantic type from someone who didn't notice you before. That can be elating!

15—Danger of financial loss is here. Guard your money, be careful with checks that are already endorsed. Do not lend anything of value. You may be tense and weary by evening and find it difficult to gain rest tonight. Take something to aid you such as warm milk.

16—Be sure to keep promises today, don't let anyone down. You may shop for small items, even a pet. Knowing what you want and getting it has a direct road today, so you are lucky in results of activities. Nothing special in work, mostly just routine to follow.

17—Do not become irritated with someone at a distance due to lack of understanding or some tendency to underestimate you. Keep good natured when talking on the telephone long distance. Value friendship which shows generosity and the wish to please you in many ways.

18—You can have your mind on entertainment about which you are in a happy mood of anticipation. Impulse to buy something new to wear should be handled carefully. Avoid extravagance and keep shopping well within the budget. They you'll enjoy making a good impression with appearance.

19—A neighbor may arouse your ire but you must not show this emotional state. Remain calm and pleasant; all will pass over and good humor be restored. Do not look upon others with a critical eye today. Make allowances for those who have troubles, try to help with comfort.

20—You may want to stay around home all day and have a feeling of no responsibility. This can be very restful and give you a chance to catch up on some light reading. Discourage someone who calls with a plan for dining out; you'd find this dull under present circumstances.

21—Don't be too generous today, you may not be appreciated and might be imposed upon. Someone may share a confidence with you; be very loyal in observing silence about this. You may be irritated with a member of the family this evening but saying so will do no good.

22—Surprises may take over the day and you may yield to a trend for giving up plans in favor of just accepting what comes. You can be delighted with some of the unexpected events of this cycle and may come out of it with a new romance that can bring enduring love to you.

23—Be tolerant with others and realize that they cannot know things about you unless you tell them. This applies particularly to someone who may take up your time this evening under the impression it relieves you of loneliness when actually you begrudge your time to anyone.

24—Be firm about avoiding a mood for pleasure-seeking. An irresponsible person might try to lure you on a spree which would be most unwise. Be practical, industrious, thrifty and carefull of all you do, also of companionship in the evening. Guard your reputation closely.

25—Go slow with work today, each item should be checked for errors. You may find a health problem developing in the afternoon. Don't panic. When diagnosed this trouble could be quite minor. Don't become angry with anyone who laughs when you think laughter inappropriate.

26—You may find a bargain when out shopping today but it can be a good idea to get the approval of a lifemate before you buy. If unmarried you will profit from the attitude of a romantic companion to this expenditure. Be very understanding and kindly in social life tonight.

27—Gossip may be going on in the neighborhood and the little you hear may make you feel it is about you. You may be wrong so do not become disturbed. Deception is in the air but you can escape its bad effects by going your own way, paying little heed to speech of others.

28—Something may come through the mail from an older relative who is willing to help you with an ambition. You can make your plans for a venture today. Be very firm in attitude about this project in which you are getting help. It can mean affluence for the future.

29—Avoid communications as far as possible. Many misunderstandings can arise through speech or writing that do not take all facts into consideration. Also avoid making any romantic promise or even thinking about such a matter.

30—A work associate may seem slothful to you and you may also feel this person is too favored by a boss. Showing such an attitude will bring down the accusation of being envious upon your head. This could be the fact; better check your own motivations in such a matter.

JULY

1—You may hear some truth that is difficult to accept. Asking the wrong question can bring an embarrassing expression of someone else's opinion. Keep family affairs within the family and don't expect help for emotional troubles from friends. Be very loyal to a loved one in public and at home.

2—A chance you want to take with money may not get off the ground. Fast developments in financial matters can deprive you of an opportunity. Don't let temper flare about such things. Have a sense of humor and even spend a little extra to entertain tonight and show you're light-hearted.

3—Do not make remarks about the personal life of someone else. It is not your mission to tell others how to change their lives for the better according to your lights. Interference can only bring trouble as usual. Go about your home chores, avoid large crowds tonight, stay on the quiet side.

4—Someone may be watching you when you don't know it. On the other hand, to be self-conscious is not wise. Dress most becomingly and then go about your life calmly. Something interesting and exciting may come your way by evening. It's a peculiar type of day with a charm all its own that you'll remember.

5—Don't let a telephone call in the morning upset you. You may incline to make a mountain out of a molehill today, particularly where personal emotions are concerned. Be friendly but make it plain that you have no romantic feeling for a person who professes to love you. Get unpleasant things settled.

6—A sermon can enrich your thought, particularly if you visit someone else's church. It is a good afternoon for getting outdoors, giving a picinc for youngsters or a dinner for older ones. You will not want to be alone today, so let your out-going spirit have its way, keep surrounded by people.

7—An older relative may need care and you may have to make new arrangements about this matter. Do not let a neighbor get in your way when you have plans completed. You'll be busy and have no time for idle gossip. Also you won't want to talk about family difficulties only you can solve.

8—A fine cycle for anything you want to do involving finances. Buy, sell, invest, save, take on more insurance or open a new savings account. Your credit picture is very good and you may get a special offer due to this. You might sell real estate at a price that will please you immensely now.

9—Be tolerant and kindly toward a younger neighbor who needs a good friend. A conversation about changing times can be pleasant and may bring you more up to date. Good to discard some outmoded ideas that haven't a chance of being revived again in public life. An evening for enjoyment is here.

10—Surprise visitors may irk you, keep you back from tasks you intended to do. Better to be good natured, take what comes, postpone things that aren't really in need of rush treatment. Your ability to entertain casually will come in handy tonight and your home may see a merry gathering of friends.

11—Someone whose intentions are generous may irritate you by doing some good for which you have no use. There is quite likely to be a big flare-up on your part and you may lose a good friend. If you want to guard your interests today, use good nature and wit. You'll get it across that you don't want advice.

12—Romantic matters may come to a strange pass. You may begin to realize that you simply must give up a certain relationship and yet be unhappy about doing so. Whichever way your thoughts turn you find unhappiness. Perhaps if you take a crucial step in separating, you'll be glad you did it.

13—Be responsive to a younger person who comes to you with a unique problem. You can help this person and at the same time make a new and loyal friend for yourself. Family news may be displeasing today but showing anger about it would be silly. Go your way and let others go theirs throughout the cycle.

14—Health is not at its best and you may have to take time to see a physician before things can improve. Your emotions can be playing more of a role than you realized. Rest for a few days may be mandatory. Don't worry about things that are not getting done while you take needed time to get well.

15—An unpleasant person may criticize something you do. Don't take this to heart; ignore it. If you take it seriously you could begin a lengthy hostility. Go along as easily as possible today, read some light material. Don't try to deal with the more serious side of life or worry about financial matters.

16—A relative may displease you a lot. You can be far too vociferous in making your opinion known. If you will be intellectually honest, you may see where you have a part in the results that you are getting now. Your own views enter into the matter strongly; don't try to deny this fact or make excuses.

17—You may be asked to do a favor for a person who is just trying to use you. The more you do, the more you'll be asked to do. Best to keep relationships of this type off your agenda. See friends, go shopping, make a telephone call or two. Not very good for social life but give it a chance.

18—Give sympathy to a friend rather than harsh blame for an error that was made. Be as generous of spirit as possible today. In work matters you may be considered for a higher and very responsible position. Do not allow envy to creep into your attitude toward a younger work associate this afternoon.

19—You may meet someone new and quite different. You can admire the frank and honest expression of this person, but if you look a little deeper and listen more closely, you'll find out all is not what it seems. Be cheerful, keep your own talk the pleasant type about current events and general abstractions.

20—Difficult work may face you but your ingenuity will win out by the end of a rugged day. Don't expect much appreciation at present; rewards will roll in later. People are preoccupied and much is expected of you automatically. Plan to stay at home this evening and let nothing change it.

21—You may make a delightful new friend, someone whose appearance charms you and whose speech arouses your admiration. Be sure to give this person credit which is due. Don't let any doubts enter your mind about sincerity. Financial troubles may have to be coped with on solid plane tonight.

22—If married you may have a major problem with your lifemate. There is a lot of emotional difficulty in your chart now where marriage is concerned. If single, don't even think of having a wedding date set for today. Travel is poorly aspected and could be costly, inconvenient and frustrating.

23—Show your good will to someone who is very sensitive and has doubts about your affection. Keep your behavior very conventional, avoid romantic talk which you know could lead to trouble, and be obliging to friends who need small favors done. Evening is good for small time social affairs outside home.

24—Do some thinking about style and some window shopping to see what you might like to buy after you've made new plans for refurbishing your appearance. A good day for the attractive side of life in a superficial way, to plan to add more glamor to your personality by appearance change.

25—A chance to talk to an influential person may be brief. Don't be angry just because someone else's time is so much in demand. State your case briefly and concisely. You may get help you need but patience will also be needed. Count on the good will of others about a major project you are working on.

26—Work may be dull, time may seem not to move at all, and associates can seem indifferent, even harsh. Don't express your views, someone may just be waiting to start an argument. Avoid trouble with the law; if you drive use every precaution. Check things at home for safety and order repairs.

27—You may take a risk and lose. That's up to you. The day shows money activity in your chart but it's on small scale. You may find it delightful to chat with a new acquaintance of the opposite sex, but if there is a taboo note about it, don't let things get to a personal stage. Be very discreet.

28—You may be completing plans for a vacation and be quite excited about it. Money alloted for this purpose must not be touched except under most demanding emergency. A small child is important in your life just now and you may have to make a decision connected with the child by evening.

29—Big things can happen in your family life. The unexpected, even the alarming can take place. You'll need your philosophy and strength of will to get through the day without some emotional eruptions. If married, trust your lifemate to make a proper decision and carry things out wisely.

30—Very good news comes through and last minute help is all you need to see you through a tight squeeze. You may be starting your vacation at some odd hour such as midnight or even a couple of hours after that. There will be no trouble with travel except for minor mechanical matters.

31—A big day and a happy one. You may feel like singing just for jovial spirits. Let yourself go, have fun, be youthful and up to date. A loved one at your side may have a lot to talk about, so be a good listener when required. This evening you may find a wonderful new place to enjoy a happy crowd.

AUGUST

1—Be thoughtful and unselfish about an older friend who is ill. Some nice little gesture aside from visiting is desirable. Choose something with a bit of practicality to it as a gift. You can delight your friend with your ingenious inspiration. Evening goes well for happy relaxation and rest.

2—You may receive an unusual telephone call from an unusual person. There may be a tricky catch to a financial venture you are invited to join. You're better off independent in any possible investment. Think of young relatives and do something to insure their welfare and future security.

3—Don't be slow to show gratitude. You may be treated very affectionately by others and yet find your own personality one of complaining and fretting over minor matters. This isn't like you so turn the whole thing into something amusing and get on the road with more important, consequential matters.

4—If you feel unclear about what you are supposed to do at work, ask about it immediately. Don't be so proud you hate to ask important questions. Shopping is favored today and you begin to get the basis of your new season wardrobe gathered together. Good to get the fresh things for coming season.

5—Luck is not with you today. It would not be wise to try any kind of risk. If a neighbor has an idea about sharing cost of a desirable item, turn it down flat. Be independent about what you spend, firm about what you won't spend. Evening finds you needing early retirement.

6—A very mysterious person may enter your life and charm you, arouse your curiosity and while seeming quite friendly may actually be quite superficial. You may find this person unwilling to talk about anything except abstract subjects. A good companion with whom to practice refusal to gossip.

7—You may swing back to a former romantic companion. Looking forward to an evening of romance with this person can be more pleasing than you thought it would. Chances are your companion wants to make you happy. Don't object to a little criticism which is meant well to improve your appearance.

8—Temperamental trends can take over in your nature and you may be difficult to get along with. If you have romantic companionship today, it could end explosively. Also, you may be unjust and critical about the ideas of a friend. You tend to refuse to let those around you have their rights of opinion.

9—An aggravating occurrence in connection with your health is only indication of a drastic step you must take soon. You'll bore people if you harp on this trouble which is not really major. Do your best at work, make no excuses for errors, strive to be right at the top when it comes to flawless work.

10—Take the most optimistic view possible of everything that comes to your attention. Do not resent the behavior of a child of your own or be angry that someone else's authority was placed before yours. It is not a very pleasant spectacle to see a parent intent upon ruling a child's life.

11—Good news from a distance can sweep away your worries and doubts. Although this may only mean a postponement of an event, still it gives you more time and hope. A good day to keep your thinking on more philosophical plane and leave room for the spiritual to enter relationships.

12—Someone may inconvenience you thoughtlessly. You can find plans broken up by an inconsiderate person. There is much possibility of a temper storm from your direction. This would be nonsensical. Why not just speak out clearly but pleasantly about having other plans that must go through?

13—Don't become intimate with a neighbor who is older and may be just looking for trouble to stir up. There is a humorous side to the day and you may in the future be able to make the whole thing into one of your gripping anecdotes of wit and wisdom about ridiculous situations to be laughed at.

14—Let no one threaten you today. Someone who has always taken a high hand and has the nature of a bully strongly implanted may threaten you most unpleasantly. You will be right and wise to be indignant and show your scorn for threats and the type of person who makes them frequently.

15—You may have a drive on schedule to visit some older relatives at a distance. You can please these people very much due to special considerations that are new in the family. You may inadvertently injure the feelings of someone else, but even when you realize this, you won't do anything about it.

16—Good bargains, bright ideas about how to add accessories to clothes or to revamp some item of apparel so that it takes on an entirely new look from some little item you buy to dress it up. Your cleverness, thrift and artistic talent bring you much praise and approval from those who count most.

17—Someone will be pleased to hear from you. Filling in gaps in information will help those whom you contact. You are generous of spirit and optimistic about being able to aid others with your special insight. Do not let a romantic companion antagonize you tonight with some harmless teasing.

18—You could become cruel in your attitude toward a person who has been a good and loyal friend, never harmed you in any way. You are urged not to pry and probe, not to turn over stones to try to find something beneath them. Let things go without interference, observe the Golden Rule.

19—Make friends with a new neighbor. Be helping with some of the usual things that go with moving into a new place. A nice idea to have a small dinner for your new neighbor, start the relationship off with pleasant and generous offers. You won't go wrong on this honorable person.

20—Someone who is a legacy hunter or willing to walk over town to save a dollar may irritate you. Much chance that you will let off steam about this and say something scathing. If this person doesn't know you well, you may assume that your relationship will never improve after this.

21—Be industrious in the home, clear away clutter, shine up what is dull, be ready to welcome visitors to an informal but lavish evening party. Make up some of your own appetizers of unique type that take a lot of work and cleverness. You'll really get some praise from all this and you'll just love it.

22—Avoid being a judge about an older person. Make your speech kindly to all. Show esteem and respect for older relatives even though you do not agree with them at all. Take good care of your health today, eat lightly. Don't let anyone tempt you to a wildly pleasurable afternoon and evening.

23—A telephone call can be startling. However, do not voice your immediate reaction. You may have extra work demands and can become exhausted early in the afternoon. Slow down; also do not brood silently on the ways of an associate who irritates you. Get your thoughts on the pleasant side.

24—Travel is favored and you will probably go somewhere that you will have a delightful time. Some of your skills may be called upon to please others, so get busy and you'll hear rewarding words for your efforts. Relax later in the day and you'll feel a very refreshing breeze blowing through your life.

25—Legal matters may come to your attention today. If you give advice about such things to younger relatives, you can cause trouble, injure a person who deserves only kindness from you. You're just a little too tricky, so sharp you may cut someone—probably yourself in the long run.

26—Financial matters please you greatly. Property you acquire today, important documents you sign are all to the good for your affluence. Treat a younger person of intelligence in a wise way and do not become flustered at any remark such a person makes. Be wary about a romance that is appearing.

27—A pronouncement you make in connection with a member of the family may be the beginning of the end of your romance or marriage unless something interferes to stop this. And it may. If unmarried, you may separate for good from a romantic companion who is unreliable and just using your generous nature.

28—Try to keep very calm, go about duties in a diligent way, think of things to make your home brighter. Shop a little by yourself, don't seek companions today. Someone may visit you this evening but you can be on your high horse and may turn such a person away with a few imperious words.

29—Make a telephone call to ask a question. You may be amazed at results you get. You may make a new friend, one who will always be kind to you but one who will also never remember anything you say or give you credit for what you do. This can be an aggravating type of relationship.

30—New conditions in your work environment can dismay you but only for a short time. Actually you'll soon find health improving due to a change of associates working around you. A personality clash is out of the way and you will be surrounded with cordial, amiable personalities from now on.

31—Some interruptions can make it difficult to get your work accomplished. You'll just have to go on a little later with it. Be particularly sociable tonight.

SEPTEMBER

1—Bright skies and happy hours for Capricorn. You will win new popularity, perhaps financial profit in the long run from contributing your talents to a newly organized group. Excellent auspices for career and personal happiness combine to make this a worthwhile day.

2—A day for important decisions. Consult the family and you will be happiest. Make plans for the future. Perhaps for a radical change in environment. Consideration of others will bring great improvement to your own life. Save the evening for romantic moments.

3—Cheerful social trends, new acquaintances will ripen into lasting affections, and conversation will bring many ideas. You may meet one who will be financially very important to you in the future. Imagination and initiative will be high during evening hours.

4—A brisk day with much accomplished in your personal life. Splendid vibrations for shopping and picking up unusual bargains. You might plan a unique entertainment for this evening. Gaiety becomes very noticeable with the advance of the day. A surprise visit tonight.

5—Best not to go out unless necessary. People will irritate you and your short temper may start serious conflict. Intolerance is in the air today and companionship will be poor even within the family. Plan on quiet, solitary pursuits and an evening with a book or TV.

6—Promising influences of the day will enable you to solve personal problems which have been pending for some time. All will be harmonious on the domestic scene and in-laws will be more congenial than ever. Save the evening for society, but don't keep late hours.

7—Happy hours will fulfill your desire for new experience and adventure in the realm of people. You will meet someone very interesting and find that conversation brings you delight. A lifelong friend may be made under these influences. Be particularly sociable tonight.

8—Bright moments for business schemes. Get together with someone who can give solid financial backing and is willing to listen. You will win your way now wherever you are determined and use your powers of speech. The evening is splendid for new romantic interests and joy.

9—Sympathy, affection and kindliness are in the air. You will feel deeply the friendship which means most to you. Enjoy human relationships today, and don't let money matters concern you too much. Make a point of doing something special for your family this evening.

10—Money and prestige are both on their way to you today. You may be asked to perform a special service and from it you will win new popularity and eventually gain of a material nature. Your personality is at its best, so make use of every hour. Accept an invitation for tonight.

11—A quarrelsome mood which can lead to serious consequences. Avoid speaking freely to neighbors and friends. If you have visitors try to be courteous and do not speak the truth even when you feel intelligence demands it. Avoid making visits yourself or using the telephone.

12—Excellent spiritual inspiration, serenity of emotions and affectionate impulses. Follow your urges for kindliness. Visit people who are lonesome, ill, or in some type of trouble. Make it clear that you are loyal and will help as needed. The evening will bring splendid rewards.

13—Physical health is important today. You may be tempted to excesses which are definitely not good for you. Be on guard against accidents, also, and make sure that there are no defective appliances which can trip you up. Best to stay at home this evening and retire quite early.

14—Take a back seat today. Avoid conversation, particularly where gossip is going around. Temptation to run down an old friend may cause you to say things you will regret quickly. A victious circle can be started now and continue for years of unhappiness. Retire very early.

15—Brisk work and many worthwhile projects. A meeting during the day will bring profitable results and renew an old friendship. Happy hours in which you can pursue successfully the plans which have been made in the past. Litigation will turn out favorably at this time. Sign papers.

16—You will find yourself in a very good position to gain what you want. Let charm rule, and avoid the impulses to be domineering. All will go your way without special effort. Make a point of being very kind to a friend who bores you, and you will be more than repaid by night.

17—Rather good hours for sheer enjoyment of life and the feeling of fitting in and being part of the scheme of the universe. Don't be too energetic, let things come to you rather than make the attempt to force issues. Those who sit and wait today will be happy with what comes.

18—Favorable trends for emotional happiness under today's auspices. A romance may get started or result in engagement. Marriage is also highly favorable today. Make it a day for pursuit of personal matters, forget work and look to the domestic scene. A social evening.

19—Some of the brightest hours you have ever known. Plan an outing today. A barbeque or any kind of a picnic will come out marvelously well, if you engineer it. Capricorn is slated for new and increased popularity. Your ingenuity will win laurels, honor and friends.

20—Another good day for accepting trends rather than being active. Your personality will impress with its natural affection and interest in people. Leave the rest to benevolent influences which can bring you surprising results. A party tonight will be romantic and pleasant.

21—Troubles in the family circle may consume time and thought. Demands will seem very unjust. Selfishness will probably predominate so stand up for your own rights. You may be criticized and condemned by in-laws. Do not let your tongue become too sharp, and do speak for yourself.

22—A splendid time to wind up transactions, make decisions, have conferences. Keep busy on projects which will increase your income. The family and associates will be harmonious. Clear skies ahead for all your ventures. Save the evening for close friends and be generous of spirit.

23—A good day for scheduled activities. Have your actions planned ahead of time and you can be sure of winning co-operation. The hours may hold problems, but you can solve them with your philosophical wisdom. Good friends will make the latter part of the day glow with affection.

24—Mischievous talk may be rampant today. If you take your part in this festival of malicious gossip, you will be in for a long siege. Avoid people, have lunch alone, read as much as possible. Avoid trends for trouble by going your way and being industrious throughout.

25—Serious moments when you may feel that you would be wise to give up all that you are now holding onto. Think twice, take a walk around the block. Do not yield to impulses today. If you talk to neighbors, be very solemn, and do not let them see that you have any weakness or flaw.

26—A real financial bonanza is coming your way. You may profit from investments beyond your expectation or receive news of a legacy which is a considerable amount. Keep all under control, avoid your tendency to spend wildly, and the day will show great fortune for the future.

27—Messages may make your time worthwhile. Take time out to think. Decisions made now can be beneficial if they have solid reasoning behind them. Buy new clothes, take care of grooming and plan for a big evening out tonight. Engagement or a new romance promised.

28—Avoid any contacts with people who may try to talk you into a change of plan. Keep your own counsel and do not confide in friends. There may be much disapproval in the air, and people trying to interfere in your private concerns. In romance, be particularly aloof and untalkative.

29—This period is a very auspicious one for your financial ventures and career hopes. Be sure to keep active, get in on every opportunity which is going around. The day is packed with significant incidents. Your willingness to take on new responsibility may count much. Entertain tonight.

30—Almost everything will go wrong. Mistakes and accidents are many. Try to keep an even keel. Do not let temper interfere with your routine duty. Stick to the job no matter what happens. Cancel all important appointments or social matters for the evening. Stay at home and retire.

OCTOBER

1—If you wish to avoid a fracas, exercise self-restraint. If you are placed suddenly in a disadvantageous position that challenges your poise and your reputation, try to remain unruffled. Attend to current needs and allow the exotic to pass by.

2—A day to be cautious rather than aggressive. A false move can topple over your best laid plans. If you value your reputation, preserve an inner calm and you should discover a psychological contentment. Do not try to extricate yourself from a tight place without expert assistance. Rout foolish notions.

3—Do not be disappointed because someone you hold in esteem shows a clay foot. All you need do is readjust your point of view and hold no grievances against relatives so that there is no need for continued recriminations and suspicions. Give the other fellow the benefit of doubt.

4—You may be in accord with the opinions of people you regard highly, but avoid long drawn-out conversations. The accent is on disagreement, defeat and dissension. Avoid making a promise that you know would be difficult to fulfill. Extra rest is suggested.

5—Resist the temptation to pass the day in pleasure because, according to the influences, amusement would be a waste of time. Work quietly to develop an idea to augment your earning power, but do not discuss your plans. Tidy up your room. Put things where they belong.

6—Shun hazardous speculation and refrain from entering games of chance. Be careful of money that is entrusted to your care. Do not suggest curtailing of expenses at home, and postpone discussions about the budget. There is too much chance of encountering antagonism.

7—If your plans have been up in the air, or if you are doubtful of what path to follow, come out of your shell today and try to arrive at a point from which a new mental departure may be made. Concentrate on self-development while powerful aspects exist.

8—Up betimes, as a homespun philosopher said, and be ready for a fruitful day. There are favorable influences generated. Don't be namby-pamby in what you attempt. Splendid cycle for a motor trip, buying furniture for the home, replenishing your wardrobe and beauty treatments.

9—Initiative, cleverness and ingenuity are the right ingredients to mix with force and determination to lift yourself above the crowd. Write letters; go shopping; see people in authority; put zip into your efforts. By nightfall you may have more money than what you began the day with.

10—If you need a job look for a colorful occupation such as art, drama, or literature, provided you know something about these professions. Employment with or for physicians, lawyers, or educators, also is on the favored list. Waste no precious time today. Do something to further your assets.

11—Aspects are adverse today, so be careful to walk around pitfalls lest you fall into trouble. There is need for careful management in employment matters, domestic affairs, travel plans, using chemicals, handling sharp instruments, participating in indoor sports and tinkering with electrical gadgets.

12—Listen to the bugle call of optimism where your finances are concerned. But more than that, do what you can to carry them out. The time is favorable to make this a vital day to use ingenuity and courage for a special objective. Get going.

13—Keep out of contests and business competition if you have any reason to doubt the integrity of the project. Do a little detective work to trace the weak link in your armor. You might discover much while in the current aspects.

14—Maybe you will be fortunate enough to attract some unlooked-for good luck or happiness under today's harmonious rays. Or a cherished desire may come to pass by an unexpected turn of events. But retain your poise even when Lady Luck smiles.

15—Think about your immediate needs. Analyze and formulate plans. Clarity of thought may pave the way for success. Give useful counsel and if necessary take it, yet be careful of the kind of philosophy you sponsor. Fine cycle to buy books, electrical gadgets, novelty jewelry.

16—Planetary magic prevails today, favoring traveling, singing, acting, sewing, writing, working, preaching, broadcasting, listening, competing, sculpting, drawing, modeling, dancing, teaching, learning, conversing and loving. Get your due share.

17—If your ambition is connected with writing, publishing or advertising, or if you aspire to intellectual achievement, try to do something definite today toward the fulfillment of your wishes. An admirable cycle to do mental work, handle literary matters, buy imported items, talk to executives and meet new friends.

18—There may be a tendency toward financial extravagance and mental exaggeration, due to the influences generated. Stick to the accepted rules of propriety. Keep away from fast-moving traffic, and don't get involved in a family quarrel.

19—Do nothing today that is unusual, for there are cosmic drawbacks. The aspects have psychological rather than material effects. Stand pat, and your mental perspicacity may find the right answer to each question. Spend part of the evening reading, or listening to music. Or catch up on your rest.

20—With discordant influences, beware of hidden deceits that may lie behind innocent exteriors. Place little trust in anyone or anything with which you are not familiar. It would be wiser to cultivate a philosophy about better things to come. Just be practical today.

21—Avoid fault finding. Look for the best in people and events. There are adverse influences so do not underestimate the value and strength of faith and rectitude. It is important to differentiate between the practical and impractical. Relax, because oncoming rays favor you.

22—Concentrate on poetry, or art, or music rather than on your woes and lacks. The planetary influences signify the possibility of unusual but pleasant news from afar. Steady judgment, mental elation, the glow of happiness and romance, and useful decisions today.

23—Be tolerant of the faults of others even if the temporary setback you meet up with is rather irritating. The equilibrium of your temper and moods depends on patience and poise. There is little use in getting excited, sarcastic or annoyed. Postpone large scale shopping expeditions.

24—The opposition is pulling a camouflage over the truth. But inasmuch as the fundamental laws of life will never change, do not permit temporary problems to alter your faith in the opportunities for the future. If you find it necessary to prod a laggard, do so gently. Stay at home tonight.

25—Do everything accurately in order to minimize insecurity. Do not overtax your mind, nor tell your problems to others. Self-pity may create irritation and annoyance. Watch out for the health of older people, and check windows and doors before retiring.

26—Even if something should not work out as you wish, do not make hasty demands on your friend to help you steer the course on which you have determined, because the influences generated are not propitious for assistance. If you are resentful, it might precipitate a quarrel.

27—It is important that you be careful of your appearance and that you polish lax ideas of etiquette. Otherwise, your behavior or remarks are likely to be misconstrued. Since you are a stickler for freedom, you may resent any attempt to enforce a special code. Try not to rebel today.

28—Don't take words at face value, particularly if the coloring—figuratively speaking—is daubed on thick enough to hide the blemishes. If there is any debunking to be done, be the first to do it. The aspects are good for factual and productive work at this time.

29—Do not be too powerful with words while the aspects are opposed. The atmosphere is laden with antagonism. The day is unfavorable for traveling by air, tinkering with unfamiliar electrical gadgets, asking for special favors, demanding special attention from friends and for neglecting duty.

30—Give a family party to iron out any little feuds if they do exist. It is a gift to be a competent peace maker. One of your dominant characteristics is that of working behind the scenes to create harmony. The day also favors shopping for food delicacies, linens, cutlery, and imported fabrics.

31—Be indulgent rather than critical of others' errors, made while the aspects are opposed. Your own shortcomings may in turn become targets of heated discussion. Instead, clear up odds and ends at home and lay out a productive program for work. Then you will be ready to meet up with the dynamic influences.

NOVEMBER

1—Be realistic in your approach, and do not take action on emotional problems. Let things remain the way they are rather than risk disappointment. Be exacting in your efforts, and avoid working in a hurry to show progress.

2—Do not allow discouraging thoughts expressed by others today to depress you. Your aggressive action may help you to overcome an obstacle that has been annoying you. Control your restless feelings, and devote your efforts to something practical.

3—Complete difficult tasks before attempting to coast along with the easy ones. Be practical in matters concerning finances, and do not let your emotions interfere with your decisions. Keep discussions on an impersonal basis to avoid discord.

4—Be guided only by established facts and no sudden impressions during the influences prevalent in this period. Work diligently toward the fulfillment of a cherished ambition. Make effective use of your time and opportunities that are available to you.

5—You may encounter many obstacles that can impede your progress today unless you stick to purdent procedures. Work on a project that can help you to increase your income and make your future secure. Settle pending matters regardless of personal inconvenience.

6—Accept conditions as you find them since any attempt to make changes may only create an unfavorable reaction. Insure a harmonious atmosphere by making allowances for the temperaments of others. Stick to routine tasks which can be completed rapidly and efficiently.

7—Your willingness to sacrifice a small amount of time and money may bring better results than you expected. You can reap the benefits of a job well done by being persistent in your efforts. Arrange to do something that can give you a feeling of pleasure as well as a sense of accomplishment.

8—Organize your time carefully if you expect to accomplish everything effectively and in a minimum amount of time. Wait for problems to resettle, with the help of others, and do not try to force an immediate solution. Guard against letting anyone take advantage of you and refuse to be imposed upon.

9—You should be able to overcome restrictions by making careful plans and carrying them out in a firm manner. Slow, unhurried action can prove more effective now than forcefulness and haste. Take care of your own responsibilities rather than entrust them to others.

10—Do things on a small scale, rather than engage in a lavish display. Maintain a neutral attitude and refuse to become upset about the difficulties of another. What you accomplish now will depend on the enthusiasm and the initiative you display.

11—Do something different for a change by seeking as much variety in your work today as possible. Do not let your emotions interfere with decisions that require an impartial approach. Be careful while working with electrical equipment or while driving.

12—Despite opposition from others, do what you think is necessary to achieve your aims. Break away from circumstances that have been hampering you, but avoid antagonizing others. Although you may feel irritated, sharp words could only make the situation worse.

13—Undertake to perform only those tasks which you are certain you can accomplish. Make arrangements to put defective mechanical and electrical equipment into good working order. Remain silent rather than arouse resentment by expressing words of criticism.

14—Before spending money, see that your cash reserves are adequate to meet expected needs. Enjoy your surroundings and seek recreation, but steer clear of arguments. Maximum progress is possible now by working in cooperation with others.

15—Keep things running as smoothly as possible today by giving others an opportunity to express their views. Do not allow your enthusiasm to dwindle even though some phases of your work may be laborious. Leave things as they are rather than force changes.

16—Give attention to existing responsibilities rather than make an attempt to escape them. Instead of worrying about your faults, make the most of your abilities. Depend on your own resources and avoid having to rely on the use of borrowed cash.

17—Maintain a patient attitude even though events may be contrary to your expectations. Make repairs and purchase items necessary to keep your household running efficiently. Avoid taking any chances that can jeopardize your present position.

18—Guard against jeopardizing a friendship today for a temporary financial gain. Give the benefit of your view and experiences to someone who can gain from them. Steer clear of arguments and heated discussions since emotional friction can flare up.

19—Organize your time so that you can accomplish your work with maximum efficiency this day. Making hasty changes could result in efforts that have to be repeated. Arrange to do something pleasant this evening for relatives or someone you love.

20—Do not act hastily on guesswork or indirect information today. Be willing to make compromises and changes necessary to achieve your goals. Be careful that you do not lose or break things through carelessness. Entertain lightly in the evening.

21—Be sure of all of your facts before making statements or taking any action. Do not let the pessimistic outlook of another discourage you. Forget worrisome situations, and try to make this an enjoyable day.

22—Participate in projects that will enable you to enlarge the scope of your activities. Seek pleasure and recreation close to your own neighborhood rather than look far afield. Make your plans well ahead of time to prevent disappointing results.

23—Profitable and practical results are obtainable through persistent effort. Hold on to what you already have with tenacity despite momentary dissatisfaction. Diplomacy, rather than applying forceful pressure, would prove more practical now.

24—Arrange to spend time with associates who appreciate the same interests as you. Fulfill your responsibilities without delay instead of deferring action for a later period. Maintain harmonious situations by keeping away from emotional or argumentative persons.

25—Be patient even though you may be burdened with duties that take up most of your leisure time. Make rapid decisions if the circumstances require it, but allow for the possibility of changing your mind. Attack irksome chores with vigor and get them out of the way.

26—Listen attentively to the suggestions of others, even though you may not intend to act on them immediately. Discuss your future prospects with someone who is in a position to give you practical assistance. Concentrate on clearing up the odds and ends of your work to make room for new ventures.

27—Be cheerful today, if only to keep those around you in a pleasant mood. Do things which you can adequately take care of yourself rather than seek assistance. Check over every phase of your work for accuracy; leave nothing to chance.

28—Do not be bashful about asking for a favor or a privilege to which you feel you are entitled. Do not be too eager to have your own way if you meet with determined opposition. You should be able to get along well with others by displaying your cheerful disposition.

29—Make every effort to solve your own problems and avoid depending on others today. Find a stimulating source of diversion to escape from customary routines. Take care of personal and home problems before involving yourself with the difficulties of others.

30—Try to concentrate on thoroughness and accuracy in your work rather than speed during this period. Keep personal plans to yourself to help ward off resentment or interference. Face issues squarely, but do not purposely create antagonism.

DECEMBER

1—Look for new horizons and fields to conquer. This is not the time to rest on your past accomplishments. Aim for continued progress, regardless of the position you now maintain.

2—Keep a steady rein on your temper, particularly in matters which concern your work. Also, guard against arousing the anger of someone who is in a position to give you orders or block your plans. A bold attitude now may lead to restrictions later.

3—Personal sacrifices that you make for a relative or friend who is experiencing setbacks may benefit all involved. Assistance given now may help avoid serious trouble later. Altruistic projects are particularly highlighted.

4—This a good time to clear up household obligations and duties which are potential sources of trouble. If you are looking for diversions, group pursuits are favored. Get together with friends who share the same hobbies or who have similar interests.

5—Tempers are likely to be frayed and your self-control put to test. Make every effort to promote harmony on the domestic scene. Control an impulse to act without forethought, and do not be rash in your remarks.

6—An alert mind and unhesitating action can be important factors in getting events to work out to your advantage. You can do much to overcome adverse situations by quick thinking. A certain amount of caution is necessary, however, in the way you handle your present responsibilities.

7—Take it slow and easy. You may pave the way for a multitude of unnecessary mistakes and erroneous impressions if you move at any accelerated pace. Instead of forcing issues let the passage of time solve this situation.

8—To get things done you will have to do them yourself. Do not rely on others since outside help might prove to be an expensive hindrance. Also, steer clear of secretive arrangements, and guard against the attempts of another to deceive.

9—Plan each move you make wisely, whether at work or at home. Do not leave anything to chance; make sure that the goals for which you are striving are practical and worthwhile. Splendid headway can be made now, provided you employ a policy of caution.

10—Personal prestige and popularity can be in jeopardy if you are too outspoken in your opinions. Therefore, avoid putting pressure on those whose viewpoints do not coincide with yours. Let others do the talking and acting while you remain silent.

11—Avoid scenes of discord. Make a point of keeping away from anyone who appears to be in a contrary mood. Ignore remarks and subtle innuendoes which are purposely meant to annoy you. Overcome emotional tension by developing an optimistic outlook.

12—Take stock of your skills and latent talents, and consider how you might capitalize on them. Whether you focus your energies on a hobby or embark upon a new field of endeavor, you should obtain surprisingly favorable results. However, guard against overburdening yourself.

13—Money spent for social activities and recreation should prove of full value. Successful results are indicated for most things you contemplate doing. Help to promote happiness and congenial understanding among the people with whom you associate.

14—Carefully consider the consequences before making a promise that concerns your money. Regardless of how tempting it may appear, do not take chances on a speculative enterprise. It would be easy now to take on a responsibility that could place you under financial hardship.

15—Rather than rely on someone else to get things done, depend on your own resources. Do not feel sorry for yourself if things go wrong; rather, seek new ways of correcting them. Things should be easier if you work out a definite program of accomplishment and adhere to it.

16—This is an adverse day for adventuresome undertakings. Do not be impetuous. Keep your opinions to yourself. Refrain from fault finding or criticizing what others have done since tempers may flare up dangerously.

17—You should be able to clear up annoying situations by being both practical and cheerful. Complete each task before you tackle a new one. Also, encourage others who need a lift. Pessimism you encounter may drag you down and diminish your enthusiasm.

18—Regardless of how well meant it may be, do not overrate another's advice about money. You cannot be too cautious in making business agreements. Also, cash purchases should be made with care.

19—Sponsor a party or arrange to have a get-together with several of your friends. Regardless of what you do, you should find that this can be an interesting and stimulating day. You may discover a new recreation you will enjoy.

20—Despite restrictions which you feel are holding you back, do not resort to extreme measures. Instead, adhere to conservative policies. This is not a good day for being aggressive or insisting on having your own way.

21—Keen thinking and able planning should take the spotlight now. Make every effort to advance your present position. Push ahead in your work by consistently keeping your shoulder to the wheel. You can achieve the results you want if you follow a well thought-out course of action.

22—Take part in friendly activities. Pleasure and duty can be combined with favorable results. You should be able to use your imagination effectively along directions that can help you to move ahead professionally.

23—Be especially prudent concerning the disposal of your cash. Refrain from giving in to extravagant whims. Since there is such a thing as too much caution, do not deny yourself articles required for efficient operation. Purchase things which give you pleasure, but remain within your budget.

24—Do not become too discouraged if your plans to achieve a specific goal fail to materialize immediately. A persistent attitude may prove helpful in getting what you want. Do something tangible toward increasing your success.

25—Beam on this holiday with all your brightness and verve for getting things done—and done in fine style. Faith will help you to find your way to truth.

26—You should have all the incentive and inspiration you need to sustain you, regardless of how difficult a program you undertake. Employment and household matters should prove satisfying in all phases. Although events may move at a rapid pace, you should find that they are working out to your advantage.

27—Use imagination in putting across your viewpoints to others; you should have little difficulty in coming out on top in a battle of wits. This is also a favorable day in which to attend to insurance policies, annuities, real estate and other property matters.

28—All your diplomacy may be required to smooth over a delicate emotional situation that can crop up. Your calm poise and smooth manner may help to avoid a display of temperament. Subtle persuasion should prove more effective than belligerence.

29—Put a feeling of restlessness to profitable use. If you feel bored with your present routine, think of ways to vary or improve it. Use your cleverness to advantage, and participate in new and interesting ventures.

30—Direct your attention toward work that must be completed immediately rather than dwell on future recreational pleasures. Unless you concentrate on what you are doing now, you may have to redouble your efforts later. Also, devote time to personal and home needs that have been neglected.

31—The end of the year is asupicious for you! Count on good news, good friends and good times. Let good will prevail as you welcome the New Year. Believe in a happy future, and it will come to you.

Aquarius

January 20th—February 18th

You are happiest
when needed by others
and being successful
with helping them.
You like to sponsor
causes for freedom and equality,
help make it possible for all people
to know the good things of life.
A career
in which you can alleviate bad conditions
will make you happy.
You love to study
in philosophical regions or occult lore.
You are an idealist
with large dreams
but find happiness
only when you can
make them come true
at least to some extent.
When friends
or a loved one
share your interests
and good discussion takes place,
you are in your element for joy.
Creative work makes you happy,
attaining ideals is a goal.

Aquarius

JANUARY

1—Keep antagonistic thoughts to yourself, although the tempers of those around you may be frayed. Arrange for a change of scenery, even if only for a few hours. Use particular care in selecting topics of conversation.

2—Ignore feelings of apprehension and take steps to gratify present wishes. Give careful consideration to any decision that might place you under a heavy obligation. Ignore distracting influences that might tend to mar your happiness.

3—Keep all activities and transactions open and aboveboard so that there will be little likelihood of your being criticized. This not a favorable period for asserting an independent attitude. Draw conclusions from facts rather than let your emotions guide you.

4—Move at a pace slow enough to insure a minimum of errors. Your failure to compromise may result in a complete upheaval of your plans. Arrange to have fun with congenial companions so that you can temporarily forget normal job worries.

5—Avoid any occasion where you would be required to mix business with pleasure. Adjust yourself rapidly to present situations rather than fight drawbacks. Carelessness and selfishness may be encountered now; do not allow them to upset you.

6—Keep yourself busy with the completion of required tasks. Dispose of obligations without delay so that you will have ample time to devote to more pleasurable activities. Take a realistic view of your problems, in order to eliminate unnecessary worry.

7—A patient attitude may be helpful when you deal with domestic duties. Analyze arrangements from all angles and then take whatever action you feel is necessary. Let your achievements speak for themselves instead of boasting about what you have done.

8—Avoid saying anything that might culminate in a severe clash of emotions. Employ an aggressive manner and demonstrate to others exactly how you want things done. Temporarily defer disposing of possessions or selling property at this time.

9—Temper your words carefully so that a few careless remarks will not set off a serious quarrel. Make effective use of your time by reading and writing letters to loved ones. Carefully-planned changes in your home may prove beneficial.

10—There should be little need for pessimism if you pursue your tasks vigorously. Grant favors or make agreements from which you feel you may derive benefits. Get your plans organized and adhere closely to a well regulated schedule.

11—Spend time on assignments you find enjoyable, but strive for practical accomplishments. Refrain from buying anything that might place you under heavy obligation. Give heed to emotional needs rather than devote all your attention to practical matters.

12—Let events move along at their own speed, without trying to hasten their pace. Be careful in your work; prevent unnecessary difficulties from arising. Let others do the talking and acting instead of attempting to dominate the scene yourself.

13—Work on assignments from which you may derive increased prestige and income. Insure an enjoyable period by keeping your conversation clear of business and financial subjects. Keep up with local events and people by spending some time with neighbors.

14—Adhere to prudent procedures, since what you do now may help to build a solid foundation for your future security. Careful attention to detail should prove effective in getting the results you desire. Offset boredom by instituting innovations that may add interest to routine tasks.

15—Fill your mind with optimistic thoughts rather than worry about what has happened in the past. Give attention to the development of latent skills and abilities. Even though you may be regulated by a strict budget, seek outside diversion.

16—Resourcefulness and well-planned aggressiveness may pay off well today. Patience rather than criticism may help correct a misunderstanding. Diplomacy and compromise are essential if you are to get along well with those around you.

17—Display your talents on projects from which you may receive financial gain. Work at your most efficient pace, without wasting time on inconsequential gains. Much can be accomplished by superior production efforts.

18—Do not get stirred up about tribulations, although domestic responsibilities may dominate your activities. Act on a hunch if you feel it is the right thing to do. Despite the pressure of your work, maintain a cheerful and optimistic attitude.

19—Exercise the utmost care in matters pertaining to financial disbursement. Avoid any activity where there is the possibility of your receiving unfavorable publicity. Stress efficiency and practicality in whatever you do.

20—Give consideration to new channels of activity in the application of your skills. Refrain from being too hasty while dealing with others. Better results may be obtained through correspondence than by making personal calls.

21—This may be a period of satisfaction and enjoyment despite the existence of minor problems about money. Before undertaking new tasks, make certain that the loose ends of all pending assignments are cleared up. You may overcome obstacles and problems by determination and well-organized effort.

22—Yielding to the feelings of restlessness may result in unanticipated difficulty. Ignore trivialities and concentrate on things you find pleasurable or profitable. Undertaking a variety of tasks simultaneously may result in confusion and wasted effort.

23—You may only arouse stubborn opposition if you insist on having your own way. Decisions concerning your livelihood may have a lasting effect. Pay attention to the important issues that confront you.

24—Regardless of the project undertaken, do not sacrifice accuracy for speed. Arrange to get away from usual surroundings for a while and enjoy sights and friendships outside your neighborhood. Take a firm stand in matters that involve your personal wishes; do not let anyone impose on you.

25—Arrange to tear down barriers that may be upsetting the harmony in your home. Drastic action in anything should be avoided at this time. Make constructive improvements in your living quarters where you feel they are needed.

26—Do not be in too much of a hurry where money matters are concerned. Apply your thinking and efforts to whatever projects you find enjoyable. Sincerity and helpfulness on your part may be successful tools in obtaining the results you desire.

27—Keep busy with tasks that can provide you with mental as well as physical stimulation. Do things that have worth-while objectives but do not hold yourself down to specific time limits. See that extravagant impulses do not place you in an embarrassing position.

28—Try out new products and methods that can help you to keep things in your home running at a more efficient pace. Prevent unnecessary complications and misunderstandings by following a prearranged program. See that your efforts to achieve a major ambition do not become bogged down through careless mistakes.

29—Maintain a flexible work schedule and be prepared for things to happen quickly. Avoid making an issue of troublesome and complex matters. Do not become so engrossed in your own whims that you neglect the needs of others.

30—Although you may not find it easy to obtain what you want, you should be able to manage things in a satisfactory manner. Arrange to take time out for fun, friendship, and romance. Try to enjoy recreations although you feel pressed for time.

31—Attempts to evade irritating conditions may only lead to further trouble. Regardless of what you are called on to do, try to produce what is expected of you. Give careful consideration to contracts before you sign anything.

FEBRUARY

1—It can be difficult and irksome to get those domestic chores done, but take care of family needs. Be adult about all this and don't fret about pleasure being missed. It can be most fortunate if you don't go anywhere today.

2—An in-law can do something that irks you greatly. Tension can rise between you. Do not let yourself erupt and bring on a big quarrel. Strive to avoid being arrogant, high and mighty.

3—A generally good day, but one you may live through without much feeling or vividness. You'll stay with routine and be pleasant, but actually your mind may be on far-off things and hopes you've been cherishing lately.

4—A pleasing gift may arrive and set up a happy mood for the day. Someone who likes to see you brightly-arrayed may have chosen just the right apparel as a gift. Look forward to wearing this on a date this evening.

5—Happy circumstances show that all will be clear for your vacation as planned. You'll have a better financial outlook than you expected. Someone has been helping you save money when you didn't even realize this was going on.

6—Good news arrives, and it's a fine day for enterprise, planning a move of residence or starting a vacation. Travel for business can really bring in more than expected. Your eager activity wins you esteem which will pay off soon.

7—A problem you have may be difficult to solve. You have little to go on when trying to judge another's true temperament. Strive for subtle ways of learning what you need to know through indirect questions and the like.

8—A letter that arrives today may demand a rather swift answer due to pressing circumstances in the life of another. You need to think carefully and analyze emotions clearly before you respond to any communication now.

9—You may be bored with most things open to you today and may turn down invitations because you are tired of the companionship of certain people. Try not to show this in your tone of voice or the attitude you take.

10—An excellent day for a new romance, a journey, some venture with money. Doing what is new will give you pleasure and bring unusual rewards. Be cautious, though, not to get too wound up and restless for the evening.

11—A time-consuming task may be yours and it can have some details that are both exhausting and unnecessary as far as you're concerned. You may be granted a favor when you ask outright instead of hinting about it.

12—Fortune smiles and you will be happy with news today. You may be able to buy something you've wanted for a long time—a large item. You may also shop for clothes that are a sheer joy for a vacation wardrobe.

13—Be careful how you estimate people now. You might think you could get by with something because an older person is dim-witted, but you could be quite wrong. If you are sneaky now, you'll be embarassed about it soon.

14—A big time in the family, and events will keep you busy. You won't have enough time to realize whether you're happy or sorry. Evening may bring a romantic telephone call that puts you high among the clouds of love.

15—Keep an even pace; don't let anything stop you from carrying out plans. You may have an advantage over someone you'd like to conquer and this is the day to use it. However, be good-natured and kindly.

16—You can be somewhat exhausted and chores may seem too much. Maybe you can get a little help with something you have promised to do, such as giving a family dinner. Appeal to the affections of those close to you.

17—You may find yourself having a marvelous time on a journey. Relaxation and comfort may be here and you can just let your head sink back and dream. Keep up your faith and courage today about a loved one.

18—Do not ask too many favors. Be very cautious with anything connected with a pet. Do not risk climbing on pieces of furniture that are old and falling apart. Keep the evening quiet and be content with a good rest.

19—You can be tempted toward a bold and unscrupulous act that injures a loved one—or one who loves you, rather. In fact, you may see clearly today that love is all a matter of "take" on your part. Not too surprising.

20—You can find a problem too much for you. Seeing a physician may be the best answer. If something goes against the grain with you, try it anyhow. You may be surprised at the benefit from medication today.

21—Be polite and gracious with an in-law, help out however you can. There may be some financial good news, perhaps a gift of value coming to you. If on vacation now, you may receive good news from your home town.

22—You may discover a secret today and be quite enthused about the matter. You'll enjoy keeping news to yourself until a dramatic moment arrives. Social life tonight may be a little wild; watch out for the excess!

23—Avoid looking for someone to blame for an accident that involves you. Be very honest about any such situation. The day and evening hold mixed aspects; pleasure and a little pain both come your way today.

24—You may be contented to relax with routine and take a leisurely view. Avoid being out too long or eating heavily. A good time to start a diet, in fact. Cut out some food you may like but that you know is increasing your weight.

25—A tiff with a relative may find you winning, but this does not mean your future will be happier. Beware of wanting to win just for the sake of the victory. Be thoughtful and not emotional during this cycle.

26—You may meet someone quick-witted and sharp of speech. Don't take offense, just enjoy this new personality. There could be a happy friendship brewing from it. Avoid jealousy in romance or married life this evening.

27—If you criticize anyone you will get back more than you give in the exchange. It's a good day to grasp the chance to be quiet and give up the chance to lose your temper. Keep family matters smooth and harmonious.

28—A decision may have to be made and you can become quite angry about this responsibility falling on your shoulders. If you are not truly in love, say so. Avoid letting any deception continue or a new one develop now.

29 (Leap Year Only)—Unexpected incidents will add brightness to the atmosphere. Surprise gifts and messages, help from relatives and sudden agreement with your plans and ideas will bring more joy than you hoped for. A splendid day to be active.

MARCH

1—Help someone who feels rejected, someone who is very depressed. Your light manner and ease in talk can be excellent for lifting the spirits of others. Your quick intelligence can go right to the root of the problem.

2—What you do today is very important for your future welfare. Avoid letting impulses take you off on tangents, concentrate on the work at hand. You'll get good news late in the day and feel you are free to celebrate a little.

3—Work slowly, keep as relaxed as possible. You may do a little special shopping for something new to wear tonight. Perhaps you have a big date. It can be very promising for the future and romantic happiness.

4—You can be in the mood to meditate and may feel quite slothful about chores. At least try to get started on home decoration or if you are planning a trip, get all your needs lined up. Even get a start at packing.

5—News that comes today may free you for a course you believed was blocked. Difficult to realize your good fortune now, so just be happy with it and it may make you even more happy in the near future. Much love is here.

6—A person who is very obstinate can anger you by being totally unreasonable. Don't let a big fuss get started at this time of the year when all should be warmly affectionate. Make peace and obstinacy may vanish.

7—Someone selfish and set in ways may be impolite, brush you off with a harsh word. This should tell you to avoid the person in the future, when you might like to try to improve the person instead. You'd get nowhere with this.

8—You may shop for some last-minute things but it will probably not work out very well. An older relative may arrive today for a visit. Be considerate and make sure all is in order for this person's comfort and happiness.

9—You can find it difficult to go on today; you may feel tired, lack of spirit to rise to occasion. If you are traveling you can be very uncomfortable. If you travel it is best to find a swift mode of transportation.

10—Keep leisurely ways, do not let anyone disturb you. Plan to look around at the stores and their decorations. If you are visiting at a distance this can be pleasant. Do something special for a child whom you love at this time.

11—It is best to ignore urges to get in touch with someone from the past. Even though quite near you would probably be disappointed and find the relationship strained if you make contact. Take the present and be optimistic.

12—You'll meet new people, experience some new events, but you may find it difficult to enjoy anything. You could be coming down with something such as a virus. Help out all you can in family plans and festivities though.

13—Your spirits are better and you will love being part of a little wonderland created for children. You probably will be free of the hard time that goes for a big family meal, but do help out in some small way as a token.

14—You can feel somewhat dismayed and gloomy today. The weather can be at least partially to blame. You can have a mystic feeling that all is not well with those you love. You may be right but don't encourage this feeling.

15—Be very kind and generous with an in-law who needs a little freedom from work. Be helpful so that others may relax and have their spirits cheered. If you are back at work do something to show affection for associates.

16—You may have a special invitation and look forward to an evening of utterly new experience. This could be as a romantic matter. Be slow to come to any conclusions about a companion during the evening hours. Listen and learn.

17—You can be quite weary today, unable to feel inspired about anything. Your personal life is in a transition period and you're waiting although you don't know it for some new trend to take your interest and attention.

18—Some very self-important people may irritate you today. Make sure there is no envy in your attitude. If you want to be more well-known in the community, undertake more work for it. Avoid empty and shallow brooding.

19—Try to make this period one of moderation for spreading good cheer, doing things that are sociable but not boisterous. Best to seek the most sensible of your friends for companionship, and avoid those who raise a lot of fuss at parties.

20—You can want to be a big spender today and may buy some luxury wardrobe items that will be much disapproved by others in your family. Even your taste is not up to standard. Best to avoid shopping by using a will of iron.

21—Get in touch with someone who might help you with an important concern. It is a good day for beginning of business ventures, real-estate transactions and success at a distance. You can be quite excited this evening.

22—More thought may be required than you are prepared to give. Make sure your grooming is perfect, select the right color for your outfit, make a good impression through appearances; this will make up for other lacks.

23—Avoid being too ambitious with any project. You can become so weary that you make errors and might even have to see a physician due to emotional difficulties. Be moderate but steady in all you do today and tonight.

24—There may be a circumstance that interests you but if you pursue it further you can get into quite an inconvenient situation. It is well to let all that happens today pass right on over. Avoid social life if possible.

25—There is no use trying to play a bit of mischief with a neighbor who has a total recall of memory. You could put a strain upon your relationship by an attempt at falsehoods, so best to be open and honest today.

26—Go to movies or a concert, drive around, have dinner out and make it a happy, healthy day. No obstacles seen and all relationships will have a charming harmony. You can learn from conversation and might even discover an advantage through it.

27—A busy day and you'll have to concentrate on details. You may become so weary by evening that you are not in good condition for a telephone call that offers an opportunity. You could lose out so try to be sharp.

28—A younger person may cheer you and make your life seem good today. A compliment you receive from this person will be sincere. Much congenial chatter is around and there is an atmosphere of healthy, happy mirth.

29—You could be inclined to worry about someone at a distance and this would be very bad for emotional health. If you can't make a contact as you wish, be patient, for you'll make it late in the day and be happy.

30—Someone from your past may return in interesting fashion. The relationship will not be picked up again, though, so do not count on anything but an ephemeral happening. Discuss a wish of yours with members of the family.

31—Avoid aggressive actions, keep busy with your own life and don't intrude on others. If courage is called for, master it for yourself and don't bring another in on the matter. Try to keep a serene mood throughout the evening.

APRIL

1—You may look with a very critical eye on someone new in your environment either at home or work. This relationship may be destined to become important romantically. However, it can take you some time to overcome your first impression.

2—Your financial affairs can be a matter of interest to a snoopy neighbor. You may be more amused than anything else, but you'll be a little angered too. Chances are a brief and biting remark will prevent further snooping. Don't hold back in self-expression if wit inspires you to be outright.

3—The day can seem slow, long and unendurable where work is concerned. For once, the diligent Aquarius nature finds too much triviality, too many boring details. Be pleasant with associates; chances are everyone feels the work load is tedious and not very constructive at this time.

4—Take your time about a decision connected with your job and money. You may have it in mind to lay down an ultimatum to an executive. Be slow to do this, put if off until the weekend is over, anyhow. Tonight friends will be cheerful and a new romance may get a small start.

5—News in the mail can be upsetting. Members of your family may have done something impractical and this is a jolt for you since you know you are the one who may have to pay. Don't be cross and irritable with those near you. Get out and shop, forget troubles that haven't come yet.

6—You may find yourself delightfully and totally in rapport with a new romantic companion. Every minute together seems precious and when you're out of sight your intuition will be telling you things. Family talk today can antagonize you. Try to let it go in one ear, out the other. Rise above it!

7—Don't hold yourself to a difficult schedule. Ease up on work and other demands. If you can help someone solve a problem without becoming too personal about it, go ahead and do so. Little chance that your wishes will be realized today, but keep your fingers crossed. Go on hoping. Be optimistic.

8—A younger person of the same sex may strike you as quite original in clothes and style. Give credit and praise where it is due. Overlook small flaws. If you have the chance you might point out an essential fact and be quite helpful by giving this person something new to think about.

9—Let the best of philosophical and religious doctrine guide you in all you do and in every relationship. You may receive a chance to invest in a rather new concern. Sleep on this matter. It may be you need your money just where it is rather than tied up in any dubious venture at this time.

10—A mistake of the past may be brought to your attention today and make you very unhappy. You'll need to redouble efforts in order to amend this situation. A loved one can be very helpful this evening and have a reassuring manner that is just what you need to get you over this bad situation.

11—A dream may come true in a strange, gradual and yet entirely natural way. Something you wanted long, long ago may now be yours. Be happy and full of pleasant talk today; your personality is at its best and you will enliven the scene this evening. It may be a very romantic date!

12—Do not tie yourself down by any promises. Follow your instincts and impulses today. If you visit anyone keep your personality pleasant though what you see may anger you. Temptation to criticize a family member tonight must be warded off. Romance may have a small letdown due to an obstacle.

13—Do all you can to make the day a worthwhile one. A church service is good to start with, friendliness with an aging person continues a good trend and finally a telephone call to a distance may please one who loves you. Then relax in the evening and sum up your situation about ambitions.

14—Someone may be too harsh in attitude, expect too much of you and others in your vicinity. If you say anything you can make matters worse. Don't let grouchy, irritable people get on your nerves, just survey them objectively and see how unhappy they make themselves by their attitudes.

15—Show appreciation for an executive who is always honest and forthright with you. You can give real pleasure by giving serious compliments and showing esteem. For evening you may have plans that have to be changed in order to attend a meeting of importance for the community welfare.

16—Delay is the trouble this morning. You can be nervous by lunchtime due to inability to proceed with work until a certain situation is untangled. Avoid shopping today; your taste isn't up to standard. Also, avoid a romantic invitation for evening; you need to relax, be free from companions.

17—A surprise gift may come through the mail and cheer you a lot. This is a favorable day for investments, starting to buy your own home or for selling a piece of real estate. Someone may try to influence your judgment this evening, but don't let this subtle person get to first base.

18—Work is difficult but you can measure up to it just by resolving to do your best. Have a pleasant, serene companion for lunch time. Afternoon can bring a joyous surprise and evening will be glamorous. Be quite thoughtful about what you wear, for the evening's impressions are important.

19—This is one of those days you may wish you were as pleasure-seeking as most people are. You may fret inwardly as you give due attention to basic chores. It is best not to entertain in your home tonight, for you do not have the proper spirit to create happiness for others in this cycle.

20—You may be quite jolted from serenity by remarks you hear at church today. Perhaps it is good to have such a shake-up to revitalize your thought. Do not jump to conclusions about meanings or motivations of anyone else. Keep to yourself later in the day and do some needed analyzing.

21—Chaos and startling events can keep the morning from amounting to much. You may be asked to take a special role in getting things cleared up. A duty you take on this afternoon may lead to a major promotion. Those in charge are inclined to admire you all the way, including your appearance.

22—A time to turn on some of your glamorous aspects, dress the part and play it well for those around you. Some may find charm in your personality that they never before realized was there. Center efforts on winning others in this way and you'll have a happy success by evening.

23—An older person may seem too serious to you and you may try to bring cheer into this life. You may not know what you are getting into. If you are wise you will keep all conversation impersonal. Keep evening for a quiet walk, meditation, reading something instructive in magazines.

24—A neighbor may become angered at something you never dreamed would displease anyone. Well, that's the way it goes and you'll have to accept what happens. You may get a type of apology a bit later, though. Be very gracious and act as though nothing has happened. Skies will clear.

25—Someone might become a little too familiar with you on short acquaintance. Best to squelch such a relationship and look ahead to the evening when you will be with trusted friends or a loyal romantic companion. Don't risk your reputation in any way or put your future in jeopardy.

26—Shopping is favorably indicated and you may buy large items for home. If you need something basic such as living room furniture, it's a good day for your judgment to select the best. Let members of the family have a voice in any such matters. Take evening for rest, avoid lengthy talks.

27—An older relative may do something that displeases you and makes life difficult for you. Little you can do to stop the progress of this opinionated and belligerent individual. Your life may be somewhat torn up and you can be angered by the circumstances you find surrounding you now.

28—Gloom may continue on until an executive asks for a conference and helps you out in emotional ways. You can be very serene after such a talk. Your work will pick up speed and efficiency in the afternoon. Make some plans this evening about a vacation that is due to arrive soon.

29—Be sure to give credit to those who are honorable and act with courtesy. It is a good day for relationships and new understanding in both love and friendship. Such a peaceful mood can descend around you by evening that you will just love basking in quiet, solitary comfort at home.

30—One of those times when unbelievable accidents can happen. If working with any heavy object around the home, be cautious that it does not fall on you. When coming out of stores, be cautious of your steps. In a crowd, be on guard against loss of money and in the evening avoid going anywhere.

MAY

1—Someone may try to get by with a large imposition; don't let this happen. Shopping can be tiring and you may need rest early in the evening. Social life offers trouble and you can be better off at home tonight. However, a long telephone talk can also be troublesome, vexing.

2—Be kindly in estimates of others, overlook their flaws. You can win new affection if you will be generous of spirit, considerate of others and willing to praise people instead of criticizing. Keep the day calm and pleasant, avoid any strenuous activity or pleasure-seeking.

3—Someone with grandiose ideas may offend you in a minor way. Overlook this haughty action or manner and go your way without anger. You can soar above petty things, be forgiving and tolerant. Do what is required but do not take on any new tasks or make promises of any kind.

4—You can be kept busy, scarcely have a chance to sit down. Be sure to eat a wholesome lunch, take your time with it in spite of demands. Avoid thinking about personal matters now, concentrate on work. You can win honors when you don't expect it and all will please you by evening.

5—People may be inconsiderate, even cause you expense. Airing your dissatisfactions will not help. It's a bleak time to get through but you'll do it. Make no plans or arrangements for evening. You won't feel sociable and had best keep to yourself after the work day.

6—The light-and-easy touch does it today. Do not be too serious about anything or anyone, including yourself. A chance to get in on a good investment may come along during casual conversation. Investigate this further; you might find it just what you want financially.

7—You may have to pursue a course you would rather not follow. Look at things with most practical and thrifty view, also take time and convenience into consideration in all decisions. Keep secrets about your motivations and let others do some guessing if they want to analyze matters.

8—Good news in the mail can change your whole day to sunshine. Get out and shop, buy new clothes, do things to make your beauty and charm more apparant. Follow new trends in all you buy and don't be too conservative about styles. Social life is really delightful tonight.

9—Give time to a new acquaintance who seeks you out in friendly fashion. Put aside some of your personal pursuits and plans in order to help such a person. Do some figuring in financial matters this evening and you may see your way clear to buying something you need.

10—Handle all mechanical objects with care, be cautious with sharp implements. Take no chances with dangers or health risks. Work slowly but surely, keep all your activities quiet. Evening might provide a moment of high emotion which could rather terrify you unexpectedly.

11—Unfortunate conditions prevail and bad news may come about family matters. Don't let worry build up, relax when you realize you cannot help in such affairs. Keep to yourself and avoid idle chatter with those around you. Pursue a hobby this evening for relaxation.

12—An executive may not see things your way and can be critical. Avoid a temper flare-up. Resolve to change your position may be wise but go slow about this trend. Shop for small items and you'll win a more calm view of your situation. Keep your diet very light this evening.

13—You may meet someone who is soon to become a romantic companion. First impressions may be in error; give the person a chance to show personality on further acquaintance. You may fall quite heavily in love eventually, so do not underestimate today's offerings in this area.

14—Handle money cautiously, particularly that which is not yours. If you do some banking make sure all is in good order. You may anticipate a happy social evening and then find there is tension and discord in the air at a party. Do not share in dubious conversation.

15—Things will go smoothly if you just follow plans and escape interruptions. Avoid unfamiliar places, extravagance and urging of irresponsible people. Outdoors is healthful and a walk in the neighborhood this evening can be pleasant. Quiet meditation is encouraged now.

16—Give attention to family matters, make long distance calls, offer help within reason. Your most dutiful traits are in the highlight now and following them will make you feel emotionally serene. A romantic discussion this evening may lead nowhere due to unexpected obstacles.

17—Be very honest with yourself in a relationship that is troubled. Be courteous to older people, show esteem for those with more experience. In financial matters a bit of advice can put you on the road to affluence if you follow it wisely. Serious matters are emphasized tonight.

18—Your love for precision will win compliments today. Some excitement may come due to a conversation with a friend who shares an idea with you. You're ready for a big change and today will give you the direction for it. Toss cares to the wind and think happily of new plans.

19—You may be restricted temporarily due to some real-estate matters that must be settled. Don't be in a rush about any such business. If you feel that someone is treating you badly speak out about it and end the situation. Be decisive in all actions and you'll win what you want.

20—Work is difficult, time seems to stretch on forever. You can feel discouraged about tasks you've set for yourself after work, for exhaustion may overwhelm you by mid-afternoon. Best to compromise and don't go on to the point of exhaustion. Relax at home, postpone chores.

21—You may feel a strong intuitive bond with a new romantic companion. Much intensity may enter a romance and make it the only thing you can think of. Devotion to a loved one comes first in your consideration. Accept circumstances and don't fight your own emotions about this.

22—You can become very nervous due to family conditions that put pressure on your financial standing. If you feel you cannot help any more, simply say so. Be affectionate but not too lenient with younger relatives. Keep the evening for a good friendship or romantic companionship.

23—One of those days when nothing seems to work out right. Plans can be upset and you may be left alone in the long run. You may feel somewhat ill this afternoon and it can be difficult to attain a needed feeling of calm. Companionship over the telephone is better than nothing.

24—Travel is in your picture today and it can be the beginning of a new phase in your life. You are favored in health, money and romantic matters but make no new decisions. Mingle pleasure with everything you do, be eager about your expectations and share good fortune with loved ones.

25—Think twice before you follow a psychic urge. A trend for the mysterious is here and it is difficult to judge what the consequences may be. If you ask advice be sure to go to an expert for it. Avoid heeding the advice of friends who mean well but do not have experience.

26—There may be a change in romantic trend that can lead to engagement before the day is over. You may be enchanted with the personality of a loved one and do little thinking beyond that fact. Good to visit an old friend this evening and share your happy news honestly.

27—Be sure to follow instructions on everything you use, take no risk with accidents, stay within the law. Avoid argument with anyone, don't make accusations. The day is a troubled one and you need to evade the influences which could cause serious blight on your happiness.

28—Do not turn down an opportunity which comes to you from an unusual career. Do not be timid about your talents and asserting them for gain. You'll make a good impression if you value yourself high today.

29—Be attentive to the needs of another person, give your services gladly. You'll make a new friend, show more generous spirits than you realized you had. A happy time this evening with social matters and friendships that have weathered many years. Romance is here also.

30—Best to stay at home, walk a bit but don't drive or ride with anyone else. Be inactive, build up health through good meals, enjoy a restful atmosphere. A family member may ask a small favor, grant it quickly. It is wisest to be helpful and kindly with anyone who has need.

31—Protect your finances from inroads of extravagant shopping trends. You're not at your practical best. Work requirements can be tremendous and your nerves can be on edge with them. Try to keep all things accurate and in good order. A friend will cheer you during evening conversation.

JUNE

1—Some interesting events may take place in your area. This is a good time for becoming acquainted with a new person. Accept invitations given today and you'll find reasons to be glad you did. Generosity will be shown to you because of affections others feel for you.

2—A good day to consolidate financial plans and come to a major decision about them. You may be through checking over an investment desire and ready to act. The family will show much approval of your course. It's generally a profitable and pleasant day for your Sign.

3—Take it easy, avoid rush about anything. Don't encourage a new acquaintance too much for you could find your time taken up by such a person and that could mean too much interruption. Be cheerful but don't linger long in any conversation. Aim at early retirement tonight.

4—Inconsiderate neighbors may cause you a bad time today. Complaint will probably get you nowhere. It might be up to you to consider moving your residence to avoid unpleasant people. However, do not make any move which depends entirely on emotional trend of the day.

5—Don't try too hard today. It's one of those times when things turn out better if you have a casual attitude toward them. Entertaining at home tonight can be pleasant but keep the guest list down to no more than four people. Avoid too much work for the party you give.

6—New ideas may come and be quite appealing but you may be too much inclined for change for its own sake. You'll be wiser to let time show you where your thoughts of today are not really desirable for action. Keep a slow pace, welcome an unexpected visitor this evening.

7—The financial picture is dim today. You can have extra expenditures due to things breaking down in the home, requests from relatives and general obstacles that interfere with plans for saving. A resigned attitude and following the course of necessity will be best.

8—Do nothing to disturb a romantic relationship now. Even though you have doubts about loyalty and sincerity, be quiet about it. Expressing yourself to a loved one now can make things even worse. Avoid arguments and quarrels, be harmonious and willing to compromise widely.

9—You may be asked to join an organization that is popular but think twice about the group this would throw you in with. Chances are the situation is not really congenial and you would not find activities worthwhile. Get some exercise in the outdoors tonight if possible.

10—You may get news about a minor change in your career. Although you are not happy about this today, the future can show many benefits from the trend. Don't delay or complain about the request of an executive. You may be learning something new of much value.

11—Someone very congenial may appear on your scene and friendship might start up from the beginning. Let conversation develop as it will. An enjoyable atmosphere is present and you may happily anticipate evening activity. Make a good impression with appearance.

12—A bright day for relationships, happy shopping with a friend or loved one, some festive dining out. Keep going and you'll win a sense of gratification. You may be in a rather large group this evening; don't let the bright lights keep you up too late for good health.

13—Romance is stressed in your chart. You may receive some objections from close relatives but that may only serve to prove to you how much in love you really are. You'll listen to your own inner conscience mostly and take your cues from the way you truly feel about love.

14—Work can be difficult and intrusions may anger you when you find yourself falling behind. You may have to be blunt about avoiding intruders but try to show a little affection too so that you lessen the weight of irritability that is present. Avoid strenuous activity tonight.

15—Make it a restful day with calm meditation. You can find much to be happy about in your entire situation. A younger relative may call with news that is quite surprising. A new trend may be starting in your own life due to this news of the day.

16—Someone with many prejudices may attack an attitude you reveal. Don't let anyone sway you to be narrow of view. Your objectivity is needed in dealing with all matters intelligently. Avoid showing partiality in a situation where it could cause subtle difficulties.

17—Getting in touch with someone at a distance can be helpful to your career. You may get volunteer aid you didn't really expect. Go out of your way to do something nice for a person who has always been very loyal. Remember that where there's a will there is a way.

18—Work may slacken and you can find yourself in the midst of a group that gossips too much. Find something to do to escape this atmosphere. Be cautious about social life tonight; much diplomacy may be needed. You may be called upon to comfort someone's injured feelings.

19—A neighbor may impose upon you and then show ungrateful spirit about the whole thing. Let this be the end of a relationship that is generous on your behalf but has grown troublesome to you. You'll be busy with friends tonight, enjoy entertainment in someone's home.

20—A fine cycle for shopping in almost any line. Buying things for enduring pleasure is stressed. Don't hesitate to buy a large item of some expense and a bit of luxury. Make the home more comfortable and convenient, your wardrobe more vivid through purchases now.

21—Avoid speech that is boastful even in a minor way. Choose your words carefully, don't give the impression of being a know-it-all. You may be associating with someone quite intelligent but in a different manner from what you are. Keep the evening free from plans; accept what comes.

22—There can be a major personality clash and the only way to mend matters can be to leave. Such a situation may force you to make a beneficial decision which otherwise you would have postponed or entirely avoided, so all is well, follow your natural instincts, intuition.

23—Be cautious of food and drink, keep good order in your life and make sure that good health prevails. You could get emotionally disturbed if you let the hours turn chaotic. Be right on schedule with everything. Discourage someone who seems bent on long conversation tonight.

24—Good news about financial activities can come in and you can anticipate affluence. Be quietly happy about this and do not discuss it with work associates. Seek out good friends or a loved one this evening to share your good news and be a little festive in providing refreshments.

25—Make sure all mechanical devices are in good working order. Handle such things cautiously. Protect yourself from accident when walking, by keen alertness. Unfortunate circumstances are present for social life and there might be a quarrel with someone you love dearly.

26—Avoid talking to anyone about a person who is no longer in your vicinity. Someone might try to draw you out, get you to disclose secrets. Use your wisdom in all relationships. Keep shopping to a minimum, observe health rules this evening if you are at a big party.

27—Someone may visit unexpectedly and show desire to become a good friend. This can be a relationship of mixed feelings, one in which you do not know exactly what is right to do. Best to be charitable, take everything in a good light and be happy with companionship.

28—You may have a fine idea about a financial investment. Don't mention this to anyone for someone else might beat you to the draw and gain property you want yourself. Be a little aloof, show no disposition to talk of plans. Make them more complete and detailed tonight.

29—You may encounter someone you haven't seen for a long time. This can be a relationship that it would be unwise to renew. Try to be on your own way soon. You may be surprised at the generosity of a work associate late in the day. Accept an invitation.

30—A good day to act upon plans, go in for a major transaction. Papers can be signed and bring benefit, all will go well for your big financial interests. If you see a loved one this evening be cautious not to take a domineering attitude due to high spirits you are feeling.

JULY

1—Let nothing sway you from your present course. A business acquaintance may offer quite an opportunity when it comes to investment. Although attracted you would not be wise to engage in this matter. Seek security and solid things rather than some intangible future benefit.

2—Make sure you are understood by those around you today. If things are not clear a quarrelsome tension may develop. Social life may occupy your mind late in the day. You can be quite excited about an event at which you know you will meet new people of the opposite sex.

3—It's best not to do a favor for a neighbor even though you feel guilty about it. Continued imposition would develop if you're willing to help today. You are in with someone whose whole philosophy is that of using other people. Ignore the matter, turn to your friends this evening.

4—You will be very thoughtful today and launch several large changes you may want to make in your life as a result. You may turn in a new direction for your business activity. There is no good in staying with a situation where you feel you are not being treated honestly.

5—One of these days when you may be just uncomfortable and find no real reason for it. Don't get into lengthy conversations for they will be boring. Steer clear of a person you know always wants to talk over emotional and romantic matters. Quite all right to be aloof and reserved just now.

6—Things may be topsy-turvy and chaotic. You can be dismayed at the direction things take. Sit down quietly, close your eyes a few moments and you will find serenity to help you tackle things and straighten them out. You may be admired for your role on this bad day, so there's some good in it.

7—Shop carefully, do not accept any substitutes or any second-best in quality. Know what you want. Look around until you find it. The evening can hold an unusual romantic situation and you may not know what is best to do about it. You're the one who must do the deciding.

8—A younger associate may say something that can startle you. There isn't much doubt about it; you need to bring your attitudes more up-to-date or you're going to be in for more shocks of this kind. Save a little humor for these matters and you'll find it a big help in catching up.

9—Your personal life may bring a disappointment. A letter may be a response you did not want. A telephone call may cancel out a hope you cherished. You'll need your stoic attitude in readiness for today's negative events. Social life tonight can be unpleasant, quarrelsome, undesirable.

10—Much better spirits and actually a sense of adventure about a new opportunity. You may be taking a long drive to investigate a special educational opportunity. Thinking of your future financial benefits is right in line with getting more training; today may strengthen this resolve.

11—Don't get into a dispute with an older neighbor who is critical and blames you unjustly. Let nothing put a dent in your pleasant personality. There are some mysterious trends shaping up in your neighborhood. It is wisest not to become involved with a new neighbor any further than you are.

12—One of those days when people jump to conclusions, don't seek facts and don't care much about the truth! You can be quite angry and distressed with this careless way. Make your way through the cycle industriously. Spend the evening with a thoroughly trustworthy loved one or relative.

13—Make a wise decision today. Take your time about it, and don't talk to others about it. A long distance call to a loved one could help you make up your mind. You'll want to do what is right and not injure anyone else. However, you do have yourself and your own happiness to consider, also.

14—A good day to take a calm attitude toward work. Pay little heed to those around you. Avoid haste in all you do. Be cautious in the home, particularly if you have a pet you might trip over or a child who leaves toys lying around. Make no plans for evening; you'll want to retire early.

15—An unexpected opportunity for a higher position may come to you this morning. There can be strings attached but be brave and accept. Your prestige can go up in a few days when you begin to master a new routine. You are just the person to handle things which need absolute perfection in all details.

16—You may be debating about an invitation and may intend to cancel it. Think twice. Even though you're a bit weary and would like to be at home tonight, it could pay you to go out and shine in society a bit. Keep your conversation this evening showing a trend of interest and concern for others.

17—Someone quite unusual may come along and make a definite bid for your attention. Through a letter or long distance telephone call you can get news that disturbs you. The day may be one of emotion rather than mental trend. Difficult to control what happens or how it affects you but try.

18—An executive may ask you to take on a particularly difficult and complex assignment. It is not like you to turn it down or even hesitate, so go right ahead. You may have troubles with this and your conscientious approach can bring you a tension headache. Not much profit in this matter.

19—The news is all good about a project you have tackled recently. It is perfection up to now and you may get the word to go ahead. Don't let your high standards cause you to become tense for then your work might not be so good. Make sure you have a quiet evening and it is best not to go out shopping.

20—Try to get to church even though you are not quite up to it in physical energy. Someone may want you to linger afterward and have dinner together. This might not be wise. If you are at home you may receive an important message. Best to stay near home after 2:30 P.M. to receive what comes.

21—You can be dull and lethargic, may need to see a physician. Avoid dosing yourself from the medicine cabinet. News you get about your health may call for quite a bit of expenditure but it is worth it to put things right. Not much accomplished today but you'll know where you stand.

22—You may be ready to give up hope about a venture you thought might bring you new affluence. There could be a sudden change in affairs and your hopes may revive even higher than before. Be very tolerant of the personal lives of those around you today. No room for the intolerant and prudish.

23—Someone may ask a favor which it will be wisest for you to turn down. You must steer clear of a person who is malicious, self-centered and without scruples. Try to cheer up this afternoon and get in the party spirit a bit for entertainment you are giving this evening. Keep the guests few.

24—Give thought to yourself and improving appearance. Buy something to wear that will add a glamorous note. This could be something connected with the hair. You may meet someone whom you fall in love with almost instantly. The night promises to be a glamorous and romantic one you'll remember.

25—You may be asked to travel for a special purpose. The mission entrusted to you can seem a bit out of your line, but obviously an executive depends upon you and has analyzed your ability, so trust in this encouragement to help you through. A romantic telephone call tonight may surprise you.

26—A new angle of looking at your career may bring a new decision about it. You're in the mood to try something different, something that could increase your chances quickly. You may win admiration for courage and faith today. Love can take over your interest tonight but don't let it rush you into a promise.

27—You can become quite angry about a neighbor who is bold in prying into your affairs. Perhaps this person wants to help and thinks it possible. In that case you've just a prying, busy-body to deal with so you can laugh a little. Solve your own problems, be silent but pleasant.

28—Something you buy today for the home can make all the difference in the world with convenience. Go ahead and be ultramodern in initiating something to lessen work greatly. You can make up for the expensive item by gradual sacrifices and minor cuts here and there in spending.

29—A new acquaintance may turn into a very good friend before long. You may be justified in trusting this person without making any lengthy test of character. Much to be thoughtful about is in the air. Evening can be busy with family matters. If married, you may find demands of a lifemate heavy.

30—Don't be too materialistic in your outlook today. If you are generous you will do much good for a person who needs your help. Be on the alert for possible accident. Don't cross any streets without looking. If you drive make sure you are exact about the law. Avoid all arguments in social life tonight.

31—An unusual event can bring you unusual good fortunes. You may travel today and find happiness at a distance from home. A somewhat gala spirit may reign where you are. Enter into festivities, take part in tests of skill. Being active is healthy today so don't be lazy or just all intellectual.

AUGUST

1—This is an excellent day for activity of any kind with real estate. Looking at property, letting others view property and making an agreement to be signed soon are all to the good. Your personal relationships are not so favorable. In a romantic matter you might come to the parting of the ways.

2—A happy mood can be contagious and you may be the one to start this ray beaming. Good conditions at work please you and you may hear rumors of some even better ones coming soon. One of the rare days on which you can put some trust in hearsay and what seems like beneficial new trends.

3—Expense can be considerable. You may be in the mood to spend too much and also inclined to help others beyond what your pocketbook tells you is sensible. If you are wise today you will bring in a moderating curb to act as protection. Subject all money activity to solid reason.

4—Don't live on a petty and trivial beam today, get on to one of the major trends and stay with it. Ask for promotion, more money, buy a home, furnish a home, pick out appliances. Do not let money stand in your way. Inconvenience is not desirable; pleasure is.

5—If you forget a fact you were told recently, it can be somewhat expensive. Worse than that you will blame yourself for an error and that feeling can nag you, mercilessly. Good news from a distance may come over the telephone tonight. Be ready with your answer to a special problem that is new.

6—You can be in the mood for buying clothes, getting your hair done elaborately, spending a lot on new cosmetics, perhaps even a hair piece. If you think all this will contribute to your chances and bring more happiness, by all means go ahead with it. It is a time when money can attract money.

7—Any mathematics you get into today can make you unhappy. You may be drawn toward trying to solve some budget problems that are quite difficult to deal with. You will be wise to give up such a project quickly and have more faith in the future. Be sensible though in all shopping you do.

8—You may come to a decision today and will need to be firm about keeping it. Someone who has been saying insolent things to you may need to be dealt with in a different fashion. Don't be too lenient with one person when you are not sure of the intent of remarks and they may be made to "bait" you.

9—There may be a costly error made but not by you even though you have to pay the expense. It will do no good to try to back out of this or to resent it. Just take it as life itself comes—unpredictable and mostly quite difficult to understand. Find some cheery company for the evening and relax.

10—A tendency to droop, be unhappy and unsociable is here. Your mood comes suddenly and can make you unfriendly at a moment's notice. If you honestly want to discourage this dull and lacklustre trend, stop it at the beginning. However, you may need much rest tonight so count on that.

11—You may have to call an end to a certain project that has become impractical and expensive. Don't go on longer on hopes that are far-fetched. You may be given erroneous information about a communication you are trying to make. A good idea to hold out for yourself and for self-protection.

12—Much affection may spring up for a younger neighbor, but don't intrude. Let others come to you today. Someone may be trying to will you to make a telephone call. Avoid all outside influences and trust your own impulses when they seem very strong and clear. That's the way it works.

13—Be cautious about all legal matters. You might be committing something that could bring legal action when you don't even realize it. Stay entirely within limits today. Your personality can be fine for a party tonight but just as long as it is given by someone else and not in your residence.

14—You can become quite intolerant of out-moded fashions and ways. When your practical nature is directed toward the modern, you can expect some real fireworks. You may go through your wardrobe and discard things at an amazing rate. Slow down a little; you could be making trouble.

15—Be very practical today even though it calls for some harsh attitudes. Neighbors can be inconsiderate, some business deals may be disadvantageous. It is up to you to be firm about these matters. You'll gain more respect by letting it be seen that you cannot be imposed upon by others.

16—You may get different information from two varying sources. This puts you in the middle with a problem to solve. Where finances are concerned, solve everything on the realistic order; where other things are involved have due respect for their significance which may be of an inner type for you.

17—The day is mostly cheerful but your path can be crossed by a person who is extremely false. From eyelashes to boots you may be dealing with someone seeking sophistication and snobbishness in the most unrealistic ways possible. Try to avoid too long a conversation with such a person but be tolerant.

18—It may be necessary to act in an unusual manner in order to keep self-respect going. However, do not enter into any falsehood, deception or "act" when dealing with others. Do not let yourself be down-graded or belittled by anyone. Show your spark of temper if the occasion calls for it.

19—Someone from your past may reappear and have a message that seems psychic. You may need help and this person may have heard your call over distances and much time. Be very pleasant and gracious with such a person. However, in the long run do not let this person influence your future.

20—Guard the pennies and the nickels will take care of themselves. Guard the nickels and dimes and the dollars will take care of themselves. You need things that require money, so save up for that reason and avoid foolish extravagance. Do not be too outspoken with a neighbor who is new tonight.

21—You may be on a journey today, have happy anticipations about visiting someone you love. Be generous, outgoing and ready for any kind of fun. There may be a slight delay in your travel program but don't let that bother you. Keep calm and be ready for happy social life.

22—Someone may criticize you for taking a slightly off-beat way of life as your own now. You may find a way to hint in gentle but witty fashion that this person is far off-base in trying to direct your life. There are signs of sparkling electric output just now due to personalities.

23—You can feel rather down in the dumps, your spirit may not be in tune with the day. Seeing a friend who has calm and certain ways can help you even though you consider this friend's attitude as nonsense most of the time. One of those days it is difficult to tell just what will win.

24—There is little that can go wrong today. Your money needs will be met and your personal joy can be considerable. A romance which has been slow to get underway can turn out to bring much pleasure. Avoid any boasting or seeming too happy among neighbors who may not wish you well now.

25—The hard work that you are accustomed to do may pile up today. You may not even think of resenting what is put on your shoulders but actually you can be bearing an unfair load due to the malingering and laziness of someone else. It is best to speak up when you know things are wrong.

26—A long distance telephone call can be baffling. You may not get news you were supposed to have due to a snag in communications. The day requires patience. In the meantime, keep busy spirits at work doing some shopping for things that please. Buying a pet is a good idea now.

27—If you under-estimate anyone near you, you can lose out on a good thing. Be particularly perceptive of your lifemate's ways and do not make a misjudgment in this relationship. If unmarried, do not imagine that your romance companion is stupid for you could find that you are the one to bear that title.

28—You can be very pleased with your mail today and a long distance telephone call can bring everything into line just perfectly. Today can be a red-letter day in your life and you may want to celebrate it in your own way. If a loved one does not fit in with this pattern, love may take a new direction.

29—You might be in a mood to brood over finances, relationships, various aspects of your personal life. This will do no good but it will do good to acquaint yourself with the law about certain family matters. Get your thoughts onto a legal level, talk with friends and you may be ready to carry out a legal matter.

30—Someone very inconsiderate can put an obstacle in your way without really having any hostility toward you. This inconvenience must be taken care of and you must guard against its occurrence in the future. You may have a romantic date tonight but your chart shows little encouragement for a new romance.

31—Word from a distance may be just what you want. A day is here when you get a lot of support. If you make any promises about finances, it is important that you keep them strictly confidential. Be considerate of other family members. Travel started now can be pleasurable, and offbeat vacations are favored today.

SEPTEMBER

1—Soaring spirits, romantic interest and vivid events will make this a long-remembered day. The atmosphere has all anyone could ask of pleasure and dreams come true. Be dressed most attractively and use your personality. By evening you may find a surprising change in your life.

2—You may pick up interesting bits of news. Read widely, listen carefully, be sociable. The air is full of opportunities, but they may have to be sifted out. A busy but cheerful time in which work will go quickly and seem easy. An invitation for evening is accented.

3—Favorable auspices for receiving money which was unexpected. Litigation may turn out well, and debts long due be paid to you finally. A gift from a relative or interested person may brighten your day. Conferences with executives tend to bring financial rewards.

4—Domestic pursuits favored, and neighborly kindness will be noted. A feeling of leisurely happiness in which you can go shopping with pleasure, choose carefully and come home with good investments in clothing, jewelry or household items. Entertain a few friends this evening.

5—Physical illness may confine you most of the day, but it will be of a minor and fleeting nature. You should begin to feel better late in the afternoon. Best not entertain or go out, however, for you will need rest. Social atmospheres are charged with nervous tension, too.

6—The aspects bring a certain amount of happiness of a personal nature. Watch out for trickery, however. Be prepared to turn down investments and new plans proposed by acquaintances. Make your plans to include loved ones this evening, and there will be much joy.

7—Good nature is prevalent today. Excellent for patching strained relationships. You will see your way clearly where affection is concerned and there will be no false barriers between people. A good day to consult people about important matters, if you want sincere advice.

8—Trends favor buying and major investments. Your cautious yet swift wisdom will show you a fine opportunity. Be prepared to take advantage of this time to augment your future security. A plan which the family has for the evening will bring happiness to you.

9—A day of unselfish gestures. Many will show their desire to please you. Your own personality will be at its generous best, and your chances to perform services for others will bring lasting affection. The late afternoon will bring an unusual surprise, perhaps a visitor.

10—Your plans and schedule will work excellently. You will meet with approval when you voice your opinions. Customary reserve and hesitation will vanish, so that aggressiveness and bold speech will win new respect. A new authority in your career approach brings rewards.

11—Litigation may threaten from a most unpleasant source. This may be the time for consulting an expert, going to expense in order to prevent humiliation and long procedures. Turn to the family, also, for comfort in any unfortunate circumstance. Do not entertain.

12—Inspiration, artistic pursuits, educational opportunities are empahsized. Spend the day with people you find stimulating. Use your talents freely and offer them where there is need for group work. You may win new prestige and perhaps the start of financial increase today.

13—Enforced delays and inconveniences can put you in a poor frame of mind for sociability. Avoid having lunch with an associate for whom you have little affection. Use your own philosophical wisdom and resort to your reserved manner to avoid needless complications.

14—Extremely good auspices for church or anything that is connected with religion and philosophy. Conversations will take a pleasantly serious turn, and you may find a new point of view very stimulating and cheering to add to your own philosophy. Entertain at home.

15—Be very slow to act today. Make a leisurely start, be sure not to forget anything if you leave home to go to work. Accidents and disappointments will result from any carelessness or neglect. Be especially sure to make important telephone calls or answer letters.

16—A brisk day when surprises and changes may take you unaware, but your good disposition will make all happy. In fact, profit and pleasure will come from changes you didn't choose, graciousness and poise will win admiration, and romance may come from someone's observations.

17—Bright spirits in the morning may sag around noon, but if you can get over an unpleasant situation at lunch, the day will pick up happiness. Late afternoon may bring an urgent message which forces a decision about your career. Think carefully. The day favors wise choice.

18—Almost entirely romantic emphasis. You may spend the day shopping for something in connection with a loved one. Engagements may be the evening's surprise. Marriage commenced today brings lasting happiness to Aquarius. The aspects are auspicious for emotional serenity.

19—Energy and a new point of view will spur you on a path to success in a favorite plan. Your vitality will allow you to accomplish marvels with work which is important. The attention of an executive can be gained and kept as a result of today's influences. Social trends tonight.

20—Your plans can be followed rigidly and methodically. Good results will be seen by mid-afternoon, and you can relax then in the atmosphere which is turning very romantic. Make plans for an evening in a sparkling atmosphere of romance, dancing and good food with a loved one.

21—Surprises may come one after the other. A chain of good fortune will make you very happy. A letter from one whom you admire greatly may hold the key to the largest secret happiness. Your radiant personality will win new friends and the affection of many. Family harmony reigns.

22—Achievement of unusual nature will bring pleasure. You may be quiet about your good fortune, but the inner glow will communicate itself to others and make companionship splendid. You can cheer a friend in trouble this evening by a few quiet words. Your reward will be surprising.

23—Be slow to make decisions. A change in circumstances may put you in a position where money becomes more important than ever. Think of family and entire situation, ask for time to concentrate. The late afternoon or early evening may show you an automatic answer which is right.

24—Unfortunate personal accidents, illness, loss of valuables. Stay at home if the morning starts with exceptional difficulty. Rest and avoid conversation. You may not even feel up to reading, but if you do a light novel can help your spirits and end the day with some cheer.

25—A day when words can be quickly regretted. You may injure feelings of a loved one and create a hostile atmosphere for many hours. Try to be tolerant, avoid criticizing neighbors or gossiping to anyone. Turn to hobbies, TV or reading tonight and seek solitude for safety.

26—A day of restlessness and discontent. It may seem necessary to make a radical change, even quit your job. Do not write any letters or make any telephone calls, for you will regret them. Your temper is not likely to be under control until late evening. A break in friendship seen.

27—Friends may be emphasized today. Give yourself over to the pleasure of renewed companionship. Take time off to relax and enjoy conversation. You may be able to get out of work early. Plan a special dinner at a restaurant or at home and have a leisurely evening of enjoyment.

28—Unfortunate circumstances of a loved one may take you away from duty and bring you sorrow. Be wise and do what is most necessary. Do not consult anyone else about personal matters. Wait and an answer will be found in another way. Spend the evening where you are needed.

29—Happy results of a former plan will stimulate your present trend of thought and perhaps allow you to make a new venture. Timidity will vanish and enterprise takes its place. A day for beginning a new business, using artistic talent, making speeches which are persuasive.

30—Lack of ability to concentrate on practical matters, worry over romantic happiness, and general feeling of exhaustion can make this an unpleasant day. Do not push yourself at work, but check what you do for mistakes. Best to avoid people who irritate you or seem crude.

OCTOBER

1—Distrust might come gliding along on spidery legs and poke its unwelcome countenance into your emotional life. But tolerance is waiting, as it were, to oust this invader to happiness, so you should not become upset about trifles. Let the first day of the month go by without a quarrel.

2—You may find yourself balked during the morning hours, but later in the day you might come face-to-face with someone who is like an electrically-charged live wire and with whom it is stimulating to talk and run the gamut of experience. You may hear of an elopement in the evening.

3—There is increasing pressure from behind the scenes that may want you to do handsprings, but be sure the floor is well padded, or you may land with a bump. At any rate, play around with light and power rather gingerly, so there is no chance of being scorched, theoretically.

4—This is a favorable day for Aquarius. In other words, you can add much to what you already have in personality, charm, popularity and graciousness. There is zest and swing to the day that may lead you to pleasant directions. Good rays to take up a hobby, or to begin lessons in a creative art.

5—Find your way through the maze alone. Don't entrust anything of value to others. Be your own courier. However, follow the lead of dear ones who beckon you to take a short trip for business or pleasure. Regulate everything with an eye toward maintenance of health, poise and personal welfare.

6—If you invest the gold of your labor in the bottomless pit of another's ignorance, you might as well be prepared to part with it forever. But don't whine. Get down to the job again. Make up for the loss by working harder. The aspects denote risk, fraud and deception.

7—Intensely ambitious and creative ideas might overwhelm you today, demanding instant self-expression. Don't hesitate, nor wait, nor compromise. This is the time to put your thoughts into action. But be sure that what you conceive is for the good of many.

8—Assistance might come in a rather pleasant way; not in money, perhaps, but in the form of useful counsel. Or you may know where it is to be found and go after it, becoming an inspired wayfarer in search of life's golden grail. The planetary influences are your supporters today.

9—It is wise that modern philosophy veers toward altruism because it gives Aquarius a chance to serve humanity with enthusiasm, either directly or indirectly. A few words of advice today would be as serviceable as a bushel of grain at any other time.

10—You have need of friendly contacts today, so mingle with others. You might feel lonely if left to your own ideas. There should be a bountiful supply of mental liveliness under the stimulating planetary influences today.

11—To be contentious, one needs an opponent, and as you know it would hurt your popularity to begin a quarrel, so fight your battle in private. If that doesn't suffice, take some strenuous physical exercise, and towards the evening you might feel relaxed sufficiently to mingle with others.

12—Unless it is absolutely imperative to make a decision, don't come to final conclusions. Your judgment is not likely to be at its best and with other conditions sodden and heavy because of adverse influences, it is better to hold matters in abeyance.

13—You may be crowded by solicitations for favors which you cannot grant, but instead of becoming excited or anxious, plant a seed of kindliness in the spot where suspicion and selfishness flourish. The Great Law of Nature is unbreakable, love begets love and hatreds sear even the innocent.

14—Get the best out of your work and recreation. Traveling, selling, shopping and literature are vitalized by the current aspects. Look for bargains, read advertisements, listen to fashion analysts on the radio so as to make sure you are getting good value for your cash.

15—The rays are favorable for friendship, altruism, surprises, ambitions, social matters and rechecking details. Career activities look promising. An excellent cycle for the end of mid-month. Take in a movie tonight, or call on a friend you haven't seen lately.

16—Literally and figuratively, pull open the doors of closets where old thoughts and possessions are stored. Discard whatever has become useless and moldy. Do not be afraid of "rattling skeletons." Throw away accumulated debris and make room for modern ideas and belongings.

17—Criticism can be turned frequently to good account, so do not waste time resenting well-intentioned comment. It might be the start of some needed self-analysis. Do not become involved in excitement that hovers near you and prevent distractions from upsetting your normal routine.

18—Be persistent in effort, and thus decide accurately between advantages and disadvantages, because the aspects are adverse now. Take things easy. You may accomplish more without strain or worry, than if you are anxious or apprehensive.

19—Let the constructive side of your nature predominate. Weigh each thought and notion with cool logic and systematic reason. Don't let expediency or the assumption that it doesn't matter cause you to resort to anything faulty or questionable. Get some extra rest tonight if possible.

20—Every day cannot be a perfect one, so if things do not go exactly the way you want them, do not allow worry to dominate your thinking. You are prone to construct imaginary houses of discord. There are better things to do than waste your time on such unprofitable occupations.

21—Interference seems to meet you at every corner, and obstacles block every doorway. The reason for all is obscure to you, and you may be puzzled about the next step to take. Accept this condition for the moment until the planetary influences fade away and you can see the way out.

22—Be generous in your relationships with others. Maintain an optimistic viewpoint and at the same time keep active your faith in your own ability and your right to the benefits of life. The friendly influences in force today may help you find new friends.

23—This may be a period of friction. Do your best to minimize the difficulty and make order out of chaos. There is nothing to be gained by giving way to unbridled excitement. Get into the proper mood early, and work hard the rest of the day.

24—Let circumstances follow their own path instead of attempting to control them. If home matters are in a state of excitement, do not make too much of an effort to quiet them. They will calm themselves, with no real harm done. In the evening be a good listener—not a loud dissenter.

25—It would be better if you did not try to preach today. Be the advised instead of the advisor. Do not be misled by your wishes. Look behind the glitter of each golden promise. Analyze each hope to make sure that you are not being tricked by false attraction.

26—Mind your valuables and papers. You may find yourself in the midst of activity requiring the quick use of your wits and information. Be sure everything is quickly adaptable to the situation; otherwise there could be a loss. Expected fun may turn out to be a dud.

27—Try not to discuss your problem with youngsters or anyone who is unreasonable and stubborn. Do not write letters or sign documents that pertain to business. Misunderstandings may arise, and you might be the loser in the end. The aspects being in opposition calls for intuitive diplomacy.

28—Give your plans and desires momentum and impetus to ride over obstacles whether they are self-made or the result of conditions beyond your control. Work diligently but subject each hunch to a thorough scrutiny so that no inspiration can escape its proper purpose.

29—Put your money into the bank rather than buy speculative stock which promises to increase your income a thousandfold overnight. Not only are instant returns problematical, but the safety of your capital also may be in jeopardy. The aspects in opposition today are adverse for all kinds of risks.

30—Augment your popularity and enhance your business attainments. The aspects create the kind of cycle that makes it possible to do a great deal of work in less time than usual. Splendid for starting on a pleasure trip and for buying beautiful clothes.

31—Let your deepest wishes remain just where they are. Be willing to abandon, outwardly, your pursuit of the ideal, because you may not be able to get it in the form that would please you. Don't be sorry for yourself and blame fate for being fickle. She has numerous surprises for you, as time goes by.

NOVEMBER

1—Do not allow stubborness to cause you to ignore practical suggestions from others. Maintain a freindly disposition, and display your sense of humor if only to keep others in a cheerful frame of mind. Face problems squarely rather than evade issues which confront you.

2—Be cautious about making hasty or impulsive decisions concerning a job matter. Keep away from people who are intent on venting their anger on you. Although tempers may be frayed and your self-control strained, keep antagonistic thoughts to yourself.

3—Refrain from taking chances with your money even though a promising deal looks safe. Overlook minor annoyances rather than let them mar the serenity of the day. Trying to rush matters may prove costly so let events work out of their own accord.

4—Be very careful today while dealing with others since emotions are likely to get out of hand. This can be a good day to settle an argument or a clash of opinion. Make certain that what you speak or write today will be clearly understood by all.

5—Show little hesitation in asking for the things you need or doing the things you want. Arrange a detailed schedule for the use of your time, and do your best to adhere to it. Do not jump to conclusions regardless of what others say or how they act.

6—Control any inclination to rush headlong into action on a project which is unfamiliar to you. Instead of becoming irritated because of opposition to your ideas, use constructive criticism to advantage. Use your leisure time to work on a hobby you like.

7—Clear up the ends of pending duties so that nothing can hold you back from accomplishing your aims. Gratify your desires provided they do not act as an imposition on others. Temporarily forget about worrisome situations and concentrate on being happy.

8—An argument that you foster now could have undesirable repercussions. Avoid taking any action that is likely to increase the burden of your present duties. Refrain from starting any project now unless you are certain you can complete it satisfactorily.

9—Arrange to do something today that is different from your routine work if only to offset a feeling of boredom that you have. Work on the development of aptitudes and skills which you feel you can use to advantage.

10—Regardless of disappointments, do not surrender to doubts or let others discourage you this day. This can be a favorable period to clear up all the loose ends and miscellaneous details of work that have been neglected for some time.

11—Do not stir up an unnecessary fuss, and keep away from situations where trouble is likely to develop. Unless present assignments require prompt attention, devote your efforts toward practical future achievements. Methodical and well-coordinated efforts should pay off, provided you do not give in to periods of temporary laxity.

12—Arrange to pay bills and collect debts even though such action may not be to your liking. Do not take anything for granted regardless of what others promise. Rather than take part in solitary endeavors, seek the enjoyment possible through spending time with congenial companions.

13—Ignore financial and business worries and enjoy the recreation and companionship that are available to you. Arrangements which you make concerning your livelihood can have a favorable and lasting effect. Before taking on new endeavors, make sure you are up-to-date with your present assignments.

14—Avoid taking chances, particularly where your income or future security is concerned. Do not participate in any activity that would be considered startling or unconventional. Regardless of how irritated you may feel, try to prevent any cause for a dispute in your home.

15—Make this a progressive day by concentrating on tasks from which you can derive financial benefit. Avoid making trouble merely to have your own way. Faster progress can be made now through slow and careful action rather than by a hasty approach.

16—Demonstrate your willingness to accept guidance from someone who is in a position to give you a helping hand. Do not discount any ideas as being impractical until you have given them a chance. Arrange to make additions to your wardrobe or get something that can enhance the decorative appearance of your home.

17—Treat contrariness and selfishness you find in others with a diplomatic attitude despite your irritation. Spending money for personal needs can give you a stimulating feeling of inner satisfaction. You can accomplish much now, provided you do not waste time worrying about minor problems.

18—Considerable self-control may be needed now to keep your spending within budgetary limits. Keep thoughts to yourself, especially in a business or job matter. Make arrangements designed to increase the efficiency of systems employed in your home or at your job.

19—Quarrels and bitter clashes of emotion are likely unless you are conservative in your actions. Regardless of setbacks, do not relent in your efforts to achieve desired goals. Exert every effort to fulfill promises and obligations for which you are responsible.

20—Keep your thinking and actions on a realistic level, regardless of how well your plans are developing. Plan in detail each move you intend to make and discuss your arrangements only with those whom you trust. Listen to what others have to say rather than continue a discussion that will intensify differences of opinion.

21—Adjust yourself to the current trend of thinking so that you can make the most of existing opportunities. Do not be so stubborn in your attitude that you ignore the wishes of others. Organize a program designed to protect and increase your income.

22—Do not let your sympathetic inclinations interfere with matters that pertain to your job or business. This can be a somewhat discordant period unless you take things easy and refuse to be hurried. Friendly contacts that you make now may lead to considerable social gains.

23—Counteract present difficulties by observing prudent policies and adhering to conservative practices. Discord can be turned into harmony, but you must make a definite effort to do so. Prepare yourself for tasks you consider important and get started on them.

24—Exert every effort to advance your present position and increase your financial assets. Press for the results you wish to obtain in a quiet but relentless manner. Do not take anything for granted, particularly when dealing with people who are unfamiliar to you.

25—Stick to a simple plan of action in your work; do not embark on a complicated program. Conflicting relations can make this an annoying day unless you go all-out to keep things running smoothly. Avoid experimenting and stick to accustomed surroundings and routines.

26—Regardless of how interested you are in what is going on, refrain from becoming involved in a controversial issue. Fill you mind with altruistic motives, and do everything you can to carry them out. Emphasize patience and proper planning if you expect to achieve desired success.

27—Do not let an accumulation of routine duties encroach on your hours for leisure. Social matters can prove enjoyable and take up a good part of your time and attention. Even though you may be swamped with work, take time out for refreshing relaxation.

28—Guard against creating obstacles for yourself or taking on more than you can comfortably handle. Do not let domestic or personal matters interfere with decisions you have to make. Use your resourcefulness and ingenuity rather than allow them to remain dormant.

29—Regardless of doubts you may have optimistic and encouraging dealings with others. Rash and impetuous action may lead to more difficulty than expected. Contact people personally rather than depend on the telephone for correspondence.

30—Keep your temper under control and you may find that many problems will work out their own solutions. A sudden shift from your normal goals at this time might have undesirable results. A strong feeling of satisfaction can be obtained through doing something thoughtful for a loved one.

DECEMBER

1—Do not risk an emotional clash by contradicting someone whose viewpoints differ from yours. Instead, listen courteously to what others have to say, and keep out of useless controversy. Steer clear of any situation which can stir-up dissension in your home.

2—Proceed carefully in matters which concern your income and financial standing. Do not let domestic or personal matters interfere with decisions you have to make. Also, refrain from participating in any activity where there is likelihood of receiving a public reprimand.

3—Your impatience to get things done in a hurry may cause trouble. Be prudent in your actions, and remain within the limits of your abilities. Guard against creating obstacles for yourself. What you do now can have an unfavorable effect on future progress.

4—Social matters should prove enjoyable and take up a good part of your time and attention. Utilize opportunities to be with friends and relatives whose companionship you find enjoyable. Meeting new people and establishing congenial relationships may help your career along.

5—Refrain from saying or writing anything that, if repeated, could be held against you. Someone may purposely use your words to place you in an embarrassing position. Adhere closely to diplomatic practices.

6—Although some of your current plans may bog down under unexpected complications, do not give up hope. Despite temporary disappointments, assistance that you receive now should enable you to overcome them.

7—Go out of your way to promote a feeling of harmony and friendliness among your family and friends. What you say and do now can have a favorable and lasting effect. Remove animosity and dissension by injecting humorous remarks into your conversation.

8—Regardless of how arduous a work program you are following, do not become so engrossed that you ignore your own wants and those of others. Even though you may be swamped with work, take time out for refreshing relaxation. Look around and get acquainted with people whom you have ignored because of lack of time.

9—You can make more effective use of gentle, persuasive methods than forceful demands. If you attempt to put pressure on someone, your efforts may get very little gain. Also hasty action will probably prove harmful to any plan you are trying to put over.

10—Though you may feel that your capabilities fall short of what is expected of you, guard against giving the impression that you are apprehensive and lack confidence in yourself. Make effective use of your resourcefulness and ingenuity.

11—Stick to a simple plan of action in your work, rather than embark on a comprehensive program of accomplishment. Establish sound approach to get what you want, and do not allow yourself to become entangled in complicated procedures. Make every effort to keep confusion and time-wasting activities to a minimum.

12—Devote time to shopping and clearing up neglected household duties. Pave the way for recreational pleasure by disposing of tasks that would otherwise occupy your time. Do not let an accumulation of routine chores encroach on your leisure hours.

13—Your intuition can prove as sound as logic in making a decision on a business matter. Use your hunches effectively without wasting time rationalizing your actions. Increased harmony and happiness, as the result of financial gain, are indicated.

14—Seek and make good use of competent advice which is available to you. By doing so, you may be able to remove a major financial obstacle that threatens your security. It would be a wise policy to pay attention to the words and guidance of someone who is interested in seeing you get ahead.

15—Conflicting emotions can make this an annoying day unless you go all out to keep things running smoothly. Regardless of how vexed you may about your own shortcomings or the faults of another, keep your temper under control. Blowing off steam now can upset friendly relationships.

16—This is not a particularly good day to be aggressive in your job or to start on new enterprises. Keep rigid control on your enthusiastic friends, even though you may be restless. Stick to accustomed surroundings and routines. Avoid experimenting.

17—This can be an interval of satisfaction and substantial advancement in your work. Since relationships with others should prove congenial, it should be easy for you to reach agreements with others. Work on projects that require mutual cooperation. Your mind ought to be working at top speed and in the right direction.

18—An attempt to gain a business advantage through social contacts may prove a serious blunder. Even though you may feel you are giving up favorable opportunities, do not mix business with pleasure. Instead, attend to each during the proper time and in the right place.

19—This can be a stimulating day with regard to household matters. Family relationships should be on the sunny side, thus making it easy for domestic harmony. Your happiness and popularity can be increased by your generosity and understanding.

20—Limit your program for the day to quiet discussions and careful planning. Take things slowly so that you can get an accurate perspective of existing situations. When you reach a decision, do not let sentiment effect the logic of your judgment.

21—A desire to take a short trip or vacation from arduous duties can be intense during this period. Gratify this wish if possible, and make such a break from your regular routine. This would be an ideal time for a change of scenery and a visit to new places.

22—Even though you may be annoyed by the complaints of someone who is having a difficult time, demonstrate your sympathy and understanding. Rather than show impatience, do what you can to be of assistance. However, avoid becoming obligated for responsibilities that are not yours.

23—To insure a profitable day in every respect, make your program flexible to cope with unexpected situations. Be prepared to make quick changes and instantaneous decisions when the occasion makes them necessary. You can keep things moving forward at a satisfactory pace.

24—Regardless of your interest in what is going on, refrain from becoming involved in quarrelsome situations, particularly where the issue does not concern you. Your attempt to smooth things over might be considered as interference. Let well enough alone and give consideration to your own problems.

25—"Don't give up hope," is your Christmas star message. Even though you are forced to smile in the face of an emotional problem, know that your Star will shine again. Pray. Dine well this evening.

26—Repaying favors and doing good turns for those who have aided you can help to make this a splendid day. Such gestures at this time can be instrumental in cementing the bonds of friendship. Fill your mind with altruistic motives and do everything in your power to carry them out.

27—Well-planned changes in your home or business can be more beneficial then first anticipated. Keep your mind alert for new ideas that you think will be helpful in achieving your aims. Revise antiquated procedures, and place emphasis on modern innovations and efficiency.

28—Banish worries about previous difficulties and anticipated problems. Be optimistic in your attitude about the present, as well as the future. You should find it possible to solve financial problems and work out budget matters satisfactorily.

29—Although you should be able to get along well in dealings with people, avoid arousing unfavorable reactions from anyone who is in a position to affect your income. Also, do not take unnecessary risks in a business matter.

30—Reduce the possibility of error and confusion in your work by doing one thing at a time and in proper order. Emphasize patience and proper planning. Keep alert since mistakes made now through carelessness can prove quite costly.

31—Stress your ambitions. Excellent results are possible, provided you undertake no more than you can comfortably handle. Be willing to make compromises that will keep things running harmomiously. It will also insure a Happy New Year!

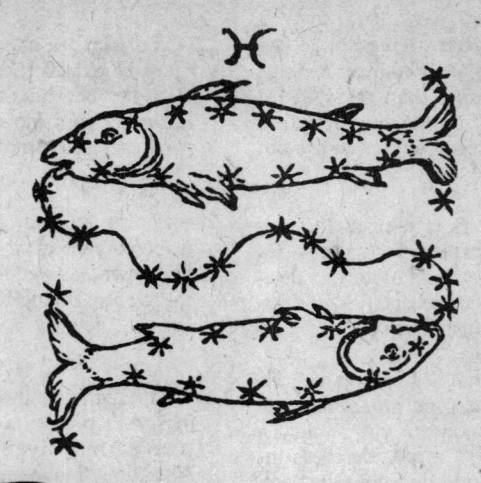

Pisces

February 19th—March 20th

You like
the quiet happiness
of knowing
you are loved and understood.
You need to be appreciated
and your emotions
must be treated with great sympathy.
You also like
to advance the lot of others,
bringing more justice to the world
pleases you,
and if you can
work in medical fields
to relieve suffering
you will know
great happiness.
Giving your attention to the underprivileged
can make you happy.
You must find friends
who share your interests in expansive causes
and are cheerfully active
to bring about better conditions.
Developing an artistic skill
can bring new happiness;
if you haven't done this
it is time to take such a step.

Pisces

JANUARY

1—Put your ingenuity and creative ability to practical use. Much can be accomplished, provided you do not let others sway your opinions or alter your goals. Take advantage of opportunities that can prove helpful in augmenting your income.

2—Concentrate your efforts on new and profitable projects from which you can gain financially. Regardless of what program you would like to put into effect, do it with a minimum of publicity. Encourage others to talk about themselves rather than direct attention toward yourself.

3—Make effective use of your leisure time by completing neglected household duties. Arrange to take part in a consistent savings plan to build up your cash reserve. Tempers can be frayed and mixed emotions may prevail unless you remain calm.

4—Take the initiative and get things done rather than wait for others to make the first move. Unnecessary tension and worry can be eliminated, provided you ignore interference with your plans. Realistic thinking is needed; do not take a chance on the unknown.

5—Give your complete attention to gratifying a cherished desire. Successful results are indicated through trying modern and progressive methods. Do not let anyone or any situation detract from the progress you can make.

6—Keep yourself in a cheerful frame of mind and refuse to let yourself become upset over minor problems. Emphasize efficiency and practicality in whatever project you undertake. Aim for worthwhile goals and do not relent in your efforts until you have attained them.

7—Stay away from persons who have been hindering or opposing you. Guard against lavish spending for entertainment or recreational purposes. Optimism and persistence can pay off in handsome financial rewards.

8—Caution is needed while dealing with others, whether strangers or members of your family. Move swiftly and keep up with rapidly changing events. Keep your conversations humorous and cheerful so that others will have something to smile about.

9—Do not let emotional interests interfere with matters that require logical attention. Get essential tasks done well ahead of time so that you can have ample opportunity for recreation. Make more effective use of the things you already own rather than give thought to the acquisition of new articles.

10—Using new ideas and approved methods for completing laborious tasks can bring benefits. Arrange a program that will enable you to clear up obligations and responsibilities rather than permit them to continue as burdens.

11—Gear your efforts for speed as well as quality in your work. Review your finances carefully and do not let anyone or any situation force you into making drastic changes. See that equipment and possessions are in good working order and readily available when needed.

12—Avoid doing anything outside your regular routine, since someone may openly oppose you. Do not give in to your doubts or let others discourage you, even though you may encounter a disappointing experience. Get your plans ready well in advance and adhere closely to the schedule.

13—Look for more-efficient and practical methods to handle your assignments. Do not give heed to an impulse for giving tactless expression to your thoughts. Refuse to let the insurmountable appearance of obstacles dim your outlook for expected accomplishments.

14—Let events occur at their own speed. Patience and persistence that you display now can be evidenced in future gains. Mutual assistance and cooperation should be easy for you to attain. Avoid making a rash statement or taking drastic action involving money.

15—Undertake only those projects you are sure you can complete with efficient thoroughness. Take difficult situations in stride rather than force an issue or increase present tension. Compromise on differences of opinions and promote harmonious relationships.

16—Give careful thought to each important decision you are required to make. Guard against increasing the number of your present responsibilities. Prevent situations that would force you to rush at the last minute or work at unaccustomed speeds.

17—New conditions may prove worthwhile in transforming some of your ambitions into realities. Adapt your plans to those of others rather than give the appearance of being contrary. Work diligently and strive for noticeable accomplishments.

18—Keep busy on assignments that will enable you to use your talents and skills for a good purpose. Promote congeniality among those around you by overlooking petty quarrels and differences of opinion. You may stir up confusion if you attempt to take on a largescale work program.

19—Clear and logical thinking is essential to meet obstacles and interference that you may encounter. Do your best to keep confusion and errors to a minimum. Personal pleasure and satisfaction can be derived through congenial association with others.

20—Keep your mind ready to handle current issues with which you are faced. Antagonistic feelings, particularly in matters connected with money, would be difficult to counteract. Back up your inspirations and wants with determined efforts to obtain the goals you desire.

21—Guard against giving in to an impulse to express yourself in anger. Rather than allow yourself to become upset, refrain from taking drastic action and avoid comment. Keep yourself busy and do not waste time in idleness or inefficiency.

22—Avoid doing anything that would ultimately invite antagonism. Do not let a feeling of restlessness cause you to waste your efforts on tasks of inconsequential importance. Take on arduous duties without complaint.

23—Use your knowledge and abilities to full advantage and aim for top results in everything you do. Ignore worries resulting from previous difficulties or anticipated problems. Clear up pending matters and prepare for new events and activities.

24—Be wary while dealing with others, especially where money is concerned. Let the merits of your efforts attract attention but do not openly seek to be noticed by others. Be firm but tactfully polite in speaking up for the things you want.

25—Keep your work schedule flexible so that you can revise it to cope with unexpected difficulties. Do not let sentiment or emotion affect your judgment, regardless of what issue comes up. Utilize your leisure hours to advantage around your home, and avoid unnecessary travel today.

26—Act quickly and press for developments without unnecessary delay. You can pave the way for financial security by making long-range budget adjustments. Refrain from acquiring anything new for which there is not a current or practical need.

27—Attune yourself to the tempo of things so that you can keep aware of what is going on. Concentrate on existing situations instead of worrying about future events. Do not wait for an inspirational urge—get started on an ambitious program.

28—Keep impatience under control, since impetuous action could result in needless difficulty. Handle diplomatically any situation that involves others. A combination of enterprise and personal sacrifice should enable you to achieve the results you want.

29—Arrange to do something that can give you pleasure and satisfaction. Reversals and setbacks you encounter now should prove to be of only minor importance. By exerting pressure on others you may invite interference with your plans.

30—Get started now on the accomplishment of something you have long wanted to achieve. Activities in which you can increase your personal prestige and popularity are favored. Use your time advantageously in hobbies you find enjoyable.

31—Think things over carefully before saying what is on your mind or taking action. You can ease the pressure of financial problems, but it will require much forethought. Adjust yourself to potentialities and advantages that are available to you.

FEBRUARY

1—Be early to rise, active in chores, and do not sit around and brood. Late in the day a telephone call can let you know that someone is becoming romantically interested.

2—Keep your best temper even though you feel that someone is keeping you from things you must do. The demands of friendship come first. If you mention the need for certain action, you'll be understood and all will be well.

3—An executive may want to talk to you quite seriously and will be very honest with you about the ways things stack up. You may have to make a distasteful decision, but it will mean more money and more prestige for your future.

4—Your mind may be kept busy with ideas and plans you are making for the near future. Try to take time out for the need of a child, though. The evening will be well-spent if you recognize how honorably someone has behaved toward you.

5—Try to make this a relaxed day, a time when nothing bothers you. Avoid letting emotion even get started. If an associate is obviously trying to bother and undermine you, laugh and discount the whole thing for good.

6—You may not accomplish all you want because of sluggish spirits and disillusionment. Your romantic life may seem to be breaking-up. It's best not to play too large a role in this yourself. Let the other person win.

7—A neighbor who feels very self-important will be untactful and crude. Don't allow this incident to mar your day. If you have a romantic date for tonight, it can be very glamorous. All social life is favored; enjoy it fully.

8—You'll need patience with the young today. It will do no good to show you are upset with them. Serenity will help and it may even bring them to you for advice and to show respect. Your relationship with the young is most important.

9—You may simply go for a drive or take a bus somewhere to view a place you've never seen. You have no taste to mingle with a crowd but prefer places that are quiet and almost solitary. You are seeking emotional nourishment.

10—Someone very chatty may attract you, but you can find that this person is usually quiet. There could be some ideal love existing in this relationship if you cultivate it. Nothing in the way of obstacles is seen.

11—A puzzle can come into your life and it can be difficult to get in touch with the person who can help solve it. A very pleasant person may show esteem and interest. React enthusiastically to such stimulation.

12—This is a big day for career matters. You may be asked to make a special speech and take on a new task and added responsibility. Use your creative talent and your ability to meet the public. It's all most exciting!

13—Work away steadily at your career and do not speed-up your pace. You'll do best by working quietly and avoiding involvement in any talk. A long distance call tonight may have interesting news which can change your picture.

14—You can meet someone interesting and be quite closely associated from now on, even though there is no element of romance in the connection. Someday there may be! Enjoy the lighter side of life tonight. Learn to appreciate friendships.

15—If you try to skim through things, you'll find your efforts wasted, for nothing will look right. Take your time, use energy and really polish up the home. Compliments you receive will be most pleasant.

16—An invitation may surprise but please you. Think just a little before accepting it. If you know deep within yourself that you are incompatible with a person, do nothing that will encourage the relationship at this time.

17—A good chance for real estate bargains, signing papers, forming a partnership or commencing any venture that is business-inspired. You'll be able to manage what you undertake and show strength of will and organizational talents to surprise all.

18—You can have an emotional upset, lose appetite or be on the way toward illness. You feel that you have been unjustly treated and would just like a corner to mourn in. Discovery of disloyalty can ruin the day.

19—This could be a very frustrating day, but you must cope with it and get the most out of it. Your schedule may be thrown off, but keep working. You'll at least complete the minimum of your plans; don't worry about the rest.

20—Someone you knew long ago may turn up and it will be nice to see each other again. You need have no worries about this person, for there is much affinity and silent understanding between you that will create a happy relationship.

21—You will be able to analyze a strange fact in seeing that a person who tells many lies always uses the same facial expression when telling them. One of those days with peculiarities. There will be some fun in social affairs tonight.

22—Keep on the alert for something that may occur to give you a new opportunity. If married, have a close and sincere discussion with your lifemate. Don't try to hide your aims, for you wouldn't be successful in that.

23—The day may bore you, visitors may bore you even more, and you can be longing for companionship that is denied to you now. Say nothing to disturb a person who loves you. You're in a bad mood and wish to be far away.

24—Avoid strenuous work, don't let yourself be rushed and keep all health rules in mind. Take it easy at lunch, browse through magazines and buy a few. Take time out for reading and catching up with new things tonight.

25—You can be angry about machinery you purchased and which seems to have self-destructed at far too quick a tempo. Don't show anger; be tactful, if you want help with this matter. Keep the evening open for music and romance.

26—Your poise and sophistication will come in handy today when you deal with an arrogant person. You may find it best to enforce your will and be very firm about it. You can win new distinction from your behavior now.

27—Do things efficiently and try to please someone with your speed, but don't be too speedy—that could cause troubles and set you back in the long run. The evening may be devoted to a date with a new romantic companion.

28—There is danger of that rare occurence—a Pisces who explodes in wrath. You may yield to a moment of disapproval which has been building up for a long time. The home can be the scene of turmoil because of your ire.

29 (Leap Year Only)—A good day for romantic relationships. You may meet someone new or have a refreshing conversation with an older contact. At any rate, even though you don't become engaged, you can expect some definite happiness from love. Domestic life is favored, too. But show attention to loved ones and take nothing for granted.

MARCH

1—Avoid probing and prying with questions. You may be curious and should admit this to yourself but that's no good reason to make another person feel uncomfortable. You'll have to make a decision whether you want to or not.

2—A career opportunity may show up suddenly and you can be quite excited with the choice that lies before you. There may be much financial benefit attached to one set of circumstances but you can be attracted more to the other.

3—Be sure to get in touch with a relative who expects to hear from you. There may be a family problem to live through now, one that cannot be solved due to the obstinacy of an individual. Don't worry where it is useless.

4—A busy day with domestic matters being demanding and shopping chores quite a few. You may run into someone who gives you amazing information. There may be a chance of some of your wishes coming true, due to this.

5—You can be indisposed, feel run down and generally unhappy. It all seems just too much of an effort. Your spiritual life is running slow and thus you have little ambition or positive thought. Reading may help adjust this.

6—Ambition may return and prod you to ask for a position that you know is just right for you. You'll have more aggressive power than usual today. You may receive some very affectionate telephone calls to brighten the evening.

7—An old friend may prove very loyal and help you get started with essential work. A simple word from such a person may be all you need to spur you onward. For one thing you want to live up to courageous standards for this person.

8—Avoid rushing, all that is unfamiliar, most extravagances, and people of questionable repute. There is not a great deal of good will in the atmosphere today, so just keep a business-like manner, be practical, talk but little.

9—Danger to health is here and you need all kinds of protection. Emphasize care in the vicinity of machinery, pets that are not your own, and substances that may be poisonous. A quiet evening at home is best.

10—A chance you had hoped for may fall through and you may have to turn ambition in another direction. A younger relative may get in touch by long distance and ask quite a favor. You may have to be firm in turning this down.

11—A busy day with neighbors dropping in. You can feel like giving up on your own duties and just entertaining. Well, don't worry; there is nothing to bind you so seriously that you can refuse hospitality of others.

12—Go over your financial situation, do all calculations necessary to revise the budget and find a way to get some things you need. Keep the day mostly for personal tasks you want to get done and for a little family talk.

13—Don't be the one to add more troubles to the burdens a work associate already bears. Say only what is diplimatic and kindly. Best to avoid all criticism of others now. If married, take a very affectionate view of your lifemate.

14—A good day to shop for clothes but do not get intrigued with some nice decorative articles for home. Still, it would be nice to buy a painting from a local artist trying to make his way financially with art.

15—It is a good day for financial ventures, career advancement and social life. You may be in the midst of a major financial transaction and it's all to the good. You may also move your residence favorably now.

16—Avoid asking personal questions of someone who is entirely innocent but whom you may be blaming for another's guilt. A touchy day and one on which you can lose the esteem of associates, neighbors, even of family members.

17—You can encounter a very snobbish person who decides to cultivate you due to your good grooming and precise speech. Best to turn down an invitation from anyone new. Keep to yourself quite a lot; avoid an incipient gossip campaign.

18—You may get help about a peculiar problem from someone who is in-the-know about many people. However, it isn't exactly ethical to ask about someone instead of just learning for yourself about this person's nature.

19—You can be sullen, unhappy, restless and inclined to look around for flaws and the people to blame them upon. What a day you can make for yourself and everyone else! Try to get in more laughter than tears, be wise!

20—Information that comes through the mail can cause your spirits to soar. However, you need to moderate feelings so you'll be able to keep a cool intellect concentrated on further activity. Your creative efforts really win!

21—A very unpleasant person can make it necessary for you to spend more than you expected. An in-law can kick up a fuss, be pleased with nothing, and you may have to pay for a sudden trip this person insists upon taking.

22—Show no surprise if you find a big change in your work environment. This can be all to the good. Probably a phase of change is being put into effect and it can bring about some interesting new training for you.

23—Be tactful and pleasant with someone who has been a good friend to you. If you show a snobbish attitude because you've risen a little in the past months, you'll disturb this person deeply. Be at your best, not just superficial.

24—You may be depressed over the ways of a young relative and know there is little you can do about it. Perhaps the further away you get, the better off you'll be emotionally. Entertaining lightly tonight can make you feel better.

25—You may be discontented with conditions and open to some temptations that must be resisted. You may feel alienated from someone formerly close to you. Try to live out this cycle without expressing any of these trends.

26—Be very tolerant, love your neighbor, find ways to chase any undesirable thoughts from your mind, any unloving feeling from your heart. Keep busy with quiet things; the day calls for serenity and health-giving peace at home.

27—Lots of work may be given to you to do and there is a chance you will feel some injustice in chores. Avoid any tendency to walk off and never return, don't even plead illness as a way of escape from today's pressured tempo.

28—Be very meticulous in dress, make sure grooming reflects care and good health. Take your time to have everything just right. The impression you make today may mean all the difference when it comes to new affluence.

29—Good news about a financial venture may come but it isn't a very large matter. Don't buy a luxury which might never be used or even fit in with your other home furnishings. Strive for good sense in everything this cycle.

30—Bright skies and happy feelings. For the unmarried there may be a hint of romance in the atmosphere. An unexpected telephone call this evening can open up a new hope about romance, but do not depend too heavily on it.

31—Much praise can come your way and please you a lot. You may be entrusted with a secret and you must avoid the temptation to pass it on. Be loyal to all who come to you today; don't play favorites even when it comes to old friends.

APRIL

1—You may be starting a whole new life today, everything shining and in order. Such a circumstance brings out all your desire to do the very best and you won't fail in that desire. You will find yourself welcomed in your new spot and already begin to feel at home by this evening, so rejoice.

2—A telephone call can be aggravating; if you show this reaction you can be piling up trouble for your future. It is wise to be patient and kindly with all, but make sure this is not in a condescending way. Do what is right according to your lights about an invitation for evening now.

3—You may shop favorably but loosen up a little on the purse strings for the luxurious or the whimsical. Add a dash of something entirely new and modern to your appearance. If you visit the beauty salon have a whole new style look; this will improve your personality and ego health.

4—Someone new in your neighborhood can be appreciated for honest and forthright talk. However, don't do too much talking yourself. An exchange of intimacies could be undesirable. Wait for time to prove the nature of this person more fully. Seek only old friends for pleasure and talk tonight.

5—The mail can bring you a joyous surprise which you can scarcely believe. New affluence is signified by the aspects and this could mean an inheritance or a large gift. You may go out socially tonight and be very popular for you are at your best in affectionate, wise friendship for others.

6—Be sociable at church, enjoy the coffee hour afterward. An older person can be delighted with your companionship. You may have to be at home early in order to complete some personal tasks you left unfinished yesterday. It is wisest not to have any visitor this evening; plan early retirement.

7—Take thought for a younger relative who needs a bit of help. You might even think of sharing your residence but that is not a good idea. Talk things over thoroughly with a lifemate if married; if not, think things through calmly. When your course is decided upon do not abandon it ever.

8—A health problem that has been threatening may now reach a stage you cannot ignore or neglect. This may be a dental matter. Be wise and make contacts, steel your mind to going through what must be done. Avoid bitterness over financial outlay; be glad you are independent financially at all times.

9—A favor done for you today may come as a surprise. Do not be too proud to take what is offered. Your schedule is somewhat broken up by necessities outside of work. Be as relaxed as you can, refuse to worry about work problems. Spend the evening quietly with books, music, TV.

10—This is a good day to plan for a considerable distance into the future. Set yourself quite a rugged course and know that you will follow it even though it is quite exhausting and monotonous in nature. You'll get great praise for what you do but you may take a cynical attitude toward praise.

11—Guard your eyes today, avoid handling sharp instruments if possible, and do not entertain this evening. The day holds pitfalls and much caution is needed. If you drive anywhere at all stay strictly within the law. Talk to a romantic companion on the telephone tonight; don't see this person.

12—You can feel exhausted for no real reason. A hidden infection could be responsible and it may clear up by itself. Friends who try to cheer you may succeed quite a bit, so don't drive off visitors who come to you with light hearts. Listen closely to an elderly friend of the family tonight.

13—A good day to prove that you are one of the people who do things rather than just talk about them. Your most generous spirit is at the front and you'll make a better impression than ever on neighbors, friends and everyone at the various places you go. Be active, get around, make new acquaintances.

14—You'll truly enjoy shopping today and may buy something that gives you pleasure. A pet that children can enjoy may be the best thing, if you have children. Your romantic picture is inspiring, if unmarried, and buying clothes you know will please a loved one is just right for today.

15—A sudden discontent with your earnings can cause you to start thinking along lines about increasing them. You may even head for some supervisory position you feel should be yours due to many years of experience. Be patient; results of today's ambitious trend may show up much later.

16—There can be much difficulty in settling a problem about family affairs. Living conditions may be part of the trouble; someone may be too lonely and want companionship in home life. Do not sacrifice yourself to anyone who is so selfish as not to care how others feel about these things.

17—Don't forget to pay bills, buy a gift, do anything necessary about insurance matters. Make it a day for the practical and obligations. Buy clothes for small children, see to it that the family home has the look of beauty you want for it. Splurge a little for a special decorative purpose.

18—Things may not go your way and you can get worked up to that violent temper for which you are known. You may have people staying away from you by the dozens if you show this grim side of your nature. When your mouth starts to twitch you can know you are far too angry, too tense. Relax, laugh!

19—A very skillful person may wangle a promise out of you about something you do not really want to do. This could mean signing a document that would obligate you too heavily. However there is another side to the question.

20—Avoid jumping to conclusions or making any decision of final nature. Let all things be tentative, judgment suspended. You may be viewing a new acquaintance too harshly, and you may not have the facts you need. Get out and walk, think of a new program for losing weight and start it tonight.

21—You may hear from some distant place which knows of your expert work. You could be asked to take on a job at this location and be given all kinds of financial assurance such as free travel, free accomodations, etc. Think twice before you turn this down; it can be key to your future.

22—A very prying and curious person may get into something personal of yours. If you lose your temper you will regret it because it is making a mountain of a molehill. Rise above all emotions and don't show that you feel anything wrong. This is your only way for a dignified victory.

23—Excellent cycle for financial gestures, using new information, shopping and travel. You'll be very busy and happy about it. Your energies are stirred and you anticipate the best results from all actions. Investment opportunity can be the best for many a year; be courageous about it.

24—If you turn down an invitation from a younger acquaintance, you may injure feelings. Accept the invitation and then resolve upon finding a way to put an end to your social visiting as quickly as possible. Just be too busy to spend very long at anyone's party whenever it happens to be.

25—A sudden inspiration may come to you about a work of artistic endeavor you want to take up. A training course is a good idea and all polishing of talents needed. A small investment to help your dreams and ambitions come true is certainly in order. A loved one will appreciate your efforts.

26—Don't dilly-dally about anything today. You can incline toward lethargy, brooding about certain things in your romantic life. You can become emotionally upset when you continue this trend. Get up, get out and do things, shop, stop in for a snack somewhere, see a good new show.

27—You can feel averse to companionship, be sharp and unreasonable with lifemate and children if you have them. Struggle against this mood, be pleasant and affectionate. Show understanding for flaws of others. If a child makes a mistake and causes disturbance be swiftly forgiving, willing to accept.

28—A good time to progress with work, show your best, be enthusiastic and go into depth about things that are to be done. Don't let anything be superficial and shoddy. Giving things a lick-and-a-promise is no good today. You must complete tasks and do so with perfection. Be firm with yourself.

29—For the unmarried this can be the most eventful day of the month or even the year. You may fall in love with someone you meet now and it may not take very long. There are signs of a romance of some endurance in your chart. Be cautious not to eat heavily tonight, resolve on diet.

30—Do not become too curious about a person who is new in your work area. Keep your mind dedicated to concentration on work, not people. The mail can bring a pleasant surprise and a long distance call tonight may elate you. Very favorable day when you are industrious and happy in nature.

MAY

1—You may be resentful of tasks, feel that the family is too demanding. Your sense of duty will see you through without a word of complaint. Do not be sharp of speech if you get a telephone call from a person who bores you. Keep equable temper with all around you tonight.

2—You may find ambitions nagging and desire to get away, but a refreshing change in work environment may lead you to a major decision now. You may not feel that the matter needs to be discussed but you could be wiser to bring it into the open and get cooperation that is needed.

3—There can be some gloom that is difficult to dispel this morning. Afternoon promises a bright spot due to the visit of a new acquaintance in your work area. Your efforts may be lifted from the commonplace due to praise you get from this interesting and vivid person.

4—There can be a new romantic trend developing and you may find your emotions much involved where it may be taboo for you to nurture desires. This is a matter in which much caution is needed. Be diplomatic and pleasant but avoid making any solid statements about your feelings.

5—Don't be extreme in anything today. Keep a moderate pace with work, eat wholesome, balanced meals, don't talk a great deal. There is a chance you will jump to some conclusions that are not justified by facts. Wait until you learn more about a certain person near you.

6—You may get a tip from someone about the wise way to handle a relationship that has become important to you—a good time to heed the words of one older than you. Wisdom will have an appeal that may defeat your emotional trend and that can be all to the good for you.

7—An impersonal manner gets you the most success today. Keep busy, don't have time for a long chat. Enjoy some shopping when you have time, take care of hair grooming, look your best for a social affair this evening. Don't keep hours that are too late for your health.

8—Much stimulation and excitement is in the atmosphere. You may be asked to take a big role in some community venture of worth. There is a chance you will be sought out for publicity that will be pleasing. A relative may be proud of you and show approval in a concrete way.

9—You may be doing much practical thinking today, organizing plans and getting in touch with people who will help out. You're in just the kind of situation you enjoy and will manage it all very efficiently. Take time out for a walk, enjoyment of exercise in the fresh air today.

10—Be careful not to make an error. It would be time-consuming and frustrating to have to do things over again. Be in touch with someone vital to your plans and put your cards on the table about results you want. Someone may ask for a large loan; be firm about refusing this.

11—You will be unjust if you try to force someone else to take all the blame for a matter of mutual concern that has you worried. If you're wise, you will let the day go by without making any statement which could be dubious of intention. Be very dutiful to family tonight.

12—An unreasonable request may be made and it can be obligatory to fulfill it. Don't be penny-pinching in attitude now or you can lose out on a good opportunity. Work at a steady pace for too much speed will have bad effect on nerves. Make allowance for someone with troubles.

13—You may ponder an investment and can be drawn to it more than you were formerly. Consolidating funds to enter in this business opportunity is worthwhile. A new neighbor may cultivate your friendship, make it easy for this person to get to know you and don't be mistrustful.

14—You need to take a large view of matters in business connections. Long-range benefit is worthwhile. Make a good impression during a conference this afternoon. Consider a chance to earn more by using a talent which has been rusting out. Polish up your chances diligently now.

15—You may wish you were free from all promises today but you'll need to go right along and fulfill them. Weariness can grip you and need for rest be foremost in your thoughts. Wait until the time comes this evening and then be firm about cutting short activities to retire early.

16—A neighbor may make overtures in an effort to impose. Be wise and don't take on a burden that would prove quite distasteful. Avoid spending much time with any one person today. It is a good time for creative pursuits, going over the budget, bringing neatness to wardrobe.

17—It can be difficult to exert patience today. A frustrating trend is here, delays may be the order of the cycle. There may be lack of needed equipment to handle a work demand and much time may be spent trying to get essential items. Avoid any big plans for this evening.

18—Repairs may be needed in several directions. It is a day that requires concern about safety and convenience. You may have to pay out money for an emergency situation due to mechanical failure. This is just one of those times to be enduring and strong enough to last out trends.

19—You may have trouble due to someone else's failure to consider details. A chance you will lose your temper explosively is here. It might be just as well, at that, to clear the air by self-expression and make it plain that you resent unnecessary work caused by another.

20—Health needs guarding today, avoid letting emotions build up to tension point. Be very cautious if you drive; preoccupation can cause an accident. If you are around small children watch out for toys they leave that might cause you to stumble and be injured painfully.

21—Be gentle in manner when you bring attention in an important matter to the consideration of a younger person who is not operating efficiently. You'll get better results from keeping your manner kindly. Evening holds social pleasure but also a tense moment or two.

22—Make an important contact today and you'll be rewarded, able to go ahead with a major project. Much enthusiasm for your present trend is here and you'll enjoy talking things over with an affectionate person who is concerned about you. A fine evening for romantic progress.

23—You'll fare best in quiet pursuits, perhaps an intimate talk with someone in your field of work. Plans for a vacation can also get ahead and you will meet perfect agreement with any companion who will be going with you. Read something of interest and instruction tonight.

24—Generosity is the best trend for your welfare today. Share the good things you have, cast your bread upon the waters. You'll have gratifying inner rewards from knowing that you have done the right thing. Help someone in a situation you have formerly been through yourself.

25—You may become involved in work which takes much time and is monotonous. Complaint may not achieve good results, but you may find an ingenious way to alleviate the circumstances without discussing them at all. Use your cleverness to protect yourself somewhat today.

26—Stay aloof from groups that go in for gossip or irresponsible activity. You can get in trouble from pleasure-seeking now. Save money, spend only on needs. Be firm in a family situation which calls for your help in solving a problem, don't yield to anyone who is impractical.

27—A good chance is here to use your talents and make a praiseworthy impression. You can lay the foundation for a promotion and pay increase by using initiative and showing originality of thought in work. Have faith that all will turn out as planned and be courageous about it.

28—The mail can hold a good surprise and you may find yourself relieved of a burden. You feel emotionally in the clear and may be humming a little song while you work. All is cheerful, relationships harmonious and evening can bring a bright new romantic hope with much attraction.

29—Be scrupulously ethical in all business relationships. Avoid too much intimacy with a business acquaintance, though. You can enjoy clever arrangements you create for entertainment this evening. You'll make guests comfortable and happy with the work you do for them.

30—The answer to a problem may appear out of the blue. You are favored to get ahead with plans important to your future. A telephone conversation can add a new idea which will be a money-saver in the long run. Be open to suggestions and advice from an older friend at a distance.

31—Long and arduous efforts may be needed to cope with today's routine and troublesome interruptions. You can come out of it well if you keep on diligently in spite of vexations. Keep the evening for relaxation, study of something interesting to you and early retirement for good rest.

JUNE

1—There may be a reckless attitude in your personality today. Difficult to gather together the various threads of your life—in sheer frustration you might follow an unwise course. Try to curb such trends and be particularly cautious if romantic sentiments are aroused now.

2—A boring and wearisome task can deplete your energies, bring on lethargic feelings. Avoid self-pity about any condition that is not pleasant, do not build up health worries. The temporary influences will drift on over by tonight and you can get a more firm grip on realities.

3—Good news may come from a distance. You may receive a small gift which is very welcome. Good friendship is accented now and you will realize the value of a younger friend and appreciate it more than you did formerly. Let concern for others show and be helpful.

4—Keep your career ambitions in mind. You may get a chance for a new job that will favor your talents much more. In any telephone conversation you have to be patient and understanding. The evening is good for a group of guests and informal entertainment the family will enjoy.

5—Someone new may enter your life and deserve much attention. This can develop into a very affectionate relationship that you cherish. Your most tolerant and sympathetic views are needed to achieve happiness. Be cooperative with the family during evening conversation.

6—Much sociability is in your atmosphere and you will enjoy contacts you make. Anything connected with the community or your church is favored today. Be active and you'll increase your reputation for good works and thoughtful consideration of welfare of those you can help today.

7—You may be given an unusual opportunity through the good will and loyalty of a friend. Don't turn down any chance to realize your higher aspirations. Good fortune that is not connected with your routine career work may arrive and might steer you in an entirely new direction.

8—Ignore the petty attitude of a neighbor who makes subtle remarks that show disapproval and scorn. Seek out companions who are cheerful and turn the day to one of enjoyment. Getting outdoors as much as possible is desirable for health. You can also reflect wisely during a leisurely walk.

9—You may have an intuitive nudge about the activities of someone in your neighborhood. You could do this person a favor if you persuade a change in plans for greater safety. Be open and aboveboard in talk today. Don't play games with your work associates in office politics.

10—Work will go like lightning once you buckle down. The path is clear for worthwhile accomplishment. You may get heartfelt praise that boosts your ego and encourages you in important career matters. A cloudy situation may clear up this evening; be alert to trends.

11—Excellent trends here for your financial activities. You can progress thoughtfully and may find large dividends in the future from a daring move you make now. A good idea to have family approval and then move straight ahead with determined zeal and intelligence prevailing.

12—Chores can be exhausting and there may be many demands to gratify. You can feel rushed and not very happy about affairs. A sense of duty will see you through but do call a halt early in the evening; relax and enjoy some informal entertainment or take in a good show.

13—Avoid being too self-centered. You'll benefit no one, including yourself, if you show vanity and determination to win in a purely selfish way. Shopping is well aspected if you are generous with others in the purchases you make. Buy something special for a young child.

14—You may be depressed today, feel somewhat rundown physically. Take some extra vitamins; the trend will pass over soon. You may be consulted about an important work matter and can get much pleasure due to the esteem an executive shows. Keep all talk on impersonal level.

15—Be generous with a young relative who is in need and is a hard worker. Answering the demands of necessity is always wise and beneficial. Do not take a harsh mood toward anyone or downgrade the efforts others make. A time to be just and kindly to all is here.

16—Be astute in discriminating about matters that are important and those that are not. A telephone conversation with a friend at a distance can be rewarding. Do not tire yourself for there can be bad results from too much work. Avoid mental tensions as far as possible.

17—Take full responsibility in a matter where someone else is dubious. Show your strength of character and firmness by being insistent. You'll get what you want by being bold and determined. It is possible to win a new position of honor and prestige in this cycle.

18—Do not cater too much to laziness and a slight physical ailment. Keep right on through the work day, and also take part in social life tonight. Once you get into action things will go more easily for you so keep busy and you'll forget all about a slothful mood.

19—You can be irritated by something that comes in the mail. It is not reasonable to take such a matter too seriously. Relax and smile a bit instead of becoming angry. Resist a temptation to read the riot act to a young member of the family tonight. Show affection to relatives.

20—Someone lonely may turn to you for companionship and help in emotional matters. Do not begrudge time and thought to this person. There is a good chance that you will be estimated highly by someone who never paid much attention to you formerly. Answer questions wisely.

21—Someone new in your work environment may cause you to admire appearance and manner. Be a little cautious in this relationship for it could have some dynamite you cannot discern now. Avoid romantic entanglements, be dutiful, accurate and thorough in all you do, don't daydream.

22—Deal with large matters mentally and dismiss all that is trivial. You may be asked for your opinion on some important matters in church or community life. Think twice before you make a comment. In fact, it might be wise to refuse to make a statement about this matter.

23—Much good cheer is around and you may be planning a trip you anticipate with joy. Be very pleasant with a loved one whether married or not. The evening can hold some progress for a romance that is becoming more serious with each day that passes.

24—It can be difficult to work today; you may have some trouble with nerves and emotions. There may be a physical cause for your slump in spirits and other troubles. Best to plan on a quiet evening, stay at home, seek some solitude in order to gain refreshing serenity.

25—A new neighbor may attract you but can be quite a malicious person, perhaps even enjoy baiting you or running down what you like. You'll be better off avoiding the company of such a person permanently. Protect your own interest, keep your ideas to yourself.

26—You will enjoy relationships today, find happiness in weaving a lovely and harmonious pattern. Show esteem for those you admire; win new amicable relationships. You may make a major decision in romantic matters this evening; once made, don't even think of changing it.

27—It is a fine day to shop for clothes and buy things that will increase your glamor. You can win happiness by being yourself, following your excellent taste and creating a day of pleasant activities. Don't let yourself be pennypinching in any matter during this cycle.

28—Keep all finances in good order, check over your accounts, make sure all insurance is paid up. Take up some new form of exercise, go to a health spa or other public service place where you can gain better health and enjoy new chance to lose weight as you should.

29—Anticipation is a major part of the day's benefits. However, don't allow yourself to spend money that is not in your hands yet. You may receive an interesting telephone call late in the day or during the evening. New ideas may come from this and you can feel encouraged.

30—It is best not to cultivate any new friendship today. You might find that someone to whom you give a confidence betrays it in gossip of most unpleasant type. Use your intellect to discriminate between true and false friends, turn your back on the latter for self-protection.

JULY

1—Be sure to remember and take care of obligations. Be pleasant, do what conscience demands and don't resent or complain about any of it. You can be on a special list for doing some service in your community. Best to take on such a task; you'll spread your name for good works and good will that way.

2—An announcement made today will probably displease you. If you can get out of town for a few days, the refreshment will do you much good. Don't brood about a younger person whose motives you suspect. There is danger that you are the one who is entirely in error about a matter of great importance.

3—Matters that come up for attention today can find you unprepared. Danger of losing your temper about a domestic concern that is not at all that important. Be kindly to a neighbor who turns to you for friendship but don't let too much intimacy develop. Keep the evening for family and old, trusted friends.

4—You need a restful day, preferably one not devoted to serious thought or anything that might depress you. Be lenient with a small child in the family and don't begrudge your time in helping young people whoever they are. You may turn down an invitation to have dinner out due to slight indigestion.

5—What you hear today may have no factual foundation. You can be off the track romantically, too, but since you're in an obstinate mood you won't be convinced. Your attitude can cause trouble that will last deep into the future. Better make an effort to switch your attitude, be friendly, don't borrow trouble.

6—You may receive a rare career honor. Somehow things do not sit well with you and you are not able to enjoy the benefits and rewards of life. This can be an emotional matter, perhaps one that only time will take care of. Let all your responses to others be quite conventional, avoid self-expression.

7—Someone quite a bit younger may seem insolent to you but it would not be wise to become indignant. Take the whole thing with a grain of humor and you'll feel better about it. The evening has some ideal romantic aspects in your chart. This trend can be a surprising one with much to please you.

8—Financial matters take your time and attention. It is a good day to act about an investment in either tangible or intangible property. A recent development can be a good investment if you have a friend who holds some of the important strings and can let you in by pulling them a bit now.

9—Communications from a distance are vital to your success and well being. Make long distance calls, write letters and get them in the box pronto. You stand to win considerably, to lose a lot if you are slow to act. Don't let routine demands stand in the way of making money that is far from routine.

10—Buy clothes, a new scent, have your hair done in a new way, then be ready to step out and do some special shining both socially and romantically. You have a style all your own, so display it to win laurels that belong to you now. You may find the dawn of a romance at the end of the evening.

11—Find a way to help someone in the family who is very sensitive and unwilling to ask for aid. Make the day bright for little children, take them on a picnic or similar outing. Your ways with people will be effective, your sincere affections will be recognized. Make it a quiet evening, retire early.

12—Check everything you do; don't let errors slide by. A good day for surprise rewards for former actions. You may get some news that changes the picture for you quite a lot. Work can become difficult, more monotonous than you realized. Stay on with it right through to the goals you set for yourself.

13—Make a good impression in every way possible, and this of course means hiding the seams so that no one knows you are trying to make an impression at all. Your romantic emotions may come into the spotlight suddenly late in the day. Watch out for this tricky situation; it can mean new troubles.

14—Avoid talking to executives if possible. You can find one of them in the mood to belittle you or otherwise tease and bait you. This wouldn't go well with you and might create a bad situation all around. Do your work, go home when time is ripe, keep to the family for associations this evening.

15—An unexpected gift or a large sum of money can come to you through the mail. This is a fortunate day for you, one you will not forget. Avoid worry about a romance that is in the background of your life; don't talk about it at all to anyone. The current news may be of interest to you personally tonight.

16—You may try in vain to reach a goal. The day holds interruptions, irritations, possibly some trouble with health. Emotions may become very unpleasant and intrude in all you do. You may find it necessary to leave work early, seek a physician. Rest and total relaxation are certainly needed for evening.

17—You can be bitter, wondering why you have the problems you don't believe you deserve. Try to do something about it instead of brooding. Get out and around if possible, buy some things to please the entire family. Take a brief trip with someone enjoyable. Having dinner out-of-town can be fun.

18—Make plans today, seek help from a loved one. You can see your situation clearly and know what you want to do about it. Get in touch with someone at a distance who may encourage you in a special problem you want to solve. Research may be the main topic of concern and you may get a chance at it.

19—You may not get the correct facts and may act in a way that will cause you loss. It is a time to check and recheck your information. Don't listen to the know-it-alls who always have an answer and an authoritative manner. You'll get things straight by evening and be aggravated by the time wasted.

20—A newcomer in your work area may interest you right from the first. There can be much mental compatibility here but if you test this further you may find a point at which you diverge sharply and are hostile to one another. Best not to let any new relationship of today grow in the future.

21—Health difficulties can assail you and may need professional care. Probably it's the type of thing for which there is instant help if you just get to the physician instantly. Don't imagine dire things of complex nature; such trouble may be completely lacking. But do go to a physician.

22—News may not be at all good but dwelling on it won't change or improve it. Keep busy with routine duties. If someone comes to you for help with work, don't be vexed. Be calm, kindly and sympathetic with others. While you're occupied thus some of the clouds can be lifting from your own scene.

23—Be generous and hospitable with someone new in the neighborhood. Where others may be intolerant, show your ability to be tolerant and accept things as they are. Your social life can have a touch of splendor tonight, so shine forth in your most becoming array and win the laurels for appearance.

24—Best not to try to persuade any member of the family who does not see things your way. This is a hazardous cycle for romantic affairs, even for marriage if it is a fairly new one. If you are too inflexible in view, you can find it the beginning of the end and very unpleasant at that, too.

25—Friends will be around when you need them and you can feel a lot of your emotional difficulty lifting and disappearing. You may look over possibilities for somewhere new to live and find just the right spot with the help of someone who wishes you well. Be orderly in what you do and all will go well.

26—You may reach some new conclusions about your own desires. A new degree of maturity can enter your thinking and allow you to see things better than you did formerly when romance had you blinded to the way things were. Keep relationships with all as pleasant as possible, be cooperative.

27—A major responsibility may be entrusted to you. Do not be too proud of this or you will create envy around you. Be diligent but also pleasant. Your ability to use words well may be part of your chores. Don't expect immediate recompense; this work will count toward better things in the future.

28—Many small irritations can add up to a great big one toward a person who does not deserve that from you. If you lose your temper with one who has liked and admired you, it may never be amended. There may be much more than you know to the facts. When you discover them you can be embarrassed.

29—A neighbor can be very meddlesome. Do not speak at all about your personal life. News that comes through in the afternoon can give you new hope. Your career is progressing well but you need to slow down a little today in order to protect health and keep things on a neater schedule.

30—There is an adventurous atmosphere today; it could presage trouble. Don't tempt fate in any way. This means not to invest, no matter how good things seem. It also means to avoid personal adventures such as romance. The motto for today and tonight is not "live dangerously" but "live cautiously."

31—Family affairs become a crucial matter for you. It may be necessary to resign yourself to a long journey in order to see an older relative who needs your help in straightening out a tangled, uncomfortable life. Not much pleasure here but keep disposition as pleasant as facts can allow tonight.

AUGUST

1—The day may be devoted to social life, outdoor activities and some conversation that vexes you. A younger friend may not show agreement with you on a matter which is of more importance than you may realize now. You'd do well to think about the silent disagreement that is shown.

2—You may go quite blithely about your tasks, not sensing that something is definitely wrong. This may seem a happy circumstance but actually you'd profit more if you had foreknowledge of facts shaping up in your life. Do some thinking about those who are closer to you, perhaps a lifemate.

3—A hostile neighbor may take a superior attitude. Don't let this worry you in the least; chances are you will be moving soon, anyhow. Your life is entering a new phase and you will soon have to settle down and be at your most practical about plans for your own future. Avoid all regrets.

4—Shocking information may come and your immediate reaction may be an entirely materialistic one. You may rush out to spend extravagantly as a result of what you are told today. This is not an ethical thing to do but may seem entirely justified to you. Be sure to call a younger friend.

5—A good day for financial matters. Financial arrangements you make will be successful. You meet with no obstacles in your suggestions about money. Desirable affluence is on the way and you will be able to rely upon what is said today about money. Trust someone in an official capacity.

6—Guard your possessions, particularly your prized possession such as your car. A heedless person might cause damage and it would be difficult to collect. Try to avoid public buildings, parks or parking lots. Your income may undergo a new regulation; this could mean expense you did not count upon but it may be mandatory to pay.

7—You may be indecisive. Because you want to be sure that you do the right things, you may spend most of the day trying to add up advantages and disadvantages in a drastic move. Don't let anyone deride your decisions. Be independent for it is your life that is being considered, not another's.

8—You can be aggravated with someone who telephones when you are in a hurry to go elsewhere. Don't be too abrupt, be willing to help a little with this person's emotional problems. You won't be sorry if you offer genuine friendship to make another's life smoother.

9—Not much doing today; you'll be stuck with routine and can be impatient about the length of time it takes some business matters to go through. You may be dealing with people who are too cautious and wasting time, but complaining about it will do not good. Try to find some entertainment to relax you tonight.

10—Do not be insistent or persuade someone to follow your advice. You could be in for a very unhappy time if you are determined that your will must overcome objections another person has. You may be leaping into the midst of trouble by thinking you are right and others wrong today.

11—Someone may try to borrow in order to make an unusual investment. Don't even consider a loan. It's a day that calls for self-protection in money and also for care in traffic whether walking or riding. A family member may need help; don't be resentful if you're asked to give up time.

12—Someone may accuse you of having an inflated ego. You might profit from heeding this. Your tendency to be rigidly set in your ways and unwillingness to alter your opinions amount to inflated ego when all's said and done. You listen to those who differ from you only with an amused attitude.

13—Something may happen to cause a sudden drop in your sense of superiority and know-it-all attitude. You will be very gracious about this matter and see the value of humility which is occasionally needed for those who are too high and mighty. Evening brings relaxation and love to help out.

14—An older neighbor may pry, criticize, accuse you of various things. Whether this person is right or not is beside the point. Your personal rights are being infringed upon and you are justified if you show anger. However, do not lose control of your temper for that would ruin everything.

15—A good day for the family to be together and talk of mutually interesting affairs. There may be quite a lot of discussion about buying a home of your own. Whatever is said now, you will have to make your own final decision. In the background a new romantic trend may have your attention.

16—This is a good time to travel, to start a vacation, to unwind as you get farther from home. Or you might be making an investigative trip to consider a special school in which you are thinking about enrollment in order to get a special license that would increase your earning a lot.

17—Keep your high philosophical standards in mind and let nothing cause you to act in a manner unworthy of your high principles. A younger person may be trying to "bait" you just to see that famous temper of yours erupt. It may not be easy to keep your cool but you just must do so.

18—A good time to shop for things you personally want. Pick out something gorgeous for the new season that is coming. Let a bit of the high style enter your wardrobe, also think about a new hair style that would be glamorous. Good news may come over long distance telephone during the evening.

19—Be wary of your own emotional mood. You could attract a lot of gossip if you show special attention to anyone. Be wise, prudent, conventional.

20—Keep your health under good care today. Avoid eating too much, although tempted. Also, avoid dampness, speed and the handling of sharp instruments. In social life tonight try to stay completely out of any unpleasant trend that may be underway. Show no special prejudice in favor of anyone during conversation.

21—Make it a leisurely day, do a few things in the home, go out and shop a bit. Buy something decorative such as a large potted plant. Be thrifty when it comes to family provision for meals, avoid the high-priced cuts and settle for that which is good, but medium in expense.

22—A kindness you try to do for an older relative may be turned down. This person may be almost impossible to get along with. Don't try too hard. Get busy and think about the coming week, make some plans of financial nature. The time is ripe to consider a project that has interested you for a long time.

23—Make sure your rights are protected. A neighbor may impose, use space that is not rightfully his. It might even pay you to consult the services of a professional. This could be a real eye-opener to you and your neighbor. If you allow imposition it will go on and become more pronounced.

24—Buy a small gift to show affection for a person for whom today is a special occasion. Being a little sentimental won't hurt you. If you have a new work requirement, fill it as well as you can. Don't regard yourself as inadequate for things that are new; you can find the way to do them.

25—A good day to make up your mind about discarding clutter. A massive donation to a charity or planning a garage sale could be fun and profitable. You need to create more neatness and good order around your home. Go through your wardrobe, too, and discard the outmoded and things you haven't worn for some time anyhow.

26—You may be inspired by the words of a younger person about the high quality of your work. While this is sincere, do not let it penetrate too deeply. This is a person whom it could be dangerous to concentrate upon, so accept the incident and then forget it. Otherwise, you'll be asking for trouble.

27—Work can be difficult, little cooperation is offered, and you may feel in grim spirits about the whole thing. A romantic date for tonight can erase all your worries and complaints. Forget the day once it is past and concentrate on having a wonderful time with someone you love tonight.

28—There can be tempting situations around and much desire to do things you know would be unwise. Make an effort to associate only with responsible people who are not extravagant and above all do not have a date with someone new this evening. Keep your ideals high and be wise.

29—Help you get must be given much appreciation. An older person can save you from inconvenient trouble. The day may go very slowly in the afternoon but you're better off with only the family than with others now. Be somewhat aloof and secluded this evening. A good night to complete personal chores.

30—An executive may ask you in for a conference which will be entirely about unexpected subjects. As a result of this you may change your career direction. You'll need to think along materialistic lines, financial necessities. Courage will be needed to make a decision, but once made you'll be glad.

31—A message you receive can have good financial news and some interesting family happenings. An enjoyable day is here when work is strenuous, but there is time for a pause to rest now and then as well as to enjoying developments taking place around you and in family matters of concern.

SEPTEMBER

1—Pisces can be assured of a favorable day. A new acquaintance can bring some vividness into life, be very appealing and offer ideas which may have a direct effect upon your career. Entertain any such person with unusual affection and show your interest openly.

2—A day of serious work on an important project. You may find yourself at the lead position in an organizational plan. Your sense of order and your desire to do creative work will come in handy now. Give your time and talent freely and you will win new honors. A family night.

3—An excellent time for relationships of an intimate nature. The family, relatives, friends of long-standing and new romantic interests will thrive. Forget all problems connected with work and finances. Forces are working to bring you good fortune in these fields. Entertain tonight.

4—Good hours for your personal happiness. Friendship is stressed, and you will be pleased to learn of the sincerity of a new acquaintance. Devote all the latter part of the day to sociability. Be dressed attractively and let the time take care of itself. Relax completely.

5—An unfortunate day for those who have an obstinate streak. If you yield to family wishes, go along with their plans and avoid all strife, you may come out all right. The least indication of opposition may bring a storm of protest or belligerence around your head.

6—Play it safe today, and you will find many events turning in your favor. Impulse is not favored, but the influences offer advantages to those who have planned their day and follow a schedule. Opportunity which arises should be investigated. You will enjoy the companionship of society.

7—Church or philosophical meditation will be very inspiring and you may be put at the head of a newly-organized group. Your good-will and desire to help others will be richly-rewarded today. Spend the late afternoon and evening by giving your time to a person who needs companionship and good cheer.

8—A day of sociability, romance, perhaps adventure. For those who are not married, these hours can contain a meeting which is very significant for future romantic plans. Work may take a back seat while you concentrate on personal relationship. Accept an evening invitation.

9—You can be pleased with a turn of events which means a radical change in your life. Probably you won't have to go out of your way to accept an opportunity which beckons. Swift decision will mark your activities and you will find cooperation wherever it is needed.

10—These hours can be very profitable if you investigate a chance to earn money in a way which uses a talent not formerly applied in a business fashion. Be very firm about your financial rights, and you will win new respect. Your security will be furthered by actions of today.

11—Accident and personal loss is likely. Be very careful in choosing your words. Quarrels can become bitter and give cause for emotional upsets which will influence your entire environment for the worse. Try to do as the family wants, particularly concerning plans for the evening.

12—Your personality will be especially appealing today, and you may be given a new honor mainly for this reason. There can be added work entailed, but you will be happy to do it. Show your talents and your ability to keep people working with you harmoniously. The path is open.

13—Unhappy times for those who have romantic plans. You can serve your emotional happiness best by staying away from anyone for whom you have great affection. The atmosphere is clouded with strife, suspicion, jealousy. Be sure to stay at home tonight. Be considerate.

14—An increase in salary is indicated. If this is not forthcoming, you will hear of a way to make extra money and find it very profitable. You have the ability to turn in excellent work and impress people who value your intelligence. Cause for happy celebration tonight.

15—Try to keep back any feelings of bitterness. You may have suspicions which are unfounded. Occasionally the insight of Pisces can be erroneous, and this is one of those days. Be affectionate as far as possible and avoid voicing any suspicions about friends. Retire early.

16—The day is active with swift decisions, vital matters settled beneficially. You may sign on the dotted line with firm assurance today. Buying major appliances, a new home, a car, or any luxury is favored. Make life more enjoyable and comfortable during these hours.

17—A favorable start for these hours may find you at your sociable best. However, there is a tendency to give away secrets, and by afternoon you may have reason to regret words you have spoken. Be very careful during lunch time. Do not let anyone irritate you.

18—The present influences portend good events for Pisces. You can expect romance to go well. A day when engagement may commence suddenly, you can be sure of the one in whom you are romantically interested. Beauty and love combine today to bring you the aura of romance most desirable.

19—Extremely favorable auspices for personal relationships. You can bask in the light of new affection today. Both family and friends will show their affection in certain terms. Accept the joy which comes by using the glowing, helpful personality which others love. Go out tonight.

20—You may have to be satisfied with steady, solemn work today. Progress can be made along these lines, but any adventurous enterprises may meet with defeat. A day for conventionality, domestic duties, good friendship. An evening which will be happy entertaining friends.

21—You may be very surprised at the adventures which befall you today. However, you will also be very happy, for unusual honors are coming your way. Relationships take on a new sparkle, and whether it is a matter of friendship or romance, you will find all going as you desire.

22—Unusual financial remuneration will come your way. Gifts, litigation, legacies are all favored. Keep busy, go after your own interests. A day when former generosity may be repaid. Friends can have good news which concerns your career future. Listen closely to all you hear.

23—Your creative talents are stressed today. Originality will attract others, and you may be given a new assignment which means more money in the future. Try to please those in a position to hlep you in such ways. Your willingness to do extra work will find high favor today.

24—Retreat on business matters. Postpone decisions to sign important papers. Even at the last moment change your mind and do everything to avoid commiting yourself. Turn to the family and follow their wishes rather than let personal impulse guide you today.

25—You may meet much opposition and argument today. Don't let your plans be changed by a person who nags you obstinately. Show your own ability to remain firm, even though it causes ill feeling. Follow a schedule, be careful of accidents from speed, and retire early.

26—Be very alert today, or you may find yourself involved in trouble from failure to react, observe, or respond. Avoid groups of people, and be brief with any guests or telephone calls. Temptation to write a letter may veil your desire to say something bitter. Best postpone writing.

27—Accomplishment will be pleasing. You may look forward to a pleasant evening at the home of a new friend. However, do not become too intimate with any such people. Your affection for the family will be repaid by the love they show you. Your personality is good tonight.

28—Your physical health can fall below par today, particularly if you rush around and undertake too many tasks. Do not accept new responsibility or be too helpful. Let others know they must shoulder their own work once in a while. Be firm but pleasant. Watch TV or read tonight.

29—Ask favors, for you can expect good fortune today. You may find hopes of long-standing coming true if you make a simple effort to fulfill them. Romantic dreams are also scheduled to have happy endings. You may become engaged tonight. Favorable for marriage, too.

30—Surprises will be of an unpleasant nature, and changes in plans which are forced upon you can be very vexing. Your ill temper may create new problems, and it is possible to alienate permanently one who is worthwhile. Try to control all emotional impulses to swift speech.

OCTOBER

1—With or without reason you might feel neglected and sorry for yourself. It won't do you any good to complain, or to find fault with your relatives or lifemate. Try to see the brighter side of life, particularly since this is the first day of the month. Turn on the music and dance.

2—Divert your attention from business and worries. Your nerves may be taxed and should be taken care of long before they are over-wrought. Your active mind requires more rest than the average person. There is such a thing as taking it easy. Music, drama, art and TV may soothe you.

3—Do not trust to hunches. They may play you false under the present influences. Resist the feeling of futility. It may cause you to think that nothing is worthwhile, or that success is impossible to achieve. Find comfort with the family or talk with an understanding friend.

4—The vibrations stimulate the extension of your efforts in anything that has to do with mental work. It is an excellent time to think and meditate, to study public reactions, and to analyze them for your own benefit. Work with determined persistence through the day. Have some fun tonight.

5—Prepare for an active day as the aspects charge your energies. However, it would be well for you to stay conservative in whatever you do. Be moderate, good-natured and friendly. This will prevent you from going off on an unwise tangent. Write letters and telephone your friends.

6—A dose of energy, combined with a pinch of pluck, aided by planetary aspects is the useful prescription for making this a productive day. Do not scatter your attentions over too wide a terrain. Think twice before you act once, and then act with courage and finality. Success is within reach today.

7—An unexpected and pleasing encounter with an interesting person may mark the beginning of a colorful friendship. Such an acquaintance often brings an increase of knowledge about human nature and introduces the source to a variety of unusual experiences. Wear something chic.

8—Today may be brimming with happiness for you. Entertain, or be entertained. Give the benefit of a doubt to the other person where possible. It is better to make a few mistakes by trusting than to be continually skeptical. An older person may give you advice that will help you decide wisely what you should do.

9—The sympathy of a close friend might bring you contentment and happiness. Relax and enjoy the restful company of someone who is strongly your supporter without any reservations or qualifications. If you have the time, write letters. Or take a walk through a seldom-visited locality.

10—Why seek romance afar when your own true love may cross the threshold of your home? Perhaps one of the family will bring about an introduction to a party who is destined to make your heart sing. If you are married, the aspects favor continued harmony. If you are eligible for a proposal, this may be the day.

11—Do not force issues but bear yourself with tact and diplomacy. There is no need risking a break when the storm probably will blow over soon. Watch out for a fire hazard, and keep out of the path of fast-moving traffic. Caution is necessary now.

12—It would be well for you to remain in an atmosphere where things are quiet; otherwise a restless feeling could urge you to start an unnecessary revolt. The mixed aspects could bring an illogical irritability. Don't contradict or oppose without sufficient reason.

13—Whether your major activity is at home, or selling, buying, manufacturing, working at a trade, or being busy at a profession, use your capabilities to the fullest. Under today's configurations, support your ambitions with practical effort and spontaneous enthusiasm. Get an early start.

14—This is one of those occasions when you can exercise your attractions so effectively. It might be easy for you to win in almost anything you attempt. In your home, too, you may find your efforts to obtain happiness warmly reciprocated. Keep in mind that happiness was born a twin.

15—A feeling of elation may mark your mood today. The influences favor you in friendships as well as in your work. You could go a long way in entrenching yourself in the good estimation of others. Fine cycle to buy labor-saving devices and to overcome hindering barriers.

16—This may be a day of extreme good fortune, bringing either a sudden, glamorous bit of diversion, or an unusual opportunity for a new business contact. Social matters will be both lively and interesting. Keep in step with the gleaming Stars.

17—The aspects activate now and have jurisdiction over your in-laws, journeys, ideals, religion, faith, psychic experiences, advanced education, thrilling adventures and prophetic dream messages. Think of your spiritual heritage, and contemplate the destiny of the human cavalcade.

18—If you are seeking a business partner, one with intense ambition, a scientific mind and a tremendous capacity for work, you may find that person today if you show the willingness to welcome that assistance. An old friend bringing you needed aid and counsel might be a worthy substitute, though.

19—Don't be taken in by a stranger who offers you something for nothing. There may be something unsound about it. Nor should you accept an alleged lucrative scheme that may be offered by a friend. Misinformation is rampant.

20—Do not try to apply pure logic to everything you do. Emotional reactions are much stronger than mental ones, and must be reckoned with. Do not take the chance of arousing resentment by being coldly reasoning. Light the human spark within yourself, and those you meet today.

21—Don't hold too tightly to your opinons when exchanges of ideas will help you make progress. Your fixed views are standing in your own way. Catch up on neglected obligations, but do nothing in a last-minute hurry. Pace your way calmly.

22—Business and pleasure are combining harmoniously under the current aspects. You may be able to untangle twisted viewpoints of acquaintances. Your tranquility can do much to ally the apprehensions of others. Excellent cycle for a public debut.

23—Your imagination may be working overtime but in the wrong way. It is putting shadows in your life instead of sunshine. The clouds you believe you see probably are not there at all. The influences induce camouflage, chicanery, subterfuge and illusion. Avoid the net of self-deception.

24—Things should move along smoothly, with an enjoyable day the prospect. Seek recreation, companionship and relaxation. Select the realistically interesting rather than the fantastic. Find time to purchase music records, or decide about lessons in music.

25—An emergency that challenges your best judgment may arise. Perhaps you will have to decide whether you will hold onto what you have, or let it go and start afresh. Do not risk your financial future on a sudden change, particularly while the aspects are confused.

26—It may not take much provocation to send your temper on a rampage at this particular time. Remember, others also get out of the wrong side of bed at times, so why not withhold your criticisms and complaints until you are in a better mood.

27—Do not err by being indulgent if you have young people under your charge. It is better to enforce a little discipline now than to find it necessary to be more severe later. The influences call for firm training. Watch your health today.

28—The current cycle helps you spread kindness and love in your home. This is a day suited better for a family gathering than for formal entertainment. Keep your domestic life quiet and pleasant. Also, a good time to buy attractive home furnishings and to mail out anniversary cards.

29—Do not allow the thwarting opposition to blind you to facts that you should face. If you let optimism run away with you today, you may find yourself on the negative side of the ledger. Resist large purchases. This day adverse to seeking special concessions or vouching for the integrity of an acquaintance.

30—If you are sure of yourself and know what you are talking about, assert yourself more forcefully. Faint heart never won a cause and hesitation has lost many golden opportunities. Get an early start while the aspects favor initiative. The early bird will catch the prize.

31—Do not offer suggestions to members of your family. Even though they know you wish to help, they may prefer to learn from their own mistakes. It may be difficult, but hold your tongue if you see someone headed toward error. Time and circumstances will prove the accuracy of your opinions.

NOVEMBER

1—Avoid wasting time on trivial tasks; keep busy on important assignments. Wait until you have actually accomplished what you have set out to do before making your intentions known. Accept conditions as you find them since any attempt to make changes could create confusion.

2—Be cautious when taking part in business negotiations since trickery and deception are likely. Do not worry about inconveniences you may have to endure until you actually experience them. Someone may actually throw obstacles in your way if you try to exert pressure.

3—Occupy your leisure time with a hobby or other activity that can act as a temporary release from mental strain and tension. Meet troublesome situations with the determination to straighten them out completely. Prevent discord in your household by keeping opinions about money to yourself.

4—Distinguish facts from assumptions by making a decision that involves your financial resources. Obeying an impulse to express yourself strongly may prove a detriment even though you feel justified in doing so. Spend the evening with the family.

5—You can make this a satisfying day if you do not press for achievements that are out of reach. Regardless of how boring you may consider your present work routine, do not switch to new activities now. Let others do and say as they wish if you expect to keep the atmosphere peaceful.

6—Do something from which others can derive pleasure as well as yourself. Regardless of how insignificant the task you undertake, watch out for careless errors. Utilize and appreciate what you already have instead of attempting to acquire new possessions.

7—Self-discipline and faith in your abilities should enable you to manage troublesome situations adequately. You may only cause yourself needless irritation if you focus your attention on past grievances. Be careful of what you do and say to avoid giving the wrong impression.

8—Your optimism and encouragement can do much to arouse a hopeful outlook in others. Refrain from giving opinions which are not requested, particularly about income or budget matters. Do not force an issue about a household matter regardless of what pressure or strain you may be under.

9—It may be expedient to give way to the views of others rather than insist on your own opinion. Avoid jumping to conclusions or depending on your first impressions when making a decision. Keep away from scenes of conflict since quarrels and antagonism can become contagious.

10—Show patience rather than irritation if the carelessness of an associate annoys you. Straighten out disputes as quickly as possible and do not prolong antagonism. Refrain from lending any of your cash or property unless you are certain it will be returned.

11—Work out money problems and make every effort to keep your accounts in order. Do not let a disturbing thought about your work take on exaggerated proportions. Formulate your own opinions rather than be swayed by the biased viewpoints of another.

12—Fulfill obligations for which you are responsible as quickly as possible rather than postpone them. Do not participate in any activity or project where there is the possibility of loss of harmony in your home. Do not let minor upsets which you encounter throughout the day throw you into an unhappy mood.

13—Arrange a complete work schedule for yourself, and adhere to it without variation. Remain persistent in your efforts even though the results are not as gratifying as you expect. Spend time on projects which will enable you to utilize your ingenuity and industriousness to advantage.

14—Separate important from trivial facts when making a vital decision about your job or career. Keep an accurate account of your expenses to save confusion and possible embarrassment. Refrain from entering a joint enterprise unless you are absolutely sure of the integrity of your associates.

15—You can benefit from delegating some of your responsibilities to a person you know is reliable. Start preparing well in advance for the things you want to accomplish at a later period. Remain calm even though some of your present plans may be suddenly disrupted.

16—Take extra precaution when attempting something with which you are unfamiliar. Make arrangements to reciprocate for favors which have been shown you in the past. Adhere firmly to your own opinions, and do not compromise with anyone who is intent on taking advantage of you.

17—Your generosity and careful use of your cash can have a beneficial effect. Give close attention to each detail of your work to avoid having to repeat your efforts. Let events develop at their normal speed and do not try to accomplish a multitude of things at once.

18—Look for new duties that are different from your customary routine for a stimulating change of pace. Make a strong attempt to get away from confining conditions and limitations that have been holding you back. You can pave the way for increased income by tackling a project designed to enhance personal advancement.

19—Attend to each problem as it arises instead of worrying about the future. Give special attention to needed household repairs before they pile up beyond reason. Hasty action may place your career in jeopardy so play safe, and remain silently in the background.

20—Complete unfinished jobs in their proper order to remove the burden of worry. Spend time on recreational activities that will enable you to make new friends. Stick to a cautious and exacting pace even though rapid action may prove advantageous.

21—The best way to achieve harmony now may be to remain silent and away from scenes of discord. Yielding to the pressure of emotional tension may result in unanticipated difficulty. A realistic attitude is needed so leave emotions out of everything you undertake.

22—Concentrate on the enjoyable times you may experience rather than focus your thoughts on points of difference. Give heed to your own problems rather than be concerned with responsibilities that are not yours. Any deviation you make from a carefully scheduled work program could easily develop into wasted time.

23—Quickly attune yourself to the tempo of things so that you can keep aware of what is going on around you. You should be able to make satisfactory headway provided you devote your complete attention to details. Refrain from discussing personal problems since doing so might arouse adverse criticism.

24—You may have to muster all your patience to overcome minor annoyances. Make your schedule of activities flexible enough to cope with difficulties that may arise. Do not deviate from practices you know to be sound and prudent while handling problems which confront you.

25—You can ease the burden of routine work duties through effective planning. Do what you can to solve difficulties through your own efforts rather than call for assistance. Prudent planning and action taken now can help pave the way for future job and financial security.

26—Be careful that the desire to buy an expensive article does not place you under too heavy an obligation. Refrain from making a business agreement until you are completely satisfied on all points. Avoid attempting anything with which you are unfamiliar unless you receive expert guidance.

27—Take part in a diversion which will enable you to find release from usual restraining influences. Do not let criticism or discouraging remarks of another deter you from doing what you think is correct. Demonstrate your hospitality or otherwise show your gratitude to someone who has been helpful.

28—Your personality and enthusiasm should be a big help in attaining the things you want. Resist any temptation to dig into savings without good reason. Accept a temporary reverse gracefully since resentment may only lead to further trouble.

29—Although the progress you make now may seem slow to you, your headway should be noticed by others. A tactful suggestion to another should prove more effective than force in getting what you want. Do not let your attention be diverted to any activity that would lull you into unproductive idleness.

30—Unguarded comments that you make may let you in for more difficulty than you anticipate. Despite generous impulses, devote time to your own personal needs rather than cater to the whims of another.

DECEMBER

1—Do something different from your routine work. Tackle a new assignment, read a new book, or take a short pleasure trip. You should find that a change from your usual activities will relieve a feeling of boredom and refresh your viewpoints.

2—Impatience and inexperience could prove detrimental in a business matter. Refrain from making any statements that cannot be immediately verified, and do not be impulsive in your actions. Seek competent advice and guidance from others.

3—Work on the development of mental aptitudes and creative skills which you feel you can put to advantage. It may be possible to augment your income through developing a latent talent. Have confidence in your own abilities and improve them whenever you can.

4—Do the things you have been wanting to, whether it is painting your room, repairing an appliance, or just relaxing. Practically anything you attempt should turn out to your satisfaction. Decisions can be made rapidly and your plans should materialize favorably.

5—Since problems about money are likely to be in evidence, you may find that the best thing to do is remain silent and away from scenes of discord. Do not take part in any activity that involves financial risk.

6—Acquiring a new possession should do much to put and keep you in a cheerful frame of mind. Buy something which you have wanted to own, even though you may place a slight strain on your budget. However, do not waste money in an effort to compete with the lavish display of someone else.

7—Examine your problems from a realistic viewpoint. Face the facts as they are and not through rose-colored glasses. Regardless of disappointments you may experience, do not give in to your doubts or let others discourage you.

8—Avoid dealing with people whom you do not know too well and refrain from visiting places unfamiliar to you. Since deception is likely to predominate the scene, you could easily be duped or placed in an embarrassing predicament. Offset difficulty by mingling only among those whom you know to be reliable.

9—Do not try to break away from existing conditions, regardless of how annoyed you may feel. Though you may have been restricted and hampered by pressure from others, take things in your stride. An open attempt to overcome present limitations might place you in a situation that could prove even more difficult.

10—If traveling or otherwise away from familiar scenes, be careful. The element of risk is strong. Patience and adherence to well-made plans are needed to protect yourself against entanglements and confusion.

11—Since you may encounter hasty or selfish action from others, depend on yourself to get things done. Do not delegate a responsibility to another, regardless of friendship. Touchiness and irritation can be so ripe that it would be best to expect little in the way of cooperation from others.

12—Social gatherings, entertainment and parties are favored. This is a good time to relax in the quietude of your home, as well as to take part in more active forms of diversion. Do something to make new friends.

13—Your personal popularity can be on the upswing as a result of social contacts and activities. Plan a get-together among friends whose company you find stimulating. Keep those around you in a happy mood by sponsoring activities that promote good will.

14—Avoid a display of temperament despite the fact that you may be irked at the actions of a member of your household. Keep things running on an even keel by controlling restlessness. Conservative action would be the best policy to follow.

15—Wade right in and get monotonous work assignments done before you have a chance to become bored. Rather than let a tedious task get you down, attend to it without delay. However, refrain from increasing your present expenses or taking on additional obligations.

16—Be particularly alert to prevent careless errors in your work. A mistake, even though inadvertently made, could make you a target for bitter criticism. Proceed slowly and place emphasis on accuracy, regardless of what pressure others bring on you.

17—Look for a business or job opportunity rather than wait for it to come to you. Arrangements which you make concerning your livelihood can have a favorable and lasting effect. Regardless of what you do however, make full use of your capabilities.

18—This is an unfavorable period to experiment with new methods and ideas. Instead, stick to procedures which you are sure will work out satisfactorily. Do not take chances, particularly where your income or future security is concerned.

19—You should be able to find ample encouragement and inspiration through being with others. Outings and other forms of social activities are highlighted. Join a group of friends and participate in diversions which you find enjoyable.

20—Constant alertness is needed to offset possible trouble and reverses resulting from swiftly-moving events. Even though you may think that things are transpiring at too rapid a pace for you, do not let up in your efforts. Take a firm stand in matters which involve your personal desires, and do not let anyone or any situation deter you from achieving your goals.

21—This can be a good day to clear up the loose ends and miscellaneous details of work that might interfere with more important things you might want to do. Before taking on new endeavors, however, make sure that you are up-to-date with your current responsibilities.

22—Matters pertaining to love and friendship are particularly favored. You should be able to find pleasure in all activities, regardless of where you are. However, avoid rushing, and take sufficient time to achieve the results desired.

23—Use extra caution while driving or handling mechanical equipment. Seek competent assistance if you encounter trouble rather than try to handle everything yourself. By playing a lone hand you can do an injustice to yourself, as well as to anyone who is affected by the decisions or actions you take.

24—Temporarily ignore financial and business worries. Instead, enjoy the hobbies, recreation or companionship that is available to you. Take a short pleasure trip away from familiar scenes and activities if possible. Liven things up rather than allow yourself to become bored by dull conversation or a monotonous routine.

25—Let others do the talking and planning today and you will remain on the safe side of any situation that may arise. Relax a bit during this beautiful holiday season!

26—Whether visiting or playing host in your own home, you should experience a cheerful and entertaining time. Plan to do something that is different from your routine activities to keep you from getting into that mental rut.

27—Attend to business and property matters. This is an excellent day to lay the groundwork for future projects and intended changes. Organize your plans so that you will be able to take advantage of favorable situations as they arise.

28—Although on the surface, conditions may appear to be normal, actually they may be enmeshed in a strong undercurrent. Give special attention to matters that involve emotions and personal feelings. Heed suggestions for your benefit, and do not ignore them merely because they fail to coincide with your own opinions.

29—Have plans well prepared and organized so that you will not be beset by last-minute confusion. Also, by doing this you will be able to remove snags before they occur and minimize unanticipated difficulties. Give attention to matters associated with your job promotion and the advancement that is possible for you.

30—Do not let your emotions interfere with matters which require practical consideration. Decide each issue on its merits alone and do not let prejudiced feelings sway your decisions. It would be undesirable to act on unfounded information at this time.

31—You could win an emotional point today, and you may be pleased about the return of an old friend. Toast the New Year in with good resolutions. And have faith in a happy destiny.

A TO Z DREAMS AND LUCKY NUMBERS

Refer to page 475, at the end of this section, for a guide to interpreting your dreams and using your lucky numbers.

A

ABACUS. This ancient device for counting and figuring is, when seen in a dream, a portent of financial improvement through careful attention to details and thorough, painstaking work. Seen in operation as a child's toy, it foretells success in any business deal that may be pending. 291

ABALONE. To eat this shell fish in a dream foretells an unusual experience. Whether this will be pleasant or otherwise will depend on whether or not the abalone has a pleasing flavor. A dream of the highly colored, iridescent inside of an abalone shell is a warning to be on your guard against jealous acquaintances. 315

ABANDONMENT. There are three ways of interpreting this dream, since it may have three aspects—active, as when you abandon someone; passive, as when someone abandons you; and objective, as when you see or hear of someone else's abandonment. 601

Active. To dream of abandoning evil companions, or of ceasing from a nefarious enterprise, predicts an increase in income. If in your dream you abandon your wife, husband, children or sweetheart, it portends trouble of a serious nature. 800

Passive. If you dream of being abandoned by someone for whom you have friendship or affection, it is a prophecy of illness in your circle of near relatives. 368

Objective. If in a dream you are a witness to the abandonment of a person of either sex or any age, you will be the recipient of news that will have a profound influence on your life. 900

ABASEMENT. To dream of being abased or humiliated warns one against boasting of his physical or mental prowess. One who is shamed by a superior will profit by the dream if it stimulates him to rise above his shortcomings, but if the abasement comes from a child or a person of low degree, the import of the dream is distinctly unfavorable. 343

ABBESS. If you see an abbess in your dream, the future will be bright, particularly so if she smiles at you. 095

ABBEY. In the sunlight, an abbey is propitious for the dreamer if seen from the outside. In gloom or at night it portends sadness and failure. 900

ABBOT. Long days of suffering are predicted if you dream of meeting and talking with the abbot of a monastery. If he speaks with a pronounced foreign accent, the augury is of having to be continually on the move. If his voice is high-pitched and he is an excitable person, you will have to make amends for a wrong you have done. 755

ABBREVIATION. To dream of seeing words abbreviated or hearing a person speak in abbreviations—such as *N. Y.* for New York, *Mass.* for Massachusetts, *mon.* for money, etc.—is to look forward to the loss of friends or income. 383

ABDICATION. Kings or queens abdicating portend achievement in social fields. 314

ABDOMEN. This is a fortunate omen in a dream when seen by itself; it predicts prosperity in every case where the abdomen is part of a living person. A pain in the abdomen foretells a long period of good health. 502

ABDUCTION. If you have a dream of being abducted, you will succeed in any new enterprise, whether business or social. 283

ABHORRENCE. To dream of feeling abhorrence or loathing of persons or things is a presage of danger from an unknown source. 958

ABILITY. A dream in which your own ability is recognized, even by yourself, points toward some achievement that will give you great happiness. If the dream is one in which you are impressed by the ability of someone else, you will receive a small sum of money. 858

ABJECTNESS. If you dream of a person who approaches you abjectly and you receive him or her with cordiality, you will be called upon to fill a new position at a much higher rate of remuneration. 017

ABLUTION. (See Bath.) 394

ABNORMALITY. To see in a dream a person or thing that is not normal—such as a man who walks on all fours, a cat with horns, a house built upside down, or the like—is an omen of a pleasant outcome to something that has worried you. 122

ABODE. (See Home.) 116

ABOMINATION. Beware of those who seek to do you ill if you dream of abominating anyone. 242

ABORIGINES. A dream of the primitive inhabitants of any country—Indians, Eskimos, African Negroes, etc.—points toward your being able to pay your debts. 133

ABORTION. You will not succeed in the project in which you are most interested at the time of this dream, whether it concerns love or money. 735

ABRASION. The scraping of skin off a finger or other part of the body; or the scratching of leather from a new pair of shoes or handbag predicts a succession of petty irritations. 610

ABROAD. Going abroad is a dream of excellent import. If you leave your own country on a ship or a train, the augury is of a trip in the near future with delightful companions. 053

ABSALOM. A dream of this Biblical character or of anyone who, like him, is caught by the hair in the limb of a tree, warns of approaching danger that may be avoided only by the greatest care. 612

ABSCESS. Do not engage in any enterprise involving real estate or securities if you dream of having an abscess. If someone else has it, such an affliction is an indication of a change of scene. 087

ABSENCE. If in a dream you notice particularly the absence of a friend or one of the family who would normally be present, you are likely to receive disquieting news from someone a long distance away. 553

ABSINTHE. Drinking this potent and demoralizing liqueur in a dream is a sure sign that someone you have trusted is seeking to ruin your reputation. 912

ABSOLUTION. Those who dream of forgiveness from a friend or absolution from a priest may look forward to a long period of peace of mind. 174

ABSTINENCE. Consciously abstaining from drink or anything else tempting in a dream is an augury of an accident. Abstaining through necessity or deprivation is a happy omen, particularly for women with child. 459

ABSURDITY. If what happens in a dream is contrary to all reason, it foretells happiness in love affairs, particularly if there is a humorous twist to the dream. 874

ABUNDANCE. To dream of having a great plenty of one or more things is a warning to conserve your resources against lean times to come. 334

ABUSE. Strangely enough, if you dream of abusing someone, there will be an improvement shortly in your financial condition. If someone abuses you, you will have an illness. 239

ABYSS. This is a bad dream for those engaged in either domestic service or farm work. If one falls into the abyss, he or she should wait at least a month before making a change in occupation. 748

ACACIA. The acacia tree in bloom will make any dream turn out lucky, or it will counteract any harmful omens if they are present. For lovers to dream of sitting under such a tree is an augury of marriage and a happy home.

ACADEMY. This institution of learning portends new experiences and new friends, but it warns against speculation.

ACCELERATOR. Increasing the speed of an automobile by pressing on the accelerator is an indication that by continued and sustained effort you will achieve the goal you have set for yourself. If in your dream you cannot remove your foot from the accelerator, you should regard it as a warning against vices such as gambling and drinking.

ACCEPTANCE. When a person hands you money or something else of value in a dream, your acceptance is an omen of success in love or business. Your refusal means exactly the opposite. If you accept counterfeit money, you are in grave danger.

ACCIDENT. Take warning from an accident dream, and if possible avoid the thing that figures in the accident. Thus, if you dream of an automobile crash, do not ride in a car for twenty-four hours, and be additionally careful in crossing the streets. Shun airplanes, trains or horse-drawn vehicles if the dream accident pertains to them. Avoid sharp knives or pointed instruments if you dream of cutting yourself, and if you dream of falling, watch your step. 845

ACCIDENT INSURANCE. It is an augury of a long and successful career to dream of taking out accident insurance. If the dream is of being paid an indemnity, you will probably have a setback of some kind. 695

ACCOMPANIMENT. Whether you are a musician or not, you will be fortunate in matters pertaining to the heart if you dream of playing an accompaniment to someone's singing. 590

ACCORDION. This instrument heard in a dream is a presage of sadness, which, although inevitable, will not be bitter. For one to dream that he or she is playing an accordion points toward a satisfactory and lasting love affair, but if the instrument is out of tune, there will be many trials to bear. 056

ACCOUCHEMENT. The delivery of a child, male or female, is a propitious dream for anyone. If a man or woman dreams of being a witness to the event, it foretells a long period of prosperity. A married woman who dreams of bearing a child may look forward to much happiness; but to an unmarried woman the dream is a portent of woe that should not be disregarded. 261

ACCOUNTS. A woman who dreams of keeping accounts, household or otherwise, will suffer through the indifference of her lover, but a happy outcome may be expected if her accounts appear to be straight. Men or women who dream of being bookkeepers and of having difficulty in calculating and balancing will go through a period of strenuous difficulty. To dream of correctly balancing accounts at the first trial points definitely to a profitable business deal. 348

ACCOUNTANT. For a young woman to dream that she loves an accountant means that she will not be happy in her married life, but that she will be well provided for. 462

ACCUSATION. Being accused of wrongdoing warns you to be on guard against those who will flatter you in order to obtain favors. 812

ACE. This denomination of playing cards signifies four different things, according to the suit, and in each case the portent represents the ultimate degree. An ace of hearts foretells success in love; of diamonds, good fortune in money matters; of spades, unrewarded labor; and of clubs, disgrace. 870

ACETIC ACID. The sour, vinegar-like odor of this acid portends a disagreeable experience with someone of the opposite sex. 552

ACETYLENE. To dream of seeing the intensely white light of an acetylene gas flame is a prophecy of a complete change of scene that will contribute to your contentment. If you smell the foul odor of this gas, you will be hounded by creditors. 693

ACHE. (See also Abdomen.) A dream of a headache warns you against confiding in anyone regarding your business plans. If your legs or arms ache, it is a sign that you will have this effect—a night's repost; in other words, contentment. 710

ACID. A dream of acids is usually unfavorable. To dream of taking an acid internally is a forerunner of great difficulty on account of debts. If acid is thrown in your face, you will have unsatisfactory dealings with a foreigner through an interpreter. 238

ACNE. (See Pimples.) 382

ACORNS. Seen growing or lying on the ground or in baskets, acorns may be regarded as the harbinger of the successful outcome of your plans for the future. 479

ACQUAINTANCE. To dream of making a new acquaintance or of seeing an old one whom you have not met in a long time is a sign of receiving money that is owed you. 003

ACQUITTAL. Practice relaxation with all the power at your command if you dream of being acquitted by a jury, for you are to undergo a trying experience, which will lose most of its danger if it is met in a calm spirit. 533

ADAM AND EVE. Anyone who dreams of Adam and Eve in the Garden of Eden is headed for troubles of various kinds, including operations and family difficulties. 604

ADAPTABILITY. You may rest easy regarding your financial future if you dream of adapting yourself to unusual or abnormal conditions. 060

ADDER. Poisonous snakes portend trouble. This variety indicates a family row because you are paying attentions to one who is beneath you. To kill an adder is to look forward to a solution to the problem involved. 559

ADDITION. (See also Accounts.) If you dream of adding figures, you will run into difficulties of a personal nature. If you add them correctly, you will become master of the situation. 949

ADENOIDS. A dream of having your adenoids removed points toward success in community work. 841

ADJOURNMENT. If in a dream you are present when a meeting comes to an end, you should be especially careful to avoid eating anything that is difficult to digest. 839

ADJUSTMENT. The adjustment of any kind of machinery in a dream is a sign of increasing business success. 092

ADMIRAL. This highest naval rank points to your making a success of your career, both socially and in business. A maiden who dreams of marrying an admiral will be wooed by a wealthy widower. 760

ADMIRATION. A man who dreams of receiving admiration is in danger of illness and degradation. A woman having this dream is likely to be criticized for her vanity. Honest admiration for someone else is a sign that points toward prosperity. 161

ADOBE. Houses made of this sun-dried brick are a favorable omen for seamstresses. 148

ADOPTION. If a man or woman dreams of adopting a child, there will be a year during which speculation will bring rich returns. 182

ADORATION. Religious or otherwise, this is a dream that presages quiet contentment and a useful future. 529

ADORNMENT. Women who dream of adorning themselves for the purpose of making an impression on men will be fortunate in their love affairs. 874

ADRIFT. Being adrift in an open boat without any means of propulsion, such as sails, oars or motor, presages a situation in which you will not know what to do. 837

ADULATION. (See Admiration.) 040

ADULTERY. A dream about adultery is an omen of distress and worry. Committing it in a dream portends disputes with family, friends and business associates. To be tempted and to resist is a sign of many setbacks but eventual triumph over those who seek to defame you. If one dreams of seeking an adulterous union, he or she should go slow in making new friends. 855

ADVANCEMENT. This is really a dream of improvement, and whether it concerns you or someone else, it has a fortunate significance. 097

ADVENTURE. The nature of the adventure will govern the prediction of this dream. It will follow closely according to whether it is distressing, exciting, humorous or shameful. It is always well to exercise your best judgment and care after such a dream. 205

ADVENTURER. Maidens may expect passionate wooing from a handsome, dashing man if they dream of meeting an adventurer, but they should exercise caution in their dealings with him. 051

ADVENTURESS. A woman of this type augurs no good to the man who dreams of her. He will almost certainly have to prove himself in a situation of great delicacy. 186

ADVERSARY. If you dream of making your adversary your friend, you will have an opportunity for business advancement that you should embrace. 573

ADVERSITY. Undergoing adversity in a dream means that you will eventually overcome the difficulties that beset you. 415

ADVERTISEMENTS. Reading advertisements in a dream is a sign of prosperity if they are accompanied by pictures, but if not, the portent is of hard work and a meager living. 879

ADVICE. You will have a falling out with your best friend if you dream of giving him or her advice. To dream of being advised points toward happiness in love. 173

AEOLIAN HARP. To dream of the sound of wind blowing through strings on an instrument, or through wires indicates deep emotional attachment. 801

AERIAL. If in a dream you string an aerial for a radio, you will succeed in a plan that you had believed was next to impossible. 711

AFFECTION. Signs of affection in a dream are propitious if they are within the bounds of decency and restraint. They foretell a happy outcome to love affairs and congenial married life. 691

AFFLICTION. To dream of suffering from a physical affliction is an augury of good health. 900

AFFLUENCE. This dream points to an increase in income that will go far toward solving your immediate problems. Maidens having this dream may look forward to making a good marriage. 238

AFFRONT. The prediction of a dream of receiving an affront is that you will be embarrassed by criticism of the clothes you are wearing. 989

AFRICA. Being in Africa in a dream portends being called for jury duty. If you are in the Sahara Desert, you will be called for civil suits; otherwise, for criminal cases. 666

AFTERNOON. A dream of events that happen in the afternoon is likely to have a better portent that those happening in the morning or at night. 992

AGATE. To dream of wearing an agate in a ring or other jewelry is a sign that you will be called upon to arbitrate a disagreement between two of your friends. Beware of butting in where quarrels between men and their wives are concerned. 199

AGE. It is bad luck to dream of guessing a woman's age. You are likely to get into hot water with a person of the opposite sex. 635

AGENT. A woman who dreams of dealing with an agent in negotiating for a husband is in danger of being deceived. 231

AGNOSTIC. Any implication of religious disbelief in a dream is a sign of a degrading experience with regard to the opposite sex. 706

AGONY. If you dream of suffering agony, you will be likely to meet an old friend who will be in want. To see anyone else suffering is a portent of a change of scene. The agony of an animal portends grief. 554

AGUE. This kind of sickness experienced in a dream predicts a new lover for maidens, a child for a married woman, or a new business for a man. 257

AIR BRAKE. The sound of escaping air as brakes are applied on a railroad train or automobile is a presage of woe, foretelling the miscarriage of plans. 489

AIREDALE. Dogs are lucky dreams, particularly if they appear friendly or if their bark is not menacing, and an airedale in a dream points toward a happy home life with simple pleasures. 056

AIR-GUN. Shooting an air-gun at a target predicts failure through lack of concentration. Shooting at a person is a sign that you should guard your tongue against idle gossip. 472

AIRPLANE. If you dream of piloting an airplane, you will achieve something of outstanding merit in the arts or in your business. If a passenger, you will have your income increased. If you fall from or bail out of an airplane you may expect several months of hard luck. 621

AIRSHIP. Traveling by an airship, or dirigible balloon, is a portent of a long period of indecision regarding your love affairs. 511

AISLE. An aisle in a church, theatre or other public place is a sign that you will have a decision of great importance to make. 297

ALABASTER. To see a statue or other article fashioned from alabaster, or to compare with alabaster anything seen in a dream, is to look forward to ill health or family disputes. 003

A LA CARTE. If you dream of ordering a meal a la carte in a restaurant, you will suffer a disappointment of some kind. 806

ALARM. A dream of turning in a fire-alarm portends more money in your pocketbook. To make an alarming statement in a dream is an omen of having to apologize to someone of inferior rank. To dream of hearing a clock ring an alarm predicts a profitably exciting time. 173

ALBATROSS. Seen from the deck of a ship, an albatross indicates success to those who are interested in any of the artistic pursuits. 717

ALBUM. To look at a photograph album in a dream, whether of portraits or snapshots, is a forerunner of a minor accident. 650

ALCOHOL. Dreamed of merely as a chemical, used in the arts or sciences, this is entirely favorable. As a beverage, it portends success if taken in moderation—otherwise failure. 966

ALDER. An alder tree seen in a dream is an omen of happiness for those with high ideals. 261

ALE. Drinking ale in a dream is a forerunner to a hearty enjoyment of simple pleasures. 526

ALGEBRA. Problems in algebra or formulas seen in a dream point to a misunderstanding with regard to a bill. 837

ALIBI. Any kind of an alibi given in a dream is an omen of marital discord. If you are puzzled by someone else's alibi, you will be singled out for some kind of honor. 942

ALIEN. If you dream of being friendly to an alien, or foreigner, you will find a sum of money that will lead to a succession of worth-while business deals. 309

ALIMONY. This is usually a dream of either receiving or paying alimony. Of receiving portends a visit to a doctor. Of paying is a sign of careless pleasures. 612

ALLEGORY. A dream in which the people and scenes appear to have a symbolical meaning predicts a succession of surprises, some of which will be disappointing. 028

ALLEY. Going through a dark alley in a dream is a presage of the loss of a lover. To be chased by an evil person augurs disgrace. To come to the end of a blind alley predicts the failure of a well-considered plan. 252

ALLEY CAT. The yowls and moans of alley cats heard in a dream are a prediction that you will become associated with obnoxious people. To dream of missiles being thrown at them is a sign that you will find a way out of the difficulty. 660

ALLIANCE. To dream of making an alliance by marriage or otherwise with rich and influential people foretells a disagreement with someone you love. 393

ALLIGATOR. Being attacked by an alligator in a dream is a sign that you will be laughed at by people who do not like you. Seeing alligators in a zoo is a prediction of a short journey. 981

ALLOWANCE. To receive an allowance in a dream from a husband or parent portends happiness. If a man dreams of receiving an allowance from his wife or some other woman, he will quarrel with his friends and acquaintances. 120

ALLOY. A dream of combining metals in a crucible points toward a happy marriage and healthy children. 547

ALLSPICE. The flavor of allspice, or its use in a dream, points to romance that will bring both interest and happiness. 071

ALLUREMENT. If, as you dream, you are definitely conscious of the allurement of one of the opposite sex, you are likely to receive invitations that will advance you socially. 655

ALMANAC. Women who dream of consulting the almanac will be forced to break important engagements, although this may be to their advantage. A man who has this dream will be fortunate in a business transaction. 119

ALMOND. To dream of lying under an almond tree that is in bloom is to look forward with certainty to happiness in the married state. Eating almonds predicts a journey into pleasant places. 742

ALMS. To give alms cheerfully in a dream is a good sign, but if they are given with any regret, the augury is of hard luck for a long time to come. To dream of soliciting alms is a sign that there will be an upturn in your business affairs. 230

ALMSHOUSE. This is a dream of opposites, wherein you may expect a comfortable and honorable living whether it is you or someone else who becomes an inmate. 059

ALPACA. This South American animal whose wool is woven into cloth is an omen of discontent with your surroundings. 589

ALPEN-STOCK. If you dream of climbing mountains with an alpen-stock, you are likely to suffer a setback in family or love affairs. To break an alpen-stock is a sign that you will lose money in a business transaction. 604

ALPHABET. The letters of the alphabet, either in their regular order or jumbled, point toward success as a writer, an actor, or a librarian. 055

ALTAR. As long as this dream is one in which reverence is shown, it is propitious. To dream of praying before an altar is an omen of release from pressing worries. 449

ALTAR-BOY. Performing his duties in the chancel of a church, he is a sign of good news from an unexpected source. 194

ALTERCATION. (See also Fight, Quarrel.) For a maiden to dream of having an altercation with her lover is a sign of a successful marriage. 322

ALTITUDE. To dream of looking down from a high altitude predicts danger of making a serious mistake. Shortness of breath on account of high altitude foretells an entanglement with someone who is not your equal. 752

ALUM. Tasting this tongue-puckering substance predicts a very puzzling experience to those who are in love. If the alum becomes sweet and agreeable to the taste, the outcome will be satisfactory. 382

ALUMINUM. Kitchen utensils made of this metal augur happiness to lovers if they are bright and shiny, but frustration if they are dull. 469

AMATEUR. A dream of doing things in the arts—painting, photography, literature, dramatics, and the like—merely for the love of it portends a handsome reward for something you have done for an older person. 490

AMAZEMENT. You may be sure of an exciting experience of some kind if you dream of being amazed at a sight you see or news you hear. 261

AMBASSADOR. Treachery from one you have heretofore trusted is the portent of a dream of seeing or talking with an ambassador from a foreign country. If you dream of being an ambassador from your own country to another, you should go very slowly in making any sort of an investment. 414

AMBITION. This is a favorable dream to those who are doing office work. It predicts a rise in salary and new responsibilities. 604

AMBROSIA. Dreaming of this food of the gods, or of food called by this poetic name, is a sign of misfortune through carelessness. 014

AMBULANCE. This is distinctly a warning dream. If you see one, it merely warns against being indiscreet where persons of the opposite sex are concerned. To dream of being placed in one warns against carelessness in speech or behavior. 075

AMBUSH. There is a pleasant surprise in store for you if you dream of hiding in ambush. 021

AMERICA. It is an augury of happiness in family life to dream that you have come to live in any part of America. 574

AMETHYST. This semi-precious gem prognosticates sadness through the loss of a relative or a friend. 905

AMIABILITY. You will be loved and admired by your acquaintances if you have a dream in which you display your own amiability. If others are amiable toward you, you must take care to guard your speech and actions. 917

AMMONIA. Those who are inclined to drink more than is good for them should be warned of excess by a dream in which they smell the fumes of ammonia. To dream of using it in the household is a sign of good health. 914

AMMUNITION. If you dream of buying ammunition for a hunting trip, you are likely to be called to account for something you have failed to do. To lose a quantity of ammunition is a sign that you will have a bitter quarrel with a person of the opposite sex. 959

AMOUR. Legitimate love dreams augur happiness in love, but to dream of illicit amours is a sign that you will have difficulties with a wife, husband or landlord. 269

AMPUTATION. Anyone who is dependent on legs or arms for a living may look forward with certainty to an increase of income after a dream of having one of these members cut off. 062

AMUSEMENT. (See also Games, Theatre, Movies.) If in indulging in any kind of amusement in a dream, you are conscious of enjoying yourself, the future will be a bright one. If the amusement bores you, you are almost certain to have trouble. 135

ANACONDA. This huge, dangerous snake, is a harmful augury. To dream of being attacked by one indicates a struggle to hold your position. 715

ANEMIA. To be told by a doctor that you are anemic is to look forward to a period of good health. 300

ANESTHESIA. (See Chloroform, Ether, Novocaine.) To take an anesthetic against your will points toward a painful sickness. Willingly to undergo anesthesia is a prophecy of better health. 235

ANAGRAMS. A dream of playing anagrams predicts a pleasant solution of difficulties concerned with love. 432

ANARCHIST. A man or woman who dreams of being an anarchist must beware of giving way to impulses. They should consider the possible results of any hasty actions. 339

ANCESTORS. To dream of ancestors other than parents denotes devotion to ideals that carry on tradition. You will be respected in the community where you live. 806

ANCHOR. Seen on shore, an anchor predicts a successfully completed task. On a ship, it points to an opportunity that is coming your way. To dream of being on shipboard when the anchor is dragging predicts danger from an unknown source. If you see anchors used as decorations on uniforms, clothing, or elsewhere, you have an interesting experience in store for you. 497

ANCHOR. To dream of anchoring a boat in a harbor presages a long period of freedom from anxiety. If the dream is of raising an anchor, the portent is of adventure with a spice of danger. If you dream of being on a boat that is dragging its anchor, you will have many family difficulties. 593

ANCHOVY. This small fish, alive, canned or in paste form augurs a reward for conscientious effort. 215

ANCIENTS. A dream of anything old and reputable is generally a sign that you will have the respect of those with whom you are associated. 459

ANDIRONS. In use in a fireplace holding burning logs or a grate, holding live coals, a pair of andirons is a portent of promotion to a higher position in business or the social world. Seen in a cold, empty fireplace, they are an omen of disappointment or chagrin. 509

ANECDOTE. You may look forward to attending a happy celebration if you dream of telling or hearing an anecdote. 840

ANGELS. A dream of seeing angels is none too good an omen. It betokens illness—either yours or a friend's—but it will not be fatal. 210

ANGER. The portent of a display of anger in a dream is either good or bad—good if the anger is roused by injustice; bad if merely an exhibition of temper. To dream of striking a person in anger predicts shame through an amour. 933

ANGLE-WORM. This is an omen of good luck for those who write for a living or for anyone who earns his or her daily bread in musical, dramatic or other artistic work. 981

ANGLER. (See Fisherman, Fishing.) 079

ANGORA CAT. (See Cats, Kittens.) You will be deceived or double-crossed if you dream of a friendly Angora cat, but if the cat shows signs of unfriendliness, you may expect that someone will show an honest dislike of you. 444

ANIMOSITY. For anyone to show animosity toward you in a dream means that you are likely to be surprised at someone's lack of moral sense. 137

ANKLE. To sprain an ankle in a dream, or otherwise injure it, is an omen of loss of money. For a man to dream of women's ankles predicts a love affair. 123

ANNIVERSARY. Birthday celebrations, wedding anniversaries, and similar occasions are omens of happy family reunions. 468

ANNOUNCEMENT. Usually it is a good sign to dream of receiving an announcement of a social or business event. But such an announcement portends evil if the card or letter is edged with black. 344

ANNOYANCE. A fly or mosquito buzzing around your head—a radio playing too loud—a doorbell that rings just as you are about to go to sleep. Such an annoyance experienced in a dream is a portent of a series of trials that you can overcome if you will. 502

ANNULMENT. Anyone who dreams of the annulment of his or her marriage is sure to find contentment. 808

ANT. These may be dreamed of either as examples of industry or as pests. If you dream of watching their industrious and intelligent habits, you are likely to be taken to task by someone for not performing your duty. If they are pests, overrunning your living quarters or getting in your clothing, the omen is that you will be the victim of many petty irritations, from which you can escape only by radical measures. 909

ANTARCTIC. To dream of going into the South Polar regions for any or no cause is a sign that the pet project that you have had in mind for a long time will not be successful. 508

ANTELOPE. A sudden increase in income will be received by those who dream of seeing one or more antelopes in the out-of-doors. To see them in a zoo indicates a disappointment. To shoot one is a sign that someone will persecute you. 844

ANTHEM. All music in dreams is a favorable sign if it is in tune and pleasing to the ear. Hearing an anthem sung is a particularly favorable augury, especially to those with weak hearts. 155

ANTICS. Seeing children, their elders, or paid performers doing antics is a dream that points toward a change of scene that will be accompanied by great financial profit. 925

ANTIDOTE. (See also Poison.) If you dream of taking an antidote for poison, you will find yourself in a very embarrassing situation through your own lack of foresight. 231

ANTIQUES. Seen in a shop, old pieces of furniture, clocks, brass ware, china and other antiques are signs of happiness in home life. 497

ANTISEPTIC. The use of an antiseptic in a dream portends a motor accident. 039

ANVIL. Any appearance of an anvil in a dream is a forerunner of good luck in money matters to those who work with their hands. A blacksmith hammering on an anvil is a prediction of a legacy that is unexpected. 866

ANXIETY. A feeling of anxiety in a dream, even if the cause is not apparent, portends loneliness. 108

APARTMENT. A dream of living in an apartment that is too small is a sign that you will quarrel with your immediate relatives. A large luxurious apartment predicts increasing prosperity. 124

APE. Someone is likely to make fun of you if you dream of seeing an ape. If an ape chases you, the prophecy is that you are in danger of losing your position through inattention to your work. 079

APOLOGY. If you make an apology to anyone in a dream, you will receive an apology from one of your friends. If someone apologizes to you, the chances are that you will receive a minor injury. 617

APOPLEXY. It is a sign that you will travel to foreign lands if you dream of seeing a person with an attack of apoplexy. To dream that you yourself have an attack augurs criticism from your family. 434

APOTHECARY. (See Druggist.) 521

APPAREL. (See Clothes.) 022

APPARITION. Seeing an apparition in a dream is a portent of serious illness. If the apparition is of someone you know, you should write immediately to learn if the person is all right. 715

APPENDICITIS. (See also Abdomen, Ache.) To dream of an attack of this disease predicts an improvement in your financial condition if you keep your own counsel. 487

APPETITE. One who dreams of having a good appetite may look forward with certainty to always having enough to eat. To dream of loss of appetite means a period of depression. 657

APPLAUSE. Hearing applause in a dream is a forerunner of receiving a small legacy from a distant relative. If you are a performer and the applause is meant for you, the augury is of success in an entirely new venture. For you to dream of applauding someone's performance is a prediction of good health. 037

APPLE. This popular fruit predicts happiness if it is ripe—otherwise woe. Seen on a tree, the ripe fruit is a sign that you are on the point of doing good for yourself—if green, it augurs ill. If you dream of eating a raw apple, it predicts good health and energy. Cooked apples—baked, in sauce, or in pies—are practically a promise that you will receive some merited honor. 028

APPLEJACK. A dream of this exhilarating beverage foretells embarrassment through ill-advised statements or acts. 761

APPOINTMENT. (See also Date.) To dream of making an appointment to meet a friend is a sure sign that some undercover plan of yours will be found out. 534

APPRECIATION. It is lucky to dream that you show appreciation of someone else, but if you or your acts are appreciated, you will be likely to have someone criticize your clothing. 801

APPRENTICE. It is a portent of success both in business and love to dream of being an apprentice and learning a trade of some kind. If you dream of having an apprentice under you, the augury is of having an opportunity to make a great deal of extra money. 867

APPROVAL. To express approval of a person or thing usually portends happiness but if the object of your approval is unworthy, you will have a setback of some kind. For a woman to have dresses sent to her on approval augurs deceit on the part of a friend. 892

APRICOT. Disappointment in love, but luck in money matters, will be the lot of those who dream of eating this fruit. 003

APRICOT BRANDY. If you accept a proffered drink, you will get the best of those who seek to outwit you in business. 601

APRON. A man who dreams of wearing an apron will be subject to a woman's whims and caprices. Good fortune is in store for women who dream of wearing dainty aprons. 839

AQUAPLANE. To dream of standing on a board that is being drawn through the water by a motor-boat is a sign of a threat from someone who has a reason for disliking you. For a man to dream of holding a comely girl on his shoulders while riding on an aquaplane is a prediction of a broken promise. 673

AQUARIUM. (See also Fish.) Hard going is predicted by a dream of large or small aquariums. If the fish are unusual in any way—size, shape or color—you should guard against accidents. 363

AQUEDUCT. Either an overhead or underground aqueduct points toward good health and a happy love life if there is water running through it. If dry, it portends woe. 720

ARAB. A dream of Arabs in their native haunts is a presage of romance and exciting experiences. Mounted on horses going at full gallop, Arabs give warning against jealous people of the opposite sex. 272

ARBITRATION. To dream of acting as an arbitrator between two quarreling factions predicts a dangerous situation from which you will extricate yourself with difficulty. To dream of submitting your own claims to arbitration is a fortunate omen. 701

ARBOR. Young women who dream of being under an arbor with a handsome man are likely to have success in artistic pursuits. They should beware of repeating confidences. 879

ARBUTUS. This beautiful little spring flower is a portent of happiness to lovers. 475

ARCADE. Walking through an arcade of any kind points toward temptations that you will find difficult to resist. 152

ARCH. You will be unjustly criticized by a number of people if you dream of passing under an arch. A broken arch signifies wasted effort. 918

ARCHBISHOP. Family quarrels are predicted by a dream of an archbishop in his ecclesiastical vestments. 221

ARCHDUKE. This pompous representative of royalty in dress uniform is a sign that you are likely to fail in your next business venture. 002

ARCHERY. (See Arrow, Bow.) 597

ARCHITECT. At work on plans for a building, the architect in a dream foretells a difficult task that will be completed successfully. 907

ARC-LIGHT. A sputtering arc-light seen in a dream predicts petty irritations arising from conditions over which you have no control. If the arc-light burns clear and white, you may look forward to peace and plenty. 752

ARCTIC. Progress through the ice-fields of the Arctic toward the North Pole augurs the achievement of a high ambition. 989

ARENA. If you dream of looking into an arena where a sporting event is being held, there is a strong chance of your being offered a new position. Consider it carefully before you make up your mind. 498

ARGUMENT. It is lucky to dream of arguing provided you do not lose your temper—otherwise the dream is a warning against hasty action in making decisions. 223

ARISTOCRAT. To dream of being snubbed or "high-hatted" by an aristocrat is an omen that you are due to receive an increase in the amount of your worldly goods. 880

ARITHMETIC. (See also Accounts, Addition.) Dreams of doing problems in arithmetic predict vexations that are difficult to understand but are possible of solution. 547

ARMCHAIR. Dreaming of a comfortable-looking armchair occupied by a person at ease points to a vacation and travel in a southern climate. An empty armchair is an omen of a minor mystery. Seeing a cat asleep in an armchair is a warning against loss of temper. If the cat wakes up and stretches, beware of scandalous tongues. 875

ARMHOLE. If you dream of putting your arms in the wrong armholes of a coat, you will find yourself in a position of great danger to your reputation. You are warned to be very discreet in your relations with the opposite sex. 326

ARMISTICE. When armies cease to fight, the prediction of such a dream is extremely favorable. A dream of celebrating an armistice augurs well for the future. 893

ARMOR. Suite or metal armor such as worn by the Knights of old prophesy high honors if dreamed of in an ancient castle or museum, but if you dream of wearing such armor yourself, you are warned of impending financial strain. To dream of armor on a battleship, submarine or motor car is a warning of personal danger. 809

ARMORY. This building where arms are stored and soldiers are drilled predicts a menace to your peace of mind if seen from the outside. To be alone in an empty armory or arsenal presages disappointment—if the armory is crowded with military men, the omen is of success in a business undertaking. 927

ARMS. Men bearing arms—guns, pistols, hand-grenades, or other weapons—portend an event that will mark a turning point in your life. Whether this will be for the better or worse will depend on the courage with which you meet it. A dream in which someone of the opposite sex puts his or her arms around you prophesies a period of prosperity and happiness. 482

ARMY. (See also Arms.) If you dream of an army on the march, the portent is one of worry about a mysterious occurrence. An army in battle foretells a scandal from which you can escape only through closely guarding your tongue. 935

AROMA. (See Odor.) 557

ARREST. To dream of being arrested by an officer is a warning against taking chances such as driving too fast, going through red lights, gambling, or drawing checks for more than your bank balance. If you dream that you are an officer and that you arrest someone, you will find a solution for your immediate problems. 107

ARRIVAL. Arriving at a railroad, bus or airplane terminal is a dream of the successful conclusion of a difficult task. To see others arrive is a sign of health. 470

ARROGANCE. Arrogant, overbearing people met in a dream predict an experience that will cause you both amusement and satisfaction. 621

ARROW. You should be extremely careful in your dealings with the opposite sex if you dream of arrows. To be struck by an arrow signifies disgrace. To shoot arrows at a target of any kind portends unfaithfulness. 572

ARSENAL. (See Armory.) 438

ARSON. (See also Fire, Flame.) Arson, or the willful setting fire to a house, is a dream that warns a man against associating with women of loose morals. Women who have this dream should be on their guard with men with whom they are not well acquainted. To dream of seeing a person set fire to a building is a portent of loss of reputation. 587

ART. (See Museum, Painting, Picture, Statue.) To discuss art in a dream or to look at objects of arts is an omen of advancement for those who are engaged in clerical or secretarial work. 467

ARTERY. (See Blood, Tourniquet, Vein.) It is a sign that you will be well liked for your fairness if you dream of cutting an artery. This is an especially good dream for a woman to have. 301

ARTESIAN WELL. To dream of an artesian well with a good supply of clear cold water is to be assured of a moderate but steady income. 946

ARTHRITIS. Freedom from bodily ills is predicted by dreaming of being afflicted with this painful disease. 383

ARTICHOKE. Eating this thistle-like vegetable in a dream is an omen of doing something that will make you appear ridiculous. 537

ARTILLERY. In action, large calibered cannon are an indication of futile attempts to make an impression on the world. 969

ARTISAN. An expert worker in metals, wood or stone occupied in his calling is a dream that predicts happiness in married life. 011

ARTIST. Seen in a dream painting or drawing from a nude model, an artist is an omen of gay and not altogether worthy pleasures. To dream that you are the artist betokens ill luck in business. 013

ASBESTOS. The use of asbestos gloves or clothing as a protection against fire in a dream signifies discord within the family circle. 545

ASCENT. Dreaming of making the ascent of a mountain portends an increase in salary, but if you dream of falling while making the ascent, you will suffer reverses. 248

ASCETIC. Talking to an ascetic in a dream augurs hard times, but if you dream that you are an ascetic, you will meet someone who will become a staunch friend. 562

ASH WEDNESDAY. To observe this holy day in a dream is a forerunner of contentment. 282

ASHES. Dreaming of having ashes blown on you foretells hard times ahead. Emptying ashes from a stove or furnace predicts embarrassment. Sifting ashes for pieces of good coal is an indication that you will prosper. 573

ASP. It is very bad luck to dream of being bitten by an asp. If you find an asp in the grass, and kill it, you will fall in love with an actor or actress. 956

ASPARAGUS. To dream of eating asparagus is a sign that you will have to admit that someone with whom you disagreed was absolutely right. 783

ASPEN. This tree with the quivering leaves is an augury of loneliness. To dream of an aspen that has been cut or blown down predicts the illness of a young person. 334

ASPHALT. Men at work laying an asphalt pavement are a prediction of travel to the West Indies. 478

ASPIC. To dream of eating food in aspic jelly foretells a period of luxury. If the dream is simply of looking at beautifully arranged jellied meats, fish, etc., the augury is of an invitation to a large fashionable party. 558

ASPIRIN. Someone will seek to defame you if you dream of taking aspirin. If you give it to someone else, you must be especially careful not to repeat gossip. 302

ASS. (See also Donkey, Mule.) If you dream of "making an ass" of yourself, you are likely to make new and congenial friends. To see someone else acting similarly is a sign of business success. To show disapproval of such actions is an omen of unpopularity. 204

ASSASSIN. To dream of seeing a well-known person being killed by an assassin predicts news that will be sensational though not necessarily depressing. 384

ASSAULT. (See also Arms, Army.) Grave danger is predicted by dreaming of an assault being made on a woman. If a man is the victim, the augury is of disquieting news. If you are the victim, there will be a serious altercation in your household. An assault made by troops on an enemy stronghold is a prognostication of an attack on your character. 670

ASSEMBLY. (See also Speech.) Your presence in an assembly of people is a dream that depends for its augury on the purpose of the gathering: if peaceful, the prediction is of an improvement in your personal affairs; if warlike, the opposite may be expected. 551

ASSEMBLYMAN. A dream of having dealings with an assemblyman usually means that a pet plan is in danger of being upset. 073

ASSESSMENT. (See also Taxes.) If you dream of having an assessment made on real estate, securities, or other property, you will have to take special care to avoid dealings with business men of low credit rating. 091

ASSIGNATION. (See Adultery, Amour.) 871

ASSIGNMENT. (See also Bankruptcy, Failure.) To dream of assigning one's interest in property, predicts that you will make an important change in your plans. 519

ASSISTANCE. If you receive assistance in a dream—financial or physical—you will find that you must have help in a business deal. If you give assistance you will be successful. 231

ASTHMA. There is no significance to this if the dreamer is an asthma sufferer, as the actuality is likely to be a carryover into sleep. For others, the dream signifies distress through carelessness. 305

ASTONISHMENT. To be astonished in a dream predicts selling goods below cost. To astonish others is a sign of increasing prosperity. 294

ASTRAL FORM. If you dream of seeing the astral form of either yourself or someone else, you will receive an important letter from an old sweetheart. 353

ASTROLOGY. (See also Horoscope.) To read a book on astrology in a dream is an augury of happiness and wealth that will come by patient effort. 418

ASYLUM. Illness and misfortune are the presages of a dream of being confined in an asylum. 866

ATHEIST. If you dream of yourself or another's being an atheist, you will be disappointed in the returns on investments of time and money. 569

ATHLETICS. (See Sports.) Family, school or college reunions are predicted by a dream of engaging in athletics of all kinds. It is lucky to dream of winning in such contests. If there is any injury sustained, the augury is of commendation from your business or social superiors. 854

ATLAS. (See also Globe Map.) Journeys, either long or short, are indicated by a dream of studying an atlas. A large atlas indicates travel by sea; a small one, travel on land; and maps in black and white, travel by air. 957

ATOM. Dreams in which you seem to see atoms predict that someone you have trusted will tell you a lie. To hear a person speak about atoms is a sign that for a time you will have to get along on a smaller income. 424

ATOMIZER. If a woman dreams that she is using a perfume atomizer, it is a sign that she will receive a proposal from an elderly man. If a man has the dream, it predicts that his sense of humor will help in his advancement. The use of a nose or throat atomizer in a dream is a warning against accidents. 877

ATONEMENT. Doing penance in a dream or atonement for a sin or a wrong you have done is a sign that you will break a precious heirloom. 651

ATROCITY. As with most horror dreams, an atrocity, even of extreme cruelty does not necessarily augur misfortune. The prediction is one of change, either of occupation or place of abode. 219

ATTACK. (See Assault.) 935

ATTAINMENT. It is an omen of the satisfactory conclusion of the task on which you are engaged if you dream of the attainment of an important object. 657

ATTIC. You have every expectation of a loving mate, healthy children and sufficient worldly goods if you dream of rummaging in trunks and boxes in an attic. To dream of being a child playing in the attic is an especially propitious dream for those who are past middle age. 509

ATTORNEY. (See Lawyer.) 234

AUCTION. It is a sign of a salary rise or money-making in some form to dream of attending an auction of any description, but to see yourself as auctioneer is unlucky. 415

AUCTION BRIDGE. (See Bridge.) 532

AUDIENCE. To face an audience from stage or platform predicts an intense but temporary pleasure. To sit in an audience predicts that you will be able to help out a friend. 491

AUDITOR. Going over accounts, an auditor seen in a dream is a forerunner of tangled finances. 583

AUDITORIUM. (See also Audience.) Music of any kind heard in a large auditorium is an omen of achievement unless the music is not played or sung in tune, in which case it augurs disappointment. 339

AUGER. To dream of boring a hole with an auger predicts that you will meet a tiresome acquaintance. 795

AUNT. If the aunt of whom you dream is your father's sister, the prediction is of simple pleasures in the company of old friends. An aunt on your mother's side predicts financial security. 157

AURORA BOREALIS. (See Northern Lights.) 975

AUTHOR. This dream may be one of the greatest interest. Meeting an author on terms of friendship or pleasant companionship foretells mental enjoyment and social prestige. If an author tries to borrow money from you in a dream, it predicts that you will receive a legacy. To dream that you are an author predicts financial difficulties. 881

AUTOBIOGRAPHY. You are in danger if you dream of writing your autobiography. Your wife, husband or sweetheart will suspect you if you have this dream. If you dream of reading the story that someone else has written of his life, you are likely to advance in your social or business position. 805

AUTOBUS. Riding on an autobus in a dream predicts success in your job if you stick to it in spite of disappointments and reverses. 726

AUTOGRAPHS. The collecting of autographs in a dream signifies that you will profit by the example of great men and women. You should read the lives of those who have accomplished big things. If you dream that you are a celebrity and are asked for your autograph, you will make a success of your work. 550

AUTOMAT. If you dream of obtaining and eating food in one of these coin-in-the-slot restaurants, you should follow the advice of the one you consider your best friend. 720

AUTOMOBILE. In this era of gasoline transportation a dream of going places in an automobile has no particular significance. It is the exceptional use of a car that makes the dream of importance. For instance, if you dream of driving on the left-hand side of the road, the augury is of travel to foreign lands. If the dream is of not being able to get sufficient power to go over a hill, the augury is of disappointment in love. A dream of running out of gas in an unpopulated country predicts hard labor for a meager living. 546

AUTOPSY. To dream of the examination of a corpse after a murder has been committed predicts an interesting though unprofitable experience. 312

AUTUMN. If in a dream the leaves on the trees are bright colored and slowly dropping to the ground, you will receive a gift from someone you believed to be unfriendly. 992

AVALANCHE. Guard your health with especial care if you dream of being caught in an avalanche. 210

AVERSION. (See also Hate.) If a person shows an aversion, or unfriendliness, toward you in a dream, the prediction is that you will be able to recognize an attempt at deception. 177

AVIARY. A cageful of many different kinds and colors of birds portends brilliant social achievements but a lessening income. It is a warning against spending too much time away from your business. 644

AVIATOR. For a woman to dream of being in love with an aviator predicts an early marriage. If she goes up with him in an airplane, there will be an elopement. If a man dreams of being an aviator, he will be singled out for high honors. To see two aviators having a fist fight is a portent of hard labor without reward. 723

AVOCATION. (See Hobby.) 148

AWAKENING. If you have the rare dream of waking up, you have much happiness to anticipate. To dream of an awakening of the spirit denotes many friends who will stand by you through thick and thin. 434

AWARD. Good fortune will come to you if you dream of receiving an award for work that is well performed. 947

AWE. You are warned against vanity and a tendency to show off if you dream someone stands in awe of you. If you are awe-struck by a personage of high rank, you must work harder if you are to keep your job. 687

AWL. This is a warning not to spend your time with loose acquaintances, either male or female. 247

AWNING. To dream of sitting under an awning is a sign that you will escape an expected injury. Raising an awning signifies many suitors to an unmarried woman, and children to the married. To a man it signifies happiness in marriage. Lowering an awning denotes a change of occupation that will mark a slight improvement. 228

AXE. Dreaming that you are handling a bright, keen axe is an augury of satisfaction and advancement in your work. A poor but honest lover is promised to a young woman having this dream. Those who dream of trying to use a dull axe should pay more attention to their dress. 864

AXLE. Disaster is predicted by a dream of breaking an axle on any kind of automobile, wagon or other vehicle. To dream of mending an axle or fitting a new one is a sign of improvement in conditions. 749

B

BABOON. Fortunate is the young woman who dreams of this animal. She will contract a most favorable marriage with a man of high social position. Others who dream of baboons will be lucky in business undertakings. 213

BABY. To hear a baby crying in one's dream, is a forerunner of sickness and disappointments. A sweet, clean baby, predicts a satisfied love and a host of good friends. To see a baby walking alone, foretells independence, and the will to rise above smaller spirits. A woman who dreams she is nursing a baby, receives a sign that she will be deceived by the one in whom she has the greatest confidence. To pick up a baby ill with fever is not a good sign. You will have many worries. 714

BABY CARRIAGE. To dream of a baby carriage is a sign that you will have a true friend who will plan many happy surprises for you. 922

BACCARAT. The significance of this dream is not affected by the results achieved by gambling. Win or lose, it predicts a succession of harassing experiences, one or more of which may prove to be serious. 579

BACHELOR. If a man dreams he is a bachelor, he must take warning and stay away from the ladies. If a woman dreams of a bachelor, it hints of wanton love. 302

BACK. To dream of a bare back, presages loss of power. Beware of lending money or giving advice. Sickness often follows this dream. To observe a person deliberately turn and walk away from you, points to envy and jealousy, causing unhappiness. If you dream of your own back, misfortune will befall you. 584

BACKBITING. Your fortune will change for the worse if you dream of being guilty of backbiting. If your friends indulge in backbiting, it predicts worriment from inside the home. 353

BACKBONE. You may look forward with certainty to a contented old age if you dream of seeing someone else's backbone. If you get a glimpse of your own in a mirror, it is a sign that you will make an advance in your worldly estate through your own efforts. 710

BACKGAMMON. If you dream of playing backgammon, it is a prediction that you will make a visit and encounter a lack of hospitality, but while there, you will win friendships that will be true and lasting. If you lose in the game, your affections will be unrequited, and your business will be unpredictable. 218

BACON. If you eat bacon, it is a sign of prosperity. Rancid bacon foretells dissatisfaction that will cause uneasiness. To dream of curing bacon is not a good omen; it foretells sickness. 324

BACTERIA. This dream's prediction is in the main favorable, but it should always be considered in connection with other features of the dream. 156

BADGE. Wearing a badge in a dream foretells social advancement. 483

BADGER. It is a sign of good luck to dream of a badger, especially so if you have encountered hardships. 749

BADMINTON. This game of skill played in a dream is a precursor of your having to make a decision that will have a definite influence on your future. 832

BAG. The significance of a bag depends on the material from which it is made. Of paper, it signifies danger, which can be avoided by taking ordinary precautions. Of cloth, the prediction is of success in your business. Of leather, the prophecy is of travel. Pleasant experiences are foretold by a dream of having someone carry your bag for you. 173

BAGGAGE. (See also Bag.) Trunks and other traveling luggage grouped in a home or railroad station foretell a long trip, probably to a foreign country. Seeing them handled by expressmen predicts happiness on the journey. To see a piece of baggage dropped is a bad sign. 803

BAGPIPE. To see a group in Scotch highland uniforms playing bagpipes is a generally fortunate omen. If, however, the bagpipes are being played out of tune, or if the uniforms are worn and soiled, the portent is one of misfortune. 688

BAIL. Unforeseen troubles will come to you if you dream of seeking bail; accidents may occur; and unwise alliances may be contracted. The same result is to be expected, though not as dire, if you go bail for another. 270

BAILIFF. This dream predicts the urge to be in higher places. If the bailiff attempts an arrest, or makes love, one may know that false friends are trying to get his money. 810

BAIT. Whether worms, minnows, or any other form of animal life intended for bait, the omen of such a dream is that you will be distressed at the critical illness of a dear friend. 798

BAKERY. Rows of bread loaves and pastry in a bakery, or bakers clad in white, presage an increase in the family for young married couples. 368

BAKING. A man or woman who dreams of baking bread, cake, pies or beans may look forward with confidence to a rise in their fortunes. 797

BALCONY. If sweethearts dream of an adieu on a balcony, a long separation may follow, perhaps final separation. To dream of a balcony also denotes bad news and absent friends. 653

BALDNESS. A bald-headed man seen in a dream predicts sharpers who will try to interest you in some business that will be unwise; but by keeping your eyes you will outwit them. For a man to dream of a bald-headed woman is a sign that he will have a vixen for a wife. A bald hill or mountain foretells famine and suffering in many forms. For a woman to dream of a bald-headed man is to forewarn her to be discreet and not accept her next proposal of marriage. If new babies are bald-headed it points to a happy home, a loving mate and obedient children. 571

BALE. The solution of a pressing problem is indicated by a dream of seeing well baled material, such as cotton, paper and so on. 284

BALL. This is a good omen, if well dressed people are happily dancing to the strains of good music. If you are unhappy and distressed, a death in the family may be expected. 138

BALLET. To dream of a ballet indicates infidelity in marriage, failure in business matters, and dissension and jealousy among those you love. 672

BALLOON. Adversity and unrealized hopes are indicated by this dream. Business of every sort will suffer temporary loss. If you ascend in a balloon, it foretells an unfortunate journey. 431

BALLOT. Casting your ballot at an election points to the fulfillment of a wish you had thought impossible of accomplishment. 258

BALLROOM. Empty, this signifies pain and sorrow. Crowded with dancers, it means that fate has a pleasant surprise in store for you. 631

BALSAM. It is a sign of better health to dream of being in pine woods and smelling the scent of balsam. 002

BALUSTRADE. If you dream of sliding downstairs on a balustrade, you will find yourself beset with petty annoyance in regard to money. 257

BAMBOO. To see a clump of growing bamboo in a dream is to be assured of many delightful hours in the company of a well-loved person. 179

BANANA. Eaten in a dream, this fruit betokens sickness. Seen growing, it predicts that one of your friends will prove to be a shallow individual. 394

BANDAGE. Seen in rolls by itself, bandages are a warning against betting on racehorses. In use, as on limbs or other parts of the body, bandages portend trouble. 040

BANDANNA. Hard work and worry will be the lot of one who wears a bandanna in a dream. To see a colored woman wearing a bandanna signifies a happy family life. 724

BANDIT. To dream of being held up by a bandit in a lonely place is a forerunner of stomach disturbances. If you dream of being a bandit and holding up someone else, it is a sign that you will have to apologize for something. 518

BANDSAW. Using a bandsaw in a dream means that you will win the approval of your employer before long. 477

BANDYLEGS. If in a dream you make fun of a person with bandylegs, you are certain to suffer reverses of one kind or another. If you dream of being so afflicted yourself, you will receive a small legacy from a distant relative. 060

BANISHMENT. If one dreams that he or she is banished from home or country, there is every probability of there being danger of fire. 794

BANJO. If you dream of a banjo, you will enjoy pleasant amusements. If a negro is playing one, you will meet with slight worries. For a young woman to see negroes playing their banjos is an omen she will fail in some anticipated pleasure. She will also quarrel with her lover. 681

BANK. To see vacant tellers' windows at a bank predicts business losses. Dispensing gold money foretells carelessness; receiving it, great gain and prosperity. 098

BANKBOOK. To lose a bankbook is a warning against taking part in church, business or society politics, and against gossiping about your neighbors. 121

BANKER. Loss of money usually follows a dream about a banker, even if the dream points to a profitable deal. 416

BANKNOTES. Clean, crisp banknotes predict financial independence, but if they are soiled and wrinkled, your money will be accompanied by trouble. 840

BANKRUPTCY. Here is a dream with an opposite meaning. It foretells either an inheritance or the acquisition of money by some other means. 376

BANNER. To dream of seeing one's country's flag flying in a clear sky predicts triumph over alien foes. To see it torn and bespattered is significant of wars and loss of military honors on land and sea. 849

BANQUET. It is a good omen to dream of a banquet. Friends will favor you. To dream of yourself, with many smartly-dressed guests, eating from costly plate and drinking wine of fabulous price and age, portends great gain in business of every nature, and happiness among friends. If you dream of seeing eerie faces or empty tables, in strange surroundings, it is ominous of grave misunderstandings. 975

BANSHEE. It is a prediction of death to someone you know when you dream that one of these creatures wails in the night. 488

BANTAM. If you dream of bantam chickens, your fortune will be small, but you will enjoy contentment. If the chickens appear sickly, or are exposed to wintry storms, your interest will be lessened in value. 072

BANYAN TREE. To dream of this spreading tree of India, whose branches take root as they lean to the ground, is an augury of acrimonious arguments with your relatives or in-laws. 351

BAPTISM. A dream of baptism signifies that your character needs strengthening. If you are an applicant for baptism, you will be in danger of humiliating yourself. To see John the Baptist baptizing Christ in the Jordan, indicates you will have a desperate mental struggle. 509

BAR. (See also Barroom.) Tending a bar denotes that you will stoop to some questionable way to advancement. Seeing a bar denotes community interests, good fortune and the consummation of illicit desires. 552

BARB. Catching one's clothes or a part of the body on a barb predicts that you will be disgraced unless you leave off associations with evil companions. 377

BARBARIAN. To have dealings in a dream with a savage, uncivilized person is auspicious for those engaged in business but only if the dreamer seems to have the upper hand. It is unlucky for anyone to dream of being chased or captured by barbarians. 804

BARBARITY. Looking on at any barbarous act by a savage means that you must take great care in selecting the food you eat, lest you suffer from poisoning. 176

BARBECUE. To dream of seeing animals of any kind being roasted whole is a sign that your hospitality will be abused by relatives or acquaintances. If you eat at a roadside "barbecue" stand, you will suffer a disappointment. 683

BARBER. Success will come through close attention to business if you dream of a barber. For a young woman to dream of a barber suggests that her fortune will increase, though slightly. 128

BARBERRY. Leaping over a barberry hedge means that you will surmount your difficulties in a satisfactory manner. To eat the red berries signifies loss of reputation. 210

BAREFEET. If you wander in the night barefoot with torn garments, you will be disappointed in your expectations, and bad influences will hover about your efforts for advancement. 139

BARGAIN. The achievement of a pet project is assured if you dream of taking advantage of a bargain. A bargain sale in a department store is propitious for women especially. 315

BARITONE. Hearing a baritone is a lucky dream for those who are in love if the singer keeps in tune. If he sings off key, there will be an unpleasant occurrence. 821

BARK. To pick the bark off a tree or twig does not augur well for the dreamer. Gathering pieces of bark with which to make a fire is a sign that you will have an embarrassing experience with someone of the opposite sex. It is a "watch-your-step" dream. (*Sailboat.*) To see a bark under full sail, in fair weather or foul, is a prophecy of a release from care and worry. 756

BARKING. A dog's bark may be joyous, warning or menacing; and the significance of this dream follows these qualities closely. When the barking has a menace in it, you are in grave danger. 981

BARLEY. A field of barley in the sunshine predicts happiness for lovers; under clouds, it points to unrequited love. 885

BARMAID. For a man to dream of a barmaid signifies his desire for low pleasures; he will scoff at purity. For a woman to dream that she is a barmaid denotes that she will be attracted to men of low repute, and that she will prefer irregular pleasures. 418

BARN. If the barn is filled with ripe, golden grain and perfect ears of corn, with goodlooking cattle in it, the omen is one of great prosperity. If empty, the reverse may be expected. 483

BARNACLES. Seen on the bottom of a boat or on driftwood, this marine growth indicates that your labors will be rewarded and you may look forward to a calm and peaceful old age. 851

BAROMETER. A barometer denotes that a change will soon take place in your affairs, which will be profitable to you. If the barometer is broken, you will encounter disturbing incidents in your business, coming unexpectedly. 688

BARREL. A full barrel seen in a dream foretells prosperity. An empty one is an omen of distress. 211

BARRIER. Walls, closed doors, fences and other barriers as a rule predict the frustration of your plans. 187

BARROOM. Your family and friends will give you their unswerving loyalty if you dream of being in a barroom. To dream of seeing women drinking at a bar is a portent of indulgence in indiscreet pleasures. If, in such a drinking place, you dream of becoming intoxicated, you will receive disappointing news. 694

BASEBALL. A baseball game in your dream, assures you of contentment, and your cheerfulness will make you a popular companion. For a young woman to dream of playing baseball means much pleasure for her, but no profit. 862

BASEMENT. (See also Cellar.) A dream of being in a basement foretells that you will have few chances of making money. 126

BASIN. A dream of filling a basin with clean warm water augurs happy days with a loving mate. Cold water in a basin predicts family troubles. To dream of finding a basin filled with dirty water is a sign of divorce in the family of one of your relatives. Emptying a basin predicts a season of prosperity. 871

BASKET. Carrying food or packages in a basket predicts that you will have new opportunities for advancement. If you take full advantage of these, you will go far in your work. An empty basket predicts disappointment. 831

BASS DRUM. It is a sign that you will achieve a pet ambition if you dream of thumping a bass drum. To see someone in a band playing a bass drum the prediction is of an exasperating experience. 555

BASSOON. To dream of playing the bassoon is to look forward to wasted effort of some description. 691

BASS VIOL. A happy family life, with one or more talented children, is the augury of a dream of playing this instrument. To dream of carrying a bass viol in a crowd predicts an amusing experience. To dream of losing one predicts petty irritations. 816

BASS VOICE. If you dream you have a bass voice, it points to some irregularity in your business, brought about by the deceit of one of your employees. For the lover, this dream foretells estrangements and quarrels. 407

BASTARD. If you dream that you are a bastard, you are almost certain to receive both honors and wealth. It is a sign of impending bad luck to call a person a bastard, but if another calls you by this name, you will receive a promotion of some kind. 285

BAT. To see a bat flying about is a dream that augurs ill if you are afraid of it. But if it does not bother you, it prophesies new interests that will be profitable. 121

BATH. Young, unmarried men and women who dream of taking a bath will save themselves considerable trouble if they will constantly be on guard against overindulgence in alcohol. For a pregnant woman to dream of bathing usually means a miscarriage. To a man, the dream means a temptation from an adulteress. Those who dream of bathing in the same tub with others are warned to avoid frivolous and immoral companions. Bathing in muddy water predicts slander from your enemies. Sea bathing is a prediction of prosperity. A warm bath foretells the reverse. 974

BATHROOM. For a young woman to dream of a bathroom is a sign her inclinations will turn toward dangerous pleasures and indiscretions. To see white or yellow roses in a bathroom signifies a minor sickness that will interfere with anticipated pleasure; but something good will result from this disappointment. This dream suggests caution in making changes in one's career. A woman should guard against social errors. 126

BATON. An orchestra leader's baton is a favorable sign, signifying a realization of your chief ambition. The baton carried by a drum major at the head of a parade is an augury of family squabbles. 106

BATTERY. If you dream of the storage battery in your car going dead, there will be a grave accident to one of your friends. 711

BATTLE. Dreaming of hearing the sound of battle from a distance is a warning against infection from a slight wound. To dream of winning a battle is an omen of success in love affairs. 089

BATTLESHIP. If in your dream you see a battleship alone at sea, you will find your life becoming easier yet more productive. A battleship in action, with guns being fired, predicts business difficulties. A group or fleet of battleships is a sign of success in a business deal. 749

BAUBLE. Flashy or cheap jewelry in a dream, is a forerunner of illness. On yourself it is a prediction of skin diseases, but seen on others it betokens a loss of weight, fallen arches, or some minor ailment. 031

BAY. There is pleasure in store for those who dream of sailing in a calm bay. If the water is rough, beware of false friends. To look upon a bay from a high point predicts travel. 176

BAYONET. If you jab a person with a bayonet in a dream, you must be on your guard against indiscreet behavior with persons of the opposite sex. If you dream of being jabbed, you are in danger of losing a sum of money. 318

BAY TREE. Fortunate are those who dream of bay trees beside pleasant doorways, for this tree is a prediction of sound investments and a well-ordered life. 863

BAY WINDOW. It is an augury of pleasant hours ahead if you dream of looking out of a bay window. If one or more of the windows are broken, you will change your address. 319

BEACH. To dream of lying on a beach in a bathing suit is a sign that you will have to explain some action that your friends have not understood. If you are naked on a beach, the prophecy is of a new and unusual undertaking. If you dream of dragging a boat up on the beach, you will be likely to need financial assistance. 654

BEACON LIGHT. (See also Lighthouse.) Fair weather is predicted to a sailor who dreams of a beacon light. A landsman having this dream may look forward to a prosperous undertaking. 371

BEADS. (See also Ornament, Rosary.) Some person of wealth and high position will single you out for attention if you dream of handling beads. If you string beads you will receive a sum of money that will surprise you. To count them is an augury of contentment. To drop a number of them portends discontent. 484

BEAGLE. (See also Barking.) A beagle hound seen on a crowded city street is a forerunner of many pleasant letters from friends. 887

BEAK. The beak of any bird seen in a dream is a portent of change. The beak of a bird of prey, such as an eagle or a vulture, foretells a change for the worse. A buzzard's beak portends a scandal that threatens you and can be avoided only by exercising the greatest care in your conduct. 163

BEAM. To dream of seeing a heavy beam of wood or steel being swung through the air by a derrick or crane foretells the successful termination of an important piece of work. A beam of light from a searchlight or spotlight is a harbinger of the solution of a problem that has been troubling you. 980

BEANS. In general, a dream of growing beans, whether limas, string, butter, soy, or other varieties, predicts financial security. To dream of eating baked beans is a warning against gossip, especially in social circles. 986

BEARS. A bear foretells competition in business pursuits. To kill a bear foretells release from social entanglements. If a young woman dreams of a bear she will be threatened with a rival or some other misfortune. 214

BEARSKIN. It is a sign that you will become discontented if you dream that you dress yourself in a bearskin. It is especially unfortunate in such a dream if you or someone else makes a pun on the words "bearskin" and "bareskin." 918

BEARD. To see a beard on a woman portends that an enemy will plot against you. There will be a battle for mastery, and you will lose some money. If the beard is gray, you may expect hard luck and fights with relatives. If some one pulls your beard, it means you will lose your property and friends. If a young woman admires a beard, it shows a desire to marry, and she will be threatened with an unfortunate alliance. 212

BEATING. Being beaten by an angry person, bodes no good for the dreamer. It points to family jars and discord. To see a child beaten, you will take unfair advantage of another. You are warned against the tendency to treat a child cruelly. 565

BEAU. For a young woman to dream of her beau is quite natural, but unless it is a dream of quarreling, it portends happiness. 899

BEAUTY. To dream of beauty is pre-eminently good. A lovely woman brings pleasure and good business. A beautiful child indicates reciprocated love and a happy marriage. 147

BEAVER. A beaver foretells that you will obtain comfortable circumstances by patient effort. If you dream of killing one you will be accused of fraud and misconduct. 201

BECK. To dream of being at someone's beck augurs better pay for those who work with their hands. 799

BECKONING. If it is a friendly person who beckons to you in a dream, the augury is one of good cheer and prosperous months ahead. If an enemy beckons, you may expect reverses. If a devil beckons, you should look to your moral conduct. 349

BED. A clean, white bed, foretells peace and freedom from worries. For a woman to dream of making a bed, is to expect a handsome lover. To dream of being in bed in a strange room, is an augury of unexpected friends on a visit. If you are sleeping on a bed in the open air, you will have delightful experiences and an opportunity to make a considerable amount of money. To dream of seeing one of the opposite sex lying in bed, either asleep or awake, is a sign that your mind is too much given to thoughts of pleasure, no matter how innocent. 644

BEDBUGS. Definitely bad news may be expected if you dream of seeing bedbugs. If you are able to kill them or otherwise get rid of them, you will be able to rise above misfortune. 835

BEDCHAMBER. One that is newly furnished foretells a change for the better in health, income, and happiness. It is not unlikely that you will have a vacation trip to a pleasant resort. 593

BEDFELLOW. To dream of being in bed with a strange person of the opposite sex is an indication of having to meet new emergencies. If the bedfellow is of your own sex, the prediction is of having to explain your failure to comply with someone's request. 050

BEDPAN. A sudden rise to fortune is indicated by a dream of a bedpan in any circumstances. 723

BEDTICK. If you dream that you are wearing a dress or a suit made of bedtick, you will have an experience of an unusual nature that will have a profound influence on your future. It is an unpleasant augury to dream of sewing on bedtick. 434

BEEF. This is not a propitious dream, especially if it is raw and bloody. It predicts internal disorders for women and is a warning against carelessness that may result in cuts or bruises. Cooked beef is better, but its augury is of worry and marital disturbances. 669

BEER. It is a good portent to dream of pouring or drinking beer, especially if there is foam on the top. To have a pitcher filled with beer is a sign of happiness in the family circle. To dream of beer that is flat or stale indicates disappointment in love. 017

BEES. Good luck may be expected after a dream of bees around a hive, or swarming. Even a dream of being stung by bees is a portent of a profitable undertaking. 244

BEESWAX. Burning beeswax is a sign of want. Rubbing beeswax on a pressing iron predicts an improvement in marital relations. 157

BEETLES. If they are crawling on your person, they foretell many difficulties in money matters. If you kill them, you will solve these problems. 048

BEETS. A thriving field of growing beets signifies that you will prosper through your close attention to your work. To eat them with a meal is a sign of a welcome change. To eat them raw foretells disaster. 628

BEGGAR. No good will come of a dream in which you refuse to help a beggar, but should you grant his request, you will have exceedingly good luck. 660

BEGONIA. To wear a blossom from this plant predicts that a relative will criticize you for being extravagant. A dream of a healthy begonia plant is a presage of happy hours. 410

BEHEADING. To dream of being beheaded foretells defeat in a struggle or failure in some undertaking. To see others beheaded, if blood flows, death or exile is predicted. 730

BEHIND. (See Buttocks.) 393

BELAYING PIN. Those who follow the sea are most likely to dream of belaying pins. If they are used as weapons in a fight, they augur trouble of a serious nature. 421

BELCH. This dream indicates that you will look back on happier times rather than forward to them. To dream of belching at a refined dinner is a prediction that you will lose a good friend unless you exercise great caution. 830

BELGIAN HARE. If you dream of seeing Belgian hares being raised for the market, you are bound to receive news that will be to your advantage. Eating a Belgian hare is a sign of making an advantageous contract. To dream of killing one is a sign of becoming tired of your work. 838

BELIEF. A dream in which your own or another's belief in their God is taken away is an omen of desperate times ahead. 422

BELLADONNA. Success in commercial circles will follow a dream by men of belladonna. Women will meet rivals in society; futile efforts will be made for places in men's affections. 715

BELLE. For a woman to dream that she is the belle of a ball, party or other social occasion is a sign that she will be happy in her love life. 825

BELLOWS. To work a bellows foretells a struggle, but a triumph over poverty. If you see a bellows, it shows that friends living at a great distance are hoping to see you. An old discarded bellows means that you have wasted your time by doing unimportant things. 559

BELLS. To dream of bells tolling portends the death of a distant friend, and news of wrong will annoy you. Liberty bells denote an improvement in business. 474

BELLY. (See also Abdomen.) If one dreams of a distended belly, it is a sign that illness will follow. Humiliation is predicted if one sees anything moving on the belly. A healthy belly signifies unusual desires. 983

BELT. A new belt foretells you are soon to meet and make engagements with a total stranger, who will put a brake on your rise to wealth. If the belt is not of the latest fashion, you will be criticized for rudeness to your acquaintances. 075

BELTING. It is a sign of prosperous business conditions if you dream of seeing machinery that is kept in motion with belting. If the belting breaks or gets tangled, it portends a loss of money. 314

BENCH. If you dream of sitting on a bench, beware of trusting people who owe you money and of making confidants. If you see one, there will be happy reunions between you and the friends who have been separated from you through some disagreement. 981

BENEDICTION. To dream of a priest or other clergyman pronouncing a benediction is a most favorable sign. It carries hope for those in love and for any legal enterprise. 995

BENEFACTOR. If you are the benefactor in a dream, you will be fortunate in your investments or your job. If someone gives you money, you should look out for your reputation. 893

BENZINE. Be warned against believing idle gossip if you dream of smelling the fumes of benzine. If you dream of using it for cleaning fabrics, you will have an opportunity of changing your occupation. 302

BEQUEST. A feeling of satisfaction from the knowledge of duties well done, and the health of young people are assured by this dream. 643

BEREAVEMENT. To dream of the death of a child signifies that your plans will miscarry, and where you have hoped for success, there will be failure. To see the death of relatives or friends foretells the frustration of your plans and a gloomy outlook for the future. 775

BEST MAN. A single man will marry within a year if he dreams of being best man at a friend's wedding. 028

BET. To dream of betting on the races is a warning. Do not engage in new undertakings. Your enemies are trying to distract your attention for their own advantage. To bet at the gaming tables suggests that immoral means will be used to procure money from you. Beware of loose women. 072

BEVERAGE. To dream of drinking alcoholic beverages is a sign of thoughtful occupations ahead. Other beverages predict a vacation. 367

BEWILDERMENT. You will be puzzled by a letter that you receive if you dream of being bewildered for any reason. 911

BEWITCHMENT. For a man to dream of a bewitching young woman, is a forerunner of financial disaster. 358

BIAS. To dream of cutting cloth on the bias is a sign of receiving a message of distress from a friend. 114

BIBLE. To see a Bible denotes that a position of trust will be offered you. If you dream of casting doubt on the teachings of the Bible, it denotes that you will succumb to temptation and be led astray by a false friend. 912

BICARBONATE OF SODA. It portends that you will make a short trip to a neighboring state if you dream of taking this as medicine. 273

BICKERING. You will have a quarrel with someone you love if you dream of bickering. 097

BICYCLE. To ride a bicycle uphill indicates bright prospects. To ride it downhill, if the rider be a woman, it is a caution to her to guard her good name and her health, for misfortune is in sight. 830

BID. (See also Auction.) Making a bid at an auction or other sale is a prelude to disappointment. 163

BIER. It is a sign of calamity to see a dead person lying on a bier. A personage lying in state and a line of spectators passing is a portent of war. 709

BIG GAME. To dream of tracking or shooting big game is a prediction of success in manufacturing enterprises. 170

BIGAMY. If a man commits bigamy in a dream he will suffer loss of virility and failing mentality. To a woman, it denotes that she will suffer dishonor unless she is most discreet. 921

BIGOTRY. A dream of arguing about religion or politics without due regard for another's opinions augurs humiliation by someone who is beneath you socially. 834

BILGE-WATER. It is a prediction of an automobile or airplane accident if you dream of bilge-water in a ship. 440

BILIOUSNESS. If you dream of being bilious, you will have difficulty in making ends meet. It is a warning against extravagant living. 798

BILL. To receive bills for rent, board or merchandise in a dream is a sign of impending good fortune. 213

BILLBOARD. To hide behind a billboard portends embarrassment through no fault of your own. A dream of advertising billboards predicts that someone will nag you. 090

BILLIARDS. Billiards portend imminent disaster. There will be law-suits and controversies over property rights. The dreamer is likely to be slandered. To see a billiard table and balls idle means that false friends are plotting against you. 667

BILLYGOAT. A dream of being chased by a billygoat is an omen of being late for an appointment. To be butted by this animal augurs the loss of money by gambling. 075

BINDING. If you dream of a beautiful and rich bookbinding, you may expect to find a release from worry. One who dreams of binding books need never worry about income. To tear the binding on a garment signifies an entanglement with one of the opposite sex. 536

BINOCULARS. A dream of using binoculars for spying on people or things you have no right to see predicts scandalous reports about the dreamer. If binoculars are used at a race-track, the omen is one of good fortune. 668

BIOGRAPHY. It predicts a serious illness if you dream of reading your own biography. If you write the story of your life, you will be appointed to a high position. 770

BIPLANE. (See also Airplane.) This dream predicts that you will have success through your own steady efforts. 696

BIRCH BARK. To dream of peeling bark off a birch tree is an omen of criticism that will cause you unrest. If you eat birch bark, you will be likely to suffer reverses of one kind or another. 988

BIRDS. It is a good omen to dream of birds with beautiful plumage. A rich husband and a happy marriage are predicted if a woman dreams thus. Moulting and songless birds signify crushing injustice to the unfortunate by people of wealth. To see a wounded bird foretells worry caused by willful and disobedient children. It is a sign of prosperity to see birds flying. Disagreeable surroundings will improve, as will health and fortune. To catch a bird is good luck. To hear it speak is a prediction that one will be called upon to perform tasks that demand clear understanding. To kill a bird with a gun means disaster, such as failure of crops or of business enterprises. 085

BIRD'S-EYE MAPLE. Maidens who dream of furniture made of this wood may expect a proposal of marriage before long. 751

BIRD'S NEST. To dream of seeing an empty bird's-nest presages gloom and a poor outlook for business. With eggs in the nest, good results may be expected from all engagements. If the young birds are in the nest, it denotes interesting journeys and satisfactory business dealings. If the young birds are deserted, the folly of someone in the family will cause you anxiety. 804

BIRTH. If a married woman dreams of giving birth to a child, great happiness and a large legacy are foretold. For a single woman, loss of reputation and desertion by her lover. It is a warning against careless behavior. 560

BIRTH CONTROL. This is a propitious dream for married people. The prophecy is of sturdy children who will prove a blessing to their parents. 370

BIRTHDAY. To be present at a birthday celebration predicts poverty to the young; to the old, many troubles and loneliness. 156

BIRTHDAY PRESENTS. To receive birthday surprises indicates that you will have many accomplishments. People of industry will advance in their profession. To give presents means that you will be a welcome guest at an important gathering. 875

BISCUITS. To eat or bake biscuits in a dream indicates sickness and the disruption of family peace over trivial disputes. 897

BISHOP. Teachers and authors will suffer great mental distress, caused by the study of difficult topics if they dream of a bishop. A tradesman will buy unwisely, and will incur a loss of money following this dream. To see a bishop, hard work will be required to reach the goal for which you are aiming. 818

BISON. This almost extinct animal of the western plains is a favorable omen when seen in a dream, but to kill one portends woe. To dream of seeing one in a zoo portends rejoicing on account of a marriage in your family or among your relatives. 477

BIT. To adjust a bit for boring either through wood or metal is a sign that you will face a problem but that you will solve it without too much trouble. 416

BITCH. A dream of a female dog that is gentle and kind is a precursor of happy days with your friends. The use of this word for a woman of whatever character predicts that you will find yourself in straitened circumstances. 833

BITE. To dream of being bitten forebodes ill fortune. It suggest that you will wish to undo something you have done. You will suffer losses through someone who dislikes you. 244

BITTER-SWEET. The simple joys of a well-ordered home life are predicted by a dream in which bitter-sweet appears. 409

BLACKBERRIES. Blackberries foretell setbacks. To gather them is an unlucky sign. To eat them is a forerunner of great losses. 670

BLACKBIRD. You will be called upon to show a good deal of courage if you dream of blackbirds flying. If they alight, you will be fortunate. A dead blackbird is a presage of trouble. 055

BLACKBOARD. To dream of seeing a blackboard covered with writing in white chalk, means that you will receive unhappy tidings of some friend, or that your financial security will be threatened by the unsettled condition of the stock market. 043

BLACKCAP. People of a mechanical turn of mind who dream of picking or eating blackcaps should take extra precaution against accidents. 738

BLACKSMITH. A blacksmith seen in your dreams, is an omen that you will embark on undertakings that will soon work out to your credit and advantage. 984

BLACKGUARD. To be called a blackguard in a dream is a prediction of an upset in your family life. If you call another by this name you will meet a handsome stranger of the opposite sex. 761

BLACKING. Good fortune at cards and other games will attend those who dream of blacking their own shoes. If the shoes are on someone else, it predicts luck at the races. 001

BLACKJACK. To dream of using a blackjack on an enemy is a warning against losing your temper, for it predicts an occasion on which you will wish to do someone bodily harm. 972

BLACKMAIL. If someone tries to blackmail you in a dream, you should be warned against free and easy conduct with members of the opposite sex. If you are the blackmailer, you will have general bad luck for a long period. 475

BLACK MARIA. A dream of opposites. It is a sign of better times ahead if you are carried off in this police wagon. If you dream of seeing others being taken away in a Black Maria, the augury is of sadness ahead. 012

BLACK SHEEP. To be called a "black sheep" in a dream means that you will have a temptation which, if it is not overcome, will prove that you are. Therefore this is a warning to watch your step. To dream of seeing a sheep that is actually black predicts an experience that will be both amusing and profitable. 312

BLADDER. To see a bladder, means you will have a physical setback if you are not careful of your health and the way you exert yourself. To see children blowing up bladders denotes the failure of your expectations. 846

BLADE. (See also Cut, Knife, Razor, Sword.) A bright, keen blade without a handle of any kind predicts that you are in danger of being criticized for questionable conduct. A rusty blade indicates illness. 582

BLAME. (See also Praise.) If you dream of hearing a person take the blame for something, you should look out for hypocrisy among your friends. If you are blamed, you will be fortunate in business, but if you blame someone else, your peace of mind will be threatened. 923

BLANKET. To dream of soiled or ragged blankets signifies treachery. If they are snowy white and new, success will follow where you feared failure, and a fatal illness will be avoided. 920

BLARNEY. Beware of making insincere statements, for if you dream of indulging in blarney, they will certainly react on you seriously. 750

BLASPHEMY. Blasphemy predicts an enemy who under the pretense of friendship will cause you great embarrassment. If you yourself blaspheme, it denotes evil fortune. If you are cursed by others, relief from financial troubles will follow. 562

BLAST. To dream of setting off a blast is a prediction of greater ease than you have heretofore enjoyed. 698

BLAST FURNACE. This is a fortunate dream for young men or women who are just entering on a business career. To dream of feeding a roaring blast furnace is a sign of rapid advancement. 623

BLAZE. (See also Fire.) In a fireplace a blaze foretells home comforts and obedient children. A blazing house is an omen that your friends will distrust you. 851

BLEACHING. (See also Hair.) For a young woman to dream of bleaching her hair is an omen of popularity among men. If a man has this dream, the prediction is one of shame. 675

BLEATING. Young bleating animals signify new duties and cares, but since they will be pleasant ones, this is a fortunate dream. 727

BLEEDING. Death by accident or malicious reports about you are the omens of the dream of bleeding. Fortune will desert you. 379

BLEEDING HEART. This old-fashioned flower augurs contentment when seen in a dream. To wear it in your buttonhole is an omen of good news. 519

BLEMISH. If a maiden dreams that she has one or more blemishes on her face, she will be wooed by many lovers. If her blemishes are on her legs, she will have to use extraordinary precaution to protect her reputation. 565

BLESSING. If one of the clergy or a poor person pronounce a blessing on you, your dream will portend a happy future, but if in your dream you bless another, you will have many vexations to contend with. 200

BLIGHT. To see growing things afflicted with blight is a warning against careless behavior in the company of light-hearted companions. 867

BLIMP. This form of dirigible balloon seen in a dream soaring overhead carries a portent of impending trouble. To be a passenger in fair weather augurs promotion; in stormy weather it promises trouble. 087

BLINDFOLD. If a woman dreams of being blindfolded, a disturbing influence will arise in her life. Disappointment will be felt by others on her account. 137

BLIND MAN'S BUFF. If you dream of playing blind man's buff, you will engage in some foolish venture which will humiliate you, and from which you will suffer money losses. 548

BLINDNESS. You may expect a change from comfort to poverty, if you dream of being blind. To see others who are blind denotes that some worthy person will ask you for financial aid. 785

BLINKING. A person or animal blinking his eyes points toward a situation in which you will be required to use great tact. 368

BLOCK. If you dream of seeing or handling a block of wood, stone, metal or other hard material, you are almost certain to need financial help. 941

BLOCKADE. In time of war, it is a sign of hunger ahead if you dream of your country being the object of a blockade. If you dream of blockading the ports of an enemy country, you will be mistaken for a fool by an acquaintance. 570

BLONDE. Men who dream of blonde women are in danger. Misbehavior in such a dream predicts illness, loss of reputation or money, and business reverses through inattention to work. To dream of seeing a blonde woman putting on her hat is a sign of an automobile accident. Women who dream of being admired for their blonde hair are likely to have an illness. 587

BLOOD. To dream of blood-stained garments warns of enemies who will try to destroy the successful career that is opening up for you. Beware of strange friendships after this dream. If blood flows from a wound, beware of physical deterioration and guard against business failure from disastrous dealings with foreign concerns. If blood is on your hands, you will have a long period of bad luck, unless you are careful of your person and your personal affairs. 293

BLOODHOUND. Unless they appear to be on your trail bloodhounds are a fortunate augury in a dream. They portend faithfulness on the part of a friend. If they pursue you, the omen is one of deceitfulness from a former friend. 225

BLOOD MONEY. If you dream of taking money for the betrayal of a person, you are warned against association with people with red hair. Otherwise, violent quarrels will ensue. 324

BLOOD STONE. To see a blood stone foretells disaster in your engagements. For a young woman to receive a gift of a blood stone means that she will lose a friend, but will make a new one who will more than make up for the loss. 621

BLOOD SUCKER. (See also Leech, Vampire.) Dreaming of being attacked by a blood-sucking animal is a sign that you should choose your companions more carefully. 759

BLOSSOMS. To see trees and shrubs in bloom presages a time of great prosperity and ease, both of body and of mind. 777

BLOT. It is a forerunner of sadness to dream of making an ink blot while you are writing with a pen. 612

BLOTCH. (See also Pimple.) A young man or woman who dreams of seeing a blotch of any kind on the face, arms or legs is warned against temptations to drink alcoholic beverages to excess. 416

BLOTTING PAPER. To use blotting paper indicates that you will be in danger of betraying secrets which will involve a good friend. If you see worn blotting paper, family quarrels or disagreement with friends may be expected. 346

BLOW. Beware of injury to yourself. If you receive a blow, you will be likely to get into difficulties of a serious kind. To defend yourself means a rise in business. 862

BLOWGUN. Anyone who is a skilled worker with the hands will profit greatly from a dream of a savage using a blowgun. To dream of a boy using one in school foretells many parties and entertainments. 008

BLOWOUT. If one of your automobile tires blows out in a dream, it is a warning to guard against accidents. 623

BLUDGEON. It is good luck to dream of hitting a person with a bludgeon, particularly if the person is misbehaving. To dream of being hit is a sign that people are gossiping about you. You should find out the cause and correct it. 098

BLUSHING. If a young woman dreams of blushing, she will be concerned in and shamed by lying reports. If she sees others blush, she will be in danger of making wisecracks that will displease her friends. 223

BOA-CONSTRICTOR. To dream of a snake is on a par with dreaming of the devil; it predicts hard times and ill fortune, as with Adam and Eve. Disillusionment will follow. To kill a boa-constrictor is good fortune. 459

BOAR. No one should engage in a new enterprise soon after dreaming about a boar. It is a warning to use extreme care in all matters pertaining to business. 700

BOARDING HOUSE. To see a boarding house in your dreams, predicts chaotic conditions in business, and you will probably move to a new address. 448

BOARDWALK. To dream of strolling along a seaside boardwalk in the company of an agreeable person of the opposite sex predicts an expected but long delayed legacy. 432

BOASTING. To boast in dreams presages regret for an impulsive act, which may cause trouble among your friends. To boast to a rival foretells that you will be unjust and will use questionable means to get ahead of your competitors. 505

BOAT. Signals seen from a boat forecast bright prospects, if you are upon still water. If the water is turbulent, you are threatened with many cares. If you are with a gay party aboard a sailboat, many favors will be bestowed upon you. To dream of falling overboard from a boat foretells irritations. 722

BOBBIN. A bobbin means important work for you, but your interests will be adversely affected if you neglect the proper attention to the bobbins under your care. 404

BOCK BEER. This is a good luck dream for all those who earn a living as operators of vehicles, elevators, trains or other carriers. 671

BODICE. For a girl to dream that her bodice is unfastened or slovenly is an omen that she must take care that her conduct is not open to criticism. 587

BODY. A beautiful body seen in a dream is a portent of success. A female body augurs public approval, while a male body predicts business advancement. 740

BODY SNATCHER. If you should dream of seeing anyone robbing a grave of the body buried there, you will be criticized for something that is not your fault. If you yourself are the grave robber, you are warned against taking sides in any quarrels among your friends or relatives. 096

BOG. To dream of trying to walk through a bog predicts a difficult time that you will find trouble in overcoming. You may be sure of rising above it through concentrated effort. 313

BOGY. Good luck will attend anyone who dreams of seeing a terrifying and grotesque figure of semi-human form. It predicts relief from money troubles. 208

BOHEMIAN. If you have a dream of being with artistic or literary people known as bohemians and of living an unconventional life, you are likely to get into difficulties through being misunderstood. It is a warning against making new friends too quickly. 512

BOILER. To see a rusty boiler of any kind foretells that you will suffer from disappointment. For a woman to dream that she sees a boiler in a cellar signifies that sickness and losses will come to her. 741

BOILS. It is an augury of distasteful work ahead if you dream of having a boil lanced. If you dream of picking at a boil, you will have trouble with your near relatives. 985

BOLERO. This short, sleeveless jacket, worn by a Spaniard in a dream, points to gayety that must be held in leash lest it go too far. As part of a woman's costume it predicts a hectic love affair. 189

BOLL WEEVIL. Cotton farmers who dream of this insect pest will do well to guard their reputation, for the dream is a warning against slanderous enemies. 937

BOLO. This wicked sword used by the wild Moro tribe of the Philippines is a symbol of sudden disaster when seen in a dream. In use by a savage it predicts the fulfillment of the thing you have most dreaded. 340

BOLONEY. You will be surprised by a sudden turn in your luck, either for better or for worse, if you dream of eating boloney. If you dream of hearing or using the word in a slang sense, you will have an amusing experience. 051

BOLSHEVISM. You are warned of devastating influences on your career if you dream of being affiliated with groups of people who have bolshevistic tendencies. 934

BOLSTER. One who dreams of putting a bolster on a bed will have an experience that he or she will wish to hide. To put a fresh slip on a bolster is a sign of having a new opportunity of making good. 854

BOLTS. From this dream you may expect that formidable obstacles will oppose your progress. If the bolts are broken or old, you will not succeed in your expectations. 541

BOMBARDMENT. One may look forward with confidence to security if he or she dreams of being bombarded by the guns of an enemy. 804

BOMBERS. These airplanes, seen soaring above you in a dream, predict a menace in your life that can be averted by the decisive use of your best judgment. If bombs are dropped and do not appear to explode, you are in danger of losing your position. If they explode, you will change your place of residence. 794

BOMBPROOF. It is a sign that you need not worry about the future if you dream of going into a bombproof shelter in wartime. 462

BOMB-SHELLS. Dreams of bomb-shells foretell anger and disputes, ending in lawsuits. Many upsetting incidents are likely to follow this dream. 281

BONANZA. To dream that you are a miner and strike a bonanza is a sign that you will have to work hard for a living. 912

BONBONS. If you dream of sending bonbons to a favored friend or lover, you will be accused of duplicity by a trusted friend. 230

BONDS. To receive valuable bonds in a dream augurs well for those who are connected with the building trades. 653

BONDAGE. It is unfortunate to dream of being in bondage to another person for whatever reason. 110

BONDSMAN. A sharp-featured bondsman who, in a dream, goes bail for you if you are arrested, is an augury of success in buying and selling. 114

BONES. If you dream that bones stick out from the flesh, beware of treachery. A pile of bones predicts famine or other bad influences. 858

BONESET. The use of this old-fashioned herb for medicine in a dream is a forerunner of contented family life. If you dream of burning it, you are likely to have serious arguments with good friends. 307

BONFIRE. (See also Blaze.) A large bonfire is indicative of your triumph over difficulties, unless a wind scatters sparks from it, in which case it predicts annoyances. 061

BON MOT. A bright saying—yours or another's—in a dream points toward a happy, carefree future. 704

BONNET. A black bonnet in a dream denotes much gossip and basely vile insinuations, from which a woman should defend herself. If a man sees a woman tying on her bonnet, good luck is far away, but his friends will be faithful. If a young woman's bonnet is new and of any color except black, she will engage in a harmless flirtation. Black bonnets mean false friends of the opposite sex. 773

BONUS. To dream of receiving a sum of money over and above what is due you is a sign that you are on the right track in your business career. 974

BOOBY. If there is any augury from a dream of being considered a booby, it is of an amusing experience in store for you. Altogether, it is a happy dream. 910

BOOK. To dream of books and reading denotes pleasant days and honor and riches if you study them. For an author to dream of his own manuscript going to press, means caution; he will encounter difficulties in placing it before the public. To see children at their books, predicts harmony and good behavior among young people. To dream of old books is a warning to avoid the appearance of evil. 445

BOOKCASE. To dream of a bookcase, is a sign that you will apply yourself diligently both to your work and recreation. To see an empty bookcase presages loss of position due to lack of education. 435

BOOK ENDS. The accomplishment of a favorite project is predicted by a dream in which book ends are a feature. 886

BOOKKEEPER. (See Accountant.) 396

BOOKMARK. If you dream of using a bookmark to keep your place in a book you are reading, you will be sure to keep an appointment that will be of benefit to you. 839

BOOK PLATE. It is an augury that you will lose caste through selfishness if you dream of pasting a book plate in one of your books. 049

BOOKSELLER. To dream that you earn a living by selling books predicts that you will have many friends who are both intellectual and agreeable. It is also lucky for you to dream of talking with a bookseller. 901

BOOKSTORE. If you visit a bookstore in your dream, you will become a writer, but your literary attempts will interfere with your regular work and pleasure. 752

BOOKWORM. For someone to call you a bookworm in a dream is a presage of quiet happy hours. Loss of money is predicted if you use the name for somebody else. 859

BOOM. To be struck by a boom while dreaming of being on a sailboat is a sign that you should be wary of strangers who profess friendship. 024

BOOMERANG. If you dream of throwing a boomerang and it comes back and hits you, it is a warning against making careless or unguarded statements. 763

BOOT. If you see a pair of boots on another, your place will be usurped in the affections of your sweetheart. If you wear a new pair of boots, you will be fortunate in business. If you are working for another, you will receive a higher salary. Old or worn out boots foretell sickness and trouble. 697

BOOTBLACK. If in a dream of being a bootblack, you take pride in your work, the prophecy is of many happy days to come. If you appear to be ashamed of it, you will be unhappy. 706

BOOTJACK. Easy living is predicted by a dream of using an old-fashioned bootjack for removing one's boots. 973

BOOTLEGGER. Dealings with a bootlegger in a dream foretell a change in your plans, perhaps for the better. A woman bootlegger portends gloom. 213

BOOTY. To find booty that has been hidden by pirates or thieves is a sign of prosperity at an early date. 049

BOOZE. (See Alcohol, Beer, Whiskey, Wine.) 409

BORACIC ACID. It is a sign that you will receive a message to get in touch with an influential person, either a man or woman, who will contribute to your advancement. 491

BORAX. To dissolve borax in a tub of water before taking a bath in a dream signifies that you will live to old age in comfort and good health. 455

BORDERLAND. A dream of being on the borderland between two states or countries predicts a period of indecision. 237

BORE. Look out for articles falling from high places if you have a dream of having to talk with a bore or a tiresome person. 674

BORER. If you dream of seeing this boring insect boring into plant stems or the bark of trees, you are warned to pay more attention to business and less to frivolous occupations. You may have a rival in love. 754

BORROWING. To borrow denotes loss and a smaller income. If a banker dreams of borrowing from another bank, he may expect a run on his bank and possible failure. If someone borrows from you, you are assured of assistance being given you if you are ever in need. True friends will stand by you. 051

BOSOM. If a young woman dreams that her bosom is hurt, some calamity will overtake her. If she dreams of a flat or wrinkled bosom, she may expect to be heartbroken, although many rivals will contend for her. If the bosom is creamy and voluptuous, she will inherit a fortune. If her sweetheart peers at her bosom through her sheer gown, she will fall a victim to an ardent admirer. 056

BOSS. It is a good sign to dream of being on friendly terms with the boss, but it is also a warning against loafing on the job. 175

BOSTON TERRIER. A friendly but excitable Boston terrier seen in a dream predicts financial improvement but warns against "burning the candle at both ends." 693

BOTANY. The scientific study of flowers in a dream foretells calm after storm, but not much profit. 724

BOTCH. To dream of making a botch of anything you make with your hands is a forerunner of discovery if you have anything to hide. 702

BOTTLES. It is a good sign to dream of a bottle if it is full of a transparent liquid. You will be successful in love, and prosperous in business. If the bottle is empty, you will be faced with disaster, from which you must exert great pressure to escape. 769

BOTTOM. (See also Buttocks.) If in a dream you look at the bottom of a dish, you will quarrel with a relative. 307

BOUDOIR. (See also Bedchamber, Bedfellow.) For either a man or woman to dream of a scented, luxurious boudoir is a warning against indiscriminate alliances and careless behavior. If a man dreams of an amorous intrigue in a boudoir, it warns him to be exceedingly circumspect in all his relations with women. 291

BOUILLON. (See Soup.) 628

BOULDER. If one dreams of moving a large rock or boulder with ease, it portends better business conditions. It tells of bad luck when it cannot be moved at all. A falling boulder is a sign of change. 369

BOULEVARD. To dream of driving a car along a well-paved boulevard during the daytime portends favors from your creditors. At night if it is well lighted, the prediction is of a journey to a strange locality. A dark boulevard is a sign of disappointment. 964

BOUNTY. Hunters who dream of receiving a bounty from the state for the pelt of a wolf, coyote or other animal pest are warned against plots by designing men and women. 681

BOUQUET. A fragrant bouquet of bright-colored flowers signifies a bequest from some affluent and distant relative; also festivities among the young people. If you see a faded bouquet, it denotes illness and possible death. 982

BOURBON. To drink Bourbon whiskey in a dream is a prediction of a profitable real estate deal. 330

BOUT. (See Boxer.) 734

BOW AND ARROW. To dream of shooting at a target with a bow and arrow foretells that you will make a profit at someone else's expense. If you shoot at an animal, you will meet an old friend. 240

BOWER. Romantic dream meetings in a pleasant bower of vines, trees or flowers are a forerunner of happiness to young and old. 779

BOWIE KNIFE. A desperate love affair is predicted if you dream of handling or wearing a bowie knife in your belt. 674

BOWL. An empty bowl signifies want. Filled with food, it is a generally good omen, but the nature of the contents will determine the omen. Look them up in other parts of this book, also the color of the bowl. 428

BOW LEGS. You should look to your own conduct if you dream of seeing a man, woman or child with bow legs. 507

BOWLING. You will be successful in your efforts to make a living if you dream of bowling, either in an alley or out of doors. 534

BOWSPRIT. A dream of climbing out on the bowsprit of a sailboat is a forerunner of exciting experiences. If the sea is rough, danger is ahead, but if you are not shaken off, you will come through without harm. 355

BOW-STRING. To dream of stringing a bow in preparation for the shooting of arrows is a prediction of a great social achievement, whether you are a man or a woman. 667

BOX. To open a box of household goods foretells wealth and enjoyable travels in South American countries. If the box is empty you will be disappointed in your work. If you see boxes full of money you will have freedom from care and will enjoy your business. 349

BOXER. A dream of men fighting in the prize ring is a sign of advancement through close attention to work. If you dream that you are a boxer, the augury is favorable if you hold your own against your opponent. Otherwise you will have a minor injury. 611

BOXWOOD. To jump over a boxwood hedge in a dream is an omen of a vexing problem that you will be able to solve without much difficulty. To dream of using a saw on boxwood predicts that you will help a good friend out of difficulties. 765

BOY. Boys at any kind of play are a good sign, especially if they are engaged in athletic events. Even a dream of fighting boys augurs well for the dreamer. A boy at play with a girl predicts happiness in marriage and love affairs. If one boy is at play with several girls, the prophecy is of an adventure that will turn out well. A boy at work to earn money is a fortunate omen for those who are contemplating marriage. 470

BOY SCOUT. Some wish that is close to your heart will be gratified if you dream of one or more Boy Scouts in the observance of their ritual. 329

BRACELET. If you wear a bracelet upon your arm or wrist, the dream augurs a present from your sweetheart or a friend and insures happiness in your marriage. Worn on your ankle, it predicts a scandal. If a young woman loses a bracelet she will have minor worries. If you find a bracelet you will inherit property. 108

BRACKEN. If you dream of lying among the bracken or other fern-like growth, there will be an exciting experience in store for you. Whether this will be agreeable or otherwise depends on the innocence surrounding your being there. 830

BRAGGART. A dream of hearing a person brag about his prowess in any line predicts a period of depression; but if you can put him to shame, the outcome will be hopeful. 867

BRAID. Uniforms or dresses trimmed with braid of gold or bright colors augur a promotion to a higher and better paying job. To see young girls with their hair done up in braids is a sign that you will be happy in your marriage. 276

BRAIN. To dream of your own brain foretells irritations. Your home and friends will displease you and you will become disgruntled and unhappy. If you see or eat the brains of animals you will hear profitable news from an unexpected source. 962

BRAKE. It is an omen of greater responsibilities ahead if you dream of applying the brake to a motor-car or other vehicle. If the brake does not slow down the vehicle, you must guard against making commitments that you cannot carry through. If the brake squeaks, you are in danger of being accused of a terrible crime. 506

BRAKEMAN. A woman who dreams of seeing a brakeman at work on a railroad train will live to see many changes for the better, both for herself and her friends. 351

BRAMBLES. If you are caught in brambles, beware of evil influences. Law-suits will be settled unfavorably, and you or a member of your family may suffer from disease. 143

BRANCH. The branches of a tree waving in a gentle breeze predict new interests for those who have found life dull. If the tree is in bloom, there is an augury of increasing comfort. In a gale the omen is not so good, although there is nothing to disturb the dreamer. 274

BRANDY. Brandy signifies great wealth and affluence but you probably will lack consideration for others. The people whose friendship you would like to cultivate will avoid you. 210

BRASS. The dream of brass utensils of all kinds means that you will advance rapidly in your business, but while assured of success you inwardly anticipate misfortune. 014

BRASSIERE. If a man dreams of adjusting a brassiere, he is warned against making any false steps in his association with the gentler sex. For him to dream of acting the part of peeping Tom is to expect an occurrence that may exercise a profound influence on his life. If a woman dreams of forgetting to wear a brassiere she will be likely to have an altercation with someone she knows well. If she dreams that a strap breaks when she is in the company of a man, she will have an invitation to a party. 554

BRAT. Those who are employed in industrial jobs will be able to look forward to easier conditions if they dream of being annoyed by brats. For clerical workers, the dream predicts a happy home life. 524

BRAVADO. A show of fake bravery in a dream is a forerunner of quiet enjoyment from simple pleasures. 681

BRAVERY. One who dreams of being brave under unusually distressing conditions will have an opportunity to demonstrate that he can be brave. 799

BRAWL. To be a witness of or participate in a brawl is a good sign if no injury results for the dreamer. Otherwise it foretells misfortune. 434

BRAWN. A display of brawn by yourself or others in a dream foretells physical troubles. 820

BRAY. To hear an ass bray predicts bad news. 715

BRAZIL NUT. To dream of having a battle with these large nuts is an omen that you will have to contend with unreasonable people. 273

BREACH OF PROMISE. It is a warning against light love affairs if a man dreams of being sued for breach of promise. For a woman to dream of suing indicates that she should regulate her life so as to avoid criticism for her acts. 523

BREAD. If a woman dreams of eating bread, she will be the mother of obstinate children for whom she will work hard and worry. If any one eats bread with another, he will be certain of always being well cared for. If you see stale bread, unhappiness and illness will come to you. If the bread is fresh and you eat it, the omen is a good one. You will be prosperous. 783

BREADLINE. You may look forward to good health if you dream of standing in a breadline. To see others in such a line predicts poverty and loss of friends. 266

BREAK. To break anything is a bad dream. If you break a leg or an arm, you are warned that you are mismanaging your affairs and are likely to be disappointed. To break a window foretells death. To break furniture means quarrels in the home and consequent worry. To dream of a broken finger ring warns that you will have heated arguments that will cause great unhappiness. 274

BREAKDOWN. If you dream of a breakdown in health, you are warned against being too free with your money. 620

BREAKFAST. If your work is mental, to dream of breakfast is a good sign. To see fresh milk and eggs on the table and a well-filled bowl of fruit predicts hurried but propitious changes. To eat alone means that you will be overcome by your enemies. If you eat with others, the augury is good. 963

BREAST. (See Bosom.) 782

BREASTBONE. To eat the meat of the breastbone of a chicken, duck or other fowl indicates that you will be prosperous in your old age. 902

BREASTPIN. A young woman who dreams of wearing a breastpin will marry the man of her choice. If the pin is set with diamonds, she will have a wealthy husband. If she pricks herself while putting on the pin, she will be subjected to petty annoyances. 025

BREASTWORKS. Trouble is foretold by a dream of throwing up breastworks or of fighting behind them. 454

BREATH. If you dream of a person with a sweet breath, your conduct will be above criticism and a profitable business deal will be put through. If the breath is not sweet, sickness is foretold. To lose one's breath by overexertion denotes failure where success was expected. 089

BREECHES. Women who dream of wearing breeches will have adventures that they may wish to avoid. Torn breeches signify that you will be held in contempt by someone whose good opinion you value. To dream of trying to put on breeches over a skirt foretells a minor accident. 956

BREEDING. You will have to struggle for an inheritance that is rightfully yours if you dream of breeding horses or cattle. 180

BREEZE. A strong and steady breeze felt in a dream predicts good business conditions. If it comes in gusts and then dies down, you will be worried. 589

BREVIARY. Reading this religious book in a dream is an augury of peace of mind. 254

BREWING. To dream of a brewery augurs injustice and ill treatment from public officials, but you will be exonerated and elevated to a high position. Brewing dreams point toward uneasiness at first, but they end in financial gain and contentment. 874

BRIBERY. To dream of offering a bribe is a warning against those who seek to exploit you for their own selfish ends. Accepting a bribe is a sign of serious illness. 153

BRIC-A-BRAC. It is a sign that your efforts will be wasted if you dream of collecting small ornaments and pieces of china to put around the house. You will have good fortune if you dream of breaking one or more of these. 255

BRICK. To dream of bricks foretells upset business conditions and upsets in your love life. If you manufacture bricks you will not make a great deal of money. 309

BRICKBAT. A dream in which you or others throw brickbats is the forerunner of success in the textile trades. If you are struck by a brickbat, you will meet a charming but unreliable person of the opposite sex. 828

BRICKLAYING. To dream of laying bricks foretells a slowly but surely increasing fortune. 043

BRICKYARD. Passing through a brickyard in a dream foretells years of travel before you finally settle down to a quiet life. It is a favorable sign for women who aspire to be in motion pictures. 104

BRIDAL WREATH. A maiden who dreams of this lovely flower will have many proposals and will make a very advantageous marriage. 684

BRIDE. If a young woman dreams of being a bride she will inherit money, particularly if she appears in a happy frame of mind while dressing for the wedding. If she is displeased she will be disappointed in her husband. If in a dream you kiss a bride, you will be reconciled with former enemies. If a bride kisses others, it foretells many friends and much happiness. If the bride kisses you, your sweetheart will inherit some money. If you kiss a bride who looks tired and ill, it means you will not be successful and that you will be disapproved of by your friends. For a bride to dream of being indifferent to her husband predicts a short honeymoon. 009

BRIDEGROOM. A man who dreams of going through the marriage ceremony is likely to find a sum of money that will relieve him for the time being. If he cannot find the wedding ring in time for the ceremony, he will be criticized for his conduct by his superiors. If a man dreams of being nervous while being married, he will be confronted with the necessity of making a momentous decision. 781

BRIDESMAID. For a girl to dream of being a bridesmaid foretells a happy marriage within the year. If her dress is torn, she will find that her husband is secretive. 374

BRIDGE. To dream of a long wooden bridge with holes in it means that you will suffer distress over the loss of precious possessions. To maidens and bachelors it predicts disappointments and broken engagements, as the beloved one will not live up to your ideals. To dream of crossing a bridge safely is an omen that you will eventually overcome obstacles. If a bridge falls while you are looking at it, be warned of seductive admirers. Clear water flowing under the bridge indicates wealth, but if the water is muddy, you may expect poor returns for your efforts in business. If you are seated at a table playing bridge and drop a card, you will lose money. If you win at bridge, you will receive a small legacy, but it will not last long. 632

BRIDGEWORK. Anyone who dreams of wearing dental bridgework will have to encounter several difficulties arising from failure to meet obligations. If the bridgework comes loose, the augury is of losing the friendship of an important person. 391

BRIDLE. To put a bridle on a horse in your dream means that you will undertake some unusual business that will cause you great distress, but will end profitably. If the bridle is old or broken you will encounter obstacles that are likely to defeat you. You will be deceived by some intriguing person or someone of the opposite sex will encourage you in a clandestine affair. 036

BRIDLE BITS. To dream of bridle bits is an omen that you will overcome an obstacle that has threatened your advancement. If the bits are broken, or appear to break in the dream, you will have to give in to your competitors. 696

BRIEFCASE. A business trip that will be both pleasant and successful is predicted by a dream of carrying a well-worn briefcase. If it is new and clean, it foretells disappointment resulting from lack of sufficient preparation. 622

BRIER. If you become entangled in a brier patch, it is a sign that unfriendly people are plotting to get ahead of you. Freeing yourself from the thorns predicts that friends will help you out of your difficulty. 345

BRIER PIPE. The ability to meet and solve your problems is promised if you dream of smoking a brier pipe. 461

BRIGAND. To dream of being held up and robbed by a fierce-looking brigand portends the discovery of a conspiracy to defame you. If you get the best of the brigand, the plotters will not be successful. 319

BRILLIANTINE. It is an augury of advancement to dream of putting this on your hair or mustache. 387

BRIM. A hole in the brim of a hat portends physical pain. If one dreams of a chip out of the brim of a tea or coffee cup, there will be disagreeable people to contend with. To see a bowl brimful of food foretells joy. 288

BRIMSTONE. Brimstone suggests that you have been using dishonorable business tactics that will cause the loss of many friends, if you do not turn over a new leaf. To dream of seeing brimstone fires means that you will be alarmed and suffer loss through a contagious disease in your neighborhood. 421

BRISKET. Eating brisket is a good sign for those engaged in jobs where skill in the use of figures is required. To see it in a meat store augurs an increase in income. 796

BRISTLES. If you dream of brushing your hair or your teeth with a brush whose bristles are soft and flabby, you will be disappointed in the way your fortunes will turn. If the bristles are stiff and vigorous, good luck may be expected. 982

BROADCAST. Listening to a broadcast in a dream portends success for those who aspire to go into radio of any kind. To dream that you are broadcasting means that your ideas will be treated with respect. 159

BROADCLOTH. To dream of wearing broadcloth is a presage of prosperity through a wise choice of friends. 350

BROCADE. If you dream that your garments are of rich brocade, beware of hypocrisy on the part of those with whom you associate. 285

BROGAN. Rough shoes or brogans that hurt your feet are an omen of a distasteful job ahead of you. 091

BROGUE. A dream of hearing someone speak with a brogue augurs a rise to affluence and power. 625

BROKER. No one who has a dream of a broker—whether in securities or commodities—ought to engage in speculation before a month has passed. 021

BROMIDE. It is distinctly unfortunate to dream of taking bromides to make you sleep. It foretells an accident. 932

BRONCHITIS. Bronchitis predicts that you will be prevented from carrying out your plans by illness in your immediate family. If one suffers with bronchitis in a dream, disappointment is in store and the possibility of attaining your objective will be doubtful. 916

BRONCO. No one can afford to disregard this warning against the underhanded activities of others if he dreams of being thrown by a bronco. 627

BRONZE. If a woman dreams of a bronze statue she will very likely fail to marry the man of her choice. If the statue moves or appears to be alive, she will fall in love but no marriage will take place. To see a bronze serpent or insect means that you will meet insecurity and jealousy. 830

BROOCH. (See Breastpin.) 406

BROOD. To dream of a hen with her brood of chickens foretells troubles to a woman. You will have several children under your care, and some of them will be stubborn and mischievous. If you see another kind of brood, it denotes the building up of a fortune. 472

BROOD MARE. It is an augury of definite improvement in home affairs to dream of seeing a brood mare with a young foal. A brood mare at the time of foaling predicts a happy event. 966

BROOM. To see a broom means that thrift and better luck will come to you in the near future, if the broom is new. If the broom is an old one, you will lose in the stockmarket. If a woman loses a broom she will be a cross wife and a poor housekeeper. 425

BROTH. To dream of broth predicts the loyalty of friends, who will always be true to you, and if you are in need of funds they will supply you with them. To lovers it denotes an enduring affection. If you make broth, you will govern your own and other destinies. 382

BROTHEL. It ought to be a forerunner of disgrace to dream of visiting a brothel, but instead it signifies honors and a dignified happy home life. For either a man or a woman the dream predicts an improvement in his or her condition. 153

BROTHER. A dream of loyalty and affection between brothers is a sign of increasing stability in financial and social position. 113

BROTHER-IN-LAW. If you dream of respecting your brother-in-law, you will discover that he lacks the very qualities that you had hoped to find in him. 483

BRUISE. Any accident in a dream that results in a bruise is a sign that you will be admired for your conduct in an emergency. A bruise on the leg, however, is a warning against carelessness at street crossings. 384

BRUSH. To use a hair or a toothbrush with flabby and ineffective bristles predicts disappointment, but if the bristles are stiff you will be pleased by developments in both home and business affairs. 920

BRUSHWOOD. Clearing away brushwood in a dream foretells a harrowing experience with one of the opposite sex. Burning brushwood warns against too great familiarity with chance acquaintances. 989

BRUSSELS CARPET. It is a forerunner of affluence and comfort if you dream of having this luxurious floor covering in your home. A dream of having it in the kitchen predicts an amusing experience with a new friend. 656

BRUSSELS SPROUTS. (See also Cabbage.) These little cabbages, as they are called by the French, are a sign of luxury ahead. To smell them cooking predicts a reward for work well done. To eat them signifies health and plenty. 273

BRUTALITY. A dream in which you are a witness to brutality predicts that you will revisit the scenes of your childhood. If you are the victim, you will see an improvement in income. 129

BUCKBOARD. Those who dream of riding in a buckboard may look forward with certainty to peace and comfort in their old age. With one horse it is a good dream, but if there is a team it is better. 172

BUCKET. To carry water or milk in a bucket is a sign that you will remember happier days. It foretells death if you stumble over a bucket. 629

BUCKLE. Numerous invitations will come to you to attend social functions if you dream of buckles, but you should be warned of neglecting your business or church duties. 148

BUCKSAW. A vacation is predicted by a dream of cutting wood with a bucksaw. If you dream of being very tired from this work, your vacation will be in the company of one of the opposite sex. 868

BUCKSHOT. Loading a gun with buckshot is a warning dream against giving way to bursts of ungovernable temper. 644

BUCK TOOTH. It is a premonition of sadness to dream of one or more prominently protruding teeth. On someone else it portends travel to faraway lands. 191

BUCKWHEAT. A thriving field of blossoming buckwheat is an omen of a calm but prosperous career. Buckwheat cakes signify that your ambitions will be realized, particularly in love. 525

BUDGET. A woman who dreams of budgeting her expenditures will not be popular with men. A man who has this dream will be likely to succeed in business. 742

BUFFALO. (See Bison.) 315

BUGLE. To hear triumphant blasts of a bugle portends unexpected happiness through someone who is far away. It augurs good luck to dream of blowing a bugle. If you dream of a bugler sounding "Taps", you will have a sad experience. 270

BUGS. There is likely to be an event that will disgust you if you dream of bugs. If the house is overrun with bugs, the prediction is one of serious illness or worse. If in the dream you are successful in getting rid of them, the omen is better. 577

BUILDING. To dream of seeing magnificent and imposing buildings with flower gardens and lawns is a sign that you will be wealthy and that you will be able to indulge in the luxury of travel. If the buildings are of modest size and well kept in appearance, it predicts a happy home and good business. Old and unsightly buildings predict unhappiness. 383

BUILDING AND LOAN. It is lucky to dream of saving for a home. To open an account in a Building and Loan is a harbinger of contentment and a happy family life. 581

BULL. If in a dream you are chased by a bull, you should look out for grasping competitors for your business. If a woman encounters a bull, she will be likely to receive a proposal of marriage, but she should not accept it. You are warned against borrowing money if you dream of seeing a bull goring a person. It is a good omen to see a white bull in a dream, for it predicts promotion through understanding. 340

BULLDOG. If a bulldog attacks you while you are trespassing on another's property in a dream, you are warned against infractions of the law such as disobeying motor regulations, falsifying your income tax return, etc. 223

BULLET. The whine of a bullet, shot from a pistol or gun and heard in a dream, is an indication that you are in great danger and that you should use every precaution against exposing yourself to criticism. A lead bullet thrown at you by a strange person means that you will be slandered by someone you have trusted. To dream of finding a bullet is a sign that someone is plotting against you. To dream of being struck by a bullet is a prediction of illness or disgrace, or both. 569

BULLETIN. It is an augury of momentous happenings in your country if you dream of reading bulletins in front of a newspaper office. A bulletin of the death of a president of the country predicts a period of unrest. 866

BULLFIGHT. If you dream of being at a bullfight and appear to be interested and excited by it, you are warned of a none too pleasant experience inside your home circle. If you are disgusted by the exhibition, you will travel to foreign lands. 224

BULLFINCH. A dream of seeing this interesting bird predicts a short period of prosperity. 172

BULLFROG. To hear bullfrogs in a dream augurs peace of mind. To see them predicts meeting new and interesting people. To catch them indicates that you will be deceived by someone whom you have trusted. 496

BULLOCK. If you dream of a bullock, you may look forward to the pleasant companionship of friends who are tried and true, besides which you will enjoy good health. 851

BULLSEYE. A dream of engaging in target practice with any kind of weapon is a fortunate one if you are successful in hitting the bullseye once, but if you hit it every time you shoot, you should be on your guard against enemies who are trying to frame you. 824

BULL TERRIER. This dream predicts that you will win recognition from your employer through unremitting effort in his behalf. To be attacked by a bull terrier is not a bad sign, but carries a warning to give more attention to business and less to social diversions. 443

BULLY. If in a dream you take the part of someone against a bully, you will find that the people with whom you come in contact will show you great respect. You will have bad luck for a long time if you dream of bullying someone else. 947

BUM. To dream of giving money or food or encouragement to a bum is a sign that you will advance in your social relations. To refuse assistance or to criticize a bum harshly is a forerunner of disgrace. 326

BUMBLEBEE. If a bumblebee buzzes around your head in a dream, you will be able to carry out some great ambition that you have had. To dream of being stung by a bumblebee is a sign of coming prosperity. 866

BUMP. Those who have been contemplating some action that may not be lawful or ethical should be warned to go slowly if they dream of being in any vehicle that bumps another. It is a warning to be extremely careful in your actions. 224

BUMPER. If the bumper on your automobile comes loose in a dream and rattles as you drive, you must try to make amends for any wrong you have recently done to an acquaintance. If the bumper drops off the car, it is a sign of trouble for you. 172

BUNDLE. A mystery that will be difficult to solve is indicated by a dream of seeing someone carrying a bundle. If you dream of wrapping a bundle of any kind, you will be criticized by your friends for not being frank. 496

BUNGALOW. A bungalow in a dream predicts the friendly regard of the people you meet. If you rent a bungalow, you will be successful in business, but if you build one, you will also be advanced socially. 851

BUNGHOLE. To try to look into the bunghole of a beer or whiskey barrel is a sign that you will fail to achieve the purpose for which you have been working. If you dream of filling a barrel through the bunghole, you have a long period of distress before you. Driving a bung into a bunghole is a sign of successful achievement. 824

BUNION. Pain felt from a bunion in a dream is a sign of definite comfort in old age. To dream of having a chiropodist attend to a bunion is to look forward to improved financial circumstances. 443

BUNK. It is an unfortunate augury to dream of going to bed in a bunk, either on shipboard or in a backwoods cabin. You are likely to need money very soon, and it will be difficult to obtain. 947

BUNTING. A dream of seeing buildings or large rooms decorated with bunting presages a violent love affair for women and a hectic period of business for men. If you dream of using bunting for decorating, you will find yourself in an unusual dilemma. 326

BURDEN. Carrying a heavy burden, whether it is material or spiritual, is a dream that foretells grave responsibilities. Also someone will infringe on your rights in some kind of property, and you will have difficulty in straightening out your affairs. 968

BURDOCK. To dream of getting a burr stuck in your clothes is a sign of family troubles. If the burr gets stuck in your hair, the prediction is one of disgrace that can be avoided only by the greatest circumspection in your actions. 067

BUREAU. You can be sure of a long period of freedom from care if you dream of laying away clothes in a bureau drawer. It is a sign of petty annoyances if you have to hunt for anything under a bureau. If you have to move a bureau in a dream, beware of those who flatter you. 892

BURGLARS. There is nothing to worry about after a dream about burglars, for they portend an increase in worldly goods. If a burglar points a pistol at you in a dream, the prediction is of an invitation to contribute to a charitable cause. If you are able to put burglars to flight, you will receive money due you. 367

BURIAL. To dream of attending a relative's funeral is a sign of the marriage of another relative if the sun is shining. If it is raining, you will receive news by mail of the illness of a relative. Business reverses may also follow this dream. 859

BURIAL ALIVE. You are likely to make a grave mistake if you dream of being buried alive. If at the last moment you are saved from this fate, you are warned against practices that you know to be unethical. 925

BURLAP. The use of burlap in a dream, whether for making bags or covering walls, predicts that you will make a success of the work in which you are now engaged. 840

BURLESQUE. Attending a burlesque show in a dream predicts that you will have explanations to make for something that you are not responsible for. 212

BURNS. Burns in a dream are an omen of good luck. If you burn your hand, it predicts that you will have the approval of your friends, but if you burn your feet, it predicts that you will be successful in the accomplishment of some difficult task. 261

BURR. (See Burdock.) 678

BURRO. Riding one of these patient little animals is an omen of contentment in your daily life with your family. If the burro is balky, you will have minor irritations. 431

BUS. Riding in a bus foretells difficult times ahead, especially for those who are engaged in clerical or stenographic work. If the bus has an accident, there will be a long period in which the dreamer will be financially embarrassed. 452

BUSH. It is the forerunner of a shameful experience to dream of hiding under a bush if you are being pursued. To see a burning bush in a dream predicts the receipt of surprising but not gratifying news. 550

BUSINESS. Usually it is bad luck to dream about your business. It is likely to be the forerunner of embarrassment in a public place. 734

BUST. (See also Bosom.) It is a sign of a death among the circle of friends to see a sculptured bust of a well known person in a dream. 845

BUSTLE. If a woman dreams of wearing a bustle, she will have an adventure in which a handsome man will figure prominently. 176

BUTCHER. To dream of seeing a butcher kill cattle or sheep is a portent of a long and serious illness in your family. To see him slicing meat portends that your reputation will be besmirched, and it is therefore a warning against committing yourself to anything in writing. 076

BUTLER. One may expect a sudden reversal of fortune if he or she dreams of being waited on by a butler. To dream of being a butler is a sign that you will be able to pay your debts. 821

BUTTER. To eat fresh golden butter is a sign that you will enjoy excellent health and will have the financial means to enjoy it to the full. Even if the butter is rancid, you will be able to make a decent living by hard work. If the dream is of selling butter, you will have an opportunity to make a small amount of money. 844

BUTTERCUP. Wandering through a field of buttercups in a dream foretells a loving mate and happy children. To pick buttercups is an omen of relief from pressing obligations; to throw them away indicates dread of the future. 084

BUTTERMILK. To drink buttermilk in a dream means that you will worry about some indiscretion you have committed. It is bad luck to throw it away or to feed it to swine. To make an oyster stew with buttermilk is a sign that you will be in danger of making poor investments and that you will quarrel with a good friend. 128

BUTTERFLY. A butterfly fluttering its way through a flower garden and occasionally alighting on a blossom is an augury of good fortune. This dream foretells a handsome lover and an early marriage to a maiden. 810

BUTTERNUT. If you try to crack a butternut in a dream, it is an indication that you will overcome your greatest difficulties. If you are successful in extracting the meat, you will receive a legacy. 358

BUTTER SCOTCH. There will be a wedding among your circle of acquaintances if you dream of making or eating this kind of candy. If you dream of breaking a tooth while eating it, you will hear bad news. 640

BUTTOCKS. A dream of kicking a person in the buttocks augurs being promoted to a higher position but losing the respect of those under your authority. To have one's buttocks kicked is a sign of disaster. 275

BUTTON. If you dream of sewing colored or shiny metal buttons on any kind of a uniform, you will win the love of a rich and handsome person. A young man having this dream has a good chance of receiving an appointment to a fine military school. Cloth buttons or those that have become tarnished are a portent of poor health and money losses. To lose a button from a garment is an indication that you will suffer embarrassment. 120

BUTTONHOLE. Worn buttonholes are an indication that you will have additional worries. New buttonholes predict new accomplishments. 569

BUTTONHOOK. Calm days ahead are predicted by a dream of using a buttonhook. 715

BUZZARD. This ungainly scavenger bird seen in a dream is a potent warning against repeating malicious gossip. If you dream of seeing it eat carrion, you are likely to regret some ill-advised action. 065

BUZZER. It is a sign that you will be appreciated at your proper worth socially and in business if you dream that you hear the sound of a buzzer calling you. 688

CAB. To ride in a cab foretells daily labor that you will enjoy. It will make for you a comfortable living. If you ride in the cab at night with one of the opposite sex, you will be in danger of telling your friends a secret that you should keep to yourself. If you dream of driving a public cab, you will work at manual labor with little promise of a salary, but you will enjoy yourself. 366

CABARET. It is a warning against the pride that goeth before a fall if you dream of being a member of a gay party at a cabaret. If you dream of singing or otherwise performing, you are likely to be criticized for indiscreet actions. 104

CABBAGE. It is good luck to dream of cooking a cabbage, but to eat green cabbage predicts a violation of the marriage contract. To cut a head of cabbage into shreds means that through extravagance you are in danger of want. 229

CABIN. To dream of being in the cabin of a ship points to misfortune. Trouble of a legal nature is ahead, and you are likely to lose the case through the perjury of your opponent. To dream of a cabin in the woods is a fortunate augury. 925

CABINET. To dream of putting away things in a cabinet portends that a secret of considerable importance will be revealed to you. It is a sign of improved financial conditions if you dream of locking a cabinet, but if you throw the key away, you will have to work hard for your money. It is not a good augury to dream of moving a cabinet. To take articles out of a cabinet signifies distressing news. 625

CABLE. Stretching a rope or wire cable foretells perilous work. If you accomplish it successfully, you will acquire much money and many honors. 477

CABLEGRAM. If you dream of receiving a cablegram, you will soon be the recipient of an important message that will be accompanied by unpleasant circumstances. 158

CACKLE. To hear hens cackle augurs news of the unexpected death of a neighbor amid circumstances that are not easily understandable. 382

CACTUS. If you dream of being thrown into a clump of cactus, it predicts a series of annoying occurrences. If you see a cactus plant in bloom, you may expect good luck in one form or another. To transplant cactus signifies going from bad to worse. To give a cactus plant in a pot to a friend portends a quarrel. 679

CADAVER. (See Corpse.) 871

CAFETERIA. Getting a trayful of food at a cafeteria is a dream that portends a small legacy from a deceased friend. If you dream of dropping the tray or otherwise spilling the food, you are in danger of illness. If you dream of going back to a counter for more food, you will receive good news. 192

CAGE. To dream of a cage in which many birds are flying about or roosting on perches foretells an inheritance of large size and a sizable family. If there is only one bird in the cage, the dream is a good one for a maiden, for she will marry to her great advantage. An empty cage predicts that you will see a serious accident while on your travels. 724

CAKES. To dream of pancakes shows that the future of the dreamer is secure and that a legacy and a home will be left him or her. Sweet cakes foretell advancement for the laborer and advancement for the industrious in every line. Those in love will be especially gratified. Layer cake denotes satisfaction in society or in business. If a young woman dreams of her wedding cake, it foretells bad luck. It is less fortunate to bake cakes in a dream than to eat them. Fluffy and rich icing on a cake predicts gay times. 941

CALABOOSE. (See Jail.) 318

CALENDAR. (See also Almanac.) To dream of marking off special dates on a calendar is a sign that you will have fewer things to worry about than formerly. 881

CALF. You may rest assured that your hopes will be realized if you dream of a calf receiving sustenance from its mother. To see a calf being butchered is an omen of disillusionment. For a man to dream of admiring the calf of a woman's leg is a sign that he will be hounded by his creditors. 540

CALICO. For a woman to dream of wearing a calico dress while at her housework is a sign of a delightful experience among men and women. If she wears calico at an evening party, she will receive a surprising message. 426

CALL. To dream of hearing your name called by a stranger you cannot see predicts that your financial affairs will be shaky and that you will be unable to meet your obligations promptly. If you hear the voice of a relative or friend, it augurs the sickness and possibly the death of one of them; in the latter case you may be importuned to act as guardian over a young person. For an engaged person to hear the voice of a fiance is a warning against negligence. Otherwise, the engagement is likely to be broken. Serious illness is predicted by hearing the voice of the dead. 726

CALLUS. To dream of having one or more calluses on your hands or feet predicts that you will shortly engage in a new and unusual kind of work. It will be interesting and remunerative. 615

CALM. One who dreams of a sudden calm in storms or periods of stress will have to take care of a noisy group of children. If you dream of calming an angry person, you will succeed in an important business deal. 411

CALOMEL. (See Laxative.) 642

CALUMNY. If in a dream you are the victim of calumny, your reputation will be attacked by evil-minded persons. If a woman has this dream, she should be careful to be guarded in all her acts. 634

CAMELS. To dream of camels portends that when you are beset with worries and irritations you will rise to the occasion and come through the ordeal with flying colors. You will inherit an important mining property if you dream of bringing a camel home. If you dream of seeing camels in a herd, you will be able to look forward to a bright future. 209

CAMEO. It is a sign or relief from storm and stress if you dream of seeing an old lady wearing a cameo ring or breastpin. 184

CAMERA. If you dream of taking pictures with a camera, you are warned against gossiping tongues. If the pictures are still, you will be able to rise above scandal, but if they are in motion, it will be much more difficult. A dream of taking nude pictures, either still or in motion, portends disgrace. If you use a candid camera, you will be shunned by those who were formerly your friends. 049

CAMISOLE. (See also Slip.) A girl who dreams of wearing a soiled camisole will receive attention from a man of great learning. If the camisole is torn, she will be rebuked by an older person. 400

CAMP. An outdoor camp in a dream portends a change in your occupation, and that you will have a long trip to make. To come upon such a camp while in the woods is a prediction that one of your good friends will have to g away. A maiden who dreams that she is camping will soon have to make up her mind which of two suitors she will marry. It is bad luck for a woman to dream that she is in a military camp. 630

CAMPAIGN. The dream of being concerned in a political campaign predicts family squabbles and added responsibilities. If you are engaged in a campaign to raise funds for a worthy cause, you will have a surprising letter from an old schoolmate. 948

CAMPFIRE. The cheerful blaze of a campfire is a forerunner of joy in married life. To dream of cooking over a campfire predicts great prosperity. Gay, though innocent times, are predicted by a dream of toasting marshmallows over a campfire. 934

CAMPFIRE GIRL. This dream is a sign of contentment in family life and pride in one's children. 266

CAMPHOR. If one dreams of smelling camphor, he or she will be annoyed by the attentions of one of the opposite sex. 654

CAMP STOOL. It is an augury of unexplainable conduct on the part of one of your friends if you dream of sitting on a camp stool inside a house or church. 194

CAMPUS. Walking across a college campus with one of the opposite sex predicts many petty disagreements after marriage. 640

CAN. To dream of opening a can of food is a sign that you will be shamed by someone of whom you are very fond. If you cut yourself on a can, you will lose money through a bad investment. 184

CANAL. A considerable loss of money is predicted by a dream of boating on a canal. To swim in a canal is an omen of disappointment in matters pertaining to love. To dream of seeing canal locks open and close is a sign of the unfaithfulness of a friend. 044

CANARY. If in a dream a canary bird shows signs of friendliness, you may be sure of good times ahead. If the bird is frightened, you will be beset by worries of various sorts. A dead canary is a prediction of illness. 774

CANCAN. This indelicate French dance performed by a woman in a dream is a forerunner of embarrassment in a public place. If a man dreams of being the dancer, he had better look well to his future conduct. 012

CANCER. Although it might seem to point otherwise, a dream of this disease portends an improvement in health. 146

CANDLE. To make candles in a dream promises hard work with but little reward. To light them is a sign of improvement in your home affairs. To snuff them out portends unhappiness. If you dream of eating candles, you will travel to a foreign country before long. 822

CANDLE-STICK. Candle-sticks in a dream predict joyous occasions if they are carried with lighted candles in them. To carry one in each hand portends a happy marriage in your family. If the candles are not lighted, there are troublous times ahead. Short, guttering candles are omens of new opportunities. 527

CANDOR. (See Honesty.) 153

CANDY. A maiden who dreams of making candy will have many ardent suitors. If she dreams of eating it, she will have one suitor and an early marriage. If a man gives her a box of candy, she will receive many invitations to parties. For a man to dream of eating candy is a presage of worry. 152

CANE. To dream of seeing sugar cane growing is an augury of an increasing fortune. To see it cut predicts a lessening income. Affluence is predicted if you carry a cane in a dream. If you break the cane, your luck will come to an end. A white cane predicts disaster. 797

CANKER SORE. It is a sign of a major irritation ahead if you dream of having a canker sore in your mouth. 026

CANNED GOODS. You will not only have leisure time but the means to enjoy it if you dream of stocking your larder with canned goods. To open canned goods predicts a series of enjoyable entertainments. 475

CANNERY. If the action of a dream occurs in a food cannery, the influence is a good one, no matter what the dream is about. 456

CANNIBAL. To be chased or captured by cannibals in a dream is a forerunner of dangerous events in your life. To see them cooking or eating human flesh predicts a dire happening close to home. 433

CANNON. The dream of cannon being fired predicts an achievement of which you will be proud. If you dream of pointing and firing the cannon, you will be singled out for a high honor. If a young woman dreams of hearing cannon-fire, she will marry a soldier. 595

CANNON BALL. To see a cannon ball rolling downhill in a dream augurs an accident that you can avoid by paying more attention to those who are dependent on you. A pyramid of cannon balls in a public park is a sign of delightful experiences with persons of the opposite sex. 745

CANOE. Paddling upstream in a canoe or in rough waters is a sign of your being able to overcome serious difficulties. If you dream of being in a canoe on a calm lake or of going downstream with one of the opposite sex, you may look forward to many happy and carefree hours with your sweetheart. To dream of upsetting a canoe and being thrown into the water is a portent of quarrels with those you love best. 009

CANOPY. A canopy in a dream signifies protection, so that if you are under it, you may look forward to comfort and contentment. A young woman who dreams of leaving a church under a canopy stretched over the sidewalk will contract an early and favorable marriage. 677

CANTALOUPE. Illness of a minor nature is foretold by the dream of eating cantaloupe. To see these delicious melons ripening on the vine is a sign of prosperity. 691

CANTEEN. A narrow escape is predicted if you drink from a canteen in a dream. To find a canteen empty predicts failing crops. To lose a canteen means the loss of a friend. 114

CANVAS. If a woman dreams that she is wearing garments made of canvas, it is a sign that she will be loved for herself alone. To sleep under canvas predicts good health and a suitable income. To see the sun shining on the canvas sails of a ship is an augury of safe travel. 741

CANYON. To enter a wooded canyon on foot and follow a stream toward its course is, for maidens and youths, a presage of love and happy marriage. A trip through a canyon on horseback predicts a love life beset by many worries and misgivings. To be lost in a canyon indicates that you will hear bad news. 356

CAP. It is a good sign to dream of wearing a cap, whether you are a man or a woman. You will find that your worries will cease and that you will be fortunate in your investments. For a man who is wearing a cap to dream of meeting a lady friend and having to lift his hat, the omen is of minor difficulties that can easily be overcome. 711

CAPE. Worn in a dream by a person of either sex, a cape signifies that through the exercise of caution you will be able to avoid the consequences of your bad judgment. 996

CAPER SAUCE. You will meet new and interesting people if you dream of eating sauce flavored with pungent capers on roast lamb or other meats. 247

CAPITALIST. One who dreams of being a capitalist, with unlimited money to spend and invest, may look forward to easier circumstances but not to great affluence. 790

CAPITOL. It is a sign of unrest but minor achievement to dream of a capitol building with a dome. Better circumstances are predicted by a fire in a capitol, but it is also a warning against taking too great chances. 627

CAPON. To eat a capon predicts good health. To see it running in a barnyard is an omen of disappointment. To dress a capon indicates that one of your friends will be too curious about your comings and goings. 327

CAPSULE. Taking medicine in a capsule is a sign that your next business deal with one of the opposite sex will be successful. 069

CAPTAIN. To dream that you are a ship's captain or a captain in the army portends a rise in your fortunes. If someone gives you the courtesy title of Captain, you will have a period of depression. A woman who dreams that her lover is a captain must beware of being jealous of her friends. 130

CAPTIVE. A maiden who dreams of being taken captive will be married before a twelve-month period has passed. If she dreams of making a man captive, she will be disappointed in love. A man who dreams of capturing a woman and handling her roughly is warned against boasting. If he dreams of being captured by gangsters, he is likely to be double-crossed by business associates. 729

CAR. (See also Automobile.) Riding in a railroad car or electric car in a dream is a prediction of being able to make a decent living in spite of the obstacles you will meet. 709

CARAMEL. (See also Candy.) If in a dream a caramel gets stuck in your teeth and you are unable to open your mouth, the augury is of trouble with your relatives. If you offer a caramel to another person, you will regret some hasty act. A dream of exceptionally sticky caramels predicts a scandal. 184

CARAVAN. Travel in far lands with a loving mate is predicted by a dream of seeing a caravan wending its way across the desert. 554

CARAWAY SEED. To dream of being disgusted by the taste of caraway seeds is a sign that you will be received hospitably by those whom you have distrusted. If you dream of eating them with relish, you will receive honors from an unsuspected source. 170

CARBOLIC ACID. It is a distinct warning against a foolish display of pride if you dream of drinking this poison. To throw it in a person's face portends serious illness, but to have it thrown at you is a forerunner of happy days. 795

CARBON. If a young man dreams that his automobile engine is full of carbon, he is warned against associating with loose companions. To married people it portends family troubles. 791

CARBON MONOXIDE. Obviously this is a warning against letting an automobile engine run in an enclosed space. 402

CARBUNCLE. (See Boil.) 243

CARBURETOR. If a person dreams of a flooded carburetor on any kind of a gasoline engine, the portent is of accidents that may prove to be serious. 783

CARCASE. It is a forerunner of prosperity to see animal carcases hung in a refrigerator or butcher shop, but if they show signs of deterioration, the augury is of hard times ahead. To dream of buying a whole carcase of a sheep or pig is a sign that you will be called to a higher position. 986

CARDIGAN JACKET. There will be explanations to make for your strange conduct in public places if you dream of wearing a cardigan jacket. If it is old and worn, the consequences will not be unlucky. 613

CARDINAL. This dream is unlucky if you see the cardinal in his ecclesiastical robes. You will have to face a situation that may compel you to change your place of residence. 545

CARDS. (See also Playing Cards.) If you dream of writing show cards, you will buy new clothes for a gala occasion. If the dream is of looking at show cards in shop windows, you will receive a small sum of money that you did not expect. To dream of working at a card index is a portent of suffering through the greediness of another. To buy buttons on a card is a sign that you will have to labor hard for a living. 693

CAREER. A maiden who dreams of being a career woman will have many lovers but no husband. For a man to dream of making a success in a career is a sign that he will consummate an important business deal. 380

CARESS. The significance of a dream about caresses depends on whether they are given under appropriate circumstances. For a lover to caress his sweetheart augurs happiness in marriage. For a maiden to caress her lover predicts early marriage and healthy children. It is a sign of unlucky investments if a married man dreams of caressing any woman other than his wife. 789

CARGO. To dream of loading cargo onto a ship foretells pleasant short trips and picnics. It is an augury of accident to dream of throwing cargo overboard during a storm. 818

CARICATURE. If you dream of seeing a caricature of yourself, it predicts that you will be a target for abuse from others. A dream of drawing a caricature of someone you know is a warning not to speak ill of those whom you do not like. 167

CARILLON. (See also Chime.) Joy will be yours if you dream of hearing a carillon played from a church or other tower. Hearing it over the radio or on a phonograph record portends disappointment in love. You will inherit money if you dream of playing a carillon yourself. 669

CARNATION. You will rise to great heights in business if you dream of wearing a white carnation on your dress or in your buttonhole. A pink carnation augurs success in love affairs; a red one, an exciting adventure. To pluck carnations in a dream indicates trouble for those who drive motor-cars. A dream of withered carnations foretells arguments with near relatives. 295

CARNIVAL. Attending or participating in a carnival predicts that you will be invited to many parties; but if you wear a mask or appear in costume, be warned against drinking too much. 716

CAROL. Whoever dreams of hearing Christmas carols sung by fresh young voices will be happy during the forthcoming year. Singing carols yourself predicts success in love. 402

CAROUSAL. A dream of a carousal in which men and women are drinking, laughing and singing predicts that your actions are likely to be misunderstood by your associates. 170

CAROUSEL. (See Merry-go-Round) 136

CARP. Try your utmost to avoid doing anything that may be criticized if you dream of catching, cooking or eating carp. 398

CARPENTER. One of the best auguries in all dreamland is that of being a carpenter. It predicts that you will be loved by your friends and respected by everyone. You will also have sufficient money to meet all your daily needs. 761

CARPET. To dream of walking on soft carpets denotes an easy and luxurious life in your own home. It is bad luck to dream of cleaning them with a carpet beater. 336

CARRIAGE. Drawn by a horse, a carriage in a dream predicts that you will have to answer embarrassing questions from one of your family. 104

CARRIER PIGEON. If you dream of catching one of these birds and finding a message on it, you are likely to receive astonishing news from an old and trusted friend. 037

CARROTS. A dream of raising carrots foretells a large income and good health. If a young woman dreams of eating them, she will marry early and have several healthy children. 314

CART. If you dream of riding in a cart, misfortune will follow and hard work will be necessary to care for your family. A cart foretells bad news from your relatives or friends. If you drive a cart you will be successful in your business and in your plans for the future. If lovers ride together they will be faithful to each other regardless of the interference of rivals. 975

CARTON. To dream of buying cigarettes or other packaged goods by the carton is a forerunner of prosperity. If you unload cartons of merchandise from a truck, you will be invited to a party at which you will meet influential people. If you receive a carton by mail and its contents are damaged, you will be disappointed in someone you considered your friend. 462

CARTOON. (See also Caricature, Comic Strip.) Cartoons that amuse you in a dream or that seem particularly appropriate augur success in business but bad luck in love. 563

CARTRIDGE. (See also Bullet.) To dream of slipping cartridges into a revolver or automatic pistol portends that you will be called upon to fill a much more important position than the one you now occupy. 048

CARVING. If you dream of carving a chicken, turkey, or any other kind of a fowl you will be unfortunate in your finances. Your ill-tempered friends will make trouble for you. If you carve meat, you will make unwise investments, but if you change your position, you will have greater success. 757

CASCADE. Water falling over rocks in a white cascade augurs a variety of experiences that will be not only be interesting but profitable. If a maiden dreams of a cascade, she will have difficulty in deciding which suitor to accept, but in the end she will make a wise decision. 657

CASEMENT. For a woman to dream of peering through a casement window is a portent of worry and possibility of disappointment. If she closes and locks the window, she will be lucky. 375

CASH. As might be expected, a dream of handling cash is an omen of prosperity. To dream of wrapping coins of any one denomination in paper indicates that you will be fortunate in business transactions. 801

CASHIER. If you dream of being a cashier, it is a sign that scheming people will lay claim to your property. If you owe money to a cashier, it denotes that some person of means will make things unpleasant for you. 514

CASH REGISTER. A dream of ringing up a sale and putting money in a cash register predicts an advancement in whatever work you are doing. 221

CASK. Rolling a cask aboard a ship is an omen of bad luck through association with loose-living companions. To dream of filling a cask with rum, fish or other foodstuffs predicts a period of plenty that will be followed by definitely hard times. 767

CASKET. Bad news and sadness may be expected by those who dream of a casket. If there is a body in it, the augury is of a public calamity. If the casket is empty, there will be a death among your circle of friends. 973

CASSEROLE. Food cooked and served in a casserole portends plenty of good times socially ahead. 249

CASSOCK. One will have every reason to expect a peaceful and quiet future if he or she dreams of seeing a priest or choir boy wearing a cassock. 071

CASTANETS. Physical disturbances are predicted by a

dream of a Spanish dancer using castanets. The sound of these instruments in a dream foretells upset conditions also in family life. 729

CASTILE SOAP. It is an augury of an improvement in your general welfare if you dream of washing your body with castile soap. 506

CAST IRON. Dreaming of cast iron is a warning of accidents through bad judgment. To break anything made of cast iron predicts an occurrence that will cause you continuing trouble. 502

CASTLE. If you dream of living or visiting in a castle, you will be assured of having enough money to gratify your wishes. It predicts travel and meeting people from many different countries. If it is an ancient, moss-grown castle you must curb your romantic notions and exercise discretion in your love affairs. 410

CASTOR OIL. (See also Laxative.) If you dream of giving castor oil to another, the dream is a warning that you must not forsake the friend who is trying to help you. To dream of taking castor oil predicts that you must do a difficult and disagreeable task. 173

CAT. If you dream of seeing a cat asleep in a chair, either a rocker or a straight chair, you will be able to look forward to a gratifying love life. For a maiden it means marriage with a handsome and wealthy man, and for a married woman the adjustment of family difficulties. Usually a dream of a cat means bad luck unless you kill it or chase it away. If the cat should attack you, the dream signifies that you will have enemies who will besmirch your reputation for honesty. If you chase the cat away, you will have a stroke of fortune. If you hear the cat mewing or yowling, someone who dislikes you is talking slanderously and doing harm to your reputation. If a cat scratches you, an enemy will make an attempt to cheat you. For a young woman to dream that she is holding a cat or a kitten augurs committing an indiscretion that will mar her life. 677

CATACLYSM. (See Catastrophe.) 863

CATACOMBS. It is a sign of good health and fortune to dream of walking through a catacomb where skeletons are on view. 110

CATAFALQUE. The death of a person whom you greatly admire is predicted by a dream of seeing a catafalque. If there are many people to watch it, you will receive a legacy. 593

CATALOG. If you study a catalog in a dream, you are going to receive a letter that will contain good news. If you dream of ordering from a catalog, you will receive money. 006

CATAMARAN. To dream of sailing in a catamaran denotes good luck in matters of business, unless you capsize, in which case you will have reverses. 532

CATAMOUNT. You will be able to outwit your competitors, either in business or love, if you dream of seeing a catamount. If you kill one, you will achieve a purpose that is close to your heart. To be attacked by a catamount is a sign that you will have a struggle to get along. 947

CATARACT. (See Cascade.) 622

CATARRH. This is a favorable dream for those who are in love. The more distressing the symptoms, the better is the augury. 522

CATASTROPHE. It is a sign of a radical change in your condition of life to dream that you are a witness to or a participant in a catastrophe. If you are not injured, or if you are able to help, the change will be for the better. Otherwise you are warned against taking chances. 290

CATCALL. To dream of being in an audience where there are catcalls for the performer is an augury of great embarrassment. If you dream of uttering catcalls at a public gathering, you will find yourself the object of shame. 138

CATECHISM. If you dream of the catechism it signifies that you will be offered a good paying job but that the conditions of the offer will cause you to think twice before accepting it. 058

CATERPILLAR. If you see a caterpillar, it foretells that deceitful people are about you and you must avoid false pretenses. Your business or love may be jeopardized. A caterpillar in your dream means you will be placed in a humiliating position and that there will be little respect or profit from it. 880

CATFISH. It is a portent of good luck to dream of catching or eating catfish. 329

CATGUT. This is a dream that predicts great annoyances. To dream of stringing an instrument with catgut foretells sleeplessness. 843

CATHEDRAL. A beautiful and inspiring cathedral seen in a dream is an omen that you will not be able to attain your desires but that you will be compensated for your struggle toward them. 365

CAT-O'-NINE-TAILS. It is a sign of sadness to come if you dream of seeing this instrument of punishment used in any way. If you are the one who uses it, you will have bad luck in your business for a long time and you will have family squabbles. 879

CATTLE. (See also Calf.) If you see fine-looking, well-fed cattle, contentedly chewing their cuds, your dream portends happiness and pleasant companions. If you see shaggy, underfed cattle, you will have to work hard all your life because of wasted time and inattention to details. Stampeding cattle foretell that you will attain wealth. A young woman who dreams of a herd of cattle will be happy in her love for her sweetheart. If you dream of milking cows that give their milk easily, you will make money; otherwise you will lose your sweetheart because of your coldness. 880

CAULIFLOWER. (See also Brussels Sprouts.) If you eat cauliflower, you are warned against taking your work too easily. To see cauliflowers growing means that your affairs will improve after a period of depression. 026

CAVALCADE. (See Parade.) 004

CAVALRY. A division of cavalry charging across a field predicts business promotion and personal honors. A party may be given in honor of your promotion. 739

CAVE. If you see the entrance to a deep cave in the moonlight, your business and health are in danger. If a maiden dreams of going into a cave with a man, it foretells that she will fall in love with a gangster and lose many of her friends. 774

CAVE MAN. A woman who dreams of being captured and dragged away by a cave man may look forward to happiness in her married life. 716

CAYENNE PEPPER. There is travel to strange out-of-the-way places in store for a person who dreams of the burning taste of cayenne pepper. The hotter the sensation, the more interesting the places you will visit. 319

CAYUSE. (See Bronco.) 984

CEDAR. The smell of cedar is an augury of smooth sailing through life. If in a dream you smell it while sharpening a pencil, you will have success through something you write. This will not necessarily be literary work. It may be a letter or merely a signature to a document. If you dream of smelling a cigar box made of cedar, you will have many invitations to social events. 320

CELEBRATION. (See also Party.) A dream of celebrating an anniversary of any kind is a good portent for those who have been worried about the future. The larger the group present, the better is the augury. 264

CELEBRITY. If you dream of meeting a celebrity and he or she is stand-offish, you will suffer disillusionment of some kind. If the celebrity is gracious and agreeable, you have a pleasant surprise in store for you. This applies to such celebrities as movie actors and actresses, high government officials, novelists, painters and other artists; in fact, anyone who is in the public eye. 641

CELERY. To see white, crisp celery denotes wealth and prominence. To see the celery limp or spoiling is an augury of a dire happening in your family circle. To eat celery is an omen that you will be loved for your sterling qualities. For a bachelor girl to dream of eating celery in the company of a young man is an omen of an inheritance. 908

CELIBACY. If you dream of living a life of celibacy, you will fail to accomplish something that is close to your heart. 138

CELL. Through something that you have failed to do you will lose a friend if you dream of being confined in a prison cell. 364

CELLAR. If you dream of a dank and musty cellar, you will become depressed with fear. You will not believe in your friends and will have evil presentiments from which it will be difficult to escape. If the cellar is dry and is stored with wines, liquors and canned goods, you are likely to get involved in a questionable deal. If a young woman has this dream, she will have an affair with a shady promoter. 327

CELLO. The heavy, satiny tones of a cello heard in a dream predict a strongly moving experience. If the cello is in tune, this will be something that will add depth and happiness to your life, but if it is played out of tune, there will be correspondingly discordant events. To see a beautiful woman playing a cello is a forerunner of a smooth and productive married life. A broken cello in a dream predicts severe illness. If you dream of putting new strings on a cello, you will receive good news either by mail, wire or radio. To break a string while playing the cello is an augury of a disturbing situation in a love affair. 449

CELLOPHANE. Good health is predicted if you dream of buying food, cigars, cigarettes, or other articles wrapped in cellophane. To wrap gifts in cellophane of any color is a sign that you will make new and interesting friends. 263

CEMENT. To use cement in fastening stones, bricks or porcelain together is a portent that you will keep your present position and advance to greater responsibilities and remuneration. To cement rubber or paper means that you will receive commendation for a noteworthy piece of work. 628

CEMETERY. To see an ill-kept and forsaken cemetery is a sign that you will outlive all your dear ones and will be left alone among strangers. A beautiful green burying ground is an augury of happiness. If young people dream of strolling through the quiet walks between graves, it denotes kind and loving friends but predicts that you will suffer many sorrows from which your friends cannot protect you. If a bride dreams of passing a cemetery on the way to her wedding, she will lose her husband while they are traveling. For a mother to put fresh flowers on a grave foretells good health and good fortune. For a young widow to dream of visiting a cemetery denotes that she will soon discard her widow's weeds for marriage clothes. If she is nervous and depressed, she will have other cares and rue the day she again became a bride. If you see small children gathering flowers and chasing butterflies in and out among the graves, it signifies a happy and healthy future. 286

CENSOR. If you dream of receiving a letter marked "Opened by Censor", you are likely to be criticized adversely by your associates. To dream of being a censor of books or public performances predicts that something you would prefer to have hidden will be revealed. 681

CENSURE. To dream of receiving censure by a lover is a forerunner of quarrels that will be serious unless you take it in good part and admit that it was justified. If the censure is from a superior in business, it is a warning against taking things too easily, both inside and outside of business. 961

CENSUS. If a maiden dreams that she is a census enumerator, she will be married to a hard-working and steady young man. To dream of answering census questions is a sign of moving to a new address. 915

CENT. A newly minted cent seen in a dream predicts that you will be deceived by someone in whom you put your trust. 313

CENTAUR. You will be shocked by news of one of your acquaintances if you dream of this creature that is half man and half horse. 304

CENTENARIAN. To dream of living to be one hundred years old and having your children and their progeny about you is an omen of happiness and the esteem of your friends. Two centenarians, man and wife, dancing with each other, predict a long life for you. 993

CENTERBOARD. It is a sign that you will escape the consequences of a foolish deed if you dream of letting down the centerboard of a sailboat. 394

CENTERPIECE. To spread a lace or embroidered centerpiece on a table predicts a slight increase in the amount of your income. 432

CENTIPEDE. This many-legged poisonous insect portends grief if you dream of seeing it. If it crawls upon you, the omen is sinister and warns against any kind of carelessness. 288

CENTURY PLANT. A dream of seeing one of these plants in bloom predicts that you will have a very unusual opportunity to make money. If it is not in bloom, the portent is of a slight accident. 741

CEREAL. Eating cold cereal for breakfast in a dream augurs success in a business deal, either through a rise in salary or by selling at a profit. Eating hot cereal is a sign of having to explain something you have failed to do. 239

CEREMONY. Religious, civil or fraternal ceremonies in a dream predict the sincerity of your friends. 317

CESSPOOL. Dreaming of a cesspool is a warning to avoid thoughts of evil and indiscriminate sex relationships. 391

CHAFF. To dream of seeing chaff predicts unsuccessful undertakings and that you will be the victim of ill health. For women to dream of piles of chaff warns against idle gossip and slander that will jeopardize their husbands' love. 052

CHAFING DISH. Good times are ahead for unmarried persons who dream of cooking in a chafing dish. Those who are married are assured of one or more sturdy children. 076

CHAINS. If you dream of being bound by chains, heavy burdens will be put upon you, but if you can break the chains and set yourself at liberty, you will not be worried about your debts. 272

CHAIR. To dream of sitting in a comfortable chair is a good sign in connection with any dream in which chairs appear. If the chair causes you discomfort, the sign is not propitious. 953

CHAIRMAN. If you see the chairman of a civic organization, it signifies that a well-paid position will be offered you. If a chairman looks displeased, you will be dissatisfied with your job. If you dream that you are a chairman of a meeting or committee, it predicts that you will be well liked for your fairness. 608

CHAISE LOUNGE. A dream of reclining luxuriously on a chaise lounge is a fortunate dream for a woman in love, although she should give way slowly to her suitor's advances. 151

CHALET. One of these decorative Swiss houses lived in or seen in a dream predicts that you will be able to make someone happy and thereby gain happiness yourself. 012

CHALK. The use of chalk for marking or writing is an omen that you will not succeed in your next business project. If you write on a blackboard and the chalk squeaks, you are warned against vicious animals. 653

CHALICE. If you dream of a chalice or communion cup, it signifies that happiness will come to you through your manner of meeting your troubles. If you break a chalice, you will be unsuccessful in keeping your friends. 729

CHALLENGE. If someone challenges you to fight, either with fists or weapons, you will get into difficulties and have to apologize or be very unhappy. You will have a serious disagreement with someone of the opposite sex if you dream of challenging another. 567

CHAMBER. (See Bedchamber.) 086

CHAMBERMAID. For a man to dream of really falling in love with a chambermaid presages a rise in his fortunes, but if in his dream he triffles with her affections, he will suffer a serious illness. 723

CHAMBER-POT. For a woman to dream of this homely article of furniture augurs contentment in family life. For a man it predicts a new source of income. 402

CHAMELEON. This little animal that changes color according to the color it is on is a warning to beware of false friends and strangers. 948

CHAMOIS SKIN. Used for polishing furniture or automobiles, chamois skin is an augury of improved business conditions and an increased income. A soiled and wet, soggy chamois skin warns against having family arguments in public. 473

CHAMPAGNE. A dream of drinking champagne at a party at which both men and women are present and where hilarity prevails is a forerunner of going into debt. To toast a bride and groom in champagne is good luck, especially to those who are in love. 550

CHAMPION. To dream that you have become a champion in any branch of sport is a sign that you will have a small business triumph. 943

CHANCEL. It augurs misfortune for a woman to dream that she enters the chancel of a church or chapel. A man who has the dream may look forward to promotion. 727

CHANDELIER. A dream of a brilliantly lighted chandelier is a forerunner of a rapid rise to business and social success. If a chandelier falls, it is a portent of a foolish act that you can avoid by using good judgment. To dream of anyone who hangs onto a chandelier either by the hands or feet is a portent of having a disquieting adventure outside of matrimony. 155

CHANT. To hear a choir chanting in a dream presages an achievement of which you may well be proud. 384

CHAPEL. You will repent of misdeeds if you dream of praying in a chapel. To dream of entering a chapel augurs peace of mind. 480

CHAPERON. A young woman who dreams of having an older one as a chaperon will find herself in a difficult situation. If a man dreams that the girl of his choice insists on a chaperon, he will be discomfited by someone he does not like. 711

CHARADES. It is a fortunate augury if you dream of playing charades, although it may not appear so for some time. Meanwhile you will enjoy simple pleasures. 202

CHARCOAL. A glowing fire of charcoal that is a feature of a dream exercises a beneficent influence, even if the rest of the dream points to misfortune. You will escape major difficulties. To dream of sketching with charcoal is an augury of easy living. 266

CHARIOT. Humorous developments in your love or family life are to be expected if you dream of driving a horse-drawn chariot such as the Romans used. A dream of a chariot race betokens an exciting episode in your social life, and is a warning against business upsets. 634

CHARITY. To give charity in a dream is a sign that if you refuse it to the needy, you will have bad luck for a year. If you dream of being the object of charity, your prospects are bound to improve. 634

CHARLOTTE RUSSE. It is exceedingly bad luck to dream of throwing one of these fluffy desserts at an enemy. You are likely to be covered with confusion if you attempt even a good natured argument with your friends. To get cream on your face from eating one is a sign of being pressed by creditors. 041

CHARM. One may look for betterment in every way if one dreams of meeting and associating with charming people. To dream of wearing a watch charm is a sign of prosperity and good health. 371

CHARTREUSE. This agreeable cordial, if taken in a dream, portends a hearty greeting from old friends whom you will visit. 029

CHARWOMAN. It is a sign that you will regain lost social standing if you dream of being considerate of a charwoman. For a maiden to dream that she is a charwoman augurs an elopement with a handsome and wealthy young man. 102

CHASE. If you dream of being a participant in a chase of any kind, it means that you will have to work hard for a living but that you will acquire enough money eventually to retire and live on the income. 886

CHASM. (See also Canyon.) If you dream that you are pursued and leap across a chasm, reaching the other side safely, you will be certain to solve any problems you may have that relate to finances. To fall into a chasm is a presage of woe. 614

CHASTISEMENT. A dream of being chastised is a forerunner of an upturn in your financial condition. If you dream of chastising another, you will suffer reverses. To chastise a child in a dream foretells illness. 512

CHEAT. Being called a cheat in a dream is a prediction of having a fortunate turn in your business affairs. If you call someone else a cheat, the augury is of being given a ticket by a traffic officer. 172

CHECK. It is good luck to dream of making out checks, and the larger the amount, the greater will be the fortune. You are likely both to inherit money and make large profits. 700

CHECKERS. Playing this ancient game in a dream augurs quiet pleasures and relaxation from worry. Win or lose, the augury is a good one unless you give way to an exhibition of temper, in which case the prediction is of harassing difficulties with your in-laws. If you dream of a sticky checker-board, you are likely to suffer from boils. 834

CHEESE. Eating cheese in a dream foretells that you will have a loving mate to help you weather the storms of life. As a rule, cheeses made of cows' milk are a better augury than those made of goats' milk. So-called "process" cheeses are omens of boredom, but any kind of strong-smelling cheese—such as Roquefort, Limburger or Stilton—in a dream is a prediction of great embarrassment. To dream of making cheese augurs success in any job. Cheese that is dry and crumbly is a sign of finding money. 912

CHEMISE. There is an agreeable surprise in store for the man who dreams of taking off a woman's chemise, and if it is of silk or rayon, it will be connected with the receipt of money. If the chemise is cotton, the augury is of being honored by a club group. A dream of losing one's chemise is an omen of financial failure. To dream of washing a chemise predicts attention from one of the opposite sex. To tear a chemise foretells the arrival of an unwelcome guest. 792

CHERRY TREE. Contrary to the moral of the George Washington story, it is very bad luck to dream of chopping down a cherry tree. You will lose money and reputation. To dream of picking ripe cherries from a tree is an augury of earning sufficient for your immediate needs but not enough from which to build up a surplus. 796

CHERUB. You will have many pleasing and amusing experiences in the company of children if you dream of cherubs or baby angels. 109

CHESS. Unlucky is a dream game of chess if it is played by a man and a woman. To a man it portends that the woman he marries, or to whom he is married, will "wear the pants." To a woman the prediction is of unfaithfulness on the part of her husband. If two men play chess, the augury is of a strenuous period in business. 684

CHEST. (See also Bosom.) If a maiden dreams of seeing a man, with hair on his chest, she should regard it as a warning against unladylike behavior among the masculine sex. 974

CHESTNUT. Roasting chestnuts in a dream is an omen of good fortune to those who work with their hands. To eat raw chestnuts denotes alluring associations with persons of the opposite sex. If in a dream one is opening chestnut burrs, the augury is of a problem that you will solve with difficulty. 104

CHEWING GUM. This is a dream of lucky import when the chewing is done inside one's home. It predicts pleasant and wholesome social relationships among one's family and neighbors and a measure of content in one's sphere of life. If the flavor of the gum is apparent in the dream, it is an indication that an interesting and agreeable experience is in store for you. For a man or woman to dream of chewing gum in public—on the street, in a theater, church, railroad station, elevator, or elsewhere—is a forerunner of a humiliating experience. If in a dream, you step on a wad of gum that has been thrown away by a careless chewer, you should take warning against letting your judgment be warped by fits of temper. 270

CHIANTI. Serving chianti from the straw-covered bottle at a meal is a sign that you should be more reserved with people you do not know well. To spill chianti on a tablecloth is an omen of social misfortune. 582

CHICKEN. (See Hen.) 809

CHICKEN POX. Minor disappointments are indicated by a dream of having this disease. To dream that your child is ill with it is a sign that he or she will have a brilliant future. 191

CHIFFONIER. (See also Cabinet.) To dream of looking for articles in a chiffonier and not being able to find them predicts quarrels with your family or the receipt of a puzzling letter. 405

CHILBLAINS. To dream of suffering the itching pain of chilblains is a sign that very shortly you will have relief from a condition that has been giving you much concern. If you dream of having a doctor treat you for chilblains, you will find several bills of large denomination, but you will have to return them to their owner. 403

CHILDBIRTH. (See also Labor.) For a man or woman to dream of being present at the birth of a child is a warning against putting things off that should be done immediately. Wills should be made, crops should be planted, bills paid, etc. It foretells ease of body and mind for a woman to dream of giving birth to a child, but a man who has this dream has a dark outlook in both business and social affairs. 567

CHILDREN. (See also Boy, Girl.) It is a fortunate augury to dream of having children. A single person may look forward to having a large and loving family. 719

CHILE CON CARNE. If this highly seasoned Mexican dish appears in a dream, it is a sign of upset love affairs. To eat it points toward trouble of one kind or another. 383

CHILL. You will have difficulty with your creditors if you dream of having a chill. 306

CHIME. (See also Carillon.) Chimes rung in tune are an augury of peace in the family circle and happy times for lovers. Out of tune, they predict the opposite. 480

CHIMNEY. If smoke is coming out of a factory or home chimney, the augury of your dream is of an increase in your earning capacity, but if sparks are rising, you will have family quarrels. A cold chimney predicts a change of occupation, perhaps for the better but not necessarily so. 743

CHIN. For a man to dream of kissing his sweetheart on the chin foretells that he will marry a nagging woman. To dream of striking a person on the chin is a portent of winning at cards; if you receive a blow on the chin, you will have surprising news. If you dream of being in a gymnasium and chinning yourself on a horizontal bar, it is a sign of being able to meet almost any situation with success. 769

CHINA. If you break china in a dream, it foretells good luck if you break it purposely, but bad luck if you break it by accident. 862

CHINESE. It is a fortunate augury if you dream of the Chinese people if they appear to be friendly. If they are hostile, you will have disquieting news from a source that will surprise you. 120

CHIROPODIST. The attentions of a chiropodist in a dream point to success in a new field of endeavor. Either you will get a better job at an increased salary or you will have an easier job in a different line at the same salary. If you dream that you are a chiropodist, you will receive news that will at the same time disgust and amuse you. 896

CHIVALRY. A dream in which a man shows evidences of chivalry to a woman—giving her his seat in a public conveyance, taking off his hat while talking with her, standing aside to allow her to precede him, assisting her to alight from a car—foretells success in the business world. 823

CHLORIDE OF LIME. The odor of this chemical used for disinfecting is an unfortunate augury in a dream. It predicts sad happenings within the family circle, and warns against infection from contact with diseased persons. To dream of using it without being conscious of the odor foretells the same things in a lesser degree. 314

CHLOROFORM. Grief will come to those who dream of using chloroform to deaden pain. The dream also warns against association with people whom you distrust. 150

CHOCOLATE. To eat or drink chocolate in a dream is an augury of illness. Chocolate candies predict a large income, much of which will be spent on hospital bills. Chocolate ice-cream sodas foretell headaches, both physical and spirtual. 282

CHOIR. A dream of singing in a choir is a forerunner of being honored for some service to your community. If you dream of singing a solo part, you will be happy in your love life. To dream of listening to a boy choir means that you will have an opportunity to distinguish yourself in one of the artistic lines of endeavor. 380

CHOLERA. This is a dream of opposites. It predicts a season in which you will be successful over a period of many months, but it also warns against spending too freely while you are fortunate. 083

CHOP. A thick juicy chop, broiled to a turn, is a lucky augury for anyone in a dream, but if it is thin and either underdone or burned, the prediction is of illness or loss of money. 170

CHOPHOUSE. To dream of eating well in a chophouse foretells that you will have ready money, especially if in the dream you are with jovial companions. 299

CHOPSTICKS. You are due to have a series of misunderstandings with people whom you like if you dream of trying to eat with chopsticks. To see Chinese people eating with them predicts a satisfactory unraveling of tangled affairs. 891

CHOP SUEY. You will solve a mystery if in a dream you eat chop suey in a Chinese restaurant. If you eat it at home, your chances for advancement are slight. 176

CHORUS. While it is a fortunate portent to dream of a chorus singing in tune, the augury is of death if you hear it singing off-key. A school or college chorus predicts that you will find something of value; a theatrical chorus, that you will lose it. 532

CHOW MEIN. (See also Chop Suey.) A dream of eating chow mein in a Chinese restaurant is a warning against a temptation by a glamorous person of the opposite sex. 116

CHRIST. Peace of mind through adjusting yourself to your condition in life and to the people with whom you have to live is predicted by a dream of our Lord. 951

CHRISTMAS. Most dreams of this holy season point toward advancement and prosperity. To dream of happiness among children at Christmas is a forerunner of satisfaction and repose. 323

CHRONOMETER. (See also Clock.) It is not a good augury to hold a person to strict time such as a chronometer tells. If you dream of this, you will be criticized by many people for your bigotry. To dream of consulting a chronometer on shipboard is to be warned that one of your friends or family is liable to be seduced. 709

CHRYSANTHEMUM. Dreaming of the scent of chrysanthemums is a forerunner of the fulfillment of a hope for the future. To pick these flowers in a garden or a greenhouse portends parties at which you will meet the right people. To give a bunch of them to a young lady foretells an understanding mate. 009

CHUCKLE. It is good luck to hear a chuckle in a dream if it is the result of pure amusement, but if it is cynical or gloating, it predicts a painful illness. 303

CHURCH. In general, a dream of going to church, of no matter what religion or denomination, augurs something better for you. If the dream is in the spirit of praise, the prediction is of improved circumstances surrounding love affairs. If it is merely fulfilling a duty, it predicts a humdrum existence with no change for the better. A dream of church social activities is a forerunner of depression in spirits. To see a church building in a dream foretells financial stability. If there is ivy growing on it, you may expect enduring love from your family. If you dream of seeing a church burning, you will lose a friend who has been tried and true. 961

CHURN. A maiden who dreams of using a churn will shortly marry a man who is a good provider. If she upsets a churn, she will be disappointed in him. If the butter comes quickly, she will have many pleasant journeys. 440

CIDER. Drinking sweet cider in a dream predicts a slight illness; but if the cider is hard, the augury is of a boisterous party at the home of a friend. To dream of working in a cidermill is a sign that you will forget an important duty. To spill cider on your clothing predicts that you will win a prize in a lottery. Carbonated cider poured from a bottle into a champagne glass presages an invitation to a weekend party at which you will meet several worth-while people. 584

CINDER. An old friend is in trouble of some sort if you dream of getting a cinder in your eye. To shovel or sprinkle cinders is a sign that you will receive an unexpected gift from an admirer. 158

CINNAMON. Used on food with which it is appropriate, cinnamon is a good augury, predicting enjoyable times. On such food as eggs, oysters or in soup it foretells heartaches. 813

CIPHER. A cipher may be a nought, o, or it may be a code. A dream in which the nought figures is a sign of failure to achieve something on which you have set your heart. If you dream of sending or receiving a message in cipher (code), the augury is of being deceived or double-crossed. 256

CIRCLE. To dream of drawing a perfect circle, either freehand or with the aid of a compass, is a prediction of the satisfactory working out of your plans and ambitions. 900

CIRCUMCISION. You will enjoy good health and success in business if you dream of being circumcised. If you dream of being present at the circumcision of an infant, it is a sign that you will make new friends who will help you toward advancement. 352

CIRCUS. If you dream of going to a circus, you are likely to receive good news from a person you see frequently. It is a warning against taking chances in motor-cars if you dream of being a circus performer. If you dream of taking a child to a circus, you will be lucky with investments. 282

CISTERN. You will receive exciting news from someone you have not seen for years if you dream of getting water out of a cistern. If the cistern is empty, or foul, you will be likely to hear bad news. 321

CITRONELLA. It is an augury of serious family difficulties if you dream of using or smelling citronella. To use it as a guard against mosquitoes is an omen of sadness. 552

CITY. A person who lives in the country and dreams of going to the city to live may look forward with certainty to many surprising adventures, especially with persons of the opposite sex. 954

CIVIL SERVICE. It is a sign that you will never be in want if you dream of getting a civil service job. To dream of working on a civil service job augurs good health and contentment. 061

CLAIRVOYANCE. You are likely to have a succession of difficulties in your love life if you dream of consulting a clairvoyant about your past or future. 957

CLAM. To open clams in a dream is an augury of a difficulty ahead that can be overcome by exercising great care and forethought. A dream of eating clams predicts relief from attacks by those who wish to do you harm. 579

CLAMBAKE. A dream of being present at a clambake predicts good times with your friends, but if you cannot eat a large quantity of food, you will be unhappy. 192

CLARET. Simple pleasures are foretold by a dream of drinking claret, but if you drink it from a bottle, you will be disappointed in love. 701

CLARINET. Those who dream of playing the clarinet have little more to look forward to than the applause they will receive for parlor tricks. It is an instrument that carries no particular rewards or penalties so far as dreams are concerned. 974

CLASSROOM. Maidens who dream of being in a classroom are likely to marry a man whom they have known in childhood. A man who has this dream will meet and possibly marry an old school friend. 056

CLAY PIGEON. Shooting at clay pigeons augurs difficulties in your job. To fail to hit them is a sign that you will not succeed in your daily work. 170

CLEAVER. It is a fortunate sign if you dream of having some meat chopped with a cleaver at a butcher shop. If in a dream you attack someone with a cleaver, you will have bad luck in business for a long time. To dream of seeing a person's head cut off with a cleaver portends misfortune. 366

CLERGYMAN. A dream of a clergyman is a sign that you will need to explain your actions to a great many people. If you dream that you are a clergyman, the prognostication is one of family achievements. 348

CLIMBING. Anyone who dreams of climbing, either mountains or stairs, will have opportunities to better himself or herself financially. 569

CLINIC. You may look forward to excellent health if you dream of going to a clinic. 781

CLIPPER SHIP. If a young man dreams of being aboard a clipper ship, he will find that he is dissatisfied both with his job and his family. A maiden who dreams of this vessel will have arguments with her sweetheart. For an elderly man it is an augury of comfort and many friends around him. 725

CLOCK. To hear the ticking of a clock in a dream denotes that you should not waste your time on unimportant matters. If you hear a clock strike, it is a sign that someone is waiting for you to make a decision. To wind a clock augurs happiness in love. 010

CLOISTER. To dream of walking through a cloister is a sign that you will have relief from your most pressing cares. A cloister in ruins augurs grief. 034

CLOTHES. A maiden who dreams of buying new clothes will have a new admirer. If she dreams of putting on her clothes, she will be invited to many parties. If she dreams of taking off her clothes, she will have proposals that will offend her. If a man dreams of dressing or undressing, he should beware of those who seek to undermine his reputation for morality. 661

CLOUD. To dream of seeing a cloud obscure the sun is a sure sign that your fortunes will improve. If you dream of piloting an airplane through a bank of clouds, you will be likely to have interesting, although possibly innocent, experiences with the opposite sex. 134

CLOVE. A dream of eating cloves or using them as a spicy flavoring is a presage of relief from worry. To use oil of cloves for toothache portends petty irritations. 912

CLOVER. A clover field in a dream is a fortunate augury, especially if the clover is in bloom. Bees in a clover field augur prosperity and contentment. 884

CLUB. For a married man to dream of going to a club for men only portends an argument with his wife. For women to dream of club activities is a forerunner of disquieting news. It is a sign of happy love affairs to dream of being hit by a club, but new responsibilities are augured by your hitting someone else with a club. 224

CLUTCH. A slipping or damaged clutch on an automobile portends that you will become estranged from an old friend. 822

COACH. To dream of riding in a coach drawn by two or more horses predicts the fulfillment of an ambition to be wealthy. If the dream is of driving the coach, the omen is of happiness in married life. If the coach overturns, you will make a change in your occupation and your place of residence. 119

COAL. To dream of buying coal means that your income will be doubled within the following few weeks. It is a sign of social advancement if you dream of delivering coal. Putting coal on a fire predicts business success. 467

COAL-HOD. Filling a coal-hod in a dream is an omen of being accused of a misdemeanor. To dream of carrying a coal-hod up a flight of stairs presages an addition to your family. To spill the contents of a coal-hod is a good sign if you do not give way to a display of temper, but if you swear, it foretells many petty vexations. 551

COAL MINE. A dream of working in a coal mine is a forerunner of an increase in wages to those engaged in manual labor. 493

COAST GUARD. If you dream of seeing the coast guard in action, you will be likely to be involved in a dispute with your neighbors. A maiden who dreams of a lover who is in the coast guard will receive news that will cause her grief. 696

COAT. If you dream of putting a coat on a hanger in a closet, you will receive the approval of someone whose opinion you value highly. To wear a ragged coat in a dream is a portent of riches and easy living. To help someone to put on a coat is a sign of lending money to a friend; but if another helps you to put on a coat, you will have to borrow. To lose a coat foretells that your feelings will be hurt by someone you admire. To throw away a coat is an omen of the loss of a friend; but to give one away predicts making new friends. 768

COAT OF ARMS. To dream of having a pretentious coat of arms framed on the wall, engraved on stationery, or embroidered on clothing predicts that you will incur jealousy through vanity. 434

COBBLER. (See Shoemaker.) 329

COBBLESTONE. If you rumble in a horse-drawn cart or truck over a street paved with cobblestones, you will lose money through gambling. If you walk with difficulty over cobblestones, your dream portends that your work will bring you in contact with disagreeable people. To throw a cobblestone at someone or through a pane of glass means that you will suffer keen regret through forgetting to do something important. 207

COCA-COLA. Drinking coca-cola in a dream is a sign that you will succeed in the enterprise closest to your heart. 410

COBRA. Misfortune will follow a dream of this deadly snake, and unless you are constantly on guard, you will meet with accidents. To dream of a snake-charmer with a cobra denotes a painful illness. 258

COBWEB. (See also Spider.) It is bad luck to dream of seeing cobwebs on any article that should be kept bright with use, such as a Bible, toothbrush, etc. It is good luck to dream of cobwebs on bottles of wine. 075

COCAINE. Used in a dream as an antidote for pain, cocaine foretells an increase in income. If it is used because a habit has been formed, the augury is of depression and sorrow. 467

COCKADE. Wearing a cockade in a dream is a sign that you should be more self-assertive if you expect to succeed in business or social affairs. To tear a cockade off of another person's hat portends an encounter with someone who will be more than a match for you; it is a warning not to start anything you cannot finish. 340

COCK-CROW. The crow of a cock heard in a dream foretells that you will make a lucky discovery. It is a particularly fortunate dream for those concerned in mining enterprises. 406

COCKER SPANIEL. A dream of one of these gentle and lovable dogs foretells happiness with one's friends and an easy living. 204

COCKTAIL. The augury of drinking or mixing cocktails depends on the base with which they are made. If they are made of gin—martinis, clover club and the like—the portent is of unfortunate occurrences in your family. Made of whisky or rum, cocktails foretell pleasant diversions with your friends. 369

COCOA. To serve cocoa to friends in a dream is a sign that you will keep your friends through thick and thin. 788

COCONUT. Eating coconut in a dream foretells that when adversity comes to you, you will meet it with great fortitude. If you dream of opening a coconut, you will find a small sum of money. 421

CODE. To receive a message written in code betokens a long period of puzzlement over the behavior of a near friend. To send a message in code is a warning against trying to deceive people. 811

COD-LIVER OIL. It is a good augury to dream of taking cod-liver oil. It foretells an increased income, and to those who are in love, peace and fulfillment. 529

COFFEE. If you dream of drinking a good cup of coffee, you will receive encouraging news from a surprising source. If the coffee is weak or bitter, you will be disappointed by one of your friends. To dream of grinding coffee beans is a sign of happiness for those who are in love. To dream of spilling coffee means minor disappointments. 680

COFFEE-MILL. To dream of grinding coffee beans in a coffee-mill is an omen of success in any kind of mechanical work you may be doing. 221

COFFIN. It is good luck to dream of a coffin. If you see yourself in it, you may look forward to great peace and happiness. 421

COGNAC. This kind of brandy augurs success in social life that will lead to profitable business opportunities. To burn brandy on a plum pudding predicts a harmonious family life. 788

COGWHEEL. Those who are in love are likely to have slight disagreements if they dream of cogwheels in smooth motion. If a tooth on one of the wheels is broken it predicts disaster to a love affair. 270

COIN. To give one or more coins in payment for an article or service is a forerunner of a delightful experience with one of the opposite sex. To receive coins is a sign that your reputation is in jeopardy. To have a coin returned to you with the statement that it is a counterfeit is an augury of ill health. 207

COKE. A dream of shoveling coke presages that you will meet with great difficulties in your daily work, but these will not be insurmountable. 274

COLD. You are warned against having arguments with relatives if you dream of having a cold. If you dream of suffering with the cold or low temperatures, you may be certain of a change for the better in the position you occupy. 495

COLIC. It is a sign that you will shortly receive a legacy from someone for whom you have done a favor if you dream of having colic or cramps. 686

COLLAR. Having difficulty in putting on a collar is a dream that portends difficulties with your landlord. 599

COLLECTING. A dream of collecting stamps, bird's eggs, old furniture, etc. foretells meeting celebrities of the screen, stage and radio. 993

COLLEGE. Lovers' quarrels are predicted by a dream of going to college. If you dream that you are a college professor, you will meet new friends who will contribute to your advancement. 534

COLLISION. (See Crash.) 805

COLOGNE. A married man who dreams of using cologne will have a serious falling out with his wife. Maidens, wives or widows will meet interesting men, with whom they will have to exercise great discretion. 883

COLONEL. A woman who dreams of meeting a colonel socially will be much sought after by men. If a man dreams that he is a colonel, he will be successful in business. 128

COMB. Problems that have bothered you will be solved to your satisfaction if you dream of running a comb through your hair. For men to dream of combing a woman's hair is a warning against flirtations. 806

COMEDY. Dreams in which there is humor or fun are lucky, and so if you dream of seeing a comedy in a theater or movie house, you will be gratified by happenings that will eventually contribute to your advancement. 483

COMET. To see one of these tailed stars streak across the night sky is an augury of sudden and unexpected good fortune. To lovers it predicts early marriage and a congenial home life. 607

COMIC STRIP. Looking at a comic strip in a dream foretells more leisure and more money. 004

COMMAND. Giving commands in a dream portends a promotion if the commands are obeyed, but if no attention is paid to them, you will lose money. 444

COMMANDMENT. To dream of Moses holding the tablet of stone on which are the ten commandments is a warning to mend your ways. 558

COMMENCEMENT. The successful conclusion of a piece of work on which you are engaged is predicted by a dream of being present at a school or college commencement. 242

COMMITTEE. Being appointed to a committee in a dream is a presage of having to make a contribution to a public cause. If you are made the chairman, there will be an upheaval in your business affairs. 514

COMMUNION. It is a fortunate augury to dream of attending communion in any church, for it points toward a long period of peace and quietude. 431

COMMUNIST. You will be misunderstood and shunned by your friends if you dream of being a member of the Communist Party, or of attending their meetings. 672

COMPACT. If a girl dreams of using make-up from a compact in a public place, she will be disappointed in her lover. If a man should dream of carrying a compact, he will be shamed by his fellows. 269

COMPANION. The enjoyment of one or more pleasant companions of either sex in a dream predicts triumph over one's enemies. 183

COMPASS. Upset conditions, both in the home and in business, will follow a dream of using a compass whose needle will not point to the north. 539

COMPLAINT. To dream that you make a complaint against conditions that do not please you is a sign that you will make new and influential friends. If a complaint is lodged against you, the augury is of a quarrel with in-laws. 377

COMPLETION. It is a sign of easier living conditions to dream that you have completed a job on which you have been working. 226

COMPLEXION. A woman who dreams that she has a perfect complexion is likely to be courted by two men at the same time. If her complexion seems to be blemished, she will be in danger of malicious slander. 189

COMPLIMENT. To receive a compliment in a dream means that you will make a success of the work you are now doing. To give a compliment presages that you will be chosen to fill a position of trust. 250

COMPOSITION. Writing a composition in a dream as you did when you were a child at school foretells meeting an old friend whom you have not seen for years. 608

COMPRESSED AIR. The sound of escaping compressed air is a dream augury that you will be censured for something that was not your fault. It is a lucky sign if you dream of compressing air with a pump, as, for instance, inflating an automobile tire. 233

COMRADE. (See Companion.) 100

CONCEPTION. For an unmarried woman to dream of having conceived a child foretells that she will have a proposal of marriage from a much older man. A married woman who has this dream will make new friends with whom she will be congenial. 315

CONCERT. If a young woman dreams of going to a concert with a man, she will be able to embrace an opportunity to go on the stage or into the movies. A dream of a tiresome concert, or one in which the music is off-key, predicts family quarrels. 295

CONCH SHELL. Strange but gratifying news from a far distant place is predicted by a dream of listening to the "roar of the sea" in a conch shell. 721

CONCUBINE. (See Mistress.) 731

CONDEMNATION. If you dream of being a judge who is condemning a murderer to death, you will be slow to attain the goal that you have set for yourself. To dream of being condemned is an assurance that your friends will remain loyal to you. 778

CONDOLENCE. To offer condolences to a bereaved person foretells the unraveling of tangled threads. To dream of receiving them is a sign of happier days to come. 271

CONDUCTOR. Having an argument with the conductor of a train, street car or bus is a dream that portends an adventure in a foreign land. To dream that you are the conductor of a public carrier augurs a new responsibility. If you dream that you are the conductor of an orchestra, you will find a sum of money. 460

CONE. (See also Ice Cream.) A dream of anything shaped like a cone foretells pleasant experiences with a person of the opposite sex. 363

CONFECTIONERY. (See Candy.) 097

CONFERENCE. Sitting in a conference with a group of business or professional persons is an augury of news that you will be able to turn to advantage. A religious conference betokens social advancement. A political conference portends hard and unremunerative work. 761

CONFESSION. If in a dream you make full confession of one or more misdeeds, you are likely to buy a new and more comfortable home within a year. If you dream of hearing a confession, you are warned against gossipping. 580

CONFETTI. Throwing confetti at a carnival or other party is a dream that foretells a fantastic adventure with an actor or actress. 093

CONFIDENCE. If you dream of someone's showing confidence in you, you will be fortunate in your business relations, but in love you will be less lucky. To show confidence in another, especially a person who has not warranted your confidence, predicts the making of new and valued friends. 195

CONFINEMENT. It is good luck for a maiden to dream of her approaching confinement, but if such a dream follows an indiscretion, it foretells loss of reputation. For a married woman or a widow to have this dream foretells happiness. 069

CONFIRMATION. To attend a confirmation in a church is a dream that foretells understanding on the part of your friends. To be confirmed predicts calm days to come. To dream of confirming an order predicts business success. 115

CONFLAGRATION. (See Fire.) 240

CONFUSION. It is a sign that you will have a well-ordered life if you dream of being annoyed by confusion either at home or in public. 262

CONGESTION. (See also Constipation, Crowd.) Dreaming of a congested condition in any part of the body is a warning to take no chances with your health. 482

CONGRATULATION. To receive congratulations in a dream for any piece of work well done foretells a rise in the value of any property you may hold. If you tender your congratulations to another, it is a sign that you will succeed handsomely. 772

CONGRESS. The temporary loss of an article that you value highly is predicted by a dream of being elected to congress. To sit in congress as a spectator foretells serenity in your life. 628

CONJURER. (See Magician.) 823

CONSCIENCE. If in a dream you feel that your conscience prevents you from doing an evil deed, or impels you to make restitution, you will retain the love of your friends and the respect of the community in which you live. 969

CONSERVATORY. Young women in love are assured of an early and desirable marriage if they dream of sitting amid plants and flowers in a conservatory. To dream of studying at a conservatory of music augurs success in any professional career. 907

CONSERVE. (See Jam, Jelly.) 516

CONSPIRACY. You will be successful in club work, church affairs and neighborhood activities if you dream that you are the victim of a conspiracy. If you dream of conspiring against anyone else, be warned against accidents. 529

CONSTIPATION. (See also Castor Oil, Colic, Congestion, Laxative.) If you dream of being a sufferer from constipation, you are warned against over-indulgence in food and drink, especially beverages with an alcoholic content. It also predicts that you will regret your own selfishness. 993

CONSUL. Through no fault of your own you will get into trouble with the authorities if you dream of going to a consular office in another country than your own. To dream of being a consul in a foreign city is an augury of success in business undertakings. 637

CONSUMPTION. (See Tuberculosis.) 553

CONTAGIOUS DISEASE. It is a hopeful sign to dream of having a contagious disease, because it foretells that you will be able to distinguish between true friends and false. 815

CONTEMPT. If a person shows contempt for you or your judgment in a dream, you will make a success of your job. If you show contempt for another, you will fail. 449

Astrology, Horoscope, and Dreams

CONTENTMENT. While it does not foretell unhappiness, a dream of contentment is a warning against smugness and a lack of interest in the trials of others. 468

CONTEST. (See Struggle.) 812

CONTORTIONIST. Embarrassment in both social and business life is predicted by a dream of seeing a contortionist perform. It is bad luck for lovers. 064

CONTRACT. You are likely to get a good civil service position if you dream of signing a contract. If your dream is of tearing up a contract, you will be advanced at the expense of someone else. 048

CONTRADICTION. It is a sign of bad luck in any enterprise connected with the sale of goods to dream of contradicting a person. If someone contradicts you, the portent is of forgetting an important engagement. 661

CONTRIBUTION. If you dream of soliciting funds and someone makes a contribution, you are due to become a participant in a romantic episode. If you make a contribution to a worthy cause, you will be able to command the respect of others. 795

CONTROVERSY. (See Argument, Dispute.) 354

CONVALESCENCE. To dream of getting well after an illness is a sign that you will travel to countries that have a warm climate. 809

CONVENT. Dreaming of studying in a convent is a fortunate augury for women, for it portends freedom from worry and insures the friendship of many desirable people. 031

CONVENTION. There is a vigorous struggle in store for you if you dream of attending a convention. At the time it will seem vitally important for you to subdue your adversary, but even if you lose, you will eventually be reconciled to the outcome. 145

CONVERSATION. General conversation heard in a dream has no particular significance, but if it is conducted in loud, highpitched tones, it augurs aggravated discontent. A conversation in a language you cannot understand predicts that you will be snubbed by your relatives. 208

CONVERT. If you dream that you made a convert to your religion or politics, you will be worried for a long time about your own future. To dream of being converted augurs not only peace of mind but interesting business connections. 165

CONVICT. You will make a success as a musician or a singer, perhaps in opera, if you dream of being a convict. If you wear stripes, you are likely to become a composer of songs. 297

CONVULSION. Dire happenings may be expected if you dream of seeing anyone, baby or grown person, having a convulsion. It is a warning not to enter into any business or social agreements for at least a month. If you dream of having a convulsion yourself, you should check with your lawyer to see that your personal and business affairs are in order. 016

COOK. A dream of being a cook, either male or female, is one of the luckiest anyone can have. It foretells that you will soon be waited on by willing servants and loved by an adoring mate. 866

COPPER. (See also Cent.) One who dreams of mining copper will have a substantial income through his or her own efforts. To dream of receiving a large number of copper pennies in change is a sign of petty annoyances. To see bright copper dishes on serving tables or hung on a kitchen wall foretells a comfortable home life. To a maiden it predicts marriage. 321

COPPERSMITH. A dream of seeing a coppersmith at work predicts that you will be invited to join a high-class social organization in your vicinity. 611

COPYING. It is good luck for a young man or woman to dream of making a typewritten copy of anything, but if the copy is made in handwriting, the augury is of censure from an older person. 617

COQUETTE. (See also Flirt.) A woman who dreams of coquetting with men will be invited out by a man she does not like. A man who dreams of a coquette who is unattractive will be offered a money-making proposition. 870

CORAL. Wearing red coral ornaments in a dream foretells happy days in the company of delightful people of the opposite sex. White coral is a prediction that you will have to take greater pains with the work you are doing. 029

CORD. (See also Rope, String.) Tying a package with a cord foretells accomplishment. Untying a knot in a cord predicts trouble through an incident with one of the opposite sex. To break a cord implies a serious accident. 876

CORDIAL. It is a happy augury, foretelling pleasant social relations, to dream of drinking a cordial, but if you spill it you will get into a jam with your associates. 806

CORDIALITY. A dream of being met cordially by a person of note is an omen of release from worry or pain. If you show cordiality to others in a dream, you will receive a message from a wealthy acquaintance that will give you much pleasure. 252

CORDUROY. If a young woman dreams that she is wearing corduroy breeches, it points toward gayety in a night club with lively companions. A man who dreams of wearing corduroy clothing will have a promotion. 096

CORK. To draw a cork from a bottle of wine or other liquid signifies that a puzzling mystery will be solved. If there is a pop when the cork is removed, the solution of the mystery will be accompanied by sorrow. It is a prediction of a light amour to dream of inserting a cork into a bottle. 805

CORKSCREW. A warning not to trifle with another's affections is contained in a dream of using a corkscrew. If the dream is of hurting yourself with a corkscrew, you will have to defend your honor. 819

CORN. (See also Chiropodist.) Happiness in married life is foretold by a dream of a field of green corn. If there are many ears on the stalks, you will have attractive children. To eat corn from the cob is a forerunner of profitable business. If you pop corn in a dream, it presages good times if the kernels burst into fluffy white, but if they burn, look out for trouble. To dream of having corns on your feet is a sign that scandal-mongers are seeking to ruin your reputation. 754

CORNCOB. A pile of corncobs seen in a dream portends divorce in your close circle of acquaintances. To smoke a corncob pipe denotes that by meeting adversity with a stout heart you will accomplish your ambitions. To use a corncob for cleaning silverware is an omen of more money in your pocket. 284

CORNED BEEF. Eaten with cabbage in a dream, corned beef is an augury of meeting new and pleasant people who will have interests similar to your own. In a sandwich it is an omen of discontent. 803

CORNER. To dream of waiting for someone on a corner means that you will make a date with a red-headed girl or man. 859

CORNET. To dream of playing the cornet in a band is a sign of having a proposition made to you that you should consider carefully. It is a sign of grief to dream of listening to someone practicing on a cornet. 431

CORNMEAL. Cooking or eating cornmeal in a dream is a sign that your health will improve and that you will have a corresponding increase in earning power. 954

CORONATION. Seen in a dream, the pomp and circumstance of a coronation are omens of a long pleasure trip in foreign lands. If you dream that you are being crowned, you are likely to make a great deal of money that will bring you added responsibilities and worry. A dream of a coronation scene in a play portends a succession of small successes. 822

CORPORAL. If a young woman dreams of going out with a corporal, she will be criticized for her boldness. A man who dreams of being a corporal is warned against being extravagant and wasteful. 215

CORPSE. (See also Dead Person.) A full life is predicted by a dream of seeing a corpse you cannot identify, for death precedes life just as surely as life precedes death. Such a dream is nothing to alarm anyone. Frequently it is an augury of success and happiness. 508

CORPULENCE. A dream of many corpulent people, all of whom are fat to the point of grossness, means that you are in danger through intemperate habits. 266

CORRAL. A dream of horses or other animals in a corral portends exciting adventures in and out of doors, probably in mountainous regions. 408

CORRESPONDENCE. (See Letters.) 244

CORRESPONDENT. For a woman to dream of being named as correspondent in a divorce suit is a warning against even the appearance of being indiscreet with men. 328

CORSET. If a man dreams of seeing a woman with nothing on but a corset, he is likely to receive a letter containing shocking news. If he dreams of helping a woman to lace or otherwise adjust a corset, he will be able to solve his financial problems. 817

COSMETICS. It is a thoroughly good augury for a woman to dream of using cosmetics—rouge, lipstick, eyeshadow, etc.—if she does not dream of using them in public places. Otherwise it augurs discontent and an end to any love affairs. A man who dreams of the use of make-up is in danger of losing his reputation and his business. 870

COSSACK. To dream of a cavalry charge by a Cossack regiment forecasts danger from an unknown source and is a warning to be continually on your guard. 506

COSTUME. Wearing a fancy costume in a dream portends a happening that no one would have suspected. Whether it is fortuitous or not depends on the spirit of the occasion for which you wear the costume. 944

COT. It is a forerunner of good luck to dream of sleeping on a cot, unless the cot breaks down, in which case you are slated for trouble. 309

COTTAGE. For young people to dream of marrying and living in a cottage augurs a happy mating and a congenial wedded life. If there is a vine on the cottage, there will be healthy children to bless the union. 210

COTTON. It is a sign that you will never go hungry if you dream of picking cotton. To walk through a field of ripe cotton foretells ease unless you are accompanied by an undesirable companion, in which case the portent is of worry. To put medicated cotton in an aching tooth means that you will have a visitor. To see a cotton-gin at work is a sign that you will suffer a disability. 258

COTTON-GIN. If you dream of this machine separating seeds from cotton fiber, you are likely to be appointed to a position of trust and honor at a very satisfactory salary. 652

COTTONTAIL. To see a cottontail rabbit out of doors portends a vacation in pleasant surroundings, but to shoot one is an augury of disappointment. 014

COUCH. You will be unable to achieve success in a pet project if you dream of hiding under a couch. To dream of sleeping on a couch is a sign that you will be successful in buying and selling operations. If you dream of sleeping on a couch with a person of the opposite sex, you will be criticized by an employer for inattention to your work. 544

COUGH. It is a portent of impending disaster, such as flood, fire or physical disability, if you dream of having a cough. 872

COUNCIL. To sit in a council and discuss weighty matters is a dream that foretells a misunderstanding with one of your best friends. 404

COUNSEL. (See Lawyer.) 429

COUNTENANCE. (See Face.) 800

COUNTER. Working behind a counter in a dream foretells comfort in your old age and a family that will be a credit to you. 587

COUNTERFEIT. Deceit from a person whom you have trusted is predicted by a dream of trying pass a counterfeit. It is good luck to dream that you destroy a counterfeit that you have received. If you dream of making or helping to make counterfeit money, you are in danger from an unknown enemy. 570

COUNTERPANE. A fresh, clean counterpane on a bed is an omen of harmonious life in the home. A soiled counterpane is an augury of discontent. 409

COUNTESS. If the countess you meet in a dream is young and beautiful, you will find it necessary to make excuses for something you have done. If she is elderly, you will receive an invitation that will help you in your social life. 610

COUNTING. Counting money in a dream predicts that you will have a larger income than formerly. Counting sheep portends family squabbles. Counting people is a good sign for those in show business. 306

COUNTRY. It is a pleasant omen to dream of being in the country in warm, sunny weather. In the rain, or when the landscape is covered with snow, the forecast is of arguments with retail merchants. 675

COUPON. To dream of clipping coupons from a bond or of saving coupons given away with merchandise is a sign that you will be under close scrutiny and possible criticism from your superiors. 188

COURT. If you dream of being a defendant in a court of law, you are likely to be called upon to explain a statement or an act. If you are a plaintiff you will find yourself in an embarrassing position. 418

COURTESAN. (See Prostitute.) 385

COURTESY. If in a dream someone is courteous to you in a manner that is unexpected, you will find an article that you had believed was lost. To dream of extending a courtesy to another is a sign that you will meet a new and charming person of the opposite sex. 668

COURT-PLASTER. To apply court-plaster, either cloth or liquid, to a wound in a dream augurs a lessening of the high regard you have had for a friend. 123

COURTSHIP. It is a sign that you will have new and agreeable experiences if you dream of courtship. 704

COUSIN. A full life, a happy life and contentment are predicted by a dream of being in love with a cousin. To dream of being friends with cousins is an omen of freedom from worry. 386

COW. (See also Calf.) Chewing her cud, a cow is a portent of physical well-being. An ugly cow predicts dissension within the family circle. 952

COWARD. To dream of being a coward predicts that you will not be wanting when there is an occasion to prove your worth. 906

COWSLIP. To dream of picking a cowslip is a warning against association with people of doubtful reputation. You should watch your step. 241

COYOTE. The howls of this prairie wolf heard in a dream are an omen of criticism from your family. To dream of killing a coyote is a sign that you will achieve something very worthwhile. 360

CRAB. Be on the lookout for designing persons of the opposite sex after a dream of fishing for crabs or crawfish. To catch a crab and then lose it foretells that you will be criticized for failing in your duty to a friend. To cook crabs predicts a slight accident; to eat them, good luck at gambling. 179

CRABAPPLE. Eating crabapples off the tree signifies a disagreeable experience with a post-office employee. A dream of making or eating crabapple jelly is a forerunner of happiness in love and family life. 081

CRACKER. To dream of stepping on a cracker predicts a very annoying situation in connection with a fraternal organization. If the dream is of eating crackers in bed, the augury is of marital squabbles. To see a baker making crackers signifies good fortune and happy days. 746

CRADLE. Rocking a cradle in which there is a baby foretells a successful marriage and profitable business. If there are twins in the cradle, the augury is of a change of scene. An empty cradle presages illness. 226

CRAMP. (See Colic.) 894

CRANBERRY. Eaten raw, cranberries portend an encounter with a police officer. Sauce or jelly, they are a presage of your being involved in political disturbances. 020

CRANE. A lifting crane seen being used in a dream signifies that you will be relieved of worries and burdens. To see a broken crane augurs hazardous undertakings. To operate a crane means that you will be asked to fill an important job. The bird known as the crane is a good portent if in the dream you see it flying; if it is standing still, you are likely to have upsets in business or in love. 853

CRAPE. Hanging on a door to denote a death in the house, crape in a dream is a portent of a series of accidents. 456

CRASH. From whatever cause, a crash in a dream portends an achievement of some kind. If you are driving a car that crashes, the portent is not a happy one, but it does not necessarily point to tragedy. 604

CRAVING. A dream of an intense longing or craving for either pleasures or material things foretells that you will be offered a splendid position. 962

CRAWFISH. (See Crab.) 323

CRAYON. To dream of drawing pictures with crayon is a sign that you will have to make excuses for overlooking something that was expected of you. 953

CREAM. A maiden who dreams of skimming cream from the top of a pan of milk will have many admirers and one good husband. If anyone spills cream, the portent is not favorable to new enterprises. 298

CREDIT. If you dream of buying luxuries on credit, there will be dire happenings in your family circle. To dream of making a bank deposit to your own credit signifies increased earnings and added respect from your friends. To give a person credit for some worthy deed is to look forward to a season of prosperity. 139

CREEK. A dream of swimming in a creek is an augury of excellent luck in business and love. 521

CREMATION. Witnessing the cremation of a dead body in a dream portends a long journey with an interesting companion. 253

CREST. (See Coat of Arms.) 047

CRETONNE. Women who dream of a bedroom in which the hangings and bed covering are of cretonne are assured of advancement both socially and financially. 975

CREVASSE. You are warned against ill-advised behavior if you dream of falling into a crevasse in a glacier. To cross safely over a crevasse is a sign that you will overcome obstacles. 378

CRIB. (See also Cradle.) It is a pleasant augury of success in married life to dream of putting a sleepy child in a crib. 358

CRIBBAGE. Playing cribbage in a dream predicts many good friends throughout your life and an interesting job, although not very much money. 968

CRICKET. Indoors, a cricket seen in a dream is an omen of many family blessings. To hear crickets sing predicts long life. A game of cricket is an omen of health, but if you dream of simply watching it and not playing, it augurs boredom in social affairs. 498

CRIME. If you dream of committing any serious crime, you are warned to guard your actions and hold your temper in check. 281

CROCHETING. A woman who dreams of crocheting will have many admirers. To drop a stitch and have to undo one or more rows predicts an altercation with relatives. 298

CROCKERY. (See also Dish.) To dream of hearing the rattle of crockery in a kitchen is a forerunner of nervous exhaustion. The crash of breaking crockery predicts an international calamity with connections in the Orient. 794

CROCODILE. Good luck will follow a dream of being chased by a crocodile, but if he catches you, the augury is of a very painful accident. If you kill him, you will be successful beyond your expectations. 909

CROCODILE BIRD. (See Birds.) 868

CROCUS. In a dream, a crocus is a harbinger of pleasant days to come, as it is a forerunner of springtime in reality. 739

CROIX DE GUERRE. To dream of seeing a soldier wearing this high military decoration foretells an encounter, either physical or otherwise, with someone whom you dislike. If you dream of wearing the croix de guerre, you will be lucky in your investments. 042

CROP. A small and disappointing crop in a dream augurs a setback in your business affairs, but a bumper crop is a sign that you will increase your holdings and build a competence. 619

CROQUET. Playing croquet is a dream that precedes wholesome and enjoyable pleasures among one's own circle of acquaintances. If it is played on a green lawn, the augury is better than if played on a dirt ground. 200

CROSS. (See also Crucifixion.) Any dream of a cross, of whatever description, portends a successful struggle, but one that will be accompanied by grief. 635

CROSS-EXAMINATION. If you dream of being cross-examined by a lawyer during a trial in court, you will be called upon to testify to the character of someone about whom you know damning things. 931

CROSSROADS. To dream of standing at the crossroads is a portent of a great change in your life that may bring you either happiness or sorrow. 706

CROUP. To see a baby with the croup in a dream is a sign that you will have to raise some money speedily. 048

CROW. The sight or sound of this black bird in a dream augurs a disappointment in love, but if you shoot it, the outcome will be satisfactory. 800

CROWD. (See also Mob.) It is a portent of profitable new associations to dream of being in an orderly or good-natured crowd. To be in a crowd that is reading bulletins of war outside a newspaper office predicts a business victory that will be unexpected. 509

CROWN. It is distinctly bad luck to dream of wearing a crown if you are in a palace, but if it is a paper crown in a masquerade or play, it simply means that you will be tempted. Be on your guard against yielding. 060

CRUCIFIX. You will have peace and comfort in your daily life, to say nothing of many true friends, if you dream of having a crucifix or of kneeling before one. 874

CRUCIFIXION. Hope for the future is promised by a dream of the crucifixion of Jesus Christ. 638

CRUELTY. (See also Brutality.) Either mental or physical cruelty in a dream is not propitious, whether you or another is the sufferer. 981

CRUISER. To dream of sailing in a cruiser for pleasure is an omen of having success in an important business deal. If the cruiser is a naval boat, you will be likely to have an enjoyable trip to a foreign land. 196

CRUST. If you dream of eating a crust with relish, you will have a pleasant vacation before long. 206

CRUTCH. It is an augury of ease and companionship among your circle of acquaintances if you dream of walking on crutches. If you dream of seeing a cripple hit a person with his crutch, you will have a prosperous month. 609

CRYING. To dream of crying betokens a heartache over someone else's misfortune. If you dream of hearing a baby crying, you will be surprised at news you receive through the mail. 667

CRYSTAL. A crystal with the sun shining through it and casting prismatic colors is, when seen in a dream, an augury of pleasing adventures in a brilliant and clever social group. 363

CUCKOO. The song of a cuckoo heard in a dream predicts meeting a genius who will be amusing but irritating. The sound of a cuckoo clock augurs contentment in home life. 293

CUCUMBER. Eating cucumbers in a dream is a sign of death in a family with which you are well acquainted. To dream of cooking cucumbers means that you are in great danger of making a serious business mistake. 344

CUDDLING. With a person of the opposite sex, cuddling is a dream that carries a warning against promiscuous relationships, but if it is between mother and child, it is an augury of contentment in the home. 075

CUFF. To write a memorandum on your cuff is a dream that should make you careful to avoid arguments with people who are in authority. To roll up the cuffs so that they will not become soiled predicts that your investments will require careful watching. 601

CULTIVATOR. Using a cultivator in a dream portends an improvement in your personal affairs. For a farmer it predicts good returns from his crops and livestock. 365

CULTURE. A dream of mingling with cultured people signifies that you will become esteemed for your bright conversation and your good manners. 011

CULVERT. If you dream of hiding from an enemy in a culvert, you will have trouble with your landlord and other creditors. 611

CUP. To drink out of a cup in a dream foretells pleasurable experiences with professional men and women. It also predicts success in the arts, such as painting, writing, and music. 536

CUPBOARD. A bare cupboard in a dream predicts a lean period in business, but if it is well stocked with food, you will have much success with your enterprises. 761

CURBSTONE. It is an augury of a hazardous occupation to come if you dream of sitting on a curbstone. 603

CURL. For a maiden to admire her own curls in a dream means that she will be disappointed in her lover. For a man to dream of having his curls admired foretells disaster to his reputation. To dream of cutting off curls is a sign of better times. 907

CURRANT. Ripe, red currants are an augury of a splendid new opportunity, but if they are dry and dark, there will be a long period of unrest. 143

CURRY-COMB. Using a curry-comb on a horse in a dream is a sign of satisfaction because of a successful business deal. 026

CURSE. To utter a curse on anybody or anything in a dream is a prediction of destruction to your fondest hopes. To use curses indiscriminately fortells the loss of a friend's respect. 217

CURTAIN. Lowering a curtain means that you will not succeed in the enterprise that interests you most. Raising a curtain is an indication of the reverse. If a curtain snaps suddenly up to the top of a window, you will have a surprising message. 710

CUSHION. It is a sign of affluence to come if you dream of sitting or lying on a cushion. To throw cushions about is a portent of having to apologize for something. To tear a cushion indicates that you will be criticized for a misdeed. 405

CUSPIDOR. Spitting into a cuspidor in a dream is an augury of new friends if you do not miss the mark; otherwise it indicates the loss of friends. 351

CUSTARD. Eating custard in a dream is an omen of having to be in the company of uninteresting people whom you must not offend. To spill custard on your clothes is a sign of distress. 727

CUSTOM HOUSE. To dream of transacting business in a custom house presages good fortune in your dealings with high officials. 940

CUT. To dream of cutting yourself with a knife, razor, or any other sharp edge is a sign of the loss of money or friends. 447

CUTAWAY COAT. It is a prediction of good fortune through close attention to business if you dream of wearing a cutaway coat at a social function. 863

CUTWORM. (See Borer.) 101

CYCLONE. A major catastrophe is predicted by a dream of being in a cyclone. You are warned to be careful at all times of your behavior, and to avoid taking any unnecessary risks to your person. 349

CYMBAL. An amusing experience is in store for you if you dream of playing cymbals in a band or orchestra. It is likely to be with someone of the opposite sex. 320

CYNIC. You will lose some money if you dream of hearing a cynic talk. If he is cynical about women, you will find it difficult to meet a note. 408

D

DACHSHUND. If you dream of one of these quaint, lovable dogs, you will be successful in business, love and family life. 881

DADDY LONGLEGS. An amusing experience is predicted by a dream of anyone being frightened by one of these ungainly but harmless insects, but if you dream of trying to frighten a person by putting one on him or her, you will be unfortunate. 871

DAFFODIL. At any time of year, but especially in springtime, a dream of daffodils is an augury of hope, no matter what problems are besetting you. To dream of a field of daffodils in bloom is an especially good omen for those who are in love. 186

DAGGER. To dream of seeing a dagger is a warning to beware of your enemies. You will be embroiled in some heated argument and be mixed up in an unpleasant affair. To see a person stabbed with a dagger signifies a conquest over your enemies, but it warns you to watch your behavior carefully and keep it above reproach. 315

DAGUERREOTYPE. To see your own likeness in a daguerreotype is a prognostication that you are slipping into lazy habits that will mean your downfall if you persist in them. To look at daguerreotypes of your ancestors is a sign that you will make progress in the work you are doing. 503

DAHLIAS. To dream of seeing colorful dahlias in a vase foretells success in money matters, especially if they are in an old-fashioned farmhouse. 089

DAIRY. Peace and contentment in your home and with your friends are foretold if you dream of seeing a dairy. To see pats of golden butter and small cheeses in a dairy means that you will have fine, healthy children and a comfortable home. 114

DAIRYMAID. If you dream of a pretty dairymaid with rosy cheeks and bright eyes, you will enjoy good health and pleasant surroundings. For a bachelor to dream of kissing a dairymaid augurs a happy love affair. 781

DAIS. (See also Platform.) To dream of a dais denotes a secret ambition to go on the stage or into the movies. A successful screen career is predicted. 730

DAISY. The dream of walking through a field of daisies foretells a gift—something you have always wanted and never expected to have. A white daisy in a dream means that your love is true to you. If you dream of a yellow daisy (black-eyed Susan), beware of a rival. To pick apart a daisy in a dream, saying "He loves me, he loves me not," is a fortunate augury for young women in love no matter how it comes out. A parallel dream is lucky for young men. 697

DAM. To dream of seeing turbulent waters rushing over a dam is a bad omen. You will encounter losses suffered through lack of serious consideration before committing yourself to action. To see a dam across a calm water course foretells success if the sun is shining upon it; otherwise, failure. 707

DAMASK. Spotless white damask table coverings are a dream portent of a dignified, successful and worthy life. If the damask is soiled or spotted, or shows signs of having been used for a long time, it indicates that you will be severely criticized by your in-laws. 537

DAMNATION. (See Condemnation.) 465

DAMPNESS. A dream of dampness is either a lucky or an unfortunate dream according to circumstances. If it follows extreme thirst or drought, it is lucky, but if it is a mildewy, continuing dampness, it predicts disintegration. 767

DANCERS. To dream of seeing beautiful ballet dancers in a gorgeous setting foretells that you will make new friends and that you will enjoy many social activities. 567

DANCING. If young people dream of dancing with partners of the opposite sex, it denotes a happy conclusion to their love affairs. If married people dream of dancing, it signifies marital happiness and bright, healthy children. Ballroom dancing signifies the announcement of an engagement. 569

DANCING SCHOOL. To dream of going to dancing school portends several love affairs and an entanglement that you will later on regret. 207

DANCING TEACHER. If a girl dreams that her fiance is a dancing instructor, she may well suspect a rival for his affections. If a man dreams of a woman dancing teacher, he will find it hard to choose between two loves. 209

DANDELION. To dream of yellow dandelions dotting the lawn in the springtime is a good sign for those in love. If the blossoms have gone to seed and the fluff blows in the wind, beware of trouble in store for you. If you wear a dandelion in your buttonhole, you will be laughed at and humiliated. 637

DANDRUFF. If you dream of seeing dandruff on someone's coat collar or on a dress, it augurs misunderstandings and a warning to walk the straight and narrow path. 513

DANGER. For one in love to dream of being in danger presages heartaches and jealousy, for it implies a broken engagement. If you dream of physical danger to yourself, the prediction is of the necessity to *go slow,* be moderate in everything, watch your accounts, your investments, your business and your heart interest. 149

DANGLING. If you dream of dangling from a high precipice or from a dangerous elevation, the dream foretells uncertainty in your business dealings. Be cautious, and look before you leap. 773

DAREDEVIL. To see someone taking undue chances with his life or happiness is a sign of hazardous undertakings. 229

DARKNESS. If in a dream the day grows suddenly dark or if there is an eclipse of the sun or the moon, it foretells what may appear to be supernatural happenings and telepathic messages. It may be the news of the passing of an old friend just as you are discussing him or her with another. 012

DARKROOM. Dreaming of working at photography in a darkroom predicts the unraveling of a mystery that has long given you trouble. 813

DARNING. If you dream of darning socks or a tear in a garment, it signifies new and pleasant companions. A maiden who has this dream will marry shortly. 116

DARNING NEEDLE. A dream of seeing the beautiful insect known as a darning needle is an augury of travel to far-off lands. 527

DART. If you dream of taking part in an archery meet, or placing your darts in your bow, the dream foretells great ambitions happily realized. If you dream of the darts reaching their mark, you will know undreamed-of success. If the dart is broken or falls very short of the bull's-eye, failure is predicted. 322

DATE. To eat dates in your dream foretells a marriage among your friends. You may be the fortunate one. To make a date is a bad omen; your sweetheart will forsake you for another. If you see dates growing on a palm tree, you will become prosperous. 748

DAUGHTER. To dream of your daughter or daughter-in-law is a sign that some dependent will lean heavily upon your resources and may take advantage of you if you are not careful. 890

DAVENPORT. To dream of a new handsomely upholstered davenport foretells improvement in your business and social standing. If the davenport is shabby and old, disappointment and loneliness will be your lot. 496

DAVID. If you dream of David, the Biblical character, fighting with the giant Goliath, you will prevail over those who seek to do you harm. 487

DAVIT. (See Lifeboat.) 059

DAWN. To dream of the sun rising and the dawn of another day denotes the offering of a splendid opportunity to better your prospects. If it dawns gray and rain threatens, you will lose a large contract for which you have been working a long time. 956

DAYBREAK. A dream of seeing it grow light at the end of night is an augury of hope for those who are distressed. 453

DAZE. If you dream of walking about in a daze, you are warned against false rumors that people are saying things about you of a scurrilous nature. 900

DEACON. A dream of seeing a church deacon cutting capers is an indication that you will be severely criticized for your actions. If the deacon is walking toward the church and seems intent upon his thoughts, the dream augurs belated blessings. 115

DEAD FOLK. (See also Corpse.) If you dream of being dead, it signifies a release from your troubles and recovery from illness. To dream of conversing with dead people is a propitious omen, signifying strength, courage, and a clear conscience. 571

DEAD LETTER. It is a warning against carelessness to dream of receiving a letter from the Dead Letter Office. 393

DEAFNESS. To dream of being afflicted with deafness is to expect a happy solution of your troubles. To try to talk with a deaf mute is to experience disillusionment. 495

DEBATE. (See also Argument.) If a man dreams of engaging in a debate with a woman, the augury is of failure to achieve his purposes. If his opponent in the debate is a man, he will win promotion through close attention to the problems of his business. A woman who dreams of debating will find that she must exert herself more in order to keep her friends. 898

DEBAUCHERY. Any form of debauchery indulged in in a dream is an augury of family and social derangements. Such a dream is a warning against association with loose companions. 268

DEBTS. If you dream of paying your debts, it is a good omen. If you are in debt and dream of not being able to meet your obligations, business worries are bound to come. 732

DEBUTANTE. A charming and winsome debutante seen in a dream denotes the beginning of a new project, either business or social, that will reflect credit on you. For a woman to dream that she is a debutante predicts pleasant love affairs. 774

DECADENCE. It is a sign that you will have difficulty in explaining some of your actions if you dream of decadent art, poetry or music. 021

DECAY. No good may be expected from a dream of decay, whether it is of animal or vegetable matter. If one dreams of eating decayed food, the augury is of trouble that will be hard to bear. 615

DECEASE. (See Corpse, Dead Folk.) 720

DECEIT. It is fortunate to recognize deceit in a dream, for it predicts that you will be able to make a large sum of money through buying and selling. If you are caught in a deceitful action or statement, things will go hard with you. 700

DECENCY. Evidences of decency on the part of persons from whom you would not normally expect it presage a reconciliation with someone from whom you have been estranged. 337

DECIMALS. To dream of mathematical calculations in which you use decimals points toward the receipt of a message for which you had hoped but which you had not expected to receive. 087

DECK. For lovers to dream of being together on the deck of a large ocean liner is good luck. To stand, sit or walk on the deck of a ship, either under sail or power, is a good omen if the sea is calm. The prediction is that you will contribute some invaluable discovery to mankind. To dream of a deck of cards foretells deceit and loss of valuable property. 431

DECOMPOSITION. (See Decay.) 454

DECORATING. If you dream of decorating a house, room or clothing for some gala occasion, it foretells gay and festive times. 460

DECORATION. A dream of decorations that please you, whether they are inside a house, outside a building or elsewhere is a portent of success in artistic lines of all descriptions. 314

DECOY. Any kind of decoy seen in a dream, whether it is intended for animals or for people, denotes the deceit of someone for whom you have had affection. 808

DEDICATION. To be present in a dream at the dedication of a church, public institution, or other building or enterprise is a sign that you will rise to an influential position among your contemporaries. 336

DEDUCTION. It is a pleasant augury to dream of making a successful deduction in the manner of a detective. You will have increased confidence in yourself and will be able to make a satisfactory business deal. 121

DEED. To sign a deed in your dream presages legal action that will probably be unfavorable to you. To see someone perform a good deed, in the manner of a Boy Scout, for instance, or to give assistance to an elderly, infirm person, denotes that many unexpected personal kindnesses will be done for you. 574

DEER. For married people to dream of a deer foretells going to war or being called into court, or disagreeing with a best friend over a slight matter. For lovers to dream of deer or fawns denotes deep affection for one another and an early marriage. For a young man or woman to dream of killing deer indicates a broken engagement. 049

DELAY. Women who dream of anything or anybody who is delayed are not likely to enjoy peace of mind for some time. To dream of a train or bus that is delayed is an omen of trouble in connection with money. A delayed check portends family arguments. 060

DELIGHT. If you dream of the delight occasioned by the attentions of your sweetheart, it denotes unexpected pleasures. 091

DEMAND. (See also Command.) To dream of someone demanding that you do or give something is a sign that you will be in a position to refuse to comply with a demand from a person who believes that he or she is your superior. 959

DENTIST. To dream of having a dentist work on your teeth is a portent of receiving a letter that will give you much concern. If you have a tooth pulled, it means a loss of money. 498

DEPOT. To dream of seeing a depot means a change of residence or that you will live in some foreign country. A depot signifies change. 734

DERBY. If you dream of the Kentucky Derby and your horse wins, it foretells your ability to carry out successfully your business or social affairs. If your horse loses or there is an accident on the turf, it predicts failure in every direction. To wear a derby hat foretells advancement. 428

DERELICT. To see a derelict boat or person denotes discouragement in your business, but by using good judgment and common sense you will profit. 706

DERRICK. To dream of a derrick signifies hope and the achievement of your wishes. A derrick is an omen of optimism, realized ambitions and thanksgiving. 955

DESERT. If you see the sands of the desert, bleak and baked by a burning sun, your dream denotes meditation and long hours spent alone with your books or your work. You will be very content if you have a resourceful nature. If there is a caravan on the desert, with camels and Arabs, the dream signifies long journeys by yourself into foreign lands. 547

DESERTER. For a man to dream of being a deserter from the army or navy is bad luck. He is likely to be severely criticized for some mistake he made a long time ago. If he dreams of standing before a firing squad, he is warned to be exceedingly careful of his conduct. 642

DESIGN. A dream of seeing designs, whether in color or black and white, and either simple or intricate, is a sign that one will be likely to have new responsibilities saddled on him or her. 021

DESIRE. (See Craving.) 906

DESK. To dream of working at a desk predicts irksome family affairs. To dream of cleaning out an old desk is a portent of new and interesting friends. 301

DESOLATION. To dream of being in a desolate house or neighborhood means that you will collect a group of articles that will increase in value as the years go by. 042

DESPAIR. If you dream of being in desperate circumstances either through danger or lack of money, it is a sign that your fortunes will improve before long. 189

DESPERADO. Meeting with a desperado in a dream portends that you will be dunned by your creditors. If you are able to capture or otherwise humiliate the man, you will collect money that is due you. 214

DESPERATION. (See Despair.) 293

DESPOTISM. To dream of living in a country whose ruler is a despot, or of working for a despotic and tyrannical boss, is an augury that you will be able to solve your most pressing problems. 425

DESSERT. If you eat a rich dessert in a dream, you will be able to indulge in some luxury that you have not had for a long time. Simple desserts augur quiet contentment. 170

DESTITUTION. (See Poverty.) 399

DESTRUCTION. Dreaming of the destruction of a building or a country by natural causes, war or other vandalism warns you against being too quick to take offense. 189

DETAIL. A dream in which the small details stand out is a forerunner of many perplexities. These details may be those of a person's face, manners or clothing; or the intricate parts of a mechanism; or of any other variety. 964

DETECTIVE. (See also G-Man.) You may expect very irritating troubles if you dream of being a detective, but if you are successful at the job, you will be able to overcome your difficulties. 046

DETOUR. It is a sign of a new job in the offing, with new responsibilities and problems, if you dream of having to make a detour from the main road you are driving over. 542

DEUCE. (See Playing Cards.) 632

DEVIL. To dream of seeing a devil tormented and tortured signifies that the dreamer is in immediate danger of being punished by the law. If you dream of striking the devil and overpowering him, it is a sign that you will overcome your enemies to your satisfaction. To meet the devil on friendly terms augurs death, melancholia, anger, disagreements, or sudden illness. To dream that the devil speaks to you signifies that you will have a great temptation. 208

DEVILMENT. Innocent devilment indulged in, in a dream, augurs pleasant diversions in the company of well-bred people. 675

DEVOTION. To dream of devotional services or devotion in other ways foretells a faithful and loving mate. 706

DEW. To dream of seeing dew sparkling on the grass denotes marriage to a person of means. For a maid or bachelor to walk barefooted in the dew presages a happy marriage in the near future. 475

DEXTERITY. (See Skill.) 352

DIAGRAM. (See also Map.) Drawing a diagram in a dream is a fortunate augury if the drawing is made with a pencil, but if pen and ink are used, it predicts complications in affairs of the heart. 746

DIAL. To break the dial of a watch or a clock indicates the necessity of inquiring into the stability of the bank where you keep your money. If you dream of calling a telephone number by using the dial, you will inherit a small sum of money from an old friend. 682

DIAMONDS. For a girl to dream of diamonds is a good omen; it indicates marriage to a man of distinction and great wealth. If a young man dreams of giving diamonds to his love, he must exercise great care in the choice of a wife. He must look for a girl who is a good home-maker rather than a social butterfly. To one who dreams of wearing diamonds there is an unpleasant experience in store with one whom they believed to be a friend. 492

DIAPER. If a man dreams of changing a baby's diapers, he will have a long and happy married life, but for him to refuse to do so predicts that he will have to spend many hours of overtime at his job. If a maiden dreams of diapers it is an augury of marriage with a commercial traveler who will be away from home for long stretches. 048

DICE. If a woman dreams of her fiance throwing dice, it is a sign that he will be guilty of dishonorable actions. Anyone who dreams of throwing a lucky combination will have a fleeting financial success, but there will be unhappiness for someone in the family circle. 630

DICTAPHONE. To dream of using a dictaphone foretells wealth and an executive's position of trust and honor. To dream of seeing one in an office means that you may hope for a rise in salary or a betterment of your position. 064

DICTATION. To dream of giving dictation to a stenographer is a sign of complicated affairs in social life. If one dreams of taking dictation, the portent is of advancement in business. 259

DICTATOR. (See Despotism.) 063

DICTIONARY. To dream of seeing a dictionary denotes a wordy argument with an opinionated person. To dream of looking up a word in a dictionary means that you have a thirst for knowledge only that you may impress your superiors. 653

DICTOGRAPH. To dream of a dictograph denotes whisperings and gossip about you by your associates. 227

DIFFICULTY. If you dream of having difficulty with a simple task, you are likely to quarrel with a friend of long standing. 126

DIGESTION. If you dream that your stomach is upset and that your digestion is poor, the warning is to keep away from temptation or you will get into trouble. Don't turn the night into day. 827

DIGGING. To dream of digging signifies that hard work is in store for you, but it will bring its reward if you dig with a shovel. Digging signifies an inquiring mind, and if you follow the dream by applying yourself diligently to the study of your problem, you will succeed. 327

DIKE. To dream of a dike denotes repression. You fear that some catastrophe will befall you, and you might fight against it with all your might and main or it will ruin you. To dream of seeing the dikes and windmills of Holland is a good omen. You will know contentment and in a small way live in financial security. 232

DIME. To dream of seeing a shiny new dime means that you will be criticized for being mercenary. If you pick up a dime and give it away, you will receive an unexpected gift by air mail. 473

DIME NOVELS. To dream of seeing someone reading a dime novel out of doors signifies a release from your worries. You will enjoy many happy outings in the country with friends. If you dream of seeing a dime novel on a newsstand, the dream denotes freedom from care. 499

DIMPLES. To dream of seeing a pretty girl with dimples or a man with a dimple in his chin foretells summer flirtations and several affairs of the heart that will be soon forgotten. 077

DINNER. If you dream of eating your dinner in a hotel or cafe with friends, a quarrel is predicted. If you dine alone with your sweetheart, it foretells an early marriage. 338

DIPLOMA. To dream of students being given diplomas at graduation exercises is a good omen. You will become an honored person of wealth and distinction. For a girl to dream of a diploma predicts that her pride will have a downfall. 607

DIPLOMAT. To dream of seeing a diplomat or some one in the diplomatic service foretells a delicate situation that will arise and will require in handling all the tact and skill of which you are capable. To say and do exactly what is expedient in the given circumstances is the warning of the dream. 691

DIPPER. There will be a family wrangle in which you will come off second best if you dream of drinking from a dipper. It is a warning to hold your tongue even when you have provocation otherwise. 961

DIRECTORY. To dream of seeing a telephone or business directory foretells participation in a game of chance, such as dice, numbers, and either horse or dog races. For a young woman to dream of looking in a directory also signifies an invitation to dinner with an admirer. 122

DIRGE. To hear a funeral dirge is, contrary to what one would expect, not always an unfavorable prediction. It foretells sympathetic understanding and helpful suggestions from a good friend. It may forewarn of a slight illness. 283

DIRIGIBLE BALLOON. (See also Airplane.) The significance of a dirigible in a dream is of achievements that will be accompanied by great hazards. 260

DIRT. (See also Earth.) The usual forms of dirt, such as dust and other accumulations of trash have an unfortunate augury if they are the result of carelessness or ill-breeding. They foretell disease and sorrow. 285

DISAPPEARANCE. To dream of seeing someone walk off in the distance and disappear from sight foretells money losses and disaster. To see an object magically disappear means that although you will be bewildered by your problems, you must face them. 298

DISAPPOINTMENT. The contrary may be expected, as to dream of disappointment presages the fulfillment of your hopes. 681

DISARMAMENT. To dream that all nations are disarming is a prediction that you will be successful in love and in other high achievements. To dream that one nation alone is disarming is a forerunner of disaster and shame. 732

DISASTER. If you dream of being in a disaster, it foretells the loss of your sweetheart either by accident or through some lover's quarrel. 454

DISCHARGE. It is a favorable omen if you dream of being discharged from your position, but at the same time it is a warning against inattention to your work. To dream of discharging an employee is a sign that you will quarrel with a person whose friendship you need more than you think at the time. 922

DISCIPLINE. To dream of being disciplined by a superior for a misdeed or an infraction of rules is a portent of a fortunate business deal. If you dream of disciplining another, the prediction is of the loss of money through unwise investments. 297

DISCOLORATION. One may look for a setback in his or her relations to social groups after a dream of seeing an eye or other part of the body that is discolored. Any color off what may be normally expected is to be regarded as a discoloration. 705

DISCORD. If you dream of discord, either in music or in daily happenings, it denotes a heated dispute between you and your fellow employees. If a young woman dreams of discord, her engagement will be broken or her marriage postponed. 232

DISCOVERY. If you discover something unexpectedly, you will inherit some property. If someone discovers you, it indicates new friends and new places. 814

DISDAIN. (See also Contempt.) Something funny is likely to occur if you dream of being treated with disdain. This dream is also a warning not to take offense at fancied slights. 758

DISEASE. Dreaming of disease in most forms is not a pleasant augury, but if the dream is regarded as a warning, it may turn out to have a fortunate aspect. 284

DISGRACE. You will encounter some difficult situations with your circle of acquaintances if you dream of being in disgrace. They will have to do with someone of the opposite sex. 455

DISGUISE. If you dream of someone disguised, it denotes treachery and underhanded dealings by your enemies. It is a warning to be perfectly open and above-board in your affairs. 330

DISGUST. If in a dream you show your disgust for a foul odor, an ungentlemanly act, or cruelty of any sort, you will be likely to be brought into contact with successful people who will help you on toward your goal. If, however, your disgust is shown for someone who is doing his best, you will lose a good and influential friend. 538

DISH. A young woman will be lucky in love if she dreams of bright, new dishes. If the dishes are soiled and broken, she will be disappointed in love. 907

DISHONESTY. If you dream of someone being dishonest, it foretells a change in your plans. You will do something you thought unwise but which will prove to be of great benefit to you and your family. If you are dishonest, the dream predicts sudden disaster and serious illness. 609

DISINFECTANT. To sprinkle disinfectant in a dream is a sign that you will be exposed to a contagious disease but that you will escape infection through exercising great care. 389

DISINHERITANCE. If a young man dreams of being disinherited, it is a sign that his parents will in good time approve of his choice of a wife. If a young woman has this dream, it signifies a happy marriage after a long engagement. To dream of disinheritance means a righting of wrongs in general. 117

DISLOCATION. If anyone has a dream of dislocating an arm, leg, or other member, he or she should go slowly in making any new business arrangements involving a change of employer. 265

DISOBEDIENCE. To dream of being disobedient to an elder foretells unrest and a change of occupation. To dream of seeing a child disobey his parents denotes a long sea voyage to another country. 447

DISORDER. A maiden who dreams that she meets a man when her hair or her dress is in disorder is warned against someone who is likely to try to take advantage of her innocence. For a housewife to dream that her house is in disorder is a sign that she will receive a letter from a former suitor. 056

DISPLEASURE. To dream of expressing displeasure to a young child is a portent of excitement over a small matter. 506

DISPUTES. To dream of having a dispute with your employer signifies a business depression and disastrous investments. If a woman gets into a dispute with a neighbor or friend she will be socially snubbed by a woman of prominence. 518

DISRESPECT. It is a fortunate augury if you dream of showing disrespect to those in authority, but if someone else shows disrespect to you, it portends a season of petty annoyances. 924

DISSIPATION. (See Debauchery.) 856

DISTAFF. If you dream of seeing a woman drawing flax from a distaff, it foretells a year of plenty and happy home surroundings. To dream of handling a distaff means that you will have to work hard for what you get, but that you will take pleasure in doing your work. 093

DISTANCE. A dream in which everything seems to be happening at a distance means that the portent will not materialize for a long time. 020

DISTILLERY. To dream of being in a distillery foretells a change in your business that will be more profitable than the one you now have. If a young woman has this dream, she will marry a man of means who is fond of the cultural things in life. 808

DISTORTION. If you dream of someone making a grimace or distorting any other part of his body, it foretells a rival, either in business or love. 723

DISTRESS. To dream of being in distress or of seeing others in distress denotes that you will have success where you feared failure. Distress is also a dream that forewarns of a slight illness. 382

DITCH. To dream of a ditch is a good sign, for it foretells that you will hurdle your obstacles with ease and will make your pastime into a business that will bring you surprising returns in a short time. A ditch signifies difficulties overcome and ultimate prosperity. 116

DIVAN. If you dream of lying on a divan it denotes loss of personal property, perhaps the robbery or theft of your pocketbook. 233

DIVE. To dream of a dive frequented by dissolute persons augurs criticism of the company you keep and that you will suffer the loss of your good name unless you reform. For a woman to dream of being in a dive predicts illicit love affairs. 106

DIVIDEND. If you dream of receiving dividends on stock, you must beware of false friends. Do not confide in anyone except those who have proved their friendship. 405

DIVING-BELL. If you dream of seeing a diving-bell, it foretells a sharp loss in the stock market followed by small gains. Being in a diving-bell denotes unrequited love. 650

DIVORCE. To dream of divorce means that one should take warning. If you are married, it means that you must make every effort to establish better understanding with your mate and that you must look into your own misdeeds. If unmarried, the dream signifies an unhappy love affair. 511

DIZZINESS. You are likely to take a transcontinental trip by plane if you dream of being dizzy. 920

DOCK. A dream of being on a dock where they are loading ships foretells good health, wealth and great happiness. To see the dock from shipboard means that a pleasant surprise is in store for you. 324

DOCTOR. To dream of consulting a doctor foretells an accident. Seeing a doctor socially is a good sign, for it means better business and happy social contacts. 170

DOCUMENT. If you dream of receiving a legal document in the mail, it foretells bad news. To dream of seeing a document lying on a table means disaster. 944

DOG. To hear a dog bark means that you will make friends out of your enemies. If a dog bites you, you will disagree with your lover. If an unmarried woman dreams of petting a small dog, it is a sign that her sweetheart is unworthy. To be frightened by a large ferocious dog foretells a love affair with a person of great mental power. If you see a white dog and he is friendly, you will be successful in business and love. 789

DOGGEREL. To read doggerel foretells you will take part in a minstrel show or some comedy on the amateur stage. To write it forewarns of a visit from an unwelcome person. 029

DOLE. If you dream of receiving dole, it denotes a betterment in your finances. If you give dole you will be connected in some way with a grocery store. 634

DOLLAR. If you see a silver dollar it means good luck. If you see a dollar bill it means misfortune. The higher the denomination the better the luck. 675

DOLPHIN. Maidens and bachelors should guard against the wiles of designing members of the opposite sex if they dream of seeing dolphins from the deck of a boat. 919

DOME. To dream of seeing a dome on a building such as the capitol or on a court-house signifies that great honors will come to you either as a government official or as a professor or president of some university. 776

DOMINOES. To dream of playing dominoes predicts taking a chance on some stock that will prove to be of small value. To see dominoes in a box denotes an offer of a worthless article which you will refuse to buy. 315

DONATION. Giving a donation in your dream signifies a change of heart. Someone whom you have always disliked will prove to be a friend in need. 261

DONKEY. If in a dream you are thrown from a donkey's back, you will be likely to quarrel with your sweetheart. To be given a donkey as a present means good luck in business, but it is a warning against evil women. If you are kicked by a donkey, you may be discovered in a clandestine love affair. A white donkey signifies success in personal matters. 047

DOOMSDAY. A dream of doomsday is a sign that you will make a success of the job you are holding down at present. 738

DOOR. To see a closed door foretells an opportunity missed. An open door through which one sees the open country denotes hopes realized; another chance will be given you to make good. 535

DOORBELL. To push the button of a doorbell in a dream augurs exciting adventures with a person of the opposite sex. 194

DOPE. Taking dope in a dream foretells a moral weakening. To see a dope addict denotes a leaning to take the easiest way instead of squaring your shoulders and making a success out of life. It is a warning to go straight. 479

DORMER-WINDOWS. Dreaming of dormer-windows is a good sign. It foretells brighter horizons. 984

DORMITORY. To see young people in a dormitory is a happy augury. To be in a dormitory means that through mental application you will arrive at your goal. 823

DOUGH. A woman kneading dough seen in your dream is a good omen. It means a season of plenty and good health. To ask for some "dough" meaning money is a sign that you will be publicly humiliated before some of your best friends. 485

DOUGHNUTS. To dream of eating doughnuts means that you will travel and circle the globe. To dream of frying doughnuts or seeing them fried by another foretells travel. If you are not careful you will become the proverbial "rolling stone." 673

DOVE. A dream of a white dove means contentment in the home and good business prospects. Seeing a flock of doves and hearing them coo foretells a trip in a plane, maybe an army plane in formation with others. 215

DOWNFALL. To dream of your own downfall foretells reverses from which you will quickly recover and profit by the lesson you have learned. Another's downfall signifies the news of friends being stricken with some muscular affliction. 458

DOWRY. For a young woman to dream of her dowry is an omen that she will marry a man of ample means. 015

DRAFT. If you dream of being drafted into the army, it predicts employment for you in work of a mechanical nature. If you dream of a draft of air, it means that you will be fooled into believing some hard luck story. Beware of panhandlers after this dream. A dream of a draft such as a money order, signifies that you will make a loan to one by whom you never expect to be repaid. 461

DRAGON. To dream of a dragon is a portent of riches and great treasures. You will have the pleasure of meeting some personage of note, possibly some member of a royal family. 637

DRAGON-FLY. A dream of seeing a dragon-fly in the garden denotes a voyage by sea to tropical lands. 305

DRAIN. A drain seen in a dream foretells sickness—such as anemia, poor blood. You must guard your strength and keep in the sunshine as much as possible. 074

DRAKE. To dream of seeing a sleek fat drake waddle across the yard denotes that festive times are in store for you. 851

DRAMA. To dream of a drama being enacted on the stage foretells a disagreeable encounter with an officer of the law. If in a dream you write a drama, you will be looked upon as a fool by your best friend. To play a part in a drama augurs success in family life. 975

DRAPERY. To dream of soft draperies signifies that you will enjoy a life of luxury. To see faded, torn draperies denotes the passing of prosperity. 030

DRAWING-ROOM. To be received in a formal drawing-room signifies high ambitions on your part that will not be realized. To lie down in a lovely drawing-room foretells jealous enemies who are plotting against you. 042

DRAW-KNIFE. Using a draw-knife in a dream presages a thrifty helpmate. If you appear to be doing a good job with it, the omen is of heartening news from a wealthy friend. If you cut yourself, you will be dunned by your creditors. 024

DREADNOUGHT. Dreaming of a dreadnought in battle presages disaster and quarrels with your relatives and in-laws. 051

DREAMS. To dream that you dreamed a dream is a sign that your dream will come true sometime in the future. 759

DRESS. For a woman to dream of seeing a pretty dress on another woman means that she will become socially prominent. To dream of a dress in a shop window signifies a social ambition or a political ambition that will benefit both you and your family. 790

DRIFT. A snowdrift seen in a dream foretells a difficult problem that you must solve or lose all that you have gained so far. Seeing the leaves drift down from the trees in the fall of the year denotes a disinclination to meet your difficulties and overcome them, but soon you will face a situation that must be solved successfully or you will regret it as long as you live. 554

DRILL. If you dream of seeing cadets drilling on the parade ground, you will be in line for a splendid position that will pay you well. If you dream of drilling, it foretells some time spent in preparing yourself for a fine opportunity either in your home town or in some large city nearby. To see a hand drill in your dreams is a sign that you will be surfeited with frivolous pleasures that will get you nowhere. 410

DRINK. To see someone drinking (anything) in your dream foretells years spent in academic learning. You will add many degrees after your name. To dream of yourself drinking to excess denotes many acquaintances who will take advantage of your easy going, indolent nature and rob you of your money. 446

DRIVING. Fast driving in a car, that is, exceeding the speed limit, foretells a hasty marriage and an unfortunate one. To dream of driving at a moderate speed through the open country implies success in a small way and much happiness. To drive a car into some object denotes frustration. You will break your engagement, or lose out in some business deal. Driving a nail bespeaks unfailing energy. You will realize your ambitions and become a prominent citizen. 853

DROMEDARY. A woman who dreams of riding a dromedary will be wise if she does not believe all that men, including her husband, tell her. If she rubs the animal's hump, she should beware of flirting with men she does not know. 208

DROOL. To dream of drooling like a baby means that you will enjoy good times with a group of young people. 050

DROPSY. A journey across the ocean is predicted by a dream of this disease. Something is likely to occur on the trip that will cause you concern. 586

DROWNING. To dream of drowning forebodes bitter sorrows. 122

DRUG. A dream of being drugged and unable to move about denotes that an enemy is watching his chance to harm you. 845

DRUGGIST. If you dream that you are a druggist, you will have to spend longer hours at your job to make the same amount of money. 127

DRUGSTORE. To dream of being in a drugstore is a sign that your investments will turn out favorably. 596

DRUM. To hear a drum in your dream is a forerunner of the long awaited success from your discovery, invention, or ideas. The muffled beat of a drum heard in the distance is a portent of dire calamities, a series of misfortunes that will overtake one of whom you are very fond. 228

DRUMMER. To see a drummer in your dream in some gala parade or orchestra signifies gay times and over-indulgence 150

DRUMSTICK. Eating a turkey drumstick in your dream means good luck. Handling wooden drumsticks is a warning against making boastful statements. 823

DRUNKARD. To dream that one is drunk is unfortunate for it signifies indiscretions and disorderly living that will cause your ruin. To dream of seeing a drunkard means loss of money through the post. 865

DUCHESS. To dream of seeing a duchess beautifully gowned and wearing a tiara foretells many social engagements, perhaps a house party where there will be distinguished guests. 635

DUCK. If you see many ducks in your dream and hear them quacking, it foretells good luck. You will have a great deal to be thankful for. 294

DUDE. To see a dude or fop in your dreams points to a disappointment in love. For a man to dream of being one augurs loss of standing. 251

DUET. To dream of hearing a duet sung predicts a happy marriage among your friends in the near future. It also foretells harmonious surroundings and freedom to work upon your hobbies. 362

DUGOUT. If you dream of being in a dugout, it foretells the need of keeping a friend's secret to your own detriment. Paddling in a dugout canoe signifies that through your own resourcefulness you will come out of an emergency unscathed. 272

DUKE. To dream of seeing or talking to a duke denotes a betterment of your circumstances. You will be looked up to by your acquaintances. 456

DULCIMER. To dream of playing the dulcimer promises sweet moments with your best beloved, but if the music sounds sour, you are warned against associating with loose characters. 438

DUMMY. A dummy seen in your dreams foretells the failure of your plans that might have meant success if you had used better judgment. 806

DUMP. A dream of a trash dump forewarns of a trying circumstance where you will be forced to bear the brunt of another's burdens. 203

DUN. It is a sign of approaching prosperity if you are dunned for money by creditors, either in person or by mail. 974

DUNGEON. To be confined in a dungeon in a dream predicts a visit from wealthy relatives whom you do not admire. 909

DUNGHILL. Scandalous things are likely to be said about you if you dream of shoveling manure on a dunghill. 480

DUSK. If you dream of the dusk gathering at the close of the day, the prediction is unfavorable. It foretells discouragement and misfortune, especially for merchants. 483

DUST. Seeing a cloud of dust denotes a new and irritating problem. Evil influences are about you. Watch your new acquaintances and your health. Seeing dust upon the furniture means that you will have an embarrassing moment. To be covered with dust signifies that you will be jilted by your sweetheart. To married people it means trouble with in-laws. 433

DWARF. To dream of a dwarf is a prediction of health and wealth. Your knotty problems will be solved as if by magic. 294

DWARF. (See also Midget.) Little people with oversized heads and hands are a sign, when seen in a dream, that your future is menaced by someone who wishes you ill. 315

DYEING. If you dream of dyeing your hair, it foretells business success. If you dream of dyeing a garment, it means social honors. 039

DWELLING. Seeing an old dwelling in a dream is a sign that you will take a trip and on the way visit school friends. If you see a new dwelling in the process of construction, the dream foretells an unexpected legacy. 637

DYNAMITE. If you dream of seeing an explosion of dynamite, your new made plans will go awry. If you see dynamite being loaded onto a ship, it means that the danger to which you have been exposed is over. 594

DYNAMO. To dream of a dynamo foretells that you will be put on night work, or that you will suffer from insomnia and will write or read a great deal during the night. 742

EAGLE. To see an eagle in a high place is a good sign. If the eagle lights upon your head, it is a sign of death; if the dreamer is carried up into the air by the eagle, a serious accident. If one dreams of seeing a dead eagle, it means a fatality to the rich, and to the poor some profit. To see an eagle flying foretells good business prospects. An eagle flying also portends the return of a good friend from a distant country. To see eaglets in the nest means that you will accept a position of trust and will be successful in your work. 899

EAR. To dream of people's ears implies startling news in the mail. To dream of pulling someone's ear signifies an altercation with your employer. 030

EARRINGS. If you dream of seeing an attractive woman wearing earrings, it foretells an affair with an adventuress. She will lead you a merry dance and leave you regretting your folly. If you wear earrings, you will win some money in a lottery. 198

EARTH. To dream of seeing the earth through a telescope means that you will inherit a large sum of money, but it will be held in litigation for some time before you will receive your share from the estate. 379

EARTHQUAKE. To see the horrors of an earthquake portends the dissolution of your affairs, but you will manage to go on, and out of your difficulties you will reap a well-deserved reward. If you are unfortunate enough to be in an earthquake, you will have troubles aplenty but will overcome them. 944

EASEL. To dream of seeing an artist painting at an easel foretells a life of ease. You will have many hobbies and live in a southern country. 075

EASTER. A dream of the lovely Eastertime portends a change of business that will be to your benefit. It means for a woman new furnishings in the home and pleasant social gatherings. If you dream of rolling Easter eggs on a green lawn, it foretells freedom from worries and the celebration of some joyous event. 793

EATING. Eating with guests in a dream portends good luck and happy times. If you eat alone, it is an unfortunate augury. 400

EAVESDROPPING. If you dream of seeing someone eavesdrop, it signifies a dilemma from which you will have difficulty in finding a way out. If you eavesdrop in your dream, you will be put on the spot and if you are not tarred and feathered, it won't be the fault of your enemies. 836

EBONY. To handle an object made of ebony, means that you will write a letter that will cause you no end of trouble and bring you unwelcome notoriety. Ebony foretells personal entanglements. 648

ECHO. To dream of hearing the echo of your voice portends a strange experience with one of the opposite sex. 015

ECLAIR. If you dream of seeing eclairs on a tray with French pastries in a restaurant or hotel diningroom, it is an omen that an old sweetheart is in town and that you will meet her or him and recall the old days. 469

ECLIPSE. To see an eclipse, either of the sun or the moon, denotes dread and forebodings of impending harm to yourself or to a member of your immediate family. 738

ECSTASY. To dream of being in a state of ecstasy signifies a proposal of marriage or the acceptance of your hand in marriage. To dream of ecstasy while dancing denotes amorous affairs and a case of "off with the old love and on with the new." 446

EDEN. If you dream of being in the garden of Eden, beware of rivals. You will be flattered but not loved. 473

EDITOR. To dream of seeing an editor at his desk is a warning to go over your accounts and balance your budget. To dream of being an editor shows dissatisfaction with your lot in life. 151

EDUCATION. To dream of working hard at your studies, trying to get an education, signifies that you will receive honors and know success but not in a cultural way. 493

EEL. To catch an eel is a good sign if it doesn't wiggle out of your hand. To dream of seeing a school of eels in the water warns you to look out for your pocketbook. 471

EFFIGY. To dream of seeing an effigy foretells the discovery of fraud in the accounts of one whom you believed the soul of honor. To see a straw effigy hanging from a tree means deceit and treachery among your acquaintances. 367

EGG. Eggs in a dream are a good omen. They portend success in any new venture. To dream of finding fresh eggs in a nest means financial profit. To eat eggs foretells good health. 391

EGGNOG. Drinking an eggnog denotes household activities, such as cleaning the house or the garage or the cellar. 065

EGGPLANT. To dream of preparing an eggplant for the table predicts social festivities and simple home entertaining. To see an eggplant growing foretells moderate success and the gift of several new books to read. 126

EGOTIST. Talking to an egotist in a dream signifies an inferiority complex that will cause you to boast of your knowledge. 919

EIGHT. To dream of seeing the number eight on an object portends disaster and disillusionment. To dream of an eight coupled with other numbers is a good augury. 283

EIGHTEEN. To see the number eighteen in a dream foretells a calamity, but you will escape unharmed. 361

EINSTEIN. To dream of the Einstein theory foretells many knotty problems in your life that will require your close attention. 723

ELASTIC. If you dream of snapping an elastic, you will encounter hazards that will try your courage but whet your appetite for more. To dream of elastic bands means that you will stretch a point to do a favor for a friend. 024

ELBOW. Elbowing your way through a crowd in a dream foretells a career in the films or on the lecture platform or in some profession where you will be before the public. To be elbowed by another who arouses your temper foretells mismanagement of your affairs and possibly a law suit. 277

ELDERBERRIES. Picking elderberries in a dream is a portent of making a friend of an old and delightful person. Making or drinking elderberry wine forecasts having to clean up the litter left by a wedding party. 976

ELDERS. To dream of your elders, that is, of being among a group of older people, signifies the coming of a momentous occasion in your life when you will be called upon to prove beyond a doubt your knowledge of a certain subject. 041

ELECTION. If you dream of celebrating an election, it foretells the offer of a small position in some department of the Government, from which you can rise to great heights if you put your shoulder to the wheel. If you dream of being elected to some office, it prophesies failure in business. 304

ELECTRICITY. To dream of seeing an electrical storm in the sky or the cross-circuiting of electric wires means the loss of property. To dream of turning electricity on and off is a sign of public acclaim; through your winning personality you will be accorded great honors. 587

ELEPHANT. To dream of seeing an elephant is an omen of good luck. To see elephants performing signifies a happy family life. Elephants at work denote a prosperous business outlook. 693

ELEVATOR. Being in an elevator with many people and going to the top of a high building augurs good luck and a bright future. To dream of descending forecasts poor investments and unsettled business conditions. Love affairs will be uncertain and unsatisfactory. 729

ELEVEN. The number eleven is auspicious. To dream of the number eleven means that good things are in store for you. Eleven is a good luck number. 512

ELK. If a man dreams of seeing or hunting elk, he will have a strong influence over women. 796

ELM. Dreaming of a beautiful elm tree predicts a carefree life, but if it is eaten with worms, you will have many annoyances. 961

ELOPEMENT. To dream of eloping with your sweetheart is a warning to take your head out of the clouds and look at realities. To dream of seeing others elope signifies that you will take a sentimental journey that will plunge you into serious difficulties. 650

ELOQUENCE. To be conscious in a dream of the eloquence of a preacher or orator is a warning not to yield to the flattery of persons who have an axe to grind. 558

EMBALMING. To dream of being engaged in embalming a body, or of looking on when an undertaker is doing this work, is a sign that a perfectly innocent action of yours will be misunderstood by your friends. 683

EMBANKMENT. To see a high embankment in your dream is a sign that you should put your pet project into cold storage for a while and await developments. 280

EMBARRASSMENT. To dream of being in an embarrassing situation means just to sit tight and avoid letting people persuade you against your better judgment. 833

EMBASSY. Being received at an embassy in a dream foretells a gay social season ahead of you. You must spring into action and not sit around waiting for things to happen. To see gentlemen at the embassy in the uniforms of their respective countries predicts social responsibilities of great importance to you and your family. 906

EMBER. To see embers, a fire of live coal, on the hearth is a good omen if the dreamer does not get burned. It signifies harmonious surroundings and a peaceful if not eventful existence. 891

EMBEZZLER. To dream of being an embezzler portends a disturbed state of mind that will respond only to an immediate discussion of your problems with those who understand them best. To dream of another person embezzling implies a secret fear that clouds your happiness and makes your progress doubtful. 479

EMBLEM. An emblem of any description in your dream foretells a journey, either to foreign countries or on a long transcontinental trip. 122

EMBRACE. To be embraced by one of the opposite sex is a sign that you will be accused of an indiscretion that will blight your good name, though there may be no truth to the rumor. To see others embrace foretells that you will be criticized to balance the praise you have received. 303

EMBROIDERY. To see a woman embroidering in your dream denotes innocent peccadilloes and good fun. To work upon fine embroidery with many bright colored silks is a sign that someone is plotting against you. 822

EMERALD. Wearing a beautiful emerald in a dream predicts a life of affluence. You will marry into a wealthy and respected old family. To dream of seeing an emerald among other jewels implies riches and social prestige. To dream of an old emerald foretells the inheritance of money and real estate coming from an unexpected source. 909

EMIGRANT. To dream of seeing emigrants from another land coming to this country aboard a ship foretells bright prospects and a change of address. To dream of being an emigrant is a sign you will be in need before the year is out. 421

EMISSARY. Seeing an emissary holding a message in his hand is a foreboding that a great calamity of national import will occur within the week. 872

EMPEROR. (See King, Queen.) 901

EMPLOYMENT. To dream of being in an employment agency predicts a happy solution to all your troubles. You will make use of something close at hand that will prove a bonanza. Offering employment to others is a sign of the opening of some project, like a mine, or oil field or something that will come out of the ground to bring you riches and great joy. 237

EMPTINESS. Opening a box, basket or bag and finding it empty when you expected to find it full, denotes futility. Do not undertake anything out of the ordinary for a while; it would prove a waste of time and a keen disappointment. 604

EMU. To dream of seeing an emu in strange surroundings is a sign you will meet a fool. 750

ENAMEL. To dream of handling enamelware foretells mistaken friendship with one whom you believed to be worthy but who will prove a thorn in the flesh. 081

ENCAMPMENT. An encampment of either soldiers or people intent on a good time is an omen of the necessity for preparedness. You must prepare for a concerted attack from the outside. Line up your assets and liabilities and balance your books. You have nothing to fear. Stand at attention. 996

ENCHANTMENT. If you dream of being enchanted by a sorceress, the prediction is that you will fall into idle ways and the society of undesirable people. 261

ENCORE. To dream of being in an audience that encores a famous artist, and of his gracious response, signifies that you will reap the reward you have worked for. If the artist fails to respond you will be disappointed. 276

ENCOUNTER. To encounter a person whom you have not seen for years is a good sign. To encounter a person or any object suddenly and unexpectedly denotes news from afar. 024

ENCYCLOPEDIA. It is a fortunate omen for all those who wish to become successful writers to dream of looking up a subject in an encyclopedia. 443

ENDIVE. Eating endives in a dream is a sign that you will become engaged to a foreigner, one who does not speak your language nor think your thoughts but who will give you much love. 743

ENEMY. To dream that you overcome an enemy is a good sign for anyone, but to dream that he or she overcomes you is a prediction of danger and a warning against taking chances. 285

ENDOWMENT. To dream of endowing a college or some other large institution denotes an undertaking that will prove to be definitely unwise. You will bite off more than you can chew and cry for help. To dream of being entrusted with an endowment foretells trouble ahead, complications that are so involved that it will seem a physical impossibility to overcome them. 962

ENERGY. Being full of pep and energy in a dream, as though you would like to tear the world up is a sign that "pride goeth before a fall." You will be guilty of a tactical error that will make your ears red. 328

ENGAGEMENT. If you dream of being engaged, you will be disappointed. Celibacy will be your lot. If you dream of breaking your engagement, you will be allergic to marriage for some time and will make of yourself a nuisance to your friends. 226

ENGINE. To dream of an engine going at top speed portends the accomplishment of an arduous task that has taken you a long time to complete but for which you will receive many honors and material awards. To dream of an engine is a good sign. You will go far in your chosen profession or job. 822

ENGINEER. Happy and successful will be the man who dreams of doing engineering work of any kind—civil, electrical, mechanical, chemical, or otherwise. 640

ENGLISH. To see and hear an Englishman speak foretells a situation that will require great diplomacy and tact. You will have to be broad-minded and look at it from all sides. 972

ENLISTMENT. If you dream of enlisting in the army or in any project of public concern, you will suffer the loss of a good friend and a home. You will become a cog in the wheel and it will be many years before you settle down. 130

ENTERTAINMENT. Dreaming of a sumptuous entertainment portends curtailment of income and pecuniary troubles. If you dream of entertaining simply in your home, it warns against extravagance; you must curb your desires, for you cannot eat your cake and have it. 735

ENTOMBMENT. If you dream of the entombment of someone you loved, you will awake to hear of the loss of some personage famed the world over for his contribution to the arts. To dream of being entombed is a warning to relax and to stop fretting over the impression you make. Forget yourself and others will remember you. 295

ENTRAILS. (See Intestines.) 372

ENTRANCE. To dream of an ornate entrance to some public building signifies the desire for higher learning. You may be an adult, but you will continue your studies to your great profit. If you are young, you will receive scholastic honors. An entrance denotes higher learning and greater knowledge. 115

ENVELOPE. Sealing an envelope in a dream foretells a happy marriage. To dream of addressing an envelope is a sign that you will meet the one to whom you address it very soon. 319

ENVY. To dream of envying someone his possessions foretells good fortune. To envy his or her good looks is prophetic of a marriage in which ill temper will mar the happiness of both parties. 444

EPAULET. If you dream of seeing epaulets on a uniform, it signifies the crushing of one's foes. To dream of wearing epaulets foretells a love affair with a girl who is famous on the stage. 869

EPICURE. To dream of being an epicure is fair warning to restrain your desires and be more discreet with acquaintances of the opposite sex. 073

EPIDEMIC. If you dream of being in an epidemic, it denotes mental disturbances. It would be well to consult a doctor and to observe the rules of health, regarding diet and exercise. 480

EPISTLE. If the epistle is delivered by hand, it indicates a troubled conscience. If it is written in colored ink, it is a portent that you will separate from your mate or break your engagement to your sweetheart. To dream of hiding an epistle is a warning to beware of a fair-haired rival. 829

EPITAPH. To see epitaphs on tombstones in a cemetery is a sign that you will become interested in work concerned with a library, either as librarian, recorder, or some research work. If the epitaphs are plainly discernible, you will overcome all the obstacles that confront you. 008

EQUATOR. If you dream of crossing the Equator it denotes a certain indecision about you. You are unsettled in your mind as to the best course to pursue. If it touches heart interests, consider well your choice. If it relates to living with your in-laws, ponder well. Your finances require close attention. If you approach the Equator in your dream and do not cross, you will rue the day you let a good opportunity slip through your fingers. 354

EQUESTRIAN. To dream of seeing equestrians in riding togs surrounded by hounds and going to the hunt, you will in the near future receive an unexpected dividend from stock that you feared was worthless. To dream of being an equestrian is a good sign, for you will meet your Prince Charming or the Beautiful Lady within the year. 495

ERASER. An eraser foretells that a close friend will suffer from loss of memory and will disappear from his usual haunts. To use an eraser on paper or on the blackboard foretells a broken heart. You will be jilted by your sweetheart and made to face your rival socially. 802

ERIN. To dream of Erin, the land of the shamrock is a happy omen. Like a prince or princess in a fairy tale, you will ride through life on the wings of success and be well loved for your priceless gift of humor, always seeing the silver lining in every cloud. 060

ERMINE. Ermine in your dream bespeaks quite the reverse from what one would expect. It implies a life of sackcloth and ashes unless one gives it to another, in which case you will wear diamonds. To wear an ermine wrap augurs cold and famine. 833

ERRANDS. To be sent on an errand in your dream means that you will lose your loved one through your selfishness. If someone comes to you on an errand it is prophetic of future interest in politics. 203

ERROR. If you dream of committing a slight error, it betokens a happy adjustment of your difficulties. If you see someone in error, the dream denotes an unfortunate affair in which you will be mixed up with a lot of silly busybodies. 724

ERUPTION. To dream of an eruption on your face or body foretells the breaking away from old beliefs and joining a new cult or group of agitators. To dream of the eruption of a volcano is a forerunner of disaster and calamity. 590

ESCALATOR. An ascending escalator signifies new hopes and ambitions, new friends and new places. A descending escalator means probable defeat that you must fight against and turn into success. 629

ESCAPE. To escape from some danger implies a speedy recovery from what will threaten to be a serious illness. To see someone escaping from a fire or an explosion, or some dire disaster foretells a check in the mail. 227

ESCORT. To escort a fair lady to the opera or theater or some other place of amusement is a good omen. You will be taken into the partnership of your concern. To be escorted denotes material help in the time of need to promote your business interests. 383

ESKIMO. Eskimos dressed in their native costumes, riding on dog sleds or standing in the snow, foretell a rebuff to your request for a loan of money. To be with Eskimos is a sign that you will meet a cool reception at the home of your best girl. 449

ESSAY. To write an essay denotes an ambition to be acclaimed by the public as a conquering hero. To read an essay foretells success as an executive or leader of men. 448

ESTATE. Grand estates, large green lawns, gabled castles, swimming pools and tennis courts, point to the necessity of your facing the realities of life. To become the owner of a small estate is a forerunner of unpleasant circumstances that could be avoided if you forgot yourself and though of others for a while. 718

ETCHINGS. Etchings, either in a shop window or in a museum or on the walls of your home denote a refinement of taste that will serve you well in your profession or job. Etchings when admired by the dreamer foretell cultural connections. 510

ETHER. To smell ether in your dream and see an operating room in a hospital implies a great change in your life for the better. 913

ETIQUETTE. To dream of not observing the rules of etiquette among a group of strangers is a warning to overcome your inferiority complex or it will get you down and you will miss out in a great many ways. Being over punctilious in your behavior foretells a public snubbing from one of social prominence whom you hoped to number among your friends. 386

EULOGY. To dream of being eulogized signifies the receipt of an expensive gift from some temple in a foreign land. To dream of eulogizing another points to hypocrisy on your part that will ultimately carry you to defeat. 443

EUROPE. If you dream of being in Europe when it is at peace, it is a happy augury; but if the continent is at war, it is the opposite. 419

EUNUCHS. To see eunuchs in a harem denotes a separation. It implies pain and sorrow and misunderstanding. 379

EVANGELIST. To dream of an evangelist is a foreboding of illness either in mind or body. 742

EVE. To dream of an eve, as the night before a great occasion, such as Christmas Eve or New Year's Eve, is a sign of discontent and the desire to outshine your friends. To dream of Eve in the Garden of Eden is a sign of fecundity and plenty. 822

EVENING. If your dream is concerned with a summer's night luminous with moonlight, it signifies a case of love at first sight. If you see the evening star in the sky and make a wish, happiness will be yours and the future will be very rosy. 734

EVERGLADE. To dream of walking in the everglades denotes an entanglement with one of the opposite sex that will cause you grave concern. 358

EVERGREEN. Any evergreen shrub or tree seen in a dream is a sign of lasting friendship. 345

EVICTION. An eviction is not a pleasant dream, It foretells financial troubles and wraps your problems in a blanket of fog compelling you to wait for the sun. But it will shine, as it always has. 065

EVIL SPIRITS. To dream of evil spirits around you shows that you will be prevented from realizing your ambitions but will find happiness and contentment in another channel. If you dream of seeing evil spirits about you, grotesque faces that appear and disappear, unaccountable situations will develop that will confuse and mystify you. 560

EWER. If you dream of seeing an old-fashioned ewer, it is a good sign. You will be talked about, but pleasantly, and compliments will be tossed your way like nosegays to a star performer. 007

EXCHANGE. To dream of exchanging goods at the store signifies a change of heart. To make an exchange denotes a rearrangement of your plans. 412

EXECUTION. A prolonged illness is predicted if one dreams of an execution by either hanging or electrocution. 530

EXILE. To dream of being an exile in a foreign land predicts difficult times ahead. Your most honorable intentions will be misunderstood, and you will be subject to calumny. 264

EXPEDITION. To go on an expedition to a strange and fearsome land foretells marriage to one you have known only a short while. You will marry and travel by boat a great distance and make your home among strangers. Whoever dreams of going on an expedition will handle strange merchandise to his great profit. 749

EXPLOSION. The terrific report of a high explosive heard in a dream is an augury of permanent improvement in your finances and health—unless it is from a death-dealing gun, which is a forerunner of the opposite. Explosions for useful purposes are of lucky import. 662

EXTRAVAGANCE. To dream of being extravagant when those about you are in want foretells a scandal in which you will be the center of interest. 639

EYE. To see eyes dancing around in space and not related to any particular face signifies an improvement in your financial condition and a hankering to play the stock market. 734

EYEBROWS. To see a face with heavy eyebrows is a sign the dreamer will be honored and esteemed by all. The dark, heavy, well-arched eyebrow is called the mandarin eyebrow and denotes aristocracy and cultural background. If the eyebrows are thin and colorless, the dreamer may expect little success either in his business or in his love affairs. 482

EYEGLASSES. If you dream of seeing your sweetheart wearing eyeglasses, you may be sure it means an end to your love affair. 622

EYELASHES. Long, silken eyelashes predict the sharing of a secret that disconcerts you and makes you appear at a disadvantage. 264

FABLE. To dream of reading a fable predicts that someone will give you a sharp lecture regarding your shortcomings. 541

FABRICS. To dream of handling beautiful fabrics, noting and feeling their color and texture, draping the material into graceful folds, foretells a bright career in some one of the arts. 397

FACE. A sweet, happy, smiling face signifies new friends and pleasures to which you are unaccustomed. Faces distorted or seemingly grotesque denotes disaster, privations and possible death. To wash your face and dry it on clean linen is a sign you will repent of your sins. To see a black face means a long life. Faces that grimace at you denote a quarrel with your sweetheart. If you dream of seeing your own face, the prediction is great unhappiness. 392

FACIAL. To dream of having a facial at a beauty parlor implies the need to scurry about and cover up some indiscretion of which you are ashamed. Don't be so selfish. Think of the other fellow for a change and see what happiness it will bring you. 232

FACT. To dream of recording facts or searching for facts denotes a law-suit and unpleasant notoriety. 622

FACTORY. A factory, full of busy, contented employees portends splendid business prospects. To dream of working in a factory signifies that you will be rewarded for your service and share in the proceeds. 982

FAD. A new and interesting fad in your dream portends a series of adventures that will take you far afield. 093

FAGOT. To dream of a bundle of fagots is a sign of homesickness, nostalgia for the old days. You will before the year is out journey back to your childhood home and visit the few old friends who are left. If you are a young person, you will return to your birthplace and see there someone who may become your future mate. 193

FAILURE. If you are in love and dream that your sweetheart refuses to marry you, it is a reminder to pursue your suit with great diligence, for if you do, you will succeed and live happily ever afterward. To dream of a failure assures success in your affairs. 564

FAINTING. To dream of fainting is a warning to stop and consider your frivolous ways and renounce the questionable associates you now call your friends. If you see a beautiful girl faint and you rush to her assistance, beware of designing women. Don't let a pair of blue eyes cause your downfall. 985

FAIR. For a young woman to dream of being at a fair means that she will marry a good-natured man of fine principles who will provide well for her. To dream of attending a country fair augurs well for you. You will enjoy life to the full. 317

FAIRY. You will have an opportunity of making children happy if you dream of the elves, pixies and gnomes of forest and field that you have read about in fairy-tales. If your dream is of imagining yourself a fairy or being recognized as such, you are warned to guard your conduct against possible misunderstanding. 654

FAIRYLAND. To dream of being in the land of the fairies peopled with elfin sprites signifies unexpected riches that will come to you through some simple invention of yours that is needed in the commercial field. To dream of fairies coming into this workaday world and of your talking to them denotes an artistic talent that you will make use of to your great profit and gratification. 528

FAITH. A dream of an abiding faith in someone or of faith in yourself means that you will finally make some decision that has long hung fire and that has prevented you from going ahead with your plans. The decision will be to your advantage and you will be free to carry on. A dream of faith always predicts a happy ending. 722

FAITHFULNESS. If a married person dreams of the faithfulness of his or her mate, the augury is one of peace and prosperity. 915

FAKE. To dream of a fake, something that isn't what it seems, or of some person who pretends to be other than what he is, predicts a situation that will occur in which you must be on your guard and not jump to conclusion. Don't gamble. Stop, look, and listen, and then, don't do it, whether it concerns love or business. 751

FAKIR. These East Indian holy men met with in a dream are a forecast of being disgusted by the behavior of one of your close relatives. 126

FALCON. The dream of seeing a falcon poised for flight is a good omen, it signifies honor. If you hunt with a falcon on your wrist, beware of thieves and robbers. If a young woman dreams of catching a falcon, it indicates that her desires will be fulfilled but that she will have a rival. 714

FALLING. To dream of falling is not propitious, for sickness, failure, and disappointments in love are foretold. If one dreams of falling and actually crashes to earth, the ominous prediction is death or a prolonged illness. 884

FALSEHOOD. It is good luck to dream that someone tells you a lie. If you dream of telling a lie to someone, you will suffer some physical injury. 532

FALSETTO. To hear someone singing in a falsetto voice is auspicious. To those in love it means an early marriage and happy dreams come true. 509

FAME. If you dream of becoming famous and accepting the adulation of the people, it signifies a turn for the worse in your affairs. Keep plodding along. Don't reach for the fruit on your neighbor's tree. If you dream of seeing a famous person, it means that help will come to you from some unexpected source. 977

FAMILY. To see a large and happy family in your dream predicts a holiday spent alone in some strange city far from home. To see a family of animals nuzzling at their mothers breast signifies a pickup in business. To see a destitute family augurs an upheaval in national affairs. 201

FAMINE. To see a country in the throes of a famine predicts unsettled conditions from which you will suffer but eventually struggle through to enjoy days of peace and contentment. To be encircled and made to endure the privations of a famine augurs troublesome times and searching for the leadership of the right man. 366

FAN. To dream of seeing a pretty girl fanning herself foretells a broken engagement and jealous heartaches. To dream of receiving a lot of fan mail is a sure sign that you are regarded as a light of love and have too many strings to your bow. To fan yourself predicts a love entanglement. To lose a fan means that your lover is becoming cold. 433

FANATIC. Meeting a fanatic in a dream predicts a long period of illness whether the fanaticism is on religion, politics or any other subject concerning which there may be conflicting opinions. 257

FANCY WORK. For a woman to dream of doing fancy work such as embroidery, knitting, crocheting, or drawn work is an augury of the renewal of an old romance. 697

FAN DANCING. A teasing exhibition by a fan dancer seen in a dream predicts the realization of an unworthy ambition. 847

FANFARE. To dream of being greeted by a fanfare of trumpets is a sign that jealous parties are seeking to do you harm by ridiculing you. 456

FANG. Seeing the fangs of an animal in a dream is a warning to pack your bags and leave before you are kicked out. Fangs foretell trouble with your in-laws. 377

FANTASY. It is a forerunner of a fortunate business adventure if you dream of a fantastic occurrence in your love life. 925

FARCE. To sit in a theatre and watch a farce on the stage presages an uncomfortable visit with people whom you dislike, where you will be ridiculed and belittled to the point where you will protest and cause a scene. 061

FAREWELL. If you bid farewell to your lover in a dream, very shortly he will become indifferent to your love. If someone bids you farewell, you will be looking for a new job. 490

FANG. Seeing the fangs of an animal in a dream is a warning to pack your bags and leave before you are kicked out. Fangs foretell trouble with your in-laws. 377

FANTASY. It is a forerunner of a fortunate business adventure if you dream of a fantastic occurrence in your love life. 925

FARCE. To sit in a theatre and watch a farce on the stage presages an uncomfortable visit with people whom you dislike, where you will be ridiouled and belittled to the point where you will protest and cause a scene. 061

FAREWELL. If you bid farewell to your lover in a dream, very shortly he will become indifferent to your love. If someone bids you farewell, you will be looking for a new job. 490

FARM. To see a carefully tended farm in your dreams means a life of plenty, simple joys and good health. To own an unprofitable farm and see poor crops and lean cattle augurs a run on the bank and a small loss of money. 645

FASCIST. A dream of living under a Fascist regime foretells having to admit being in the wrong regarding something that happened many years ago. 690

FASHION. To dream of being dressed in the height of fashion foretells a season of social activities and of your taking a prominent part in them. To dream of being out of fashion predicts all work and no play, if you do not exert yourself and meet your friends at least halfway. 465

FASTDAY. To dream of observing a fastday means that you will right a wrong and be much happier for it. 466

FATNESS. If you dream of being exceedingly fat and very uncomfortable, you will have few worries and many friends. 346

FATALIST. To dream of being a fatalist shows a troubled conscience. Brush out the cobwebs and begin a new day.

You will be given an opportunity to do this very soon; take advantage of it. 334

FATE. If you dream that fate has played you a shabby trick, you may rest assured that good luck is coming your way. If you dream that fate has played into your hands, you will marry the one you love and build the home you want. 972

FATHER. To dream of one's father presages a change of environment. If you are a city resident, you will move to the country; if you live in a rural community, you will move to the city or into another state. If you dream of being a father with your children about you, it foretells a rise in your fortune and a change in business that will be to your advantage. If a wife dreams of the father of her children she will get a new dress. 544

FATHER TIME. To dream of Father Time augurs a national crisis in which you will play a prominent part. You will be chosen to carry burdens of state and because of your aptitude for supervision you will direct the work of others and be honored and revered. The dream of Father Time predicts participation in public affairs. 454

FATIGUE. It is a fortunate augury to dream of being tired. You will enjoy good health and an income that will be sufficient for your needs. 493

FAUCET. To dream of a dripping faucet means that you will be guilty of divulging a secret of great importance so that it will change your entire future and not to your liking. To dream of a new, shiny faucet signifies a great happiness that will come to you unsolicited. 225

FAULT. You will be delighted by news that you will hear if you dream of admitting a fault. Finding fault with another person in a dream prophesies that you will win a promotion. 851

FAVOR. To dream of asking a favor of someone predicts loss of face or social standing. To dream of conferring a favor means that you will receive a compliment from someone you esteem. 052

FAWN. To see a fawn in your dream portends a serious disagreement with one you love; it may result in a broken engagement or the divorce court. 113

FEAR. To experience the sensation of fear in your dream foretells a decision that you alone must make, and upon it hinges your future happiness. To dream of allaying the fears of another presages a righting of wrongs and a clearing of the atmosphere from petty annoyances that threaten your peace of mind. 976

FEAST. To dream of feasting is propitious. It indicates a period of plenty, during which you will enjoy the good things of life. 076

FEATHER. Dreaming of eagle feathers denotes success, the realization of your ambitions. To dream of ostrich feathers predicts a fortunate business transaction. To dream of a cloud of feathers as though they were coming from a pillow means unprecedented good fortune that will please your pride as well as your purse. 620

FEMALE. A sex disturbance of some kind is foretold by a dream of using the word "female" as a substitute for *woman, lady* or *girl.* 321

FENCE. If you dream of building a fence, you will be lucky in love. If the fence falls, you will lose your sweetheart. If you dream of climbing a fence, you will reach the height of your ambitions. To have dealings with a fence, or buyer and seller of stolen goods, is a dream that portends failure in business. 952

FENDER. To dream of a broken fender on an automobile signifies that your pride will take a fall. A fender in front of a fireplace denotes family unity. 667

FERMENTATION. A dream of the fermentation of wines predicts a temporary mental disturbance. If you dream of fermented canned goods or preserves, you will receive gratifying news. 086

FERN. A bank of fresh ferns seen in a dream predicts a threat of coolness between you and one of your friends. To gather ferns foretells an adventure of a startling nature that will be both enjoyable and thrilling. 257

FERRET. To dream of one of these little animals is a prognostication of disease either in your immediate family or among your circle of acquaintances. 628

FEEBLENESS. If you dream of being feeble and infirm, you are likely to be approached by a solicitor of funds for a charitable cause. 352

FEEDING. A dream of feeding animals foretells a journey. Feeding a baby denotes a happy family reunion. Feeding a family predicts the undertaking of some civic project that will bring you great personal satisfaction. 544

FEET. To dream of bathing the feet foretells a pleasant relief from anxiety. If you dream of seeing your own feet, it means that your position is insecure. To dream of seeing many feet walking along a pavement portends material loss. 437

FELICITATIONS. To dream of being felicitated denotes a marriage in the near future. Offering felicitations to another augurs the celebration of some big event. 007

FELON. To dream of a felon or crook indicates that your secret fears will interfere with your plans unless you bring them into the open and crush them. 795

FERRY. Being ferried across a river in a dream means that you will accomplish what you have set out to do, and your rewards will be commensurate with the labor you have expended. 259

FERTILITY. A new and unexpected source of income is predicted by a dream that indicates either fertility of the soil or of the body. 307

FERTILIZER. It is auspicious to dream of putting fertilizer on any field or garden. It predicts an increase in income and good fortune in love. 622

FESTIVAL. If you dream of participating in a festival where there is much gayety, you will rejoice at the good fortune of a friend. To dream of attending a musical festival predicts the introduction of a new interest into your life, either a rare friendship or a fascinating hobby that will make you famous. 231

FESTOON. To dream of seeing ribbons or greens festooned about a room foretells a happy occasion among friends and relatives. 554

FETLOCK. If you dream of grasping a horse's fetlock, it forecasts new business hazards. 958

FETTER. To dream of being fettered with chains, ropes or conditions predicts a new and successful love affair. 466

FEUD. A person who dreams of taking part in a feud can look forward to a long period of contentment. 791

FEVER. If you dream that you have a fever, you are likely to have upsets in your love life. Your love affairs will take a sudden turn for the worse. 683

FIASCO. A dream of a ridiculous failure or of any sudden reversal of your fortunes denotes the ability to pay your debts and hold up your head. 320

FICTION. (See Novel, Story.) 012

FIDDLE. (See Violin.) 741

FIDELITY. (See Faithfulness.) 940

FIELD. It is a sign of great perturbation just around the corner if you see one person running across a field. If there are several, you will find yourself in legal difficulties. To see animals pastured in a field predicts easier work. 616

FIEND. If you have the misfortune to dream of a fiend from hell, you will be liable to punishment for some misdeed that you would prefer to forget. 567

FIESTA. (See Festival.) 340

FIFE. To play or hear a fife in a dream is a portent of an upset in love affairs. If accompanied by drums, however, it foretells an easy conscience. 263

FIG. Shame will come to you if you dream of eating figs. If you pick figs from a tree, your difficulty will be with a member of the opposite sex. 886

FIGHT. If you dream of being in a fist fight, you are likely to find that people will regard you highly. If you see others fighting, you will find happiness in your own sphere. 105

FIGHTING COCK. If you dream of attending a show of fighting cocks, some covetous person will try to get hold of your possessions. A dream of putting a fighting cock into a ring signifies a gain of minor proportions. 208

FIGURE. (See also Accounting.) To dream of a hodgepodge of unrelated figures is a sign that you will meet a combative person and come off second best. For a man to notice a woman's figure in a dream forecasts pleasant and innocent diversions out of doors. 053

FIJI ISLANDER. If you dream of seeing one of these natives of the South Seas in his or her simple native costume, the augury is that you will be advanced in your position. If the native is in European dress, you will be demoted. 323

FILBERT. Trouble and anger are the portents of a dream about eating filberts. To buy a bag of them indicates that you will take a short trip. 714

FILE. Using a file on wood in a dream is an augury of criticism from a person older than yourself; on iron or steel it portends a reconciliation with an enemy. Used on one's fingernails, it predicts the fulfillment of expectations. 330

FILET OF SOLE. You will be disturbed by the actions of someone you know who will avoid you if you dream of eating filet of sole. To cook it augurs worries of a personal nature. 703

FILIGREE. It is an augury of receiving a package in damaged condition if you dream of handling silver or gold filigree work. 449

FILING CABINET. Unless one is searching for a lost letter, it is good luck to dream of working at a filing cabinet. Where a letter is lost it portends a lowering of moral standards. 801

FILIPINO. After dreaming of a native of the Philippine Islands, one should be on guard against accidents and contagious diseases. 408

FILLING STATION. Buying gas at a filling station predicts an increase in your income, but to dream of buying anything else is a portent of illness. To visit the washroom of a filling station is a sign of less worry than you have been undergoing. 330

FILLY. You will have more leisure time for your avocations if you dream of seeing a filly in a pasture. If she is inclined to be friendly, you will make money in your spare time. 983

FILM. To dream of threading a film into a motion-picture projector is a sign of being able to buy new clothes. To load a camera with a roll of film signifies gratification of a love for jewelry. To make prints from photographic film is an augury of disappointment. 709

FILTH. If you are not constantly on your guard, circumstances will work toward your degradation after a dream of filth, either actual or mental. 996

FIN. A dream of seeing a fish wave its fins is an augury of freedom from detestable work. If, in preparing a fish for cooking, you cut off the fins, you will lose a valuable trinket and have great difficulty in finding it. 633

FINANCIER. It is a sign that you will have bad luck with your money affairs if you dream of being a financier. To dream of meeting on equal terms with financiers is a sign of good luck in buying and selling. 198

FINE. No good will come of a dream of having to pay a fine, no matter what the offense, even if it is for failure to return a public library book on time. You will have an altercation with one of your neighbors and you are likely to have to apologize. 873

FINERY. Girls who dream of wearing finery will be certain to have plenty of attention from men, probably men twice their age. 500

FINGER. (See also Thumb.) Scornfully to point your finger at another person in a dream is to look forward to being neglected by those whom you had considered your friends. To blow a kiss from your fingers to a person of the opposite sex is an augury of finding a new and exciting friend. To cut your finger predicts a long season of discontent. To dip your finger into food for the purpose of tasting it foretells jealous relatives. 196

FINGER BOWL. Someone will criticize you for snobbishness if you dream of using a finger bowl after a meal. To drink out of a finger bowl predicts money from a surprising source. 915

FINGERNAIL. To dream of trimming your fingernails is an augury of greater usefulness to the community in which you live. If you trim them too close, you will have troubles that will take some time to overcome. To bend back a fingernail predicts a period of unrest caused by critical relatives. For a woman to redden her fingernails is a sign that she will be criticized for her conduct. 657

FINGER PRINT. A friend will come to your aid in trouble if you dream of being finger-printed by the authorities. To dream of finger prints on light-colored woodwork signifies financial distress. 604

FINGER WAVE. Young women who dream of getting a finger wave at a beauty parlor will meet new and intriguing men of whom they should be extremely careful. 435

FINISH. It is a prediction of a new association, either in business or social life, if you dream of finishing a job. 798

FINN. To dream of one or more of the natives of Finland is an augury of good health, honor and a large income. 718

FIORD. You may look forward to calm, peaceful days in a happy home if you dream of sailing on a fiord of Norway or on any other narrow bay with mountains on either side. 219

FIR. It is a sign of disaster if you dream of cutting down a fir tree, but to walk through a forest of fir trees is a forecast of good fortune, especially when you can smell the piney odor. 567

FIRE. This is a bad sign when it burns you, but an auspicious one when it provides comfort. To build a fire portends an adventure with a person of the opposite sex. To dream of setting fire to a building is a sign of impending harm. If you dream of putting out a fire, you will overcome your enemies. Looking at a building that is on fire means that you will have a call on your sympathy. 081

FIREARMS. (See Gun.) 683

FIREBOAT. In action, with jets of water spraying from its nozzles, a fireboat is a presage of nervous disorders that should receive medical care. 152

FIREBRAND. To dream of snatching a brand from a fire is a prediction of being able to save somebody from death. If the dream is of throwing a firebrand into a house or any other inflammable material, you will have to make amends for a misdeed. 575

FIRECRACKER. The sight and sound of the explosion of firecrackers in a dream portend irritations of a serious nature. If you dream of setting off firecrackers, you will have an interesting experience that will not be wholly to your liking. 781

FIRE ENGINE. Good luck in money matters will be yours if you dream of seeing any kind of fire apparatus on its way to a fire. To be at a fire-house when the engine is leaving is especially good luck, but to see it returning forebodes evil days. 640

FIRE ESCAPE. It presages pressure on you from your creditors if you dream of being on a fire escape either through necessity or for relaxation. 637

FIREFLY. Young men and women who dream of seeing fireflies in a summer garden should take warning that their conduct will be severely criticized by their elders. 227

FIREMAN. A man who dreams of being a fireman will be invited to an exclusive stag party composed of influential citizens. If you dream of driving a fire-engine, you will have a narrow escape from accident. To dream of saving the life of a woman at a fire presages amorous adventures under very peculiar circumstances. 082

FIREPLACE. (See also Fire.) It is an augury of home comforts to dream of sitting in front of a fireplace in which a fire is burning, but if there is no fire, it predicts an upset in love affairs. 714

FIREWOOD. To gather firewood predicts a happy family life with the girl or man of your choice. To split firewood augurs success in the affairs of your community. 634

FIREWORKS. Skyrockets, Roman candles, pinwheels and other such displays forecast lack of success in the accomplishment of the work you have planned. 070

FIRST AID. To dream of administering first aid to a disabled or wounded person predicts that you will be called upon to fill a high position. 386

FISH. A dream of fish predicts a death in your family or among your circle of friends. To catch fish with hook and line is a forerunner of illness; if with a net, it foretells an accident. 042

FISH-HOOK. Baiting a fish-hook in a dream is a fortunate prediction for men and women in love, no matter what their age. To get a fish-hook into any part of the body foretells a long period of distress through family troubles and lack of money. 399

FISH-MARKET. Dreaming of a fish-market in which the fish are attractively displayed foretells a pleasant vacation. If the fish appear to be spoiling, you are likely to have to pay a large income tax. 992

FISHNET. The use of a fishnet in a dream is a lucky omen only when the net is empty; if it has fish in it, there will be a mortal illness in your family or in your immediate circle of acquaintances. 597

FISH STORY. If in a dream someone tells you a "fish story"—one that you cannot believe—and you say that you do not believe it, you will find yourself in a difficult love tangle. 418

FIST. (See also Fight.) Success in love and business will come to those who dream of doubling up a fist. 163

FIT. If a person dreams of seeing another in a fit, he or she will be in a quandary over family problems. To see a dog, cat, or other animal in a fit is a sign of vexation on account of one's work. 763

FIZZ. Young women who dream of taking any kind of drink that fizzes are likely to be held to account for unseemly behavior. 604

FLAG. You may be sure of pleasant association with friends if you dream of seeing the flag of your country floating in the breeze. To dream of hoisting one on a flagpole is a forerunner of an increase in your worldly estate. If you dream of saluting your country's flag, you will win acclaim for an outstanding achievement. To lower a flag at sunset predicts finding a large sum of money. 111

FLAKE. A dream of any kind of flakes—corn, snow or what not—presages a difficult situation in which you will have to use more than ordinary discretion in order to keep from making a serious mistake. 218

FLAME. (See Fire.) 395

FLAMINGO. This long-legged, web-footed red bird is an augury of exciting adventure far from home when seen flying in a dream. If it is standing or walking, it predicts worry. 281

FLASH. A flash of light that occurs in a dream portends that you will cash in on an idea and be able to live in comfort. 920

FLASHLIGHT. To use an electric flashlight indoors foretells that you will have a strong temptation to do wrong. It is therefore a warning to be on your good behavior. To use a flashlight out of doors is a sign that you will make a new and valuable friend. 183

FLATTERY. You are warned against repeating reports that are damaging to another if you dream of being flattered. If you dream of flattering someone else, you will have an illness. 543

FLATULENCE. A dream of being flatulent in the company of others is a presage of a violent quarrel with one of your best-liked associates. If the flatulence is that of someone else, you will go on an extended journey. 534

FLAVOR. To taste any definite or pronounced flavor in a dream portends good luck if it is to your liking. Otherwise it is a sign of petty annoyances. 267

FLAW. If you dream of finding a flaw in an otherwise perfect thing, you are likely to be blamed for something for which you are not responsible. If someone else points out the flaw, it predicts an altercation with a traffic officer. 969

FLAX. Growing in a field, flax is an augury of being admired for your sterling qualities. 073

FLEA. To dream that you are a flea, with the flea's great power as a jumper, is a warning against going into business deals without very careful consideration. If you dream of being bitten by fleas, it is a sign that you will be harassed by your creditors. Better luck will follow a dream of killing a flea. 359

FLEECE. You will have to go through a period of depression if you dream of wearing garments or gloves lined with fleece. 800

FLEET. A fleet of battleships at anchor in river or bay betokens freedom from the worries that beset you. Steaming out to sea, they predict travel. A fleet of fishing boats seen in a dream augurs worry if they are putting out to sea—contentment if they are returning to a harbor. 802

FLESH. (See also Meat.) A dream of human flesh, if it is regarded from the personal standpoint, is an omen of distress through ill-advised behavior with one of the opposite sex. 349

FLEUR-DE-LIS. (See Iris.) 160

FLIGHT. (See also Airplane.) For a person to dream of flying like a bird is a sign that he or she is in some way attempting the impossible; but if the dream is of flight in an airplane, the augury is a good one. 194

FLINT. Young people who dream of striking fire with flint and steel will have love affairs that will probably lead to early marriage. 758

FLIRT. (See also Coquette.) For a man or woman to dream of meeting a flirt and encouraging him or her predicts a short and unsuccessful love affair. 439

FLOAT. A dream of lying on a float in a bathing suit is a portent of a heavy disappointment. To step out of a boat onto a float is a sign of making up after a quarrel. 376

FLOCK. Birds seen in a flock are usually a propitious augury in connection with other items in a dream. 499

FLOGGING. After a dream of seeing a person flogged you will have an opportunity to be revenged on someone who has done you wrong. Be warned, therefore, against all ill-advised acts. 119

FLOOD. This is a dream that should put you on your guard against crooks, gangsters and other evil persons. If you are swept away by a flood, you are in danger of losing your head over some unscrupulous person of the opposite sex. 726

FLOOR. To dream of laying a new floor in a house is a sign of activity and profit in business. To lie on a floor predicts an alliance that will cause you misery. To sweep a floor foretells a journey that will bring you much pleasure. 277

FLOORWALKER. A maiden who dreams of a floorwalker in a store will receive flowers and other simple gifts from an admirer. 858

FLOP-HOUSE. You are on the point of having to decide whether to go to a distant city if you dream of sleeping in a flop-house. 726

FLORIST. To dream of being in a florist's shop forecasts a romance for the unmarried, but for those who have wives or husbands it foretells a scandal. 304

FLOSS. Any flossy material seen or handled in a dream is a forerunner of backbiting and ugly gossip. 798

FLOUNDER. It is a sign that a pet project will fail to materialize if you dream of catching or eating flounder. 641

FLOUR. Any dream in which flour is used for baking is a forerunner of contentment in the home. 104

FLOW. Any kind of gentle flow is an augury of peace of mind to those who dream of it. 133

FLOWER. Luck will follow dreams of most of the garden flowers. Wild flowers predict adventure. 388

FLU. (See Grippe.) 733

FLUKE. To dream of an achievement made through a lucky fluke is an omen of a rise in salary or a small legacy. The flukes of an anchor betoken misery, but the flukes of a whale's tail are a sign of freedom from worry. 288

FLUME. A dream of a flume down a slope through a forest is a portent of increasing good fortune through the years. 088

FLUNKEY. You will be likely to have a humorous experience with one of the opposite sex if you dream of being a flunkey in uniform. To dream of having flunkeys in your employ portends embarrassment. 217

FLURRY. A flurry of snow or dust in a dream is an omen of temporary prosperity. 089

FLUTE. The sound of a flute in a dream augurs peace and contentment in family life. To dream of playing a flute predicts being caught in an embarrassing situation. 698

FLY. A dream of being annoyed by common house-flies portends a variety of difficulties with which you will have to contend. You are warned against losing your temper. If you dream of killing flies with a swatter, you will have good fortune of a minor sort. If you see flies that have been caught on flypaper, your future will be beset with many annoyances. 062

FLYING. (See Flight.) 229

FLYING FISH. Travel to the Eastern Hemisphere and a variety of odd experiences are predicted if you dream of seeing flying fish from the deck of a boat. 440

FLYPAPER. To see or use flypaper in a dream augurs getting into a jam through repeating gossip. You should regard it as a warning. To dream of seeing a cat walk across a sheet of flypaper predicts that someone will

Astrology, Horoscope, and Dreams

laugh at you for attempting the impossible. If you dream of sitting on flypaper or of getting your hands in it, you will be accused of taking advantage of someone. Getting it in the hair is a sign of having to defend yourself in a court of law. 576

FLYSPECK. A disgusting episode is likely to occur if you dream of seeing flyspecks on any place that is connected with the preparation or the serving of food. 192

FOAL. (See also Filly.) It is a sign that you will hear interesting news, some of which will prove advantageous, if you dream of seeing a foal. If it is accompanied by a mare, the augury is especially lucky. 479

FOAM. (See also Soapsuds.) On a glass of beer or other beverage, foam seen in a dream indicates that you will have pleasure with light-hearted (and perhaps light-headed) companions. The foam generated by the propeller of a ship or motor-boat is an omen that you will travel both for business and pleasure. 743

FOOD. (See also separate items of food.) In general a dream of seeing or eating food is auspicious; a dream of wanting it, the reverse. 679

FOOL. If you dream of playing the fool, the augury is directly along the line that the foolishness takes. You will reap according to the manner in which you sow. 840

FOOT. Looking at your own bare foot in a dream is a sign that you will laugh before you will cry and suggests that you should cultivate the habit of looking on the bright side of life. Seeing the bare foot of another signifies a new acquaintance who will prove to be an excellent friend. If the foot is deformed, you will hear disturbing news. Stocking feet betoken a mystery; with shoes on them, they point to new experiences in the company of one of the opposite sex. If someone steps on your foot, you are warned to guard your tongue lest you get into trouble. 588

FOOTBALL. You are headed toward a large sum of money if you dream of playing football before spectators. If you dream of witnessing a football game, you are warned against making friends too easily. 546

FOOTLIGHTS. Beware of entanglements with those in public life after a dream of seeing a row of footlights either from backstage or from the audience. To dream of seeing them go out predicts disaster. 666

FOG. If you dream of being in a fog at sea, there will be disturbing occurrences that will require your utmost patience and skill to overcome. If the fog lifts, the outcome will be entirely favorable. A dream of being in a fog on land is an indication of a coming dilemma that will cause you and your family much concern. 226

FOGHORN. To those who are harassed by worry and poverty a dream of hearing a foghorn offers hope of speedy relief. 887

FOLIAGE. If the foliage of trees, flowers or vegetables is fresh and green, seeing it in a dream is a pleasant augury for those who are in love. If it is brown or eaten by worms, there will be quarrels and perhaps broken engagements. 813

FOLK-SONG. As a rule, a dream of hearing people sing folk-songs forecasts much pleasure in the company of your family and friends. 625

FOLLY. A dream of folly that is not vicious indicates a calm period during which you will have an opportunity to readjust your finances so as to better your condition. 349

FOGHORN. To those who are harassed by worry and poverty a dream of hearing a foghorn offers hope of speedy relief. 887

FOLIAGE. If the foliage of trees, flowers or vegetables is fresh and green, seeing it in a dream is a pleasant augury for those who are in love. If it is brown or eaten by worms, there will be quarrels and perhaps broken engagements. 813

FOLK-SONG. As a rule, a dream of hearing people sing folk-songs forecasts much pleasure in the company of your family and friends. 625

FOLLY. A dream of folly that is not vicious indicates a calm period during which you will have an opportunity to readjust your finances so as to better your condition. 349

FOOD. (See also separate items of food.) In general a dream of seeing or eating food is auspicious; a dream of wanting it, the reverse. 679

FOOL. If you dream of playing the fool, the augury is directly along the line that the foolishness takes. You will reap according to the manner in which you sow. 840

FOOT. Looking at your own bare foot in a dream is a sign that you will laugh before you will cry and suggests that you should cultivate the habit of looking on the bright side of life. Seeing the bare foot of another signifies a new acquaintance who will prove to be an excellent friend. If the foot is deformed, you will hear disturbing news. Stocking feet betoken a mystery; with shoes on them, they point to new experiences in the company of one of the opposite sex. If someone steps on your foot, you are warned to guard your tongue lest you get into trouble. 588

FOOTBALL. You are headed toward a large sum of money if you dream of playing football before spectators. If you dream of witnessing a football game, you are warned against making friends too easily. 546

FOOTLIGHTS. Beware of entanglements with those in public life after a dream of seeing a row of footlights either from backstage or from the audience. To dream of seeing them go out predicts disaster. 666

FOOTMAN. (See Flunkey.) 536

FOP. (See Dude.) 245

FORCEPS. (See also Dentist.) To have forceps used on your teeth during a dream is a forerunner of a difficult period from which you will emerge triumphant. 881

FORECAST. To dream of hearing or reading a forecast of events is a warning to exercise great care in your behavior and your investments. 025

FOREHEAD. (See also Headache.) You may expect difficulties of a serious nature if you dream of looking at your own forehead. If the dream is of smoothing the forehead of another, you will be happy with your mate. A wrinkled forehead seen in a dream is an augury of security and peace. 519

FOREIGNER. If he or she is inclined to be friendly, a foreigner in a dream, whatever the nationality or race, is an auspicious augury. 174

FOREMAN. It betokens good tidings about money if you dream of being a foreman in a shop or of a jury. 547

FOREST. If in a dream of being in a forest you are alone and frightened, it foretells that someone will break a solemn promise made to you. 128

FOREST. If you dream of being lost in a forest, you are likely to receive a puzzling and disturbing message about an old wrong. 555

FORFEIT. To have to forfeit anything in a dream—money, honor, even a kiss—is a sign of having to make amends for a wrong you have done. 519

FORGE. It is a sign that you will make definite progress if you dream of seeing a blacksmith working at a forge. 276

FORGERY. Dire misfortune is likely to follow a dream of committing a forgery. If you dream of having your name forged to a check or document, you are warned against trusting strangers. 292

FORGETFULNESS. A dream of forgetting things is an admonition to younger persons to be kind and considerate to their elders. 672

FORGIVENESS. One may look forward to a long period of relaxation and comfort if he or she dreams of forgiving a wrong. To dream of being forgiven has much the same augury. 501

FORK. It is a sign of relief from pain if one dreams of eating with a fork. To dream of stabbing a person with a fork is a prediction of the loss of one's position. 719

FORM. A dream about the beautiful form of one of the opposite sex indicates that you will find it possible to invent a gadget that will bring you much fame and a little money. 534

FORMALITY. Any occasion in a dream that is accompanied by great formality is likely to be followed by an increase in your worldly estate. 159

FORMULA. It is a good sign for lovers if they dream of making up solutions and preparations from formulas. 164

FORNICATION. (See Adultery.) 433

FORSYTHIA. Joy of living is predicted by a dream of seeing a yellow forsythia bush in bloom. To make a bouquet of it foretells a happy love love affair. 528

FORTIFICATION. A dream of fortifications is an excellent augury because these indicate defense against an enemy. To dream of being in command of a fortification is a sign of increasing responsibility and commensurate reward. 100

FORTITUDE. If in a dream you show bravery and strength of character, you are warned that these qualities will be required of you in the near future. 315

FORTUNE. A dream of a large legacy or a fortunate turn in your business affairs is a forerunner of conditions in which it will be necessary for you to exercise the best judgment at your command. 117

FORTUNE-TELLING. Having your fortune told in a dream points to a successful love life, whether or not the fortune is a favorable one. 047

FOSSIL. To find a fossil in a dream is a warning against taking things too easily in your job. If someone calls you a fossil, it is a warning against carelessness. 220

FOUNDATION. Working on the foundation for a building or a bridge is a dream that presages good over a long period. 476

FOUNDLING. To dream of finding a baby that has been abandoned by its parents and seeing that it is taken care of is an augury of peace of mind over a long period. If a maiden has this dream, she may look forward to a happy wedded life. 305

FOUNDRY. Achievement is the forecast of a dream of working in any kind of a metal foundry. 515

FOUNTAIN. Frustration is predicted by a dream of a dry fountain, but if it is playing and the water spurts, it augurs a contented and fruitful married life. 882

FOUNTAIN PEN. If you have any literary aspirations, a dream of using a fountain pen assures you of success. 021

FOWL. (See also Hen.) Any kind of fowl—hens, geese or ducks—seen in a dream are a sign of being able to hold up your head among the best people. 197

FOX. Beware of those who are seeking to do you harm if you dream of seeing a fox. If you dream of a fox hunt on horseback, you will be likely to receive an invitation for a week-end party. 182

FOX TERRIER. Nervous disorders are indicated by a dream of a fox terrier, but you will have good luck in your financial affairs. 468

FRACTION. It is a prediction of vexatious circumstances if you dream of figuring in fractions. 457

FRAGRANCE. Any pleasing odor in a dream is a harbinger of delight to those who are in love. 516

FRAME. The successful completion of a job or project is foretold by dreaming of putting a picture into a frame. 815

FRAME-UP. If you dream of being a party to any kind of a frame-up, you are likely to be asked for money by your creditors. If you dream of being "framed", you will find that your friends will rally round you in time of need. 046

FRANKFURTER. Eaten at a roadside stand, frankfurters predict grievous misunderstandings, but a dream of eating them at a picnic is a sign that you will work out your problems satisfactorily. 612

FRATERNITY. If a man dreams of being in a fraternity or brotherhood of any kind, he will be likely to meet influential people. 669

FRAUD. A dream of fraud perpetrated on yourself, is a warning against having a too trusting nature. If you dream of being the perpetrator, you will lose a valued friend. 221

FRECKLE. Young men or women who dream of having freckles are sure to find successful and steady-going mates. 074

FREEDOM. The sensation of freedom, felt in a dream, is a presage of contentment with the man or woman of your choice. 899

FREE LANCE. There is inspiration and an augury of happiness in a dream of being a free lance and earning your living by writing books and magazine articles, or by painting and drawing pictures. 196

FREE LOVE. (See also Adultery.) Everyone who has a dream of indulging in free love must make up his or her mind whether it is love or lust. If it is free *love,* the augury is of better days through closer attention to personal and business duties. This dream does not condone marital relations outside of marriage, but it does point toward better contacts with life. 520

FREE MASONRY. You will have many loyal friends if you dream of taking part in any of the rites of free masonry. 724

FREIGHT TRAIN. Improved business conditions may be confidently expected if you dream of riding on or seeing a freight train. 530

FRIAR. In person or in a picture, a friar seen in a dream is an augury of a pleasant, comfortable existence. 198

FRICASSEE. Whether of chicken or of veal, a fricassee in a dream is a sign that you will find it hard going for the next few weeks. 511

FRICTION. In general, a friction element in a dream predicts a heartache. 878

FRIEND. Anything in a dream that goes to prove that a person is a real friend is a wholesome and heartening prediction. 498

FRIGATE. Love affairs will come to a happy ending if you dream of seeing a frigate under full sail. At anchor, it predicts adventure of a dangerous sort. 061

FRIGHT. Things will turn out for you better than you had feared they would if you dream of being frightened; but if you dream of purposely frightening another person, you will suffer reverses. 195

FRITTER. Eating fritters—corn, clam or other varieties—is a dream that forecasts amazing adventures both with men and women. To dream of making them portends new work without additional compensation. 550

FRIVOLITY. (See Folly.) 805

FROCK COAT. A man will be criticized for loose behavior if he dreams of wearing a frock coat. You are warned against indiscretions. 615

FROG. Frogs in a dream are an omen of restfulness in your life. To hear them is an augury of steady and quiet progress in your business and community life. To eat their legs predicts that your friends will understand and love you. 266

FROLIC. It is an auspicious augury if you dream of frolicking either with children or grown-ups. You will have good luck at home and abroad. 080

FRONTIER. (See Borderland.) 844

FROST. It is an augury of an exciting experience to dream of seeing frost in patterns on a window. 991

FROST BITE. If you dream of being frostbitten, you are warned against doing things that will endanger your health or your reputation. 925

FROSTING. There is a sermon on frivolity in a dream about the frosting on a cake—a simple warning against taking things the easiest way—going for the sweet things of life first without thinking of those which are more lasting. 825

FROTH. (See Foam.) 514

FROWN. You will be pretty certain to have a humorous experience if you dream of seeing a person frown. If you dream of frowning yourself, you are likely to have an encounter with a law officer. 021

FROZEN FOODS. You will take a pleasure trip to a warm climate if you dream of eating or preparing frozen foods. 927

FRUGALITY. (See also Stinginess.) It is a sign that you will not want for creature comforts if you dream of practicing frugality in your home. 773

FRUIT. Generally speaking, fruit in a dream augurs good health if it is ripe; if it is green, the reverse. 612

FUCHSIA. This old-fashioned flower is not a good sign for those who are afflicted with skin diseases. 411

FUDGE. A warning to save money against an evil day is contained in a dream of making or eating fudge. One who dreams of buying it will have upsets in his or her love life. 473

FUGITIVE. Dreaming of being a fugitive from justice foretells a violent altercation with a member of your immediate family. To dream of helping a fugitive escape augurs money troubles. 450

FULLBACK. A maiden who dreams of the fullback on a football team had better be on her guard against unscrupulous men. 830

FUN. Good clean fun in a dream foretells general good luck; but fun at the expense of others' feelings predicts loss of money and health. 166

FUNERAL. The death of either a relative or a friend is foretold by a dream of going to a funeral. To dream of being at your own funeral portends a national calamity. 982

FUNGUS. You are pretty certain to have tooth trouble if you dream of seeing fungus growths on trees. It is a sign that you should guard against conspiracies of your competitors if you dream of fungus on any part of your body. 974

FUNNEL. Using a funnel in your dream to pour liquid from a container into a bottle is a sign that you will receive a message that will be difficult to understand. 946

FUNNY-BONE. It is not a funny dream where hitting the funny-bone is concerned, for it portends dismay at a sudden downward turn in your fortunes. 005

FUR. A woman who dreams of wearing luxurious furs is warned against the appearance of evil in her relations with men. If the furs are worn and ratty, she will be singled out for honors. A man who dreams of wearing a fur overcoat may look forward to a long season of prosperity. 830

FURLOUGH. A dream of being on a furlough from military or naval duty is a forecast of relief from pressing financial obligations. For a maiden to dream of meeting a soldier on furlough presages a happy love affair. 917

FURNACE. (See also Coal.) A cold furnace seen in a dream is an omen that you will be able to add to your savings account. With a fire in it, the augury is that you will be invited to social functions. 115

FURNITURE. (See Bed, Chair, etc.) 572

FURROW. (See also Plow.) A straight furrow in a dream portends hard but productive work. If the furrow is crooked, it is a sign of new problems. 641

FURY. A dream of being in a fury foretells that you are in danger of doing something that will make you appear ridiculous. If someone else is in a fury, you are warned against loose companions. 637

FUSE. It is a sign that you are wasting your time on a useless project if you dream of having to replace an electric fuse that has blown out. 863

FUSELAGE. (See also Airplane.) You will be likely to find a sum of money if you dream of climbing in or out of the fuselage of an airplane. 804

FUTURE. Good tidings from a person you have not seen in many years may be expected from any dream that looks ahead into the future. 986

GABLE. To dream of a house with many gables is a sign that you will go adventuring. You will visit strange places, both in your own land and in foreign countries. 575

GAITER. To dream of wearing gaiters portends that you will go on a shopping tour on which you will spend more money than you had intended. If you see someone else wearing gaiters, you will be cold-shouldered by someone whom you admire greatly. A pair of gaiters in a shop window is a warning to relax and take life easy for awhile so that you will the more readily reach the goal you have set for yourself. 069

GALE. If you dream of going through a devastating gale, it indicates that you will have a series of misfortunes that may be partially averted if you take care in every step you take. If, aware of your own security, you dream of watching a gale, you may expect financial difficulties, but you will emerge from these battered but undefeated. 748

GALLEON. An old-time Spanish galleon, well manned and riding the waves, signifies a blessed escape from your troubles if it is seen in a dream. You will enjoy a period of peace and plenty. 545

GALLERY. Visiting an art gallery in a dream denotes a happy climax to the project on which you have set your heart. If the paintings are by the fine old masters, you will renew an old and pleasing acquaintance, but if they are of the modern school, the friends you will make will lead you a merry chase. 218

GALLOWS. To dream of seeing a gallows is an omen of a broken engagement or a divorce. If there is a victim hanging on the gallows, you will have to overcome a great obstacle before you will be happy. 790

GALLSTONES. A dream of having gallstones foretells a bright future in spite of obstacles. 192

GALOSHES. Wearing galoshes in a dream is a forerunner of being able to save a considerable sum of money. If they are too large for you, the augury is even better, but if they leak and allow your feet to get wet, you are in danger of being called to account for some sin of omission. 042

GAMBLING. To dream of sitting in at a game of chance surrounded by gamblers of a vicious nature foretells that opportunity is on the point of knocking at your door and that you must prepare yourself to embrace it. If you dream of having losses at gambling, it portends a healthy readjustment of your mode of living; if you dream of winning, it is simply a warning against gambling. 576

GAME. Playing any game in a dream is an omen of a proposal of marriage or of a love affair that will bring you the greatest possible job. 902

GAMEKEEPER. It is a thoroughly heartening dream to see a gamekeeper because it means that you will check up on all your affairs and adjust yourself to the manner of living that will be most advantageous to you, both spiritually and financially. 943

GAMIN. To dream of a poor little gamin, an Arab of the streets, foretells an election to public office in which you will be able to help others to help themselves. 374

GANDER. (See also Goose.) A gander in a dream warns you to watch your weight lest you become too heavy for your height. To catch and hold a gander means that you have a happy surprise in store for you. 035

GANG. If you dream of being one of a gang, it portends a weak submission to your lot and a warning against having too little initiative. To be the head of a gang foretells a curtailment of your income. To see a threatening gang of ruffians signifies a period of unrest ahead of you. You must exercise great will power to rid yourself of despondency and to force yourself to do the things that make for a successful career. 905

GANGRENE. It is a sign that you will have a nagging wife or husband if you dream of a gangrenous wound. 023

GANGSTER. A dream of gangsters is an augury of easy money but a terrible catastrophe resulting therefrom. If you are captured and tortured by gangsters, you are likely to go through a long period of distress. To dream of being a gangster yourself predicts many difficulties of a financial nature. 510

GANGWAY. To dream of a gangway from a boat filled with gay, chattering, happy tourists denotes a stage of transition in your life—a change of occupation, a new home and pleasant associates. You will slip from a difficult past into an easy future. If the gangway is crowded with harassed, jostling refugees, or of people worried and fearsome of their destiny, the dream foretells a change for the worse, but it does not mean there will be a tragedy. 826

GANTLET. Fine new gantlets worn in a dream predict a smooth sailing love affair. If your gantlets are shabby and worn, your love will be unrequited. To dream of flinging down a gantlet as a signal that you wish to fight is an omen of an argument with your landlord. 082

GARBAGE. Strange as it may seem, a dream of garbage is a good omen. From a small beginning you may reasonably expect to develop a big future. 758

GARDEN. Lucky is he or she who dreams of a garden in bloom, for it is a portent of happiness, not only in love and married life, but in the things of the spirit. The opposite may be expected from dreams of a garden neglected and gone to seed, for it foretells adversity and misfortune. 294

GARDENIA. To dream of the heavy-scented gardenia is a forerunner of passionate embraces from the one you love best. 363

GARGLE. Some distasteful task is predicted by a dream of gargling. You are warned that you must make the best of it and exercise sportsmanship. 505

GARGOYLE. To see a gargoyle in your dream signifies a humorous experience that will temporarily get you into hot water. 992

GARLAND. A garland of flowers is a good sign. It signifies unity of purpose. By putting your thinking cap on you will meet and jump a hurdle with ease and come out of a difficulty with flying colors. 075

GARLIC. To dream of smelling garlic foretells some achievement that will bring you recognition in the field of sports. If in your dream you use garlic as a seasoning, you will receive a letter that for a time will give you much concern. 017

GARMENT. If you wear a new garment in your dream and receive many compliments about it, you will have an invitation to spend the week-end with some new and wealthy friends. If you dream of wearing an unbecoming or torn garment, it foretells a disappointment or a pleasure that you must forego. 982

GARNET. To wear jewelry with garnets in it is not a propitious dream. Garnets are harbingers of hard work and little to show for it. To see garnets worn by others denotes a futile longing for old times. You must forget the past, and live for today. 327

GARRET. An orderly garret seen in a dream is a good sign, and it foretells family gatherings, pleasant home interests and contentment. If the garret is used as a catch-all for trunks and boxes, and is covered with dirt and cobwebs, the dream is a warning to renew your home ties before it is too late. 690

GARRISON. A garrison of troops seen in a dream is a sign that you should put your affairs in order. Don't be caught napping, but prepare for the future. A deserted garrison foretells disaster. 945

GARTER. To dream of your garters being unfastened indicates that you will come to grief unless you signify your disapproval of loose morals. To dream of finding a pretty feminine garter is a sign that you are at the present time skating on thin ice and you are likely to go through. For a man to dream of putting a garter on a young woman is a warning against taking chances. 190

GARTER SNAKE. It is a sure sign that someone is talking behind your back if you dream of seeing a garter snake in the out of doors. To dream of handling a garter snake is a warning against repeating ugly rumors. 497

GAS. The smell of escaping gas in a dream is a warning not to interfere in the business of other prople. Seeing a victim overcome by gas predicts a scandal. Lighting a gas stove or other kind of outlets foretells the necessity to go slow in making commitments. 770

GASH. To dream of seeing a person with a deep gash in his or her body is a sign that your feelings will be hurt. It is a warning not to harbor grudges over personal slights, but to speak kindly of others even if you do not like them. 972

GAS LOG. If in a dream you see a gas log burning cheerily on the hearth, it forecasts a party at which there will be conviviality and simple good times. 146

GAS MASK. Calamity is foreboded by a dream of a person wearing a gas mask. If you dream of wearing one yourself, you will find that your creditors will be on your trail. 346

GAS METER. Seeing a man read your gas meter in a dream portends the receipt of a bill that does not concern you but which will cause you considerable inconvenience. 192

GATE. To dream of coming to an open gate predicts that there are opportunities for you ahead. A closed gate indicates that you will be thwarted in your plans for the immediate future. 095

GAUZE. Applying a gauze bandage to a cut or other wound in a dream foretells relief from harassing mental upsets. To dream of seeing a willowy young woman in a gauze dress predicts that you will be invited to an exhibition of famous paintings and sculpture. 195

GAVEL. A gavel, seen or used in a dream, portends the righting of a wrong. You will doubtless have a great deal of trouble, but if you remain firm and keep your own counsel, you will come through with flying colors. 204

GEEZER. To dream of seeing an old geezer who is interested in everybody's business but his own is an augury of being likely to have to explain an innocent but unusual act of your own. 786

GEHENNA. (See Hell.) 595

GELATINE. Gelatine used in a salad or dessert foretells a long walk through open country with a congenial companion of the opposite sex. If you dream of seeing powdered gelatine in a package, you will be likely to meet a famous dancer with whom you will have much in common. 993

GEM. (See also separate items.) Seeing many beautiful gems in a dream predicts fantastic happenings and a possible psychological upset. On the other hand, something unusual and unexplainable will possibly happen that will cause you much delight. 550

GENEALOGY. If you dream of studying your genealogy, you are likely to marry beneath you and rue the day. 768

GENEROSITY. A dream of being generous to your family and others predicts many honors to be showered on you. You are assured of an exalted position and more than the usual share of worldly goods. 500

GENII. Genii of the fairy tale variety seen in a dream are a sign of difficult but successful struggles with the world. 323

GENIUS. To dream of a genius with extraordinary talents foretells an unpleasant episode caused by your jealousy. Be warned against losing a friend. 255

GENTIAN. The lovely blue gentian in its native setting is a dream promise that you will return to live in the country and enjoy again the pleasures of life close to nature. For a woman to wear a blossom is a sign that she will marry her true love. 519

GENTLEMAN. To dream of a gentleman, a man with courtly manners and kindly spirit, a man set apart and above the rest, means an invitation to the opera, a concert or some classical entertainment by someone you have not known for long but for whom you have the greatest admiration. 757

GEOGRAPHY. If you dream of studying geography, you will soon have an opportunity to visit foreign lands. 135

GERANIUMS. Geraniums in bloom in a dream foretell a journey in a trailer or some large overland bus. 211

GERMS. To see germs through a microscope denotes pleasure through the study of the things closest to you. To dream of being afraid that germs will attack you is an augury of a visit from distant relatives. 815

GERMANY. Dreaming of Germany and of the German people at peace denotes a full larder in your home and peace of mind through the use of the mind. 359

GESTURE. If you see a group of people making strange gestures, the dream foretells a successful career on the stage or in the movies. 606

GIDDINESS. If you dream of feeling giddy, you will soon be called upon to make a momentous decision concerning your future and that of two near relatives. 545

GIFT. To offer a gift in a dream foretells happy responsibilities. To receive a gift denotes unexpected pleasures of a social nature. 921

GIGGLE. A dream of giggling in the midst of a solemn gathering foretells that you must pay your debts to save your honor. To see a group of giggling schoolgirls is a sign that you will be invited to see one of the current plays by an admirer. 808

GIMLET. To dream of using a gimlet assures you of a new outlook on life and, as a result, much contentment. 932

GIN. Drinking gin in a dream foretells that a surprise is in store for you. To see others drinking gin denotes an unsettled state of affairs that will cause you much worriment. 341

GINGER. Tasting or smelling ginger in a dream signifies a passionate romance that may or may not turn out to your liking. 790

GINGERBREAD. To eat gingerbread in a dream portends a wedding. To bake it foretells a happy family life. 142

GINGHAM. To dream of bright-colored gingham, either in a dress or upon the counter, is a sign you have come to the crossroads. You must make a decision between two loves. 670

GIPSY. A gipsy dream augurs an illicit love affair that will light from a small spark, flare up for a short time, and go out suddenly. 349

GIRAFFE. To see a giraffe in your dream is a warning to keep out of other people's affairs. 793

GIRDER. Trouble ahead and danger to your reputation are indicated by a dream of seeing a girder swung into place on a new building under construction. 302

GIRDLE. To dream of a girdle is a good sign. It means that you will accomplish the job that you have set out to do. 752

GIRL. To dream of a pretty girl means love, of course, but following the old adage that the course of true love never did run smooth, you will have your ups and downs. If you dream of a homely girl, proffered love will be refused. The standard of beauty in a dream is your own taste. 188

GLACIER. If you dream of seeing a glacier on a slope or mountainside, you will go on an extended tour of northern countries. 724

GLADIOLUS. In a dream, this beautiful flower signifies that someone will make you a straightforward proposition to take on new responsibilities with added compensation. 989

GLAMOUR. Since this means so many things to different people, it can only be said that in general a glamourous person in a dream is a warning against indiscretion. 767

GLAND. The dream of a swollen and painful gland foretells worries over nothing in particular—worries that are perhaps foolish and unnecessary. 965

GLASS. Glassware for the table or bar, used or seen in a dream, a short, sharp and unfortunate argument with a person of the opposite sex. To dream of breaking glass indicates a change in your condition of life. To dream of putting a glass pane in a window is an augury of contentment. 968

GLASS-BLOWER. Seeing a glass-blower at work in a dream presages promotion in your job, and additional compensation. 482

GLASSES. You will be fortunate in your family life if you dream of wearing glasses—either eyeglasses or spectacles—and you will find a way to clear up all of your obligations. 389

GLEN. To dream of being in a mountain glen portends the recurrence of an old ailment if you are alone. If you are accompanied by one of the opposite sex, you will be able to look forward to better relations with your family. 053

GLIDER. In a glider, or airplane without an engine, riding the winds is a portent of regaining the respect and co-operation of a business friend who will wish you to help revive a dormant business. 586

GLOBE. Dreaming of a globe of any material—metal, glass, wood, etc.—foretells a great many new diversions and the wherewithal to enjoy them. A globe map is an omen of wide travel and adventure. 490

GLOOM. If in any dream there appears to be an atmosphere of gloom, you are likely to be afflicted with severe headaches. 675

GLOVE. (See also Gantlet.) Gloves worn in a dream portend security, marital happiness and pleasant surroundings. New gloves, never worn, assure one of promotion to a higher-salaried position. 467

GLUE. To dream of spilling glue on your clothing is a sign that you are likely to be held up by a robber. If you dream of using glue to mend anything, you will lose money through unwise investments. 673

GLUTTON. Seeing a glutton eat in a dream signifies that you will be snowed under with invitations to social functions. You should try to accept as many of these as possible, for they will help you in your business career. If you dream of acting the part of a glutton, you will be successful but not popular. 236

GNAWING. Much trouble that will be your own fault is predicted by a dream of gnawing a bone. 699

GNOME. The augury of a dream in which gnomes and other unreal people are figures is that you will have to face a certain problem and that the sooner you do so, the better off you will be. 598

GNU. To see one of these animals in your dream is a warning to spend more time out of doors. 237

GNASHING. If you dream of gnashing your teeth in rage, it is a sign that you will become embroiled in some low affair, and that you will suffer humiliation. 168

GNAT. To dream of gnats is to be warned against investing in any proposition that you have not thoroughly investigated. 194

GOAL. Reaching the goal you have set for yourself is a dream that augurs success. If you dream of playing a game in which there is a goal, and you are successful in reaching it, you will find that new friends and new opportunities will come to you. 492

GOAT. Grazing goats seen in a dream are a warning against associating yourself with any enterprise in which there is the slightest suspicion of graft. General irritations will follow a dream of milking a she-goat. 923

GOATEE. To dream of a man wearing a goatee is a warning against taking chances with your health. If you wear one yourself, the omen is of scandal. 971

GOBLET. To dream of drinking water out of a goblet portends a quarrel with someone you know but slightly. If the goblet holds beer, you will be welcomed into the homes of wealthy people. To break a goblet is an omen of losing a small amount of money. 238

GOD. Any dream in which you seem to be standing in the presence of God is an augury of new opportunities to be of service to the world. It is also a promise of peace through adjustment to circumstances. 057

GODPARENT. If you dream of being a godfather or a godmother, you will be enabled to engage in a new business under propitious circumstances. 758

GOGGLES. Wearing goggles or sun-glasses in a dream signifies that you will be called a light-o'-love and taunted for your boldness. 841

GOITER. To dream of having a goiter indicates that you will have petty anxieties that will be depressing to you but that can easily be overcome. 353

GOLD. To dream of gold is an indication that you are avaricious, and that because of your miserly inclinations you will suffer the loss of many good friends. To dream of mining for gold signifies dissatisfaction with your home surroundings. 883

GOLD BRICK. If you foolishly buy a gold brick in your dream and are chagrined, it denotes a secret shame that you are trying to hide from the world. 016

GOLDENROD. To dream of seeing goldenrod growing by the roadside is a warning to stop meddling in your friends' affairs. To gather goldenrod denotes a new friend who will teach you many things that are worthwhile. 920

GOLDEN RULE. If you dream of following the golden rule, you will be able to learn to play some stringed instrument. 691

GOLDFISH. A woman who dreams of seeing goldfish in a bowl or aquarium is warned to make sure that her shades are drawn when she retires to her room. Peeping Toms will be seeking to look in on her. 799

GOLF. To play golf in your dream means that you will turn over a new leaf and be able to right a wrong. 137

GONDOLA. To dream of a gondola on one of the canals of Venice signifies a honeymoon on foreign shores. 066

GONG. To hear a gong clanging in your dreams is a warning to go back to your former occupation. If you do this, you will make a success of it. 779

GOOD FRIDAY. If you dream of going to church on Good Friday, you will be rewarded for the patience and care you have given to one of your family. 294

GOOSE. To dream of seeing a goose in a barnyard is a sign that you should watch the scales. Correct your diet, either to reduce or put on weight, according to the doctor's orders. It is a sign that you will enjoy good health if your diet includes plenty of goose-grease. 314

GOOSEBERRY. Eating gooseberries from the bush in a dream is a forecast of being derided in public for some folly for which you are not directly responsible. To make or eat gooseberry jam is a sign that you will get a ticket from a traffic officer on a highway. 685

GOOSEFLESH. If gooseflesh breaks out all over your body in a dream, you will fall in love with a good-natured fat person who is not particularly moral. 655

GOPHER. If you should see one of these little rodents in a dream, the augury is of poor business and troubles within the family circle. 282

GORE. (See Blood.) 555

GORILLA. A dream of a terrifying gorilla that haunts you even after you are awake is a portent of an embarrassing moment in which you will be misunderstood and unjustly criticized. 380

GOSPEL. If you dream of reading the gospel, you will soon be able to confer a favor on someone who is in a position to do you a great deal of good. 259

GOSSIP. To dream of being the object of malicious gossip, you will quarrel in some public place with strangers who are likely to have the better end of the argument. If you dream of idly gossiping about another, you will be involved in the love affair of another person. 786

GOSSIP. If you dream of being with people who are gossiping, you are bound to have disagreements over one or more wills in which you are mentioned. If you dream of being accused of malicious gossip by a person of either sex, you are warned against repeating confidences. 807

GOULASH. A merry weekend party if foretold by a dream of eating Hungarian goulash. 197

GOURD. A gourd used or seen in a dream, is a sign of friendship, amiable companions and comfort. 403

GOUT. To dream of having the gout foretells postponement of a long anticipated visit to old friends. It is also a warning to cut down on your consumption of alcoholic beverages. 906

GOVERNOR. If you dream of seeing or meeting the governor of your State, you will be able soon to buy a new automobile. 707

GOWN. A new gown in a dream denotes to a woman a desire to be the center of interest. You will be, but it will not be entirely satisfactory to you. A dream of wearing an old and ragged gown is a sign that a skeleton will be dragged out of the closet. 486

GRACE. To say grace in a dream before partaking of food is an omen of receiving a handsome gift that you will always treasure. 675

GRADUATION. To dream of being present at a graduation, whether as a participant or a spectator, denotes a rise in fortune and a much better position in business and social life. 963

GRAFTER. To dream of being approached by a grafter is a sign that you contemplate some questionable undertaking. You are warned against trying to make easy money. 007

GRAIL. A dream of the Holy Grail foretells that you will be called upon to share your estate with others. This omen is one that should be taken very seriously. 333

GRAIN. Feeding grain to horses or cattle in a dream is a sign of prosperity for you and your family. Handling bags of grain portends a visit from relatives. 544

GRAMMAR. It is bad luck to dream of correcting another person's grammar, but good luck if someone else corrects yours. 816

GRAMOPHONE. If you hear or see a gramophone in your dream, it is a sign of a one-sided, half-hearted love affair. 694

GRIDDLE CAKES. If you dream of making griddle cakes, the portent is that your love will be sought by at least two ardent suitors. To eat griddle cakes in a dream means that you will have a love affair with the next dark-eyed person you meet. 528

GRIDIRON. A football gridiron in a dream, if a game is being played, is a sign that you will have an interesting time with one of the opposite sex. 952

GRIEF. To dream of being grief-stricken portends a slight digestive disturbance that may lead to a more serious ailment if not given proper attention. 378

GRILL. Being in a grill and surrounded by many people of both sexes points toward an affair of the heart with a married person. 974

GRIN. It is a sign, if in your dream you see a person grin, that you will be sent tickets for a high class concert or stage performance. If you grin at someone else, you are likely to achieve some success as an amateur actor or actress. 180

GRINDSTONE. To dream of turning a grindstone is a sign that you will encounter hazards in your business but that through attention to the ins and outs you will overcome them. 989

GRIPPE. Suffering from the grippe in a dream predicts that you will shortly be able to take a long rest under pleasant circumstances. 029

GRIT. If you dream of eating grit in your food—spinach, asparagus or what not—you will be compelled to retract some statement that you have made about another person. 588

GROAN. To groan in your dream signifies that your last year's income tax is likely to be investigated. If in your dream you hear another person groan, the augury is of an unfulfilled wish. 601

GROCERY. To dream of a grocery store well stocked with goods is a sign that you will meet with success and be able to take time out for a pleasant vacation. 338

GRANARY. To dream of a full granary is a sign that your wishes will be fulfilled. To see an empty granary foretells a lonely heart. 847

GRAND JURY. A lawyer who dreams of seeing a grand jury in session is likely to be accused of malpractice. Any one who dreams of sitting on a grand jury is in danger of being accused of double dealing. 201

GRANDPARENT. If you dream of your grandfather, you will receive high honors from the community in which you live. A dream of your grandmother is an omen of plenty. 485

GRANGE. If you dream of being a member of a grange, you will be called to officiate at a meeting of a community group. 725

GRANITE. To dream of blocks of granite portends sickness and a slow recovery. 192

GRAPES. A dream of picking grapes and eating the luscious fruit augurs well for you. You will be appointed to a high position and will be able to set aside enough money for a rainy day. 349

GRAPEFRUIT. Golden grapefruit eaten in a dream foretells a division of interests. Your love affairs, business and sports will draw you in varying directions. 334

GRASS. If you dream of green grass bordering a flower garden, you will make money at the same time that you are making love. Brown, sunburned grass, neglected and gone to seed, predicts that you will have to work very hard for what you get. 068

GRASSHOPPER. To dream of grasshoppers foretells unsettled times ahead. You will be bewildered by the complexities of life. You are advised to take advice from your elders. 840

GRATE. If you dream of sitting before an open grate with a brisk fire burning, you will have many convivial companions and not a few good friends. 540

GRAVE. A grave freshly banked with flowers is an omen of a broken vow. A forsaken grave means that unkept promises will cause you many a heartache. 901

GRAVEL. If you dream of driving a car over coarse gravel, you will court a girl who is on the stage, and you should beware of skidding. 411

GRAVESTONE. (See also Grave.) To dream of seeing a new gravestone in a lot where the other stones are moss covered is an omen of having a new chance to make good. Old gravestones in a rural cemetery are a sign that you will meet a long lost friend at an opportune time. 639

GRAVY. If you dream of passing a bowl of gravy at a dinner party, you are likely to overlook an opportunity that might have brought you fame and fortune. If you dream of making gravy, you are sure to select the lucky number in a lottery. 787

GREASE. Getting grease on your clothes in a dream portends a stupid blunder that will make you simply sit down and think things over. You are warned to use the judgment with which you were endowed. To dream of greasy pots and pans or dishes predicts that you are likely to rush in where angels fear to tread. Be advised especially against giving advice where it is not asked—and then be careful. 943

GREAT LAKES. To dream of flying over the Great Lakes or motoring around them or sailing on them is an augury that you are likely to be stuck in one position all your life. It is a warning to get out of the rut you are in. 924

GREEK. To dream of either modern or ancient Greeks is a sign that you will be very successful in your business ventures. 261

GREEK CROSS. Good luck may be confidently expected after a dream in which the Greek cross figures. 612

GREENBACK. If you dream of finding a greenback of whatever denomination, you will be likely to ask a friend for a loan. If you dream of having a pocketful of greenbacks, it is a sign that you will soon be in need of financial assistance. 912

GREENHOUSE. To dream of being in a greenhouse, smelling the damp earth and vegetation therein, is a sign of a bright future. Love, laughter and adventure will be yours. 760

GREEN ROOM. If you dream of an actors' green room, you will soon be able to rest on your laurels and enjoy the satisfaction of your art. 133

GRENADE. (See Hand Grenade.) 507

GREYHOUND. To dream of seeing a greyhound running foretells a sudden collapse of your plans for the future. 369

GROOM. Seeing a groom in a dream currying a horse means that you will make an overland trip within a fortnight. A man or woman who dreams of a bridegroom will not be married within the year. 392

GROTTO. A grotto deep in the earth, or a religious retreat in a mountainside, foretells an illness of a muscular nature that will be cured through faith and taking good care of your health. 641

GROUND HOG. If you dream of seeing a ground hog, you are apt to fall in love with a genius. This may or may not be a fortunate dream. 830

GROVE. To dream of a grove of trees is a sign that you will preside over a meeting where there will be many people who will hold different opinions. 374

GROWL. Hearing a dog growl in a dream means that you are likely to have an encounter with a person whom you have never liked but who never gave you any real cause for actual criticism. 751

GRUNT. Hearing an animal grunt in a dream means that you will have to consider changing the kind of work that you are doing. If you dream of grunting yourself, you will be likely to have a troublous experience. 883

GUARD. If you dream of seeing a police guard for any kind of valuables, it foretells the loss of some sort of valuables. If the dream is of your being on guard, the prediction is of an increase is salary. 119

GUARDIAN. To dream of being made guardian of a young person forecasts many worries arising from both financial affairs and the criticism of your friends. 770

GUERNSEY. To dream of Guernsey cattle signifies that someone will ask you for a small loan. 678

GUEST. Entertaining guests in a dream is an augury of great satisfaction through an achievement. To dream of being a guest in another's home is a sign that you will shortly take a trip to a city you have never visited before. 439

GUIDE. If you dream of being a guide to someone from out of town, you will have an opportunity to make money through a new invention. If you are the one to be guided, the augury is of a discovery that is likely to make a great deal of money for you. 948

GUIDE BOOK. Referring to a guidebook in a dream signifies that you will attend a cocktail party at which there will be many famous people present. 786

GUILLOTINE. You will have a serious misunderstanding with a friend if you dream of seeing a person brought to the guillotine. If you dream of being the victim, you are in great danger of an illness that may prove fatal. 037

GUITAR. To dream of playing a guitar is a sign that you are apt to have your pocket picked. Listening to a guitar in a dream is a portent of pleasant love affairs. 803

GULL. If you dream of seeing gulls flying, you are very

likely to have adventure of an exciting but innocent nature. 236

GUM. Chewing gum in a dream is a sign that your best girl will break a date with you; or, if you are a woman, it warns against too much familiarity with men you have but recently met. 235

GUM DROPS. To dream of gum drops means that you will see a friend or a relative whom you have not seen for many months or years. 897

GUN. Injustice either to you or to one of your family or friends is foretold by a dream of firing a gun—a pistol, rifle, shot-gun, or large-calibered cannon. To hear the sound of guns in a dream is a sign of unrest. 928

GUTTER. A dream of lying in a gutter predicts a period through which you will pass in which you will have many things to explain. Trying to clean out a gutter in a dream is a sign that you will be successful in the next job you undertake. 930

GYMNASIUM. Gymnasium exercises in a dream augur invitations to functions on the same date, and consequent embarrassment. 007

GYPSY. Amorous adventures are predicted by a dream about gypsies. If a gypsy tells your fortune, you are likely to find a mate. 408

H

HABERDASHERY. Clean haberdashery—shirts, collars, neckties, scarves—is a fortunate augury when seen in a dream. If these articles are soiled, the omen is of business failure. 267

HABIT. To dream of having formed a habit—drink, tobacco, drug, etc.—is a portent of difficulty in social relationships. 477

HABITATION. (See Home.) 884

HADDOCK. Lovers may look forward to unhappiness but eventual marriage if they dream of eating this kind of fish. 152

HADES. (See Hell.) 494

HAG. No good comes of a dream of a hag. Men will find themselves snubbed by their sweethearts, and women will have disillusioning experiences. 962

HAGGIS. This Scotch pudding is an augury of plenty when seen or eaten in a dream. If one dreams of sticking a knife into a haggis, he or she is warned against behaving indiscreetly. 519

HAIL. A hailstorm in a dream is a forerunner of a succession of grievous occurrences. 264

HAIR. Combing one's hair in a dream signifies a solution of annoying problems. To comb another's hair indicates that you will be called upon to help a friend, and if you are wise, you will help him or her. If you comb the hair of a person of the opposite sex, you will be able to solve any sex problems that you may have. To have your hair cut is a sign of success in a new sphere of life. To cut another's hair is a warning against those who are unfriendly to you. To braid your own hair signifies that someone will make an explanation to you; to braid another's is a sign that you will have to explain something. For a woman to wave her hair portends new men friends, but if a man dreams of waving his hair, it is an omen of shame. 884

HAIRDRESSER. A woman who dreams of going to a hairdresser should guard against repeating any scandalous gossip she may hear. 647

HAIRPIN. Happy is the man who dreams of seeing a woman arranging her hair with hairpins. If there are hairpins in her mouth, so much the better. He can look forward to a calm and fruitful married life. It is also a good sign to dream of making minor repairs to machinery with hairpins. 175

HAIR SHIRT. Better times are in store for the person who dreams of voluntarily wearing a hair shirt, but dire happenings will follow a dream of forcing another to do so. 832

HALF-BREED. If you dream of a half-breed Indian, you are likely to have an exciting adventure, but you should be on guard against treachery. 128

HALF COCK. To dream of carrying a gun or pistol at half cock is a warning against losing your temper. If you dream of such a weapon going off half-cocked, you are bound to regret a hasty action. 880

HALF DOLLAR. If you dream of receiving a bright new silver half dollar in change or for payment, you are likely to have a disappointing experience. 590

HALF-MAST. A flag at half-mast seen in a dream is a sign of calamity, although it does not necessarily portend death. 920

HALF MOON. In a clear sky a half-moon is an omen of travel to foreign lands. If the sky is partially obscured by clouds, the portent is one of dissatisfaction with your position. Guard against complaining to your boss. 303

HALITOSIS. To dream of seeing a person turn away from you in disgust because you have halitosis is a warning against too great self-assertiveness. If you dream of another person's having it, the omen is of either a business or social obstacle that will have to be overcome. 879

HALL. You may as well make up your mind to be ready for a long period of fear and worry if you dream of being alone in a long hall. 962

HALLELUJAH. This exclamation of joy, heard or spoken in a dream, is a portent of the successful culmination of an ardent love affair. 308

HALLOWE'EN. To dream of high jinks on Hallowe'en presages increased influence in club, church, lodge or community life. 143

HALLUCINATION. If you dream of having hallucinations, you will be called upon to testify in behalf of a friend. Be on your guard against perjuring yourself. 891

HALO. To see a person wearing a halo in a dream predicts a death among your circle of close friends. If the halo is on someone you know, it foretells a death in your family. If it is on yourself, it predicts travel to a far-off land. If you dream of taking off a halo, you will have business advancements. 754

HALTER. Putting a halter on a horse in a dream is a sign that you will be able to control your own destiny in spite of the forces that seem to be working against you. 299

HALYARD. To dream of halyards breaking while a boat is in motion is a presage of having an experience that will make you change your plans radically. 838

HAM. Smoking hams in a dream is a sign of a year of plenty. To dream of baking a ham augurs a difficult time that will work out to your ultimate good. If you dream of eating ham in any form—smoked or fresh—you will be lucky in business affairs. 456

HAMLET. A dream of a hamlet, or small village, is an augury of defeat in a project that is close to your heart. To dream of Shakespeare's play "Hamlet" predicts that you will have much comfort in the bosom of your family. 806

HAMMER. Using a hammer in a dream, whether for driving a nail or for other purposes, predicts an achievement for women and an accident for men. 294

HAMMOCK. Sitting in a hammock alone in a dream foretells a succession of irritations arising from a selfish attitude. If you are with a person of the opposite sex, it predicts wholesome recreations. 778

HAMPER. It is a sign that you will make progress if you dream of putting soiled clothing into a hamper. 989

HAND. A dream of any beautiful hands is an augury of satisfaction in life. A dream of busy, skillful hands predicts recreation after toil. If you dream of bent and gnarled hands, you will find relief from your financial worries. Waving hands predict separations. Caressing hands foretell romance and marriage. 444

HANDBAG. A mystery is predicted if you dream of a lady's handbag. To dream of a woman or girl opening and looking through a handbag foretells an episode in which all your sympathies will be brought into play. 039

HANDBALL. It is a sign that you will have varying fortunes for a period but final success if you dream of playing handball. 669

HANDBILL. A dream of distributing handbills is an augury of great content in your everyday life. To dream of seeing handbills strewn around the street is a prophecy of an upset condition. 926

HANDCUFF. If you dream of having handcuffs snapped on your wrists, there is no need to worry about an encounter with the law, but a man who has this dream will have mother-in-law complications if he is married, and if he is single, he will be likely to be criticized by his boss. A woman having the dream should guard her good name. If you dream of putting handcuffs on another, the augury is of an unexpected promotion. 993

HAND GRENADE. The deepest shame may be expected after a dream of throwing a hand grenade. It is also a warning not to do anything against your better judgment. 222

HANDICAP. To succeed in a dream in spite of a handicap is a sign that you will have a better position offered to you. If you dream of receiving a handicap in any kind of contest, you will be very likely to make a success in business. 995

HANDICRAFT. It is a fortunate augury of better times if you dream of being skilled in handicrafts such as weaving, wood-working, book-binding, printing and the like. You will always be able to make a living. 917

HANDKERCHIEF. To dream of using the handkerchief for blowing the nose is a prophecy of an increase in your income; for wiping perspiration from your forehead, release from worry. If you wave your handkerchief to someone, you will have an interesting though not passionate love affair. To wash a handkerchief is a sign of losing money. 911

HAND ORGAN. Hearing a hand organ in a dream foretells a pleasant vacation amid unfamiliar but beautiful surroundings. To dream of playing one is a prophecy of rollicking adventure. 343

HANDSPRING. Maidens who dream of doing handsprings had better keep a watchful eye on their behavior while in the company of young men. A man having this dream should be careful to keep his mind on his work. 518

HANDWRITING. It is a sign that you will succeed in business undertakings if you dream of trying to decipher "blind" handwriting in a letter or document. To dream of reading handwriting of the "copperplate" variety means that you must be on your guard against deception. 374

HANDY MAN. Enlisting the services of a handy man in a dream for any sort of cleaning or repairs portends a series of difficulties with your landlord. 520

HANGAR. You are certain to have a rise in your fortunes if you dream of being locked in a hangar where airplanes are kept, but if the hangar is empty, you will suffer disappointment and chagrin. 649

HANGER. It is a sign of freedom from care if you dream of putting away a suit of clothes or a dress on a hanger in a closet. 875

HANGING. To be present at the hanging of a condemned person in a dream is a prophecy of having to give an alibi of some sort. 563

HANGMAN. You will have worries aplenty if you dream of fulfilling the duties of a hangman. It is a distinct warning against being too critical of your friends. 432

HANGNAIL. An ailment that, unless it is given prompt and careful attention, may lead to serious consequences is predicted by a dream of having a hangnail. If you dream of pulling it off, the dream signifies an even worse state of affairs. 637

HANGOVER. This is a serious dream for a maiden to have. She must be very careful not to make any false moves where young men are concerned. For men or married people the dream portends relaxation from worries regarding their financial affairs. 699

HAPPINESS. After a dream in which you get the impression of happiness, you are advised to take particular care not to do anything that may impair your health. A dream of happy children is a pleasant augury. 051

HARA-KIRI. This Japanese method of suicide by disembowelment is a sign of distressing circumstances both in your personal and business life. 374

HARANGUE. You will have difficulties with your relatives if you dream of delivering a harangue to several persons. If you dream of listening to a harangue, you will be likely to be given a civil service job. 247

HARBOR. To dream of coming into a harbor in a sailboat or steamship denotes that you will be successful in meeting your obligations. If the ship is leaving a harbor, you will doubtless take a trip abroad. 817

HARDTACK. Eating hardtack in a dream portends rough going in love affairs. You should be warned against losing your temper in an argument. 672

HARDWARE. Many items of hardware seen in a dream is an omen of general good fortune in business. 940

HARE. To kill a hare in a dream predicts a change of occupation. To eat a hare is an omen of good times. To prepare a hare for the table forecasts pleasant family surroundings. 770

HAREM. A maiden who dreams of being a member of a harem is apt to have upsets in her love life. A man who dreams of keeping a harem had better watch his step, or he will be criticized. 387

HARLEQUIN. Dancing in a pantomime with the fair Columbine, Harlequin in a dream is an augury of happy hours in the company of your best-beloved. 386

HARLOT. Dreaming of harlots is a sign of impending illness for a man, but if a woman dreams of being a harlot, she will be likely to have good news from an unexpected source. 576

HARMONICA. Played in tune and with a vivacious lilt, a harmonica in a dream portends pleasant hours spent in the company of one's best beloved. 588

HARMONY. There can be no other interpretation of a harmony dream than that harmony in your life is predicted. 064

HARNESS. (See also Halter.) It is an augury of an interesting achievement of a minor nature if you dream of putting a harness on a horse or other animal. 642

HARP. Playing a harp in a dream portends a reawakening of your spiritual life. If you see a beautiful woman playing a harp, you will find that someone will do you a favor of considerable importance. 334

HARPOON. To dream of having a harpoon buried in your body is an omen of great distress over the loss of money. Using it on a large fish or a whale portends increased earning capacity and a better place in which to live. 264

HARPSICHORD. A tuneful harpsichord on which is played refined music is a favorable augury to those in love. Jazz or swing music played on a harpsichord portends a puzzling experience. 159

HARVEST. It is a sign of good circumstances if you dream of gathering a satisfactory harvest, but if it is disappointing, you are likely to have difficulties in business. 888

HARVEST MOON. Lovers will come into their own if they dream of a large harvest moon. If it becomes obscured by mist, the augury is of quarrels that should not be allowed to become serious. 254

HASH. A dream of hash predicts that something will happen that for a time will be unexplainable. To make hash in a dream is a sign of having trouble with machinery; to eat it portends a mystery. 467

HASHISH. (See Marihuana.) 072

HASSOCK. To dream that you are a child sitting on a hassock at the feet of someone you love is an augury of peace after a period of distress. 052

HASTE. To do anything in a great hurry in a dream augurs difficulties that you could have avoided by exercising a little forethought and care. You are warned against doing your work in a slap-dash manner. 153

HAT. For a gentleman to dream of lifting his hat to a lady is a sign of promotion in business. If he dreams of keeping his hat on under such circumstances, he will meet with a puzzling problem that will require skillful handling. To dream that your hat is blown off by the wind portends irritations in business. It is a sign of good fortune that will arrive soon if you dream of buying a new hat. To wear a hat that is much too small for you predicts a heartache; if it is too large, you will be called to account for an indiscretion. 060

HATCHET. It is an augury of disturbances both at home and in the business world to dream of cutting down a tree with a hatchet. To split kindling wood with a hatchet predicts that you will make up any differences you may have with your family. It is a sign of an increased income if you dream of sharpening a hatchet. 124

HATE. Sad happenings are forecast if you dream of hating anyone, but if you dream that someone hates you, the augury is of an improvement in your affairs. 481

HAUGHTINESS. Woe betide you if you dream of acting in a haughty manner to another person, but if someone similarly tries to "high-hat" you, there will be a mildly amusing experience in the near future. 967

HAVOC. For whatever cause—wind, rain, fire or other disaster—a dream of the havoc that has been wrought bespeaks a new opportunity for you before long. 516

HAWAIIAN. (See also Hula Hula.) If they are in their native costumes, Hawaiians seen in a dream foretell stirring adventures in love. Dressed in European clothes, they are an augury of boredom. 196

HAWK. A hawk flying augurs new business opportunities. Otherwise it foretells a period of depression. 038

HAWSER. Reaching from a large boat and made fast to a dock, a hawser is an augury of a secure future for yourself and family. To dream of seeing a hawser break foretells dire happenings from the effect of which you will find it difficult to escape. 252

HAY. Contrary to what might be expected, to dream of making hay under sunny skies is a sign that you will lose money and get into debt. If it is cloudy, the dream is of better import, for you will receive money that you never expected to get. It is a good sign to dream of playing in a haymow; it is a presage of happy love affairs to young men and women. 664

HAY FEVER. No good will come of a dream of suffering from hay fever unless you take it as a warning to guard your health. 238

HEAD. A disembodied head seen in a dream is a sign of a new situation in your life that must be met with fortitude and good sense. 600

HEADACHE. To dream of suffering from a headache indicates that if you will keep your own counsel regarding your job and your investments, you will make a success of a pet project. 751

HEADCHEESE. A house which dreams of making headcheese will have a happy time visiting with an old friend. To eat headcheese in a dream is an augury of getting an important letter. 887

HEADDRESS. (See also Hat.) An opportunity will be offered for you to make progress in your community if you dream of seeing a striking headdress on a woman of the Old World. 795

HEAD HUNTER. A dream of being captured by headhunting savages is a prediction that you will have a chance to retaliate for a wrong that has been done you. It is also a warning against associating with wild company. 322

HEADLIGHT. One or more glaring headlights coming toward you in a dream, either on an automobile or a railway locomotive, are a portent of a disaster that you can avert only by quick and decisive action. 953

HEADLINE. To dream of seeing your name in a newspaper headline is an augury of an unpleasant occurrence in your neighborhood. 741

HEADSTONE. If you dream of erecting a headstone on a grave, you will have to call upon a friend to help you out of trouble. A headstone that has fallen over portends a narrow escape. To dream of reading your own name on a headstone is an omen of exciting news from afar—perhaps to your great advantage. 766

HEALTH. Accent on health in a dream portends joy to the dreamer. 639

HEARSE. It is a sign of increasing responsibilities if you dream of being asked to ride with the driver of a hearse. To dream of occupying the interior of a hearse predicts a sudden business trip. 414

HEART. The augury of a dream of losing one's heart to a person of the opposite sex is of meeting a new and eligible person. To dream of having a heart attack augurs many years of happy and productive living. 513

HEARTACHE. For whatever reason, a heartache in a dream predicts better times through a release from worrisome responsibilities. 667

HEARTBURN. An attack of heartburn felt in a dream presages a return to simpler pleasures than those to which you have become accustomed. 594

HEARTH. (See Fireplace.) 432

HEAT. To dream of suffering from heat is a portent of having to apologize to someone for an ill-advised action or remark. 759

HEATER. (See Furnace.) 653

HEATHEN. Unfortunate is he or she who dreams of referring to a person of another faith as a heathen. 468

HEATHER. Lying in the heather under a sunny sky is a dream that portends simple but lasting pleasures. If the sky is cloudy, the portent is of hard work and little reward. Heather at night predicts sorrow. 069

HEAT STROKE. To dream of passing out because of extreme heat is a presage of difficulties of a physiological nature. 696

HEAVEN. Dying and going to heaven in a dream portends a new and more difficult job; and it may be a better one for you. 715

HEBREW. (See Jew.) 238

HEDGE. It portends good luck to dream of clipping a hedge; bad luck to dream of jumping over one. If you dream of crawling through an opening in a hedge, you will snubbed by a society matron. 871

HEDGEHOG. (See Porcupine.) 180

HEEL. If you dream of losing a heel from one of your shoes, you will find yourself at odds with long-established friends. To dream of nailing a heel on one of your shoes is a portent that you will make a social error. A dream of rubber heels is an omen that you will be deceived. 573

HEIFER. (See Calf, Cow.) 625

HEIR. A small sum of money will be yours if you dream of falling heir to a large fortune. 721

HEIRLOOM. The significance of an heirloom in a dream is one of dignity in your association with the people you meet. 332

HELIOTROPE. This old-fashioned purple flower predicts a quiet and sensible love affair to the unmarried and a secure future to all who dream of it. 626

HELIUM. Safe and profitable investments are forecast by a dream of this gas used for inflating dirigible balloons. 546

HELL. A dream of the orthodox hell described by Dante and the great religionists of old and illustrated by Dore and such artists is a sign that you will have an easier time financially but that you will have disagreements with your neighbors. If you dream of going through "hell on earth", you are warned that you should try harder to understand people you do not like. 145

HELL-CAT. An augury of a succession of annoyances is contained in a dream of calling a woman a hell-cat. 592

HELMET. If you dream of seeing soldiers wearing steel helmets, you will have an internal disturbance that may prove serious. To wear a helmet yourself portends better health. 289

HELP. A dream of calling for help is a sign that you will shortly need help, and get it. If you dream of hearing a call for help and answer it, you will find that you are in a good position to make money. 897

HEM. To stitch or sew a hem on a garment or other piece of cloth denotes the completion of a creditable job. 556

HEMORRHAGE. Any kind of a hemorrhage seen in a dream—whether it is yours or another's—is a warning against over-exertion in both manual and mental work. 859

HEMORRHOIDS. A dream of this affliction, commonly known as piles, is a warning against foolishly exposing yourself to physical danger or contagious diseases. 747

HEMP ROPE. (See also Rope.) The successful termination of a long and arduous job is portended by seeing a coil of new hemp rope. To uncoil it presages the beginning of an important piece of work. To make a noose with a hemp rope is a prediction of misfortune. A mystery will be unraveled for you if you dream of seeing the manufacture of hemp rope. 867

HEMSTITCHING. A woman who dreams of doing hemstitching will be happy in love. If a man has this dream he will win the respect of his associates. 063

HEN. General comforts in life varied by ups and downs and family worries are predicted by a dream of feeding hens. To dream of seeing a hem sitting on eggs is a sign of plenty. Killing a hen in a dream signifies a visitor. Plucking a hen means that you will have to spend more money than you had planned to. 765

HENNA. New scenes and new friends are promised the woman who dreams of putting henna on her hair. 415

HEN-PECKING. A man who dreams of being hen-pecked is warned thereby against losing his temper. 655

HERALD. To dream of seeing a young man in the costume of a herald delivering a message of importance is a forecast of an advance in your fortunes. 909

HERALDRY. (See Coat of Arms.) 378

HERB. Contentment in your daily life, in love and in marriage are predicted by a dream of growing herbs in a garden. The pungent, unusual aroma of herbs in a dream is a sign of new and pleasing adventures. 393

HERESY. A dream of being accused of heresy foretells that you will assert yourself in your community and thereby make greater progress than formerly. 976

HERITAGE. (See Legacy.) 676

HERMAPHRODITE. You will have many disquieting experiences if you dream of being a hermaphrodite. If you dream of seeing one, you must behave with more circumspection in the company of the opposite sex. 886

HERMIT. To dream of visiting a hermit in his retreat portends the early solution of a vexing problem. If he or she shows anger, this solution will cause you no end of trouble. 850

HERNIA. (See Rupture.) 086

HERO. If in a dream you appear to play a hero's part by doing brave acts in the face of death, you are likely to be criticized by someone younger than yourself or called to account by your employer for unseemly actions. To dream of seeing a heroic act performed by another is a sign that you will engage in a new business deal and make a handsome profit. 521

HEROIN. (See also Marihuana.) You will be despised by someone whose good opinion you value highly if you dream of experimenting with this drug. 797

HERON. Things will move faster in your business career if you dream of herons, and the gains will be greater than the losses. 104

HERRING. Smoked herring eaten in a dream are a portent that warns against over-indulgence in wines and hard liquors. To buy herring foretells that people will be suspicious of your actions. 934

HERRING. Smoked herring eaten in a dream is a portent that warns against over-indulgence in wines and hard liquors. To buy herring foretells that people will be suspicious of your actions. 934

HICCOUGH. A dream of hiccoughing seldom comes except in connection with liquour, and therefore it is to be regarded as a warning against drinking too much. 952

HICKORY. Using the wood of the hickory tree in a dream foretells hard going in your business. Eating hickory nuts predicts that you will succeed in the job you are doing. 500

HIDE. A dream of the hides of animals is a sign that you will be invited to take a vacation with a wealthy friend. 164

HIEROGLYPHICS. Dreaming of making an attempt to read the hieroglyphics or inscriptions on ancient Egyptian monuments is an augury of making a discovery that will bring you renown. 930

HIGHBALL. To drink one highball in a dream—either Scotch or rye—is a good augury. To drink two or more forecasts an argument with an associate. 101

HIGHBROW. If someone calls you a highbrow in a dream you will be shamed by a person for whom you have little regard. To dream of a person who shows evidences of being a highbrow portends that you will distinguish yourself by an intellectual achievement. 876

HIGH JINKS. If the high jinks in your dream are conducted among low company, you are likely to be successful in business dealings with people of inferior intelligence, but you will get no personal satisfaction therefrom. 084

HIGH SCHOOL. To dream of being back in your high school days is a sign of a love affair that will be both exciting and disturbing. 642

HIGH TIDE. There is great promise in a dream of high tide. You should take the greatest possible advantage of any opportunities you may have offered after such a dream. 121

HIGHWAYMAN. Being held up on a lonely road and robbed of your valuables by a highwayman portends losing your head over a person younger than yourself. 019

HILARITY. If you dream of being hilarious at a gathering of men and women, the augury is of time-wasting festivities. 460

HILL. To dream of climbing a hill augurs some small success. Standing or sitting on the top is a sign of an established income and contentment. 140

HINDU. A mysterious but enjoyable person will come into your life if you dream of associating with one or more Hindu men or women. 409

HINGE. A rusty hinge in a dream foretells difficult times in connection with personal affairs. One that speaks is a prediction that someone will be cruel to you, either physically or mentally. 867

HIP. For a man to dream of a woman who is carrying a burden of any kind on her hip is a portent of a love affair in a foreign land. To dream of the naked hips of a person of the opposite sex betokens a succession of small troubles. 750

HIPPOPOTAMUS. You will soon have to run to escape danger if you dream of a hippotamus in its native lair. If it is seen in a zoological park, you will run the risk of being very much bored by people from whom you cannot escape. 171

HISS. To hear a snake hiss in a dream portends that you will make a grave mistake through not controlling your temper. It is an augury that you will be held in contempt if you dream of hissing at an actor or a speaker. To dream of being hissed predicts slow but sure progress in your work. 837

HISTORY. If in your dream your mind goes back over historic episodes, you will be likely to have an opportunity to better yourself financially by showing good judgment. This dream is a warning to be ready. 029

HITCH-HIKING. You will be criticized for your dependence on others if you have a dream of hitch-hiking. If you dream of taking on a hitch-hiker while driving a car, it is a sign that you will have to have a show-down with your creditors. 988

HIVE. A beehive in a dream is a sign of freedom from worry, but if you overturn it or otherwise damage it and set the bees loose, your dream will have exactly the opposite import. 421

HIVES. This skin eruption in a dream portends unexplainable occurrences that will cause you no end of concern but that will not be serious if you do not allow them to become so. 556

HOARHOUND. This medicinal herb is a good sign in any dream. The candy known as hoarhound predicts ease of life for a long period. 123

HOARSENESS. If you dream of being hoarse and unable to speak above a whisper, you are likely to have an affair that will put you in an embarrassing situation. 803

HOAX. To perpetrate a hoax in a dream, even if it is an innocent one, presages that you will have explanations to make for apparently strange actions. 694

HOBBY HORSE. It is a fortunate augury if you dream of riding a hobby horse. This may be the kind of hobby horse you had when a child or it may simply mean following a hobby such as collecting things, photography, or other recreations. 542

HOBGOBLIN. Hobgoblins in a dream are not to be taken seriously by themselves. They seldom mean anything more than indulgence in too rich food before going to bed. 498

HOBO. Easy times are ahead if you dream of being a hobo, but if you are concerned in nefarious actions, the augury is anything but auspicious. You are likely to be shamed in public. 194

HOCKEY. A rough game of hockey in a dream is a portent of success through close attention to business. This is true whether the game is played on the ice or elsewhere. 412

HOCKSHOP. (See Pawnbroker.) 869

HOE. The use of a hoe in a dream portends good fortune in the sale of farm and dairy products. 093

HOG. A dream of a clean, well-groomed hog forecasts an unusual experience in connection with a factory of some sort. If a hog is in a wallow, the portent is success in a new business enterprise. 303

HOGSHEAD. If you dream of being pushed into a hogshead and having the cover put on, you will have an altercation with a woman in which you will not make a good showing. To dream of packing a hogshead with foodstuffs indicates that you will have success through your ability for organization. 283

HOLDUP. (See Highwayman.) 712

HOLE. A hole in a garment predicts better luck in financial affairs. If you dream of seeing a bullet hole in a body, you are warned against believing what strangers tell you. 944

HOLIDAY. A dream of having a holiday and being able to rest from your labors is a sign that you will have to work even harder but that your efforts will be effective in procuring for you greater rewards. 585

HOLINESS. It is an augury of peace and understanding with family and friends if you dream of the holiness of any particular person. 968

HOLLAND. The countryside of Holland, with its windmills and its people in wooden shoes, is the setting for a dream that will bring you content in your family circle and in your community. 041

HOLLY. If in a dream you hang wreaths of holly in windows or on a door, you will have good luck in both material ways and in your friendships. 279

HOLLYHOCK. This old-fashioned flower seen in a dream is a portent that you will be happy in spite of present poverty. 209

HOLY COMMUNION. To partake of Holy Communion in a dream points toward making a friend who will stand by you through life. 430

HOME. If the dream is of happy home life, it portends success of small dimensions and great contentment. 262

HOME RUN. You may be sure that your next business venture will be successful if you dream of making a home run in a baseball game. 215

HOMESICKNESS. This dream is a sign that you will receive good news from an old and valued friend and that you will use this news to good advantage. 076

HOMICIDE. (See Murder.) 401

HOMINY. Dull days are predicted by a dream of eating hominy. Eaten cold, it also predicts illness. 309

HONESTY. It is a particularly fortunate augury in a dream if someone whom you believed to be dishonest turns out to be honest. To dream that you yourself are honest means nothing, for that should be the normal expectation. 749

HONEY. Going will be slow and difficult if you dream of eating honey. Hard times are predicted if you dream of getting your fingers sticky with it. If you call someone "Honey", you will be placed in an embarrassing position. 461

HONEYMOON. To dream of being on your honeymoon is a sign of wedded bliss. 544

HONEYSUCKLE. The sweet scent of honeysuckle in a dream is an augury of love to the unmarried, To pick sprays of it indicates real contentment in home life and among your neighbors. To others it is a sign that you will be able to make the most of your opportunities. 984

HOOD. It is not a good sign to wear a hood in a dream. You will be deceived by those whom you have trusted. 099

HOODLUM. Unfortunate is he or she who dreams of hoodlums. It signifies that you will be shamed and held up to public scorn. 195

HOOF. The hoof of a horse, cow or other animal, seen in a dream, indicates that you are in danger of being swindled. If the hoof is cloven, the augury is of complications in love affairs. 694

HOOK. To be caught on a hook of any kind in a dream presages difficulties that will give you much concern. If you are able to wriggle free, it will be at the expense of much sorrow and grief. 139

HOOP. If you dream of rolling a hoop as you did when you were a child, you are likely to hold your present job as long as you wish to. 881

HOPE. Any dream that seems to hold out hope in the face of difficulties is to be regarded as a good dream in the long run. 505

HOPS. Picking hops in a dream prophesies love affairs that will carry you away for the time being and then suddenly cease. 761

HOPSCOTCH. If the game of hopscotch you play in a dream gives you pleasure, the augury is of an entertainment in store for you; otherwise it means a defeat of some kind. 202

HORIZON. To see a far horizon in a dream is a sign of success in your business life and your love affairs, If the horizon seems close at hand, the augury is of incidents that are likely to give you much concern for a long time. 968

HORIZONTAL BARS. Exercising on horizontal bars in a dream is a sign that you will be called upon to exhibit courage in the face of danger. 584

HORN. The sound of a horn heard in a dream has different meanings according to circumstances. An automobile horn is, of course, a warning against danger. A fish horn is a sign of gay times ahead. A horn in an orchestra or band predicts family difficulties. 525

HORNET. To dream of being stung by a hornet is, strangely enough, a forerunner of good luck in your next business undertaking. 497

HOROSCOPE. The best of luck may be expected from a dream of having your horoscope read by an expert. 769

HORROR. This note in a dream should be interpreted in connection with the other elements that figure in it. It is not necessarily unfortunate. 303

HORS D'OEUVRES. Your expectations are good after a dream of being served with hors d'oeuvres at a restaurant or a bar. They predict that you will make progress with your business associates. 502

HORSE. In general, dreams about horses portend acts of faithfulness on the part of your friends. If you dream of riding horseback, the omen is of achievement in affairs relating to your community. To dream of breaking a horse is an augury of resistance from someone you want to be friendly with. If you dream of being kicked by a horse, it is a warning against over-confidence in strangers. Seeing two horses fighting in a dream portends ill luck. 030

HORSE CHESTNUT. You are likely to have a short illness if you dream of eating horse chestnuts. To dream of throwing them at an enemy is a sign of failure in business. 641

HORSEFLY. Minor annoyances are portended by a dream of being bitten by a horsefly. 593

HORSESHOE. (see also Quoits) To dream of nailing a horseshoe over a door augurs a series of happenings that appear to be unlucky but that will add up to something extremely good for you. 657

HORSERADISH. If you dream of eating horseradish, you will be beset by doubts of the fidelity of your friends. 402

HORSE-TRADING. To dream of trading horses is a sign of having to contend with a trying business situation that will require careful handling. 044

HORSEWHIP. (See Flogging.) 229

HOSE. (See also Stockings.) Squirting a hose in a dream portends new adventures, perhaps of a dangerous nature. If it is directed on a fire, the adventures will be in a foreign land. Playing with a hose on a lawn predicts new friends. 735

HOSIERY. (See Stockings.) 885

HOSPITAL. Dreaming of being taken to a hospital means that although you will get into difficulties, you will overcome them and be ahead of where you were before. 210

HOSPITALITY. If you are shown hospitality in a dream, the augury is of a comfortable home life. To show it to others is a sign of increased income. 869

HOST. To dream of being the host or hostess to visitors or guests at a dinner party points toward successful handling of your financial affairs. 680

HOSTILITY. If it is directed at you, hostility in a dream betokens keen regret for some unworthy action. If you show it to others, you are likely to find yourself in a compromising situation. 484

HOTBED. Working with plants in a hotbed is a dream that foretells delightful experiences with new friends. 543

HOT DOG. (See Frankfurter.) 218

HOTEL. A dream of registering at a hotel is a sign of increasing responsibilities in your job if you are alone in the dream. If you are accompanied by one of the opposite sex, it is a portent of having to meet an emergency. 249

HOTHOUSE. (see Conservatory.) 539

HOUND. Riding to hounds in a dream is an omen that you will have much leisure time but by the same token it is a warning that you should make good use of it and not waste it in gay parties. To dream of being pursued by bloodhounds is a sign that unless you slacken the pace at which you are going, you will suffer a breakdown. 748

HOUR-GLASS. It is a portent of woe resulting from wasted opportunities if you dream of looking at an hour-glass with the sand running through. 933

HOUSE. Dreaming of building a house portends good fortune in business; of buying a house, a short and mad love affair. 809

HOUSEBOAT. A dismal outlook for those in love is predicted by a dream of living on a houseboat. If the houseboat slips its moorings, the augury is one of disquieting adventure with loose companions. 734

HOUSEKEEPER. For a woman to dream of being a housekeeper for a wealthy man is a prophecy of an increasing income but much criticism from the world at large. 212

HOUSEMAID. If a man dreams of companionship with a pretty housemaid, he is likely to be invited to a school reunion. If he dreams of kissing her, he will be dunned by those to whom he owes money. 037

HOUSEWIFE. A maiden who dreams of being a housewife will be likely to marry an actor or some other professional man who must be more or less constantly on the move. 381

HOVEL. You will not want in your old age if you dream of living in a hovel. If the hovel burns down, however, you will hear good news. 601

HOWLING. The sound of howling in a dream—either from an animal or a human—portends misery and pain. 359

HUBBUB. A dream of being in the center of a hubbub foretells a great many vexatious occurrences inside your family group. 480

HUCKLEBERRY. A warning to investigate all unsanitary conditions around you is contained in a dream that in any way concerns huckleberries. To dream of picking them augurs a slight illness. 688

HUCKSTER. To dream of hearing a huckster call his wares forecasts a period of freedom from pressing worries. To buy vegetables or fruit from a huckster is an augury of good health. 831

HUG. A warm hug, if unaccompanied by passion, is a fortunate portent in a dream by young persons. It points toward a happy marriage and healthy children. If the hug is lacking in innocence, the augury is of a trip around the world. 397

HULA HULA. This highly insinuating dance, performed by grass-skirted Hawaiian girls in a dream foretells stirring adventures with persons of the opposite sex. 573

HUM. The sound of humming in a dream is a forerunner of disaster. If it seems to stop for no particular reason, the augury is one of shame. 802

HUMBUG. Showing up a humbug in a dream is a good sign. It foretells success in your work and the respect of your fellow workers. 127

HUMIDITY. Great embarrassment is foretold by a dream of suffering from the humidity. 531

HUMILITY. To display humility in a dream is a warning against being bigoted and arrogant when in the company of others. 577

HUMOR. (See Fun.) 575

HUNCHBACK. It is a sign that you will be financially fortunate if you dream of seeing a hunchback. 405

HUNGER. Better times are sure to come if you dream that you are hungry. To dream that you satisfy the hunger of another predicts that you will receive a legacy and be able to take a long vacation. 541

HUNTING. If you dream of hunting for something you have lost, you will be talked about scandalously by your enemies. To dream of hunting for game is a sign of impending physical danger. 724

HURDY-GURDY. The sound of a hurdy-gurdy heard in a dream portends a new opportunity to make good. If you dream of turning the handle of one, you will have interesting adventures with strange but likable people. 252

HURRICANE. (See Cyclone.) 961

HURRY. The cause for hurrying in a dream has a bearing on its significance. If it is selfish, it predicts worries, if it is to help others, the portent is auspicious. 727

HURT. To dream of being hurt is a warning against carelessness in crossing streets or roads. 750

HUSBAND. If a maiden dreams that she has a husband and yields to his embraces joyously, she will be married within a year. 440

HUSKING BEE. Love affairs will go well for those who dream of attending a husking bee. 886

HUSSY. To dream of a young woman who has the reputation of being a hussy is a sign that you are laying yourself open to criticism by your behavior. 610

HUSTLE. (See Hurry.) 533

HUT. (See Hovel.) 563

HYACINTH. Growing out of doors in a garden, hyacinths portend visitors whom you have not expected and who are not entirely welcome. In pots, hyacinths are a sign of improvement in finances. 042

HYDRANT. To dream of a hydrant that is flowing is a sign of good luck to those who are oppressed. Seeing one burst denotes a large fortune in the distant future. If you dream of a fireman attaching a hose to a hydrant, you are likely to have a disquieting experience. 967

HYDRO-AIRPLANE. Whether landing on or taking off from the water, a hydro-airplane in a dream foretells a successful outcome to a perplexing situation. 952

HYDROPHOBIA. Sad happenings are predicted by a dream of seeing a dog with hydrophobia. 287

HYENA. To be attacked by a hyena in a dream augurs ill unless you kill the animal or put it to flight. To see hyenas pacing back and forth in a cage is a sign that you will be afflicted with boils. 435

HYMN. To hear a hymn being sung in a dream portends new and constructive occupations in connection with your life in the community where you live. 670

HYPNOTISM. Being hypnotized in a dream and doing what someone wills you to do is a portent of having to account for something you would rather keep hidden. If you dream of hypnotizing someone else, you will have difficulty in meeting your debts. 710

HYPOCRITE. If in a dream you seem to discover that one of your friends is guilty of hypocrisy, you are warned against jumping too quickly at conclusions. If it is you who acts the part of a hypocrite, the augury is of illness. 942

HYSTERIA. Sorry consequences may be expected by the man who dreams of a woman having a fit of hysteria. He will suffer business losses and have family troubles. Mob hysteria in a dream forcasts national calamities. 418

ICE. This is a contrast dream in most of its phases. To sit on a cake of ice foretells comfort in daily living, while to slip on the ice is a sign that you will have a vacation in a warm climate. If you dream of ice skating, you will merit applause for some worthy action, but a dream of skating with a person of the opposite sex is a warning against unseemly behavior. To put ice into drinks foretells discomfort during warm weather. 427

ICE-CREAM. Eating ice-cream in a dream foretells a happy experience in which children will figure prominently. 487

ICICLE. A dripping icicle seen in a dream portends trouble unless you arrange to save a certain sum each week. To eat an icicle foretells sickness. 665

IDEA. Getting what appears to be a brilliant idea in a dream foretells great irritation of mind unless you can remember the idea when you awaken. Then it is excellent luck. 951

IDEAL. If a man dreams of a girl as his ideal, he is warned against making a fool of himself in the company of women. 280

IDIOT. Grave trouble is foretold by dreaming of trying to talk with an idiot. 431

IDLENESS. If you dream of doing nothing while others about you are busily working at their jobs, you will find that you will have to make explanations to your associates. 434

IDOL. To dream of seeing a person worshiping an idol is a sign that you are due for an increase in income. If in the dream you are the worshiper, you are likely to have differences with your employer. 290

IGNORANCE. If you are disgusted in a dream at a person's ignorance of any well known fact, you are in danger of being exposed for doing something that you would prefer to keep hidden. If your own ignorance is shown up, you will have a rise in salary. 142

ILLEGIBILITY. Trying to decipher illegible handwriting in a dream is a sign of having to prove your identity in a court of law. 910

ILLNESS. Arguments with those you love are predicted by any dream of being ill; if it is others who are ill, the augury is of distress through worry. 563

ILLITERACY. To meet in your dream a grown person who is unable to read or write is a sign that you will take on added responsibilities in connection with your job. 204

ILLUMINATION. Any brilliant illumination in a dream—by whatever means—presages the solution of a perplexing problem. 374

ILLUSION. If in a dream you are aware that what you are seeing is an illusion, you will be able to discover secrets of considerable value. 020

ILLUSTRATION. To be interested in an illustration for a story in a dream is a sign that your love will be requited. 622

IMAGE. (See Idol, Picture, Statue.) 825

IMAGINATION. In a dream if you come in contact with a display of imagination, such as that of a writer, poet, artist or inventor, the portent is likely to be of an inspiration that will make money for you. 564

IMBECILE. (See Idiot.) 658

IMITATION. A dream of finding out that something you treasure is only an imitation of what you thought it was prophesies being disillusioned by someone in whom you believed. 524

IMMODESTY. A dream by men of women being immodest in behavior, speech or dress is a portent of making errors that will cause shame and heartaches. 424

IMMORALITY. A warning is contained in a dream of immorality to be on guard against judging others until you are sure that your own conduct is above reproach. 651

IMMORTALITY. Dreaming of immortality, either of the body or soul, is a portent that you will have to put additional energy into the work you are doing. 380

IMP. (See Devil.) 535

IMPACT. (See Crash.) 845

IMPATIENCE. A dream in which you show impatience with someone who is doing his or her apparent best foretells a grievous condition within your immediate circle of friends. 900

IMPERFECTION. (See Flaw.) 618

IMPERSONATION. For whatever purpose the impersonation is made—disguise, masquerade, or theatrical performance—if you dream of impersonating another, you will have to make excuses for being remiss in your duty. If you dream of being fooled by an impersonation, you are likely to make new friends unexpectedly. 703

IMPLEMENT. (See Tool). 373

IMPOSTOR. To dream of being swindled by an impostor is a portent of hard times in your business. 405

IMPRISONMENT. (See Prison.) 976

IMPUDENCE. If you have a dream in which you are impudent to someone who normally would have a much higher business or social rank, or whose authority is undeniable, you will find yourself in line for advancement in business. 438

IMPURITY. Discovering impurities in food, drink, or anywhere else where they are a menace is a sign of happiness in love affairs and married life. 988

INAUGURATION. It is a lucky portent to dream that you are present at the inauguration of the president of a republic. 809

INCANTATION. Humorous experiences may be expected if you dream of hearing a person uttering incantations at a weird ceremony. 135

INCENSE. You may be certain of pleasing adventures with persons of the opposite sex if you dream of burning incense or seeing it burned. To smell the odor in a dream foretells travel. 198

INCEST. A dream of incest is a warning against lowering the standards of your life for any reason whatever. 348

INCISION. To dream of showing another person where the incision was made for an appendicities operation is a sign that you will show increasing efficiency in your job. If you dream that you are a surgeon and make an incision in a patient, you are likely to have trouble with the authorities. 242

INCOHERENCE. If you dream of hearing a person talk without being able to understand what he is driving at, you will be in danger of having to explain something that will embarrass you. 549

INCOME. To dream of an increase in your income is a sign that you will have additional worries. If the dream is of a smaller income than that to which you have been accustomed, you are likely to have a rise in salary. 824

INCOMPATIBILITY. For a married person to dream of incompatibility with his or her mate is a warning against loss of temper that may lead to serious consequences. 784

INCUBATOR. Baby incubators seen in a dream are portents of better health for you and your family. Chicken incubators are an omen of being able to meet your obligations. 604

INCUBUS. For a woman to dream of an incubus is an augury of discontent and foreboding. 089

INDELIBLE INK. Marking clothes with indelible ink in a dream is a sign of a new accumulation of money, but if you dream of trying to erase indelible ink, you will have trouble with your landlord. 735

INDEMNITY. There will be little peace during the following month for the person who dreams of levying an indemnity on another. 523

INDEPENDENCE. To feel or show your independence in a dream is a warning against being too sure of yourself in the next business deal on which you are working. 538

INDEX. To search for an item in the index of a book is a sign that a man will have a better understanding of women and vice-versa. If you dream of indexing a book, you will advance to a higher and more lucrative position. 626

INDIAN. Either North or South American Indians seen or met within a dream are a good sign if they are friendly, but if they appear to be hostile, the dream is a warning against placing too great trust in your business associates. 098

INDIFFERENCE. If you dream that someone you love is indifferent to you, it is a sign that you should exert yourself to make yourself more agreeable to others. If you dream of showing indifference to others, you will find yourself in want. 001

INDIGESTION. A dream of indigestion is usually the effect of either over-eating or over-drinking, so it seldom has any meaning other than that you should be more discreet. 636

INDIGO. Dreaming of this shade of blue is a presage of a cruise in southern waters. 368

INDUSTRY. A dream in which you are conscious of the industry of others foretells new responsibilities both in your business and your home. If you dream of being industrious, you may look forward to a period of rest and relaxation. 870

INFANT. (See Baby.) 056

INFANTRY. On the march, infantry in a dream foretells adventure and, for the unmarried, love affairs that are short-lived. 019

INFECTION. It is a warning against taking chances if you dream of having even a small wound infected. 662

INFERIORITY COMPLEX. Friends will stand by you if you dream of strutting by reason of an inferiority complex. 428

INFERNO. (See Hell.) 984

INFIDELITY. A man or woman who dreams of being unfaithful to his or her mate is warned to be extremely careful in their dealings with the opposite sex. 083

INFIRMARY. If you dream of going to an infirmary to be treated for some sickness or disability, the chances are that one of your friends will do something nice for you. 543

INFIRMITY. If in a dream you notice and comment on someone else's infirmity, you will have to explain a misdeed to someone outside of your family. 211

INFLUENCE. To dream that a person of either sex has an influence over your actions portends that mischief makers will plot against you. 971

INFLUENZA. To dream of being ill with influenza is a forerunner of a vacation during which you will have an opportunity to travel. 328

INFORMALITY. This dream depends for its import on whether there is occasion for formality or not. If one dreams of being informal at a very impressive occasion, the augury is of disgrace through unworthy actions. If, however, a great dignitary meets you with informal charm, the augury is of advancement in social life. 986

INHERITANCE. Receiving an inheritance in a dream usually foretells receiving one in real life. 981

INITIATION. Being roughly handled by your fellows in an initiation ceremony is a forerunner of sound friendship and good times. 191

INJURY. No dream of receiving a physical injury has a good portent, but if the injury is to your reputation, it is a sign that you will be well thought of. 887

INK. Spilling ink in a dream is nothing to cry about, but to write with ink is a warning to go slowly in giving confidences even to your best friends. 163

INKSTAND. Filling an inkstand in a dream means that soon you will pack your luggage and leave home for an extended trip to distant points. 095

INN. (See Hotel.) 455

INNOCENCE. A dream of taking advantage of another's innocence is an augury of defeat in all your undertakings. 714

INOCULATION. You may rest easy regarding your most insistent creditors if you dream of being inoculated against any disease. 061

INQUEST. To be present in a dream at an inquest over a dead body foretells that very soon you will have to assume a new responsibility. 270

INQUIRY. If in a dream an inquiry is made that you are unable to answer, the portent is of sorrow through someone's leaving you. If you are able to answer the inquiry, you will receive an important letter. 129

INQUISITION. You will be subjected to the closest supervision of your employer if you dream of having to submit to an inquisition. It is a warning against loafing on the job. 655

INSANITY. A dream of an insane person forecasts an uncomfortable session with hostile relatives. If you dream that you are insane, the omen is of good news. 943

INSCRIPTION. Reading the inscription on a gravestone or monument is a sign that you will be promoted to a higher and more difficult position. 265

INSECT. Indoors, insects portend annoyances through minor afflictions and skin irritations. 867

INSOLENCE. If you dream of being insolent to an inferior, you will have to answer for a misdeed to a superior. If a young person is insolent to you, it is a warning not to lose your temper. 729

INSOLVENCY. If you dream that you are insolvent, either personally or in business, you will be much better satisfied with the job you now hold. 219

INSURANCE. A dream of taking out life or accident insurance portends a difficult time with your financial affairs. If an insurance salesman approaches you in a dream, you are likely to be offered a new job. 334

INTEMPERANCE. Dreaming of being intemperate in the use of liquor, in eating, or in other ways augurs that you are likely to lose one or more staunch friends. 291

INTERPRETER. If in a dream you have to speak with a foreigner through an interpreter, you are likely to have difficulties with your investments. 133

INTERRUPTION. To dream of being interrupted either in your work or while speaking, is an augury of discontent in your marital relations or the upsetting of a love affair. 548

INTESTINES. A definite warning against overexertion is contained in a dream of your own intestines. If there is excruciating pain, it is a sign that you will be ill unless you are checked by your physician. 921

INTOLERENCE. If you dream of being intolerant of anyone else's views on religion, politics or other controversial subject, you will be disappointed in the attitude adopted by your warmest friends. If others are intolerant of your viewpoint, you will have a small legacy. 020

INTRIGUE. To dream of being a party to a love intrigue means that people will discuss your personal affairs to your detriment. 183

INUNDATION. (See Floods.) 795

INVALID. If you dream of taking care of an invalid, you are certain to receive good news through the mail. 873

INVENTION. Good news is in store for you if you dream of working on an invention. It portends that you are likely to receive the thing for which you have hoped the most. 592

INVENTOR. To dream of being an inventor foretells good fortune. If in the dream you invent something that seems to be successful, it is a protent of success in whatever business you are engaged in. 178

INVITATION. A dream of receiving an invitation of any description forecasts additional expense that you probably do not wish to incur. 274

IODINE. Swallowing iodine in a dream is a warning to snap out of your depression and a forerunner of better times. 857

IPECAC. If you dream of taking ipecac as an emetic, you will receive news that will at first disgust you and then amuse you. 443

IRIS. This beautiful purple or yellow flower is a harbinger of peace and plenty when seen in a dream. If it is bordering a pool, you will realize your fondest wish for a faithful mate. 767

IRON. From a dream of iron in any form one may expect a slow but steady progress to prosperity. 475

IRONING. For a woman to dream of ironing clothes is an omen that she will be relieved of burdens she has borne for a long time. If a man has this dream, it portends an increase in salary. 153

ISLAND. If you dream of living on an island, you are liable to find that for a time things will not go well with you but if you keep your chin up, you will win through. For a man to dream of being alone with a girl on an island is an omen of exciting and dangerous adventures. 901

ITCH. Unimportant but irritating troubles are predicted by a dream in which any part of the body itches. 997

IVORY. To dream of hunting ivory in African jungles foretells that a wealthy relative will make you an offer which you should accept. If you dream of carving ornaments and objects of art out of ivory, you will make a reputation for your honesty and ability. 974

IVY. The constancy of those you love is insured by a dream of a fine, healthy growth of ivy on a wall or building. Tearing it off in a dream portends woe and disappointment. Planting it is a presage of good times to come. 730

J

JAB. If you dream of being given a jab, you will soon suffer an imagined wrong due to your super-sensitiveness. It will make you and others miserable unless you can rise above it. 349

JACKASS. A jackass in a dream portends that you will be made a fool of in the company of someone whose esteem you crave. 586

JACKET. Wearing a fine jacket in a dream foretells that you will be invited to a select dancing party where attractive favors will be handed to the guests. A worn jacket is a sign that you will not have a good time at the next party you attend. 755

JACK-KNIFE. To dream of a jack-knife is a sign that you will be accused of being two-faced. 773

JACK-POT. Winning the jack-pot in a poker game is a portent of going to the races and placing a bet on a dark horse. If you lose the jack-pot and see another take it, you will not get married this year. 200

JADE. Dreaming of beautiful jade set in gold foretells that you will be asked to contribute to some relief fund. Buying a rare piece of jade in a dream means that you will have visitors from another city. 213

JAG. If you dream of going on a jag, you will have to answer to your employer's criticism that you are paying too much attention to the opposite sex. 937

JAGUAR. To dream of one of these tiger-like South American animals is a warning to beware of some catty woman's slanderous tongue. 960

JAIL. To go to jail in a dream is a sign that you will be caught in a white lie to your great embarrassment. To see prisoners being committed to jail foretells that you are in danger of infection by a contagious disease. 562

JAILER. If you are a jailer in a dream, you will be called to account for some infraction of the motor laws. For a woman to dream that she marries a jailer is a sign that she is in danger from an unknown source. 483

JAM. To get in a jam—traffic or personal—in a dream where there seems to be no possible way out augurs a quarrel with someone whose friendship you should cultivate. To put up jam and put it in jars signifies that you will be invited to a neighborhood party. 521

JANITOR. A disagreeable task is sure to be assigned to you if you dream of being the janitor of an apartment house or public building. 138

JAPAN. If you dream of being in Japan and seeing the Japanese people, you will have an unusual experience, doing something quite apart from your everyday pattern of living. 820

JAR. A row of jars on a shelf, seen in a dream, means that you will find pleasure in social activities. A family "jar" or quarrel is a sign of illness. 146

JARDINIERE. To dream of a colorful jardiniere with a plant in it signifies a new romance to those who are unmarried, but it is a warning to others to watch their step. An empty jardiniere is an indication of adventure. 728

JASMINE. Maidens and youths who dream of jasmine will win their hearts' desire. 269

JAUNDICE. Your efforts at making money will come to naught if you have a dream that you are afflicted with jaundice. 669

JAUNT. A dream of taking a jaunt or short trip is a favorable sign for those who are in love. 163

JAVELIN. Broken friendships are foretold by a dream of throwing a javelin at a human being, but if it is thrown as a pastime in athletics, the augury is favorable to business men. 087

JAW. Dreaming of one's own jaw portends a humiliating experience, but another's jaw is a sign of a rise in salary. 992

JAYWALKER. Seeing a jaywalker in a dream means that you will be called to account for a slight infraction of the law. If you are the jaywalker, you will have a serious altercation with an officer. 680

JAZZ. A dream of hearing jazz music is a forerunner of gayety that will cost you more money than you can afford. Dancing to jazz music with a good-looking partner foretells that you will have to borrow carfare shortly. 689

JEALOUSY. To dream of being jealous of a person of the opposite sex means that you will have a burst of despondency or at least a fit of the blues. If you can snap out of it, it will be much better for your future. 682

JEER. Being jeered at in a dream portends that someone will cancel an engagement with you. If you jeer at another, your sweetheart will quarrel with you. 438

JELLY. (See Jam.) 773

JERUSALEM. If you dream of the city of Jerusalem, you will suffer an injustice and know the misery of loneliness. Visiting Jerusalem in a dream means that a relative will come to stay with you. 531

JESSAMINE. Happy will be the person who dreams of this fragrant flower. It portends health, wealth, and peace of mind. 509

JEST. (See Joke.) 855

JESTER. To dream of a jester at the court of an ancient king portends adventures among strange and amusing people. 662

JESUS. To dream of Jesus augurs peace of mind and contentment. 645

JET. (See also Fountain.) Pieces of polished black jet on a woman's dress portend the enjoyment of a luxury that will not be good for you. A burning gas jet, seen in a dream, signifies a love affair with a person of wealth. 124

JEW. The presence of Jewish people in dreams presages a career that will be varied both in occupation and place of abode. 075

JEWELRY. A display of jewelry seen in a dream signifies social activity among community-minded persons. To dream of buying jewelry is a sign that you will have to answer for peccadillos that you believed you could keep hidden. 634

JEW'S-HARP. If you play a jew's-harp in a dream, you are likely to visit some eastern country within a year. Hearing a jew's harp played is an augury of having to choose between two loves. 375

JIG. To dance a jig in your dream is a good sign. You will win the favor of an elderly person who will leave you his money. 466

JIGSAW. Dreaming of using a jigsaw portends a broken engagement. 588

JILT. If you jilt your sweetheart in a dream, you are in danger from failing to keep an important appointment. If you are the jilted one, your investments will yield a larger return. 229

JINGLE. To dream of hearing someone repeat a silly jingle is a sign that you will receive a wedding announcement from a long forgotten acquaintance. The jingling of bells heard in a dream foretells a pleasant outing with a person of the opposite sex. If you hear money jingle, you will lose an opportunity of a semi-business nature. 380

JINRICKISHA. Riding in a jinrickisha is a portent of travel to a country you have never visited. If you dream of pulling a jinrickisha, you will have to meet an emergency that no one could have predicted. 843

JITNEY. If you dream of riding in a jitney bus; you will be likely to have a visitor whom you will have to take on a sightseeing trip. 865

JITTERS. Having the jitters in a dream signifies that you will have an important part in amateur theatricals. 931

JIU-JITSU. Your carefully conceived plans for the future are in danger of collapsing if you see someone in a dream practicing jiu-jitsu. To take an active part in this form of self-defense foretells a successful business trip. 812

JOB. To dream of finally getting a job after many discouragements is a sign that you will find a purse with a large sum of money in it, personal belongings, and the name and address of the owner. If you dream of losing a job, you must be on your guard against losing your temper with those to whom you are responsible. 167

JOCKEY. Young people who dream of seeing a jockey ride a horse in a race will shortly take a civil service examination in which they will make a satisfactory showing. 648

JOHN BULL. If you dream of this symbol of England, it denotes that you will have a better than ordinary chance of success if you decide to try for the consular service. 323

JOHN DOE. If you dream of hearing a person describe himself as John Doe when booked in a police court, it is a warning against participation in a questionable racket. 002

JOHNNY CAKE. If you eat Johnny Cake in your dream, you will meet a charming Southerner. 530

JOKE. Hearing a joke in your dream and laughing heartily at it means that you will have an unwelcome visitor, perhaps your mother-in-law. If you dream of telling a joke that makes a hit with your audience, the omen is of successful business; if no one laughs, you will be disappointed in someone you have trusted. 268

JOKER. To dream of holding the joker in a card game presages loss of business due to the efforts of a competitor who is more energetic than you. 111

JONAH. If Jonah and the whale get all mixed up in your dream, it means that you will have a family dispute over money matters. If you dream of being a "Jonah", you will be made to apologize for a remark you have made about a friend's wife. 286

JONQUIL. Yellow jonquils in a dream foretell the receipt of a passionate love letter. 009

JOSS HOUSE. To dream of a joss house filled with idols and smelling of incense is a sign that you will fall in love with someone from another country whose religious beliefs are different from yours. 663

JOSS STICKS. Burning joss sticks in a dream denote the desire for higher learning. You will attend a night school or take some course in some professional branch. 139

JOURNAL. If you dream of reading a journal, you will receive a telegram. If you buy a journal, you will receive word that a dividend has been declared on a stock you believed worthless. 937

JOURNEY. To dream of going on a journey foretells a nervous affliction that will require medical attention. 416

JOWLS. If you dream of a person whose cheeks, or jowls, are heavy and pendulous and thickly bearded, you will meet with a narrow escape on the road. 024

JOY. A dream of joy, whether yours or another's, is a prophecy of happiness in the home circle. When it is the joy of children, the prophecy is much better. To dream of being joyous on an occasion that is not creditable is a sign that you will have to answer for something that you would prefer to forget. 714

JOY RIDE. Going on a joy ride in a dream presages that you will abandon yourself to circumstances. You may, however, turn defeat into an amazing success if you give your problems proper attention. 719

JUBILEE. To celebrate with a jubilee portends recognition of long and faithful service. You will receive either a sum of money or a vacation with all expenses paid. 408

JUDAS. If you dream of a false friend (a Judas), you will turn your hand to a new trade. Go slowly. 811

JUDGE. To dream of appearing before a judge in a courtroom is unlucky for married men. It forecasts having to explain satisfactorily an absence from home. If you dream of passing judgment upon another, you will be assigned a thankless task that entails much work. 563

JUDGMENT DAY. Dreaming about appearing on Judgment Day foretells a robbery. 135

JUG. Days in the country are predicted by a dream of drinking out of a jug. 702

JUGGLER. To dream of a juggler practicing his art is a sign that you will compete in some popular contest where the prize is of considerable value. 200

JUGULAR VEIN. You will have an illness and require a change of climate if you dream of having your jugular vein cut. 912

JUICE. Financial help will be forthcoming if you dream of drinking vegetable or fruit juices. To serve these to your guests is a sign that you will come to the aid of another. 883

JULEP. To dream of drinking a mint julep is a portent that you will be host to a group of old friends. 264

JULY. It is a sign that you will meet your fate at a post-office if you dream of going on a vacation in July. 878

JUMPER. If you dream of a horse in the jumping class going over high hurdles, you are likely to find leisure to go on a hunting trip. 416

JUMPING. If you dream of jumping over obstacles, you will be able to meet your difficulties with assurance and overcome them. 566

JUMPING-JACK. A dream of a jumping-jack being played with by either a child or a grown-up person augurs new agreeable companions. 091

JUNE. A thrilling success will be yours if you dream of being married in June. If you dream of a girl with this lovely name, you will be married within a year. To dream of attending a June wedding is an augury of advancement in your job. 237

JUNIOR. Naming a child Junior in a dream is an omen that you will forget to mail an important letter and thereby bring trouble upon yourself. 816

JUNIPER. To cut down a juniper tree in a dream is a portent of good luck. To pick the berries warns against associating with loose characters. 264

JUNK. A pile of junk in a dream predicts that you will be confused regarding a decision you will have to make shortly. 931

JURY. To dream of sitting on a jury foretells a serious difference of opinion with your sweetheart. It is possible to arbitrate the matter, but unless you use considerable tact and discretion, you will be unhappy, 473

JUSTICE. In a dream if you are of the opinion that justice is being done, the augury is of a successful future. If you are the person who metes out the justice, you will be subject to criticism by your neighbors. 396

JUVENILE COURT. Being present in a dream at a session of a juvenile court means that you will fail to keep a promise and thereby be in danger of losing a good friend. 119

K

KALEIDOSCOPE. To dream of looking into a kaleidoscope and watch with interest the ever-varying pattern before you signifies that you will take a new interest in your dress and in the creation or designing of new costumes. 335

KEG. To see a new keg in your dream means that you will attend a masquerade party where there will be much hilarity and a great deal too much to drink. 624

KELP. Gathering kelp on the seashore in a dream is a sign that you will visit a naval academy and see the cadets on parade. 436

KENO. To be in on a game of keno in your dream is an excellent portent. You will meet Lady Luck in the person of a blue-eyed blond and embrace her heartily. 632

KANGAROO. Dreaming of a kangaroo jumping nimbly about foretells a journey by airplane. If the kangaroo is a female and has one of its young in her pouch, the journey will be full of adventure. 262

KATYDID. To hear the summer song of a katydid denotes a visit to a Spanish or Mexican night club where you will dance to music punctuated by castanets. 814

KEEPSAKE. If you are given a keepsake in your dream by one of the opposite sex, it augurs a serious illness in your immediate family. 146

KERNEL. To dream of feeding kernels of corn to a flock of birds is a sign that you will be ecstatically thanked. 315

KEROSENE. To fill lamps or stoves with kerosene in your dream portends a walking tour through a country with an understanding companion. 424

KETCHUP. To season your food with tomato ketchup is a sign that you will be kept guessing by a handsome and intriguing person of the opposite sex. 001

KETTLE. Dreaming of a kettle boiling on the stove points toward a pleasant and enjoyable family life. A kettle that boils dry is a sign of woe. 790

KETTLEDRUM. If you play the kettledrum in an orchestra, you are in danger of overindulgence in both food and drink. 024

KEY. Dreaming of having a key in your hand foretells a mild flirtation. If you dream of putting a key in a lock, you are very likely to be rebuked by someone you like very much. 206

KEYHOLE. Peeping through a keyhole in a dream is a prophecy of shame. To put a key in a keyhole predicts an amorous adventure. 758

KHAKI. Domestic troubles are foretold by a dream of seeing anyone wearing clothes made of khaki. 524

KICK. You will be reprimanded by a superior if you dream of being kicked either by man or beast. This is a warning against loafing on the job, for you are in danger of having your salary docked on account of infractions of office discipline. 697

KID. To see a young goat or kid in your dream presages the meeting of a bearded man of great learning and influence. 364

KIDNAPING. If you are kidnapped in your dream, you should watch your step. You are likely to marry great wealth, but it will bring you no happiness and much shame. To dream of kidnaping someone means that thieves will steal your most treasured possession. 574

KIDNEY. To dream of your own kidneys indicates that you are in danger of investing in worthless stock. It is a sign of physical deterioration if you dream of eating kidney stew. 537

KILLING. If someone is killed in your dream and you are a terrified witness to the crime, you will change your place of abode and be sorry for it. To dream of killing a person, whether purposely or by accident, is an omen that you will be criticized for bad manners. 409

KILT. To see a Scotchman wearing kilts in a dream is an indication that you will have to buy new luggage in preparation for a long trip. 967

KIMONO. Pretty Japanese girls wearing kimonos in your dream are a sign of attending a festival at which you will meet your fate. To dream of a woman wearing a faded and soiled kimono is a portent of a love affair that you will some day wish to forget. 806

KINDERGARTEN. To dream of seeing little children in a kindergarten is a sign that maidens and youths will marry early and have healthy progeny. 350

KING. (See also Queen.) If a man dreams that he is a king, the interpretation is similar to that for a woman who dreams of being a queen. 280

KISS. The portent of a kiss in a dream depends on the circumstances surrounding it. Kisses between married people are an omen of content; between unmarried people they predict happiness. A maiden who dreams of kissing an old man will suffer disappointment. To dream of kissing a baby indicates success in a difficult undertaking. Kisses given in hypocrisy or contrary to the moral code are a sign of illness or disgrace. 077

KITCHEN. If one dreams of being the happy possessor of an attractive modern kitchen, it is an omen of being the host or hostess to a group of congenial dinner guests. A dream of a dirty, cluttered-up kitchen is a portent of having to make a visit to the doctor. 970

KITE. To fly a kite in your dream is an augury of trying a job that will be too much for your capabilities. If the kite-string breaks, the omen is of bad luck in business. 064

KITTEN. For a maiden, playful kittens in a dream portend a suitor who will be more interested in dalliance than in the serious side of love-making. A man who dreams of kittens is in danger of being played with by the object of his affections. 786

KLEPTOMANIAC. If in a dream you have the urge to steal things that you do not need, it is a sign that there are people who seek to work your undoing. It is a warning against the appearance of evil. 972

KNAPSACK. A full knapsack denotes a pleasant journey. An empty knapsack denotes hard going financially. 782

KNAVE. To dream of holding the knave of any one of the four suits indicates that you will be tricked into doing something against your better judgment. 948

KNEADING. Kneading dough for bread is a sign that you will be visited by your female relatives. 923

KNEE. If you dream that your knees are quaking, it is a sign that you should kneel on them for the sins that you have committed. For a man to dream of dimpled knees is a portent of a liaison with a foreigner. 956

KNEELING. To see a person kneeling in prayer in an incongruous setting, such as a streetcar or in a cafe, is a sign that you are in danger of breaking at least two of the ten commandments. 995

KNELL. To hear a funeral knell in a dream is an ill omen. You will miss an opportunity to better yourself. 976

KNIFE. An open knife in a dream is a sign of strife to come. A closed knife indicates that someone is trying to swindle you. A very dull knife portends difficult times in making a living. 237

KNIGHT. Knights of old dressed in full armor presage the discovery of valuable family papers that will be turned to advantage. 230

KNITTING. Plying the knitting needles in a dream is a good sign. You will be blessed with children and grandchildren who will love you. 472

KNOB. To dream of a door-knob indicates that you are likely to enter a new business. The augury is of success if you go slowly. 424

KNOCK. If you hear a knock in your dream and then hear it repeated several times, it denotes that you will come in contact with a mysterious stranger whom you will never get to know. 437

KNOT. Dreaming of tying knots in a string or rope without any particular purpose is a warning against riding horseback, for you are likely to fall. To knot a necktie in a dream forecasts a meeting with a charming person of the opposite sex. 259

KODAK. Taking pictures with a Kodak in a dream is a portent of hard work with little or no remuneration. 271

KOHINOOR. To dream of seeing the famous Kohinoor diamond is a sign of an approaching engagement. If you dream of handling it and wearing it, you will have a lucky turn through speculation. 255

KOSHER. Kosher foods, eaten and relished in your dream, portends good business and good health. 913

KOWTOWING. To see a Chinaman kowtowing in your dream foretells that you will agree to some plan of which you heartily disapprove. 124

KU KLUX KLAN. Dreaming of hooded figures in white gathered about a fire at night is a warning against sacrificing the good name of a friend for the purpose of furthering your own interests. 909

KUMMEL. To drink this liqueur flavored with caraway seed is a sign that you will be elected to membership in a select club or society to which you had despaired of ever becoming elected. 771

LABEL. To dream of paying special attention to the label on a bottle, can, jar or garment is a forerunner of success in a business enterprise. 708

LABOR. Solid achievement is predicted by a dream of laboring on construction work. To dream of being affiliated with a labor party is an omen of better living and working conditions. To be ashamed of honest and productive labor is a sign of the deterioration of the mental faculties. If a maiden dreams of having labor pains, she may expect an early marriage and a large family. If a married woman dreams of having labor pains, she may expect to become pregnant in the near future. 869

LABORATORY. You will unravel a mystery of long standing if you dream of working in any kind of a laboratory. 165

LABYRINTH. To lose your way in the tangled paths of a labyrinth is a portent of having to untangle a problem of your own making. If there appear to be wild beasts in the labyrinth, you will be beset by difficulties purposely thrown in your way by enemies. 697

LACE. Women who dream of lace will be loved for their feminine traits. Lace on women's undergarments dreamed of by a man foretells an episode that has possibilities for either good or ill. It warns against using bad judgment in casual social relations with women. A dream of lace on a man's underwear is a sign that you will make money in a questionable manner. Lace curtains in a dream are a portent of easy living. Lace made of paper portends accidents. 838

LACERATION. Painful lacerations of your flesh suffered in a dream portend a combination of circumstances that will cause you both discomfort and embarrassment. 475

LACKEY. (See Flunkey.) 739

LACQUER. Using lacquer in a dream to cover furniture or a floor predicts a whirlwind love affair with a foreigner. 009

LACROSSE. To dream of seeing a game of lacrosse played is a warning against giving credence to superstition. If you play the game yourself, you should guard against accidents. 465

LADDER. If in a dream you are climbing a ladder and a rung breaks, you will not need to worry about your financial future. If a ladder falls on you, the augury is of malicious gossip about you. To dream of entering a house by way of a ladder predicts a message that will cause you some concern. 147

LADLE. Using a ladle in a dream—serving soup or other food—portends visitors who will impose on your hospitality. 259

LADY. If you dream of meeting a woman with the title of Lady—Lady Vere de Vere, Lady Montmorency, Lady Chichester or the like—the augury is good or bad according to whether or not she acts like a lady. 372

LADY-KILLER. The dream spectacle of a man who behaves as if he thought all women were crazy about him portends an experience that will be as profitable as it is amusing. 094

LAGER BEER. (See Beer.) 669

LAGOON. Boating alone on a quiet lagoon in your dream predicts danger from traffic accidents. If you are accompanied in the boat by one or more people, you will meet an old friend under surprising circumstances. 816

LAIR. Discovering the lair of a wild animal in a dream portends a struggle. If the animal is present, you will overcome the difficulty; if not, you will not be successful. 541

LAKE. Dreaming of a stormy lake predicts a disaster that, if you do not let it overwhelm you, will lead to eventual triumph. If you are sailing on it and are overturned, you will have family troubles as well. To sail on the calm waters of a lake in fine weather is an augury of peace and interest in life. Sailing on a lake by moonlight portends happy love affairs. 548

LAMB. (See also Sheep.) New lambs in a dream predict an experience that will soften you and make you a better man or woman. To dream of lambs playing together is an omen of happy family affairs. If you dream of eating lamb chops or roast spring lamb, you will be able to turn a fortunate business deal. 278

LAMENESS. If in a dream you feel sympathy for a lame person, or if you give assistance to a lame person, the prediction is one of good health. If you dream of being lame yourself, you will have to go slow in any enterprise that you are considering. Bad times are ahead for one who dreams of pushing or crowding a lame person. 892

LAMENTATION. Hearing the lamentations of one or more persons in a dream foretells a season of unhappiness. 080

LAMP. The interpretations of these dreams relate to oil, gas or electric lamps, but not to neon signs. To light a lamp signifies that someone to whom you have done a kindness will reciprocate. To put out a lamp is a sign that you will be able to take a long needed vacation. To hang a lamp so that it will guide people predicts that you will have a piece of good luck. To break a lamp is an omen that someone will distrust you. 682

LAMPBLACK. A dream of getting smudged with lampblack is a forerunner of disgrace. 501

LAMP-POST. To dream of leaning against a lamp-post in a state of inebriation is an omen of trouble in the family circle. If you dream of a lamp-post that has been broken, you are likely to have a serious quarrel with a neighbor. 395

LANCE. If you dream of being a doctor and using a lance on a patient, you will find that friends will avoid you for some unexplainable reason. To dream of having a boil lanced is a sign that you will have trouble with your in-laws. 925

LANDING. A landing of any kind in a dream, whether in connection with an airplane or a boat, denotes the successful completion of a hard job. 491

LANDLADY or **LANDLORD.** To dream of being asked for the rent by your landlady or landlord is a sign that you will have a lucky strike in business and buy your own home. 951

LANE. Young men and maidens who dream of meeting each other in a shady lane will be fortunate in love if they are discreet in their actions. 894

LANGUOR. Active participation in games is predicted by a dream of relaxation and languor. 876

LANTERN. (See also Lamp.) A dream of trying to signal a railroad train by swinging a lantern is a presage of grave danger through designing women. If your lantern is blown out by the wind, you are likely to have trouble with a law officer. 832

LAP. Sitting on the lap of a person of the opposite sex predicts love affairs of a passionate nature. To dream of falling off a person's lap signifies the loss of a good position. 161

LAPDOG. If you dream of being bitten by a lapdog, you are likely to have difficulties with jealous women. A dream of a dead lapdog foretells prosperity within a short time. 152

LAPIS LAZULI. This beautiful blue gem is an augury of blessed content when seen in a dream. If you receive it as a gift, you will be able to take a long and enjoyable trip to the Orient. 038

LAP-ROBE. You will get into difficulties with a person of the opposite sex if you dream of holding hands under a lap-robe. 637

LARCENY. (See Stealing.) 097

LARD. Dealings with people of doubtful morals are predicted if you dream of using lard in your cooking. 274

LARDER. (See Pantry.) 639

LARIAT. (See Lasso.) 907

LARK. The song of a lark heard in a dream presages joyous experiences of an innocent nature. If you kill a lark in a dream, it is a forerunner of an agonizing experience. 422

LARYNGITIS. A dream of having laryngitis is a sign of having to endorse a note for a friend. If it results in making you lose your voice, you will be unlucky in gambling. 541

LASHING. (See Flogging.) 836

LASSO. To throw a lasso in a dream is a good augury for married people if it is a successful throw. To have the rope looped about you presages embarrassment among your friends. 783

LATIN. To dream of anyone speaking in the Latin tongue augurs a long period during which you will be forced to give way to others. 656

LAST SUPPER. To dream of being a witness to the Last Supper portends the making of a new friend who will prove to be invaluable. 046

LATCH. If in a dream you leave the latch off, you will have delightful experiences in the company of the opposite sex. 961

LATHE. Working at a lathe in a dream portends working out an idea that will be of immense value to you. 972

LATHER. If you dream of lathering your face or underarms for shaving, you are likely to solve a pressing problem. Lathering the body in the bath forecasts getting good news by mail. 360

LATRINE. Business affairs will come to a satisfactory conclusion if you dream of visiting a latrine. 217

LATTICE. Opening a lattice window onto a summer garden is a portent of ease and contentment. 839

LAUDANUM. (See Opium.) 031

LAUGHTER. (See also Comedy, Fun.) If you dream of laughing, the augury can be nothing but good. To hear a good joke that provokes your laughter means that you will have good luck over a long period. To make another person laugh indicates profitable investments. 384

LAUNCH. To see a boat launched in a dream foretells exciting and profitable adventures. If you dream of sailing in smooth waters in a launch, you will have a satisfactory love affair. 289

LAUNDRY. To dream of being in a laundry is a sign of meeting a person on a train, bus or airplane and finding that you have friends in common. To dream of sending soiled linen to a laundry sounds a sharp warning against gossiping. 840

LAUREL. This lovely flower seen on bushes in a dream portends success in an important enterprise. 604

LAVA. Issuing from a volcano in eruption, lava seen in a dream warns you that unless you pay stricter attention to your work, you will be discharged. If it is sweeping over the countryside, destroying houses and trees, it is a sign of illness. 987

LAVATORY. Visiting a lavatory or washroom in a dream foretells a sharp altercation with a tradesman. To slip on the floor of a lavatory is a sign that you are in danger of forgetting to execute an important commission. 206

LAVENDER. The scent of lavender in a dream foretells pleasant companions in whose company you will improve your mental status. Lavender-colored dresses portend exciting adventures with members of the opposite sex. 773

LAW. To dream of being in the toils of the law presages many harassing experiences in your business. If you retain a lawyer to bring suit against a person or a company, you are warned against carelessness. To dream of winning a lawsuit foretells that you will lose money. To dream of laying down the law to another person is a portent of success in business. 781

LAWN. A fine green lawn seen in a dream foretells contentment in your home life. If you dream of mowing a lawn, you will be invited out by one of your neighbors. A lawn that is brown and gone to seed portends illness. 946

LAWN TENNIS. (See Tennis.) 705

LAWYER. A maiden who dreams of marrying a lawyer is likely to be caught in an embarrassing predicament. Here is a warning against loose morals. 790

LAXATIVE. Taking a laxative in a dream is an omen that someone whom you believed to be stingy will treat you with great generosity. 400

LAZINESS. (See also Leisure.) Being lazy in a dream is a good augury, but if someone takes you to task for it, you will have family difficulties. 743

LEAD. Grievous troubles will beset your path if you dream of carrying a load of lead. To dream of moulding bullets out of lead, you will have a serious accident. To hit a person with a length of lead pipe portends business upsets. 046

LEAF. (See also Foliage.) One leaf remaining on a tree is a sign of pleasure in the company of people older than yourself. To press a leaf between the pages of a book foretells having to answer embarrassing questions. To tear a leaf out of a book is a warning against repeating rumors. 616

LEAK. A leaky faucet in a dream is a forerunner having to account for something you have said about another. Leaky overshoes portend illness. A boat that is leaking is a forecast of accidents. 203

LEAP. To dream of leaping over a fence is a sign that you will overcome an obstacle that has been in your way for some time. If you dream of leaping over a house or some other impossible object, you will attain social prestige. 854

LEARNING. People in dreams who display their learning in an obnoxious manner are an augury of a prolonged illness. If you dream of seriously trying to learn a new trade, language or some difficult subject, you will discover a new friend in whom you may place your trust. 863

LEASE. To lease a dwelling-house, building, or plot of ground in a dream is a sign that you will increase your income. 232

LEATHER. Leather in a dream augurs advancement by hard unremitting toil. To dream of working with leather is a sign of having to meet some overdue bills. 156

LEAVE. (See also Furlough.) If you dream of being on leave from a job without pay, you have a good chance of having your salary raised. 649

LECTURE. Anyone who dreams of going to a lecture by an important figure in politics, literature or art will be fortunate in love affairs. If you dream of being a lecturer, you will take an extended trip. 931

LEDGER. (See Accounting.) 625

LEECH. To dream that a leech is sucking your blood predicts that demands will be made upon you by relatives. 759

LEG. Dreaming of a single leg is a portent of failure to accomplish your ambition. Crooked legs in a dream foretell that you will suffer from a lack of capital with which to further an enterprise. Beautiful, shapely legs are a sign of success in social enterprises. To break a leg signifies discontent. 059

LEGACY. A dream of receiving a legacy foretells pleasant days if it does not come as the result of death in your immediate family. Otherwise, it portends woe. 587

LEGERDEMAIN. (See Magic.) 946

LEI. This garland of flowers that the Hawaiians hang on the necks of their friends is a fortunate augury in a dream. It foretells happiness to lovers. 951

LEISURE. To dream of spending your leisure in quiet and dignified pursuits is a sign of an increase in your fortune and respect in your community. 279

LEMON. Sucking a lemon is a dream predicts that you will be unpopular among professional people. To squeeze a lemon for use in making mixed drinks portends difficult times ahead. 992

LEMONADE. Making lemonade in a dream is a portent of making new friends who will stand by you in time of need. Drinking lemonade is a forerunner of being looked up to by your friends. 581

LENTIL. A maiden who dreams of cooking lentils will thereby be assured of winning a handsome husband and a happy home. To eat lentils portends several healthy children. 920

LEOPARD. To be attacked by a leopard in a dream predicts trying experiences, but if you succeed in killing it or putting it to flight, you will achieve your ends. 266

LEPER. Difficult times are ahead for the person who dreams of associating with lepers. 371

LETHAL CHAMBER. If you dream of being led into a lethal chamber for execution, you are warned against investing your money without making a thorough investigation of its honesty. To see another person go into a lethal chamber means that you will make money by buying and selling. 719

LETTER. In any dream regarding letters the portent varies according to whether they contain good or bad news or simply routine information. To dream of receiving good news by mail—and that of course includes money—is an augury of good business prospects. Letters in which the news is either distressing or disappointing portend a battle to protect your good name. To receive a batch of unimportant letters is a sign that you will be harried by your creditors. To dream of writing an impassioned love letter is an augury of regret for a wrong you have done someone long ago. To dream of tearing up or burning a letter before you have read it predicts a money loss. Shame is the portent of reading a letter intended for another. It is a sign that your fondest wish will come true if you dream of dropping a letter into a mail-box or mailing it at the post-office. 015

LEWDNESS. A dream of being present when people are behaving in a lewd manner augurs new opportunities to make money, but in a questionable manner. 602

LIAR. If you dream of calling a person a liar, you will have to defend yourself against a vicious attack on your character. To be called a liar by someone else in a dream is a portent of quarrels. To dream of calling yourself a liar presages illness of a serious nature. 971

LIBEL. To dream of being libeled is a warning against any actions that you are well aware may cause criticism. To libel another is a portent of continuing hard luck. 855

LIBRARY. You will be applauded for your cleverness if you dream of going to a library. It is a particularly fortunate dream for those who are engaged in creative work. 146

LICENSE. Being asked by a traffic officer in a dream to show your license is an omen of good fortune in love unless you are unable to produce the license, in which case the omen is of family squabbles. To dream of buying a license for a dog presages a long period of home comfort. 618

LICKING. (See Flogging.) 389

LICORICE. It is a sign that you will begin to go places in your business life if you dream of eating licorice. 500

LIE. It ought not to be so, but a dream of telling a lie is a forerunner of good luck in financial affairs. If a married man dreams of telling his wife a lie, he will have to buy her an expensive present, but he will be able to. If you dream of having someone tell you a lie, you will fail in an important enterprise. If you tell a lie to save someone shame or embarrassment, you will have good luck socially. 424

LIFEBOAT. Launching a lifeboat in a dream means that you will embark on a new venture that may be either business or love. As long as the lifeboat is steady, the venture will be successful, but if it overturns, the opposite may be expected. 472

LIFEBUOY. If you dream of being taken off a wreck by means of a lifebuoy, you are in danger of being put to great inconvenience by a member of the opposite sex. 140

LIFEGUARD. A maiden who dreams of being rescued by a lifeguard at a bathing resort will meet a likeable sort of fellow with whom she will have many good times. 316

LIFE INSURANCE. To dream of being turned down for life insurance after you have been examined by the physician predicts a long and happy life. Paying a premium on your life insurance in a dream is an augury of new opportunities to make money. 527

LIFT. (See Elevator.) 318

LIGHT. Light in a dream is always a more favorable augury than darkness. To turn on an electric light indicates a pleasant party. Lighting a candle augurs a happy meeting. 658

LIGHTHOUSE. Seen from the deck of a ship at night, lighthouse in a dream signifies good going in love and in business. A lighthouse in the sunshine with waves breaking about its base is a portent of travels abroad. 652

LIGHTNING. Accompanied by rain and thunder, streaks of lightning seen in a dream are a forerunner of disaster. Heat lightning foretells pleasant days with one's friends. 950

LIGHTNING-ROD. It is a sign that you are in danger from a mysterious source if you dream of seeing a lightning-rod on a house or other building. 266

LILAC. A lilac bush in bloom, either lavender or white, predicts illness of a young friend, but it will turn out for the best. 601

LILLIPUTIAN. (See Midget.) 299

LILY OF THE VALLEY. A dream of picking this sweet-scented spring flower augurs happiness for lovers. 927

LIMA BEAN. Canned lima beans predict business disappointments, but if they are fresh, they foretell solid achievement. 629

LIMBURGER CHEESE. There is a forecast of embarrassment in any dream in which this foul-smelling cheese figures. 769

LIME. If you dream of squeezing limes for limeade or cocktails, you are likely to meet a person who is in some way peculiar or outlandish. To dream of mixing mortar with lime is an augury of a promotion in business. 989

LINEN. Clean linen in a dream predicts easy living. Bed linen is an augury of romance. Table linen is a sign of social distinction. 841

LINER. An ocean liner lying at a dock foretells adventure. For a woman to dream of seeing people off on a trip and being carried away on the liner portends a new lover. To dream of being on a liner in mid-ocean is an omen that someone will distrust you. 161

LINGERIE. (See also Lace.) Men who dream of lingerie— of silk, fine linen or rayon—are warned to guard against loose talk while in the company of the opposite sex. For a woman to dream of lingerie foretells social advancement. Black lingerie predicts adventurous companions in night clubs. 326

LINIMENT. Rubbing lame parts of the body with liniment foretells a legacy consisting of valuable personal effects. 298

LINOTYPE. To dream of this typesetting machine is a good omen for all persons who are interested in creative art of any kind, but especially for those who write. 438

LINSEED OIL. A dream of mixing paint with linseed oil predicts success in a difficult undertaking. 431

LION. You will be looked up to by your associates if you dream of being on friendly terms with a lion. If a lion attacks you and you overcome him, you will develop greater leadership socially and in business. 272

LIP. (See also Kiss, Mustache.) To dream of the lips of an old person is a sign that you will have a problem to solve. Deeply reddened lips portend illness and loss of business. Thick, sensual lips foretell disappointment in love. 153

LIPSTICK. To dream that you see a woman using a lipstick in a public place is a portent of defeat in a struggle. You will be the butt of a practical joke if you dream of seeing a man use lipstick. 138

LIQUOR. Drinking hard liquors in a dream is a warning against over-indulgence in alcohol. 240

LITERATURE. (See Reading.) 698

LITIGATION. (See Law.) 290

LIVE-OAK. Peaceful days are assured if you dream of live-oak trees, but if they are hung with moss you will have to stay pretty close to home for one reason or another. 595

LIVER. If you appear to be having trouble with your liver in a dream, you are likely to find a purse full of money. To eat liver in a dream is a sign of good health. Taking cod or halibut liver oil predicts a love episode that will make you happy. 082

LIVERY STABLE. A dream of going to an old-fashioned livery stable where horses and carriages are rented is an omen of courtship and marriage. 688

LIZARD. This reptilian creature seen in a dream is an augury of being caught in some unimportant misdemeanor. It is chiefly a warning to watch your step. 174

LLAMA. A dream of a llama carrying its burden in the Andes of South America is a forerunner of success in business where merchandise is dealt in. If you dream that a llama spits at you, the augury is one of great perturbation. 337

LOAD. Carrying a load of any kind in a dream is an omen of having to begin work early and continue until late. 136

LOAN. Dreaming of getting a loan from a bank or other moneylending institution is a portent of hard going in business that will eventually work out to your financial benefit. Making a loan to another presages a new and lasting friendship. 790

LOBSTER. A live lobster in a dream portends petty difficulties. To eat lobster in any form is a sign that you will receive some money that has been long overdue. 208

LOCK. To lock a door or a box, trunk or other container in a dream indicates that someone will be suspicious of you. To pick a lock with a skeleton key or piece of wire presages great embarrassment. If you dream of finding a padlock on the door of your home, you are likely to run afoul of the law. To be locked in a room or prison cell predicts being called upon for a speech at a public gathering. 011

LOCKET. For a woman to dream of wearing a locket in which there is a man's picture predicts a love affair of a warm and passionate nature, 152

LOCKJAW. You will have little peace for a long time if you dream of having lockjaw. 597

LOCOMOTIVE. Driving a locomotive in a dream is a portent of realizing an ambition. To ride in the cab of a locomotive is an augury of promotion in business. 028

LOCUST. The whirring sound of locusts heard in a dream predicts grief through the loss of a friend. To dream of a plague of locusts is a forerunner of business losses. 293

LODGER. If you dream that you are a lodger in a rooming or boarding house, you will see an improvement in your affairs before the week is out. 983

LOG. To dream of sitting on a log is a signal of contentment on a small but steady income. You will have leisure to follow your favorite hobby. Sawing logs for use in a fireplace predicts new home comforts. To see logs floating in a river is a portent of a business opportunity that you should not overlook. A log jam predicts failure. To enter a log cabin is a forerunner of honor among your fellows. To build one presages satisfaction through hard work. 827

LOLLYPOP. If in a dream someone hands you a lollypop as a pacifier, you will be elected to office in some social group such as a club, church organization, lodge or community association. To dream of sucking a lollypop in church, school or other public place portends embarrassment. 123

LONELINESS. A dream of being lonely is a sure indication that you will have company. 072

LONGSHOREMEN. Seeing longshoremen in a dream loading or unloading a ship is a prophecy that you will have a job offered you within a month—a job that you should accept. 238

LOOKING-GLASS. (See Mirror.) 584

LOOM. To dream of weaving cloth on a loom foretells pleasant days doing constructive work. If the loom breaks or the threads get twisted, there is trouble in store for you, but with patience it can be straightened out. 480

LOON. A dream of seeing a loon diving under water is a sign that you will travel to faraway lands. 728

LOOT. If you have a dream of coming upon a quantity of loot left by burglars, you are warned against being too grasping in your dealings with business men and women. 835

LORD'S PRAYER. You will meet a most interesting person of means and refinement if you dream of reciting the Lord's Prayer. 172

LOSS. Losing anything in a dream is an unfortunate augury unless you find it again. The loss of reputation portends sickness and death. 788

LOTTERY. To dream of buying a lottery ticket is a sign that you will be held up to ridicule by someone you have always liked. If you dream of winning in a lottery you will get into a jam with your relatives. 480

LOTUS. Lotus blossoms seen in a dream predict romance to the unmarried. To inhale their fragrance at dusk is a sign that you will have ecstatic happiness. 045

LOUD SPEAKER. A blaring loud speaker on a radio is a portent of woe, but if you dream of turning down the volume, you will have good luck in community affairs. 738

LOUNGE. In a cafe or theatre, a lounge is a prophecy of luxury. To meet your friends there portends difficulties in business that can be overcome by hard work. 691

LOUSE. Being afflicted with lice in a dream is a sign that you are going to be approached by an unscrupulous person who will propose an alliance for dishonest purposes. To see lice on another foretells a keen disappointment. 918

LOVE. Dreams of honest love foretell happiness and contentment. Illicit love affairs foretell disappointment. The greater the passion in a love dream, the greater the possibilities for reaching the heights or the depths. To dream of witnessing the love-making of others is a sign that you will succeed in the project on which you are at present engaged. 829

LOZENGE. Taking a throat lozenge in a dream means that you will be taken to task for talking too much. If you swallow a lozenge whole, you will have to do a disagreeable job that you have been putting off for some time. 609

LUBRICANT. (See Oil.) 990

LUCK. To dream of having luck is a sign that you will be lucky, but it is also a warning against taking things too easily. 577

LUGGAGE. (See Baggage.) 023

LUMBER. Piles of lumber seen in a dream augur prosperity through increasingly good business. To see lumber carelessly strewn about a yard betokens harassing family squabbles. 894

LUNACY. (See Insanity.) 047

LUNCH. If you dream of eating lunch from a box or basket in the out of doors, you will find that your health will improve and you will gain weight. To eat lunch in a restaurant at a table is an indication that you will have difficulty with your employer. Eating at a lunch counter is a sign of a rise in salary. 764

LUNG. To dream of having your lungs congested or otherwise affected is a warning to guard both your conduct and your health. 083

LUST. If you are not additionally careful of your conduct, you are in great danger if you dream of giving way to lustful impulses. 888

LUTE. Playing this old-fashioned stringed instrument in a dream portends happy love affairs. 429

LUXURY. Any dream of luxury is a warning against indolence. Keep your mind on your job during working hours and let nothing interfere with your advancement. 407

LYE. To dream of using lye in cleaning or making soap is a forerunner of being investigated for your integrity. 929

LYING. (See Liar.) 397

LYNCHING. Death is predicted by a dream of taking part in a lynching; disgrace if you are simply a witness. 191

LYNX. A young woman who dreams of having a fur piece made of lynx will marry a handsome editor or author. 285

LYRE. To dream of playing this ancient stringed musical instrument presages an adventure in a garden of love, but if you break a string, it is probable that evil days will befall you. A lyre that is out of tune predicts a menace in your life. 190

LYSOL. Peace of mind is the portent of dreaming of the use of lysol for disinfecting, but if it is used as a poison you will have much to regret. 625

M

MACADAM. To drive or walk along a macadam road is a pleasant augury for middle-aged people. 259

MACARONI. Dreaming of eating macaroni in an Italian restaurant is a sign that you will soon take your sweetheart to a rousing musical screen show. To dream of cooking macaroni at home means that you will have relatives to visit you. 931

MACAROON. Macaroons served with ice cream or other dessert in your dream foretell days spent in a large and luxurious hotel. 803

MACAW. A macaw of birght plumage hopping about a cage, denotes an escape from an unpleasant and boring conference. 035

MACHETE. To wield a sharp machete in hacking your way through a hot, sticky jungle is a sign that you must guard against speaking unkindly of your close relatives. 165

MACHINERY. (See also Cogs, Wheels.) If in a dream you see machinery in motion and it is clean and well cared-for, you will make good with your employer. If the machinery is idle or rusty, you will have difficulties with your car, your employer or your family. 451

MACKEREL. A dream of catching fresh mackerel from a small boat points toward a short vacation with your family. 660

MACKINAW. To wear a bright plaid mackinaw in a dream foretells taking enjoyment in outdoor sports. If the mackinaw shows signs of hard wear, you are warned against accidents. 470

MAD DOG. It is bad luck to dream of being bitten by a mad dog, but if you are able to put him to flight, the augury will be of good import. 329

MADNESS. (See Insanity.) 573

MADONNA. A picture or a statue of the Madonna is a propitious omen. You will win the love of a gifted and beautiful child. 934

MAGAZINE. To see many magazines on a newsstand portends a budding romance with a foreigner who does not speak your language. To write for a mazagine in a dream is an augury of success in literary work. 697

MAGGOT. Dreaming of maggots in cheese or other food is a forerunner of a disturbed mental condition. You will harbor a grudge against someone. Forget it. 622

MAGIC. Magic in any form in a dream foretells a strange coincidence. To see a magician at work and to be mystified by his tricks foretells meeting someone whom you never expected to see again. 481

MAGISTRATE. If you dream of having to appear before a magistrate for some infraction of the law, it is a sign that you are burning the candle at both ends and should go more slowly. 862

MAGNET. To dream of the attractive power of a magnet portends many palpitating love affairs and much admiration from the opposite sex. 030

MAGNIFICENCE. (See also Luxury.) Good things may come of a dream of magnificence if you do not take it too seriously. You must regard it as a dream that will give you something to live up to as regards your conduct. 083

MAGNIFYING GLASS. You will have more money to spend if you dream of examining articles with a magnifying glass. 387

MAGNOLIA. To dream of a beautiful magnolia tree in bloom foretells to unmarried folk a happy spring wedding. To wear a magnolia blossom indicates that you will lose your heart to a Southern beau or belle. 610

MAGPIE. If magpies fly into a tree in your dream and chatter among themselves, it is a sign that it will be sheer idiocy on your part to pursue any longer a love that is dead. 740

MAHARAJAH. If you dream of one of the fabulously wealthy majarajahs of India bedecked with jewels and living in a home surrounded with houris of devastating beauty, it is a sign that you should be more discreet in your contacts with persons of the opposite sex. Mend your ways, and do not let your conceit be your undoing. 652

MAHOGANY. To admire a beautiful piece of mahogany furniture in a dream is a sign that you will inherit a house and property from a distant relative. To dream of polishing mahogany predicts better living conditions. Trying to saw or otherwise cut mahogany is a portent of doing productive work. 746

MAIDEN. Pretty, graceful maidens seen in a dream are a portent of innocent happiness. To have a maiden confide in you foretells a respected place in your community. 301

MAIDENHAIR FERN. To dream of the dainty maidenhair fern growing in a bosky dell signifies that you will have a partnership interest in a country home where your children and your children's children will be happy. 750

MAIL. If you dream of calling for mail at the post-office, it is a sign that you will buy a new piece of furniture. If you receive mail, it predicts a good buy; if not, you will not get a bargain. To dream of mailing a letter predicts a better than ordinary chance of making money. 004

MAILMAN. (See Postman.) 685

MAILBOX. To drop a letter into a mailbox and have difficulty in getting it in is a sign that the answer will be No to anything you propose. 757

MAJOR. If in your dream you meet a major in uniform and recognize him as such, it means that you will have an invitation to join a civic association. 223

MAKEUP. (See also Cosmetic, Lipstick, Rouge.) If you dream of making up for the stage, you will be asked to solicit funds for a community chest. If in making up for some social engagement you get powder on your gown, you are likely to make a faux pas at a party. If you dream of making up someone else, you are in danger of burning a hole in your clothes with a cigarette. 139

MALARIA. To dream of having malaria means that you will fail to get a hoped-for position. 160

MALICE. A display of malice in a dream, whether it is shown by yourself or another, is a sign of having to make amends of some kind to a much younger person than yourself. 474

MALLET. Handling a mallet in your dream portends a labor disturbance in which you will have a part. It may be in the office or factory where you work or it may be in your own kitchen. 600

MALTESE CAT. To fondle a maltese cat in your dream and hear him purr with delight at your attentions is a sign that a woman whose reputation is not of the best will make advances to you. 890

MAN. To dream of man in the abstract is a warning against too much brain work. For a woman to dream of a man foretells a meeting with an interesting person who will be a platonic friend. 751

MANAGER. To call the manager of a hotel, store or telephone exchange in your dream augurs a visit to the dentist that may result in considerable pain. If in a dream you appear to be the manager of an organization, you are likely to hear good news by letter, wire or radio. 826

MANDOLIN. A maiden who dreams of hearing the strumming of a mandolin is promised a short whirlwind courtship and a very happy marriage. 013

MANE. A horse's mane seen in a dream, whether it is black, white or roan, foretells a telephone call and an invitation. 528

MANGE. If you dream of your dog having the mange, it is an indication that you will be beset by family troubles. 761

MANGER. To dream of the Christ child in a manger is a happy omen. You will inherit property and be happy in your married life. 714

MANIAC. One is likely to have a nightmare if one dreams of seeing a maniac. One is likely to be falsely accused of appropriating another's belongings. 873

MANICURE. To be manicured in your dream by a beautiful operator is a prediction that you will have to cut down on your expenses. To dream of having a manicurist make advances to you is a portent of having to arrange to meet additional expense. 276

MANNERS. Being conscious in a dream of the good manners of someone present portends better circumstances surrounding the main interpretation; bad manners suggest the reverse. 576

MANNIKIN. If in a dream one sees a fashionably dressed mannikin parading before a group of women, it signifies that you will have a dispute with one of the opposite sex. 068

MANOR HOUSE. To visit a manor house and be entertained there as an honored guest is a sign that the dreamer will receive favorable word from overseas, either from friends or relatives. 673

MANSION. To dream of living in a mansion and enjoying all the luxuries that go with it is a sign that you will travel with the mate you have selected. 548

MANTILLA. To dream of a woman wearing a mantilla forecasts a flirtation that will cause you considerable perturbation. It is a warning to be discreet in the company of persons of the opposite sex, especially when you are away from home. 735

MANUFACTURING. A dream of being engaged in manufacturing of any kind augurs respect from the community in which you live. 092

MANURE. Dreaming of soil that has been richly manured is a sign that you will discuss a promotional plan with an associate whose sound advice and financial cooperation will enable you to proceed with the work. 354

MANUSCRIPT. Typing and editing a manuscript for publication in a dream means that you will be likely to be called for jury duty. To dream of submitting a manuscript to an editor augurs probable disappointment. 424

MANX CATS. Tailless, green-eyed Manx cats in your dream foretell trouble with a neighbor over the behavior of one of your family, probably a child. 443

MAP. To consult road maps and colored plates in a world atlas portends a marriage alliance with a person of another race and creed. 010

MAPLE. Maple furniture in a dream is a good sign. It indicates that you will have happy family connections and home life. 364

MAPLE SUGAR. To be present at an old-fashioned sugaring off is a sign that you will sell your city property and buy a farm in the country. If you dream of eating maple sugar as a confection, you will be fortunate in your dealings with the opposite sex. 509

MARASCHINO CHERRY. If you dream of tipping your cocktail glass to get the cherry in it, you will be fortunate in business. 485

MARATHON. Watching a marathon race or dance in a dream is a portent of nervous strain. If you dream of being a contestant you are in danger of having to answer for a misdeed that you did not intend. 980

MARBLES. Playing a game of marbles in a dream signifies that if you meet a former suitor, you will find his sentiments unchanged. 475

MARCEL WAVE. To be given a marcel wave in a dream and be concerned about the results is a sign that you will have an opportunity to compete for the favor of a newcomer to your circle. 298

MARDI GRAS. You will sign an important document if you dream of celebrating Mardi Gras, and the chances are that this will make you independent for life. 684

MARE. (See Horse.) 049

MARIGOLDS. Marigolds seen by a woman in a dream are a sign that she will wear a new hat to her next party. 251

MARIHUANA. A dream of smoking this drug foretells a serious illness coupled with disgrace. 451

MARIONETTES. To stage a marionette show for the entertainment of the children foretells much joy in family life. 136

MARK. If you dream of having a birthmark on your person, it predicts a meeting with someone who will be both interesting and profitable to you. If you dream of someone who cannot write and sign a check or document with his mark, you are likely to have a strange experience. 195

MARKET. Dreaming of an outdoor market in which all sorts of foodstuffs are temptingly displayed is an omen of prosperity, but if the food is wilted or otherwise spoiled, it predicts hard times. 185

MARMALADE. Eating marmalade in a dream betokens an invitation to visit a friend or relative. 794

MARRIAGE. A dream of being happily married and proud of your mate portends a quarrel with a lover. If a maiden dreams of being a bridesmaid at the wedding of a friend, it is a sign that she will have a whirlwind courtship and marriage within a year. A divorce is indicated if a marriage ceremony is accompanied by many tears from those assembled. 647

MARS. Looking at the planet Mars through a telescope in a dream foretells a serious argument with a business acquaintance. 571

MARSEILLAISE. To hear the Marseillaise played or sung in your dream is a portent of the news of a birth, probably to one of your friends or relatives. 285

MARSH. To walk through marshy ground in a dream is a sign that you will go through a period of bad health. 655

MARSHMALLOWS. Toasted or served from the box, marshmallows portend the introduction of a tall, handsome man into your circle. He will be popular among the feminine members of your group. 154

MARTYR. If you dream that you are being made a martyr, it augurs that your doctor will recommend a diet that will be good for you but very distasteful. 813

MASCOT. To see a mascot paraded before a crowd of people at any kind of game is simply a portent that you will have a serious argument with a taxi driver. 375

MASK. The interpretation of a dream in which one wears a mask is that you will be deceived by someone you trusted. 052

MASON. To be employed as a mason and expert in your work is a sign that you will get a small rise in salary and work fewer hours. 432

MASQUERADE. To dream of attending a gay masquerade party with sprightly music and amusing companions predicts that there is a surprise in store for you—probably concerning a fascinating person of the opposite sex. 416

MASS. For a person to attend mass in a dream is a good augury. He or she will be blessed with fine, healthy children. 493

MASSACRE. A painful visit to the dentist is foretold by a dream of being present at a massacre. 936

MASSAGE. A facial or body massage in a dream is a portent of going to a party where you will have a good time but where you will lose some important belonging. It is a lucky augury if you dream of massaging a sick friend. 299

MASTICATION. If you dream of carefully masticating or chewing your food, so much so that you jaws ache and your patience is exhausted, it is a sign that you will, through sheer determination, win an arugment of long standing. 108

MASTOID. To dream of being threatened with a mastoid operation is a warning against eavesdropping lest you hear your own shortcomings discussed. 713

MAT. Going to the mat with anyone in your dream and fighting it out denotes overconfidence in your abilities. To lay a mat in front of a door foretells visitors. 417

MATADOR. To dream of seeing a matador in a bull fight is a sign that you will find a very interesting friend from one of the Latin-American countries. If the matador is injured in the ring, you will be disappointed in love. 549

MATCH. If you strike a match in your dream, the portent is one of good luck. You will fall in love, and what is more, your love will have what it takes to create a happy home. 725

MATCHMAKER. Woe betide the person who dreams of being matchmaker. He or she will be held responsible for a great many things over which they have had no control whatever. 813

MATE. If a maiden dreams of matching things up—such as a pair of stockings, gloves or shoes—she will be married shortly and have identical twins, If you dream of your mate, fearful that he or she is lost or hurt, it is a reminder that there is an anniversary of some kind that you should remember. 460

MATERNITY. A dream concerning maternity is a forerunner of increasing responsibility. 502

MATHEMATICS. To work on a mathematical problem in your dream and despair of its solution is an indication that you have no hope of fulfilling your plans. 081

MATINEE. If you dream of attending a matinee in the company of light-hearted and pleasure-seeking people, it foretells a lapse from the straight and narrow path. 311

MATTING. A dream of laying matting on a floor portends that some people you do not know are conspiring to do you harm. 478

MATTRESS. To be lying on a soft mattress in your dream, luxuriating in its comfort and ease, is a sign that you are in danger of losing your initiative. If you have a companion of the opposite sex, you will have to look to your conduct. 473

MATZOTH. If you dream of eating this Jewish unleavened bread you will be likely to go hungry so that you may feed your friends. 105

MAUSOLEUM. To walk in a cemetery and see magnificent mausoleums in memory of the dead warns against unworthy attentions to a wealthy relative in the hope of inheriting his money. 326

MAXIM. To dream of reading maxims and being impressed by them portends self improvement and an increased income through home study. 351

MAYONNAISE. Making mayonnaise dressing in your dream and serving it on salads is a portent of opening a tea-room. 550

MAYOR. If you dream of becoming the mayor of your city and being acclaimed by the citizens, you are likely to be called for jury duty. 412

MAYPOLE. Dancing about a maypole in a dream is a good omen for lovers. It predicts an early marriage and healthy progeny. 405

MAZE. (See Labyrinth.) 498

MEADOW. Meadows and rich pasture lands in a dream foretell a season of plenty during which you should provide for the future. If there is a stream flowing through the meadow, your fortune will be that much better. 203

MEALS. (See Dinner, Eating, Lunch.) 383

MEASLES. You will have to make amends to someone for a slight if you dream of being afflicted with the measles. 498

MEAT. To dream of buying meat foretells that you will be very busy in your work for a long time, with but little opportunity for recreation. 247

MECHANIC. A maiden who dreams that her lover is a mechanic will have a struggle to hold him, but she should consider it worth while. 237

MEDAL. Wearing medals in a dream is an omen that you will be given some distinction for work that you have accomplished. Seeing medals on others is a warning against showing jealousy. 702

MEDDLER. To dream of a meddler—one who is poking his nose into other people's affairs or handling articles that do not concern him—means that you should not allow yourself to be drawn into squabbles that are other people's business. 830

MEDICINE. Taking medicine in a dream augurs good health, but to give it to another is a sign of disappointment. 528

MEDICINE BALL. Tossing a medicine ball portends a pleasure trip to a warm section of the country. 157

MEDIUM. To dream of visiting a spiritualist medium foretells learning something about your forebears that you never knew before. It may or may not be to your advantage. 256

MEDUSA. You are warned against illicit love if you dream of this mythical woman whose hair was changed into snakes. Be very circumspect in the company of the opposite sex. 057

MEERSCHAUM PIPE. If you dream of breaking a new white meerschaum pipe, you will be saved much trouble in the nick of time. Smoking an old and richly colored meerschaum is a portent of comfort. 758

MEGAPHONE. A night-club singer crooning through a megaphone is a sign of disturbances that will annoy you for some time. Dreaming of a megaphone used out of doors is a good portent for young people in love. 660

MELANCHOLY. You may look forward to calm happiness if you dream of being sad and melancholy, but if you dream of living with someone similarly affected, the portent is of unsatisfactory business conditions. 127

MELODRAMA. Blood and thunder episodes in a dream are a good portent if they seem to be part of a play or motion picture. 774

MELODY. Hearing a melody in a dream is a good portent. If it seems new, you are likely to meet influential and agreeable people. If it is a melody that you recognize, there will be a meeting with a well-loved friend of long standing. 144

MELON. A dream of eating any kind of melon predicts a slight upset of the digestive tract. Raising melons for the market portends surprising incidents in connection with your business affairs. 731

MEMORANDUM. To make a memorandum of a coming appointment in a dream is an augury of being blessed for a kindly act. To lose an important memorandum foretells a dwindling income. 843

MEMORIAL. Pausing in a dream to do homage to a great man or woman in front of a memorial is a forerunner of deceit on the part of one of your acquaintances. 294

MEMORIAL DAY. You will be loved by your friends and respected by your neighbors if you dream of taking part in Memorial Day services or of putting flowers on the graves of those who have gone before. 015

MEMORY. If you can remember in a dream something that has eluded you in your waking hours, you will have an easier and more lucrative job offered you. 741

MENACE. Anything that is a menace to your personal safety in a dream warns you against taking chances in crowded thoroughfares. 459

MENAGERIE. (See Zoo.) 982

MENDICANT. (See Beggar.) 325

MENDING. To dream of mending hosiery or other clothing forecasts a new means of making money that will add a considerable amount to your income. 575

MENU. To dream of studying the menu or bill of fare in a restaurant is an omen that you need not worry about having plenty for comfortable living. 716

MEPHISTOPHELES. (See Devil.) 331

MERCHANT. If you dream that you are a merchant and are prospering through the buying and selling of necessary and staple goods, you are assured of hard work but a reasonably good income. 173

MERCURY. Dreaming of mercury, or quicksilver, is a definite warning against careless behavior in the company of the opposite sex. 892

MERCY. Showing mercy to a person who has wronged you in a dream predicts a long and happy life with the object of your affections. If you dream of being at the mercy of a brute, you will have to answer publicly for a misdeed. 591

MERINGUE. Eating this frothy mixture of eggs and sugar in a dream predicts an adventure with some person of a lighthearted disposition. 475

MERMAID. A dream of discussing matters of general interest with a mermaid indicates that you will suffer a keen disappointment. 286

MERRIMENT. (See Frolic, Fun.) 784

MERRY-GO-ROUND. If you dream of riding with happy children on a merry-go-round or carousel, you will have an experience that will change your life for the better. 834

MESH. (See Net.) 363

MESS. To dream of making a mess of things is a sign that you will have an argument with near relatives. Eating at the officers' mess in the Army or Navy is a forerunner of promotion. 119

MESSAGE. (See Letter.) 411

MESSENGER. Acting as a messenger in a dream is a sign of making money in real estate. To send a package or letter by a messenger augurs the success of a pet project. 675

METAL. (See Gold, Iron, Platinum, Silver, Steel.) 191

METEOR. To dream of a streaming meteor flashing across the sky denotes sudden success that will be of short duration. 641

METER. Reading a gas or electric meter in a dream is a portent of having to listen to good advice that you ought to follow. 156

METRONOME. To dream of playing the piano or other musical instrument to the clicking of a metronome is a forecast of having to do a disagreeable task. 665

MEW. The sound of a cat or kitten mewing in a dream is an augury of accidents in which you will receive several superficial wounds. 944

MICROBE. If you have the unusual dream of seeing a single microbe, you are warned against driving your car when the roads are snowy, wet or otherwise slippery. 483

MICROSCOPE. Looking at objects under a microscope in a dream is an omen of being surprised at the behavior of someone you thought you knew well. If you dream of breaking a microscope and being greatly worried thereby, you will fail to persuade someone of your good intentions. 720

MIDDLE AGES. To dream of living in a walled city of the Middle Ages and wearing the picturesque costume of the time is a portent of an exciting love affair, especially if there is fighting in your dream. 098

MIDDLEWEIGHT. If a girl dreams of being in love with a pugilist in the middleweight class, she is likely to marry a man of literary or artistic tastes. 997

MIDGET. To dream of one or more midgets foretells making the acquaintance of a man connected with books and pictures who will prove to be a good friend. 515

MIDWIFE. (See also Childbirth.) A man who dreams of calling a midwife in to deliver a child is likely to suffer for his extravagant habits. If a woman dreams of officiating as a midwife, she will have a quarrel with her husband about money. 481

MIGNONETTE. To wear a sprig of mignonette in a dream is an omen of meeting dainty women or fascinating men. 460

MIGRATION. Dreaming of the migration of birds predicts freedom from worry; of the migration of animals, a new opportunity in business. 493

MIKADO. Japanese rulers in a dream are a portent of light-hearted diversions in unusual surroundings. 625

MILDEW. Disappointment in love or the loss of a friend is forecast by a dream of finding mildew on clothing. You are also warned against placing too much confidence in strangers. 064

MILE-POST. A succession of mile-posts seen in a dream portends a long and enjoyable cross-country motor journey. 647

MILITIA. To dream of serving in the militia is a sign that you will be respected in your neighborhood. If you are called out on active duty, you are likely to have an advancement in your position but not necessarily with an increase in salary. 810

MILK. A dream of milk is one of the luckiest dreams you can have, for it foretells lasting happiness that is the result of the right kind of a marriage and calm, peaceful home life. To drink cows' milk in a dream predicts good health! to drink goats' milk, business progress. If one dreams of milking a cow or a goat, the augury is comfort and prosperity through hard work. 294

MILKY WAY. You will be successful in acquiring further education if you dream of gazing at the Milky Way. 788

MILL. If it is driven by water-power, a mill in a dream portends happy hours with the person you love. If the mill is large like a factory, the augury is of money acquired through the toil of others. 252

MILL DAM. You will make progress in your chosen work if you dream of high water in back of a mill dam. If the water is low or stagnant you are warned to take precautions against making unwise commitments. 289

MILLER. A miller at work is a sign of greater industry on your part and corresponding higher wages. 222

MILLIONAIRE. To dream of being a millionaire and spending money lavishly on the things you have always wanted to have is a portent of receiving money in a roundabout way for a service you had rendered and forgotten. To dream of helping out your less fortunate friends with your money is a sign of good fortune just around the corner. 717

MIMIC. To see a mimic imitating the peculiarities of a worthy person is a warning not to place too great confidence in casual acquaintances. If you dream of mimicking another, you are likely to have great difficulty with your work. 570

MINARET. If you dream of seeing the minarets of a Mohammedan mosque, you will have many opportunities to travel and meet interesting people. If there is someone on the minaret calling to prayer, you will be financially fortunate. 248

MINCE PIE. You will have almost insurmountable difficulties with your in-laws if you dream of eating mince pie. To dream of making it is an augury of revenge upon someone who has done you wrong. 777

MIND READER. Nothing but bad luck can come from a

dream of visiting and paying money to a mind reader. 203

MINE. (See also Bomb.) To dream of working in a mine—coal, gold, silver or other metal—predicts that you will make a great deal of money through your own efforts. To feel suspense and fear from mines while on shipboard in the area of warring countries augurs worry from some indiscreet remark or action. If the ship is blown up, it is a sign that you should be constantly on your guard in all your dealings with strangers. 290

MINERAL WATER. If you drink sparkling mineral water in a dream, the prophecy is of having a good time in the company of old and trusted friends. 104

MINISTER. If in your dream you talk over your troubles with a minister of the gospel, you will be able to clear up all your outstanding obligations, both financial and social. To dream of social contacts with a minister from a foreign government is a sign of increasing prosperity. 384

MINK. If a maiden dreams of acquiring a mink coat, she should regard it as a warning against unscrupulous men. To dream of trapping minks for their furs is an augury of having to work hard for a small return. 034

MINNOW. Catching minnows with the hand in a dream is a sign of success in making others do your bidding. Using minnows for bait in fishing augurs increasing popularity among your associates. 308

MINSTREL. A dream of attending an old-fashioned minstrel show predicts that you will meet a valued friend whom you have not seen for years. Minstrels of the Middle Ages in a dream foretell meeting fascinating companions of the opposite sex. 686

MINT. The flavor of mint in a dream predicts that your next trip will be in a northerly direction. 567

MINT JULEP. To mix or drink a mint julep in a dream foretells enjoyment through making an effort to understand the viewpoint of others. 791

MINUET. Dreaming of a dignified minuet performed by ladies and gentlemen of the old school portends definitely better prospects for your social future. To listen to the music for a minuet predicts that you will be invited to a party. 330

MINX. To call a girl a minx in a dream, meaning that she is pert and saucy, is a sign that you will have a difficult time with your dentist. 767

MIRACLE. If in a dream you witness a miracle, or something that could not happen without Divine intervention, you have every reason for looking toward the future with confidence. 055

MIRAGE. A mirage or scene that fades away as you watch it is an augury that you will be confronted with an apparently hopeless task. Do not, however, fail to try it; for you are likely to succeed. 237

MIRE. Being stuck in the mire—on foot, horseback or in a motor-car—is a dream that foretells a difficult situation arising from failure to meet obligations. 559

MIRROR. You will be unfortunate in your love affairs if you dream of breaking a mirror. To dream of seeing yourself in a mirror is a sign that you will be admired by one of the opposite sex. 953

MIRTH. (See Fun.) 251

MISCONDUCT. (See Adultery.) 180

MISER. A dream of a miser counting his money and gloating over it is a portent of getting riches in a manner of which you would be ashamed if you did not heed the warning. 434

MISSIONARY. You will fail in an important enterprise if you dream of being a missionary. If you dream of being converted by a missionary, you will be successful in business. 110

MIST. (See Fog.) 508

MISTAKE. Making a mistake in a dream is a generally good portent if you admit your error and apologize for it, but to try to cover up a mistake or blame it on another augurs ill luck in an important project. 704

MISTLETOE. (See also Kiss.) Young people who dream of kissing under the mistletoe have much to look forward to. A maiden who dreams of hanging mistletoe will win a charming and ardent lover. 089

MISTRESS. A married man who dreams of keeping a mistress is warned against yielding to the lures of designing women. A woman who dreams of being mistress to a man, whether married or single, will have difficulty in meeting her debts. 763

MITTEN. Wearing mittens in a dream foretells trouble to anyone who drives a car or works with machinery. A man who dreams of being "given the mitten," or refused by the girl of his choice, will have much to be thankful for. 292

MOAN. The sound of a moan heard in a dream is a forerunner of illness in your family. If you dream of moaning, you will be pestered by bill collectors. 758

MOB. If in a dream you are pursued by a mob, you are in danger from one of the social group with which you associate. Do not be suspicious, but be careful. 203

MOBILIZATION. To dream of the mobilization of troops

for war is a sign of temporary affluence and then hard times. 404

MOCCASIN. On an Indian in a dream, moccasins portend disappointment in a friend whom you trusted. If you are wearing moccasins, you will be given a job supervising others. 453

MOCKING BIRD. The night song of a mocking bird heard in a dream foretells a long period of rest and contentment. 919

MODEL. Dreaming of mechanical or shop models portends commendation for a job well done. Artists' models in a dream are an omen that you will be distrusted by the people who know you best. 991

MODERN ART. This dream is of weird pictures or statuary that have little or no relation to life and that are bizarre or illogical in arrangement. It predicts a period of worry concerning your health. 417

MODESTY. Any exhibition of modesty in a dream, whether it is by a maiden or a reprobate, is a sign that has a good influence on other factors in the dream. 074

MOHAMMEDAN. To dream of a person of this faith in the performance of his or her religious duties is a sign that you will have an opportunity to travel in foreign lands. 780

MOLASSES. Eating molasses in a dream foretells that you will be censured for some ill-advised statement you have made concerning another person. 065

MOLD. (See also Mildew.) A dream of finding mold on meat, jelly or other food is a warning against careless habits that are likely to get you into serious trouble. To find mold on the covers of a Holy Bible warns against loose living. 027

MOLE. Burrowing into the ground, a mole in a dream is an augury of success in work that is in any way connected with engineering. To wear a mole-skin coat predicts unwelcome attention from the opposite sex. 303

MONARCH. (See King.) 789

MONASTERY. (See also Monk.) It is a sign of bad luck generally if a woman dreams of being in a monastery. She will be accused of deception by persons of rank. For a man to have this dream is a portent of smooth sailing in his affairs. 193

MONEY. If it is come by honestly, money in a dream is a sign that you will develop your resources to the point where you will have ample for your needs. To give money away is a forecast of having an interesting job but a small income. 838

MONK. (See also Monastery.) It is an augury of good fortune to dream of talking things over with a monk. You will have easier work and an easier mind. 537

MONKEY. To dream of keeping a monkey as a pet indicates that you are going to meet with treachery. A chattering monkey denotes that people will gossip about you and your personal habits. Monkeys in a cage at the zoo are a portent of coming trouble with hostile competitors. 034

MONKEY WRENCH. You will be able to solve a pressing problem if you dream of using a monkey wrench on a piece of machinery or an automobile. 124

MONOCLE. Wearing a monocle in a dream predicts uproariously amusing experiences. If you dream of laughing at another who is wearing this kind of eyeglass, you will have to apologize for some shortcoming. 664

MONOPLANE. (See Airplane.) 550

MONUMENT. (See Memorial.) 976

MOON. To dream of looking at the new moon over your left shoulder augurs a month of good luck. A clear, silvery moon in a cloudless sky foretells that you will devote your energy to a new and worthwhile project, but if it becomes clouded over, you will have many discouragements. A full moon denotes success in love affairs, particularly if you see it reflected in water. To dream of the harvest moon is an omen of excellent returns on your investments. 293

MOONSTONE. If someone hands you a moonstone in a dream, either in a setting or not, you will be mystified by the behavior of one of your friends. 047

MOOSE. If you dream of seeing a moose in the wild out of doors, you will find that a new avenue of enjoyment and profit will be opened up for you. To shoot a moose is a sign of impending trouble with your family and other relatives. If you see a baby moose, you will be invited to go on a trip with a wealthy friend. 440

MOP. Using a clean new mop in a dream foretells favorable comment on some of your work. Seeing an old and dirty mop in a pail of filthy water is a warning not to repeat evil rumors that you hear. 331

MORALS. To question the morals of your friends in a dream is a direct warning that you should look to your own. Keep to your own high standards and let them judge their own acts. 219

MORASS. (See Mire.) 083

MORGUE. To dream of looking through a morgue and finding the dead body of someone you are acquainted with is a forerunner of disaster and a warning to guard your health in every possible manner. If you dream of being a corpse and lying in a morgue, you will soon be called upon to perform a disagreeable duty. 654

MORMON. It is bad luck to dream of speaking in disparagement of a Mormon because of his or her religious beliefs. To dream of being converted to Mormonism augurs success in a venture that will require courage and hard work. 260

MORNING AFTER. If you have the experience of dreaming of having what is inelegantly called a "hangover" or "katzenjammer," due to overindulgence in alcohol the night before, you are likely to be reprimanded by someone who has authority over you. This may be your employer or your wife. 754

MORNING GLORY. This bright-colored climbing vine in bloom seen in a dream foretells carefree lazy days. 459

MORPHINE. If you dream of taking morphine in any shape, form or manner, you are warned that you must not shrink from facing a disagreeable duty. You will save yourself and others a heartache if you seize the bull by the horns. 413

MORTAR. Mixing mortar in a dream for use in bricklaying portends the successful accomplishment of a difficult job. Carrying mortar in a hod or other receptacle foretells a better position. 590

MORTGAGE. Great hardship is predicted by a dream of paying off a mortgage, but if you dream of foreclosing one, you will be fortunate in business. To put a mortgage on a house or other piece of property foretells a lucky business turn. 057

MOSLEM. (See Mohammedan.) 236

MOSQUE. (See also Minaret.) To dream of a mosque with its domes and minarets in the bright sunshine or moonlight is an omen that you will take renewed interest in the affairs of your own particular religion. 328

MOSQUITO. To dream of being bitten or annoyed by mosquitoes buzzing around your head or person is an augury of sadness unless you are able to kill them, in which case you are likely to find contentment. 015

MOSS. Soft green moss in a dream is an omen of happy, fruitful romance and married bliss, but dry gray moss predicts disillusionment. 885

MOTH. Slanderous statements will be made about you and your family if you dream of trying to catch a moth. If you succeed in getting it and killing it, you will overcome your enemies. If you find clothing full of moths, there will be sadness in your family. 706

MOTHER. If you dream of a mother who has gone to her reward, you will have many happy hours in the company of tried and true friends. If you dream of being a child and being hugged to your mother's bosom, the omen is a fortunate one, for your family and friends will rally to your aid in time of trouble. To see a new mother with her babe at her breast betokens peace and security for the future. 982

MOTHER-IN-LAW. For a man or woman to dream of having an altercation with a mother-in-law is a portent of a situation that will require skill and patience to adjust. For a woman to dream of being a mother-in-law is a sign that she will have to apologize for angry words. 860

MOTION PICTURE. If in a dream of being at the movies, the picture gives you great pleasure, you will overcome an obstacle that is in your way. If the pictures are depressing or disgusting, you will lose a piece of jewelry. 501

MOTOR. Any motor seen in a dream, be it electric or gasoline, is a sign of progress. If you cannot make it function as it should, the portent is of trouble ahead. 918

MOTOR BOAT. Freedom from business and family cares is predicted by a dream of operating your own motorboat. If you race with another power boat and win, you will have business worries that will cause you concern for only a short time. If you lose the race, you will make new friends. 131

MOTOR CAR. (See Automobile.) 840

MOTOR CYCLE. For a woman to dream of riding on a motor-cycle behind a young man predicts that she will have an adventure that may lead to serious consequences. It is a warning not to be careless of appearances. 094

MOUNTAIN. Climbing a mountain in a dream foretells a promotion in business, but it also warns you not to say you can handle a job unless you are sure that you can do so. If the mountain is very steep or if it is covered with ice and snow, you will be likely to succeed in spite of great difficulties that will be put in your way. 669

MOURNING. It may seem strange, but a dream of being in mourning is a portent of better times to come. If one dreams of seeing a city or community in mourning, the omen is of happenings that will be hard to bear but that will work out to a good end. 619

MOUSE. For a woman to dream of being frightened by a mouse is an augury of being put to shame by a younger person. If she kills the mouse, she will be able to buy new clothes and millinery. To catch a mouse in a trap is a sign that you will receive a letter from someone you do not like. 654

MOUTH. (See also Lip.) Cruel mouths seen in a dream are a warning against being too quick to criticize the actions of others. If the teeth show, you are likely to be hurt by base insinuations from those whom you had trusted. A beautiful mouth is a portent of great happiness for lovers.

The mouth of a baby is a sign that the person you had trusted least will turn out to be a firm and lasting friend. 829

MOVIES. (See Motion Picture.) 816

MUCILAGE. Using mucilage in a dream is an indication that your present work will not be permanent and that it will not be satisfactory to you. 520

MUCK. Dire consequences are predicted by a dream of falling down in the muck of a barnyard. You are warned against evil companions. 935

MUD. To get mud on your clothes in a dream is a sign that someone who wishes you ill is trying to influence people against you. To drive in a car through a muddy lane presages trouble with people to whom you owe money. 043

MUFF. If a man dreams of putting his hands into a muff that is being carried by a woman, he will have to answer for an ill-advised act or statement. For a maiden to dream of carrying a muff is a sign of spinsterhood over a long period. 912

MUFFIN. Eating tasty hot muffins in a dream foretells pleasant family relations. To dream of baking muffins is a sign that you will receive a small legacy. 291

MUFFLER. It is a sign of illness if you have a dream in which you put on a muffler. For a girl to dream of knitting a muffler for her boy friend is a sign that she is likely to lose his affection. 315

MULE. Driving one or more mules in a dream is a portent of loss of reputation through talking out of turn at a social gathering. If a mule kicks you in a dream, you are likely to get into business difficulties. To see a mule kick another of his kind is a sign of a pick-up in business. 601

MUMMY. To dream of discovering a mummy in an underground tomb predicts new and unusually prosperous undertakings. If you unwrap the mummy, you are liable to be talked about by people who do not like you. 800

MUMPS. If you dream of having mumps, the augury is of a long vacation at your employer's expense. 368

MURDER. It is distinctly bad luck to dream of committing murder, the more so if the victim is a baby or young person. This is a dream that warns you against loss of temper, association with people of little or no moral scruples, and extravagance. 900

MUSCLE. If you dream of displaying your muscles to an admiring audience, you are likely to be snubbed by someone you would like to have for a friend. 343

MUSEUM. Good luck in your social contacts will follow a dream of going through a museum of art or science and studying the exhibits. 095

MUSH. To eat mush in a dream foretells a visit to the dentist. To throw it, either playfully or in anger, portends misunderstandings with a friend. To eat it fried is a sign of being invited to go on a trip with a school friend. 900

MUSHROOM. To pick mushrooms in a dream is an indication that through taking intelligent chances you will make considerable money. To eat them signifies achievement in social life that will help you financially. 343

MUSIC. Hearing music in a dream portends good luck so long as it is played or sung in tune; otherwise it means that you will have reason to be discouraged. 095

MUSK. Dreaming of the odor of musk is a forerunner of exciting love affairs. 755

MUSKRAT. To trap or kill muskrats in a dream is a prophecy of want. To wear a coat made of the skins of muskrats is a sign of irritations from a relative who wishes to regulate your life. 383

MUSSEL. It is a sign that you will lead a carefree, contented life if you dream of gathering mussels on the shore. To eat them is a presage of popularity in your social circle. 314

MUSTACHE. For a maiden to dream of kissing a man who wears a mustache is a forerunner of discontent with her surroundings. If a man dreams of shaving off his mustache he will lose a valuable feminine friend. 502

MUSTANG. For a maiden to dream of kissing a man who wears a mustache is a forerunner of discontent with her surroundings. If a man dreams of shaving off his mustache he will lose a valuable feminine friend. 283

MUSTANG. (See Bronco.) 958

MUSTARD. Putting mustard on a sandwich or frankfurter in a dream portends a new interest in which will figure a person of the opposite sex. To see mustard growing predicts happiness in love. 858

MUTINY. If you dream that you are an officer on a ship and the crew mutinies, you are in danger of being accused of double-dealing. Be on guard against those who seek to do you harm. 017

MUTTON. Eating mutton in a dream foretells comfort with one's family. If it is served with caper sauce, the augury is of a celebration. 394

MYRRH. The scent or taste of myrrh in a dream betokens unusual experiences through social contacts. 122

MYRTLE. Young men and women who dream of myrtle trees will have many lovers. 116

MYSTERY. Any dream in which you are introduced to a mystery is a portent of worry over an unimportant matter that will eventually be straightened out. 242

MYTH. You will be fortunate in love if you dream of being a character in one of the great myths of the ages. 133

N

NAGGING. If you have a dream in which someone nags you for something you have done or left undone, the augury is of having to visit either a doctor or a dentist. 735

NAIL. To drive nails in a dream means that you will accomplish a task that you had believed was beyond your powers. 610

NAKEDNESS. To dream of finding yourself naked in a mixed group of dignified people is a portent of being found out in some minor deception of which you have been found guilty. 053

NAME. If in a dream you meet someone whom you know perfectly well and cannot remember his or her name, you will have trouble in explaining your conduct to your family. 612

NAP. To dream of lying down to take a nap during the daytime is an augury of having plenty of money to spend. 087

NAPKIN. Using a napkin in a dream, whether to wipe off your mouth or your hands, indicates that you will complete in a satisfactory manner a job that has been assigned to you. If you fold a napkin, you will receive an invitation to a house to which you have long wished to go. 553

NAPOLEON. If you dream of seeing Napoleon, you are likely to be restless for a long time. If you dream of being Napoleon, you will suffer from the criticism of your fellow men. 912

NARCISSUS. Your friends are likely to make fun of you if you dream of this lovely flower. It is a warning against self esteem. 174

NASTURTIUM. A dream of picking nasturtiums is an augury of meeting with interesting people through whom you will achieve advancement. Eating the stems of nasturtiums in a dream is a sign of pleasant adventure. 459

NAUSEA. Being sick at one's stomach in a dream portends a situation in which you will be suspected of stealing a sum of money. Be on your guard against a frame-up. 874

NAVEL. To dream of having a sore navel indicates that you will visit the scenes of your childhood. To look at your own navel is an omen that you will win the respect of your associates. To look at another's is a sign of a coming adventure. A dream of Buddha contemplating his navel portends a season of excellent luck. 334

NAVIGATION. There will be problems in your life that will be difficult but not impossible to solve if you dream of being the navigating officer of either a ship or an airplane. To dream of studying navigation portends traveling through many parts of the world. 239

NAVY. If you dream of being in the navy, you will have many admirers of the opposite sex. 748

NECK. Dreaming of a pain in the neck is a sign that someone who does not like you will try to make you uncomfortable. Seeing a woman's beautiful neck predicts social advancement; if her neck is thin and scrawny, you will lose money in business. 174

NECKING. It depends on what is in your mind in your dream of necking whether this is a good or a bad portent. Innocent love-making portends happiness in married life, but if the necking is casual, there will be grief in your family. 877

NECKLACE. A woman who dreams of wearing a necklace will meet a distinguished gentleman and spend many happy hours with him. If a man dreams of giving his sweetheart a necklace, he will find that he will be fortunate. 303

NEGRO. To dream of being friends with a Negro is a portent of good luck in business. If you dream of highhatting a Negro, you will be made uncomfortable by your superiors. 043

NEIGHBOR. You are warned against losing your temper too quickly if you quarrel with your neighbors in a dream. If you dream of helping a neighbor who is in any kind of trouble, you will receive a legacy that you never expected. 045

NECROMANCY. (See Magic.) 695

NEON LIGHT. A dream of neon lights of any color predicts that you will be prodigiously bored by the conversation of a new acquaintance. To dream of smashing a neon light is an augury of a rise in salary. 590

NEPHEW. To dream of being asked for money by a nephew forecasts many calm and happy hours among genial companions. 329

NERVE. It is a sign of coming good fortune to dream of having a nerve removed from a tooth by a dentist. To dream of tortured nerves predicts that you will find contentment in your family circle. 748

NEST. Birds building a nest are an augury of marriage to the young and of happiness in home and children to their elders. It is a portent of woe if you dream of stealing a bird's nest, especially if there are eggs in it. 173

NET. Maidens who dream of wearing a net dress must be on their guard when they are being courted by suitors. To use a fishnet in a dream augurs an experience with the opposite sex that you would rather forget. For a man to buy a hairnet for his wife predicts that his family life will be smooth and happy. 877

NETTLE. To dream of being irritated by a nettle is a sign that there will soon be an occasion on which you should assert yourself in no uncertain terms. Stand up for your rights and you will get them. 303

NEURALGIA. Family upsets are predicted if you dream of having an attack of neuralgia. 043

NEWS. (See also Letter.) To dream of receiving news is a sign of good fortune if the news is in any way encouraging; otherwise it portends distress. 845

NEWSPAPER. To buy a newspaper in a dream augurs a surprise, although it may be an unhappy one. To dream of using newspapers as a means of procuring warmth is a sign of good health. 695

NEWSPAPER REPORTER. You will have many petty annoyances if you dream of being interviewed by a newspaper reporter. If the dream is of being a reporter, you will make a success in your business and love life. 590

NEW YEAR. If you dream of seeing the New Year come in, you may look forward to hopeful developments in your career. Gay New Year's eve parties in dreams portend happiness. 056

NICKEL. To hand a nickel to a beggar in a dream is a prophecy of making a lucky turn in business. To drop a nickel into a slot machine portends a disappointment with regard to financial affairs. 261

NICKNAME. For a man to dream of calling his wife by a nickname—or vice versa—predicts happy days in the out of doors. To dream of familiarly addressing a dignified person by a nickname is a sign of great prosperity.

NIGHT-CAP. To dream of wearing a night-cap augurs an altercation with a husband, wife or sweetheart. If you dream of taking an alcoholic drink as a "night-cap" you are sure to be able to relax for a period.

NIGHTINGALE. The song of a nightingale heard in a dream is a happy portent for lovers. For married people it prophesies social advancement.

NIGHTMARE. It is unusual to dream of having a nightmare, but it is not unheard-of. It portends serious trouble of a kind that you have never experienced before.

NIPPLE. If a grown person dreams of taking sustenance through a nipple, the augury is of worry about personal debts.

NOBEL PRIZE. To dream of winning the Nobel Prize is a warning against too great satisfaction with your own achievements.

NOISE. If in a dream one hears noises that do not readily lend themselves to any particular happening, the portent is of having to meet bills of long standing.

NOMINATION. If you dream of being nominated for any sort of office, you will be likely to have a season of difficulties in business and family life.

NOODLES. Dreaming of eating crisp noodles such as those served with chow mein portends a change of address to a quieter location. If the noodles are of the soft variety, you will be enabled to carry out a plan on which you have set your heart.

NORMAL SCHOOL. A girl who dreams of going to normal school is sure to meet the man whom she will marry within a few weeks. If a man should dream of going to normal school, he will be in danger of gossiping tongues.

NORTHERN LIGHTS. If you see this brilliant electrical display in a dream, and the sky shows many bright colors, you are assured of great success in your work.

NOSE. For a man to dream of tweaking a girl's nose is a sign that he will be married within twelve months. If a girl dreams of kissing a young man on the nose, the augury is of trouble with her relatives. Blowing one's nose in a dream predicts relief from the pressure of creditors.

NOSEDIVE. For a person to dream of piloting an airplane and going into a nosedive is a portent of an exceedingly interesting experience with a member of the opposite sex. 348

NOTARY. It is a sign that you will be asked for a contribution to a worthy charity if you dream of taking a document to be attested by a notary. 462

NOUGAT. Eating the candy known as nougat in a dream portends coming in contact with a group of exotic persons whom you will not understand at first and whom you will never quite like. 812

NOVEL. It is bad luck to dream of writing a novel, but to read one is a prophecy of happy hours in congenial company. 870

NOVOCAINE. Having novocaine administered in a dream foretells that you will be given a vacation, but it will be at your own expense. 552

NUDITY. If in a dream of nudity you are aware of the beauty of the human body, it is a sign of happiness for lovers. If it is accompanied by libidinous thoughts, the augury is one of discontent. 693

NUGGET. To find a nugget of gold in a dream augurs a new set of friends and new occupation. 710

NUMBERS. (See chapter "How to Find a Number to Correspond With Your Dream.") 238

NUN. To dream of seeing and talking with nuns is a sign that you will be able to square yourself with the world and your problems. 382

NUPTIAL. (See Marriage.) 479

NURSE. A uniformed and trim looking nurse seen in a dream is a portent of a new source of income. For a man to dream of falling in love with a nurse predicts a lucky break in his business. 003

NURSING. It is good luck in family life to dream of seeing a mother nursing her child. If a young woman dreams of being a trained nurse, she will marry a rich and handsome man. 533

NUT. To crack a nut in a dream augurs success in whatever project you are working on. Eating nuts is a sign that you will be tempted and that you will yield unless you are exceptionally strong willed. 604

NUTMEG. Grinding nutmeg in a dream portends a party at which you will enjoy great popularity because of your joviality. The taste of nutmeg is an omen of missing a date that will cause you great embarrassment. 060

NYMPH. To dream of a nymph wearing a flowing diaphanous robe is a sign of a strange but enjoyable experience in the out-of-doors. 559

O

OAK. Lovers who dream of oak trees may be certain of a long, happily wedded life and a suitable number of healthy children. If oak is used in the construction of a building or furniture, the prediction is sound health, a comfortable income, and more than usual harmony in the family group. 415

OAR. To dream of breaking an oar while rowing is an omen that you will get into trouble that, by using your brains, you can get out of. 879

OASIS. To arrive at an oasis after a hot, tiresome trip across the desert is an augury of great importance to the dreamer, for he may expect forthwith phenomenal success in a new venture quite outside of his usual line of endeavor. 173

OATH. It is a good sign to take an oath in a dream if it is to help an innocent person to escape suffering. 801

OATS. Whether growing in the field or prepared for the breakfast table, oats in one's dream are a prelude to a fortunate and prosperous business season. 711

OBEDIENCE. A dream in which there is a display of obedience to a higher power portends a better understanding with a former enemy. 691

OBELISK. An obelisk in a dream foretells that you will plan a tour of foreign countries, gathering pamphlets and information, and getting advice from those who have traveled, but it is probable that your trip will have to be deferred for some time. 900

OBESITY. If you dream of being too fat, it is a warning against over-indulgence in food and drink. 238

OBLIGATION. To dream of being under an obligation to someone is a sign of distress, but if you are able to meet your obligations, you will be given a long vacation with pay. 989

OBITUARY. To read an obituary in a dream and to be startled by it is a sign that an old friend will have decided to move to a distant city. 666

OBOE. Playing an oboe in your dream, or hearing one played, is a definite warning to be cautious of your eyes and ears. 992

OBSERVATORY. To look out from an observatory and see a beautiful panorama of the countryside is a good omen. You will not only enlarge your business but you will find great content in the friendships you have made. 199

OBSTETRICS. Any dream of the delivery of a child is an augury of good fortune. To dream of assisting a doctor in an obstetrical operation predicts that you will have good luck in whatever projects you engage in that relate to family matters. 635

OCCULT. If you dream of attending a spiritualist meeting or any other gathering of investigators of the occult, you will find that your friends will be likely to criticize you for being over-sensitive. 231

OCEAN. An ocean voyage in your dream denotes an escape from a troublesome person. To swim in the ocean is a portent of an opportunity to relax from your cares and worries. To look on the ocean when it is calm is an augury of prosperity, but if the sea is angry, it foretells business depression. 706

OCULIST. To visit an oculist in your dream is an augury of having to meet a serious situation in your family life. 554

ODOR. A pleasant odor permeating your dream is auspicious, and you will meet no opposition from your lover. A stench is the reverse. You will run into difficulties wherever you go and you will, moreover, be suspected by members of the opposite sex. 257

OFFENSE. To be offended in a dream and show every evidence of resenting the behavior of another means that you are likely to speak in haste and repent at leisure. If you give offense in your dream and are taken to task for it, the portent is that you will lose a friend and make an enemy. 489

OFFERTORY. To dream of being in church as the offertory is being played on the organ is an omen of embarrassment. To dream of forgetting to bring any money with you is a sign that you will be called on to pay the check the next time you are dining at a restaurant. 056

OFFICER. To be bawled out by a traffic officer for some infraction of rules for driving foretells the receipt of a check that will bounce back at you. 472

OGLER. A girl who dreams of being ogled will be likely to have a flirtation with a sailor who is just off a ship. 621

OGRE. If you dream of a terrifying ogre, you are in danger of doing something that will prey on your conscience so that you cannot sleep. 511

OIL. Money in your pocket is foretold by a dream of a rich oil field. To oil machinery is a sign that you will receive commendation for your work. To purchase oil from a roadside service station foretells a telephone call from a sweetheart who is worried about you. To sell or try to dispose of oil is an omen of being approached by someone who will try to get you to cooperate in a crooked deal. 297

OILCLOTH. Bright, new, shiny oilcloth laid upon a table in your dream denotes that you will have a rendezvous with a member of the opposite sex. Guard against any illicit love affairs and you will be happy. 003

OIL PAINTING. A fine oil painting in a heavy gold frame, if it is hung on the wall of your home, is a dream that warns against false pride. Accept the invitation that you will receive, for it may mean that you will meet people who will be able to do you much good. 806

OILSKINS. If you dream of wearing oilskins in a dream, be sure to wait a full week before drawing any money out of your savings account. 173

OINTMENT. The use of ointment in a dream, whether it is rubbed on your own or another's body, is a sign that you are in danger of flattering the wrong person. Be discreet in your dealings with anyone of the opposite sex. 717

OLD-FASHIONED. Dreaming of drinking an old-fashioned cocktail foretells that you will live in a small town and be a member of a select group of people. 650

OLD GLORY. If you dream of seeing Old Glory, the American flag, waving from a flagpole, you will acquit yourself with honor in a difficult task. 966

OLD MAID. To dream of being an old maid is a sign that you will marry a fiery black-eyed musician. 261

OLD TESTAMENT. To read the Old Testament in a dream or hear someone quote passages from it portends a welcome visit from an elderly and well-loved relative. 526

OLIVES. Juicy ripe olives eaten in a dream portend an unexpected experience in kissing. Green olives are a sign of meeting someone of an unusual type. Stuffed olives are a warning against talking with people you do not know. 837

OLIVE OIL. To dream of using olive oil in salad dressing is an omen of falling in love at first sight. Using it for deep frying predicts pleasure in a house party. 942

OMELET. Young people who dream of eating light, fluffy omelets portend a swift courtship that will make the head spin but which will result in a happy marriage. A flat, heavy omelet predicts that you will have to kiss someone as a matter of duty. 309

OMNIBUS. (See Bus.) 612

ONION. (See also Halitosis.) If you dream of peeling this vegetable and shedding oniony tears, you are likely to go to a circus or some other kind of joyous entertainment. To eat boiled onions signifies good health; fried onions indicate the making of an enemy. 028

ONYX. To be given an onyx ring or brooch in your dream foretells that you will change your mind on some important question. To break an onyx table signifies good fortune. 252

OPAL. Contrary to the popular belief that opals portend bad luck, to dream of them is a sign of both prosperity and popularity. 660

OPERA. To dream of going to the opera and enjoying it is a portent of being tempted to deceive a friend. 393

OPERA GLASSES. To gaze through opera glasses at a well-known person in a dream presages meeting a theatrical manager who will prove to be a good friend. Using opera glasses as a peeping Tom is a sign that you will be accused of deception. 981

OPERA HOUSE. If you dream of going into a darkened opera house, wandering about through the aisles and backstage, you will suffer a keen disillusionment through the perfidy of an old acquaintance. 120

OPERATION. You will have an ordeal of some kind to meet if you dream of being operated on by a surgeon. This may be either physical or mental. You should have an understanding with a friend and agree on some sort of procedure. To dream of being a witness to an operation is a portent of the satisfactory completion of an important and difficult job. 547

OPIUM. Opium administered to another or to yourself in a dream warns you against associating with people of loose morals and convivial habits. 071

OPOSSUM. An early celebration of some accomplishment is predicted by a dream of eating this animal roasted. 655

OPTICIAN. To dream of going to an optician for eyeglasses is a portent of worry about the possible loss of your position. It is a good dream, however, for the extra effort you will put forth will insure your keeping it. 119

OPULENCE. (See Money.) 742

ORACLE. To consult an oracle in your dream is a sign that you should not allow yourself to be tied to a woman's apron strings. If the oracle predicts dire happenings, you will find that your fortunes will pick up. 230

ORANGE. Eating an orange in your dream foretells happy days ahead. To pick oranges from the tree is a sign of a love affair that you will never forget or regret. Squeezing an orange and drinking the juice means that you will lead a happy-go-lucky existence. To see oranges graded, sorted and boxed in a packing house is a portent of a slowly increasing income. 059

ORANG-OUTANG. The best advice on a dream about this great ape is: don't dream about him. A ruthlessly cruel person will seek to destroy your credit, your home and your happiness. 589

ORATION. To be bored in a dream by a long and stupid oration is a sign that you will submit to an injustice to save the honor of another person. To deliver a lengthy oration in your dream is an augury of having to make good on an old promise. 604

ORCHARD. Lucky is he who dreams of an orchard in bloom. He will be blessed with a happy home and a full larder. 055

ORCHESTRA. To hear a jazz orchestra in a dream predicts gay times, especially if there is swing music played. A symphony orchestra is a portent of being entertained at a fine home in the suburbs. 449

ORCHIDS. Dreaming of orchids worn as a corsage denotes that you will be accused of extravagance by someone who has no business to do so. To present your lady love with orchids is a sign that you will borrow money to pay the rent. 194

ORGAN. Listening to the strains of organ music in a dream foretells being loved by someone of the opposite sex. If you play the organ, you will be a bridesmaid or best man at a wedding. 322

ORGY. If you dream of being in a drunken orgy, it is a sign that you should be more careful of the company you keep. You are likely to run afoul of the law unless you take great care after this dream. 752

ORIENT. To dream of being in an Oriental country and mingling with the common people is a prophecy that you will try to deceive an associate to further your own interests. You are warned not to yield to the temptation. 382

ORIOLE. These black and gold songbirds foretell a change of abode to a higher altitude. You will live up in the hills or perhaps in a higher apartment than the one you now occupy. 469

ORNAMENT. (See also Decoration.) You will be successful in a selling proposition if you dream of applying ornaments to anything. 490

ORPHAN. To dream that you are a child in an orphanage is a warning against self-pity that will make you tiresome to your friends. If you dream of adopting an orphan, you will be the victim of jealousy from your neighbors. 261

OSTEOPATH. If you are treated by an osteopath in a dream and feel as if your bones are being cracked, you should take special care in crossing streets because an accident is indicated. 414

OSTRICH. An ostrich dream is a good sign, particularly if the great bird kicks you. You will carry a bankroll and have many friends. 604

OTTER. In the water or out, an otter in a dream signifies a period of financial stress. Save now for the future. 014

OTTOMAN. To dream of putting your feet on an ottoman foretells that young people of different foreign origins will visit you and fall in love. 075

OUIJA BOARD. Someone of the opposite sex will divulge a secret that you have shared if you dream of getting messages by means of a ouija board. 021

OUTBOARD MOTOR. If you dream of sailing in a boat with an outboard motor, you will be the victor in a dispute with a disagreeable person. If your outboard motor stalls, it is a sign that you will lose a sum of money. 574

OUTLAW. If you dream of harboring an outlaw, you are likely to be made a tool by an unscrupulous group of persons. To bring an outlaw to justice means that you will have an opportunity to make money. Do not fail to grasp it. 905

OVEN. To use a hot oven for cooking in your dream predicts that you will be made an officer in a church or community organization. A cold oven is a sign of yearning for days and people who can never return. 917

OVERALLS. For a man to dream of wearing overalls is a sign that he will buy a new suit of evening clothes which he will wear to important social functions. Women who dream of wearing overalls will be admired by men in the army or navy. 914

OVERCOAT. It is a sign of upset business conditions to dream of buttoning up your overcoat against an icy wind. To lose an overcoat betokens adversity. 959

OWL. An owl in a dream portends evil, but if the dreamer is able to scare it away, the prophecy is of improved circumstances. To dream of an owl coming into your room predicts a visit to quarreling relatives. 269

OXEN. The simple life is predicted by dreaming of a yoke of oxen, but though you will be poor in the world's goods, you will have many friends. 062

OXYGEN TENT. To dream of being put in an oxygen tent predicts that you will overcome the obstacle that is hindering you most. 135

OYSTER. Eating oysters in a dream shows that you are too modest and self-effacing for your own good. You can overcome this if you always put your best foot forward. To open oysters and eat them from the shell warns against someone who is trying to cheat you. 715

P

PACIFIC OCEAN. To dream of cruising on the Pacific Ocean or of crossing it for the first time is a sign that you will invest in oil stocks. 300

PACKAGE. If you carry a package in your dream, it indicates that you will shoulder a heavy responsibility that should be shared by another member of your family. To wrap up a package carefully denotes the finishing of a job with which you have taken infinite care to bring to a satisfactory conclusion. 235

PADDLE. If you dream of being dextrous with a canoe paddle, you will be able to handle your own affairs with great success. You may be placed in the position of mentor or guardian over young people. 432

PADDLE-WHEEL. To dream of seeing an old boat with a paddle-wheel is a sign that you will venture forth from your home in quest of fortune. You are warned not to take too many chances. 339

PADDOCK. Horses in a paddock attended by their grooms are a dream portent of being able to provide handsomely for your family. 806

PADLOCK. If you dream of trying to open a padlock on a door or chest, your ambitions will be thwarted and you will have a long season of discontent. 497

PAGE. Turning the pages of a book or magazine in your dream indicates that you will make a sound investment and reap a rich reward. To dream of handsome young pages in uniform is a forerunner of better business. 593

PAGEANT. A dream of trying to open a padlock on a door or chest, your ambitions will be thwarted and you will have a long season of discontent. 215

PAGODA. If you see a Chinese pagoda in your dream, it is a sign that you will plant a lovely garden. 459

PAIL. To carry a pail in your dream implies that you will move to a better neighborhood. Shiny milk pails in a row are a portent that you will take a trip and have to make an early start. 509

PAIN. To feel pain in any part of the body in a dream means that someone will try to defame you. Watch your step. 840

PAINT. To see a house being painted in a dream is an augury that someone is keeping news from you that you ought to hear. If you dream of painting anything, you will have to hide something from your best friend. 210

PAINTINGS. To dream of having paintings of your ancestors hung in your home, framed in heavy gilt, is a sign that you will receive a small inheritance from a relative you believed to be hostile to you. 933

PAJAMAS. Luxurious pajamas worn in a dream for the purpose of impressing others foretell a sordid affair with a very common person. Taking your ease in lounging pajamas in the comfort and privacy of your home is a forerunner of a mild flirtation. 981

PAL. Dreaming of having a real pal, one who goes everywhere with you, shares your secrets, and enjoys the things that you like, is a sign that you will have general good luck for a long time to come. 079

PALACE. Living in a dream palace, surrounded by much pomp and ceremony, augurs marriage with a wealthy old person with one foot in the grave. 444

PALETTE. Seeing an artist's palette smeared with colors is a portent that you will be a guest at a tea or cocktail party where there are people who represent all the arts. 137

PALISADES. To dream of seeing beautiful and imposing palisades against a sky brilliant with the colors of sunset is an omen that you will go on a western trip for a visit. 123

PALLBEARER. If you dream of being a pallbearer at a funeral, you will be promoted to a higher position. 468

PALMIST. Having your palm read in a dream presages a period during which you will do considerable worrying about your home life and finances. 344

PALM SUNDAY. To dream of attending church on Palm Sunday dressed in new spring finery is a sign that you will have a religious argument with a well-loved friend. 502

PALM TREE. If in a dream you try to climb a palm tree, you are likely to fail in an enterprise that you have in mind. To cut down a palm tree augurs deceit on the part of one whom you believed to be your friend. 808

PALSY. If you see someone suffering from palsy in your dream, you are likely to outlive your children. 909

PAN. A dream concerning the god Pan is a good omen for young and old of either sex. It foretells that you will bring a sense of humor to bear on your troubles and thereby minimize them. To use a frying pan or other kind of pan used in the kitchen is a sign of coming prosperity. 508

PANAMA HAT. Wearing a Panama hat in a dream indicates that you will be invited to engage in recreations that you cannot afford. 844

PANCAKES. Making pancakes in a dream foretell an invitation to a sumptuous banquet where you will meet worthwhile people. Eating them portends being called upon to make a speech. 155

PANHANDLER. (see Beggar.) 925

PANIC. If you dream of being caught in a panic-stricken crowd, you are warned against losing your temper when your work is criticized by your employer. 231

PANSY. To wear pansies in a corsage or in your buttonhole foretells a dinner date with people who are not quite normal. To pick pansies in a garden is a forerunner of a misunderstanding with a person of the same sex. 497

PANTHER. A panther seen in a dream portends misfortune through a neighbor who is a busybody and a gossip. If you kill the panther or put it to flight, you will make a large sum of money. 039

PANTOMIME. If you dream of watching a pantomime, either on the stage or between two people who cannot talk, you are likely to meet some very interesting people of the stage or screen. 866

PANTRY. Dreaming of a well-stocked pantry means that you will be well loved. You will have a schoolteacher for a visitor if you dream of someone robbing your pantry. 108

PAPER. The broad significance of paper in dreams is of exertion. White paper portends the possibility of success, while colored papers are an omen of wasted effort. Paper that is ready to be thrown out or burned is a sign of new opportunity. 124

PAPOOSE. To see an Indian papoose in your dream is a prophecy of a broken engagement. 079

PAPRIKA. Using paprika to season your food predicts a heated argument with someone of the Latin race. 617

PARABLE. (See Fable.) 434

PARACHUTE. To dream of bailing out from an airplane in a parachute, having difficulty in making it open, means that you will be criticized severely by someone you love. If the parachute opens easily and you float down to a safe landing, you will have a smooth and happy love life. 521

PARADE. You are likely to be elected to public office if you dream of leading a parade. If you are simply one of the rank and file, you will find that relatives will visit you and overstay their welcome. To watch a parade and be thrilled by the music and pageantry is a sign of an increase in income. 022

PARADISE. To dream of being in Paradise, a place more beautiful than you believed possible, in the companionship of charming people, portends a state of both spiritual and material happiness. 715

PARAFFIN. Using paraffin for covering jars of jelly or preserves is a dream that signifies making a call on a new neighbor. If you dream of chewing paraffin, you will make a change in your occupation. To use a paraffin candle indicates that you will receive money. 487

PARALYSIS. Temporary disability is predicted by a dream of being paralyzed. It is a warning to avoid danger so far as possible. 657

PARASOL. For a maiden to dream of carrying a pretty parasol in the bright sunshine is a protent of a love affair at a summer resort. To open a parasol in the house predicts a visit to a savings bank for the purpose of depositing money. 037

PARCEL. To carry parcels in a dream prophesies discontent but eventual success in your work. To receive a parcel by mail or express is a prophecy of profitable ventures. 028

PARCEL POST. To send a package by parcel post in your dream and have to wait in line to have it weighed and stamped is a sign that you will receive a gift from across the water. To receive a parcel post package by insured mail denotes a surprising experience with a person of the opposite sex. 761

PARCHMENT. Dreaming of an ancient and yellowed parchment manuscript presages that you will make a discovery of great value in a bookshop that specializes in first editions. Parchment lampshades portend a release from pain and sorrow. 534

PARENTAGE. A dream concerning doubt as to the parentage of a child augurs quarrels among your family circle. 801

PARIS. If you dream of visiting or living in Paris, you will be likely to find happiness and success in the study of art. To imagine that you are a French resident of Paris, dressed in the latest style, is a sign that you are in danger of making a purchase that will be very extravagant and disappointing as well. 867

PARK. Someone will give you a young puppy if you dream of walking alone in a public park. To dream of a sentimental meeting with a person of the opposite sex in a park is a sign of love affairs that will prove exciting. If flowering trees are in bloom, it foretells marriage. 892

PAROLE. Dreaming of talking with a person of either sex who has been released from prison on parole, and being interested in helping that person, is an indication that you will have an opportunity to do newspaper work. 003

PARROT. To dream of hearing a caged parrot using profane, abusive or disgusting language is a sign that you will have to defend your name against calumny. A group of noisy, squawking parrots foretells having to attend a gathering composed chiefly of women. 601

PARSLEY. Pleasant social relations in your neighborhood are predicted by eating parsley that is used as a garnish. 839

PARSNIPS. Parsnips in a dream portend a broken friendship. If they are the only available food, you are warned against being too easily satisfied. 673

PARSON. If you dream of talking with a parson in his church, you will come under the spell of a foreign missionary. A parson in his shirtsleeves is a sign of being disappointed in a friend. 363

PARTNER. You will be financially successful if you dream of having an agreeable partner, and this relates to marriage as well as business. It portends bad luck if you are suspicious of him or he of you. 720

PARTNERSHIP. To dream of going into a business partnership predicts buying a home and being a power in the community; but to dream of dissolving a partnership augurs misfortune. 272

PARTRIDGE. (See Quail.) 701

PARTY. A dream of going to a party connotes either pleasure or distress, according to the character of the party and its guests. 879

PASSENGER. Being a dream passenger in any wheeled vehicle is a sign of slow but steady improvement in your work. 475

PASSPORT. To dream of going through all the formalities of obtaining a passport predicts travel in foreign lands and a chance to make money as well. Losing a passport is a sign that someone will belittle your best efforts. 152

PASSWORD. Going into some forbidden place by giving a password is a dream that prophesies many new friends. 918

PASTRY. (See also Cake, Pie.) Rich pastries eaten in a dream are a portent of having to miss an important engagement. 221

PASTURE. (See Meadow.) 002

PATCH. To dream of having a patch on the seat of your trousers or on some other conspicuous part of your clothing is an omen of luck in games of chance. A patch worn over an eye predicts adventure in foreign lands. Seeing a patch on a beautiful woman's face is a forerunner of an adventure that you will not tell your grandchildren. 597

PATCHWORK. (See Quilt.) 907

PATENT. To dream of receiving a patent for something you have designed or invented is a sign that you will win at card-playing and the races. 752

PATENT LEATHER. Wearing shoes of patent leather and suffering because they draw the feet is a prediction that you will have to make excuses to a wife, husband or sweetheart. 989

PATENT MEDICINE. Any dream of buying or taking patent medicine is a forecast of getting into a situation that will make you appear ridiculous. 498

PATH. (See also Trail.) To walk down a shady path in your dream is a prediction that you will keep a love tryst. To shovel a path through the snow portends that you will meet people of extraordinary charm. 223

PATIO. To be welcomed into the patio of a Mexican or other Latin-American home and entertained as a guest is a sign that you will be invited to a party where you will meet celebrities of the motion-picture world, artists, writers and dancers. 880

PATTERN. If you dream of seeing fantastic patterns formed with kaleidoscopic colors that change as you watch them, you will have a succession of surprising adventures with a radical person of the opposite sex. They will be diverting, but they are likely to be as dangerous as they are alluring. 547

PAUPER. If you have a dream in which you are a pauper and resort to begging, you are in danger of becoming a very selfish miser. 875

PAVEMENT. Driving a car over a pavement full of depressions and bumps is a sign that you will feel badly because your best friend is more fortunate than you. Resist feelings of envy if you value your peace of mind. 326

PAW. If a dog or cat gives you a paw in a dream, it is a prophecy that someone you do not like will make friendly advances. If a young woman dreams of being "pawed" by a man, she is thereby warned not to engage in conversation with strangers. 893

PAWNBROKER. To go to a pawnbroker in a dream and get a loan on one of your treasured possessions is a sign that you will have an upturn in fortune within a short time. 809

PEA. For a man to dream of shelling peas means that he will meet a dark-haired, blue-eyed woman who will be the means of his climbing high on the ladder of success. A woman who shells peas will have a talkative visitor. To work in a garden of peas signifies that you must apologize to someone for your thoughtlessness. To open a can of peas augurs a family disagreement that will soon be straightened out. 927

PEACE. To dream of a world at peace is a presage of having a spiritual uplift that will help you and others in your daily life. 482

PEACH. Eating ripe peaches in a dream is a portent of a leisurely trip by automobile to the places you have long wished to visit. Green peaches are a sign that unless you right an injustice, you will suffer great regret. 935

PEACOCK. A dream of peacocks strutting about a large estate spreading their beautiful tail feathers fanwise indicates that you will be criticized for your manner toward someone less fortunate than yourself. 557

PEANUT. Eaten from the shell or salted, peanuts in a dream indicate that you will be invited to a party by people whom you have known only a short time. Eating peanut butter is a sign of regret for a white lie you have told. 107

PEAR. Seen in a dream in connection with other fruits, pears foretell a pleasant picnic in the country or in the woods. To eat fresh pears foretells hearing a scandal; canned pears, a church supper. 470

PEARL. New friends of wealth and social position are foretold by a dream of wearing pearls. You may meet one of the nobility or a distant relative of the royal family. 621

PEBBLE. A pebble tossed into water in a dream is a warning against being careless with jewelry when you bathe either at home or on the beach. If you dream of walking barefoot on pebbles, you will have an opportunity for revenge on someone who has misused you. You should weigh the consequences. 572

PECANS. Eating pecan nuts in a dream is an augury of an invitation to a delightful dinner party. 438

PEKINESE DOG. To own or care for a Pekinese dog in your dream is a portent of being complained of by your neighbors for having your radio turned on too loud. 587

PELICAN. To dream of pelicans means that you will be invited to dinner by a friend who has returned from a fishing trip with a full creel. 467

PEN. (See also Fountain Pen.) Dreaming of using a pen that spatters ink on the page is a sign you are in danger of hurting your reputation by associating with a person of doubtful character. 301

PENCIL. Trying to write in a dream with a very blunt, badly sharpened pencil portends being criticized for slovenly dress. To dream of breaking a pencil point while you are writing is a warning to look out for accidents to your person. 946

PENITENTIARY. (See Jail.) 383

PENNY. To give a child a penny in a dream foretells pleasant experiences in the woods and fields. 537

PENSION. If you dream of receiving a pension from a corporation or the government, you will be likely to receive a position doing some kind of manual work that will be both agreeable and profitable. 969

PENTHOUSE. To dream of living in a penthouse from which you have a view over a large area and in which you entertain your friends lavishly is an indication that the next place you live in will be a basement. If you dream of being a house-guest in a penthouse, you are warned against living beyond your means. 011

PEPPER. (See also Cayenne.) To dream of shaking pepper on your food and sneezing because of its pungency is a sign that you are likely to lose your temper in a manner that will bring you regret. 013

PEPPERMINTS. Eating peppermints from a paper bag in a dream is a prophecy that a distant relative will leave you all his money and heirlooms. 545

PERCOLATOR. Dreaming of making coffee with a new percolator signifies that you will move into another house; but if the percolator is old and battered, it means that your present quarters will be re-decorated. 248

PERFUME. For a woman to dream of spraying or dabbing perfume on herself predicts that she will meet a man who will fall in love with her. If a man has this dream, he will be misunderstood by both men and women. To smell a heady perfume is a prophecy of an exciting taxi ride with a person of the opposite sex. Delicate perfume that stirs pleasant emotions foretells meeting a young and beautiful woman. 562

PERISCOPE. To dream of looking through a submarine periscope is a portent of receiving a letter containing news that will cause you great concern. 282

PERMANENT WAVE. Admiring one's own permanent foretells approaching marriage to a maiden and social success to a married woman. To dream of having one's hair waved is a prediction of the receipt of money. 573

PEROXIDE BLOND. A dream of a blond whose hair has obviously been chemically treated is an omen that you will be invited to a dinner party and draw a partner who will bore you stiff. 956

PERSIAN LAMB. To dream of wearing Persian lamb predicts trouble with people in the educational field, either professors, teachers, principals or members of the board of education. 783

PERSIMMON. Eating a persimmon in a dream is an augury of an unexpected holiday. If the persimmon is unripe, you will not have a good time. 334

PERSPIRATION. (See Sweat.) 478

PESSIMIST. It is a sign that your fortunes will improve if you dream of being with a person who looks on the dark side of life. To dream that you are a pessimist is a warning against taking the burdens of the world on your shoulders. 558

PET. (See Cat, Dog, Etc.) 302

PETAL. To pull the petals from a rose or other flower in your dream is a portent of a broken engagement or friendship. 204

PETROL. (See Gasoline.) 384

PETROLEUM. (See Oil.) 670

PETTICOAT. (See Slip.) 551

PETTING. (See also Necking.) Petting an animal in a dream foretells pleasant home affairs. For young people to dream of "petting" is a sign that they must learn to be discreet in their social contacts. 073

PETUNIA. A man who dreams of wearing a petunia in his buttonhole is likely to be disappointed in love. To set out petunias in a flower bed portends an enjoyable party in the near future. 091

PEWTER. You will enjoy the friendship of an older person if you dream of having pewter dishes and utensils in your home. 871

PHANTOM. (See Ghost.) 519

PHARMACIST. (See Druggist.) 231

PHEASANT. To hunt pheasants in a dream foretells that for a short time you will have easy going, but it is also a warning to save your money for a rainy day. Eating roast pheasant portends a new source of income. 305

PHONE. (See Telephone.) 294

PHONOGRAPH. (See also Record.) Hearing your own voice from a phonograph in a dream is a portent of being disillusioned about your ability to impress others. To listen to phonograph music predicts a new kind of adventure that may or may not be agreeable. 353

PHOSPHORESCENCE. It is an augury of a strange and exciting experience to dream of seeing the glow of phosphorous at night upon the sea or in the woods on decaying tree stumps. 418

PHOTOGRAPH. (See also Camera.) To dream of looking over old photographs and renewing your youth thereby predicts that you will meet an old school friend who has made a great success. To see a photograph of a former sweetheart whom you had almost forgotten is a sign of content in your present life. 866

PHYSIC. (See Laxative.) 569

PHYSICIAN. (See Doctor.) 854

PIANO. To dream of being able to play the piano with ease and enjoyment, even if you have never taken lessons, is a forerunner of success in drawing, painting or writing. You will stand a good chance of making your mark as a movie actor or actress if you dream of being a piano tuner. To dream of lifting a piano presages a long period of achievement and good health. To hear an artist play the piano beautifully is a promise of more money in your pay envelope; but if it played out of tune, you are likely to be discharged. 957

PIAZZA. (See Porch.) 424

PICK. (See also Toothpick.) You are likely to have hard going in your work if you dream of using a pick, but in this dream there is a promise of better times if you will persist in trying to better yourself in education. 877

PICKEREL. Catching this kind of fish in a dream augurs an exciting experience with a member of the opposite sex. If a pickerel bites you with his saw teeth, you will have trouble with an acquaintance you had trusted. 651

PICKET. In climbing a fence in a dream, if you get caught on a picket you will have to answer for a minor misdeed. If you dream of picketing a factory or a shop for being unfair to union labor, you will win admiration for the completion of a difficult job. 219

PICKLE. Eating pickles in a dream denotes being satisfied with the state of your health and your bank account. 935

PICKPOCKET. If you dream of catching someone who is picking your pocket, you are likely to have an altercation with a person to whom you owe a sum of money. 657

PICK-UP. A man who dreams of picking up a girl on the street is in danger of severe criticism from his employer. If a girl dreams of being picked up, she will marry in haste and repent all her life. 509

PICNIC. (See also Camp, Frolic.) Dreaming of going on a picnic portends joyous association with friends. 234

PICTURE. (See Motion Picture, Painting, Photograph.) 415

PIDGIN ENGLISH. To hear Pidgin English spoken in a dream is a sure sign that you will travel in Oriental countries. 532

PIE. (See Cake, Pastry.) 491

PIER. (See Quay.) 583

PIG. A dream of pigs in a sty predicts a comfortable home, children, and plenty to eat and drink. 339

PIGEON. To dream of pigeons wheeling through the air is a prophecy of family trouble. Feeding pigeons in a dream portends distractions on account of business conditions. 795

PILE. (See also Hemorrhoids.) To put articles into a pile in a dream is a sign of having to account for an omission of duty. 157

PILGRIMAGE. Dreaming of a pilgrimage to a shrine of some kind portends good luck both in business and social life. 975

PILGRIM FATHERS. You will find that you can enjoy life better after a dream of the austere and unbending Pilgrim Fathers of New England. 881

PILL. To take a pill in a dream is a sign that you will move to a new address. 805

PILLORY. This old-fashioned means of punishment seen in a dream is a forerunner of great embarrassment. If you dream of being pilloried, you will have to pay a debt that you had believed was outlawed. 726

PILLOW. To dream of laying your head in comfort upon a soft pillow is a prophecy that you will not have to worry about your ability to make a living. If the pillow seems hard and uncomfortable you will have difficulty in meeting your just obligations. 550

PILOT. If you dream of being a pilot of either a ship or an airplane, you will be asked for advice by a person who is much older than you are. 720

PIMPLE. Being annoyed by a pimple in a dream augurs difficulties with people to whom you owe money. If you pick a pimple in a dream, you are apt to be ill for some time. 546

PIN. To dream of hearing a pin drop is an augury of contentment. Sitting on a pin prophesies a pleasant surprise. If you dream of pinning up a dress, the augury is of embarrassment at an evening party. 312

PINAFORE. It is a wholly pleasant augury if you dream of seeing little girls who are wearing pinafores. 992

PINCHERS. To dream of trying to make repairs on machinery with a pair of pinchers is a prediction of success in your business. 210

PINCUSHION. A maiden who dreams of making a pincushion for her dressing table will have many invitations to parties from interested men. 177

PINE. A pine tree in a dream is a sign of health and well-being whether it is a large or small one. 644

PINEAPPLE. Love adventures in tropical lands are predicted by a dream of working in a field of pineapples. Drinking the juice portends a successful business career. Eating the fruit is a forerunner of social success. 723

PINE CONE. Long life is presaged by a dream of picking up pine cones in a forest. To burn them portends the birth of a son to one of your friends. 148

PINFEATHERS. To dream of picking pinfeathers off a chicken or other fowl foretells ease and plenty for a housewife and good business for a man. 434

PING-PONG. If you dream of playing a fast game of ping-pong with the odds about even, you will have new responsibilities given you and a corresponding increase in your weekly remuneration. 947

PIN MONEY. A woman who dreams of being given pin money by a husband or lover will be likely to inspire jealousy in one of her acquaintances. 687

PINOCHLE. Good friendship and conviviality in your social circle is predicted by a dream of playing this card game whether you win or lose. 247

PIONEER. To dream of pioneering in an uncultivated country points to success in your chosen work. 228

PIPE. For a man to dream of smoking a pipe augurs eventual success and an adequate income. For a woman to have this dream is an augury of being publicly rebuked for an indiscretion. 864

PIRATE. Armed to the teeth and dressed in eighteenth-century clothes, pirates in a dream portend a motor-car accident. You are warned to exercise great caution. 749

PISTACHIO NUT. To eat this green-colored nut in a dream augurs a loving friend of the opposite sex. A dream of its use as flavoring and coloring for food is a prophecy of social entertaining. 213

PISTOL. (See also Gun, Revolver.) It is bad luck to dream of pointing a pistol at anyone, even if it is only a toy pistol. It prophesies that you will suffer from some physical ailment. To shoot at a target with a pistol foretells success if you score a hit; otherwise failure. 714

Astrology, Horoscope, and Dreams

PITCH. To dream of getting pitch on your hands or your clothing is a sign that unless you select your friends with greater care, you will be involved in a scandal. 922

PITCHER. Pouring from a pitcher in a dream is a sign of plenty. To break a pitcher augurs foot trouble. To piece together a broken pitcher foretells a party where there will be considerable drinking. 579

PITCHFORK. Handling a pitchfork for hay or barnyard uses is a forerunner of good health. To dream of being chased by a devil or a human being holding a pitchfork augurs worry over money affairs. 302

PITH HELMET. You will visit a tropical country if you dream of wearing a pith helmet. 584

PITY. If you pity another in a dream, you will have to share your home with an in-law. If someone pities you, the omen is good for business. 353

PLACER MINING. This form of mining by the playing of a stream of water to loosen the ore in a hill portends new expenses that will be difficult but not impossible to meet. 710

PLAGUE. To dream of a terrible plague visiting the city or community in which you live is a sign that you should have a physician check up on your health. 218

PLAID. Wearing plaid materials in a dream means that an old and trusted friend will visit you and make you much happier than you have recently been. To see a Scotch highlander in a plaid kilt is a sign of a whirlwind love affair. 324

PLAN. To dream of going over the plan of your house with an architect or contractor is a forerunner of getting some new and becoming clothes. If you dream of drawing your own plans, you are likely to be cheated in a land deal. 156

PLANE. (See Airplane.) 483

PLANK. To dream of walking on a plank predicts that you will be in danger of being robbed. If the dream is of being made to "walk the plank" by pirates, you must also guard against personal injury. 749

PLASTER. Mixing plaster in a dream foretells a lucky break with a lottery ticket. Applying it to a wall is an omen of continued prosperity. 832

PLATE. (See Dishes.) 173

PLATE GLASS. If you dream of passing a plate glass window and seeing your reflection in it, you should be warned against flirtations. To break a plate glass window is a sign of your having to relieve somebody's distress. 803

PLATFORM. You will be called upon to make a public address if you dream of standing on a platform. You may have an offer from a lecture manager from across the pond. 688

PLATINUM. For a maiden to dream that, she will meet the man of her choice and that he will lead her shortly to the alter. To lose a platinum ring is an omen of having to apologize for forgetting an important duty. 270

PLAY. Seeing a play in your dream is a good portent if it gives you enjoyment but if it is sad or disagreeable, you will be dunned by your creditors. 810

PLAYER. (See Actor.) 798

PLAYGROUND. To dream of happy, noisy children in a playground forecasts a vacation with an old school friend. 368

PLAYING CARDS. (See also Cards.) If you dream of playing cards, you will have a falling out with the one you love best. This interpretation holds whether you win or lose; but if you dream of winning, you will have good fortune with regard to money affairs. 797

PLAYMATE. You will receive an important and interesting communication in regard to property if you dream of an old playmate of childhood. 653

PLEDGE. If you make a pledge in a dream, you will have to sacrifice one of your treasured possessions to help out a relative. 571

PLOT. Bad luck in a variety of ways will follow if you dream of being a party to a plot to injure another. If you discover a plot against yourself you will be able to pay your debts and save money. 284

PLOW. To use a plow drawn by horses or mules foretells slow but sure progress in business and love. A tractor plow augurs a lucky turn in real estate. 138

PLUM. Eating a fresh plum in a dream and having the juice trickle down your chin indicates that you will be appointed to a position of honor. Canned plums augur a disappointment. Plum pudding is a sign of danger from gossip. 672

PLUMBING. Bright new chromium plated plumbing seen and used in a dream forecasts leisure and the means to take a short pleasure trip. Old leaky plumbing portends great irritation from nagging relatives. 431

PNEUMONIA. There will be difficult times ahead if you dream of having this disease, but you can make your own destiny by avoiding any course of which your better judgment would disapprove. It is a particular warning to guard your health. 258

POCKET. A dream of being surprised at what you find in your pocket is a promise of an easy-going mate who will bear with you in your peculiarities and shortcomings. A dream of having a hole in a coat pocket predicts loss of prestige among your neighborhood group. 631

POCKETBOOK. If a man dreams of looking through a woman's pocketbook and finding a great variety of articles, he will be confronted with a problem he cannot solve. For anyone to dream of having a pocketbook full of money means that an increase in salary is on the way. 002

POEM. To dream of writing a poem that pleases you is a sign that you will be approached by a motion-picture concern to do special character parts. Reading another's poem in a dream portends popularity among church members. 257

POET. If you dream of being on friendly terms with a poet, one of your friends will ask you for a loan or will suggest coming to live with you. A poet with long hair signifies unusual experiences. 179

POINTER. Good news may be confidently expected after a dream of seeing a pointer in the hunting field. 394

POISON. A dream of taking posion portends that someone will ridicule you for your strange views on behavior. To dream of poisoning an animal signifies distressing events in your family life. 040

POISON IVY. Suffering in a dream from contact with poison ivy is a forerunner of misunderstandings with a very good friend of the opposite sex. 724

POKER. A game of poker played in a dream foretells pleasant relaxation with good friends. The augury is much the same whether you win or lose. Using a fire poker to chase an animal or robber is a sign that you will have to explain an ill-advised action. 518

POLAR BEAR. Seen in a zoo, a polar bear portends misery from the loss of treasured possessions, but if you dream of seeing it in its native habitat of ice and snow, it is an omen of improved living conditions for yourself and family. 477

POLECAT. (See Skunk.) 060

POLICE. It is good luck to dream of the police unless you are trying to escape from them. To stop and ask directions from a traffic officer portends a visit to wealthy friends. To be stopped by a traffic officer for some minor infraction of the law predicts that you will apologize to some friend. 794

POLICE DOG. To dream of being attacked by a police dog is a forerunner of being called upon to contribute to a cause in which you do not believe. A friendly police dog is a good augury for people who enjoy outdoor sports. 681

POLICY. If certain numbers recur in your dreams, it is a sign that you will be fortunate in playing policy and other games of chance. 098

POLITENESS. (See Courtesy.) 121

POLITICS. Talking politics in your dream is a sign of success in business if the conversation is between members of the same sex and there is no bitterness in it. It is bad luck for a man to talk politics with a woman, or vice-versa. Listening to a political speech during a campaign betokens a row with your in-laws. Making a speech of this kind is a sign that you will receive a small sum of money. 416

POLKA. It is a prediction of good times in the company of quiet, well-bred people to dream of dancing the polka or of watching other people dance it. 840

POLO. You will be remembered in some wealthy person's will if you dream of playing polo or watching others play. 376

POLYGAMY. To dream of having several wives is a sure sign of worries and regrets. 849

POMEGRANATE. To pick and eat the seeds of a pomegranate in a dream augurs pleasant hours in the company of one of the opposite sex. 975

POMPADOUR. Wearing your hair a la pompadour in a dream foretells a light adventure with a member of the opposite sex. 488

PONCHO. If you dream of putting a poncho over your head to keep off the rain or to keep you warm, the augury is of someone coming to your aid in time of great need. 072

POND. (See also Lake.) A clear pond in which there are swans portends wealth through industry. To see the reflections of trees and clouds in a pond indicates that you will develop a genius for addressing audiences. A muddy pond seen in a dream is a sign of a hilarious time with professional people. 351

PONIARD. (See Dagger.) 509

PONY. (See Filly, Horse.) 552

POODLE. You will have amusing experiences in business if you dream of seeing a French poodle clipped according to the fashion for these dogs. 377

POOL. A pool in a garden in which are growing water lilies, lotus and other aquatic plants is a harbinger of contentment for lovers. To play pool in a dream predicts that you will acquire much skill in reading character. 804

POOP. To dream of standing on the raised deck in the stern of a vessel is a splendid augury in almost any circumstances. 176

POPCORN. Eating fresh, white crisp popcorn in a dream portends money, leisure and enjoyment of life. If it is limp and stale and full of unpopped kernels, you are likely to be disagreeably surprised by a letter that you will receive. 683

POPGUN. Shooting a toy gun in a dream and making only a loud pop warns you that someone will make a derogatory remark about your personality. Check up on your personal faults. 128

POPLAR. Bending before a stiff breeze, poplar trees in a dream are an indication of adventures with people who value neither their lives nor their reputations. Cutting down a poplar augurs temporary financial embarrassment. To plant one is a sign of good returns on a small investment. 210

POPPY. A short but passionate love affair is predicted by a dream of red poppies in a garden. California poppies in a field are an augury of sentimental delight. To dream of picking poppies betokens disappointment. 139

PORCELAIN. Fine, dainty porcelain, whether new or old, seen or used in a dream foretells meeting people of social importance under pleasant circumstances. To break a porcelain dish augurs making a good friend. 315

PORCH. Maidens who dream of sitting on a porch with a young man will have a proposal within a short time, but they should not be too quick to accept it. Anyone who dreams of sleeping on a porch will have to explain the reason for what appears to be a definitely crazy act. 821

PORCUPINE. You will be advanced in your position if you dream of being stuck by quills on a porcupine, but you will have a serious argument with one of your friends. 756

PORK. In any form—fresh, salted or smoked—a dream of eating pork foretells that you will obtain a better job, either with the same employer or a different one. You will need it, however, for you will have added responsibilities. 981

PORRIDGE. Cooking or eating porridge in a dream is a good augury for the unmarried, for it predicts many friends among both sexes. 885

PORT. Dreaming that you drink port wine foretells that you will entertain your friends with your sparkling conversation and behavior. Reaching a port in a sailing vessel or steamship augurs the successful completion of a pet project. 418

PORTER. To have a porter carry your luggage in a dream is an omen of going on a trip that will add to your success. To dream of drinking porter predicts better health. 483

PORTFOLIO. If you dream of carrying a portfolio, you will be asked for advice by an important and influential personage. This is a dream that suggests that you try to improve your mind through study and reading of the newspapers. 851

PORTHOLE. To dream of looking through the porthole of a ship and seeing another ship is a sign of approaching adventure in which you will meet a friend whom you have not seen in years. 688

PORTRAIT. Having your portrait made in a dream, either by photography or painting, is a sign of disillusionment. To see another person posing for a portrait portends being invited to a select social gathering. 211

POSTAGE. (See Stamp.) 187

POSTCARD. Writing a message on a postcard in a dream foretells being accused of an indiscretion. To dream of receiving a postcard written in fine handwriting that is hard to decipher is a prediction of being harassed by debt. 694

POSTERIOR. (See Buttocks.) 862

POSTMAN. To dream of receiving mail matter from a postman—letters, circulars or parcels—augurs the receipt of good news from an old friend. 126

POSTPONEMENT. To dream of the postponement of your wedding prophesies a long trip by airplane. Postponing an outdoor event on account of rain presages bad weather and a delayed vacation. 831

POT. Whether of crockery or metal, a pot in a dream forecasts an upset condition of mind from which you should make a determined effort to get away. To break a pot augurs grief through the lack of consideration of one of your friends. 555

POTATO. Peace of mind and a comfortable income are predicted by a dream of eating potatoes in any form. Hoeing in a potato field is a sign of a lucky business deal. 871

POTTER. To dream of a potter fashioning a vase on a revolving potter's wheel is an omen of meeting someone who will become a true friend and who will have a good influence over you. 691

POTTERY. Dreaming of fine pottery in a shop or home portends the beginning of a new order of things in which you will be able to live the kind of life to which you have aspired. 816

POULTICE. Applying a poultice in a dream portends the development of an idea that will bring you riches. 407

POUT. Dreaming of a pretty girl with a pout on her face is a sign of having to break an engagement of long standing. 285

POVERTY. A dream of poverty is unlucky only if it is accompanied by dirt or degradation. Otherwise it is a forerunner of better times. 121

POWDER. A man who dreams of seeing his sweetheart or wife powdering her nose in a public place is warned against women who are both vain and lacking in the niceties of behavior. A woman who dreams of dropping a box of face powder on the floor will have a series of minor accidents that will keep her in a state of turmoil. 974

PRAIRIE. Being alone on a great flat prairie in a dream is a prophecy of having a struggle with your conscience. 126

PRAISE. If you dream of being praised for your accomplishments, you will find a new and profitable interest in life. 106

PRANK. To dream of playing a prank on a friend is a sign of having to account for something you have left undone. If you are the victim of a prank and take it good-naturedly, you will be likely to have an honor conferred on you. If you show irritation in your dream, prepare for family troubles. 711

PRAYER. A dream of praying for Divine guidance or help augurs good fortune in both your spiritual and material condition. To listen to the prayer of another, especially a child, is a forerunner of making a friend who will remain faithful through life. 089

PREACHING. (See Sermon.) 749

PREDICTION. If you dream of making a prediction and of its coming true, you are likely to find that people will begin to ask your advice on all sorts of matters. 031

PREFACE. Reading a book's preface in a dream is a sign that you will shortly begin a new and successful project. 176

PREGNANCY. For a woman to dream that she is pregnant foretells that she will have the means to buy many new pretty clothes. If a man should have this dream, it augurs an adventure in which there will be considerable danger. 318

PRESCRIPTION. Having a prescription filled by a druggist in a dream is a sign that you will have an illness that will be the result of your own carelessness. 863

PRESENT. To receive a present in a dream foretells good luck in gambling; to give one, the receipt of money by mail. 319

PRESENTIMENT. Having a presentiment of death in a dream is a sign that you should take especial care not to do anything involving risk. 654

PRESERVES. A woman who dreams of making preserves in her kitchen will be invited to become a member of a prominent woman's organization. Eating preserves is a fortunate dream for those connected with the grocery business. 371

PRESTIDIGITATOR. (See Magic.) 484

PREVARICATION. (See Lie.) 887

PRICK. Giving your finger a prick in a dream is a portent of what will appear to be supernatural happenings. If blood is drawn, there will be general misunderstandings and matters that will cause you perturbation. 163

PRICKLY HEAT. A dream of having prickly heat forecasts a major operation for yourself or one of your friends. 980

PRIEST. Whatever the denomination, a priest in a dream is usually a good sign. 986

PRIMA DONNA. To dream of meeting socially a prima donna of the dramatic or operatic stage prophesies a succession of adventures with a glittering circle of people. To see her perform on the stage predicts an escapade that will make you a little ashamed of yourself. 214

PRIMER. To dream of seeing a child reading out of a primer is a sign that you will take up the study of a new language. If you dream that the child is yourself, you will have happy adventures. 918

PRIMROSE. A dream of sending a primrose plant to a person of the opposite sex is a forerunner of a love affair that is not likely to turn out happily. 212

PRINCE. A woman, young or old, spinster or wife, who dreams of meeting a prince at a social function will find that she will have increasing influence in her community, but she should guard against arousing jealousy among other women. 565

PRINCESS. The interpretation for this dream is for a man, and is a parallel to that in the preceding. 899

PRINTING. A person who dreams of being in the printing business or trade will be received in the best society and much respected for being well-informed on most subjects. It is a fortunate dream for those who aspire to write magazine articles and books. 147

PRISON. (See Jail.) 201

PRIVACY. A dream of having your privacy invaded by a person of the opposite sex predicts a happening that will be upsetting but amusing. 799

PRIVET HEDGE. (See Hedge.) 349

PRIVY. To dream of an old-fashioned country privy foretells the inheritance of property but litigation with other claimants for it. You may or may not finally receive it; but if you do, it will be of much less value because of lawyers' fees and other legal expenses. 644

PRIZE. To dream of being awarded a prize in any kind of a contest indicates that you will be successful in your work. If you give someone a prize in a dream, you will be left a small legacy by a friend who has passed on. 835

PRIZE-FIGHTER. For a young woman to dream of being wooed by a prize-fighter is a prophecy of quarrels with her suitor. If she dreams of seeing him go down for the count in the prize ring, it means that she will be married within a month. If a man dreams of being a prize-fighter, he will have a raise in salary before long, 593

PROCESSION. (See Parade.) 050

PRODIGAL. If you dream of the Biblical story of the Prodigal Son, you will have an opportunity to forgive an enemy and thereby make a friend. 723

PRODIGY. A dream of a very young person who is accomplished far beyond his or her years—such as a violinist, pianist, or other kind of musician or artist—points toward your being bored by the people with whom you mingle every day. 434

PROFANITY. Hearing profanity from a man in a dream portends a drop in the value of your securities and real estate holdings. If the swearing is done by a woman, you are going to have an embarrassing experience with one of the opposite sex, and if you are not careful it will develop into something quite serious. 669

PROFIT. If you dream of making a business deal and thereby turning a profit, you are warned to keep your counsel during the following few weeks. 017

PROHIBITION. To dream that prohibition is in force in your country or state is a sign that you will be taken to task by an officer of the law. 244

PROMISSORY NOTE. If in a dream you have a note coming due and have no resources with which to meet it, you are warned against over-extravagance in spending. To dream of meeting a note when it is due augurs success in business and a good income. 157

PROPAGANDA. Trying to influence public opinion in favor of or against certain things is a dream that predicts a lack of trust on the part of your acquaintances. If it appears to be in wartime, you will be falsely accused of irregularities in the conduct of your business. 048

PROPELLER. It is a sign that you will fail in work that has been given you to do if you dream of being on a boat that has lost its propeller. 628

PROPOSAL. A maiden or widow who dreams of having a proposal from an eligible man will be given much attention by men older than they will admit. A man who dreams of proposing will have increased power of making money; but if he is rejected he will spend everything he gets. 660

PROSTITUTE. If the prostitute of whom you dream is an object to inspire sympathy, the augury is of success as a worker for the downtrodden. If she is brazen and unscrupulous, you will suffer a short illness. 410

PRUDE. (See also Plum.) Dried prunes eaten in a dream signify a change of address. Stewed prunes predict better health than you have enjoyed for years. 730

PTOMAINE POISONING. To dream of suffering from ptomaine poisoning is a direct warning against gluttony, especially in restaurants and other public eating places. 393

PUBLISHER. For a man or woman to dream of meeting a publisher is a sign that unless he or she is very careful, there will be a loss of money sustained. To dream of signing a contract with a publisher is an augury of great wealth. 421

PUDDING. Eating pudding in a dream is an indication that you will have a proserous but uneventful life. If it is plum pudding, however, there will be many ups and downs. 830

PUDDLE. It is a sign that you will have a disagreeable experience if you dream of being splashed by muddy water from a puddle. 838

PUKE. (See Vomit.) 422

PULLMAN CAR. Riding in a Pullman car in a dream is a forerunner of prosperity and time for travel to places you have never seen. The augury is similar whether the Pullman is a chair car, sleeper, diner or observation car. 715

PULPIT. You will be suspected of double-dealing if you dream of delivering a sermon from a pulpit. 825

PULSE. To dream of feeling the wrist pulse of a sick woman warns of being too confidential with people whom you have met recently. If in a dream your own pulse quickens either at emotion or danger, you will find that there will be a new interest in your life. 559

PUMP. Drawing water from a pump in a dream is a sign of a successful career in banking lines. To push a pump handle back and forth without getting any water predicts disappointment in a business deal. To find a pump frozen up means that you will have to work hard for little money. To prime a pump portends temporary prosperity. 474

PUMPERNICKEL. Eating pumpernickel in a dream foretells the ability to buy a new automobile and new and fashionable clothes. 983

PUMPKIN. You will have a smooth and happy family life if in your dream you eat pumpkin in any form. To see yellow pumpkins at harvest time in a cornfield predicts a season of plenty and comfort. 075

PUN. To dream of making a pun that amuses you but offends others foretells the loss of a friend. 314

PUNCTURE. If you dream of being without a spare tire and having a puncture, you will go a long time in your automobile without having an accident. Trying to repair a puncture in a dream is a prophecy of an argument with husband, wife or sweetheart. 981

PUPPY. It is a good portent for married people to dream of having one or more puppies playing on the floor. To dream of a dead puppy foretells sorrow. 995

PURGE. (See also Laxative.) To dream of a purge in the sense of killing politically undesirable people by a despotic government points toward a situation in which you will be called upon to save a relative or friend from disgrace. 893

PURSE. (See Pocketbook.) 302

PUS. Dreaming of a wound from which pus is issuing foretells an accident from which you are likely to carry scars for the rest of your life. 643

PUSHBUTTON. Pressing a pushbutton in a dream and hearing a bell ring in the deep recesses of the house portends a surprise that will probably be pleasant. 775

PUTTY. You will be able to influence your business associates if you dream of moulding putty with your hands. To use it in putting a pane of glass in a window augurs satisfaction through a business deal. 028

PYGMY. (See also Midget.) These small denizens of the jungle seen in a dream are a prophecy of distress through the suspicion of your best friend. This is true whether they are hostile or friendly. 072

PYRAMID. A dream of an Egyptian pyramid foretells travel to eastern countries, but if the pyramid appears to be inverted and resting on its apex, you will lose your money and have to live with relatives. 367

PYTHON. To dream of this large boa-like serpent is a sign that someone will try to intimidate you. Hold your ground and you will win out. 911

Q

QUACK. To dream of finding out that you have asked the advice of a quack doctor is a portent of better health. 358

QUADRILLE. You will go to a rather stupid party and be thoroughly bored if you dream of dancing in a quadrille. 114

QUAGMIRE. (See Mire.) 911

QUAIL. If you flush a covey of quail in a dream, you are likely to have a surprising and altogether agreeable experience. To dream of eating quail predicts an increase in your income and greater comforts in your daily life. 273

QUAKER. Peace and comfort will be your daily lot if you dream of associating with Quakers. 097

QUARANTINE. Being held in quarantine in a dream augurs misery unless you can show a clean bill of health. 830

QUARREL. For a girl to dream of quarreling with her suitor is an omen of an early marriage. A man who dreams of quarreling with a woman will come off second best in an argument with his boss. A dream of quarreling with your neighbors portends travel by bus. A family quarrel foretells that you will move to other living quarters. 163

QUARRY. If you dream of working in a quarry, getting out pieces of rock, you will have to work hard for a meager living. 709

QUARTETTE. To dream of singing in a quartette denotes a lessening of influence with people whom you formerly controlled. 170

QUARTZ. To find a beautiful piece of quartz in a dream is an augury that someone will try to cheat you. You must be alert to everything that is going on or you will lose money. 921

QUAY. You will go on a vacation trip to foreign shores if you dream of seeing ships lying alongside a quay. 834

QUEEN. If a woman dreams that she is a queen and inspires awe and reverence among her subjects, she is in great danger of being asked for money that she owes. To dream of kneeling before a queen is an omen of promotion to a better job; but if you kiss her hand you will be the victim of office or church politics. Seeing a queen go by in a carriage or automobile signifies honor, happiness and prosperity. 440

QUEST. (See Searchlight.) 798

QUESTION. In general, it is good luck to ask questions in a dream; but if someone questions you and you are unable to answer, the augury is not propitious. 213

QUESTIONNAIRE. Petty irritations are foretold by a dream of replying to a long list of questions in a questionnaire. 090

QUEUE. To dream of standing in a queue in front of a theatre or other place of amusement portends a disappointment. To see a Chinaman wearing a queue is a sign of approaching good luck. 667

QUICK. You will hear disparaging remarks about yourself if you dream of cutting a fingernail or toenail down to the quick. 075

QUICKSAND. A dream of sinking in quicksand is a sharp warning against prying into the affairs of other people. To help another out of quicksand foretells increasing income. 536

QUIET. If you dream of being in an absolutely quiet place, you are likely to undergo some nervous shock. A sudden change from a noisy to a quiet place is a portent of a trip. 668

QUILL. Plucking a quill from a bird of any kind foretells the writing of an important letter that will bring you luck. 770

QUILT. To dream of covering yourself with a patchwork quilt predicts a reunion with several members of your family. A down quilt is a sign that you will soon be able to afford more luxury. 696

QUINCE. Someone will accuse you of being stupid if you dream of eating ripe quinces. Jelly made from this fruit portends meeting a person whom you will not understand. 988

QUININE. Taking this medicine in a dream is a sign to engaged couples that their ardor will cool sooner or later. If the bitter taste is apparent, there will be a sharp quarrel and a broken engagement. 085

QUINSY. You will lose an important argument if you dream of having an attack of quinsy sore throat. 751

QUINTUPLETS. It is a favorable augury to dream of seeing a group of quintuplets of any age or sex. An early marriage is predicted to lovers and a happy home life to those who are married. It is a portent of obstacles overcome for a woman to dream of giving birth to quintuplets. 804

QUIP. You will meet a new and interesting person if you dream of making a clever quip. To hear one made signifies that you will be invited to a gay party. 560

QUIRT. A disagreeable argument with a traffic officer is prophesied by a dream of carrying a quirt. 370

QUIVER. You must make up your mind to avoid alcoholic liquors if you dream of a quivering face. A quiver full of arrows is a portent that if you pay a little more attention to your job, your salary will be raised. 156

QUIZ. If you dream of answering questions in a quiz, the augury is good or bad according to whether you give the right or wrong answers. 875

QUOITS. If you dream of answering questions in a quiz, the augury is good or bad according to whether you give the right or wrong answers. 897

QUOITS. Young people who dream of playing quoits will have delightful love affairs. To get a "ringer" in a dream predicts an early marriage and a long honeymoon.

QUOTATION. Hearing well-known quotations in your dream—such as lines from Shakespeare, maxims from the Bible and similar sources—predicts success in literature, art, music and the drama.

R

RABBI. If you are of the Jewish faith and dream of consulting a rabbi, you will be prosperous in business. If you are of another faith, you will make a new friend who will help you toward the goal you have set for yourself. 818

RABBIT. Many rabbits seen in a dream signify that you will have several children who will be a credit to you. To go rabbit hunting predicts meeting an interesting person of the opposite sex on a trip by bus, rail or plane. To wear a rabbit fur coat is a sign that you will be able to wear mink. 477

RABIES. If in a dream a mad dog attacks you and you get the rabies, it is an indication that you have an unsuspected enemy who is talking behind your back. 416

RACCOON. Raccoons seen in their native haunts foretell the purchase of a new saddle horse. To go on a 'coon hunt is a sign of good crops for the farmer and good business in general. To wear a raccoon coat is a sign that you will go further with your education. 833

RACE. To watch a race being run—on foot, horseback, in an automobile or airplane—is a fortunate augury if you win money on the result. Lovers will come together in a happy marriage, and important business deals will be consummated. If you dream of running in a footrace, you will have a new position offered to you whether you win or lose. To dream of hating any race other than your own augurs bad luck in your business or social life. 244

RACKET. Hearing a loud racket in your dreams is a sign that you will be criticized for talking out of turn. To dream of playing tennis with a racket portends an argument that will cause ill feelings. 409

RACKETEER. Be on your guard against false friends after a dream of being made a proposition by a racketeer. You will be tempted to do something against your better judgment. If you are threatened with physical harm by a racketeer, you are likely to suffer an illness. 670

RADIATOR. Dreaming of a radiator that is hissing and pounding with steam is a sign that there will be an attempt at blackmail. Be warned not to do anything to warrant it. A cold radiator betokens regret for thoughtlessness. If you dream of your car radiator boiling, there will be difficulties to smooth out in your love life. 055

RADIO. To dream of hearing a radio playing gently in your dream is a portent of peaceful days spent at home with your family, among your books and hobbies. A blaring radio that annoys others foretells an attack of rheumatism or arthritis. 043

RADISH. If you eat a radish in your dream, you will be flattered by a designing person of the opposite sex. 738

RADIUM. Handling a particle of radium in your dream is a sign that you will acquire a large amount of money but that it will give you little happiness. If you dream that it burns you, you are warned against motor-car accidents. 984

RAFFLE. Winning a raffled article in a dream foretells luck in bingo, sckeeno, or bank night. 761

RAFT. To dream of floating on a raft on a slow-moving, sluggish river indicates that your indolence is causing you to fall behind in the procession of life. If in your dream you build a raft and launch it on swift, bright waters, you will have reason to feel encouraged about the future. 877

RAG. Dirty rags in a corner indicate the probability of illness. To fold clean rags and put them away for use in cleaning is a dream that portends a prosperous season. Ragged clothes worn in a dream are a sign that you are on the verge of receiving a legacy. 001

RAGE. If you dream that you fall into a rage and are so beside yourself with temper that you are ready to go to any lengths to be revenged on one or more individuals, it is a sign that you will be snubbed by someone whose favor you would like to enjoy. To dream of trying to pacify another person who is in a rage foretells that you will have hard luck in the work you are doing. 972

RAID. To dream of being in a city that is being raided by enemy airplanes portends the loss of property. If you dream of making a raid, you will make a small sum of money outside your regular income. 475

RAILWAY. Riding on a railway in a dream foretells that you will find a new and pleasant hobby. To dream of seeing a streamlined railway train whiz by you indicates that someone will help you get out of a tight place. 012

RAIN. To be out in the rain and drenched to the skin in your dream foretells a cool reception from the person you

Astrology, Horoscope, and Dreams

love. To watch the rain from indoors or other sheltered spot predicts a disappointment in business. 312

RAINBOW. You may chase rainbows even in your dreams. You may search for the pot of gold at the foot of the rainbow, and the interpretation is ever the same—trouble of various kinds, followed by the greatest happiness that you have ever known. 846

RAISIN. To eat raisins in a dream foretells that you will develop strength of character that will stand you in good stead when you are tempted to go wrong. 582

RAKE. To dream of using a rake on the lawn or in the garden is an omen that you and your family are due for a good time together. To step on a rake and have the handle come up and hit you is a sign of an approaching agreeable surprise. 923

RAM. If you dream of being chased or butted by a ram, it is time that you thought of giving up loose companions with whom you have been associating. 920

RANCH. If you dream of owning and living on a western ranch, you will make many new friends in the show business and newspaper circles. Being a guest at a dude ranch in a dream is a sign of getting into trouble through repeating an accusation that you have heard. 750

RANGER. A fit of homesickness is portended by a dream of seeing forest rangers at work. 562

RANSOM. To be held for ransom in a dream portends the receipt of a large sum of money from someone who has wronged you and wishes to make amends. 698

RAPE. A dream of rape in any form is a warning to anyone to avoid the appearance of evil. 623

RASPBERRY. Seen on the bush in a dream, raspberries foretell a day of leisure; eaten from a dish, they are an omen of a day of pleasure. 851

RAT. Sickness of an epidemic nature is foretold by a dream of rats. It is a warning to avoid crowds and to guard your health. 675

RATTLE. You will sit at the head of your own table if you dream of a baby's rattle. A rattle in your automobile that is hard to locate predicts worry for the safety of your relatives. 727

RATTLESNAKE. A warning against people whom you do not trust is contained in a dream of encountering a rattlesnake; you will likely suffer a severe illness if it bites you. 379

RAT TRAP. To set a rat trap in a dream foretells release from a menace that you have feared. To dream of catching a rat in a trap is an omen of better fortune. 519

RAVEN. (See Crow.) 565

RAVIOLI. Eating ravioli in an Italian restaurant foretells that you will meet a family of foreigners who are in some way connected with army or navy life. 200

RAZOR. If you dream of using the old type of razor with an unguarded blade for shaving, it presages a meeting with an old-fashioned girl. To shave with a safety razor in a dream portends winning esteem from your employer through your close attention to work. If you cut yourself with either type of razor, you will have to answer for a misdeed that you did not expect to be discovered. To dream of fighting and slashing with a razor portends years of poverty. 867

READING. Reading aloud from a magazine or newspaper in a dream is a portent of meeting a rich man who will help you to succeed. Reading a book foretells comfort. Reading in a dream is always a good sign, unless it is bad news. Reading books foretells peace of mind in the home life. 087

REAL ESTATE. A dream concerning the purchase or sale of real estate predicts an inheritance of both money and securities. 137

RECEPTION. To attend a reception, large or small, in a dream indicates that you will be asked to make a speech before a church or school gathering. To dream of giving a reception is a portent of being received into the social group that is of greatest interest to you. 548

RECIPE. Exchanging recipes in a dream is a sign that you will receive a valuable gift in return for a favor you have done. 785

RECORD. If you dream of playing records on a phonograph, it indicates that you will reach a position of honor. To keep a record of your daily movements, expenses, etc., predicts good fortune, but if you lock them up in a chest or closet, you will unearth a family skeleton. 368

RED. If red is the outstanding color in your dream, it will have a disturbing influence. 941

RED CROSS. To dream of seeing Red Cross nurses in action during a war or other disaster is a forerunner of your being called upon to relieve the distress of one of your family or friends. 570

REDHEAD. If a man dreams of a red-headed girl he will be in danger from indiscreet actions. A woman who dreams of a red-headed man will have a quarrel. 587

REFORMATORY. A dream of being sent to a reformatory for either boys or girls is a warning to avoid low companions. 293

REFRIGERATOR. Putting food away in an electric refrigerator is a sign that you will be prosperous and that you will give many popular parties. To take food out of one portends a visitor who will stay a long time. 225

REFUGEE. Dreaming of refugees from a war-torn country predicts a national disaster. If you harbor one or more of them in your home, someone will criticize you unjustly for a deed that was misunderstood. 324

REGIMENT. To see a regiment marching by in your dream is a sign that you will be asked to take an active interest in civic and state affairs. This is good luck dream if you will make it so. 621

REINDEER. What you had believed to be worthless securities will prove to be valuable if you dream of seeing reindeer either in the open country or hitched to Santa Claus' sleigh. 759

RELIEF. To dream of being on relief is a sure sign that easier and happier days are just ahead of you. 777

RELIGION. If you seem to be deeply religious in your dream and get a spiritual uplift from it, you will take a growing interest in all kinds of church and social work. 612

RENT. Someone will shortly invite you out to lunch or dinner at an excellent restaurant if you dream of being unable to pay rent. If you dream of trying to collect rent from someone else, you will have a long visit from a maiden aunt. 416

REPTILE. (See Alligator, Asp, Boa, Python, Rattlesnake.) 346

RESERVOIR. To dream of approaching a reservoir that is protected by a fringe of evergreen trees and shrubs is an omen that you will be able to buy an entirely new outfit of clothes. 862

RESOLUTION. In a dream if you make good resolutions and then break them portends mental torture for someone you love. 008

RESORT. Summer or winter resorts visited in a dream indicate that you will have a passing fancy for one of the opposite sex, an amusing flirtation, and a sharp rebuke. 623

RESTAURANT. To dream of eating alone in a cheap restaurant, studying the prices of the foods rather than the foods themselves is a prediction that you and your mate will have a comfortable little house in the country. If you are with others, and "going Dutch," you will suffer some kind of embarrassment. 098

RETIREMENT. If you dream of retiring from business, you will have your salary raised, but it is a warning that you will have to increase your working speed to keep up. 223

REUNION. Family, school or college reunions in a dream signify that you will have cooperation of a kind that will help you to further your ambitions. 459

REVEILLE. To dream of hearing reveille played by the bugler in a camp at daybreak means that you have a chance to go way ahead of your fellow-workers if you "step on the gas." 700

REVENGE. Any dream of having revenge on an enemy is a bad sign, especially for women and girls. It portends accidents and illness. 448

REVOLUTION. You will have to rearrange all your affairs if your dream centers about a revolution in which there is blood and carnage, but if the revolution is bloodless, there will simply be a change in your position. 432

REVOLVER. Shooting a revolver in a dream warns you not to yield to blind jealousy, for if you do, it will warp your whole future and make you and others very unhappy. 505

REVOLVING DOOR. To dream of being caught in a revolving door and have to push and fight your way out is a sign that until you take stock of your resources your luck will be at a standstill. 722

REVUE. If you dream of being in the cast or the chorus of a theatrical revue, it is an indication that you should follow your bent for acting, dancing or singing. You will be successful, but it will be hard work. 404

REWARD. To offer a reward of any kind in a dream means that you are unlikely to win your next lawsuit. If you are rewarded for some act of honesty, kindness or heroism, it predicts a surprisingly good streak of luck. 671

RHEUMATISM. If you dream of having rheumatism, it is a warning not to fall down on any promises you have made. 587

RHINESTONE. Worn on yourself or admired on others, rhinestones in a dream foretell that someone whom you asked for a reference will not give you a good one. 740

RHINOCEROS. You will be snowed under with bills if you dream of seeing a rhinoceros in a jungle. Seen in a menagerie or zoo it portends that a person of the opposite sex will seek your company. 096

RHUBARB. Eaten or picked from the garden in your dream, rhubarb foretells better health. Taken as a medicine, it is an omen of a move to new quarters. 313

RIBBON. Ribbons worn by a girl in a dream augur catching a new boy friend. To dream of losing a ribbon hatband is a forerunner of an accident through carelessness. 208

RICE. Boiled rice served in a dream portends a visit to a bazaar or fair held for charity. Seeing rice growing in paddies is a forerunner of a long trip to strange and unfamiliar lands. If you throw rice at a dream wedding and it goes on the bride and groom, you will hear good news about one of your own family. 512

RICHES. (See Money.) 741

RIDDLE. Riddles asked and answered in a dream are an omen of a lukewarm love affair that will be strung out for a long time. 985

RIDE. To ride a horse in your dream signifies that you will reap the reward of another's labor. To ride in any vehicle is a sign that you will have news of a distant friend. 189

RIFLE. (See Arms, Gun, Pistol, Revolver.) 937

RIGGING. To dream of busying yourself about the rigging of a boat means that you will engage in some sort of transaction with a person of a different race. 340

RING. If someone of the opposite sex places a ring upon your finger in a dream, you will have some very disquieting moments in your love life. If you find a ring, you will find another object of your affection. To lose one foretells good luck in business. 051

RINK. Skating on ice rink in a dream portends a party with happy-go-lucky friends. Roller skating rinks imply a disappointment of a minor kind. 934

RIOT. To dream of being in a riot is a warning against luxurious excesses and sensual indulgence. Beware of being too free with persons of the opposite sex. 854

RIVAL. To have a hated rival in your dream and proceed to do him or her harm foretells that you are in great danger through loss of temper. It is a warning to be on your guard against hasty actions. 454

RIVER. Sitting on the bank of a river in a dream and watching boats of all kinds is a portent that you are headed in the right general direction and that if you will try to correct your faults, you will succeed handsomely. 541

ROAD. To dream of seeing a long straight road ahead with little traffic on it foretells good luck and smooth going. If the road twists and turns and you have difficulty in driving, you will encounter many discouragements before you meet with the success you will have. 804

ROAST. To carve a large roast in your dream points toward a celebration to which you will be invited. 794

ROBBERY. If you dream that a robbery is committed in your home and you lose something that you have treasured, it is a sign that someone will give you a present that will give you great satisfaction. To dream of a robber tying you up predicts a visit to a good show. 462

ROBIN. Hearing a robin sing in a dream promises a new opportunity to make good in every way. Robins pulling worms out of the ground or building nests portend that your income will be sufficient to meet your daily needs. 281

ROCKER. To sit in a rocking chair and rock back and forth in your dream foretells that you will not need to worry for a long time. To rock an empty rocking chair is a portent of misfortune to yourself and family. 912

ROCKET. (See Fireworks.) 230

RODEO. To dream of watching cowboys and cowgirls whooping it up in a rodeo is a sign that you will be invited to a reunion of your classmates and that you too will celebrate with wine and song. 653

ROGUES' GALLERY. Looking through a rogues' gallery in a dream and finding there a picture of yourself portends a narrow escape from being involved in a public scandal. To see a photograph of a friend or relative is a portent of censure from someone whose authority you respect. 110

ROLLING PIN. Using a rolling pin in a dream for the purpose of thinning pastry dough is an omen of pleasant times with your family. If you throw a rolling pin at someone you will regret a display of temper. 114

ROLLS. (See Bread.) 858

ROLLS ROYCE. If you dream of riding in a Rolls Royce automobile, you will have the best opportunity that has ever been offered you. Take it, and make your fortune. 307

ROMAN CANDLE. (See Fireworks.) 061

ROMANCE. (See Love.) 704

ROOF. To climb on a roof in your dream implies that you will have a better understanding with your family and friends. To see a roof on fire is an omen of living in dread of an unlikely catastrophe. To dream of nailing shingles on a roof predicts new sources of income. 773

ROOM. To dream of opening a door and going into a room is a warning not to trifle with the affections of one of the opposite sex. If the room is furnished, the omen is that someone will be jealous of you; if unfurnished, you are likely to be sued. If you dream of occupying a small room and being slowly suffocated, you will have a narrow escape from a major catastrophe. 974

ROOSTER. (See also Cock-crow.) Dreaming of seeing a rooster lording it over his harem in a barnyard is a good sign for men, but it denotes hard work and much responsibility for women. 910

ROPE. Handling a coil of rope in a dream indicates that you will find a good friend for whom you will be willing to make sacrifices. 445

ROSARY. Counting the beads of a rosary in a dream is a forerunner of great peace of mind and easier living conditions than formerly. 435

ROSE. Roses of any color in a dream portend love between a man and a woman. Faded roses imply the loss of a dear friend. Artificial roses are an omen of deceit on the part of someone you had trusted. 886

ROUGE. (See also Cosmetics, Lipstick, etc.) To notice rouge on the check of a young girl covering her natural beauty and coloring is a sign that you will be criticized for narrow-mindedness regarding things that do not concern you. If you see an ederly woman who is heavily rouged, you will develop a more optimistic viewpoint toward life in general. Dreaming of women applying rouge to their faces in public places is a sign that an adventuress will come into your life and make trouble for you. 396

ROULETTE. A woman who dreams of playing roulette at a fashionable gaming resort will doubtless fall in love with a playboy and live to regret it. A man who spins the wheel in a dream will be lucky in gambling. 839

ROYALTY. (See King, Prince, Queen.) 049

RUBBER. In any form, rubber in a dream foretells that by taking proper precautions you will enjoy good health and freedom from worry. Wearing rubbers and sloshing through the wet is an omen that you should protect your interests with proper insurance. 901

RUBBISH. To dream of seeing piles of rubbish indoors or out is an omen that you will have a visitor and will have to do housecleaning in anticipation. 752

RUBY. If a girl dreams of wearing one or more rubies, she will soon have many ardent suitors. 859

RUFFLES. A dream of ruffles on a dress or on dainty curtains is a sign that your attitude toward your friends is narrow and biased. You are warned to act more sensibly. 024

RUG. If you dream of walking on large, luxurious velvety Oriental rugs, you will inherit a fortune when you least expect it. But you will have to make a dollar go a long way if your dream is of rugs that are worn and full of holes. 763

RUIN. To dream of standing in the midst of ruin, desolation and suffering, presages the receipt of bad news by post or telegraph. 697

RUMMAGE SALE. If you go to a rummage sale in a dream and buy a lot of miscellaneous goods, you will be able to make a small amount of money in a stock transaction. 706

RUPTURE. You will be afflicted by many family worries if you dream of suffering from rupture. It is a sign of many trials for either sex to dream of being ruptured. It is also a warning against over-exertion of all kinds. 973

RYE. To see rye growing in a dream, or to dream of harvesting it, is an omen of stirring adventures in the company of good companions. 213

RYE BREAD. Eating sandwiches of rye bread in a dream is a portent of meeting someone of a peculiar character who will become a fast friend. 046

RYE WHISKEY. (See Whiskey.) 409

S

SABBATH. If you dream of keeping the Sabbath according to the tenets of your religion, you will be invited to participate in an important public ceremony. If you dream of making the Sabbath a day of revelry, you will be likely to be charged with a serious offense. 491

SABLE. Rich sables worn or admired in a dream portend the coming of a mysterious woman into your life. 455

SABOT. If you dream of seeing a person wearing wooden shoes or sabots, clopping along on the pavement, it is a sign that you will cultivate the friendship of an influential citizen who will help you to advance in every way. 237

SABOTAGE. Being concerned in sabotage, or the wrecking of machinery and other property belonging to your employer, is a dream that predicts a disastrous collision. 674

SACHET. You will meet a sweet, motherly woman to whom you may go for comfort and advice if you dream of putting sachet bags away with your clothing or linens. 754

SADDLE. If you ride horseback in a dream and feel that the saddle is slipping or otherwise uncomfortable, it is a sign that you are not paying careful enough attention to your work. 051

SAFETY RAZOR. (See Razor.) 056

SAFFRON. If you dream of eating saffron, you should guard against yielding to momentary sex urges that are bound to get you into trouble if followed out. This is a warning dream. 175

SAGE. Dreaming of desert sagebrush portends homesickness for friends and things that are no more. To dream of the odor after rain is a sign of good luck and good times to come. 693

SAILOR. A dream of sailors ashore is a warning to boys and girls that they will lose their sweethearts. Sailors aboard ship portend adventure away from home. 724

SAINT. You will have a sin to confess if you dream of seeing or talking with a saint. 702

SALAD. Appetizing salads eaten in your dream foretell that you will go to a party where you will not know anyone. You will be ill at ease until you force yourself to unbend. 491

SALARY. If you dream that your salary is raised and you immediately begin to spend money recklessly, it predicts a cut instead of a rise in salary. If you dream of asking to have your salary raised and it is refused, you will receive added money from an outside source. If the request is granted, you must be careful not to loaf on the job. 455

SALE. (See also Auction.) To attend a bargain sale in your dream and to be pushed and mauled by frenzied women is a sign that you will be given some old family silverware and other heirlooms. The sale of any of your personal belongings augurs a better income in the future. 237

SALMON. To dream of eating canned salmon is a sign that you will have an adventurous career somewhere east of Suez. Fresh salmon portends lovers' quarrels and reconciliation. If you dream of fishing for salmon, you will make new friends in an unconventional manner. 674

SALOON. If you dream of drinking at a bar or table in a saloon, and the atmosphere is decent and reasonably quiet, you will be asked by someone in your neighborhood to join the church or lodge. If the saloon is peopled by noisy, drunken characters, you will find it necessary to go with a relative to a gathering of tiresome people. 754

SALT. Sprinking salt on food in a dream portends a mild attack of food poisoning. To dream of putting salt on a bird's tail augurs an amusing experience with a member of the opposite sex. 051

SALVATION ARMY. To stop and listen to a meeting of the Salvation Army in a dream is a portent of your doing a good deed for someone less fortunate than yourself. 056

SAMPLE. To dream of receiving samples of food from your grocer is a sign of having to pay a bill that you incurred unwillingly. 175

SAND. A dream of sand in your spinach, on the seashore, or in an hour-glass predicts that you will be annoyed by a presumptuous person who will try to use you to advance his or her own interests. 724

SANDALS. To wear sandals in a dream predicts, if they are comfortable, a romance by moonlight. If they chafe your feet, the augury is of an altercation with someone to whom you owe a small amount of money. 702

SANDBAGS. A dream of using sandbags as a defense against bombs or as a bulwark against a flood foretells that you will have a burglary in the house where you live. 769

SANDWICH. To dream of eating a sandwich is a prophecy of an opportunity to better your condition. Indoors, eating sandwiches at a lunch counter warns against casual conversations with people you do not know. A toasted sandwich foretells an adventure that you may wish to forget. Sandwiches at a picnic portend a love affair that is liable to backfire. Be on your guard. 307

SANITARIUM. If you dream of being a patient in a sanitarium, it is a warning to take better care of your health and to avoid being alarmed too easily. 693

SAPPHIRE. You will regret a hasty action if you dream of wearing sapphires set in either a ring or a brooch. If you see them but are not wearing them, you will be introduced to a person of rank. 291

SARDINE. To dream of opening a sardine can is an omen of distress of mind. Eating sardines portends that you will be defamed by someone who is jealous of your mental attainments. 628

SATAN. (See Devil.) 369

SAUERKRAUT. Good sauerkraut eaten in a dream is a forerunner of an invitation to listen to a fine musical program. Drinking sauerkraut juice predicts good health. 964

SAUSAGE. You are likely to be accused of stealing another's love if you dream of eating sausage. To see a variety of sausages hanging in a meat store or delicatessen shop augurs a fortunate turn in business. 681

SAW. It is a sign that you will change your political beliefs if you dream of using a handsaw in a factory or the home. To dream of a buzz saw in operation is a portent of approaching danger to your reputation and your credit. Using a hacksaw to cut metal predicts that you will have to devote more time to the job you are doing, but with extra pay. 982

SAXOPHONE. Heard in a dream, a saxophone is a forerunner of a gay dancing party with much liquor flowing. To dream of playing it is an omen of a quarrel with someone living in your immediate vicinity. Good luck is predicted by a dream of losing a saxophone. 330

SCAFFOLD. A hangman's scaffold seen in a dream is an omen of a dreadful happening close to home. It can be averted only by your walking the straight and narrow path for a long time to come. Wooden or iron scaffolding erected in connection with building operations predicts new business opportunities. 734

SCALES. To weigh food upon scales is a sign that you will have plenty to eat. To dream of weighing yourself presages disappointment and worry. To scrape the scales off a fish in a dream portends the discovery of a plot to discredit you. 240

SCALLOPS. Dreaming of having a plate of freshly cooked scallops served to you forecasts a change to a more desirable place of abode. Raw scallops predict a vacation by the sea. 779

SCANDAL. To dream of being mixed up in a scandal implies that you should clear your conscience of something that has been bothering you. Otherwise you will have much regret. To dream of talking scandalously about other people predicts that you will be accused of dishonesty. 674

SCAR. It is a sign of difficulty in meeting the wishes of your employer if you dream of seeing a woman whose face is disfigured with a prominent scar. If the scar is on your own face or body, you will try to hide something of which you are ashamed. 428

SCARF. Wearing a bright scarf in your dream foretells the best of luck in a heartfelt love affair. 507

SCENARIO. If you dream of writing a movie scenario, you are likely to be successful in a writing or acting career. 534

SCENERY. Beautiful natural scenery, whether on land or at sea, is a good augury, and if you enjoy it with a person of the opposite sex, your friends will soon have reason to buy wedding gifts. Theatrical scenery presages missing a good time through a minor illness. 355

SCHOOL. To dream of being young and going to school predicts an enjoyable encounter with an old friend who lives a long distance from you. If the schoolhouse burns in your dream, you will have a temporary streak of luck, during which you should save as much money as possible. 330

SCIENTIST. If you dream of being a great scientist and making a tremendous discovery of benefit to all mankind, you will be called upon to join a group of amateur actors. If you see a scientist in a laboratory making experiments with intricate apparatus, the augury is of meeting a high official who will look with favor upon you. 734

SCISSORS. Cutting with a pair of scissors in a dream indicates that you will be the victim of a humorous prank. To dream of using a left-handed pair of scissors foretells that you will make a discovery of interest. 240

SCOLDING. Dreaming of being scolded by a parent or employer is a warning against being too sure of yourself in arguments. You will profit by a suggestion from a younger person. 779

SCORE. If you dream of keeping the score for any outdoor game and there is a dispute as to the manner in which you keep it, you will be closely watched by a jealous mate. 674

SCORPION. To dream of a scorpion is a sign of warning against over-confidence in yourself. Enough is plenty. Try to take other people's advice occasionally if you value your peace of mind. 428

SCOTTISH TERRIER. To own a Scottish terrier and play with it in your dream, is a sign that you will be invited by a charming spinster to a cocktail party. 507

SCOUT. (See also Boy Scout.) It is a sign that you will go on a diet to reduce your weight if you dream of scouting in the wilderness or in a battle area. 534

SCRAPBOOK. To busy yourself with a scrapbook in a dream and paste in it clippings and pictures of subjects in which you are interested is a sign that points two ways: you will be a success in whatever you attempt, and you will have a loving mate. 355

SCRAPBOOK. You will be fortunate financially and in your family life if you dream of keeping a scrapbook. 667

SCREAM. A bloodcurdling scream heard predicts that you will be afraid of having a family skeleton revealed. But you should remember that you are not responsible for anything your forebears have said or done. If you dream of screaming, it is a sign that you will join a movement for the betterment of the aged and infirm. 349

SCREWBALL. If you dream of calling someone a screwball, you are likely to find that you will not have good luck in your business. 611

SCULPTOR. To admire the work of a sculptor in your dream signifies that you will have a temptation to meddle with someone's personal affairs. Therefore it is a warning to mind your own. To dream of seeing a sculptor at work presages embarking on a new and interesting enterprise. 765

SEA. (See Ocean.) 470

SEAHORSE. To dream of seeing a tiny seahorse grow to a gigantic size augurs traveling in a motor caravan. A dream of harnessing a seahorse predicts pleasant adventures. 329

SEAL. A fishing trip is predicted by a dream of many seals disporting themselves on a rock. To kill a seal is an augury of hard going in business. A sealskin coat worn in a dream foretells prosperity. 108

SEANCE. To attend a spiritualistic seance in a dream and be conscious of being skeptical of it is a portent that you will turn down someone's offer of help and live to regret it. 830

SEARCHLIGHT. To dream of being in the direct beam from a powerful searchlight is an omen that you will get your heart's desire, but you will have to go through fire and water for it. To see many searchlight beams playing in the sky indicates coming danger from your enemies. Be prepared. 867

SEAWEED. Dreaming of seaweed that is tangled about you while you are trying to swim denotes that a very strong-willed person will try to persuade you to do something against your better judgment. 276

SECRET. Intrigue among people whom you have trusted is foretold by hearing a secret in a dream. If you repeat a secret that has been told you in strict confidence, you will be annoyed by malicious gossip. 962

SECRETARY. To dream that you are a beautiful young secretary and that the boss is in love with you is a sign that you are going to have trouble in getting along. For a man to dream of kissing his secretary augurs criticism from his relatives. To dream of being elected secretary of a corporation or other organization portends an increase in salary. 506

SEDUCTION. (See Rape.) 351

SENATOR. For a man to dream that he is a senator at Washington indicates that someone among his acquaintances will ask him for a favor. A woman will achieve social prominence if she dreams of having a senator make love to her. 143

SERENADE. A maiden who dreams of being serenaded by a young man will have a proposal within a month. If she throws him a flower from her window, it foretells a happy marriage and lovely children. 274

SEWING. Look to the future and provide for it if you dream of anyone sewing. If it is you who sews, an opportunity for advancement will come shortly. 210

SEX. Few dreams there are that have no connection with sex, for all living things are created male and female. Therefore as such, it has little significance. Dreaming of the biological functions of sex in the manner in which they should be used portends a long and happy life. 014

SHAKING HANDS. A dream of shaking hands with a firm hearty grasp augurs new friends, but if the grasp is weak and flabby, the omen is of failure in some important enterprise. 554

SHAME. If you dream of being shamed, you have every reason for looking forward to the respect of your friends and your employer. To shame another in a dream portends a motor accident on a highway. 524

SHAMPOO. Having a shampoo either at home or at a hair-dresser's is a sign that you will be admired by a stranger who will find some way of meeting you socially. To dream of giving a shampoo to another indicates that you will receive good news. 681

SHAMROCK. You will receive three party invitations for the same date if you dream of seeing the green shamrock of Saint Patrick. 799

SHAVING. (See also Razor.) To dream of seeing a woman shaving her face augurs an experience that you will not understand for a long time. If she is shaving under her arms, there is the probability of your being taken on a trip by a wealthy friend. For a man to dream of shaving means that he will have to keep an appointment. 434

SHAWL. To dream of wearing a shawl over your head is a warning against being careless in your manners. A shawl over your shoulders is an indication that you will have difficulty in cashing a large check. 820

SHEARS. (See Scissors.) 715

SHEEP. Counting sheep in a dream is a portent of petty irritations and temporary setbacks. If you dream of shearing the wool from sheep, you will be moderately prosperous. 273

SHEET. Putting clean sheets on a bed in a dream is a portent of more ease and comfort than you have had before. To dream of being tangled in bedsheets is a sign of worry over a love affair. To escape from a high window by tying bedsheets together augurs a business difficulty from which you will emerge after a period of unrest. 523

SHELL. Gathering sea-shells in a dream is an omen of going to a spiritualist meeting. To crack the shell of a coconut or any other variety of nut, augurs success in an undertaking. A shell used as ammunition for a gun of any size predicts a siege with a dentist. 783

SHERBET. Eating a sherbet at a dinner party in a dream foretells a situation with a person of the opposite sex in which you will need to exercise great restraint. To spill sherbet on your gown or suit is an omen of being distrusted by someone you like. 266

SHERIFF. If you dream of having the sheriff on your trail, someone whom you have offended will demand an apology. It is a sign of bitter wrangling with your relatives if you dream of seeing a sheriff make an arrest. 274

SHERRY. To drink sherry in your dream denotes a new association with a high grade group of people. 620

SHIP. To dream of ships, powered either by sail or steam, is an augury of an adventure that will be productive of profit and satisfaction. To be on a ship that is wrecked is a portent of having to struggle to save your good name. To build a model of a ship in a dream foretells that you will love someone madly and marry within the year. 963

SHIRT. To put on a clean shirt in a dream is a sign of good luck, but if there is a button missing, you will have trouble with members of your family. To lose a shirt augurs a long period of grief. 782

SHOE. New shoes worn in your dream portend short journeys. Shoes that are old and comfortable are a phophecy of home relaxations and good friends. To dream of losing one of your shoes prophesies new activities that will come to naught. To throw an old shoe at a wedding is a sign that you will have family worries. 902

SHOEMAKER. To dream of a shoemaker working at his last is an omen of finding someone who will be able to finance a business deal for you. 025

SHOP. (See Store.) 454

SHORE. If you walk along the seashore in a dream and watch the tide creep in, you will be called a hero or heroine for some worthy action. If the tide is going out, you will make money through some transaction involving food or real estate. 089

SHORTHAND. (See also Secretary.) If in a dream your employer dictates a letter and you take it down in shorthand, you will receive an advance in salary; but if you dream that you cannot read your own notes, the prophecy is definitely inauspicious. 956

SHOVEL. An increase of responsibility is augured by the use of a shovel in a dream of any kind. 180

SHRIMP. A maiden who dreams of eating cooked shrimps will soon step out with a new suitor who will be able to entertain her royally. For others, the dream portends pleasant adventures with highly respectable people. 589

SIGNATURE. Putting your signature to a legal paper in a dream means that you will work at a desk for a small salary. To sign a check in a dream foretells moderate prosperity, but many worries. 254

SILK. A dream of wearing silk next to the skin is a fortunate augury for women of all ages, for it portends all the necessities of life and many of the luxuries. To wear silk gowns in a dream predicts that your neighbors will gossip about you on account of something they do not understand. For a man to dream of wearing silk underwear or pajamas is a sign that he will be singled out for promotion by his employer. A dream of raw silk or a bolt of silk yardage prophesies election to a position of honor and trust. 874

SILO. Taking ensilage out of a silo in a dream is a sign that you must avoid overindulgence in whiskey, gin and other hard liquors. A silo on fire is a warning against waiting too long before paying your bills. 153

SILVER. To dream of possessing a large quantity of table silver and having to work hard to keep it bright augurs a long visit from critical relatives. Silver money in a dream is an omen of plenty but with great responsibility. 255

SIN. (See Adultery, Robbery, etc.) 309

SINGING. To dream of singing a solo before a large audience implies a desire for solitude, and you are likely to go away for a vacation in a small place where you are not known. To join in the singing of a chorus or congregation indicates good companionship and merry times with your friends. 828

SISTER. It is an ill portent to dream that your sister is in any kind of difficulty. To dream of hating a sister is a sign that some stupid person will tell you lies about a friend. 043

SKATING. (See also Ice, Rink.) Good times are predicted by a dream of either ice or roller skating. To fall while skating is a sign of being asked to contribute to a fund for underprivileged children. 104

SKELETON. A dream of a human skeleton found in a closet or chest is a sign that you will be ridiculed for being afraid of what might happen. Seen in an anatomical display, it augurs new and interesting friends who are of a scientific disposition. 684

SKIDDING. If in a dream you are driving a car that skids, you are in danger of making a grave error of judgment that has great possibilities for danger to yourself and your family. To get out of a skid is a sign that you will make a favorable business turn. 009

SKIRT. If a woman dreams that her skirt is either too short or too long in a dream, it is a sign that she will be unhappy over something that is relatively unimportant. For a man to dream of seeing a woman wearing a skirt that shows practically all of her legs is a portent that there will be a rise in his worldly forutnes. 781

SKULL. (See also Skeleton.) To dream of handling a skull is a portent of success in either literary work or dramatic acting. If in digging you unearth a skull, you are likely to have an adventure that will at first puzzle you and then give you delight. 374

SKUNK. To smell or see a skunk in a dream is a sign that you will not receive an invitation to a party you expected to attend. To kill a skunk augurs sadness through homesickness. 632

SKY. A dream of a colorful sky either at sunset or sunrise portends a hectic love affair that will come to nothing. A sky that is leaden and gray is a prediction of making a good friend who will stick by you through thick and thin. 391

SLANG. To dream of hearing a precise and dignified person using picturesque slang is a portent of attending a gathering of substantial and likeable people. If your dream is of slang that you cannot understand, there will be a deep and fascinating mystery in your life. 036

SLAUGHTER HOUSE. To dream of working in a slaughter house portends criticism of a serious nature from your employer. 696

SLED. Sliding downhill on a sled in a dream is an omen of happy times with young people. If the sled overturns and you are thrown off in the snow, you will be called upon to take a comedy part in an amateur theatrical performance. 622

SLIP. For a maiden to dream of making a slip portends an early marriage and a trousseau of many silken underthings. 345

SMALLPOX. If you dream of having smallpox, you are slated for an experience that will be serious but not fatal. It is a sign that you will make many new friends if you dream of taking care of a smallpox patient. 461

SMOKE. (See also Cigar, Pipe.) To dream of smelling smoke and not know where it is coming from augurs worry for a long period. To see smoke coming from a fire or a chimney is a sign of an increase in income. 319

SMUGGLER. A dream in which you or another person is trying to smuggle articles into your country predicts that you will be called upon to explain something that you would rather keep hidden. 387

SNAIL. Eating snails in a dream is an omen of happiness in love and married life. To gather them prophesies success to those who work with their hands. 288

SNAKE. (See Adder, Asp, Rattlesnake.) 421

SNEEZE. Sneezing in a dream foretells good health and a satisfactory income. To hear others sneeze portends danger through infection. 796

SNOW. Dreaming of a snowstorm and wading through deep drifts means that you will work long and hard upon a project but that you will eventually make it a big success. A wet snow that sticks to the branches of trees is a sign that you will make money on your investments. Shoveling snow is an augury of having words with a person who has the power to do you either good or harm. 982

SNOWSHOES. Young people who dream of traveling on snowshoes may look forward to a complete understanding with their sweethearts. To dream of putting on snowshoes is a portent of being rewarded for a good deed. 159

SNUFF. (See also Sneeze.) It is a sign of a healthy and contented old age if you dream of taking snuff. 350

SOAP. Scented toilet soap used in a dream portends moonlight and roses with the one you love. Soap-flakes, kitchen or laundry soap indicates that you will have to struggle before you will achieve a competence. Any antiseptic soap is a sign that you will be ill at ease in company. 285

SOCKS. (See Stockings.). 091

SODA. Drinking ice-cream soda in a dream foretells that you will meet an outstanding celebrity in the motion- picture world. 625

SOFA. To dream of sitting on a sofa with your sweetheart and making earnest love denotes that you will be called upon to make a hurried business trip that will help you toward success. If you dream of having a slipcover made for a sofa, you are likely to have visitors with children. A sofa with a broken spring is a sign of distress. 021

SOLITAIRE. Playing solitaire in a dream predicts that you will engage in some work that will tire you both physically and mentally. If you dream of winning, you will receive a large amount of money that you did not expect. 932

SON. A man who dreams of his son or a woman who dreams of her son is sure to achieve happiness through his or her own efforts. 916

SORE. It is a sign of unpleasant times ahead if you dream of having sores on your body. If you dream of sores on another person or on an animal, you are likely to receive disquieting news. 627

SOUP. To dream of hearing a person make a noise while eating soup foretells that you will receive an invitation to a dinner party. 830

SPAGHETTI. Dreaming of difficulty in eating spaghetti, getting it on your chin and clothes, is a portent of good times in the company of your friends. 472

SPANIEL. Any type of spaniel in a dream is an augury of pleasant home associations. To dream of seeing a spaniel getting his ears in his food predicts a humorous experience with a school teacher. 966

SPARROW. To dream of English sparrows in the city indicates that you will have to get along with a lean purse and have unpopular children. It is a lucky omen to dream of chasing these birds away. 425

SPATS. A man who dreams of wearing spats is likely to have an offer of a new and better position. To wear only one spat is a sign of losing your job. 382

SPEECH. Making a speech in a dream augurs success in business and social life. 153

SPEEDBOAT. Driving a speedboat through the water in a dream is a portent of accomplishing an important job to the satisfaction of your employer. 113

SPELLING BEE. If you dream of taking part in a spelling bee, you will receive an invitation to compete for a valuable prize. To dream of misspelling a simple word is a sign of a minor disgrace. 483

SPHINX. Bathed in moonlight, the sphinx seen in a dream is a portent of meeting someone whom you like immensely but do not understand. 384

SPICE. Pungent aromatic spices used in a dream are a forerunner of a trip that will lead toward far eastern countries. Hearing spicy conversation foretells danger from unscrupulous people of the opposite sex. 920

SPIDER. Encouragement is predicted by a dream of seeing a spider in his web, for it is an omen that through industry and skill you will achieve the end for which you have been working. 989

SPINACH. Good health and enjoyment of life is foretold by a dream of eating spinach so long as you find no grit in it. But if you bite on a grain of sand, the augury is of meeting a group of thoroughly detestable people. 656

SPIRE. To dream of seeing a church spire outlined against the sky is an augury of the blessings of friendship and love. If the spire leans away from the perpendicular, it means that you will have many difficulties before you finally achieve the end toward which you have been working. 273

SPIRIT. You should take warning against certain people who will try to deceive you if you dream of seeing or talking to the spirit of someone who has passed on. 129

SPIT. To dream of seeing meat being roasted on a spit is a sign of being invited to be a guest at a big dinner. If you see someone spit in your dream, you are likely to be offended by a friend. 172

SPITE. If you dream of an act being committed for spite, you will have occasion to censure one of your friends. To be spiteful in a dream augurs physical pain. 629

SPLINTER. It is a sign of an acrimonious dispute with relatives if you dream of getting a splinter in any part of your body. To remove a splinter from anyone else forecasts the loss of an important letter or document. 148

SPONGE. To wash your body with a sponge predicts a sea voyage; to wash an automobile is a forerunner of being commended for good work that you have done. Squeezing the water out of a sponge is a portent of greater earning power. Trying to squeeze water out of a dry sponge is a dream that warns against gambling at cards or in lotteries. 868

SPOOL. If in a dream you step on a spool lying on the floor, and fall down, you are warned against indiscreet relations with a person of the opposite sex. To unwind thread from a spool predicts embarking on a new enterprise that is almost certain to bring you profit. 644

SPOON. To dream of eating with a spoon something that ordinarily would be eaten with a fork—such as meat, potatoes, salad, etc.—is a sign that you will get yourself talked about for your informal behavior. To lose a silver spoon in a dream predicts a loss of money through an unlucky business deal. 191

SPORTSMANSHIP. Any display of sportsmanship is a good portent. You will be much sought after by people of refinement and influence. 525

SPOTLIGHT. (See also Searchlight.) A dream of being on a stage and having a spotlight thrown on you indicates that you will be singled out of a large group to receive an award or other honor. 742

SPRAIN. If you dream of spraining an ankle, wrist, your back or other part of your body, you will be approached by a committee who will ask you to run for office. 315

SPRAY. A spray from a hose, atomizer or other source in a dream is an indication of good times with your friends. 270

SPRING. A dream of springtime, with budding trees, blossoming flowers and birds singing is a favorable omen to lovers and to those starting a new business. 577

SPRUCE. Better health is the portent of a dream in which spruce trees figure. Chewing spruce gum foretells meeting an overbearing person whom you must not take too seriously unless he or she gets the advantage over you. 383

SPUR. Spurs in a dream predict that you will be nagged by someone who has some sort of authority over you. 581

SPY. To dream that you are a spy in the service of your country augurs being elected to an honorary position that you do not want. If you dream of being spied on, you are warned to be more circumspect in your behavior. 340

SQUALL. A sudden short storm at sea in a dream predicts a coming difficulty that you can overcome if you use good sense. 223

SQUASH. A good opportunity will be given you to make money if you dream of preparing or eating squash. 569

SQUINT. Eyes that squint in a dream portend concern over the condition of a sick relative or friend. 866

SQUIRREL. Feeding nuts to a squirrel in a dream is an augury of pleasant times in the company of your friends. A squirrel in a cage, running on a revolving wheel, predicts a hopeless love affair. To see squirrels chasing each other among the branches of a tree is an omen of trouble through unpaid bills. 224

STADIUM. To dream of looking at a football game or other athletic contest in a stadium foretells a round of parties with friendly and worthwhile people. 172

STAG. An antlered stag seen in a dream is an omen of exciting adventures outside of your everyday experience. If the animal is brought to bay by staghounds, your adventures will be dangerous as well. 496

STAGE. (See also Actor.) If you dream that you are on the stage, you may regard it as a distinct sign of encouragement to continue in any efforts along dramatic or literary lines. It is a good omen for those who write poetry. 851

STAGECOACH. Being a passenger in a dream stagecoach drawn by horses is a portent of a stirring love affair that will depend on its innocence for its success. To dream of driving a stagecoach prophesies an adventure that will be something to tell your grandchildren about. 824

STAGGER. If you walk with a stagger in a dream, it is a warning against being influenced by flattery. To see another person staggering augurs a cry for help from one of your friends. 443

STAIN. If a woman dreams of staining her gown, she is warned not to accept the attentions of men much older than she is. To dream of a stain on one's family name is a sign of honors in store for you. 947

STAIR. To fall upstairs in a dream augurs peace of mind for the unmarried, but a short period of trouble for married folk. To fall downstairs is a sign that you will be drawn into a conspiracy unless you have the good sense to keep out of it. To sweep or scrub a flight of stairs is a prophecy of improved living conditions. 326

STAKE. To dream of driving a stake into the ground for a tent or other purpose predicts starting a new and probably successful enterprise. If you dream of being present while someone is being burned at the stake, you will have an opportunity to assert yourself in no uncertain terms to a person who tries to bully you. 968

STALL. Dreaming of putting a horse into a stall indicates that you will win approval for your work from your employer. If you dream that someone ties you in a stall, you will win a prize in a lottery. 067

STAMP. To put a stamp on a letter in a dream is a prophecy that you will receive money and commendation for a job well done. To buy stamps at the post-office is an omen of better business. Collecting postage stamps of all countries in a dream is a prophecy of meeting high-grade people socially and being able to advance yourself through knowing them. If you dream of finding a rare stamp on an old envelope that you had forgotten, you will have good luck financially for a year or more. 892

STAR. To dream of a certain bright star predicts that through the help of a friend of the opposite sex you will be able to achieve an ambition of long standing. 367

STARCH. Using starch in a dream is a portent of carrying out a project that will net you a round sum. If you dream of eating starch, you will get into trouble through being too sure of yourself. 859

STARE. If a person of the opposite sex stares at you in a dream, you are likely to have to make an abject apology for a mistake you have made. 925

STARFISH. Finding a starfish on the shore in a dream is a prophecy of meeting an influential person who, if properly approached, will help you to an excellent position. 840

STARVATION. Dreaming of being starved is an ill omen. You are warned to curtail your expenses and save as much money as possible. It is a sign that you will have many unhappy days if you dream of seeing other people starving. 212

STATEROOM. Going into a stateroom aboard ship portends an adventure that may or may not be to your advantage, according to whether you are alone or in company with one of the opposite sex. 261

STATIC. To dream of hearing static on your radio is a prophecy of being called to account for something irregular about your behavior. 678

STATIONERY. Buying stationery in a dream—paper, typewriter ribbons, pencils, pens, ink, etc.—is a sign that you will be increasingly successful in your business. 431

STATUE. Carving a statue in a dream is a sign of a new opportunity to advance yourself in your career. To look at statues in a museum foretells meeting an interesting group of people who will stimulate you to do better work. 452

STEAK. To dream of broiling a steak presages popularity in your community. You will be asked to join a select club or society that you have wished to be associated with. If you dream of eating steak you are likely to have an offer to go with a new concern that will pay you an excellent salary. 550

STEALING. If you dream of stealing, you are warned to go slowly in making investments. To dream of being caught is good luck. 734

STEAM. The sound of escaping steam in a dream is a sign that you will have an altercation with a person who has some authority over you. To turn off the steam indicates that you will succeed in accomplishing a task that you had thought was impossible. If you dream that you are burned by steam, you should be on the lookout for evidences of underhanded work against you. 845

STEAMROLLER. Operating a steamroller in a dream augurs success in any enterprise that you have embarked on. If you dream that a steamroller runs over you, look out for those who wish you ill. 176

STEAMSHIP. (See Ship.) 076

STEEL. If you dream of steel being used for a constructive or worthy purpose, the augury is of increased value to the community and corresponding reward for your labors. If it is used for destructive purposes, such as guns, swords, etc., you are warned against evilly disposed persons. 821

STEEPLE. Maidens who dream of church steeples will have exciting experiences with young men whom they do not know but who wish to make their acquaintance. A dream of a broken steeple is an augury of thwarted ambitions. 844

STEEPLECHASE. Horses in a race in which they jump hurdles are an omen of much social excitement involving theatres, night clubs and cocktail parties. If any of the horses fall with their riders, the portent is of having to foot the bill at the next party. 084

STENCH. A foul odor in a dream foretells much grief over an innocent mistake. It is a warning against making jokes at the expense of your friends. 128

STENOGRAPHER. (See also Secretary.) If a man dreams of making love to his stenographer, he will have to answer to either his wife or his employer for something he has forgotten. A young woman who dreams of being a stenographer is likely to be married with the year. 810

STEREOSCOPE. Travel in your own country and abroad is predicted by a dream of looking at pictures through a stereoscope. 358

STETHOSCOPE. To dream of a doctor listening to your chest with a stethoscope presages an accomplishment of which your family and friends will be proud. 640

STEW. Eating stew in a dream portends a reunion with old friends. To dream of making stew is an indication that there will be a birth in the family of one of your near relatives. 275

STILETTO. If you should happen to stab someone with a stiletto in a dream, you are quite likely to make a rash statement that will get you into serious trouble. Guard your tongue lest you hurt yourself as well as others. 120

STILTS. Walking on stilts in a dream is a warning against pride, for pride goeth before a fall. If you dream of falling, it is a good sign because it will make the warning more potent. 569

STINK. (See Stench.) 715

STOCK FARM. If you dream of being on a stock farm and having charge of the care and breeding of animals, you may look forward to a successful business career. 065

STOCKING. Putting on one's stockings in a dream portends the beginning of an adventure that is likely to lead to a profitable contract for services. To find a hole in one's stocking is a sign that you will have to explain an absence from duty. To mend stockings is an omen of hard work that will give you satisfaction but no financial reward. If you dream of hanging up a stocking at Christmas, you will have many friends but not much money. 688

STOMACH. To dream of having a belly-ache and calling it a stomach-ache is a sign that you will be embarrassed by the revelations of a friend. Beware of showing jealousy of anyone if you dream of having a sour stomach; it will react on you unfavorably. 366

STORAGE BATTERY. Bad luck will follow you for a long time if you dream that your storage battery goes dead while you are driving in traffic. 104

STORE. One may expect an increase in income if he or she dreams of working in a store. If the dream is of being the proprietor, the augury is better. 229

STORM. To dream of being caught in a storm, either rain or snow, portends a season of discontent from which you will emerge only when you have found that you can control your own destiny. 925

STORY. To dream of reading a story portends happy days. To dream of writing one is a sign of heartaches. 625

STOVE. (See Furnace.) 477

STRAIT-JACKET. Struggling to free yourself from a strait-jacket in a dream foretells a time during which you will have difficulty in getting your debts paid. If you release yourself, or if someone else releases you, the outcome will be propitious. 158

STRAWBERRY. Picking strawberries in a dream is a prophecy of a luxurious vacation that will be paid for by a wealthy friend. Eating strawberries prophesies happy days in the company of your favorite companion. 382

STREETCAR. If you dream of riding on a streetcar with people of your own kind, you will be able to buy a new automobile within a short time. If the streetcar runs off the track, it portends exciting experiences. 679

STRIKE. To dream of going on strike against unfair treatment by your employer is a sign that you will make progress in the work that you are engaged in. 871

STRING. A dream of saving string taken from packages predicts that you will be laughed at for being fussy or prim. 192

STRING BEAN. Eating string beans in a dream foretells gay and unrestrained parties where you will meet many people who are engaged in artistic pursuits. To prepare string beans for the table is a sign of receiving word that will cause you to seek another position. 724

STRIP TEASE. You had better watch your conduct if you dream of being at a performance where a young woman does a strip tease act, for it portends disgrace through an indiscretion that can and should be avoided. 941

STRUMPET. (See Prostitute.) 318

STUDIO. Any dream transpiring in a studio predicts association with artists, writers, actors and musicians. 881

STUNT. To dream of being among a group of people who are doing stunts is a portent of a joyous reunion with people you have known since childhood. 540

STUTTER. If in your dream you talk with a person who stutters, and you have difficulty in following him or her, you will have trouble with a relative who is critical of you and your actions. 426

SUBMARINE. Being on a submarine in a dream predicts having to explain your absence from a gathering at which you were supposed to be present. To dream of firing a torpedo from a submarine portends an occurrence in connection with a friend of the opposite sex that will have a profound influence on your life. 726

SUBWAY. Dreaming of riding on a crowded subway foretells a succession of irritating incidents that will be likely to cause you no end of trouble unless you keep a stiff upper lip. A wreck in a subway is a sure potent of disaster. 615

SUFFOCATION. You are warned to avoid large gatherings of people if you dream of being suffocated. Keep out in the open air as much as you can. 411

SUITCASE. To pack a suitcase in a dream does not augur a trip as might be supposed. It portends a visit from a tiresome busybody of a relative who will stay a long time. 642

SUITOR. A young woman who dreams of her suitor will be happy with him if the dream is a pleasant one; otherwise the engagement will be broken. 634

SUNDAE. To dream of eating a luscious and drippy sundae is a portent to women that their men friends are thinking of them. It is a good sign if one dreams of spilling a sundae on clothing, but a sign of sorrow if the ice cream is sour. 209

SUN DIAL. It is a distinctly pleasant dream if there is a sun dial in it, especially if it is in a garden with blossoming flowers. If you can tell time by the dial, your best hopes will come true. 184

SUNFLOWER. Wearing a sunflower in your buttonhole or as a corsage predicts that you are in danger of making a spectacle of yourself by some unusual action. Guard against being too informal. To eat sunflower seeds is a portent that you will meet old friends when you least expect to. 049

SUNRISE. If you dream of seeing the sunrise, you are likely to have success in the work that you are doing. A red sunrise portends a struggle through which you will emerge triumphant. 400

SUNSET. Gorgeous colors in the sky at sunset are a prophecy of a new opportunity to make good with your wife, husband, sweetheart or employer. 630

SUNSHADE. (See Parasol.) 948

SURF. A dream of watching surf beat upon the seashore is a sign that you will receive encouragement. This may be in a love affair or in your work. 934

SURGEON. To dream of being a surgeon and performing delicate operations prophesies that you will change your occupation to one that is connected with the newspaper business. If you dream of being operated on by a surgeon, the augury is of an improvement in health. 266

SUSPENDERS. A maiden who dreams of her lover wearing suspenders will be disillusioned through his lack of manners. If a man dreams of losing his suspenders, he will win a prize in a public contest. 654

SWAMP. Being lost in a swamp in a dream is an augury of bad luck in financial matters. It also predicts family squabbles. 194

SWAN. Graceful white swans gliding over smooth waters in a dream foretell a happy married career to maid and matron alike. Swans flying portend healthy children and a satisfactory income. 640

SWASTIKA. A dream of this prehistoric symbol of good luck is a forerunner of eventual riches and in the meantime a well-ordered life among people with culture and a sense of humor. 184

SWEARING. (See Profanity.) 044

SWEAT. To dream of sweating, either in winter or summer, predicts a comfortable living through hard work. If the sweat gets into your eyes, you will worry for the health of your loved ones. 774

SWEATER. Wearing a sweater in a dream portends harsh criticism for a deed that you did not intend to be harmful. 012

SWEETHEART. A pleasant dream of your sweetheart is always a good augury, but if you dream of a quarrel, the omen is of having to make amends for an unintentional wrong. 146

SWIMMING. The best of luck in fortune and friends may be expected if you dream of swimming in the nude. If you wear a bathing suit, you will be taken to task for failing to recognize someone whom you have recently met. To dream of teaching another how to swim is a prophecy of an increase in income. 822

SWINE. (See Pig.) 527

SWISS CHEESE. (See Cheese.) 153

SWITCHBOARD. To dream of working at a telephone switchboard is a portent of making a new acquaintance who will take a keen interest in you. Give him or her a chance. 152

SWORD. Wearing a sword in a dream is a presage of being called upon to fill a higher position either in your community or office. To fight a duel with a sword foretells a quarrel with someone whose good will you should cultivate instead. 797

SWORDFISH. To angle for swordfish in a dream predicts that you will struggle to attain an object which, after all, is hardly worth fighting for. If the battle is a tiring one, you will be laughed at for your pains. To eat swordfish in a dream foretells a vacation at the seaside. 026

SYNAGOGUE. To dream of seeing people going into a synagogue predicts prosperity for those in mercantile lines. Attending a service in a synagogue is a forerunner of progress of an intellectual nature. 475

SYRUP. Using syrup on food in a dream is a prophecy of delight in the company of young people. You will be able to further their love affairs and make them and yourself happier thereby. If you get your hands sticky the portent is so much the better. 456

T

TABASCO. Using this very hot and peppery condiment on food in a dream portends an exciting encounter with a romantic person of the opposite sex. To burn your mouth with it predicts that through an indiscretion you will come to grief. 433

TABBY. (See Cat.) 595

TABERNACLE. (See Church.) 745

TABLE. Sitting at a table has many meanings in a dream. A library table with a lamp and books on it portends a promotion in your work through home study. A dining-table is an omen of convivial times ahead. A card table augurs a new opportunity to make money. A kitchen table predicts hard work at a small salary. 009

TABLE D'HOTE. To dream of eating a table d'hote luncheon or dinner foretells smooth sailing in your business and home affairs. Your chances for making good investments are excellent. 677

TACK. Driving a tack with a hammer in a dream indicates that you will be called upon by a friend for a small service that you will perform willingly. For a woman to dream of driving a tack with the heel of her shoe is an augury of a man's awakening interest. Pulling out a tack prophesies arguments with your employer. To dream of placing a tack on a chair for someone to sit on predicts danger of a grave error in judgment. 691

TAIL. If you dream that you have a tail, it is a prophecy of having to apologize for the actions of one of your relatives. To pull the tail of a cat or dog in a dream is an omen of sickness. 114

TAILOR. To be measured for a suit by a tailor in a dream foretells an answer to a letter that you have written concerning a position. A dream of seeing a tailor sitting cross-legged at his work signifies travel on another continent. 741

TALCUM POWDER. To dream of using talcum powder after shaving or bathing portends a charming person of the opposite sex. 356

TALLOW. Eating tallow in a dream is a portent of war. To throw it away predicts hunger. To burn a tallow candle is a forerunner of sorrow. 711

TAMALE. If you eat tamales in a dream, there is a strong probability that you will be asked to go on a hunting or fishing trip. 996

TAMBOURINE. A dancing girl with a tambourine in a dream is a sign of having to explain an absence from home to one of your family. It is a warning to be discreet. Trying to play a tambourine augurs hearing a rumor that will cause you concern. 247

TANAGER. This scarlet bird in a dream portends a pleasant house party where you will meet many interesting people. To dream of killing a tanager portends distress. 790

TANGERINE. Eating a tangerine in a dream is a sign of better health and good friends. 627

TANGLE. To dream of tangled threads, either actual or in your personal affairs, augurs a distressing situation that will cause you much embarrassment. 327

TANGO. Dreaming of the dance known as the tango predicts that you will spend too much money in night clubs and other places of amusement. 069

TANTRUM. If you dream of seeing one of the opposite sex in a tantrum, and you are at your wits' end to know what to do, you will get into a predicament through carelessness in your speech. 130

TAPESTRY. To dream of being in a room hung with tapestry is a prophecy of having to deal with a plot against your reputation. Hanging worn tapestry portends mental distress. 729

TAPEWORM. To dream of having a tapeworm presages the inheritance of a large amount of miscellaneous material from a deceased friend. 709

TAPIOCA. Pudding made of tapioca eaten in a dream forecasts a season of regret for a lost opportunity. 184

TAPROOM. (See Barroom.) 554

TARANTULA. Guard against menaces to your health and your personal safety if you dream of a tarantula. If this large spider bites you, the augury is of a ghastly experience. 170

TART. (See Pastry.) 795

TASSEL. To dream of curtains or other hangings with tassels on them is a sign of having to do a difficult job without any remuneration. 791

TATTOOING. Being tattooed in a dream is an augury of travel on sea and land. To dream of seeing odd designs on a person's body predicts hearing a story that you cannot repeat. 402

TAVERN. (See Hotel.) 243

TAX. If you dream of being oppressed with taxes, you are likely to have a new opportunity to make money. 783

TAXICAB. Riding in a taxicab with a person of the opposite sex prophesies that your love life will be beset with difficulties and misunderstandings. Riding alone presages an inheritance from someone you have met only once. 986

TAXIDERMIST. To dream of seeing a taxidermist at work mounting a bird or animal is a sign that you will be sought for your good companionship. 613

TEA. Drinking tea in a dream, iced or hot, is a presage of pleasure among your church or club friends. To pour tea from a pot predicts that you will have a visitor. 545

TEACHER. If you dream of meeting a former schoolteacher socially, it is a sign that you will be asked to contribute to a charitable fund. To dream of being a teacher portends headaches, both physical and mental. 693

TEAR. To shed tears in a dream augurs happiness to come within a very short time. To see others shed them and to try to give comfort means that you will be made happy by a kind act from someone else. 380

TEAR GAS. A dream of seeing a crowd dispersed with tear gas predicts that you will be greatly concerned over the fate of one of your friends. 789

TEASING. (See also Strip Tease.) If you dream of being teased by someone of the opposite sex, you are likely to have trouble in making one of your actions understood by your friends. 818

TEETOTALER. To offer a drink to a person in a dream and have him or her refuse it on the ground of being a teetotaler is a prophecy that you will lose an important argument with one of your family. 167

TELEGRAM. To dream of receiving a telegram depends for its meaning on the nature of the message it contains. If it is good news, the augury is of money; otherwise it means that you will get into hot water through tax evasions. 669

TELEPATHY. If you dream of receiving a message through the medium of telepathy, or through transference, you will receive good news by mail. 295

TELEPHONE. The ringing of a telephone bell in a dream portends trouble and sickness. To dream of using a telephone is a sign that you will meet an old friend unexpectedly after several years. If in a dream you try to use a dead telephone you will receive news of the serious illness of one you love. 716

TELEVISION. To dream of seeing an important public event by television—an inauguration, coronation, Olympic games, etc.—portends greater activity and more profits in your business. It is bad luck to dream of seeing a hanging or electrocution by television. 402

TEMBLOR. (See Earthquake.) 170

TEMPLE. (See Church.) 136

TEMPTATION. Dreaming of being tempted by one of the opposite sex has a good or bad augury according to the extent of the temptation and whether or not you yield to it. The dream is a warning not to get into a situation where you will be tempted. 398

TENNIS. (See also Racket.) Watching a tennis game in a dream is a portent of increasing activity in business. To play tennis, whether you win or lose, augurs social advancement. 761

TENOR. To dream of singing tenor is a sign that you will lose a valued possession. Hearing a tenor take an exceptionally high note portends a trip to the mountains. 336

TENT. (See also Camp.) To pitch a tent in a dream is a prognostication of relief from personal and business worries. To dream of being in a tent when it is blown down by a storm is a forerunner of disaster. 104

TERRAPIN. Eating terrapin in a dream foretells a long period of financial success. Catching them predicts grief. 037

TERRIER. Beware of letting yourself get into a nervous condition after a dream of any kind of a terrier. This is a warning. 314

TERROR. To dream of being in the midst of any terrorizing experience foretells that you should be on your guard against those who are trying to get your means of support away from you. 975

TESTAMENT. (See Bible.) 462

TEXTBOOK. Studying a textbook in a dream predicts that you will have an opportunity to fill a higher position than the one you occupy. 563

THANKSGIVING. Giving thanks to God in a dream augurs contentment. Dreaming of eating a Thanksgiving dinner, with turkey, cranberry sauce and all the rest of the fixings, is a portent of a happier and more prosperous life. 048

Astrology, Horoscope, and Dreams

THATCHED ROOF. A dream of a cottage with a thatched roof is a fortunate augury for those who are in love. It points toward happiness with family and children. 757

THEATRE. If a performance is going on, a dream of a theatre predicts happy hours in the company of people who are energetic in the pursuit of pleasure. A dark theatre portends a period of boredom. 657

THERMOMETER. To be surprised in a dream by looking at the thermometer is a sign that you will be embarrassed in public by finding something unbuttoned or a hole in a garment. 375

THIEF. Seeing a thief caught in a dream foretells that you will be given a vacation with pay. If you dream that you are called a thief, the augury is of having to exercise great economy in your daily life. 801

THIMBLE. To dream of losing a thimble predicts a slight injury. For a man to dream of giving a thimble to a woman as a present prophesies that he will have a love affair that will come to a happy climax. 514

THIRD DEGREE. If you dream of being given the "third degree" at police headquarters, it is a warning to avoid dissolute companions. A dream of taking the third degree in a fraternal initiation foretells the making of new and lasting friendships. 221

THIRST. Being thirsty in a dream is a prophecy of an invitation to visit relatives in another part of the country. To slake your thirst at a well or spring augurs the receipt of money for a service rendered. To drink alcoholic liquors when you are thirsty for water is a presage of accident. 767

THORN. To catch your clothing or person on a thorn in a dream is a signal that you are heading for trouble through the company you have been keeping. If you see a bird or animal impaled on a thorn, you will suffer for an error of judgment. 973

THOROUGHBRED. Be it horse, dog or human being, a dream of a thoroughbred augurs a step upward in your social relationships and your financial condition. 249

THREAD. (See also Spool.) To dream of picking a thread off someone else's clothing portends getting into a slight difficulty of a humorous nature. Harassing experiences are predicted by a dream of trying to thread a needle. 071

THRESHING. To be present in a dream at the threshing of wheat or other grain is a sign of happiness and prosperity. 729

THRIFT. To dream of exercising thrift in your buying is a sign that you are in danger of committing some extravagance. Putting money away in a bank predicts receiving a remittance by air mail. 506

THRILL. Being thrilled in a dream by a play, movie, music or a brave act is a forerunner of an invitation to spend a weekend with wealthy friends. 502

THROAT. For a man to dream of a woman's throat is a sign that he will be irritated by a woman's caprice. If a woman dreams of a man's throat including his Adam's apple, she is warned to pay more attention to her personal appearance. 410

THRONE. (See also King, Queen.) To dream of sitting as a ruler on a throne prophesies that if you are not more willing to take chances, you will lose out in the race for fame and fortune. 173

THROTTLE. If you have a dream of opening the throttle of a steam locomotive, you are warned against any kind of dissipation. To open the throttle of a motor-car predicts that you will be supported in your course of conduct by the most influential people of your neighborhood. 677

THRUSH. Hearing the song of a thrush in a dream is a sign of delight and happiness to lovers and of peaceful content to those of advanced years. 863

THUD. To hear a thud in a dream presages a surprising communication about a slight infraction of the law. It is a warning to drive carefully at all times. 110

THUG. (See Gangster.) 593

THUMB. A sore thumb in a dream indicates coming prosperity. To "thumb" rides on a highway is a warning to watch your conduct. 532

THUMBNAIL. (See Fingernail.) 947

THUNDER. (See also Lightning.) If thunder rolls and growls in your dream, be warned of treachery from acquaintances whom you have suspected of double dealing. If it cracks, booms, and crashes, it presages the solution of pressing problems. 622

TIARA. (See also Crown.) For a woman to dream of wearing a jeweled tiara on her head foretells being upset by the jealousy of her female friends. 522

TICKET. To dream of arriving at a theatre or other place of amusement and of having forgotten to bring tickets is a forerunner of a quarrel with the person you love best. To dream of losing a railroad ticket is a sign of misfortune and regret. 290

TICKLE. You are warned against indiscreet behavior with a person of the opposite sex if you dream of tickling anyone or being tickled. 138

TIDAL WAVE. A dream of the devastating effects of a tidal wave portends death in your own family or that of one of your close friends. 058

TIDE. An incoming tide in a dream predicts increased financial resources; an ebbing tide is a sign of added worry. 880

TIGER. To be attacked by a tiger in a dream is a portent of a family quarrel that will have far-reaching results. If you succeed in killing the tiger or putting it to flight, the outcome will be in your favor. 329

TIGER LILY. Making a bouquet of tiger lilies in a dream augurs invitations to a round of rather stupid and boring parties. 843

TIME CLOCK. If you dream of punching a time clock, you will find that your work is appreciated by your employer. To dream of seeing someone trying to tamper with a time clock is a sign that you will be tempted by a smooth stranger. 365

TINSEL. Any dream in which tinsel is used in decorating is a forerunner of having to explain what has appeared to be an unworthy act. This applies to Christmas trees as well as anything else. 879

TINTYPE. For a young person to dream of having a tintype taken with one of the opposite sex is a sure sign of approaching marriage. To look at old tintypes is a prediction of happiness in family life. 880

TIRE. To dream of changing an automobile tire on a country road is an augury of having to meet a bill that you thought was outlawed. To have a tire blow out when you are driving is a portent of danger from jealous business associates. To buy a new tire augurs peace of mind. If you dream of losing your spare tire you will have family outcries. 026

TISSUE PAPER. Using tissue paper for wrapping up packages is a portent of good luck through investments. For any other purpose tissue paper is a sign of relief from worry. 004

TOAD. If you dream of stepping on a toad, you will castrate a plot to harm you. To pick a toad up in a dream predicts that you will suffer a slight but annoying incident. 739

TOADSTOOL. (See also Mushroom.) To dream of picking a toadstool and eating it raw is a sign of impending disaster. To hand it to another person augurs an enmity that you will have to combat. 774

TOAST. Making toast in a dream is a fortunate augury unless you allow it to burn, in which case it predicts great annoyances. To eat toast is a sign of being invited to a dinner party with a group of old friends. To butter toast in a dream is a portent of increased expenses. 716

TOASTMASTER. It is a portent of a new opportunity to make a place for yourself in the community and in your business if you dream of being the toastmaster at a banquet. 319

TOBACCO. (See also Cigar, Cigarette, Pipe.) To smoke tobacco in a dream augurs content. To chew tobacco is a sign of trouble with one of the opposite sex. 984

TOBOGGAN. A dream of an exhilarating slide on a toboggan down a steep slope is a prophecy of having money left you by someone you had always distrusted. If the toboggan overturns and dumps you into a snowbank, you are due for disturbing news from your employer. 320

TODDY. Drinking a toddy alone in a dream denotes that you will meet a selfish woman. Drinking in company portends meeting jovial companions. 264

TOILET. For a woman to dream of making her toilet predicts a date with a young man. To dream of seeing a person going to a toilet is a sign of receiving a request for money that you cannot ignore. 641

TOMATO. Eating tomatoes, either fresh or canned, in a dream foretells having an offer made to you that will entail considerable enjoyable travel. To drink tomato juice predicts travel by airplane. 908

TOMB. A dream of entering a tomb signifies that your enemies will fail to do you harm. Being locked in a tomb augurs disease. 138

TOM-TOM. (See also Drum.) Hearing the rhythmic beat of a savage tom-tom in a dream is a forerunner of a disagreeable experience that will be hard to understand. 364

TONGUE. To eat ox-tongue in a dream predicts being invited to go on a picnic in the country. To dream of seeing a person stick out his or her tongue at another is a sign that your personal affairs will be discussed in an unkindly manner by your close neighbors. 327

TONSILS. If you dream of having your tonsils removed, the augury is of the loss of a treasured heirloom. Swollen tonsils in a dream portend grief through the loss of a friend. 449

TOOL. To dream of using tools of any kind is a sign of a rise in your weekly salary. If you dream of losing a tool and hunting high and low for it, you will have an opportunity to advance yourself by not losing your temper. 263

TOOTH. An aching tooth in a dream portends family squabbles and upset business conditions. To dream of having a tooth filled by a dentist is a sign that you will soon hear agreeable news. Having a tooth extracted signalizes a good opportunity to make investments or a change in your business. 628

TOOTHBRUSH. Dreaming of using a toothbrush predicts a wedding to the unmarried. If one of the bristles gets

Astrology, Horoscope, and Dreams

wedged between your teeth, you will be happy with your mate and children. 286

TOOTHPICK. Bad luck will follow you for many days if you dream of picking your teeth with a toothpick. Be on your guard against false friends. 681

TORCH. Carrying a torch in a dream forecasts a love affair under strange circumstances. You are likely to be discomfited by the way it turns out. 961

TOREADOR. If you dream of attending a bull-fight and seeing a toreador strut about the ring, you are warned against underhanded dealings by a person of the opposite sex. 915

TORPEDO. (See also Bomb, Mine.) To dream of being on a submarine or warship and helping to launch a torpedo is a sign that you will have to fight against competition that bids fair to ruin you. If you dream of being on a ship that is torpedoed, you are likely to receive distressing news. 313

TORTURE. (See also Third Degree.) A dream of seeing a person or animal tortured foretells nervous disorders. If you are the one to be tortured, the augury is that you are unjustly suspicious of someone. 304

TOURNIQUET. To dream of stopping the flow of blood by applying a tourniquet to one of the limbs predicts a stroke of good luck through an old friend. 993

TOTEM POLE. These Alaskan Indian memorials seen in a dream foretell meeting a distant relative whom you have never seen before. It will result in a happy association. 394

TOWEL. To dry your hands and face on a cloth towel in a dream predicts prosperity and good health, but if the towel is of paper, the augury is the reverse. If you are disappointed by finding that the towel is wet and soggy, you are due to receive disquieting news. To strike another person with a wet towel in a dream, portends danger of losing your position. 432

TOWER. To dream of seeing a tall tower from a far distance augurs wasted effort in a love affair. Looking at the top of a tower from its base is a sign that you are in danger of being swindled by an unscrupulous person. 288

TOY. To dream of playing with toys forecasts new friends; new children to young married people. If you make a child happy by giving it a toy, you will be greatly beloved by your family and friends. 391

TRACTOR. Driving a tractor in a dream portends engaging in a enterprise that will prosper. A dream of a tractor that will not run is an omen of inconstancy on the part of a lover. 052

TRAFFIC. Watching the traffic in the city or on the highway is a dream that augurs a new and vexing problem connected with your business. To drive through traffic successfully predicts the solution of business and family problems, but a traffic jam foretells serious difficulties. 076

TRAIL. To dream of following a trail, either afoot or on horseback forecasts success through perseverance. To lose the trail is a sign that you will have an adventure with one of the opposite sex. 272

TRAILER. Dreaming of going from place to place in a trailer equipped for housekeeping predicts that you will soon move your place of abode. 953

TRAIN. Travel by train in a dream means that you will accomplish more both for your employer and yourself if you will give greater attention to your work. 608

TRAITOR. You must make up your mind to passing through a lean season if you dream of a person who is a traitor to his or her country. 151

TRAMP. To be asked for food by a tramp in a dream and to refuse it portends that you will work hard for a meager living. If you provide food for the tramp, you will have good fortune in connection with the settling of an estate. To dream that you are a tramp foretells easier living. 012

TRAP. It is a fortunate augury if a young man dreams of setting out traps. He will meet a beautiful girl who will become his wife and the mother of his children. To dream of being caught in a trap is a warning to avoid people who meddle in other persons' affairs. 111

TRAPEZE. If a woman dreams that she is a trapeze performer, swinging high over the heads of an audience in a circus tent or theatre, she will meet a handsome and agreeable man who will eventually propose marriage. To dream of falling from a trapeze is an omen of making a grave mistake; therefore it is a warning to use caution. 086

TRAVEL. By whatever means—motor-car, train, bus, steamship, airplane, or even foot—travel for pleasure or rest in a dream foretells that you will have a sudden and large increase in your income. 723

TRAY. Carrying a tray loaded with dishes is a dream that portends good fortune, but if you drop the tray and break dishes, you will get into trouble. 402

TREACHERY. (See also Traitor.) A dream of treachery from one you had considered friendly is a forerunner of losing a sum of money through the failure of a business. 948

TREADMILL. A foreigner is likely to cheat you if you dream of walking on a treadmill. If your dream is of an animal generating power by a treadmill—a dog, horse or mule—you will make a small amount of money by a lucky turn. 943

TREASURE. Finding treasure in a dream predicts travel and adventure that will bring you pleasure but not much money. Digging for treasure is an omen of good health; diving under the sea for it is an augury of receiving a gift. 747

TREE. To plant a tree in a dream is a fortunate omen for those who are in love; it augurs a June wedding, a blissful honeymoon, and a serene and happy married life. Beautiful trees in the forest or elsewhere have an auspicious influence on the interpretation of any dream. To cut down a tree is an omen of misfortune in love. 480

TRIAL. If you dream of being on trial in a courtroom, you will be confronted with a problem that will have to be approached with the greatest care lest you do or say the wrong thing. It is a warning to be cautious in all your dealings with professional people. 711

TRICK. (See also Magician.) Dreaming of a trick that you cannot explain is a portent of a day's excursion full of interesting and innocent amusements. If you dream of doing tricks to amuse one or more persons, you will receive an invitation to join a church organization. 202

TRIP. (See Travel.) 371

TRIPE. Prepared in any way, tripe is a good augury for business and health, but it is a warning to exercise great discretion in matters of the heart. 029

TRIPLETS. (See also Quintuplets.) A dream of baby triplets being wheeled in a wide carriage predicts that you will have good luck at cards. A woman who dreams of giving birth to triplets will have many admirers. 102

TROPHY. If you dream of winning a trophy in any athletic contest, you will profit greatly in buying and selling. 512

TROPICS. To dream of being in a tropical land foretells being presented with oranges, grapefruit or tangerines. Being on friendly terms with the natives of the country augurs an adventure with someone of the opposite sex, but there will be no romance connected with it. 700

TROUSERS. For a man to dream of finding himself on the street or in another public place without his trousers is an omen of having to make amends for a breach of courtesy. To dream of pressing a pair of trousers foretells an increase in income. 912

TROUSSEAU. A maiden who dreams of getting together a trousseau may look forward to happy hours in the company of her lover. For a widow to dream of a trousseau augurs a marriage for companionship. 796

TRUANT. To dream that you are playing hookey from school is an omen of making a friend who will be faithful through life. 974

TRUCK. A good living and a dignified place in the community is foretold by a dream of being a truck driver. To dream of running a truck over an embankment forecasts an attack on you by a thug. 104

TRUMPET. Blowing a trumpet in a dream predicts a surprise in which you will be gratified by the result of something you have accomplished. If you dream of an angel blowing a trumpet, you will suffer from rheumatism. 808

TRUNK. To dream of packing a trunk foretells travel; unpacking a trunk is a sign of a change of address. If you dream of carrying a heavy trunk on your back, you will have to assume a new responsibility. 405

TUB. (See also Bathtub.) Trees or other large plants growing in tubs are a dream sign that you will be invited to a large and brilliant social gathering. Packing butter or other food in a tub foretells a visit from a cousin, uncle or aunt. 403

TUBERCULOSIS. A warning is contained in this dream to take better care of your health. It is not necessarily a prediction that you will contract the disease. 719

TUGBOAT. Dreaming of a tugboat towing a steamship or a long line of barges predicts that you will have to work longer hours but at a higher wage. To dream of being a passenger or one of the crew of a tugboat is a sign that you will be involved in labor troubles. 383

TULIP. If you dream of a row of bright-colored tulip blossoms in a garden, you will be kissed by a handsome person of the opposite sex. To gather tulips implies a round of gayety. To plant tulip bulbs foreshadows disappointment. 306

TUNA. Fishing for tuna in a dream predicts an exciting adventure in the out-of-doors. Eating tuna in any form is a forerunner of disillusionment. 480

TUNNEL. To dream of going through a dark tunnel predicts a period of difficult going before you finally achieve your heart's desire. 962

TURKEY. (See also Thanksgiving.) A flock of gobbling turkeys seen in a dream foretells a position in which you will have to go to many public meetings. To kill a turkey is a portent of good luck; to dress one is an omen of plenty. 120

TURKISH BATH. You will have a strenuous and upsetting experience connected with your business or your job if you dream of taking a Turkish bath. 823

TURNSTILE. Going through a turnstile in a dream warns you to get the advice of a lawyer before committing yourself to any new business arrangement. 314

TUXEDO. Wearing a tuxedo in a dream is a sign that someone will ask you for money. To dream of wearing a white tie with a tuxedo portends being scandalously gossiped about. 150

TWEEZERS. Women who dream of having their eyebrows plucked with tweezers will meet new and agreeable men. 282

TWINE. (See String.) 380

TYPEWRITER. If you dream of using a typewriter, the augury is of advancement so long as it does not get out of order. If the ribbon sticks or the keys jam, you may look for disquieting news. It is bad luck to dream of writing love letters on a typewriter. 170

TYPIST. (See Secretary, Stenographer.) 299

TYRANT. If a woman dreams that her husband is a tyrant, she may look forward to a peaceful and comfortable home life. To dream that the ruler of your country is a tyrant augurs a political upset that will definitely affect your career. 532

UKULELE. To hear a ukulele strummed in your dreams foretells an avowal of love from an old friend whom you have not suspected of being sentimental. To play a ukulele and have a string break is a sign of having a short period of hard luck. 116

ULCER. (See Sore.) 951

ULTRA VIOLET RAYS. If you dream of lying beneath a sun lamp, basking in the health-giving ultra violet rays, you will be compelled to take a deferred vacation, but the postponement will be to your advantage. 709

UMBRELLA. To dream of carrying an umbrella in a downpour is a sign that you will meet with reverses. To be burdened with an umbrella when the sun shines presages startling news that will have a definite effect in changing your plans for the future. 009

UMPIRE. If you dream that you are umpiring a game of baseball and a heated argument occurs regarding your decision, it denotes a rift at home. Family differences will be the means of your having to leave for another address. To criticize the umpire harshly at a game foretells a season during which you will be under the close scrutiny of a critical relative who may have money to leave to you. 303

UNDERTAKER. To see a solemn, unctuous undertaker in your dream augurs that someone will try and cheat you of your birthright. Guard, therefore, both birth and marriage certificates and keep your personal papers under lock and key. 440

UNDERTOW. If you dream of sea-bathing and of being drawn seaward by the undertow, it indicates that you will share in the sorrows of another. 594

UNDRESSING. To dream of seeing a person of the opposite sex undressing is a warning to go very slowly in placing your trust in any new person you may meet. 813

UNIFORM. To dream of wearing a smart military or naval or police uniform is a sign that you will be honored for a kind or heroic deed for women or children. 900

UNION. If you dream of being active in a trade union of any description, you will be able to look forward to prosperity and the respect of your fellow men. 552

UNIVERSITY. If you attend a university in your dream, the portent is of a bright outlook in business and a strong political pull. 061

UPHOLSTERY. To dream of heavily upholstered furniture in your home is a sign that you will inherit a number of shares of stock that have as yet never paid a dividend. 192

URN. If in a dream an urn is filled with fresh plants or flowers, the augury is of calm happiness, but if the urn is empty or the flowers are faded, there will be sad times for you ahead. A funeral urn holding the ashes of the dead is a dream that presages a voyage to strange but interesting lands. 701

USHER. If you dream of being an usher in a theatre, you will have the pleasure of meeting someone with social and business influence. To fall in love with an usher is a good augury for a maiden. 974

VACATION. To dream of taking a vacation at the expense of your employer is a portent of increased earning capacity, but if it is at your own expense you will be able to retire in a few years. 056

VACCINATION. If you dream of being vaccinated, you are in a fair way to make a great success in the work that you like best. 366

VACUUM CLEANER. Using a vacuum cleaner in a dream and walking with it from room to room foretells success with projects concerned with persons of the opposite sex. If a fuse blows out while you are at work, you must guard your conduct while in their company. 010

VAGABOND. To dream of being a rollicking, devil-may-care vagabond portends a season of relaxation during which you will not be bothered by care or worry. 034

VALENTINE. If you receive a valentine decorated with lace and perfumed, you will kiss someone of the opposite sex. 912

VALET. To dream of having a valet to lay out your clothes, shave you and keep you in fit condition for social events is a sign that you will be asked to take a position of high honor in your community.

VAMPIRE. You will have many disquieting experiences if you dream of being attacked by a vampire bat, but if you are able to kill it, you will have a season of good fortune, especially with persons of the opposite sex.

VAN. If you dream of having your household goods piled into a moving van, you will soon make a change in your position and your address that will be for the better. If you dream of riding in a van you will have a chance to make a large amount of money.

VANILLA. Smacking your lips over any food flavored with vanilla in a dream is a sign that you will have a party given for you on the occasion of a birthday or other anniversary.

VARNISH. To dream of putting varnish on a piece of furniture or a floor indicates that you will try to excuse a flagrant mistake that you have made. It is therefore a warning against making errors that could have been avoided.

VASE. If you dream of filling a vase with flowers, you are likely to find that friends will come to your rescue when you most need their help.

VAUDEVILLE. A dream of vaudeville is a sign that you will have friends that are true but of the type known as screw-ball. To dream that you are a vaudeville actor portends many friends of a professional type.

VAULT. To dream of being entombed in a subterranean vault denotes a nerve-wracking lawsuit and much litigation.

VEGETABLE. Eating vegetables in a dream is a sign that you will have to pay for a pleasure that is long past. To dream of raising vegetables in a garden portends good health and pleasure with your family.

VEIL. If you wear a veil in your dream you will be able to defy fate. Seeing a bride who is wearing a veil means that you will transgress but you will not have to repent.

VEIN. To dream of cutting a vein is a sign of distressing news from an old friend.

VELVET. Wearing velvet in a dream indicates that you will do a deed that you will have to live down. If you make a velvet dress, you will meet a handsome man who will court you with great ardor.

VENEER. If you dream of seeing a piece of furniture with the veneer coming off, you will be surprised at the behavior of one whom you believed to be your friend.

VENETIAN BLINDS. After a dream of Venetian blinds you must behave with great circumspection unless you are willing to take the consequences of ill-advised acts.

VENISON. Eating venison in a dream predicts that you will go to a party without an escort and be criticized for an act that is considered a breach of etiquette.

VENTRILOQUIST. To be amused by a ventriloquist in a dream is a sign that someone whom you do not like will make uncomplimentary remarks about you. 224

VERANDA. (See Porch.) 467

VERMIN. Suffering from vermin in a dream predicts disappointment in some project you had believed to be favorable. 551

VERTIGO. Dreaming of a sudden attack of vertigo is a warning to unmarried persons against designing people of the opposite sex. 207

VEST. If your vest is unbuttoned in your dream you will make a glutton of yourself. If you dream of wearing a vest in a loud and striking pattern it is a sign that you will be criticized for drinking too much. 258

VETERAN. To dream of seeing a veteran of a war marching in line or selling poppies on the street is an augury of trying to explain why duties have been unfulfilled. 075

VETERINARIAN. To watch a veterinarian skillfully administer help to some unfortunate animal is a sign that you will have a slight accident such as a fall or a jar. 340

VICAR. If you dream of a vicar in the pursuit of his duties you are likely to be invited to a party where women will dominate. 406

VINE. To dream of seeing an old building covered with vines fortells that a bearded man will enter your life and bring great happiness. 204

VINEGAR. You will have to account for being away from your accustomed haunts if you dream of tasting vinegar. To put vinegar into a salad dressing portends good fortune in family life. 788

VINEYARD. Dreaming of a vineyard laden with ripe fruit indicates that you will have a good year in which to try experiments. If the vineyard is stripped of its vintage, you are warned to look before you leap—do not try to engage in new businesses that are hazardous. 811

VIOLET. Pleasant company is promised by a dream of picking violets. For a woman to dream of wearing a corsage of violets is a prophecy of social advancement. 529

VIOLIN. If you dream of playing a violin, you will be criticized for having queer ideas about life and religion, but you will be loved for your generosity and your friendliness. 680

VIRGIN. If a woman dreams of being a virgin, she will have many good friends of the male sex. For a married women to dream of being a virgin is a sign that she will have disquieting episodes in her life. 421

VISION. You will have strange premonitions if you dream of having visions. If they are pleasant you are due for a happy surprise; otherwise you will be harassed by debt. 788

VISITOR. To dream of having a visitor is a sign of receiving a gift of silver. If you dream of being a visitor at the house of a relative or friend, it is a sign that you will be a guest at a house party. 270

VOLCANO. If you see an active volcano in your dream belching forth molten lava, it predicts an experience with a neighbor that will give you some concern but will be harmless. 207

VOMIT. It is a prognostication of better conditions in your business and home life if you dream of vomiting. 495

VOODOOISM. A dream of voodooism is a sign that you will be subject to nervous disorders. If you dream of being a party to voodoo rites you will have difficulty in your business life. 599

VOTE. A dream of voting indicates that you will be likely to express yourself in public when it would have been better if you had kept silent. 993

VOW. If you take a solemn vow in a dream, it foretells a happy solution of any problem that you may have concerning your love life. 534

VOYAGE. To dream of going on a voyage to countries that you have seen before portends living again the scenes and events of your childhood. It is one of the happiest auguries that you could have. 607

WAFFLE. Eating waffles in a dream portends having to break an engagement with a person of the opposite sex. To cook them is a sign of being called upon to entertain a small child who will annoy you considerably. 431

WAGER. (See Bet.) 183

WAGES. A dream of receiving wages is a sign of a chance that will be offered you to take a higher position with additional responsibility. 269

WAGON. Riding on a wagon in a dream foretells that you will attend an auction sale. Young women who dream of riding on a hay-wagon will have offers of matrimony. 226

WAIST. If a woman dreams that her waist is too large for the prevailing style, she will be distracted by social demands on her time and energy. If she dreams that a man puts his arm around her waist, she will have an embarrassing experience with a minister. A man who dreams of a woman's waist will have to pay an overdue bill. 250

WAITER. Tipping a waiter or waitress in a dream is an augury of losing a piece of jewelry. To dream of having a waiter spill soup or other food on your clothing portends being misunderstood by your best friend. If you are kept waiting a long time for your food in a dream, you will have trouble with your landlord. 608

WALKING-STICK. (See Cane.) 100

WALLET. If you dream of losing your wallet, you will be caught in a rainstorm. Finding a wallet containing money portends a deferred vacation; an empty wallet is a sign that you will be honored for an achievement. 315

WALL-FLOWER. For a girl to dream of being a wallflower at a dance, experiencing the bitterness of unpopularity, is a sign that she will buy a new gown that will attract much favorable attention. 721

WALL PAPER. To dream of papering a wall and making a mess of it foretells the coming of a house-guest. If you dream of the job being done by a professional paperhanger, you will be invited to attend the opening night of a theatrical performance. 731

WALNUT. A dream of shelling and eating walnuts portends a comfortable income. If the meats come out of the shells without breaking, the augury is favorable to your love life. 460

WALTZ. For a man to dream of hearing a dreamy waltz foretells that he will fall hard for a debutante with red hair. A woman who has this dream will receive a letter from a stranger asking for a date. Dancing the waltz in a dream is a forecast of having to make an explanation. 363

WAND. To wave a fairy wand in a dream and achieve the fulfillment of a wish signifies that you will play an important part in amateur theatricals. 099

WAR. (See Arms, Army, Battle, Submarine, Torpedo, etc.) 069

WARDEN. If you see the warden of a prison in your dream, it foretells that you will be under a nurse's care for a few days. 262

WARDROBE. To dream of having a large wardrobe and of selecting your clothes with great care for every occasion is a sign that you will be called for jury duty. If you dream of finding only one suit or gown in a wardrobe, someone will send you two theatre tickets. 628

WAREHOUSE. It is a good omen to dream of being in a warehouse that is crowded with stocks of various kinds. You will not need to worry about the future. 195

WART. If you dream of having a wart on any part of your body, you are likely to get into hot water by trying to be helpful to others. A dream of a beautiful woman with a wart on her face portends grief. 516

WARWHOOP. To dream of hearing a warwhoop from a painted Indian predicts an amusing experience with an effeminate dandy. 529

WASHBOWL. It is a sign that you will have an agreeable visitor if you dream of washing your hands or face in a washbowl. To break a washbowl augurs undesirable company who will be hard to get rid of. 993

WASHING. If you dream of washing clothes in a tub, it presages that you will be called upon to act as peacemaker between quarreling lovers. Washing clothes in a machine portends a vacation with pay. To dream of washing your body is a sign of success in a new venture. If you wash a baby in a dream, you will find happiness in your home. 637

WATCH. Wearing a fine watch in your dream is a sign that some influential person is keeping his eye on you. An old-fashioned watch foretells that you will be made the guardian of a young person. 553

WATER. (See also Brook, Ocean, Pond, etc.) A dream of drinking cold water is a lucky omen for man, woman or child; but throwing it on anyone portends that you will be unpopular. If you dream of hot water in any form, it predicts a season of great trouble, both socially and in business. 815

WATERFALL. To see a beautiful waterfall in your dream is a sign that you will be introduced to a handsome and gracious man or woman who will be exceedingly kind to you. 449

WATER LILY. (See Lily.) 468

WATERMELON. Eating watermelon in a dream points toward a cruise in southern waters. If you dream of snapping the seeds at another person, you will find a small sum of money. A watermelon on the vine portends a moonlight tryst at which you should be on your guard. 064

WAVE. To dream of seeing high waves dashing on the shore predicts the futility of your love affair. 661

WAX. (See also Beeswax.) Lighted wax candles in a dream foretell that you will meet small, dainty women. To walk on waxed floors is a sign that you will fail to keep an important appointment. 354

WEALTH. If you dream of possessing great wealth, you will have a financial upset that may have beneficial results. 809

WEAVING. To watch a weaver at his or her loom foretells that you will make much progress in your chosen work. To dream of weaving portends a peaceful and prosperous life. 031

WEB. (See also Spider.) Beware of getting mixed up with any kind of intrigue after a dream of a spider spinning its web. 145

WEDDING. To dream of going to your own wedding is a forerunner of happiness in love; another's wedding predicts meeting new friends. Eating wedding cake portends long life with a loving partner. 208

WEEDS. Weeds in a flower garden warn you to protect your good name by denying a scandalous act that has been attributed to you. 165

WEEK-END. Dreaming of a week-end visit to a great country estate predicts that you will be able to open a bank account. 297

WEEPING. (See Tear.) 378

WEIGHING. To dream of weighing yourself and finding that you are either overweight or underweight is a sign that you will be gossiped about by your neighbors. 321

WELSH RAREBIT. If you make a welsh rarebit in a dream and it is a success, you will find a sum of money in unexpected spot. If the rarebit is tough and rubbery, it is an augury of being embarrassed in a public place. 611

WET NURSE. The significance of a wet nurse in a dream is of renewed hope for those who are depressed. If a woman dreams of being a wet nurse, she will receive good news from an old friend. 617

WHALE. If you dream of getting a whale on a fishline, you can make up your mind that there will be an improvement in your relations with your acquaintances. 029

WHARF. If you dream of tying a boat to a wharf, you will buy a piece of jewelry for one of the opposite sex. Standing on a wharf and watching a boat leave predicts sadness. 876

WHEAT. A dream of seeing a wheatfield ready for reaping foretells prosperity and well-being. Wheat in sheaves is a sign of accomplishing an arduous task. 805

WHEEL. To dream of seeing wheels turning portends hard labor that will be productive of good results. Adventure is predicted by a dream of having a wheel come off your car while driving. An old wheel by the side of the road foretells disappointment. 754

WHEELBARROW. Pushing a loaded wheelbarrow in a dream is a forerunner of a delightful companionship with one of the opposite sex. To draw a wheelbarrow predicts a sad happening to one of your friends. Seeing a wheelbarrow upside down is a sign that you will bear a heavy burden. 803

WHIP. (See also Flogging.) To whip an animal in a dream foretells that someone will take pleasure in making you uncomfortable. 431

WHISKERS. To wear whiskers in a dream predicts that you will attend a masquerade party and win the prize. For a woman to dream of being kissed by a man wearing whiskers is a sign that she will be made love to by a beardless youth. 954

WHISKEY. To drink whiskey in a dream denotes a busy season in business but no great profit from it. 822

WHISTLE. If in a dream you whistle a tune you will find that you can buy something that you have always wanted. To whistle for a taxicab is an omen of prosperity; for a policeman, poverty. 215

WHITE SLAVE. To dream of being connected with the white slave traffic is a warning against going into business with a certain person who has designs on you. For a woman to dream of being a white slave foretells that she will be the target of scandalous gossip. 266

WHITEWASH. If you dream of using whitewash on any kind of wall or fence or building you will be called upon to get a friend or relative out of trouble. 408

WIDOW. For a man or woman to dream of being a widower or widow is a sign that money will arrive in the mail. 244

WIG. To dream that you wear a wig foretells having a new and better position offered you. If the wig is blown off or otherwise removed in public, you will have to answer an embarrassing question. 817

WIGWAM. If in a dream you enter an Indian wigwam and feel at home, you will be given a handsome present of considerable value. 870

WIND. To hear the wind howling in a dream is a portent of woe. If at the same time you feel it in your face, it indicates that you will be required to do work that you despise. 506

WINDOW. Opening a window in a dream foretells better health. Closing a window is a portent of having a visitor. To enter a house through a window indicates that someone will libel you. To break a pane of glass in a window augurs a period of poor health. 944

WINDPIPE. It is a sign that you will have troubled times on account of your creditors if you dream of having something stuck in your windpipe. 309

WINE. If you dream of drinking wine, you are likely to meet a clergyman who will appeal to your imagination. Be on your guard against giving away a secret if you dream of becoming intoxicated on wine. 210

WING. A bird with a broken wing in a dream means that you are going to have trouble in attaining the goal you have set for yourself. To dream of seeing an airplane wing crumple while in the air presages having to atone for an old sin. 258

WINK. To dream of winking at a comely person of the opposite sex is a sure forerunner of distress. It is a warning to use discretion every day of your life. 652

WIRELESS. (See Radio.) 014

WISHBONE. Making a wish and breaking a wishbone with a person of the opposite sex foretells the receipt of a sizable legacy. 544

WISTARIA. An arbor covered with wistaria in bloom is a dream that predicts happiness to lovers and married folk. 872

WITCH. Dreaming of witches riding broomsticks forecasts a good time in the company of your friends. 404

WOLF. To be pursued by wolves in a dream is an augury of having to borrow money temporarily on which to live. If you are able to kill them or put them to flight, you will overcome all your obstacles. 429

WOODEN SHOE. (See Sabot.) 800

WOODPECKER. Hearing the sound of a woodpecker in a dream is an omen of war. To see him boring holes with his beak is a forerunner of a family row. 587

WOODPILE. It is a fortunate augury for a man to dream of working on a woodpile, especially if the day is sunny. Women who have this dream are likely to have a short illness. 570

WORSHIPER. To dream of seeing one or more people at worship in church predicts that you will meet people who will work for your advancement. 409

WREATH. Hanging a wreath of flowers or holly is a dream that foretells being invited to attend a dinner or other celebration as the guest of honor. 306

WRECK. To be a witness of an automobile, airplane, train or shipwreck predicts a round of disturbances in business and in love. To be injured in a wreck is a warning to drive with caution. 385

WRESTLER. A dream of wrestlers in action portends that you will win the next bet you make. 668

WRIST WATCH. (See Watch.) 123

WRITER. To dream of being a writer of books, magazine articles, poetry and the like is a sign that you will accumulate a library of good books and enjoy life. 952

XYZ

X-RAYS. To dream of having an X-ray photograph taken of your teeth or other part of the body is a forerunner of a mysterious occurrence in the life of one of your friends. If you dream of looking at your own bones by means of the X-ray, you will be called to account for an indiscretion you have committed. 906

XYLOPHONE. Playing a xylophone or hearing one played in a dream is a portent of taking part in a pageant of historical interest. If the xylophone is played out of tune, it foretells an accident. 241

YACHT. Being entertained on a yacht in a dream is a sure sign of improvement in your financial condition. If the water is rough and you are seasick, you may look forward to a lucky stroke in business. To talk with people of the opposite sex on a yacht foretells a happy love life. 360

YAM. Eating yams in a dream predicts an increase in your weight. It is therefore a warning to fat people. 179

YARDSTICK. To measure anything with a yardstick in a dream is a portent of being criticized for your conduct. To break a yardstick augurs good luck for salespeople. 081

YARN. If you dream of winding yarn off a hank into a ball, you will increase the number of your friends. Using yarn for knitting or crocheting forecasts marriage to maidens and widows. 746

YAWL. Sailing a yawl in a dream predicts progress as long as the sea is calm; if not, you will suffer a setback both in love and business affairs. 226

YAWN. To dream of yawning or seeing another person yawn is a portent of catching a contagious disease. 894

YEAST. Eating yeast in a dream is a sign that you are slated to receive a high honor. Mixing it for use in bread or biscuits predicts receiving the adoration of your beloved. 020

YELL. To emit a yell in your dream presages being discovered in an unworthy plot. To hear the yell of another is a prediction of being able to help an old friend. 853

YODEL. It is a lucky sign, particularly for those who are in love, to hear a singer yodeling in the open air. It points to marriage and happiness. 456

YOKE. To wear a yoke of any kind in a dream portends hard labor under an exacting taskmaster. To dream of seeing a yoke of oxen is an omen of a new address quite distant from your present place of abode. 604

YOUTH. For an elderly person to dream of his or her youth is a portent of continuing ease and comfort. 962

YUCCA. Dreaming of a yucca plant in full bloom predicts love and matrimony to young people, love and comfort to the married, and an appreciation of spiritual values to all. 323

YULE LOG. To dream of cutting and bringing in a yule log at Christmas time foretells true friends and much simple comfort. 953

ZEBRA. If you dream of one of these striped, horse-like animals, you are likely to visit good friends who live in the country. A dead zebra portends that one of your acquaintances is in danger of having to serve a prison sentence. 298

ZEPHYR. A dream of a warm, gentle breeze, or zephyr, is a forerunner of peace through a loving family and moderate prosperity. 139

ZERO. Dreaming of zero temperature and of suffering from the cold is a prophecy of having a present of a new gown or suit of clothes. 521

ZIPPER. To dream of fastening one's clothes with a zipper is a sign that you will preserve your dignity in the face of great provocation to do otherwise. If you dream of a zipper getting stuck, you will be chagrined by the actions of one of your friends. 047

ZITHER. Playing the zither in a dream foretells peace of mind and a host of friends. 378

ZOO. You will travel to far-off places if you dream of looking at the animals in a zoo. If you take a child to the zoo, you will make a great deal of money. 968

A TO Z DREAMS AND LUCKY NUMBERS

How to Interpret Your Dreams

To use the dream section of this book to the best advantage, you must bear in mind that dreams are usually made up of several elements besides the one that fixes it in your memory. There is one, of course, that is most important, and that should be looked up first; but the references to the others should be found and considered in interpreting the dream.

For example, for a dream about a printing press, it is likely that, besides that item, you will have to look up Wheel, Gears, Paper, Ink, and so on, before you can work out its meaning satisfactorily. If you dream of taking a bath, perhaps you will have to look up Tub, Shower, Soap, Sponge, Towel and Bath mat. None of these minor considerations should be overlooked, for they may have a definite influence on what you may expect in the future.

Dreams that follow overindulgence in rich food, alcohol and such seldom mean anything as far as the future is concerned. It is only the dreams that come to people in normal sleep that have any significance.

The results of a lifetime study of dreams have gone into this book. Thus you will find not only references that are common to all time, but also things that are as new as this evening's newspaper or the latest radio broadcast.

Please regard this as a friendly book, even if at times it might point to disaster through one of its interpretations. By heeding a warning you can often avert trouble. After all, you may control your own destiny; and "Forewarned is forearmed."

How To Use Your Dream Number

It is not intended in this chapter to outline the science of numerology. The purpose is merely to make it possible for you to discover a *friendly* number in connection with every dream.

It is easy to use the number that goes with any dream. It may or may not be favorable so you must use your own judgment as to whether or not to use it. You need not be surprised if a favorable dream proves to have an unfavorable number. On the other hand, an unfavorable dream may have a favorable number. The number does *not* affect the dream interpretation, nor does it have any direct effect on the dreamer unless he or she uses it for some particular purpose.

You may simply choose to use the lucky number associated with your dream just as it appears, to place a bet, play the lottery, or the like. Or, you may decide to analyze your number a bit further.

Use your dream number wisely, as the choices are always yours. For a deeper look at numbers and how to use them to your best advantage, refer to the Numerology section of this book. Good luck!

GLOSSARY

Alignment: in graphology, indicates amount of balance.
Aspects: measurements of celestial longitude by which any two celestial bodies are separated. These measurements are forces that give energy to the original meaning of the sign, house, planet combination.
Astrological dial: determines the earth's position to see the scheme of things, at a particular time, using longitude and latitude.
Astrology: the science of the influence of cosmic forces emanating from celestial bodies upon human character and destiny.
Basic numbers: in numerology, the devices through which the vibrations of all the forces in the universe are communicated.
Beginning strokes: in graphology, indicates amount of emotional stability.
Bracelets: see Racettes.
Capital letters: in graphology, indicates amount of modesty.
Child lines: in palmistry, indicates person's feelings about children.
Connectedness: in graphology, indicates continuity of thought patterns.
Conscious self: in numerology, the number that shows what you dream about and your impression on others.
Croix Mystique: see Mystic Cross.
Destiny: in numerology, this number shows what the soul is to accomplish.
Dots: in graphology, indicates amount of logical thinking.
Eight: in numerology, a successful person.
Elaborations: in graphology, an indication of idealism and optimism.
Expression of force: in graphology, concerns both writing pressure and writing slant.
Fate line: in palmistry, indicates amount of independence.
Fingerprints: in palmistry, the loops and arches that modify the qualities of the fingers.
First finger: in palmistry, the finger that is ruled by Jupiter and indicates awareness of the surrounding world.
Five: in numerology, an adventurous person.
Fluency: in graphology, an indication of creativity.
Four: in numerology, a steadfast person.
Girdle of Venus: in palmistry, indicates mood-swings.
Graphology: science of character delineation through the study of a person's handwriting.
Head Line: in palmistry, indicates amount of intelligence.
Heart Line: in palmistry, indicates amount of emotional stability.
Holistic: a gestaltic, inter-connected, approach to life.
Horoscope: a chart representing the position of the planets at the moment of birth.
Individualized forms: in graphology, indicates independence and creativity.
Inspiration: in numerology, the number that shows the person's abilities and vocation, along with how the self is expressed.
Life Line: in palmistry, indicates quality of life.
Line of Health: see Line of Mercury.
Line of Hepatica: see Line of Mercury.
Line of Liver: see Line of Mercury.
Line of Mercury: in palmistry, indicates intuition and possibly state of health. Also called the Line of Health, Line of Hepatica, and Line of Liver.
Line of Perception: in palmistry, indicates insight.
Line of Venus: in palmistry, indicates sunny disposition.
Lines of Marriage: in palmistry, indicates deep emotional attachment.

Loops: in graphology, indicates intellectual imagination.
Margins: in graphology, indicates amount of communication powers.
Mount of Jupiter: in palmistry, rules the position in life.
Mount of Luna: in palmistry, rules psychic ability and emotional stability.
Mount of Mercury: in palmistry, rules commerce and medicine.
Mount of Pluto: in palmistry, rules psychology and viral diseases.
Mount of Saturn: in palmistry, rules service to others.
Mount of Venus: in palmistry, rules success in the arts.
Mystic Cross: in palmistry, indicates psychic powers.
Negative writing: in graphology, a messy and disorganized pattern of writing.
Nine: in numerology, an idealistic person.
Numerology: the study of the esoteric value of numbers and their relation to the universe.
Occult: esoteric, or hidden, knowledge.
One: in numerology, an ambitious person.
Palmistry: divination through the study of the natural lines and mounts of the hands.
Planets in houses: an indication of destiny.
Planets in signs: an indication of character.
Positive writing: in graphology, a neat and harmonious pattern of writing.
Racettes: in palmistry, the three lines that separate the wrist from the palm. Also called the Bracelets.
Rhythm: in graphology, indicates amount of consistency in the writing movement.
Rigidity: in graphology, indicates lack of spontaneity and flexibility.
Ring finger: in palmistry, the finger that is ruled by Venus and indicates creativity and success.
Ring of Solomon: in palmistry, indicates wisdom.
Second finger: in palmistry, has to do with service to others since it arises out of the Mount of Saturn. It is referred to as Medius.
Seven: in numerology, a philosophical person.
Sign: a portent.
Signature: in graphology, indicates the writer's self-concept.
Simplicity: in graphology, indicates clarity of thought.
Six: in numerology, a responsible person.
Spacing: in graphology, indicates amount of ease in relationships.
Subconscious self: in numerology, the number that gives the soul's motivation.
Symbol: a condensed cuneiform of information to stimulate the mind to all information associated with a particular planet; a key word.
Terminal strokes: in graphology, indicates the writer's attitude and motivation.
Three: in numerology, an artistic person.
Thumb: in palmistry, indicates purpose and direction in life.
Two: in numerology, an emotionally balanced person.
Via Lascivia: in palmistry, indicates lax morals.
Writing size: in graphology, indicates the writer's view of his/her world.
Zodiac: the astrological divisions, or signs, of the heavens consisting of constellations which are assigned thirty degrees each, to make up the full circle of three hundred sixty degrees.
Zonal balance: in graphology, the vertical height of individual small letters.